The New Library of International Accounting

Series Editor: Christopher W. Nobes

PricewaterhouseCoopers Professor of Accounting, University of Reading, UK

1. Developments in International Accounting – General Issues and Classification
   Christopher W. Nobes

2. Developments in Country Studies in International Accounting – Europe
   Sally Aisbitt and Lisa Evans

3. Developments in Country Studies in International Accounting – Americas and the Far East
   Gary K. Meek

Future titles will include:

Developments in the International Harmonization of Accounting
Christopher W. Nobes

Developments in Financial Reporting by Multinationals
Clare B. Roberts

Wherever possible, the articles in these volumes have been reproduced as originally published using facsimile reproduction, inclusive of footnotes and pagination to facilitate ease of reference.

For a list of all Edward Elgar published titles visit our site on the World Wide Web at
www.e-elgar.com

Developments in Country Studies in International Accounting – Americas and the Far East

Developments in Country Studies in International Accounting – Americas and the Far East

Edited by

Gary K. Meek

Oscar S. Gellein/Deloitte and Touche Professor of Accounting
Oklahoma State University, USA

THE NEW LIBRARY OF INTERNATIONAL ACCOUNTING

An Elgar Reference Collection
Cheltenham, UK • Northampton, MA, USA

Published by
Edward Elgar Publishing Limited
Glensanda House
Montpellier Parade
Cheltenham
Glos GL50 1UA
UK

Edward Elgar Publishing, Inc.
136 West Street
Suite 202
Northampton
Massachusetts 01060
USA

A catalogue record for this book is available from the British Library.

ISBN 1 84376 272 2

Printed and bound in Great Britain by MPG Books Ltd, Bodmin, Cornwall

Contents

B Japan

C Other Asian Countries

Acknowledgements

The editor and publishers wish to thank the authors and the following publishers who have kindly given permission for the use of copyright material.

American Accounting Association for articles: Stephen A. Zeff (1995), 'A Perspective on the U.S. Public/Private-Sector Approach to the Regulation of Financial Reporting', *Accounting Horizons*, **9** (1), March, 52–70; Mark H. Lang and Russell J. Lundholm (1996), 'Corporate Disclosure Policy and Analyst Behavior', *Accounting Review*, **71** (4), October, 467–92; Christine A. Botosan (1997), 'Disclosure Level and the Cost of Equity Capital', *Accounting Review*, **72** (3), July, 323–49; Paquita Y. Davis-Friday and Juan M. Rivera (2000), 'Inflation Accounting and 20-F Disclosures: Evidence from Mexico', *Accounting Horizons*, **14** (2), June, 113–35; Ronald A. Dye and Shyam Sunder (2001), 'Why Not Allow FASB and IASB Standards to Compete in the U.S.?', *Accounting Horizons*, **15** (3), September, 257–71; Stephen P. Baginski, John M. Hassell and Michael D. Kimbrough (2002), 'The Effect of Legal Environment on Voluntary Disclosure: Evidence from Management Earnings Forecasts Issued in U.S. and Canadian Markets', *Accounting Review*, **77** (1), January, 25–50.

Blackwell Publishing Ltd for articles: Tatsuo Inoue and Wayne B. Thomas (1996), 'The Choice of Accounting Policy In Japan', *Journal of International Financial Management and Accounting*, **7** (1), Spring, 1–23; T.E. Cooke (1996), 'The Influence of the Keiretsu on Japanese Corporate Disclosure', *Journal of International Financial Management and Accounting*, **7** (3), Autumn, 191–214; Lynn Rees and Pieter Elgers (1997), 'The Market's Valuation of Nonreported Accounting Measures: Retrospective Reconciliations of Non-U.S. and U.S. *GAAP*', *Journal of Accounting Research*, **35** (1), Spring, 115–27; Russell Craig and Joselito Diga (1998), 'Corporate Accounting Disclosure in ASEAN', *Journal of International Financial Management and Accounting*, **9** (3), October, 246–74; Ben-Hsien Bao and Lynne Chow (1999), 'The Usefulness of Earnings and Book Value for Equity Valuation in Emerging Capital Markets: Evidence From Listed Companies in the People's Republic of China', *Journal of International Financial Management and Accounting*, **10** (2), Summer, 85–104; Andreas Charitou, Colin Clubb and Andreas Andreou (2000), 'The Value Relevance of Earnings and Cash Flows: Empirical Evidence for Japan', *Journal of International Financial Management and Accounting*, **11** (1), Spring, 1–22; Don Herrmann, Tatsuo Inoue and Wayne B. Thomas (2000), 'The Persistence and Forecast Accuracy of Earnings Components in the USA and Japan', *Journal of International Financial Management and Accounting*, **11** (1), Spring, 48–70; Joseph Aharony, Chi-Wen Jevons Lee and T.J. Wong (2000), 'Financial Packaging of *IPO* Firms in China', *Journal of Accounting Research*, **38** (1), Spring, 103–26; In-Mu Haw, Daqing Qi and Woody Wu (2000), 'Timeliness of Annual Report Releases and Market Reaction to Earnings Announcements in an Emerging Capital Market: The Case of China', *Journal of International Financial Management and Accounting*, **11** (2), Summer, 108–31; Edward B. Douthett, Jr. and

Kooyul Jung (2001), 'Japanese Corporate Groupings (*Keiretsu*) and the Informativeness of Earnings', *Journal of International Financial Management and Accounting*, **12** (2), Summer, 133–59; Elizabeth A. Gordon (2001), 'Accounting for Changing Prices: The Value Relevance of Historical Cost, Price Level, and Replacement Cost Accounting in Mexico', *Journal of Accounting Research*, **39** (1), June, 177–200; Don Herrmann, Tatsuo Inoue and Wayne B. Thomas (2001), 'The Relation Between Incremental Subsidiary Earnings and Future Stock Returns in Japan', *Journal of Business Finance and Accounting*, **28** (9 and 10), Nov/Dec, 1115–39.

Canadian Academic Accounting Association for article: Mary E. Barth and Greg Clinch (1996), 'International Accounting Differences and Their Relation to Share Prices: Evidence from U.K., Australian, and Canadian Firms', *Contemporary Accounting Research*, **13** (1), Spring, 135–70.

Elsevier Science for articles: Kam C. Chan and Gim S. Seow (1996), 'The Association Between Stock Returns and Foreign GAAP Earnings versus Earnings Adjusted to U.S. GAAP', *Journal of Accounting and Economics*, **21** (1), February, 139–58; Donna L. Street and Kimberley A. Shaughnessy (1998), 'The Evolution of the G4 + 1 and Its Impact on International Harmonization of Accounting Standards', *Journal of International Accounting, Auditing and Taxation*, **7** (2), 131–61; Joseph H. Godwin, Stephen R. Goldberg and Edward B. Douthett (1998), 'Relevance of U.S.-GAAP for Japanese Companies', *International Journal of Accounting*, **33** (5), 589–604; Mary S. Harris and Karl A. Muller III (1999), 'The Market Valuation of IAS versus US-GAAP Accounting Measures Using Form 20-F Reconciliations', *Journal of Accounting and Economics*, **26** (1–3), January, 285–312; A. Rashad Abdel-khalik, Kie Ann Wong and Annie Wu (1999), 'The Information Environment of China's A and B Shares: Can We Make Sense of the Numbers?', *International Journal of Accounting*, **34** (4), 467–89; Roger C. Graham and Raymond D. King (2000), 'Accounting Practices and the Market Valuation of Accounting Numbers: Evidence from Indonesia, Korea, Malaysia, the Philippines, Taiwan, and Thailand', *International Journal of Accounting*, **35** (4), 445–70; Hollis Ashbaugh (2001), 'Non-US Firms' Accounting Standard Choices', *Journal of Accounting and Public Policy*, **20** (2), Summer, 129–53; W.R. Singleton and Steven Globerman (2002), 'The Changing Nature of Financial Disclosure in Japan', *International Journal of Accounting*, **37** (1), 95–111; Joseph P.H. Fan and T.J. Wong (2002), 'Corporate Ownership Structure and the Informativeness of Accounting Earnings in East Asia', *Journal of Accounting and Economics*, **33** (3), August, 401–25.

Every effort has been made to trace all the copyright holders but if any have been inadvertently overlooked the publishers will be pleased to make the necessary arrangement at the first opportunity.

In addition the publishers wish to thank the Marshall Library of Economics, Cambridge University, the Library of the University of Warwick and the Library of Indiana University at Bloomington, USA for their assistance in obtaining these articles.

Introduction

Gary K. Meek

This volume contains articles published from 1995 to the middle of 2002. The previous edition, *Country Studies in International Accounting – Americas and the Far East*, included articles published through 1994. Most of the articles in the previous edition had a US focus, reflecting the nature of the research literature at the time. It was noted in the introduction that international accounting research on issues of interest to Asia was growing, but still rather slight overall. In addition, there was almost no international accounting research in English dealing with Latin America. Research on Asian countries, especially China and Japan, has expanded significantly since then. Unfortunately, there is still scant English-language literature on Latin America.

The previous edition contained articles dealing with foreign currency translation and geographic segment reporting by US multinationals. A companion volume in the series, *Financial Reporting by Multinationals*, also contained articles on these two subjects. For the current series, the editors decided to include all papers on foreign currency translation and segment reporting in the companion volume. Thus, the reader should see *Developments in Financial Reporting by Multinationals* for articles on these two topics.

This volume is arranged into three major sections: accounting regulation and policy choice, the Americas, and the Far East. The Americas section includes articles focusing on the United States, Canada, and Mexico, and the Far East section includes articles on China, Japan, and other Asian countries. The articles in the Americas and Far East sections cover three broad areas: disclosure practices, the properties of accounting earnings, and the value relevance and informativeness of accounting information. Studies on disclosure practices deal with actual corporate reporting practices and their causes or their effects. Studies on the properties of accounting earnings are concerned with such issues as earnings management and the persistence of earnings components. Studies of the value relevance and informativeness of accounting information focus on the relation between accounting measurements (such as the book value of stockholders' equity and earnings) on securities prices and returns. Table 1 cross-references the articles in the Americas and the Far East sections to these three topical areas. An analysis of the articles in the three sections follows.

Accounting Regulation and Policy Choice

Accounting regulations are the rules that must be followed in preparing financial statements. In many countries, these include laws and statutes and they are sometimes called *generally accepted accounting principles* (GAAP). The accounting regulatory process differs greatly around the world, but it is becoming increasingly global in nature. Accounting regulations

Table 1 Topical Areas of Articles on the Americas and Far East

	Disclosure Practices	Properties of Accounting Earnings	Value Relevance and Informativeness of Accounting Information
Americas			
• USA	6: Lang and Lundholm [1996] 7: Botosan [1997]		8: Barth and Clinch [1996] 9: Harris and Muller [1999] 10: Rees and Elgers [1997] 11: Chan and Seow [1996]
• Canada	12: Baginski et al. [2002]		
• Mexico			13: Gordon [2001] 14: Davis-Friday and Rivera [2000]
Far East			
• China	15: Haw et al. [2000]	16: Aharony et al. [2000]	17: Abdel-khalik et al. [1999] 18: Bao and Chow [1999]
• Japan	19: Cooke [1996] 20: Singleton and Globerman [2000]	21: Herrmann et al. [2000]	22: Godwin et al. [1998] 23: Charitou et al. [2000] 24: Douthett and Jung [2001] 25: Herrmann et al. [2001]
• Other Asian Countries	26: Craig and Diga [1998]		27: Graham and King [2000] 28: Fan and Wong [2002]

Note: Numbers refer to article numbers.

typically contain a set of policies from which a company may choose. The first three papers in the section are about accounting regulation, while the last two concern the incentives behind the accounting policies chosen by companies.

An important development during the 1990s was the establishment of the G4+1. Reflecting an 'Anglo-Saxon' emphasis on fair presentation and full disclosure, the G4+1 comprised the standard setters of Australia, Canada, the United Kingdom, and United States, with the secretariat of the International Accounting Standards Committee as observer. Later, the New Zealand standard setter joined. All had similar conceptual frameworks and the discussion papers issued helped to coordinate the standard setting efforts of the group. G4+1 activities ended in 2001 when the new International Accounting Standards Board (IASB) was appointed. Street and Shaughnessy (Chapter 1, this volume) review the history and work of the G4+1 and assess the impact of the group's work on the standards published by its member bodies. The G4+1 clearly had the result of converging accounting standards in the member countries.

Zeff (Chapter 2, this volume) provides insights into the functioning of the US financial reporting regulatory system. The US system is arguably the best known, but its actual functioning is often misunderstood outside the United States. US accounting is regulated by a private sector body (the Financial Accounting Standards Board, or FASB), but a governmental agency (the Securities and Exchange Commission, or SEC) underpins the authority of its standards. Even though the SEC has the legal authority to prescribe accounting and reporting standards for public companies, it relies on the private sector to set them. Despite the fact that the FASB and the SEC work closely together, conflicts have occurred. At times, the SEC has delayed or overruled pronouncements or has imposed its own requirements. Zeff also contrasts the European and US regulatory environments.

An issue in the US regulatory environment is whether the standards promulgated by the IASB should be an acceptable substitute for those of the FASB. The SEC requires listed companies to use US GAAP in their SEC filings. Dye and Sunder (Chapter 3, this volume) discuss arguments for and against allowing companies a free choice between IASB or FASB rules. The result of such a free choice would be to introduce competition into the accounting standard setting process in the United States. Interestingly, this paper appeared just before the 2001–2002 US accounting scandals. Some of the arguments presented in this paper (for example, 'if it's not broken, don't fix it') are likely to be viewed differently in light of these scandals.

The final two papers in this section deal with accounting policy choices by companies. In Chapter 4 of this volume, Ashbaugh investigates the factors associated with the choice of International Accounting Standards (IAS) or US GAAP by non-US companies. She first investigates why these companies choose either IAS or US GAAP over their domestic GAAP in preparing financial statement information. She then assesses the choice between IAS and US GAAP. The paper uncovers certain incentives behind these choices and, to some extent, informs the debate in Chapter 3.

Inoue and Thomas (Chapter 5, this volume) is about accounting policy choice in Japan. Specifically, the authors examine hypotheses about income increasing or income decreasing accounting policy choices by Japanese companies. Certain factors found to have influenced such accounting policy choices in the United States are examined, but the authors also tailor their hypotheses to the Japanese environment. Some of their results are surprising. For example, company size – typically viewed as a proxy for political costs – is found to be a significant variable. Given the close relationship between Japanese business and the government, one would not expect Japanese companies to face political costs the way US companies do. As the authors point out, size probably represents a more general characteristic than political costs in the Japanese context. This paper shows how empirical studies from one national setting can be adapted to another.

Americas

USA

The first two papers in this section focus on the disclosure practices of US companies, specifically the benefits of increased disclosure. Companies must meet minimum disclosure requirements set by accounting regulations, but they often voluntarily disclose additional information beyond the requirements. Even for mandatory disclosures, there can be substantial variation in the informativeness and amount of detail provided.

In Chapter 6 of this volume, Lang and Lundholm investigate the effects of disclosure on analyst following and the accuracy of their forecasts. Based on a survey of analysts, they measure the informativeness of a company's disclosure policy, divided into three categories: the annual report, other published information such as quarterly filings and press releases, and investor relations. The disclosure scores across these three categories are highly correlated, suggesting that companies adopt overall strategies for informing the public. The authors find that companies with more forthcoming disclosures have a greater analyst following, more consensus among analysts' earnings forecasts, more accurate forecasts, and less variable forecast revisions. The results imply that by disclosing more, companies can enlarge their potential pool of investors and improve investors' evaluations of past performance and expectations about future performance.

Botosan (Chapter 7, this volume) examines the effect of disclosure level on the cost of equity capital, an issue of considerable importance to the financial reporting community. A significant benefit of improved disclosure should be a lower cost of capital. Voluntary annual report disclosures are used to measure disclosure level and the cost of equity capital is estimated using the so-called Edwards-Bell-Ohlson valuation formula. She finds that greater disclosure is associated with a lower cost of capital for firms with low analyst following, but no evidence of an association for firms with high analyst following. Despite the mixed results, this paper is important because it provides a direct empirical link between better disclosure and lower capital costs.

An issue that has continued to occupy the attention of researchers is the so-called value relevance of restatements of accounting measurements from non-US to US GAAP. The previous edition had papers by Bandyopadhyay, Hanna and Richardson and Amir, Harris and Venuti. These papers examined the value relevance of foreign firms' restatements to US GAAP in their SEC filings. Barth and Clinch (Chapter 8, this volume) extend this line of research. Bandyopadhyay, Hanna and Richardson focused exclusively on Canadian companies and Amir, Harris and Venuti's sample was a cross-section of companies from 20 countries, excluding Canada. Barth and Clinch look at Australian, Canadian and UK firms. They find that earnings restatements and stockholders' equity restatements are incrementally value relevant for Australian and UK firms, but generally not, for Canadian companies. The non-result for Canadian companies is therefore consistent with Bandyopadhyay, Hanna and Richardson.

Harris and Muller, in Chapter 9, this volume, examine the value relevance of the restatement between International Accounting Standards and US GAAP. The SEC has been considering for some time whether to allow companies to use IAS in lieu of US GAAP in their Form 20-F filings. They find that the earnings restatement is value relevant but the stockholders' equity restatement is not. Further, they find that IAS amounts are more highly associated with prices than US GAAP amounts, but that US GAAP amounts are more highly associated with returns. Despite their inconclusive results, some evidence is provided supporting the SEC's traditional position that reconciliations to US GAAP, even from IAS, provide useful information to the market.

One reason for the mixed evidence on the value relevance of restatements is that investors may be able to anticipate (some or all of) the restatement information through alternative information sources, such as domestic financial statements and interim earnings announcements. This is the premise behind Rees and Elgers (Chapter 10, this volume). First-time SEC filers must provide earnings restatements for the previous three years and stockholders' equity restatements for the previous two years. These retrospective restatements to US GAAP provide an opportunity to test for the existence of alternative information sources. Finding an association even before the initial disclosure suggests that the Form 20-F is not the exclusive source of this information. This is what Rees and Elgers find, though they do not identify the alternative sources of information.

The literature on the value relevance of restatements has distinguished the incremental information content and the relative information content of alternative GAAP. The former focuses on the value relevance of the restatement given domestic GAAP, while the latter is concerned with which GAAP's information is more value relevant than the other. The previous studies have all been about the incremental value relevance of restatements to US GAAP. Chan and Seow (Chapter 11, this volume) are concerned with the relative information content of home versus US GAAP earnings (but not stockholders' equity). Their findings indicate that foreign GAAP earnings have greater information content than US GAAP earnings. This result questions the SEC requirement for US GAAP information. Overall, the mixed evidence on the value relevance of restatements does not resolve the debate on the efficacy of the SEC's requirement for them.

Canada

Why do companies from some countries disclose more voluntary accounting information than companies from other countries? In Chapter 2, this volume, Zeff argues that the litigiousness of American society contributes to the volume and detail of US GAAP. Baginski, Hassell and Kimbrough (Chapter 12, this volume) test the hypothesis that this litigiousness also dampens the amount and character of voluntary disclosure by US companies. One type of voluntary disclosure is the management earnings forecast. They compare earnings forecasts between Canada and the United States, two otherwise similar business environments with different legal regimes. They find that the frequency and characteristics of voluntary earnings forecast disclosures differ across the two countries. Canadian managers disclose more earnings forecasts in periods of both 'good' and 'bad' news, and their forecasts are more precise and of longer range. US managers also behave differently in the face of bad news: their forecasts are more frequent, less precise, and of shorter horizon.

Mexico

Inflation-adjusted accounting is a key difference between accounting in Mexico, and that in the United States and Canada. The next two papers examine the value relevance of Mexican inflation-adjusted accounting information. Gordon (Chapter 13, this volume) examines the value relevance of historical cost, price level, and replacement cost accounting (in the context of Mexican GAAP) using a sample of Mexican firms from 1989 to 1995. Until 1997, Mexican GAAP required price level accounting, and allowed replacement cost accounting in the main accounts. After 1997, replacement cost accounting was no longer allowed. These different bases of accounting can be gleaned from disclosures in the companies' annual reports. Gordon tests both the incremental and relative value relevance using Mexican share price data. She finds that price level and replacement cost accounting adjustments are value relevant beyond historical cost. Replacement cost adjustments are relatively and incrementally relevant beyond both historical cost and price level measures while price level adjustments are incrementally value relevant beyond historical cost measures. One implication of the results is that discontinuing replacement cost eliminated value relevant information.

In Chapter 14, this volume, Davis-Friday and Rivera focus on the difference between Mexican and US GAAP. The sample consists of US-listed Mexican companies and uses their US share prices for analysis. They examine the relationship between share prices and Mexican versus US GAAP net income and stockholders' equity. They find that both Mexican and US GAAP accounting measures are individually value relevant, but that the SEC Form 20-F reconciliation between the two is not. In other words, once you have one set of numbers, either Mexican or US GAAP, there is no incremental gain to adding the second set. In essence, this paper adds to the 'mixed evidence' referred to earlier on the value relevance of the SEC required restatement from non-US to US GAAP.

Far East

China

It is a well-documented phenomenon in developed capital markets such as Australia and the United States that companies accelerate the release of good news and delay the release of bad news. In Chapter 15, this volume, Haw, Qi and Wu examine whether this phenomenon occurs on the Chinese stock market. They find that it does. 'Good news' firms tend to release their annual reports earlier than 'bad news' firms, and loss firms release their annual reports the latest. Firms also accelerate the release of their annual reports when they have good news to report and they delay the release when there is bad news. The study also finds share price reactions to the release of the annual report for both early and late reporting firms. This implies that Chinese GAAP accounting information provides useful information to investors.

The process of listing Chinese state-owned enterprises began in the early 1990s. Aharony, Lee and Wong (Chapter 16, this volume) examine the earnings properties of the first initial public offering (IPO) firms available to foreign investors. These firms are classified as 'protected' or 'unprotected.' Protected companies are large monopolies under direct supervision of the state. Because of their close ties to the state bureaucracy, they receive special treatment from the state regulatory agencies for public listing and they face less stringent profitability requirements for listing than other ('unprotected') firms. Unprotected firms have professional managers, have more freedom to set prices and face more competition than protected firms. The authors hypothesize that there will be greater earnings management by unprotected firms than by protected firms. In addition, some IPOs occurred on the Chinese markets while others were on the Hong Kong exchange. Their evidence indicates that Chinese IPO firms engage in earnings management, and that the pattern of earnings management depends on the firm's relationship with the government and where its shares are listed.

The next two papers examine the value relevance of accounting measurements reported by Chinese companies. In Chapter 17, this volume, Abdel-khalik, Wong and Wu focus on the information environments represented by Chinese A-shares and B-shares. A-shares are only sold domestically to locals and only adopt Chinese accounting standards. Here, the information environment is relatively unstructured and informal. By contrast, B-shares are sold only to foreign investors, and companies offering B-shares must prepare financial statements using IAS and audited by international CPA firms. The information environment is relatively more arm's-length and reliable. The A-share information environment is viewed as 'low quality' while the B-share information environment is viewed as 'high quality'. The authors hypothesize that the disclosure of earnings for A-shares will not affect securities prices while the disclosure of earnings for B-shares will. The results are actually the opposite. The explanations of their counter results offer some good lessons for researchers importing methodologies from developed capital markets to developing capital markets.

In Chapter 18, this volume, Bao and Chow use an approach similar to Chan and Seow (Chapter 11, this volume), to assess the relative information content of earnings and book value based on Chinese GAAP versus IAS. Their sample consists of B-share firms, required to issue financial statement information under both sets of accounting standards. The results show that earnings and book value reported using IAS have greater information content than those based on Chinese GAAP. These results are inconsistent with the B-share results reported in Chapter 17. Taken overall, the studies in this section provide some, but not conclusive, evidence of the value relevance of accounting measurements under both Chinese GAAP and IAS.

Japan

The next two papers examine the disclosure practices of Japanese companies. These practices are generally perceived as being secretive, reflecting cultural norms of Japanese society. Cooke (Chapter 19, this volume) examines whether disclosure levels vary based on whether or not the company is part of a *keiretsu*. Given that *keiretsu* are characterized by stable, cross-shareholdings in which information is shared within their respective networks, it is hypothesized that firms in a *keiretsu* will disclose less information than those not in one. Firms in a *keiretsu* face fewer pressures and economic incentives for the disclosure of information than their non-*keiretsu* counterparts. In essence, *keiretsu* and non-*keiretsu* represent two corporate governance systems operating in Japan. Cooke develops a disclosure index of required and voluntary disclosures to test his hypothesis. He finds no evidence that companies belonging to a *keiretsu* disclose significantly less information than non-*keiretsu* companies.

In Chapter 20, this volume, Singleton and Globerman investigate whether Japanese companies changed their disclosure practices over the 1990s in response to the changing economic environment of the Japanese economy. The pre-1990 period is characterized as a 'bubble' economy, followed by adjustments in the first half of the 1990s in which bankruptcies and business failures increased, and asset prices began to fall. The Japanese economy was in a major recession in the second half of the 1990s; the bubble finally burst. The authors hypothesize that the pressure for Japanese corporate disclosure intensified over the 1990s, reflecting increased global competition and a banking crisis that forced many firms to seek capital outside Japan. They use Botosan's disclosure index (Chapter 7, this volume) to capture voluntary disclosures. They find that disclosures increased over the 1990s, consistent with the economic incentives tied to changing market conditions.

Herrmann, Inoue and Thomas (Chapter 21, this volume) compare the persistence and forecast accuracy of increasingly disaggregated components of earnings of both Japanese and US companies. Persistence is the extent to which an earnings component maps into future earnings. If the components of earnings differ in persistence, then disaggregation of these earnings components should increase the ability to forecast future earnings. They find differences in the persistence of earnings components for Japanese and US companies. The forecast accuracy of earnings also improves with increased disaggregation for both Japanese and US companies. However, the improvement in accuracy is greater for US than for Japanese companies. This result is consistent with more detailed US guidelines for reporting earnings components producing a better differentiation in the persistence of these components.

The next set of papers focuses on different aspects of the value relevance and informativeness of accounting information provided by Japanese companies. In Chapter 22, this volume, Godwin, Goldberg and Douthett examine the incremental information content of US GAAP information (over Japanese GAAP) for Japanese companies. Similar to other studies of this type (see the earlier discussion under the USA) they find mixed evidence of the value relevance of US GAAP. Overall, the value relevance results are stronger for stockholders' equity than for earnings. One limitation of this study is its small sample size.

Charitou, Clubb and Andreou (Chapter 23, this volume) provide empirical evidence on the association of earnings and cash flows with securities returns. Their evidence shows that cash flows are incrementally value relevant given earnings and that earnings are incrementally value relevant given cash flows. Further, they find that the value relevance of earnings decreases and cash flows increases as earnings become more transitory. Their evidence is broadly consistent with empirical evidence from the United States and supports recent changes in Japanese financial reporting requirements for additional cash flow information.

Chapter 24, this volume (Douthett and Jung) is concerned with the informativeness of earnings for *keiretsu* and non-*keiretsu* firms. They find that the informativeness of earnings is greater for *keiretsu* firms than non-*keiretsu* firms. Within *keiretsu* firms, informativeness increases with the strength of the *keiretsu* relationship. Given that disclosures are comparable between *keiretsu* and non-*keiretsu* firms (see Chapter 19, this volume), the results support the idea that the *keiretsu* relationship improves the monitoring of managerial performance.

In Chapter 25, this volume, Herrmann, Inoue and Thomas examine the pricing of parent-only and subsidiary earnings of Japanese companies. A widely held view is that parent-only data provide a more reasonable basis for valuing Japanese companies than consolidated data. They investigate the extent to which parent-only earnings and subsidiary earnings persist in next year's consolidated earnings and then examine whether the securities market understands these time-series behaviors. Their results indicate that the Japanese stock market adjusts correctly for the persistence of parent-only earnings, but the market appears to underestimate the persistence of subsidiary earnings in current stock prices. Even though they show the value relevance of consolidated information, their results indicate that the Japanese stock market misprices this information on a timely basis. Recent changes in Japanese financial reporting regulations have promoted consolidated data over parent-only data. The mispricing documented in this study may disappear in time.

Other Asian Countries

The remaining papers focus on several Asian countries rather than individually on China or Japan. In Chapter 26, this volume, Craig and Diga compare disclosure regulations and annual report disclosure practices of five Asian countries: Singapore, Malaysia, Indonesia, the Philippines and Thailand. They find a high degree of consensus among the five countries in terms of shared disclosure requirements. However, there is substantial variation across the countries in terms of compliance with these requirements. Company size and industry affiliation also influence disclosure practices. Curiously, foreign owned companies tend to disclose less than locally owned companies. Social and nonfinancial disclosures are minimal.

Graham and King (Chapter 27, this volume) compare the value relevance of accounting earnings and book values in six Asian countries: Indonesia, South Korea, Malaysia, the Philippines, Taiwan and Thailand. They find that accounting measurements are value relevant in all six countries but that the value relevance differs across these six countries. These differences in value relevance are generally consistent with differences in their requirements in terms of conservatism and clean surplus accounting.

Concentrated ownership and insider control are characteristics of the business environment in most East Asian countries. In Chapter 28, this volume, Fan and Wong examine the effect of these characteristics on the value relevance of accounting earnings in seven Asian countries: Hong Kong, Indonesia, Malaysia, Singapore, South Korea, Taiwan and Thailand. They find that earnings become less informative, in terms of the earnings-return relationship, as ownership concentration and insider control increases. An implication of their findings is that the mere adoption of more transparent accounting standards and disclosure rules (such as IAS) will not necessarily result in more informative accounting in these countries.

Part I
Accounting Regulation and Policy Choice

[1]

The Evolution of the G4 + 1 and Its Impact on International Harmonization of Accounting Standards

Donna L. Street
Kimberley A. Shaughnessy

This research consists of a historical review of the formation and work of the G4 + 1 and an assessment of the impact of the group's work on the standards published by its member bodies. From the perspective of the user-driven model of financial reporting, the research supports the view that a significant achievement of the IASC is its successful efforts to build relationships with national standard setters, particularly the Anglo-Americans that comprise the G4. During the 1990s, the G4 + 1 has reaped substantial benefits from its cooperative endeavors and has contributed much to accounting thought and regulation.

Criticisms of the G4 + 1 are also explored. Specifically, some argue the G4 + 1 is an effort to maintain Anglo-Saxon dominance of accounting. Others fear the IASC's continuing existence and dominance as the international accounting standard setting body may be threatened by the G4.

In concluding, the future of the G4 + 1 is considered in relation to the restructuring of the IASC. An argument is made that if the restructuring proposal is modified to address G4 concerns continued cooperation between the G4 and IASC is likely. However, if the restructuring plan is implemented in its present form, the G4 and IASC may begin working independently with the result being the development of two competing sets of internationally recognized standards.

Key Words: *G4 + 1; IASC; harmonization of accounting standards*

INTRODUCTION

Throughout the twentieth century, the world's industrial economies have experienced dramatic growth and change. Unprecedented increases in foreign invest-

Donna L. Street and **Kimberley A. Shaughnessy** • James Madison University, School of Accounting, Harrisonburg, VA 22807.

Journal of International Accounting, Auditing & Taxation, 7(2):131-161 ISSN: 1061-9518

ment, the formation of regional economic groups (such as the European Union), and the desire of multinational enterprises to provide capital for their operations has intensified the importance of developing comprehensive methods to manage public finances and enhance financial information comparability (Radebaugh and Gray 1997). Such a global business focus has caused companies throughout the world to change the way they do business (Carsberg 1996). According to Mogg, Director-General of the European Commission (EC), when different countries "establish commercial relationships and exchange capital flows, the need arises to be able to understand and use the financial information produced by their counterparts." Moreover, that information must be deemed both reliable and relevant.

The international business community has thus been forced to commit to and undertake the daunting task of reconciling the accounting practices of different nations in an effort to improve the comparability of financial information. There are three feasible approaches to achieve this objective: mutual recognition of accounts, reconciliation with national standards, or harmonization (Cairns 1995). The current focus is on achieving harmonization. Many look to the International Accounting Standards Committee (IASC) to play a major role in this endeavor.

The IASC was created in 1973 through the diligent efforts of the professional accountancy bodies in the United Kingdom (UK), United States (US), Australia, and Canada, among others. Numerous objectives underlying the goal of accounting standard harmonization have been achieved in the ensuing 25 years. While several groupings of national standard setting bodies have cooperated to promote harmonization and at times issue comparable standards, perhaps the most significant contributions towards harmonizing accounting standards internationally have been associated with the "Group of 4" (or G4). The G4 initially consisted of national standard setters from the UK, Australia, Canada and the US. Currently, New Zealand (NZ) is also a member. With the addition of the IASC, the group is referred to as the G4 + 1. The G4 + 1 meets four times a year to discuss key financial reporting issues with the aim of ensuring that future accounting standards are harmonized among its members. Given the potential global impact of the work produced by the G4 + 1, the group's individual and collective philosophies and strategies merit investigation, especially in light of the IASC's current restructuring plan.

The current research consists of a historical review of the formation and work of the G4 + 1 and an assessment of the impact of the group's work on the standards published by its member bodies. Prior to discussing the G4 + 1, a brief history of the IASC is provided followed by a review of the current harmonization policies of the G4 members.

A Brief History of International Standard Setting

When classifying accounting systems, researchers often refer to the Anglo-American accounting model. The model can generally be described as one that emphasizes investors and creditors in a private standard-setting environment (Beresford 1992). Anglo-American accounting is practiced not only in the UK and US, but also in other countries where the UK has had a major colonial influence including Canada and Australia. The Anglo-American model has significantly affected the philosophy and objectives of the IASC, particularly in recent years. According to the G4 + 1, its member bodies "share an objective of providing quality financial standards for the primary purpose of providing information useful to capital market participants" (Paul 1997).

The International Accounting Standards Committee

Numerous accountancy bodies, including those in the UK, US, Australia and Canada, have recently arrived at the conclusion that a large majority of accounting problems could be better resolved at an international, rather than a national, level (Carsberg 1996). A critical first step towards attaining some degree of similarity in accounting standards at the international level was taken in 1966 when the Accountants' International Study Group was formed through the cooperative efforts of professional accountancy bodies in the US, the UK, and Canada.

Significant progress toward the development of a set of international accounting standards (IASs) began to be made in 1972 when an agreement was formed to establish the IASC at the World Congress of Accountants. In 1973, through an agreement made by professional accountancy bodies from Australia, Canada, France, Germany, Japan, Mexico, the Netherlands, the UK, Ireland, and the US, the IASC commenced operations. The IASC was founded with two stated objectives:

a. to formulate and publish in the public interest accounting standards to be observed in the presentation of financial statements and to promote their worldwide acceptance and observance and,
b. to work generally for the improvement and harmonization of regulations, accounting standards, and procedures relating to the presentation of financial statements.

Three Stages of the IASC's Development. The IASC has passed through three distinct stages (Epstein and Mirza 1997). Stage one encompassed the early years, from 1973 through 1982, when the IASC attempted to promulgate a common body of standards through the examination and evaluation of the treatments used for all the major accounting issues. Essentially, the IASC ended up endorsing practically all of the conventional methods used by the major nations. As a result, the IASs produced during this period generally permitted numerous alternatives with no obvious conceptual basis. Despite this lack of clear leadership, the period was significant as it served to establish the IASC's legitimacy as an international standard setting body.

During stage two, which began in 1983, the IASC decided to obtain a first hand view of the accounting standard processes in place throughout the world. The IASC established a goal of visiting the standard setting bodies in each board member's country. By the time the IASC had embarked on its Comparability and Improvements project with the issuance of Exposure Draft (E) 32 in 1989, the IASC had visited the standard setting bodies in each board member's country (except Taiwan) in addition to 15 other countries (Cairns 1997a). Via the Comparability Project, the IASC reduced the number of alternatives allowed in ten IASs to facilitate comparability and promote harmonization. Stage two marked the culmination of a successful period in the IASC's history. By establishing relationships with national standard setting bodies, the IASC was able to further its own harmonization agenda, which is viewed by some to be among the IASC's most significant achievements to date (Cairns 1997a).

The IASC is now in the third stage of its evolution. The era is marked by the pursuit of harmonization objectives and the endorsement of major stakeholders, such as the International Organization of Securities Commissions (IOSCO). The IASC has embarked on an aggressive timetable to conclude a work program that will culminate in the issuance of a core set of standards. In accordance with a 1995 agreement, IOSCO will then review IASs and consider whether the standards are acceptable for cross-border securities registrations (*CA Magazine* 1995). Such an endorsement would represent a clear milestone for the IASC.

IASC Today. As of 1998, the IASC comprised 122 members and six associate or affiliate members, representing 91 countries including the founding members. Most of the founding members (including the major English-speaking nations of the US, UK, Canada, and Australia) currently maintain membership on the governing board and retain a significant measure of influence over its direction. The IASC's first chairman, Lord Benson, predicted in 1973 that the impact of the IASC would not be radical or immediate, but, rather, would rise to commanding importance in the preparation and presentation of financial statements by about the year 2000 (Cairns 1993). His predictions have proved prophetic.

In addition to issuing 38 IASs, the Board has completed a *Framework for the Preparation and Presentation of Financial Statements*. This framework facilitates the Board's efforts in developing future IASs and reviewing existing standards. The IASC relies on the precepts in the framework when discussing issues with other standard setting bodies (Cairns 1995). This is particularly evident regarding the IASC's recent endeavors with the G4.

As part of a strategy review, an IASC working party currently is considering a new structure for the IASC (Cairns 1997b). Carsberg, Secretary General of the IASC, has noted that the purpose of this most recent IASC strategy review is to establish a new relationship between the IASC and national standard setters. Preliminary indications are that the G4 will play a major role in the IASC's future in that, along with standard setters from a few other countries, this group of national standard setters will draft IASs. The proposed IASs may then be subject to approval of the IASC Board. The latter issue is currently the subject of debate.

G4 Member's Harmonization Objectives

UK. During the brief history of the UK's Accounting Standards Board (ASB), Financial Reporting Standards (FRSs) have been developed with due regard to international developments (Davies, Patterson and Wilson 1994). Reflecting its support of the IASC's harmonization effort, the ASB generally forges national standards that conform with IASs. Tweedie, ASB Chair, has stated that the Board will follow IASs unless there is a specific reason not to do so. Currently, the ASB Chair serves as a UK representative on the IASC Board.

Australia. Prior to completion of the IASC Comparability Project, compliance with Australian GAAP guaranteed compliance with IASs. However, modifications to the ten revised IASs yielded significant differences with Australian standards. In 1996, the Australian Accounting Standards Board (AASB) and the Public Sector Accounting Standards Board of the Australian Accounting Research Foundation (AARF) issued Policy Statement 6. The objective of the statement was to change Australian accounting standards and to influence the development of and changes to IASs so that an Australian reporting entity complying with Australian accounting standards would also be complying with IASs (Peirson and McBride 1997). When a conflict between the Australian standard and the IAS exists, the AASB, the AARF and IASC will work together to identify an acceptable approach to remove the incompatibility. Issuance of the 1996 International Harmonization Policy commits the AASB to a strategy designed to assist in the development of an internationally accepted set of accounting standards which can be adopted in Australia (AARF 1997). The program is expected to yield approximately 20 revised AASB standards.

The Australian government proposed new arrangements for the setting of accounting standards in September 1997 (Cairns 1997c; and *Double Entries* 1997). The new structure would include wider adoption of IASs in Australia "when they have been accepted for reporting purposes in major capital markets."

Canada. Because of the connection between the US and Canadian capital markets, Canadian financial reporting practices generally are not markedly different from the US. As more foreign subsidiaries and multinational entities conduct business in Canada, efforts to internationalize accounting standards have taken on greater importance. In 1975, the Canadian Institute of Chartered Accountants

(CICA) Handbook first included a Recommendation on conformity with or deviations from IASs (Murphy 1986). Handbook Section 1501, which was issued in 1996, states that the Canadian Accounting Standards Board (AcSB) supports the objective of international harmonization and notes that the Board will work with the IASC to minimize differences between IASs and corresponding Canadian Recommendations. Whenever a significant difference between Canadian GAAP and an IAS is discovered, a project is initiated to modify the CICA Handbook, unless disagreement exists with the IAS (Skinner 1987). The AcSB (or its predecessor) has often utilized an IAS as the basis of a new or revised accounting rule.

> Recently, the Inter-Institute Vision Task Force Report, recommended that a key goal should be to:
>
> harmonize accounting and auditing standards globally with a particular focus on developing common standards on an integrated basis (including developing new standards and responding to emerging issues), first in North American and then internationally" (Hillier and Smith 1996).

One of the objectives included in the 1993–1997 five-year plan of the AcSB was "to work with IASC and FASB with the aim of harmonizing accounting standards, and consider adopting IASC and FASB standards." In a 1997 report, the CICA Task Force on Financial Reporting recommended that Canada continue to make contributions to the global standard setting process.

US. The FASB (1997) formulated its first strategic plan for international activities in 1991. Overall, the FASB desires to achieve greater comparability between US accounting standards and those issued by other national standard setting bodies and by the IASC. The FASB concedes that the IASC is the logical focal point for harmonization efforts. Currently, the FASB serves on the IASC Consultation Committee, and a Board member attends IASC meetings as an observer. In addition, the FASB intends to engage in joint multinational standard-setting projects on mutually selected topics. The goal of these projects will be to arrive at separate national standards that are in substantial agreement with one another. The FASB also states that it will compromise and consider adopting IASC, or foreign national, standards that are deemed to be superior to their US counterparts. Beresford, then FASB Chair, stated that the US plans to move its standards "a little closer to the IASC and UK way of doing things" in order to have broad standards requiring more professional judgment in their application (Kelly 1997).

An Era of Cooperation–the Formation and Evolution of the G4 + 1

During the "third stage" of its evolutionary process, the IASC has faced great pressure to complete a set of high quality core standards that would make possible an IOSCO endorsement. To achieve, and possibly accelerate its harmonization goals, the IASC has become more cognizant of the need to work with national standard setters. According to Carsberg (1996), a cooperative effort among the most influential and organized accounting standard setters, whose high professional standards are universally recognized, must be initiated to facilitate the goal of international standard harmonization. Among the likely candidates to participate with the IASC in such an endeavor are the accounting standard setters from the US, the UK, Australia, and Canada, especially in view of each entity's keen interest in and commitment towards harmonizing standards and their strikingly similar conceptual frameworks.

Prior to the 1990s, the IASC's history of cooperative efforts had been limited. The initial structure of the IASC required that contact between the Board and the national standard setting bodies be made through the professional accountancy bodies (the IASC member bodies). Accordingly, contact and coordination between the IASC and other standard setters left much to be desired. For example, Cairns (1997a) states that during the early 1980s, the IASC was almost destroyed by the efforts of standard setters in Canada, the UK, and the US to find a common solution to foreign currency accounting. The French and Germans were annoyed that while they were putting forth considerable effort and funding into the IASC, the AcSB, UK Accounting Standards Committee (the ASB's predecessor), and FASB were making private agreements outside the IASC. The problem was compounded by the fact that France and Germany disagreed with the accounting proposals advocated by Canada, the UK, and the US.[1]

In November 1980, the IASC passed the following resolution.

> Because members have agreed that IASC is the appropriate forum for the development and publication of International Accounting Standards, the Board of IASC requests Member Bodies to use their best endeavors to ensure that the IASC Board is kept fully informed of all initiatives within their country towards the development of accounting standards and that, when any discussions on accounting standards are proposed between two or more countries that do not share common legislation, *IASC is invited to participate*[2] therein on the understanding that any such participant does not have the authority to commit IASC in such discussions without the express authority of the Board of IASC. (IASC 1993a)

Following its 1980 resolution, the IASC engaged in a few cooperative endeavors with other standard setters. For example, in 1981 the IASC formed a working party of standard setting bodies in the Netherlands, the UK, and the US to review the possibility of greater harmonization on accounting for corporate taxes. The working party's output formed the basis for a draft version of a revised IAS on Accounting for Income Tax (IASC 1993a). Four years later, the IASC arranged a meeting of standard setting bodies in Canada, the UK, and the US to discuss accounting for pension costs.

These early cooperative endeavors can be viewed as limited successes at best. Regarding income taxes, harmonization between the IASC and the US, Canada, and Australia was only recently achieved (Street and Shaughnessy 1998).[3] The UK continues to endorse an alternative treatment (partial allocation). However, the ASB (1997a) argues that with the issuance of IAS 12, revised, comprehensive allocation has become the only internationally accepted method. Thus, the ASB is consulting interested parties, and a financial reporting exposure draft (FRED) consistent with IAS 12, is expected in late 1998.

Although pension accounting also continues to represent an area of divergence, the January 1998 revision of IAS 19 brings the IASC and US and Canadian standards closer together. The UK ASB (1997a) is reconsidering pensions but has noted that the IASC approach differs from the UK's preferred approach. And, Australia, which was hoping to develop a standard based on the revision of IAS 19, has expressed dissatisfaction with IAS 19 Revised (AASB and AARF 1998a). The position taken by the UK ASB in its forthcoming FRED and by the AASB will determine the degree of harmonization among the G4 + 1 in the area of pension accounting.

In 1993, the IASC confirmed its 1980 resolution (IASC 1993a) within the context of further concerns about joint activities among national standard setting bodies. Cairns (1997a) argues that it is this resolution which emphasizes the importance of the IASC's participation in the work of groups of standard setters such as the G4.

In 1990, the IASC approved a five-year plan that included the objective of working for:

> ...greater comparability between national accounting requirements (whatever their form) and International Accounting Standards and the removal of existing differences between those requirements and International Accounting Standards (IASC 1990).

The 1991–1995 plan placed greater emphasis on contact between IASC and national standard setting bodies. To accomplish this goal, the IASC agreed to:

- continue visits to national standard setting bodies;
- establish task forces with national standard setting bodies on those topics for which there was further scope for the improvement or harmonization of existing requirements; and
- to hold a conference of national standard setting bodies to discuss appropriate accounting issues.

As early as 1987, the IASC had proposed a regular meeting of standard setting bodies. Following adoption of the new five-year plan, the first such meeting was organized by the IASC and the FEE (the European accountancy profession) in June 1991. Similar meetings followed on an annual basis. The G4 and the IASC conceived the notion of the "future events" project at the second such conference of world standard setters. At the third conference, the G4 and the IASC first exposed the position paper *Future Events* to a large audience. The 1991–1995 five-year plan truly set the stage for the IASC to increase its interaction with national standard setters such as the G4.

Birth of the G4 + 1 and the Future Events Position paper

In 1992, the UK ASB Chair visited the FASB offices, and the Canadian AcSB Chair was invited to join the discussions (D.P. Tweedie, personal letter May 15, 1997). During the meeting, it became apparent that all three standard setters had problems with provisioning (e.g., UK-the big bath provision and US-environmental/decommissioning provisions). The standard setters agreed to work jointly on provisioning issues. This agreement represented the first step in the development of the G4 working group.

In the spirit of the 1991 conference hosted by the IASC, the FASB hosted a meeting of world standard setters following the 1992 World Congress held in Washington, DC. Topics of discussion included cooperative efforts to improve accounting standards and future attempts towards harmonization. During that meeting, the UK, US, and Canadian standard setting bodies made a general invitation for other national standard setters to join their working group (D.P. Tweedie, personal letter May 15, 1997). The Dutch and Australians volunteered to participate, although the Dutch later dropped out.

Following the conference, the G4 continued to work on provisions and proceeded to commence development of a series of cases addressing the recognition and measurement of future events. The immediate objective was to produce a position paper to be presented at an upcoming meeting of world standard setters (IASC 1993b). Thus, both the initial meeting of the Chairs of the US, UK, and Canadian standard setters at the FASB offices and the subsequent agreement of the G4 (along with the IASC) to work on the future events project marked the beginning of the G4 meetings (D.P. Tweedie, personal letter May 15, 1997).

Comments made at the 1992 Washington World Congress of Accountants and the subsequent meeting of world standard setters hosted by FASB raised concerns regarding the level of cooperation between national standard setters. Primarily, the main issue centered on the IASC's involvement, or apparent lack of involvement, in such arrangements (IASC 1993a). At the world standard setters meeting, IASC Chairman Sharpe revealed that the IASC had recently agreed to consider a formal strategic plan supporting cooperative endeavors. During a March meeting, the IASC also considered how it might lead, or otherwise be involved in, cooperative efforts between national standard setting bodies.

An invitation to participate in the future events project had been extended to the IASC because the G4 did not wish others to believe that the major

TABLE 1
Future Events: A Conceptual Study of Their Significance for Recognition and Measurement (1994) Principal author: L. Todd Johnson (FASB)

- First G4+1 output.
- Addresses two primary issues:
  1) Whether and/or when to recognize such events as assets or liabilities, and,
  2) the most appropriate measurement criteria to employ.
- Measurement issues focused on:
  1) the role of future events that are probable,
  2) future economic events, and
  3) future legal requirements.
- Considerable consensus was gained throughout the study, however, measurement criteria relating to probable future events received dissenting viewpoints.
- Recognition issues centered on:
  1) the relationship between costs and future benefits,
  2) the relationship between obligations and future sacrifices,
  3) the role of management intent, and
  4) perceptions of the past event and probable future benefit or sacrifice.

English-speaking standard setters were keeping secrets from the rest of the world. According to D.P. Tweedie (personal letter May 15, 1997), then G4 Chair, "By inviting the IASC to participate, the G4's intentions should be apparent to others." The IASC's new strategic plan was consistent with its decision to work on the future events project with the G4.

Following an IASC board meeting in Oslo, the UK ASB hosted a Conference of Standard-Setting Bodies in London in November 1993 (FASB 1994; IASC 1994). At the conference, which was held under the auspices of the IASC, the G4 and IASC working group (now dubbed the G4 + 1) exposed its future events case to a larger audience representing 18 countries and three international organizations (ASB 1994a).

Because each member of the G4 + 1 was of the opinion that concepts should play a principal role in the setting of accounting standards, the issues addressed in the study were considered from a conceptual basis. In addition, the viewpoints of the participating individuals were purely their own and had not been deliberated previously by the accountancy bodies represented (Johnson 1994). At a debriefing following the future events debate, the G4 + 1 (FASB 1996):

- Agreed to jointly publish the future events paper
- Agreed to continue to meet as a group
- Agreed to meet twice a year (with different hosts, at either free-standing meetings or linked to meetings such as an IASC Board Meeting)
- Committed to harmonization within group
- Committed to achieving efficiencies for members

The cases and views of the working group were summarized in 1994's *Future Events: A Conceptual Study of Their Significance for Recognition and Measurement* (see Table 1). Announcing *Future Events*, the FASB (1994) argued that the publication represented a "milestone in international cooperation." The FASB stated that the purpose of the study was "to help standard setters worldwide to develop a common conceptual foundation on which they can base accounting standards for their respective countries concerning issues that involve future events."

Introducing *Future Events*, the UK ASB (1994a) asserted that the research study reflected increasing international cooperation between accounting standard setters. The ASB Chair stated:

> This thought-provoking study explores some major problems that affect all five of the bodies that took part. The study shows that there was wide agreement between the members of the working group, reflecting the similarity of the principles on which we base our work. The study is an excellent example of the benefits of international cooperation. I believe that it will help standard-setters across borders and thus make an important contribution to international harmonization.

The IASC was also pleased with the outcome of future events endeavor and sought to continue to coordinate agendas with the G4, and other standards setters, in an effort to adopt common solutions (Carsberg 1996).

During April 1994, the FASB (1994) hosted a G4 + 1 meeting. The group agreed that given the success of the future events project, the G4 + 1 should meet on a more regular basis with the goal of analyzing new case studies encompassing financial reporting dilemmas. Topics of discussion at the April meeting included financial instruments, joint ventures, and goodwill.

With its members committed to future endeavors, the G4 + 1 further developed its goals. The group initially viewed its purpose as ensuring that standards were harmonized among its members. During its first years, the G4 + 1 did not actually set accounting standards but attempted to agree the broad principles and then encourage each member to then prepare its own national policy (D.P. Tweedie, Personal letter May 15, 1997).

Other G4 + 1 Joint Position Papers

Major Issues Related to Special Hedge Accounting. During 1995, the G4 + 1 experienced a fruitful year. In its revised plan for international activities, FASB (1995) noted that the "accounting concepts working group" would continue to meet regularly and that such meetings would lead to the identification of common problem areas which would benefit from joint consideration. In May, the G4 + 1 met in conjunction with the World Standard Setters meeting in Amsterdam. At this meeting, the FASB led a discussion on hedge accounting

TABLE 2
Major Issues Related to Hedge Accounting (1995)
Principal authors: Jane B. Adams and Corliss J. Montesi (FASB)

- Outlines the arguments and raises a number of questions related to:
  1) the definition of risk and measuring the exposure to risk,
  2) methods of managing risk and reducing exposure, and
  3) accounting for the effects of risk management, including deferral of gains and losses, options, and cash and synthetic instrument accounting.
- Only achieved concurrence on recognizing and measuring derivative financial instruments using fair value.
- The publication provides a discussion of four broad alternatives so that readers can have a context for assessing the issues discussed.
- The alternatives presented provide standard setters with the opportunity to analyze different approaches that could be used to resolve the issue in their own jurisdiction.

based on a G4 + 1 project (IASC 1995a). Following the conference, the G4 + 1 published its second position paper, *Major Issues Related to Special Hedge Accounting* (Adams and Montesi 1995, see Table 2).

Prior to the publication, the IASC and G4's individual standards provided limited guidance centering on the recognition and measurement of hedging instruments. The objective of the hedge accounting project was to facilitate understanding, not provide resolution, of significant issues. Members of the G4 + 1 did agree, however, that derivative financial instruments should be recognized and measured at fair value.

Borrowing from the G4 + 1 position paper, 1998's SFAS 133 requires that all derivatives be recognized at fair value. Changes in fair values are to be reported either in net income or comprehensive income (another G4 + 1 project) depending on the classification of the derivative.

The G4 + 1 position paper has also been utilized by the IASC financial instruments steering committee in developing proposals on hedging (IASC 1995b). An IASC Draft Statement of Principles (DSOP), that was prepared jointly with Canada, was published in 1997. The IASC DSOP argued that all financial assets/liabilities should be measured at fair value and that all changes in fair value should be presented as income/expense (see Cairns 1997d).

The Australian Society of CPAs (ASCPA 1997) welcomed the IASC DSOP noting that the proposals provide a sound basis for the development of a truly international standard. The ASCPA has requested that the AASB issue the IASC DSOP as an Australian discussion paper.

A 1996 UK discussion paper on derivatives and other financial instruments concludes that present measurement practices are no longer adequate and proposes that all financial instruments should be measured at current values (ASB 1996a).

In September 1997, the G4 + 1 (with NZ) announced its members would work together to complete national and international standards requiring the use

TABLE 3
Provisions: Their Recognition, Measurement, and Disclosure in Financial Statements (1995)
Principal authors: Andrew Lennard and Sandra Thompson (UK ASB)

- Provisions should be recognized when:
  1) an enterprise has a present obligation to transfer economic benefits as a result of past events. A present obligation exists when the enterprise has little or no discretion to avoid the transfer of economic benefits; and
  2) a reasonable estimate of the amount of the obligation can be made.
- The amount provided for provisions should be the best estimate of the expenditure that will be required to settle the obligation that existed at the balance sheet date.
- The G4+1 argues that the amount provided for should be discounted if this has a material effect.
- Disclosures should include the following:
  1) a brief description of the nature of the obligation, and
  2) if there is significant uncertainty over the amount or timing of the expenditure that will be made, the factors that are relevant to determining them, and
  3) the amount provided for and, if estimated, the basis on which the estimate has been made.
- In addition to discussing the general principles for reporting provisions, their specific application in two circumstances where provisions are often recognized are discussed:
  1) future operating losses, and
  2) restructuring costs.

of fair values for all financial instruments (Cairns 1997e; AARF and AASB 1998b). The (then) Chair of the G4 stated that the project represents the first time the group will be developing a standard rather than a position paper.[4]

In October 1997, the IASC Board voted against a staff recommendation that as an interim step the Board adopt all US standards on financial instruments. Alternatively, the Board decided that IASC should join with national standard setters to develop "an integrated and harmonized international accounting standard on financial instruments" (IASC 1997a).

With the addition of representatives from France, Germany, Japan, and five Nordic countries to the G4, the Financial Instruments Joint Working Group (JWG) has now replaced the IASC financial instruments steering committee. The JWG aims to produce an international standard by 2000 (IASC 1998). The JWG will report to the G4 + 1, the IASC, and the participating standard setting bodies.

Provisions: Their Recognition, Measurement, and Disclosure in Financial Statements. In 1995, the G4 + 1 issued a position paper on the very topic that had motivated the Chairs of the US, UK, and Canadian standard setting boards to conceive the G4, *Provisions: Their Recognition, Measurement, and Disclosure in Financial Statements* (Lennard and Thompson 1995, see Table 3). The G4 + 1 elected to address provisions because the member bodies' existing standards clearly provide little guidance regarding the most appropriate accounting treatment (see Street and Shaughnessy 1998; Skinner 1987; Davies et al. 1994;

and AARF 1997). Such guidance is critical because related transactions often are material to a reporting entity's financial position.

The aim of the G4 + 1 position paper is to develop a common conceptual understanding of the issues to enhance the prospect of international harmonization (IASC 1995c). Such an understanding was viewed as vital because Canada, the UK, and the US were in the process of developing standards on some or all of the issues covered in the study. In addition, the IASC was scheduled to begin a project on provisions and contingencies. At the time of publication, each of the five standard setting bodies were expected to utilize the publication when developing or revising their individual standards on provisions. This has definitely been the case for the IASC and UK ASB.

In 1996, the IASC added provisions and contingencies to its agenda as a joint project with the UK. The ASB Chair was appointed Chair of the IASC Steering Committee, and the committee drew from the G4 + 1 position paper (IASC 1996a). During 1997, IASC E 59 and FRED 14 were issued. Consistent with the G4 + 1 position paper, these EDs argue that provisions (including product warranties, environmental liabilities, future operating losses, and restructuring costs) are liabilities and should be recognized if, and only if, there is a present obligation to transfer economic benefits as a result of past events. Provisions should be carried at the best estimate of the amount required to settle the obligation that existed at the balance sheet date (IASC 1997b and ASB 1997b). The IASC and ASB are soon expected to issue similar standards. In April 1998, Australia's ED 88 set forth proposals consistent with the IASC and UK proposals (AASB and AARF 1998c).

Accounting for Leases: A New Approach. During 1996, the G4 + 1 met in Toronto, Edinburgh, and Norwalk, Connecticut (IASC 1996a). In addition, the working group met via video conferencing. Early in 1996, the G4 appointed the UK ASB Chair to serve as its first Chair. While some viewed the appointment as a threat to the IASC (Cairns 1996), the new G4 Chair insisted the move was "purely administrative" and not a threat to the IASC (*Accountancy* 1996). Tweedie also stated that the G4 meetings were "very open"[5] and that the group was not planning to take on the IASC at is own game. He continued, "We find the meetings very useful. It saves a lot of time if we can argue out the issues first."

Also during 1996, NZ participated in the preparation of the G4 + 1 position paper, *Accounting for Leases: A New Approach* (McGregor 1996, see Table 4). The position paper discusses the limitations of current leasing standards (see Street and Shaughnessy 1998; Skinner 1987; Davies et al. 1994; and Godfrey and Warren 1995) and advocates new approach whereby all non-cancelable leases would be capitalized.

Initially, the IASC intended to utilize the G4 + 1 position paper as a basis for performing a limited review of IAS 17. However, leasing represents a critical

TABLE 4
Accounting for Leases: A New Approach (1996)
Principal author: Warren McGregor (AARF)

- Spotlights similarities in:
  1) the definitions of assets, liabilities, equity, revenues, and expenses, and
  2) in the recognition criteria found in the conceptual frameworks of the G4+1 (including NZ).
- Examines whether existing lease accounting standards ensure that financial statements include relevant and reliable information about assets and liabilities arising under lease contracts.
- Resulted in the development of the following "different" approach to accounting for leases:
  1) A lease contract conveys a contractual right to a lessee to use the economic benefits embodied in the lease property during the lease term, and creates a contractual obligation on the lessee to compensate the lessor for use of property.
  2) Such assets and liabilities arise under both operating and finance leases.
- The new approach:
  1) removes the distinction between operating and finance leases (a key feature of current leasing standards)
  2) recognizes in the financial statements of lessees all material rights and obligations arising under lease contracts that meet the conceptual framework definitions of assets and liabilities
  3) avoids many problems currently encountered in applying leasing standards.
- Implementation issues addressed include:
  1) the distinction between "non-cancelable" leases, giving rise to rights and obligations, which meet the definitions of assets and liabilities, and "cancelable" leases,
  2) the treatment of contingent rentals, renewal options, and sale and leaseback transactions,
  3) the economic distinctions between a lease and similar contractual commitments, i.e., purchase commitments and executory contracts, and
  4) the implications for lessor accounting.

aspect of the IOSCO agreement (IASC 1996b) and, facing a self-imposed 1998 deadline, the IASC decided to limit its review of IAS 17 to issues IOSCO considers essential. Accordingly, initial changes to IAS 17 Revised, which was approved in October 1997, focus on enhanced disclosure for lessees and lessors and eliminates the current free choice of methods for lessors to recognize finance lease income.

Executory contracts and leases were revisited by the G4 + 1 during its March 1997 meeting in Sydney, Australia. Specifically, the problem of distinguishing leases from executory contracts was addressed as the G4 + 1 considered case studies prepared by Australia. The cases were designed to assist the group in identifying the key issues related to the existence and nature of rights and obligations arising from executory contracts and how those rights and obligations should be recognized and measured. The G4 + 1 is developing a paper aimed at identifying the principal characteristics of executory contracts that will address alternative accounting treatments (Cairns 1997f).

Also at the March 1997 meeting, Australia and the UK agreed to coordinate activities on the new approach to leases (Cairns 1997f). Australia will look at

TABLE 5
International Review of Accounting Standards Specifying a Recoverable Amount Test for Long-Lived Assets (1997)
Principal author: Jim Paul (AARF)

- Identifies differences between accounting standards that specify a recoverable amount test and major issues requiring resolution.
- Reviews the following competing models:
  1) SFAS 121
  2) IASC E 55, and
  3) UK ASB FRED 15.
- These models differ in that the US does not allow discounting when conducting the test for impairment. The UK and IASC model requires discounting.
- The US model prohibits reinstatement of previously recognized impairment write-downs; however, the IASC and UK provide for reinstatement.
- Consensus views achieved:
  1) Profit-seeking entities should apply a recoverable amount test to long-lived assets held for future use.
  2) Accounting standards need a screening mechanism based on indicators of potential impairment because estimating the impairment recognition trigger of each asset or group of assets each reporting period is too costly.
  3) An assertion that a loss in value is "permanent" should not be a required condition for an impairment write-down.
  4) Accounting for impairment requires estimates of net cash flows for determining the impairment recognition trigger and sometimes for re-measuring assets. Those estimates should be based on the expected selling prices for the asset's products over the asset's remaining useful life, using reasonable and supportable assumptions and projections.
  5) Expected net cash flows from future use that are used to measure the impaired value should be discounted using a current market-determined rate of discount.
  6) When estimating cash flows, assets should be grouped at the lowest level for which there are identifiable net cash inflows that are largely independent of the net cash inflows of other groups of assets.
  7) When assessing assets obtained via a business acquisition for recoverability, goodwill should be attributed to assets or groups of assets as reliably as possible. When an impairment write-down is recognized for a group of assets including goodwill, it should be applied to any physically impaired assets first, to goodwill second, and to other assets thereafter.
- Also discusses issues on which a consensus could not be reached and provides a basis on which harmonization can be pursued while developing needed improvements to those standards.

scope, and the UK will address other issues related to lease accounting. At a September 1997 meeting, the G4 + 1 discussed the recognition of revenue on executory contracts. Australia will explore the implications in a series of case studies for a future group meeting.

According to Cairns (1997f), FASB representatives at the March 1997 meeting appeared more interested in the new approach than they had in the past. Australia and the UK are focused on developing an accounting standard, and the IASC is also committed to the new approach. The IASC's interest may be linked to IOSCO's suggestion that the IASC should consider, as a long term project, a new approach such as that explored in the G4 + 1 position paper (IASC 1996b). Currently, there is some discussion among the G4 + 1 members regarding the possibility of developing a joint discussion paper on leasing with an indication of future direction in all member countries (D.P. Tweedie, personal letter April 1, 1998).

International Review of Accounting Standards Specifying a Recoverable Amount Test for Long-Lived Assets. Australia has been leading a G4 + 1 project directed at minimizing differences in members' standards regarding asset impairment (Street and Shaughnessy 1998). The G4 + 1 discussed impairment at the group's March 1997 meeting. The impetus behind the discussions centered on a paper prepared by Australia relating to differences among members' standards. A key area of contention centers on the appropriate base for identifying or measuring the impaired asset. The G4 + 1 did agree, however, that the time value of money should be considered whenever the impaired asset is revalued (Cairns 1997f). In late 1997, a position paper that summarizes the G4 + 1 views was published (see Table 5). This position paper, entitled *International Review of Accounting Standards Specifying a Recoverable Amount Test for Long-Lived Assets*, provides a basis on which harmonization of accounting standards can be pursued while developing needed improvements.

In the preface to the position paper, the G4 + 1 sets forth its objectives. The G4 + 1 organizations share the objectives of (Paul 1997, iii):

- providing quality financial standards for the primary purpose of providing information useful to capital market participants
- seeking common solutions to financial reporting issues. A single, quality financial reporting approach is more useful to capital market participants than multiple approaches.

The position paper further stated that the G4 + 1 organizations seek to:

- learn more about the timing and approach of standard setting agenda projects in other countries. That knowledge can help them identify and take advantage of opportunities to coordinate their efforts and thereby further their shared objectives
- further their shared objectives by exchanging new ideas and approaches to financial reporting issues and standard-setting processes that can be applied in their own countries
- further their shared objectives by pooling resources and ideas in joint research efforts.

TABLE 6
Reporting Financial Performance: Current Developments and Future Directions (1998)
Principal authors: L. Todd Johnson (FASB) and Andrew Lennard (UK ASB)

- Discusses the components of financial performance that should be reported and sets out two broad approaches that might be pursued by standard-setters:
  1) The dual approach incorporates a conventional measure of earned/realized profit.
  2) The single perspective approach focuses on comprehensive income, which defines financial performance as encompassing all recognized transactions and events other than those with owners.
- The large majority of the Group favored the comprehensive income approach.

Reporting Financial Performance: Current Developments and Future Directions. In early 1998, the G4 + 1 (with NZ) published *Reporting Financial Performance: Current Developments and Future Directions* (Johnson and Lennard 1998, see Table 6).

While recently issued standards of the G4 + 1 members (i.e., FRS 3, SFAS 130, and IAS 1 Revised) require the reporting of comprehensive income, several areas of debate remain. Thus, the G4 + 1 has agreed to undertake Phase 2 of its comprehensive income project. During this phase, the group is addressing issues relating to reporting financial performance that were either not addressed or not resolved in the first phase (AARF and AASB 1998b). The Group has agreed to consider:

- How should the main components of financial performance identified in Phase 1 (Operating Activities, Financing and Other Treasury Activities, and Other Gains and Losses) be interpreted?
- How should corrections of errors be presented?
- How should the effects of changes in accounting policies and changes in accounting estimates be presented?
- How should continuing/discontinuing activities be presented?
- How should reclassification (recycling) adjustments be presented?

The above issues were debated at a January 1998 G4 + 1 meeting in London and later in 1998 at a meeting in Wellington, New Zealand. Currently, the UK ASB is writing a paper on comprehensive income that may be exposed as a joint discussion paper with an indication of future direction in all member countries (Tweedie 1998). The G4 + 1 expects to publish the joint discussion paper in early 1999.

G4 + 1 Forthcoming Publications

Joint Ventures. At the March 1997 meeting, the G4 + 1 considered a Canadian paper that identifies the unique characteristics of joint ventures and reviews the current accounting standards and proposals of the group members (Cairns 1997f; also see Street and Shaughnessy 1998). The Canadian paper addresses the diversity of accounting alternatives and presents the arguments regarding each. Based on its discussion of the paper, the G4 + 1 gained consensus concerning the use of equity accounting for joint ventures, "including those in which the venturers have an undivided interest in the assets of the joint venture." An anticipated G4 + 1 publication, tentatively titled "*Bases of Reporting Interests in a Joint Venture: Conceptual, Methodological, and Practical Issues*," will discuss the pros and cons of the alternative treatments for accounting for joint ventures.

The UK ASB's recent project on associates and joint ventures reflects the Board's commitment to harmonization with its G4 + 1 partners. A discussion paper (ASB 1994b) acknowledged that joint ventures have become an increasingly common feature of business and there is at present "a good deal of uncertainty as to how they should be treated in the accounts." While the Board stated a preference for the equity method in its discussion paper, FRED 11 (ASB 1996b) stated that either the equity method or proportional consolidation should be used based on the characteristics of the joint venture. Yet following the March 1997 G4 + 1 meeting, the ASB modified the proposals set forth in FRED 11 and moved in line with the G4 + 1 consensus. FRS 9 (ASB 1997c) states that joint ventures are to be included in the venturer's consolidated financial statements using the gross equity method.[6]

Government Grants. The G4 + 1 brought up the issue of government grants during its March 1997 meeting after reviewing a paper prepared by NZ. This paper addressed measurement and recognition issues centering on Government Grants and contributions (Cairns 1997f). The issue was further discussed at a September 1997 meeting. There is general agreement among the G4 + 1 that unrestricted contributions as well as contributions with restrictions attached should be recognized as revenue by the recipient when control is obtained by the entity (AARF and AASB 1998b). However, there is disagreement over the treatment of contributions with contributor-imposed conditions. The G4 + 1 plans to further discuss government grants at its August 1998 meeting in Edinburgh and aims to publish a paper during late 1998.

Other G4 + 1 Ongoing Projects

Business Combinations and Goodwill. In 1996, the FASB added business combinations to its agenda. In a Special Report (Johnson and Yokley 1997) the FASB notes that its decision was influenced by the SEC's view that APB Opinions 16 and 17 need to be modified. Another rationale for the project flows from the need for accounting standards to be comparable internationally. Many of the FASAC members who supported undertaking the project cited promoting international comparability as the most significant reason.

In March 1997, members of the G4 + 1 expressed concerns about the widespread use of pooling in the US (Cairns 1997f). Concern was also expressed over the disparity that exists among the G4 + 1 membership in accounting for purchased goodwill (see Johnson and Yokley 1997 for a review of the G4 + 1 individual member standards; see also Street and Shaughnessy 1998; Hillier and Smith 1996; Epstein and Mirza 1997; and Tweedie 1996). Similarities among the AcSB, ASB, and IASC business combination standards might provide a basis for promoting comparability (ASB 1996c; Johnson and Yokley 1997). The approach set forth in the UK's FRED 12 (now FRS 10) and FRED 15 could serve as a possible basis for promoting comparability in accounting for purchased goodwill. Because the ASB and IASC were involved in projects related to business combinations and the FASB was adding its project, it was agreed that a unique opportunity existed to further international comparability.

At the March 1997 meeting, the FASB was skeptical regarding the Canadian, IASC, and UK approach of permitting the pooling method only when the acquirer cannot be identified (Cairns 1997f). However, the FASB stated that it intended to tighten the rules under which pooling is permitted. A further threat to harmonization surfaced at the meeting when the AcSB stated that it is under pressure to relax its requirements (Cairns 1997f). Some Canadian-based companies have threatened to move to the US to benefit from the FASB's more relaxed criteria for pooling. The G4 + 1 further discussed business combinations at a September 1997 meeting and agreed to retain the topic as an agenda item and to exchange information between meetings.

Recent events suggest FASB may indeed tighten up on pooling. In discussing a recent FASB project on goodwill, Larson of the FASB stated that the Board is trying to "come up with an answer on goodwill that's less likely to impact earnings. Then maybe people won't be so concerned if poolings go away" (in MacDonald 1998). The FASB (1998a) has stated, however, that international comparability of standards for business combinations will not dominate the Board's considerations.

Goodwill standards are not harmonized among the G4 + 1 members (Street and Shaughnessy 1998). Currently, the IASC is revisiting goodwill. IASC E 60 reasserts support for the capitalization and amortization of goodwill (IASC 1997c). Given the issuance of FRS 10 in the UK and a FASB press release (see MacDonald 1998) supporting the UK approach, the IASC is requesting feedback regarding whether goodwill always should be subject to amortization. Grant (1996) argues that Australia will likely follow the approach eventually adopted by the IASC.

The UK's FRS 10 presents an alternative to the "capitalize and amortize" approach. FRS 10 holds that goodwill need not be amortized if the value of goodwill is significant, expected to be maintained indefinitely, reliably measured in the future, and an impairment review indicates no diminution in value (ASB 1998 and Johnson and Yokley 1997). However, if the life is expected to be limited, goodwill should be amortized on a systematic basis, that is restricted to 20 years. And, FASB has recently announced that it is considering a very similar approach under which:

> Purchased goodwill that has a limited and determinable useful life would be amortized over the weighted average of the useful lives of its discernible elements.
>
> Purchased goodwill that has a useful life that is not determinable would not be amortized but would be subject to an impairment review. (FASB 1998b)

If the FASB adopts the UK approach, the IASC may reconsider its position. In which case, given their commitment to harmonize with IASs, Australia and Canada would likely consider adopting the capitalization without amortization approach for goodwill. In the meantime, with the issuance of FRS 10, the G4 + 1 now concur that goodwill should be capitalized but continue to disagree regarding amortization policy.

Discounting and Pensions Costs. Movements towards harmonization with respect to discounting are gaining momentum, although several areas of disagreement currently exist. Chief among the areas of contention is pension cost accounting (ASB 1997d). The G4 + 1 discussed discounting initially at its March 1997 meeting as a result of the review of UK and US publications regarding the appropriate bases for discounting cash flows relating to assets and liabilities (Cairns 1997f).

In 1997, the UK ASB published *Discounting in Financial Reporting*. The paper presents a coherent approach to discounting by addressing measurement issues on such long term assets and liabilities as provisions, pension costs, and impairment of fixed assets (ASB 1997d). The working paper underscores the relevance of recording long term items using the time value of money and the notion of how misleading such statements can be when these items are not discounted.

A FASB discussion memorandum was issued in December 1990, and, in February 1996, a Special Report entitled *The FASB Project on Present Value Based Measurements: An Analysis of Deliberations and Techniques* was disseminated. In 1997, an ED of a proposed Statement of Financial Accounting Concept (SFAC) was released which supported the use of the expected cash flow approach. The US and UK's preliminary documents differ in key aspects. Thus, the G4 + 1 effort to promote harmonization among members is of paramount importance.

At a September 1997 meeting, the G4 + 1 discussed a paper "Measurement of Pension Obligations" prepared by FASB staff members (AASB and AARF 1998b). The objective of the paper is to assist the G4 + 1 members in arriving at agreement on some of the basic underlying principles of pension accounting and to explore members' views on the discounting of future cash flows. The G4 + 1 has experienced significant difficulty in reaching agreement on the appropriate discount rate for measuring pension obligations.

The paper addressed three approaches to the measurement of future cash flows arising in relation to pension obligations. The three approaches are also discussed in the recent FASB ED *Using Cash Flow Information in Accounting Measurement.* The majority of the G4 + 1 members viewed the approach that determines the fair value by the present value of the future cash flows that an entity expects to pay to settle the obligation over its life as being conceptually superior or as a practical alternative.

At its September 1997 meeting, the G4 + 1 then agreed that there are three components to the measurement of the pension obligation under the above mentioned approach which are:

- The expected cash flows, discounted at the risk-free rate
- An adjustment for risks, such as mortality and liquidity, that are not correlated with market returns
- An adjustment, if possible, for risks that may be correlated with market returns.

The G4 + 1 has agreed to further develop the paper for discussion at future meetings.

Recognition in Financial Statements. At its September 1997 meeting, the G4 + 1 decided to update the 1982 FASB Research Report *Recognition in Financial Statements: Underlying Concepts and Practical Conventions* in that many issues discussed in the report are still relevant today and no country has fully developed principles for recognition (AASB and AARF 1998b). The G4 + 1 agreed to extend the Report to address new issues, such as accounting for executory contracts and leasing and to update some of the terminology and examples. The G4 + 1 also discussed a number of cases dealing with recognition issues and agreed to continue their deliberations at future meetings.

IASC Restructuring

At recent meetings the G4 + 1 has discussed the structure of the IASC, which has become a source of considerable concern among the G4 members. Some G4 members have commented that the present IASC structure is too "cumbersome" and "gives too much influence to countries with a second ranking technical expertise" (Cairns 1996). The G4 has proposed a reduction in the IASC Board size to no more than nine members. The Board would be supported by a "general assem-

TABLE 7
IASC Restructuring Proposal Main Proposed Changes Main Structural Changes

Main Structural Changes

- A Technical Committee of National Standard-Setters would replace IASC Steering Committees.
- Representation on the IASC Board would be widened.
- The IASC Foundation would replace the Advisory Council.

Main Procedural Changes

- The Technical Committee, rather than the IASC Board, would set the IASC's standard-setting priorities and agenda.
- IASC projects would be carried out as joint projects with national standard setters rather than being undertaken as separate projects.
- The responsibility for review of detailed technical content of final standards would be transferred from the IASC Board to the Technical Committee.
- Many of the responsibilities of the part-time IASC Chairman would be redistributed to the full-time chairman of the Technical Committee.
- Whereas the Advisory Council had its powers delegated by the IASC Board, the IASC Foundation's powers and responsibilities would be assigned by a revised IASC Constitution.
- The IASC Foundation, rather than the Advisory Council, would appoint IASC Board members, members of the Technical Committee and the IASC Foundation. The IASC Foundation also would appoint individual representatives to the IASC Board and chairpersons of the IASC Board and Technical Committee.
- The IASC Foundation would not participate in technical decisions of the IASC Board and would do nothing to impair the independence and objectivity of the Board.

Source: AARF and AASB 1998b.

bly involving more countries and interests" (Cairns 1997f). With a reduced Board size, the influence of the G4 over IASC actions would likely increase significantly, a fact which has led some to question whether the G4 has a hidden agenda. Cairns (1996) argues that "any threat to the IASC from the G4 + 1 is potentially much more significant because there would be little need for international accounting standards if national standard setting bodies could agree to common improvements in their national requirements."

An IASC working party currently is considering a new structure (see Table 7). Based on the current proposal, a standing committee consisting of national standard setters will take over the development of IASs (AARF and AASB 1998b; Cairns 1997b). Issuance of standards will be contingent upon approval of the IASC Board. The standing technical committee will have a full-time Chair and approximately ten other members. The committee will follow due process and will likely meet monthly in public.

The proposal was discussed at the G4 + 1 September 1997 meeting (AARF and AASB 1998b). The G4 are generally supportive of the new structure but have expressed concern about the proposed IASC Board veto over standards developed by the standing committee. According to the G4, the standing committee should have the power to issue IASs on its own authority. The IASC Board should be an advisory, not a supervisory, body.

Carsberg has noted that the purpose of the most recent IASC strategy review is to establish a new relationship between the IASC and national standard setting bodies. The modified structure will also improve the IASC's operating efficiency while continuing to allow a large number of countries to participate in the IASC's work. An exposure draft of the proposed changes is expected in late 1998. If the proposal becomes a reality, the importance of the G4 may increase exponentially.

PROGRESS TOWARDS HARMONIZATION

According to Cairns (1997a), among the most significant achievements of the IASC is its successful efforts to build relationships with national standard setting bodies during the 1980s and 1990s. Viewed from the perspective of the user-driven model of financial reporting endorsed by the G4 and the IASC, our historical review supports Cairns' contentions, particularly in regard to the Board's recent endeavors with the group of national standard setters known as the G4. Given the proposal regarding a new structure for the IASC, the IASC's liaisons with national standard setters, particularly members of the G4, will become even more crucial to the successful operation of the IASC.

In a 1993 presentation to the International Section of the American Accounting Association (AAA), McGregor, Executive Director of the AARF, stated that bilateral and multilateral cooperation between national standard setting bodies represents a growing trend (IASC 1993a). To gain real support at the national level, the IASC must include national standard setters in this process and, while the involvement of the FASB and the EC is important, the IASC must go further. McGregor further argued that the high level of exchange of technical information between national standard setting bodies should continue. He stated that standard setting bodies should investigate the possibility of joint research at the very beginning of a project and at staff interchanges. McGregor encouraged the IASC to become actively involved with these cooperative efforts and coordinate its work program to benefit directly from the product of such synergetic efforts.

At the same meeting, Denman of the CICA noted that one key benefit of accounting standard harmonization and the increased cooperative efforts of standard setters would be the cost savings that could be realized as the level of duplication decreased (Schweikart 1994). Standard setters had discovered during round table discussions in 1992 (the year the G4 was formed) that many countries were addressing the same issues concurrently without benefiting from each other's efforts. Taking up the challenge, numerous standard-setting bodies began to work in earnest towards reducing duplicate efforts and embarking on joint projects to accomplish the objectives of their individual and collective agendas.

In the years following McGregor's address, considerable progress has been achieved. The G4 and the IASC have reaped substantial benefit from their cooperative endeavors. While several groupings of national standard setting bodies have cooperated to achieve harmonization objectives during the 1990s, the efforts of the G4 must be deemed as the most significant. By focusing on the common threads inherent within each nation's conceptual frameworks and adopting a philosophy based on cooperation and teamwork, the G4, in cooperation with the IASC, has made a tremendous contribution towards harmonizing international accounting standards. The impact of the G4 + 1 efforts is only beginning to manifest itself in the actual accounting rules of the member bodies. Examples include the IASC's and UK's forthcoming standards on provisions and contingencies and the members' decision to work together to complete national and international standards requiring the use of fair values for all financial instruments.

In the near future, more significant movements toward harmonization are likely. For example, the group's work will likely result in minimizing differences in the members' standards on comprehensive income and impairment of long-lived assets. Collectively, the G4 + 1 may achieve improvements in financial reporting that would be very difficult, if not impossible, for any one of the standard setters to accomplish individually. For example, for any one standard setter acting alone, it would be unlikely that compliance could be achieved for an accounting standard requiring that all non-cancelable leases be capitalized.

The G4 + 1 maintained a relatively low profile throughout its initial years, yet, the working group is deemed responsible for the acceleration of the development of accounting thought and regulation, which endorses substantive change and facilitates the goal of reducing the amount of time necessary to promulgate new accounting standards. In fact, the due process time period has been reduced for the IASC. Its Steering Committees now rely significantly on the joint publication papers produced by the G4 + 1[8] and benefit greatly from other cooperative endeavors with national standards setters. An example being the forthcoming IAS on provisions which is based on a G4 + 1 position paper and a joint project with the UK. The effort to produce standards in an efficient manner may prove even more successful under the revised IASC structure, as national standard setters assume the responsibility for drafting IASs. Again, expectations are that the G4 will play a highly significant role in this endeavor.

Despite the G4 + 1's initial success stories, observers at the G4 + 1's first open meeting in March 1997 noted that the G4 + 1 gatherings have become notable for the frequency with which member viewpoints differ with respect to the best accounting practice to adopt (Curran 1997). For example, significant divergence was evident on issues such as measurement and comprehensive income. This observation is further evidenced by the lack of consensus apparent in the group's joint paper on International Review of Accounting Standards Specifying a Recoverable Amount Test for Long-Lived Assets. In this position paper, the G4 + 1 lists six major areas where the working group was unable to achieve consensus. Such differences serve as a reminder to the G4 + 1 members that, going forward into the twenty-first century, conceptual accounting issues such as ordinary income, realized profits, recognition and reliability will have to be revisited (Curran 1997). If the members can overcome their differences and master the art of compromise, the G4 + 1 will be poised to gain greater international influence.

G4 Viewed as a Threat

While the momentum behind the G4 + 1's continued presence is building as its multilateral endeavors are gaining wider notoriety, reaction to the IASC's involvement with the G4 has been mixed. Some fear that the IASC's continuing presence and dominance as the international accounting standard setting body may be threatened by the G4. For example, the host country initially chaired G4 + 1 meetings (*Accountancy* 1996). In 1996, however, the G4 appointed Tweedie its first chairman, a move that is deemed by some to be a clear indication of the group's objective to gain influence over the IASC (Cairns 1996).

Tweedie has denied that the G4 poses any threat to the IASC and commented that the position was designed primarily to ensure the group remained focused on the achievement of its objectives (Perrin 1996). The former G4 Chair (as of January 1998 the position has been held by Ken Spencer Chair of the AASB) envisions three basic future roles for the IASC:

1. producing standards for those countries that have no standards of their own
2. assisting in the reduction of diverse national practices; and
3. acting as an umbrella organization for national standard setters who will be working together on developing issues to produce common principles which could then be turned into international standards by the IASC (Schweikart 1994).

Clearly, the G4 can be viewed as the primary vehicle for fulfilling the third role.

Critics also claim the G4 + 1 is merely attempting to "maintain Anglo-Saxon dominance of accounting standards" (Cairns 1997g). In that the G4 + 1 represents a serious threat to those who support an alternative view of financial reporting such as Continental European members of the EU, the EU has recently increased its efforts to participate actively in IASC endeavors, primarily to counter the strong influence of the G4. *Accountancy* (1998) reports that the "European accounting heads have formed a think tank to give a more forceful voice to European concerns and rival the G4 + 1." Known as the E5 + 2, the group includes European board member from the Netherlands, France, Germany, Norway, and the UK, and representatives from the EC and the Federation des Experts Comptables Europeans.

The IASC has attempted to downplay criticism of the G4 + 1 and issued the following invitation in its 1995 Annual Review:

> We particularly want to extend the involvement of national standard setters to the non-English speaking countries where national standard setters may have a different constitution but an equally important contribution to make. (IASC 1995d)

Despite criticism of the G4 + 1, Cairns (1996) argues that the increased collaboration among standard setting bodies and the IASC has represented a significant change for the better. And, while there are those who might view these cooperative endeavors as a threat to the IASC, they are an important buttress for both the IASC and national initiatives.

THE FUTURE OF THE G4 + 1

As the IASC enters what may be referred to as its fourth stage of development, concerns regarding the threat posed by the G4 may significantly increase. Although the G4 is expected to play a major role in the new IASC structure, the group has expressed concern about the proposed IASC Board veto over IASs developed by the standing technical committee (Cairns 1997b). As key members of the IASC technical committee, the G4 members would contribute much to the development of IASs. A veto by the IASC Board could be followed by each G4 member adopting the proposal drafted by the technical committee as its national standard. Repeated episodes of this nature could result in the creation of two competing sets of internationally recognized accounting standards, G4 endorsed standards and IASs.

Alternatively, if the IASC Board has veto power, some, if not all, members of the G4 may refuse to serve as members of the IASC technical committee. Under this scenario, the G4 may elect to focus its resources on the development of harmonized accounting standards for G4 member nations. Again, this would yield a second set of internationally recognized standards to compete with IASs. This second scenario would be particularly problematic for the IASC if the G4 membership were to expand to include national standard setters from countries such as Germany, France, and Japan. Formation of a working group of national accounting standard setters representing most of world's market capitalization could mark the end of the IASC.

In conclusion, given the IASC's commitment to a user-driven model, cooperative endeavors with the G4 appear to represent the best way forward. If the IASC restructuring plan is revised to address the concerns of the G4, the outlook for continued cooperation between the G4 and IASC is more likely. Together the G4 + 1 members can continue to reap much benefit from their cooperative endeavors and contribute significantly to accounting thought and practice. The alternative scenario is less attractive whereby the IASC and G4 work independently to develop competing sets of internationally recognized standards.

NOTES

1. In SFAS 52, FASB (1981, par. 76) stated: "The Board maintained close liaison with representatives of the International Accounting Standards Committee and the accounting standards-setting bodies in Canada and the United Kingdom and Ireland as this Statement was developed. Representatives from each of these groups were active participants with the Board's foreign currency task force." Accordingly, following passage of its 1980 resolution, the IASC did eventually become an active participant in this cooperative endeavor.
2. Emphasis added.
3. ED 87 will bring Australia more in line with IAS 12 Revised.
4. Prior to the decision to develop a comprehensive financial instruments standard, the G4 + 1 did not engage in standard setting. However, various G4 + 1 members have cooperated in joint standard setting projects. One example is the IASC/UK provisions project, which is discussed in the next section. Others include: an US and IASC project on earnings per share which resulted in SFAS 128 and IAS 33; a US and Canada project on reporting disaggregated information which ran parallel to an IASC project which yielded SFAS 131, Canadian Handbook Section 1701, and IAS 14 Revised; and a Canadian and IASC project on financial instruments which resulted in IAS 32 and Canadian Handbook Section 3860.
5. In March 1997, the G4 + 1 held its first open meeting.
6. This new method of accounting expands the net amounts included under the equity method to show the venturer's share of its joint venturers' turnover, gross assets, and gross liabilities. Thus, the gross equity method gives more information about joint ventures than would be provided by the traditional equity method.
7. The decrease in time is also impacted by the 1998 IOSCO deadline.

REFERENCES

Accountancy. 1996, May. Tweedie to Chair G4, p. 15.

______. 1998, January (International Edition). E5 + 2: A Rival to G4 + 1, p. 8.

Accounting Standards Board (ASB). 1994a, October 3. Future events—Publication of collaborative research study. ASB Press Release: PN 53.

______. 1994b, July 28. Associates and joint ventures and the reporting entity: Publication of ASB Proposals. ASB Press Release: PN 49.

______. 1996a, July. Derivatives and other financial instruments. *Inside Track*, pp. 2-3.

______. 1996b, April. FRED 11 associates and joint ventures. *Inside Track*, p. 1.

______. 1996c, June 27. Publication of exposure draft (FRED 12) on goodwill and intangible assets. ASB Press Release: PN 76.
______. 1997a, January. Other current projects. *Inside Track*, p. 3.
______. 1997b, June 12. Provisions and Contingencies/Impairment of Fixed Assets and Goodwill Exposure Drafts Published. ASB Press Release: PN 92.
______. 1997c, November 27. Issue of FRS 9 associates and joint ventures. ASB Press Release: PN 105.
______. 1997d, April 17. Discounting in financial reporting – ASB document issued. ASB Press Release: PN 75.
______. 1998, January. Goodwill and Intangible Assets (Accounting Standard Issued). *Inside Track*, p. 1.
Adams, J.B. and C.J. Montesi. 1995. *Major Issues Related to Hedge Accounting*. AASB, AcSB, IASC, UK, ASB, FASB.
Australian Accounting Research Foundation (AARF). 1997. *Australian Company Financial Reporting*, J.B. Ryan and C.T. Heazlewood (Eds.): 113.
Australian Accounting Research Foundation and Australian Accounting Standards Board (AARF and AASB). 1998a, March 23. Australian boards disappointed with IASC standard on employee benefits. Media Release, AARF and AASB World Wide Web.
______. 1998b, February. G4 + 1 meeting. *The Standard*, pp. 31-34.
______. 1998c, February. Progress report on the IASC harmonisation program. *The Standard*, pp. 3-8.
Australian Society of CPAs (ASCPA). 1997, April 3. CPAs welcome international financial instruments proposals. ASCPA Media Release.
Beresford, D.R. 1992, June 30. The international scene from a U.S. perspective. *FASB Viewpoints*, pp. 6-10.
CA Magazine. 1995, October. IASC and IOSCO reach agreement, p. 13.
Cairns, D. 1993, July. The IASC–20 more years of vision and commitment. *Accountancy*, pp. 72-74.
______. 1995. *A Guide to Applying International Accounting Standards*. The Institute of Chartered Accountants in England and Wales: Central Milton Keynes.
______. 1996, May 16. Time for turf warriors to reach a peace accord. *Financial Times*.
______. 1997a. The future shape of harmonisation: A reply. *European Accounting Review* 6(2): 305-348.
______. 1997b, October. A new IASC. *FT World Accounting Report*, p. 4.
______. 1997c, October. New standard setting regime. *FT World Accounting Report*, p. 9.
______. 1997d, April. Fair values for all instruments. *FT World Accounting Report*, p. 4.
______. 1997e, October. IASC, G4 + 1 and U.S. Congress. *FT World Accounting Report*, p. 3.
______. 1997f, April. G4 + 1 – First open meeting. *FT World Accounting Report*, p. 13.
______. 1997g, April. Survey G4 + 1. *FT World Accounting Report*, p. 11.
Carsberg, B. 1996. The role and future plans of the international accounting standards committee. In I. Lapsley (ed.). *Essays in Accounting Thought: A Tribute to WT Baxter* (pp. 68-84). Edinburgh: The Institute of Chartered Accountants of Scotland.
Curran, B. 1997, April. G4 + 1A personal impression. *FT World Accounting Report*, p. 12.
Davies, M., R. Patterson, and A. Wilson. 1994. *UK GAAP: Generally Accepted Accounting Practice of the United Kingdom*, (4th ed.). Great Britain: MacMillian.
Double Entries. 1997. Proposals to reform Australian accounting standard setting 3 (28).
Epstein, B.J., and A.A. Mirza. 1997. *IAS 97: Interpretation and Application of International Accounting Standards*. New York: Wiley.
Financial Accounting Standards Board (FASB). 1981. *Statement of Financial Accounting Standards No. 52: Foreign Currency Translation*. Norwalk, CT: FASB.
______. 1994, August. *FASB Status Report*, FASB to Publish Special Report on Future Events, p. 1.

______. 1995, March 31. *FASB Status Report*, FASB's Plan for International Activities, pp. 6-10.
______. 1996, March 21. G4 + 1 Overview: A presentation at the AAA & KPMG Peat Marwick International Accounting Research Conference. Montvale, NJ.
______. 1997. *FASB's Plan for International Activity*. World Wide Web.
______. 1998a, April 13. Business combinations. *Financial Accounting Series Status Report*, pp. 8-9.
______. 1998b. Business Combinations (Project Update), World Wide Web.
Godfrey, J.M., and S.M. Warren. 1995. Lessee reactions to regulation of accounting for leases. *Abacus* 31 (2): 201-228.
Grant, S. 1996. Goodwill the debate that never ends. *Australian Accountant* 18: 20-21.
Hillier, D., and S. Smith. 1996, October. Global standard bearers. *CA Magazine*, pp. 50-53.
International Accounting Standards Committee (IASC). 1990, October. *IASC News*, p. 6.
______. 1993a, March. Cooperation by standard setting bodies. *IASC Insight*, p. 1.
______. 1993b, December. What is the role of future events in financial reporting. *IASC Insight*, pp. 6-7.
______. 1994, September. The significance of future events. *IASC Insight*, p. 3.
______. 1995a, May. *IASC Update*.
______. 1995b, September. Hedging. *IASC Insight*, p. 15.
______. 1995c, December. Provisions: Discussion paper issued. *IASC Insight*, p. 3.
______. 1995d. *Annual Review*, p. 4.
______. 1996a. *Annual Review*.
______. 1996b, September. Accounting for leases—time for a change. *IASC Insight*, p. 18.
______. 1997a, November. Financial instruments. *IASC Update*, p. 1.
______. 1997b, March. Provisions. *IASC Insight*.
______. 1997c, October. Intangible assets and goodwill: The solution. *IASC Insight*.
______. 1998, March. Plans for an integrated international standard. *IASC Update*, p. 7.
Johnson, L.T. 1994. *Future Events: A Conceptual Study of Their Significance for Recognition and Measurement* (pp. iii-vi, 1-56). AASB, AcSB, IASC, ASB, FASB.
Johnson, L.T., and B.D. Yokley. 1997, June. *Issues Associated with the FASB Project on Business Combinations*. Norwalk, CT: FASB.
Johnson, L.T., and A. Lennard. 1998. *Reporting Financial Performance: Current Developments And Future Directions*. AASB, AcSB, IASC, NZASRB, ASB, FASB.
Kelly, J. 1997, April. IASC/IOSCO—a hand on the brake. *FT World Accounting Report*, pp. 2-4.
Lennard, A., and S. Thompson. 1995. *Provisions: Their Recognition, Measurement, and Disclosure in Financial Statements*. AASB, AcSB, IASC, UK ASB, FASB.
MacDonald, E. 1998, April 27. FASB may change M&A accounting to favor cash over all-stock deals. *Wall Street Journal*, pp. A3 and A24.
McGregor, W. 1996. *Accounting for Leases: A New Approach*. AASB, AcSB, IASC, NZ ASRB, NZ FRSB, UK ASB, FASB.
Murphy, G.J. 1986. A chronology of the development of corporate financial reporting in Canada: 1850 to 1983. *The Accounting Historians Journal* 13 (1): 31-62.
Paul, J. 1997. *International Review of Accounting Standards Specifying a Recoverable Amount Test for Long-Lived Assets*. AASB, AcSB, IASC, NZFRSB, ASB, FASB.
Peirson, G., and P. McBride. 1997, April. More on international harmonization in Australia. *CPA Communiqué*. Australian Society of CPAs.
Perrin, S. 1996, April. IASC Backs Tweedie's role in G4. *Accountancy Age*, p. 24.
Radebaugh, L.H., and S.J. Gray. 1997. *International Accounting and Multinational Enterprises*. New York: Wiley.
Schweikart, J.A. 1994. Progress and impediments to world accounting harmonization: Comments from accounting standard-setters at the american accounting association annual meeting. *Journal of International Accounting Auditing & Taxation* 3 (1): 1-15.

Skinner, R.M. 1987. *Accounting Standards in Evolution.* Holt, Rinehart and Winston of Canada, Limited.

Street, D.L., and K.A. Shaughnessy. 1998. The quest for international harmonization: A Review of the accounting standard setting agendas of the IASC, US, UK, Canada, and Australia, 1973–1997. *International Journal of Accounting* 33 (2): 179-209.

Tweedie, D.P. 1996. The conceptual framework and the Accounting Standards Board. In I. Lapsley, (ed.), *Essays in Accounting Thought: A Tribute to WT Baxter* (pp. 41-67). Edinburgh: ICAS.

[2]

Accounting Horizons
Vol. 9 No. 1
March 1995
pp. 52–70

COMMENTARY

Stephen A. Zeff

Stephen A. Zeff is Herbert S. Autrey Professor of Accounting at Rice University and is Professor of Accounting at the State University of Limburg, The Netherlands.

A Perspective on the U.S. Public/Private-Sector Approach to the Regulation of Financial Reporting

INTRODUCTION

Today, companies or securities legislation in numerous countries either prescribes accounting and disclosure standards that must be reflected in company financial reports or authorizes a public-sector or private-sector agency to promulgate such standards. In some countries, such as Germany, legislation prescribes accounting and disclosure standards, but does not designate a standard-setting agency. In others, such as the United States, legislation does not prescribe standards but instead authorizes a government agency to do so. In still others, such as the United Kingdom, legislation prescribes standards and also makes provision for a private-sector agency to set standards. In Australia, legislation prescribes standards and explicitly authorizes a federal statutory board to set further standards.

Yet comparatively little attention has been given in most countries to securing actual compliance with the standards. Curious extremes may be cited in this regard. It has been alleged that "more than 90 percent of German limited liability companies refuse to publish their accounts" (Van Hulle 1993, 390), notwithstanding a statutory requirement that they do so. Since the German government has apparently not taken any action against these delinquents, the European Union has instituted an infringement procedure against Germany.

In the Netherlands, the Enterprise Chamber, established in 1970 as the court in which interested parties could challenge a company whose annual financial report is believed to be in violation of the law, is no longer attracting any cases. SOBI, the public interest group that had brought almost half of the financial reporting cases since the early 1970s, has withdrawn from the field, and no financial reporting cases are currently reported to be in the pipeline. Hence, unless one accepts that the financial reporting by all Dutch companies complies fully with the law, the enforcement mechanism seems no longer to be effective.

In the United Kingdom, the private-sector Financial Reporting Review Panel has been authorized by the Government to institute civil proceedings against companies whose annual financial statements reflect departures from applicable accounting standards when it believes they do not give a "true and fair view," unless

The author is grateful to several commentators for their valuable suggestions on an earlier draft: J. T. Ball, John C. Burton, Charles T. Horngren, Benjamin S. Neuhausen, David Solomons, and Arthur R. Wyatt. Useful comments on the European scene sere provided by Christopher Nobes, Karel Van Hulle, Allan Cook, and Henk Brink. In an earlier version, this paper served as the basis for the author's Inaugural Address as professor of accounting at the State University of Limburg, The Netherlands, on June 3, 1994. The responsibility for its contents is entirely his.

the companies enter into an agreement to issue revised financial statements. Whether the courts will find that departures from applicable accounting standards *ipso facto* detract from a "true and fair view" in particular cases is not yet known, since all of the actions so far taken by the Review Panel have led to company agreements to issue revised financial statements.

The oldest and best known compliance system is the one practiced in the United States. Yet there is evidence that the actual functioning of the U.S. system is frequently misunderstood.

It is the author's aim in this paper to provide insight into the functioning of the U.S. compliance system, in the context of the overall regulatory system for financial reporting. As a central element in that regulatory system, a federal government agency collaborates with a private-sector standard-setting body. At the outset of the paper, this collaborative system is described, following which there is a discussion of the means used by the government agency to secure compliance with its norms. At the close of the paper, a discussion of some contrasts between the European regulatory environment and that in the U.S. is intended to bring out some of the distinctive features of the latter.

STANDARD SETTING

The SEC—An Introduction

To understand the U.S. regulatory system is to understand the working of the Securities and Exchange Commission (SEC) and its relation to the accounting standard-setting body. The SEC is an independent federal regulatory agency that was established in 1934 by Congressional legislation.[1] Under the securities legislation approved by Congress in 1933–34, the SEC possesses authority to prescribe the form and content of financial statements contained in registration statements (i.e., prospectuses) accompanying an offer to sell securities to the public and in subsequent periodic reports filed with the Commission.[2] In the 1960s, the SEC, through its proxy regulations, also began to exercise active surveillance over the form and content of financial statements contained in corporate annual reports to shareholders. The approximately 12,000 companies (known as registrants) subject to the SEC's jurisdiction are those that are listed on national securities exchanges (such as the New York Stock Exchange), are traded in the over-the-counter market, or have issued securities in interstate markets and have met certain minimum size tests.[3] Federal securities legislation became necessary to regulate the flow of information to investors since the corporation laws of the several states did not effectively regulate such communications.[4] The states compete with one another to attract corporations to become domiciled (and thus pay fees and taxes) in their respective jurisdictions, and in many states there has been a tendency to minimize the burdens imposed on corporations' boards of directors (known in some quarters as a "race to the bottom"). Prior to the 1930s, quite a number of states attempted to enforce securities legislation (known as "blue sky laws"), but these laws were largely ineffective.

The SEC is composed of five full-time members (known as Commissioners) who are appointed by the President and confirmed by the Senate. Not more than three Commission-

[1] For a history of the SEC, see Seligman (1982). For a critical analysis of the effectiveness of the SEC's accounting disclosure regulations, see Benston (1969), and for a dialogue on Benston's argument concerning the efficacy of the Securities Acts, see Benston (1974) and Sommer (1974).

[2] The SEC also exercises supervisory authority over auditing standards and procedures, including the standards of auditor independence. The SEC imposes penalties on auditors whose audits are not conducted in accordance with the norms established by the SEC and by the Auditing Standards Board of the American Institute of Certified Public Accountants (AICPA). Other than in Article 2 of Regulation S-X (see below), which concerns audit reports and independence, and in its Accounting and Auditing Enforcement Releases, the Commission has not set auditing standards. The SEC's auditing role will not be discussed in this paper.

[3] In addition to administering the Securities Act of 1933 and the Securities Exchange Act of 1934, the SEC also administers the Public Utility Holding Company Act of 1935, Trust Indenture Act of 1939, Investment Company Act of 1940, Investment Advisers Act of 1940, and Securities Investor Protection Act of 1970.

[4] In the U.S., corporations are formed under state law, not federal law.

ers may be members of the same political party. Of the some 75 individuals who have served on the Commission during its first 60 years, more than two-thirds have been lawyers, while others have typically been drawn from the ranks of economists, investment bankers, and financial executives. Only three have been certified public accountants.[5] The current Chairman, Arthur Levitt, Jr., is a former chairman of the American Stock Exchange. The SEC has a full-time staff in excess of 2,600. The chief accountant is the principal adviser to the Commissioners on accounting and auditing matters, and the Division of Corporation Finance reviews registration statements and periodic reports for conformity with the norms accepted by the Commission.

When the SEC came into being there was no program in either the public or private sector for issuing regular pronouncements on accounting principles.[6] In effect, the public-sector regulator, including a compliance mechanism, was installed even before a private-sector standard-setting body was established—in part, a reversal of the timing sequence that has been experienced in several other countries.

GAAP and "Present Fairly"

Before proceeding, a discussion of two important terms, "generally accepted accounting principles" and "present fairly," would be useful.

In 1934, a committee of the American Institute of Accountants (AIA), which was renamed the American Institute of Certified Public Accountants (AICPA) in 1957, introduced the first standard form of the auditor's report, which stated that the financial statements "fairly present, in accordance with accepted principles of accounting" the company's position and the results of its operations. In 1939, the phrasing was modified to state that the financial statements "present fairly" the position of the company and the results of its operations, "in conformity with generally accepted accounting principles," the language that has survived to the present day. Two key phrases are "present fairly" and "generally accepted accounting principles," or GAAP. As to GAAP, the terminology is misleading. In reality, "principles" has come to include practices, methods and procedures, not solely principles. Originally, "accepted" meant that one or more practices were actually being used by corporations, and "generally" was added to make it evident that the acceptance of a particular practice by one or a few corporations was not sufficient to endow it with authoritative support: the practice had to be "generally accepted" among corporations. Subsequently, "accepted" came to mean that a given practice was accept*able* to the private-sector standard setter, and also to the SEC.[7] It began as a descriptive notion but eventually took on a normative character, even though the terminology, "generally accepted accounting principles," remained unchanged.

The term "present fairly" is more difficult to explain. The adverb "fairly" was initially proposed for inclusion in the auditor's report in 1934 by the AIA committee mentioned previously.[8] While either "fairly present" or "present fairly" has appeared in the Institute's standard form of the auditor's report since 1934, the test that has been applied by the SEC is the conformity of a company's finan-

[5] The CPA Commissioners were Donald C. Cook (1949–53; chairman 1952–53), Edward T. McCormick (1949–51), and James J. Needham (1969–72). Cook was also a lawyer. Of the three, only Needham joined the Commission from an audit firm.

[6] In 1932–33, prior to the establishment of the SEC, a committee of the American Institute of Accountants (AIA), in correspondence with the New York Stock Exchange, proposed a framework by which listed corporations could choose "detailed methods of accounting" falling within the limits of five "broad principles of accounting which have won fairly general acceptance." Those five principles, together with a sixth added by another committee, were approved by the Institute's membership in 1934 (*Audits of Corporate Accounts 1932–1934* 1934). Once the SEC had entered the picture, the AIA seemed reluctant to continue furthering the development of accounting principles. Thereupon, the American Accounting Association, the organization of accounting academics, launched its own program for creating an authoritative literature on accounting principles (see Zeff 1972, 119–134).

[7] This evolution occurred over a period from the 1940s to the mid-1960s, and culminated in the historic decision by the AICPA's Council in 1964 to support a proactive role for the standard setter (see Carey 1970, chaps. 4–6; and Zeff 1972, 180–202).

[8] It is a curious fact that the originator of the use of "fairly" in this context was Richard Whitney, the president of the New York Stock Exchange, who in 1938 pleaded guilty to grand larceny and was expelled from the Exchange (Seligman 1982, 169).

cial reporting with GAAP.[9] The overriding criterion used by the SEC has been whether a registrant's financial statements would be misleading if a particular accounting or disclosure practice were (or were not) followed.[10] Under Rule 203 (adopted in 1973) of the AICPA's Code of Professional Ethics, members may give an opinion that a company's financial statements are presented in conformity with GAAP even though they contain a departure from an accounting principle promulgated by the body designated by the Institute's Council to establish such principles, but only if it can be shown that the statements would have been misleading in the absence of the departure. Observe that "fairly" is nowhere mentioned, while "misleading" is. In 1975, the AICPA's Auditing Standards Executive Committee (AudSEC, predecessor of the Auditing Standards Board) declared that

> The independent auditor's judgment concerning the "fairness" of the overall presentation of financial statements should be applied within the framework of generally accepted accounting principles. Without that framework the auditor would have no uniform standard for judging the presentation of financial position, results of operations, and changes in financial position in financial statements (para. 3).[11]

Interestingly, in 1978 the AICPA's Commission on Auditors' Responsibilities recommended that the term "present fairly" be deleted from the auditor's report, as it was probably confusing to the average reader (1978, 14, 74), and in 1980 the Auditing Standards Board (ASB) actually recommended the adoption of an auditor's report with "fairly" excluded. Owing, however, to the negative reaction from commentators, the ASB's proposed elimination of "fairly" was withdrawn (Carmichael and Winters 1982, 17–18). Hence, "present fairly" is a term that was developed in the private sector but which seems not to be invoked in professional or regulatory circles. Today, discussions within the major public accounting firms, and between the firms or corporations and the SEC's accounting staff, over the propriety of accounting or disclosure practices revolve about the question, "is it GAAP?"

While GAAP seems to dominate considerations of "present fairly" among the technical specialists, sometimes "present fairly" is seen to be an essential quality by jurists, financial journalists, members of Congress, and other lay commentators. In the famous Continental Vending case in the 1960s,[12] the trial judge instructed the jury that

> the "critical test" was whether the financial statements "fairly presented the financial condition of Continental as of September 30, 1962" and whether they "accurately reported the operations for fiscal 1962." He instructed the jury to consider proof of compliance with professional standards [e.g., GAAP] as "evidence which may be very persuasive but not necessarily conclusive" that the financial statements "were not materially false or misleading"(Rosenfield and Lorensen 1973, 16–17).

The SEC's Liaison with the Private-Sector Standard Setter

Although the SEC possesses authority to prescribe accounting standards, it embarked upon a policy in 1937–38 which had the effect of entreating the accounting profession to provide the Commission with "substantial authoritative support" for sound accounting practice, or GAAP. The private sector responded by establishing a standard-setting program that passed through three stages, as follows:

Committee on Accounting Procedure (1939–59), composed of 21 part-time members

---

[9] When, from 1946 to 1962, Arthur Andersen & Co. followed a policy of giving separate opinions on fairness of presentation and conformity with GAAP in its reports to clients, Carman G. Blough was alone in filing a public dissent to the practice, and the SEC's accounting staff did not take exception. See Zeff (1992) and Blough (1958).

[10] The SEC's administrative policy expressing this overriding criterion appears in Accounting Series Release No. 4, issued in 1938.

[11] John C. Burton, then the SEC chief accountant, took issue with AudSEC's position on "fairness" (as contained in an exposure draft). He argued (1975) that it is necessary for the auditor to make subjective judgments about "fairness" in order to promote the effective communication of business results to the investing public. In its non-mandatory Statement No. 4, the APB (1970, para. 189) also viewed "fairness" as playing an important role. Clearly, all of the weight is not on one side.
AudSEC's 1975 position on "fairness" continues to be Institute policy (see Auditing Standards Board 1992, para. 3).

[12] United States v. Simon, 425 F.2d 796 (2d Cir. 1969), cert. denied 397 U.S. 1006 (1970).

drawn from public accounting and academe, which was a committee of the AIA/AICPA. Its pronouncements were known as Accounting Research Bulletins.

Accounting Principles Board (APB) (1959–73), composed of 21 part-time members drawn from public accounting, industry, the financial community and academe, which was a committee of the AICPA. Its pronouncements were known as Opinions (mandatory) and Statements (advisory).

Financial Accounting Standards Board (FASB) (since 1973), composed of seven full-time members, which is supported and overseen by the trustees of an independent Financial Accounting Foundation (FAF), which in turn is sponsored by eight major professional associations that have an interest in the quality of financial reporting.[13] Its principal pronouncement, which is produced only after extensive "due process" procedures, is known as a Statement of Financial Accounting Standards.

While the pronouncements of this succession of standard-setting bodies have been promulgated without explicit reference to the SEC, one should not conclude that the SEC has been a passive bystander during the standard-setting process. The SEC's accounting staff has kept a close watch over the issues, agendas, priorities, and tentative positions of the standard setter, and has not been reluctant to intervene with its views.[14]

The two bodies have been in almost daily contact, in writing and orally, on all phases of the development of each standard. Since 1973, the SEC chief accountant has attended the quarterly meetings of the FASB's advisory council, and he gives a report on recent SEC developments. Each quarter, representatives from the FASB's staff brief the SEC chief accountant and his staff on the status and progress of FASB projects. In addition, over the years, SEC chief accountants and members of the successive standard-setting bodies have voiced their opinions in numerous speeches, many of which have been published in professional or academic journals. SEC Commissioners have visited the offices of the FASB, and FASB members have paid calls on the SEC. Since 1979, the SEC Commissioners and FASB members have held a joint meeting in most years. Hence, each side has had ample opportunity to know what the other is thinking, although, as will be noted below, open conflicts do occur.

Trading Places

In addition to the continuing communication between the SEC's accounting staff and the standard setter, there has been a movement of personnel between the two bodies. Most of the SEC chief accountants, following their service with the Commission, have come to occupy important positions on the private-sector standard-setting side. Carman G. Blough, the SEC's chief accountant from 1935 to 1938, became the AIA's first full-time Director of Research in 1944, and remained until 1961. In that role, Blough was the staff director of the Committee on Accounting Procedure, and from 1947 to 1963 he wrote a monthly column on accounting and auditing in the Institute's magazine, the *Journal of Accountancy*, which earned him a reputation as the foremost U.S. authority on GAAP. William W. Werntz, the SEC chief accountant from 1938 to 1947, became a member of the Com-

13 The current sponsors of the FAF are the AICPA, American Accounting Association, Institute of Management Accountants, Financial Executives Institute, Association for Investment Management and Research, Securities Industry Association, Government Finance Officers Association, and National Association of State Auditors, Comptrollers and Treasurers. In 1984, the FAF set up a Governmental Accounting Standards Board, which explains the appearance of the last two sponsoring bodies in the foregoing list. Today, the FASB has a professional staff of about 45 and an annual budget of about $15 million. About two-thirds of the FASB's financial support comes from publication sales, and the balance is donations from sources in the private sector. A limit is placed on the amount of any single donor's annual contribution in order to avoid the fact or appearance of undue influence. For further information about the operation of the FASB, see Miller et al. (1994). For the report of the AICPA study group that recommended the setting up of the FASB, see *Establishing Financial Accounting Standards* (1972).

14 While the SEC's accounting staff may comment on a private-sector standard setter's tentative positions, "the commission does not make formal responses to FASB proposals, because the commission's statutory authority is such that it can't express an official view on a standard and then accept a significantly different result" (Burton 1982, 46).

mittee of Accounting Procedure in 1950 and served as its chairman from 1956 to 1959. In 1958, when the Institute president appointed a special committee whose report led to the establishment in 1959 of the APB, to succeed the Committee on Accounting Procedure, three of its nine members were the sitting SEC chief accountant, Andrew Barr, and two of the preceding chief accountants, Blough and Werntz. These three were also made members of the advisory committees for the formative research studies on postulates and broad accounting principles published in 1961–62 under the auspices of the APB (Moonitz 1961; Sprouse and Moonitz 1962), and their harsh criticisms had much to do with the APB's rejection of the two research studies. Blough also was a member of the APB from 1959 to 1964.

In 1971, when the APB was under heavy criticism and the AICPA appointed a blue-ribbon committee to propose a new regime (which became the FASB), the chairman of the committee was Francis M. Wheat, a former SEC Commissioner. Once the FASB succeeded the APB, Andrew Barr, the SEC chief accountant from 1956 to 1972, became a member of the FASB's advisory council for the period from 1973 to 1976. John C. Burton, the SEC chief accountant from 1972 to 1976, served on the advisory council from 1977 to 1981. A. Clarence Sampson, the SEC chief accountant from 1978 to 1987, was an FASB board member from 1988 to 1993, and, moving in the opposite direction, Walter P. Schuetze, who was on the FASB board from 1973 to 1976, became the SEC chief accountant in 1992. Hence, this movement back and forth (especially forth) between the SEC's accounting staff and the sphere of the private-sector standard setter surely would have sensitized each party to the aims and thinking in the other.

ASR No. 150

Since the late 1930s, the SEC has generally adhered to a policy of relying on the private sector for leadership in establishing and improving accounting principles. But, prior to 1973, this policy had not been stated by the Commission in any of its releases. In that year, with the advent of the independent and well-endowed FASB, the SEC publicly announced, in Accounting Series Release (ASR) No. 150, that, for purposes of its administrative policy enunciated in ASR No. 4 (1938), "principles, standards and practices promulgated by the FASB in its Statements and Interpretations will be considered by the Commission as having substantial authoritative support, and those contrary to such FASB promulgations will be considered to have no such support" (SEC 1973, footnotes omitted). The Commission made it clear, however, that it alone possesses the statutory authority to set accounting standards under the Acts that it administers. While this formal recognition of the FASB as the primary accounting standard-setting body on which the SEC relies was welcomed by the FAF as "a significant and unprecedented step" (Financial Accounting Foundation 1974), it has not, as noted below, foreclosed the SEC from taking initiatives in the setting of accounting standards.

Tension and Disagreements

All has not been smooth between the SEC and the private-sector standard setter. During the 1940s and early 1950s, when the two parties were learning how to relate to each other, the SEC took issue with the Committee on Accounting Procedure on several matters: interperiod tax allocation (i.e., deferred taxes), all-inclusive v. current-operating-performance concept of the income statement, stock options, and upward asset revaluations. During the 1960s, the SEC succeeded in pressing the APB to "narrow the areas of difference" in accounting practice on such topics as pensions, extraordinary items, and deferred taxes.[15] Sounding a note that had been heard from the Commission since the 1930s, SEC Chairman Manuel F. Cohen said in 1964 that "an immediate and pressing objective is to eliminate the use of alternative accounting principles underlying financial statements not

[15] For an article by a member of the SEC accounting staff on the early evolution of the Commssion's "tutorial role" in the development of accounting principles, see Pines (1965).

justified by different circumstances."[16] A leader of the accounting profession interpreted this charge from the SEC to mean "that the APB should recommend accounting practices which will make like things look alike, and unlike things look different" (Trueblood 1966, 189). To the SEC, the comparability among corporations' financial statements has always been an over-arching concern, and the unrestricted availability of alternative accounting practices has been seen as incompatible with comparability.[17]

From 1963 to 1971, the Administrations of three successive U.S. Presidents blocked the APB from putting into effect its recommended accounting for the investment credit (i.e., a credit against a business entity's income tax equal to a percentage of the cost of newly purchased equipment and machinery), because the Government believed that a deferral of the income-statement effect of the credit, by way of amortizing the credit as a cost reduction over the life of the fixed assets, would not serve as a sufficient inducement for companies to invest in such assets, in comparison with taking the full amount of the credit immediately into accounting net income. Since the APB supported only the deferral approach, the SEC, under behind-the-scenes pressure from the Treasury Department in President John F. Kennedy's Administration, prevented APB Opinion No. 2, issued in 1962, from going into effect. Evidence suggests that the SEC probably would have rejected the APB's recommendation even without the Administration's pressure, since it was troubled by the considerable dissension within the public accounting profession over the Opinion. In 1967, when the investment credit was reintroduced by the Lyndon B. Johnson Administration and the APB sought to reassert the position it had taken in Opinion No. 2, the Treasury Department—openly, this time—intervened to prevent the APB from working its will. In 1971, when the investment credit was reintroduced a final time, the SEC announced that it would abide by the APB's recommendation. After the APB again made it known that it favored the deferral approach, the Treasury Department under President Richard M. Nixon obtained Congressional approval for income tax legislation providing that no taxpayer shall be required to use "any particular method of accounting for the credit" in its financial statements.[18] This was the first evidence that a Goverment department (i.e., a ministry), abetted by Congress, would intervene in the accounting standard-setting process (see Moonitz 1966; and Zeff 1972, 178–180, 201–202, 219–221).

In the mid-1960s, as well as on several earlier occasions, the SEC made it known that, if the private-sector standard setter failed to "narrow the areas of difference," the SEC would step in and do so itself. This threat of direct SEC intervention has always hung over the standard setter's head, and leaders of the accounting profession and in the corporate community have strongly opposed a government determination of accounting principles.[19] Among the leaders of the major public accounting firms there had been philosophical disagreements since the 1940s over the desirability of "uniformity" vis-à-vis "flexibility" of accounting principles, and in the 1960s, a decade of highly competitive capital markets, corporate executives had begun to appreciate the benefits of flexible accounting.[20]

It was in the 1970s that the SEC seemed to single out disclosure as the area in which it would take the standard-setting lead, leaving

---

[16] As quoted in Zeff (1972, 189). Other historical material in this paper is drawn from Storey (1964), Zeff (1972, chap. 3), Carey (1969, 1970), Moonitz (1974), Chatov (1975), Previts (1978, 1981), Solomons (1986b, chap. 2), Van Riper (1994), and the several articles contained in the Centennial Issue of the *Journal of Accountancy*, issued in May 1987.

[17] In 1972, SEC Chairman William J. Casey said that "the desirability of making earnings statements as comparable and as uniform as possible [should] gain priority over the frequently conflicting objective of affording management choice and flexibility in the way it keeps score" (1972, 73).

[18] Sec. 101(c) of the Revenue Act of 1971, P.L. 92–178, 85 Stat. 499 (1971).

[19] Chatov (1975, esp. chap. 17) and Kripke (1979), both lawyers, argue that the SEC should take on a much stronger role in establishing accounting principles.

[20] See the papers included in "Uniformity in Financial Accounting" (1965) and Zeff (1984).

measurement issues to the FASB (Burton 1974b). This was when the SEC was expanding the coverage of Management's Discussion & Analysis (MD&A), an extensive narrative disclosure that is required to be appended to the financial statements (see Dieter and Sandefur 1989).[21]

A long-standing policy of the SEC, which began to be abandoned in the 1970s, was an opposition to departures from historical cost in the determination of net income (see Walker 1992). This posture was a reaction to unsubstantiated asset revaluations by corporations during the pre-regulation 1920s, and in general it exemplified the SEC's concern over highly subjective information that could be misleading to investors, including the possibility of deliberate management manipulation. This policy had led it to disallow the inclusion of management projections and forecasts in filings with the Commission. In 1973, for the first time, the SEC permitted such representations in its filings (Burton 1974a). Later in the 1970s, a decade of high inflation, the SEC abruptly entered the standard-setting arena by requiring about a thousand large registrants to report selected replacement cost information in an appendage to their annual financial statements (SEC 1976). In this action, the SEC rejected an FASB exposure draft favoring a general price-level accounting (GPL) approach. Soon thereafter, a chastened FASB issued Statement of Financial Accounting Standards No. 33 (1979a), which called for both current cost and constant dollar (GPL) information to be reported in a supplementary disclosure, in a move calculated to reassert its position as the prime standard setter.[22]

In 1978, the SEC announced a decisive break from the its decades-long opposition to departures from historical cost accounting in the income statement itself. Despite the SEC chief accountant's professed expectation that the FASB and the SEC "will have to operate on the principle of mutual non-surprise if their joint efforts are to be maximized" (Burton 1974, 271),[23] the SEC shocked the FASB by advocating "reserve recognition accounting," an application of current value accounting to the proven reserves of oil and gas producers, in preference to the FASB's recommended successful efforts costing (on a historical cost basis) to reflect exploration activity.[24] In its release, the SEC nonetheless reaffirmed its support of private-sector standard setting in general and of the FASB in particular, and explained that, under the Energy Policy and Conservation Act, approved by Congress in 1975, the SEC "was required to conduct a review of [the FASB's standard] that is unique with respect to the Commission's traditional role in the process of establishing financial accounting standards" (SEC 1978).[25]

Some of these tensions and disagreements, and others not mentioned here, have been precipitated by pressures applied by powerful business lobbies, elements in the financial community, departments of the Government, and members of Congress to promote one or another accounting practice that would favor special interests. The FASB and its predecessor bodies have endeavored to make their recommendations conducive to the unbiased information that would be useful to investors and creditors, but other forces in society have sometimes prevented the private-sector standard setter from acting on principle.

---

[21] In 1969 and 1977, the SEC completed extensive studies of its policies and role in the corporate disclosure system (see SEC 1969; and *Report of the Advisory Committee* 1977).

[22] For a discussion of these initiatives, see Tweedie and Whittington (1984, chap. 7).

[23] Burton held this view from the beginning of his term as chief accountant (see Pacter and Nolan 1973, 26).

[24] See Horwitz and Kolodny (1982, 102–108), Gorton (1991), Zeff (1993, 137–140), and Van Riper (1994, chap. 4) for discussions of the episodes in this drama. As noted below, beginning in 1990, SEC Chairman Richard C. Breeden argued for "mark-to-market" accounting for investments in debt and equity securities (see Wyatt 1991). On these two occasions (i.e., oil and gas, and marketable securities) when the Commissioners became directly involved in standard-setting issues, they favored current value accounting over historical cost accounting. As noted above, the Commissioners are themselves rarely accountants, and they thus are not steeped in historical cost accounting as are most accountants who are educated in U.S. business schools.

[25] Two years later, in ASR No. 280, the SEC seemed to make a special point of again reaffirming its support for private-sector standard setting and the FASB.

Even the SEC has not been impervious to pressure.[26] In 1981, the major oil and gas producers forced the SEC to back down on the use of "reserve recognition accounting" in the primary financial statements (SEC 1981), and in 1986 the same industry defeated an attempt by the SEC chief accountant to require the use of successful efforts costing for all exploration activity (Zeff 1988, 21).

An SEC Embargo

In 1974, the SEC put a stop to an emerging trend by some corporations of capitalizing, instead of expensing, their annual interest costs. This practice had long been followed by regulated public utilities (e.g., electricity supply monopolies), but, for companies in other industries, the SEC regarded it as not being within the tradition of the "conventional accounting model." In ASR No. 163, it prohibited companies (other than those that had already so acted) from adopting an accounting policy of capitalizing interest costs until the FASB were to issue a standard. The SEC release appeared at a time of steeply rising interest rates, when the capitalization of interest costs could substantially increase a registrant's annual net income. Five years later, the FASB (1979b) issued a standard that allowed interest capitalization in defined circumstances, and the SEC rescinded its moratorium.

Conceptual Framework

In the 1970s and 1980s, the FASB invested a great deal of energy and resources into fashioning a conceptual framework. Although the project got off to a promising start, it eventually foundered when difficult decisions on recognition and measurement were addressed. In the end, the FASB's conceptual framework failed to fulfill expectations that it might constitute a powerful intellectual force for improving financial reporting (see Rappaport 1977; Horngren 1981; Solomons 1986a, 1986b; and Gore 1992).

SEC Oversight of the FASB

Annually since 1978, in response to a request from a Senate committee, the SEC has rendered a report to Congress on its oversight of the accounting profession, including the standard-setting activities of the FASB. The first three reports were issued as separate documents. Subsequent years' reports have been included in the Commission's annual report to Congress. As a practical matter, this oversight role does not seem to have altered the nature of the SEC's relationship with the FASB.

AcSEC

When the FASB succeeded the APB in 1973, the AICPA formed the Accounting Standards Executive Committee (AcSEC) as its senior technical committee on accounting matters. Its 15 members have been drawn predominantly from public accounting firms, but usually also include one or two representatives from industry and an academic. For some time, AcSEC and the FASB have had an arrangement under which AcSEC takes up certain issues, typically along narrower lines involving single industries or specialized transactions, for resolution under FASB oversight (see Rodda 1993). The SEC accounting staff also oversees AcSEC projects, and sometimes participates in the deliberations of the subcommittee handling a particular project.

Concluding Note

Whatever one's judgment about the effectiveness of the special relationship forged by the SEC and the standard setter, there is no doubt that both parties have worked diligently to make the relationship work.[27] One party is a government agency with a legislative mandate to establish accounting principles and practices for registrant companies, while the other is a private-sector body whose mission is to provide the government agency, as well as the preparers, auditors and users of accounting information, with expert opinions on

[26] For discussions of "economic consequences" in standard setting, see Horngren (1973), Moonitz (1974), Solomons (1978), Zeff (1978, 1993), Kelly-Newton (1980), Bromwich (1985), and Van Riper (1994).

[27] For a dozen papers that reflect on the SEC's performance of its accounting role, presented at a conference commemorating the 50th anniversary of the Commission, see Mundheim and Leech (1985).

those principles and practices. While an SEC chief accountant has generously depicted the relationship between the SEC and the private-sector standard setter as a "partnership,"[28] an APB member during its final days preferred a very different characterization: the SEC is "top management power" and the APB is "lower management: analyzer, formulator, implementer" (Horngren 1972, 38).[29] Without question, the agendas of the successive standard setters and many of their pronouncements have been powerfully shaped by signals emanating from the SEC. The number of FASB standards statements issued thus far (more than 120) and the extensive detail found therein respond to the expressed needs of a government regulator.[30]

THE SEC AS AN ENFORCEMENT AGENCY

From its inception in 1934, the SEC has applied a heavy hand to enforcement. Once accounting and disclosure standards have been set, the SEC regards it as essential to the credibility of corporate financial reporting that full compliance with those standards be enforced.

Procedures

In comparison with the task facing some countries' enforcement agencies that deal with the accounting rules used by perhaps hundreds of thousands of companies, the SEC's concern is with the approximately 12,000 companies subject to the federal securities legislation that it administers.[31] These are a tiny fraction of the approximately 3.7 million U.S. corporations, and it is therefore unnecessary for the SEC and the private-sector standard setter to be concerned about the costs that accounting and disclosure standards might impose on middle-sized and small companies that have elected not to enter the securities market.[32] Apart from the companies subject to the SEC's jurisdiction and others (such as financial institutions) that are regulated by other agencies, most remaining companies are not required by statute to issue periodic financial statements. Typically, they would issue (but not publish) financial statements in accordance with the terms of bank loan agreements, or as information to co-venturers, but these financial statements may not need to be audited. The legislatures of nine states have approved laws requiring all corporations to furnish shareholders with annual financial statements, but the use of GAAP is not prescribed, nor is an audit required. In most other states, corporations are required to furnish such statements only upon written request (Zeff et al. 1992, 357, ftn 47). It is widely understood, however, that audited financial statements in this unregulated sector would need to be prepared in accordance with the

---

28 Interview with John C. Burton (Pacter and Nolan 1973, 26).

29 During the tenure of the APB, it was not unknown for the APB itself, as well as its task forces and committees, to seek feedback informally from the SEC chief accountant in the course of their deliberations. Thus, it is not difficult to appreciate some of the source of Horngren's "top management, lower management" characterization. The FASB, however, has adhered to a policy of not allowing outsiders, including the SEC, access to its internal documents.

30 In fairness, it must be pointed out that about one-third of the FASB's standards statements have been supplements or amendments of earlier statements, yet each was given a new number in the series. By contrast, under the numbering scheme followed by the U.K./Irish Accounting Standards Committee between 1970 and 1990, an amendment or supplement would have led to the reissuance of the original standard as revised, retaining the original number. Also, included in the contents of each U.S. standards statement is a discussion entitled "Basis for Conclusions," which does not form part of the standard itself. The "Basis for Conclusions" appearing in most of the standards statements is actually longer than the standard.

Since 1974, the FASB has issued some 40 Interpretations intended "to clarify, explain, or elaborate on" previously issued standards. The process for issuing Interpretations is less elaborate than for standards.

31 Two primers on the authority and procedures of the SEC are Skousen (1991) and Afterman (1994). Two handbooks on the SEC's financial reporting and disclosure requirements, as well as its procedures, are Murray et al. (1993) and Afterman (1994).

32 The FASB has, nonetheless, taken an interest in the costs imposed on "closely held" (i.e., private) companies. See the report of the AICPA Committee on Generally Accepted Accounting Principles for Smaller and/or Closely Held Companies (August 1976) which was reproduced in FASB (1980). The FASB has suspended the application of certain standards in regard to "nonpublic enterprises" (FASB 1978a), and in several major standards statements it has deferred the effective date of the new standard for such entities (e.g., FASB 1985, para. 76; and FASB 1990, para. 108).

same GAAP that applies to corporations filing with the SEC. In court cases, a heavy burden would fall on those who would use other standards.

The SEC has broad powers and a large and competent staff to require registrants to provide the securities market with adequate and timely financial information. Within the SEC, 17 accountants work in the Office of the Chief Accountant, and the Division of Corporation Finance (DCF) is served by 120 accountants, as well as by an equal number of lawyers and a small number of financial analysts. A further 20 accountants, together with several hundred lawyers, work in the Division of Enforcement. Registration statements by first-time issuers are scrupulously examined by the DCF, whereas the registration statements of established reporting companies and periodic reports (including quarterly reports) are subjected to selective review. If the DCF were to raise any questions about the form or content of the financial statements or with respect to the MD&A, a "letter of comment" (referred to colloquially as a deficiency letter) would be sent to the registrant. Unless these questions can be resolved by amendments made to the filing or by clarifications or other explanations given by telephone to the SEC's staff, it will be necessary for the registrant and the auditor to attend a conference with the DCF's staff, which is usually preceded by the submission of a position paper by the registrant addressing the unresolved issues. In the event of continuing differences between the parties, the DCF might, in the case of a registration statement, refuse to accelerate its effective date, which may place considerable pressure on the registrant to concede the points at issue in order to take advantage of a favorable market for its securities. If that tactic is unavailing or if a periodic report is at issue, a further conference would be held, this time with the chief accountant and his staff. The chief accountant will make the final judgment. If the differences between the staff and the registrant persist, the Division of Enforcement may be asked to conduct an inquiry or investigation and perhaps subpoena certain documents from the registrant.[33] An unwillingness by the registrant to accept the chief accountant's judgment may lead to a Commission decision to file for injunctive or administrative action (such as "cease and desist") to require restatement and future compliance. A more severe Commission action would be the issuance of a "stop order," preventing the registration statement from becoming effective (and thus precluding the public issuance of securities) or, in the case of a periodic report, preventing further transactions in the registrant's securities in whatever public market in which they are traded. Few registrants are likely to submit to such a penalty: the black mark alone on the corporate escutcheon would take years to erase, and the registrant's shareholders would lose liquidity for their holdings. So the chief accountant's decision is virtually always final (unless, in very rare cases, the Commission were to disagree). In fact, most disputes between the SEC and a registrant are settled without the need for formal action.

Unlike the publicity attending communications in the U.K. between the Financial Reporting Review Panel and companies whose financial reports it believes are defective under the law, discussions between the SEC and a registrant are held entirely in confidence.[34] Occasionally there is comment in the press when a financial report is revised and reissued by the registrant,[35] but the SEC would not divulge any of the proceedings (or even their existence) unless a "stop order" or other enforcement or disciplinary action were instituted. In the U.K., the Review Panel lacks the legal standing of the American SEC, and relies on press publicity to achieve its desired result. In the U.S., the SEC has the full power to secure conformity without recourse to the press. Ironically, in the open American society the process for securing compliance is se-

[33] When the Commission receives intelligence from outside sources that certain information in a registrant's filings may be misleading, the Division of Enforcement will initiate an inquiry.

[34] Certain factual information, however, may be available under the Freedom of Information Act.

[35] See, for example, Loomis (1982) and Hwang (1994).

cret, while in a society known for guarding its secrets the process is played out in public.

It is not uncommon for registrants or auditors to sound out the SEC's accounting staff on novel or controversial accounting implementation issues prior to the submission of a registration statement or of a periodic report. Again, such inquiries are held in confidence. Similar pre-filing inquiries are made of the FASB's technical staff. Since 1979, the FASB has issued a series of Technical Bulletins, involving limited "due process" when compared with standards statements, in order to communicate the views of its staff on implementation issues on which there have been many inquiries. The identities of the corporations or auditors making such inquiries are not disclosed.

A further important role played by the SEC chief accountant in implementation/compliance matters is his participation at meetings of the FASB's Emerging Issues Task Force (EITF). Formed in 1984 (and since imitated in Canada, the U.K. and Australia), the EITF seeks to reach a consensus on difficult implementation issues raised by companies, public accounting firms or the SEC. As might be expected, financial instruments have occupied a great deal of the EITF's attention. Abstracts of the EITF's consensus positions are published by the FASB. The EITF draws its 13 voting members from the Big 6 firms, other public accounting firms, and corporations and banks, and it is chaired by the FASB's director of research and technical activities. The SEC chief accountant attends as an observer, and he takes part in the deliberations. Significantly, the SEC chief accountant generally has accepted EITF consensus positions as authoritative support in filings with the Commission (Miller et al. 1994, 159). But he has also occasionally announced his conclusions and forestalled further EITF discussion of an issue (see FASB 1993c).

Publications

The SEC regularly publishes its accounting positions. From 1937 to 1982, it issued 307 Accounting Series Releases announcing the Commission's opinions and decisions on accounting and auditing matters, about one-third of which arose out of enforcement actions taken against auditors. In 1982, the series was divided into two: Financial Reporting Releases, expressing the Commission's positions on accounting and auditing principles and practices; and Accounting and Auditing Enforcement Releases, which communicate enforcement actions taken against auditors.

In 1975, the DCF and Office of the Chief Accountant instituted a series of Staff Accounting Bulletins, which convey their interpretations and practices in administering the disclosure requirements of the federal securities laws. The Staff Accounting Bulletins do not, however, represent rules or interpretations of the Commission, nor do they bear the Commission's official approval.

When the SEC proceeds to enforce compliance with a newly issued FASB standard, it does not give public notice of its action, unless it were to issue a release, for example, changing the effective date given in the FASB statement.

Two Commission documents synthesize most of its disclosure rules and requirements. Regulation S-X, first issued in 1940, contains substantially all of the Commission's financial reporting requirements. Regulation S-K, instituted in 1977, is intended to standardize all of the Commission's nonfinancial disclosure requirements.

Finally, the SEC reviews the major accounting and auditing developments during the year in a section of its annual report to Congress.

Some Reflections on the SEC's Enforcement System

An unhappy consequence of the SEC's rigorous enforcement system has been to inhibit desirable innovations in financial reporting (see Solomons 1986b, 194–198). The SEC has engendered a "climate of conformity," which has been hostile to experimentation with non-standard approaches to measuring and reporting accounting information in the audited financial statements. A securities commission understandably has a difficult balance to strike between encouraging informative financial reporting and censoring misleading practices. An excessive emphasis on the latter can lead to an ossification of financial reporting development, and perhaps was a reason why the FASB felt unable to point the way toward improved financial reporting in its conceptual framework. The FASB board members' own experiences are necessarily rooted in the tradition of U.S. financial reporting practice, and the members may perhaps be excused if they cannot recall a time when financial reporting was not tightly prescribed, and the prescriptions not strictly enforced.

During its first four decades, the SEC was more concerned with the potential of financial information to mislead than to inform. In the 1970s, however, the SEC began to call for expanded disclosures in flexible formats, to place the financial statements in an informational context (Burton 1981). An important example is the MD&A, which is intended to complement the formalistic financial statements with "soft," interpretive information that would not be allowed in the financial statements themselves.

FACTORS THAT HELP EXPLAIN THE U.S. APPROACH TO THE REGULATION OF FINANCIAL REPORTING

Some of the distinctive elements in the U.S. approach to financial reporting regulation can be more clearly seen against the relief of other countries' approaches. Furthermore, it is useful to be reminded that the institutional environment varies from country to country, which necessarily influences the role accorded to financial reporting and its regulation. The factors discussed in this section are (1) the varying breadth of the user group across countries; (2) the conditions prevailing in the U.S. that lead to a great deal of specificity in enunciated standards; (3) the effects of differential takeover climates on the intensity of lobbying of the standard setter; and (4) the impact on the standard-setting process of the rigorous enforcement of standards by the SEC.

1. Breadth of the User Group

The FASB's primary focus is on the use of financial reporting by "present and potential investors and creditors and other users in making rational investment, credit, and similar decisions" (FASB 1978b, para. 34). Since the *raison d'être* of the FASB is to provide the SEC with "substantial authoritative support" for GAAP, and since the SEC is charged with regulating a broad securities market with emphasis on "full and fair disclosure" to all participants, the FASB's focus on investment and credit decisions is understandable.

In the U.K., even with the Government's recent decision to exempt 500,000 companies from the statutory requirement to prepare audited financial statements, some 600,000 companies are still subject to the audit requirement (Jack 1993; Hurst 1994). Hence, the U.K. Accounting Standards Board needs to be much more attentive than does the FASB to the cost imposed by its standards on middle-sized and small companies that have not entered the securities market, and several U.K. standards contain exemptions for smaller companies. Furthermore, in the U.K., where there is no government securities commission, the users of financial statements are very broadly defined by the Accounting Standards Board to include "present and potential investors, employees, lenders, suppliers and other trade creditors, customers, governments and their agencies and the public" (1991, para. 9). Yet, judging from the backgrounds and affiliations of the Accounting Standards Board's members (which are similar to the backgrounds of the FASB's members), as well as from the general thrust of the work thus far achieved, there seems to be a great deal in common between the U.S. and U.K. standard-setting programs. As in the U.S., the focus of the Accounting Standards Board's work seems to be on investors and creditors as the most important users.

On the European continent, where the statutory accounting rules apply to all limited liability companies, not just the small set of companies whose securities are publicly traded, the breadth of the user group would appear to be as large as the characterization cited above in the U.K. Equity capital markets, especially those in which there are widespread individual holdings, are a much less important source of financing than in the U.S. or the U.K. In their place, funds are raised from banks and other financial institutions, from family sources, and from the state: parties who, as members of boards of directors, have an "inside" access to company financial information. And financial reporting is, in most countries, much influenced by, if not actually linked to, income tax rules (for a German view, see Haller 1992). Conservatism in financial reporting is paramount. Creditor protection is more important, and the interests of employees are, in several countries, taken into consideration. In contrast to Anglo-American countries, transparency, i.e., full candor in financial reporting, is not accepted as a premise (see Nobes and Parker 1991), in the sense of fully satisfying the information needs of investors. There may well be, however, a sufficient degree of transparency for other users.[36] On the European continent, therefore, the difference in financial reporting climate from that in the U.S. would seem to be considerable.

2. Influences on the Number and Detail of Standards

It was mentioned above that the requirements of a government regulator, the SEC, help explain the extensive detail in the FASB's standards. Two other factors that contribute to the volume of standards and other technical literature emanating from the FASB are the litigiousness of American society and the feverish competition among public accounting firms for clients. In regard to the weight of litigation, auditors, as a defense in potential lawsuits, want to be able to cite express provisions of GAAP in support of their clients' financial reporting. As to the heightened competition among firms, there has been a spate of "opinion shopping" incidents beginning in the 1970s. Auditors have been confronted with clients who claim that they know of other public accounting firms that would be more "flexible" on certain accounting treatments. This has led public accounting firms to call for a means of stemming the deterioration of standards and, even more importantly, the consequent loss of clients. In essence, the auditors urged the standard setter to provide more detailed rules so as to avoid being individually responsible for making judgments based on the existing rules. The establishment of the EITF was one such response.

In the U.S., as was noted above, the standard of quality in financial reporting is *conformity with GAAP*. There is no subjective override, such as "true and fair view" in the U.K. (see Parker and Nobes 1994). For this reason, together with (a) the SEC's rigorous enforcement of compliance with FASB standards, (b) the litigious environment, and (c) the "opinion shopping" climate, FASB statements are rule-oriented and numerous.

3. Effect of Differential Takeover Climates

A common characteristic of the U.S. and U.K. financial environments is the frequent occurrence of contested takeovers. Executives are acutely aware that the image of profitability projected by their company's financial reporting may play a role in precipitating an unwanted takeover and, not long thereafter, their dismissal from the enterprise. In such an environment, company executives would have strong feelings about a standard setter's attempt to narrow the range of alternative accounting choices, thus making it more difficult to "tell their story." Experience has shown that they will lobby the standard setter to avert that outcome. On the European continent, however, contested takeovers, owing to a variety of legal and structural barriers, are rare. Consequently, the climate in which accounting standards or guidelines are established is much less politically charged than in Anglo-American countries (see Zeff et al. 1992, 352, 370–371, 380).

[36] For a clash of views on the U.S. and German financial reporting climates, see "Mutual Recognition" (1993).

4. Effect of SEC's Enforced Compliance with Standards

Owing to the SEC's comparatively strict enforcement of compliance with GAAP, U.S. corporate executives have come to realize that the "court of last resort" is the private-sector standard setter. Once the standard setter issues a pronouncement, the SEC expects compliance. Hence, in the United States the amount and intensity of lobbying of the standard setter is understandably much greater than in countries where the compliance operation is more relaxed. One implication of this differential behavior is that the quality of the standards issued by the FASB may sometimes be diluted by the need to compromise with powerful forces opposing the Board. An excellent example during the last few years was the FASB's heavily compromised standard on accounting for certain investments in debt and equity securities (FASB 1993a), notwithstanding the strong advocacy by the SEC Chairman (with the apparent support of the Commission) of "mark-to-market" accounting. The banking community was unified in its opposition to "mark-to-market" accounting, and lobbied the Board relentlessly (see Worthy 1992).

An even more recent example is the unprecedented Congressional pressure (evidently on behalf of small business interests) on the FASB to retreat from its tentative position to require explicit income-statement recognition of the compensation implicit in employee stock options (see FASB 1993b; *Employee Stock Options* 1994; Norris 1994; and Van Riper 1994, 151–155).

The fervent lobbying of the standard setter and, on occasion, even the SEC has succeeded in deflecting some proposed revisions of the financial statements into the footnotes or other disclosures. An excellent example was the SEC's reluctant decision in 1981 (mentioned above), following three years of special pleading by the major oil and gas producers, that its proposed "reserve recognition accounting" should be shown in a supplementary disclosure than as part of the primary financial statements. In the U.S., it is not unusual for executive bonus plans or loan agreements to be keyed to profits or debt/equity ratios reflected in the financial statements. When companies sense that a proposed accounting standard might adversely affect the interpretation of these contracts, they will tend to favor additional disclosures over an actual revision of financial-statement figures.

Probably owing to motivations suggested in points 3 and 4, a powerful body of chief executive officers of more than 200 of the largest corporations and banks, known as The Business Roundtable, has, through its Accounting Principles Task Force, lobbied the FASB and the SEC since the mid-1980s both on substantive accounting issues and on the Board's procedures (see Loomis 1988; Miller et al. 1994, 167–169; and Van Riper 1994, chap. 9). The Task Force has sought to impose controls on the FASB's agenda, and probably was a factor behind the decision taken in 1990 by the FAF's board of trustees to revert to a 5-2 vote instead of a simple majority when the FASB approves standards. In addition, the Task Force has a seat on the FASB's Emerging Issues Task Force, at least one seat on the FASB's advisory council, and a *de facto* seat on the FAF's board of trustees.

A Final Note

Is the U.S. standard-setting environment anchored in the private sector with benign SEC oversight, or is it a government enterprise with the private-sector standard setter as the cat's paw? The answer, as is usually the case when comparing polar positions, is somewhere in between. The SEC is not benign, and the private-sector standard setter has not been a cat's paw. Each has influenced the other in unanticipated ways. The cautiousness and conservatism of the SEC prior to the early 1970s undoubtedly restricted the range of substantive issues that the standard setter could effectively take up. On the other side, the exhortations by the SEC's Chairmen and chief accountants have driven the standard setter to tackle controversial accounting issues that it might not otherwise have addressed. The large question that confronts both parties is how they will perform in the face of intense political lobbying against proposals that special interests find to be obnoxious even though the proposed reforms are seen as serving the interests of financial statement users. The private-sector standard setter will take the brunt of the lobbying pressure, but the SEC must take risks in supporting the standard setter on matters of principle.

REFERENCES

Accounting Principles Board. 1962. *Accounting for the "Investment Credit."* Opinion No. 2. New York, NY: AICPA.

———. 1970. *Basic Concepts and Accounting Principles Underlying Financial Statements of Business Enterprises*. Statement No. 4. New York, NY: AICPA.

Accounting Standards Board. 1991. *The Objective of Financial Statements & the Qualitative Characteristics of Financial Information*. Statement of Principles—Exposure Draft. London, U.K.: ASB.

Afterman, A. B. 1994. *Handbook of SEC Accounting and Disclosure*. New York, NY: Warren, Gorham & Lamont.

———. 1995. *SEC Regulation of Public Companies*. Englewood Cliffs, NJ: Prentice Hall.

Auditing Standards Board. 1992. *The Meaning of "Present Fairly in Conformity With Generally Accepted Accounting Principles" in the Independent Auditor's Report*. Statement on Auditing Standards No. 69. New York, NY: AICPA.

Auditing Standards Executive Committee. 1975. *The Meaning of "Present Fairly in Conformity With Generally Accepted Accounting Principles" in the Independent Auditor's Report*. Statement on Auditing Standards No. 5. New York, NY: AICPA.

Audits of Corporate Accounts 1932-1934. 1934. New York, NY: American Institute of Accountants.

Benston, G. J. 1969. The effectiveness and effects of the SEC's accounting disclosure requirements. In *Economic Policy and the Regulation of Corporate Securities*, edited by H. G. Manne, 23–79. Washington, D.C.: American Enterprise Institute for Public Policy Research.

———. 1974. Evaluation of the Securities Exchange Act of 1934. *Financial Executive* 42 (May): 28–36, 40–42.

Blough, C. G. 1958. Implications of "present fairly" in the auditor's report. *Journal of Accountancy* 105 (March): 76–77.

Bromwich, M. 1985. *The Economics of Accounting Standard Setting*. London, U.K.: Prentice Hall International in association with The Institute of Chartered Accountants in England and Wales.

Burton, J. C. 1974a. Forecasts: A changing view from the Securities and Exchange Commission. In *Public Reporting of Corporate Financial Forecasts*, edited by P. Prakash and A. Rappaport, 81–98. Chicago, IL: Commerce Clearing House, Inc.

———. 1974b. The SEC and the accounting profession: Responsibility, authority, and progress. In *Institutional Issues in Public Accounting,* edited by R. R. Sterling, 265–275. Lawrence, KS: Scholars Book Co.

———. 1975. Fair presentation: Another view. In *The Emanuel Saxe Distinguished Lectures in Accounting 1974-1975*, 27–39. New York, NY: The Bernard M. Baruch College, City University of New York.

———. 1981. Emerging trends in financial reporting. *Journal of Accountancy* 152 (July): 54–56, 58, 60–62, 64, 66.

———. 1982. The SEC and financial reporting: The sand in the oyster. *Journal of Accountancy* 153 (June): 34, 36, 38, 40, 42, 44, 46, 48.

Carey, J. L. 1969. *The Rise of the Accounting Profession: From Technician to Professional, 1896–1936*. New York, NY: AICPA.

———. 1970. *The Rise of the Accounting Profession: To Responsibility and Authority, 1937–1969*. New York, NY: AICPA.

Carmichael, D. R., and A. J. Winters. 1982. The evolution of audit reporting. In *Auditing Symposium VI*, edited by D. R. Nichols and H. F. Stettler, 1–20. Lawrence, KS: School of Business, University of Kansas.

Casey, W. J. 1972. Toward common accounting standards. *Journal of Accountancy* 134 (October): 70–73.

Chatov, R. 1975. *Corporate Financial Reporting: Public or Private Control?* New York, NY: The Free Press.

The Commission on Auditors' Responsibilities. 1978. *Report, Conclusions, and Recommendations*. New York, NY: The Commission on Auditors' Responsibilities.

Dieter, R., and K. Sandefur. 1989. Spotlight on Management's Discussion and Analysis. *Journal of Accountancy* 168 (December): 64–66, 68, 70.

Employee Stock Options. 1994. Hearing before the subcommittee on securities of the Committee on Banking, Housing, and Urban Affairs, United States Senate, 103d Congress, 1st Session (October 21, 1993), S.Hrg. 103–359. Washington, D.C.: U.S. Government Printing Office.
Establishing Financial Accounting Standards. 1972. New York, NY: AICPA.
Financial Accounting Foundation. 1974. *Report/July 1, 1972-December 31, 1973*. Stamford, CT: FAF.
Financial Accounting Standards Board. 1978a. *Suspension of the Reporting of Earnings per Share and Segment Information by Nonpublic Enterprises*. Statement of Financial Accounting Standards No. 21. Stamford, CT: FASB.
———. 1978b. *Objectives of Financial Reporting by Business Enterprises*. Statement of Financial Accounting Concepts No. 1. Stamford, CT: FASB.
———. 1979a. *Financial Reporting and Changing Prices*. Statement of Financial Accounting Standards No. 33. Stamford, CT: FASB.
———. 1979b. *Capitalization of Interest Cost*. Statement of Financial Accounting Standards No. 34. Stamford, CT: FASB.
———. 1980. *Financial Statements and Other Means of Financial Reporting*. FASB Invitation to Comment. Stamford, CT: FASB.
———. 1985. *Employers' Accounting for Pensions*. Statement of Financial Accounting Standards No. 87. Stamford, CT: FASB.
———. 1990. *Employers' Accounting for Postretirement Benefits Other Than Pensions*. Statement of Financial Accounting Standards No. 106. Norwalk, CT: FASB.
———. 1993a. *Accounting for Certain Investments in Debt and Equity Securities*. Statement of Financial Accounting Standards No. 115. Norwalk, CT: FASB.
———. 1993b. *Accounting for Stock-based Compensation*. Proposed Statement of Financial Accounting Standards. Norwalk, CT: FASB.
———. 1993c. *EITF Abstracts: A Summary of Proceedings of the FASB Emerging Issues Task Force*. Issued annually. Norwalk, CT: FASB.
Gore, P. 1992. *The FASB Conceptual Framework Project 1973–1985: An Analysis*. Manchester, U.K.: Manchester University Press.
Gorton, D. E. 1991. The SEC decision not to support SFAS 19: A case study of the effect of lobbying on standard setting. *Accounting Horizons* 5 (March): 29–41.
Haller, A. 1992. The relationship of financial and tax accounting in Germany: A major reason for accounting disharmony in Europe. *The International Journal of Accounting* 27 (4): 310–323.
Horngren, C. T. 1972. Accounting principles: Private or public sector? *Journal of Accountancy* 133 (May): 37–41.
———. 1973. The marketing of accounting standards. *Journal of Accountancy* 136 (October): 61–66.
———. 1981. Uses and limitations of a conceptual framework. *Journal of Accountancy* 151 (April): 86, 88, 90, 92, 94–95.
Horwitz, B., and R. Kolodny. 1982. *Financial Reporting Rules and Corporate Decisions: A Study of Public Policy*. Greenwich, CT: JAI Press Inc.
Hurst, K. 1994. Small company audits: The end of the line. *Accountancy* 114 (December): 140–141.
Hwang, S. L. 1994. Borden to reverse, reclassify 40% of 1992 charge. *The Wall Street Journal* (March 22): B7 (Southwest Edition).
Jack, A. 1993. Last call for smaller company annual audits. *Financial Times* (December 2): 16.
Kelly-Newton, L. 1980. *Accounting Policy Formulation: The Role of Corporate Management*. Reading, MA: Addison-Wesley Publishing Company.
Kripke, H. 1979. *The SEC and Corporate Disclosure: Regulation in Search of a Purpose*. New York, NY: Law & Business, Inc./Harcourt Brace Jovanovich, Publishers.
Loomis, C. J. 1982. Behind the profits glow at Aetna. *Fortune* 106 (November 15): 54–58.
———. 1988. Will "FASBEE" pinch your bottom line? *Fortune* 118 (December 19): 93, 94, 100, 104, 106, 108.
Miller, P. B. W., R. J. Redding, and P. R. Bahnson. 1994. *The FASB: The People, the Process, and the Politics*. Burr Ridge, IL: Irwin.
Moonitz, M. 1961. *The Basic Postulates of Accounting*. Accounting Research Study No. 1. New York, NY: AICPA.
———. 1966. Some reflections on the investment credit experience. *Journal of Accounting Research* 4 (Spring): 47–61.
———. 1974. *Obtaining Agreement on Standards in the Accounting Profession*. Studies in Accounting Research #8. Sarasota, FL: AAA.

Mundheim, R. H., and N. E. Leech, eds. 1985. *The SEC and Accounting: The First 50 Years*. 1984 Proceedings of the Arthur Young Professors' Roundtable. Amsterdam: North-Holland.

Murray, R. J., W. E. Decker, Jr., and N. W. Dittmar, Jr. 1993. *The Coopers & Lybrand SEC Manual*. Englewood Cliffs, NJ: Prentice Hall.

Mutual recognition of financial statements in international capital markets. 1993. *IASC Insight* (December): 10–12.

Nobes, C., and R. Parker. 1991. Introduction, and causes of differences. In *Comparative International Accounting*, edited by C. Nobes and R. Parker, chap. 1. Hemel Hempstead, Herts: Prentice Hall International (U.K.) Ltd.

Norris, F. 1994. As accounting enters politics, watch out. *The New York Times* (June 12): Sec. 3, 1.

Pacter, P., and J. Nolan. 1973. Paper shuffling and economic reality. *Journal of Accountancy* 135 (January): 20, 26, 28.

Parker, R. H., and C. W. Nobes. 1994. *An International View of True and Fair Accounting*. London: Routledge.

Pines, J. A. 1965. The Securities and Exchange Commission and accounting principles. *Law and Contemporary Problems* 30 (Autumn): 727–751.

Previts, G. J. 1978. The SEC and its chief accountants: Historical impressions. *Journal of Accountancy* 146 (August): 83–91.

———, ed. 1981. *The Development of SEC Accounting*. Reading, MA: Addison-Wesley Publishing Company.

Rappaport, A. 1977. Economic impact of accounting standards—implications for the FASB. *Journal of Accountancy* 143 (May): 89–90, 92, 94, 96–98.

Report of the Advisory Committee on Corporate Disclosure to the Securities and Exchange Commission. 1977. Committee on Interstate and Foreign Commerce, U.S. House of Representatives, 95th Congress, 1st Session. Committee Print 95–29. Washington, D.C.: U.S. Government Printing Office.

Rodda, A. K. 1993. The AICPA role in standard setting. *Journal of Accountancy* 175 (February): 67–68, 70.

Rosenfield, P., and L. Lorensen. 1973. *Independent Auditors' Responsibilities and the Audit Report*. Technical Research Report 1. New York, NY: AICPA.

Securities and Exchange Commission. 1938. *Administrative Policy on Financial Statements*. Accounting Series Release No. 4. Washington, D.C.: SEC (April 25).

———. 1969. *Disclosure to Investors: A Reappraisal of Federal Administrative Policies under the '33 and '34 Acts*. The Wheat Report. Chicago, IL: Commerce Clearing House, Inc.

———. 1973. *Statement of Policy on the Establishment and Improvement of Accounting Principles and Standards*. Accounting Series Release No. 150. Washington, D.C.: SEC (December 20).

———. 1974. *Capitalization of Interest by Companies Other than Public Utilities*. Accounting Series Release No. 163. Washington, D.C.: SEC (November 14).

———. 1976. *Notice of Adoption of Amendments to Regulation S-X Requiring Disclosure of Certain Replacement Cost Data*. Accounting Series Release No. 190. Washington, D.C.: SEC (March 23).

———. 1978. *Adoption of Requirements for Financial Accounting and Reporting Practices for Oil and Gas Producing Activities*. Accounting Series Release No. 253. Washington, D.C.: SEC (August 31).

———. 1980. *General Revision of Regulation S-X*. Accounting Series Release No. 280. Washington, D.C.: SEC (September 2).

———. 1981. *Financial Reporting by Oil and Gas Producers*. Accounting Series Release No. 289. Washington, D.C.: SEC (February 26).

Seligman, J. 1982. *The Transformation of Wall Street: A History of the Securities and Exchange Commission and Modern Corporate Finance*. Boston, MA: Houghton Mifflin Company.

Skousen, K. F. 1991. *An Introduction to the SEC*. Cincinnati, OH: South-Western Publishing Co.

Solomons, D. 1978. The Politicization of Accounting. *Journal of Accountancy* 146 (November): 65-72.

———. 1986a. The FASB's conceptual framework: An evaluation. *Journal of Accountancy* 161 (June): 114–116, 118, 120–122, 124.

———. 1986b. *Making Accounting Policy: The Quest for Credibility in Financial Reporting*. New York, NY: Oxford University Press.

Sommer, Jr., A. A. 1974. Financial reporting and the stock market: The other side. *Financial Executive* 42 (May): 36–40.

Sprouse, R. T., and M. Moonitz. 1962. *A Tentative Set of Broad Accounting Principles for Business Enterprises*. Accounting Research Study No. 3. New York, NY: AICPA.

Storey, R. K. 1964. *The Search for Accounting Principles: Today's Problems in Perspective*. New York, NY: AICPA.

Trueblood, R. M. 1966. Accounting principles: The Board and its problems. *Empirical Research in Accounting: Selected Studies 1966. Journal of Accounting Research* 4 (Supplement): 183–191.

Tweedie, D., and G. Whittington. 1984. *The Debate on Inflation Accounting*. Cambridge, U.K.: Cambridge University Press.

Uniformity in Financial Accounting. 1965. *Law and Contemporary Problems* 30 (Autumn).

Van Hulle, K. 1993. Harmonization of accounting standards in the EC: Is it the beginning or is it the end? *The European Accounting Review* 2 (September): 387–396.

Van Riper, R. 1994. *Setting Standards for Financial Reporting: FASB and the Struggle for Control of a Critical Process*. Westport, CT: Quorum Books.

Walker, R. G. 1992. The SEC's ban on upward asset revaluations and the disclosure of current values. *Abacus* 28 (March): 3–35.

Worthy, F. S. 1992. The battle of the bean counters. *Fortune* 125 (June 1): 117–118, 122, 124, 126.

Wyatt, A. R. 1991. The SEC says: Mark to market! *Accounting Horizons* 5 (March): 80–84.

Zeff, S. A. 1972. *Forging Accounting Principles in Five Countries: A History and an Analysis of Trends*. Champaign, IL: Stipes Publishing Company.

———. 1978. The rise of "economic consequences." *Stanford Lectures in Accounting 1978*. Stanford, CA: Graduate School of Business, Stanford University: 11–19.

———. 1984. Some junctures in the evolution of the process of establishing accounting principles in the U.S.A.: 1917–1972. *The Accounting Review* 59 (July): 447–468.

———. 1988. Setting accounting standards: Some lessons from the US experience. *The Accountant's M gazine* 92 (January): 20–22.

———. 1992. Arthur Andersen & Co. and the two-part opinion in the auditor's report: 1946–1962. *Contemporary Accounting Research* 8 (Spring): 443–467.

———. 1993. The politics of accounting standards. *Economia Aziendale* 12 (August): 125–142.

———, F. van der Wel, and K. Camfferman. 1992. *Company Financial Reporting: A Historical and Comparative Study of the Dutch Regulatory Process*. Amsterdam: North-Holland.

[3]

© 2001 American Accounting Association
Accounting Horizons
Vol. 15 No. 3
September 2001
pp. 257–271

Why Not Allow FASB and IASB Standards to Compete in the U.S.?

Ronald A. Dye and Shyam Sunder

Ronald A. Dye is a Professor at Northwestern University and Shyam Sunder is a Professor at Yale University.

SYNOPSIS: This paper discusses arguments for and against introducing competition into the accounting standard-setting process in the U.S. by allowing individual corporations to issue financial reports prepared in accordance with either FASB or IASB rules. The paper examines several arguments supporting the status quo, including (1) the FASB's experience and world leadership in making accounting rules; (2) the increased risk of a "race to the bottom" under regulatory competition; (3) the inability of most users of financial reports to understand the complex technical issues underlying accounting standards; (4) the possibility that IASB's standards will be diluted to gain international acceptance, allowing additional opportunities for earnings management; (5) the risks of the IASB being deadlocked or captured by interests hostile to business; (6) the costs of experimentation in standard setting; and (7) economies from network externalities. Arguments examined on the other side include how competition will (1) help meet the needs of globalized businesses; (2) increase the likelihood that the accounting standards will be efficient; (3) help protect standard setters from undue pressure from interest groups; (4) allow different standards to develop for different corporate clienteles; (5) allow corporations to send more informative signals by their choice of accounting standards; (6) protect corporations against capture of regulatory body by narrow interests; and (7) not affect network externalities at national or global scales.

Keywords: accounting standards; regulatory competition; international.

INTRODUCTION

This essay is written in the form of a debate between two individuals, M and C, over the appropriateness of introducing competition into the accounting standard-setting process. It is motivated by current discussions over whether standards promulgated by the International Accounting Standards Board (IASB) should be an acceptable substitute for those developed by the Financial Accounting Standard Board (FASB) in the U.S. At present, the Securities and Exchange Commission effectively allows the FASB to take the lead in formulating financial accounting standards for U.S. businesses.

We benefited from comments of two anonymous referees, Bryan Carsberg, Karel van Hulle, Edmund Jenkins, James Leisenring, Katherine Schipper, Stephen A. Zeff, and workshop participants at Carnegie Mellon University, Hong Kong University of Science and Technology, and Nanyang Technological University. We alone are responsible for the paper.

Submitted: March 2001
Accepted: May 2001
Corresponding author: Shyam Sunder
Email: shyam.sunder@yale.edu

Expanding the set of acceptable standard-setting bodies will significantly change the financial-reporting environment.

The desirability of introducing competition in standard setting varies with the issue being evaluated. We evaluate the pros and cons of competition by organizing this discussion between M (for monopoly) and C (for competition) around several of the major issues commonly raised. We provide section labels to demark the discussion of distinct issues.

IF IT'S NOT BROKEN, DON'T FIX IT

M1: The FASB has done a good job of dealing with many complex accounting issues over the past quarter century. It is the unquestioned leader in setting financial accounting standards in the world. Its standards serve as the model for a large number of other countries; some countries adapt its standards to suit their local conditions. The FASB standard-setting process is "open," encouraging participation by all interested constituencies. The FASB does not shy away from taking up difficult, even unpopular, stands on tough issues. Even many opponents of its proposals came to support its actions. It has acknowledged expertise; it has an established tradition; it has a worldwide reputation for visionary leadership in setting standards. Why change things now?

THE WORLD HAS CHANGED

C1: I agree with much of what you said. The FASB's pronouncements are often used as a model by many other countries, as well as by the IASB itself. No other standard-setting body in the world comes even close to matching the FASB's achievements. An argument for change now need not be read as a criticism of the FASB's past accomplishments and leadership. However, we must also look at the present and into the future.

The economic map of the world has changed over the past quarter century, and it continues to change. The U.S. economy, its capital markets, and U.S.-based multinational corporations are still the largest in the world. However, even though the U.S. economy continues to grow, faster growth in other parts of the world elevates the relative importance of other economies, their capital markets, and corporations based outside the U.S. In addition, capital flows more freely across national boundaries now than in the past. As a result, an increasing proportion of the holders of securities reside outside the legal jurisdiction in which the issuers of the securities reside. For example, a corporation chartered in the state of Delaware has shareholders, plants, employees, customers, and vendors scattered all over the globe, diluting the meaning and relevance of its national identity.

If we assume that certain standards are useful for promoting commerce, cross-boundary commerce requires cross-boundary standards. This is what the IASB is trying to do in the field of accounting, for the U.S. and for the world economy. There are parallels between the IASB's efforts and the federal laws that regulate interstate commerce and securities in the U.S. Over a century ago, the state of New York dominated the U.S. economy, and the laws and practices of that state influenced business conventions throughout the country.[1] As the economies of the

[1] See, for example, Carey's (1970) discussion of the importance of New York State's role in the development of accounting and auditing standards.

other parts of the U.S. developed, the national role of the state of New York diminished. Given the continuing development of the world economy, the FASB may not be able to continue its predominant role in determining national and international accounting standards.

I could make many arguments why it is desirable to allow the IASB to take the lead in formulating accounting standards in the U.S. Instead, I propose a more conservative course of allowing both the FASB and IASB standards to operate in the U.S. for five to ten years. With the insights generated by this experience, we could then decide whether to depend on either the FASB's or the IASB's standards, or to allow the standards developed by both to continue to operate in parallel.

COMPETITION MAY INDUCE A RACE TO THE BOTTOM

M2: Let us consider the suggestion that the U.S. allow each reporting organization to choose whether it wishes to publish its financial reports according to the FASB's or IASB's accounting standards. Presumably, firms will not be allowed to pick and choose among individual standards, and financial reports will be clearly labeled to inform the reader of the set of standards they conform to. However, I doubt if the average reader of financial reports has the accounting and financial expertise to distinguish between the information provided by financial reports prepared under the two sets of standards. How many people understand the meaning and implication of the UL (Underwriters Laboratories) stamp at the bottom of their toaster? And, using a toaster is easier than reading financial statements. I fear that allowing two sets of standards will induce a "race to the bottom," and erase the hard-won gains of financial reporting in the U.S. over the past half-century.

C2: What do you mean by a "race to the bottom"?

M3: A "race to the bottom" is a degradation of the quality and/or quantity of standards resulting from competition between standard-setting bodies.[2] It is closely linked to Gresham's Law—bad money drives out good money—and it applies to many forms of regulation. For example, in their quest to compete for depositors, countries such as Switzerland and the Cayman Islands simplified their banking regulations. Consequently, their banks became havens for illegitimately obtained money from all over the world. Similarly, some U.S. states and municipalities gave such large tax breaks to attract new businesses that their financial viability was threatened.

The same may happen to accounting standards if alternatives to FASB rules are permitted in the U.S. The financial reports of public corporations are prepared by their managers. Viewing accounting standards as a burden, managers prefer to comply with the least rigorous and demanding standards available. Requests for new accounting standards rarely originate from corporate executives who prepare financial reports. Whenever the FASB proposes a new standard, one can be reasonably sure that the Financial Executives International will resist the idea.[3] Moreover, managers seem to exploit whatever flexibility exists in accounting standards to present themselves, or their firms, in better light than indicated by their underlying performance.[4]

---

[2] See Monks and Minow (1995) or Easterbrook and Fischel (1991) for further discussion of the "race to the bottom."

[3] See Parfet (2000, 484).

[4] As an example of analytical model of managers' demand for earnings management, see Dye (1988).

Moreover, the FASB pays for many of its operating costs through the sale of publications, and through contributions from various constituents, including firms subject to FASB's rules. Given the freedom to choose between alternative sets of standards, firms are likely to buy the publications of, and make contributions to, the body whose standards they adopt. In addition to this link between the adoption of standards and the revenues of the standard-setting bodies, there is also the question of the respect and authority that derives from having many firms comply with a given body's standards. In their attempt to attract a larger following, and knowing that the firms prefer the least-demanding standards, the standard-setting bodies will tend to issue standards that pander to the reporting firms. What is worse, you won't have to wait for arrival of actual competition among standard setters before observing a reduction in the quality of accounting standards; even the anticipation of competition will lower the quality of standards.[5]

C3: Won't standard setting actually improve with increased competition?

M4: It is difficult for me to imagine that FASB's Standard No. 106, *Other Post Retirement Employee Benefits,* for example, could have been issued in a competitive environment. It was fought tooth and nail by business firms, even though many critics of that proposal are now glad that the FASB persevered in spite of their original objections.[6]

The argument that competition is good because it pushes organizations to be more responsive to their constituents can be taken only so far. In some instances, markets break down, and the consequences of competition can be worse than monopoly. If air pollution standards were set locally by individual municipalities, each might seek to attract industry by lowering its own standards with the expectation that a significant part of the cost of pollution will be borne by the residents of neighboring towns. In order to avoid this "race to the bottom," these standards are set by the federal government at the national level.

In any case, as I mentioned earlier, the process for setting accounting standards in the U.S. already has many desirable attributes: it is transparent and subject to detailed public scrutiny. Moreover, it is highly responsive to its constituents, which include both the investing public and the business community. Making the process more responsive, by allowing competition between standard-setting bodies, is only likely to create inappropriate pressure for lowering standards.

COMPETITION NEED NOT BE EQUATED TO "RACE TO THE BOTTOM"

C4: After hearing your argument, I agree that unbridled market competition is not a perfect solution to the problem of standard setting. We should look at the restraints that exist in the system to keep the potentially undesirable consequences of free competition under control. We also need to review the benefits of a limited amount of competition in this field.

If we allow competition in the creation of accounting standards, we will not do so in a vacuum. Acceptance of IASB standards in other countries is subject to the approval of local authorities. So is the approval of any changes in GAAP in the

[5] This is similar to how the threat of competition from firms not presently in a market can discipline the prices set by firms already in the market. See, e.g., Baumol et al. (1982).

[6] See Parfet (2000, p. 484).

U.S. Even today in the U.S., the SEC reviews all proposals and pronouncements of the FASB before deciding to support them. We will certainly continue this process if we allow IASB standards to compete with those of the FASB. If the SEC judges that either body is trying to "race the other to the bottom," it can withdraw its support and undermine the credibility of the offending standard setter. This threat will restrain the tendency of standards to "race to the bottom."

Moreover, all markets do not necessarily "race to the bottom." Competing bodies for standardization and certification of products and membership exist in many fields, such as engineering and education, in virtually all countries. The resulting standards are not necessarily watered down.[7] Producing sloppy standards enhances neither the reputations of those who set or comply with the standards nor the demand for their services. The same is true of competition among the 50 states in the U.S. with respect to corporate charters (see Dodd and Leftwich 1980).

I am also not convinced that managers always prefer or select the most aggressive reporting behavior permitted under prevailing rules. Conservatism has a long-standing and respected tradition among accountants and managers. Some firms and their managers attach considerable value to being known for reporting "high quality" earnings and are rewarded by the capital markets with lower cost of capital. In 1993, Daimler-Benz of Germany chose to adopt the stricter and more transparent U.S. standards in the hope of gaining these benefits.[8] Firms that adopt aggressive reporting behavior often experience large drops in value when the investing public becomes aware of their aggressiveness, and the managers of such firms sometimes get fired. Managers have substantial incentives to protect their reputations by adhering to conservative reporting practices. In short, there is an implicit demand by managers of public corporations for quality accounting standards and disclosures.[9]

M5: Although some of the details of your argument make sense to me, I want to return to the analogy between competition among accounting standard setters and competition among jurisdictions in setting pollution standards mentioned previously. In both cases, the problem is the existence of "externalities," or "spillover" costs or benefits arising when one party's actions result in uncompensated gains or losses to other parties. Pollution creates an externality except in those rare instances where the polluter reimburses those harmed by the pollution.[10] When individual jurisdictions set pollution standards, they capture the benefits of relaxed pollution

[7] There is historical evidence that competition for members among accounting groups need not destabilize membership standards. In the United Kingdom, and in Canada, three institutes of accountants compete in overlapping markets. The membership requirements of these institutes do not seem to be progressively slackening over time. This should not be surprising: these institutes must worry about the reputation of their members and the demand for their services when setting the height of the bar for admission. Setting the bar low enhances neither their reputations nor the demand for their services.

[8] "[Y]ou have to have access to global capital. That means listing on the leading stock markets. And it means presenting your financial accounts to the standards of the transparency demanded by investors" (Jürgen Schrempp, Chairman of Daimler Benz to Graham Bowley ([1997]).

[9] William Parfet (2000, 481–482), the chairman and CEO of MPI Research, Inc., said about managers' behavior in preparing firms' accounting reports, "To use a sports analogy, we want to win, but we want to win playing by the rules."

[10] When no individual has property rights over the fish in a body of water, unregulated competitive fishing leads to depletion of stocks. This is a classic example of inefficient use of a resource in presence of an externality, and often goes by the name "the tragedy of the commons." See, e.g., Stiglitz (1997).

restrictions. These benefits include attracting businesses seeking to avoid the costs of complying with pollution-related regulations, without bearing any of the costs imposed by pollution outside of their jurisdictions. The net result is too much pollution. There is a similar externality produced by standard-setting bodies. In evaluating General Motors, an investor looks not only at GM's financial statements, but also compares them to the financial statements of Ford. If Ford chooses to comply with a different set of reporting standards, then evaluation of GM becomes more difficult and less precise. Externalities of this sort pose problems only when there are multiple, competing jurisdictions. Why introduce this problem into the U.S. financial-reporting environment by inviting the IASB to compete with the FASB in the U.S.?

C5: It is interesting that you present the example of why there are national, and not municipal, standards for air pollution. Just as air travels from one municipal jurisdiction to another—making air quality difficult to control satisfactorily by local standards—capital also travels across national boundaries, making it difficult to control by national standards. This argument lies at the heart of the case for giving the IASB a fair trial in the U.S.

Achieving the right balance in air pollution controls is not a trivial problem. However, neither is choosing the right level of accounting standards. The most difficult problem in developing accounting standards, it seems to me, entails determining the right balance between "excessive" and "insufficient" standardization. The value of financial reporting is diminished at either extreme. Insufficient standards make it difficult for financial statement readers to identify the principles firms applied in constructing the statements. Excessive or inordinately narrow standards may prevent firms from selecting a reporting procedure that accurately conveys the substance of their economic situation.

Competition can help the economy "zero in" on the right level of accounting standards. It is difficult to conduct a social cost-benefit analysis of proposals for new standards, or for eliminating existing ones. Estimates of the economic consequences of such proposals are notoriously inaccurate. Asking firms or others to furnish their own estimates of the economic consequences of an accounting proposal runs into two problems. First, only those people or firms whose individual gains or losses are sufficiently large respond to such solicitations, resulting in a selection bias. Second, when they do respond, firms and other interested parties have obvious incentives to exaggerate their estimates in the hope of influencing the adopted policy.

Because accurate social cost-benefit analyses are difficult to conduct, accounting rules actually implemented may be inappropriate. Moreover, the difficulties attending the assessment of standards makes standard-setters susceptible to the so-called Law of the Instrument;[11] that is, standard setters may recommend the promulgation of increasingly more standards even when better alternatives exist. The resulting standards do not achieve the best social outcomes. This may account for the explosive growth of standards during the years since the creation of the FASB.

---

[11] "I call it *the law of the instrument*, and it may be formulated as follows: Give a small boy a hammer, and he will find that everything he encounters needs pounding" (Kaplan 1964, 28) (emphasis in the original).

Competition among standard-setting organizations can eliminate some of these problems and increase the efficiency of standards. Reactions to competing standards furnish each standard-setting organization with real feedback from their constituents. Instead of posturing as they often do at present, firms will "vote with their feet" in adopting or rejecting standards.[12] Competing standard-setting organizations are likely to be more responsive to demands for better standards than is a monolithic standard setter. If one set of standards is deficient relative to another, then competition will eliminate the former. Both insufficient and excessive standard setting will be curtailed as a consequence.

SURVIVAL OF THE FITTEST AND VOTING BY FEET

M6: Your argument seems to be a variation on the Darwinian "survival of the fittest" line of reasoning. Following this logic, one can make a case for not having any standards at all. After all, standards are a form of social norm or custom, and customs tend to evolve to efficient forms over time. This is the basic premise of the law and economics movement championed by Posner (1992) and others: the common law will eventually lead to socially efficient rules of behavior over time. Since the law does not face competition from other laws in a society, but is presumed to become efficient eventually, why shouldn't we expect accounting standards to become efficient over time, also—with or without competition?

C6: I agree that, like all social norms, accounting standards may converge to efficient rules over time with or without competition. However, and also like social norms, the evolution of accounting standards toward efficiency is neither rapid nor certain. Under rapid and continual change, accounting standards can permanently lag behind current business conditions, causing resources to be misallocated. Thus, there is a demand for organizations that develop financial-reporting standards. If we must have some formal standard-setting body, it is sensible not to allow any single body to have monopoly control of this process. A single source of accounting standards doesn't allow firms to "vote with their feet," and hence increases the chance of errors being perpetuated over the long term.

PEOPLE MAY NOT KNOW WHAT IS GOOD FOR THEM

M7: This "voting by their feet" argument assumes that people who make these decisions have sufficient understanding of the alternatives on hand to know the consequences of each option and to choose correctly what is in their best interest. I know that it sounds like an elitist argument, but years of experience with standard setting lead me to a different conclusion. The issues involved in setting accounting standards are technically quite complex, and it is not realistic to expect more than a handful of people to make the effort to gain more than superficial understanding of these issues. People do not always know what is in their own best interest when it comes to accounting. I already gave the example of the FASB's standard, *Other Post-Retirement Employee Benefits,* and there are many other examples. If the FASB could ever get its original proposal for a new standard on accounting for employee stock options approved, I believe firms will then ultimately understand that it was in their own best interest to recognize these expenses. The FASB has

[12] See Tiebout (1956) for the effects of competition between jurisdictions on the efficiency of the provision of local public goods. See, also, Tjiong (2000) for some counterarguments.

little chance of reaching that stage in such a politically charged issue. In any case, that is the reason why we need panels of experts like the FASB and IASB rather than referendums to set accounting standards.

C7: Your concern about the receptivity of business to new accounting standards such as those involving accounting for stock options or post-retirement benefits actually provides another reason for allowing competition between standard-setting bodies. Let's take the debate on accounting for derivatives. Alan Greenspan, Chairman of the Federal Reserve Board, agreed with the major banks' objections to mark-to-market accounting for derivatives. It was not until Congress introduced legislation to intervene in this matter, citing his position, that Mr. Greenspan reiterated his support for the independence of the FASB's process. With multiple sets of standards, the political pressures on the FASB, or any other standard-setting body adventurous enough to propose significant new reporting requirements, would be lower. That body could say, "Look, if you don't like these standards, opt out and select another set." The net result of introducing competition in standard setting might be just the opposite of what you call a "race to the bottom." Competition could reduce the lobbying pressure on any single standard-setting body compared to the present regime in which a single authoritative accounting body is subjected to considerable political pressure whenever it proposes an accounting innovation.

THE U.S. IS DIFFERENT (BETTER?) THAN THE REST OF THE WORLD

M8: Your argument implies that the IASB could serve as a foil for the FASB. Think about the specifics of how international accounting standards are set. Instead of developing in a vacuum, they respond to specific institutional settings. German accounting rules, for example, permit a plethora of "reserve" accounts. Lack of disclosure about these accounts makes it difficult for the reader to assess the value of a firm from its financial statements. Yet, this opacity of financial reports presents no problem for German banks—historically the principal source of capital for German firms. As lenders, these banks are privy to additional information not available to the general readers of German firms' financial statements. A representative of the bank often sits on the firm's board of directors. Under this financing and corporate governance structure, German GAAP does not hinder financing of German firms. However, financing and corporate governance structures in the U.S. are different. Individuals and other "nonbank" financial institutions hold much of the equity and debt issued by U.S. firms. Allowing U.S. firms the freedom to issue opaque statements loaded with reserve accounts will not work well because the providers of capital do not have access to the information hidden behind the reserve accounts.

Moreover, international accounting standards necessarily gloss over the variations in the functioning of national capital markets. They tend to be based on one of two strategies. One strategy is to base the international standards on standards already in force someplace. If sufficient support is not forthcoming for any existing standard, then a new standard is drafted. The new standard needs to gain substantial support from countries with diverse accounting practices and institutions. Often, the outcome of this process is a "minimum common denominator standard," which is just another way of phrasing "the race to the bottom" we discussed earlier. Unless the standards chosen are modeled after the practices of a country with a strong bias in favor of equal access to information, the outcome will be a step backward for investors. Since the U.S. is the leader in standard setting, forcing U.S. standard setters to compromise their principles for the sake of international harmonization will only have the effect of watering down U.S. GAAP. This is not the best outcome for participants in the U.S. securities markets.

C8: We both agree that business environments vary across countries. Let us also agree that in an ideal world it might be best to develop a unique set of ideal accounting standards for each environment. However, even within a legal jurisdiction, organizations of different sizes operate in different industries and in regions with different business environments. In fact, one could make a good argument that there is less difference between the business environments of Exxon and British Petroleum than between Exxon and Paradise Inc., a small Florida confectioner traded on the NASDAQ. So the problem you rightly point to is not unique to international accounting standard setting.

Fortunately, the resolution on the table leads to a reasonable solution to the problem. Under a competitive standard-setting system, the harmonization of reporting standards across the globe can proceed at a voluntary pace determined by local conditions. Firms with local clientele and little or no international exposure may find comfort in conforming to locally optimized standards written by their domestic standard-setting body, such as the FASB in the U.S. Other firms with international clienteles will choose to conform to international standards if they believe they are better off by doing so. This two-tiered system allows more freedom of choice to firms in all countries. Instead of suppressing it, such an approach will actually promote the legitimization of local standard-setting bodies. Within the U.S., for example, various stock exchanges compete by setting their own standards for listing firms. This competition creates a multitiered market that is healthy for the securities industry. It led to an equilibrium in which the New York Stock Exchange coexists with the NASDAQ, several regional exchanges, and even the Vancouver Stock Exchange with its reputation for trading highly speculative securities. Introducing competition between the IASB and local standard-setting bodies will encourage similar healthy competition in setting accounting standards.

Moreover, the possibility of segmentation of accounting standards is not new to the U.S. There has been much discussion about the "Little GAAP, Big GAAP" controversy over adjusting reporting standards for clientele effects. Competition between IASB and the FASB will respond to clienteles on a global scale. In short, I agree that, while there may be a problem resulting from IASB standards not being directly competitive with U.S. GAAP, there is a simple resolution of the problem—just introduce more competition!

BROADER AGREEMENT MEANS WEAKER STANDARDS

M9: You turned my own argument against me. But it is not that simple. Because the IASB must gain approval from a much larger constituency, the number of things they can agree on must be smaller than what the FASB agrees on. A possible result is lax standards compared to those of the FASB. Lax IASB standards allow firms more opportunity to manage their earnings, making financial reports less useful to investors. One of the costs associated with reaching the political consensus necessary to get international standards adopted is that the standards must be constructed relatively broadly and less specifically. Broad standards create more ambiguities and enhance chances that opportunistic, if not illegal, accounting treatments are blessed by generally accepted accounting principles. Earnings and balance-sheet management is one consequence of this vagueness. Earnings management misleads and harms investors who read and rely on the financial statements of culpable firms. A firm may be made to look more profitable and less risky. This practice injures not only the investors in the culpable firm, but also harms investors in other firms who may make invalid comparisons among the financial statements of firms that do/do not manipulate their earnings.

UNIFORMITY OF FORM OR UNIFORMITY OF SUBSTANCE

C9: Achieving uniformity and comparability of financial reports across firms and across time is a difficult problem in financial accounting. Contrary to popular belief, more detailed and more rigid or "uniform" standards that allow fewer options to managers do not make financial reports more comparable, or more informative. Statement of Financial Accounting Standards No. 2 is a good example. It requires all research and development outlays to be expensed, allowing managers no discretion when accounting for such costs. As a consequence, two firms that spend equal amounts on research report identical financial results, even when one's research is successful and the other's research yields no usable results. The idea that detailed rules lead to uniform and comparable results can be easily rejected on the basis of the exponential growth of the Internal Revenue Code, and the public dissatisfaction with the inequities of the tax burden and the administration of the Code.[13]

When you permit firms to choose from a set of accounting alternatives, firms do not necessarily reduce the amount of information they reveal to the readers of their reports, as long as the method they choose is also disclosed in the reports. Their choice among methods reveals what they know to the discriminating reader, just as the choice of an auto insurance policy with a low deductible reveals a policyholder's private information to an insurance company (see Levine 1996). By choosing a low-deductible policy, the policyholder reveals his/her high driving risk and high aversion to financial risk. Financial analysts continually scrutinize the choice of accounting methods by firms to assess the quality of firms and the quality of their management. Nothing generates a faster sell decision by an experienced analyst than a financial report in which management enlists all possible accounting tricks to burnish the report. Managers cannot resort to such methods without also revealing to knowledgeable readers that their firm is in a desperate condition. By eliminating such options in favor of "tight" standards, we also close off yet another channel of communication from the firm to the investing public.

Besides, managers who wish to be in the good graces of shareholders and analysts, and have confidence in the prospects of their firm, always have the option of revealing more than the applicable standards require. Adding IASB to FASB standards will not change any of this.

[13] Also see Havighurst (1965); Sunder (1997, 143–145).

INTERNATIONAL STANDARDS BODY MAY BE CAPTURED BY NONBUSINESS INTERESTS

M10: I want to step back to an earlier point about how the nature and extent of lobbying might be affected by competition between standard setters. You think that introducing competition will take the heat off a single standard-setting body and so, in principle, induce that body to be more adventurous in choosing innovative, even aggressive, standards. Contrary to your conjecture, I think competition will exacerbate, not relieve, lobbying pressures. We know how children try to play one parent against the other to get what they want. Competition between standard setters to attract client firms will only make them more susceptible to such pressures. It is easier to take a hard line when you are the only game in town.

Moreover, I worry about the pressures that could be brought to bear on the IASB. In the U.S., some accountants complain about the excessive influence of the Financial Executives International and the Business Roundtable in the standard-setting process. However, lobbying pressure from nonbusiness interests could be even worse. Think of the IASB as the United Nations of accounting boards. It is a voluntary association created by accounting organizations across 114 countries. If environmental or governmental interests in enough countries dominate business interests, then the IASB might be induced to issue standards unacceptable or irrelevant to business firms. International labor unions, various governmental groups, environmental and consumer groups may all try to sway IASB standards. One possible result of all this pressure is for the business community to stay away from IASB standards entirely. The conflicts among business, accounting, and other groups I mentioned could produce a deadlocked, paralyzed IASB—a paper tiger.

C10: Early in this conversation, you argued against more than one standard-setting body because the resulting competition would pose a serious challenge to the FASB, and that is undesirable. Now, you're saying that it is undesirable to have more than one standard-setting body because it wouldn't create viable competition. You can't have it both ways.

The possibility of IASB standards being co-opted by nonbusiness interests is remote. Even if that happens, the business community will not sit and watch from the sidelines any more than they did when the FASB's standards became mandatory in the U.S. Business will have a significant voice in all standard-setting decisions. Moreover, when businesses can choose which set of standards to adopt, neither the IASB nor any other standard-setting body can afford to write standards that alienate the business community. Even if your worst fears came true, and the IASB were captured by interests hostile to business, under the proposal we are debating the business community could simply ignore those standards and carry on.

My overall argument is simple: either IASB would be a viable alternative or it wouldn't; let's experiment by giving it a chance! The costs of conducting the experiment aren't that high. How can you lose?[14]

[14] The importance of "experimenting," or taking an action that may not be the best possible given current information, in hopes of making improved future decisions based on additional information collected today, has been the subject of intense study in the statistics literature. These problems have been classically referred to as "bandit" problems. See Berry and Fristed (1985) for an overview. This literature occasionally receives attention in economics as well. See, e.g., Grossman et al. (1977) for the earliest such treatment in economics. An interesting discussion about how successful firms may be averse to innovating, and consequently lose what made them successful, may be found in Christensen (1997).

THE COST OF STANDARDS AND EXPERIMENTATION

M11: The cost of failed experimentation with accounting standard-setting mechanisms is not low. Let's go through the list. Costs of standards include: (1) the costs incurred by the standard-setting body and the constituents in the formulation of standards; (2) the direct costs of implementing the standards by firms preparing the financial statements; and (3) the indirect costs of various agents adjusting their behavior to the new standard, and the economic consequences of the altered behavior. Most of our debate so far has centered on the third category. However, the costs in the first two categories are not small. Indeed, much of the opposition from business to new proposals for accounting standards is based on business' beliefs that their benefits do not exceed their costs.

The duplication of effort in evaluating competing standards is inevitable and wasteful. On top of this, firms may incur significant implementation costs if they decide to switch between competing standards. In addition, competing standard-setting groups lack the incentives to engage in due diligence when developing standards. Since the output of a standard-setting body is what economists call a "public good," a competing standard-setting body can use the concepts and ideas underlying a standard for free without incurring the cost of developing it. A developer of standards has no enforceable property right to its ideas and concepts. In contrast, a monopoly standard-setting body has the appropriate incentives to do due diligence without wasteful duplication.

C11: Keeping your three cost categories in mind, I agree that it is easier to estimate the costs in the first and second categories than in the third.[15] But the third category of costs is an order of magnitude higher than the other two. In a competitive environment, the standard-setters have reasons to minimize the sum of all three costs—essentially minimizing the third element. This inherent tendency of a competitive system is absent in a monopoly regime.

While your schema of costs is quite comprehensive, it is difficult in practice to provide reasonably precise estimates of any but the most trivial of these costs. Consider just one of the costs that is difficult to evaluate: the cost of obtaining "representative" standards board members. No standard-setting body can perfectly represent of all its constituencies. Limitations on the feasible size of such a body, and the large number of interests in society on which its actions may impinge, ensure that the constitution of such bodies must be less than perfectly representative. Competition among standard-setting bodies reduces the import of such imperfections. It ensures that such bodies must take into account the interests of various constituents even if they are not directly represented on the body itself. Disgruntled interests can shift their allegiances to the competition. This argument is invoked against federal chartering of corporations in the U.S. All 50 states of the union compete vigorously in the market for corporate charters, and Delaware seems to have won a lion's share of the market by designing laws, or

[15] Accounting and management generally are plagued with instances in which decisions are based on the easily assembled or computed information, rather than information most relevant to the decision at hand. A classic example is the emphasis on the "total costs of quality," consisting of appraisal, prevention, internal failure, and external failure costs (see, e.g., Kaplan and Ittner 1988). While the existence of these costs cannot be denied, they probably are an order of magnitude smaller than the effects of quality on customer demand.

"standards," attractive to various corporate constituents. In the 1980s, when some states tried to pass laws in support of corporate takeover defenses, economists argued that such laws only drive business away from the states that enact them. In brief, the composition of a standard-setting body becomes less critical when standard-setting bodies have to compete.

As I mentioned earlier, the costs of setting standards are difficult to quantify. To evaluate a monopoly standard-setter, one needs to know the magnitude of various costs. With competition among standard setters, there is less of a need to make such judgments. Competition helps ensure that the right amount of time, money, and effort is devoted to each of the activities the various standard setters engage in.

M12: There are other costs of competition. Economists study network externalities—the benefits of having multiple customers adhere to the same standard.[16] The telephone and facsimile machine provide classic examples of network externalities. One telephone, or one facsimile machine, is not of much use by itself. The usefulness of a telephone, or facsimile machine increases with the number of others who use compatible machines. Accounting standards also have network externalities. Using or interpreting financial reports to infer a firm's economic condition and performance is prone to error. If multiple firms adhere to the same set of standards, readers can compare across firms and interpret the reports better. This is a big advantage of having a single set of standards, and hence a single standard setter. I can only imagine the consequences if each firm reported by its own unique set of "standards."

As another example, think about the rationale for a single set of health and sanitation standards for restaurants in a city. Diners could go into a restaurant and ask themselves, "Is the set of health standards used here appropriate for what I would like to order for lunch today?" Instead, they prefer to have experts set uniform standards to ensure that all food served in all restaurants is safe. Analogously, investors don't want to have to wade into technical arguments about variations in GAAP when interpreting a firm's financial reports. You win investors' trust, and eliminate their confusion, by having all financial reports prepared in accordance with one GAAP.

C12: I agree that network externalities apply to accounting standards. Without such externalities, each firm could follow its own rules and there will be little need for standards (see Sunder 1997, chap. 11). The critical issue is how the magnitude of network externalities of accounting standards changes with the number of conforming firms. The economics literature typically assumes that the benefit of using a common standard increases with the number of consumers, according to some functional relationship. We do not know this function. It is possible that the rate of increase in benefit drops significantly as the numbers grow, in which case the advantage of adhering to a single set of standards in a large economy is minimal.

Let's consider the following thought experiment for the network externalities associated with telephones. Suppose everyone in the U.S. has a phone, but no one in Russia does. Under this hypothetical situation, it is not clear that most U.S. residents would get much added benefit if all Russians were given phones. We

[16] See Farrell and Saloner (1985) for an early reference.

should expect the incremental network externalities associated with more users to become small at some point. While network externalities may be important, we should not overstate their magnitude.

If the potential benefits from network externalities diminish rapidly with the number of firms adhering to the standards, then competing standard setters may do as well as a monopolist standard setter. This is true even without considering the other benefits of competition I mentioned earlier.

Your analogy with uniform sanitation code is inappropriate. First, investors do not have to know the details of GAAP, only their investment advisors do. People order and eat their meals without professional advisors at their side. Second, U.S. GAAP already permits many financial-reporting alternatives, forcing investors and analysts to cope with the different choices firms make.

M13: Perhaps the largest of the costs of accounting standards we haven't discussed yet is their effect on the risks borne by investors and the risk premium investors demand when pricing securities. Reporting standards cannot reduce the risk arising from the covariance between the market and firm returns. They can affect portrayal of the risk associated with the firm's cash flows. A monopoly standard setter, concerned with the risk borne by the shareholders of firms that adhere to its standards, could attempt to minimize this latter risk premium in the aggregate. Would competition among several standard setters do as well?

C13: I believe that competitive standard setters would do better. If the only objective of standard setters is to minimize the "informational" risk premium, then there will be no difference in the disclosures proposed by a monopoly standard setter and a set of competitive standard setters.[17] However, socially concerned standard setters must also consider whether increased disclosures result in firms' disclosing proprietary information to their competitors. When such proprietary costs are taken into account, it is very difficult to determine efficient or optimal standards. As I stated above, competitive standard-setting bodies are more likely to make the right choices in such tough decision-making circumstances.

SUMMARY

M14: I think we have put as many issues on the table as is possible in one debate, so let me summarize. I do not believe we need to fix something that is not broken. You believe in laissez faire competition, even in fields where the presence of externalities mitigates against the advantages of competition. As a practical matter, the SEC will never countenance the "choice" solution you propose. As a regulatory agency, the SEC has low tolerance for ambiguity and always champions the cause of uniformity over flexibility, even when, in your opinion, such uniformity is more a matter of form than substance. It is the least likely body to accept a regime under which companies subject to its jurisdiction can choose their own accounting standards. Of course, that does not mean that we shouldn't discuss and debate it. Do you have any final thoughts?

[17] See Dye (1990).

C14: Informed by a wider debate of this kind, we could make a better decision about opening the U.S. to the IASB standards. I wish we could elicit the best arguments by inviting more people to participate in this debate, even offering a prize to the person who makes the most persuasive case. However, I guess to be consistent with the philosophical position you advanced throughout this debate, you prefer a debate with only one person present, whose assertions are final and binding.

REFERENCES

Baumol, W., J. Panzar, and R. Willig. 1982. *Contestable Markets and the Theory of Industry Structure*. New York, NY: Harcourt, Brace and Jovanovich.

Berry, D., and B. Fristedt. 1985. *Bandit Problems: Sequential Allocation of Experiments*. London, U.K.: Chapman and Hall.

Bowley, Graham. 1997. Corporate culture and a community contribution. *Financial Times* (October 31): 16.

Carey, J., 1970. *The Rise of the Accounting Profession: To Responsibility and Authority 1937–1969*. New York, NY: AICPA.

Christensen, C. 1997. *The Innovator's Dilemma*. Cambridge, MA: Harvard Business Press.

Dodd, P., and R. Leftwich. 1980. The market for corporate charters: "Unhealthy competition" versus federal regulation. *Journal of Business* 53: 259–283.

Dye, R. 1988. Earnings management in an overlapping generations model. *Journal of Accounting Research* 26 (Autumn): 195–235.

———. 1990. Mandatory vs. voluntary disclosures: The cases of real vs. financial externalities. *The Accounting Review* 65 (January): 1–24.

Easterbrook, F., and D. Fischel. 1991. *The Economic Structure of Corporate Law*. Cambridge, MA: Harvard University Press.

Farrell, J., and G. Saloner. 1985. Standardization, compatibility, and innovation. *Rand Journal of Economics* 16 (Spring): 70–83.

Grossman, S. J., R. E. Kihlstrom, and L. J. Mirman. 1977. A Bayesian approach to the production of information and learning by doing. *Review of Economic Studies* 44 (October): 533–547.

Havighurst, Clark C., editor. 1965. *Uniformity in Financial Accounting. Law and Contemporary Problems*. Vol. XXX. Durham, NC: Duke University.

Kaplan, A. 1964. *The Conduct of Inquiry: Methodology for Behavioral Science*. San Francisco, CA: Chandler Pub. Co.

Kaplan, R., and C. Ittner. 1988. *Texas Instruments: Cost of Quality (A)*. HBR Case Studies. Boston, MA: HBS Publishing.

Levine, C. 1996. Conservatism, contracts and information revelation. Doctoral dissertation, Carnegie Mellon University.

Monks, R., and N. Minow. 1995. *Corporate Governance*. Oxford, U.K.: Blackwell.

Parfet, W. U. 2000. Accounting subjectivity and earnings management: A preparer perspective. *Accounting Horizons* 14 (December): 481–488.

Posner, R. 1992. *The Economic Analysis of Law*. 4th edition. Boston, MA: Little Brown and Company.

Stiglitz, J. E. 1997. *Economics*. Second edition. New York, NY: W. W. Norton.

Sunder, S. 1997. *Theory of Accounting and Control*. Cincinnati, OH: Thomson Learning.

Tiebout, C. M. 1956. A pure theory of local expenditures. *Journal of Political Economy* 64 (October): 416–424.

Tjiong, H. I. T. 2000. *Breaking the Spell of Regulatory Competition: Reframing the Problem of Regulatory Exit*. Bonn, Germany: Max-Planck-Projektgruppe Recht der Gemeinschaftsguter.

[4]

ELSEVIER Journal of Accounting and Public Policy 20 (2001) 129–153

Journal of Accounting and Public Policy

www.elsevier.com/locate/jaccpubpol

Non-US Firms' Accounting Standard Choices

Hollis Ashbaugh *

School of Business, Grainger Hall, University of Wisconsin at Madison, 975 University Avenue, Madison, WI 53706-1323, USA

Abstract

My study investigates the factors associated with non-US firms voluntarily reporting financial information prepared in accordance with International Accounting Standards (IAS) or United States (US) Generally Accepted Accounting Principles (US-GAAP). Documenting the factors associated with non-US firms' disclosures of IAS or US-GAAP financial information is important in that many equity market regulators are now allowing, or considering allowing, registrants to report under alternative sets of accounting standards. The annual reports of 211 non-US firms listed with the London Exchange are examined to determine firms' disclosure of IAS or US-GAAP financial information. Using multivariate logit regression, I found systematic differences in firm characteristics associated with non-US firms disclosing IAS or US-GAAP financial information rather than or in addition to financial information prepared in accordance with their domestic generally accepted accounting principles (domestic-GAAP). The results are consistent with the hypotheses that non-US firms are more likely to disclose IAS or US-GAAP financial information as their shares trade in more equity markets. In addition, I found that firms are more likely to disclose IAS or US-GAAP financial information when by doing so they can provide more standardized financial information relative to the information generated via their domestic-GAAP. I also found that firms are more likely to report IAS financial information when they participate in seasoned equity offerings and when US-GAAP requires more accounting policy changes relative to what is required under firms' domestic-GAAPs. These results suggest that non-US firms report IAS financial information to receive some benefits of providing more standardized financial information at costs less than what are incurred to implement US-GAAP. © 2001 Elsevier Science Ltd. All rights reserved.

* Tel.: +1-608-263-7979; fax: +1-608-265-9412.

E-mail address: hashbaugh@bus.wisc.edu (H. Ashbaugh).

0278-4254/01/$ - see front matter

PII: S0278-4254(01)00025-4

1. Introduction

This study investigates the factors associated with non-United States firms reporting financial information prepared in accordance with International Accounting Standards (IAS) or United States (US) Generally Accepted Accounting Principles (US-GAAP). IAS promulgated by the International Accounting Standards Committee (IASC) are a set of accounting standards intended to be used as a basis for cross-border capital raising and listing purposes in global markets (e.g., International Accounting Standards Committee, 1995). A competing international accounting regime, US-GAAP is derived from a hierarchy of US standard setting organizations, including the Financial Accounting Standards Board (FASB). The objective of an international set of accounting standards is to standardize firms' financial disclosures and accounting method choices among different nations (Ashbaugh and Pincus, 2001; Financial Accounting Standards Board, 1996, pp. 16–19). Proponents of international standards claim that if all firms follow the same set of accounting standards, firms' external financial reports would provide more uniform disclosures and accounting variables would be more useful to investors (Purvis et al., 1991, p. 43). It is also claimed that firms, in addition to investors, would benefit from disclosing financial information prepared in accordance with an internationally acceptable set of accounting standards (see e.g., Financial Accounting Standards Board, 1996, p. 3), i.e., IAS or US-GAAP. However, the majority of non-US firms do not disclose IAS or US-GAAP financial information (Speidell and Bavishi, 1992, pp. 58–66). This suggests that for the majority of non-US firms the costs associated with reporting IAS or US-GAAP financial information outweigh the benefits.

The scope of my study is to document factors associated with non-US firms voluntarily reporting IAS or US-GAAP financial information in their annual financial reports. Identifying the firm-specific characteristics associated with firms' disclosure of IAS or US-GAAP financial information is important in that many equity market regulators are now allowing, or considering allowing, registrants to report under alternative sets of accounting standards. For example, German laws were changed in 1998 to allow listed firms to prepare their consolidated financial reports in accordance with IAS or US-GAAP (Eggert, 1998, pp. 61–62) and the US Securities and Exchange Commission (SEC) is currently reviewing IAS as an alternative reporting regime for foreign registrants (Securities and Exchange Commision, 2000). Documenting the factors associated with non-US firms voluntarily reporting IAS or US-GAAP financial information contributes to our understanding of firms' financial reporting strategies in the global market.

Non-US firms listed with the London Exchange and quoted on the Stock Exchange Automated Quotation System (SEAQ) International Equity Market of London in 1993 are used to investigate the factors associated with non-US firms' IAS or US-GAAP reporting. I use this setting for several reasons. First, the London Exchange (1994a, pp. 35–40) allows foreign registrants to prepare financial reports in accordance with IAS, US-GAAP, UK-GAAP, or firms' domestic generally accepted accounting principles, i.e., domestic-GAAP. Second, as the largest international equity market (Zeff, 1998, p. 74), SEAQ International provides a more generalized setting to examine firms' accounting standard choices than a national equity market. Third, the London Exchange was the first to specifically identify IAS as an internationally acceptable set of accounting standards (International Accounting Standards Committee, 1992, p. 4). Since 1993 many domestic standard setters have incorporated IAS, or a subset of IAS, into their set of generally accepted accounting principles (International Accounting Standards Committee, 1995, pp. 8–10) suggesting that in periods after 1993, firms' choices may be influenced by their domestic standards alignment with IAS.

I examined the annual reports of 211 non-US firms to determine firms' accounting standard choices. Less than half of my sample firms (43.6%) disclose IAS or US-GAAP financial information in their annual reports. [1] After controlling for relative firm size and US-listings, the results of the multivariate logit regression indicate that the probability of disclosing IAS or US-GAAP financial information is positively associated with the number of foreign equity markets in which a firm's shares trade. The results also indicate that IAS or US-GAAP reporting is positively associated with the number of accounting measurement methods and disclosure changes imposed by the international accounting regimes relative to firms' domestic-GAAP. These results suggest that non-US firms use IAS or US-GAAP to disseminate standardized financial information to diverse financial information users.

To better understand why non-US firms disclose IAS financial information, I repeated the logit analysis excluding firms that report US-GAAP financial information. I found a positive association between firms' disclosures of IAS financial information and the number of foreign equity markets in which their shares trade. In addition, firms are more likely to disclose IAS financial information when IAS requires more financial disclosures and restricts their accounting method choices relative to their domestic-GAAPs. I also found that non-US firms are more likely to disclose IAS financial information when they are raising additional capital via the issuance of equity shares, i.e., participating

[1] The firms identified as disclosing IAS (US-GAAP) financial information state that the financial information that they are presenting complies with IAS (US-GAAP). Street et al. (1999) suggest that non-US firms do not implement IAS on a consistent basis. Ashbaugh and Olsson (2001, pp. 10–15) indicate that their sample of non-US firms reporting under IAS have done so for more than five years and, in addition, contract with the large international auditing firms, suggesting that non-US firms do apply IAS on a consistent basis. It is beyond the scope of this study to attest to my sample firms' compliance with IAS or US-GAAP.

in seasoned equity offerings. These findings are consistent with the suggestion that non-US firms voluntarily disclose IAS financial information in an attempt to lower the information asymmetry component of their costs of capital (Leuz and Verrecchia, 2001).

My study's final analysis investigates the firm-specific characteristics associated with non-US firms voluntarily reporting IAS or US-GAAP financial information in their annual reports. The majority of my sample firms reporting US-GAAP financial information in their annual reports are required to file such information with the SEC because their shares trade in the New York, American, or NASDAQ market. However, 33.3% of my sample firms reporting US-GAAP financial information have no SEC filing requirements. While the results of the logit analysis indicate that non-US firms are more likely to disclose IAS financial information when they do not have to file US-GAAP financial information with the SEC, the results also indicate that non-US firms are more likely to disclose IAS financial information when they trade in fewer equity markets relative to US-GAAP firms. Furthermore, I found that non-US firms are more likely to disclose IAS financial information when the disclosure requirements and accounting method constraints of US-GAAP increase relative to IAS and their domestic-GAAP. Collectively, these findings suggest that non-US firms not required to adhere to the stringent reporting standards of US-GAAP prefer IAS as the means to provide standardized financial information because IAS allows greater flexibility in firms' accounting measurement choices and requires fewer disclosures relative to US-GAAP.

My study provides evidence on the factors associated with non-US firms deviating from their traditional reporting practices, i.e., domestic-GAAP, and reporting financial information prepared in accordance with IAS or US-GAAP. These factors proxy for some of the benefits associated with non-US firms reporting financial information prepared in accordance with IAS or US-GAAP. The fact that not all non-US firms voluntarily report IAS or US-GAAP financial information implies that firms incur non-trivial costs to report financial information prepared in accordance with an internationally acceptable set of accounting standards. The remainder of the paper is organized as follows. Section 2 develops the hypotheses and Section 3 sets forth the research design. The results are presented in Section 4. Section 5 concludes the study.

2. Factors influencing firms to disclose IAS or US-GAAP financial information

Welker (1995) suggests that firms engage in differential disclosure practices, and that firms' disclosure strategies and changes thereof can impact capital market participants. Firms have discretion over the financial disclosures they provide to capital markets (Lang and Lundholm, 1996). The annual report is one mechanism firms use to disseminate discretionary financial information

(Botosan, 1997, p. 326). My general hypothesis is that non-US firms will disclose financial information prepared in accordance with IAS or US-GAAP when the benefits related to such disclosures outweigh their costs. More specifically, I posit three factors that proxy for the benefits associated with non-US firms voluntarily disclosing IAS or US-GAAP financial information in their annual reports.

2.1. To communicate with foreign financial information users

With the globalization of capital markets and the increase in world trade, firms are more likely to communicate with foreign as well as domestic financial information users. Firms acknowledge the importance of providing useful financial information to foreign as well as domestic investors (see e.g., Bayer, 1997, p. 60). Firms conducting business outside their native country are also concerned with communicating with diverse suppliers and customers. Such firms have used foreign listings as a mechanism to gain public recognition in a foreign market (Saudagaran, 1988, p. 106). Managers have identified the increase in company visibility as a benefit of foreign listings (Mittoo, 1994, pp. 33–35). Furthermore, as a firm's securities trade in more foreign equity markets, there is a wider distribution of equity shares and a greater demand for financial information (Biddle and Saudagaran, 1991, p. 71). [2] Therefore, I hypothesize that the greater the number of foreign equity markets in which a firm's shares trade, the more likely it is that the firm discloses IAS or US-GAAP financial information. [3] Formally, the first hypothesis is (in alternative form):

H1: The probability of disclosing IAS or US-GAAP financial information is positively related to the number of foreign equity markets in which a firm's shares trade.

---

[2] The proportion of equity shares held by foreign investors may be an alternative measure of foreign financial information users. However, this measure does not address the diversity of foreign shareholders or capture the other potential users of firms' financial reports. For example, suppose two French firms each have 20% of their stock held by foreign investors. Assume the first firm's foreign investors reside in Germany because this firm is listed on the Frankfurt exchange. Assume the other firm has a uniform distribution of foreign investors residing in Sweden, Switzerland, the UK, Norway, Finland, and Germany because this firm is listed on six foreign exchanges. It is assumed the latter firm is more likely to present internationalized financial information in its annual report.

[3] Recall that the London Exchange was the only exchange to specifically accept IAS as a basis for financial reporting in 1993. Since then, more exchanges are accepting IAS as a basis for financial reporting (Choi et al., 1999, 255–266). Thus, a tangential benefit firms may currently receive by reporting IAS or US-GAAP financial information is the minimization of financial reporting costs across equity markets.

2.2. To facilitate raising equity capital

Prior research suggests that firms benefit from providing voluntary disclosures (Welker, 1995; Botosan, 1997). Moreover, prior research suggests that firms time their voluntary disclosures to preempt investors' private information search activities (Choi, 1973). For example, Cooper and Grinder (1996, pp. 470–472) report US firms have significantly higher information flows in the month prior to announcing new equity offerings. I hypothesize that non-US firms incorporate the reporting of IAS or US-GAAP financial information into their disclosure strategies to facilitate raising equity capital. That is:

H2: The probability of disclosing IAS or US-GAAP financial information is positively related to the occurrence of firms' stock issuances.

2.3. To provide more standardized financial information in the annual financial report

Fishman and Hagerty (1989, pp. 635–642) demonstrate that firms expend more resources on disclosure than is socially optimal because firms must compete for the attention of traders since it is too costly for a trader to study the disclosures of every firm. In the context of this study, firms may choose to provide standardized financial disclosures and measures of accounting variables (e.g., net income, stockholders' equity) to reduce traders' information processing costs related to understanding alternative domestic-GAAP. If so, firms preparing financial information in accordance with IAS or US-GAAP may be better able to attract the attention of traders and increase the efficiency of the market prices of their securities.

2.3.1. Disclosure requirements

In some countries, domestic-GAAP varies from IAS and US-GAAP because there are fewer disclosure requirements and/or firms have more discretion in the informativeness of the disclosures provided in their annual reports (Coopers and Lybrand, 1993, pp. 1–37). Table 1 reports the comparisons between eight IAS (11 US-GAAP) disclosures in force in 1993 to the 1993 disclosure requirements of domestic-GAAP of countries in which the firms used in the empirical analysis are domiciled. The disclosure items, while not all-inclusive, represent the more significant variation in financial disclosure requirements across national boundaries (International Accounting Standards Committee, 1993, pp. 6–7). A domestic-GAAP is considered less stringent than IAS or US-GAAP in its disclosure requirements if (1) it has no re-

Table 1
Matrix of required disclosures: IAS and US-GAAP compared to domestic accounting standards[a]

	Addition disclosures required under IAS[b]									Additional disclosures required under US-GAAP			
Country[c]	1	2	3	4	5	6	7	8	IASDIS[d]	9	10	11	USDIS[d]
Australia					X[e]				1				1
Belgium		X				X		X	3		X		4
Bermuda									0			X	1
Denmark					X	X			2			X	3
Finland	X		X	X	X	X	X		6	X		X	8
France	X			X	X	X			4			X	5
Germany	X				X	X			3		X	X	5
Hong Kong	X				X		X		3			X	4
Japan				X	X				2	X			3
Luxembourg	X			X	X		X		4		X	X	6
Netherlands	X				X				2		X	X	4
New Zealand				X	X				2			X	3
Norway	X	X		X	X	X	X	X	7		X	X	9
Singapore	X			X					2				2
Spain				X	X		X		3	X	X		5
Sweden	X			X	X	X		X	5		X	X	7
Switzerland	X			X	X			X	4		X	X	6

[a] *Sources*: Coopers and Lybrand (1993) and Price Waterhouse (1996).
[b] Disclosure items: 1 = required statement of funds/cash flows; 2 = required disclosure of accounting policies; 3 = required disclosure of effect of change in accounting policy; 4 = required disclosure of effect of change in accounting estimate; 5 = required disclosure of prior period adjustment; 6 = required disclosure of post balance sheet events; 7 = required disclosure of related party transactions; 8 = required disclosure of segmental information; 9 = required disclosure of discontinued operations; 10 = required disclosure of earnings per share; 11 = required disclosure of allowance of doubtful accounts.
[c] The countries examined are based on where the firms used in the empirical analysis are domiciled.
[d] IASDIS and USDIS are the sum of the additional disclosures required under IAS and US-GAAP, respectively, relative to a country's GAAP disclosure requirements.
[e] X = when (1) domestic-GAAP has no disclosure requirement or (2) the domestic-GAAP requirement is less stringent than IAS or US-GAAP.

quirement or (2) the requirement is less restrictive than the IAS or US-GAAP requirement. [4]

The IASDIS (USDIS) value in Table 1 is the sum of differences in the disclosure requirements of a domestic-GAAP relative to IAS (US-GAAP). IASDIS (USDIS) represents the increasing standardization of firms' required financial disclosures by choosing to comply with IAS (US-GAAP) rather than their domestic-GAAP. In general, firms domiciled in Finland, France, Luxembourg, Norway, Sweden, and Switzerland provide more standardized financial disclosures by complying with IAS than by complying with their domestic-GAAP. [5] Because US-GAAP has more stringent disclosure requirements than IAS, i.e., USDIS, firms domiciled in these countries would also provide more standardized financial disclosures by complying with US-GAAP.

2.3.2. Accounting method restrictions

Choi and Levich (1992) suggest that the differences in the number of accounting measurement methods within and across domestic-GAAP result in disparities in information across markets. Ashbaugh and Pincus (2001) document that the differences in domestic-GAAP relative to IAS are positively associated with analysts' forecast errors. The differences in accounting measurement methods across domestic-GAAP potentially impacts other users of firms' financial reports as they may find it too costly to become (and remain) informed about alternative domestic-GAAP accounting measurement methods. Hence, firms have incentives to provide more standardized measures of net income and stockholders' equity.

Table 2 compares four IAS (seven US-GAAP) accounting measurement rules in force in 1993 to the 1993 domestic-GAAP measurement rules for countries where my sample firms are domiciled. IAS (US-GAAP) is considered to be more restrictive than domestic-GAAP when IAS (US-GAAP) has fewer acceptable methods of accounting for an economic event relative to the

[4] For example, IAS requires post-balance sheet events having evidence of existence at the balance sheet date to be disclosed in the footnotes to the financial statements (Coopers and Lybrand, 1993, pp. IAS-8–IAS-9). French-GAAP only requires disclosure if the going-concern assumption might be affected by the post-balance sheet event (Coopers and Lybrand, 1993, pp. F-39-F-40). Thus French-GAAP is considered to be less stringent that IAS.

[5] Since the public accounting profession in Bermuda was governed by the Institute of Chartered Accountants of Bermuda, which was formally affiliated with the Canadian Institute of Chartered Accountants, firms domiciled in Bermuda in 1993 generally followed Canadian-GAAP (Price Waterhouse, 1996, p. 2). As such, the Bermuda indices reported in Tables 1 and 2 are based on comparisons between Canadian-GAAP and IAS (US-GAAP).

Table 2
Restriction of accounting measurement choices: IAS and US-GAAP compared to domestic accounting standards[a]

	Accounting measurement restrictions under IAS[b]					Accounting measurement restrictions under US-GAAP			
Country[c]	1	2	3	4	IASCON[d]	5	6	7	USCON[d]
Australia			X[e]	X	2	X		X	4
Belgium	X		X	X	3	X			4
Bermuda					0			X	1
Denmark		X		X	2		X		3
Finland	X	X	X	X	4	X	X		6
France	X	X	X		3	X	X	X	6
Germany	X				1				1
Hong Kong				X	1	X	X	X	4
Japan		X	X		2				2
Luxembourg			X	X	2		X		3
Netherlands			X		1	X	X	X	4
New Zealand				X	1	X	X	X	4
Norway			X		1	X	X	X	4
Singapore					0	X	X	X	3
Spain			X		1		X	X	3
Sweden		X	X		2	X	X		4
Switzerland	X	X	X	X	4		X	X	6

[a] *Sources*: Coopers and Lybrand (1993) and Price Waterhouse (1996).
[b] Accounting measurement restrictions; 1 = domestic-GAAP allows firms to report additional depreciation that has been recorded to reduce firms' tax liability or to setup replacement reserves; 2 = accounting for leases; 3 = accounting for pensions; 4 = accounting for research and development costs; 5 = required use of historical cost accounting for property, plant, and equipment; 6 = accounting for intangible assets other than research and development; 7 = accounting for investments.
[c] The countries examined are based on where the firms used in the empirical analysis are domiciled.
[d] IASCON and USCON are the sum of the accounting measurement constraints under IAS and US-GAAP, respectively, relative to a country's GAAP measurement methods.
[e] X = when adopting IAS restricts the accounting measurement choices relative to the accounting measurement choices available under domestic-GAAP.

methods acceptable under domestic-GAAP. [6] IASCON (USCON) represents the increasing restrictions on a firm's accounting measurement choices by complying with IAS (US-GAAP) rather than the domestic-GAAP of its country of domicile. IAS compliance results in greater restrictions on accounting measurement choices for firms domiciled in Belgium, Finland, France, and Switzerland. Firms from these countries will report more standardize measures of net income and stockholders' equity by complying with US-GAAP.

It is reasonable to conjecture that firms incur differential costs to disclose IAS or US-GAAP financial information since not all firms report such information in their annual reports. The more restrictive IAS or US-GAAP is in its accounting measurement methods relative to domestic-GAAP, the more costly it is to report standardized measures of net income and stockholders' equity. Explicit costs are due, in part, to the information collection and processing costs associated with the number of changes needed to convert a domestic-GAAP accounting system into a system that produces earnings and stockholders' equity in accordance with IAS or US-GAAP (see e.g., Biddle and Saudagaran, 1991, p. 71). The increase in required standardized disclosures can also impose costs on firms. Firms incur out-of-pocket costs to produce the additional disclosures if the data are not already produced for internal reporting purposes. The additional disclosures may also impose implicit costs on a firm if such disclosures place a firm at a competitive disadvantage when competitors do not publish similar information. Hence, for some firms the costs will dominate the perceived benefits associated with reporting IAS or US-GAAP financial information. Since the costs and benefits of reporting IAS or US-GAAP financial information is unclear due to the variation in domestic-GAAP, the following hypothesis is tested:

H3: The probability of disclosing IAS or US-GAAP financial information is associated with the financial reporting requirements of a firm's domestic-GAAP.

3. Research design

The sample selection is as follows. The London Exchange provided me the names of all 484 non-US/non-UK firms admitted to listing as of March 31, 1994. Of these, 184 firms were eliminated because they were not in the *Global Vantage*

[6] For example, a French firm may elect to capitalize leases in its consolidated financial statements (Coopers and Lybrand, 1993, pp. F-43–F-44). IAS requires leases to be capitalized when substantially all the risks and rewards incident to ownership are transferred to the lessee (Coopers and Lybrand, 1993, pp. IAS-11–IAS-12). Thus, lease accounting under IAS is judged to be more constrained than under French-GAAP.

database, the source of financial and market data, and 15 firms were eliminated because they were approved for listing but did not trade on SEAQ International in 1993. [7] I deleted eight Italian firms and 26 South African firms because IAS was the basis for those countries' domestic-GAAP in 1993 (International Accounting Standards Committee, 1995, p. 9). Letters were sent to the remaining 251 SEAQ International firms requesting a copy of their 1993 and 1994 annual reports. Annual reports of 211 firms were received (an 84.1% response rate). [8]

Based on my examination of their annual reports, firms were classified as IAS firms, US-GAAP firms, or domestic-GAAP firms. [9] Non-US firms are classified as IAS (US-GAAP) firms if it was stated in their summary of accounting policies or audit reports that the financial statements were prepared in accordance with IAS (US-GAAP). [10] Firms providing IAS (US-GAAP) footnote reconciliations are also classified as IAS (US-GAAP) firms. [11] The domestic-GAAP firms use the accounting standards of their country of domicile. Table 3 presents the distribution of the three categories of sample firms by country. The majority of IAS firms are domiciled in France (11 firms), Finland (8), Switzerland (8), and Sweden (7). [12] The US-GAAP firms are domiciled primarily in Japan (16 firms), France (6), and Sweden (4). [13]

[7] The London Exchange did not identify any Canadian firms as being listed with the Exchange and quoted on SEAQ International in 1993.

[8] The London Exchange's listing requirements require non-UK firms listed with the Exchange to prepare their annual report in English (London Exchange, 1994a, p. 34).

[9] None of the firms used UK-GAAP.

[10] Details on how firms implement IAS are provided in the Appendix.

[11] To gain some insight into the impact of adopting IAS or US-GAAP, I calculate the changes in net income and stockholders' equity for the few firms that provide footnote reconciliations from domestic-GAAP to either IAS ($n = 9$) or US-GAAP ($n = 17$). The median change from domestic-GAAP net income to IAS (US-GAAP) net income is 0% (−12%), although the changes range from −367% to 372% (−79 to 185%). The median change from domestic-GAAP stockholders' equity to IAS (US-GAAP) stockholders' equity is 22% (6%). Overall, the variation in earnings and stockholders' equity measured in accordance with an internationally acceptable set of standards suggests the implementation of IAS or US-GAAP may differentially impact firms' financial statements.

[12] There are five firms that are domiciled in Bermuda where firms generally follow Canadian accounting standards (Price Waterhouse, 1996, p. 12.1). I performed two sensitivity tests related to these firms. First, I set SET (USSET) equal to 12 (18) under the assumption that Bermuda firms would have to make all the changes to adhere to the disclosure requirements and accounting standards choices under IAS (US-GAAP). Second, I deleted Bermuda firms from the statistical analyses. The results reported in Tables 5, 6, and 8 are robust to these two sensitivity tests.

[13] To provide some evidence about business operations, I examined firms' SIC codes (not tabled). The distribution of SIC codes appears similar across the three types of firms. Regardless of accounting standard choice, the majority of firms are engaged in manufacturing operations. Descriptive statistics of other firm-specific characteristics (e.g., sales, total assets) are dependent on firms' accounting standard choices and as such are not prepared.

Table 3
Distribution of firms by country of domicile

	Accounting Standard Choice							
	IAS		US-GAAP		Domestic-GAAP		Total	
Country	*n*	%	*n*	%	*n*	%	*n*	%
Australia	5	9	1	3	13	11	19	9
Belgium	1	2	1	3	3	3	5	2
Bermuda	5	9	0	0	0	0	5	2
Denmark	1	2	1	3	0	0	2	1
Finland	8	14	0	0	1	1	9	4
France	11	20	6	16	11	9	28	14
Germany	0	0	0	0	22	18	22	11
Hong Kong	1	2	1	3	8	7	10	5
Japan	5	9	16	43	34	28	55	26
Luxembourg	0	0	1	3	0	0	1	0
Netherlands	0	0	2	6	14	12	16	8
New Zealand	0	0	1	3	1	1	2	1
Norway	3	5	1	3	5	4	9	4
Singapore	1	2	0	0	0	0	1	0
Spain	0	0	1	3	1	1	2	1
Sweden	7	12	4	11	5	4	16	8
Switzerland	8	14	0	0	1	1	9	4
Total	56	100	36	100	119	100	211	100

Accounting Standard Choice classifications are based on the examination firms' 1993 annual report prepared in English in accordance with the London Exchange's listing requirements (London Exchange, 1994b, pp. 8–9).

Firms were classified as IAS firms if (1) they prepared financial reports in accordance with IAS as described in the summary of significant accounting policies or the audit report or (2) they prepared financial reports in accordance with their domestic-GAAP and provided IAS footnote reconciliations; Firms were classified as US-GAAP firms if (1) they prepared financial reports in accordance with US-GAAP as described in the summary of significant accounting policies or the audit report or (2) they prepared financial reports in accordance with their domestic-GAAP and provided US-GAAP footnote reconciliations; Firms were classified as Domestic-GAAP firms if their financial reports were prepared in accordance with the generally accepted accounting principles of their country of domicile and they did not provide any IAS or US-GAAP financial data in their financial reports.

The factors hypothesized as being associated with firms' decisions to disclose IAS or US-GAAP financial information are tested using the following logit regression:

$$\text{P(CHOICE)} = \beta_0 + \beta_1\text{NMARKETS} + \beta_2\text{ISSUE} + \beta_3\text{SET} + \beta_4\text{RELSIZE} + \beta_5\text{USXCH} + \varepsilon, \quad (1)$$

where Choice equals one if a firm reports IAS or US-GAAP financial information in its 1993 annual financial report ($n = 92$) and zero if a firm reports only domestic-GAAP financial information ($n = 119$), NMARKETS is the number of foreign equity markets in which a firm's shares are traded, ISSUE equals one if a firm issues stock in 1993 or 1994, and zero otherwise, SET is the sum of IASDIS and IASCON from Tables 1 and 2, respectively, RELSIZE is the market value of a firm's shares listed on its domestic exchange divided by the total capitalization of its domestic equity market at December 31, 1993, USXCH equals one if a firm is required to file Form 20-F and zero otherwise.

The number of foreign equity markets in which a firm's shares are traded, NMARKETS, is identified through the *Bloomberg Financial Services* database. [14] Firms raising capital through equity offerings, i.e., ISSUE = 1, are identified by reading the firms' 1993 and 1994 financial reports. Equity offerings in 1993 and 1994 are considered because my sample firms adopted IAS prior to 1993. Specifically, 5.4%, 19.6%, and 75.0% of the IAS sample firms adopted IAS in 1990, 1991, and 1992 respectively. The value assigned to SET represents the potential number of accounting policy changes firms made by providing IAS financial information. SET reflects the fact that each set of domestic-GAAP is a unique combination of disclosure and accounting measurement policies (Ashbaugh and Pincus, 2001). [15] The same classifications are assumed for firms using US-GAAP in this phase of the analysis.

---

[14] It could be that firms decide jointly to change their financial reporting strategies and list on foreign exchanges. If so, the number of foreign exchanges may not be exogenous to the model of accounting standard choice. To test for exogeneity, I applied the Hausman test (Hausman, 1978) as follows. First, I used absolute firm size as the instrumental variable in the first stage regressions where the dependent variable is NMARKETS. Absolute firm size is defined as the firm's market value of equity. The market value of equity is statistically significant (at the 0.01 level, two-tailed test) in each model and the R^2s range from 0.10 to 0.22. Second, the predicted values from the first stage regressions are added as instrumental variables (call the variable NMARKET-HAT) to the original logit equations. The results of the second stage regressions fail to reject the hypothesis that the coefficients on NMARKET-HAT are zero. Thus, the number of exchanges can be considered an exogenous variable.

[15] Doupnik and Salter (1993) argue that countries' legal classifications are aligned with countries' accounting objectives, suggesting that common law countries' domestic-GAAP objectives are to produce transparent financial information. In this sense, domestic-GAAP from common law countries would be similar to IAS since IAS are intended to produce information that allows users to properly value firms (International Accounting Standards Committee, 1999, pp. 38–46). Using the common versus code law country classifications reported in Haskins et al. (1996, p. 19), I found the SET variable to be highly positively correlated with a categorical variable, coded 1 for firms domiciled in countries classified as having a code law legal system and one for firms domiciled in countries classified as having a common law legal system. As a sensitivity test, I substituted the legal classification categorical variable for SET in my regression analyses and obtained quantitatively similar results.

Two control variables are included in the regression equation. RELSIZE is a relative size measure where the numerator is equal to a firm's price per share multiplied by the number of shares outstanding as of December 31, 1993. The denominator of RELSIZE is the total equity market capitalization of the firm's country of domicile as reported in the *London Exchange 1994 Fact Book* (1994b, p. 36). Wyatt (1992, p. 13.9) suggests that non-US firms will use IAS to facilitate the cross-border flow of capital when they exhaust their ability to raise capital in their home markets. I use RELSIZE to proxy for a firm's demand for foreign capital (Saudagaran, 1988, p. 108). USXCH controls for firms' required filing of US-GAAP financial data with the SEC when they trade on a major US exchange.

4. Results

Table 4 presents summary statistics. Likelihood ratio χ^2 tests indicate that IAS/US-GAAP firms (1) trade in more foreign equity markets than domestic-GAAP firms, (2) issue more equity in 1993 or 1994 than domestic-GAAP firms, (3) provide more standardized information by complying with IAS or US-GAAP relative to their domestic-GAAP, and (4) more often file Form 20-F than domestic-GAAP firms. The mean value of RELSIZE for IAS/US-GAAP firms is significantly larger (at the 0.01 level in a one-tailed test) than the mean value of RELSIZE for domestic-GAAP firms. [16]

The results of logit regression (1) are reported in Table 5. Overall, the model is highly significant ($\chi^2 = 62.93$; significance level <0.001) and has a Pseudo R^2 of 0.22. [17] The positive and significant coefficient on NMARKETS (at the 0.02 level, one-tailed test) indicates that firms are more likely to disclose IAS or US-GAAP financial information when their shares trade in more foreign equity markets. The positive and significant coefficient on SET (at the <0.01 level, two-tailed test) indicates that firms from countries with less stringent reporting requirements are more likely to report financial information prepared in accordance with an internationally acceptable set of accounting standards. The positive and significant coefficient on ISSUE (at the 0.08 level, one-tailed test) indicates that firms seeking additional equity capital are more likely to disclose IAS or US-GAAP financial information. The coefficients on the control variables RELSIZE and USXCH are also

[16] Spearman correlations (not tabled) for the explanatory variables range from −0.258 to 0.392. In general, the pattern of significant correlations is similar across the three firm classifications.

[17] The Pseudo R^2 is calculated as $1 - (\log L_{UR} / \log L_R)$ (Maddala, 1988, pp. 277–279).

Table 4
Summary statistics

Variable	IAS/US-GAAP firms ($n = 92$)				Domestic-GAAP firms ($n = 119$)			
	Mean	Median	S.D.	Min./ Max.	Mean	Median	S.D.	Min./ Max.
NMARKETS++	3.64	3.00	1.99	1/9	2.77	2.00	1.68	1/8
ISSUE++	0.35	0.00	0.48	0/1	0.21	0.00	0.41	0/1
SET+++	5.93	5.00	2.38	0/10	4.76	5.00	1.55	3/10
USXCH+++	0.35	0.00	0.47	0/1	0.07	0.00	0.25	0/1
RELSIZE	0.03***	0.01###	0.04	0.00/ 0.24	0.01	0.00	0.01	0.00/ 0.05

Variable descriptions: NMARKETS is the number of foreign markets in which a firm's shares are traded in 1993. ISSUE equals 1 if a firm issues stock in 1993 or 1994 and 0 otherwise. SET is the sum of IASDIS and IASCON from Tables 1 and 2, respectively. USXCH equals 1 if a firm is required to file Form 20-F and 0 otherwise. RELSIZE is the market value of a firm's shares listed on its domestic exchange divided by the total capitalization of its domestic equity market at December 31, 1993.

++ Likelihood ratio χ^2 tests reject the hypotheses of no difference in the values of the discrete and binary variables across IAS/US-GAAP and domestic-GAAP firms (significant at the 0.05 level).

+++ Likelihood ratio χ^2 tests reject the hypotheses of no difference in the values of the discrete and binary variables across IAS/US-GAAP and domestic-GAAP firms (significant at the 0.01 level).

*** A *t*-test rejects the hypothesis of no difference in the means of RELSIZE for IAS/US-GAAP and domestic-GAAP firms (significant at the 0.01 level, one-tailed test.)

A Wilcoxon rank sum test rejects the hypothesis of no difference in the distributions of RELSIZE (significant at the 0.01 level, one-tailed test).

positive and significant (at the 0.09 and <0.01 levels, respectively, one-tailed tests). These results suggest, in general, that non-US firms with culturally diverse shareholders, less demanding domestic reporting practices, and relatively large domestic market capitalization perceive benefits associated with reporting financial information prepared in accordance with an internationally acceptable set of accounting standards.

To investigate the characteristics that are associated with firms disclosing IAS financial information, I re-estimate Eq. (1) excluding US-GAAP firms from the analysis. Specifically, I code the dependent variable in Eq. (1) as 1 if the firm discloses IAS financial information in its annual report ($n = 56$) and 0 if a firm reports only domestic-GAAP financial information ($n = 119$). The results are reported in Table 6. The model is significant ($\chi^2 = 38.41$; significance level < 0.001; Pseudo $R^2 = 0.18$).

The positive and significant coefficient on SET (at the 0.01 level, two-tailed test) indicates that firms from countries with less stringent reporting requirements are more likely to use IAS, suggesting IAS is viewed as a mechanism to disseminate more standardized financial information than what is provided under the firms' domestic-GAAP. The significant coefficient on ISSUE (at the

Table 5
Probability of disclosing IAS or US-GAAP financial information

	Explanatory variable	Predicted sign	Parameter estimate	Standard error
	Intercept	Unsigned	−3.676###	0.691
H1	NMARKETS	+	0.227**	0.104
H2	ISSUE	+	0.510*	0.365
H3	SET	±	0.375###	0.094
	RELSIZE	+	15.782**	9.441
	USXCH	+	1.706***	0.468

Maximum likelihood estimates		Goodness-of-fit measures	
χ^2	62.93	Pseudo R^2	0.22
Significant level	0.00	Concordant	80%

Dependent variable: Probability of IAS or US-GAAP, coded 1 for firms that disclose IAS or US-GAAP financial information in their annual reports ($n = 92$) and 0 otherwise ($n = 119$). NMARKETS is the number of foreign markets in which a firm's shares are traded in 1993. ISSUE equals 1 if a firm issues stock in 1993 or 1994 and 0 otherwise. SET is the sum of IASDIS and IASCON from Tables 1 and 2, respectively. RELSIZE is the market value of a firm's shares listed on its domestic exchange divided by the total capitalization of its domestic equity market at December 31, 1993. USXCH equals 1 if a firm is required to file Form 20-F and 0 otherwise.

Significant at the 0.01 level (two-tailed test).

* Significant at the 0.10 level (one-tailed test).

** Significant at the 0.05 level (one-tailed test).

*** Significant at the 0.01 level (one-tailed test).

0.01 level, one-tailed test) indicates a positive relation between IAS reporting and seasoned equity offerings. Recall that my sample of IAS firms adopted IAS in 1990, 1991, or 1992, i.e., the years immediately preceding the analysis period. This result suggests firms incorporate IAS into their disclosure strategies in order to increase their externally reported information flows prior to issuing additional shares. [18] The positive and significant coefficient on NMARKETS (at the 0.08 level, one-tailed test) indicates that non-US firms more likely to adopt IAS as their shares trade in more foreign equity markets, suggesting that firms view IAS financial information as being useful to foreign financial

[18] Due to data limitations, I was not able to discern from the financial reports if firms were issuing stock in their domestic or in foreign equity markets. However, anecdotal evidence suggests firms have incentives to standardize and/or increase their disclosures to meet the information needs of both domestic and foreign shareholders. For example, prior to 1991, domestic institutional investors in Switzerland were not as active in their domestic equity market as their US counterparts. Evidence suggests, however, that after 1992, domestic institutional investment has increased in Switzerland due, in part, to the improvements in corporate disclosures by Swiss companies (Euromoney, 1994, pp. 29–30).

Table 6
Probability of disclosing IAS financial information

	Explanatory variable	Predicted sign	Parameter estimate	Standard error
	Intercept	Unsigned	−3.690###	0.747
H1	NMARKETS	+	0.163*	0.118
H2	ISSUE	+	0.943***	0.388
H3	SET	±	0.321###	0.099
	RELSIZE	+	22.777**	11.351
	USXCH	unsigned	0.480	0.610

Maximum likelihood estimates		Goodness-of-fit measures	
χ^2	38.41	Pseudo R^2	0.18
Significant level	0.00	Concordant	76%

Dependent variable: Probability of IAS, coded 1 for firms that disclose IAS financial information in their annual report ($n = 56$) and 0 for firms that disclose only domestic-GAAP financial information ($n = 119$). NMARKETS is the number of foreign markets in which a firm's shares are traded in 1993. ISSUE equals 1 if a firm issues stock in 1993 or 1994 and 0 otherwise. SET is the sum of IASDIS and IASCON from Tables 1 and 2, respectively. RELSIZE is the market value of a firm's shares listed on its domestic exchange divided by the total capitalization of its domestic equity market at December 31, 1993. USXCH equals 1 if a firm is required to file Form 20-F and 0 otherwise.

Significant at the 0.01 level (two-tailed test).

* Significant at the 0.10 level (one-tailed test).

** Significant at the 0.05 level (one-tailed test).

*** Significant at the 0.01 level (one-tailed test).

statement users. Turning to the two controls variables, the coefficient on RELSIZE is positive and significant (at the 0.04 level, one-tailed test) whereas the coefficient on USXCH is now insignificant.

Recently, the debate over the acceptability of IAS has centered on the US capital markets (Pownall and Schipper, 1999). The SEC requires foreign registrants to prepare US-GAAP financial information if their equity shares trade in the New York, American, or NASDAQ markets. Instead of preparing their annual report in accordance with US-GAAP, firms can elect to provide a reconciliation of domestic-GAAP earnings and stockholders' equity to US-GAAP earnings and stockholders' equity as a supplement to their domestic-GAAP annual report. The SEC is considering allowing registrants' financial information to be prepared in accordance with IAS without reconciliation to US-GAAP (Securities and Exchange Commision, 2000, p. 1). Non-US firms trading or wanting to trade their equity shares in the US capital markets may prefer IAS to US-GAAP because they perceive US-GAAP to be too restrictive in its accounting method choices and/or too demanding in its disclosure requirements. Non-US firms may use IAS as the mechanism to report more standardized financial information until they have to bear the additional costs of preparing US-GAAP financial information for the SEC. [19]

Table 7 reports the sample distribution of IAS and US-GAAP firms across US equity markets (domestic-GAAP firms are included for completeness). Of the 88 firms using IAS or US-GAAP, 23 (26.2%) did not trade equity shares in the US. A larger proportion of IAS firms (29.6%) than US-GAAP firms (9.1%) traded American Depository Receipts (ADRs) in the Over-the-Counter Bulletin Board market. [20] Of the 39 sample firms required to file US-GAAP financial information with the SEC, because they traded their ADRs in the New York, American, or Nasdaq markets, 24 elected to report US-GAAP information in their annual report while seven firms elected to report IAS financial information. A likelihood ratio χ^2 test rejects the null hypothesis of no difference in the frequencies of US equity market listings across IAS and US-GAAP firms. The distribution suggests that the required filing of Form 20-F influences a firm's choice between reporting IAS or US-GAAP information, but does not dictate the choice.

Recall that Tables 1 and 2 summarize the additional disclosures and accounting measurement restrictions of US-GAAP relative to IAS when a firm deviates from its domestic-GAAP. For the majority of firms, preparing US-GAAP financial reports results in two additional required disclosures beyond IAS requirements. In addition, US-GAAP materially restricts most firms' accounting measurement choices relative to the choices available under IAS (Financial Accounting Standards Board, 1996, pp. 25–37). The additional reporting requirements of US-GAAP suggest that US-GAAP reporting may be a more costly disclosure strategy for non-US firms than the strategy of disseminating IAS financial information.

To investigate the firm-specific characteristics of IAS versus US-GAAP firms, the following logit regression is estimated:

[19] Anecdotal evidence consistent with this conjecture can be found. For example, Saga Petroleum (1993, p. 45) applied IAS in its 1993 financial report by providing a footnote reconciling Norwegian GAAP net income and shareholders' equity to IAS net income and stockholders' equity. However, in 1994, Saga presents a footnote reconciling its domestic-GAAP to US-GAAP because of the company's interest in obtaining a New York Stock Exchange listing during the next year (Saga Petroleum, 1994, p. 49). Prior to having to file US-GAAP financial information with the SEC, Saga arguably believed financial information prepared in compliance with IAS to be beneficial to the readers of its 1993 financial report. Because Saga incurred costs to generate US-GAAP financial information for 1994, it may not have been worth the additional cost to prepare its annual financial reports using IAS.

[20] The Over-the-Counter Bullettin Board market is an electronic quotation system sponsored by Nasdaq. Non-US firms trading ADRs on the Bulletin Board in 1993 were not required to file financial information with the SEC (Frost and Lang, 1996, pp. 98–99).

Table 7
Distribution of firms across US equity markets

	Not traded in the US	US Bulletin Board market[a]	US Form 20-F market[b]	Total
IAS firms				
Frequency	19	26	7	52[c]
Percent of total	21.6	29.6	7.9	
Row percent	36.5	50.0	13.5	
US-GAAP firms				
Frequency	4	8	24	36
Percent of total	4.6	9.1	27.3	
Row percent	11.1	22.2	66.7	
Domestic-GAAP firms				
Frequency	53	58	8	119
Percent of total	25.6	28.0	3.9	
Row percent	44.6	48.7	6.7	
Total	76	92	39	207

A likelihood ratio χ^2 test rejects the hypothesis of no difference in the frequencies of equity market listings across IAS and US-GAAP firms (significant at the 0.01 level).
Accounting Standard Choice classifications are defined in Table 3.
[a] Non-US firms that trade American Depository Receipts in the Nasdaq's Over-the-Counter (OTC) Bulletin Board market did not have to file US-GAAP financial information with the SEC in 1993 (Frost and Lang, 1996, pp. 98–99).
[b] Non-US firms trading in the New York, American, or NASDAQ markets must file Form 20-F with the SEC.
[c] Four IAS firms were deleted from the analysis because they also reported US-GAAP reconciliations in their annual reports.

$$P(\text{IAS}^*) = \beta_0 + \beta_1\text{NMARKETS} + \beta_2\text{ISSUE} + \beta_3\text{USSET} + \beta_4\text{RELSIZE} + \beta_5\text{USXCH} + \varepsilon, \quad (2)$$

where IAS* equals 1 if a firm discloses IAS financial information in its annual financial report ($n = 52$) and zero if the firm chooses US-GAAP ($n = 36$), USSET is the sum of USDIS and USCON from Tables 1 and 2, respectively.

Table 8 presents the results of estimating multivariate logit regression (2). The model is significant ($\chi^2 = 58.86$; significance level < 0.001; Pseudo $R^2 = 0.49$). As expected, the negative and significant coefficient on USXCH (at the 0.01 level, one-tailed test) is consistent with the notion that firms are more likely to disclose IAS financial information when they are not required to file US-GAAP financial information with the SEC. The negative and significant coefficient on NMARKETS (at the 0.02 level, two-tailed test) indicates that IAS firms' shares trade in fewer equity markets relative to firms that disclose US-GAAP financial information in their annual reports. The negative and

Table 8
Probability of disclosing IAS versus US-GAAP financial information

Explanatory variable	Predicted sign	Parameter estimate	Standard error
Intercept	Unsigned	6.310###	1.666
NMARKETS	Unsigned	−0.493##	0.220
ISSUE	Unsigned	2.571###	0.834
USSET	±	−0.602###	0.180
RELSIZE	Unsigned	20.633##	9.302
USXCH	–	−3.142***	0.808
Maximum likelihood estimates		Goodness-of-fit measures	
χ^2	58.86	Pseudo R^2	0.49
Significance level	0.00	Concordant	92%

Dependent variable: Probability of IAS, coded 1 for firms that disclose IAS financial information in their annual reports ($n = 52$) and 0 for firms that disclose US-GAAP, ($n = 36$). Four IAS firms were eliminated from the analysis because they also reported US-GAAP reconciliations in their annual reports. NMARKETS is the number of foreign markets in which a firm's shares are traded in 1993. ISSUE equals 1 if a firm issues stock in 1993 or 1994 and 0 otherwise. USSET is the sum of USDIS and USCON reported in Tables 1 and 2, respectively. RELSIZE is the market value of a firm's shares listed on its domestic exchange divided by the total capitalization of its domestic equity market at December 31, 1993. USXCH equals 1 if a firm is required to file Form 20-F and 0 otherwise.

Significant at the 0.05 level (two-tailed test).

Significant at the 0.01 level (two-tailed test).

*** Significant at the 0.01 level (one-tailed test).

significant coefficient on USSET (at the 0.01 level, two-tailed test) documents that firms are more likely to disclose IAS financial information when US-GAAP requires more disclosures and restricts accounting measurement methods relative to the policies of their domestic-GAAP. [21] The positive and significant coefficient on ISSUE (at the 0.01 level, two-tailed test) indicates that firms are more likely to disclose IAS financial information when they are issuing seasoned equity.

The positive and significant coefficient on RELSIZE (at the 0.02 level, two-tailed test) indicates that relatively larger firms, in terms of domestic market capitalization, are more likely to disclose IAS financial information than US-GAAP financial information. Recall that RELSIZE is a size measure that proxies for a firm's demand for foreign capital (Saudagaran, 1988, p. 108). It could be that such relatively large firms demand more foreign capital because their domestic markets are smaller or less sophisticated than other countries' capital

[21] One of the criticisms of IAS is that the IAS accounting measurement choice set is too large (Financial Accounting Standards Board, 1996, pp. 34–37). The IASC has had two major overhauls of the set of standards comprising IAS. The first was the Comparability Project implemented in January 1, 1995 (International Accounting Standards Committee, 1993, pp. 8–9). The second was the Core Project completed in 1998 (Zeff, 1998, pp. 67–70).

markets and reporting IAS financial information is the first step in providing more standardized financial information to capital market participants. [22] To investigate this conjecture, I partitioned my sample firms into quartiles based on RELSIZE. Examining the upper quartile (where the expectation is that 25% of the sample firms from each country would appear), I found that 60.0%, 50.0%, 66.7%, 70.0%, 55.6%, 100%, 50.0%, 31.3%, and 33.3% of the sample firms from Belgium, Denmark, Finland, Hong Kong, Norway, New Zealand, Spain, Sweden, and Switzerland, respectively, have RELSIZE upper quartile values. In general, the number of listings and trading volume in these countries' equity markets are less relative to other countries represented in my sample, e.g., France, Germany, Japan (Euromoney, 1994, pp. 9–10, 11–13, 55–57, respectively). [23]

Alternatively, large firms, in absolute terms, may have incentives to disclose IAS or US-GAAP financial information because there is a greater demand for information about large firms (Lang and Lundholm, 1993, pp. 250–251). I explored the incentives large firms have to disclose IAS or US-GAAP financial information by re-estimating the regression equations using an absolute size measure; the market value of a firm's shares listed on its domestic exchange at December 31, 1993, measured in millions of US dollars. The estimated coefficients on the absolute size variable (not reported) were insignificant in each analysis. This suggests that absolute firm size does not influence a firm's decision to disclose IAS or US-GAAP financial information.

5. Conclusions

My study develops and tests hypotheses explaining why non-US firms voluntarily report financial information prepared in accordance with IAS or US-GAAP. The evidence presented in this paper indicates that non-US firms are more likely to disclose IAS or US-GAAP financial information when their equity shares trade in more foreign equity markets and when IAS or US-GAAP results in more standardized financial information relative to their domestic-GAAP reports. The results also document that firms are more likely to disclose IAS financial information when they are participating in seasoned equity offerings. I also found that firms are more likely to disclose IAS financial information when US-GAAP requires more disclosures and restricts accounting measure methods relative to the policies of their domestic-GAAP. Overall, the factors documented as being associated with non-US firms' ac-

[22] I thank a reviewer for positing this explanation of the positive association between non-US firms' disclosure of IAS financial information and their relative size.

[23] The remaining countries (Australia, Bermuda, France, Germany, Luxemburg, Japan, Netherlands, and Singapore) had relatively equal distribution of sample firms across the RELSIZE quartiles.

counting standard choices suggest that non-US firms select increasingly stringent sets of accounting standards when the expected benefits exceed the expected costs.

Documenting the factors associated with non-US firms' accounting standard choices is important because market regulators, accounting standard setters, accounting researchers, and capital market participants are interested in the quality of accounting standards. One characteristic of high quality accounting standards is that the standards result in transparent and comparable financial information (Securities and Exchange Commision, 2000, pp. 3–4). However, firms' implementation of accounting standards can influence the transparency and comparability of the resulting financial statements. Without knowing what motivates non-US firms to report IAS or US-GAAP financial information, it is difficult to assess the comparability of the alternative sets of standards because firms' incentives may influence the implementation of the standards. To this end, the results of my study provide insights into what motivates non-US firms' to deviate from their domestic-GAAP and implement an internationally acceptable set of accounting standards. Further research can assess whether the factors documented in my study as being associated with non-US firms' reporting of IAS or US-GAAP financial information result in differential implementation of the sets of standards and, ultimately, differential transparency and comparability of firms' financial information.

Acknowledgements

This paper is based on my dissertation titled Non-US Firms' Accounting Standard Choices in Accessing Foreign Capital Markets. I thank my chair, Morton Pincus and other members of my dissertation committee, Tom Carroll, Dan Collins, Amy Dunbar, George Neumann, and Grace Pownall, for their comments. In addition, I appreciate the comments of Robert Dosch, W. Bruce Johnson, Tom Linsmeier, Per Olsson, Mohan Venkatachalam, R.S. Olusegun Wallace, Terry Warfield, and workshop participants at the American Accounting Association/KPMG 1997 International Accounting Research Conference, Purdue University, Ohio State University, Oklahoma State University, and the University of Wisconsin–Madison. I also thank the Ernst & Young Foundation for their funding of this project.

Appendix A. IAS implementation

Firms implement IAS differently and, in general, the cost of IAS implementation is dependent on a firm's domestic-GAAP. Firms from developing countries where IAS have become the national standards do not incur any incremental costs to report IAS financial information because they can prepare financial reports that conform with national and international requirements (International Accounting Standards Committee, 1995, pp. 8–9). In some developed countries, IAS is the basis for domestic-GAAP (Cairns, 1995, pp. 53–56), suggesting that firms incur minimal incremental costs in preparing IAS financial information. In countries with sets of financial reporting standards that are independent of IAS, firms can incur substantial incremental costs to report IAS financial information (Leuz and Verrecchia, 2001). These firms can provide footnote reconciliations of domestic-GAAP net income and shareholders' equity to IAS-based net income and shareholders' equity (see e.g., Bergesen, 1997, p. 25) or they can provide two sets of financial statements within the annual report; one prepared in accordance with domestic-GAAP and the other prepared in accordance with IAS (see e.g., Huhtamaki, 1997, pp. 24–26). Alternatively, a firm can apply IAS to the financial statements taken as a whole and disseminate only IAS financial statements to capital market participants (see e.g., Bayer, 1997). The incremental costs of reporting IAS financial information are assumed to be minimized when firms choose the subset of measurement and disclosure practices that meet their domestic requirements and that also comply with IAS. [24]

References

Ashbaugh, H., Olsson, P., 2001. An exploratory study of the valuation properties of cross-listed firms' IAS and US-GAAP earnings and book values. The Accounting Review (forthcoming).

Ashbaugh, H., Pincus, M., 2001. Domestic accounting standards, International Accounting Standards, and the predictability of earnings. Journal of Accounting Research (forthcoming).

Bayer, 1997. Annual Report. Bayer AG, Germany.

Bergesen, 1997. Annual Report. Bergesen ASA, Norway.

Biddle, G., Saudagaran, S., 1991. Foreign stock listings: Benefits, costs, and the accounting policy dilemma. Accounting Horizons 5 (3), 69–80.

Botosan, C., 1997. Disclosure level and the cost of equity capital. The Accounting Review 72 (3), 323–349.

Cairns, D., 1995. A Guide to Applying International Accounting Standards. Accountancy Books, London.

Choi, F., 1973. Financial disclosure and entry to the European capital market. Journal of Accounting Research 11 (2), 159–175.

Choi, F., Levich, R., 1992. International accounting diversity and capital market decisions. In: Frederick, C. (Ed.), Handbook of International Accounting. Wiley, New York, pp. 7.1–7.29.

[24] For example, 1993 IAS require firms to expense all research costs but allow firms to capitalize some development costs (International Accounting Standards Committee, 1994, pp. 140–146). Norwegian-GAAP permitted firms to capitalize research and development costs (Coopers and Lybrand, 1993, pp. N-91–N-92). By capitalizing only its development costs, a Norwegian firm can comply with its domestic-GAAP and IAS.

Choi, F., Frost, C., Meek, G., 1999. International Accounting, third ed. Prentice-Hall, Englewood Cliffs, NJ.

Cooper, D., Grinder, B., 1996. Voluntary information disclosure during periods of stock price vulnerability. Journal of Business Finance and Accounting 23 (3), 461–472.

Coopers & Lybrand, 1993. International Accounting Summaries, second ed. Wiley, New York.

Doupnik, T., Salter, S., 1993. An empirical test of a judgmental international classification of financial reporting practices. Journal of International Business Studies 28 (1), 41–60.

Eggert, R., 1998. German corporate law and accounting legislation. International Tax Review 9 (7), 61–62.

Euromoney, 1994. World Equity Markets, Euromoney, London.

Financial Accounting Standards Board, 1996. The IASC-U.S. Comparison Project: A Report on the Similarities and Differences between IASC Standards and U.S. GAAP, Financial Accounting Standards Board, Norwalk, CT.

Fishman, M., Hagerty, K., 1989. Disclosure decisions by firms and the competition for price efficiency. The Journal of Finance 44 (3), 633–646.

Frost, C., Lang, M., 1996. Foreign companies and US securities markets: Financial reporting policy issues and suggestions for research. Accounting Horizons 10 (1), 95–109.

Haskins, M., Ferris, K.. Selling, T., 1996. International Financial Reporting and Analysis. Irwin, Chicago.

Hausman, J., 1978. Specification tests in econometrics. Econometrica 46, 1251–1271.

Huhtamaki, 1997. Annual Report 1997. Huhtamaki Oy, Finland.

International Accounting Standards Committee, 1992. IASC Annual Review 1991/1992, International Accounting Standards Committee, London.

International Accounting Standards Committee. 1993. IASC Insight: December, International Accounting Standards Committee, London.

International Accounting Standards Committee, 1994. International Accounting Standards 1994, International Accounting Standards Committee, London.

International Accounting Standards Committee, 1995. IASC Annual Review 1994, International Accounting Standards Committee, London.

International Accounting Standards Committee, 1999. International Accounting Standards 1999, International Accounting Standards Committee, London.

Lang, M., Lundholm, R., 1993. Cross-sectional determinants of analyst ratings of corporate disclosures. Journal of Accounting Research 31 (2), 246–271.

Lang, M., Lundholm, R., 1996. Corporate disclosure policy and analyst behaviour. The Accounting Review 71 (4), 467–492.

Leuz, C., Verrecchia, R.. 2001. The economic consequences of increased disclosure. Journal of Accounting Research (forthcoming).

London Stock Exchange. 1994a. A listing in London, second ed. The International Stock Exchange of the United Kingdom and the Republic of Ireland, London.

London Stock Exchange. 1994b. Fact Book 1994. The International Stock Exchange of the United Kingdom and the Republic of Ireland, London.

Maddala, G., 1988. Introduction to Econometrics. Macmillan, New York.

Mittoo, U., 1994. Evaluating the foreign listing decision in a capital budgeting framework. Managerial Finance 20 (8), 22–35.

Pownall, G., Schipper, K.. 1999. Implications of accounting research for the SEC's consideration of international accounting standards for U.S. securities offerings. Accounting Horizons 13 (3), 259–280.

Price Waterhouse. 1996. Doing Business in Bermuda, Price Waterhouse, NJ.

Purvis, S., Gernon, H., Diamond, M., 1991. The IASC and its comparability project: Prerequisites for success. Accounting Horizons 5 (2), 25–44.

Saga Petroleum. 1993. Annual Report. Saga Petroleum, Norway.

Saga Petroleum, 1994. Annual Report. Saga Petroleum, Norway.
Saudagaran, S., 1988. An empirical study of selected factors influencing the decision to list on foreign stock exchanges. Journal of International Business Studies 19 (1), 101–127.
Speidell, L., Bavishi, V., 1992. GAAP arbitrage: Valuation opportunities in international accounting standards. Financial Analysts Journal 48 (6), 58–66.
Street, D., Gray, S., Bryant, S., 1999. Acceptance and observance of International Accounting Standards: An empirical study of companies claiming to comply with IASs. The International Journal of Accounting 34 (1), 11–48.
United States Securities and Exchange Commission (SEC), 2000. SEC Concept Release No. 1215: International Accounting Standards, Securities and Exchange Commission, Washington, DC.
Welker, M., 1995. Disclosure policy, information asymmetry, and liquidity in equity markets. Contemporary Accounting Research 11 (2), 801–827.
Wyatt, A., 1992. International Accounting Standards and organizations: Quo Vadis? In: Frederick, C. (Ed.), Handbook of International Accounting. Wiley, New York, pp. 13.1–13.20.
Zeff, S., 1998. The IASC's core standards: What will the SEC do? Journal of Financial Statement Analysis 4 (1), 67–78.

[5]

Journal of International Financial Management and Accounting 7:1 1996

The Choice of Accounting Policy In Japan

*Tatsuo Inoue**
Kwansei Gakuin University

*Wayne B. Thomas**
University of Utah

Abstract

The purpose of this study is to investigate factors which potentially influence Japanese managers' choices of accounting policies. Several factors have been posed to affect the choice of accounting policy of U.S. managers (e.g., Watts and Zimmerman's (1986) positive accounting theory). However, the general business characteristics of the U.S. environment differ, sometimes drastically, from those in Japan. Factors affecting the choice of accounting policy in the U.S. may not similarly affect the choice of accounting policy in Japan. At the same time, new factors may be identified in the Japanese business environment.

Income strategy models are developed for each firm according to the type (income increasing or income decreasing) of accounting policies employed. The results suggest that both the size and debt/equity hypotheses are significant, even for keiretsu firms. These results are surprising given (1) the close relationship between firms and the government, (2) regulations of the commercial code which serve to protect the interests of debtholders, and (3) the tight relationship between banks and firms within keiretsu groups which protects firms from bankruptcy and takeover. Variables representing firms' effective tax rate, ability to finance operations internally, and foreign political costs are also shown to significantly affect Japanese managers' choices of accounting policy. The bonus hypothesis is not significant in the Japanese environment. Furthermore, the choice of accounting policy is explained more by individual firm characteristics than by keiretsu membership or industry membership.

I. Introduction

The purpose of this study is to investigate factors (i.e., economic, institutional, and cultural phenomena) which potentially influence Japanese managers' choices of accounting policies. A distinct characteristic of the Japanese environment, which makes an investigation of accounting policy choices particularly appealing, is the conformity of the financial and tax reporting systems. In general, expenses cannot be deducted for tax purposes unless they are also deducted for financial reporting purposes. Thus,

* The authors gratefully acknowledge the many helpful comments made by the reviewers. Earlier versions also benefitted from comments received by Don Hansen, Don Herrmann, Daniel Tilley, participants at the University of Tulsa Research Symposium, and participants at the 1995 American Accounting Association annual meeting.

with the apparent impetus to minimize income, the fact that many Japanese managers choose income increasing accounting policies (and forego the tax savings) suggests that choices of accounting policies do have economic consequences on the firm.

Relatively little research has attempted to explain accounting policy choices in foreign environments because of data limitations and differing research styles in foreign countries. This paper provides a first attempt at investigating the factors that influence Japanese managers' accounting policy choices. A unique database was built by gathering the accounting policy choices from the footnotes of approximately 2,000 firms listed on stock exchanges in Japan. Income strategy models are then developed for each firm according to the type (income increasing or income decreasing) of accounting policies chosen.

This study considers six factors which potentially affect the choice of accounting policy in Japan: size, debt/equity ratio, existence of bonus plan, effective tax rate, ability to finance operations internally, and foreign political costs. The ability of variables such as firm size, debt/equity ratio, and existence of bonus plan to explain the choices of accounting policies for U.S. firms has been extensively tested and generally confirmed (Christie 1990). Ceteris paribus, larger U.S. firms tend to choose income decreasing accounting procedures in an attempt to become less visible and thereby avoid increased political costs, U.S. firms with higher debt/equity ratios tend to choose income increasing accounting procedures to avoid debt covenant violations, and U.S. managers whose bonus compensation is tied to earnings tend to choose income increasing accounting procedures to maximize their wealth. These variables are discussed and tested within the context of the Japanese environment. The remaining three variables are chosen because of unique Japanese business conditions.

Despite the differences in the U.S. and Japanese business environments, the results indicate that the firm size and debt/equity hypotheses remain valid in the Japanese environment, even for keiretsu firms. These results may suggest that these proxies have more general meanings than political cost and debt contracting costs. Bernard (1989, p. 80) criticizes this line of research and states, "The variables that most frequently appear significant in this literature are the debt-equity ratio and firm size; these variables could proxy for any number of factors that are totally outside the theory." The bonus plan hypothesis does not explain Japanese managers' choices of accounting policies. In addition, firms' effective tax rates have a significant influence on accounting policy choices. The results also suggest that Japanese managers' choices of accounting policies are influenced by the firm's ability to finance operations internally and the firm's vulnerability to foreign political costs. Furthermore, the choice of accounting policy appears to be explained more by individual firm characteristics than by keiretsu membership or industry membership.

The study proceeds as follows. Section II discusses the environmental characteristics in Japan and formally states the hypotheses to be tested. Section III provides the data and research design used in this study. Section IV reports the results by individual accounting choices, income strategies, keiretsu membership, industry membership, and firm size. Section V summarizes the results and provides conclusions.

II. Hypotheses and the Japanese Environment

Political Costs

Political costs refer to the costs imposed on firms by politicians via taxes and regulations. Prior studies have most commonly used firm size to represent political costs. Alchian and Kessel (1962, p. 162) suggest that large firms fear greater government action, especially if their profits are large, and therefore tend to defer profits. However, one might expect political costs via regulations to be low in Japan because of the close relationship between businesses and the government. For example, Japan's Fair Trade Commission estimates that products under government regulation account for 41% of total value-added manufactured in all industries. Despite numerous liberalization packages, the number of products regulated by the state exceeds 10,000, and there are numerous laws that serve primarily to protect the interests of Japanese firms (Bowring and Kornicki 1993, p. 331). The first hypothesis to be tested is the size hypothesis. The hypothesis is stated below in its traditional form with the expectation that it will not hold because of the factors discussed above.

> **H1:** The larger the firm, the more likely the manager is to choose income decreasing accounting procedures, i.e., shift reported income from current to future periods.

Taxes represent another means by which political agents can impose costs upon firms. Unlike the U.S., the tax and financial reporting systems in Japan are very closely related. In general, expenses cannot be deducted for tax purposes unless they are also deducted for financial reporting purposes. Ceteris paribus, more profitable Japanese firms directly incur higher political costs (i.e., higher taxes). For Japanese firms, a one dollar decrease in reported income increases present cash flows by the effective tax rate. The effective tax rate is measured as income taxes paid, divided by income before taxes and depreciation. The second hypothesis to be tested is the tax hypothesis.

H2: Managers of firms with higher effective tax rates are more likely to choose income decreasing accounting procedures, i.e., shift reported income from the current period to future periods.

Debt Covenants

In the extreme, owner-managers have incentives to liquidate the assets of the firm in the form of dividends and leave the debtholders with nothing but the shell of the firm. However, a rational market will price the debt according to the probability of being left with the shell of the firm. According to the theory of accounting choices, to reduce the debt contracting costs, owner-managers have incentives to offer debt covenants which restrict some of their actions.

However, in Japan, debtholders are likely to receive more protection from the requirements of the commercial code than from debt covenants. The Japanese commercial code places requirements on a firm's mandatory legal reserve and the maximum dividend payments. Such requirements serve to protect the interests of debtholders. The commercial code requires that an amount equal to at least 10% of the total appropriated amount paid and exactly 10% of interim cash dividends paid be appropriated as a legal reserve until the reserve equals 25% of the capital stock account. This reserve may be used to reduce a capital deficit or it may be transferred to paid-up capital by appropriate legal procedures. And the commercial code permits a firm to distribute profits by way of annual or interim dividends out of the excess of its net assets over the aggregate of: (a) the stated capital, (b) the capital surplus, (c) the accumulated legal reserve, (d) the legal reserve to be set aside in respect of the annual appropriation or interim dividend concerned, and (e) the excess, if any, of the unamortized pre-operating expenses and unamortized deferred research and development expenses over the aggregate of the amounts refereed to in (b), (c) and (d) above (JICPA 1986, pp. 24–25). Therefore, debt covenants made between the firm and debtholders are likely to have less influence on accounting policy choices in Japan than in common law countries.[1]

Also, in Japan, the relationship between the owner-manager and the debtholder is thought to be tight. The typical corporate group (*keiretsu*) in Japan consists of an intricate web of cross holdings with no dominant parent company, and at the middle of this corporate group lies a main bank that serves not only as the primary lender for group members, but also as a significant owner of each member's outstanding stock (Lowe 1990). Prowse (1989) argues that many of the agency problems of borrowing can be circumvented in Japan because banks are allowed to take large debt and equity positions in the same firm. It is also common practice for group members to lend to one another. In times of financial distress, main banks and other group members do not cutoff financial support and force the distressed firm into bankruptcy, but instead provide additional financial support (Hoshi *et al.* 1990). This practice suggests that because of the tight agency relationship between debtholders and firms, and therefore the low contracting costs, the debt covenant hypothesis may not hold in the Japanese environment, at least in keiretsu groups.

These factors suggest that the debt covenant hypothesis is not likely to hold in Japan, at least for firms in keiretsu groups. The third hypothesis tested is the debt/equity hypothesis. The hypothesis is stated below in its traditional form with the expectation that it will not hold in the Japanese environment.

H3: The larger the firm's debt/equity ratio, the more likely the manager is to choose income increasing accounting procedures, i.e., shift reported income from future periods to the current period.

Bonus Plans

The bonus plan hypothesis suggests that managers whose bonus payments are determined based on the level of the firm's income have an incentive to increase income through accounting procedures. This proposition is based on the simple assumption that managers maximize their utility by maximizing their compensation which directly depends on reported income. In Japan, some firms pay bonuses based on operating income or ordinary income while other firms use the difference between actual and budgeted sales as the measure of profit to share. Therefore, Japanese managers may be able to increase the present value of their compensation by choosing income increasing accounting procedures, indicating that the bonus compensation plan hypothesis should hold in the Japanese environment.

However, we believe that bonus plans are not likely to have a significant influence on accounting policy choices in Japan because firms tend to pay relatively constant and/or small bonuses to directors. Compared with management compensation in other major industrialized countries, the compensation of Japanese executives is quite modest. Morais *et al.* (1993) report that the 20 best-paid U.S. executives earned on average $4,800,000 in cash salary and bonus in 1992, versus an estimated $530,000 in Japan. The average CEO of a large U.S. firm makes 35 times (and in several cases 1,000 times) as much as the average U.S. manufacturing employee. In Japan the ratio is only about 15 to 1 (Nelson-Horchler 1990). In place of high salaries and bonus payments, Japanese managers benefit more by keeping their social status and spending the firm's entertainment expense account (*kousaihi*). High social status allows many Japanese CEOs to have a significant impact on government policy. Thus, when Japanese managers select accounting policies, bonus compensation plans, which are often for a fixed amount, are not likely to be a significant influence. The fourth hypothesis tested in this paper is the bonus plan hypothesis. The hypothesis is stated below in its traditional form with the expectation that it will not hold.

H4: Managers of firms with bonus plans are more likely to choose income increasing accounting procedures, i.e. shift reported income from future periods to the current period.

Internal/External Financing

Most Japanese firms maintain a low dividend payout ratio and instead reserve large amounts of income in the form of appropriated retained earnings. For the sample of firms in this study the average ratio of appropriated to unappropriated retained earnings is 4.19 with 93.6% having a ratio exceeding one. Appropriated retained earnings serve as reserves for activities such as future investment and research and development and allow firms to rely on internal financing rather than external financing. The ability of Japanese firms to rely more on internal financing instead of external financing, the more costly of the two, gives them a comparative operating advantage over firms from other countries.

In addition, Japan's historically low real interest rates and flourishing capital markets have provided Japanese firms the use of external financing at a low cost. In the 1970s and late 1980s, many believed Japanese firms had an unfair advantage in the form of lower cost of capital, and empirical research generally confirmed this to be true.[2] However, the time period of this study coincides with a sharp rise in the interest rates in Japan and a severe decline in the Japanese stock markets. As a result, the ability of Japanese firms to finance operations internally through retained earnings, as opposed to external through debt or equity, has become more important in recent years.

Japanese firms commonly appropriate retained earnings for activities such as future research and development, overseas investments, special depreciation, exchange rate fluctuation, and other general matters. A low level of appropriated retained earnings would be indicative of a firm which is more apt to rely on external, and therefore more costly, methods of financing. To reduce financing costs (i.e., costs of capital) these firms are more likely to choose income increasing accounting procedures in an attempt to signal a stronger financial position for the firm. The fifth hypothesis tested is the internal/external financing hypothesis.

H5: The greater the firm's need to finance operations externally, the more likely the firm's manager is to select income increasing accounting procedures, i.e., shift reported income from future periods to the current period.

The ratio of appropriated retained earnings to net assets is used as a measure of the firm's ability to finance operations internally (FIN).

$$\text{FIN} = \frac{\text{Appropriated Retained Earnings}}{\text{Net Assets}}$$

This ratio represents the proportion of net assets that are appropriated for internal financing. An inverse relationship should exist between the firm's income strategy and FIN. As FIN decreases, the manager is more likely to select income increasing accounting policies to reduce the firm's cost of financing.[3]

Foreign Political Costs

The Japanese economy is highly dependent on foreign trade. Consequently, individual Japanese firms are likely to be affected by their dependence on foreign trade and the extent of their operations in other countries. In addition to any domestic political costs, firms operating in foreign countries, and therefore under foreign governments, potentially face additional political costs. For example, Japan's trade surplus with the U.S. in 1993 was $44 billion. Consequently, many U.S. firms lobby for anti-dumping taxes, import restrictions, and higher tariffs for Japanese imports. In fact, foreign political costs may be much greater than domestic political costs. Because of the strong sense of nationalism and patriotism that exists in most countries, politicians may receive greater utility by transferring wealth from foreign firms to domestic services. As a result, foreign firms may attempt to reduce their political costs by decreasing income through accounting policy choices. The sixth hypothesis tested is the foreign political costs hypothesis.

H6: Managers of firms that are more vulnerable to foreign political costs are more likely to choose income decreasing accounting procedures, i.e., shift reported income from the current period to future periods.

The foreign sales ratio (foreign sales/total sales) is used to represent the vulnerability of the firm to foreign political costs. Japanese firms with larger ratios of foreign sales to total sales will attempt to avoid foreign political costs by decreasing reported income.

III. Data and Research Design

The data were collected from two sources, the CD-ROM database published by the Ministry of Finance in Japan and the NEEDS/MICRO database.[4] The NEEDS/MICRO database provided financial data for each firm. CD-ROM was used to gather each firm's accounting policy choices disclosed in the footnotes of the annual reports. Firms were excluded from the study if they were banks or insurance companies, had changed their closing dates in 1991, were not listed on CD-ROM, or did not have sufficient financial data. The resulting sample consists of 1,489 Japanese firms with closing dates between October 1990 and September 1991. This sample covers 74% of all listed Japanese firms.

In this study, we use the income strategy model developed by Zmijewski and Hagerman (ZH 1981). ZH use the firm's overall income strategy as the dependent variable in an ordered probit analysis. In the simplest case, income strategy is defined as the number of income increasing accounting procedures in the firm's portfolio of accounting procedures. ZH examine the accounting policies for depreciation, inventory, amortization of past pension costs, and investment tax credit. Accounting for inventory is not included in this study because of the common use of the average cost method in Japan and because many firms employ a combination of the inventory costing methods. Very few firms employ exclusively FIFO and LIFO. The amortization period of past pension cost is also not used because in Japan the amortization period is much shorter and the actual data are difficult to obtain. Accounting for investment tax credit is not used because it does not exist in Japan. These three accounting policies are replaced with the accounting policies for marketable securities, for research and development costs, and for employees' retirement allowances. The following paragraphs describe the Japanese generally accepted accounting principles (GAAP) for the relevant accounting policies.

Japanese GAAP

Depreciation: Similar to U.S. GAAP, either straight-line or accelerated depreciation is allowed for financial reporting purposes in Japan. The most frequent change in choice of accounting policy in Japan is that for depreciation. Firms using both accelerated and straight-line depreciation methods were omitted from the study.

Marketable Securities: Japanese GAAP allow both the lower of cost or market value method or the cost method to account for marketable securities.

Research and Development: U.S. GAAP require that all research and development expenditures be expensed as incurred except in special situations.[5] In Japan, any research and development costs can either be amortized over a period of time not exceeding five years or be expensed immediately.

Retirement Allowance: Most Japanese firms establish an allowance to provide for employees' retirement, the benefits of which are usually determined based on the reason for termination, length of service, and current salary. Japanese GAAP allow firms to record this liability at 100% of the amount which would be required if all employees voluntarily terminated at the end of a fiscal year. However, tax regulations allow only up to 40% of the liability to be treated as tax deductible. Therefore, recording the liability for any amount above 40% of the possible amount would decrease income without any additional tax benefit.

Table 1. *Classification of Income Increasing and Income Decreasing Accounting Policies*

Policy	*Income Decreasing* *0*	*Income Increasing* *1*
Depreciation	Accelerated	Straight line
Retirement Allowance	Greater than 40% of possible amount	40% of possible amount
Marketable Securities	Lower of Cost or Market	Cost
Research and Development	Immediate expensing	Capitalizing

Table 2. *The probit model for individual accounting choices*

$$\text{CHOICE}_i = \alpha_0 + \alpha_1\text{SIZE} + \alpha_2\text{LEV} + \alpha_3\text{BONUS} + \alpha_4\text{TAX} + \alpha_5\text{FSALE} + \alpha_6\text{FIN} + \varepsilon$$

CHOICE	=	1 if an income increasing method is chosen, 0 if an income decreasing method is chosen.
i	=	The accounting policy for depreciation, research and development costs, employees' retirement allowance, or marketable securities.
SIZE	=	Log of net sales.
LEV	=	Leverage (total debt/total assets).
BONUS	=	Bonus to directors (directors' bonuses/ordinary income).[6]
TAX	=	Effective tax rate (income taxes paid/(income before tax + depreciation)).[7]
FSALE	=	Proportion of foreign sales (foreign sales/total sales).
FIN	=	Internal/external financing (appropriated retained earnings/net assets).

Income Strategy Models

Individual probit analyses are run for each of the four accounting policies used. The dependent variable in the individual probit analyses has a value of 1 if the firm chooses an income increasing policy and a value of 0 if the firm chooses an income decreasing policy. Straight-line depreciation, the cost method for marketable securities, capitalizing research and development costs, and recording the retirement allowance for less than or equal to 40% of the possible amount represent income increasing accounting policy choices. Accelerated depreciation, the lower of cost or market value method for marketable securities, immediately expensing research and development costs, and recording the retirement allowance for greater than 40% of the possible amount represent income decreasing accounting policy choices (Table 1). The probit model for individual accounting choices is shown in Table 2.

Table 3. *The ordered probit model for income strategies*

$$STRAT_i = \alpha_0 + \alpha_1 SIZE + \alpha_2 LEV + \alpha_3 BONUS + \alpha_4 TAX + \alpha_5 FSALE + \alpha_6 FIN + \varepsilon$$

STRAT	= income strategy: 0 if no income increasing policies are chosen, 1 if one income increasing policy is chosen, 2 if two income increasing policies are chosen, and so on.
i	= Income strategy Model 1 or Model 2.

All other variables are defined as above.

Next, the combination of the firm's accounting methods are used to develop each firm's income strategy. As ZH explain, a stronger test can be provided by observing the portfolio of choices made by the firm. For this we use two different ordered probit models. Model 1 uses the accounting methods for depreciation, provision for employees' retirement allowance, marketable securities, and research and development and has a sample size of 288 firms. This study assumes that the effects on income of all four accounting methods are equal. ZH found that the effects of weighing accounting policies differently in the income strategy model did not significantly change the results.

Model 2 uses the accounting policies for depreciation, provision for employees' retirement allowance, and marketable securities. Research and development is dropped from this model because a large number of firms either do not incur research and development costs or do not disclose such costs. As a result, the sample size for Model 2 increases to 979 firms. Assuming that all accounting methods have the same effect on income, Model 2 results in four possible income strategies. The ordered probit model for income strategies is shown in Table 3.

IV. Results

We first determine, whether the independent variables are strongly correlated. As Table 4 shows, little correlation exists among the independent variables. In no case are the independent variables correlated at a magnitude greater than .23 and in most cases are below .10. The highest correlation is –.223, between the ratio of total assets to total liabilities and the ratio of appropriated retained earnings to net assets. The low correlations imply that there is sufficient variation among the independent variables to estimate discrete effects. Table 5 shows the frequency of income increasing and income decreasing accounting policy choices and income strategies for the sample of Japanese firms.

12 *Tatsuo Inoue*

Table 4. *Correlation Matrix for the Independent Variables*[a]

	1	*2*	*3*	*4*	*5*	*6*
1. Size	1.00					
2. Leverage	.192	1.00				
3. Bonus	–.167	–.028	1.00			
4. Effective Tax Rate	.101	–.052	–.031	1.00		
5. Foreign Sales	.156	–.053	–.055	–.158	1.00	
6. Internal/External Financing	.020	–.223	.031	.003	–.070	1.00

[a] This matrix represents the correlation between the independent variables of the 979 firms used in Model 2. The correlation matrix of the independent variables of the 288 firms used in Model 1 reveals even less correlation.

Table 5. *Choice of Individual Accounting Policy and Income Strategy*

Income Effect	*Depreciation*	*Retirement Allowance*	*Marketable Securities*	*Research & Development*
Decreasing	1,139	497	733	335
Increasing	84	725	756	79
Total # of Firms	1,223	1,222	1,489	414

Income Strategy[a]	*Model 1 4 Accounting Policies*	*Model 2 3 Accounting Policies*
0	80	259
1	105	381
2	68	291
3	26	48
4	9	NA
Total # of Firms	288	979

[a] Income strategy is the number of income increasing accounting procedures in the firm's portfolio of accounting choices.

Individual Accounting Policies

Before reporting the results of the overall income strategy models, we first report results for each individual accounting policy choice in Table 6.[8] Size and leverage are significant at the .01 level for all accounting policy choices. These results suggest that the size and debt/equity hypotheses help to explain Japanese managers' choices of accounting policies. Bonus

Table 6. *Probit Analysis on Individual Accounting Choices*

Independent Variables	*Predicted sign*	*Depreciation*	*Retirement Allowance*	*Marketable Securities*	*R & D*
Size	(–)	–.1490[a]	–.1562	–.1771	–.3345
		(–3.159)**	(–5.110)**	(–6.720)**	(–4.916)**
Leverage	(+)	1.1233	2.0566	1.7759	1.5552
		(3.543)**	(8.959)**	(9.234)**	(3.572)**
Bonus	(+)	–2.9998	2.1446	–.2926	–.8885
		(–.983)	(1.148)	(–.443)	(–.555)
Effective Tax Rate	(–)	–.3786	–.6797	–.4639	–.8718
		(–1.457)	(–2.917)**	(–2.461)**	(–1.709)*
Foreign Sales	(–)	–.3618	–1.4993	–.4813	–.0598
		(–.799)	(–4.793)**	(–1.894)*	(–.106)
Internal/External	(–)	–1.1976	–1.6613	–.5034	–1.2432
Financing		(–3.705)**	(–8.005)**	(–2.793)**	(–3.234)**
Constant		–.0313	1.5185	1.2150	2.4407
		(–.059)	(4.270)**	(4.100)**	(3.173)**
Probit Analysis:					
X^2 with 6 d.f.		51.27	252.40	161.12	55.70
% Classified Correctly		93.0%	68.9%	63.4%	81.4%
Sample Size		1223	1222	1489	414

[a] Coefficient (asymptotic t-statistic)
* significant at the .05 level
** significant at the .01 level

is never significant, which suggests that the bonus compensation plan is not an important explanatory variable in the Japanese environment.[9]

The internal/external financing variable is significant at the .01 level for all four accounting policies. Effective tax rate is significant at the .05 level or better for three of the four accounting choices. The foreign sales ratio is significant at the .05 level or better for two of the four accounting policies. All four models are significant at the .0001 level. Proper classifications for the sample observations are 93.0% for depreciation, 68.9% for retirement allowance, 63.4% for marketable securities, and 81.4% for research and development. Only the probit models for retirement allowance and marketable securities significantly outperform the naive model of choosing the most common accounting policy choice.

As ZH mention, interpreting the results from individual analyses has limitations. Managers are likely to select accounting policies to form an overall income strategy. Therefore, stronger evidence can be obtained by examining the results of overall income strategies.

Table 7. *Ordered Probit Analysis on Income Strategy*

Independent Variables	*Predicted Sign*	*Model 1 4 Accounting Policies*	*Model 2 3 Accounting Policies*
Size	(–)	–.2881[a]	–.2059
		(–4.870)**	(–7.416)**
Leverage	(+)	2.1738	2.1554
		(6.051)**	(11.032)**
Bonus	(+)	.1958	.1201
		(.058)	(.115)
Effective Tax Rate	(–)	–.5914	–.6546
		(–1.188)	(–3.003)**
Foreign Sales	(–)	–1.0467	–.9070
		(–2.053)*	(–3.454)**
Internal/External Financing	(–)	–2.0154	–1.3955
		(–4.752)**	(–6.911)**
Constant		3.6545	2.4407
		(5.347)**	(7.671)**
Probit Analysis: X^2 with d.f.		106.51	256.60
% Correctly Classified		43.4%	47.5%
Sample Size		288	979

[a] Coefficient (asymptotic t-statistic)
* significant at the .05 level
** significant at the .01 level

Income Strategies

The results of the overall income strategy for both Model 1 (four accounting policies) and Model 2 (three accounting policies) are shown in Table 7. These results are generally consistent with the results of the individual analyses. Size and leverage are significant at the .01 level for both models. Bonus is not significant in either model. Foreign sales ratio and the internal/external financing variable are significant at the .01 or .05 level in both models. The effective tax rate is significant at the .01 level for Model 2. Both Model 1 and Model 2 are significant at the .0001 level.[10] Proper classifications for the sample observations are 43.4% for Model 1 and 47.5% for Model 2. Model 1 and Model 2 provide significantly better predictions at the .01 level than the naive models which assume either an equal probability for each strategy or that the most common income strategy is always chosen.

A hold-out sample is also used to test the models. For Model 1, approximately one-half of the sample firms are used to estimate coefficients, and then the estimated coefficients are applied to the remaining hold-out sample firms. The same procedure is used for Model 2. Proper classification of hold-out sample firms is 43.3% for Model 1 and 46.6% for Model 2. Neither of these percentages differs significantly from the full sample proper classification.

Keiretsu Analysis

One of the most unique features of the Japanese business environment is the corporate group (keiretsu). As discussed previously, members of keiretsu groups are typically assumed to share very close relationships. As such, the choices of accounting policies may depend more upon the choices of accounting policies made by other firms in the same keiretsu rather than upon individual firm characteristics. To investigate this possibility, the sample was split into two subsamples: keiretsu and non-keiretsu. In addition, within the keiretsu subsample, keiretsu firms were split according to their specific keiretsu membership. *Industrial Groupings in Japan* (Dodwell Marketing 1992) was used to identify the firms included in the eight major horizontally-connected keiretsu groups.

Table 8 shows the average income strategy and average individual accounting policy choices for the subsample of non-keiretsu firms, for the subsample of keiretsu firms, and for each keiretsu group. Evidence that keiretsu membership (or nonmembership) affects accounting policy choices is assumed if the average income strategy (or individual accounting policy choice) of a particular subsample differs from the average of the overall sample. The overall sample average is assumed to represent the expected income strategy (or individual accounting policy choice). This methodology is similar to the one used by Christie and Zimmerman (1994). A paired difference test was used to test for statistical differences in averages.

As Table 8 shows, most of the sample averages do not differ significantly from the averages of the overall sample. There does not appear to be a strong keiretsu effect on the choices of accounting policies. One particularly interesting finding, however, is that the keiretsu subsample has a significantly higher average income strategy. Perhaps one reason for this is that keiretsu firms have, on average, much higher debt ratios than do non-keiretsu firms. However, the close relationships that keiretsu members have with the main bank and other firms in the keiretsu suggest that most of the agency costs associated with borrowings should be minimal, and accounting policy choice would have little affect. In fact,

Table 8. *Analysis of Income Strategy and Individual Accounting Policy Choices for Keiretsu and Non-keiretsu Firms*

	Income Strategy						Depr	Mkt Sec	Ret All
	n	*0*	*1*	*2*	*3*	*average (t-stat)*[b]	*average*[a] *(t-stat)*[b]	*average*[a] *(t-stat)*[b]	*average*[a] *(t-stat)*[b]
Overall sample	979	259	381	291	48	1.13	.077	.492	.562
Subsamples:									
Non-keiretsu	614	179	235	176	24	1.07	.059	.487	.528
						(−1.67)	(−1.89)	(−.27)	(−1.69)
Keiretsu	365	80	146	115	24	1.23	.107	.501	.643
						(2.14)*	(1.87)	(.34)	(2.25)*
Keiretsu Groups:									
Mitsubishi	66	13	29	18	6	1.26	.136	.500	.621
						(1.17)	(1.40)	(.124)	(.99)
Mitsui	45	12	11	18	4	1.31	.178	.556	.578
						(1.24)	(1.75)	(.844)	(.21)
Sumitomo	61	18	29	11	3	.98	.066	.279	.639
						(−1.39)	(−.35)	(−3.69)**	(1.25)
Fuyo	59	12	16	26	5	1.41	.153	.644	.610
						(2.32)*	(1.61)	(2.41)*	(.76)
Dai-Ichi	55	9	24	19	3	1.29	.091	.618	.582
Kangyo Bank						(1.46)	(.37)	(1.90)	(.30)
Sanwa	53	13	25	13	2	1.07	.057	.377	.642
						(−.50)	(−.62)	(−1.71)	(1.20)
Tokai	15	3	7	5	0	1.13	.000	.533	.600
						(.01)	.NA*	(−.31)	(.29)
Industrial Bank	11	0	5	5	1	1.64	.091	.727	.818
of Japan						(2.48)*	(.16)	(1.67)	(2.10)

[a] Firms choosing income increasing procedures are assigned a value of 1 and firms choosing an income decreasing procedure are assigned a value of 0. Thus, the averages represent the percentage of firms choosing income increasing procedures.
[b] t-statistic was computed based on a paired difference test between the particular subsample and the overall sample.
* significant at the .05 level
** significant at the .01 level
.NA = t statistic cannot be computed because there is no variance in policy choice.

based on contracting theory, we would expect debt contracting costs to have a greater effect on accounting policy choice for the non-keiretsu group than for the keiretsu group, but this is not the case.

The effects of keiretsu membership on the choices of accounting policies are also tested by splitting the sample of firms used in Model 2 into a keiretsu subsample and a non-keiretsu subsample, and then estimating Model 2 for each subsample. Table 9 shows that the estimates

Table 9. *Probit Analysis on Income Strategies of Keiretsu and Non-keiretsu Firms*

Independent Variables	*Predicted sign*	*Non-keiretsu*	*Keiretsu*	*Model 2*
Size	(–)	–.2002[a]	–.2385	–.2135
		(–5.420)**	(–5.315)**	(–7.447)**
Leverage	(+)	1.8215	2.8106	2.1259
		(7.597)**	(7.625)**	(10.811)**
Bonus	(+)	.1787	.9161	.1453
		(.166)	(.259)	(.141)
Effective Tax Rate	(–)	–.7172	–.6148	–.6365
		(–2.505)**	(–1.517)	(–2.921)**
Foreign Sales	(–)	–.6566	–1.5204	–.9055
		(–2.027)*	(–3.050)**	(–3.470)**
Internal/External Financing	(–)	–1.1451	–1.8834	–1.3627
		(–4.661)**	(–5.053)**	(–6.708)**
Inclination				.0360
				(1.284)
Constant		2.4208	2.6992	2.4920
		(5.616)**	(5.290)**	(7.694)**
Probit Analysis: X^2 with 6 d.f.[b]		132.30	130.30	258.41
% Classified Correctly		45.3%	50.7%	47.3%
Sample Size		614	365	979

[a] Coefficient (asymptotic t-statistic)
[b] Model 2, with the inclination variable, is tested using a X^2 with 7 d.f.
* significant at the .05 level
** significant at the .01 level

from the ordered probit models are virtually identical for the keiretsu and non-keiretsu subsample with one exception. The effective tax variable is significant only for the non-keiretsu subsample. However, the estimated coefficient on effective tax rate for the non-keiretsu subsample is not significantly different from the estimated coefficient on effective tax rate for the keiretsu subsample.

The effect of keiretsu membership is also investigated by noting the extent of involvement of each firm within a keiretsu group. *Industrial Groupings in Japan* ranks the degree of "inclination" of each firm to the group on a scale of 1 to 4. A rank of 1 indicates that the firm has a weak relationship with other keiretsu members and a rank of 4 indicates a strong relationship. We include an additional independent variable to determine whether firms' degrees of inclination to their keiretsu groups contributed to the explanation of accounting policy choices. Non-keiretsu firms were assigned a value of 0. As Table 9 shows, the degree of inclination does not seem to affect accounting policy choices. The inclination variable is not significant and all other variables remain virtually unchanged from the results obtained for Model 2 in Table 7.[11]

Industry Analysis

We also test for the effects of industry on accounting policy choice. Perhaps the choice of accounting policy is determined more by industry membership than by individual firm characteristics. The 979 firms used in Model 2 are classified by their two-digit industry code. All industries containing 30 or more firms are included in the analysis. Thirteen industries met this criterion. We test for an industry effect by assuming that the overall sample average represents the expected income strategy. Evidence of an industry effect is assumed if the average income strategy (or individual accounting policy choice) of an industry differs from the overall sample average. A paired difference test was used to test for statistical differences in averages.

Table 10 shows the average income strategy and average individual accounting policy choices for the overall sample and for each of the 13 industries. There does not appear to be much of an industry effect. The average income strategy and average individual accounting policy choices for most industries do not differ significantly from the overall sample averages. Firms in the chemical industry choose, on average, more income increasing accounting policies than would be expected given the averages of the sample. Two reasons for this may be that firms in the chemical industry typically have low ratios of appropriated retained earnings to net assets and low effective tax rates. Such firms may tend to choose income increasing accounting policies because of the need for external financing and the relatively lower tax effect of higher income.

Firms in the electric equipment and motor vehicles industries choose, on average, more income decreasing accounting policies than would be expected. Firms in the motor vehicle industry are larger than average and firms in the electric equipment industry have lower than average debt/equity ratios, both of these factors indicate a tendency to choose income decreasing accounting policies. In addition, firms in both industries have, on average, very high foreign sales ratios. Therefore, in an attempt to avoid greater foreign political costs, these firms may reduce income through accounting policy choices.

Table 10. *Analysis of Income Strategy and Individual Accounting Policy Choices by Industry*

		Income Strategy					*Depr*	*Mkt Sec*	*Retire*
Industry	*n*	*0*	*1*	*2*	*3*	*average (t-stat)*[b]	*average*[a] *(t-stat)*[b]	*average*[a] *(t-stat)*[b]	*average*[a] *(t-stat)*[b]
Overall sample	979	259	381	291	48	1.13	.077	.492	.562
Construction	92	23	37	29	3	1.13 (.000)	.033 (−2.36)*	.457 (−.68)	.641 (1.58)
Food Processing	56	10	29	16	1	1.14 (.13)	.054 (−.75)	.446 (−.68)	.643 (1.25)
Textile	41	7	16	16	2	1.31 (1.46)	.049 (−.81)	.537 (.56)	.732 (2.43)*
Chemicals	74	11	26	25	12	1.51 (3.50)**	.311 (4.32)**	.635 (2.53)*	.568 (.10)
Glass, Clay	30	7	14	9	0	1.07 (−.47)	.033 (−1.29)	.467 (−.27)	.567 (.05)
Metals	52	14	20	14	4	1.15 (.18)	.115 (.87)	.538 (.66)	.500 (−.88)
Machines	100	29	38	32	1	1.05 (−.99)	.010 (−6.66)**	.470 (−.44)	.570 (.16)
Electric Equipment	109	37	45	25	2	.93 (−2.65)**	.037 (−2.20)*	.422 (−1.47)	.468 (−1.95)
Motor Vehicles	31	15	13	2	1	.65 (−3.58)**	.032 (−1.37)	.226 (−3.49)**	.387 (−1.96)
Other Manufacture	33	9	12	9	3	1.18 (.31)	.091 (.28)	.545 (.60)	.545 (−.18)
Trading Company	73	21	28	24	0	1.04 (−.97)	.000 .NA**	.452 (−.68)	.589 (.47)
Retail	44	11	17	14	2	1.16 (.22)	.045 (−.98)	.454 (−.49)	.659 (1.35)
Services	36	10	13	10	3	1.17 (.23)	.139 (1.07)	.444 (−.57)	.583 (.26)

[a] Firms choosing income increasing procedures are assigned a value of 1 and firms choosing an income decreasing procedure are assigned a value of 0. Thus, the averages represent the percentage of firms choosing income increasing procedures.
[b] t-statistic was computed based on a paired difference test between the industry and the overall sample.
* significant at the .05 level
** significant at the .01 level
.NA = t statistic cannot be computed because there is no variance in policy choice.

Large and Small Firms

ZH (p. 144) state, "The management compensation variable would be more important for firms facing low political costs than those facing high political costs. Likewise, other variables should be more important for the

Table 11. *Probit Analysis on Income Strategy of Large and Small Firms*[a]

Independent Variables	*Predicted Sign*	*Large Firms*	*Small Firms*
Size	(–)	–.2065[b]	–.1793
		(–3.592)**	(–2.435)**
Leverage	(+)	2.4691	1.9209
		(7.461)**	(7.398)**
Bonus	(+)	–.5882	.0969
		(–.138)	(.090)
Effective Tax Rate	(–)	–.8081	–.5755
		(–2.665)**	(–1.531)
Foreign Sales	(–)	–.8908	–1.0171
		(–2.819)**	(–2.062)*
Internal/External Financing	(–)	–1.7507	–1.1259
		(–5.217)**	(–4.333)**
Constant		2.4397	2.1908
		(3.415)**	(2.930)**
Probit Analysis: X^2 with 6 d.f.		133.55	97.98
% Correctly Classified		48.9%	45.1%
Sample Size		489	490

[a] The results are obtained from using Model 2 (3 accounting policies).
[b] Coefficient (asymptotic t-statistic)
* significant at the .05 level
** significant at the .01 level

high political cost firms than for low political cost firms." We test this statement in the Japanese environment. The sample used for Model 2 is partitioned by size. Those above (below) the median size are classified as large (small) firms. Table 11 shows the results of the ordered probit analyses for the large and small subsamples. All independent variables, except the bonus variable, are significant at the .01 level for the large firm model. The results are weaker for the small firm model. Only the size, leverage, and internal/external financing variables are significant at the .01 level. The foreign sales ratio is significant at the .05 level and effective tax rate is not significant. The large firm model correctly classifies 48.9% of the sample observations while the small firm model correctly classifies only 45.1% of the sample observations. This difference is significant at the .05 level. These results suggest that the model is more appropriate for large firms.

V. Summary and Conclusions

The purpose of this study is to investigate factors which potentially influence Japanese managers' choices of accounting policies. Using the income strategy model established by Zmijewski and Hagerman (1981), variables affecting Japanese managers' choices of accounting policies for depreciation, marketable securities, employee retirement allowance, and research and development costs are examined. This study shows that while the bonus plan hypothesis does not significantly explain Japanese managers' choices, the size and debt/equity hypotheses do, even for firms in keiretsu groups. Because of the close relationship between Japanese businesses and the government, one may question whether size is accurately reflecting political costs or partially reflecting some other factor. The debt/equity hypothesis also holds in the Japanese environment. This result is surprising given the improbability that simple manipulations of income through accounting policy choices can actually reduce debt contracting costs when the relationships between businesses and debtholders are thought to be very close and stable.

There are two possible interpretations of these results. First, Japanese firms and the business environment in Japan are more similar to those in the U.S. than typically assumed. Second, debt/equity and firm size are proxying for any number of factors that are totally outside the theory of accounting choices (Bernard 1989, p. 80). The second interpretation seems to be more reasonable than the first since the debt/equity and firm size hypotheses hold as well for keiretsu firms as for non-keiretsu firms. Keiretsu firms should have less contracting costs than non-keiretsu firms. Nevertheless, firm size and debt/equity ratios do appear to be empirical regularities in the explanation of accounting policy choices in Japan. This suggests that firm size and the debt/equity ratio represent more general characteristics than political costs and debt contracting costs, respectively.

Other factors are also found to significantly influence Japanese managers' choices of accounting policies. Taxation has a significant effect on Japanese managers' choices because of the tight relationship between the Japanese tax and financial reporting systems. The extent of foreign sales explains the influence of foreign political costs on Japanese firms. The firm's ability to finance operations internally as opposed to externally is also shown to significantly influence Japanese managers' choices of accounting policies.

This study is not meant to be conclusive but merely the first step in understanding the income strategies of Japanese firms. Future research could further develop the contractual and agency relationships in Japan, as well as in other countries. Research on accounting policy choice in foreign environments can only stand to enrich researchers' understanding of accounting policy choice in their own environment.

Notes

1. The Ministry of Finance requires firms to maintain certain financial constraints when issuing unsecured bonds. Common financial constraints include constraints on maximum dividend payments, level of secured debt, minimum maintenance of net assets, and *minimum maintenance of income*. However, in 1990, the Ministry of Finance relaxed these requirements because of liberalization of the bond markets and the effect of the market crash. After 1990, a company issuing unsecured bonds can avoid to constrain on minimum maintenance of income under the new requirement.

2. See Frankel (1991) for a survey of the Japanese cost of finance.

3. Alternative proxies for the internal/external financing hypothesis were considered (e.g., the ratio of appropriated retained earnings to unappropriated retained earnings and the ratio of the difference between appropriated and unappropriated retained earnings to net assets). However, these ratios fluctuate according to changes in unappropriated retained earnings even though the amount of appropriated retained earnings remains constant. A decrease in unappropriated retained earnings because of low levels of income may cause a higher ratio, but higher ratios do not necessarily indicate greater amounts of appropriated retained earnings. Therefore, these ratios are not used.

4. NEEDS/MICRO database was obtained from Kwansei Gakuin University Information Processing Research Center and CD-ROM was obtained from Kwansei Gakuin University Institute of Industrial Research.

5. Research and development costs for materials, equipment and facilities, and purchased intangibles that have alternative future uses are capitalized. Also some types of computer software development costs are capitalized.

6. Bonus compensation plans of managers are not disclosed in Japan. Instead, Japanese companies only disclose total bonus amounts paid to directors. Two other variables also were used to test the bonus plan hypothesis: 1) a dummy variable with 1 if bonuses were paid to directors within the last three years, 0 otherwise and 2) the ratio of bonus payments to unappropriated retained earnings. Using either of these two variables instead of the one chosen did not qualitatively change the results.

7. We also tested the tax hypothesis using the ratio of income taxes paid, divided by sales minus cost of goods sold (Zimmerman, 1983). Using this variable instead of the one chosen did not qualitatively change the results.

8. All probit analyses are conducted using LIMDEP 6.0. Binomial probit models are used for testing individual accounting policies and ordered probit models are used for testing income strategies.

9. Holthausen, Larcker, and Sloan (1994) show that annual bonus schemes do not affect US managers' manipulation of earnings, which contrasts with the findings of Healy (1985).

10. To determine whether the change in sample influences the results, Model 2 was rerun with the 288 firms from Model 1. The results are qualitatively similar to those of Model 1.

11. We also used a 0/1 dummy variable with 0 for nonkeiretsu firms and 1 for keiretsu firms for the inclination variable. The results were qualitatively similar to those obtained.

References

Alchian, A. and R. Kessel, "Competition, Monopoly and the Pursuit of Money," in *Aspects of Labor Economics* (Princeton: Princeton University Press, 1962).

Bernard, V. 1989. Capital Market Research in Accounting During the 1980s: A Critical Review, in *The State of Accounting Research as We Enter the 1990's*, T. J. Frecka, ed. (University of Illinois, Urbana-Champaign, IL), pp. 72–120.

Bowring, R. and P. Kornicki, eds, "The Cambridge Encylopedia of Japan," (New York, Cambridge University Press, 1993).

Christie, A., "Aggregation of Test Statistics: An Evaluation of the Evidence on Contracting and Size Hypotheses," *Journal of Accounting and Economics* 12 (1990), pp. 15–36.

Christie, A. and J. Zimmerman, "Efficient and Opportunistic Choices of Accounting Procedures: Corporate Control Contests, *The Accounting Review* (October 1994), pp. 539–566.

Frankel, J., "The Japanese Cost of Finance: A Survey," *Financial Management* (Spring 1991), pp. 95–127.

Healy, P., "The Impact of Bonus Schemes on the Selection of Accounting Principles," *Journal of Accounting and Economics* 7 (1985), pp. 7–34.

Holthausen, R., D. Larcker, and R. Sloan, "Annual Bonus Schemes and the Manipulation of Earnings," Working Paper at the University of Pennsylvania (1994).

Hoshi, T., A. Kashyap, and D. Sharfstein, "The Role of Banks in Reducing the Costs of Financial Distress in Japan, NBER Working Paper No. 3435 (October 1990).

Japanese Institution of Certified Public Accountants, *Corporate Disclosure in Japan: Overview*. The Japanese Institution of Certified Public Accountants, Tokyo, Japan, 1989.

Lowe, H., "The Shortcomings of Japanese Consolidated Financial Statements," *Accounting Horizons* (September 1990), pp. 1–9.

Morais, R., G. Eisenstodt and S. Kichen, "The Global Boss' Pay: Where (and How) the Money is," *Forbes* (June 7, 1993), pp. 90–98.

Nelson-Horchler, J., "The Pay Revolt Brews," *Industry Week* (June 18, 1990), pp. 28–36.

Prowse, S., "Firm Financial Behavior in the U.S. and Japan: The Role of Agency Relationships," NBER Working Paper (August 1989).

Watts, R. and J. Zimmerman, *Positive Accounting Theory*. Englewood Cliffs, NJ: Prentice-Hall, Inc., 1986.

Zimmerman, J., "Taxes and Firm Size," *Journal of Accounting and Economics* (1983), pp. 119–149.

Zmijewski, M. and R. Hagerman, "An Income Strategy Approach to the Positive Theory of Accounting Standard Setting Choice," *Journal of Accounting and Economics* (1981), pp. 129–149.

Part II
Americas

A
USA

[6]

THE ACCOUNTING REVIEW
Vol. 71, No. 4
October 1996
pp. 467–492

Corporate Disclosure Policy and Analyst Behavior

Mark H. Lang
University of North Carolina at Chapel Hill
Russell J. Lundholm
University of Michigan

ABSTRACT: This paper examines the relations between the disclosure practices of firms, the number of analysts following each firm and properties of the analysts' earnings forecasts. Using data from the *Report of the Financial Analysts Federation Corporate Information Committee* (FAF Report 1985–89), we provide evidence that firms with more informative disclosure policies have a larger analyst following, more accurate analyst earnings forecasts, less dispersion among individual analyst forecasts and less volatility in forecast revisions. The results enhance our understanding of the role of analysts in capital markets. Further, they suggest that potential benefits to disclosure include increased investor following, reduced estimation risk and reduced information asymmetry, each of which have been shown to reduce a firm's cost of capital in theoretical research.

Key Words: *Financial analysts, Discretionary disclosure, Analysts' forecasts, Capital markets.*

Data Availability: *The FAF data used in this study are available from the authors on request.*

I. INTRODUCTION

Financial analysts are an integral part of the capital market, providing earnings forecasts, buy/sell recommendations and other information to brokers, money managers and institutional investors. Much of the information analysts use in their evaluations is

We thank Mary Barth, Amy Sweeney, Katherine Schipper, Tom Stober, anonymous reviewers and workshop participants at the University of Arizona, the University of California at Berkeley, Duke University, Columbia University, Harvard University, Michigan State University, University of North Carolina, Notre Dame University, University of Oregon, Pennsylvania State University, Stanford University, University of Waterloo, the National Investor Relations Institute and the American Accounting Association annual meeting for helpful comments, and IBES Inc. for providing the analyst forecast data.

Submitted September 1994.
Accepted April 1996.

provided directly by the firm.[1] Although all publicly traded firms must meet minimum disclosure requirements set by the SEC, firms vary substantially in the amount of additional information they provide to the capital markets. Even for mandatory disclosures, such as those found in annual financial statements, firms have substantial discretion in the informativeness of the disclosures and the amount of detail provided.[2] Discretion in disclosure is even more pronounced for press releases and direct contact with analysts. In this paper, we investigate the association between disclosure practices and the number of analysts following the firm and the properties of their forecasts. We document significant associations and interpret those associations to suggest that analysts respond to firms' disclosure practices. Our conclusions suggest that firms can attract analysts, improve the accuracy of market expectations, reduce information asymmetries and limit market surprises by adopting more forthcoming disclosure practices. Although not addressed directly by this study, theory indicates that such results may be associated with a lower cost of capital for firms adopting those strategies.

We use data from the FAF Report (1985–89) as a comprehensive measure of the informativeness of a firm's disclosure policy.[3] In the FAF report, analysts evaluate the complete range of a firm's disclosures, summarizing their evaluations by a score in each of three categories: annual published information, other published information (including quarterly filings, press releases and proxy statements) and investor relations. Our dependent variables are the number of analysts following the firm and the accuracy, dispersion and variability of their forecasts. We control for other variables that previous research has shown to be related to our variables of interest and find that, within their industry, firms with more forthcoming disclosure practices have a larger analyst following, more accurate analyst earnings forecasts, less dispersion among individual analyst forecasts and less volatility in forecast revisions. In addition, these results hold after controlling for potential simultaneity between firms' disclosure choices and analysts' following.

Overall, our results indicate that company-provided disclosure is an important determinant of analyst following and the characteristics of their forecasts. In addition, our finding that more analysts follow firms with more informative disclosure practices is consistent with the notion that firm-provided information is not a substitute for analyst services. Finding greater consensus among analysts for firms with more informative disclosure practices suggests that different analysts make different forecasts primarily because of differences in non-firm-provided information, rather than differences in interpretation of common information.

Nichols (1989) and Schipper (1991) suggest that the behavior of analysts provides insight into the activities and beliefs of investors that cannot be observed directly. To the extent that analysts may be viewed as either representing or influencing investor beliefs, our results also provide insight into the effect of disclosure on investor following and the characteristics of their

---

[1] Based on surveys of financial analysts, Lees (1981) finds their sources of information, in order of importance, are: (1) interviews with company executives, (2) 10-Ks and other reports to the SEC, (3) annual and interim stockholders' reports, (4) management forecasts (if disclosed), and (5) formal presentations by company executives. Knutson (1992) also argues that companies are a primary source of information for analysts and identifies various communication channels.

[2] As an example, firms have discretion in the number of segments they report, how they aggregate operations into segments and whether they include segmental data in quarterly reports.

[3] We use the term "disclosure policy" to refer to the overall informativeness of a firm's discretionary disclosures, as measured by their score in the FAF Report. The FAF Report (1985–89) measures "the firm's effectiveness in communicating with investors" and the extent to which the firm provides information "so that investors have the information necessary to make informed judgments" across all types of disclosure. Section IV contains a more complete discussion of the data.

beliefs.[4] The effects of enhanced disclosures are of interest to accounting professionals who are involved in preparing and attesting to firm-provided disclosures, corporate managers and regulators. Benefits described by the AICPA Special Committee on Financial Reporting (AICPA 1993), and echoed by investor relations authors Marcus and Wallace (1991) and Mahoney (1991), include reduced uncertainty, lower information asymmetry among stock market participants, fewer extreme earnings surprises and greater investor following. Theoretical research echoes similar benefits to disclosure, including increased investor following (Merton 1987), reduced estimation risk (Barry and Brown 1985), and reduced information asymmetry (Glosten and Milgrom 1985), each of which reduces the cost of capital. Our results suggest that increased disclosure is associated with increases in analyst following and forecast accuracy, reductions in forecast revision volatility and dispersion and which hence, may reduce the cost of capital.

In the next section we discuss the related literature, and in section III we present our hypotheses. In section IV, we present the data and empirical analysis and, in section V, summarize our results and conclusions.

II. RELATED LITERATURE

Our research is related to two streams of the extant literature: (1) research on determinants of analyst following, and (2) research on the determinants of forecast accuracy and dispersion. Most of the empirical research on the determinants of analyst following focuses on firm characteristics other than disclosure policy. In a cross-sectional study, Bhushan (1989) finds that the number of analysts following a firm is increasing in firm size, institutional ownership, and return variability. In a time-series study, O'Brien and Bhushan (1990) find that analyst following increases when a firm's return volatility has declined, increases more for firms with smaller prior analyst following, and increases more for firms in industries with more stringent disclosure requirements and increasing numbers of firms. Brennan and Hughes (1991) find that analyst following is greater for firms with lower share prices after controlling for size, return variability and past returns, and that the number of analysts increases after a stock split. Perhaps closest to our study, Byrd et al. (1993) document a short-term increase in analyst following after CEO presentations to analyst societies and Healy et al. (1994) find that firms in the top quintile of FAF ratings' changes over a 12-year period experience a significant increase in their analyst following, although the firms in the bottom quintile of ratings' changes do not experience a significant decrease in their analyst following. Healy et al. (1994) also find that the firms in the top quintile of FAF ratings' increases are more likely to experience management changes, undertake major business restructurings, access capital markets, repurchase stock and announce stock splits, making it difficult to attribute the increase in analysts solely to the increase in disclosure.

Although there is substantial literature on the properties of analyst forecasts (see Brown et al. 1985 and Brown 1993 for reviews), relatively few papers consider how discretionary disclosure affects analysts' forecasts. Baginski and Hassell (1990) and Jennings (1987) provide evidence that analysts revise their forecasts in response to management earnings forecasts, and Williams (1996) suggests that the magnitude of the adjustment is a function of the usefulness of

[4] Survey evidence in SRI International (1987) suggests that analyst reports are a primary source of information to buy-side investors, and Marcus and Wallace (1991) argue that analysts are an important source of information for individual investors, either directly or through brokers. This view underlies the use of analyst expectations as a proxy for investor expectations in a large body of capital markets research (see Brown (1993) for an overview).

managements' previous forecasts. Similarly, Waymire (1986) finds that the accuracy of analyst earnings forecasts increases slightly after a management earnings forecast is released. While management earnings forecasts have the advantage of being concrete disclosure events, the FAF data represent a more comprehensive measure of firm disclosure by incorporating important aspects of disclosure which are difficult to quantify (e.g., new product announcements, management discussion and analysis, qualitative discussions with management) and reflect the perceptions of some of the primary users of financial statement data.[5] As an alternative to management earnings forecasts, Kross et al. (1990) use inches of print in the *Wall Street Journal Index* to test whether the accuracy of analyst forecasts increases as the amount of media coverage increases. However, media coverage captures the impact of exogenous events and editorial policy as well as the effect of disclosure policy.[6]

III. HYPOTHESES

We focus on two aspects of analysts' behavior—their choice of which firms to follow as measured by the number of analysts providing earnings forecasts for a firm, and characteristics of their earnings forecasts as measured by the forecast accuracy, the degree of dispersion among forecasts and the variability of forecast revisions during the year.[7]

Disclosure and Analyst Following

In Bhushan (1989), the equilibrium number of analysts is determined by the intersection of the aggregate demand and supply curves for analyst services. The model describes how various firm characteristics affect the intersection of these curves and, consequently, the equilibrium supply of analysts. Applied to our study, the issue is how firm-provided information affects the supply and demand for analyst services.

If it is less costly to receive information from the firm than to acquire it independently from other sources, increased disclosure will shift the analyst supply curve to the right, increasing aggregate supply. All else equal, this effect increases the equilibrium number of analysts.[8] The effect of additional disclosure on the demand for analyst services depends on the role that analysts play in the capital market. If analysts are primarily *information intermediaries*—the principle flow of information goes from the firm to the analysts, who process the information and transmit

---

[5] It is not clear whether management earnings forecasts are representative of other types of disclosure. The *ex post* accuracy of earnings forecasts is publicly validated or refuted in relatively short order while the validity of other types of disclosure is not as easily assessed. As a result, managers perceive more legal risk associated with earnings forecasts than with other types of disclosure (Lees 1981). Skinner (1994) suggests that concern about potential litigation creates incentives to issue earnings forecasts preempting bad earnings news; however, incentives for "softer" disclosure which is not validated as quickly or precisely are not as clear.

[6] In terms of mandatory disclosures, Brown and Han (1992) find that the consensus of analyst long-range forecasts increases around earnings announcements, and Swaminathan (1991) finds that consensus increases following the adoption of segmental reporting requirements. Baldwin (1984) finds that analysts' forecast accuracy increases for multisegment firms after the adoption of segmental reporting requirements. Brown and Rozeff (1979) find that analyst forecasts of annual earnings become more accurate following interim accounting reports, and Critchfield et al. (1978) find that forecast accuracy increases through the fiscal year but the dispersion among analysts' forecasts remains unchanged. Finally, Brown et al. (1987) show that forecast accuracy (relative to a random walk) is positively associated with firm size and negatively associated with the dispersion of analyst forecasts.

[7] By focusing on earnings forecasts, we ignore other functions of analysts such as issuing buy/sell recommendations and generating trades. It is unclear how analysts weight these different activities, but we assume that the choice of which firms to cover and what to forecast for earnings is a significant part of their job.

[8] In an investor relations context, Nichols (1989) describes how a lack of disclosure leads to a low supply of analyst services. He quotes Robert Dunlap of Irving Trust, "I don't follow Pullman because they won't tell you enough about their business to allow you to get a handle on it.... If they change and become more open with the street, there is no doubt that I'd take more of an interest in Pullman."

it to the capital market—then an increase in firm-provided information means the analyst has a more valuable report to sell. In this case, increased disclosure increases aggregate demand for analyst services. This effect in isolation will increase the equilibrium number of analysts.[9] Consistent with this prediction, the analyst community has consistently come out in favor of increased firm-provided disclosure.[10]

However, if analysts are primarily *information providers* who compete with firm-provided disclosures made directly to investors, then an increase in firm-provided information will substitute for the analyst report. In this case, increased disclosure reduces the aggregate demand for analyst services. This effect in isolation will decrease the equilibrium number of analysts.

In sum, increased firm-provided disclosure is expected to increase the supply of analyst services, but it may either increase or decrease the demand for analysts, so the net effect depends on the relative importance of these potentially competing forces. An observed negative relation between disclosure levels and the number of analysts implies that analysts are primarily information providers, and firm-provided disclosure is a substitute for their services.[11] An observed positive relation implies that either analysts are primarily information intermediaries or else, if they are information providers, the effect of reduced information production costs outweighs the effect of reduced demand.

Since the direction of the effect of disclosure on analyst following is unclear, we test the following non-directional hypothesis (stated in the null form):

H1: The number of analysts following a firm is unrelated to the informativeness of the firm's disclosure policy.

The direction of causality between a firm's disclosure level and the number of analysts is debatable. Specifically, an observed positive relation could reflect either the fact that analysts are attracted to firms which disclose more or that analysts are able to apply pressure on firms which they follow for other reasons to increase their disclosure levels. Evidence presented in Section IV suggests that the direction of causality runs from disclosure policy to analyst following.

Disclosure Policy and Forecast Characteristics

In addition to affecting the number of analysts following the firm, additional disclosure is likely to affect the properties of analysts' earnings forecasts. We consider three characteristics—forecast dispersion, accuracy and volatility.

Dispersion

The effect of increased disclosure on the dispersion of analyst forecasts depends on whether differences in forecasts are due to differences in information or differences in forecasting models. If analysts have a common forecasting model and observe the same firm-provided disclosures but possess different private information, they will place less weight on their private information as the informativeness of firm-provided disclosure increases, increasing the consensus among their forecasts. Alternatively, if analysts have the same firm-provided and private information but

---

[9] Fishman and Hagerty (1989) and Merton (1987) make similar predictions for investor following. In these models, investors can only follow a limited number of firms and prefer to follow firms that provide the most valuable information.

[10] Knutson (1992) and AICPA (1993), for example, discuss analysts' positions on increased disclosure.

[11] To the extent that firms have an incentive to increase analyst following (as they would in Merton (1987) and Fishman and Hagerty (1989)), it may seem unlikely that they would engage in discretionary disclosure that reduces analyst following. However, as discussed in the introduction, other incentives for disclosure exist (e.g., reductions in information asymmetry, risk, earnings surprises, etc.) which would be balanced in determining disclosure policy.

differ in the weights they place on components of firm-provided disclosure in forecasting earnings, additional disclosure may increase the dispersion of analyst forecasts.[12]

Therefore, an observed negative relation between disclosure and forecast dispersion implies that analysts differ primarily in their private information. Observing a positive association implies that analysts have different forecasting models, so they draw different conclusions from the same observed disclosures and, as the disclosures become more precise, their forecasts become more dispersed. Since the direction of the effect of disclosure on dispersion in analyst forecasts is unclear, we test the following non-directional hypothesis (stated in the null form):

H2: The dispersion of analysts' earnings forecasts is unrelated to the informativeness of a firm's disclosure policy.

Accuracy

The likely relation between disclosure and forecast accuracy is more clear. To the extent that firm-provided disclosure is informative about future earnings, analysts' forecast accuracy will increase with the informativeness of a firm's disclosure policy. Although a firm's disclosures may be useful to analysts without providing information about next period's earnings, it is difficult to imagine scenarios (short of fraudulently misleading disclosures) in which additional disclosure systematically reduces the accuracy of analysts' earnings forecasts. However, the strength of the relation between firm-provided disclosures and the accuracy of analysts' forecasts is an empirical issue. This leads to the following hypothesis:

H3: The accuracy of analysts' earnings forecasts is positively associated with the informativeness of a firm's disclosure policy.

Revision Volatility

The volatility of forecast revisions in the time period leading up to an earnings announcement is likely to be reduced by a more forthcoming disclosure policy. In assessing the informativeness of a firm's disclosure practice, the FAF considers the timeliness of information releases and firms that disclose information on an ongoing basis are judged to have more informative disclosure practices than those that withhold information until a mandatory disclosure is required. Over time, events occur with implications for the firm's future earnings. The firm has the option of disclosing them as they occur (with analyst revisions made after each announcement) or waiting and disclosing them all at once (with only one analyst revision). The latter will result in more extreme expectation revisions when the information is disclosed. The notion that more timely disclosure may be valuable in reducing the magnitude of forecast revisions is consistent with Mahoney (1991) who argues that disclosure is beneficial, in part, because it reduces the incidence of significant surprises for investors and analysts.[13] Our fourth hypothesis (stated in alternate form) is:

H4: The volatility of analyst earnings forecast revisions is negatively associated with a firm's disclosure policy.

---

[12]Harris and Raviv (1993) and Kandel and Pearson (1995) present models in which investors differ in their interpretation of publicly-disclosed data, and in which additional disclosure can result in divergence of beliefs.

[13]Mahoney (1991) states that "surprises are anathema to analysts and investors, and thus to investor relations practitioners as well. They are to be avoided. How? By keeping analysts and investors informed..."

IV. EMPIRICAL ANALYSIS

Disclosure Data

The informativeness of firms' disclosures is measured by FAF ratings. The analysis in the FAF Report (1985–89) is conducted by industry-specific subcommittees composed of leading analysts and contains evaluations of the informativeness of a firm's disclosures along three dimensions: annual published information, quarterly and other published information, and investor relations and related aspects.[14] The assessment factors include both the content of a firm's disclosure and its timeliness. Briefly, in the "Annual Published Information" category, analysts assess the clarity and candor of the financial highlights and president's letter, the amount of detail about the corporate officers, the corporation's goals and product and geographic segments, and the overall level of detail in the financial statements and footnotes. In the "Quarterly and Other Published Information" category, analysts consider the depth of coverage in quarterly reports and the availability and timeliness of other written material, such as press releases, proxy statements, summaries of the annual meeting proceedings and presentations to analyst groups, and statistical supplements. In the "Investor Relations" category, analysts assess how knowledgeable and responsive the company contact is to analyst questions, the accessibility of management and their candor in discussing corporate developments, and the frequency and content of presentations to analysts.

The industry subcommittees meet first to agree on the firms to be reviewed and the criteria and weights to be applied in evaluating companies in the industry. The larger firms in the industry are generally reviewed, and the set remains relatively constant over time. Individual committee members later complete evaluations of each firm, which are returned to the subcommittee chairperson. The subcommittees generally meet a second time to summarize the scores, prepare a written explanation and decide whether to recommend any companies for an "Award for Excellence in Corporate Reporting." Each subcommittee report is reviewed by the Corporate Information Committee for consistency and fairness, and a final report is prepared containing a detailed evaluation of each firm. The evaluation assigns a score in each category and a total company score which is a weighted combination of the three category scores. The report is mailed to all the firms surveyed, the FASB, the SEC and other interested parties. In many cases, the subcommittee meets individually with company representatives to discuss the results.[15] A typical year's report covers 460 firms in 27 industries, with an average of 13 analysts in each industry providing the evaluations.

Our primary sample of FAF ratings is taken from the 1985–89 FAF reports. For the investor relations, other publications and total score categories, we use these data as our measure of disclosure that took place during the company's fiscal year. However, the annual report is not

[14]A comparison of the analysts included on the subcommittees with those selected for the *Institutional Investor* All-American Research Team (1988) suggests a substantial overlap. For example, in 1988, 3 of the 5 airline subcommittee analysts and 10 of the 18 chemical subcommittee analysts were members of the 1988 All-American Research Team. In discussions with analysts, a primary motive for serving on a subcommittee is visibility and an indication of status in the analyst community.

[15]The stated goal of the evaluation process is to measure the forthcomingness and effectiveness of communicating with investors. The FAF's "Checklist of Criteria for Evaluating Financial Communications Effort" emphasizes that the evaluation is based on communication with both analysts and shareholders. However, since the evaluation is conducted by analysts (although both the buy and sell sides are included), the criteria may reflect the effectiveness in communicating with analysts more than with investors. Given that our dependent variables are based on analyst followings and characteristics of their forecasts, a disclosure measure which focuses on the ability of disclosure to satisfy analysts' needs is appropriate.

released until after the company's fiscal year end, so for this disclosure category we use the FAF annual report ratings from 1984–1988, matching the analyst dependent variables for a fiscal year to the lagged disclosure data.[16] Descriptive statistics on the disclosure data are based on 1985–1989.

The FAF data represent a cross-section of industries, including service, manufacturing, financial, transportation and extraction.[17] Because approximately nineteen percent of the industry subcommittees (covering 38 percent of the firms) report only the overall company scores, the composition of the sample varies depending on whether the total score or individual category scores are used.[18] Re-estimating the results for the total score variable including only those industries with complete data on each of the disclosure components yields similar conclusions to those reported.

Although disclosure policy is likely to be correlated across the three categories, we include each separately, as well as the total score, because firms may vary in their choice of disclosure media and because the effect of disclosure policy may vary by the media employed.[19] For example, because much of the disclosure included in the investor relations category is targeted specifically at analysts, this category may have the most influence on the willingness of analysts to follow the firm but, to the extent that periodic press releases are important sources of information on material developments for the firm, the other publications category may be a more important determinant of forecast accuracy.

The FAF data contain a potential sample of 751 firms (732 with COMPUSTAT data) that are rated in at least one of the five FAF reports during 1985–1989. In total, there are 2272 firm-years in the sample, with each firm evaluated approximately three times in the five year period. Panel A of table 1 provides descriptive statistics for the three category scores and the total company score as a percentage of total available points. As seen in the table, each category has considerable variation; the difference between the 1st and 99th percentiles is highest for the investor relations variable (75 percent) and lowest for the annual report variable (58 percent), which may suggest that firms can more clearly differentiate their investor relations efforts than their annual report disclosures, perhaps because annual reports are more closely regulated.

A primary advantage of the FAF data is that the scores capture all aspects of disclosure which are viewed as important by analysts rather than focusing on a single aspect, such as the existence of a management earnings forecast. Further, the scores quantify qualitative disclosure (e.g., management's discussion and analysis) and disclosure which may not have been reflected in published financial statements or the media (e.g., conference calls to analysts). In addition, the measures are prepared by analysts who are primary users of financial statements, are familiar with the firms' disclosures through their use of them during the year and invest substantial time and effort in preparing the FAF reports.

A potential problem with the FAF data is that the scores reflect analysts' perceptions of firms' disclosure policies rather than the disclosure policies themselves. However, the FAF is clearly aware of this possibility and the FAF's evaluation process is specifically designed to enhance the objectivity of the evaluations in several ways. First, only summary measures for a subcommittee

---

[16]For example, we use the 1988 FAF annual report score and 1989 FAF investor relations, other publications and total scores as explanatory variables for 1989 analyst following and forecast characteristics.

[17]See table 1 in Lang and Lundholm (1993) for a summary of industries.

[18]Most prominently, the banking industry provides 20 percent of the total score observations, but this industry subcommittee does not report individual category scores. As a result, the banking industry affects the analysis of total scores, but not the individual disclosure categories.

[19]Marcus and Wallace (1991) and Mahoney (1991) discuss the relative advantages and disadvantages of various disclosure media.

TABLE 1
Descriptive Statistics for the Raw FAF Disclosure Scores, Analyst Dependent Variables and Control Variables

Panel A: Disclosure Variables

					percentile		
Variable	*n*	*mean*	*1%*	*25%*	*50%*	*75%*	*99%*
Annual Report	1324	.73	.37	.64	.75	.83	.95
Other Publications	1392	.70	.30	.60	.72	.83	.96
Investor Relations	1392	.74	.25	.64	.77	.87	1.00
Total Score	2272	.70	.32	.62	.72	.80	.95

Panel B: Dependent Variables

					percentile		
Variable	*n*	*mean*	*1%*	*25%*	*50%*	*75%*	*99%*
Number of Analysts	2175	17.6	2.4	9.9	16.7	24.3	39.8
Standard Deviation of Forecasts	2141	.014	.001	.003	.005	.010	.150
Accuracy	2164	–.042	–.619	–.025	–.008	–.003	.000
Revision Volatility	2211	.010	.000	.001	.002	.005	.137

Panel C: Control Variables

					percentile		
Variable	*n*	*mean*	*1%*	*25%*	*50%*	*75%*	*99%*
Market Value ($ millions)	2215	2438	33	433	1072	2538	20794
Std(Return on Equity)	2022	.021	.001	.005	.015	.028	.111
Return-Earnings Correlation	1952	.316	–.590	.090	.360	.590	.895
Earnings Surprise	2166	.076	.000	.009	.019	.044	.842
Percentage New Forecasts	2169	.267	.102	.208	.263	.318	.457

The four disclosure variables are the analysts' ratings of disclosure from the FAF report measured as the percent of possible points received in each category. The dependent variables, percentage of new forecasts and earnings surprise are all calculated from the IBES Summary Tape. Other control variables are from COMPUSTAT. In total there are 751 firms with at least one year of FAF data during the years 1985 through 1989.

are presented, thereby reducing the opportunity for individual analysts to curry management's favor by providing a more positive evaluation than is warranted. Second, a primary motive for having subcommittee members meet both before and after the evaluation process is to reduce subjectivity and ensure that all members use the same basic criteria in their evaluations. Further, because each subcommittee report includes a written justification of each firm's score, and the report is frequently presented to the firm orally, subcommittee members cannot capriciously make their evaluations. Finally, the Corporate Information Committee's review of the subcommittee reports helps ensure fairness and consistency.

Because each industry is evaluated by a different set of analysts, we industry-adjust the dependent and independent variables. Therefore, the tests explain intra-industry variation in the number of analysts and their forecast properties by the intra-industry variation in the disclosure and control variables. This approach controls for potential cross-industry variation in scores due to differences in subcommittee composition, but ignores cross-industry variation in scores due to legitimate differences in disclosure policy across industries. The results for measures that are not industry-adjusted are consistent with those reported in the paper.[20]

Dependent Variables

All analyst data are taken from the IBES Summary Tape. The four dependent variables we consider are:

Number of Analysts	=	the number of analysts providing an annual earnings forecast;
Std. Dev. of Forecasts	=	the inter-analyst standard deviation of forecasts deflated by stock price;
Forecast Accuracy	=	the negative of the absolute value of the analyst forecast error, deflated by stock price (i.e., $-(\lvert EPS_t - AF_t \rvert)/P_t$, where EPS_t, AF_t and P_t are earnings per share, the median analyst forecast of earning per share and price per share in period t, respectively); and
Revision Volatility	=	the standard deviation of the changes over the fiscal year in the median forecast from the preceding month, deflated by the stock price as of the beginning of the fiscal year.

We deflate the forecast measures by the stock price to facilitate comparisons across firms. We define forecast accuracy as the negative of the (scaled) absolute forecast error so that more accurate forecasts are represented by higher values. The revision volatility measures the smoothness with which analysts' expectations change during the period.[21]

We are interested in assessing the impact of disclosure generally, rather than at a particular announcement date. Further, there is no single time during the year when one would expect investor relations or other publication disclosures to have the most significant effect on analysts. Even though the annual report is issued at a single point in time, it is difficult to identify the date

[20] A related concern is that the individual analysts in a subcommittee may vary across years so that scores may not be strictly comparable across years. The FAF formalizes the evaluation process in part to mitigate such variation. To the extent that it remains, it will add noise to the disclosure variables. Results are consistent when estimated on a year-by-year basis, suggesting that variation in committee composition over time is not of serious concern.

[21] Disclosure policies might also affect the bias in analyst forecasts. For example, analysts might bias earnings forecasts to reward firms who were particularly forthcoming. However, Lang and Lundholm (1993) provide evidence that positive forecast errors are associated with more disclosure. Although this result could imply that analysts bias their forecasts downward for firms who disclose more, a more likely explanation is that firms are more willing to report good news than bad news.

on which the annual report information reaches the market, and the informativeness of the annual report will influence the forecast accuracy and other variables over the entire year. Consequently, the number of analysts, the standard deviation of forecasts and the forecast accuracy are computed as the simple average of the measure across the twelve monthly reporting periods on the IBES tape during the company's fiscal year. Revision volatility is computed as the standard deviation of forecast changes over the twelve months of the fiscal year. Each dependent variable is based on forecasts of annual earnings made during the fiscal year to which the forecasts pertain.[22] As a practical matter, results are robust to changes in the period over which the dependent variables are measured and are very similar using measures computed based on data for a single month computed at fiscal year-end or at six months prior to fiscal year-end.

Panel B of table 1 reports descriptive statistics on the dependent variables. The median firm-year in the sample is followed by 16.7 analysts, has a standard deviation of forecasts equal to 0.5% of its share price, has an analyst forecast error that is 0.8% of its share price and a standard deviation of forecast revisions equal to 0.2% of its share price. Each variable also exhibits considerable variation across the sample, as evidenced by the inter-quartile ranges.

Control Variables

The hypothesized relations between disclosure and the analyst variables are based on the assumption that other variables are held constant. In practice, however, other factors are likely to vary systematically with both the dependent variables and disclosure scores, creating the possibility of an omitted/correlated variable problem. For example, firm size has been shown to be related to both the number of analysts and a firm's FAF disclosure score. If we did not control for firm size in the regression, a significant relation between the number of analysts and disclosure could be observed even if size were the true explanatory variable. Therefore, in addition to simple correlations, we also estimate multiple regressions including five control variables which prior research suggests may affect analyst following and forecast properties, and may be correlated with the variables of interest.

For the analyst-following regression, we include firm size, the standard deviation of return on equity and the historical returns-earnings correlation as control variables. Bhushan (1989) and Brennan and Hughes (1991) provide empirical evidence of a positive association between the number of analysts following a firm and both firm size and performance variability. Waymire (1986) and Lang and Lundholm (1993) suggest that firm size and performance variability are also likely to be correlated with disclosure policy. King et al. (1990) argue that analyst following is likely to be positively associated with returns-earnings correlation because it is easier to predict future stock price based on earnings forecasts for those firms. Lang and Lundholm (1993) document a negative correlation between the level of return-earnings correlation and the firm's disclosure level, with the interpretation that a low returns-earnings correlation indicates that earnings does a relatively poor job of capturing valuation-relevant information, so additional forms of disclosure are necessary.

---

[22]For example, the number of analysts following a December 31 year-end firm for the 1985 observation is computed as the sum of the number of analysts providing forecasts of 1985 annual earnings at the IBES reporting date for each of the months January through December 1985, divided by 12. As a result, forecasts of 1985 earnings made prior to the announcement of 1984 results may not be strictly comparable with those made later in the year because, for example, some analysts may only begin forecasting 1985 earnings when 1984 results are known. However, the predicted relation between disclosure and analyst behavior holds regardless of whether the forecast variables are measured before or after 1984 results are announced.

The control variables for the number-of-analysts regressions, computed from COMPUSTAT, are:

Market Value	=	the market value of the firm's equity at the beginning of the fiscal year;
Std. Dev. of ROE	=	the historical standard deviation of return on equity computed over the preceding ten years; and
Return-Earnings Correlation	=	the historical correlation between annual returns and earnings computed over the preceding ten years.

We also include the preceding control variables in the regressions examining the forecast dispersion, accuracy and revision volatility. Firm size, returns-earnings correlation and standard deviation of ROE are likely to affect forecast characteristics because, as argued above, they affect analysts' incentives to gather information about the firm and, consequently, are likely to affect their forecast characteristics.[23]

In addition to the control variables listed above, we include additional control variables, earnings surprise and the percent of new forecasts, in our forecast characteristic regressions. The earnings surprise, measured as the random walk forecast error deflated by price, controls for the fact that forecast characteristics are likely to be affected by the magnitude of the earnings information to be disclosed. Consider a firm's introduction of a major new product. Realized earnings are likely to deviate substantially from expected earnings, consensus among analysts is likely to be low, and there are likely to be significant revisions in analyst forecasts. Inclusion of a measure of earnings surprise as an independent variable should control for such factors.

The percentage of new forecasts mitigates the possible effect of stale IBES forecasts. Analyst forecasts which were not updated in a given month are still included in IBES's computation of summary statistics on analyst forecasts, and it is not possible to determine whether the forecast was not revised because it still reflected the analyst's best estimate or because the analyst opted to not reestimate earnings. As a partial control for cross-sectional differences in the staleness of forecasts, we include the average monthly percentage of new forecasts for the year. Controlling for the percentage of new forecasts should reduce any systematic variation across observations in the IBES forecast characteristics which is due solely to differences in the proportion of recently revised forecasts.[24]

We define earnings surprise and percent new forecasts as follows:

Earnings Surprise	=	the absolute value of the difference between the current year's earnings per share and last year's earnings per share, divided by the price at the beginning of the fiscal year; and
Percent New Forecasts	=	the number of forecasts revised during the month plus the number of first-time forecasts issued during the month divided by the number of forecasts at the month-end, averaged over the twelve months in the firm's fiscal year.

[23]We also performed three specification checks for alternative control variables in the number-of-analysts regressions. First, we included the number of institutional investors and the percent of shares outstanding held by institutions in 1987, reflecting Bhushan's (1989) evidence that analyst following is increasing in institutional ownership. Second, we included the firm's share price, based on Brennan and Hughes' (1991) result that the number of analysts is higher for firms with lower share prices. Finally, we included the other three dependent variables as independent variables in each regression. The results are not sensitive to any of these variations.

[24]We have also conducted the analysis for the quartile of observations with the highest percentage of new forecasts (where staleness should be less of an issue) and find consistent results. However, the possibility of stale forecasts cannot be dismissed entirely.

Panel C of table 1 presents descriptive statistics on the control variables. The sample firms are generally large, as indicated by a median firm-year market value in excess of $1 billion; however, market value ranges from $33 million in the 1st percentile to over $20 billion in the 99th percentile.[25] For the median firm-year, the standard deviation of return on equity is 1.5%, the earnings/returns correlation is 36.0%, the absolute value of the change in earnings per share from the previous year is 1.9% of the share price, and 26.3% of the forecasts are new each month.

Simple Correlations

Because we do not predict a particular functional form for the relation between the dependent and independent variables, we base our analysis on ranked data. We rank the dependent and independent variables within their industry-year and convert the ranks to percentiles: (rank – 1)/(number of firms – 1). The conversion yields the percentile of the firm's rank within its industry-year, so the lowest-ranking firm receives a zero and the highest-ranking firm receives a one.

Table 2 presents correlations between pairs of independent variables after they have been converted into percentiles. As one would expect if firms coordinate disclosure policy across media, the three disclosure categories are positively correlated at levels ranging from 0.46 to 0.83. Disclosure categories have correlations that are considerably less than one, suggesting that different categories may capture different aspects of disclosure. The correlations among the control variables are relatively low, ranging from 0.28 to –0.25, as are the correlations between the disclosure variables and the control variables, suggesting that multicollinearity among disclosure and control variables is not likely to be a significant issue in the multiple regressions. As reported in Lang and Lundholm (1993), firms with higher disclosure scores are generally characterized by larger market values, lower standard deviations of past return on equity, and lower past return/earnings correlations. Further, higher disclosure scores are associated with a larger proportion of forecast revisions, suggesting that a more forthcoming disclosure policy is associated with more frequent forecast revisions.

Table 3 presents simple correlations between pairs of analyst variables, and between pairs of analyst variables and independent variables. Panel A displays the associations of primary interest in this study, the relations among analyst following and forecast characteristics and the disclosure variables. The associations are consistent across all three disclosure categories, with correlations significant at the 0.01 level. The number of analysts is positively correlated with the informativeness of a firm's disclosure practices, and firms with more informative disclosure practices have less dispersion in analyst forecasts, the forecasts are more accurate, and there is less volatility in the sequence of forecast revisions.

Table 3, panel B reports the correlations between the analyst variables and the control variables. The number of analysts is most closely associated with market value (0.70). The standard deviation of forecasts and the revision volatility are both highly positively correlated with the earnings surprise and the standard deviation of past return on equity suggesting that, for firm-years with high past and present uncertainty, there is more dispersion and volatility in analysts' forecasts. Similarly, forecast accuracy is negatively correlated with earnings surprise, suggesting that analysts are less accurate when there has been a significant change from last period's earnings.

[25]Because the sample firms are large on average, care should be taken in generalizing the results to other populations. Marcus and Wallace (1991) and Mahoney (1991) suggest that, because of the competition for analyst attention and limited alternate sources of information, disclosure policy is likely to have a greater impact for small firms than for large firms.

TABLE 2
Correlations among the FAF Disclosure Score Variables and Control Variables

	Disclosure Variables			*Control Variables*				
	Other Pub.	*Inv. Rel.*	*Total Score*	*Mkt. Value*	*SD of ROE*	*R-E Corr*	*Earnings Surprise*	*Percent New*
Disclosure Variables:								
Annual Report	.622	.463	.825	.230	–.113	–.115	–.073	.048
	.0001	.0001	.0001	.0001	.0001	.0001	.0100	.0906
Other Publications		.494	.804	.169	–.079	–.106	–.017	.069
		.0001	.0001	.0001	.0050	.0002	.5451	.0121
Investor Relations			.737	.188	–.101	–.099	–.031	.009
			.0001	.0001	.0003	.0005	.2657	.7560
Total Score				.245	–.085	–.083	–.018	.031
				.0001	.0002	.0003	.4079	.1525
Control Variables:								
Market Value					–.247	–.113	–.125	.061
					.0001	.0001	.0001	.0050
Std. Dev. of ROE						.111	.186	.058
						.0001	.0001	.0099
Returns-Earnings Correlation							.126	.038
							.0001	.0949
Earnings Surprise								.275
								.0001

All variables are computed by ranking the unranked variables in table 1 within their industry-year and converting the ranks to percentiles: (rank – 1)/(number of firms – 1). Listed below each correlation is the p value. The number of observations ranges from 1047 to 2125.

TABLE 3

Correlations Among the Dependent Analyst Variables and the FAF Disclosure Score Variables and Control Variables

	Dependent Variables			
	Number of Analysts	*Std. Dev. of Forecasts*	*Forecast Accuracy*	*Revision Volatility*
Panel A: Disclosure Variables				
Annual Report	.267 .0001	–.174 .0001	.081 .0080	–.142 .0001
Other Publications	.228 .0001	–.095 .0005	.086 .0018	–.113 .0001
Investor Relations	.267 .0001	–.177 .0001	.156 .0001	–.200 .0001
Total Score	.331 .0001	–.123 .0001	.106 .0001	–.146 .0001
Panel B: Control Variables				
Market Value	.701 .0001	–.255 .0001	.182 .0001	–.270 .0001
Std. Dev. of ROE	–.190 .0001	.303 .0001	–.172 .0001	.267 .0001
Return-Earnings Correlation	–.116 .0001	.152 .0001	–.128 .0001	.107 .0001
Earnings Surprise	–.071 .0009	.454 .0001	–.458 .0001	.404 .0001
Percent New Forecasts	.079 .0002	.407 .0001	–.475 .0001	.507 .0001
Panel C: Dependent Variables				
Std. Dev. of Forecasts	–.149 .0001			
Forecast Accuracy	.131 .0001	–.615 .0001		
Revision Volatility	–.197 .0001	.764 .0001	–.670 .0001	

All variables are computed by ranking the unranked variables in table 1 within their industry-year and converting the ranks to percentiles: (rank – 1)/(number of firms – 1). Listed below each correlation is the p value. The number of observations ranges from 1047 to 2125.

Table 3, panel C reports the correlations between the dependent variables. The highest correlation is between forecast revision volatility and standard deviation of forecasts (0.76) suggesting that forecast revisions tend to be more volatile in cases in which there is less consensus among analysts. Forecast accuracy is positively correlated with the number of analysts, possibly because the median forecast becomes a more accurate estimator as the number of observations increases.

Given the relatively high correlations among the analyst following and forecast characteristic variables, the control variables and the disclosure variables noted above, inference drawn from the simple correlations may be misleading. Specifically, our interest is in the marginal effect of disclosure on analyst following and forecast characteristics. In the next section, we assess the marginal effect of disclosure holding other variables constant.

Regression Results

Table 4 reports the results of regressions of the number of analysts on the control and disclosure variables.[26] With respect to H1, results for the total score category indicate a significant relation between disclosure policy and analyst following, suggesting that analyst following is a function of disclosure policy.[27]

To test whether each category has explanatory power incremental to that in the other categories, we estimate the regression including all three categories together. The collinearity among the disclosure variables discussed earlier can result in inflated sampling variances and unstable coefficient estimates. Nevertheless, when all three components of disclosure are included, coefficients on both the other publications and investor relations categories are significantly positive, while the coefficient on the annual report variable is insignificant.[28] The significant positive coefficients for the investor relations and other publications variables are consistent with Lees' (1981) survey finding that analysts rely heavily on direct contact with firms and with the notion that, although the securities laws prohibit disclosure of material nonpublic information to selective subsets of the analyst population, a firm's willingness to communicate with analysts is an important factor in their willingness to follow a firm.[29] The significant result when the annual report variable is included separately and the correlations across disclosure categories suggest that increased disclosure in the annual report is part of an overall disclosure strategy that increases analyst following. However, the fact that annual report loses significance when all three categories are included indicates that the other disclosure variables capture the

[26]Iman and Conover (1979) provide a discussion of rank regression. This ranking mechanism produces larger differences between percentiles for small industries than for large industries. For example, in an industry with only two firms, one will have a disclosure score of 1.0 and the other of 0.0 where, if those firms were in an industry with many firms, their values would probably be less extreme. As a result, observations in industries with fewer firms will tend to have slightly higher variances. We have re-estimated the regressions with unranked data and with data ranked across all firms (not adjusted for industry) with similar results to those reported in the paper, suggesting that this effect does not affect our conclusions.

[27]Significance levels should be interpreted with caution because some firms are included in the analysis for consecutive years, which may induce auto-correlation in the residuals. We have conducted specification checks which take first order auto-correlation into account with very similar results. As a more extreme check, we also conducted the analysis using only one observation per firm with very similar results. A firm appears in our sample on average three times, so at most the number of independent observations is overstated by a factor of three, causing the t-statistics to be overstated by at most a factor equal to the square root of 3. Unless otherwise stated, we refer to a result as "significant" if the p-value for a two-tailed test is less than 0.01.

[28]Collinearity between disclosure categories is an issue in all of the sets of regressions which follow. In every case, each disclosure category is statistically significant with a consistent sign in explaining forecast characteristics when included alone, but generally one or more are not significant when the other categories of disclosure are included.

[29]The fact that the coefficient on the total score is higher than that on any of the components reflects the fact that the relation tends to be stronger for the industries for which the subcommittees did not provide scores for the individual disclosure categories (principally banking).

TABLE 4
Regression of the Number of Analysts Following the Firm on Disclosure Scores and Control Variables

$$\textit{Number of Analysts} = \alpha + \beta_1 \textit{Annual Report} + \beta_2 \textit{Other Publications} + \beta_3 \textit{Investor Relations} + \beta_4 \textit{Total Score} + \beta_5 \textit{Market Value} + \beta_6 \textit{Standard Deviation of ROE} + \beta_7 \textit{Return-Earnings Correlation} + \varepsilon$$

α	β_1	β_2	β_3	β_4	β_5	β_6	β_7	N	R^2
0.11				0.17	0.66	–0.01	–0.02	1868	0.52
(6.2)				(10.1)	(38.6)	(–0.8)	(–1.5)		
0.17	0.02	0.07	0.10		0.59	–0.05	–0.06	998	0.45
(6.1)	(0.8)	(2.3)	(3.5)		(23.0)	(–1.8)	(–2.7)		

Regressions are estimated using ordinary least squares, with all variables ranked and then computed as percentiles within the industry-year. T-statistics are noted in parentheses below each coefficient estimate. Annual Report, Other Publications, Investor Relations and Total Score are the annual report, other publications, investor relations and total score, respectively, based on the FAF scores for each category of disclosure. Number of Analysts is the average number of analysts on IBES providing an estimate of annual earnings over the 12 months of the company's fiscal year. Market Value is the market value of outstanding equity at the beginning of the fiscal year. Standard Deviation of ROE is standard deviation of net income divided by shareholders' equity and Returns-Earnings Correlation is the correlation between annual returns and earnings, each calculated over the 10 years prior to the observation. N is the number of observations and R^2 is the adjusted R^2 for the regression.

effect of the disclosure strategy, and the score for the annual report does not have incremental explanatory power.[30]

The positive relation between the number of analysts and the FAF scores suggests that firm-provided disclosures complement rather than substitute for analyst activities. Consequently, information intermediation (processing firm-provided information) appears to be a significant aspect of the analyst function in capital markets. As argued earlier, if analysts were primarily information providers—in competition with firm disclosures provided directly to investors—then more firm-provided disclosures should diminish the value of analyst services and the number of analysts following the firm.

The coefficient on firm size is positive and significant, consistent with the results reported by Bhushan (1989). The standard deviation of past return on equity and the correlation between annual returns and earnings are significantly negative in the regression including all three categories of disclosure separately but are not significant in the regression including only the total disclosure score, providing weak evidence that analysts are more likely to follow firms with low performance variability and firms for which earnings are not highly correlated with returns. The negative coefficient estimate for performance variability in the regressions including all three

[30]The fact that we measure analyst following as an average over 12 months while the annual report is released at one point in time may bias against results for the annual report variable. However, results are not sensitive to time period over which the analyst-following variable (or other analyst variables) are measured.

categories of disclosure is consistent with that documented by Bhushan (1989) and Brennan and Hughes (1991), but the negative association between analyst following and the return-earnings correlation runs counter to the intuition from King et al. (1990) that the incentives for private information acquisition will be greater when the returns-earnings correlation is high. The explanatory power of the regressions is substantial, with an adjusted R^2 of 0.52 for the regression including the total score and 0.45 for the regression including all three of the disclosure categories.

Direction of Causality

Our hypotheses assume firms choose their disclosure policies partly to influence the activities of analysts. Thus, we view the informativeness of disclosure as "causing" the observed level of analyst following. It is possible, however, that the direction of causality is the opposite (i.e., a larger analyst following causes the firm to increase its disclosures) or that analyst following and the informativeness of disclosures are simultaneously determined by other exogenous variables.

One approach to investigating the direction of causality is to examine the association between changes in disclosure scores and changes in the lead and lag number of analysts. There are several problems with this approach. First, while the FAF attempts to maintain consistency from year to year, the evaluation process is designed to make comparisons among firms at a point in time, rather than comparisons of the same firm through time. The composition of the industry subcommittees and the specific criteria and weights vary from year to year, so changes in disclosure scores may reflect changes in subcommittees or criteria over time. Second, the disclosure policy of a firm and the number of analysts following it are likely to change only slowly over time because of the fixed costs to a firm of substantially changing disclosure policies or the fixed cost to an analyst of adding or deleting a firm. Therefore, we include changes computed over time periods of up to four years. However, because a given firm may have been evaluated in only a subset of the sample years, the number of observations for longer intervals is significantly reduced.

We compute the rank-order correlations between changes in disclosure scores and changes in both lead and lag analyst following. The change in lead (lag) analyst following is the change in the number of analysts following the firm computed over the time period following (preceding) the period over which the change in disclosure is computed. If changes in the number of analysts following the firm *precede* changes in disclosure policy, then the correlation between changes in disclosure and changes in the lagged number of analysts should be positive; if changes in the number of analysts *follow* changes in disclosure policy, then the correlation between changes in disclosure and changes in the lead number of analysts should be positive. As seen in table 5, all but one of the correlations for the lagged number of analysts are negative (although many are not significant), rejecting the hypothesis that changes in the number of analysts precede changes in disclosure. In addition, all the correlations for the lead number of analysts are positive, (although only a subset are significant) supporting the hypothesis that changes in the number of analysts follow changes in disclosure. Although a chronological ordering of events does not conclusively establish causality, these results provide limited evidence that disclosure policy changes cause changes in the number of analysts; we observe no evidence that causality runs in the opposite direction.

An alternate approach is to estimate a simultaneous equations model to investigate whether a firm's disclosure score and the number of analysts following the firm are jointly determined by a set of exogenous variables. The simultaneous equations approach potentially controls for bias in the OLS estimates when the error term is correlated with the independent variables, as is the case when a truly endogenous variable is treated as an exogenous (independent) variable. To implement this model, we estimate a first stage regression of FAF scores on a set of instrumental

TABLE 5

Correlations between Changes in FAF Disclosure Score Variables and Lag 1 and Lead 1 Changes in the Number of Analysts Following the Firm, Computed over Window Lengths of 1 to 4 Years

	ΔAnnual Report	*ΔOther Pubs*	*ΔInvestor Relations*	*ΔTotal Score*	
		4 Year Window			
Δ in lead 1	0.11908	0.29018	0.11076	0.23833	*correlation*
# of analysts	0.1494	0.0003	0.1802	0.0001	*p value*
	148	148	148	265	*number of obs.*
Δ in lag 1	−0.00767	0.05087	−0.13693	−0.01944	
# of analysts	0.9270	0.5435	0.1005	0.7569	
	145	145	145	256	
		3 Year Window			
Δ in lead 1	0.02421	0.14201	0.04560	0.05948	
# of analysts	0.6578	0.0083	0.3985	0.1594	
	337	345	345	561	
Δ in lag 1	−0.04320	−0.02268	−0.11085	−0.08039	
# of analysts	0.4300	0.6751	0.0399	0.0607	
	336	344	344	545	
		2 Year Window			
Δ in lead 1	0.11373	0.17181	0.05293	0.07938	
# of analysts	0.0091	0.0001	0.2135	0.0171	
	525	554	554	902	
Δ in lag 1	−0.03703	−0.01245	−0.10952	−0.05556	
# of analysts	0.3972	0.7708	0.0102	0.0999	
	525	550	550	878	
		1 Year Window			
Δ in lead 1	0.05136	0.06131	0.00597	0.02076	
# of analysts	0.1461	0.0715	0.8608	0.4361	
	802	865	865	1409	
Δ in lag 1	−0.04702	−0.02555	−0.03657	−0.03731	
# of analysts	0.1846	0.4561	0.2861	0.1680	
	798	853	853	1367	

ΔAnnual Report, ΔOther Pubs, ΔInvestor Relations and ΔTotal Score are the changes in the annual report, other publications, investor relations and total disclosure scores from the FAF data. Δ in lead 1 # of analysts and Δ in lag 1 # of analysts are the changes in the number of analysts over the period following and over the period preceding the window over which the change in disclosure scores is computed respectively. The window over which both variables are computed is noted at the top of each panel.

variables; we then use the predicted value from this regression in place of the actual disclosure score in the number-of-analysts regression. Whether the coefficient estimates from this approach are more or less biased than the OLS estimates depends on whether the instrument variables are indeed exogenous (i.e., independent of the error term) and the portion of the variation in disclosure score that is captured in the first stage regression (Bound et al. 1993). In the context of our analysis, the difficulty is identifying instrumental variables that are highly correlated with FAF scores, but are uncorrelated with the error from the number of analysts regression.

Our source of instruments is Lang and Lundholm (1993), who model disclosure scores as a function of the firm's structural environment (market value and standard deviation of past return on equity), performance (market-adjusted returns and analysts' earnings forecast errors) and activity in the public capital market (security offering in the current or following two years). While the explanatory variables are statistically significant, the resulting first-stage regressions have very low adjusted R^2s, ranging from 0.05 to 0.09, which suggests that significant measurement error may have been introduced in the first stage of the analysis.

To assess statistically whether the two equations are simultaneously determined, we apply the Hausman test (Hausman 1978). We regress the number of analysts on the exogenous variables (i.e., the control variables), the instrument for disclosure score (i.e., the predicted value from the first-stage regression) and the actual disclosure score. If the disclosure score is truly exogenous, the coefficient on the instrumented disclosure score will equal zero. The results from this test fail to reject the hypothesis that the coefficient is zero for all four disclosure score variables, suggesting that simultaneity is not an issue. The p-value for two-tailed t-test is 0.19 for the annual report, 0.18 for other publications, 0.62 for investor relations and 0.77 for the total score.

Results from estimating the second-stage regressions using the instruments estimated in the first stage (not reported) are consistent with those reported earlier. While the statistical significance of the disclosure scores is reduced somewhat relative to the results in table 4, all remain significant at less than the 0.10 level. The reduced significance may reflect the effects of simultaneity, but it also likely reflects the low R^2 in the first-stage regressions.

In summary, the analysis for number of analysts suggests a significant relation between the firm's disclosure policy and the number of analysts following the firm. Further, there is limited evidence that changes in firms' disclosure policies cause changes in analyst following; there is no evidence of the opposite direction of causality.[31]

Forecast Dispersion and Disclosure

Table 6, panel A provides evidence on H2 with respect to the relation between forecast dispersion and disclosure. In the regression including the total disclosure score, the coefficient on the total score is significantly negative, suggesting that more forthcoming disclosures decrease dispersion among analyst forecasts. This result is consistent with additional disclosure reducing the divergence of beliefs across analysts by increasing the precision of their shared information. In the regression including all three categories of disclosure, coefficients on both the annual report and investor relations variables are significantly negative, but the other publications variable is not significant.

The relation between the standard deviation of analyst forecasts and market value is negative, indicating that analyst dispersion is lower for larger firms. The relations between the standard

[31]We do not control for simultaneity of other dependent variables because forecast characteristics in a given period are unlikely to affect contemporaneous disclosure ratings (e.g., firms are unlikely to increase disclosure because analyst forecasts are very accurate). It is possible that analysts' perceptions of disclosure are affected by forecast characteristics, but the FAF designs the evaluation process to mitigate this bias.

TABLE 6
Regression of Forecast Characteristics on Disclosure Scores and Control Variables

Forecast Characteristics = $\alpha + \beta_1$*Annual Report* + β_2*Other Publications* + β_3*Investor Relations* + β_4*Total Score* + β_5*Market Value* + β_6*Standard Deviation of ROE* + β_7*Returns-Earnings Correlation* + β_8*Earnings Surprise* + β_9*% New Forecasts* + ε

Panel A: Standard Deviation of Analyst Forecasts

α	β_1	β_2	β_3	β_4	β_5	β_6	β_7	β_8	β_9	N	R^2
0.19				–0.07	–0.18	0.17	0.06	0.31	0.33	1850	0.38
(8.7)				(–3.6)	(–9.1)	(8.8)	(3.3)	(15.9)	(17.4)		
0.28	–0.08	0.01	–0.06		–0.25	0.18	0.07	0.27	0.33	989	0.42
(8.6)	(–2.7)	(0.2)	(–2.2)		(–9.2)	(6.7)	(2.6)	(10.5)	(13.0)		

Panel B: Forecast Accuracy

α	β_1	β_2	β_3	β_4	β_5	β_6	β_7	β_8	β_9	N	R^2
0.79				0.06	0.14	–0.03	–0.05	–0.33	–0.40	1858	0.38
(35.4)				(3.4)	(7.2)	(–1.4)	(–2.5)	(–17.0)	(–20.6)		
0.73	–0.01	0.06	0.07		0.19	–0.02	–0.03	–0.32	–0.41	994	0.38
(21.4)	(–0.4)	(1.9)	(2.3)		(6.5)	(–0.7)	(–1.2)	(–12.2)	(–15.7)		

(Continued)

TABLE 6 (*Continued*)

Panel C: Volatility of Forecasts Revisions

α	β_1	β_2	β_3	β_4	β_5	β_6	β_7	β_8	β_9	N	R^2
0.24				–0.09	–0.21	0.12	0.02	0.23	0.45	1858	0.41
(11.0)				(–5.1)	(–10.8)	(6.6)	(1.0)	(12.0)	(24.5)		
0.33	–0.03	0.01	–0.10		–0.27	0.12	0.02	0.19	0.44	994	0.42
(9.9)	(–1.1)	(–0.4)	(–3.4)		(–9.9)	(4.5)	(1.0)	(7.6)	(17.5)		

Panel title indicates the forecast characteristic dependent variable in the regression. Regressions are estimated using ordinary least squares, with all variables ranked and then computed as percentiles within the industry-year. T-statistics are noted in parentheses below each coefficient estimate. N is the number of observations and R^2 is the adjusted R^2 for the regression.

deviation of forecasts and the standard deviation of past ROE, the past returns-earnings correlation, earnings surprise and the percentage of new forecasts are all significantly positive, suggesting that the dispersion among analysts is higher when the past earnings series is volatile and strongly related to past returns, and when there is a large earnings surprise and frequent forecast revisions. The proportion of variation explained in the regressions is substantial, with adjusted R^2s of 0.38 for the regression including total score and 0.42 for the regression including all three disclosure categories.

Forecast Accuracy and Disclosure

Table 6, panel B presents results from the regressions of forecast accuracy on the disclosure scores, providing evidence on H3. The coefficient on the total disclosure score is significantly positive when it is included as an explanatory variable, confirming that firm disclosure is an important determinant of the accuracy of analyst forecasts. When all three disclosure categories are included, coefficients on both the other publications and investor relations categories are significantly positive, consistent with the notion that ongoing communication with companies is an important source of information to analysts in forecasting earnings.

Accuracy is positively associated with market value, suggesting that analysts' forecasts are relatively more accurate for larger firms. The coefficients on the standard deviation of past return on equity are negative but insignificant. The standard deviation of past forecasts was significantly negatively correlated with accuracy in the simple correlations, so it appears that inclusion of other measures of uncertainty such as earnings surprise and market value have rendered this variable insignificant. Coefficients on the earnings-return correlation, earnings surprise and percent of new forecasts are generally significantly negative, suggesting that forecasts tend to be less accurate in cases when there is a large earnings surprise, when analysts are frequently revising their forecasts and when the past association between returns and earnings is low. The significant negative coefficients on the percent of new forecasts suggest that its inclusion is, at best, a partial control for stale forecasts. The regression explains a significant proportion of the variation in forecast accuracy, with adjusted R^2s of 0.38 for both the regression with total score and the regression including all three categories of disclosure.

Volatility of Forecast Revisions and Disclosure

Table 6, panel C presents evidence on H4 from the regression of forecast revision volatility on disclosure scores. The coefficient on the total score is significantly negative when it is included in the regression. When all three disclosure categories are included, only investor relations is significant, consistent with the notion that a firm can reduce the likelihood of large revisions in analysts' expectations through its investor relations effort.

The volatility of forecast revisions is decreasing in market value, suggesting that there are fewer extreme expectation revisions for large companies. The relation between variability of forecast revisions and the standard deviation of past ROE, earnings surprise and percentage of new forecasts are all positive, suggesting that revisions in expectations tend to be volatile when there is a large earnings surprise, there are frequent forecast revisions and the past earnings series is volatile. The coefficient on the correlation between returns and earnings is insignificant, suggesting that the past relation between returns and earnings is not a significant determinant of forecast revision volatility. The explanatory power of the regressions is high, with adjusted R^2s of 0.41 for the regression with the total disclosure score and 0.42 for the regression including all three categories of disclosure.

V. CONCLUSIONS

The results of this paper indicate that, after controlling for size, the earnings surprise and other attributes of the information environment, firms with more forthcoming disclosures in their industry have a greater analyst following, more consensus among analysts' earnings forecasts, more accurate forecasts and less variable forecast revisions. Of the three categories of disclosure considered, investor relations is consistently a significant determinant of analyst behavior even after controlling for other categories of disclosure, confirming existing survey and anecdotal evidence that direct contact with the company is a primary source of information for analysts.

Overall, these results are consistent with the view that more forthcoming disclosure policies, particularly in the investor relations area, attract more analysts, either because these disclosures increase the demand for analyst reports or because they reduce analysts' costs of supplying them. The fact that an increase in firm-provided information increases analyst following suggests that analysts are not in direct competition with firm disclosures provided directly to investors. The results are also consistent with the view that analysts possess both firm-provided and privately-acquired information, but that increases in disclosure and timeliness reduce the weight analysts place on other information in their forecasting models and smooth the forecast revision process by expediting the resolution of uncertainty.

To the extent that the behavior of analysts captures that of investors more generally, these results are consistent with motivations for disclosure given in the investor relations literature and have implications for management as it sets disclosure policy, for the SEC and Congress as they establish securities laws and for the FASB as it proceeds with its project on "Disclosure Effectiveness." While there has been a great deal of discussion about the costs of increased disclosure, potential benefits have received less attention.[32] Although the evidence is indirect, this study finds relationships between firms' disclosure policies and factors that have been linked to a reduced cost of capital. The results for analyst following suggest that firms that disclose more have a larger pool of potential investors; the results for forecast accuracy suggest that their investors have more accurate beliefs about future performance; the results for forecast dispersion suggest that there is less asymmetry in investors beliefs about their performance; and the results for revision volatility suggest that investor expectations about their earnings change more smoothly over the year.

[32]The FASB laments in SFAS No. 1 that, "the benefits from financial information are usually difficult or impossible to measure objectively, and the costs often are."

REFERENCES

American Institute of Certified Public Accountants, The AICPA Special Committee on Financial Reporting (AICPA). 1993. *The Information Needs of Investors and Creditors*. New York: AICPA.

Baginski, S., and J. Hassell. 1990. The market interpretation of management earnings forecasts as a predictor of subsequent financial analyst forecast revision. *The Accounting Review* 65 (January): 175–190.

Baldwin, B. 1984. Segment earnings disclosure and the ability of security analysts to forecast earnings per share. *The Accounting Review* 59 (July): 376–389.

Barry, C., and S. Brown. 1985. Differential information and security market equilibrium. *Journal of Financial and Quantitative Analysis* 20 (December): 407–422.

Bhushan, R. 1989. Firm characteristics and analyst following. *Journal of Accounting and Economics* 11 (July): 255–274.

Bound, J., D. Jaeger, and R. Baker. 1993. The cure can be worse than the disease: A cautionary tale regarding instrumental variables. NBER technical paper # 137, Boston, MA.

Brennan, M., and P. Hughes. 1991. Stock prices and the supply of information. *Journal of Finance* 46 (December): 1665–1691.

Brown, L. 1993. Earnings forecasting research: Its implications for capital markets research. *International Journal of Forecasting* 9 (November): 295–320.

———, and J. Han. 1992. The impact of annual earnings announcements on convergence of beliefs. *The Accounting Review* 67 (October): 862–875.

———, and M. Rozeff. 1979. The predictive value of interim reports for improving forecasts of future quarterly earnings. *The Accounting Review* 56 (July): 585–591.

———, G. Richardson, and S. Schwager. 1987. An informational interpretation of financial analyst superiority in forecasting earnings. *Journal of Accounting Research* 25 (Spring): 49–67.

Brown, P., G. Foster, and E. Noreen. 1985. *Security Analyst Multi-Year Forecasts and the Capital Market*. Sarasota, FL: American Accounting Association.

Byrd, J., M. Johnson, and M. Johnson. 1993. Investor relations and the cost of capital. Working paper, University of Michigan, Ann Arbor, MI.

Critchfield, T., T. Dyckman, and J. Lakonishok. 1978. An evaluation of security analysts' forecasts. *The Accounting Review* 53 (July): 651–668.

Financial Analysts Federation. 1984–89. *Report of the Financial Analysts Federation Corporate Information Committee*. New York, NY: FAF.

Fishman, M., and K. Hagerty. 1989. Disclosure decisions by firms and the competition for price efficiency. *Journal of Finance* 44 (July): 633–646.

Glosten, L., and P. Milgrom. 1985. Bid, ask, and transaction prices in a specialist market with heterogeneously informed traders. *Journal of Financial Economics* 26 (March):71–100.

Harris, M., and A. Raviv. 1993. Differences in opinion make a horse race. *Review of Financial Studies* 6: 473–494.

Hausman, J. 1978. Specification tests in econometrics. *Econometrica* 23 (November): 1251–1271.

Healy, P., K. Palepu, and A. Sweeney. 1994. Disclosure strategy changes: What prompts them and what are their capital market consequences? Working paper, Harvard University, Boston, MA.

Iman, R., and W. Conover. 1979. The use of rank transformation in regression. *Technometrics* 21 (November): 499–509.

Institutional Investor. 1988. The All-American Research Team. October: 98–184.

Jennings, R. 1987. Unsystematic security price movements, managerial earnings forecasts, and revisions in consensus analyst earnings forecasts. *Journal of Accounting Research* 25 (Spring): 90–110.

Kandel, E., and N. Pearson. 1995. Differential interpretation of public signals and trade in speculative markets. *Journal of Political Economy* 103 (August): 831–853.

King, R., G. Pownall, and G. Waymire. 1990. Expectations adjustments via timely management forecasts: Review, synthesis, and suggestions for future research. *Journal of Accounting Literature* 9:113–144.

Knutson, P. 1992. Financial reporting in the 1990s and beyond: A position paper of the Association for Investment Management and Research. Working paper, University of Pennsylvania, Philadelphia, PA.

Kross, W., B. Ro, and D. Schroeder. 1990. Earnings expectations: The analysts' information advantage. *The Accounting Review* 65 (April): 461–476.

Lang, M., and R. Lundholm. 1993. Cross-sectional determinants of analyst ratings of corporate disclosures. *Journal of Accounting Research* 31 (Autumn): 246–271.

Lees, F. 1981. *Public Disclosure of Corporate Earnings Forecasts*. New York, NY: The Conference Board.

Mahoney, W. 1991. *Investor Relations: The Professional's Guide to Financial Marketing and Communications*. New York, NY: New York Institute of Finance.

Marcus, B., and S. Wallace. 1991. *Competing in the New Capital Markets: Investor Relations Strategies for the 1990s*. New York, NY: HarperBusiness.

Merton, R. 1987. Presidential address: A simple model of capital market equilibrium with incomplete information. *Journal of Finance* 42 (July): 483–510.

Nichols, D. 1989. *The Handbook of Investor Relations*. Homewood, IL: Dow Jones-Irwin.

O'Brien, P., and R. Bhushan. 1990. Analyst following and institutional ownership. *Journal of Accounting Research* 28 (Supplement): 55–82.

Schipper, K. 1991. Analysts' forecasts. *Accounting Horizons* 4 (December): 105–121.

Skinner, D. 1994. Why firms voluntarily disclose bad news. *Journal of Accounting Research* 32 (Spring): 38–60.

SRI International. 1987. *Investor Information Needs and the Annual Report*. Morristown, NJ: Financial Executives Research Foundation.

Swaminathan, S. 1991. The impact of SEC mandated segment data on price variability and divergence of beliefs. *The Accounting Review* 66 (January): 23–41.

Waymire, G. 1986. Additional evidence on the accuracy of analyst forecasts before and after voluntary management earnings forecasts. *The Accounting Review* 59 (January): 129–142.

Williams, P. 1996. The relation between a prior earnings forecast by management and analyst response to a current management forecast. *The Accounting Review* 71 (January): 103–115.

[7]

THE ACCOUNTING REVIEW
Vol. 72, No. 3
July 1997
pp. 323–349

Disclosure Level and the Cost of Equity Capital

Christine A. Botosan
Washington University

ABSTRACT: The effect of disclosure level on the cost of equity capital is a matter of considerable interest and importance to the financial reporting community. However, the association between disclosure level and cost of equity capital is not well established and has been difficult to quantify. In this paper I examine the association between disclosure level and the cost of equity capital by regressing firm-specific estimates of cost of equity capital on market beta, firm size and a self-constructed measure of disclosure level. My measure of disclosure level is based on the amount of voluntary disclosure provided in the 1990 annual reports of a sample of 122 manufacturing firms. For firms that attract a low analyst following, the results indicate that greater disclosure is associated with a lower cost of equity capital. The magnitude of the effect is such that a one-unit difference in the disclosure measure is associated with a difference of approximately twenty-eight basis points in the cost of equity capital, after controlling for market beta and firm size. For firms with a high analyst following, however, I find no evidence of an association between my measure of disclosure level and cost of equity capital perhaps because the disclosure measure is limited to the annual report and accordingly may not provide a powerful proxy for overall disclosure level when analysts play a significant role in the communication process.

Key Words: *Voluntary disclosure, Cost of equity capital, Corporate disclosure strategy.*

Data Availability: *Contact the author.*

This paper is dedicated to the memory of Victor L. Bernard. It is based in part on my dissertation at the University of Michigan. I wish to thank the members of my dissertation committee for their many insightful comments and suggestions: Vic Bernard and Russ Lundholm (Chairs), David Hirshleifer, Phil Howrey and Doug Skinner. I would also like to thank Nick Dopuch, Carol Frost, Mahendra Gupta, Bob Holthausen, Ron King and two anonymous reviewers for their comments. I benefited from the input of workshop participants at the University of British Columbia, the University of Colorado, Duke University, Harvard University, the University of Kansas, the University of Michigan, Michigan State University, Northwestern University, University of Pennsylvania, Stanford University, Vanderbilt University, Washington University, the University of Waterloo and Wilfrid Laurier University. I am grateful for the financial support of the Institute of Chartered Accountants of Ontario, the Social Sciences and Humanities Research Council of Canada, the Horace H. Rackham School of Graduate Studies, the Paton Accounting Center and the University of Michigan Business School.

Editor's Note: This paper is the winner of the 1996 AAA Competitive Manuscript Award.

Submitted October 1995.
Accepted February 1997.

I. INTRODUCTION

The extent to which firms benefit from increased disclosure remains a controversial issue. Several models of asset pricing suggest increased disclosure reduces cost of equity capital but little empirical evidence exists to support these claims. This absence of evidence fuels an ongoing debate among practitioners regarding the benefits of enhanced disclosure. For example, the Special Committee on Financial Reporting of the American Institute of Certified Public Accountants (1994) (i.e., Jenkins Committee) states that an important benefit of greater disclosure is a lower cost of equity capital. In rebuttal, the Financial Executives Institute (Berton 1994) argues that the enhanced disclosures called for in the Committee's report are targeted to stock traders which would add to share price volatility thereby increasing risk and leading to a higher cost of equity capital.

Theoretical research supporting a negative association between disclosure level and cost of equity capital has followed two related thrusts. The first is that greater disclosure enhances stock market liquidity thereby reducing cost of equity capital either through reduced transactions costs or increased demand for a firm's securities. This stream of research includes Demsetz (1968), Copeland and Galai (1983), Glosten and Milgrom (1985), Amihud and Mendelson (1986) and Diamond and Verrecchia (1991). The second stream of research which includes Klein and Bawa (1976), Barry and Brown (1985), Coles and Loewenstein (1988), Handa and Linn (1993), Coles et al. (1995) and Clarkson et al. (1996) suggests that greater disclosure reduces estimation risk arising from investors' estimates of the parameters of an asset's return or payoff distribution. That is, greater uncertainty exists regarding the "true" parameters when information is low. If estimation risk is nondiversifiable, investors require compensation for this additional element of risk. However, no consensus has been reached on the diversifiability of estimation risk (Clarkson et al. 1996).

Although existing empirical research tends to support a negative association between disclosure level[1] and cost of equity capital, the authors of the Jenkins Committee (1994, 38) report admit that the evidence to date does not present "an empirical case that informative disclosure lowers the cost of capital." This is because prior research has examined the impact of disclosure on variables that are expected to be positively related to cost of equity capital[2] and not on cost of equity capital itself. Prior research has adopted an indirect approach because appropriate cost of equity capital estimates for an investigation of the impact of disclosure on cost of equity capital are difficult to obtain. That is, traditional methods of estimating cost of equity capital either provide no role for information (this is the case with the traditional Capital Asset Pricing Model) or yield measures of this cost that demonstrate little or no relation to market beta (the most well accepted measure of firm risk) and are difficult to defend as a result.

In this study I estimate the cost of equity capital using an accounting based valuation formula developed by Edwards and Bell (1961), Ohlson (1995) and Feltham and Ohlson (1995). I show that these estimates are both increasing in market beta and decreasing in firm size. I then test for the association between disclosure level and the cost of capital itself after controlling for market beta and firm size and document a negative association between cost of equity capital and voluntary disclosure level for firms that attract a low analyst following. The magnitude of the effect is such that a one-unit difference in the disclosure measure is associated with a difference

---

[1] Disclosure quality is also important but very difficult to assess. As a result, researchers tend to assume quantity and quality are positively related. This assumption seems justified given the importance of managers' reporting reputations and the constraints placed on managers by legal liability.

[2] See for example, Healy et al. (1995), Byrd et al. (1995), Frankel et al. (1995), Healy and Palepu (1995) and Welker (1995).

in the cost of equity capital of 28 basis points, on average, for these firms. However, I find no evidence of an association between my measure of disclosure level and cost of equity capital for firms with a high analyst following. This may be because my disclosure measure is limited to the information provided in the annual report and accordingly may not yield a powerful proxy for overall disclosure level when a substantial amount of information is disseminated through financial analysts.

The remainder of the paper is organized as follows. I develop the hypotheses in section II. My sample selection procedures and descriptive statistics for the sample are provided in section III. Procedures used to estimate firms' cost of equity capital and level of disclosure are described in section IV followed by the empirical results in section V. Conclusions, limitations and suggestions for future research appear in section VI.

II. HYPOTHESIS DEVELOPMENT

Theoretical support for a negative association between disclosure level and cost of equity capital is provided by two streams of research. The first is represented by Amihud and Mendelson (AM) (1986) and Diamond and Verrecchia (DV) (1991). AM (1986, 228) claim that the cost of equity capital is greater for securities with wider bid-ask spreads because investors demand compensation for added transactions costs. By disclosing private information firms can reduce the adverse selection component of the bid-ask spread and reduce their cost of equity capital. DV suggest that greater disclosure reduces the amount of information revealed by a large trade thereby reducing the adverse price impact associated with such trades. As a result, investors are willing to take larger positions in a particular firm's stock than they otherwise would. This increases demand for the firm's securities and raises the current price of the firm's stock, thus reducing the cost of equity capital.[3]

The second stream of theoretical research suggests that greater disclosure can reduce cost of equity capital by reducing nondiversifiable estimation risk. Klein and Bawa (1976) were perhaps the first to consider estimation risk but, more recent work includes Barry and Brown (1985), Coles and Loewenstein (1988), Handa and Linn (1993), Coles et al. (1995) and Clarkson et al. (1996).

These researchers recognize that the parameters of a security's return or payoff distribution must be estimated by investors based on a firm's return history and/or other information about the firm. Barry and Brown (1985), Handa and Linn (1993) and Coles et al. (1995) use a Bayesian approach which recognizes that investors form predictive distributions that reflect their uncertainty about the true parameters. They conclude that estimation risk is nondiversifiable, is not reflected in the traditional CAPM formula for market beta (which is derived under the assumption that the parameters of the distribution are known) and that estimates of market beta are systematically too low for low information securities because market beta fails to incorporate estimation risk.

Clarkson et al. (CGT) (1996), state that estimation risk has a significant nondiversifiable component if resolution of uncertainty about low information securities affects the return earned on the market portfolio. CGT also argue, however, that the breadth of modern securities markets allows the correlation of returns induced by the resolution of uncertainty to be diluted to the point that any nondiversifiable component of estimation risk is immaterial. Nevertheless, CGT (1996, 79) conclude that "...the extent of the impact of estimation risk remains, fundamentally, an empirical question."

---

3 DV also show that when reduced information asymmetry results in rapid exit from market making the opposite result obtains. However, the conditions that give rise to this finding are described as "less typical."

The research discussed above, motivates the following hypothesis (stated in alternative form):

H1: There is a negative association between cost of equity capital and disclosure level.

Existing evidence indicates that firms coordinate their disclosure policies across different media. For example, using the set of corporate disclosure rankings produced by the Association for Investment Management and Research (AIMR), Lang and Lundholm (LL) (1993) document a significant rank-order correlation between annual report and other publication disclosure rankings (coefficient of 0.62) and between annual report and investor relations disclosure rankings (coefficient of 0.41).[4] This suggests that a measure of disclosure level produced by examining any one aspect of corporate reporting could proxy for the general level of disclosure provided by a firm. I rely on this assumption when using the amount of voluntary information found in a firm's annual report alone to serve as a proxy for the amount of disclosure provided by a firm across all avenues.

If firms perfectly coordinated their disclosure policies across various avenues, this assumption would not introduce additional measurement error into the analyses. However, as LL indicate, the correlation, while significantly positive, does not approach one, particularly with respect to the correlation between annual report disclosure rankings and investor relations rankings. As a result, my measure of disclosure level which is limited to disclosure provided in the annual report may not provide a powerful proxy for overall disclosure level when firms are followed by a large number of analysts and presumably use these analysts to communicate with the market. For firms with fewer analysts, however, measurement error arising from the limited scope of the disclosure measure should be less severe because the annual report plays a much larger role in the communication process. For example, Previts et al. (1994, 67) observe, "The parties who have an interest in (small publicly traded companies) appear to be left to their own resources and to *general purpose statements* [emphasis added] to ascertain information, since analysts do not provide a ready source of guidance." This suggests that the association between cost of equity capital and my measure of disclosure level may not be as significant for firms with a large analyst following. This is restated as hypothesis two.

H2: The association between cost of equity capital and disclosure level is less significant for firms that attract a greater number of analysts.

III. SAMPLE SELECTION AND DESCRIPTION

Sample Selection

Two factors are critical to the power of my empirical analysis: (1) sufficient cross-sectional variation in disclosure levels and (2) a sufficiently large sample. A sufficiently large sample could be provided in the disclosure rankings produced by the AIMR which provides a readily available source of a relatively long time series of disclosure rankings across a broad spectrum of industries. However, the AIMR sample tends to be limited to the largest most heavily followed firms in an industry.[5] Since disclosure levels are positively correlated with firm size (Lang and Lundholm

[4] Each year the AIMR selects a small number of firms from a variety of different industries and provides a within industry ranking of firms' corporate reporting along three dimensions: annual reports, quarterly and other published reports and investor relations. These rankings are published annually in The Association for Investment Management and Research, Report of the Corporate Information Committee.

[5] Based on a sample of 751 firms with at least one year of AIMR data during the period 1985 to 1989, Lang and Lundholm (1996) report that the average firm in this sample is followed by approximately eighteen analysts and has a market value of equity of approximately $2.4 billion.

1993), AIMR firms are unlikely to display sufficient cross-sectional variation in disclosure levels.[6]

An alternative to using the AIMR sample is to select a sample of firms characterized by greater variation in firm size and analyst following but for which disclosure rankings are not readily available. The advantage of obtaining potentially greater cross-sectional variation in disclosure level comes at the cost of a limited sample size and a more narrowly defined measure of disclosure level due to the difficulty of constructing a data base of disclosure rankings. I chose to adopt this latter approach and limit the sample to one year and one industry to maximize statistical power, as discussed below. I also test hypothesis two to address the possibility that an association between cost of equity capital and my disclosure measure might be attenuated when financial analysts play a significant role in the communication process.

I limit the analysis to one year because firms' disclosure policies appear to remain relatively constant over time. For example, Healy et al. (1995) are able to identify only 90 large and sustained increases in AIMR disclosure rankings in a sample of 595 firms in 23 industries over the period 1980 to 1990. Since this suggests that year-to-year disclosure observations for a given firm are not independent, I chose to increase sample size by adding cross-section observations as opposed to observations over time. Fiscal year 1990 was chosen because it was recent enough to ensure reasonable access to firms' corporate reports yet still ensure other post-sample year data would be available.

One industry was selected because different industries display different patterns of disclosure. For example, firms in the pharmaceuticals industry tend to provide much more disclosure about their research and development activities than do firms in other industries. Using different disclosure measures for firms in different industries necessitates a *within* industry analysis resulting in smaller intra-industry samples so I chose instead to select firms for which the same disclosure measure is expected to be appropriate. Specifically, I examine firms in the machinery industry broadly defined to include firms with primary operations in the following SIC codes: 3312–3399 (primary metals), 3411–3499 (fabricated metal products, except machinery and transportation equipment) and 3511–3569 and 3581–3599 (industrial and commercial machinery).[7]

Firms in this particular industry appear to display a sufficient amount of variation in disclosure practices. This is evidenced by the within industry variation in disclosure scores assigned by the AIMR during 1985–1989. For all AIMR industries with a full five years of data, I computed the cross-sectional standard deviation of AIMR scores assigned to firms within a particular industry for a given year.[8] Standard deviations for each industry were then averaged across time, and rank ordered. The machinery industry was selected for analysis because its mean standard deviation fell in the top quintile of the distribution and it is a large industry.[9]

The 1994 edition of Ward's Business Directory lists 372 publicly traded companies in the SIC codes of interest. Seventy-one of these firms were dropped from the sample because at least 24 of the 60 monthly return observations in the five-year period ended May 31, 1991 (the data needed to estimate beta) were not available in the Center for Research in Security Prices (CRSP) 1993

---

[6] Evidence to suggest that this may indeed be the case is provided later in this section.

[7] Electronic components manufacturers (SIC codes 3571–3579) are excluded because their disclosure practices may be influenced by the high technology nature of these firms which is quite different from the other firms included in the analysis.

[8] The banking and insurance industries are excluded because their disclosure practices are heavily influenced by regulatory requirements.

[9] The lowest mean standard deviation of total disclosure scores is 5.5 and is associated with the retail industry. The highest is 11.8 and is associated with Publishing and Broadcasting. The mean standard deviation of total disclosure scores for the machinery industry is 10.2.

stock return files. All of the remaining firms were contacted to request a copy of their 1990 annual report to shareholders. Of these, 87 failed to send the requested report. However, annual reports for 40 of these 87 were collected from other sources, such as *LaserD* (distributed by Disclosure Information Services), yielding a total sample of 254 annual reports. During fiscal 1990, four of these firms were reorganizing under Chapter 11, two were not primarily engaged in manufacturing activities, and one underwent a major merger. Since the disclosures made by firms engaged in such activities are likely to differ from the norm, they were excluded from the analysis. One hundred and twenty-five firms not followed by Value Line were also excluded because I need the forecast data provided by Value Line to estimate cost of equity capital.[10] As shown in table 1, the sample selection procedures yielded a final sample of 122 firms.

Sample Description

Descriptive statistics for the sample are provided in table 2. ANALYST is the maximum number of analysts reported either in the 1991 edition of *Nelson's Directory of Investment Research* or in any of the 12 monthly IBES reports issued during 1990. BETA is estimated via a market model regression of at least 24 of the 60 monthly return observations in the five-year period ended May 31, 1991 on a market index defined in terms of equally weighted NYSE/AMEX returns. MVAL is the market value of equity at the end of 1990 in millions of dollars. ASSET is the book value of total assets, PPE is the net book value of property, plant and equipment and SALES is total sales, all for the fiscal year ended 1990, and all in millions of dollars. NUMEMP is the number of employees reported in the fiscal year end 1990 annual report or 10-K. DSCORE is the firm's disclosure score. A discussion of this measure is provided in section IV.

[10]Other forecasting services such as IBES, Nelson Publications and Zacks do not provide long-term forecasts of book value, earnings and future price; key inputs into the cost of equity capital formula described in section IV.

TABLE 1
Summary of Sample Selection Procedures

	Number	*Percent*
Public firms in SIC codes 3312–3599 (excluding 3571–3579)	372	124%
Firms with insufficient CRSP data	(71)	(24)
Firms contacted for 1990 annual report	301	100%
Firms failing to respond	(87)	(29)
Annual reports received	214	71%
Annual reports collected from alternative sources	40	13
Total annual reports	254	84%
Firms in Chapter 11	(4)	(1)
Firms not primarily engaged in manufacturing	(2)	(1)
Firms undergoing a major merger during 1990	(1)	(0)
Firms not followed by Value Line	(125)	(42)
	122	40%

The data indicate a wide range of firm size with market value of equity of $18.5 million at the first percentile compared to $5.9 billion at the ninety-ninth percentile of the distribution. The range associated with several other measures of firm size—ASSET, PPE, SALES and NUMEMP—also suggest substantial cross-sectional variation in firm size. Mean (median) market value of equity is $713.4 million ($209 million). In contrast, the average firm ranked by the Machinery Industry Subcommittee of the AIMR (Subcommittee) in 1990 was twice as large with mean (median) market value of equity of $1.2 billion ($543.9 million).

The average sample firm is followed by approximately eleven analysts. One-quarter of the firms attract the attention of five or fewer analysts compared with the firms in the upper quartile which are followed by 15 or more analysts. In comparison, the mean number of analysts following the sample of firms examined by the Subcommittee in 1990 was 18.

Compared to the sample employed in this study, virtually all of the Subcommittee's firms fall in the upper half of the distributions of firm size and analyst following. The most lightly followed firm included in the Subcommittee's sample in 1990 attracted the attention of eight analysts while the market value of equity of the smallest firm was $189 million. Thus, expanding the sample of firms beyond those ranked by the AIMR yielded a final sample characterized by a broader distribution of firms with respect to firm size and analyst following. Since disclosure is positively correlated with firm size, this should lead to greater variation in disclosure level which appears to be the case. Of the 24 firms included in the AIMR sample and in the sample employed here, 67 percent fall in the top two quintiles of my disclosure rankings.

Hypothesis two is tested by dividing the sample into firms followed by less than the median number of analysts and those followed by more than the median number and estimating the association between cost of equity capital and disclosure level for the two resulting subsamples. Splitting the sample into only two subsamples still ensures a reasonable number of observations in each subset. The low analyst following subsample includes 62 firms with nine or fewer analysts. Sixty firms with ten or more analysts are included in the high analyst following subsample. Panels B and C of table 2 present descriptive statistics for the two subsamples.

On average a firm in the low analyst following subsample attracts the attention of five analysts.[11] The corresponding figure for firms in the high analyst following subsample is 18. On average the firms in the low analyst following subsample are smaller with mean market value of equity of $129.5 million compared to $1.3 billion for the firms in the other subsample. This difference is statistically significant at the 1 percent level using a t-test or Wilcoxon rank-sum test. Finally, the mean market beta for the high analyst following subsample is significantly greater than the corresponding average market beta for the low analyst following subsample.

IV. EMPIRICAL PROXIES

The Disclosure Index

In this section I describe my disclosure index and provide evidence supporting its reliability and validity. As noted earlier, I base my index on the information firms provide in their annual reports to shareholders. Although the annual report is only one means of corporate reporting, it should serve as a good proxy for the level of voluntary disclosure provided by a firm across all disclosure avenues. This is because annual report disclosure levels are positively correlated with the amount of disclosure provided via other media (Lang and Lundholm 1993). The annual report

[11]Although a firm must be followed by Value Line to be included in the sample, three firms reportedly have no analyst following. This discrepancy arises because analyst following is determined by the number of analysts reported in either Nelson's Directory of Investment Research or IBES. Since neither source is comprehensive some understatement of analyst following is to be expected.

TABLE 2
Descriptive Statistics

Panel A: Full Sample of Firms

Variable[a]	n	Mean	Percentile 1%	25%	50%	75%	99%	Standard Deviation
ANALYST	122	11.5	1.0	5.0	9.0	15.0	41.0	9.3
BETA	122	1.14	0.66	0.94	1.11	1.30	2.05	0.28
MVAL	121	713.4	18.5	89.3	209.0	593.9	5865.4	1244.3
ASSET	122	1408.6	68.9	206.4	413.8	1104.7	15918.3	2898.2
PPE	122	489.4	11.2	57.6	124.5	383.9	6596.0	1085.4
SALES	122	1493.9	69.0	241.4	559.6	1438.2	14511.0	2847.5
NUMEMP	122	10362.4	351.0	2056.0	3945.0	10700.0	63700.0	20279.7
DSCORE	122	30.0	12.0	25.0	29.6	35.0	46.0	7.7

Panel B: Low Analyst Following Subsample of Firms

Variable[a]	n	Mean	Percentile 1%	25%	50%	75%	99%	Standard Deviation
ANALYST	62	4.8	0.0	3.0	5.0	7.0	9.0	2.6
BETA	62	1.09	0.56	0.89	1.07	1.27	1.75	0.26
MVAL	61	129.5	9.0	45.1	90.7	170.6	624.9	120.1
ASSET	62	350.4	57.3	148.1	217.9	361.6	2516.7	423.9
PPE	62	115.2	11.2	43.7	65.5	110.5	1025.6	161.7
SALES	62	422.9	69.0	197.8	280.8	461.7	1858.0	383.5
NUMEMP	62	3448.1	351.0	1684.0	2277.5	3930.0	18860.0	3599.7
DSCORE	62	26.5	11.4	22.0	27.0	30.4	42.0	6.5

Panel C: High Analyst Following Subsample of Firms

Variable[a]	n	Mean	Percentile 1%	25%	50%	75%	99%	Standard Deviation
ANALYST	60	18.4**	10.0	12.0	15.0	22.5	42.0	8.6
BETA	60	1.20*	0.67	1.01	1.19	1.38	2.09	0.28
MVAL	60	1307.2**	40.1	320.6	592.3	1555.6	6095.6	1556.6
ASSET	60	2501.9**	68.9	438.1	1025.9	2690.2	19034.0	3827.4
PPE	60	876.1**	5.9	150.9	311.1	796.6	6747.0	1445.6
SALES	60	2600.7**	67.1	617.4	1397.4	3140.5	21442.0	3745.1
NUMEMP	60	17507.2**	230.0	4130.0	9800.0	20330.5	192600.0	26979.6
DSCORE	60	33.6**	17.0	29.4	33.9	37.8	50.5	7.2

* Difference between the low and high analyst following samples is significant at the 5 percent level using either a t-test or Wilcoxon rank sum test (two-tail test).

** Difference between the low and high analyst following samples is significant at the 1 percent level using either a t-test or Wilcoxon rank sum test (two-tail test).

[a] ANALYST is the maximum number of analysts following the firm reported in either the 1991 edition of *Nelson's Directory of Investment Research* or any of the 12 monthly IBES reports issued during 1990. BETA is estimated via a market model regression using at least 24 of the 60 monthly return observations in the five-year period ended May 31, 1991, and MVAL is the market value of equity at the end of 1990 in millions of dollars. ASSET is the book value of total assets, PPE is the net book value of property, plant and equipment and SALES is total sales, for the fiscal year ended 1990, all in millions of dollars. NUMEMP is the number of employees reported in the fiscal year end 1990 annual report or 10-K. DSCORE is the firm's disclosure score. See table 3 for a summary of the major items included in DSCORE and section IV for a discussion of this measure.

is the focus of my disclosure index because the annual report is generally considered to be one of the most important sources of corporate information. For example, Knutson (1992, 7) states, "At the top of every analyst's list (of financial reports used by analysts) is the annual report to shareholders. It is the major reporting document and every other financial report is in some respect subsidiary or supplementary to it."

The purpose of my disclosure measure (which I refer to as DSCORE) is to produce a cross-sectional ranking of disclosure levels based on the amount of voluntary disclosure provided by firms in their annual reports. The selection of items included in the index was guided by recommendations provided in the American Institute of Certified Public Accountants (1994) study of business reporting (i.e., the Jenkins Committee report), the SRI International (1987) survey of investor information needs, and the Canadian Institute of Chartered Accountants (1991) study of the annual report.[12] The items included in DSCORE reflect five categories of voluntary information identified by investors and financial analysts as useful in investment decision making: background information, summary of historical results, key non-financial statistics, projected information and management discussion and analysis. Table 3 summarizes just the major elements of DSCORE; the entire instrument is available from the author upon request.

Background Information

Background information such as management's objectives and business strategy, the competitive environment, the principal products produced and the principal markets served is useful to investors because it provides a context within which to interpret other detailed information about the firm. Firms were awarded one point for each background item disclosed. One additional point per item was given if the information provided included quantitative data not recoverable from the basic financial statements, such as the total size of the market in units or a corporate goal stated in terms of a numerical target (e.g., minimum return-on-equity of 16 percent).

Summary of Historical Results

Ready access to historical summaries of quarterly and annual financial results provide information useful in trend analysis. Historical summaries present information on a consistent basis, reflecting restatements due to acquisitions, discontinued operations, stock splits and stock dividends. According to the SRI International Survey (1987), 46.2% of the individual investors and 69.6% of the professional investors surveyed rate the historical summary of operating results as important or extremely important.

Typically, firms present five or ten years of annual data. However, ten years of data is preferable due to the long cyclical trends characteristic of the machinery industry.[13] Accordingly my scoring procedure awarded twice as many points for a summary of ten or more years (or the maximum number of years possible for firms in existence less than ten years), than for a summary of shorter duration. The points awarded were based on the availability of information to compute basic profitability ratios such as return-on-assets, net profit margin, asset turnover and return-on-equity.

[12]Additional sources that guided the selection of items included in the index were Merton (1987), King et al. (1990), Healy and Palepu (1993), the Corporate Information Committee Reports of the AIMR, the AIMR Machinery Industry Subcommittee's rating sheet, conversations with the members of this committee and prior research employing disclosure indices including Cerf (1961), Singhvi and Desai (1971), Buzby (1975) and Chow and Wong-Boren (1987).

[13]The Machinery Industry Subcommittee of the AIMR's scoring sheet indicates that firms are awarded ten points if ten years of data are presented. If fewer than ten years are disclosed, they are given a score of zero for this item. Since 25 percent of the total points available are allocated to this one item, firms are severely penalized by the Subcommittee for not providing a full ten years of data.

TABLE 3
Summary of the Major Elements of DSCORE

I. Background Information:
- i. Statement of corporate goals or objectives
- ii. Barriers to entry are discussed
- iii. Competitive environment
- iv. General description of the business
- v. Principle products
- vi. Principle markets

II. Ten- or Five-Year Summary of Historical Results:
- i. Return-on-assets or sufficient information to compute return-on-assets (i.e., net income, tax rate, interest expense and total assets)
- ii. Net profit margin or sufficient information to compute net profit margin (i.e., net income, tax rate, interest expense and sales)
- iii. Asset turnover or sufficient information to compute asset turnover (i.e., sales and total assets)
- iv. Return-on-equity or sufficient information to compute return-on-equity (i.e., net income and stockholders' equity)
- v. Summary of sales and net income for most recent eight quarters

III. Key Non-Financial Statistics:
- i. Number of employees
- ii. Average compensation per employee
- iii. Order backlog
- iv. Percentage of sales in products designed in the last five years
- v. Market share
- vi. Units sold
- vii. Unit selling price
- viii. Growth in units sold

IV. Projected Information:
- i. Forecasted market share
- ii. Cash flow forecast
- iii. Capital expenditures and/or R&D expenditure forecast
- iv. Profit forecast
- v. Sales forecast

V. Management Discussion and Analysis:
- i. Change in sales
- ii. Change in operating income
- iii. Change in cost of goods sold
- iv. Change in gross profit
- v. Change in selling and administrative expenses
- vi. Change in interest expense or interest income
- vii. Change in net income
- viii. Change in inventory
- ix. Change in accounts receivable
- x. Change in capital expenditures or R&D
- xi. Change in market share

The above is a partial list of the items included in DSCORE. The entire instrument is available from the author on request.

Key Non-Financial Statistics

The Jenkins Committee Report (AICPA 1994) suggests that non-financial statistics about a company's business activities that are not recoverable from the financial statements and related disclosures provide users with important information. Moreover, the SRI International Survey (1987) indicates that 73.7% of professional investors surveyed believe that the annual report should include company performance statistics and ratios. The non-financial statistics category of the index includes items such as market share, units sold, order backlog and average compensation/employee. Firms were awarded two points for each non-financial statistic disclosed.

Projected Information

The Jenkins Committee Report (AICPA 1994) also indicates that information about opportunities and risks and management's future plans is important to professional investors and analysts. However, these individuals do not consider forecasted operating and financial data to be necessary or even desirable, preferring instead to develop their own forecasts. This sentiment is echoed by Lees' (1981) finding that 65 percent of analysts surveyed oppose mandatory disclosure of management earnings forecasts. In both studies, participants question the objectivity of management forecasts and believe that users' needs for forecast information are adequately served by the analyst community. Of course this sentiment may merely reflect a bias against management forecasts motivated by analysts' self-interest. Accordingly, I decided to incorporate forecasts of sales, profits and capital expenditures, and disclosure of future opportunities, risks and plans into my index. The scoring procedure assigned two points for each directional prediction and three points for a point estimate.

Management Discussion and Analysis

The management discussion and analysis (MD&A) section of the annual report is intended to convey information about year-to-year changes that is not recoverable from the basic financial statements. This information is valued by financial analysts. For example, Knutson's (1992, 7) position paper for the AIMR states, "Other than the financial statements themselves, perhaps the most useful single part of the annual report is the management discussion and analysis...." Similarly, the Jenkins Committee report includes the MD&A in its list of important information. However, the participants in the Jenkins study caution that the MD&A provided by managers is often superficial and one-sided. As a result, the scoring procedure assigned one point for each item discussed, provided a detailed explanation that was not recoverable from the basic financial statements or footnotes was given for the change. One additional point per item was awarded if the explanation included quantitative data also not recoverable from the basic financial statements or footnotes.

Weighting of Items Included in the Index

A major concern is that large firms could achieve higher scores because they have more disclosure opportunities due to the complexity of their organizational structures. For example, if a company operates in several different industries, it may selectively disclose forecasts or other types of voluntary information for some industry segments while withholding this information for others. However, if a firm operates in only one industry segment, it does not have the same opportunity to strategically disclose or withhold forecast or other information for particular segments. Several steps were taken in the design of my disclosure index and scoring procedures to circumvent this problem. First, projected sales and earnings information provided by multi-segment firms was weighted by the proportionate contribution of the segment being forecasted to consolidated earnings or sales for fiscal year end 1990. Hence, multi-segment firms earned all of the points allocated to projected information only if they provided a forecast for all segments or an overall forecast for the consolidated entity. Second, I limited the disclosure index to items that all sample firms could choose to disclose and I did not award multiple points for multiple references to the same disclosure item.[14] Quantitative information was weighted more heavily in the disclosure index than qualitative information because precise information is more useful and may enhance management's reporting reputation and credibility.

The total points earned by a given firm is computed by the following formula:

$$DSCORE_j = \sum_{i=1}^{5} SCORE_{ij}. \tag{1}$$

Summing the total number of points awarded to firm j for category i across all categories i=1,5 produces an ordinal measure of disclosure level (DSCORE) for each firm. All of my primary statistical analyses are based on the ranks of the disclosure measure, and non-parametric tests are conducted when feasible.

A disclosure score that places equal weight on each of the five disclosure categories was also examined. This disclosure score was computed by:

$$ESCORE_j = \sum_{i=1}^{5} \frac{SCORE_{ij}}{\max(SCORE_i)} \times 20\%. \tag{2}$$

Where $\max(SCORE_i)$ is the maximum score awarded to any sample firm for a given category. The results reported in the tables employ DSCORE since none of the conclusions change when ESCORE is used.

Descriptive Statistics Pertaining to DSCORE

Table 2 presents descriptive statistics pertaining to DSCORE for the full sample and the two subsamples. Cascade Corporation's disclosure score of 12.0 marks the first percentile of the distribution. In its 1990 annual report, Cascade Corporation provides no discussion of its principle products or markets and presents a very limited, five year summary of historical results. The only key non-financial statistic disclosed is the number of individuals employed by the company, and no forecast information is included in the report. Its management discussion and analysis discusses the change in sales, net income, capital expenditures and market share in qualitative terms only. At the opposite end of the distribution, Cummins Engine Co., received one of the highest scores, 46.0, for its 1990 annual report disclosures. Cummins' report provides a detailed discussion of its principle products and markets with specific quantitative information, a comprehensive ten year summary of historical results and several key non-financial statistics such as number of employees, average compensation per employee, market share statistics and units sold. In addition, Cummins' management discussion and analysis deals with more items than Cascade's and incorporates quantitative information not recoverable from the financial statements and footnotes. Finally, Cummins' report includes profit and sales projections, a discussion of the future impact of existing industry trends, and a capital expenditure budget for the coming

[14]The disclosure index does not include a category for segment data because it is very difficult to assess whether non-disclosing firms are simply withholding this information or are truly single segment entities. Approximately one-half of the sample firms identify themselves as single-segment companies.

year. Hence, the range of scores reported in table 2 reflects a substantial amount of variation in the underlying documents.

The range of disclosure scores awarded to the firms in each of the two subsamples is quite similar. Specifically, disclosure scores range from 11.4 to 42.0 (first and ninety-ninth percentiles) for the sample of firms with low analyst following, as compared to a range of 17.0 to 50.5 for firms with high analyst following. The null hypothesis that the sample variances are equal cannot be rejected at conventional levels of significance.

Consistent with Lang and Lundholm's (1996) finding that larger numbers of analysts are attracted to more forthcoming firms, the average disclosure score for firms with a high analyst following is 33.6, compared to 26.5 for firms with a low analyst following. This difference is statistically significant at the 1 percent level (two-tail test). Notwithstanding a positive correlation between analyst following and DSCORE, however, partitioning the sample by analyst following does not also partition the sample by disclosure level. For example, a firm with 30 points on the disclosure index would fall in the upper quartile of the distribution of the low analyst following subsample and in the second quartile of the distribution of the subsample of high analyst following.

Assessment of Validity of DSCORE

Prior studies that use disclosure indices to investigate the determinants of corporate disclosure levels have documented consistently strong and corroborative results.[15] This prior work demonstrates that disclosure indices are a useful research tool. However, financial disclosure level is not easily measured because the development and application of a disclosure index requires subjective assessments by the researcher applying the technique. As a result, it is important to assess the validity of the resulting measure.

An examination of the internal consistency of DSCORE provides some insight into the reliability of my measure and its possible limitations. Since disclosure strategies are coordinated across various avenues, I expect the components of the disclosure index to be positively correlated with one another, the number of *Wall Street Journal* articles written about the firm during 1990 and the number of financial analysts following the firm during that year—two other potential proxies for availability of corporate information. Each of these correlation coefficients is positive and statistically significant at the 2 percent level or better.

Cronbach's coefficient alpha (Cronbach 1951), is a measure of internal consistency that uses repeated measurements (in this case the various categories of the disclosure index) to assess the degree to which correlation among the measurements is attenuated due to random error. Coefficient alpha takes on a maximum value of one when the correlation between each pair of variables is one. Computed with standardized data, Cronbach's coefficient alpha, for the five categories of the disclosure index is 0.64. There is no standard test of significance for this statistic. As a general rule, an alpha of 0.8 indicates that the correlation is attenuated very little by random measurement error (Carmines and Zellner 1979). Thus, a coefficient alpha of 0.64 suggests that random measurement error could reduce the power of the empirical tests that follow.[16]

[15]For example, Cerf (1961), Singhvi and Desai (1971), Buzby (1975), Chow and Wong-Boren (1987) and Lang and Lundholm (1993) examine the association between disclosure level and firm specific characteristics and document similar results. Also, see Ball and Foster (1982), Marston and Shrives (1991) and Ahmed (1995) for reviews of accounting research employing disclosure indices.

[16]A factor analysis including DSCORE, the number of *WSJ* articles and the number of analysts indicates that all variables load on the same factor. However, consistent with the relatively low coefficient alpha, the amount of variation explained is only about 48 percent. These results support the conclusion that DSCORE is a reliable measure of disclosure level although random measurement error in the disclosure index may reduce the power of subsequent empirical tests.

Ahmed (1995) provides a meta-analysis of the results of 23 separate studies of the association between annual report disclosure level and firm characteristics. He finds that the following four variables have a statistically significant positive association with disclosure level: firm size, exchange listing status, audit firm size and leverage. If my disclosure index measures disclosure level, it should be correlated with these characteristics.

Panel A of table 4 presents Spearman correlation coefficients between DSCORE and firm size, leverage and exchange listing status. Audit firm size is not examined because all but two of the sample firms are audited by a Big 6 firm. The results are very similar to those reported by Ahmed in terms of direction and magnitude. Each firm characteristic variable is positively correlated with DSCORE and the magnitude of the coefficients fall within the 95 percent confidence intervals presented by Ahmed (1995) for leverage and exchange listing status and just outside of this interval for firm size.

Although the studies considered by Ahmed (1995) tend not to use multivariate analyses, panel B presents the results of a rank regression of DSCORE on firm size, leverage and exchange listing status. Firm size and leverage continue to be positively associated with disclosure level while listing status is no longer statistically significant. Approximately twenty-five percent of the variation in DSCORE rank is explained by the variables included in the model.

I also computed the rank-order correlation between DSCORE and the annual report disclosure scores assigned by the AIMR (ASCORE) during 1990/1991 for the *24* firms appearing in both samples.[17] Initially, I find that DSCORE and ASCORE are not significantly correlated. However, this result is sensitive to the inclusion of two extreme observations. When these observations are excluded the positive correlation between DSCORE and ASCORE is statistically significant. The correlation coefficient is 0.37 with a p-value of 0.04 (one-tail). Even with these two observations, the rank-order correlation between ASCORE and (1) the summary of historical results category score (HIST) and (2) the projected information category score (FORE) is significantly positive at less than a 5 percent level of significance (one-tail). The correlation coefficients between ASCORE and HIST and ASCORE and FORE are 0.43 and 0.37, respectively.

The correlation between ASCORE and these specific categories may reflect the relatively heavy weight the Machinery Industry Subcommittee of the AIMR (Subcommittee) places on these types of disclosures in its scoring procedures. The percentage of total points allocated by the Subcommittee to the ten-year historical summary and to future outlook statements are 25 percent and ten percent of the total, respectively.

In summary, the validity of DSCORE is supported by four different sets of analyses: (1) the correlation among the components of DSCORE, number of analysts and number of *WSJ* articles, (2) Cronbach's coefficient alpha, (3) the correlation between DSCORE and firm characteristics identified in prior research to be associated with disclosure level, and (4) the correlation between DSCORE and annual report disclosure scores assigned by the AIMR to the 24 firms in both samples. The results suggest that extending the main hypothesis to include individual category scores, the number of *Wall Street Journal* articles and/or the number of analysts might provide insights in addition to those revealed by an examination of DSCORE alone.

Cost of Equity Capital

Several alternative approaches to estimating the cost of equity capital were considered. One approach estimates this cost using average realized returns. However, average realized returns

[17]These results should be interpreted cautiously for several reasons. First, statistical power is limited by the small number of firms common to both groups. Second, there is no basis for judging what the magnitude of the correlation between DSCORE and ASCORE should be before DSCORE is deemed a valid measure of disclosure level relative to ASCORE. Finally, the analysis assumes ASCORE is an appropriate benchmark which may not be the case.

TABLE 4
Correlation Analysis of Disclosure Scores and Firm Characteristics

Panel A: Univariate Analysis

	MVAL[b]	*DERATIO*	*STATUS*
correlation	0.4443	0.2647	0.2172
p-value	0.0001	0.0034	0.0163
# of observations	121	121	122

Panel B: Multivariate Analysis[a]

	Intercept	*MVAL*	*DERATIO*	*STATUS*
coefficient[c]	0.1368	0.4261	0.2625	0.0329
t-statistic	2.059	5.167	3.267	0.560
p-value	0.0418	0.0001*	0.0007*	0.2884*
adj. R^2	24.7%			
Prob. > F	0.0001			

* One-tail test.
[a] The fractional rank (rank divided by the number of observations) of each variable (including DSCORE) is included in the analysis. White's (1980) test does not indicate the presence of heteroscedasticity. The results have been checked for the presence of influential data points using Cook's D statistic. No influential data points were detected.
[b] MVAL is the market value of equity at the end of 1990 in millions of dollars, DERATIO is the debt-to-equity ratio at the end of 1990 and STATUS is a dummy variable set equal to one if the firm is listed on the NYSE or AMEX exchange and zero if the firm is listed on NASDAQ.
[c] Estimated with 120 observations.

provide an extremely noisy measure of cost of equity capital. Indeed, prior research employing average realized returns has had difficulty establishing a significant association between returns and market beta, the most widely accepted measure of risk (Fama and French 1992). Recently Lakonishok (1993) concluded that at least *70 years* of data would be required to show that even market beta is a statistically significant risk factor if average realized returns are used to proxy for the cost of equity capital. Hence, it is unlikely that this approach would provide a powerful test of the disclosure hypothesis, especially given the limited sample employed in this study.

Practice and prior research suggest other alternatives that may incorporate less noise than realized returns. One is to estimate cost of equity capital with the Capital Asset Pricing Model (CAPM) which defines expected return as the sum of the expected risk free rate $(E(R_f))$ and the product of a firm's estimated market beta $(\hat{\beta})$ and the expected risk premium $(E(R_m - R_f))$. The premise of my study, however, is that cross-sectional variation in disclosure level explains variation in cost of equity capital. In contrast, the CAPM assumes that cross-sectional variation in market beta alone drives variation in the cost of capital. As a result, the CAPM approach provides no role for disclosure level, unless one assumes cross-sectional variation in disclosure level induces variation in beta, a notion that has no theoretical support.

The earnings-to-price ratio adjusted for growth and dividend payout is a measure that has been used in the past by academics and practitioners to estimate cost of equity capital that does not impose such restrictions.[18] This approach defines cost of equity capital as follows:

[18]For an excellent discussion of various approaches used in practice to estimate cost of equity capital see Ehrhardt (1994) and Gitman and Mercurio (1982).

$$r_j = K_j(1+g_j)\left(\frac{E_t}{P_t}\right)_j + g_j \text{; for firm j.} \tag{3}$$

In this model cost of equity capital, "r_j", is a function of a constant rate of dividend payout, "K_j", a constant rate of growth, "g_j", and the earnings-to-price ratio $\left(\frac{E_t}{P_t}\right)_j$. If one assumes zero growth and a 100 percent dividend payout rate, cost of equity capital is equal to $\frac{E_t}{P_t}$. Since these restrictions are not valid for many firms, a more sophisticated approach involves estimations of g and K for each firm.

Penman (1993) argues that the E/P ratio may be used to estimate the cost of equity capital only in the rare situation where expected future earnings is current earnings adjusted for growth at a rate equal to the cost of capital. He points out that prior research fails to find a connection between the E/P ratio and measures of risk because E/P ratios reflect cross-sectional variation in the ability of firms' current earnings to predict their future earnings more than they reflect cross-sectional variation in cost of equity capital. Consistent with this, I find no statistically significant association between the cost of equity capital estimates generated by equation (3) and market beta for my sample of firms.[19]

None of the above approaches provide viable estimates of cost of equity capital in the context of this study so I adopt an alternative approach using the accounting based valuation formula developed by Edwards and Bell (1961), Ohlson (1995) and Feltham and Ohlson (1995) (i.e., the EBO valuation formula). The derivation of the EBO valuation formula is briefly outlined below, beginning with the well known dividend discount formula:

$$P_t = \sum_{\tau=1}^{\infty} (1+r)^{-\tau} E_t[d_{t+\tau}]. \tag{4}$$

This model states that the market price of a firm's stock (P_t) is equal to the sum of expected dividends $\{E_t(d_{t+\tau})\}$ discounted at the cost of equity capital (r).[20] Ohlson (1995) shows that as long as all gains and losses that affect forecasted book value flow through forecasted earnings (i.e., clean surplus accounting holds) equation (4) can be rewritten as a function of current book value plus the discounted sum of expected abnormal earnings. This leads to equation (5):

$$P_t = b_t + \sum_{\tau=1}^{\infty} (1+r)^{-\tau} E_t[x_{t+\tau} - rb_{t+\tau-1}]. \tag{5}$$

---

[19] I estimated cost of equity capital for my sample firms using four different specifications of the formula given by equation (3). The first two specifications adjusted for growth but assumed a constant dividend payout: (1) earnings-price ratio adjusted for growth in earnings and (2) earnings-price ratio adjusted for growth in dividends. The next two specifications adjust for growth and dividend payout: (3) earnings-price ratio adjusted for growth in earnings and dividend payout and (4) earnings-price ratio adjusted for growth in dividends and dividend payout. I also estimated cost of equity capital using two other approaches found in practice: average return-on-equity and the Gordon Growth model (also known as the Constant or Perpetual Growth Valuation Model). Consistent with prior research, I found no correlation between the cost of equity capital estimates produced by any of these methods and market beta. As a result, these estimates are not considered further in the analysis.

[20] It should be noted that both the EBO valuation formula and the dividend discount formula were developed assuming that the expression arguments to be discounted are risk-adjusted and discounting takes place at the risk-free rate. However, in application the dividend discount formula is typically stated in terms of unadjusted dividends discounted at the cost of equity capital. A similar substitution in the EBO valuation formula does not require any assumptions in addition to those already implicit in the risky discount rate form of the dividend discount formula (Bernard 1995, 743).

Equation (5) specifies price per share entirely in terms of accounting numbers—current and future book values (b_t and $b_{t+\tau}$) and future earnings ($x_{t+\tau}$). It can be written in terms of a shorter horizon by recognizing that equation (5) is equivalent to:

$$P_t = b_t + \sum_{\tau=1}^{T}(1+r)^{-\tau}E_t\left[x_{t+\tau} - rb_{t+\tau-1}\right] + \sum_{\tau=T+1}^{\infty}(1+r)^{-\tau}E_t\left[x_{t+\tau} - rb_{t+\tau-1}\right]. \tag{6}$$

The infinite horizon term in equation (6) can then be rewritten as:

$$\sum_{\tau=T+1}^{\infty}(1+r)^{-\tau}E_t\left[x_{t+\tau} - rb_{t+\tau-1}\right] = (1+r)^{-T}\sum_{\tau=T+1}^{\infty}(1+r)^{-\tau+T}E_t\left[x_{t+\tau} - rb_{t+\tau-1}\right]. \tag{7}$$

The summation term on the right-hand side of equation (7) is equal to the excess of forecasted price over forecasted book value at time T (i.e., $E_t(P_T - b_T)$, see equation (5)). Substituting this into equation (7) and the result into equation (6) yields the short horizon form of the valuation equation:

$$P_t = b_t + \sum_{\tau=1}^{T}(1+r)^{-\tau}E_t\left[x_{t+\tau} - rb_{t+\tau-1}\right] + (1+r)^{-T}E_t(P_T - b_T). \tag{8}$$ [21]

I set T in equation (8) equal to four and solve the resulting fourth-degree polynomial equation for cost of equity capital, $r_{E/BV}$. Using *Mathematica* software, I identified four unique closed form solutions for $r_{E/BV}$. (In general, an nth-degree polynomial equation has exactly n solutions (Chiang 1984).) The formulas are not reproduced here due to their extraordinary length, however, each defines $r_{E/BV}$ as a function of the same set of variables.

$$r_{E/BV,i} = g_i\begin{pmatrix} p_t, E_t(p_{t+4}), b_t, E_t(b_{t+1}), E_t(b_{t+2}), E_t(b_{t+3}), \\ E_t(b_{t+4}), E_t(x_{t+1}), E_t(x_{t+2}), E_t(x_{t+3}), E_t(x_{t+4}) \end{pmatrix} \tag{9}$$

where:

$r_{E/BV,i}$ = cost of equity capital estimate i (i=1,4)
$g_i(\circ)$ = the function operator i (i=1,4)
p_t = price at date t
$E_t(\circ)$ = the expectations operator
b_t = book value at time t
x_t = earnings for year t.

Forecasts of earnings and book value for fiscal years 1991 and 1992 and long-range forecasts of earnings, book value, P/E ratio, maximum price and minimum price for 1994 were collected from forecasts published by Value Line during the second quarter of 1991.[22] Since Value Line does not provide a forecast for 1993, I interpolate between 1992 and 1994 to obtain estimated forecasts of earnings and book value for 1993. Current stock price is the stock price reported by

[21]The derivation sketched out via equations (6) to (8) is drawn from Abarbanell and Bernard (1994).

[22]Value Line forecasts earnings, book value and stock price. Other sources such as IBES, Nelson Publications and Zacks do not provide forecasts of all of these variables. As a result, restrictive assumptions regarding future growth in earnings beyond year T and growth in book value would be necessary if non-Value Line sources are used. The potential measurement error induced by these restrictions would further reduce the statistical power of the tests.

CRSP on June 30, 1991 and current book value is the book value reported by the company at the end of fiscal year 1990. I use the price implicit in the long-run P/E ratio forecast as the forecast of price in year four.[23]

Using the data described above I solved the four closed form solutions for each firm. In each case, two of the four solutions were undefined and one was unrealistic (a negative number typically in the neighborhood of −2). The remaining estimate (denoted $r_{E/BV}$) became my estimate of the firm's cost of equity capital.

Table 5 provides descriptive statistics pertaining to the cost of equity capital for the entire sample and for the two subsamples. For the full sample, the mean $r_{E/BV}$ is 20.1% while the corresponding figures for the low and high analyst following subsamples are 22 percent and 18 percent, respectively. Although 20.1% may appear inflated, it is reasonable. Ehrhardt (1994) indicates that estimates of the risk free rate range between 6.0% and 9.25% with associated market risk premiums ranging between 8.2% and 7.8%. Using Ehrhardt's median values and the sample average beta of 1.146 the CAPM estimate of cost of equity capital is 17.4%. This crude approximation suggests that, on average, information risk might add about 2.7% to the cost of equity capital.

The inter-quartile range of 11.4% indicates that the distribution of the cost of equity capital estimates is relatively tight. However, six of the 122 estimates fall more than two standard deviations from the mean (i.e., six estimates are either less than three percent or greater than 40 percent).[24] The primary analyses have been estimated with and without these observations. The

[23] An alternative would be to use the average of the minimum and maximum long-run price forecast. Both approaches yield virtually identical estimates of future price. The difference between the price implicit in the long-run P/E ratio forecast and the mid-point of the long-run price forecast is less than 15 percent of the price implicit in the long-run P/E ratio forecast in all cases. It is ten percent or less for all but two firms and five percent or less for 113 of the 122 sample firms.

[24] All six firms are members of the low analyst following subsample. The four cost of equity capital estimates that are "too high" appear to be caused by overly optimistic forecasts of future stock price on the part of Value Line that have not been impounded into current stock price. For example, one company is currently trading at about $1.125 with a market-to-book ratio of 0.72. Value Line is forecasting a stock price four years into the future of $9.00 with a market-to-book ratio of 2.9. It takes a very high cost of equity capital to equate these high forecasted values back to the low current price. In one of the two cases with a low cost of equity capital estimate, Value Lines notes that its forecasts of earnings may be understated because the company is actively involved in an acquisition program. If Value Line's forecasts are understated relative to the market's assessment of future earnings, the discount rate that falls out of the formula is understated. The remaining low cost of capital estimate is associated with a company whose current stock price peaked during the months of May to August 1991. The unusually high stock price used in the computation lowered the estimated cost of equity capital figure.

TABLE 5
Descriptive Statistics for Cost of Equity Capital Estimates

			Percentile					
	n	*Mean*	*1%*	*25%*	*50%*	*75%*	*99%*	*Standard Deviation*
Full Sample	122	20.1%	2.3%	13.3%	19.0%	24.7%	51.0%	10.0%
Low Analyst Following	62	22.1	−2.7	15.0	20.4	27.1	65.2	11.7
High Analyst Following	60	18.2*	4.6	11.6	17.8^	24.0	35.6	7.3

^ Difference between low and high analyst following samples is significant at the ten percent level (Wilcoxon Rank Sum Test, two-tail test)

* Difference between the low and high analyst following samples is significant at the five percent level (T-test, two-tail test). Cost of equity capital is estimated using the earnings/book value approach with Value Line forecasts for expected earnings, book value and future stock price.

results documented in the tables exclude them because model fit is improved and, for the most part, the conclusions drawn are not affected. Where this is not the case, I discuss in the footnotes the impact of including these observations.

Assessing the Validity of $r_{E/BV}$

A valid measure of cost of equity capital should be increasing in risk as measured by market beta. Moreover, we might also expect it to display the well known "size effect." The results of a regression of $r_{E/BV}$ on market value and market beta are presented in table 6. BETA is estimated by the market model using a minimum of 24 monthly return observations over the five-year period ended May 31, 1991, and an equally weighted NYSE/AMEX market index return. MVAL is the market value of outstanding common equity at December 31, 1990.

As expected $r_{E/BV}$ is increasing in market beta and decreasing in firm size. In addition, the magnitude of the coefficient on beta suggests a market risk premium of approximately seven

TABLE 6

Regression of $r_{E/BV}$ on Market Value and Beta

$$r_{E/BV,i} = \gamma_0 + \gamma_1 beta_i + \gamma_2 ln(mval_i) + \varepsilon_i$$

Panel A: Simple Regression Including Beta[b]

	Intercept	*Beta*[a]
coefficient	0.1094	0.0738
p-value	0.0003	0.0020*
adj. R^2	6.3%	
Prob. > F	0.0039	

Panel B: Simple Regression Including MVAL[c]

	Intercept	*MVAL*
coefficient	0.2879	–0.017
p-value	0.0001	0.0003*
adj. R^2	8.8%	
Prob. > F	0.0007	

Panel C: Multiple Regression Including Beta and MVAL[c]

	Intercept	*Beta*	*MVAL*
coefficient	0.2050	0.0661	–0.0155
p-value	0.0001	0.0037*	0.0007*
adj. R^2	13.7%		
Prob. > F	0.0001		

* One-tail test

The log of market value is included in the analysis. White's (1980) test does not indicate the presence of heteroscedasticity. All regression results have been checked for the presence of influential data points using Cook's D statistic. No influential data points were detected.

[a] $r_{E/BV}$ is the estimated cost of equity capital produced using the earnings/book value approach. Beta is estimated via the market model based on a minimum of 24 monthly return observations over the five-year period ended May 31, 1991 with the market index defined in terms of the equally weighted NYSE/AMEX return. MVAL is the market value of equity at 12/31/90.

[b] Estimated with 116 observations.

[c] Estimated with 115 observations.

percent, very close to the historical average market risk premium of approximately eight percent referred to earlier. These results support the validity of $r_{E/BV}$ as a measure of the cost of equity capital.

It is apparent from the R^2s reported in table 6 (six percent to 14 percent depending on the specification) that substantial variation in cost of equity capital is left unexplained by market beta and firm size. This could reflect noise in the cost of equity capital estimates, noise in the risk measures, and/or missing risk factors (such as estimation risk). The next section examines the effect of expanding this model to include disclosure level.

V. EMPIRICAL RESULTS

Empirical Analysis of Hypothesis One

Table 7 provides Pearson correlation coefficients between cost of equity capital, market beta, market value, disclosure level and analyst following.[25] DRANK is computed by dividing the rank of a firm's DSCORE by the number of firms included in the sample and is increasing in disclosure level. All other variables are computed as discussed earlier.

The correlation between $r_{E/BV}$ and DRANK is –0.143, significant at the 6.3% level using a one-tail test. Before controlling for any other variables, this result is consistent with the claim that cost of equity capital is decreasing in disclosure level. As documented earlier, cost of equity capital correlates positively with BETA and negatively with market value, and DRANK is positively correlated with firm size and analyst following. All of the correlation coefficients are less than 0.80 except for the correlation between analyst following and firm size. This suggests that multi-collinearity should not be a problem unless both of these variables are included in the same model.

[25]One hundred and fifteen observations are used in all analyses involving market value because market value of common equity as of December 30, 1990 is missing for one sample firm. (i.e. One hundred and twenty-two observations less six extreme observations and less one with missing firm size data.)

TABLE 7
Pearson Correlation Coefficients

Variable[a]	$r_{E/BV}$	*DRANK*	*BETA*	*MVAL*	*ANALYST*
$r_{E/BV}$	1.000				
	0.0				
DRANK	–0.143	1.000			
	0.1254	0.0			
BETA	0.266	0.149	1.000		
	0.0039	0.1098	0.0		
MVAL	–0.310	0.404	–0.096	1.000	
	0.0007	0.0001	0.3070	0.0	
ANALYST	–0.059	0.457	0.118	0.819	1.000
	0.5258	0.0001	0.2042	0.0001	0.0

The p-values quoted above are for a two-tail test of statistical significance.
The log of market value is included in the analysis.
[a] $r_{E/BV}$ is the estimated cost of equity capital produced using the earnings/book value approach. DRANK is the fractional rank of the firm's disclosure score. BETA is estimated via a market model regression using at least 24 of the 60 monthly return observations in the five-year period ended May 31, 1991, with the market index defined in terms of the equally weighted NYSE/AMEX return. MVAL is the market value of equity at the end of 1990 in millions of dollars and ANALYST is the maximum number of analysts following the firm reported in either the 1991 edition of *Nelson's Directory of Investment Research* or any of the 12 monthly IBES reports issued during 1990.

Hypothesis one is tested by regressing cost of equity capital on market beta, fractional disclosure rank and the log of market value measured at the end of 1990.[26] That is,

$$r_{E/BV,i}=\gamma_0+\gamma_1 BETA_i+\gamma_2 DRANK_i+\gamma_3 MVAL_i+\varepsilon_i. \quad (10)$$

Market value is included in the analysis because evidence presented earlier indicates a significant association between market value and cost of equity capital, as well as between market value and disclosure level suggesting that market value would be a correlated omitted variable if excluded from the analysis.

The results are presented in table 8. The market risk premium implied by the statistically significant coefficient on beta of 7.0% is comparable to the historical average risk premium discussed earlier and the coefficient on MVAL is significantly negative as expected. The coefficient on DRANK, however, while negative is not statistically significant. These results indicate that, for the full sample of firms, cost of equity capital is not decreasing in DRANK after controlling for cross-sectional variation in market beta and firm size.

Specification Tests

I assessed the sensitivity of these results to model specification by estimating two other specifications of equation (10). The first regresses fractional rank of cost of equity capital on each of the fractional ranks of market beta, disclosure level and market value. The second specification allows the disclosure measure to enter the model via two categorical variables (DHI, set equal to one if the firm is a high disclosing firm, zero otherwise; and DMED, set equal to one if the firm is a moderate disclosing firm, zero otherwise). This specification allows the level of cost of equity capital to vary with high, medium and low disclosure level after controlling for firm size and beta. If cost of equity capital is decreasing in disclosure level the coefficients on DMED and DHI should

[26]The conclusions drawn from this analysis are not altered if common equity at the beginning of 1990 is used in place of ending market value.

TABLE 8
Regression Results Based on Full Sample

	Intercept	*BETA*[a] (+)	*DRANK* (–)	*MVAL* (–)
coefficient[b]	0.201	0.070	–0.021	–0.014
t-statistic	4.879	2.831	–0.812	–2.624
p-value	0.0001	0.0028*	0.2093*	0.0050*
adj. R^2	13.5%			
Prob. > F	0.0003			

* One-tail test.
The log of market value is included in the analysis. White's (1980) test does not indicate the presence of heteroscedasticity. All regression results have been checked for the presence of influential data points using Cook's D statistic. No influential data points were detected.

[a] $r_{E/BV}$ is the estimated cost of equity capital produced using the earnings/book value approach. DRANK is the fractional rank of the firm's disclosure score. BETA is estimated via a market model regression using at least 24 of the 60 monthly return observations in the five-year period ended May 31, 1991, with the market index defined in terms of the equally weighted NYSE/AMEX return, and MVAL is the market value of equity at the end of 1990 in millions of dollars.

[b] Estimated with 115 observations.

be negative with the coefficient on DMED greater than the coefficient on DHI. The results (not reported in tables) do not differ significantly from those reported in table 8.

Empirical Analysis of Hypothesis Two

Hypothesis two states that the association between DRANK and the cost of equity capital may be diluted for firms with a large analyst following. To address this possibility, I constructed a categorical variable (DU) set equal to one if the number of analysts is less than or equal to the median of nine and zero otherwise, and allowed DU to enter the model on its own and in interaction with DRANK. This model allows the slope coefficient associated with DRANK and the intercept to vary for low versus high analyst following. A significantly negative coefficient on the interaction variable (in equation (11) below) indicates that the association between cost of capital and DRANK is stronger for firms with fewer analysts. The full model is given below:

$$r_{E/BV,i}=\gamma_0+\gamma_1 DU_i+\gamma_2 BETA_i+\gamma_3 DRANK_i+\gamma_4 DRANK_i{*}DU_i+\gamma_5 MVAL_i+\varepsilon_i. \qquad (11)$$

The results obtained from estimating regression equation (11) are presented in table 9. The coefficient on BETA is significantly positive, the coefficient on MVAL is significantly negative and the coefficient on DRANK is insignificant suggesting that, for firms with high analyst following, cost of equity capital is increasing in market beta, decreasing in firm size and is unrelated to disclosure level as measured by DRANK. The coefficient on DRANK*DU is significantly negative, however, suggesting that the association between cost of equity capital and disclosure level is significantly more negative for the subsample of firms with low analyst following even after controlling for firm value and market beta. An F-test of the sum of the slope coefficients associated with DRANK and DRANK*DU suggests that, for firms with low analyst following, the association between disclosure level and cost of equity capital is significantly negative at the one percent level or better (one-tail test).

The magnitude of the coefficients on DRANK and DRANK*DU indicate that among the firms with low analyst following, the *most* forthcoming firm enjoys about a 9.7% reduction in its cost of equity capital relative to the *least* forthcoming firm. Alternatively, estimating the model with DRANK replaced by DSCORE indicates that a one-unit increase in DSCORE results in a reduction in cost of equity capital of 0.28% for these firms.

A perspective on the magnitude of this effect is provided by the following examples. Walbro Corporation's score of 12.0 was the highest score awarded to any sample firm in the low analyst following subset for the forecast information category. In its 1990 annual report, Walbro provided a discussion of the potential impact of anticipated risks and existing opportunities facing the firm, provided directional predictions of future profits and sales, and gave a point estimate forecast of capital expenditures. One interpretation of the results discussed above would imply that by providing this information Walbro Corporation reduced its cost of equity capital by approximately 3.4% (i.e., 12.0 × 0.28%) relative to a firm with low analyst following that provided *no* forecast information, holding all else equal. The results could also be interpreted to imply, other things equal, that a firm with low analyst following could reduce its cost of equity capital by 2.0% (i.e., maximum points for historical summary information of 7.0 × 0.28%) relative to a non-disclosing firm by providing a ten-year summary of historical data and eight quarters of interim sales and profit information.

The preceding discussion is provided to place the magnitude of the effect in context. However, the discussion should be interpreted with caution for two different reasons. First, the standard error associated with the slope coefficients is large, such that a 95 percent confidence interval around the 28 basis-point figure indicates that the "true" reduction in cost of equity capital

TABLE 9

Regression Results for Low vs. High Analyst Following

	Intercept (?)	*DU*[a] (?)	*BETA* (+)	*DRANK* (−)	*DRANK*DU* (−)	*MVAL* (−)
coefficient[b]	0.140	0.069	0.082	0.035	−0.132	−0.012
t-statistic	2.063	2.002	3.130	0.994	−2.460	−1.725
p-value	0.0415	0.0477	0.0011*	0.8387*	0.0078*	0.0437*
adj. R^2	16.5%					
Prob. > F	0.0001					

* One-tail test.

The log of market value is included in the analysis. White's (1980) test does not indicate the presence of heteroscedasticity. Regression results have been checked for the presence of influential data points using Cook's D statistic. No influential data points were detected.

[a] $r_{E/BV}$ is the estimated cost of equity capital produced using the earnings/book value approach. DRANK is the fractional rank of the firm's disclosure score. DU is a categorical variable set equal to one if the number of analysts is less than or equal to the median and zero otherwise. DU*DRANK refers to the interaction of DU with DRANK. BETA is estimated via a market model regression using at least 24 of the 60 monthly return observations in the five-year period ended May 31, 1991, with the market index defined in terms of the equally weighted NYSE/AMEX return, and MVAL is the market value of equity at the end of 1990 in millions of dollars.

[b] Estimated with 115 observations.

may fall somewhere in the range of less than one basis point to slightly in excess of 66 basis points. Second, the analysis conducted relates cross-firm differences in cost of capital to cross-firm differences in disclosure level. Such a cross-firm analysis will not necessarily provide accurate predictions about how within-firm changes in disclosure level will change a firm's cost of capital.

Analysis of Individual Disclosure Categories

Specifically what type of disclosure reduces cost of equity capital is an interesting and important question; it is also a difficult one to address. This is because firms coordinate their disclosure policies across various avenues (see Lang and Lundholm (1993)) so any correlation between "alternative" measures of disclosure obscures the relative importance of individual types of disclosure. This is the case here since the five categories that comprise DSCORE are positively correlated with one another, the number of analysts following the firm, the number of *Wall Street Journal* articles published about the firm and with DSCORE itself. Moreover, the sample size is small, particularly when split into high and low analyst following subsamples resulting in a small number of observations (55 to 60) with which to estimate the seven to nine regressors included in the model depending on the specification.[27] Hence, the results that follow should be viewed as exploratory.

Depending on the subsample examined, coefficients on three of the five categories that comprise DRANK are negative and statistically significant after controlling for firm size and market beta (results not reported). With respect to the subsample of firms with low analyst following, cost of equity capital is decreasing in the level of forecast information (FRANK) and key non-financial statistics (SRANK) provided by a firm. The magnitude of the coefficient on each variable implies that the most forthcoming firm has a smaller cost of equity capital by approximately six percent relative to the least forthcoming firm. The p-values associated with the

[27] To aid in interpretation, separate regression equations were estimated for the low versus high analyst following subsamples in this section. The results of these analyses are not reported in tables but are discussed in the paragraphs that follow.

coefficients on FRANK and SRANK are 0.07 and 0.09, respectively (one-tail). For the subsample of firms with high analyst following the coefficient on the historical summary category (HRANK) is negative and statistically significant with a p-value of 0.05 (one-tail). The magnitude of the coefficient on HRANK indicates that the most forthcoming firm's cost of equity capital is smaller by approximately six percent relative to that of the least forthcoming firm.

Evidence presented in the SRI International Survey (1987) may provide a partial explanation for these results. According to the survey, individual investors value financial projections in the annual report to a greater extent than analysts or portfolio managers ("professional investors") while the opposite relation holds with respect to historical summary information. The survey indicates that 61.5% of individuals favor including forecast information in the annual report as compared to 54.5% of professionals. In contrast, only 46.2% of individual investors view the historical summary as important, compared to 69.6% of professional investors. Hence, forecast information may be particularly important when a firm is not followed by a large number of analysts because individual investors rely on management forecasts when analyst forecasts are more scarce. When a large number of analysts follow a firm, however, firms benefit more by providing historical summary information which is valued by financial analysts.

Analyses Incorporating Analyst Following and Number of WSJ Articles

I altered the model estimated in table 9 to include two additional potential proxies for disclosure: ARANK (the fractional rank of analyst following) and WRANK (the fractional rank of the number of *Wall Street Journal* articles). I also estimated a model that includes the five categories of DRANK, along with ARANK and WRANK. None of the conclusions drawn from the previously reported results are changed. In some cases, however, the condition index is high indicating the presence of multi-collinearity, probably due to the high correlation between analyst following and firm size.

Finally, I estimated the following regression equation with the full sample:

$$r_{E/BV,i}=\gamma_0+\gamma_1 BETA_i+\gamma_2 DRANK_i+\gamma_3(DRANK_i{*}ANALYST_i)+\gamma_4 ANALYST_i+\gamma_5 MVAL_i+\varepsilon_i. \quad (12)$$

The results from estimating regression equation (12) are consistent with those arising from the analyses reported in table 9. Specifically, the coefficients on BETA and MVAL remain significantly positive and negative, respectively. The coefficient on DRANK is significantly negative while the coefficient on the interaction term is significantly positive. This suggests that cost of equity capital is decreasing in disclosure level as measured by DRANK, but at a decreasing rate as analyst following increases. The coefficient on ANALYST is not statistically significant.

VI. SUMMARY AND CONCLUSION

The effect of disclosure level on the cost of equity capital is a matter of considerable interest and importance to the financial reporting community. However, the ongoing debate between proponents and opponents of greater disclosure has been unproductive because the benefits of greater disclosure are not well established and are difficult to quantify. This paper provides direct evidence of an association between cost of equity capital and disclosure level, and an indication of the magnitude of its effect. For a sample of firms with relatively low analyst following, the evidence suggests that greater disclosure is associated with a lower cost of equity capital, holding cross-sectional variation in market beta and firm size constant. For firms with high analyst following, no significant relation between disclosure level, as measured by DRANK, and cost of equity capital is observed.

My study also provides some preliminary evidence on the types of disclosure that seem to play an important role in reducing cost of equity capital. Specifically, for firms with low analyst following, disclosure of forecast information and key non-financial statistics is particularly important while for firms with high analyst following, disclosure of historical summary information is beneficial. Questions remain, however, that could be examined in future research. Given the high correlation among various types of disclosure, initial attempts may choose to focus on a limited number of broad categories of disclosure such as those contained in the AIMR rankings.

Finally, my study demonstrates a procedure for estimating cost of equity capital that could be applied in other contexts in which firm-specific cost of equity capital estimates are required and analyst forecast data is available. In addition to being negatively associated with disclosure level, the cost of equity capital estimates produced by my approach are increasing in market beta and decreasing in firm size.

The analyses and results reported here are based on observations for firms in one industry, for one year. Hence, the results may not be generalizable to other industries and/or time periods. This issue could be addressed in future research by applying the same techniques to a different industry or time period. However, the advantage of achieving greater cross-sectional variation in disclosure levels, must be weighed against the need to create a data set of disclosure rankings. An alternative would be to use the disclosure rankings produced by the Association for Investment Management and Research which covers a broad spectrum of industries and time periods and offers a more comprehensive measure of disclosure level. However, the AIMR sample restrains cross-sectional variation in disclosure to the upper end of the distribution potentially limiting the power of the analysis.

REFERENCES

Abarbanell, J., and V. Bernard. 1994. Is the U.S. stock market myopic. Working paper, University of Michigan.

Ahmed, K. 1995. The effect of corporate characteristics on disclosure quality in corporate annual reports: A meta-analysis. Working paper, Victoria University of Wellington, New Zealand.

American Institute Of Certified Public Accountants (AICPA). 1994. *Improving Business Reporting—A Customer Focus: A Comprehensive Report of the Special Committee on Financial Reporting*. New York, NY: AICPA.

Amihud, Y., and H. Mendelson. 1986. Asset pricing and the bid-ask spread. *Journal of Financial Economics* 17: 223–249.

Ball, R., and G. Foster. 1982. Corporate financial reporting: A methodological review of empirical research. *Journal of Accounting Research* 20 (Supplement): 161–248.

Barry, C., and S. Brown. 1985. Differential information and security market equilibrium. *Journal of Financial and Quantitative Analysis* (December): 407–422.

Bernard, V. 1995. The Feltham-Ohlson framework: Implications for empiricists. *Contemporary Accounting Research* (Spring): 733–747.

Berton, L. 1994. Companies pressure accounting panel to modify demands for more data. *Wall Street Journal* (August 16): A2.

Buzby, S. 1975. Company size, listed versus unlisted stocks, and the extent of financial disclosure. *Journal of Accounting Research* (Spring): 16–37.

Byrd, J., M. Johnson, and M. Johnson. 1995. Investor relations and the cost of capital. Working paper, University of Michigan, Ann Arbor, MI.

Canadian Institute Of Chartered Accountants. 1991. *Information to be Included in the Annual Report to Shareholders*. Toronto, Ontario: CICA.

Carmines, E., and R. Zellner. 1979. *Reliability and Validity Assessment*. Newbury Park, CA: Sage Publications, Inc.

Cerf, A. 1961. *Corporate Reporting and Investment Decisions*. Berkeley, CA: University of California Press.

Chiang, A. 1984. *Fundamental Methods of Mathematical Economics*. New York, NY: McGraw-Hill, Inc.

Chow, C., and A. Wong-Boren. 1987. Voluntary financial disclosure by Mexican corporations. *The Accounting Review* (July): 533–541.

Clarkson, P., J. Guedes, and R. Thompson. 1996. On the diversification, observability, and measurement of estimation risk. *Journal of Financial and Quantitative Analysis* (March): 69–84.

Coles, J., and U. Loewenstein. 1988. Equilibrium pricing and portfolio composition in the presence of uncertain parameters. *Journal of Financial Economics*: 279–303.

Coles, J., U. Loewenstein, and J. Suay. 1995. On equilibrium pricing under parameter uncertainty. *Journal of Financial and Quantitative Analysis* (September): 347–364.

Copeland, T., and D. Galai. 1983. Information effects on the bid-ask spread. *The Journal of Finance* 36: 1457–1469.

Cronbach, L. 1951. Coefficient alpha and internal structure of tests. *Psychometrika* 16: 297–334.

Demsetz, H. 1968. The cost of transacting. *Quarterly Journal of Economics* 82 (February): 33–53.

Diamond D., and R. Verrecchia. 1991. Disclosure, liquidity and the cost of equity capital. *The Journal of Finance* (September): 1325–1360.

Edwards, E., and P. Bell. 1961. The theory and measurement of business income. Berkeley, CA: University of California Press.

Ehrhardt, M. 1994. *The Search for Value: Measuring the Company's Cost of Capital*. Boston, MA: Harvard Business School Press.

Fama, E., and K. French. 1992. The cross-section of expected stock returns. *Journal of Finance*: 427–465.

Feltham, G., and J. Ohlson. 1995. Valuation and clean surplus accounting for operating and financial activities. *Contemporary Accounting Research* (Spring): 689–731.

Frankel, R., M. McNichols, and G. P. Wilson. 1995. Discretionary disclosure and external financing. *The Accounting Review* (January): 135–150.

Gitman, L., and V. Mercurio. 1982. Cost of capital techniques used by major U.S. firms: Survey and analysis of Fortune's 1000. *Financial Management*: 21–29.

Glosten, L., and P. Milgrom. 1985. Bid ask and transaction prices in a specialist market with heterogeneously informed traders. *Journal of Financial Economics*: 71–100.

Handa, P., and S. Linn. 1993. Arbitrage pricing with estimation risk. *Journal of Financial Economics* (March): 81–100.

Healy, P., and K. Palepu. 1993. The effect of firms' financial disclosure strategies on stock prices. *Accounting Horizons* (March): 1–11.

———, and ———. 1995. The challenges of investor communications: The case of CUC International, Inc. *The Journal of Financial Economics* (June): 111–140.

———, ———, and A. Sweeney. 1995. Do firms benefit from expanded voluntary disclosure? Working paper, MIT Sloan School of Management, Cambridge, MA.

King, R., G. Pownall, and G. Waymire. 1990. Expectations adjustment via timely management forecasts: Review, synthesis, and suggestions for future research. *Journal of Accounting Literature*: 113–144.

Klein, R., and V. Bawa. 1976. The effect of estimation risk on optimal portfolio choice. *Journal of Financial Economics* 3: 215–231.

Knutson, P. 1992. *Financial Reporting in the 1990's and Beyond*. New York, NY: Association for Investment Management and Research.

Lakonishok, J. 1993. Is beta dead or alive? In *The CAPM Controversy: Policy and Strategy Implications for Investment Management*. New York, NY: Association for Investment Management and Research.

Lang, M., and R. Lundholm. 1993. Cross-sectional determinants of analyst ratings of corporate disclosures. *Journal of Accounting Research* 31: 246–271.

———, and ———. 1996. Corporate disclosure policy and analyst behavior. *The Accounting Review* 71 (4): 467–492.

Lees, F. 1981. *Public Disclosure of Corporate Earnings Forecasts*. New York, NY: The Conference Board, Inc.

Marston, C., and P. Shrives. 1991. The use of disclosure indices in accounting research: A review article. *British Accounting Review* 23: 195–210.

Merton, R. 1987. A simple model of capital market equilibrium with incomplete information. *The Journal of Finance* (July): 483–510.

Ohlson, J. 1995. Earnings, book value, and dividends in security valuation. *Contemporary Accounting Research* (Spring): 661–687.

Penman, S. 1993. The articulation of price-earnings ratios and market-to-book ratios and the evaluation of growth. Working paper, University of California at Berkeley, CA.

Previts, G., R. Bricker, T. Robinson, and S. Young. 1994. A content analysis of sell-side financial analyst company reports. *Accounting Horizons* (June): 55–70.

Singhvi, S., and H. Desai. 1971. An empirical analysis of the quality of corporate financial disclosure. *The Accounting Review* (January): 129–138.

SRI International. 1987. *Investor Information Needs and the Annual Report.* Morristown, NJ: FERF.

Welker, M. 1995. Disclosure policy, information asymmetry and liquidity in equity markets. *Contemporary Accounting Research* (Spring): 801–828.

White, H. 1980. A heteroskedasticity-consistent covariance matrix estimator and a direct test for heteroskedasticity. *Econometrica* 48 (May): 817–838.

[8]

International Accounting Differences and Their Relation to Share Prices: Evidence from U.K., Australian, and Canadian Firms*

MARY E. BARTH *Stanford University*

GREG CLINCH *University of New South Wales*

Abstract. We synthesize and extend research exploring differences between U.S. and other countries' Generally Accepted Accounting Principles (GAAP) by investigating whether differences between domestic and U.S. GAAP for U.S.-listed U.K., Australian, and Canadian firms are associated with firms' returns and prices. The accounting differences we investigate include goodwill, asset revaluations, income taxes, pensions, interest capitalization, foreign currency, and extractive industries accounting. We conclude that goodwill is priced as an asset; that asset revaluations, successful efforts accounting for extractive industries, and immediate recognition of foreign currency exchange gains and losses on long-term assets and liabilities are generally uncorrelated with the information that investors consider relevant; that U.K., U.S., and Australian tax accounting methods do not recognize 'enough' tax expense or liability; and that accrual pension accounting and, in some specifications, interest capitalization add explanatory power beyond Australia's cash-based method. Our findings suggest that the U.S. Securities and Exchange Commission's (SEC's) required GAAP reconciliation reflects information useful to investors for U.K. and Australian firms, and to a more limited extent, for Canadian firms.

Résumé. Les auteurs font la synthèse des travaux actuels portant sur l'analyse des différences entre les PCGR des États-Unis et ceux des autres pays; ils poussent plus loin les recherches en s'interrogeant sur la relation possible entre les différences des PCGR de divers pays par rapport à ceux des États-Unis, d'une part, et le rendement et le cours des actions d'entreprises du Royaume-Uni, de l'Australie et du Canada, inscrites en bourse aux États-Unis. Les différences comptables qu'ils étudient ont trait, entre autres, à l'achalandage, aux réévaluations de l'actif, aux impôts sur le bénéfice, aux régimes de retraite, à la capitalisation des intérêts, aux devises et aux méthodes comptables de l'industrie

* Accepted by Gordon Richardson. This paper was presented at the 1995 *Contemporary Accounting Research* Conference, generously sponsored by the following agencies: **Alberta's Chartered Accountants** through the **Accounting Education Foundation of Alberta**, the **Canadian Institute of Chartered Accountants**, the **Ernst & Young Foundation**, the **CGA Canada Research Foundation**, the **Peat Marwick Thorne Educational Foundation**, the **Society of Management Accountants of Canada**, and the **University of Alberta**.
We appreciate helpful comments and suggestions from Philip Brown, Dick Dietrich, Deborah Hackett, Sanjay Kallapur, Gordon Richardson (the editor), Amy Sweeney, Greg Whittred, and Ian Zimmer, from workshop participants at the Boston Accounting Research Colloquium, 1995 *CAR* Conference, University of Illinois, Macquarie University, Monash University, University of Western Australia, the American Accounting Association (AAA) annual, Northeast Regional and AAANZ meetings (especially Stephen Taylor), and the Securities and Exchange Commission Office of Economic Analysis, and from two anonymous reviewers. We also appreciate the data collection assistance of Partha Mohanram, Christine Murphy, and Sarah Woolverton. Funding by the Division of Research, Harvard Business School and the Australian Graduate School of Management is gratefully acknowledged.

minière. Les auteurs concluent que l'on traite l'achalandage à titre d'élément d'actif; les réévaluations de l'actif, la capitalisation du coût de la recherche fructueuse dans l'industrie minière et la constatation immédiate des gains et pertes de change sur les éléments d'actif et de passif à long terme ne présentent généralement aucune corrélation avec l'information que les investisseurs jugent pertinente; les charges fiscales ou les impôts à payer que permettent de constater les méthodes comptables appliquées aux fins fiscales au Royaume-Uni, aux États-Unis et en Australie ne sont pas «suffisantes»; la comptabilisation de la charge de retraite sur la base des prestations constituées a un pouvoir explicatif supérieur à celui de la méthode basée sur la comptabilité de caisse en vigueur en Australie et, à certains égards, c'est aussi le cas de la capitalisation des intérêts. Les constatations des auteurs laissent croire que le rapprochement des PCGR exigé par la SEC livre de l'information utile aux investisseurs en ce qui a trait aux entreprises du Royaume-Uni, de l'Australie et, dans une moindre mesure, du Canada.

The U.S. Securities and Exchange Commission (SEC) requires that non-U.S. registrants provide a reconciliation between their home country's (domestic) Generally Accepted Accounting Principles (GAAP) and U.S. GAAP, generally for income and shareholders' equity. This provides a rare opportunity to compare two sets of accounting methods for the same firms. We exploit this opportunity to investigate whether the differences in accounting methods reflect information used by investors in setting share prices. Specifically, for a sample of firms domiciled in the United Kingdom, Australia, and Canada and trading shares in U.S. markets, we compare financial results reported under their domestic GAAP with results reported using U.S. GAAP and investigate how the differences are associated with firms' share returns and prices.

Our analysis provides insight into several accounting issues currently, or recently, under consideration by standard setters in the countries we study. These include accounting for goodwill, asset revaluations, income taxes, and pensions, among others. For each issue, accounting standard setters must choose an appropriate accounting measurement method, and different countries often choose different methods. Our research provides evidence on one aspect of these choices: how the different accounting measures relate to information used by investors in determining share prices. We do this by estimating the relation between market returns, or prices, and reported domestic GAAP net income and/or shareholders' equity, and the major individual differences in firms' accounting numbers under domestic and U.S. GAAP. Because our analysis reflects the extent to which U.S. GAAP numbers capture information used by investors and incremental to information contained in domestic GAAP, our results also relate to the potential usefulness of the SEC's domestic to U.S. GAAP reconciliation requirement.

As discussed more fully in the next section, we contribute to research addressing similar issues by synthesizing and extending several related studies, including, for example, separate investigation of U.K. and Australian GAAP differences and the use of a potentially more powerful research design. Although our findings are generally consistent with related studies, some differ. We also provide (in the Appendix) a simple model to aid in interpreting our findings, investigate whether investors weight equally discretionary differences that increase and decrease net income and shareholders' equity, and investigate whether investor composition, as reflected by the relative importance on each firm's share register of domestic and U.S.-based shareholders, influences the extent of association between different GAAP regimes and share prices.

Our results suggest several inferences: (1) Goodwill amortization under U.K., Australian, and U.S. GAAP all result in too little amortization expense, and share prices act as if goodwill were an asset, but value it at a discount relative to other assets. (2) U.K. revaluations are not positively correlated with information investors use in setting share prices. Because we expect revalued amounts to be value relevant, this finding suggests that revalued amounts are unreliable, perhaps attributable to management discretion over timing, estimated amounts, and which assets to revalue. We also find that Australian revaluations are not viewed by investors as assets, but clear interpretation of the Australian revaluation findings is hampered by aggregation of tangible and intangible asset revaluations and a small sample size. (3) Neither the U.S., U.K., nor Australian income tax method recognizes "enough" tax expense or liability, perhaps reflecting investors' beliefs about increased future tax rates or recognition of tax benefits that are not likely to be realized. (4) Accrual-based pension accounting methods reflect information used by investors beyond that reflected in Australian GAAP's cash-based method. (5) U.S. GAAP's successful efforts accounting for extractive industries and recognizing immediately foreign currency exchange gains and losses on long-term assets and liabilities have no significant explanatory power incremental to Canadian GAAP's extractive industries' accounting and deferral of foreign currency exchange gains and losses. (6) Investors weight less heavily discretionary differences that increase net income and shareholders' equity than those that decrease them. (7) The extent of association between different GAAP regimes and share prices does not differ systematically with investor composition.

We begin in the next section by reviewing related research. In the second and third sections, we set out the estimation equations and describe the differences between U.S. and U.K., Australian, and Canadian GAAP and develop predictions for our empirical work. The fourth and fifth sections present our empirical findings and describe our sensitivity checks. The final section concludes the paper.

Related research

Our research shares many characteristics with the large literature comparing alternative accounting methods for U.S. firms.[1] Fewer examine international accounting differences. Some recent studies compare the explanatory power of a particular country's GAAP with U.S. GAAP for a matched sample of firms (e.g., Harris and Lang 1992 for Germany; Hall, Hamao, and Harris 1992 for Japan; and Niskanen, Kinnunen, and Kasanen 1992 for Finnish GAAP as compared with International Accounting Standards [IAS]). They generally report mixed findings as to whether U.S. or IAS GAAP is aligned more closely with returns than the GAAP of the country investigated. However, they are unable to compare directly different countries' GAAP for a common set of firms.

In contrast, several recent studies investigate the relation between share prices and the SEC-required domestic to U.S. GAAP reconciling items for non-U.S. firms whose shares trade in U.S. equity markets. Pope and Rees (1992) investigate the information content of earnings calculated under U.K. and U.S. GAAP for the 1987 to 1990 period. They find that U.K. GAAP earnings changes have greater power in explaining U.K. share returns than do U.S. GAAP earnings changes, but U.K. GAAP earnings levels have no explanatory power incremental to U.S. GAAP earnings levels after controlling for earnings changes. Amir, Harris, and Venuti (1993) investigate the value relevance of the reconciling items for earnings and shareholders' equity, in the aggregate and separately, for four major reconciling items within a sample of firms from 20 countries, excluding Canada. They also report findings for their components analysis for a combined U.K. and Australian subsample. For this subsample, they find that the GAAP differences in goodwill and revaluation shareholders' equity (changes in revaluation income) provide significant explanatory power in their price (returns) specification incremental to domestic shareholders' equity (net income). Bandyopadhyay, Hanna, and Richardson (1994) investigate the magnitudes and information content of U.S. and Canadian GAAP earnings differences for the period 1983 to 1989. Even though U.S. and Canadian GAAP are similar for many items, Bandyopadhyay et al. document that the differences between U.S. and Canadian GAAP can be large in magnitude. However, despite the magnitude of the differences, they find no significant association between the differences and the returns.

McQueen (1993) also uses the SEC-required reconciliations to investigate the explanatory power of U.S. GAAP earnings relative to domestic GAAP earnings for a sample of firms from a variety of countries from 1987 to 1991. She provides some evidence that domestic GAAP earnings and the aggregate difference between domestic and U.S. GAAP earnings are associated with security returns measured over long and short intervals using specifications that include either domestic earnings and the GAAP difference or changes in domestic earnings and the GAAP difference.

We contribute to the related research in several ways. (1) We investigate separately net income and shareholders' equity component differences between domestic and U.S. GAAP for U.K., Australian, and Canadian firms. Pope and Rees (1992) and McQueen (1993) investigate only aggregate differences for net income, McQueen pools firms from many countries, and Amir et al. (1993) pool U.K. and Australian firms. Investigation by individual country permits us to gain more insight into specific accounting methods than is possible when two or more countries' GAAP are aggregated. (2) We synthesize related research by investigating differences between U.S. and U.K., Australian, and Canadian GAAP, using the same difference components, estimation equation specifications, and sample period. (3) We use a potentially more powerful estimation technique. (4) Because one of our primary interests is in gaining insights into the market's perception of different accounting methods, we provide a simple model to aid in interpreting our findings. (5) Because most U.K. and Australian GAAP differences are discretionary, we investigate whether investors weight equally differences that increase and decrease net income and shareholders' equity. (6) We investigate whether investor composition, as reflected by the relative importance on each firm's share-register of domestic and U.S.-based shareholders, influences the extent of association between different GAAP regimes and share prices.

Estimation equations

We begin by estimating the following equation for each of the countries in our sample:

$$RET_{it} = \alpha_0 + \alpha_1 NI_{DOMit} \times \alpha_2 NI_{DIFit} + e_{it} \qquad (1)$$

where i and t denote firms and years, respectively, RET is the 15-month share return ending three months after fiscal year-end, NI_{DOM} is domestic GAAP net income, NI_{DIF} is U.S. GAAP net income minus domestic GAAP net income, and e is the regression error term.[2] We estimate equation (1) by pooling observations cross-sectionally and over time, with each independent variable deflated by beginning-of-year price. Finding that α_2 differs significantly from zero indicates that the aggregate net income GAAP differences (or equivalently, U.S. GAAP net income) provides explanatory power incremental to domestic GAAP net income. Because U.S. GAAP net income equals NI_{DOM} plus NI_{DIF}, rejecting the hypothesis that $\alpha_1 = \alpha_2$ is evidence that domestic GAAP net income provides explanatory power incremental to U.S. GAAP net income.[3]

To address analogous questions for shareholders' equity, we estimate the following equation for U.K. and Australian firms (Canadian firms generally do not report shareholders' equity differences in their SEC filings):

$$PRICE_{it} = \beta_0 + \beta_1 SE_{DOMit} + \beta_2 SE_{DIFit} + u_{it} \qquad (2)$$

where $PRICE$ is share price, SE_{DOM} is per-share domestic GAAP shareholders' equity, SE_{DIF} is per-share U.S. GAAP shareholders' equity minus per-share domestic GAAP shareholders' equity, and u is the regression error term. The estimation approach is the same as for equation (1) except that, to mitigate heteroscedasticity, all variables are deflated by the number of American Depository Receipts (ADRs) outstanding.[4]

In the United States, most accounting rules articulate the statements of income and financial position by requiring that changes in assets and liabilities be recognized in income. However, U.K. and Australian GAAP require a clean surplus less frequently than do U.S. GAAP. Thus, equation (1) is not strictly a first-difference version of equation (2). This also implies that estimation equations based on the clean surplus assumption (e.g., Ohlson 1989) are less appropriate in this international setting. Nevertheless, to facilitate comparison of our findings with those of Pope and Rees (1992), Amir et al. (1993), and Bandyopadhyay et al. (1994), we also report findings estimated from expanded versions of equations (1) and (2) and based on Ohlson's clean surplus model. Specifically, we estimate:

$$RET_{it} = \alpha_0 + \alpha_1 NI_{DOMit} + \alpha_2 NI_{DIFit} + \alpha_3 \Delta NI_{DOMit} + \alpha_4 \Delta NI_{DIFit} + e_{it} \qquad (1')$$

$$PRICE_{it} = \beta_0 + \beta_1 SE_{DOMit} + \beta_2 SE_{DIFit} + \beta_3 NI_{DOMit} + \beta_4 NI_{DIFit} + u_{it} \quad (2')$$

where Δ denotes annual change. In a later section, we also investigate our findings' robustness to alternative specifications, including some that consider "dirty surplus."

Our initial focus on aggregate differences between U.S. and domestic GAAP differences is primarily descriptive. Although we expect domestic GAAP net income (shareholders' equity) to be related positively to returns (prices), without a model that maps the specific accounting methods underlying domestic and U.S. GAAP on the share valuation characteristics relevant to investors, it is not possible to develop precise predictions for the coefficients in equation (1) ([2]). However, estimating equations (1) and (2) provides evidence on whether U.S. GAAP numbers are correlated with information used by investors in setting share prices incremental to information reflected in domestic GAAP numbers, and vice versa.

To investigate the individual accounting differences described in the next section, we estimate the following equations:

$$RET_{it} = \gamma_0 + \gamma_1 NI_{DOMit} + \sum_{j=2}^{9} \gamma_j NI\_ITEM_{jit} + e_{it} \quad (3)$$

$$PRICE_{it} = \delta_0 + \delta_1 SE_{DOMit} + \sum_{j=2}^{8} \delta_j SE\_ITEM_{jit} + u_{it} \quad (4)$$

where *NI_ITEM* and *SE_ITEM* are, respectively, the specific net income and shareholders' equity GAAP differences that we investigate. As with equations (1) and (2), we also estimate expanded specifications of equations (3) and (4) to facilitate comparison with related research:

$$RET_{it} = \gamma_0 + \gamma_1 NI_{DOMit} + \sum_{j=2}^{9} \gamma_j NI\_ITEM_{jit} + \gamma_{10} \Delta NI_{DOMit} + \sum_{j=11}^{18} \gamma_j \Delta NI\_ITEM_{jit} + e_{it} \quad (3')$$

$$PRICE_{it} = \delta_0 + \delta_1 SE_{DOMit} + \sum_{j=2}^{8} \delta_j SE\_ITEM_{jit} + \delta_9 NI_{DOMit} + \sum_{j=10}^{16} \delta_j NI\_ITEM_{jit} + u_{it}. \quad (4')$$

We base our reported findings for each of the preceding equations on joint Seemingly Unrelated Regression (SUR) estimation of two equations, where the dependent variables are U.S. and domestic returns, or prices, and the coefficient estimates are constrained to be equal across equations. Our objective in using SUR estimation is to increase the power of our tests. As Pope and Rees (1992) discuss, with trading frictions and microstructural factors absent, one would expect the prices in each market to differ only because of currency differences. However, observed prices are less than perfectly correlated, and thus, can be viewed as measures of the "true" price with noise, leading to potential efficiency gains through the use of SUR estimation.[5]

GAAP differences and empirical predictions

Our objective is to investigate whether information implicit in share returns and prices is captured by the various accounting methods used in the countries we study. Table 1 summarizes the major differences between U.S. and U.K., Australian, and Canadian GAAP. Later in this section, we develop predictions for our empirical tests relating to equations (3) and (4), by determining how we expect each difference between domestic and U.S. GAAP to relate to returns and prices based on prior research and the accounting methods' characteristics. We summarize our predictions in Table 4, which presents the findings for the difference components estimation.

If a difference is to reflect information that is used by investors in setting share prices but is not reflected in domestic GAAP, then we expect the difference component coefficient to be positive. If not, then we expect it to be zero. Tests of our predictions are joint tests of the generalizability of prior research findings (when available) to our sample of firms and to our analysis of the GAAP methods.[6] Error in accounting measurements can also result in findings that differ from our predictions (see, e.g., Barth 1994). In particular, even if the economic construct purportedly represented by an accounting measure is relevant to investors in valuing firms' equity, it will not be reflected in share prices or returns if it is not sufficiently reliable. Consequently, observing estimated coefficients that differ from our predictions can be interpreted as evidence for the measures' reliability.

We limit our predictions to coefficient signs because we believe it is too ambitious in the face of measurement error to predict their magnitudes. However, the Appendix presents a simple measurement-based model that can assist in interpreting the magnitudes of the estimated coefficients, particularly relative to the domestic GAAP coefficients, under certain assumptions about the measurement errors' covariance structure.

Goodwill (GW)

Most U.K. firms write off goodwill immediately to shareholders' equity, resulting in zero amortization expense and no goodwill asset. As a result, for goodwill, the difference between U.S. and U.K. GAAP net income equals U.S. GAAP amortization expense, and the shareholders' equity difference equals the goodwill asset recognized under U.S. GAAP. If investors view goodwill as a depreciable asset, then the coefficient on the net income and shareholders' equity difference components will be positive. Observing a positive coefficient is consistent with Jennings, Robinson, Thompson, and Duvall (1993), who investigate the relation between market value of equity and firm assets, including goodwill, for a sample of U.S. firms and conclude that investors view goodwill as an asset.

Australian GAAP accounting for goodwill is similar to U.S. GAAP, except that, in Australia, amortization is required over no more than 20 years (vs. 40 years in the United States). We have no priors on whether 20 or 40 years is appropriate for goodwill amortization. Moreover, often the Australian goodwill difference component also includes differences related to other intangibles not amortized under Australian GAAP. Descriptive statistics reported in the next section indicate that most Australian GAAP net income goodwill differences are negative, a finding consistent with intangibles as a dominant factor, and the shareholders' equity differences vary in sign. Because our ability to predict the signs of the Australian goodwill difference components' coefficients is hampered

TABLE 1
Summary of GAAP by country for major items of U.K., Australian, or Canadian GAAP that differ from U.S. GAAP.

ITEM	U.S.	U.K.	Australia	Canada
Goodwill and other intangibles (*GW*)	For purchase business combinations, positive or negative goodwill and intangible assets are amortized to income over a period not to exceed 40 years (*APBO 16, 17* and *SFAS No. 72*).	For purchase business combinations, amortization of positive goodwill and intangible assets to income and direct write off to shareholders' equity are permitted (the latter is more common). Negative goodwill is credited directly to shareholders' equity (*SSAP 22*).	All acquisitions are purchases and positive goodwill is amortized to income over a period not to exceed 20 years. As with U.S. GAAP, negative goodwill is first applied to reduce noncurrent assets, but any excess is recognized in income as a gain. Intangible assets often are not amortized (*AASB 1013*).	Similar to U.S. GAAP (*CICA Handbook, Section 1580*).
Asset revaluation (*REV*)	With few exceptions, recognizing assets in excess of amortized cost is prohibited (*APBO 6*).	Revaluations of classes of assets, normally fixed assets, are permitted when certain criteria are met. Frequency and method of determining the amount of revaluation is not specified. Revaluation increments are recognized in a shareholders' equity reserve. Income is affected by (1) revised depreciation charges based on the revalued amount, (2) a downward revaluation when it exceeds a previously recognized upward revaluation of the same asset, or (3) on disposition when gains and losses are recognized based on the asset's carrying amount, including associated revaluation reserve (*Companies Act, 1985, Sch. 4*).	Similar to U.K. GAAP except that the portion of the revaluation reserve realized through asset disposal cannot be taken back to earnings (*AASB 1010*).	Revaluations are not permitted unless the entire balance sheet is revalued as part of a reorganization (*CICA Handbook, Section 3060*).

Deferred taxes (*TAX*)	For most of the sample period, a comprehensive deferral method was required (*APBO 11*). Even under newly adopted *SFAS No. 96* and *109*, which use a liability approach, possible changes in future tax rates are not considered.	Liability approach is used with provision for deferred taxes required only to the extent that tax liabilities are expected to become payable in the foreseeable future, i.e., no deferred taxes are provided on nonreversing "core" timing differences. Expected changes in future tax rates are considered. Test for deferred tax assets is less restrictive than for U.S. GAAP (*SSAP 15*).	A comprehensive liability approach that recognizes all timing differences at expected future tax rates subject to a "beyond reasonable doubt" test for future tax benefits is required (*AASB 1020*).	Similar to U.S. GAAP prior to SFAS No. 109, except for classification of deferred tax balances of an acquired company (*CICA Handbook, Section 1580*).
Pensions (*PEN*)	Pension cost is based on accrual accounting reflecting actuarial assumptions. Recognized pension liability is the difference between pension cost and contributions to the pension plan. Effective in 1989, the recognized liability is no less than the pension plan's accumulated underfunded amount. If an additional amount is recognized to state the liability at this specified minimum, a corresponding intangible asset is also recognized. Annually, pension assets and liabilities are remeasured and critical assumptions are subject to change (*SFAS No. 87*).	Similar to U.S. GAAP, pension expense is based on an actuarial method that recognizes expected pension costs over the service lives of employees, but U.K. GAAP permits more flexibility: (1) several actuarial methods are permitted, (2) assumptions such as pension liability discount rate, which under U.K. GAAP equals the assumed rate of return on plan assets, are not adjusted frequently, and (3) pension revaluations are required only every three years. Recognized pension liability is the difference between cumulative pension costs and contributions to the pension plan or directly paid pensions. There is no minimum liability or related intangible asset (*SSAP 24*).	No liability is recognized for an underfunded pension plan, and pension expense is based on cash contributions to the pension fund.	Similar to U.S. GAAP, except that no minimum liability is specified (*CICA Handbook, Section 3460*).

continued on p. 144

TABLE 1 *continued*
Summary of GAAP by country for major items of U.K., Australian, or Canadian GAAP that differ from U.S. GAAP.

ITEM	U.S.	U.K.	Australia	Canada
Interest capitalization (*INT*)	Interest costs incurred to finance construction of long-lived assets are capitalized as part of the asset's cost and are depreciated over the completed asset's useful life (*SFAS No. 34*).	Interest capitalization is optional (*Companies Act 1985*, as amended by *Companies Act 1989*).	Interest capitalization is optional.	Interest capitalization is optional (*CICA Handbook, Section 3850*).
Foreign currency (*FOR*)	Income statements of foreign subsidiaries whose functional currency is other than the U.S. dollar are translated at the average rate for the period, and balance sheets are translated at the end-of-period rate. The net difference is a separate component of shareholders' equity. For subsidiaries whose functional currency is the U.S. dollar, historical translation rates are used to translate both financial statements, and translation gains and losses are included in income (*SFAS No. 52*).	The method for translating foreign subsidiaries' financial statements, depends on whether the subsidiary is self-sustaining or integrated (i.e., financially or operationally dependent on the parent company). Although similar, the U.K. and U.S. classifications differ. U.K. and U.S. GAAP are similar when self-sustaining subsidiaries do not use the parent company's currency as their functional currency. However, U.K. GAAP permits the translation of income statements, using either the average or end-of-period translation rate. Treatment of integrated subsidiaries is similar to U.S. GAAP when the subsidiary uses the parent company's currency as the functional currency, i.e., all non-monetary balance sheet items and related depreciation are translated at historical rates, with transactions gains and losses reflected in the income statement (*SSAP 20*).	Similar to U.K. GAAP except that an average rate is required to translate income statements of self-sustaining subsidiaries (*AASB 1012*).	Similar to Australian GAAP except that foreign long-term debt exchange gains and losses are deferred and amortized over the life of the instrument for both integrated subsidiaries and foreign long-term debt issued by the Canadian parent (*CICA Handbook, Section 1650*).

continued overleaf

Extractive industries (*EXT*)	Either full-cost or successful-efforts method is used. If full cost is used, there is an upper limit on the amount capitalized based on the present value of projected net cash flows using a stipulated 10 percent discount rate. Cost centers cannot extend beyond country boundaries (*SFAS No. 19*).	Similar to U.S. GAAP.	Full cost is the predominant method, although both it and successful efforts are permitted. However, allowable geographical areas over which successful efforts are capitalized is less restrictive than under U.S. GAAP (*AASB 1022*).	Full-cost method with upper limit on capitalization, calculated with no required discounting of estimated future cash flows is permitted. Cost centers can be worldwide.

AASB is Australian Accounting Standard; *APBO* is *Accounting Principles Board Opinion*; *CICA* is *Canadian Institute of Chartered Accountants*; *SFAS* is *Statement of Financial Accounting Standards*; *SSAP* is *Statement of Standard Accounting Practice*.

by the potentially confounding effects of the two items, we make no predictions.[7]

Asset Revaluation (REV)

The revaluation difference component effectively reverses out revaluations recognized under U.K. or Australian GAAP. Because, measurement issues being absent, we expect revalued amounts to be relevant to investors, we also expect a zero coefficient on the U.K. and Australian revaluation difference components. Observing a zero coefficient is consistent with Easton, Eddey, and Harris (1993), who report evidence that Australian revaluations are value relevant.

Deferred Taxes (TAX)

U.K. and Australian GAAP use liability approaches to recognize deferred taxes and capture the impact of tax rate changes. Because we do not expect the U.S. deferral-based amounts to reflect information that is used by investors to set share prices but is not reflected in the liability-based amounts, we expect zero coefficients for U.K. and Australian deferred-tax difference components. The observation of a zero coefficient is consistent with Givoly and Hayn (1992), who report that, for a sample of U.S. firms, although investors view deferred taxes as a liability, they appear to discount it according to the timing and likelihood of the liability's settlement.

Pensions (PEN)

Australian GAAP pension expense is based on cash contributions to the pension fund, whereas U.S. GAAP uses an accrual-based approach. Prior research (e.g., Dhaliwal 1986; Landsman 1986; Barth 1991; and Barth, Beaver, and Landsman 1992, 1993; among others) provides evidence that accrual-based pension amounts are related significantly to share prices for samples of U.S. firms. Thus, we expect U.S. accrual-based pension accounting to reflect information that is useful to investors but is not reflected in the Australian cash-based method, and so, we expect a positive coefficient for the Australian pension difference components. Because U.K. GAAP also uses an accrual approach for pensions, it is difficult to predict the signs of the U.K. pension difference components' coefficients.

Interest Capitalization (INT)
If the cost of financing long-term production of an asset is viewed as part of its cost and if cost and value are similar for new assets, then asset amounts that include capitalized interest should reflect relevant information that is not reflected in the amounts that exclude it. If not so viewed, the coefficient will be zero. Bowen (1981) finds positive economic value for interest capitalization for a sample of U.S. utility firms; thus, we expect a positive coefficient.

Foreign Currency (FOR)
Unlike U.S. GAAP, Canadian GAAP allows the impact of foreign exchange rate movements on long-term liabilities to be capitalized and amortized over future periods. Because we presume exchange rate movements flow immediately into investors' pricing decisions, we expect, measurement issues aside, a positive coefficient on the Canadian GAAP foreign currency difference component.[8] Because of its similarity to U.S. GAAP, we are unable to predict the signs of the difference components' coefficients for U.K. GAAP.

Extractive Industries (EXT)
Canadian GAAP permits recognition of exploration costs using the full-cost method, whereas successful efforts are often required under U.S. GAAP. Because Canadian GAAP permits the capitalization of costs based on a worldwide cost center and does not require the discounting of future cash flows to determine the capitalization limit, it is possible that costs with no future benefit are deferred. Moreover, Harris and Ohlson (1987) find that book value per equivalent barrel of oil has greater power to explain imputed market values for a sample of U.S. successful-effort firms than for full-cost firms. Thus, we expect U.S. GAAP for extractive industries to reflect information that is relevant to investors but is not reflected in Canadian GAAP, and so, we expect a positive coefficient for the Canadian extractive industries difference component coefficient.

Other (OTH)
There are other differences between U.S. and domestic GAAP for the countries we investigate. We aggregate these differences into other items because we have insufficient observations to investigate them separately. Such differences include capitalizing research and development, LIFO (last-in, first-out) inventory costing, and lease accounting for U.K. firms, accounting for investments, employee stock plans, and dividend provisions for Australian firms, and deferral of start-up costs and minor pension accounting differences for Canadian firms.[9]

Empirical results

Data and sample firms

The sample includes all firms that (1) were incorporated in the U.K., Australia, and Canada, (2) traded equity shares in U.S. securities markets and thus were included in COMPUSTAT as of January, 1992, and (3) presented in their Form 20-F, Form 10-K, or annual report a reconciliation from domestic to U.S. GAAP. Criteria (1) and (2) resulted in, respectively, an initial sample of 55 U.K., 16 Australian, and 242 Canadian firms. Applying criterion (3) and data requirements for estimating equations (1) and (2) resulted in two final samples over 1985 to 1991. For equation (1), using U.S. (domestic) returns as the dependent variable, we found 115, 24, and 261 (135, 32, and 236) U.K., Australian, and Canadian firm-year observations, respectively. For equation (2), using U.S. (domestic) prices as the dependent variable, we found 153 and 36 (180 and 47) U.K. and Australian firm years, respectively.[10] Availability of domestic and U.S. returns and prices results in different numbers of observations for estimating the two versions of each equation. However, because SUR estimation is possible only on common observations, the final sample consists of 98, 22, and 229 returns observations for U.K., Australian, and Canadian firms, and 139 and 36 price observations for U.K. and Australian firms, respectively. The return (price) firm-year observations are generated by 29, 8, and 48 (36, 10 and 0) firms, respectively, for the United Kingdom, Australia, and Canada.

We collect the differences between domestic and U.S. GAAP from disclosed SEC-required reconciliations and obtain or calculate from COMPUSTAT data, the returns, prices, and accounting variables. We obtain domestic returns and prices primarily from COMPUSTAT's Global Vantage database, but obtain some data from the *Australian Financial Review* and the *Financial Times*. We calculate returns over 15 months beginning with the first month of the fiscal year and use prices as of three months after fiscal year-end. We use returns and prices extending three months beyond fiscal year-end to ensure that the domestic to U.S. GAAP reconciliation disclosures are in the public domain. However, the analyses reported in the Sensitivity Checks section demonstrate that the findings are insensitive to the price and return date. Because of the cross-equation coefficient constraint, we translate domestic prices into U.S. dollars using the contemporaneous (fiscal year-end) spot exchange rate.[11] When domestic returns and prices are the dependent variable, we adjust them for exchange movements in the domestic currency relative to U.S. dollars.[12]

Finally, it is important to recognize that self-selection can affect our ability to generalize our inferences beyond our sample of cross-listed firms. Firms with large differences between domestic and U.S. GAAP-reported results may choose not to list their securities on U.S. exchanges if the differences otherwise would not be in the public domain. Also, firms that choose to list securities on U.S. exchanges can make accounting choices to reduce differences between domestic and U.S.-GAAP reported results. Nevertheless, because our sample firms are typically large multinational corporations, they represent, at a minimum, firms of major interest in their own right.

TABLE 2
Descriptive statistics for variables used in regressions of returns on net income and/or its components and of price on shareholders' equity and/or its components and number of positive and negative GAAP differences, pooled over 1985–1991 sample years.

	U.K.						Australia						Canada					
	N	mean	med	sd	# pos	# neg	*N*	mean	med	sd	# pos	# neg	*N*	mean	med	sd	# pos	# neg
NI_{DOM}	98	791.2	595.0	847.3	—	—	22	417.5	377.7	320.5	—	—	229	71.3	16.5	225.5	—	—
NI_{US}	98	741.7	395.0	826.4	—	—	22	365.1	302.1	307.0	—	—	229	65.2	9.6	229.2	—	—
NI_{DIF}	98	-49.5	-26.7	140.4	20	78	22	-46.4	-17.6	109.6	6	16	229	-6.0	0.1	40.4	115	113
SE_{DOM}	139	3996.4	1224.4	5224.1	—	—	36	3227.6	2830.3	2482.4	—	—	—	—	—	—	—	—
SE_{US}	139	4296.9	1784.0	4619.7	—	—	36	2274.8	2060.0	1643.0	—	—	—	—	—	—	—	—
SE_{DIF}	139	300.5	117.8	1955.4	83	59	36	-952.8	-380.0	1534.8	6	30	—	—	—	—	—	—
NI_ITEM:																		
GW	86	-53.2	-29.2	70.4	0	86	13	-46.5	-16.0	60.1	1	12	—	—	—	—	—	—
TAX	85	-27.9	-6.5	102.0	27	58	11	3.5	10.7	52.5	8	3	—	—	—	—	—	—
REV	28	16.4	4.4	28.4	28	0	29	23.6	15.3	39.4	19	1	—	—	—	—	—	—
PEN	46	20.3	6.5	47.0	29	17	10	-29.3	0.2	78.4	6	4	—	—	—	—	—	—
INT	28	26.3	13.2	39.8	24	4	—	—	—	—	—	—	33	1.6	1.5	6.9	24	9
FOR	29	-6.6	-1.1	33.3	11	18	—	—	—	—	—	—	127	1.4	0.1	20.7	68	59
EXT	—	—	—	—	—	—	—	—	—	—	—	—	53	-16.6	-1.6	46.6	24	29
OTH	70	2.3	-0.9	125.1	31	39	19	-19.9	-5.5	67.3	5	14	162	-5.0	-0.5	29.9	67	95
SE_ITEM:																		
GW	124	861.5	431.8	1259.2	121	3	21	59.6	5.0	252.4	12	9	—	—	—	—	—	—
TAX	121	-803.4	-89.8	1587.7	3	118	23	1.2	-2.8	81.9	6	17	—	—	—	—	—	—
REV	80	-358.4	-103.4	686.5	0	80	33	-592.8	-358.8	827.4	0	33	—	—	—	—	—	—
PEN	59	27.3	9.7	149.2	40	19	18	-12.2	3.6	75.4	14	4	—	—	—	—	—	—
INT	40	259.3	134.0	281.4	40	0	—	—	—	—	—	—	—	—	—	—	—	—
FOR	11	6.8	5.8	27.6	9	2	—	—	—	—	—	—	—	—	—	—	—	—
OTH	135	361.2	50.3	1042.7	106	29	31	-537.1	-21.3	898.4	6	25	—	—	—	—	—	—
% ADR	35	0.10	0.04	0.15	—	—	9	0.04	0.01	0.05	—	—	—	—	—	—	—	—

Descriptive statistics

Table 2 presents descriptive statistics for the net income and shareholders' equity GAAP differences. All amounts are in millions of U.S. dollars, except the percentage of ADRs to total shares outstanding. This latter statistic indicates that on average 10 percent of U.K. and 4 percent of Australian sample firms' shareholdings are traded in the United States; Canadian firms do not trade ADRs.

Consistent with related research, Table 2 reveals that the mean total differences between U.S. and domestic GAAP net income are large, representing 7, 13, and 8 percent of the mean U.S. GAAP net income for U.K., Australian, and Canadian firms, with U.S. GAAP net income lower than domestic GAAP for all three countries' firms. Except for Canadian firms, the standard deviation of U.S. GAAP net income is also smaller than that of domestic GAAP. Similarly, the shareholders' equity differences are large, representing 7 and 42 percent of U.S. GAAP shareholders' equity for U.K. and Australian firms. As with net income, for Australian firms, average U.S. GAAP shareholders' equity is lower than domestic GAAP shareholders' equity. For U.K. firms, however, the relation is reversed. That is, although on average U.S. GAAP net income is lower than domestic GAAP net income, average U.S. GAAP shareholders' equity is higher than that based on U.K. GAAP. This highlights the fact that differences in accounting rules across countries affect differently net income and shareholders' equity.

Table 2 also presents descriptive statistics for individual reconciling items, after omitting differences equal to zero. The largest item for U.K. firms is goodwill. On average goodwill differences are 7 percent of the mean U.S. GAAP net income and 20 percent of the mean U.S. GAAP shareholders' equity. For

TABLE 2 *notes*

Initial sample comprises 55, 16, and 242 firms from the U.K., Australia, and Canada, respectively. The number of firm-year observations for each variable (*N*) differs, reflecting missing data. # pos and # neg indicate the number of positive and negative differences. med and sd denote median and standard deviation.

N_{DOM}	= domestic GAAP net income.
NI_{US}	= U.S. GAAP net income.
NI_{DIF}	= U.S. GAAP net income minus domestic GAAP net income.
SE_{DOM}	= domestic GAAP shareholders' equity.
SE_{US}	= U.S. GAAP shareholders' equity.
SE_{DIF}	= U.S. GAAP shareholders' equity minus domestic GAAP shareholders' equity.
NI_ITEM	= reconciling items between domestic and U.S. GAAP net income.
SE_ITEM	= reconciling items between domestic and U.S. GAAP shareholders' equity.
GW	= goodwill and other intangibles.
TAX	= deferred taxes.
REV	= asset revaluation.
PEN	= pensions.
INT	= interest capitalization.
FOR	= foreign currency translation.
EXT	= extractive industries.
OTH	= other.
% ADR	= percent of equity traded in U.S. markets represented by ADRs.

TABLE 3
Summary statistics for regression of returns on domestic net income and the difference between U.S. and domestic GAAP net income, and of price on domestic shareholders' equity and the difference between U.S. and domestic GAAP shareholders' equity, for three samples of non-U.S. firms whose equity shares trade in U.S. markets: 1985–1991.

Panel A: $RET_{it} = \alpha_0 + \alpha_1 NI_{DOMit} + \alpha_2 NI_{DIFit} + \alpha_3 \Delta NI_{DOMit} + \alpha_4 \Delta NI_{DIFit} + e_{it}$

	U.K				Australia				Canada			
coef	est	*t*	est	*t*	est	*t*	est	*t*	est	*t*	est	*t*
α_0	0.24	5.75	0.23	5.37	0.06	1.08	0.21	2.41	0.07	2.56	0.06	2.35
α_1	0.42	2.64	0.46	2.38	1.05	4.11	– 0.38	– 0.51	0.64	6.75	0.63	6.11
α_2	2.08	4.19	2.44	4.05	3.01	2.20	1.31	0.57	–0.08	–0.50	–0.87	–1.87
α_3	—	—	0.04	0.13	—	—	2.34	2.74	—	—	0.01	0.22
α_4	—	—	–0.59	–0.72	—	—	2.47	1.93	—	—	0.72	1.90
nobs		98		96		22		22		229		229
χ^2 (*p* value) for test of:												
all slopes = 0		17.63 (0.00)		18.33 (0.00)		18.96 (0.00)		39.43 (0.00)		45.83 (0.00)		40.57 (0.00)
$\alpha_1 = \alpha_2$		16.76 (0.00)		13.53 (0.00)		2.12 (0.25)		0.57 (0.45)		12.38 (0.00)		13.01 (0.00)
$\alpha_3 = \alpha_4$				0.66 (0.42)				0.01 (0.91)				4.95 (0.03)
$\alpha_1 = \alpha_2$ & $\alpha_3 = \alpha_4$				17.08 (0.00)				2.82 (0.24)				7.96 (0.00)

continued overleaf

Panel B: $PRICE_{it} = \beta_0 + \beta_1 SE_{DOMit} + \beta_2 SE_{DIFit} + \beta_3 NI_{DOMit} + \beta_4 NI_{DIFit} + u_{it}$

	U.K.				Australia			
coef	est	t	est	t	est	t	est	t
β_0	9.90	2.65	10.49	3.03	13.22	4.78	12.77	5.99
β_1	1.11	4.38	1.01	2.49	0.56	2.88	0.13	0.57
β_2	0.63	4.01	0.55	2.75	0.64	2.51	0.16	0.57
β_3	—	—	0.30	0.17	—	—	3.36	3.52
β_4	—	—	−1.68	−0.25	—	—	4.17	1.89
nobs		139		139		36		36
χ^2 (p value) for test of:								
all slopes = 0		20.45 (0.00)		36.75 (0.00)		8.37 (0.02)		45.03 (0.00)
$\beta_1 = \beta_2$		7.77 (0.01)		1.25 (0.26)		0.53 (0.47)		0.06 (0.81)
$\beta_3 = \beta_4$				0.11 (0.74)				0.09 (0.76)
$\beta_1 = \beta_2$ & $\beta_3 = \beta_4$				1.53 (0.46)				0.16 (0.93)

Initial sample comprises 55, 16, and 242 firms from the United Kingdom, Canada, and Australia, respectively. The number of observations for each regression differs, reflecting missing data. Net income variables are deflated by beginning-of-year price. Shareholders' equity variables are deflated by the number of ADRs outstanding. t is t-statistic based on White (1980) standard errors. The χ^2 statistics are also based on White (1980) standard errors. Regressions are estimated using Seemingly Unrelated Regression (SUR) on two equations with domestic and U.S. returns or prices as the dependent variable. We report a χ^2 statistic to test all slope coefficients equal to zero, rather than a regression R^2, because of the SUR joint estimation.

RET	= fifteen-month share return, ending three months after fiscal year-end.
PRICE	= price per share three months after fiscal year-end.
NI_{DOM}	= domestic GAAP net income.
NI_{DIF}	= U.S. GAAP net income minus domestic GAAP net income.
SE_{DOM}	= domestic GAAP shareholders' equity.
SE_{DIF}	= U.S. GAAP shareholders' equity minus domestic GAAP shareholders' equity.
Δ	denotes annual change.

Australian firms, the largest net income item is also goodwill and other intangibles, but the largest shareholders' equity item is asset revaluation.[13] The largest item for Canadian firms is accounting for extractive industries.

The Table 2 statistics also indicate that the aggregate net income and shareholders' equity differences vary in sign for all three countries' firms and that some individual items increase U.S. GAAP net income and shareholders' equity relative to domestic GAAP, whereas others decrease them. However, as expected, goodwill and revaluation for U.K. and Australian firms generally have the same sign across firms. For net income, almost all goodwill differences are negative (i.e., the amortization of goodwill and other intangibles is higher under U.S. GAAP than under U.K. or Australian GAAP), and almost all revaluation differences are positive (i.e., revaluation depreciation exceeds U.S. GAAP depreciation). For shareholders' equity, the reverse holds true. That is, almost all goodwill differences are positive (i.e., there is less recognized goodwill under U.K. GAAP than under U.S. GAAP), and the revaluation differences all are negative (i.e., assets are revalued upward under U.K. and Australian GAAP, but are not revalued under U.S. GAAP). Australian firms' goodwill shareholders' equity differences' signs are more variable because this reconciling item includes intangibles. Intangibles differences are typically negative (i.e., intangibles under Australian GAAP are larger than under U.S. GAAP), because intangibles often are not amortized under Australian GAAP, but amortization is required under U.S. GAAP. Conversely, under Australian GAAP, goodwill must be amortized over a period not longer than 20 years, which typically is shorter than the U.S. GAAP amortization period.

Differences in interest capitalization for U.K. and Canadian firms follow a somewhat different pattern. As expected, because interest capitalization is optional, all shareholders' equity differences are positive (i.e., a smaller asset is recognized under U.K. GAAP than under U.S. GAAP). Yet, most net income differences are also positive, suggesting that, in our sample firm-years, U.K. and Canadian firms incurred more current period interest expense than would have been amortized had interest capitalization and amortization been the accounting policy.

Regression results for aggregate differences in GAAP

We first investigate aggregate GAAP differences and Table 3, panel A (B), presents regression summary statistics from estimating equations (1) and (1′) ([2] and [2′]).[14]

Looking first at the findings from estimating equation (1), panel A reveals that for all three countries, domestic GAAP net income is significantly correlated with information used by investors in setting share returns, incremental to that reflected in the difference between domestic and U.S. GAAP net income, that is, the α_1 estimates differ significantly from zero. For U.K. firms, but not for Australian, the null hypothesis that $\alpha_1 = \alpha_2$ is rejected at less than the 0.01 level, indicating that U.K. GAAP net income provides explanatory power incremental to U.S. GAAP net income. For U.K. and Australian firms, panel A also reveals that the difference between U.S. and domestic GAAP (or, equivalently, U.S. GAAP net income) provides explanatory power incremental to domestic GAAP net income, that is, the α_2 estimates differ significantly from zero. For Canadian firms, U.S. GAAP net income provides no explanatory power incremental to Canadian GAAP net income. Estimating equation (1′) results in inferences about the incremental explanatory power of the two GAAP net income measures that are similar to those from estimating equation (1), although for Australian firms, the change variables are significant, but not the levels variables. Also, the coefficient on NI_{DIF} (ΔNI_{DIF}) is significantly negative (positive) for Canadian firms.

The panel A findings generally are consistent with Amir et al. (1993). However, they contrast with Pope and Rees (1992), who find that for a sample of U.K. firms, neither net income measure provides explanatory power incremental to the other, nor does the difference between the two measures. Also, Pope and Rees find that U.K. earnings changes have more explanatory power than U.S. earnings changes. Pope and Rees investigate 1987 to 1990, whereas we investigate 1985 to 1991. However, repeating our analysis on Pope and Rees's sample period does not resolve the differences. Our findings also contrast with Bandyopadhyay et al. (1994), who find no association between U.S. and Canadian GAAP differences and share returns. Bandyopadhyay et al. investigate 1983 to 1989, whereas we investigate 1985 to 1991, and supplemental analysis indicates that the differences in findings are attributable to differences in the sample period.[15] Together, Bandyopadhyay et al. and our findings suggest that there is no conclusive stable evidence that NI_{DIF} and ΔNI_{DIF} provide incremental explanatory power, although our findings provide evidence of some incremental explanatory power that is not provided by Bandyopadhyay et al.

Estimation of equation (2) in panel B reveals that the difference between U.S. and domestic GAAP shareholders' equity (and, equivalently, U.S. GAAP) provides explanatory power for share prices for U.K. and Australian firms, incremental to domestic GAAP, that is, β_2 differs significantly from zero. It also reveals that domestic GAAP shareholders' equity provides significant explanatory power incremental to the difference in GAAP, that is, β_1 differs significantly from zero. As with net income, domestic GAAP shareholders' equity provides explanatory power incremental to U.S. GAAP shareholders' equity, that is, $\beta_1 = \beta_2$ is rejected, only for U.K. firms. Inferences from estimating equation (2′) are similar. However, in this specification, the Australian inferences result from the net income variables, rather than the levels variables.

Regression results for specific reconciling items

The total difference between domestic and U.S. GAAP is the sum of the individual differences described in the previous section. In this section, we permit each major difference to have its own coefficient. We report in Table 4 regression summary statistics from estimating equations (3), (3′), (4), and (4′), although the small number of observations precludes us from estimating equations (3′) and (4′) for Australian firms.

TABLE 4

Summary statistics for regressions of returns (price) on domestic net income (shareholders' equity) and major U.S. and domestic GAAP differences, for three samples of non-U.S. firms whose equity shares trade in U.S. markets: 1985–1991.

Panel A: $RET_{it} = \gamma_0 + \gamma_1 NI_{DOMit} + \gamma_2 GW_{NIit} + \gamma_3 TAX_{NIit} + \gamma_4 REV_{NIit} + \gamma_5 PEN_{NIit} + \gamma_6 FOR_{NIit} + \gamma_7 INT_{NIit} + \gamma_8 EXT_{NIit} + \gamma_9 OTH_{NIit} + \gamma_{10}\Delta NI_{DOMit} + \gamma_{11}\Delta GW_{NIit} + \gamma_{12}\Delta TAX_{NIit} + \gamma_{13}\Delta REV_{NIit} + \gamma_{14}\Delta PEN_{NIit} + \gamma_{15}\Delta FOR_{NIit} + \gamma_{16}\Delta INT_{NIit} + \gamma_{17}\Delta EXT_{NIit} + \gamma_{18}\Delta OTH_{NIit} + e_{it}$

	U.K.						Australia				Canada					
	pred. sign	est	t	$\gamma_1 = \gamma_i$ p value	est	t	pred. sign	est	t	$\gamma_1 = \gamma_i$ p value	pred. sign	est	t	$\gamma_1 = \gamma_i$ p value	est	t
γ_0	?	0.24	5.15	—	0.24	4.31	?	0.11	1.91	—	?	.07	2.61	—	0.07	2.41
γ_1	+	0.48	2.59	—	0.49	1.93	+	1.03	4.10	—	+	.65	6.64	—	0.68	6.40
γ_2	+	2.33	4.09	0.00	3.65	4.22	?	16.14	7.98	0.00	—	—	—	—	—	—
γ_3	0	2.73	2.59	0.01	2.54	2.02	0	–4.44	–0.71	0.38	—	—	—	—	—	—
γ_4	0	0.99	0.40	0.84	–2.83	–0.79	0	18.28	8.81	0.00	—	—	—	—	—	—
γ_5	?	1.65	0.47	0.73	4.44	0.94	+	–0.93	–0.67	0.16	—	—	—	—	—	—
γ_6	?	1.11	0.29	0.87	7.23	1.29	—	—	—	—	+	.21	.13	0.77	–0.11	–0.66
γ_7	+	3.52	0.37	0.75	11.18	0.86	—	—	—	—	+	.62	.13	0.99	0.09	0.02
γ_8	—	—	—	—	—	—	—	—	—	—	+	.36	.91	0.49	0.37	0.78
γ_9	?	1.86	2.09	0.30	2.47	1.31	?	4.23	3.85	0.00	?	–.20	–.70	0.01	–0.21	–0.66
γ_{10}	—	—	—	—	0.18	0.71	—	—	—	—	—	—	—	—	–0.02	–1.27
γ_{11}	—	—	—	—	–1.76	–2.01	—	—	—	—	—	—	—	—	—	—
γ_{12}	—	—	—	—	0.78	0.91	—	—	—	—	—	—	—	—	—	—
γ_{13}	—	—	—	—	2.51	0.94	—	—	—	—	—	—	—	—	—	—
γ_{14}	—	—	—	—	–2.01	–1.25	—	—	—	—	—	—	—	—	—	—
γ_{15}	—	—	—	—	–4.01	–1.40	—	—	—	—	—	—	—	—	–0.02	–0.12
γ_{16}	—	—	—	—	–11.66	–1.94	—	—	—	—	—	—	—	—	1.43	2.18
γ_{17}	—	—	—	—	—	—	—	—	—	—	—	—	—	—	0.09	1.17
γ_{18}	—	—	—	—	–0.54	–0.61	—	—	—	—	—	—	—	—	–0.05	–1.00
nobs			98						22				229			
χ^2 (p value) for test of:																
all slopes = 0				20.14		45.23			101.30	46.35				56.70		
				(0.01)		(0.00)			(0.00)	(0.00)				(0.00)		
$\gamma_2 = \gamma_3 = \ldots = \gamma_9$				2.59					70.47					0.85		
				(0.86)					(0.00)					(0.84)		

continued overleaf

Panel B: $PRICE_{it} = \delta_0 + \delta_1 SE_{DOMit} + \delta_2 GW_{SEit} + \delta_3 TAX_{SEit} + \delta_4 REV_{SEit} + \delta_5 PEN_{SEit} + \delta_6 FOR_{SEit} + \delta_7 INT_{SEit} + \delta_8 OTH_{SEit} + \delta_9 NI_{DOMit} + \delta_{10} GW_{NIit} + \delta_{11} TAX_{NIit} + \delta_{12} REV_{NIit} + \delta_{13} PEN_{NIit} + \delta_{14} FOR_{NIit} + \delta_{15} INT_{NIit} + \delta_{16} OTH_{NIit} + u_{it}$

	U.K.						Australia			
	pred. sign	est	t	$\delta_1 = \delta_i$ p value	est	t	pred. sign	est	t	$\delta_1 = \delta_i$ p value
δ_0	?	13.34	5.02	—	12.96	4.98	?	4.64	2.41	—
δ_1	+	0.99	2.72	—	1.00	1.71	+	1.63	7.99	—
δ_2	+	0.49	2.99	0.06	0.19	0.47	?	1.19	1.72	0.53
δ_3	0	−0.27	−0.32	0.02	−0.08	−0.10	0	−28.40	−5.94	0.00
δ_4	0	3.18	2.63	0.02	3.66	2.06	0	2.47	6.60	0.00
δ_5	?	4.26	1.39	0.25	4.65	0.57	+	13.95	6.80	
δ_6	?	0.19	0.00	0.99	−20.90	−0.96	—	—	—	—
δ_7	+	1.41	0.31	0.93	7.49	1.38	—	—	—	—
δ_8	?	0.05	0.10	0.14	−0.01	−0.01	?	1.71	3.53	
δ_9	—	—	—	—	−0.38	−0.17	—	—	—	—
δ_{10}	—	—	—	—	−8.78	−0.76	—	—	—	—
δ_{11}	—	—	—	—	−2.39	−0.15	—	—	—	—
δ_{12}	—	—	—	—	2.21	0.08	—	—	—	—
δ_{13}	—	—	—	—	7.94	0.29	—	—	—	—
δ_{14}	—	—	—	—	15.27	0.29	—	—	—	—
δ_{15}	—	—	—	—	−36.69	−0.96	—	—	—	—
δ_{16}	—	—	—	—	−3.33	−0.65	—	—	—	—
nobs			139			137			36	
χ^2 (p value) for test of:										
all slopes = 0			308.78 (0.00)		464.29 (0.00)			73.30 (0.00)		
$\delta_2 = \delta_3 = \ldots = \delta_9$			41.40 (0.00)					62.59 (0.00)		

Initial sample comprises 55, 16, and 242 firms from the United Kingdom, Canada, and Australia, respectively. The number of observations for each regression differs, reflecting missing data. Net income variables are deflated by beginning-of-year price. Shareholders' equity variables are deflated by number of ADRs outstanding. Regressions estimated using Seemingly Unrelated Regression (SUR) on two equations with domestic and U.S. returns or prices as the dependent variable. t is t statistic based on White (1980) standard errors. The χ^2 statistics test for equality of the difference components' coefficients and are also based on White (1980) standard errors. We report a χ^2 statistic to test all slope coefficients equal to zero, rather than a regression R^2, because of the SUR joint estimation.

- *RET* = fifteen–month U.S. share return, ending three months after fiscal year-end.
- *PRICE* = price per share three months after fiscal year-end.
- NI_{DOM} = domestic GAAP net income.
- SE_{DOM} = domestic GAAP shareholders' equity.
- *GW* = goodwill and other intangibles.
- *TAX* = deferred taxes.
- *REV* = asset revaluation.
- *PEN* = pensions.
- *INT* = interest capitalization.
- *EXT* = extractive industries.
- *OTH* = other.

NI or *SE* subscript denotes effect of difference on net income or shareholders' equity. Δ denotes annual change.

Net income differences

Table 4, panel A, presents the findings for the net income GAAP differences. Estimation of equation (3) indicates that restricting all GAAP differences to having the same coefficient is inappropriate for the Australian, but not for the U.K. or Canadian firms—equality of coefficients is rejected at $p = 0.00$, $p = 0.86$, and $p = 0.84$ —although the findings indicate that the lack of rejection for U.K. firms is attributable to large standard errors for some coefficient estimates. As expected, the coefficients on domestic net income are significantly positive for all three countries' firms.

The component analysis indicates that goodwill and other intangibles differences, GW_{NI}, are significant in explaining share returns for U.K. and Australian firms (est. = 2.33 and 16.14, $t = 4.09$ and 7.98, respectively). U.K. taxes, TAX_{NI}, and Australian asset revaluations, REV_{NI}, differences also are significant (est. = 2.73 and 18.28, $t = 2.59$ and 8.81, respectively), whereas U.K. revaluation, interest capitalization, and foreign currency translation; Australian taxes; and U.K. and Australian pension differences coefficients insignificantly differ from zero.[16] Estimated coefficients that are indistinguishable from zero indicate that U.S. GAAP (or the difference between U.S. and domestic GAAP) provides no explanatory power beyond domestic GAAP. The variable that combines several less pervasive differences, OTH_{NI}, is also significantly different from zero for both U.K. and Australian firms (est. = 1.86 and 4.23, $t = 2.09$ and 3.85, respectively). The insignificant difference components findings for Canadian firms might be expected from the Table 3 findings. They suggest that successful efforts accounting for extractive industries, the recognition of foreign currency exchange gains and losses on long-term assets and liabilities, and interest capitalization have no significant explanatory power incremental to their Canadian GAAP counterparts (full cost accounting, deferral of foreign currency exchange gains and losses on long-term balance sheet items, and lack of interest capitalization). Inferences from estimating equation (3′) are similar to those from equation (3) in that the significance levels for the levels variables are similar. However, changes in goodwill and interest capitalization differences are significant for U.K. firms, as is interest capitalization for Canadian firms.

Our findings for Canadian firms generally are consistent with Bandyopadhyay et al. (1994), who find no individual GAAP differences to provide significant explanatory power, although we find such power for changes in interest capitalization differences in the equation (3′) specification. Our findings contrast somewhat with Amir et al. (1993). For their combined U.K. and Australian sample, Amir et al. find that only changes in revaluation and deferred tax differences provide incremental explanatory power. We find that, for U.K. firms, levels of goodwill, deferred taxes, and other differences and changes in goodwill and interest capitalization differences provide significant explanatory power. For Australian firms, we find also that levels of goodwill, revaluations, and other differences provide significant explanatory power.

Note that in the equation (3) specification, all U.K. and Australian difference coefficients differing significantly from zero except OTH_{NI}, also significantly exceed those on NI_{DOM}, that is, the adjustment required under U.S. GAAP for these items receives a larger multiple in the returns relation than does net income measured under domestic GAAP. Table 2 indicates that goodwill differences are always negative for U.K. and Australian firms, and tax differences are generally negative for U.K. firms. Thus, finding that these component coefficients are positive and significantly larger than those on domestic net income, while recalling that NI_{DOM} plus the difference components equals U.S. GAAP net income, indicates that for goodwill (U.K. and Australian firms) and taxes (U.K. firms) domestic *and* U.S. income are higher than the amount implicit in returns. For goodwill, this suggests that the zero amortization for U.K. firms, 20-year amortization for Australian firms (or no amortization in the case of intangibles) and 40-year amortization under U.S. GAAP, all result in too little amortization expense. This interpretation is consistent with the shareholders' equity findings in panel B. For taxes, the findings suggest that neither the U.S. nor U.K. income tax method generally recognizes "enough" tax expense, perhaps reflecting investors' beliefs about increased future tax rates or managers' recognition of tax benefits that are not likely to be realized. This interpretation is consistent with finding that TAX_{NI} provides no explanatory power incremental to Australian GAAP net income. Australian GAAP for deferred taxes differs from U.S. and U.K. GAAP by including expectations about future tax rates and recognizing tax assets only when assured "beyond a reasonable doubt."

Because Table 2 indicates that the Australian revaluation differences are positive, finding a significantly positive coefficient on the Australian revaluation net income difference reliably larger than the one on domestic net income suggests that income including revaluation depreciation (i.e., domestic net income) is lower than the amount implicit in returns, but so also is U.S. GAAP net income (because it equals domestic net income plus the revaluation difference). Because U.S. GAAP net income includes no revaluation depreciation, this suggests that there are offsetting income items unrecognized in both countries and correlated with the revaluation amounts. For U.K. firms, the coefficients on domestic and U.S. GAAP net income for revaluations are indistinguishable, suggesting that investors ignore revaluation depreciation for U.K. firms.

Shareholders' equity differences

Regression summary statistics from estimating equation (4) in Table 4, panel B, reveal that goodwill, revaluations, deferred taxes, and pension shareholders' equity differences provide significant power in explaining share prices incremental to domestic GAAP. The goodwill and revaluation differences have a positive relation to price, although only marginally significant for Australian goodwill (est. = 0.49 and 1.19, t = 2.99 and 1.72 for goodwill; est. = 3.18 and 2.47, t = 2.63 and 6.60 for revaluations), as does the Australian pensions difference (est. = 13.95, t = 6.80). The Australian taxes difference has a significantly negative coefficient (est. = –28.40, t = –5.94), and the coefficients on U.K. interest capitalization, taxes, foreign currency translation, and pension differences are indistinguishable from zero.

Regression summary statistics from estimating equation (4′) for U.K. firms are similar to the equation (4) statistics except that the level of goodwill does not provide significant explanatory power. None of the net income reconciling differences provide incremental explanatory power. Our findings differ slightly from Amir et al. (1993): for their combined U.K. and Australian subsample, they find that only goodwill and revaluations have incremental explanatory power.

Looking again at the equation (4) statistics, we see that the coefficient on the goodwill difference, GW_{SE}, for U.K. firms is marginally significantly smaller than that on SE_{DOM} ($p = 0.06$). Because U.S. GAAP goodwill exceeds U.K. GAAP goodwill, this suggests that share prices act as if goodwill were an asset, but at a discount relative to other assets. This finding is consistent with the goodwill income component findings that suggest U.S. GAAP goodwill amortization is slower than that implicit in returns, and thus, a smaller goodwill asset amount is implicit in price.[17] It also suggests that by electing to write off goodwill, U.K. managers reduce the relevance of reported asset amounts. For Australian firms, the goodwill difference coefficient is not significantly different from that on SE_{DOM} ($p = 0.53$), suggesting that Australian GAAP for goodwill does not add explanatory power over U.S. GAAP.

The coefficient on the U.K. revaluation difference is also significantly different from that on SE_{DOM} ($p = 0.02$). However, it is significantly greater. This is evidence that revalued assets are not positively correlated with the information that investors use in establishing share prices. In fact, because the revaluation difference is always negative, the evidence suggests that investors discount equity of U.K. firms in a way that is correlated with the write-off of revaluation amounts to conform to U.S. GAAP. Moreover, the income component findings in panel A of Table 4 indicate that U.K. GAAP for revaluations has no explanatory power incremental to U.S. GAAP—additional depreciation attributable to the revalued amount is not associated with returns. Because our priors are that revaluations are relevant to investors, these findings suggest that estimation error is potentially an important factor. This is plausible because U.K. GAAP permits considerable management discretion over revaluations; our findings suggest that permitting such discretion impairs the revaluation amounts' relevance.

For Australian firms, the revaluation difference coefficient is significantly larger than that on SE_{DOM} ($p = 0.00$), indicating that reported revaluation increments are not perceived as assets by investors. This is consistent with the net income difference results, discussed previously, that indicate adjustments to U.S. GAAP for revaluation depreciation expense are priced. These findings are inconsistent with Easton et al. (1993). However, our Australian revaluation reconciliation item includes revaluations of tangible (e.g., property) and intangible (e.g., mastheads in the case of newspaper companies) assets (see footnote 13), whereas Easton et al.'s do not. It is possible that revaluation of these two types of assets is perceived differently by investors and that our finding relates to one, but not to the other. Unfortunately, our data do not permit us to distinguish directly between them. Investigation of the potential effects of aggregation is also limited by the small Australian sample size.

The coefficients on the income taxes differences, TAX_{SE}, also differ significantly from those on SE_{DOM} for U.K. and Australian firms ($p = 0.02$ and 0.00, respectively). However, when viewed in conjunction with the tax findings in panel A of Table 4, the findings are inconclusive for both sets of firms.

Sensitivity checks

Alternative estimation specifications

We estimated equations (1) through (4) using several other alternative specifications to explore our findings' robustness. All yielded results similar to those reported, although in some cases the significance levels were somewhat higher. (1) We estimated a fixed effects model that assumes the error term has two components: year-specific and random. The small number of observations per firm did not permit us to include a firm-specific error term component. (2) Our regression equations include observations obtained from disclosures of previous years' data even though contemporaneous disclosures were not available. This potentially introduces error if the amounts were restated from those reported the prior year. We re-estimated all equations using only contemporaneous disclosures. (3) We included only firms with market value of equity greater than $100 million. (4) U.S. dollar returns include effects of changes in exchange rates. Thus, we included the annual change in the respective exchange rate as an additional explanatory variable in the returns regressions. None of our findings are affected, and the exchange rate variable is significant only for the Australian sample. (5) We included, as additional explanatory variables, proxies for growth (three and five year growth in sales), size (beginning and end-of-year market value of equity), market return, and lagged domestic earnings. (6) We used weighted least squares to account for potential heteroscedasticity where the weights were based on time-series monthly market-model regression residual variances for each firm. (7) We estimated the equations with no deflator.

In our reported estimations, we use 15-month returns and prices three months after fiscal year-end because, although a Form 20-F is due six months after year-end, many U.K. and Australian firms report the domestic to U.S. GAAP reconciliation in their annual reports (see, e.g., Pope and Rees 1992). Canadian firms typically file a Form 10-K, which is due three months after year-end. Moreover, McQueen (1993) presents evidence that much of the reconciliation information is impounded in share prices before the 20-F filing date. The use of prices and returns calculated as of six months after year-end, twelve month returns ending with the firm's fiscal year-end, and prices as of fiscal year-end does not affect our inferences, although, as expected, and consistent with Pope and Rees, statistical significance is somewhat lower using the fiscal year-end market information. Amir et al. (1993) report findings similarly insensitive to the price date. Also, using twelve-month returns ending three months after the firm's fiscal year-end yields similar findings, except that the aggregate Australian difference in equation (1) is no longer significant. We also estimated the equations with 12- and 15-month returns obtained from Center for Research in Security Prices. Although this resulted in the loss of a large number of observations, the findings were similar to those reported.

Also, as noted previously, U.K. and Australian GAAP do not require articulation of the financial statements as frequently as U.S. GAAP does. The inclusion of changes in net income in the returns equation is motivated by the Ohlson (1989) model, which is based on articulation, or "clean surplus." As Pope (1993) points out, a "dirty surplus" specification might be more appropriate for U.K. and Australian firms. Thus, for these two samples, we estimated equation (1) including the change in the shareholders' equity goodwill and revaluations components, after subtracting the associated net income difference components. Of the additional variables, only the coefficient on the revaluation difference for Australian firms significantly differs from zero. The coefficients on NI_{DOM} and NI_{DIF} are similar to those reported in Table 3. The Australian revaluation finding is consistent with Easton et al. (1993), who also estimate a somewhat different "dirty surplus" equation and conclude that increments to the revaluation reserve provide incremental explanatory power for securities returns.[18]

Sensitivity of reported findings to partitioning GAAP differences by sign
Pope (1993) suggests investigating areas where management has discretion differentially across GAAP regimes. As noted in the Descriptive Statistics section, there are patterns in the signs of several GAAP differences. Moreover, our description of GAAP differences indicates that most domestic versus U.S. GAAP differences are discretionary.[19] Thus, if investors are concerned about managers exercising their discretion to increase reported income, we might expect a different relation between share prices and those GAAP differences that increase or decrease domestic income or shareholders' equity relative to U.S. amounts. The findings are consistent with this scenario.

Table 5, panel A, presents summary statistics from estimating equation (1) after partitioning NI_{DIF} into NI_{DIFPOS} and NI_{DIFNEG}, where NI_{DIFPOS} equals NI_{DIF} if NI_{DIF} is positive, and is zero otherwise; and NI_{DIFNEG} equals NI_{DIF} if NI_{DIF} is negative, and is zero otherwise. Panel B presents analogous summary statistics for equation (2) after similarly partitioning SE_{DIF}.

Panel A reveals that for U.K. firms in both specifications, only the negative differences are related significantly to share price. Thus, when U.K. GAAP income exceeds U.S. GAAP income, U.S. GAAP income provides explanatory power incremental to U.K. GAAP income. This is not the case when U.S. GAAP income exceeds U.K. GAAP income. For Australian firms, the findings are similar in the equation (1) specification. For Canadian firms, similar to the Table 3 findings, neither difference coefficient differs significantly from zero. The findings in panel B are similar to those in panel A for Australian firms—only the negative differences are significantly related to share prices. For U.K. firms, the positive differences are significantly related to stock prices, but the negative differences are not.

Possible effects of different investor composition
Evidence presented in the Empirical Results section indicates that some differences in accounting rules across countries are associated with share prices and

returns. Moreover, the relations are consistent across domestic and U.S. markets. However, it remains possible that investor composition influences the extent of the association. Specifically, if investors rely on their domestic GAAP because, for example, they understand it better than U.S. GAAP, then the pricing of international accounting differences will be influenced by the relative importance

TABLE 5
Summary statistics for regression of returns (price) on domestic net income (shareholders' equity) and the difference between U.S. and domestic GAAP net income (shareholders' equity), partitioned by sign, for three samples of non-U.S. firms whose equity shares trade in U.S. markets: 1985–1991.

Panel A: $RET_{it} = \phi_0 + \phi_1 NI_{DOMit} + \phi_2 NI_{DIFPOSit} + \phi_3 NI_{DIFNEGit} + e_{it}$

	U.K.		Australia		Canada	
coef	est	t	est	t	est	t
ϕ_0	0.24	5.62	0.08	0.92	0.05	2.01
ϕ_1	0.45	2.75	1.00	3.49	0.66	6.74
ϕ_2	1.01	0.54	0.50	0.10	0.90	1.13
ϕ_3	2.18	3.87	3.36	1.84	−0.22	−1.12
nobs		98		22		229
χ^2 (p value) for test of $\phi_2 = \phi_3$:						
		0.32		0.22		1.80
		(0.57)		(0.64)		(0.18)

Panel B: $PRICE_{it} = \varphi_0 + \varphi_1 SE_{DOMit} + \varphi_2 SE_{DIFPOSit} + \varphi_3 SE_{DIFNEGit} + u_{it}$

	U.K.		Australia	
coef	est	t	est	t
φ_0	10.34	3.07	13.76	4.34
φ_1	1.13	4.07	0.54	2.64
φ_2	0.63	4.03	−0.74	−0.61
φ_3	1.23	1.26	0.64	2.47
nobs		139		36
χ^2 (p value) for test of $\varphi_2 = \varphi_3$:				
		0.44		1.55
		(0.51)		(0.21)

Initial sample comprises 55, 16, and 242 firms from the United Kingdom, Canada, and Australia, respectively. The number of observations for each regression differs, reflecting missing data. Net income variables are deflated by beginning-of-year price. Shareholders' equity variables are deflated by number of ADRs outstanding. t is the t statistic based on White (1980) standard errors. The χ^2 statistics are also based on White (1980) standard errors. Regressions are estimated using Seemingly Unrelated Regression (SUR) on two equations with domestic and U.S. returns or prices as the dependent variable. We report a χ^2 statistic to test all slope coefficients equal to zero, rather than a regression R^2, because of the SUR joint estimation.

RET	= fifteen-month share return, ending three months after fiscal year-end.
$PRICE$	= price per share three months after fiscal year-end.
NI_{DOM} (SE_{DOM})	= domestic GAAP net income (shareholders' equity).
NI_{DIF} (SE_{DIF})	= U.S. GAAP net income (shareholders' equity) minus domestic GAAP net income (shareholders' equity).
NI_{DIFPOS} (SE_{DIFPOS})	= NI_{DIF} (SE_{DIF}), if positive.
NI_{DIFNEG} (SE_{DIFNEG})	= NI_{DIF} (SE_{DIF}), if negative.

on each firm's share-register of domestic versus U.S.-based shareholders. This argument parallels similar analyses relating to the potential impact of distinct clienteles of investors on the pricing of firms' securities (see, e.g., Scholes, Wilson, and Wolfson 1990 for tax clienteles). In effect, we explore the possibility that clienteles based on geographic location influence the pricing of international differences in accounting rules. We do not seek to explain why the relative shareholder base varies across firms.

We use two proxies for the relative influence of domestic versus U.S. shareholders. The first is the percentage of a firm's outstanding shares that are in the form of ADRs that can be traded in U.S. markets. This percentage is generally available in Form 20-Fs for U.K. and Australian firms. It is not available for our Canadian firms because they typically trade common shares, not ADRs. The second proxy is the ratio of U.S. to domestic trading volume, after adjusting for the ADR to common share ratio. This variable is unavailable for many Australian firms.[20] Table 6 presents regression summary statistics for equations (1) (panels A1 and A2 for the ADR and trading volume proxies) and (2) (panels B1 and B2) estimated to permit different slope coefficients on the difference between U.S. and domestic GAAP to reflect different relations depending on investor composition.

The findings in Table 6 indicate that there is generally no significant differential relation between share returns or prices and the difference between domestic and U.S. GAAP, dependent on investor composition. The exceptions are U.K. net income and Australian shareholders' equity differences, using trading volume and the percentage of shares that firms traded as ADRs as the investor-influence proxy. The large negative coefficient on the trading-volume proxy ($NI_{DIF \cdot VOL}$, est. = –5.36, t = –2.04) suggests that the higher the U.S. trading volume, the lower the coefficient on NI_{DIF}. This is inconsistent with our conjectures. The large positive coefficient on the ADR interaction variable ($SE_{DIF \cdot ADR}$, est. = 7.88, t = 2.38) suggests that the significant coefficient on the difference variable in Table 3 is primarily attributable to U.S.-based investors. However, this is not supported by the net income findings in panel A1. As always, insignificant findings, particularly with a small sample size (nobs = 17), are difficult to interpret. The remaining findings in Table 6 indicate the general lack of significance, using either influence proxy. Thus, we document little evidence that our finding of significance for the difference variables (or, equivalently, for U.S. GAAP) is attributable to the influence of U.S.-based shareholders.

Summary and concluding remarks

We investigate the relation between share returns and prices and the differences between U.S. and domestic GAAP net income and shareholders' equity for samples of U.K., Australian, and Canadian firms that trade shares in U.S. securities markets. Our primary objective is to provide insight into several accounting issues currently, or recently, under consideration by standard setters in the countries we study, including accounting for goodwill, asset revaluations, income taxes, and pensions, among others.

TABLE 6
Summary statistics for regression of returns on domestic and U.S. GAAP net income and of price on domestic and U.S. GAAP shareholders' equity for three samples of non-U.S. firms whose equity shares trade in U.S. markets: 1985–1991, permitting different slope coefficients depending on the influence of U.S.-based shareholders.

Panel A

A1: $RET_{it} = \theta_0 + \theta_1 NI_{DQMit} + \theta_2 NI_{DIFit} + \theta_{22} NI_{DIF \cdot ADRit} + e_{it}$

	U.K.		Australia	
coef	est	t	est	t
θ_0	0.22	4.08	0.00	−0.06
θ_1	0.61	2.35	1.76	5.49
θ_2	2.92	3.53	10.84	3.64
θ_{22}	−0.59	−0.19	−32.89	−1.57
nobs		81		17

A2: $RET_{it} = \theta'_0 + \theta'_1 NI_{DOMit} + \theta'_2 NI_{DIFit} + \theta'_{22} NI_{DIF \cdot VOLit} + e_{it}$

	U.K.		Canada	
coef	est	t	est	t
θ'_0	0.19	3.28	0.07	2.45
θ'_1	0.62	2.27	0.47	3.30
θ'_2	4.21	4.10	0.22	0.75
θ'_{22}	−5.36	−2.04	−1.22	−1.04
nobs		62		225

Panel B

B1: $PRICE_{it} = \vartheta_0 + \vartheta_1 SE_{DOMit} + \vartheta_2 SE_{DIFit} + \vartheta_{22} SE_{DIF \cdot ADRit} + u_{it}$

	U.K.		Australia	
coef	est	t	est	t
ϑ_0	9.93	2.04	15.01	5.36
ϑ_1	1.09	3.30	0.32	1.52
ϑ_2	0.54	1.84	−0.72	−1.22
ϑ_{22}	0.35	0.41	7.88	2.38
nobs		105		27

B2: $PRICE_{it} = \vartheta'_0 + \vartheta'_1 SE_{DOMit} + \vartheta'_2 SE_{DIFit} + \vartheta'_{22} SE_{DIF \cdot VOLit} + u_{it}$

	U.K.	
coef	est	t
ϑ'_0	8.51	1.44
ϑ'_1	1.09	3.41
ϑ'_2	0.68	2.51
ϑ'_{22}	−0.10	−0.14
nobs		77

Initial sample comprises 55, 16, and 242 firms from the United Kingdom, Australia, and Canada, respectively. Number of observations for each regression differs, reflecting missing data. Net income (shareholders' equity) variables are deflated by beginning-of-year price (number of ADRs outstanding). t refers to t-statistic based on White (1980) standard errors. Figures are based on SUR estimation of regressions with U.S. and domestic returns and prices as dependent variables.

RET = fifteen-month share return, ending three months after fiscal year-end.
PRICE = price per share three months after fiscal year-end.
NI_{DOM}, SE_{DOM} = domestic GAAP net income (*NI*) or shareholders' equity (*SE*).
NI_{DIF}, SE_{DIF} = U.S. GAAP net income (*NI*) or shareholders' equity (*SE*) minus domestic GAAP net income or shareholders' equity.
$NI_{DIF \cdot X}$, $SE_{DIF \cdot X}$ = NI_{DIF} or SE_{DIF} times percent ADRs or ratio of U.S. to domestic trading volume.

Our results indicate that in addition to domestic net income and shareholders' equity, differences in accounting for goodwill, asset revaluations, deferred income taxes, and pensions (or, equivalently, the U.S. GAAP for these items) provide incremental power in explaining share returns or prices for either, or both, U.K. and Australian firms. Only the interest capitalization difference is significant for Canadian firms. We interpret our findings as follows. (1) Goodwill amortization under U.S., U.K., and Australian GAAP is "too small" relative to the expense reflected in returns, and a portion of U.S. GAAP goodwill is priced as an asset, suggesting that, by electing to write off goodwill, U.K. managers reduce the relevance of reported balance sheet amounts. (2) U.K. asset revaluations are not positively correlated with the information that investors use in setting share prices, suggesting that estimation error affects the relevance of revalued assets. This is plausible because U.K. GAAP permits management discretion in revaluations as to timing, estimated amounts, and choice of assets to be revalued. We also find that Australian revaluations are not viewed by investors as assets, but clear interpretation of the Australian revaluation findings is hampered by the aggregation of tangible and intangible asset revaluations and by small sample size. (3) Neither the U.S., U.K., nor Australian income tax method recognizes "enough" tax expense or liability, perhaps reflecting investors' beliefs about increased future tax rates or the recognition of tax benefits that are not likely to be realized. (4) Accrual pension accounting adds explanatory power beyond cash-based pension accounting. (5) Interest capitalization provides no incremental explanatory power for U.K. and Australian firms.

The Canadian findings suggest that successful efforts accounting for extractive industries and foreign currency exchange gains and losses on long-term assets and liabilities have no significant explanatory power incremental to their Canadian GAAP counterparts. Because U.S. and Canadian GAAP are similar for many items, the SEC considered permitting Canadian firms to trade shares in the United States without providing a GAAP reconciliation. However, recently the SEC decided to continue the reconciliation requirement for Canadian firms. Although we provide limited evidence that U.S. GAAP reflects the information that investors use in establishing share prices beyond that reflected in Canadian GAAP, the evidence is unstable, and thus inconclusive, a finding that is consistent with Bandyopadhyay et al. (1994).

We also find evidence that investors weight less heavily discretionary differences that increase net income and shareholders' equity than they do those that decrease them and that the extent of association between different GAAP regimes and share prices does not differ systematically with investor composition.

Although we provide no evidence that the SEC-required domestic to U.S. GAAP reconciliation itself is used by investors, our evidence indicates that it is correlated with information used by investors in establishing share prices for U.K. and Australian, but not for Canadian firms. Correlation is a necessary condition for informativeness, and it alone might be sufficient for standard setters or regulators whose objective is to require disclosure of summary statistics that capture relevant information.

Appendix

To guide our interpretation of the estimated coefficients further, we employ a simple measurement error-based model. Under its assumptions, the model permits us to interpret the coefficients' magnitudes, particularly relative to the domestic GAAP coefficients, to provide insights into the relation between the accounting measures and an underlying valuation construct and the reliability of the accounting measures. Of course, our interpretations depend on the validity of the underlying assumptions. Our model is consistent with Miller and Modigliani (1966), Beaver, Lambert, and Morse (1980), Beaver, Eger, Ryan, and Wolfson (1989), and Barth (1991, 1994), among others. The model expresses NI_{DOM} and NI_{US} as measuring with error a common underlying construct reflecting information of value to investors, X:

$$NI_{DOM} \equiv X + e_{DOM}$$
$$NI_{US} \equiv X + e_{US}$$

where e_{DOM} and e_{US} are errors in NI_{DOM} and NI_{US} induced by domestic and U.S. GAAP measurement rules. We use an analogous model based on shareholders' equity to interpret findings from our price regressions.

To retain simplicity, we assume that e_{DOM} and e_{US} can be correlated with each other, but are uncorrelated with X.[21] Consistent with a large body of accounting research, we also assume that share returns are increasing and linear in X:

$$RET = a + bX + u$$

where a and b are valuation parameters, $b > 0$, and u is a random error term. Under these assumptions, it is straightforward to show that because NI_{DIF} equals NI_{US} minus NI_{DOM}, the coefficients in equation (1), $RET_{it} = \alpha_0 + \alpha_1 NI_{DOMit} + \alpha_2 NI_{DIFit} + e_{it}$, are:

$$\begin{bmatrix} \alpha_1 \\ \alpha_2 \end{bmatrix} = \begin{bmatrix} k(\sigma^2_{DOM} + \sigma^2_{US} - 2\sigma^2_{DOM,US}) \\ k(\sigma^2_{DOM} - \sigma_{DOM,US}) \end{bmatrix} \tag{A1}$$

where σ^2_{DOM} and σ^2_{US} are the variances of e_{DOM} and e_{US}, $\sigma_{DOM,US}$ denotes the error covariance, and $k > 0$ is determined by X's variance, the covariance matrix of NI_{DOM} and NI_{DIF}, and b.

The expressions in equation (A1) provide a guide to interpreting estimated coefficients in equation (1). The interpretations of possible coefficient estimates and relations are listed in the following table and provide the basis for our interpretations of the coefficients in the text.

coef. relation	interpretation
$\alpha_2 < 0$	Measurement error in NI_{DOM} is less than in NI_{US}; errors are positively correlated (i.e., $\sigma^2_{DOM} < \sigma_{DOM,US} < \sigma^2_{US}$).
$\alpha_2 = 0$	NI_{US} reflects no information relevant to investors that is not reflected in NI_{DOM}.
$(\alpha_2 \neq 0)$	(NI_{US} reflects information relevant to investors but not reflected in NI_{DOM}.)

$0 < \alpha_2 < \alpha_1$ Both NI_{US} and NI_{DOM} reflect information that is not provided by the other. The sign of any correlation between errors is indeterminate.

$\alpha_2 = \alpha_1$ NI_{DOM} reflects no information relevant to investors that is not reflected in NI_{US}.

$\alpha_2 > \alpha_1$ Measurement error in NI_{US} is less than in NI_{DOM}; errors are positively correlated (i.e., $\sigma^2_{US} < \sigma_{DOM,US} < \sigma^2_{DOM}$).

Note that α_1 is non-negative under conditions of the measurement model and that the preceding table is presented in terms of the net income regression. The interpretation of the coefficients is analogous for the shareholders' equity regression.

The model indicates that comparing estimated coefficients on NI_{DOM} and NI_{DIF} reveals characteristics of the measurement error in domestic and U.S. GAAP net income relative to information used by investors in determining share returns. For example, if the coefficient on NI_{DIF}, α_2, is greater than that on NI_{DOM}, α_1, then the measurement error variance is less under U.S. GAAP than under domestic GAAP, and the errors are positively correlated. Such a finding could reflect, for example, that the depreciation expense recognized under U.S. GAAP is closer to the depreciation expense assessed by investors than the depreciation expense under domestic GAAP is (which, e.g., includes depreciation of revalued assets), but that both accounting depreciation expenses are still too low.

Endnotes

1 See, for example, those studies comparing current and replacement costs disclosed under *Statement of Financial Accounting Standards* (*SFAS*) *No. 33* and *Accounting Series Releases* (*ASR*) 190 with historical costs (e.g., Beaver and Landsman 1983; Bublitz, Frecka, and McKeown 1985; Bernard and Ruland 1987), reserve recognition accounting with historical costs for oil and gas firms (e.g., Magliolo 1986; Harris and Ohlson 1987), fair values with historical costs for banks' investment securities (e.g., Barth 1994), and various accounting measures of pension assets and liabilities (e.g., Dhaliwal 1986; Landsman 1986; Barth 1991).

2 Our definition of the difference variable is consistent with Amir et al. (1993) and Bandyopadhyay et al. (1994). Pope and Rees (1992) define their difference variable as U.K. GAAP minus U.S. GAAP. The two specifications are econometrically equivalent, except for the sign of the difference.

3 This follows from noting that equation (1) is econometrically equivalent to $RET_{it} = \alpha_0 + \psi_1 NI_{DOMit} + \alpha_2 NI_{USit} + e_{it}$, where $\psi_1 = \alpha_1 - \alpha_2$.

4 In the United States, Australian and U.K. firms typically trade ADRs, rather than common shares, and thus, the number of ADRs is the deflator. For each firm, one ADR represents a specified number of common shares and entitles its holder to voting rights and dividends in proportion to the rights attributable to the underlying common share equivalent. See Amir et al. (1993) for further discussion.

5 The magnitude of the potential gain depends on the correlation between the residuals of the two equations. The correlations are 0.93, 0.81, 0.91, 0.92, and 0.92 for the U.K. returns and prices, Australian returns and prices, and Canadian returns specifications, respectively. Also note that the independent variables in our returns regressions differ by the choice of deflator (U.S. or domestic beginning-of-year price), whereas those in our price regressions are the same across equations. Without cross-

equation coefficient restrictions, SUR estimation of the price regressions would be equivalent to separate ordinary least squares (OLS) estimation of the two equations. However, with such restrictions, there can be efficiency gains even with identical independent variables. We checked the appropriateness of the coefficient restrictions by testing for equality between corresponding coefficients in separately estimated U.S. and domestic regressions. In only one case—when prices were regressed on shareholders' equity items for U.K. firms—was equality of coefficients rejected. Separate estimation of the equations yields similar results to those reported in Tables 3 and 4.

6 We do not base our predictions on Amir et al. (1993) or Bandyopadhyay et al. (1994) because their data are similar to ours.

7 Another potentially confounding effect is that the current goodwill accounting requirements became mandatory in 1988. Before that, Australian GAAP allowed multiple approaches—including directly writing off goodwill to shareholders' equity, as in the U.K., or through income. Some companies wrote off previously recognized goodwill just prior to implementing the current amortization requirement. Thus, for some firms, the difference between net income under U.S. and Australian GAAP reflects a *reduction* in amortization for recently acquired goodwill and an *increase* in amortization for goodwill written off prior to the introduction of the amortization requirement. The net effect varies across firms and can be negative or positive.

8 The possible existence of natural revenue hedges across business units in Canadian firms represents a potential source of measurement error in the Canadian foreign currency difference component.

9 Extraordinary income item classification also varies across the GAAP regimes we investigate, with U.S. GAAP generally more restrictive in permitting extraordinary item classification than the other countries. We investigate net income and thus do not investigate extraordinary item classification differences. We use net income, rather than another summary measure such as income before extraordinary items or operating income, because these are not available for a large number of our sample firms, nor are the domestic GAAP income components related to the difference variable.

10 These sample sizes are after eliminating observations with returns greater than 300 percent or with extreme residuals: four observations from the Canadian U.S. returns regression, two from the Canadian domestic returns regression, and two from the Australian domestic returns regression. Exclusion of these data points had little effect on our reported results except for regressions involving U.S. returns for Canadian firms, where one observation with a return in excess of 700 percent (more than six standard deviations from the sample mean) had a marked influence on several estimated coefficients.

11 Bandyopadhyay et al. (1994) also translate domestic prices into U.S. dollars. Our primary objective is to state both U.S./domestic prices and reconciling items in the same units of currency to permit equating coefficient estimates. This is also necessary because some firms state their domestic to U.S. GAAP reconciliation in U.S. dollars, whereas others state it in domestic currency. Our translation into U.S. dollars using the fiscal year-end exchange rate is consistent with the approach used by companies in our sample that perform the translation themselves, an approach which implicitly adopts a U.S. investor view. We believe that this is appropriate because the 20-F reconciliation is required for U.S. investors.

12 Prior to calculating returns, where relevant we restate domestic prices and dividends to U.S. dollars using contemporaneous foreign currency exchange rates. To implement this procedure, we adjust dividends using the exchange rate at the end of the quarter in which they were paid. In almost all cases, we do not have access to the actual dividend *ex* date.

13 For Australian firms, some shareholders' equity effects from accounting for intangibles are included in the revaluation reconciliation item because Australian GAAP allows revaluation of separately identifiable intangible assets. Easton et al.'s (1993) Australian revaluation data exclude intangibles, thus hampering a direct comparison between our Australian revaluation findings and theirs.

14 We calculate all t statistics using White (1980) standard errors, even though the White test for heteroscedasticity and correct model specification cannot be rejected at conventional levels for any regression. Barth and Kallapur (1995) provide evidence that White standard errors closely approximate true standard errors, regardless of whether the regression error variances are heteroscedastic. We also verified that the regressions contain no outliers, as identified by the Belsley, Kuh, and Welsch (1980) influence diagnostics. We use the term *significant* to denote significance levels less than 5 percent. Also, we report a χ^2 statistic to test all slope coefficients equal to zero, rather than a regression R^2, because of the SUR joint estimation.

15 Bandyopadhyay et al. (1994), Table 3, reports separate year regression summary statistics for their sample and reveals that the 1983 findings differ noticeably from those of the other years. Omitting 1983 from their analysis, the averages over the remaining six years of the estimated coefficients on NI_{DIF} and ΔNI_{DIF} are –0.37 and 0.52, respectively, compared with the 0.66 and 0.02 that they report. Estimating our coefficients for our sample on a similar period (1984–1989) results in similar estimates: –0.59 for NI_{DIF} and 0.51 for ΔNI_{DIF}. Moreover, these estimates differ insignificantly from zero. Thus, it appears that 1983 pulls the findings towards zero and insignificance, whereas 1990 and 1991 do the opposite.

16 The Australian findings are somewhat sensitive to one outlier identified by the Belsley et al. (1980) influence diagnostic. Eliminating the observation results in the revaluation (pension) coefficient being insignificant (significant), although the pension coefficient is negative.

17 This interpretation is consistent with Amir et al. (1993) for their combined U.K. and Australian subsample. However, Jennings, Robinson, Thompson, and Duvall (1993) present mixed findings on the relative pricing of goodwill and other assets for their sample of U.S. firms. The time-series mean of annual estimated coefficients on goodwill exceeds that of other assets, but the goodwill coefficient in a fixed-effects model suggests goodwill is discounted by investors relative to other assets.

18 Specifically, Easton et al. (1993) also include changes in earnings and exclude a separate goodwill variable.

19 This is consistent with assertions made in the popular financial press. For example, WPP Group is cited as using asset revaluations to increase shareholders' equity: "Owing to WPP's aggressive acquisition strategy and U.K. GAAP, which allows goodwill to be charged to the balance sheet's equity account as opposed to amortized through the earnings statement, WPP's balance sheet has not been representative of the financial strength or underlying values of the company ... Recently the company has addressed this cosmetic financial problem by incorporating a subjective value of its brands on the balance sheet. This cosmetic revaluation ... allowed the company to show a positive net worth ..." (PanMure Gordon and Co. Ltd., March 30, 1990, analyst report on WPP Group Company Report, R. Sanderson). Also, the *Wall Street Journal* (February 9, 1989) points out: "British firms used brand values primarily to boost their balance sheets; by recording brand values as intangible assets, they could magically increase their assets while drawing attention to their important brands. U.S. accounting rules didn't allow any such advantages." Similarly, *Business Review Weekly*, an Australian business publication, notes that: "In so many cases, the experience in Australia of revaluing intangibles has proved it is not reliable."

20 The relative trading volume measure also is missing for many U.K. and Canadian firm-year observations. To enable sample sizes of sufficient size for reliable estimation, we form the variable as an average over available years for each firm, rather than a separate value for each firm year. This average is then applied as an interaction variable in each available firm year. Although this approach depends on stationarity assumptions, it results in a greatly increased number of observations. Estimation with the reduced set of firm-year trading volume observations does not alter the tenor of our results, but does reduce their statistical significance.

21 This assumption is not necessary; allowing the errors to be correlated with the underlying valuation construct does not alter our inferences.

References

Amir, E., T.S. Harris, and E.K. Venuti. A comparison of the value-relevance of U.S. versus non-U.S. GAAP accounting measures using form 20-F reconciliations. *Journal of Accounting Research* (Supplement 1993), 230–275.

Bandyopadhyay, S.P., J.D. Hanna, and G. Richardson. Capital market effects of U.S.-Canada GAAP differences. *Journal of Accounting Research* 32 (1994), 262–277.

Barth, M.E. Relative measurement errors among alternative pension asset and liability measures. *The Accounting Review* 66 (1991), 433–463.

——, Fair value accounting: evidence from investment securities and the market valuation of banks. *The Accounting Review* 69 (1994), 1–25.

——, W.H. Beaver, and W.R. Landsman. The market valuation implications of net periodic pension cost components. *Journal of Accounting and Economics* 15 (1992), 27–62.

——, ——, and ——. A structural analysis of pension disclosures under SFAS 87 and their relation to share prices. *Financial Analysts Journal* (January/February 1993), 18–26.

———, and S. Kallapur. The effects of cross-sectional scale differences on regression results in empirical accounting research. Working paper. Stanford University, Graduate School of Business, 1995.

Beaver, W.H., C. Eger, S. Ryan, and M.A. Wolfson. Financial reporting and the structure of bank share prices. *Journal of Accounting Research* 27 (1989), 157–78.

——, R. Lambert, and D. Morse. The information content of security prices. *Journal of Accounting and Economics* 2 (1980), 3–28.

——, and W.R. Landsman. *Incremental information content of statement 33 disclosures.* FASB, 1983.

Belsley, D.A., E. Kuh, and R.E. Welsch. *Regression Diagnostics.* John Wiley & Sons, 1980.

Bernard, V., and R. Ruland. The incremental information content of historical cost and current cost numbers: time series analysis. *The Accounting Review* 62 (1987), 701–722.

Boreham, T. Australia: Accountancy – the Rocky Road to World Standards. *Business Review Weekly.* August 30, 1991.

Bowen, R.M. Valuation of earnings components in the electric utility industry. *The Accounting Review* 56 (1981), 1–22.

Bublitz, B., T.J. Frecka, and J.C. McKeown. Market association tests and FASB statement no. 33 disclosures: a reexamination. *Journal of Accounting Research* 23 (Supplement 1985), 1–23.

Dhaliwal, D. Measurement of financial leverage in the presence of unfunded pension obligations. *The Accounting Review* 61 (1986), 651–661.

Easton, P.D., Eddey, P.H., and T.S. Harris. An investigation of revaluations of tangible long-lived assets. *Journal of Accounting Research* (Supplement 1993), 1–38.

Financial Accounting Standards Board. Statement of Financial Accounting Standards No. 33, Financial Accounting and Changing Prices. Stamford, Connecticut, 1979.

Givoly, D. and C. Hayn. The valuation of the deferred tax liability: Evidence from the stock market. *The Accounting Review* 67 (1992), 394–410.

Hall, C., Y. Hamao, and T.S. Harris. A comparison of relations between security market prices, returns and accounting measures in Japan and the United States. Working paper. Columbia University, 1992.

Harris, T.S., and M. Lang. Relations between security market prices, returns and accounting measures in Germany. Working paper. Stanford University, 1992.

——, and J.A. Ohlson. Accounting disclosures and the market's valuation of oil and gas properties. *The Accounting Review* 62 (1987), 651–670.

Jennings, R., J. Robinson, R.B. Thompson II, and L. Duvall. The relation between accounting goodwill numbers and equity values. Working paper. University of Texas, 1993.

Landsman, W. An empirical investigation of pension fund property rights. *The Accounting Review* 61 (1986), 662–691.

Lipman, J. British Value Brand Names – Literally. *Wall Street Journal.* February 9, 1989, p.84

Magliolo, J. Capital market analysis of reserve recognition accounting. *Journal of Accounting Research* 24 (Supplement 1986), 69–108.

McQueen, P.D. The information content of foreign and U.S. GAAP earnings in SEC Form 20-F. Working paper. New York University, 1993.

Miller, M.H., and F. Modigliani. Some estimates of the cost of capital to the electric utility industry, 1954–57. *The American Economic Review* 56 (1966), 333–391.

Niskanen, J., J. Kinnunen, and E. Kasanen. The association of stock returns with international accounting standards (IAS) earnings: evidence from listed Finnish firms. Working paper. Helsinki School of Economics, 1992.

Ohlson, J.A. Accounting earnings, book value, and dividends: the theory of the clean surplus equation (part 1). Working paper. Columbia University, 1989.

Pope, P.F. Discussion of a comparison of the value-relevance of U.S. versus non-U.S. GAAP accounting measures using form 20-F reconciliations. *Journal of Accounting Research* (Supplement 1993), 265–275.

Pope, P.F., and W.P. Rees. International differences in GAAP and the pricing of earnings. *Journal of International Financial Management and Accounting* 4 (1992), 190–219.

Scholes, M.S., G.P. Wilson, and M.A. Wolfson. Tax planning, regulatory capital planning, and financial reporting strategy for commercial banks. *The Review of Financial Studies* 3 (1990), 625–650.

Securities and Exchange Commission. ASR No. 190, Notice of Adoption of Amendments to Regulation S-X Requiring Disclosure of Certain Replacement Cost Data. Commerce Clearing House, March 23, 1976.

White, H. A heteroskedasticity-consistent covariance matrix estimator and a direct test for heteroskedasticity. *Econometrica* 48 (1980), 817–838.

[9]

ELSEVIER Journal of Accounting and Economics 26 (1999) 285–312

JOURNAL OF Accounting & Economics

The market valuation of IAS versus US-GAAP accounting measures using Form 20-F reconciliations[1]

Mary S. Harris, Karl A. Muller III*

Smeal College of Business Administration, Pennsylvania State University, University Park, PA 16802, USA

Received 1 September 1997; received in revised form 1 December 1998

Abstract

We investigate the market valuation of earnings and book value amounts prepared under IAS and US-GAAP to provide evidence for the debate between the US SEC and NYSE on whether foreign firms should be allowed to list in the US using IAS. We find that the US-GAAP earnings reconciliation adjustment is value-relevant and that US-GAAP amounts are valued differently for market value and return models, but not a price-per-share model. We also find that IAS amounts are more highly associated with price-per-share than US-GAAP amounts, and that US-GAAP amounts are more highly associated with security returns than IAS amounts. © 1999 Elsevier Science B.V. All rights reserved.

JEL classification: M41; G15

Keywords: Capital markets; International Accounting Standards; US-GAAP; Form 20-F

* Corresponding author. Tel.: 814/865-0601; fax: 814/863-8393; e-mail: kam23@psu.edu.

[1] We thank Eli Amir (the referee), Anne Beatty, Dick Dietrich, Glen Hansen, David Harris, Irene Karamanou, S.P. Kothari (the editor), Jim McKeown, K. Ramesh, Judy Rayburn, Phillip Stocken, Mohan Venkatachalam (the discussant), Elizabeth Venuti, Jerold Zimmerman and participants at the 1997 Big-10 Summer Research Conference for their helpful comments and suggestions. We also thank Shawn Davis and Shouli Zhang for their excellent research assistance.

PII: S0165-4101(99)00003-8

1. Introduction

The US Securities and Exchange Commission (SEC) is the only regulatory authority in the world to require foreign registrants to reconcile their home country accounting numbers to local accounting principles (i.e., United States generally accepted accounting principles (US-GAAP)). Foreign firms listing their securities on US exchanges are required to file a Form 20-F, the equivalent of a US firm's 10-K, within six months of fiscal year end. This form includes a reconciliation of earnings and book value of owners' equity to US-GAAP from home-country accounting principles.

Since the early 1990s, the New York Stock Exchange (NYSE) has pressured the SEC to permit foreign firms listing on US exchanges to either avoid the reconciliation requirement or to reduce their required disclosures (Salwen, 1991; Jarrell, 1992; Freund, 1993). The SEC has rejected the suggestion that foreign firms be allowed to list in the US with financial statements prepared under *Foreign*-GAAP based on two policy considerations: investor protection and avoiding a two-tiered disclosure system, one for domestic registrants and a second, lower one, for foreign registrants.

Recently, the debate between the SEC and NYSE has shifted to permitting foreign equity listings in the US without a US-GAAP reconciliation if the firms adopt International Accounting Standards (IAS) in their primary accounts. In April 1996, the SEC announced that, if the International Accounting Standards Committee (IASC) successfully completes an agreed-upon-work-plan, it will consider allowing foreign firms to list in the US using IAS without a reconciliation to US-GAAP (SEC, 1996).[2] However, as the former Chief Accountant of the SEC points out, "it is important to remember that the Commission has *not* already agreed to accept filings prepared in accordance with IASC standards" (Sutton, 1997, p. 101, emphasis added) and that acceptability of IAS to US investors and investment analysts "will depend on how well IASC standards measure up when compared to US standards" (Sutton, 1997, p. 99). Although there has been considerable debate about the quality of IAS, whether or not reconciliations to US-GAAP provide useful information to investors, and the effect of different accounting systems on market quality and efficiency, the lack of research on the comparability of IAS to US-GAAP is often cited as a hindrance to these debates (Bayless et al., 1996; Frost and Lang, 1996; Sutton, 1997). As IAS are typically viewed as being closer to US-GAAP than Foreign-GAAP (Harris, 1995; Ashbaugh, 1997), prior research investigating the reconciliation of Foreign to US-GAAP (Amir et al., 1993; Pope and Rees, 1993; Bandyopadhyay et al., 1994; Barth and Clinch, 1996; Chan and Seow, 1996) cannot be used for

---

[2] The International Organization of Securities Commissions (IOSCO) has also agreed to consider a core set of international accounting standards for cross-border listings around the world.

the current policy debate between the SEC and NYSE. Consistent with this, US standard setters, regulators, and academics have called for research on the comparability of IAS and US-GAAP (Bayless et al., 1996; Frost and Lang, 1996).

To provide such evidence, we investigate the market valuation of IAS and US-GAAP amounts as prepared and reported by foreign firms using market value, price-per-share, and return models. Our sample consists of foreign firms listed in the US that prepare their home country financial statements using IASC standards and reconcile from IAS to US-GAAP in their Form 20-F filing. Thus, in contrast to prior research investigating the reconciliation of Foreign to US-GAAP or comparing IASC and US standards as written, we are able to *directly* compare the association between firm value and IAS and US-GAAP accounting measures as they are implemented by foreign firms listed in the US.

Our results indicate that both the mean and median reconciliation amounts from IAS to US-GAAP are smaller than the reconciliation amounts from Foreign to US-GAAP reported in other studies, suggesting that IAS earnings and book values are closer to US-GAAP for our sample firms. Despite these smaller differences, we find evidence that the US-GAAP earnings reconciliation adjustment is value-relevant after controlling for IAS amounts for the market value and return models. In addition, we find evidence that IAS and US-GAAP earnings amounts are valued differently for both the market value and return models. However, these inferences must be tempered by the fact that we do not find a significant association between US-GAAP reconciliation amounts and prices-per-share. Finally, we test which accounting method, IAS or US-GAAP, produces amounts that are more highly associated with market values, prices-per-share, and returns. We find evidence that IAS amounts are more highly associated with prices-per-share than US-GAAP amounts, and that US-GAAP amounts are more highly associated with returns than IAS amounts. Our test of a greater association between market values and either IAS or US-GAAP amounts are inconclusive. The inconsistent nature of our levels-based specification results may be due to coefficient bias and heteroskedasticity arising from scale differences (Barth and Kallapur, 1996; Easton, 1998). One may wish, therefore, to place greater weight on the return specification results which should be affected less by such concerns (Christie, 1987). Taken together, for the firms examined, our results provide limited evidence consistent with the current SEC position that reconciliations to US-GAAP, *even from IAS*, provide useful information to the market.

Our results and inferences are subject to the following caveats and limitations. First, as is common of tests that examine associations with market value metrics, US-GAAP reconciliation amounts may not provide the market with new information as investors may be able to independently derive US-GAAP amounts from alternative information sources. Second, as foreign firms are likely to choose IAS and list in the US because of some net benefit, our analysis could be affected by a sample selection bias. However, sensitivity analysis using the two-stage switching regression procedure suggested by Heckman (1979) indicates that the impact of self-selection on our results and inferences is minimal. Finally, as IASC standards are currently being revised, our results may not extend to the future when new, more harmonized, standards are adopted. However, sensitivity analysis indicates that our results and inferences are similar for the period after enactment of the IASC's Comparability and Improvements Project. In addition, evidence on how managers implement current IASC standards is informative for the current debate between the SEC and the NYSE and provides a benchmark to which the value-relevance of future IASC standards can be compared.

The remainder of the paper is organized as follows. Section 2 discusses prior research, our sample selection, and briefly describes the major differences between IAS and US-GAAP. Section 3 discusses our research design. Section 4 reports our empirical results. Section 5 provides a discussion of the sensitivity of our results. Section 6 concludes the paper.

2. Prior research, sample selection, and GAAP differences

The SEC's reconciliation requirement is often perceived as a major deterrent to foreign firms listing in the United States; it is claimed to be costly, unnecessary to protect shareholders' interests, and potentially misleading to investors (Edwards, 1993). In the early 1990s, the New York Stock Exchange (NYSE) began pressuring the SEC to permit foreign firms to list on US exchanges using Foreign-GAAP (Salwen, 1991; Jarrell, 1992; Freund, 1993). Consistent with the SEC's concern, prior research investigating the value-relevance of US-GAAP reconciliation amounts reported in Form 20-F filings focused on reconciliations from Foreign-GAAP to US-GAAP and found support for the hypothesis that such reconciliation amounts are value-relevant (Amir et al., 1993; Pope and Rees, 1993; Bandyopadhyay et al., 1994; Barth and Clinch, 1996; Rees and Elgers, 1997). However, as IAS typically restricts accounting measurement choices and requires more extensive disclosures than Foreign-GAAP (Harris, 1995; Ashbaugh, 1997), the evidence in these studies cannot be used to address the current policy debate.

In contrast to research using 20-F reconciliations between Foreign and US-GAAP, Harris (1995) provides evidence that accounting measures under IAS, depending on which methods are chosen, can produce results similar to US-GAAP. His sample consists of eight multinationals with data for 1992 or 1993, for which he adjusts their reported Foreign-GAAP amounts to IAS and then to US-GAAP using company supplied information. He concludes that firms complying with revised IAS "provide accounting measures that are essentially consistent with US-GAAP" (p. 2). One advantage of the case study method used by Harris is that he is able to investigate adjustments from both Foreign-GAAP to IAS and IAS to US-GAAP. However, one of the primary complaints regarding IAS is the wide latitude managers are allowed in implementing the standards (Bayless et al., 1996). Because Harris (1995) calculated the adjustments from Foreign-GAAP to IAS and US-GAAP himself, he is unable to provide evidence on the comparability between US-GAAP and IAS as actually implemented or to investigate the market valuation of these alternative accounting measures. Thus, our evidence on the value-relevance of IAS amounts prepared and reported by management extends Harris', analyses and uses a larger sample from a more recent time period.

Ashbaugh (1997) provides evidence on how *stated* IAS compare to Foreign-GAAP and why firms adopt IAS. She finds that IAS is more restrictive with respect to accounting measurement choices in 16 of the 17 countries she examines and requires more disclosures than Foreign-GAAP in every country, suggesting that firms adopting IAS are meeting higher recognition and disclosure standards than required under their domestic GAAP. Ashbaugh also compares foreign firms that adopt IAS to those that choose Foreign-GAAP using a logit analysis. She finds that the probability of adopting IAS is higher for firms in countries with lower disclosure requirements and where IAS more severely restricts their measurement choices, after controlling for firm size, the number of markets in which the firm is listed, and future equity offerings, suggesting that these firms adopt IAS to improve their disclosures. In addition, listing in the US had no effect on the choice between IAS and Foreign-GAAP, suggesting that foreign firms adopt IAS to improve disclosures to shareholders whether or not they are listed in the US.

Ashbaugh and Pincus (1998) test whether the adoption of IAS improves the usefulness of accounting information for predicting future earnings. Specifically, for a sample of non-US firms that adopted IAS between 1990 and 1993, they find a significant increase in the accuracy of analysts forecasts in the year after adoption of IAS relative to the year before. Their results are also consistent with a greater improvement in forecast accuracy the more restrictive IAS is relative to domestic GAAP, after controlling for analysts following and firm size.

In contrast to these prior studies, we investigate the association between firm value and IAS amounts as prepared and reported by foreign firms which reconcile from IAS to US-GAAP in their Form 20-F filing during the years 1992–1996. We begin our investigation in 1992 for two reasons. First, we identified only eight firms listed in the US that prepared their primary financial statements using IAS between 1989 and 1991.[3] Second, as with US-GAAP, IASC standards are constantly being revised and improved. Thus, our focus

[3] The 20-F data file on Lexis/Nexis, our data source, currently only extends back to 1989.

on a recent period is likely to reflect higher quality IASC standards and greater efforts toward harmonization. In addition, evidence on current standards is likely to be more useful to the SEC in evaluating the acceptability of IAS.

The IASC completed its Comparability and Improvements Project in 1993 with ten new standards becoming effective on 1 January 1995.[4] Thus, our sample period includes observations before and after the implementation of these new standards. The purpose of the Comparability and Improvements Project was to improve disclosure requirements and reduce the number of alternative accounting treatments. In Section 5, we discuss the sensitivity of the reported results to implementation of these new standards.

Our sample consists of all foreign firms on the Lexis/Nexis database with accounting policies that conform to IAS and reconcile to US-GAAP in their Form 20-F filing.[5] Compliance with IAS is usually stated in the audit opinion. The cost of compliance varies depending on the degree of similarity between the firm's domestic accounting standards and IAS. For example, in countries with few restrictions on accounting measurement choices, firms can comply with IAS by choosing IAS standards that are also acceptable under domestic GAAP. However, evidence in Harris (1995), Ashbaugh (1997) and Ashbaugh and Pincus (1998) is consistent with IAS compliance significantly altering firms' reported amounts and disclosures.

Because foreign (i.e., home-country) stock exchanges accept annual reports prepared under IAS and do not require reconciliations from IAS to Foreign-GAAP, our sample firms report only IAS and US-GAAP earnings and book values. Hence, we are unable to determine what amounts these firms would have reported under their home-country GAAP. However, we are able to provide anecdotal evidence for one firm as Harris' (1995) sample includes Broken Hill Proprietary (BHP), one of our sample firms. For 1993, the adoption of IAS by BHP eliminates items that otherwise would be required in a reconciliation from Australian-GAAP to US-GAAP. Specifically, according to Harris (1995), adjustments for the following four items are not included in the US-GAAP reconciliation after adoption of IAS: equity method accounting, accrual basis for pensions, exclusion of minority interests from shareholders' equity, and the classification of a loan to an ESOP. Thus, even in Australia, where the accounting system is very similar to that in the US, the adoption of IAS reduces the number of US-GAAP reconciliation adjustments.

---

[4] The primary changes in these standards are summarized later in this section.

[5] In contrast, Amir et al. (1993) examine Form 20-F reconciliations from Foreign-GAAP to US-GAAP for the period 1981–1991. Their sample consists of 101 firms from 20 countries. The Amir et al. sample likely includes the previously discussed eight firms that used IAS prior to 1992, which are excluded from our study due to our examination of a later time period. The overlap between our sample and other prior 20-F studies examining reconciliations from Foreign-GAAP to US-GAAP is similarly very limited.

Table 1
Distribution of observations by country and year

The sample consists of all non-US firms adopting International Accounting Standards in their primary accounts with a reconciliation to US-GAAP in their Form 20-F filing during the period 1992–1996.

Country	Observations	Firms	Year	Observations
Australia	15	4	1992	12
Bermuda	2	2	1993	18
Canada	19	5	1994	23
China	3	2	1995	23
Colombia	1	1	1996	13
Finland	3	1		
			Total	89
France	11	3		
Israel	2	1		
Italy	20	8		
Luxembourg	3	1		
Mexico	5	1		
Netherlands	1	1		
Portugal	4	1		
Total	89	31		

Panel A of Table 1 displays the final sample consisting of 89 observations representing 31 firms from 13 countries. Consistent with the findings of Ashbaugh (1997) that the probability of adopting IAS is higher for firms whose home country GAAP is relatively less restrictive than IAS, our sample is comprised of firms from countries with relatively less developed accounting practices than the US (e.g., China, Colombia, Finland, Israel, Luxembourg, Mexico, and Portugal). In addition, the representation of firms from the other countries is not surprising, with the possible exceptions of Canada and the Netherlands. For instance, France permits firms to follow IAS for consolidated reporting purposes, Italy has adopted IAS in the absence of a standard by the National Councils of the Italian Accounting Profession, and the Australian Accounting Standards Board has undertaken a project to harmonize Australian accounting standards with IAS. Thus, the distribution of our sample firms by country does not appear to be random. However, as the SEC's mandate is to ensure investor protection, and, thus, enforce minimum disclosure requirements for all firms, evidence of an association between the US-GAAP reconciliation adjustment and market value metrics for these firms, after controlling for IAS amounts, is of interest from a policy perspective. In addition, our sample firms should be of primary interest to the SEC, as these firms would be among the first to report under IAS-GAAP if the SEC were to abandon the US-GAAP reconciliation requirement for firms adopting IAS in their primary accounts. Panel B shows that the number of observations per year varies from a high of 23 in 1994 to a low of 12 in 1992.

The US-GAAP earnings and book value reconciliation amounts were collected from firms' 20-F filings. To provide information about the magnitude of the major reconciliation adjustments (i.e., adjustments with at least 10 observations), we grouped them into six categories of common reconciliation adjustments: goodwill, deferred income taxes, foreign exchange adjustments and transactions, research and development expenditures, pensions, and tangible asset revaluations. Reconciliation adjustments not fitting into one of these major classifications were classified as 'other' adjustments. These classification categories are similar to those used in research investigating the value-relevance of Foreign to US-GAAP reconciliation adjustments (Amir et al., 1993; Bandyopadhyay et al., 1994; Harris, 1995; Barth and Clinch, 1996; Rees and Elgers, 1997). A description of the major differences between IAS and US-GAAP before the implementation of the IASC's Comparability and Improvements Project is as follows (effects of the implementation of the Project are discussed below):[6]

Goodwill. For our sample firms, under IAS No. 22 (revised 1983) (IASC, 1993g), goodwill could be capitalized and amortized, or charged directly to owners' equity in the year of acquisition. Under US-GAAP, (APB Opinion 17 (APB, 1970)), firms are required to capitalize and amortize goodwill over its expected useful life, which may not exceed 40 years.

Deferred income taxes. Under IAS 12 (1979, reformatted IASC, 1994), deferred income taxes can be recognized under a partial allocation method which allows managers to *not* recognize deferred tax assets and liabilities if the book/tax difference is not expected to reverse in the foreseeable future. IAS 12 also allows managers to choose whether or not to adjust deferred tax amounts for changes in tax rates and laws. SFAS 109 (FASB, 1992) requires recognition of deferred income taxes on a comprehensive basis for *all* temporary differences (with a valuation allowance for certain deferred tax assets) and requires the use of tax rates that reflect future tax rates and laws in determining the deferred tax amount.

Foreign exchange adjustments. Numerous differences exist between IAS 21 (IASC, 1993f) and SFAS 52 (FASB, 1981). However, the most significant differences are those concerning forward exchange contracts, hedge accounting and the accounting for goodwill and fair value adjustments on the acquisition of

[6] This synopsis is based on information contained in firms' US-GAAP reconciliation disclosures, *International Accounting Standards* (IASC, 1997), *The IASC-US Comparison Project: A Report on the Similarities and Differences between IASC Standards and US-GAAP* (FASB, 1996), and *Coopers & Lybrand International Accounting Summaries* (Coopers and Lybrand, 1993).

foreign subsidiaries. International Accounting Standards also presently do not cover accounting for forward exchange contracts and hedging. Thus, any accounting method is accepted for IAS. Under US-GAAP, foreign exchange gains and losses on forward contracts and hedges are recognized in net income or as a component of equity in the period in which they occur. IAS 21 permits a choice between current and historical exchange rates when translating goodwill and fair value adjustments on foreign acquisitions. SFAS 52 requires use of the current exchange rate.

Research and Development expenditures. IAS 9 (IASC, 1993b) allows capitalization of development costs if certain criteria are satisfied. US-GAAP (SFAS 2 (FASB, 1974)) requires that all research and development costs be expensed as incurred.

Pensions. For defined benefit pension plans, IAS 19 (IASC, 1993e) permits the use of both accrued-benefit and projected-benefit valuation methods and requires the use of long-term assumptions. Under the accrued-benefit valuation method, service cost is measured as the present value of benefits payable in the future as a result of current period service. Under the projected-benefit method, service cost is based on both current and future service. In contrast, SFAS 87 (FASB, 1985a) and SFAS 88 (FASB, 1985b) require the use of the accrued-benefit method and current market-based assumptions. In addition, SFAS 87 requires recognition of a minimum pension liability for underfunded plans. IAS 19 has no such requirement.

Tangible asset revaluations. Revaluations of property, plant and equipment and investments are permitted under IAS 16 (IASC, 1993d), with upward adjustments to the historical cost values reflected in a revaluation reserve, which is part of shareholders' equity. In the case of property, plant and equipment, the depreciation charged against income increases as a direct result of such a revaluation. US-GAAP does not permit property, plant and equipment to be valued above historical cost.

As a result of its Comparability and Improvements Project, the IASC issued ten revised accounting standards effective from 1 January 1995 that generally reduce the number of acceptable alternative accounting treatments and increase disclosure requirements. In this project, the IASC identified twenty four issues with alternative accounting treatments, sixteen of these were eliminated and several other methods were designated as acceptable alternatives rather than as the preferred accounting method. Depending on whether or not the accounting methods eliminated are acceptable under US-GAAP, these revisions in IAS may increase or decrease the difference between IAS and US-GAAP earnings and book value amounts.

The major changes in acceptable IAS accounting methods resulting from the Comparability and Improvements Project are as follows (see Pereira (1994) for

Table 2

Descriptive statistics for IAS to US-GAAP earnings and owners' equity reconciliation components

The sample consists of all non-US firms adopting International Accounting Standards in their primary accounts with a reconciliation to US-GAAP in their Form 20-F filing during the period 1992–1996.

Panel A: IAS earnings and US-GAAP reconciliation components for earnings ($n = 86$)[a]

	$\frac{E^{IAS}}{BV^{IAS}}$[b]	$\frac{GW}{BV^{IAS}}$[c]	$\frac{DFTX}{BV^{IAS}}$	$\frac{FOREXCH}{BV^{IAS}}$	$\frac{R\&D}{BV^{IAS}}$	$\frac{PENSION}{BV^{IAS}}$	$\frac{REVAL}{BV^{IAS}}$	$\frac{OTHER}{BV^{IAS}}$	$\frac{E^{US-IAS}}{BV^{IAS}}$
Mean	7.67%	− 0.18%	0.52%	0.01%	− 0.07%	− 0.01%	0.26%	− 0.54%	0.28%
Standard deviation	16.94%	0.63%	3.84%	0.71%	0.67%	0.14%	0.62%	5.84%	4.92%
25th percentile	1.40%	0.00%	− 0.12%	0.00%	0.00%	0.00%	0.00%	− 0.50%	− 0.87%
Median	11.29%	0.00%	0.00%	0.00%	0.00%	0.00%	0.00%	0.00%	0.00%
75th percentile	16.09%	0.00%	0.23%	0.00%	0.00%	0.00%	0.05%	0.53%	1.00%
IASC Comparability and Improvements Project[d]									
Pre-adoption mean	5.45%	− 0.25%	0.72%	− 0.04%	0.00%	− 0.02%	0.16%	0.13%	0.62%
Post-adoption mean	11.24%	− 0.05%	0.21%	0.09%	− 0.18%	0.00%	0.43%	− 1.62%	− 0.28%
Means test (t-statistic)	1.55	1.44	0.60	0.87	1.23	0.73	2.00	1.36	0.82

continued overleaf

Panel B: US-GAAP owners' equity and US-GAAP reconciliation components for owners' equity (n = 86)[a]

	$\frac{BV^{US}}{BV^{IAS}}$[b]	$\frac{GW}{BV^{IAS}}$[c]	$\frac{DFTX}{BV^{IAS}}$	$\frac{FOREXCH}{BV^{IAS}}$	$\frac{R\&D}{BV^{IAS}}$	$\frac{PENSION}{BV^{IAS}}$	$\frac{REVAL}{BV^{IAS}}$	$\frac{OTHER}{BV^{IAS}}$	$\frac{BV^{US-IAS}}{BV^{IAS}}$
Mean	100.21%	1.83%	1.10%	− 0.21%	− 0.12%	0.04%	− 1.81%	− 0.62%	0.21%
Standard deviation	21.32%	5.18%	8.49%	0.85%	0.66%	0.60%	6.02%	18.93%	21.32%
25th percentile	98.09%	0.00%	0.00%	0.00%	0.00%	0.00%	− 0.73%	− 1.84%	− 1.91%
Median	99.96%	0.00%	0.00%	0.00%	0.00%	0.00%	0.00%	0.00%	− 0.04%
75th percentile	103.40%	0.00%	1.58%	0.00%	0.00%	0.00%	0.00%	1.97%	3.40%
IASC Comparability and Improvements Project[d]									
Pre-adoption mean	97.69%	2.51%	1.38%	− 0.32%	− 0.04%	0.09%	− 2.33%	− 3.60%	− 2.31%
Post-adoption mean	104.25%	0.74%	0.65%	− 0.04%	− 0.24%	− 0.05%	− 0.97%	4.16%	4.25%
Means test (t-statistic)	1.40	1.55	0.39	1.49	1.32	1.11	1.02	1.87	1.40

[a] Positive reconciliation amounts reflect additions to IAS amounts to arrive at US-GAAP amounts.

[b] E^{IAS} (BV^{IAS}) is earnings (owners equity) reported by firms calculated using IAS; E^{US} (BV^{US}) is earnings (owners equity) reported by firms calculated using US-GAAP.

[c] US-GAAP reconciliation adjustments: *GW* is goodwill; *DFTX* is deferred income taxes; *FOREXCH* is foreign exchange; *R&D* is research and development; *PENSION* is pensions; *REVAL* is tangible asset revaluations; and *OTHER* is all other adjustments.

[d] The IASC completed its Comparability and Improvements Project in 1993 with ten new standards becoming effective 1 January 1995.

a more detailed discussion). In IAS 2 (IASC, 1993a), FIFO and weighted average cost became the preferred inventory methods; LIFO was designated an acceptable alternative. In IAS 9 (IASC, 1993b), development expenditures meeting the criteria for capitalization can no longer be expensed at management discretion but must be recognized as assets and amortized. In IAS 11 (IASC, 1993c) the completed contract method of accounting was eliminated as an alternative method. In IAS 16 (IASC, 1993d), historical cost became the preferred method for property, plant, and equipment; fair value was designated an acceptable alternative. In IAS 19 (IASC, 1993e), the accrued-benefit valuation method became the preferred method for measuring pension service costs; the projected benefit method was designated an acceptable alternative. Finally, in IAS 22 (IASC, 1993g), the option to immediately charge goodwill to equity was eliminated, instead, goodwill must be capitalized and amortized. In addition, negative goodwill is now reduced by the fair value of non-monetary assets, with any remainder being recognized as a liability and amortized into income over its expected life. Changes were also made to IAS for the reporting of discontinued operations, foreign currency translations, and borrowing costs.

Descriptive information about IAS earnings and US-GAAP book values and about the US-GAAP reconciliation components, deflated by IAS owners' equity, is presented in Table 2. Influential observations excluded from later empirical tests are also excluded from the descriptive information presented in Table 2. As can be seen from panel A, the aggregate earnings reconciliation adjustment averages 0.28% of IAS owners' equity. Similarly, the aggregate owners' equity reconciliation adjustment averages 0.21% of IAS owners' equity (panel B, Table 2). Although the magnitudes of the aggregate reconciliation adjustments appear on average to be relatively small, this is likely due to the fact that some adjustments are generally negative (e.g., goodwill amortization), while other adjustments are generally positive (e.g., tangible asset revaluation depreciation adjustments). Consistent with this, the standard deviations of the aggregate adjustments are much larger, 4.92% of owners' equity for earnings adjustments and 21.32% of owners equity for equity adjustments.

Although a separate investigation of the US-GAAP reconciliation components might be interesting, because of the limited number of independent observations available, we do not attempt to examine the association of each component with market values, prices-per-share, or returns. However, we do examine the distribution of the components before and after the implementation of the IASC's Comparability and Improvements Project, which affected financial statements beginning on or after 1 January, 1995. As can be seen in Table 2, the distribution of the components appears quite similar. Tests of differences in the means were insignificant, with the exceptions of the reconciliation adjustment from IAS earnings for asset revaluations (t-statistic = 2.00) and the reconciliation adjustment from IAS owners' equity for other reconciliation items (t-statistic = 1.87). Whether the aggregate US-GAAP reconciliation amounts are value-relevant is examined next.

3. Research design

We investigate the value-relevance, incremental, and relative association of IAS measures of earnings and owners' equity versus US-GAAP measures with market value, price-per-share, and return models. To facilitate comparison with prior research examining Foreign-GAAP and US-GAAP (Amir et al., 1993; Barth and Clinch, 1996; Rees and Elgers, 1997), we adopt the following market value model which relates a company's earnings and book value measured under IAS and the US-GAAP reconciliation amounts to its market value:

$$MV_{jt} = \alpha_0 + \alpha_1 BV_{jt}^{\mathrm{IAS}} + \alpha_2 E_{jt}^{\mathrm{IAS}} + \alpha_3 BV_{jt}^{\mathrm{US-IAS}} + \alpha_4 E_{jt}^{\mathrm{US-IAS}} + \alpha_5 SHR_{jt}^{+} \varepsilon_{jt}, \tag{1}$$

where

MV_{jt} = market value of owners' equity for firm j six months after fiscal year-end of period t,
BV_{jt}^{IAS} = the book value of owners' equity calculated under IAS for firm j at time t,
E_{jt}^{IAS} = the earnings calculated under IAS for firm j at time t,
$BV_{jt}^{\mathrm{US-IAS}}$ = the difference between US-GAAP and IAS book value of owners' equity for firm j at time t,
$E_{jt}^{\mathrm{US-IAS}}$ = the difference between US-GAAP and IAS earnings for firm j at time t, and
SHR_{jt} = number of shares outstanding for firm j at time t.

Consistent with the suggestions of Barth and Kallapur (1996), Eq. (1) is estimated undeflated with White's (1980) correction for heteroskedasticity and a separate variable to proxy for scale is included, number of common shares outstanding (SHR_{jt}). However, in order to examine the robustness of our results to alternative specifications, we also estimate Eq. (1) using the number of shares outstanding as a deflator (i.e., a price-per-share specification). Eq. (1) is estimated using a pooled sample.[7]

[7] To control for possible autocorrelation in the pooled sample, we also estimated Eq. (1) using only the most recent observation per firm. In unreported tests, our inferences are identical to those discussed in Section 4, with the exception that IAS amounts are no longer more highly associated with prices-per-share than US-GAAP amounts.

US-GAAP earnings and book value reconciliation amounts were collected from firms' 20-F filings.[8] Earnings, book value of owners' equity, dividend, number of shares outstanding and market value information was collected from Datastream International. IAS reported accounting measures collected from the 20-F filing were checked against the Datastream data for consistency. Home-country market values were selected for our empirical tests.[9] As discussed in Amir et al. (1993), home-country and US security prices should be equal assuming no arbitrage.[10]

To ensure that the market has access to the information in the Form 20-F filing, the market value of owners' equity is measured six months after fiscal year-end because foreign registrants typically wait until the end of the 180 days they have to file their Form 20-F with the SEC (Amir et al., 1993). For Canadian firms the market value of owners' equity is measured three months after fiscal year-end because Canadian registrants have 90 days to file their Form 10-K with the SEC. All variables are measured in firms' domestic currencies. A positive coefficient on the E_{jt}^{IAS} (BV_{jt}^{IAS}) variable would indicate that IAS earnings (book value) reflect value-relevant information. The coefficients for the $E_{jt}^{\text{US-IAS}}$ and $BV_{jt}^{\text{US-IAS}}$ variables provide tests of whether the US-GAAP reconciliation adjustments are incrementally valued by the market after controlling for IAS amounts (i.e., it provides a test of the composition of earnings and book value that is valued by the market). In addition, the specification of Eq. (1) allows us to examine whether the market values IAS and US-GAAP amounts differently by testing whether the coefficients for the IAS and US-GAAP variables are equivalent. This test provides evidence on whether IAS and US-GAAP amounts are interpreted differently by the market. The market may interpret IAS and US-GAAP amounts differently as the earnings amounts may reflect items that differ in their persistence and book value amounts may be measured with differing amounts of error relative to their underlying economic values. We also use Eq. (1) to compare the relative association of IAS

---

[8] In Italy, IAS are adopted in the absence of a standard under the National Councils of the Italian Accounting Profession. For the Italian firms, we checked each US-GAAP reconciliation adjustment for its conformance to IAS. If IAS and US-GAAP were the same, we removed this adjustment from the reconciliation amount and added it to the IAS measure as this represents an adjustment from Italian GAAP to IAS rather than IAS to US-GAAP. We made seven such adjustments for four firms.

[9] Home-country market values were unavailable for three firms. US amounts were collected for these firms and converted to the firms home country currency.

[10] Amir et al. (1993) provide support for this assumption by investigating the correlation between translated home country and US security prices. The Pearson (Spearman) correlations for their sample were 0.998 (0.999) for fiscal year end prices and 0.988 (0.992) for six months after fiscal year end prices.

versus US-GAAP amounts with firm value. Similar tests have been adopted to investigate the relative association of foreign versus US-GAAP (Chan and Seow, 1996) and accounting earnings versus cash flows (Biddle et al., 1995; Dechow, 1994) with security returns. Thus, this test will provide evidence on the question of whether IAS or US-GAAP provide relatively better summary measures as indicated by market values.

To investigate the relative association of IAS versus US-GAAP amounts with market values we use the recently developed Siegel and Biddle (1994) test. The Siegel and Biddle (1994) measure is a test of competing nonnested models, in this case IAS versus US-GAAP. Alternative methods for testing relative association include those described by Davidson and MacKinnon (1981) and Vuong (1989). In contrast to these alternatives, the Siegel and Biddle test is finite sample exact and can be used in conjunction with White's (1980) correction for heteroskedasticity. Thus, this test, given our sample size, potentially provides a more powerful test of which GAAP, IAS or US, is more highly associated with market values.

Following Kothari and Zimmerman's suggestion (Kothari and Zimmerman, 1995) (p. 34) that "use of both return and price models has the potential to yield more convincing evidence", and because scale and heteroskedasticity problems are largely mitigated in return estimations relative to levels-based specifications (Christie, 1987; Easton, 1998), we adopt the following return model to complement our levels-based analysis and conduct the same tests as discussed above:

$$R_{jt} = \beta_0 + \beta_1 \frac{E_{jt}^{\mathrm{IAS}}}{MV_{jt-1}} + \beta_2 \frac{\Delta E_{jt}^{\mathrm{IAS}}}{MV_{jt-1}} + \beta_3 \frac{E_{jt}^{\mathrm{US-IAS}}}{MV_{jt-1}} + \beta_4 \frac{\Delta E_{jt}^{\mathrm{US-IAS}}}{MV_{jt-1}} + \eta_{jt}, \tag{2}$$

where

R_{jt} = stock return (inclusive of dividends) for firm j during year t,
E_{jt}^{IAS} = earnings calculated under IAS for firm j at time t,
$\Delta E_{jt}^{\mathrm{IAS}}$ = the change in IAS earnings for firm j from period $t-1$ to period t,
$E_{jt}^{\mathrm{US-IAS}}$ = the difference between US-GAAP and IAS earnings for firm j at time t, and
$\Delta E_{jt}^{\mathrm{US-IAS}}$ = the change in the difference between US-GAAP and IAS earnings for firm j from period $t-1$ to period t.

The form of Eq. (2) is identical to that used in Amir et al. (1993), and Barth and Clinch (1996) to investigate the value-relevance of reconciliations from Foreign-GAAP to US-GAAP. Consistent with previous research, returns are measured over the 12 month period ending six months after fiscal year end to coincide with the Form 20-F filing deadline. For the Canadian firms in our sample, returns are measured over the 12 month period ending three months after fiscal year end to coincide with the 10-K filing deadline.[11] All coefficients in Eq. (2) are expected to be positive. Of particular interest are the variables E_{jt}^{US-IAS} and ΔE_{jt}^{US-IAS}. If the aggregate US-GAAP reconciliation adjustments are valued by the market, after controlling for IAS earnings and the change in IAS earnings, then we expect both coefficients to be positive. We also investigate whether the market values IAS and US-GAAP amounts differently by testing the equality of the IAS and US-GAAP earnings coefficients and the change in earnings coefficients. Finally, we test whether IAS or US-GAAP is more highly associated with returns using the Siegel and Biddle (1994) test.

4. Empirical results

Panels A and B of Table 3 report the descriptive statistics for the variables included in Eqs. (1) and (2). The descriptive statistics and regression results reflect the removal of observations determined to be influential. Observations were considered influential if the absolute value of their R-student ratio (see Belsley et al., 1980) measured in Eqs. (1) and (2) were greater than three. This procedure resulted in the deletion of three observations from the market value and price-per-share samples, and four from the returns sample.[12]

From panel A, the mean (median) market value for the sample firms is \$4,262.4 (\$1,480.5) millions of US dollars and there is a great deal of variation in firm size. Earnings, calculated under IAS and measured in millions of US dollars, have a mean of \$189.7 and a median of \$46.0. For comparison, in unreported analyses, the mean (median) of the market-to-book ratio, with book value calculated using IAS, is 2.56 (1.74), which is quite similar to that reported in Amir et al. (1993) and Rees and Elgers (1997) in their investigation of Foreign versus US-GAAP. From panel B, the mean (median) difference between US-GAAP and IAS earnings deflated by lagged market value of − 0.002 (0.000) is smaller than the difference between Foreign and US-GAAP reported in Amir et al. (1993), mean (median) − 0.006 (− 0.005). In addition, the standard deviation of the difference between US-GAAP and IAS earnings deflated by lagged price of 0.032 is smaller than the standard deviation of the difference between Foreign and US-GAAP reported in Amir et al. (1993) of 0.12. Thus, the difference

[11] To investigate the sensitivity of our results, we also measure returns over the 15 month-period ending 6 months after fiscal year end (three months for Canadian firms). A similar returns window is adopted by Chan and Seow (1996) in their investigation of Foreign versus US-GAAP. Our inferences remain unchanged relative to those reported in Section 4.

[12] Our inferences remain unaffected by the removal of outliers in the levels-based analyses. However, our results appear much more reasonable after the removal of outliers in the returns analysis; the adjusted R^2 for Eq. (2) before (after) the removal of outliers was 58.76% (17.28%).

Table 3
Descriptive statistics for regression variables

The sample consists of all non-US firms adopting International Accounting Standards in their primary accounts with a reconciliation to US-GAAP in their Form 20-F filing during the period 1992–1996.

Panel A: Descriptive statistics for variables in Eq. (1), in millions of US dollars, except SHR_{jt} which is in millions, number of observations = 86

Variable	Mean	Median	Standard deviation	Minimum	Maximum
MV_{jt}	4,262.4	1,480.5	7,163.5	13.1	40,777.0
BV_{jt}^{IAS}	2,313.0	636.2	3,403.4	8.7	14,968.0
E_{jt}^{IAS}	189.7	46.0	568.6	− 1,123.3	2,812.6
BV_{jt}^{US-IAS}	53.5	− 0.1	389.5	− 860.0	1,937.6
E_{jt}^{US-IAS}	8.7	0.0	119.1	− 778.1	367.3
SHR_{jt}	825.7	113.9	1,595.5	1.7	7,999.2

Panel B: Descriptive statistics for variables in Eq. (2), deflated by lagged market value, number of observations = 54.

Variable	Mean	Median	Standard deviation	Minimum	Maximum
R_{jt}	0.191	0.138	0.337	− 0.451	1.042
E_{jt}^{IAS}	0.044	0.049	0.070	− 0.158	0.198
ΔE_{jt}^{IAS}	0.018	0.009	0.086	− 0.255	0.382
E_{jt}^{US-IAS}	− 0.002	0.000	0.032	− 0.188	0.082
ΔE_{jt}^{US-IAS}	− 0.005	0.000	0.042	− 0.176	0.120

MV_{jt} = market value of owners' equity for firm j six months after fiscal year-end of period t,
BV_{jt}^{IAS} = book value of owners' equity reported under IAS for firm j at time t,
E_{jt}^{IAS} = earnings reported under IAS for firm j at time t,
BV_{jt}^{US-IAS} = the difference between US-GAAP and IAS book value of owners' equity for firm j at time t,
E_{jt}^{US-IAS} = the difference between US-GAAP and IAS earnings for firm j at time t.
R_{jt} = annual stock return (inclusive of dividends) for firm j for the period ending six months after fiscal year-end of period t,
ΔE_{jt}^{IAS} = the change in IAS earnings for firm j from period $t-1$ to period t,
ΔE_{jt}^{US-IAS} = the change in the difference between US-GAAP and IAS earnings for firm j from period $t-1$ to period t, and
SHR_{jt} = number of shares outstanding for firm j at time t.

between IAS and US-GAAP earnings, for our sample firms, is generally smaller than the difference between foreign and US-GAAP earnings observed in previous research. Consistent with this, the book value reconciliation amounts between IAS and US-GAAP, mean (median) 0.0021 (− 0.0004) deflated by IAS book value, reported in panel B of Table 2, are also smaller than those reported in Amir et al. (1993).

Panel A of Table 4 reports results from estimating Eq. (1) with all observations pooled across time. The first set of results in panel A are from estimating

Table 4
Tests comparing the association of IAS and US-GAAP measures of earnings and book value with market values ($n = 86$), prices-per-share ($n = 86$) and stock returns ($n = 54$)

The sample consists of all non-US firms adopting International Accounting Standards in their primary accounts with a reconciliation to US-GAAP in their Form 20-F filing during the period 1992–1996 (t-statistics in parentheses)[a].

Panel A: $MV_{jt} = \alpha_0 + \alpha_1 BV_{jt}^{IAS} + \alpha_2 E_{jt}^{IAS} + \alpha_3 BV_{jt}^{US-IAS} + \alpha_4 E_{jt}^{US-IAS} + \alpha_5 SHR_{jt} + \varepsilon_{jt}$

Variable	Market value		Price-per-share	
INTERCEPT	190.28	259.68	14.64	19.13
	(0.90)	(1.21)	(1.65)	(1.53)
BV_{jt}^{IAS}	1.07	0.90	1.34	1.33
	(4.81)	(4.62)	(10.13)	(9.80)
E_{jt}^{IAS}	4.63	5.69	4.77	4.71
	(5.53)	(6.70)	(3.58)	(3.45)
BV_{jt}^{US-IAS}		– 1.12		0.06
		(– 1.10)		(0.59)
E_{jt}^{US-IAS}		11.17		3.56
		(3.94)		(1.38)
SHR_{jt}	0.86	0.97		
	(2.09)	(3.61)		
R^2_{adj}	87.96%	90.62%	35.36%	34.49%
Test equality of coefficients				
Difference in α_1 and α_3		2.02		1.27
		(1.88)		(6.59)
Difference in α_2 and α_4		5.48		1.15
		(2.13)		(0.39)
Comparison of IAS vs. US-GAAP[b]				
Siegel–Biddle χ^2		1.83		7.70
p-value		0.18		0.01

Panel B: $R_{jt} = \beta_0 + \beta_1 \dfrac{E_{jt}^{IAS}}{MV_{jt-1}} + \beta_2 \dfrac{\Delta E_{jt}^{IAS}}{MV_{jt-1}} + \beta_3 \dfrac{E_{jt}^{US-IAS}}{MV_{jt-1}} + \beta_4 \dfrac{\Delta E_{jt}^{US-IAS}}{MV_{jt-1}} + \eta_{jt}$

Variable		
INTERCEPT	0.14	0.14
	(2.47)	(2.67)
E_{jt}^{IAS}	1.18	1.11
	(1.25)	(1.41)
ΔE_{jt}^{IAS}	– 0.11	1.81
	(– 0.19)	(2.03)
E_{jt}^{US-IAS}		0.52
		(0.20)
ΔE_{jt}^{US-IAS}		4.83
		(1.92)
R^2_{adj}	1.47%	17.28%

Table 4, Panel B (*continued*)

Variable	
Test equality of coefficients	
Difference in β_1 and β_3	0.59
	(0.40)
Difference in β_2 and β_4	3.02
	(2.03)
Comparison of IAS vs. US-GAAP[b]	
Siegel–Biddle χ^2	3.74
p-value	0.05

MV_{jt} = market value of owners' equity for firm j six months after fiscal year-end of period t,
BV_{jt}^{IAS} = book value of owners' equity reported under IAS for firm j at time t,
E_{jt}^{IAS} = earnings reported under IAS for firm j at time t,
$BV_{jt}^{\text{US-IAS}}$ = the difference between US-GAAP and IAS book value of owners' equity for firm j at time t,
$E_{jt}^{\text{US-IAS}}$ = the difference between US-GAAP and IAS earnings for firm j at time t,
SHR_{jt} = number of shares outstanding for firm j at time t,
R_{jt} = annual stock return (inclusive of dividends) for firm j for the period ending six months after fiscal year-end of period t,
$\Delta E_{jt}^{\text{IAS}}$ = the change in IAS earnings for firm j from period $t-1$ to period t, and
$\Delta E_{jt}^{\text{US-IAS}}$ = the change in the difference between US-GAAP and IAS earnings for firm j from period $t-1$ to period t.

[a]Reported t-statistics are White (1980) adjusted.
[b]The Siegel–Biddle χ^2 statistic compares earnings and book values computed using IAS to earnings and book values computed using US-GAAP as competing nonnested models. Reported probability levels are based on a two-tailed test.

Eq. (1) undeflated, with a separate scale proxy variable (e.g., number of shares outstanding) and White (1980) standard errors. The second set of results are from using the number of shares outstanding as a deflator (i.e., a price-per-share specification). For comparison, the results of estimating Eq. (1) using only IAS earnings and book value amounts are also presented for both specifications.

For the market value estimation, when only IAS amounts are included in the model, the adjusted R^2 is 87.96% and the estimated coefficients on earnings and book value are both significantly positive at the 1% level indicating that IAS book values and earnings reflect value-relevant information. When the reconciliation amounts between IAS and US-GAAP are included, the adjusted R^2 increases to 90.62% and the estimated coefficients on IAS earnings and book value remain significantly positive. More importantly, the estimated coefficient on the US-GAAP earnings reconciliation adjustment amount, $E_{jt}^{\text{US-IAS}}$, is significantly positive at the 1% level (coefficient = 11.17, t-statistic = 3.94). This is consistent with the US-GAAP earnings reconciliation adjustment being incrementally associated with market values after controlling for IAS amounts. In addition, the estimated coefficient on the $E_{jt}^{\text{US-IAS}}$ variable is significantly more than the estimated coefficient on the E_{jt}^{IAS} variable (difference = 5.48, t-statistic = 2.13), indicating that US-GAAP earnings amounts are valued as having greater persistence than IAS earnings amounts by the market. However, the estimated coefficient on the aggregate book value reconciliation, BV_{jt}^{US-IAS}, is not significantly different from zero (coefficient = − 1.12, t-statistic = − 1.10), and the estimated coefficient on BV_{jt}^{IAS} is greater than the estimated coefficient on BV_{jt}^{US-IAS} (difference = 2.02, t-statistic = 1.88). The estimated Siegel and Biddle (1994) test value is positive and insignificant ($\chi^2 = 1.83$) with a p-value of 0.18 (two-sided test). Thus, we do not find evidence that US-GAAP amounts are more highly associated with market values than IAS amounts.[13]

For the price-per-share estimation, when only IAS amounts are included in the model, the adjusted R^2 is 35.36% and the estimated coefficients on earnings and book value are both significantly positive at the 1% level indicating that IAS book values and earnings reflect value-relevant information. In contrast to the market value estimation results, when the reconciliation amounts between IAS and US-GAAP are included, the adjusted R^2 decreases to 34.49%. Consistent with this, the estimated coefficient on the US-GAAP earnings reconciliation adjustment amount, E_{jt}^{US-IAS}, is not significantly positive at conventional levels (coefficient = 3.56, t-statistic = 1.38). In addition, the estimated coefficient on the E_{jt}^{US-IAS} variable is not significantly different than the estimated coefficient on the E_{jt}^{IAS} variable (difference = 1.15, t-statistic = 0.39). Thus, for the price-per-share estimation we do not find evidence that the US-GAAP earnings reconciliation is value-relevant or incrementally associated with security prices.[14] The

[13] In contrast to our findings, Amir et al. (1993) find evidence that both the US-GAAP reconciliation adjustments for shareholders' equity and earnings are value-relevant. However, as reconciliations to US-GAAP from IAS and Foreign-GAAP do not measure earnings and book value in the same manner and as our firms do not provide a reconciliation to IAS from Foreign-GAAP, a direct comparison of our results with those of Amir et al. (1993) is not possible.

[14] As the issue of the appropriate deflator for levels-based research designs is currently unresolved (e.g., Christie, 1987; Barth and Kallapur, 1996; Easton, 1998), we also examine the robustness of our tests to the use of book-value of equity as the deflator. The use of book value of equity has commonly been used in levels-based regressions investigating the value-relevance of US-GAAP reconciliation amounts (Amir et al., 1993; Barth and Clinch, 1996; Rees and Elgers, 1997). In addition, the use of book value of equity is consistent with the recommendations of Easton (1998), who further cautions on the use of the price-per-share value metric to mitigate scale effects. In untabulated tests, the use of either US-GAAP or IAS book value of equity as deflators yield inferences identical to the results from the undeflated market valuation estimation of Eq. (1) in Table 4. In order to obtain some insight into which deflator, number of shares outstanding or book value of equity, best explains the nature of the heteroskedasticity in Eq. (1), we use White's (1980) test to directly examine the nature of the heteroskedasticity. Such an investigation reveals that either US-GAAP or IAS book value explains the nature of the heteroskedasticity in Eq. (1) better than the number of shares outstanding, and thus are preferable deflators to mitigate the impact of heteroskedasticity. Specifically, the R^2 from regressing the squared residuals from the undeflated market valuation estimation of Eq. (1) on the square of shares outstanding is only 5.97%, whereas the R^2 from regressing the same squared residuals on the square of US-GAAP book value (IAS book value) is 21.72% (25.20%).

estimated coefficient on the aggregate book value reconciliation, BV_{jt}^{US-IAS}, is again not significantly different from zero (coefficient = 0.06, t-statistic = 0.59), and the estimated coefficient on BV_{jt}^{IAS} is again greater than the estimated coefficient on BV_{jt}^{US-IAS} (difference = 1.27, t-statistic = 6.59). In contrast to the market value estimation results, the estimated Siegel and Biddle (1994) test value is negative and significant ($\chi^2 = 7.70$) with a p-value of 0.01 (two-sided test). Thus, we find evidence that IAS amounts are more highly associated with prices-per-share than US-GAAP amounts.

Panel B of Table 4 reports the results of estimating Eq. (2). Again, results of regressing returns onto IAS amounts only are presented. In contrast to the results in panel A, IAS amounts alone do not explain much of the variation in returns; the adjusted R^2 is 1.47% and both estimated coefficients are insignificant. When the US-GAAP reconciliation amounts are included in the model the adjusted R^2 increases to 17.28% and the estimated coefficient on the change in IAS earnings becomes significant (coefficient = 1.81, t-statisic = 2.03). Consistent with the market value estimation results in panel A, the estimated coefficient on the change in the US-GAAP earnings reconciliation amount is significantly positive (coefficient = 4.83, t-statistic = 1.92) supporting the conclusion that the US-GAAP earnings reconciliation amounts are valued by the market after controlling for IAS amounts. Moreover, as reported in panel B, the estimated coefficient on the ΔE_{jt}^{US-IAS} variable is significantly greater than the estimated coefficient on the ΔE_{jt}^{IAS} variable (difference = 3.02, t-statistic = 2.03), again indicating that IAS and US-GAAP amounts have different valuation implications to investors. The estimated coefficient on the US-GAAP earnings reconciliation amount is insignificant. In contrast to the market value and price-per-share estimation results, the estimated Siegel and Biddle (1994) test value is positive and significant ($\chi^2 = 3.74$) with a p-value of 0.05 (two-sided test) indicating that US-GAAP amounts are more highly associated with annual returns than IAS measures. Thus, US-GAAP appears to be a better performance measure as reflected by stock returns than IAS. Because IAS are generally considered to be more stringent than foreign accounting standards, this finding appears inconsistent with Chan and Seow's (1996) finding that Foreign-GAAP measures are more highly associated with returns than US-GAAP. Unfortunately, because our sample firms do not provide a reconciliation between Foreign-GAAP and IAS, we are unable to directly examine whether IAS is a better performance measure than Foreign-GAAP.

5. Sensitivity analysis

As the decisions to adopt IAS and to list in the US are voluntary, our sample firms do not represent a random sample of foreign firms. In order to formally investigate the impact of self-selection on our reported results, we follow the two-stage switching regression procedure suggested by Heckman (1979). In the first stage, using a probit model, we analyze the decision to jointly adopt International Accounting Standards and list in the US. We match each sample firm, based on industry and size, with a comparison firm from the same country that reports using Foreign-GAAP and is not listed in the US.[15,16] We adopt a matched-pair design to control for differences in costs of adopting IAS and listing in the US, as such costs should be similar for firms of similar size from the same country and industry. Examples of such costs include competitive disadvantage costs due to recognition of IAS information and disclosure of US-GAAP amounts and accounting preparation costs due to IAS adoption and the US-GAAP reconciliation requirement. The dependent variable in our probit analysis, $CHOICE_{jt}$, equals 1 for the sample firms and 0 for the comparison firms. We include the following variables as explanatory variables in the analysis and expect all variables to be positively related to the choice to list in the US and follow IAS:

Growth ($GROWTH_{jt}$). As growing firms have greater capital needs and access capital markets more frequently, we include a variable for growth, defined as sales growth over the past five years, to proxy for firms' demand for new capital.

Number of foreign markets in which the firm's shares are traded ($NMKT_{jt}$). Because IAS may be preferred by foreign investors (e.g., IAS could be viewed as being more comparable and informative than Foreign and US-GAAP (Ashbaugh, 1997), we include a variable for the number of foreign markets in which the firm's shares are traded, excluding the US, to proxy for the information demands of foreign investors.

Relative size ($RSIZE_{jt}$). Saudagaran (1988), Biddle and Saudagaran (1989), and Ashbaugh (1997) provide evidence that because local demand for additional shares may be relatively inelastic, firms that are large by domestic standards may have a greater need to access larger foreign capital markets to reduce their cost of capital. Consistent with this, we include a variable for relative size, defined as the market value of a firm's common shares as a proportion of the total market value of the firm's domestic stock exchange, to proxy for firms' desire to access foreign capital.

---

[15] The sample selection procedure results in an oversampling of US listed foreign firms adopting IAS. This oversampling can result in biased slope coefficients in our probit model, and, thus, a biased inverse mills ratio estimate. However, our first stage results are similar using a logit model, which does not suffer from biased slope coefficients. This indicates that any bias from oversampling is likely small.

[16] We match on industry using 4-digit SIC codes. As a 4-digit match was not always available, two (five) industry matches were made using 3-digit (2-digit) SIC codes. We match on size using net sales.

Leverage (LEV_{jt}). As Botosan and Frost (1998) provide evidence that more highly leveraged, US-listed foreign firms provide greater disclosure, we include a variable for leverage, defined as long-term debt divided by common equity.

Coverage by domestic (home-country) and foreign analysts (AN_D_{jt}, AN_F_{jt}). Botosan and Frost (1998) provide evidence that greater analyst coverage is positively associated with disclosure for a sample of US-listed foreign firms. Lang and Lundholm (1996) provide similar evidence for US firms. Consistent with this, we include variables for the number of domestic and foreign analysts covering the sample and comparison firms.

Issuance of equity and debt (EQ_{jt}, $DEBT_{jt}$). Frankel et al. (1995) and Lang and Lundholm (1993) provide evidence that firms increase their discretionary disclosures when accessing capital markets. We include indicator variables for firms' issuing equity and/or debt in the current year to proxy for firms' propensities to access equity and debt markets, respectively.

Financial performance (ROE_{jt}). As Lang and Lundholm (1993) provide evidence that firms' discretionary disclosure increases with greater financial performance, we include a variable for financial performance, return on equity.

We also include an indicator variable for Italian firms ($ITAL_{jt}$) as Italian firms are required to prepare their accounts under IAS when no Italian standard exists. Financial and market information was collected from Worldscope and Datastream International. The number of foreign equity markets in which a firm's shares are traded was collected from Bloomberg Financial Services. Financial analyst coverage information was collected from Nelson's Directory of Investment Research. In the second stage of the Heckman (1979) procedure, we use the predicted probabilities from the probit estimation to construct a self-selection variable (i.e., the inverse-mills-ratio), and include it in our Eq. (1) to mitigate any bias caused by self-selection.

The results for the probit estimation for 104 observations, 52 sample and 52 comparison firm observations, are as follows (asymptotic *t*-statistics in parentheses):

$$\begin{aligned} CH\hat{O}ICE_{jt} = & -3.733 + 0.019GROWTH_{jt} + 0.266NMKT_{jt} \\ & (-3.495) \quad (2.380) \qquad\qquad (1.758) \\ & + 31.845RSIZE_{jt} + 0.003LEV_{jt} - 0.023AN\_D_{jt} \\ & \quad (1.990) \qquad\qquad (2.100) \qquad (-0.621) \\ & + 0.159AN\_F_{jt} + 0.318EQ_{jt} + 1.137DEBT_{jt} \\ & \quad (3.814) \qquad\quad (0.398) \qquad (1.557) \\ & + 0.006ROE_{jt} + 0.067ITAL_{jt}. \\ & \quad (0.908) \qquad\quad (0.085) \end{aligned}$$

As can be seen, the estimated coefficients for growth, number of foreign markets in which the firm's shares are traded, relative size, leverage, and coverage by foreign analysts are positive and significant at less than a 5% level. The explanatory power of the estimated model is relatively high, with a pseudo-R^2 of 58.63%.

In the second stage of the Heckman (1979) procedure, in unreported tests, the estimated coefficient for the inverse-mills ratio included in the undeflated market value and price-per-share estimations of Eq. (1) are significant (t-statistics = 1.762 and 2.688); however, all other estimated coefficients remain virtually unchanged and all prior inferences remain unchanged. Thus, the impact of self-selection on our results appears to be minimal.

The use of market-based accounting research techniques (which rely on the use of historical data) to investigate the value-relevance of two alternative accounting systems for the purposes of making comparisons between those standards is difficult because accounting standards under both systems are continuously being revised and new standards issued. In the case of a comparison of IAS and US-GAAP, this is especially true. For instance, the IASC's Comparability and Improvements Project which eliminated alternative accounting methods and improved the overall quality of IAS became effective for financial statements covering periods beginning on or after 1 January 1995. Furthermore, the IASC completed a core set of international accounting standards in 1998 for consideration for acceptance by the International Organization of Securities Commissions and the US SEC. In the US, the Financial Accounting Standards Board (FASB) has also issued a large number of important accounting standards in the last few years and is in the process of issuing more in the near future.

The enactment of the IASC's Comparability and Improvements Project is viewed as a significant improvement in IASC standards during the time period we study (Harris, 1995). In order to ensure that our results generalize to these more current IAS reporting requirements, we re-estimated Eq. (1) using only those observations from fiscal years beginning on or after 1 January 1995. Consistent with the evidence in Table 4, in untabulated tests, for the undeflated market value estimation of Eq. (1) the US-GAAP earnings reconciliation adjustment was value-relevant and the Siegel and Biddle (1994) relative association test statistic was insignificant. However, the US-GAAP earnings adjustment was not valued significantly different than IAS earnings. In addition, for the price-per-share estimation of Eq. (1) the US-GAAP earnings reconciliation adjustment was again insignificant; however, we no longer find that IAS amounts are more highly associated with prices-per-share than US-GAAP amounts. We were unable to re-estimate Eq. (2) over this more recent time period due to the lack of a reasonable sample size.

6. Summary and concluding comments

Our study contributes to the debate between the US Securities and Exchange Commission and the New York Stock Exchange over whether foreign firms should be allowed to list their securities in US markets without a US-GAAP reconciliation if they follow IAS. Using a sample of foreign firms that adopt IAS in their primary accounts and report a reconciliation to US-GAAP, we investigate whether US-GAAP reconciliation amounts provide information beyond IAS amounts, whether investors value these amounts differently, and whether IAS or US-GAAP is more highly associated with market values, security prices, and returns.

We find evidence that US-GAAP earnings reconciliation amounts are value-relevant after controlling for IAS amounts for market value and return models. We also find evidence that the US-GAAP earnings reconciliation adjustment is valued differently than IAS earnings for market value and return models. These inferences, however, must be tempered by the fact that we fail to find a significant association between US-GAAP earnings reconciliation amounts and prices-per-share. In tests examining which accounting method, IAS or US-GAAP, produces amounts that are most highly associated with prices-per-share and security returns, we find evidence that IAS amounts are more highly associated with prices-per-share than US-GAAP amounts and that US-GAAP amounts are more highly associated with security returns than IAS amounts. Our test of a greater association between market values and either IAS or US-GAAP amounts are inconclusive. As the inconsistent nature of our levels-based results may be due to coefficient bias and heteroskedasticity arising from scale differences (Barth and Kallapur, 1996; Easton, 1998), one may wish to place greater weight on our return-based results which are affected less by such problems (Christie, 1987). Taken together, subject to the caveat that investors may be able to obtain US-GAAP reconciliation information from sources other than the Form 20-F filing, our results provide limited evidence consistent with the current SEC position that reconciliations to US-GAAP, *even from IAS*, provide useful information to the market.

For further reading

The following reference is also of interest to the reader: Pope (1993).

References

Accounting Principles Board, 1970. Accounting Principles Board Opinion 17: intangible assets. AICPA, New York, NY.

Amir, E., Harris, T.S., Venuti, E.K., 1993. A comparison of the value-relevance of US versus non-US-GAAP accounting measures using Form 20-F reconciliations. Journal of Accounting Research Supplement 31, 230–264.

Ashbaugh, H., 1997. Non-US firms' accounting standard choices in accessing foreign capital markets. Working paper, University of Iowa, January.

Ashbaugh, H., Pincus, M., 1998. International Accounting Standards, Diversity in Accounting Standards, and the Predictability of Earnings. Working paper, University of Iowa, February.

Bandyopadhyay, S.P., Hanna, J.D., Richardson, G., 1994. Capital market effects of American-Canadian GAAP differences. Journal of Accounting Research 32, 262–277.

Barth, M.E., Clinch, G., 1996. International accounting differences and their relation to share prices: evidence from U.K., Australian, and Canadian firms. Contemporary Accounting Research 13, 135–170.

Barth, M.E., Kallapur, S., 1996. The effects of cross-sectional scale differences on regression results in empirical accounting research. Contemporary Accounting Research 13, 527–567.

Bayless, R., Cochrane, J., Harris, T.S., Leisenring, J., McLaughlin, J., Wirtz, J.P., 1996. International access to US capital markets – an AAA forum on accounting policy. Accounting Horizons 10, 75–94.

Belsley, D., Kuh, E., Welsch, R., 1980. Regression Diagnostics, Identifying Influential Data and Sources of Collinearity.. McGraw-Hill, New York, NY.

Biddle, G.C., Saudagaran, S.M., 1989. The effects of financial disclosure levels on firms' choices among alternative foreign stock exchange listings. Journal of International Financial Management and Accounting 1, 56–87.

Biddle, G.C., Seow, G.S., Siegel, A.F., 1995. Relative versus incremental information content. Contemporary Accounting Research 12, 1–23.

Botosan, C., Frost, C.A., 1998. Regulation, disclosure and market liquidity: an examination of foreign issuers in regulated versus less-regulated US equity markets. Working paper, Washington University (St. Louis).

Chan, K.C., Seow, G.S., 1996. The association between stock returns and foreign GAAP earnings versus earnings adjusted to US-GAAP. Journal of Accounting and Economics 21, 139–158.

Christie, A.A., 1987. On cross-sectional analysis in accounting research. Journal of Accounting and Economics 9, 231–258.

Coopers, Lybrand, 1993. International Accounting Summaries: A Guide for Interpretation and comparison.2nd edition. John Wiley and Sons, Inc., New York, NY.

Davidson, R., MacKinnon, J.G., 1981. Several tests for model specification in the presence of alternative hypotheses. Econometrica 49, 781–793.

Dechow, P.M., 1994. Accounting earnings and cash flows as measures of firm performance: the role of accounting accruals. Journal of Accounting and Economics 18, 3–42.

Easton, P.D., 1998. Discussion of: Revalued financial, tangible, and intangible assets: Association with share prices and non market-based value estimates. Journal of Accounting Research Supplement, Forthcoming.

Edwards, F.R., 1993. Listing of foreign securities on US exchanges. Journal of Applied Corporate Finance 5, 28–36.

FASB, 1974. Statement of Financial Accounting Standards No. 2: accounting for research and development costs. FASB, Norwalk, CT.

FASB, 1981. Statement of Financial Accounting Standards No. 52: foreign currency translation. FASB, Norwalk, CT.

FASB, 1985a. Statement of Financial Accounting Standards No. 87: employers' accounting for pensions. FASB, Norwalk, CT.

FASB, 1985b. Statement of Financial Accounting Standards No. 88: employers' accounting for settlements and curtailment of defined benefit pensions plans and for termination benefits. FASB, Norwalk, CT.

FASB, 1992. Statement of Financial Accounting Standards No. 109: accounting for income taxes. FASB, Norwalk, CT.

FASB, 1996. The IASC-US comparison project: a report on the similarities and differences between IASC standards and US-GAAP. FASB, Norwalk, CT.

Frankel, R., McNichols, M., Wilson, G.P., 1995. Discretionary disclosure and external financing. The Accounting Review 70, 135–150.

Freund, W.C., 1993. That trade obstacle, the SEC. The Wall Street Journal, August 27.

Frost, C.A., Lang, M.H., 1996. Foreign companies and US securities markets: financial reporting policy issues and suggestions for research. Accounting Horizons 10, 95–109.

Harris, T.S., 1995. International Accounting Standards versus US-GAAP reporting: empirical evidence based on case studies.. South-Western College Publishing, Cincinnati, OH.

Heckman, J., 1979. Sample selection bias as a specification error. Econometrica 47, 153–161.

IASB, 1993a. International Accounting Standard No. 2: inventories. IASC, London, England.

IASB, 1993b. International Accounting Standard No. 9: accounting for research and development activities. IASC, London, England.

IASB, 1993c. International Accounting Standard No. 11: construction contracts. IASC, London, England.

IASB, 1993d. International Accounting Standard No. 16: accounting for property, plant and equipment. IASC, London, England.

IASB, 1993e. International Accounting Standard No. 19: accounting for retirement benefits in the financial statements of employers. IASC, London, England.

IASB, 1993f. International Accounting Standard No. 21: accounting for the effects of changes in foreign exchange rates. IASC, London, England.

IASB, 1993g. International Accounting Standard No. 22: accounting for business combinations. IASC, London, England.

IASB, 1994. International Accounting Standard No. 12: accounting for taxes on income. IASC, London, England.

IASB, 1997. International Accounting Standards. IASC, London, England.

Jarrell, A., 1992. SEC crimps big board's future. The Wall Street Journal, June 19.

Kothari, S.P., Zimmerman, J.L., 1995. Price and return models. Journal of Accounting and Economics 20, 155–192.

Lang, M., Lundholm, R., 1993. Cross-sectional determinants of analysts ratings of corporate disclosures. Journal of Accounting Research 31, 246–271.

Lang, M., Lundholm, R., 1996. Corporate Disclosure Policy and Analyst Behavior. The Accounting Review 71, 467–492.

Pereira, V., 1994. Fewer alternatives permitted: the IASC has made significant amendments to certain standards. Accountancy, July, 121–122.

Pope, P., 1993. Discussion of a comparison of the value-relevance of US versus non-US-GAAP accounting measures using Form 20-F reconciliations. Journal of Accounting Research Supplement 31, 265–275.

Pope, P.F., Rees, W.P., 1993. International differences in GAAP and the pricing of earnings. Journal of International Financial Management and Accounting 4, 190–218.

Rees, L., Elgers, P., 1997. The market's valuation of non-reported accounting measures: retrospective reconciliations of non-US and US-GAAP. Journal of Accounting Research 35, 115–127.

Salwen, K.G., 1991. Breeden rejects big board plan to relax listing standards for foreign concerns. The Wall Street Journal, May, 3, C7.

Saudagaran, S., 1988. An empirical study of selected factors influencing the decision to list on foreign stock exchanges. Journal of International Business Studies 19, 101–127.

Securities and Exchange Commission, 1996. SEC Statement Regarding International Accounting Standards. Press release, April 11.

Siegel, A., Biddle, G., 1994. Comparison of regression functions in the presence of heteroskedasticity. Working paper, University of Washington.

Sutton, M., 1997. Financial reporting in US capital markets: international dimensions. Accounting Horizons 11, 96–102.

Vuong, Q.H., 1989. Likelihood ratio tests for model selection and non-nested hypotheses. Econometrica 57, 307–333.

White, H., 1980. A heteroskedasticity-consistent covariance matrix estimator and a direct test for heteroskedasticity. Econometrica 40, 817–838.

[10]

Journal of Accounting Research
Vol. 35 No. 1 Spring 1997
Printed in U.S.A.

Capsules and Comments

The Market's Valuation of Nonreported Accounting Measures: Retrospective Reconciliations of Non-U.S. and U.S. *GAAP*

LYNN REES* AND PIETER ELGERS†

1. *Introduction*

This study extends Amir, Harris, and Venuti's [1993] investigation of the association between share values or returns and reconciliations to U.S. *GAAP* as disclosed in Form 20-F, the annual report filed with the *SEC* by non-U.S. registrants.[1] While they found a highly significant association between share values and shareholders' equity reconciliations,

*Washington State University; †University of Massachusetts. We acknowledge, with thanks, the helpful comments of an anonymous reviewer and the following individuals from the *SEC*: Wayne Carnell, Richard Cohn, Paul Dodak, Richard Hohl, and other members of the *SEC* staff. Research assistance was provided by Sonny You (Barrett, You & Associates, Inc.), Carlos Mesa, and Jim Shaud (Federal Filings, Inc.). Partial funding for this project was received from the School of Management at the University of Massachusetts.

[1] Several other recent studies have also addressed the value relevance of the U.S. *GAAP* disclosures, e.g., Barth and Clinch [1996], Bandyopadhyay, Hanna, and Richardson [1994], and Pope and Rees [1993].

they argue that this evidence of value relevance does not imply the 20-F reconciliations are themselves the source of the information. In particular, short-window returns tests around the 20-F filing dates suggest that any information in the reconciliations has been impounded in prices prior to the filing dates (Amir, Harris, and Venuti [1993]).[2] Information from other sources (e.g., domestic financial statements or voluntary disclosures) may simply be captured or summarized by the 20-F reconciliations. Alternatively, reconciliation components may be sufficiently stable that investors anticipate subsequent reconciliations based on information in earlier filings (Pope [1993] and Amir, Harris, and Venuti [1993]).

We extend the work of Amir, Harris, and Venuti [1993] by analyzing income and shareholders' equity reconciliations in initial registration statements of non-U.S. registrants.[3] These initial filings provide a unique setting in which to examine the informativeness of the *SEC*-mandated disclosures since the filing firms have not previously provided U.S. *GAAP* data. The shareholders' equity (net income) reconciliations are identical to those in Form 20-F and are provided for at least the prior two (three) years for firms with a sufficient reporting history.

Retrospective reconciliations of domestic accounting reports to U.S. *GAAP* provide an opportunity to test for the existence of alternative information sources. An association between price and these retrospective reconciling items in periods *prior* to their disclosure would suggest that the *SEC*-mandated disclosures are not the exclusive source of the value-relevant information. The existence of such alternative information sources would call into question the necessity of the 20-F disclosures.

Our analysis is intended to contribute to the continuing policy debate between the New York Stock Exchange (*NYSE*) and the *SEC* (Bayless et al. [1996]). The *NYSE* has attempted to persuade the *SEC* to eliminate or change the requirement that non-U.S. firms provide U.S. *GAAP* data, based on the argument that the U.S. *GAAP* disclosures do not benefit investors (Freund [1993]).[4] Constituents of the *NYSE* also claim that the U.S. *GAAP* requirement puts U.S. security exchanges at a disadvantage in attracting more non-U.S. listings (Freund [1993] and Salwen [1991]). The *SEC* contends that the reconciliations provide important

---

[2] Amir, Harris, and Venuti [1993] argue that short-window returns tests suffer from difficulties in identifying the appropriate event window and modeling the market's expectations.

[3] The initial registration statement form depends on whether the company files under the Securities Act of 1933 (Form F-1) or under the Securities Exchange Act of 1934 (Form 20-FR).

[4] In 1990, *Staff Accounting Bulletin No. 88* released non-U.S. firms from accounting for certain items if the home country did not require accounting for that particular item. In 1991, the *SEC* conceded that Canadian firms need not provide the U.S. *GAAP* reconciliation for nonconvertible investment-grade debt and preferred stock issues. Most recently, the *SEC* has allowed non-U.S. firms to submit a cash flow statement based on *International Accounting Standard* (*IAS*) *No. 7*, in addition to accepting parts of *IAS No. 21* (accounting for hyperinflationary environments) and *IAS No. 22* (accounting for business combinations).

information to investors (Schapiro [1993]). Our results should provide additional information to policy makers about one kind of benefit derived from the U.S. *GAAP* reconciliations.

Section 2 describes the research methodology and reports our empirical results. Section 3 summarizes the findings and discusses implications.

2. *Hypotheses, Design, and Empirical Results*

2.1 HYPOTHESES

Following Amir, Harris, and Venuti [1993], we examine associations between income reconciliations and annual security returns, and associations between the shareholders' equity reconciliations and market-to-book ratios. Amir, Harris, and Venuti's annual returns test results varied widely from year to year. In contrast, results for the market-to-book models indicated value relevance for the shareholders' equity reconciliations in each period tested. Our initial tests focus on the associations between market-to-book value and the U.S. *GAAP* reconciliations, as given in expression (1), which corresponds to expression (6) in Amir, Harris, and Venuti [1993]. We estimate (1) in various time periods predating the filing of the initial registration statement:

$$\frac{P_{j,t-n}}{BV_{j,t-n}} = \beta_0 + \beta_1 \frac{E_{j,t-n}}{BV_{j,t-n}} + \beta_2 \frac{DBV_{j,t-n}}{BV_{j,t-n}} + \beta_3 \frac{DE_{j,t-n}}{BV_{j,t-n}} + e_{j,t-n} \quad (1)$$

where:

P_j is the fiscal year-end market price of firm j in domestic currency;

BV_j is the book value of shareholders' equity of firm j in domestic currency, reported in domestic *GAAP*;

E_j is the fiscal year earnings of firm j, reported in domestic *GAAP*;

DBV_j is the difference between shareholders' equity measured under U.S. *GAAP* and under domestic *GAAP* for firm j;

DE_j is the difference between the fiscal year earnings of firm j measured under U.S. *GAAP* and under domestic *GAAP*;

e_j is a random error term meeting the *OLS* assumptions;

t is a time subscript that corresponds to the fiscal year that the initial registration statement was filed; and

n ranges from one to three years.

For example, if a.December 31 fiscal year firm files its registration statement in June of 1990 and $n = 1$, the $t-1$ subscript indicates the regression variables correspond to fiscal year 1989. Each sample firm has between one and three observations in the sample depending on the number of retrospective reconciliations provided and other data availability.

Similar to previous research that investigates the association between share values and contemporaneous earnings, we expect to document a significantly positive coefficient for β_1. This result would be consistent with non-U.S. *GAAP* earnings reflecting value-relevant information. The primary coefficients of interest, however, are β_2 and β_3. The results that β_2 and/or $\beta_3 > 0$ would imply that at least part of the value-relevant information contained in the reconciliation items was available from other sources before the registration statement was filed. These results would not, however, imply that the reconciliation information was fully impounded prior to the *SEC* disclosures.[5] Evidence of an association between share values and reconciliation items before those items were actually disclosed in the registration statement does not rule out the possibility that the reconciliations provide information that assists investors in interpreting previous disclosures from other sources.

To examine this issue, we employ the following expression (corresponding to equation (3) in Amir, Harris, and Venuti) for the fiscal year that the firm filed the initial registration:

$$\frac{P_{jt} - P_{j,t-1} + d_{jt}}{P_{j,t-1}} = \beta_0 + \beta_1 \frac{E_{jt}}{P_{j,t-1}} + \beta_2 \frac{\Delta E_{jt}}{P_{j,t-1}} + \beta_3 V_{jt} + \varepsilon_{jt} \tag{2}$$

where d_j is dividends per share paid by firm j; V_j is nonrandom "other information" that explains returns for firm j; and all other variables are defined as before.

Amir, Harris, and Venuti [1993] rewrite equation (2) to include the earnings reconciliation variable as part of the other information that is contained in V_j. We follow this approach but also include the first retrospective shareholders' equity reconciliation because its initial public disclosure occurs during the returns measurement period. Accordingly, we rewrite equation (2) and estimate the following expression:

$$\frac{P_{jt} - P_{j,t-1} + d_{jt}}{P_{j,t-1}} = \beta_0 + \beta_1 \frac{E_{jt}}{P_{j,t-1}} + \beta_2 \frac{\Delta E_{jt}}{P_{j,t-1}}$$

$$+ \beta_3 \frac{DE_{jt}}{P_{j,t-1}} + \beta_4 \frac{\Delta DE_{jt}}{P_{j,t-1}} + \beta_5 \frac{DBV_{j,t-1}}{P_{j,t-1}} + \varepsilon_{jt} \tag{3}$$

where Δ represents a change in the corresponding variable and time t is the end of the fiscal year in which the registration statement was filed. All other variables are as defined earlier.

The primary coefficient of interest in expression (3) is β_5. Estimation results indicating $\beta_5 > 0$ would imply that security returns in the period of initial public disclosure were associated with the previously undisclosed

[5] We cannot know the magnitudes of coefficients β_2 and β_3 that would imply full impounding of the reconciliation items. Valuation coefficients are likely to differ across the components of the reconciliation due to attributes such as persistence, risk, and growth (e.g., Freeman and Tse [1992]).

retrospective reconciling items, which supports the *SEC*'s view that the disclosures are important to investors.[6] Results indicating β_3 and/or $\beta_4 > 0$ would be consistent with prior studies that document a significant association between the reconciling items and security returns (Barth and Clinch [1996], Amir, Harris, and Venuti [1993], and Pope and Rees [1993]), but these associations might be based on information obtained from other (nonreconciliation) sources.

2.2. SAMPLE DESCRIPTION

A 1993 survey of financial statements prepared by 528 non-U.S. registrants (*SEC* [1993]) indicates that 84 firms (mostly Canadian and Japanese) provided U.S. *GAAP* financial statements, and 158 firms did not provide a reconciliation because no material differences existed between shareholders' equity and earnings measured using U.S. and the registrant's domestic *GAAP.* The remaining 286 firms are the initial sample for this study.

We obtained registration statement data from Barrett, You & Associates, Inc. and Federal Filings, Inc., two research firms located in Washington, D.C.[7] Monthly prices and market values were obtained from *Compustat's Global Vantage* database and *Datastream.* Of the 286 candidate firms, 148 were eliminated because no reconciliation was provided at the date of initial registration[8] and/or the initial registration was dated prior to 1982; 71 companies were eliminated because of a lack of market value data.[9]

Table 1 provides descriptive information on the sample. United Kingdom and Australian firms comprise 54% of the total observations (identical to the percentage in Amir, Harris, and Venuti [1993]). Amir, Harris, and Venuti did not include Canadian firms in their analyses, while Canadian firms comprise 20% of our sample. Because previous research indicates that the earnings reconciliation for Canadian firms (Barth and Clinch [1996] and Bandyopadhyay, Hanna, and Richardson [1994]) is not value-relevant, we report results with and without Canadian firms. The yearly distribution of cases exhibits reasonable diversification over

---

[6] This model specification implicitly assumes that the level of the shareholders' equity reconciliation is correlated with the unexpected portion of the reconciliation. This assumption is similar to using the level of earnings as a proxy for unexpected earnings.

[7] The research firms provided us with copies of the reconciliations from the initial registration statements, which we used to gather the necessary data. The services of these firms and several others are available to the public for the collection of *SEC* data.

[8] These companies were included on the *SEC* list because they did provide reconciliations in certain years after the initial registrations.

[9] The final sample of 67 firms is smaller than that used by Amir, Harris, and Venuti [1993], who base their analysis on 101 firms. Our study requires the firms (1) to have registered with the *SEC* after 1982, (2) to disclose a reconciliation at the time of the *SEC* registration, and (3) to be listed on a major exchange prior to listing on a U.S. exchange.

TABLE 1

Country and Time Distribution of Observations and Summary Statistics[a]

Panel A: Distribution of Observations

By Country		By Year	
United Kingdom	52	Pre-1985	20
Australia	24	1985	17
Canada	28	1986	17
Ireland	7	1987	16
France	6	1988	18
Spain	6	1989	18
Netherlands	4	1990	19
All others	13	1991	15
Total	140		140

Panel B: Descriptive Statistics[b]

	Market-to-Book Value[c]		Aggregate Reconciliation	
	Non-U.S. Book	U.S. Book	Income[d]	Shareholder Equity[e]
Full Sample				
Mean	2.34	1.81	−.032	.294
(Std. dev.)	(2.28)	(1.77)	(.174)	(1.09)
Non-Canadian Sample				
Mean	2.43	1.75	−.032	.374
(Std. dev.)	(2.46)	(1.87)	(.178)	(1.20)

[a]The sample consists of 67 companies that filed an initial registration statement with the *SEC* during the period 1982–91 and provided retrospective U.S. *GAAP* reconciliation data.

[b]All descriptive statistics are the result of pooling the 140 firm-year observations.

[c]Total market value of common shareholders' equity divided by book value, measured at fiscal year-end.

[d]Difference between non-U.S. and U.S. *GAAP* measures of income before extraordinary items, scaled by non-U.S. shareholders' equity.

[e]Difference between non-U.S. and U.S. *GAAP* measures of common shareholders' equity, scaled by non-U.S. shareholders' equity.

time, which should reduce cross-sectional dependencies in the regression residuals.[10]

Panel B of table 1 reports descriptive statistics for the market-to-book ratios and for the aggregate income and shareholders' equity reconciliations. The market-to-book ratios using U.S. *GAAP* measurements are closer to 1.0 and have a lower cross-sectional variation than do the ratios based on non-U.S. *GAAP*. The relative magnitudes of these ratios are similar to those reported in Amir, Harris, and Venuti, who interpret this result as evidence of greater conservatism of non-U.S. *GAAP*. In addition, the mean income reconciliation reduces income by about 3.2% of non-U.S. book value for both the full sample and the non-Canadian

[10]The sample also exhibits a reasonable distribution of country observations within each year. For example, the United Kingdom sample, which comprises 37% of the total observations, has at least one observation in every year and a maximum of eight observations in any one year.

subsample, and the mean shareholders' equity reconciliation increases non-U.S. book value by about 29.4% and 37.4% for the full and non-Canadian samples, respectively (the corresponding percentages in Amir, Harris, and Venuti [1993, table 4] are −1% and +25%, respectively).

2.3 MARKET VALUATIONS OF RECONCILIATION ITEMS IN THE PRE-INITIAL-DISCLOSURE PERIOD

The results from estimation of expression (1) are presented in table 2.[11] We report both pooled and annual regression results. Similar to the full-sample results in Amir, Harris, and Venuti [1993, table 7], the earnings level and shareholders' equity reconciliation variables in our pooled sample are statistically significant at below a 1% level, and the income reconciliation item is not significant at conventional levels. These results are generally consistent for both the full and non-Canadian samples and for the separate annual regressions, except for year $t-3$ where the sample size is too small to provide powerful tests. Because the reconciliation components used in estimating expression (1) were not included in *SEC* filings until at least 3 months, with a median of 18 months, after our measurements of the dependent variable, the significance of $\hat{\beta}_2$ in the predisclosure period implies that the retrospective shareholders' equity reconciliations reported in the registration statements are correlated with information previously impounded in share prices, i.e., information available to market participants from other sources.

Table 3 extends the analysis to consider five components of the retrospective shareholders' equity reconciliations: goodwill, asset revaluations, deferred taxation, pension benefits, and "all else." For the pooled sample, the coefficients for goodwill, asset revaluations, and "all else" are significant at conventional probability levels, while the deferred taxation and pension variables are not significant. Similar analyses in Amir, Harris, and Venuti [1993] show significant results for all but the pension benefit component. Despite the reductions in sample size, all variables (except for β_7 in panel B) that are statistically significant in the pooled sample are significant in at least one annual regression. Also, variables that are not significant in the pooled sample are not significant in the annual regressions.[12]

The results in table 3 are not surprising, given the methods of accounting for goodwill and asset revaluations. For example, while British companies typically charge goodwill directly to retained earnings, it would seem to be relatively straightforward to adjust current and subsequent

[11] The results presented in tables 2, 3, and 4 are based on Ordinary Least Squares (*OLS*) regression. To adjust for possible heteroscedasticity and cross-correlations in the regression residuals, a bootstrapping procedure was used to estimate the coefficients and their standard errors (Noreen [1989]). Conclusions based on the bootstrapping procedure are qualitatively similar to those reported.

[12] Amir, Harris, and Venuti did not report separate annual results for the components of the reconciliations.

TABLE 2

Market-to-Book Regressions for Retrospective Aggregate U.S. GAAP Reconciliations in Years Preceding Initial Filings[a]

$$\frac{P_{j,t-n}}{BV_{j,t-n}} = \beta_0 + \beta_1 \frac{E_{j,t-n}}{BV_{j,t-n}} + \beta_2 \frac{DBV_{j,t-n}}{BV_{j,t-n}} + \beta_3 \frac{DE_{j,t-n}}{BV_{j,t-n}} + e_{j,t-n}$$

Panel A: Full Sample

	$\hat{\beta}_0$	$\hat{\beta}_1$	$\hat{\beta}_2$	$\hat{\beta}_3$	R^2_{adj}	N
Pooled sample	1.38	3.49	0.97	-0.66	.567	140
	(8.56)**	(5.37)**	(7.24)**	(-0.76)		
Annual regressions						
$t-1$	1.72	2.77	0.94	-0.03	.509	67
	(7.56)**	(3.33)**	(6.25)**	(-0.03)		
$t-2$	1.03	4.96	0.91	-1.51	.656	57
	(3.78)**	(3.88)**	(2.39)**	(-0.77)		
$t-3$	2.29	-5.65	1.82	-6.89	.746	16
	(5.27)**	(-2.06)	(2.28)*	(-0.69)		

Panel B: Non-Canadian Sample

	$\hat{\beta}_0$	$\hat{\beta}_1$	$\hat{\beta}_2$	$\hat{\beta}_3$	R^2_{adj}	N
Pooled sample	1.06	4.86	0.92	0.53	.620	112
	(5.01)**	(5.36)**	(6.60)**	(0.44)		
Annual regressions						
$t-1$	1.43	3.77	0.95	0.95	.563	50
	(4.51)**	(3.27)**	(6.06)**	(0.71)		
$t-2$	0.39	8.99	0.16	0.12	.744	46
	(1.03)	(4.19)**	(0.38)	(0.04)		
$t-3$	2.29	-5.65	1.82	-6.89	.746	16
	(5.27)**	(-2.06)	(2.28)*	(-0.69)		

[a]The full sample consists of 67 companies that filed an initial registration statement with the *SEC* during the period 1982–91 and provided U.S. *GAAP* reconciliation data.

P_j is the fiscal year-end market price of firm j in domestic currency;

BV_j is the book value of shareholders' equity of firm j in domestic currency, reported in domestic *GAAP*;

E_j is the fiscal year earnings of firm j, reported in domestic *GAAP*;

DBV_j is the difference between shareholders' equity measured under U.S. *GAAP* and under domestic *GAAP* for firm j;

DE_j is the difference between the fiscal year earnings of firm j measured under U.S. *GAAP* and under domestic *GAAP*;

e_j is a random error term meeting the *OLS* assumptions;

t is a time subscript that corresponds to the fiscal year that the initial registration statement was filed; and

n ranges from one to three years.

t-statistics are in parentheses.

* and ** indicate that the coefficient exceeds zero, significant at .05 and .01 alpha level, respectively, using a one-tailed test.

periods' reported net income and shareholders' equity for the effects of capitalizing and amortizing goodwill. With respect to asset revaluations, investors have access to historical costs from previous financial reports, specific price indexes, and other data that may be relevant in explaining how the asset revaluation was derived. In fact, annual reports in some countries (e.g., the United Kingdom and Australia) provide

TABLE 3

Market-to-Book Regression for Retrospective Components of U.S. GAAP Reconciliations in Years Preceding Initial Filings[a]

$$\frac{P_{j,t-n}}{BV_{j,t-n}} = \beta_0 + \beta_1 \frac{E_{j,t-n}}{BV_{j,t-n}} + \beta_2 \frac{DE_{j,t-n}}{BV_{j,t-n}} + \beta_3 \frac{GW_{j,t-n}}{BV_{j,t-n}} + \beta_4 \frac{RV_{j,t-n}}{BV_{j,t-n}} + \beta_5 \frac{TX_{j,t-n}}{BV_{j,t-n}} + \beta_6 \frac{PB_{j,t-n}}{BV_{j,t-n}} + \beta_7 \frac{OTH_{j,t-n}}{BV_{j,t-n}} + e_{j,t-n}$$

Panel A: Full Sample

	$\hat{\beta}_0$	$\hat{\beta}_1$	$\hat{\beta}_2$	$\hat{\beta}_3$	$\hat{\beta}_4$	$\hat{\beta}_5$	$\hat{\beta}_6$	$\hat{\beta}_7$	R^2_{adj}	N
Pooled sample	1.53	3.59	−0.55	0.95	2.70	0.72	−0.30	1.46	.570	140
	(8.32)**	(5.28)**	(−0.59)	(6.89)**	(2.95)**	(0.79)	(−0.07)	(1.96)*		
Annual regressions										
$t-1$	1.82	3.22	0.72	0.99	2.85	0.33	−10.02	0.13	.495	67
	(6.84)**	(3.42)**	(0.58)	(6.29)**	(1.68)*	(0.26)	(−0.57)	(0.09)		
$t-2$	1.03	5.31	−1.74	0.63	1.28	−0.76	0.65	2.39	.651	57
	(3.18)**	(4.00)**	(−0.88)	(1.43)	(0.96)	(−0.42)	(0.14)	(1.73)*		
$t-3$	2.24	−5.12	−17.13	0.70	2.88	−2.89	32.65	1.41	.570	16
	(4.80)**	(−1.52)	(−0.85)	(0.38)	(1.88)*	(−0.93)	(1.15)	(1.01)		

Panel B: Non-Canadian Sample

	$\hat{\beta}_0$	$\hat{\beta}_1$	$\hat{\beta}_2$	$\hat{\beta}_3$	$\hat{\beta}_4$	$\hat{\beta}_5$	$\hat{\beta}_6$	$\hat{\beta}_7$	R^2_{adj}	N
Pooled sample	1.09	5.40	1.44	0.90	2.25	−0.32	−0.53	1.52	.626	112
	(4.09)**	(5.50)**	(1.07)	(6.34)**	(2.26)*	(−0.31)	(−0.12)	(1.74)*		
Annual regressions										
$t-1$	1.45	4.57	2.16	0.99	2.57	−0.51	−9.43	0.60	.552	50
	(3.43)**	(3.45)**	(1.31)	(6.12)**	(1.37)	(−0.36)	(−0.46)	(0.33)		
$t-2$	−0.01	11.22	1.98	−0.25	0.01	−4.32	1.44	0.87	.764	46
	(−0.01)	(4.87)**	(0.62)	(−0.54)	(0.01)	(−2.24)	(0.34)	(0.58)		
$t-3$	2.24	−5.12	−17.13	0.70	2.88	−2.89	32.65	1.41	.570	16
	(4.80)**	(−1.52)	(−0.85)	(0.38)	(1.88)*	(−0.93)	(1.15)	(1.01)		

[a]The full sample consists of 67 companies that filed an initial registration statement with the *SEC* during the period 1982–91 and provided U.S. *GAAP* reconciliation data.

GW_{jt} is the goodwill adjustment to shareholder equity at time t (fiscal year-end);
RV_{jt} is the revaluation adjustment to shareholder equity at time t;
TX_{jt} is the tax adjustment to shareholders' equity at time t;
PB_{jt} is the pension benefit adjustment to shareholder equity at time t;
OTH_{jt} is the total of all other adjustments to shareholder equity at time t; and all other items are as defined in earlier tables.

* and ** indicate that the coefficient exceeds zero, significant at .05 and .01 alpha level, respectively, using a one-tailed test.

enough information to allow investors to calculate historical costs.[13] The results also suggest that at least some of the accounting differences in the "all else" category can be interpreted by the market before their actual disclosure. On the other hand, information needed to calculate differences in deferred taxes and pension expense (e.g., marginal tax rates, deferred tax reversal expectations, certain pension-related assumptions) are less likely to be available.

In general, the results in tables 2 and 3 show that the value relevance of shareholder equity reconciliations reported in Amir, Harris, and Venuti [1993] during periods after the initial 20-F filings was also present in periods predating firms' initial registration statements. These findings suggest that the benefits derived from the *SEC*'s requirement to provide U.S. *GAAP* disclosures may be small relative to the costs. These results, however, do not preclude the possibility that the actual measurement and reporting of 20-F reconciliations convey additional value-relevant information to the market.

2.4 MARKET VALUATIONS OF RECONCILIATION ITEMS IN THE YEAR OF INITIAL DISCLOSURE

Table 4 investigates the association between security returns and reconciling items in the year of the initial disclosure. Results presented in tables 2 and 3 indicate investors anticipate the effects of certain cross-national differences in accounting procedures before these differences are disclosed in *SEC* filings. However, if the actual disclosure of the retrospective U.S. *GAAP* reconciliations in year t contains some element that was not previously impounded in stock price, or leads investors to reinterpret previously available information, the annual return for the year of registration (year t) should be correlated with the items contained in the last retrospective shareholders' equity reconciliation (corresponding to year $t-1$) after controlling for the current period's earnings.

Expression (3) is estimated using one year of data for each firm. The reduced sample results in a greater potential for a few observations to exhibit undue influence on the parameter estimates. For this reason, and following Amir, Harris, and Venuti, we delete any observation which yields an *R*-student ratio[14] greater than three in absolute value.

The results of estimating expression (3), reported in table 4, indicate that only the earnings level stated in domestic *GAAP* is significantly asso-

[13] We are indebted to the reviewer for informing us of this point.

[14] The *R*-student ratio is recommended by Belsley, Kuh, and Welsch [1980] for identifying influential observations and is defined as follows:

$$RSTUDENT_{it} = \frac{r_{it}}{s_{it}\sqrt{1-h_{it}}}$$

where r_{it} is the residual for observation it; s_{it} is the estimated standard deviation after deleting observation it; and h_{it} is the hat matrix or $\mathbf{x}_{it}(\mathbf{X}'\mathbf{X})^{-1}\mathbf{x}_{it}'$. This procedure resulted in the deletion of four observations.

TABLE 4

Regressions of Annual Returns on Contemporaneous Earnings and Retrospective Shareholders' Equity Reconciliations[a]

$$R_{jt} = \beta_0 + \beta_1 \frac{E_{jt}}{P_{j,t-1}} + \beta_2 \frac{\Delta E_{jt}}{P_{j,t-1}} + \beta_3 \frac{DE_{jt}}{P_{j,t-1}} + \beta_4 \frac{\Delta DE_{jt}}{P_{j,t-1}} + \beta_5 \frac{DBV_{j,t-1}}{P_{j,t-1}} + e_{jt}$$

	$\hat{\beta}_0$	$\hat{\beta}_1$	$\hat{\beta}_2$	$\hat{\beta}_3$	$\hat{\beta}_4$	$\hat{\beta}_5$	R^2_{adj}	N
Coefficient	–0.05	2.82	-1.77	1.53	–0.62	–0.07	.100	63
(*t*-statistic)	(–.55)	(3.38)**	(-1.91)	(0.74)	(–0.41)	(–0.29)		

[a]Four observations were deleted from the full sample based on their *R*-student ratio exceeding three.
R_j is the fiscal year annual return for firm j;
t is the fiscal year that the initial registration statement was filed with the *SEC*;
Δ represents the change in the corresponding variable; and all other items are as defined in earlier tables.
* and ** indicate that the coefficient exceeds zero, significant at .05 and .01 alpha level, respectively, using a one-tailed test.

ciated with annual returns in the year of the initial registration statement. The disclosure of the retrospective shareholders' equity reconciliation is not associated with current-period returns. Therefore, it appears as though market participants have fully impounded *all* value-relevant portions of the reconciliation in share prices prior to non-U.S. registrants disclosing the information in their annual reports.[15]

The insignificance of $\hat{\beta}_3$ suggests that the difference between non-U.S. *GAAP* earnings and U.S. *GAAP* earnings is not relevant in explaining annual returns. This result is consistent with findings in Amir, Harris, and Venuti [1993, table 6], who document a significantly positive association between annual returns and the income reconciliation in only one of five years examined.

As an alternative test of whether the value-relevant information contained in the retrospective reconciliation is fully impounded by the market prior to its disclosure in the registration statement, we pooled observations in the year immediately prior to the reconciliation's disclosure and the year of the initial registration filing and estimated the following expression:

$$\frac{P_{j,t}}{BV_{j,t}} = \upsilon_0 + \upsilon_1 \frac{E_{j,t}}{BV_{j,t}} + \upsilon_2 \frac{DE_{j,t}}{BV_{j,t}} + \upsilon_3 \frac{DBV_{j,t}}{BV_{j,t}} + \upsilon_4 \frac{DUM_{j,t} \times DBV_{j,t}}{BV_{j,t}} + \varepsilon_{j,t} \quad (4)$$

[15] Retention of the observations that were deleted according to the *R*-student ratio criterion reduces the significance of β_1 ($t = 1.82$); all other coefficients remain statistically insignificant.

where *DUM* = 1 if *t* is the year the registration statement was filed, 0 otherwise. The coefficient υ_4 provides a measure of the difference in the association between price and the stockholders' equity reconciliation before and after the reconciliation's disclosure. Consistent with results reported in table 4, the parameter estimate for υ_4 (−0.03) is not statistically different from zero (*t*-statistic = −0.10).

3. Summary and Implications

This study evaluates the value relevance of 20-F reconciliations of shareholders' equity using retrospective reconciliations provided when a non-U.S. firm files an initial registration statement with the *SEC*. Our results indicate that market-to-book ratios in periods predating the initial *SEC* filing by at least three months are significantly associated with the shareholders' equity reconciliations disclosed in the registration statement. This result implies that at least some of the value-relevant information in the *SEC*-mandated disclosures is available to the market from other sources. Further analysis of the association between the retrospective reconciliations and annual returns for the year during which the reconciliations are disclosed to the market for the first time does not reveal an association between the reconciling items and security returns, which indicates that all of the value-relevant information captured in the reconciliation is fully impounded in prices prior to its disclosure.

Our results provide information about one aspect of the benefits of the 20-F reconciliations and do not support the *SEC*'s position of requiring non-U.S. companies to provide U.S. *GAAP* disclosures. Ultimately, whether to retain the U.S. *GAAP* disclosure requirement would require assessment of all costs and all benefits.

REFERENCES

AMIR, E.; T. S. HARRIS; AND E. K. VENUTI. "A Comparison of the Value-Relevance of U.S. versus Non-U.S. *GAAP* Accounting Measures Using Form 20-F Reconciliations." *Journal of Accounting Research* (Supplement 1993): 230–64.

BANDYOPADHYAY, S. P.; J. D. HANNA; AND G. RICHARDSON. "Capital Market Effects of American-Canadian *GAAP* Differences." *Journal of Accounting Research* (Autumn 1994): 262–77.

BARTH, M. E., AND G. CLINCH. "International Accounting Differences and Their Relation to Share Prices: Evidence from U.K., Australian, and Canadian Firms." *Contemporary Accounting Research* (Spring 1996): 135–70.

BAYLESS, R.; J. COCHRANE; T. HARRIS; J. LEISENRING; J. MCLAUGHLIN; AND J. P. WIRTZ. "International Access to U.S. Capital Markets—An AAA Forum on Accounting Policy." *Accounting Horizons* (March 1996): 75–94.

BELSLEY, D. A.; E. KUH; AND R. E. WELSCH. *Regression Diagnostics*. New York: Wiley, 1980.

FREEMAN, R. N., AND S. Y. TSE. "A Nonlinear Model of Security Price Responses to Unexpected Earnings." *Journal of Accounting Research* (Autumn 1992): 185–209.

FREUND, W. C. "That Trade Obstacle, the SEC." *Wall Street Journal* (August 27, 1993).

NOREEN, E. *Computer-Intensive Methods for Testing Hypotheses: An Introduction*. New York: Wiley, 1989.

POPE, P. "Discussion of a Comparison of the Value-Relevance of U.S. versus Non-U.S. *GAAP* Accounting Measures Using Form 20-F Reconciliations." *Journal of Accounting Research* (Supplement 1993): 265–75.

POPE, P. F., AND W. P. REES. "International Differences in GAAP and the Pricing of Earnings." *Journal of International Financial Management and Accounting* (1993): 190–219.

SALWEN, K. G. "Breeden Rejects Big Board Plan to Relax Listing Standards for Foreign Concerns." *Wall Street Journal* (May 3, 1991): C7.

SCHAPIRO, M. L. "The SEC's Open Door Policy." *Wall Street Journal* (September 23, 1993).

SECURITIES AND EXCHANGE COMMISSION. *Survey of Financial Statement Reconciliations by Foreign Registrants.* New York: Division of Corporate Finance, SEC, May 1, 1993.

[11]

ELSEVIER Journal of Accounting and Economics 21 (1996) 139–158

JOURNAL OF Accounting & Economics

The association between stock returns and foreign GAAP earnings versus earnings adjusted to U.S. GAAP

Kam C. Chan, Gim S. Seow*

Department of Accounting, University of Connecticut, Storrs, CT 06269, USA

(Received May 1994; final version received April 1995)

Abstract

This study examines the association between stock returns and foreign GAAP earnings *versus* earnings adjusted to U.S. GAAP. Using a sample of foreign firms with common stock or American Depositary Receipt (ADR) traded in U.S. exchanges, we compare the returns–earnings relations between U.S. and foreign GAAP-based earnings. Results based on the J_A test indicate that earnings based on foreign GAAP are more closely associated with contemporaneous stock returns than earnings reconciled to U.S. GAAP. We find evidence that our results may be driven by institutional factors which are specific to foreign markets.

Key words: Capital markets; U.S. GAAP; Foreign GAAP; Form 20-F

JEL classification: M41

1. Introduction

During the 1980s and 1990s, rapid globalization of capital markets has generated great interest among U.S. investors in foreign securities. In fact, trading volume in foreign stocks among U.S. investors jumped fourteen-fold to

* Corresponding author.

The authors are grateful to Ray Ball (the editor) and Gary Biddle (the referee) for their detailed comments and very constructive suggestions. Helpful comments from Dave Guenther, Jim Heintz, Rob Hoskin, Tsoung-Chao Lee, Wai-Nang Po, Hannah Wong, and the workshop participants at the University of Connecticut and Baruch College are also gratefully acknowledged. We also appreciate the research assistance provided by Hoseoup Lee and Jay Thibodeau.

SSDI 0165-4101(95)00405-8

over $253 billion annually, from 1980 to 1990.[1] According to the U.S. Department of Commerce, the market value of foreign stocks held by U.S. investors reached $714 billion by 1990. A major responsibility of the Securities and Exchange Commission (SEC) is to ensure that U.S. investors receive adequate and accurate information concerning all securities traded in U.S. markets. Under the Securities Exchange Act of 1934, foreign issuers whose securities are widely held and traded in the U.S. are subject to certain periodic reporting requirements. In particular, foreign firms with direct security listings are required to file quarterly Form 10-Q reports and the annual Form 10-K report, while those with listed American Depositary Receipts (ADRs) are required to file semiannual Form 6-K report and the annual Form 20-F report within 180 days after the fiscal yearend. In Form 20-F reports, earnings determined using foreign generally accepted accounting principles (GAAP) must be reconciled to U.S. GAAP, and material effects due to differences in accounting policies separately listed.[2] Currently, 492 foreign registrants are subject to the SEC's 10-K and 20-F reporting requirements (Edwards, 1993, p. 32).

Current SEC policy requiring 20-F reconciliations to U.S. GAAP is based on two critical assumptions. One, as expressed in Edwards (1993), is that a two-tier disclosure system allowing foreign firms to use home-country GAAP would put U.S. firms at a competitive disadvantage due to their greater disclosure costs.[3] Two, is that 'the information disclosed by foreign firms under home-country standards is *inferior to* the information disclosed by U.S. firms' (Edwards, 1993, p. 31, emphasis added). The validity of this second assumption has been questioned by many. For example, Baumol and Malkiel (1993, pp. 24–27) present evidence that institutional investors specializing in foreign equities are not able to outperform international stock indexes.[4] Their findings, together with those of Hawawini (1984) and Lessard (1990), also suggest that major

[1]Derived by the Federal Reserve Bank of Atlanta from U.S. Department of the Treasury, U.S. Treasury Bulletin, Winter 1991, Table CM-V-5; Winter 1981, Table CM-VI-10.

[2]Details on SEC disclosure and financial reporting requirements can be found in Murray, Decker, and Dittmar (1993).

[3]An important implication of this assumption is that U.S. investors would demand a higher risk premium for holding foreign equities that provide less complete information. Diamond and Verrecchia (1991) provide theoretical support for this point by showing that revealing public information to reduce information asymmetry can reduce a firm's cost of capital. This is accomplished through greater demand by institutional investors as well as increased liquidity of its securities. Clarkson and Thompson (1990) present empirical evidence that securities with relatively little information are perceived as relatively more risky because of the greater uncertainty surrounding the exact parameters of their return distributions.

[4]For a more elaborate analysis of international mutual fund performance, see Cumby and Glen (1990).

overseas markets are as efficient as those in the United States. This led Baumol and Malkiel to argue that additional disclosures in accordance with U.S. GAAP would provide little benefit to investors. Furthermore, they suggest that foreign GAAP numbers may be 'untranslatable' due to major differences in tax laws, corporate governance, intercorporate ownership of securities, and other important institutional features. Such reconciliations may, in fact, mislead U.S. investors into making unwarranted inferences.

Moreover, Biddle and Saudagaran (1989) present evidence suggesting that firms are less likely to list their securities on foreign stock exchanges that require more extensive disclosures than domestic standards.[5] Their findings suggest that many foreign firms may decide not to list their securities in the U.S. exchanges due to the stricter U.S. reporting requirements. Another impediment to listing in the U.S. is the cost of complying with the SEC rules. Biddle and Saudagaran (1991, p. 72) report that a major Japanese or U.K. firm will have to spend at least $1 million annually to comply with U.S. GAAP reporting requirements. Consequently, U.S. investors are forced to transact in foreign markets at higher costs.[6]

A major controversy has arisen between the SEC and the New York Stock Exchange (NYSE) over the reporting requirements (20-F filings) for foreign issuers (see Freund, 1993; Gumbel and Steinmetz, 1995; Siconolfi and Salwen, 1992). The NYSE argues that SEC reporting requirements for non-U.S. firms put it at a competitive disadvantage in terms of the number of foreign listings relative to foreign stock exchanges (see Wall Street Journal, 1994). However, the SEC contends that it must protect U.S. investors from inadequate disclosures by foreign firms (Freund, 1993).

The objective of this study is to compare the relative information content of reported earnings based on foreign GAAP *versus* earnings adjusted to U.S. GAAP.[7] To compare the relative information content of foreign earnings *versus* earnings adjusted to U.S. GAAP, we conduct association tests between stock returns and the two sets of earnings reported by the same firm. Our research design employs each foreign firm in the sample as its own control. Using this design, we avoid the need to match foreign firms with domestic firms as in prior studies. Therefore, this eliminates any criticism based on imperfect matching

[5]Among German and Swiss companies, Daimler–Benz is the first to be listed on the New York Stock Exchange. While supporters of the SEC policy interpret this event as a success, opponents view Daimler–Benz's submission to SEC pressure as a consequence of the German auto-maker's urgent need to raise new capital abroad (Freund, 1993; Gumbel and Steinmetz, 1995).

[6]See Siconolfi and Salwen (1992) and Freund (1993) on the current debate between the New York Stock Exchange and the SEC on whether to relax accounting and disclosure rules for foreign *versus* U.S. companies.

[7]For details on the distinction between relative and incremental information content, see Biddle, Seow, and Siegel (1995).

procedures. In particular, our research design eliminates confounding factors associated with cross-country differences due to regulatory policies, tax regimes, social and cultural structures, among others.

By providing evidence on the contemporaneous association of stock returns with foreign earnings and U.S. GAAP-adjusted numbers, this study contributes to the debate on the appropriateness of pursuing the existing disclosure and reporting requirements for foreign companies in the U.S. This study examines the validity of the maintained hypothesis that U.S. GAAP is *better than* foreign GAAP as a financial reporting standard for foreign firms. We test whether U.S. investors use foreign earnings or earnings adjusted to U.S. GAAP to value foreign firms. Empirical evidence on how U.S. investors respond to earnings under different GAAPs may be useful to both foreign and domestic companies. This knowledge will enable security issuers to make informed tradeoffs between value-added disclosures and costs associated with their production and dissemination.

The remainder of the paper is organized as follows. Section 2 discusses prior research that compares differences between U.S. and foreign GAAPs. The research hypotheses and the empirical research design are presented in Section 3. Empirical results and implications are discussed in Section 4. Section 5 provides an explanation for the results obtained in Section 4 and presents evidence consistent with those results. Conclusions and suggestions for future research are provided in the final section.

2. Prior research

Early research in international financial reporting established that there are substantial qualitative differences among countries in their financial reporting standards (see Meek and Saudagaran, 1990, for a review of research in this area). Research by Mueller, Gernon, and Meek (1991) and Nobes (1988) suggests that economic, social, and political factors influence the development of accounting standards.

In classifying financial reporting practices across countries, Nobes (1983) presents four groups: U.S. influence (U.S. and Canada); U.K. influence (U.K., Ireland, Australia, and New Zealand); macro-based with legal emphasis (Germany and Japan); and macro-based with tax emphasis (Belgium, France, Italy, and Spain). Establishing differences among financial reporting standards, however, does not imply that these differences would matter for making investing decisions.

Using a judgmental approach, several studies compare the 'quality' of U.S. GAAP with foreign GAAP. Gray (1980) develops a country index for 'conservatism' by comparing the level of reported earnings under two different GAAPs. A particular GAAP is said to be *more* conservative if, on aggregate, it provides a lower earnings level. Studies by Gray (1980), Cairns, Lafferty, and Mantle (1984), and Hellman (1993) present evidence that U.S. GAAP is *more* conservative than U.K. GAAP, thirty-two other foreign GAAPs, and Swedish GAAP, respectively. On the other hand, Aron (1990) and Weetman and Gray (1991) report that U.S. GAAP is *less* conservative than Japanese GAAP and Swedish GAAP, respectively. Findings from this research are difficult to interpret because the differences in conservatism documented may be attributed to differences in definitions, subjective measurement techniques, and different weighting schemes. Furthermore, the lack of a link to securities markets poses difficulties in making inferences on whether these differences affect the pricing of securities.

Meek (1983) finds stock price reactions to annual foreign GAAP earnings announcements made in the U.S. by foreign firms. But the magnitude of the market reaction to foreign earnings numbers is not different from the magnitude of the market reaction to U.S. earnings numbers reported by a matched sample of U.S. firms. Moreover, Meek (1983) observes no price reaction during the three-day window surrounding the 20-K (predecessor to the Form 20-F) filing date. Two feasible inferences from Meek's results are: U.S. investors find earnings based on foreign GAAP are just as useful as those based on U.S. GAAP, and that the 20-K filing may not provide incremental information for U.S. investors. However, his study does not control for the magnitude of unexpected earnings and his matching procedure for U.S. and foreign firms does not rule out structural and regulatory differences across countries as potential explanations for his results. Amir et al. (1993) also examine whether the U.S. GAAP reconciliation information in the Form 20-F provides incremental information beyond the foreign GAAP earnings in explaining stock returns. Similar to Meek's findings, Amir et al. (1993) find no evidence that the reconciliation information is associated with stock returns around the Form 20-F filing date, and provide mixed results for the association between the reconciliation information and stock returns measured over an 18-month period.

Recent work by Alford et al. (1993) investigates the information content and timeliness of earnings from U.S.- and foreign-based companies by examining the association between stock returns and reported earnings over a fifteen-month period using a matched group design. They document varying degrees of differences in the value relevance and timeliness of accounting earnings between U.S. and foreign GAAPs.

While Alford et al. (1993) find differences in information content of accounting earnings, their results may be attributable to their use of a matched group design. Prior research has found that results from matching firm analyses are sensitive to the matching procedure (see Harrison, Tomassini, and Dietrich, 1983; Murray, 1983). Our study overcomes limitations associated with the Alford et al. (1993) and Meek (1983) studies by not using a matching procedure or including U.S. firms in our sample. Each foreign firm with securities listed in the U.S. capital markets is matched with itself. For our sample of foreign firms, the association between stock returns and reported earnings based on foreign GAAP will be compared with the association between stock returns and reported earnings adjusted to U.S. GAAP.

3. Hypotheses and empirical research design

This study examines the association between accounting earnings (based on foreign and U.S. GAAP) and contemporaneous security returns. We employ the Biddle, Seow, and Siegel (1995) 'earnings levels and lagged levels' specification as presented below:

$$R_{jt} = a_0 + a_1 \cdot [X_{jt}/P_{jt-1}] + a_2 \cdot [X_{jt-1}/P_{jt-1}] + e_{jt}, \tag{1}$$

where

R_{jt} = stock return for firm j during year t,
X_{jt} = annual accounting earnings for firm j during year t,
X_{jt-1} = annual accounting earnings for firm j during year $t-1$,
P_{jt-1} = stock price of firm j at beginning of year t,
a_0 = constant intercept term,
a_1, a_2 = slope coefficients,
e_{jt} = error term.

Eq. (1) is also consistent with the earnings level and change model employed by Easton and Harris (1991) and Ali and Zarowin (1992).[8]

3.1. Sample selection procedure

An initial sample of 61 foreign companies with common stock or American Depositary Receipt (ADR) traded on the U.S. stock exchanges is identified from the Value Line Investment Survey (VL) published in the fourth quarter of 1993. An additional 69 foreign firms which filed Form 20-Fs with the SEC in 1992 and 1993 are identified from the LEXIS/NEXIS database. To be included in the final sample, the foreign common stock or ADR has to meet two sample selection

[8]The earnings level and change specification used in Easton and Harris (1991) and Ali and Zarowin (1992):

$$R_{jt} = b_0 + b_1 \cdot X_{jt}\ P_{jt-1} + b_2 \cdot [X_{jt} - X_{jt-1}]/P_{jt-1} + e_{jt},$$

may be decomposed into

$$R_{jt} = b_0 + b_1 \cdot X_{jt}/P_{jt-1} + b_2 \cdot X_{jt}/P_{jt-1} - b_2 \cdot X_{jt-1}/P_{jt-1} + e_{jt},$$

which is equivalent to our Eq. (1) with $a_0 = b_0$, $a_1 = b_1 + b_2$, and $a_2 = -b_2$.

criteria. First, earnings based on U.S. GAAP and foreign GAAP must be available either in the VL or the Standard and Poor's Stock Report (S&P) for fiscal years ending between July 1987 to June 1992. Second, returns of the foreign company's common stock or ADR must be available in the daily return files of the Center for Research in Security Prices (CRSP) tapes. The final sample in this study consists of 45 firms and 147 firm-year observations. The 45-firm sample does not lend itself to a more elaborate country-by-country analysis as performed by Alford et al. (1993). However, our sample firms are closely monitored by Value Line and Standard and Poor. This implies that these foreign firms generate sufficient interest from the U.S. investment community, and thus represent foreign companies that are most likely to be affected by the SEC's disclosure rules.

3.2. Model specifications

The main research hypothesis in this study is whether reported earnings based on foreign GAAP or earnings adjusted to U.S. GAAP is *more* closely associated with contemporaneous stock returns. This is a question of *relative* information content (Biddle, Seow, and Siegel, 1995; Dechow, 1994). We measure stock returns using both raw returns as well as market-adjusted returns. Market-adjusted return is calculated as the difference between the stock return of the firm and the contemporaneous return on the equal-weighted CRSP index. Results employing both definitions are reported in the next section.

Consistent with the prior literature, stock returns of the sample firms are regressed on accounting earnings based on U.S. GAAP divided by beginning-of-fiscal-year stock price using Eq. (1), the earnings level, and lagged earnings level model. The analysis is then repeated using earnings based on foreign GAAP.

We chose a twelve-month (fiscal year) window for our main analyses. To check the sensitivity of our results to the choice of window lengths, we also employed a fifteen-month window (starting nine months before and ending six months after the fiscal yearend) for foreign firms with ADRs that are required to file Form 20-F. For foreign firms with direct stock listings that are required to file 10-Ks with the SEC, we use a twelve-month window that commences nine months before and ends three months after the fiscal yearend. In our sample of 45 foreign firms, five of them are directly listed in U.S. stock exchanges and file 10-Ks. In terms of the number of observations, they represent seventeen firm-years.

3.3. Comparison J_A tests

To determine whether earnings based on foreign GAAP or earnings adjusted to U.S. GAAP is *more* associated with stock returns, the J_A-test is applied to the following pair of hypotheses (firm subscript omitted):

$$H_{10}: \quad R_t = a_0 + a_1 \cdot [X_{Ut}] + a_2 \cdot [X_{Ut-1}] + e_t, \tag{1a}$$

$$H_{1A}: \quad R_t = b_0 + b_1 \cdot [X_{Ft}] + b_2 \cdot [X_{Ft-1}] + n_t, \tag{1b}$$

where

R_t = stock returns during year t,
X_{Ut} = reported annual earnings of year t based on U.S. GAAP divided by beginning-of-fiscal-year stock price,
X_{Ut-1} = reported annual earnings of year $t-1$ based on U.S. GAAP divided by beginning-of-fiscal-year stock price,
X_{Ft} = reported annual earnings of year t based on foreign GAAP divided by beginning-of-fiscal-year stock price,
X_{Ft-1} = reported annual earnings of year $t-1$ based on foreign GAAP divided by beginning-of-fiscal-year stock price.

The J_A test, which was developed by Fisher and McAleer (1981) and Godfrey (1983), is a modified version of the Davidson and MacKinnon (1981) J test. The J_A test statistic is expected to have better finite-sample properties than the original J test statistic, and is considered as a more conservative test for the alternative hypothesis (Davidson and MacKinnon, 1993; MacKinnon, 1992). The J_A test is a model specification test for nonnested models. The objective of the J_A test is to assess which one of the two competing sets of independent variables is *more* closely associated with the dependent variable. In contrast, the traditional F test for the regression R^2 is a test for nested models. Therefore, the goal of the F test is to examine the incremental contributions of the additional independent variables in explaining the dependent variable. Since the research focus of this study is to examine the *relative* information content of the two sets of accounting numbers, the J_A test is used to examine the research hypotheses.

The above pair of hypotheses will be tested as follows. First, the stock return is regressed on U.S.-GAAP-based earnings to obtain a metric of predicted values of the stock returns computed using the estimated regression coefficients. Second, the predicted stock returns from the previous regression is regressed on foreign-GAAP-based earnings to obtain another metric of predicted stock returns (ZF) using the estimated regression coefficients from the second regression. In the final step, the observed stock return is regressed on the U.S.-GAAP-based earnings levels and lagged earnings levels and the predicted stock returns (ZF) from the second regression as follows:

$$R_t = c_0 + c_1 \cdot [X_{Ut}] + c_2 \cdot [X_{Ut-1}] + c_3 \cdot [ZF] + e_t. \tag{2}$$

H_{10} would be rejected if the coefficient estimate of c_3 is significantly different from zero. However, the rejection of H_{10} does not imply the validity of H_{1A} (see

Davidson and MacKinnon 1981, 1993, for a more detailed discussion). Therefore, a second pair of hypotheses stated below is also tested:

$$\text{H}_{20}\text{:}\quad R_t = d_0 + d_1 \cdot [X_{Ft}] + d_2 \cdot [X_{Ft-1}] + m_t, \tag{3a}$$

$$\text{H}_{2A}\text{:}\quad R_t = g_0 + g_1 \cdot [X_{Ut}] + g_2 \cdot [X_{Ut-1}] + h_t. \tag{3b}$$

H_{20} is tested in a similar fashion as H_{10}. This time the stock returns are regressed on foreign-GAAP-based earnings and the estimated regression coefficients are used to compute the predicted stock returns metric. Then, this predicted stock returns metric is regressed on the U.S.-GAAP-based earnings to obtain the second predicted stock returns metric (ZU) from the coefficients of the second regression. Finally, the actual stock returns is regressed on the foreign-GAAP-based earnings levels and lagged earnings levels and the predicted stock returns metric (ZU) previously obtained:

$$R_t = k_0 + k_1 \cdot [X_{Ft}] + k_2 \cdot [X_{Ft-1}] + k_3 \cdot [ZU] + m_t. \tag{4}$$

H_{20} is rejected if the coefficient estimate of k_3 is significantly different from zero. If H_{10} is rejected and H_{20} is not rejected, this would suggest that the stock returns are *more* closely associated with earnings under foreign GAAP rather than earnings adjusted to U.S. GAAP. However, if H_{20} is rejected and H_{10} is not rejected, the implication is that the stock returns are *more* closely associated with earnings adjusted to U.S. GAAP than earnings under foreign GAAP. It is possible for both or neither hypotheses to be simultaneously rejected. Rejection of both hypotheses implies that neither model seems compatible with the data, while failing to reject both hypotheses suggests that the two models are very similar or the data sets are not very informative.

4. Results and implications

Panel A in Table 1 presents the means, medians, standard deviations, minimum and maximum observations for variables used in subsequent regressions.[9] The mean and median raw stock returns during the fiscal year are 19.70% and 15.33%, respectively. During the 1988–92 period, the average annualized return for the S&P 500 portfolio was 16.66%. The mean and median raw returns for the fifteen-month window are 20.51% and 15.35%, respectively. Scaled by

[9]Statistics presented in Table 1 are based on the 144 firm-year observations used in subsequent regressions and J_A test analyses. Three observations were eliminated because they were identified as outliers based on procedures suggested by Belsley, Kuh, and Welsh (1980). The results are qualitatively similar when the outliers are included.

Table 1
Descriptive statistics of regression data and SIC's of sample firms and firm-years; number of firm-year observations = 144

Panel A: Descriptive statistics of regression data

Variable	Mean	Median	Std. dev.	Min. obs.	Max. obs.
Raw returns[a]	0.1970	0.1533	0.4231	− 0.8328	2.5025
Raw returns[b]	0.2051	0.1535	0.4333	− 0.9330	2.3012
Market-adj. returns[a]	− 0.0014	− 0.0593	0.3131	− 0.8959	1.2514
Market-adj. returns[b]	− 0.0266	− 0.0445	0.3457	− 0.9524	1.8869
X_{Ft}/P_{t-1}	0.0850	0.0880	0.0581	− 0.3560	0.1952
X_{Ut}/P_{t-1}	0.0823	0.0818	0.0669	− 0.4446	0.2261
X_{Ft-1}/P_{t-1}	0.0881	0.0843	0.0483	− 0.0809	0.2720
X_{Ut-1}/P_{t-1}	0.0867	0.0787	0.0525	− 0.0600	0.3370

Panel B: Breakdown of sample firms and firm-years by SIC code

Industry classification	No. of firms	Firm-years
1000–1999 Natural resources	10	23
2000–2999 Consumer manufacturing	13	45
3000–3999 Industrial manufacturing	7	23
4000–4999 Transportation/public utilities	8	28
5000–5999 Merchandising	2	3
6000–6999 Financial services	4	17
7000–7999 Business/personal services	1	5
Total	45	144

[a]Fiscal-year stock returns.
[b]Fifteen month stock returns (month − 9 through month + 6 from fiscal year end).

beginning-of-year stock price, the average earnings based on foreign GAAP is 8.50%, and the average earnings based on U.S. GAAP is 8.23%. A two-tailed paired t test of mean difference ((Foreign EPS − U.S. EPS)/Stock price) suggests that the difference between these two sets of numbers of 0.27% is not statistically different from zero (t-statistic = 0.9062, p-value = 0.3664). However, the mean absolute difference between the two sets of earnings numbers (|Foreign EPS − U.S. EPS|/Stock price) is 0.0228. This difference is statistically different from zero (t-statistic = 9.5425, p-value = 0.0001).

In panel B of Table 1, industry classification of the sample firms based on SICs reveal a distribution similar to that of publicly held U.S. corporations. Of the 45 firms, three are from Australia, three from Canada, one from Chile, one from Denmark, one from Hong Kong, two from Italy, one from Mexico, four from the Netherlands, one from Norway, one from South Africa, three from Spain, three from Sweden, and 21 are domiciled in the U.K. The distribution of

Table 2
Regression results using both earnings levels and lagged levels; t-statistics in parentheses; sample size = 144 firm-years

	Twelve-month returns[a]		Fifteen-month returns[b]	
Variable	Raw returns	Market-adjusted[c]	Raw returns	Market-adjusted[c]
Panel A: Earnings based on U.S. GAAP				
Constant	0.0834	– 0.0863	0.0878	– 0.1354
	(1.327)	(– 1.875)*	(1.320)	(– 2.604)**
X_{Ut}[d]	3.3648	2.5737	3.0032	2.6093
	(6.397)***	(6.679)***	(5.393)***	(5.993)***
X_{Ut-1}[e]	– 1.8832	– 1.4627	– 1.4976	– 1.2207
	(– 2.807)***	(– 2.976)***	(– 2.109)**	(– 2.198)**
Adj. R^2	0.2140	0.2296	0.1599	0.1933
Panel B: Earnings based on foreign GAAP				
Constant	– 0.0095	– 0.1574	0.0160	– 0.1912
	(– 0.133)	(– 3.066)***	(0.207)	(– 3.189)***
X_{Ft}[f]	4.0020	3.1321	3.4949	3.0584
	(7.732)***	(8.411)***	(6.228)***	(7.035)***
X_{Ft-1}[g]	– 1.5196	– 1.2528	– 1.2281	– 1.0842
	(– 2.440)**	(– 2.796)***	(– 1.818)*	(– 2.072)**
Adj. R^2	0.2936	0.3322	0.2081	0.2534

[a]Fiscal-year stock returns.
[b]Fifteen-month stock returns (month – 9 through month + 6 from fiscal year end).
[c]Stock returns are adjusted using the CRSP equal-weighted index.
[d]Earnings based on U.S. GAAP divided by beginning-of-fiscal-year stock price.
[e]Lagged earnings based on U.S. GAAP divided by beginning-of-fiscal-year stock price.
[f]Earnings based on foreign GAAP divided by beginning-of-fiscal-year stock price.
[g]Lagged earnings based on foreign GAAP divided by beginning-of-fiscal-year stock price.

Asterisks indicate significance at the 1% (***), 5% (**), and 10% (*) levels using two-tailed t tests.

our sample firms across different countries seems to reflect the cross-section of foreign firms which have securities listed in U.S. exchanges.[10]

Regression results for the raw and market-adjusted returns over the twelve-month fiscal year and fifteen-month window are shown in Table 2. In panel A,

[10]The distribution of national origins of our final sample is consistent with Wall Street Journal (1995) which ranks the U.K. and Australia as number one and two in number of ADRs listed.

the slope coefficients for the U.S. GAAP earnings level and lagged level variables are statistically significant at the 0.05 level. The adjusted R^2s range from 15.99% to 22.96%, with slightly higher R^2s for the annual window. In panel B, all slope coefficients for foreign GAAP earnings levels and lagged level are also statistically significant, with adjusted R^2s being about 7% higher than those for corresponding returns specifications in panel A. One inference drawn from the observed higher adjusted R^2s for the foreign GAAP numbers is that earnings based on foreign GAAP have greater information content than earnings adjusted to U.S. GAAP. The returns–earnings level and lagged level regression results for the sample of foreign firms, in terms of the slope coefficient estimates and their t-statistics, and the adjusted R^2s, appear consistent with empirical evidence on U.S. samples presented by Easton and Harris (1991) and Ali and Zarowin (1992).[11] Qualitatively, the returns–earnings relation for foreign firms reported here is very similar to results reported in other studies that use U.S. samples.

The J_A test results for both twelve-month and fifteen-month windows are presented in Table 3. In panel A, we maintain the U.S. GAAP as the null hypothesis and test whether earnings based on foreign GAAP is better [Eq. (2)]. In all four specifications of the stock returns dependent variable, we reject the null at the 1% level based on the t-statistics for the ZF variable. Next, we maintain the foreign GAAP as the null and test whether earnings adjusted to U.S. GAAP is better [Eq. (4)]. Results presented in panel B show that the null cannot be rejected at conventional levels of statistical significance.[12] The joint results in panels A and B suggest that foreign GAAP earnings have *greater* information content than earnings based on U.S. GAAP.

5. Why foreign GAAP earnings may be better

Results in Tables 2 and 3 present evidence that foreign GAAP earnings have *better* information content than earnings based on U.S. GAAP. The next research question is what may be causing the observed difference. In Section 2, prior studies that have compared U.S. and foreign GAAPs suggest that institutional differences in tax laws, corporate governance, intercorporate securities holdings, to name a few, may play important roles in the evolution of the foreign GAAPs. According to Baumol and Malkiel (1993), this diversity in business and/or economic environments across different countries may render earnings

[11]A replication of results shown in Table 2 without the seventeen observations from Form 10-K filers was also performed and was found to be qualitatively similar.

[12]Similar J_A test results were obtained when the seventeen Form 10-K firm-years were omitted.

Table 3

J_A test results using both earnings levels and lagged levels; t-statistics in parentheses; sample size = 144 firm-years

	Twelve-month returns[a]		Fifteen-month returns[b]	
Variable	Raw returns	Market-adjusted[c]	Raw returns	Market-adjusted[c]
Panel A				
Constant	− 0.1239	0.0050	− 0.1031	− 0.0078
	(− 1.585)	(0.108)	(− 1.134)	(− 0.126)
X_{Ut}[d]	− 0.9892	− 1.1693	− 0.3849	− 0.4028
	(− 0.842)	(− 1.387)	(− 0.306)	(− 0.418)
X_{Ut-1}[e]	1.0304	1.0643	− 0.6269	0.6035
	(1.079)	(1.547)	(− 0.632)	(0.805)
ZF[f]	1.5890	1.7847	1.3922	1.4281
	(4.094)***	(4.903)***	(2.989)***	(3.473)***
Adj. R^2	0.2930	0.3378	0.2047	0.2519
Panel B				
Constant	0.0071	− 0.1965	0.0241	− 0.2086
	(0.095)	(− 3.300)***	(0.281)	(− 2.729)***
X_{Ft}[g]	4.7817	4.1156	3.7503	3.3874
	(4.043)***	(4.844)***	(2.931)***	(3.417)***
X_{Ft-1}[h]	− 1.9143	− 1.7649	− 1.3522	− 1.2448
	(− 2.323)**	(− 2.949)***	(− 1.540)	(− 1.827)*
ZU[i]	− 0.2446	− 0.3932	− 0.0921	− 0.1354
	(− 0.733)	(− 1.287)	(− 0.222)	(− 0.370)
Adj. R^2	0.2913	0.3353	0.2027	0.2488

[a]Fiscal-year stock returns.
[b]Fifteen-month stock returns (month − 9 through month + 6 from fiscal year end).
[c]Stock returns are adjusted using the CRSP equal-weighted index.
[d]Earnings based on U.S. GAAP divided by beginning-of-fiscal-year stock price.
[e]Lagged earnings based on U.S. GAAP divided by beginning-of-fiscal-year stock price.
[f]Predicted returns metric derived from foreign-GAAP-based earnings level and lagged level.
[g]Earnings based on foreign GAAP divided by beginning-of-fiscal-year stock price.
[h]Lagged earnings based on foreign GAAP divided by beginning-of-fiscal-year stock price.
[i]Predicted returns metric derived from U.S.-GAAP-based earnings level and lagged level.

Asterisks indicate significance at the 1% (***), 5% (**), and 10% (*) levels using two-tailed t tests.

based on foreign GAAP 'untranslatable'. Results based on a survey of institutional investors, corporate issuers, and regulators led Choi and Levich (1991) to conclude that restatement is not sufficient to remove the problem of accounting diversity. They attribute this to either: (a) crude restatement algorithms, (b) ineffective implementation of restatement algorithms, or (c) no algorithm is capable of producing a proper and meaningful restatement. If foreign earnings are not easily translated into U.S. GAAP, this could explain their greater relative information content.

Recent research in international financial markets suggests that national factors may be influencing the returns correlations between different markets. Grinold, Rudd, and Stefek (1989), Beckers, Grinold, and Rudd (1992), and Drummen and Zimmermann (1992) regress firm stock returns on global, industry, and national factors and conclude that national factors dominate the explained part of stock price variances. More recently, Heston and Rouwenhorst's (1994) investigation of the country and industry structure of twelve European countries' stock returns suggests that the similarity of the economic environment may be reflected in the strength of cross-country stock returns correlation.

Based on the current research in international stock markets, the closeness of the foreign capital market to the U.S. financial market may be represented by the returns correlation between the U.S. stock index and the foreign stock index. The greater the difference in business environment between the U.S. and the foreign country, the lower the cross-country stock returns correlation. If the business environment in the foreign country is quite different from that prevailing in the U.S., some of the unique aspects of the business environment in that country may be better reflected by the foreign GAAP earnings than the earnings reconciled to U.S. GAAP. Consequently, a larger difference in the association of stock returns and the two sets of earnings should be expected for firms domiciled in countries with low stock returns correlations with the U.S.

5.1. Measuring the returns correlation coefficient

Monthly returns on various stock indexes are computed using monthly data from December 1987 through December 1992. Foreign returns are calculated in terms of the corresponding foreign currency and also after translation into U.S. dollars using the beginning- and end-of-month exchange rates. The S&P 500 Index is obtained from the S&P Security Price Index Record. The Australia All Ordinary (Australia), Toronto Stock Exchange Composite (Canada), Hang Seng Index (Hong Kong), Banca Commerciale Index (Italy), Amsterdam All Share Index (Netherlands), Oslo Stock Exchange Index (Norway), Johannesburg Stock Exchange Industrials (South Africa), Madrid Stock Exchange (Spain), Afarsvarlden General Index (Sweden), Financial Times 100 Index (United Kingdom) are collected from the 1993 Moody's International Manual. Stock indexes and exchange rates for Chile, Denmark, and Mexico are obtained from the International Monetary Fund survey. Monthly exchange rates for the other countries are obtained from the Federal Reserve Board Bulletin.

Table 4
Returns correlations between U.S. and foreign stock indexes; 1988–92

Country	In foreign currencies	In U.S. dollars
Australia	0.079	0.003
Canada[a]	0.477	0.418
Chile	0.022	0.012
Denmark[a]	0.375	0.281
Hong Kong	0.156	0.150
Italy	0.133	0.130
Mexico[a]	0.363	0.368
Netherlands	0.225	0.173
Norway	0.091	0.067
South Africa	0.137	0.128
Spain[a]	0.419	0.398
Sweden[a]	0.334	0.363
United Kingdom[a]	0.359	0.275

Data are obtained from S&P Security Price Index Record, 1993 Moody's International Manual, Federal Reserve Board Bulletin, and the International Monetary Fund survey.

[a]Countries in the high-correlation group.

Table 4 presents returns correlations between U.S. and foreign stock indexes for the 1988–92 period. Coefficients computed in foreign currencies and in U.S. dollars yield similar rankings. Six countries (Canada, Denmark, Mexico, Spain, Sweden, and the United Kingdom) with the highest correlations with the U.S. stock market are assigned to the high-correlation group, while the other seven countries are placed in the low-correlation group.

5.2. Empirical results

Regression results for high- and low-correlation groups using twelve-month stock returns are reported in Table 5. In panel A, the independent variables are the earnings level and lagged earnings level based on U.S. GAAP. The adjusted R^2s for the high-correlation group are 22.14% and 25.20% for the raw and market-adjusted returns, respectively. For the high-correlation group, the t-statistics for the U.S. GAAP earnings level (X_{Ut}) and lagged level (X_{Ut-1}) are statistically significant at 0.01 level. For the low-correlation group, the adjusted R^2s are 13.64% and 4.94% for the raw and market-adjusted returns, respectively. Only the U.S. GAAP earnings level variable (X_{Ut}) in the raw returns regression has a statistically significant t at the 0.1 level.

Panel B presents results for the foreign GAAP earnings variables. The adjusted R^2s for the high-correlation group are 29.82% and 34.68% for the raw and market-adjusted returns, respectively. The corresponding adjusted R^2s for

Table 5
Comparisons between high- and low-correlation groups using twelve-month stock returns as dependent variable; *t*-statistics in parentheses

	Twelve-month returns[a]		Twelve-month market-adjusted returns[b]	
	High corr.	Low corr.	High corr.	Low corr.
Sample size:	117	27	117	27
Panel A: Earnings based on U.S. GAAP				
Constant	0.1263	0.0127	− 0.0580	− 0.1196
	(1.593)	(0.121)	(− 1.026)	(− 1.280)
X_{Ut}[c]	3.4699	2.9081	2.6841	1.9299
	(5.910)***	(2.382)**	(6.406)***	(1.779)*
X_{Ut-1}[d]	− 2.4657	− 0.8856	− 1.8857	− 0.6273
	(− 2.711)***	(− 0.977)	(− 2.905)***	(− 0.779)
Adj. R^2	0.2214	0.1364	0.2520	0.0494
Panel B: Earnings based on foreign GAAP				
Constant	0.0069	− 0.0219	− 0.1400	− 0.1804
	(0.079)	(− 0.200)	(− 2.281)**	(− 1.926)*
X_{Ft}[e]	4.0913	3.2432	3.1806	2.6552
	(6.962)***	(3.048)***	(7.705)***	(2.910)***
X_{Ft-1}[f]	− 1.8298	− 0.5671	− 1.5292	− 0.4557
	(− 2.362)**	(− 0.619)	(− 2.810)***	(− 0.580)
Adj. R^2	0.2982	0.2252	0.3468	0.2056

[a]Fiscal-year raw stock returns.
[b]Fiscal-year market-adjusted stock returns using the CRSP equal-weighted index.
[c]Earnings based on U.S. GAAP divided by beginning-of-fiscal-year stock price.
[d]Lagged earnings based on U.S. GAAP divided by beginning-of-fiscal-year stock price.
[e]Earnings based on foreign GAAP divided by beginning-of-fiscal-year stock price.
[f]Lagged earnings based on foreign GAAP divided by beginning-of-fiscal-year stock price.
Asterisks indicate significance at the 1% (***), 5% (**), and 10% (*) levels using two-tailed *t* tests.

the low-correlation group are 22.52% and 20.56%. For the high-correlation group, the *t*-statistics are statistically significant at the 0.05 level for both the foreign GAAP earnings level (X_{Ft}) and the foreign GAAP lagged earnings level (X_{Ft-1}) variables. For the low-correlation group, only the level variable (X_{Ft}) has statistically significant *t*s at the 0.01 level. There is a larger increase in adjusted R^2s for the low-correlation group. Results from the two panels are compared using the ratio of R^2s. For instance, using the twelve-month raw returns, the ratios of adjusted R_U^2/R_F^2 are 0.742 and 0.606 for the high- and low-correlation groups, respectively. Using the twelve-month market-adjusted returns, the adjusted R_U^2/R_F^2 ratios are 0.727 and 0.240 for the high- and low-correlation groups, respectively. Both results seem to indicate that foreign GAAP earnings are better than earnings adjusted to U.S. GAAP in their associations with twelve-month stock returns, and that the improvements appear to be greater for the low-correlation group. Results using fifteen-month returns provide similar inferences. With fifteen-month raw returns, the adjusted R_U^2/R_F^2 ratios are 0.796 and 0.506 for the high- and low-correlation groups, respectively. The corresponding ratios are 0.797 and 0.399 when the fifteen-month market-adjusted returns are employed. Since the correlation coefficient employed in forming the two groups is a proxy for the difference between the U.S. and the foreign business environments, our results suggest that the greater explanatory power of foreign GAAP earnings may be due to its relevance to the specific business, economic, and legal practices in those foreign countries.

6. Conclusions

We report stronger associations as evidenced by higher adjusted R^2s for returns–earnings regressions using foreign GAAP earnings than for those using earnings adjusted to U.S.-GAAP. This suggests that earnings based on foreign GAAP may have *greater* relative information content than U.S.-GAAP-based earnings in terms of their association with stock returns. Our results are consistent with Alford et al. (1993) who report that foreign GAAP earnings in certain countries are more timely or value-relevant than earnings based on U.S. GAAP, and Meek (1983) who document market reaction to the announcement of foreign GAAP earnings.

Unlike previous research in this area, our empirical research design avoids the problems associated with sample matching procedures discussed in Harrison, Tomassini, and Dietrich (1983) and Murray (1983). By comparing foreign GAAP earnings *versus* U.S.-GAAP-based earnings for the same firm over the same fiscal year, we are able to use each firm-year observation as its own control. Thus, we rule out potential confounding effects related to firm-specific, industry, or other structural factors caused by the mismatching of firms across different countries.

Turning to the question of what may explain these results, we explore the notion of 'translatability' suggested by Baumol and Malkiel (1993). The returns correlation between a foreign stock index and the S&P 500 index is used as a surrogate for the closeness of the foreign business environment to that of the U.S. Observations are partitioned into a high- and a low-correlation group. The association between stock returns and earnings based on foreign GAAP is stronger than for earnings based on U.S. GAAP for both the high- and the low-correlation group, but the within-group difference is much stronger for the low-correlation group than for the high-correlation group. This result is consistent with the notion that the foreign GAAP rules may reflect the specific, and perhaps, idiosyncratic set of institutional features relevant to that foreign country. Among the institutional differences advanced by Baumol and Malkiel (1993), Edwards (1993), Jacobson and Aaker (1993), and Falk (1994) are those relating to tax structures intercorporate ownership, industrial relations, type of economy (e.g., agriculture-based, resource-based, manufacturing), and national, economic, and social policies.

Our overall results seem to suggest that earnings based on foreign GAAP may convey information that may be lost in the reconciliation to U.S. GAAP. In translating the foreign earnings numbers to conform with U.S. GAAP, differences reflecting contextual factors may inadvertently be overlooked, resulting in a less meaningful set of earnings numbers. Therefore, the current SEC regulation requiring foreign registrants to disclose earnings adjusted to U.S. GAAP calls for further investigation.

References

Alford, A., J. Jones, R. Leftwich, and M. Zmijewski, 1993, The relative informativeness of accounting disclosures in different countries, Journal of Accounting Research 31, 183–223.

Ali, A. and P. Zarowin, 1992, The role of earnings levels in annual earnings–returns studies, Journal of Accounting Research 30, 286–296.

Amir, E., S. Harris, and E. Venuti, 1993, A comparison of the value-relevance of U.S. versus non-U.S. GAAP accounting measures using Form 20-F reconciliations, Journal of Accounting Research 31, 230–264.

Aron, P.H., 1990, Japanese P/E multiples in an era of increasing uncertainty, Report no. 41 (Daiwa Securities America, New York, NY).

Baumol, W. and B. Malkiel, 1993, Redundant regulation of foreign security trading and U.S. competitiveness, Journal of Applied Corporate Finance 5, 19–27.

Beckers, S., R. Grinold, and A. Rudd, 1992, The relative importance of common factors across the European equity markets, Journal of Banking and Finance 16, 75–95.

Belsley, D.A., E. Kuh, and R.E. Welsh, 1980, Regression diagnostics: Identifying influential data and sources of collinearity (Wiley, New York, NY).

Biddle, G.C. and S.M. Saudagaran, 1989, The effects of financial disclosure levels on firms' choices among alternative foreign stock exchange listings, Journal of International Financial Management and Accounting 1, 55–87.

Biddle, G.C. and S.M. Saudagaran, 1991, Foreign stock listings: Benefits, costs, and the accounting policy dilemma, Accounting Horizons 5, 69–80.

Biddle, G.C., G.S. Seow, and A.F. Siegel, 1995, Relative *versus* incremental information content, Contemporary Accounting Research, forthcoming.

Cairns, D., M. Lafferty, and P. Mantle, 1984, Survey of accounts and accountants 1983–84 (Lafferty Publications, London).

Choi, F.D.S. and R.M. Levich, 1991, Behavioral effects of international accounting diversity, Accounting Horizons 5, 1–13.

Clarkson, P.M. and R. Thompson, 1990, Empirical estimates of beta when investors face estimation risk, Journal of Finance 45, 431–453.

Cumby, R.E. and J.D. Glen, 1990, Evaluating the performance of international mutual funds, Journal of Finance 45, 497–522.

Davidson, R. and J.G. MacKinnon, 1981, Several tests for model specification in the presence of alternative hypotheses, Econometrica 49, 781–793.

Davidson, R. and J.G. MacKinnon, 1993, Estimation and inference in econometrics (Oxford University Press, New York, NY).

Dechow, P.M., 1994, Accounting earnings and cash flows as measures of firm performance: The role of accounting accruals, Journal of Accounting and Economics 18, 3–42.

Diamond, D.W. and R.E. Verrecchia, 1991, Disclosure, liquidity, and the cost of capital, Journal of Finance 46, 1325–1359.

Drummen, M. and H. Zimmermann, 1992, The structure of European stock returns, Financial Analysts Journal 48, 15–26.

Easton, P.D. and T.S. Harris, 1991, Earnings as an explanatory variable for returns, Journal of Accounting Research 29, 19–36.

Edwards, F., 1993, Listing of foreign securities on U.S. exchanges, Journal of Applied Corporate Finance 5, 28–36.

Falk, H., 1994, International accounting: A quest for research, Contemporary Accounting Research 11, 595–615.

Fisher, G.R. and M.J. McAleer, 1981, Alternative procedures and associated tests of significance for non-nested hypotheses, Journal of Econometrics 16, 103–119.

Freund, W.C., 1993, That trade obstacle, the SEC, Wall Street Journal, August 27.

Godfrey, L.G., 1983, Testing non-nested models after estimation by instrumental variables or least squares, Econometrica 51, 355–365.

Gray, S.J., 1980, International accounting differences from a security analysis perspective: Some European evidence, Journal of Accounting Research 18, 64–76.

Grinold, R., A. Rudd, and D. Stefek, 1989, Global factors: Fact or fiction?, Journal of Portfolio Management 16, 79–88.

Gumbel, P. and G. Steinmetz, 1995, German firms shift to more-open accounting, Wall Street Journal March 15.

Harrison, W.T. Jr., L.A. Tomassini, and J.R. Dietrich, 1983, The use of control groups in capital markets research, Journal of Accounting Research 21, 65–77.

Hawawini, G., 1984, European equity markets: A review of the evidence on price behavior and efficiency, in: Gabriel Hawawini and Pierre Michel, eds., European equity markets (Garland, New York, NY) 3–84.

Hellman, N., 1993, A comparative analysis of the impact of accounting differences on profits and return on equity: Differences between Swedish practice and US GAAP, European Accounting Review 3, 495–530.

Heston, S.L. and K.G. Rouwenhorst, 1994, Does industrial structure explain the benefits of international diversification?, Journal of Financial Economics 36, 3–27.

Jacobson, R. and D. Aaker, 1993, Myopic management behavior with efficient, but imperfect, financial markets: A comparison of information asymmetries in the U.S. and Japan, Journal of Accounting and Economics 16, 383–405.

Lessard, D.R., 1990, The implications of market efficiency for U.S. disclosure by non-U.S. world class issuers, Working paper (M.I.T., Cambridge, MA).

MacKinnon, J.G., 1992, Model specification tests and artificial regressions, Journal of Economic Literature 30, 102–146.

Meek, G.K., 1983, U.S. securities market responses to alternative earnings disclosures of non-U.S. multinational corporations, The Accounting Review 58, 394–402.

Meek, G.K. and S.M. Saudagaran, 1990, A survey of research on financial reporting in a transnational context, Journal of Accounting Literature 9, 394–402.

Mueller, G.G., H. Gernon, and G. Meek, 1991, Accounting: An international perspective (Richard D. Irwin, Homewood, IL).

Murray, D., 1983, The effect of certain design choices on the assessment of the market's reaction to LIFO changes: A methodological study, Journal of Accounting Research 21, 128–140.

Murray, R.J., W.E. Decker, Jr., and N.W. Dittmar, Jr., 1993, The Coopers & Lybrand SEC manual, 6th ed. (Prentice Hall, Englewood Cliffs, NJ).

Nobes, C.W., 1983, A judgmental international classification of financial reporting practices, Journal of Business Finance and Accounting 10, 1–19.

Nobes, C.W., 1988, The causes of financial reporting differences, in: C.W. Nobes and R.H. Parker, eds., Issues in multinational accounting (Ethan Allan, Oxford).

Siconolfi, M. and K. Salwen, 1992, Big Board, SEC fight over foreign stocks, Wall Street Journal, May 13.

U.S. Department of Commerce, 1992, Survey of current business (DOC, Washington, DC).

Wall Street Journal, 1994, Big Board chairman seeks to boost overseas listing, Wall Street Journal, November 8.

Wall Street Journal, 1995, Japan's ADRs show investment promise, Wall Street Journal, March 28.

Weetman, P. and S.J. Gray, 1991, A comparative international analysis of the impact of accounting principles on profits: The USA *versus* the UK, Sweden and the Netherlands, Accounting and Business Research 21, 363–379.

B
Canada

[12]

THE ACCOUNTING REVIEW
Vol. 77, No. 1
January 2002
pp. 25–50

The Effect of Legal Environment on Voluntary Disclosure: Evidence from Management Earnings Forecasts Issued in U.S. and Canadian Markets

Stephen P. Baginski
John M. Hassell
Michael D. Kimbrough
Indiana University

ABSTRACT: Citing fear of legal liability as a partial explanation, prior research documents (1) managers' reluctance to voluntarily disclose management earnings forecasts, and (2) greater forecast disclosure frequencies in periods of bad news. We provide evidence on how management earnings forecast disclosure differs between the United States (U.S.) and Canada, two otherwise similar business environments with different legal regimes. Canadian securities laws and judicial interpretations create a far less litigious environment than exists in the U.S. We find a greater frequency of management earnings forecast disclosure in Canada relative to the U.S. Further, although U.S. managers are relatively more likely to issue forecasts during interim periods in which earnings decrease, Canadian managers do not exhibit that tendency. Instead, Canadian managers issue more forecasts when earnings are increasing, and their forecasts are of annual rather than interim earnings. Also consistent with a less litigious environment, Canadian managers issue more precise and longer-term forecasts. These findings hold after controlling for other determinants of management earnings forecast disclosure that might differ between

---

We thank workshop participants at the University of Georgia, Washington University, and Indiana University for comments on earlier versions of this paper. We also benefited from discussions with Jamie Pratt, Jerry Salamon, Jim Wahlen, Grace Pownall, Jim Seida, and discussants' comments by Paquita Davis-Friday and Lenny Soffer in conjunction with our presentations of this paper at the Second Globalization Conference (2000), jointly sponsored by the American Accounting Association and the British Accounting Association, and the 2000 American Accounting Association Annual Meeting, respectively. Professor Baginski thanks the Center for International Business Education Research (CIBER) at Indiana University for support of the study. We also gratefully acknowledge the contribution of I/B/E/S International Inc. for providing earnings per share forecast data. These data have been provided as part of a broad academic program to encourage earnings expectations research.

Submitted August 2000
Accepted June 2001

the two countries—firm size, earnings volatility, information asymmetry, growth, capitalization rates, and membership in high-technology and regulated industries.

Keywords: *management earnings forecasts; legal liability; voluntary disclosure.*

Data Availability: *The data used in this study are publicly available from the sources listed in the text.*

I. INTRODUCTION

This paper reports empirical evidence of differences in management earnings forecast disclosure behavior between the United States and Canada. We expect that management forecast disclosure differs between these two countries because of the substantial differences in their legal environments that affect the success of class action, securities-related litigation. Shareholders can bring lawsuits against U.S. companies under SEC Rule 10b-5. Upon observing a large stock price decline (often at an earnings announcement date), plaintiffs in these class action suits typically argue that managers failed to promptly disclose material bad news, causing plaintiffs to buy an overvalued security that declined in value after management revealed the material information.[1] Plaintiffs in the U.S. have favorably settled many of these suits out of court. In contrast, Canadian securities laws and legal interpretations make it difficult to win class action, securities-related suits, especially suits related to the secondary market for securities.

Management forecasts affect security prices (Patell 1976; Ajinkya and Gift 1984; Waymire 1984). Therefore, it is important to understand whether and how legal regimes affect forecast disclosure. On one hand, potential litigation costs associated with failure to meet a management forecast mitigate "cheap talk," and thus may enhance the credibility of publicly disclosed forecasts. On the other hand, fear of litigation may alter the conditions under which managers issue forecasts.

As an example of how litigation fears could alter *which* forecasts are released, Skinner (1994) argues that fear of legal liability relating to Rule 10b-5 suits gives U.S. managers incentive to hasten disclosure of bad news, because (1) early disclosure is a defense against shareholders' claims that management withheld adverse information, and (2) early disclosure shortens the period in which investors can qualify as members of a class action suit. Based on a sample of 93 NASDAQ firms, Skinner (1994) provides evidence that, because of asymmetric incentives to provide timely bad news disclosure, managers are more likely to issue imprecise interim forecasts during periods of large negative earnings surprises than during periods of large positive surprises. Similarly, in a sample of 565 NYSE and AMEX firms, Kasznik and Lev (1995) find that managers are twice as likely to disclose forecasts during periods of large negative earnings news than during periods of large positive earnings news. Policymakers also argue that the threat of litigation reduces a manager's tendency to provide *any* voluntary disclosure of forward-looking information because of the possibility that earnings may fall short of the forecast (e.g., Breeden 1995). In fact, Congress enacted the Private Securities Litigation Reform Act of 1995 to encourage firms to disclose forward-looking information by reducing legal exposure.

[1] Technically, management's failure to disclose material bad news that it should have released to correct misleading or inaccurate prior disclosures triggers legal liability. In practice, however, the mere existence of undisclosed bad news increases the firm's exposure to shareholder lawsuits (see Skinner [1994] and Bamber and Cheon [1998] for related arguments).

Using a sample of U.S. and Canadian firms from 1993 to 1996, we find that Canadian firms issue more management earnings forecasts than do U.S. firms. Further, although U.S. managers are relatively more likely to issue forecasts during interim periods in which earnings decrease, Canadian managers do not exhibit that tendency. Instead, Canadian managers issue more forecasts when earnings are increasing, and their forecasts are of annual rather than interim earnings. Also consistent with a less litigious environment, Canadian managers issue longer-term and more precise forecasts. These Canadian firms' different disclosure patterns persist after controlling for other conditions that might lead to differential disclosure, including firm size, earnings volatility, information asymmetry, growth, capitalization rates, and membership in high-technology and regulated industries.

Our study contributes to management forecast research by investigating the relation between legal regime and specific management forecast disclosure properties—incidence, timeliness, and precision. Although Skinner's (1994) and Kasznik and Lev's (1995) results are consistent with legal liability leading to more disclosure in bad news periods, it is not clear that the legal environment is driving U.S. firms to issue bad news management forecasts in interim periods. First, extant empirical evidence is mixed on the effectiveness of a bad news management forecast in avoiding litigation. Francis et al. (1994) find that (1) substantial declines in earnings are not sufficient to cause litigation; (2) early disclosure of adverse earnings news is not an effective deterrent to litigation, and failure to provide early disclosure of adverse earnings news does not necessarily lead to litigation; and (3) in a litigation sample of 45 observations, 28 suits were based on a management forecast or other pre-earnings release disclosure rather than on the subsequently released actual earnings announcement. Further, Skinner (1997) finds no evidence that management forecast disclosure increases the probability of lawsuit dismissal. However, he provides some evidence that, after controlling for estimated shareholder damages, timely disclosure reduces settlement amounts. Finally, Johnson et al. (2001) interpret their finding that bad news disclosure frequency increases after the Private Securities Litigation Reform Act of 1995 as inconsistent with the argument that reduced legal exposure leads to proportionally fewer bad news disclosures.

Second, with the exception of Frost (2001) and Johnson et al. (2001), prior research has not examined management forecast disclosures in different legal environments.[2] Skinner (1994, 1997), Francis et al. (1994), and Kasznik and Lev (1995) examine disclosures made in the highly litigious U.S. environment. Our finding that managers are more likely to issue forecasts (both bad and good news) in the less litigious Canadian environment is consistent with Frost (2001) and Johnson et al. (2001), who conclude that managers are more likely to issue voluntary disclosures in less litigious environments. Further, our finding that firms issue proportionally fewer bad news forecasts in the Canadian legal environment (relative

---

[2] Johnson et al. (2001) capitalize on an expected change in legal liability created by passage of the Private Securities Litigation Reform Act of 1995 in the U.S. to test whether management forecasting behavior changed. They examine 523 firms in three high-technology industries and find that managers issue more good news and bad news management earnings and sales forecasts after the Act. However, confining the analysis to high-technology firms limits the results' generalizability. The extent that the Act reduced legal exposure was likely not clear to most managers and their legal counsels. Although the rate of post-Act fraud suit dismissals increased from 40 to 60 percent (Levine and Pritchard 1998), 40 percent of the suits continued. Further, Grundfest and Perino (1997) document a shift of post-Act filings from federal to state courts, presumably to avoid the defendant's additional protections under the Federal Act.

Frost (2001) provides comparative descriptive evidence on disclosure of forward-looking information in the U.S. and several European countries for firms in the manufacturing sector. Samples of 80 firms in each country reveal that managers issue more forecasts and more precise forecasts in the non-U.S. countries where legal and regulatory environments are less stringent.

to good news forecasts) is consistent with Skinner's (1994) and Kasznik and Lev's (1995) conclusions that legal liability increases U.S. firms' incentives to disclose management earnings forecasts when earnings news is bad. However, our evidence is inconsistent with Johnson et al.'s (2001) evidence that U.S. high-tech firms do not issue proportionally fewer bad news forecasts after passage of the 1995 Private Securities Litigation Reform Act (which was intended to reduce legal liability).

The results of our study are also relevant to accounting policymakers and securities regulators who believe litigation reform can improve financial reporting. The AICPA's Jenkins Committee identified fear of litigation as an obstacle to providing forward-looking information (AICPA 1994). Managers and auditors complained about excessive and frivolous litigation; accordingly, Congress provided additional safe harbors in the Private Securities Litigation Reform Act of 1995 for parties associated with good-faith projections. Evidence on the effect of legal liability on management forecasting can help policymakers understand the costs of forecast disclosure, which is important if they expect cost-reduction strategies to create incentives for forecast disclosure.

In Section II, we develop hypotheses about how differences in legal environment are likely to affect Canadian and U.S. management forecasting. We describe the sample in Section III and the research design in Section IV. We present the primary results in Section V and the results of supplemental tests in Section VI. In Section VII, we discuss the study's limitations and provide suggestions for future research.

II. MANAGEMENT FORECAST DISCLOSURES IN THE U.S. AND CANADA

Evidence suggests that U.S. management forecasting behavior has changed over time. Patell (1976) suggested that, in the 1960s and 1970s, managers selectively released good news. In the early 1980s, Ajinkya and Gift (1984) and Waymire (1984) documented symmetric forecasting. Then, in the late 1980s and early 1990s, litigation against companies and their auditors increased. Accordingly, Skinner (1994) investigated whether legal liability creates an asymmetric incentive favoring timely management forecasting of bad news. Using a sample of U.S. management forecasts from the 1980s, his results are largely consistent with legal liability-based arguments: (1) management issues more forecasts in periods of bad earnings news than in periods of good news (evidence of asymmetric incentives); (2) bad news interim forecasts occur in imprecise form (e.g., range rather than point, open-interval rather than closed-interval); and (3) the bad news disclosures occur in interim periods. Although these findings are clearly consistent with legal-liability arguments, Skinner (1994) does not vary legal regime.

Differences between the U.S. and Canadian legal systems create a natural experiment with two different legal regimes. Clarkson and Simunic (1994) note that, unlike the U.S., (1) courts in Canada generally require unsuccessful plaintiffs to pay the costs of a successful defendant; (2) because plaintiffs have no absolute right to a jury trial in Canada, judges typically hear technical cases and are less likely to award large settlements based on emotional plaintiff appeals; (3) Canadian discovery rules limit whom the plaintiff can examine under oath; (4) Canadian provinces generally do not allow lawyers to work on a contingent-fee basis, and when allowed, the practice is not widespread; and (5) it is considerably more difficult to bring a class action suit in Canada. Clarkson and Simunic (1994) argue that auditors and managers operating in Canada are therefore likely to make decisions with the expectation of lower litigation costs than would be the case in the United States. Although McConomy (1998) notes that the Ontario Class Proceedings Act (effective in 1993) made class action lawsuits more likely, Paskell-Mede (1994, 1999) and Grossman (1996) point out that class action suits remain rare in Canada and continue to face such significant impediments that Canada is still a far less litigious environment than is the U.S.

A particularly important difference between Canadian and U.S. securities legislation is the notion of "fraud on the market" and its relation to secondary security markets (Paskell-Mede 1999). In common law actions, a plaintiff must prove that (1) a misrepresentation exists, (2) the misrepresentation was negligent, and (3) the plaintiff suffered a loss due to reliance on the misrepresentation. In U.S. courts, the "fraud on the market" concept provides a proof that the plaintiff relied on share price that efficiently reflected the misrepresentation. Judges in Canadian courts refuse to apply the "fraud on the market" concept, stating that it has no place in the Canadian legal system. Instead, Canadian law places the burden of proof on the defendant to prove that the plaintiff did not rely on the misrepresentation, but only in the case of initial security offerings. That is, once a plaintiff proves that management made a negligent misrepresentation in the prospectus, the law deems the plaintiff's reliance to have occurred unless the defendant can prove that the plaintiff did not rely on the misrepresentation when purchasing shares (often by proving that the plaintiff was aware of the misrepresentation). However, in the case of secondary trading, the burden of proving reliance remains with the plaintiff. Because plaintiffs in Canadian secondary-markets-related suits must prove individual reliance on a misrepresentation, but cannot use the "fraud on the market" argument, they face a significant barrier to successful litigation.[3]

Hypothesis Development

We test two general hypotheses. First, the concern that legal liability costs curb public disclosure of either favorable or adverse forward-looking information lies at the core of U.S. policymakers' arguments for increased forward-looking information disclosure. In addition, under economic models of symmetric belief adjustment (King et al. 1990), management forecasts increase the firm's exposure to legal liability. Our first hypothesis (stated in the alternative form) is:

> **H1:** Canadian firms, faced with a less-litigious legal environment, engage in more voluntary information disclosure relative to U.S. firms (*degree of information disclosure hypothesis*).

We define "more voluntary information disclosure" to include: (1) a higher forecast frequency, (2) more precise forecasts, and (3) forecasts over longer horizons. Accordingly, we perform three sets of tests of H1 that correspond to these three measures of information disclosure. Hypothesis 1 predicts that (1) Canadian firms are more likely to disclose management earnings forecasts because managers do not fear the legal liability associated with being inaccurate; (2) Canadian managers disclose more precise forecasts even though inaccuracy is easier to detect *ex post* in more precise forecasts; and (3) Canadian managers disclose forecasts over longer horizons even though the likelihood of inaccuracy increases in forecast horizon.

Our second hypothesis (also stated in the alternative form) relates to prior evidence suggesting that litigation exposure prompts U.S. firms to strategically base the frequency and properties of management forecasts on whether earnings are increasing or decreasing. Specifically, when earnings are decreasing (i.e., in bad news periods), U.S. firms tend to be: (1) more likely to issue a forecast; (2) more likely to issue the forecast in an imprecise form; and (3) more likely to issue the forecast over a short-horizon period. We expect

[3] Empirical evidence suggests that even the stronger Canadian laws for primary offerings do not introduce significant fear of litigation. Clarkson and Simunic (1994) note that approximately 50 percent of Canadian initial public offerings include a management forecast in the offering prospectus (a virtually nonexistent practice in U.S. initial public offerings), and these management forecasts are on average optimistic (Clarkson et al. 1992).

Canadian firms' forecast disclosure properties (frequency, precision, and horizon) to be less associated with earnings decreases:

> **H2:** Canadian firms, faced with a less-litigious legal environment, engage in voluntary information disclosure behaviors that are less related to earnings decreases than do U.S. firms (*bad-news-related behavior hypothesis*).

Because prior research has shown that U.S. firms' forecast frequency, precision, and horizon are related to earnings decreases, H2 is rejected if either Canadian forecast frequency, precision, and horizon are unrelated to the sign of earnings changes or if these Canadian forecast disclosure properties are related to earnings *increases*. In either case, Canadian firms do not engage in the kinds of forecasting behaviors that are related to fear of legal liability resulting from bad earnings news.

Country Similarities that Strengthen Internal Validity

The similar business and investment environments in the U.S. and Canada support our inferences that differences across the two countries in the frequency, precision, and horizon of management forecasts are attributable to differences in legal regimes. For example, researchers often group together U.S. and Canadian firms in international tests of value relevance of accounting data, primarily because these firms are similar on so many dimensions and because empirical evidence shows that the association between accounting data and stock prices is relatively similar in the two countries (Ali and Hwang 2000). The U.S. and Canada share important determinants of the value relevance of accounting data—a market-oriented financial system, private sector standard setting, low influence of tax rules on financial accounting measurements, and higher spending on external auditing (Ali and Hwang 2000). Although generally accepted accounting principles differ between Canada and the U.S., Bandyopadhyay et al. (1994) and Barth and Clinch (1996) find that adjustments from Canadian to U.S. GAAP are irrelevant for valuing cross-listed Canadian companies.

Investor sophistication and market efficiency with respect to the interpretation of forecasted data also appear similar in the two countries. McNichols (1989) provides empirical evidence that U.S. investors can assess the *ex ante* firm-specific bias in seasoned firms' management forecasts. Clarkson et al. (1992) find similar investor sophistication for Canadian firms' management forecasts issued in initial public offerings. With respect to market efficiency, Freund et al. (1997) conclude that the Toronto Stock Exchange (TSE) is informationally efficient. Brown et al. (1991) also document that investors privy to financial analyst forecasts could generate abnormal returns on the TSE, but that the returns are not significantly higher than transactions costs if the trading strategy is not implemented until after the forecasts become public (also see L'Her and Suret [1991] for similar findings).[4] In summary, empirical evidence suggests that revelation of Canadian managers' private

[4] Our data requirements result in a Canadian management forecast sample that is almost entirely composed of large firms listed on the TSE, approximately three-quarters of which have analyst following. The market for shares of large firms with analyst following is more likely to be informationally efficient. Further, if managers release forecasts to move stock prices, a lack of market efficiency would likely result in fewer Canadian management forecasts relative to the U.S. (a bias against the null hypothesis that we reject in tests described later). Also, a bad news management forecast would be a more beneficial legal liability-limiting strategy in Canada because the company could reap the benefits of public disclosure without the associated negative stock price reaction (a bias in favor of the null hypothesis that Canadian management forecasts exhibit the same bad news bias as do U.S. management forecasts—a null that we reject in tests described later).

information in management forecast form should lead to a relatively complete and immediate price reaction.[5]

Canadian and U.S. exchanges have similar rules on material news disclosure. The TSE's "Policy Statement on Timely Disclosure and Related Guidelines" requires firms to provide investors with equal access to all material information. Material information is "any information relating to the business and affairs of a company that results in or would reasonably be expected to result in a significant change in the market price or value of any of the company's listed securities" (TSE 2000, 1). The TSE requires "immediate disclosure" of "firm evidence of significant increases or decreases in near-term earnings prospects," although "forecasts of earnings and other financial forecasts need not be disclosed" (TSE 2000, 4). Further, the TSE encourages wide dissemination through news services (specifically mentioning Dow Jones). Exceptions to these rules allow delay for proprietary information. Guidelines and rules of law also prohibit insider trading.

Finally, differences in earnings management opportunities may exist between the two countries. However, to create an alternative explanation for our results, (1) differences in earnings management opportunities must exist between the two countries; (2) earnings management must be a successful means of limiting legal liability; and (3) when considering the menu of alternative actions to limit legal liability (e.g., engage in earnings management, issue a voluntary management forecast disclosure of bad news, do not provide a forecast that could turn out to be wrong, etc.), the action chosen must differ between the U.S. and Canada because one alternative performs better on a cost/benefit trade-off. If these conditions all hold, then a finding of, say, fewer management forecasts in the U.S. might indicate that U.S. managers can more easily manage subsequently revealed earnings, that such earnings management fools investors about firm performance, and that earnings management is more beneficial to the firm than voluntary disclosure. We are unaware of any empirical evidence on differential benefits to earnings management between the U.S. and Canada, but we cannot rule out this possibility because controlling for earnings management differences across countries is beyond the scope of our study.

In summary, many similarities between U.S. and Canadian environments strengthen the internal validity of our comparative analysis. Still, differences exist that may affect management forecasts—information asymmetry, analyst coverage, earnings volatility, firm size, membership in high-tech and regulated industries, growth, and capitalization rates. Our empirical tests control for these conditions.

III. SAMPLE

Periods Available for Forecasting

Our sample includes all quarterly and annual periods of U.S. and Canadian firms with available data on Compustat, including beginning-of-period price data, shares, earnings per share, and adjustment factors for the 1993–1996 period.[6] Table 1, Panel A reports that

---

[5] In an untabulated regression of percentage change in analyst forecasts on percentage change in expectations conveyed by management forecasts, the slope coefficient is significantly positive ($p < 0.001$). Significant differences do not exist (1) between the slope coefficient for Canadian and U.S. firms, and (2) for the Canadian firms, between locally listed firms and firms cross-listed in the U.S. These results suggest that analysts update their expectations in response to management forecasts.

[6] Like most research, our sample is limited to firms covered by Compustat, which covers only about half of the firms reporting to the SEC in the middle of our sample period. (In the 1994 manual, Compustat reports coverage of approximately 6,800 U.S. companies; Guenther and Rosman [1994] report that 13,424 firms filed with the SEC in 1994.) Although we do not have data on the number of Canadian firms in 1994, the most recent TSE web site lists 1,407 traded firms. The 1998 Compustat tape includes 674 TSE firms, nearly half of the TSE population, which according to its web site, represents 95 percent of market capitalization in Canada. Thus, Compustat Canadian firm coverage spans an important segment of the Canadian market.

TABLE 1
Sample Selection Criteria and Sample Characteristics

Panel A: Selection of 1993–1996 Firm-Quarters and Firm-Years

	U.S. Firms	*Canadian Firms*	*Total*
Firm-years available on Compustat	51,434	5,073	56,507
Missing data	(24,895)	(2,102)	(26,997)
Surviving firm-years	26,539	2,971	29,510
Firm-quarters available on Compustat	132,737	19,694	152,431
Missing data	(52,600)	(13,590)	(66,190)
Surviving firm-quarters	80,137	6,104	86,241
Total firm-years and firm-quarters sample	106,676	9,075	115,751

Distributed across Following Exchanges	*Firms*	*% of total*
NASDAQ	39,591	34.2
NYSE	34,412	29.7
OTC	25,583	22.2
American Stock Exchange	8,737	7.5
Toronto Stock Exchange	5,757	5.0
Regional exchanges	893	0.8
Vancouver Stock Exchange	378	0.3
Nonlisted Canadian	253	0.2
Montreal Exchange	147	0.1
Total firm-years and firm-quarters sample	115,751	100.0

Panel B: Selection of 1993–1996 Management Earnings Forecasts

	Issued by U.S. Firms	*Issued by Canadian Firms*	*Total*
Earnings forecasts identified by keyword search of Dow Jones News Retrieval Service	1,688	391	2,079
Lost due to changes in Compustat coverage	(281)	(78)	(359)
Listed on Compustat	1,407	313	1,720
Missing Compustat data	(74)	(36)	(110)
Complete data on Compustat	1,333	277	1,610
Forecasts of 1992 and 1997 results	(112)	(26)	(138)
Long-range (> 365 days) forecasts	(57)	(32)	(89)
Final management earnings forecast sample	1,164	219	1,383

Distributed across Following Exchanges	*Forecasts*	*% of Total*
NYSE	649	46.9
NASDAQ	376	27.2
Toronto Stock Exchange	206	14.9
Other U.S.	139	10.1
Other Canadian	13	0.9
Final management earnings forecast sample	1,383	100.0

(*Continued on next page*)

TABLE 1 (Continued)

Distributed across Firms	*Firms (%)*	*Forecasts (%)*
U.S. firms that issued:		
one forecast	398 (57.9)	398 (34.2)
two forecasts	181 (26.4)	362 (31.1)
three forecasts	64 (9.3)	192 (16.5)
four or more forecasts	44 (6.4)	212 (18.2)
	687 (100.0)	1,164 (100.0)
Canadian locally listed firms that issued:		
one forecast	38 (59.4)	38 (34.9)
two forecasts	16 (25.0)	32 (29.3)
three forecasts	5 (7.8)	15 (13.8)
four or more forecasts	5 (7.8)	24 (22.0)
	64 (100.0)	109 (100.0)
Canadian cross-listed firms that issued:		
one forecast	20 (40.0)	20 (18.2)
two forecasts	16 (32.0)	32 (29.1)
three forecasts	8 (16.0)	24 (21.8)
four or more forecasts	6 (12.0)	34 (30.9)
	50 (100.0)	110 (100.0)

56,507 firm-years and 152,431 firm-quarters are available. Periods with complete data totaled 115,751. NASDAQ was the most represented U.S. exchange (34.2 percent of all periods in the two-country combined sample), and the TSE was the most represented Canadian exchange (5.0 percent of all periods in the combined sample). In contrast to most prior legal-liability-related research and in order to enhance our results' generalizability, we do not limit our tests to periods with "large" earnings surprises.

Management Earnings Forecasts

We collected management forecasts of both interim and annual earnings from the Dow Jones News Retrieval Service (DJNRS) during the entire 1993–1996 period.[7] The DJNRS contains articles published in the *Wall Street Journal* and *Barron's*, as well as unpublished announcements appearing on the Broad Tape. The DJNRS covers the major news wires and newspapers in Canada, especially those specializing in corporate news. In addition, the TSE lists Dow Jones as a preferred means of disclosure. Therefore, we consider DJNRS a reasonable (and unbiased) source of management earnings forecasts. However, if DJNRS provides incomplete Canadian coverage, either because of the DJNRS physical location or because U.S. investors are less interested in smaller foreign firms, then the incomplete coverage would bias against our finding of greater forecast frequency for Canadian firms. We also do not limit the coverage period to only the fourth quarter because Canadian firms are required to file only the first three quarters of interim results (Frost and Kinney 1996).

[7] Our DJNRS search keywords are: "expects earnings," "expects net," "expects income," "expects losses," "expects profits," "expects results," and three similar lists with first words "forecasts," "predicts," and "sees."

Table 1, Panel B presents information about the management forecast selection. Our original search identified 2,079 forecasts. We lost 359 forecasts due to changes in Compustat coverage.[8] After deleting forecasts for periods with missing Compustat data (110), forecasts of 1992 and 1997 results (138), and long-range forecasts (89), a total of 1,383 management forecasts remain in the sample: 1,164 issued by U.S. firms and 219 issued by Canadian firms.[9]

The 1,164 U.S. forecasts are made by 687 firms (1.69 per firm). The 219 Canadian management forecasts are made by 64 Canadian firms listed only in Canada and 50 Canadian firms cross-listed on U.S. exchanges (1.92 per firm). Our primary tests do not differentiate locally listed from cross-listed Canadian firms. Pooling the locally listed and cross-listed firms reduces the power of our tests to the extent that cross-listed Canadian firms face some legal exposure in U.S. markets. However, Frost and Pownall (1994) were unable to identify a single instance of formal investigation, administrative proceeding, or court action against a foreign issuer for violation of U.S. disclosure rules. Legal analysis (Paskell-Mede 1999) also raises doubts about the extent to which cross-listed firms are exposed to liability under the U.S. legal system. Frost and Pownall (1994) cite political issues, difficulty in monitoring, and lack of cooperative agreements with other countries as barriers to enforcement of foreign-issuer compliance. Finally, Core (1997) finds that although cross-listing is associated with the magnitude of director and officer liability coverage for Canadian companies that purchase insurance, cross-listing does not explain Canadian firms' decisions to purchase the policy. In summary, cross-listing is unlikely to increase legal exposure to the level faced by U.S. firms. Accordingly, Table 1, Panel B provides descriptive data on the disclosures of the Canadian cross-listed firms vis-à-vis locally listed Canadian and U.S. firms, but our primary tests pool together the cross-listed and locally listed Canadian firms.

IV. RESEARCH DESIGN

In this section, we present our research design for tests of H1 and H2 using the three measures of information disclosure: forecast frequency, forecast precision, and length of forecast horizon.

Forecast Frequency

To test H1 and H2, we estimate the following logistic regression model for a combined sample of U.S. and Canadian companies across all potential forecasting periods (n = 115,751):[10]

$$\begin{aligned} \text{FORECAST}_{i,t} = {} & a_0 + a_1\,\Delta\text{ESIGN}_{i,t} + a_2\,\text{CANADA}_{i,t} + a_3\,\text{CANADA}_{i,t} \\ & \times \Delta\text{ESIGN}_{i,t} + a_4\,|\Delta\text{EARNINGS}_{i,t}| + a_5\,\text{LSIZE}_{i,t} \\ & + a_6\,\text{REGULATE}_{i,t} + a_7\,\text{HIGHTECH}_{i,t} + \varepsilon_{i,t} \end{aligned} \tag{1}$$

[8] A major source of data loss is a combination of CUSIP and name changes that we are unable to track. Conversations with Compustat personnel have not enabled us to recover these observations. Because the rate of management earnings forecast observation loss is higher for Canadian firms (78 ÷ 391 = 20 percent) than U.S. firms (281 ÷ 1,688 = 16.6 percent), and because we find greater forecast frequency for Canadian firms, the loss of observations does not affect our inferences for H1.

[9] Canadian forecasts represent 18.8 percent of the original sample (391 of 2,079). However, 36 percent of the discarded long-range forecasts (32 of 89) are Canadian, indicating that Canadian firms provide more long-range (> 365 days) forecasts.

[10] We also ran OLS regressions, and the results are qualitatively identical. We code single news stories containing both annual and interim earnings forecasts as two separate observations.

where:

$FORECAST_{i,t}$ = 1 if the firm issued a management earnings forecast during the period, and 0 otherwise;
$\Delta ESIGN_{i,t}$ = the sign of the earnings change, defined as 1 for $\Delta EARNINGS_{i,t} \geq 0$ (i.e., good news) and 0 for $\Delta EARNINGS_{i,t} < 0$ (i.e., bad news); where $\Delta EARNINGS_{i,t}$ = the change in earnings, defined as $(EPS_{i,t} - EPS_{i,t-k})/PRICE_{i,t-k}$, where $EPS_{i,t}$ = earnings (net income) per share for firm i in period t; $EPS_{i,t-k}$ = earnings per share for firm i in period t − 1 for annual and t − 4 for quarterly periods; and $PRICE_{i,t-k}$ = security price for firm i at the end of period t − 1 for annual and t − 4 for quarterly periods (all obtained from Compustat);[11]
$CANADA_{i,t}$ = 1 if the potential forecasting period relates to a Canadian firm (regardless of whether the firm issued a forecast in that period), and 0 otherwise (i.e., 0 when the potential forecasting period relates to a U.S. firm);
$|\Delta EARNINGS_{i,t}|$ = the absolute value of $\Delta EARNINGS_{i,t}$;
LSIZE = the log of market value of equity at the beginning of the period;
REGULATE = 1 if the firm is in a regulated industry, and 0 otherwise; and
HIGHTECH = 1 if the firm is in a high-technology industry, and 0 otherwise.

Figure 1 maps the coefficients in Equation (1) to H1 and H2. Column (1) lists the coefficient sums in earnings increase periods (i.e., good news; ΔESIGN = 1) for Canadian firms (row 1) and for U.S. firms (row 2). Column (2) provides analogous coefficients for earnings decrease periods (i.e., bad news; ΔESIGN = 0). The last row indicates the difference *between countries* in the propensity to issue forecasts in periods of good news ($a_2 + a_3$) and bad news (a_2). Hypothesis 1 predicts that Canadian firms issue more forecasts; thus, we expect both sets of coefficients to be positive ($a_2 + a_3 > 0$, $a_2 > 0$).

The last column of Figure 1 provides coefficients associated with differences between good and bad news periods (i.e., "sign-related" forecasting behavior) in Canada (row 1) and in the U.S. (row 2). The last row in the column shows that the coefficient a_3 measures the difference *between countries* in sign-related forecasting behavior. If legal-liability-created asymmetric forecast disclosure incentives in the U.S. lead to more forecasts in bad news periods, then we expect $a_1 < 0$. Hypothesis 2 predicts $a_3 > 0$, indicating that Canadian managers are less likely to skew forecast disclosure toward bad news periods. Given our focus on the differences associated with different legal regimes, we base all hypothesis tests on the difference between countries, not the conditions within a country.

The remaining variables in Equation (1) control for other potential nonlegal-liability-related differences between the two countries that could affect management forecasting behavior. Firms with more volatile earnings face greater risk of inaccurate forecasts, with

[11] Kasznik and Lev (1995) employ alternative quarterly expectation models (analyst forecasts and seasonal random-walk) and document no difference in results. To maximize sample size, results tabulated for Equation (1) are based on the random-walk (seasonal random-walk) expectations to compute annual (quarterly) earnings surprise. Replication with a random-walk for quarterly earnings does not affect our conclusions. Analyst forecast coverage is significantly greater for our U.S. firms (mean analyst coverage of 1.84) than for our Canadian firms (mean analyst coverage of 1.29, Wilcoxon rank sum test p-value < 0.001 on the difference). We were able to obtain I/B/E/S median financial analyst forecasts for 40 percent of the sample. Replication substituting I/B/E/S analyst forecasts when available and limiting the analysis to firms covered by analysts does not affect our inferences.

FIGURE 1
Mapping Equation (1) Coefficients into Hypothesis Tests[a]

	Good News Period *ΔESIGN = 1*	*Bad News Period* *ΔESIGN = 0*	*Difference across Sign of Earnings Change (column 1 – column 2)*
Canadian (CANADA = 1)	$a_0 + a_1 + a_2 + a_3$	$a_0 + a_2$	$a_1 + a_3$
U.S. (CANADA = 0)	$a_0 + a_1$	a_0	a_1
Difference between countries (row 1 – row 2)	(H1 test during good news period): $a_2 + a_3 > 0$	(H1 test during bad news period): $a_2 > 0$	Difference between countries in sign-related behavior (H2): $a_3 > 0$

[a] Equation (1): $FORECAST_{i,t} = a_0 + a_1\,\Delta ESIGN_{i,t} + a_2\,CANADA_{i,t} + a_3\,CANADA_{i,t} \times \Delta ESIGN_{i,t} + a_4\,|\Delta EARNINGS_{i,t}| + a_5\,LSIZE_{i,t} + a_6\,REGULATE_{i,t} + a_7\,HIGHTECH_{i,t} + \varepsilon_{i,t}$

To map equations (2), (3), and (4) into the hypotheses, replace the "a" coefficients with "b," "c," and "c" coefficients, respectively, and reverse the sign predictions on b_3 and c_3. Then refer to the following models:

Equation (2): $PRECISE_i = b_0 + b_1\,\Delta ESIGN_i + b_2\,CANADA_i + b_3\,CANADA_i \times \Delta ESIGN_i + b_4\,LSIZE_i + b_5\,REGULATE_i + b_6\,HIGHTECH_i + b_7\,FHORIZON_i + v_i$

Equation (3): $FHORIZON_i = c_0 + c_1\,NEWS_i + c_2\,CANADA_i + c_3\,CANADA_i \times NEWS_i + b_4\,LSIZE_i + b_5\,REGULATE_i + b_6\,HIGHTECH_i + \mu_i$

Equation (4): $ALTFHORIZON_i = c_0 + c_1\,NEWS_i + c_2\,CANADA_i + c_3\,CANADA_i \times NEWS_i + c_4\,LSIZE_i + c_5\,REGULATE_i + c_6\,HIGHTECH_i + \eta_i$

ΔESIGN = 1 for ΔEARNINGS ≥ 0 (i.e., good news), 0 for ΔEARNINGS < 0 (i.e., bad news), where $\Delta EARNINGS_{i,t} = [EPS_{i,t} - EPS_{i,t-k}] / PRICE_{i,t-k}$;
$EPS_{i,t}$ = earnings per share for firm i in period t;
$EPS_{i,t-k}$ = earnings per share for firm i in period t-k;
$PRICE_{i,t-k}$ = security price for firm i in period t-k; and
k = 1 and 4 for annual and quarterly observations, respectively.

FORECAST = 1 if the firm issued a management forecast during the period, and 0 otherwise;
PRECISE = 3 (2, 1, 0) for point (range, open-interval, general impression) forecasts;
CANADA = 1 if the potential forecasting period relates to a Canadian firm, and 0 if it relates to a U.S. firm;
NEWS = 1 if the forecast is good news, and 0 if the forecast is bad news. *Good news* disclosures include management forecast point estimates above expected earnings, range estimates where the midpoint exceeds expected earnings, and all minimum estimates. Expected earnings equals the median I/B/E/S analyst forecast when available. Otherwise, expected earnings equals the random-walk EPS for annual forecasts and seasonal random-walk for quarterly forecasts. *Bad news* disclosures include point estimates below expected earnings, range estimates where the midpoint is less than expected earnings, and all maximum estimates;
FHORIZON = the number of calendar days between the date of forecast and the end of the period being forecast;
ALTFHORIZON = the number of calendar days between the date of forecast and the end of the firm's fiscal year;
LSIZE = natural log of the market value of equity at the beginning of the period;
HIGHTECH = 1 if a firm belongs to Pharmaceuticals (Compustat SIC codes 2833–2836), R&D Services (8731–8734), Programming (7371–7379), Computers (3570–3577), or Electronics (3600–3674) industries, and 0 otherwise; and
REGULATE = 1 if a firm belongs to Telephone (4812–4813), TV (4833), Cable (4841), Communications (4811–4899), Gas (4922–4924), Electricity (4931), Water (4941), or Financial (6021–6023, 6035–6036, 6141, 6311, 6321, 6331) industries, and 0 otherwise.

the associated legal and reputational costs. We control for volatility using the absolute value of the current-period earnings change, |ΔEARNINGS|, because this captures current-period volatility and does not introduce the survivorship bias associated with an historical measure. We expect $a_4 < 0$ because managers are less willing to forecast when earnings are volatile. Prior research finds that larger firms issue more management forecasts (Cox 1985; Waymire 1985), so we control for the log of market value of equity at the beginning of the period, LSIZE, and expect $a_5 > 0$. Regulatory bodies require regulated firms to produce large amounts of information, and thus, management earnings forecasts are likely less beneficial (Kasznik and Lev 1995). Using Kasznik and Lev's (1995) classification scheme, REGULATE equals 1 when a firm belongs to Telephone (4812–4813), TV (4833), Cable (4841), Communications (4811–4899), Gas (4922–4924), Electricity (4931), Water (4941), or Financial (6021–6023, 6035–6036, 6141, 6311, 6321, 6331) industries, and 0 otherwise. We expect $a_6 < 0$ if regulated firms issue fewer forecasts. High-tech firms are riskier, and the greater value of private information may lead less-informed investors to demand more voluntary, publicly released management forecasts to level the informational playing field. On the other hand, high-tech firms may be less likely to issue a management forecast to avoid conveying proprietary information. Accordingly, we cannot predict the sign of a_7. Following Kasznik and Lev (1995), HIGHTECH equals 1 if a firm belongs to Pharmaceuticals (Compustat SIC codes 2833–2836), R&D Services (8731–8734), Programming (7371–7379), Computers (3570–3577), or Electronics (3600–3674) industries, and 0 otherwise.

Forecast Precision

King et al. (1990) argue that managers are concerned about potential litigation if a forecast turns out to be inaccurate. Less precise forecasts (e.g., a range, minimum, maximum, or general impression) are less likely to turn out to be inaccurate than are point forecasts. Accordingly, researchers have argued that, when faced with perceived higher expected litigation costs, managers will issue less precise forecasts. Empirical evidence in U.S. markets is consistent with the assertion that forecasts are less precise when the firm is performing poorly (Skinner 1994; Baginski and Hassell 1997; Bamber and Cheon 1998).

Although Canadian firm managers are subject to adverse reputation effects of inaccuracy, the Canadian legal system exacts lower legal penalties for inaccuracy than does the U.S. system. Canadian managers are therefore likely to issue more precise management forecasts (H1) and to make forecast precision choices that are less likely to depend on whether the firm is performing poorly during the period (H2). To test these hypotheses, we estimate the following ordered logistic regression model for a pooled sample of all *forecasts* issued by U.S. and Canadian firms (n = 1,383):

$$\begin{aligned} PRECISE_i = {} & b_0 + b_1\,\Delta ESIGN_i + b_2\,CANADA_i + b_3\,CANADA_i \times \Delta ESIGN_i \\ & + b_4\,LSIZE_i + b_5\,REGULATE_i + b_6\,HIGHTECH_i \\ & + b_7\,FHORIZON_i + v_i. \end{aligned} \quad (2)$$

We measure management forecast precision using an ordinal coding scheme that assigns the highest value to the most precise forecasts. PRECISE equals 3, 2, 1, and 0 for point, closed-interval, open-interval, and general impression forecasts, respectively. Hypothesis 1 predicts that Canadian firms will issue more precise forecasts because the legal penalties for inaccuracy are smaller. For earnings decreases, this suggests that $b_2 > 0$, and for earnings increases, it suggests that $b_2 + b_3 > 0$. If fear of legal liability leads U.S. firms to issue less precise forecasts when the firm is performing poorly, then $b_1 > 0$. Hypothesis 2 predicts that Canadian forecast precision is less skewed toward poor performance than is U.S. forecast precision ($b_3 < 0$).[12]

Based on Baginski and Hassell's (1997) conclusion that larger firms garner lower benefits of precise forecasting, we expect a negative coefficient on firm size ($b_4 < 0$). As in Baginski and Hassell (1997) and Bamber and Cheon (1998), we also control for forecast horizon (FHORIZON), the number of calendar days between the forecast and period-end. The longer the forecast horizon, the greater management's uncertainty about earnings, which should lead to less precise forecasts. Thus, we expect $b_7 < 0$. We continue to expect $b_5 < 0$ (less precise forecasts for regulated firms), and we make no prediction for b_6.

Length of Forecast Horizon

Longer forecast horizons provide investors with information on a timelier basis. However, longer-horizon forecasts have a greater chance of being *ex post* inaccurate and, as a result, increase the firm's legal exposure. Canadian firms are more likely to enjoy the benefits of providing investors with more timely information because Canadian firms face lower legal exposure when issuing longer-horizon forecasts. Thus, H1 predicts that Canadian firms issue longer-horizon forecasts for both good and bad news.

Skinner (1994) finds that, faced with substantial legal exposure, U.S. firms' longer-horizon annual forecasts reflect primarily good news, but their shorter-horizon interim forecasts reflect primarily bad news. Hypothesis 2 predicts that Canadian firms, facing relatively less legal exposure, are less likely to restrict bad news forecasts to short horizons.

To test these predictions, we estimate the following OLS regression models for the pooled sample of U.S. and Canadian management forecasts (n = 1,204):

$$\text{Model 1: } FHORIZON_i = c_0 + c_1\, NEWS_i + c_2\, CANADA_i + c_3\, CANADA_i \times NEWS_i + c_4\, LSIZE_i + c_5\, REGULATE_i + c_6\, HIGHTECH_i + \mu_i. \quad (3)$$

$$\text{Model 2: } ALTFHORIZON_i = c_0 + c_1\, NEWS_i + c_2\, CANADA_i + c_3\, CANADA_i \times NEWS_i + c_4\, LSIZE_i + c_5\, REGULATE_i + c_6\, HIGHTECH_i + \eta_i. \quad (4)$$

As in Baginski and Hassell (1997) and Skinner (1997), we operationalize forecast horizon (FHORIZON) as the number of calendar days until period-end, regardless of whether the period is an interim or annual forecasting period. However, viewing an interim forecast as part of an annual period suggests an alternative measure of horizon (ALTFHORIZON), the number of days until fiscal year-end. For example, a first-quarter forecast 15 days before quarter-end is 288 days before year-end. Accordingly, we estimate the model for each of the two forecast horizon definitions.

---

[12] An alternative contemporaneous measure of earnings change directly compares the management forecast to prevailing analyst expectations. However, this measure is problematic because its construction is a function of forecast precision, the dependent variable. Therefore, we use the period's earnings change in the precision tests, consistent with Bamber and Cheon (1998), who use earnings change rather than forecast-based news in their model to explain forecast precision.

When investigating the relation between legal liability and forecast horizon, Skinner (1994) defines good and bad news in terms of the change in contemporaneous expectations. Accordingly, we define a dichotomous variable, NEWS, to proxy for the sign of the news management forecasts convey relative to contemporaneous expectations. *Good news* disclosures include management forecast point estimates above expected earnings, range estimates where the midpoint exceeds expected earnings, and all minimum estimates. Expected earnings equals the median I/B/E/S analyst forecast when available. Otherwise, expected earnings equals the random-walk EPS for annual forecasts and seasonal random-walk for quarterly forecasts. *Bad news* disclosures include point estimates below expected earnings, range estimates where the midpoint is less than expected earnings, and all maximum estimates. NEWS equals 1 for good news forecasts and 0 for bad news forecasts. We discard 32 *neutral news* forecasts (point estimates equaling expected earnings and range estimates where the midpoint equals expected earnings) and all general impression forecasts.[13]

Hypothesis 1 predicts that Canadian firms will be more likely to engage in riskier longer-range forecasting for both bad ($c_2 > 0$) and good ($c_2 + c_3 > 0$) news. Given Skinner's (1994) finding that U.S. firms tend to voluntarily release good news in longer-horizon annual forecasts and bad news in shorter-horizon interim forecasts, we expect $c_1 > 0$, indicating that U.S. good news forecasts are of a longer horizon. Hypothesis 2 predicts that Canadian firms will have less tendency to choose longer forecast horizons for good news relative to U.S. firms ($c_3 < 0$). For the control variables, we expect $c_4 > 0$ (longer forecast horizons for larger firms), $c_5 < 0$ (shorter forecast horizons for regulated firms), and we make no prediction for the coefficient c_6 on high-tech firms.

V. RESULTS

Variable Distributions and Other Descriptive Statistics

Table 2, Panel A describes variable distributions for our sample of 115,751 forecasting periods used to estimate Equation (1) (forecast frequency tests). Mean and median ΔEARNINGS are slightly higher than 1 percent and 0.1 percent of share price, respectively. Mean and median |ΔEARNINGS| are approximately 8.5 percent and 1.1 percent of price, respectively. Mean earnings change is more positive for Canadian firms (2.15 percent relative to 1.13 percent for U.S. firms), but median earnings change is almost identical (0.16 percent relative to 0.14 percent for U.S. firms). A similar relationship holds for absolute earnings change.[14]

Median firm size (per observation) is nearly $87 million, which is much smaller than in Kasznik and Lev (1995), who report median firm sizes of $381 and $436 million for earnings increase and decrease periods, respectively. We do not require I/B/E/S quarterly analyst forecasts for our primary tests, so our sample includes many more small and lightly followed firms. Also, in contrast to Kasznik and Lev (1995), we include only earnings forecasts, not sales forecasts, and we sample from the full year instead of only the fourth quarter where management forecast frequency is the greatest. Not surprisingly then, Panel

---

[13] Defining minimum estimates as good news and maximum estimates as bad news is consistent with the stock price reactions to these disclosures documented by Baginski et al. (1994). We also replicated the analysis using a five-level news measure corresponding to the five categories of news in Baginski et al. (1994) with similar results.

[14] Because our hypotheses are based only on the *sign* of the surprise (ΔESIGN), skewness in ΔEARNINGS (and its absolute value) only affects the control variables. In untabulated results, we find that log transformation of |ΔEARNINGS| does not increase the variable's explanatory power, nor does it change our inferences concerning H1 and H2.

TABLE 2
Variable Distributions for 1993–1996 Sample of 115,751 Potential Forecasting Periods (Panel A) and 1993–1996 Sample of 1,236 Management Earnings Forecasts (Panel B)

Panel A: Variable Distributions for Sample of 115,571 Potential Forecasting Periods and Frequencies and Types of Forecasts Released during those Periods

Continuous Variables	*n*	*Mean*	*Standard Deviation*	*Lower Quartile*	*Median*	*Upper Quartile*
ΔEARNINGS	115,751	0.0121	0.2258	−0.0083	0.0014	0.0124
U.S.	106,676	0.0113	0.2237	−0.0082	0.0014	0.0120
Canadian	9,075	0.0215	0.2494	−0.0083	0.0016	0.0182
|ΔEARNINGS|	115,751	0.0850	0.2096	0.0027	0.0105	0.0462
U.S.	106,676	0.0838	0.2077	0.0027	0.0130	0.0452
Canadian	9,075	0.0991	0.2298	0.0033	0.0130	0.0589
SIZE (millions)	115,751	984.3	4315.3	22.5	86.7	396.1
U.S.	106,676	1001.5	4459.5	22.2	85.1	386.3
Canadian	9,075	782.3	1926.4	29.2	107.3	535.4

Classification Variables	*Yes (%)*	*No (%)*	*Total (%)*
High-tech firm (HIGHTECH = 1)	20,058 (17.3)	95,693 (82.7)	115,751 (100.0)
U.S.	18,913 (17.7)	87,763 (82.3)	106,676 (100.0)
Canadian	1,145 (12.6)	7,930 (87.4)	9,075 (100.0)
Regulated firm (REGULATE = 1)	15,116 (13.1)	100,635 (86.9)	115,751 (100.0)
U.S.	14,541 (13.6)	92,135 (86.4)	106,676 (100.0)
Canadian	575 (6.3)	8,500 (93.7)	9,075 (100.0)
Good news period (Earnings increase; ΔESIGN = 1)	67,378 (58.2)	48,373 (41.8)	115,751 (100.0)
U.S.	62,348 (58.4)	44,328 (41.6)	106,676 (100.0)
Canadian	5,030 (55.4)	4,045 (44.6)	9,075 (100.0)

Forecast Rates in Potential Forecast Periods	*Forecasts*	*Periods*	*Rate*
Canadian firms	219	9,075	2.41%
Good news periods (ΔEARNINGS ≥ 0)	150	5,030	2.98%
Bad news periods (ΔEARNINGS < 0)	69	4,045	1.71%
U.S. firms	1,164	106,676	1.09%
Good news periods	685	62,348	1.10%
Bad news periods	479	44,328	1.08%

Management Forecast Type	*U.S. Firm*	*Canadian Firm (%)*	*Total (%)*
Point	282 (24.2)	101 (46.1)	383 (27.7)
Range	292 (25.1)	32 (14.6)	324 (23.4)
Minimum	309 (26.5)	48 (21.9)	357 (25.8)
Maximum	151 (13.0)	14 (6.4)	165 (12.0)
General impression	130 (11.2)	24 (11.0)	154 (11.1)
Total	1,164 (100.0)	219 (100.0)	1,383 (100.0)

(Continued on next page)

TABLE 2 (Continued)

Panel B: Variable Distributions for 1993–1996 Sample of 1,236 Management Earnings Forecasts for which Forecast News Can Be Calculated (General Impression Forecasts Excluded)

Continuous Variables	*n*	*Mean*	*Standard Deviation*	*Lower Quartile*	*Median*	*Upper Quartile*
FHORIZON	1,236	89.2	107.4	6.0	49.0	188.0
U.S.	1,040	70.5	98.1	2.0	30.0	105.5
Canadian	196	188.1	100.3	145.0	215.0	246.0
ALTFHORIZON	1,236	152.5	111.6	63.0	160.0	245.0
U.S.	1,040	142.5	112.9	54.0	139.0	239.5
Canadian	196	205.5	87.6	197.0	228.0	258.0
SIZE (millions)	1,236	1,789.5	4,523.0	74.9	300.7	1,397.8
U.S.	1,040	1,893.3	4,862.4	66.6	280.4	1,374.9
Canadian	196	1,238.5	1,795.9	138.8	541.9	1,526.7
|ΔEARNINGS|	1,236	0.0343	0.1013	0.0023	0.0080	0.0247
U.S.	1,040	0.0347	0.1079	0.0019	0.0072	0.0221
Canadian	196	0.0324	0.0536	0.0038	0.0113	0.0361

Classification Variables	*Yes (%)*	*No (%)*	*Total (%)*
High-tech firm (HIGHTECH = 1)	211 (17.1)	1,025 (82.9)	1,236 (100.0)
U.S.	193 (18.6)	847 (81.4)	1,040 (100.0)
Canadian	18 (9.2)	178 (90.8)	196 (100.0)
Regulated firm (REGULATE = 1)	45 (3.6)	1,191 (96.4)	1,236 (100.0)
U.S.	39 (3.8)	1,001 (96.2)	1,040 (100.0)
Canadian	6 (3.1)	190 (96.9)	196 (100.0)
Interim forecast	635 (51.4)	601 (48.6)	1,236 (100.0)
U.S.	620 (59.6)	420 (40.4)	1,040 (100.0)
Canadian	15 (7.7)	181 (92.3)	196 (100.0)
Analyst following	910 (73.6)	326 (26.4)	1,236 (100.0)
U.S.	758 (72.9)	282 (27.1)	1,040 (100.0)
Canadian	152 (77.6)	44 (22.4)	196 (100.0)

Forecast News	*Total (%)*	*U.S. (%)*	*Canadian (%)*
Good news (NEWS = 1)	769 (62.2)	650 (62.5)	119 (60.7)
Neutral news (discarded)	32 (2.6)	25 (2.4)	7 (3.6)
Bad news (NEWS = 0)	435 (35.2)	365 (35.1)	70 (35.7)
Total	1,236 (100.0)	1,040 (100.0)	196 (100.0)

FHORIZON = the number of calendar days between the forecast and the end of the period being forecast.
ALTFHORIZON = the number of calendar days between the forecast and the end of the firm's fiscal year;
$\Delta EARNINGS_{i,t}$ = $[EPS_{i,t} - EPS_{i,t-k}]/PRICE_{i,t-k}$;
$EPS_{i,t}$ = earnings per share for firm i in period t;
$EPS_{i,t-k}$ = earnings per share for firm i in period t − k;
$PRICE_{i,t-k}$ = security price for firm i in period t − k; and
k = 1 and 4 for annual and quarterly observations, respectively.
ΔESIGN = 1 for ΔEARNINGS ≥ 0 (i.e., good news), 0 for ΔEARNINGS < 0 (i.e., bad news);
$|\Delta EARNINGS_{i,t}|$ = absolute value of $\Delta EARNINGS_{i,t}$;

(Continued on next page)

TABLE 2 (Continued)

SIZE = market value of equity at the beginning of the period;
NEWS = 1 if the forecast is good news, and 0 if the forecast is bad news. *Good news* disclosures include management forecast point estimates above expected earnings, range estimates where the midpoint exceeds expected earnings, and all minimum estimates. Expected earnings equals the median I/B/E/S analyst forecast when available. Otherwise, expected earnings equals the random-walk EPS for annual forecasts and seasonal random-walk for quarterly forecasts. *Bad news* disclosures include point estimates below expected earnings, range estimates where the midpoint is less than expected earnings, and all maximum estimates;
HIGHTECH = 1 if a firm belongs to Pharmaceuticals (Compustat SIC codes 2833–2836), R&D Services (8731–8734), Programming (7371–7379), Computers (3570–3577), or Electronics (3600–3674) industries, and 0 otherwise; and
REGULATE = 1 if a firm belongs to Telephone (4812–4813), TV (4833), Cable (4841), Communications (4811–4899), Gas (4922–4924), Electricity (4931), Water (4941), or Financial (6021–6023, 6035–6036, 6141, 6311, 6321, 6331) industries, and 0 otherwise.

A shows that forecast frequency is only 1.09 percent for U.S. firms and 2.41 percent for Canadian firms, compared to Kasznik and Lev's (1995) rates of between 9 percent and 21 percent.

U.S. firms report a slightly higher proportion of earnings increases (58.4 percent) during the time period sampled than do Canadian firms (55.4 percent). The U.S. also has a higher percentage of both high-tech and regulated firms. Canadian management earnings forecasts appear in the most precise point form 46.1 percent of the time, nearly twice as often as those of U.S. firms.

Table 2, Panel B presents data for the sample of 1,236 management forecasts possessing all data necessary to estimate Equations (2) through (4) (precision and horizon tests). Panel B's sample equals Panel A's sample of 1,383 management forecasts minus 154 general impression forecasts plus 7 forecasts for which an analyst forecast was available on I/B/E/S when data for constructing a random walk forecast (i.e., prior period EPS) were not available on Compustat. Comparison of Panel B (periods for which the firm issues a forecast) to Panel A (all periods regardless of whether the firm issues a forecast) reveals several expected differences. Firms issuing forecasts are on average much larger; absolute change in earnings during the period (|ΔEARNINGS|) is much lower; and regulated firms rarely issue forecasts. Panel B also shows that mean (median) forecast horizon (FHORIZON) is 188.1 (215.0) calendar days for Canadian firms but only 70.5 (30.0) days for U.S. firms. U.S. firms are much more apt to issue interim forecasts (59.6 percent of U.S. forecasts) than are Canadian firms (7.6 percent of Canadian forecasts). Even measuring forecast horizon relative to the fiscal year-end, mean (median) ALTFHORIZON is 205.5 (228.0) for Canadian firms but only 142.5 (139.0) days for U.S. firms. Therefore, Canadian firms' annual forecasts occur earlier in the fiscal year than U.S. firms' interim forecasts. In addition, 73.6 percent of the firms are covered by at least one I/B/E/S analyst. The coverage is slightly greater for Canadian firms that issue management forecasts (77.6 percent relative to 72.9 percent for U.S. firms that issue management forecasts). Finally, 62.2 percent of the forecasts are good news. The distributions of NEWS for the U.S. and Canada are fairly similar.

Primary Results: Forecast Frequency

Table 3 presents the Equation (1) logistic regression tests of H1and H2. Coefficient a_2 is significantly positive ($p = 0.006$), so Canadian firms are more likely to issue forecast

TABLE 3
Management Earnings Forecast Frequency in the U.S. and Canada

$$FORECAST_{i,t} = a_0 + a_1\,\Delta ESIGN_{i,t} + a_2\,CANADA_{i,t} + a_3\,CANADA_{i,t} \times \Delta ESIGN_{i,t} + a_4\,|\Delta EARNINGS_{i,t}| + a_5\,LSIZE_{i,t} + a_6\,REGULATE_{i,t} + a_7\,HIGHTECH_{i,t} + \varepsilon_{i,t}$$

Independent Variable (Coefficient)	*Expected Sign (Hypothesis)*	*Coefficient Estimate (p-value[a])*
Intercept (a_0)	None predicted	−5.65 (0.001)
ΔESIGN (a_1)	−	−0.14 (0.009)
CANADA (a_2)	+ (H1 for bad news)	0.33 (0.006)
CANADA × ΔESIGN (a_3)	+ (H2)	0.59 (0.001)
$|\Delta EARNINGS_{i,t}|$ (a_4)	−	−0.52 (0.007)
LSIZE (a_5)	+	0.27 (0.001)
REGULATE (a_6)	−	−1.51 (0.001)
HIGHTECH (a_7)	None predicted	−0.10 (0.149)
Coefficients $a_2 + a_3$	+ (H1 for good news)	0.92 (0.001)
n		115,751
Chi-square		764.8
p-value		(0.001)

[a] p-values are one-tailed for signed predictions.

$|\Delta EARNINGS_{i,t}|$ = absolute value of $\Delta EARNINGS_{i,t}$, where $\Delta EARNINGS_{i,t} = [EPS_{i,t} - EPS_{i,t-k}]/PRICE_{i,t-k}$;
$EPS_{i,t}$ = earnings per share for firm i in period t;
$EPS_{i,t-k}$ = earnings per share for firm i in period t − k;
$PRICE_{i,t-k}$ = security price for firm i in period t − k; and
k = 1 and 4 for annual and quarterly observations, respectively.
ΔESIGN = 1 for ΔEARNINGS ≥ 0 (i.e., good news), 0 for ΔEARNINGS < 0 (i.e., bad news);
FORECAST = 1 if the firm issued a management earnings forecast during the period, and 0 otherwise;
CANADA = 1 if the potential forecasting period relates to a Canadian firm, and 0 if it relates to a U.S. firm;
LSIZE = natural log of the market value of equity at the beginning of the period;
HIGHTECH = 1 if a firm belongs to Pharmaceuticals (Compustat SIC codes 2833–2836), R&D Services (8731–8734), Programming (7371–7379), Computers (3570–3577), or Electronics (3600–3674) industries, and 0 otherwise; and
REGULATE = 1 when a firm belongs to Telephone (4812–4813), TV (4833), Cable (4841), Communications (4811–4899), Gas (4922–4924), Electricity (4931), Water (4941), or Financial (6021–6023, 6035–6036, 6141, 6311, 6321, 6331) industries, and 0 otherwise.

disclosures during bad news periods relative to U.S. firms. The sum $a_2 + a_3$ is also significantly positive ($p < 0.001$), revealing that Canadian firms are more likely to issue forecast disclosures during good news periods relative to U.S. firms. These results support H1's prediction that lower legal liability in Canada leads to more forecast disclosure for *both* good and bad news periods.[15] These results are consistent with the higher univariate forecast rates for Canadian firms (2.41 percent) relative to U.S. firms (1.09 percent) reported in Table 2, Panel A.

With respect to H2, the results are also consistent with our expectations. The tendency to skew disclosure toward bad news periods relative to good news periods differs between

[15] Untabulated analysis reveals that forecasting frequencies for Canadian cross-listed firms (2.02 percent) are smaller than for Canadian locally listed firms (3.01 percent), but greater than for U.S. firms (1.09 percent). The ordering also holds for bad news and good news considered separately.

the U.S. and Canada. U.S. firm behavior is as expected: coefficient a_1 is significantly negative ($p = 0.009$), indicating more forecast disclosure in bad news periods relative to good news periods. Coefficient a_3, which measures the difference between Canadian and U.S. sign-related behavior, is significantly positive ($p < 0.001$), indicating that Canadian firms are less apt to skew disclosure toward bad news periods than are U.S. firms.[16] In fact, Table 3 reveals that Canadian firms skew disclosure toward good news. The sum $a_1 + a_3$ measures the extent to which Canadian forecast frequency is related to the sign of earnings changes (i.e., the sum $a_1 + a_3$ is the Canadian equivalent to coefficient a_1 for U.S. firms). This sum is positive and significant ($p < 0.001$; results not tabulated), indicating that Canadian forecasts occur more often in good news periods. The univariate forecast rates reported in Table 2, Panel A are consistent with this result.[17]

These differences between Canadian and U.S. forecasting behavior arise even after controlling for the absolute value of the earnings surprise (a_4 is significantly negative as expected, $p = 0.007$), firm size (a_5 is significantly positive as expected, $p < 0.001$), regulated industry membership (a_6 is significantly negative as expected, $p < 0.001$), and high-tech industry membership (a_7 is insignificantly different from 0).[18]

Primary Results: Forecast Precision

Table 4 presents results of estimating Equation (2). As H1 predicts, the significantly positive b_2 ($p < 0.001$) indicates that Canadian firms issue more precise forecasts in bad news periods than do U.S. firms, and the significantly positive sum $b_2 + b_3$ ($p < 0.001$) indicates that Canadian firms also issue more precise forecasts in good news periods than do U.S. firms. Coefficient b_1 on ΔESIGN is significantly positive ($p = 0.028$), indicating

---

[16] Table 3 results could also occur if DJNRS selectively judges U.S. good news as insufficiently newsworthy to report. Such a selective bias would make it appear as if (1) more Canadian forecasts existed (because some U.S. forecasts were not reported), and (2) sign-related behavior existed for U.S. firms (because editors biased reporting toward bad news), but not for Canadian firms (because the editors' bias existed for only U.S. firms). Additional analysis suggests that this alternative interpretation is unlikely to explain our results.

PR Newswire carries all subscribing company disclosures, and thus is free of editorial bias. We searched PR Newswire for one of our sample years (1993) and found 89 management forecasts for subscribing companies. Then we used DJNRS to determine whether we would pick up these forecasts. Of the 89 forecasts from PR Newswire, we located 83 (93 percent). Of the six that we could not locate, four were bad news (i.e., earnings lower than previous expectations) and two were good news (i.e., record earnings). This analysis suggests that Dow Jones picks up substantially all of the information contained in PR Newswire. To the extent that Dow Jones is missing any information, it does not appear that it is a result of an editorial bias in favor of reporting bad news. These findings suggest that our evidence is not attributable to Dow Jones editorial policies that favor the dissemination of bad news over good news for U.S. firms.

[17] In an untabulated supplemental analysis, we split the full sample into annual and interim periods, which permits a closer comparison to Skinner's (1994) U.S. results. Coefficient a_1 is significantly positive in the annual sample ($p = 0.028$), but significantly negative in the interim sample ($p < 0.001$). This result corroborates (in our larger and more diverse sample) Skinner's (1994) finding that U.S. managers are more likely to issue interim forecasts when earnings are declining, while they are more likely to issue annual forecasts when earnings are increasing. Canadian firms issue more forecasts in both good and bad news periods relative to U.S. firms only in the annual subsample ($p < 0.001$ for annual regression coefficients a_2 and $a_2 + a_3$). Canadian firms are less likely to skew forecast incidence toward earnings decrease periods (relative to U.S. firms) only in the interim sample ($a_3 > 0$; $p = 0.048$). These results suggest that Canadian firms, operating in a less litigious environment, are issuing more forecasts, but are not using interim forecasts to convey bad news.

[18] We examined other potential control variables for which data were available for subsets of our sample. Substantial differences in earnings capitalization rates affect both the costs and benefits of a publicly released forecast by affecting the price reaction to a given dollar of unexpected earnings. Consequently, we examined whether it was necessary to control for differences in earnings capitalization rates and growth using a subset of firms for which data were available (results not tabulated). Specifically, including as an additional variable ranked, leading price/earnings ratios (for firms with positive leading earnings) did not affect our conclusions. Also, proprietary information could adversely affect management's willingness to release an earnings forecast publicly. In addition to our control for high-tech firms, we added another proxy for proprietary information, expected growth (measured as market to book value of common equity), with no change in our conclusions.

TABLE 4
Determinants of Management Forecast Precision in the U.S. and Canada

Model: $PRECISE_i = b_0 + b_1\,\Delta ESIGN_i + b_2\,CANADA_i + b_3\,CANADA_i \times \Delta ESIGN_i + b_4\,LSIZE_i + b_5\,REGULATE_i + b_6\,HIGHTECH_i + b_7\,FHORIZON_i + v_i$

Independent Variable (Coefficient)	*Expected Sign (Hypothesis)*	*Coefficient Estimate (p-value[a])*
ΔESIGN (b_1)	+	0.211 (0.028)
CANADA (b_2)	+ (H1 for bad news)	1.060 (0.001)
CANADA × ΔESIGN (b_3)	− (H2)	−0.141 (0.301)
LSIZE (b_4)	−	−0.007 (0.393)
REGULATE (b_5)	−	−0.247 (0.155)
HIGHTECH (b_6)	None predicted	−0.178 (0.090)
FHORIZON (b_7)	−	−0.003 (0.001)
Coefficients $b_2 + b_3$	+ (H1 for good news)	0.919 (0.001)
n		1,383
Model Chi-square		67.13
probability		(0.001)

[a] p-values are one-tailed for signed predictions.

PRECISE = 3 (2, 1, 0) for point (range, open-interval, general impression) forecasts;
$\Delta EARNINGS_{i,t}$ = $[EPS_{i,t} - EPS_{i,t-k}]/PRICE_{i,t-k}$;
$EPS_{i,t}$ = earnings per share for firm i in period t;
$EPS_{i,t-k}$ = earnings per share for firm i in period t − k;
$PRICE_{i,t-k}$ = security price for firm i in period t − k; and
k = 1 and 4 for annual and quarterly observations, respectively.
ΔESIGN = 1 for ΔEARNINGS ≥ 0 (i.e., good news), 0 for ΔEARNINGS < 0 (i.e., bad news);
CANADA = 1 if a Canadian firm issued the forecast, and 0 if a U.S. firm issued the forecast;
LSIZE = natural log of the market value of equity at the beginning of the period;
HIGHTECH = 1 if a firm belongs to Pharmaceuticals (Compustat SIC codes 2833–2836), R&D Services (8731–8734), Programming (7371–7379), Computers (3570–3577), or Electronics (3600–3674) industries, and 0 otherwise;
REGULATE = 1 if a firm belongs to Telephone (4812–4813), TV (4833), Cable (4841), Communications (4811–4899), Gas (4922–4924), Electricity (4931), Water (4941), or Financial (6021–6023, 6035–6036, 6141, 6311, 6321, 6331) industries, and 0 otherwise; and
FHORIZON = the number of calendar days between the forecast and the end of the period being forecast.

that U.S. firms on average issue less precise forecasts when earnings are declining. However, the data do not support H2's prediction that the sign of earnings change has less effect on forecast precision in Canada (b_3 is insignificant, $p = 0.301$). These results arise after controlling for the expected negative effects of long forecast horizons on forecast precision (negative b_7; $p < 0.001$), high-tech firms that issue less precise forecasts (negative b_6; $p = 0.090$), and firm size and regulated firms (insignificant b_4 and b_5, respectively). In summary, the results reported in Table 4 indicate that Canadian firms issue more precise forecasts than do U.S. firms.

Primary Results: Forecast Horizon

Table 5 presents OLS regression estimates of Equations (3) and (4), designated Model 1 and Model 2, respectively. Hypothesis 1 predicts that Canadian firms issue longer-horizon forecasts. Consistent with H1, the significantly positive c_2 ($p < 0.001$ in both models), indicates that Canadian firms issue longer-horizon bad news forecasts than do U.S. firms, and the significantly positive sum $c_2 + c_3$ ($p < 0.001$ in both models), indicates that

TABLE 5
Determinants of Management Forecast Horizons in the U.S. and Canada

$$\text{Model 1: } FHORIZON_i = c_0 + c_1\,NEWS_i + c_2\,CANADA_i + c_3\,CANADA_i \times NEWS_i + c_4\,LSIZE_i + c_5\,REGULATE_i + c_6\,HIGHTECH_i + \mu_i$$

$$\text{Model 2: } ALTFHORIZON_i = c_0 + c_1\,NEWS_i + c_2\,CANADA_i + c_3\,CANADA_i \times NEWS_i + c_4\,LSIZE_i + c_5\,REGULATE_i + c_6\,HIGHTECH_i + \eta_i$$

Independent Variable (Coefficient)	*Expected Sign (Hypothesis)*	*Estimated Coefficients (p-values[a])*	
		Model 1	*Model 2*
Intercept (c_0)	None predicted	31.69 (0.001)	110.76 (0.001)
NEWS (c_1)	+	30.61 (0.001)	11.67 (0.050)
CANADA (c_2)	+ (H1 for bad news)	141.82 (0.001)	80.78 (0.001)
CANADA × NEWS (c_3)	− (H2)	−35.18 (0.013)	−33.34 (0.031)
LSIZE (c_4)	+	3.78 (0.004)	4.86 (0.002)
REGULATE (c_5)	−	12.35 (0.800)	20.43 (0.891)
HIGHTECH (c_6)	None predicted	−15.47 (0.038)	−18.91 (0.012)
Coefficients $c_2 + c_3$	+ (H1 for good news)	106.64 (0.001)	47.44 (0.001)
n		1,204	1,204
Adjusted R^2		0.1931	0.0556
Model F		48.97	12.80

[a] p-values are one-tailed for signed predictions.

FHORIZON = the number of calendar days between the forecast and the end of the period being forecast;
ALTFHORIZON = the number of calendar days between the forecast and the end of the firm's fiscal year;
NEWS = 1 if the forecast is good news, and 0 if the forecast is bad news. *Good news* disclosures include management forecast point estimates above expected earnings, range estimates where the midpoint exceeds expected earnings, and all minimum estimates. Expected earnings equals the median I/B/E/S analyst forecast when available. Otherwise, expected earnings equals the random-walk EPS for annual forecasts and seasonal random-walk for quarterly forecasts. *Bad news* disclosures include point estimates below expected earnings, range estimates where the midpoint is less than expected earnings, and all maximum estimates;
CANADA = 1 if a Canadian firm issued the forecast, and 0 if a U.S. firm issued the forecast;
LSIZE = natural log of the market value of equity at the beginning of the period;
HIGHTECH = 1 if a firm belongs to Pharmaceuticals (Compustat SIC codes 2833–2836), R&D Services (8731–8734), Programming (7371–7379), Computers (3570–3577), or Electronics (3600–3674) industries, and 0 otherwise; and
REGULATE = 1 if a firm belongs to Telephone (4812–4813), TV (4833), Cable (4841), Communications (4811–4899), Gas (4922–4924), Electricity (4931), Water (4941), or Financial (6021–6023, 6035–6036, 6141, 6311, 6321, 6331) industries, and 0 otherwise.

Canadian firms also issue longer-horizon good news forecasts than do U.S. firms.[19] U.S. firms forecast good news over longer horizons relative to bad news (significantly positive c_1, $p < 0.05$). Further, the data also support the H2 prediction that the sign of forecast news has less effect on Canadian firms' forecast horizon. As expected, Canadian firms are less apt to choose longer forecast horizons for good news relative to bad news (significantly negative c_3, $p = 0.031$).

VI. SENSITIVITY CHECKS

Effects of the Private Securities Litigation Reform Act on U.S. Forecasting Behavior

On December 22, 1995, Congress voted to override a presidential veto, thereby establishing the Private Securities Litigation Reform Act of 1995. One intent of the Act was to encourage firms to disclose forward-looking information by reducing legal penalties. If management forecasting behavior changed after the Act, then including post-Act U.S. forecasts in our sample biases the results in favor of the null hypothesis of no differences between U.S. and Canadian forecasting behavior. We reject the null hypothesis in each of our tests except for H2 in Table 4, where we find no difference between Canada and the U.S. in the association of the sign of the earnings change and forecast precision. Accordingly, we ran a model analogous to Equation (2) on U.S. firms only, replacing the Canadian regime indicator variable (CANADA) with a 1,0 indicator variable for whether the forecast was issued after the Act in 1996. We find that, in 1996, U.S. forecasting firms still issue less precise forecasts in periods of earnings decreases ($p = 0.022$; results not tabulated). However, running Equation (2) without 1996 U.S. forecasts does not change our inference of no significant difference between Canada and the U.S. in the association of the sign of the earnings change and forecast precision.

Information Asymmetry

The benefits of voluntary management forecast disclosure increase when private information exists (King et al. 1990). Fowler et al. (1979) and Jorion and Schwartz (1986) document thin-trading for many TSE firms, a symptom of information asymmetry.[20] If Canadian managers wish to reduce such asymmetry to decrease the firm's cost of capital (King et al. 1990), then they will be more likely to issue management earnings forecasts, and the forecasts will on average be longer-horizon. Although Canadian managers may also wish to issue more precise forecasts when faced with greater information asymmetry, their forecasts will likely be less precise because information asymmetry is strongly linked to uncertainty, and Baginski and Hassell (1997) document that management forecast precision is inversely related to uncertainty.

We replicated our entire study for the subset of firm-periods for which more than one analyst follows the firm at the beginning of the period. We use the standard deviation of these analyst forecasts as a proxy for predisclosure information asymmetry (e.g., Atiase and Bamber 1994). Specifically, we divide the standard deviation by beginning of the period price, rank the deflated variable, and include it as an additional control variable. Greater

---

[19] Cross-listed Canadian firms' forecast horizons fall in-between the forecast horizons of Canadian locally listed and U.S. firms. Horizons in calendar days for Canadian locally listed, Canadian cross-listed, and U.S. forecasts are 194, 182, and 70 days, respectively. For the alternative definition of forecast horizon relative to the fiscal year-end, the lengths are 208, 202, and 142 days, respectively.

[20] As firm size and analyst following increase, TSE thin-trading becomes a lesser issue. Fowler et al. (1979) note that of the firms in the TSE 300 index, approximately only 6 percent trade infrequently (trades on fewer than 80 percent of sampled days).

information asymmetry leads to greater forecasting benefits (i.e., removal of information asymmetry). Thus, our proxy should be associated with more management forecasts, longer forecast horizons, and due to its link to uncertainty, with less precise forecasts. The results (not tabulated) are consistent with these expectations, but our conclusions concerning H1 and H2 remain unchanged.[21]

VII. SUMMARY AND CONCLUSIONS

Policymakers regularly call for U.S. corporations to increase disclosure of forward-looking information (e.g., AICPA 1994; Breeden 1995). In this paper, we show that the frequency and characteristics of voluntary earnings forecast disclosures differ across two countries with different legal regimes. Canadian managers, faced with a less litigious environment than U.S. managers, disclose more earnings forecasts (in periods of both good and bad news), and their forecasts are more precise and of longer range. In addition, using a larger and more representative sample of firms, we confirm the findings in prior research that U.S. forecasts occur more often, are less precise, and are of a shorter horizon when earnings news is bad. In contrast, we document that Canadian forecasts are less likely to exhibit these bad-news-related tendencies. In fact, Canadian firms issue more forecasts in earnings increase relative to earnings decrease periods.

Our evidence that lower legal liability is consistent with more voluntary management forecast disclosure is consistent with evidence in Frost (2001) and Johnson et al. (2001). Our finding that Canadian firms issue proportionally more good news forecasts in the lower legal liability regime is consistent with Skinner's (1994) and Kasznik and Lev's (1995) conclusions that legal exposure leads to asymmetric incentives favoring proportionally more disclosure of bad news. However, the finding is inconsistent with Johnson et al. (2001), who fail to find a proportional decrease in bad news forecasts (or proportional increase in good news forecasts) after passage of the Private Securities Litigation Reform Act that was intended to reduce legal liability. This pattern of evidence suggests that either (1) the difference in legal exposure between the U.S. and Canada is greater than the change in legal exposure in the U.S. brought about by the Private Securities Litigation Reform Act, or that (2) post-Act behavior of firms in high-tech industries differs substantially from that of firms in other industries.

Although we are unaware of any documented biases in our data sources that could confound our analysis, sampling of periods available for disclosure and actual forecast disclosures is limited by the completeness of sources such as Compustat and DJNRS. Although our sample is from the relatively recent 1993–1996 period, our results may not be generalizable to the present. U.S. voluntary disclosure policy is constantly evolving, and managers may now have more evidence on whether the Private Securities Litigation Reform Act of 1995 actually reduces disclosure-related legal exposure.

Our evidence suggests that legal regime is associated with management forecasting behavior. Future research could assess whether lower legal liability undermines the credibility of Canadian management forecasts. To date, research on the relation between legal liability and forecast credibility focuses on the passage of the Private Securities Litigation Reform Act of 1995, and its results are mixed. Johnson et al. (2001) find no change in management forecast accuracy and bias post-Act; however, Ali and Kallapur's (2001) results suggest that shareholders reacted negatively to the Act's restrictions on their ability

---

[21] Our conclusions are also unaffected when we control for the number of analysts who follow the firm (results not tabulated).

to bring suit. Substantial difference in legal regimes across countries might provide a powerful treatment effect for detecting differences in forecast credibility and shareholders' perceptions of how their wealth is affected by protections under different legal regimes.

REFERENCES

Ajinkya, B., and M. Gift. 1984. Corporate managers' earnings forecasts and symmetrical adjustments of market expectations. *Journal of Accounting Research* 22 (Autumn): 425–444.

Ali, A., and L. Hwang. 2000. Country-specific factors related to financial reporting and the value relevance of accounting data. *Journal of Accounting Research* 38 (Spring): 1–21.

———, and S. Kallapur. 2001. Securities price consequences of the Private Securities Litigation Reform Act of 1995 and related events. *The Accounting Review* 76 (July): 431–460.

American Institute of Certified Public Accountants (AICPA), Special Committee on Financial Reporting. 1994. *Improving Business Reporting—A Customer Focus.* New York, NY: AICPA.

Atiase, R., and L. S. Bamber. 1994. Trading volume reactions to annual accounting earnings announcements: The incremental role of predisclosure information asymmetry. *Journal of Accounting and Economics* 17 (May): 309–329.

Baginski, S., J. Hassell, and G. Waymire. 1994. Some evidence on the news content of preliminary earnings estimates. *The Accounting Review* 69 (January): 265–273.

———, and ———. 1997. Determinants of management forecast precision. *The Accounting Review* (April): 303–312.

Bamber, L. S., and Y. Cheon. 1998. Discretionary management earnings forecast disclosures: Antecedents and outcomes associated with forecast venue and forecast specificity choices. *Journal of Accounting Research* 36 (Autumn): 167–190.

Bandyopadhyay, S., J. D. Hanna, and G. Richardson. 1994. Capital market effects of U.S.-Canada GAAP differences. *Journal of Accounting Research* 32 (Autumn): 262–277.

Barth, M., and G. Clinch. 1996. International accounting differences and their relation to share prices: Evidence of U.K., Australian, and Canadian firms. *Contemporary Accounting Research* (Spring): 135–170.

Breeden, R. 1995. Testimony before the Securities Subcommittee of the Senate Committee on Banking, Housing, and Urban Affairs. April 6, 1995. Washington, D.C.: Government Printing Office.

Brown, L., G. Richardson, and C. Trzcinka. 1991. Strong-form efficiency on the Toronto Stock Exchange: An examination of analyst price forecasts. *Contemporary Accounting Research* 7: 323–346.

Clarkson, P., A. Dontoh, G. Richardson, and S. Sefcik. 1992. The voluntary inclusion of earnings forecasts in IPO prospectuses. *Contemporary Accounting Research* (Spring): 601–626.

———, and D. Simunic. 1994. The association between audit quality, retained ownership, and firm-specific risk in U.S. vs. Canadian IPO markets. *Journal of Accounting and Economics* 17 (January): 207–228.

Core, J. 1997. On the corporate demand for directors' and officers' insurance. *Journal of Risk and Insurance* 64 (March): 63–87.

Cox, C. 1985. Further evidence on the representativeness of management earnings forecasts. *The Accounting Review* 60 (October): 692–701.

Francis, J., D. Philbrick, and K. Schipper. 1994. Shareholder litigation and corporate disclosures. *Journal of Accounting Research* 32 (Autumn): 137–164.

Fowler, D., C. H. Rorke, and V. Jog. 1979. Heteroscedasticity, R^2 and thin trading on the Toronto Stock Exchange. *Journal of Finance* 34: 1201–1210.

Freund, W., M. Larrain, and M. Pagano. 1997. Market efficiency before and after the introduction of electronic trading at the Toronto Stock Exchange. *Review of Financial Economics* 6: 29–56.

Frost, C., and G. Pownall. 1994. Accounting disclosure practices in the United States and the United Kingdom. *Journal of Accounting Research* 32 (Spring): 75–102.

———, and W. Kinney, Jr. 1996. Disclosure choices of foreign registrants in the United States. *Journal of Accounting Research* 34 (Spring): 67–84.

———. 2001. Characteristics and information value of corporate disclosures of forward-looking information in global equity markets. Working paper, Dartmouth College.

Grossman, B. 1996. Class rules. *CA Magazine* 129 (March): 31–33, 43.

Grundfest, J., and M. Perino. 1997. Security litigation reform: The first years' experience. Working paper, Stanford University.

Guenther, D., and A. Rosman. 1994. Differences between COMPUSTAT and CRSP SIC codes and related effects on research. *Journal of Accounting and Economics* 18 (July): 115–128.

Johnson, M., R. Kasznik, and K. Nelson. 2001. The impact of securities litigation reform on the disclosure of forward-looking information by high technology firms. *Journal of Accounting Research* 39 (September): 297–327.

Jorion, P., and E. Schwartz. 1986. Integration vs. segmentation in the Canadian stock market. *Journal of Finance* 41 (July): 603–614.

Kasznik, R., and B. Lev. 1995. To warn or not to warn: Management disclosures in the face of an earnings surprise. *The Accounting Review* 70 (January): 113–134.

King, R., G. Pownall, and G. Waymire. 1990. Expectations adjustment via timely management forecasts: Review, synthesis, and suggestions for future research. *Journal of Accounting Literature* 9: 113–144.

Levine, D., and A Pritchard. 1998. The Securities Litigation Uniform Standards Act of 1998: The sun sets on California's Blue Sky Laws. *Business Lawyer* 54 (November): 1–54.

L'Her, J., and J. Suret. 1991. The reaction of Canadian securities to revisions of earnings forecasts. *Contemporary Accounting Research* (Spring): 378–406.

McConomy, B. 1998. Bias and accuracy of management earnings forecasts: An evaluation of the impact of auditing. *Contemporary Accounting Research* 15 (Summer): 167–195.

McNichols, M. 1989. Evidence of informational asymmetries from management earnings forecasts and stock returns. *The Accounting Review* 64 (January): 1–27.

Paskell-Mede, M. 1994. What liability crisis? *CA Magazine* 127 (May): 42–43.

———. 1999. Cross-border lawsuits. *CA Magazine* 132 (April): 37–38.

Patell, J. 1976. Corporate forecasts of earnings per share and stock price behavior: Empirical tests. *Journal of Accounting Research* (Autumn): 246–276.

Skinner, D. 1994. Why firms voluntarily disclose bad news. *Journal of Accounting Research* 32 (Spring): 38–60.

———. 1997. Earnings disclosure and stockholder lawsuits. *Journal of Accounting and Economics* 23 (November): 249–282.

Toronto Stock Exchange (TSE). 2000. *The Toronto Stock Exchange's Policy Statement on Timely Disclosure.* Toronto, Ontario.

Waymire, G. 1984. Additional evidence on the information content of management earnings forecasts. *Journal of Accounting Research* 22 (Autumn): 703–718.

———. 1985. Earnings volatility and voluntary management forecast disclosure. *Journal of Accounting Research* 23 (Spring): 268–295.

C
Mexico

[13]

Journal of Accounting Research
Vol. 39 No. 1 June 2001
Printed in U.S.A.

Accounting for Changing Prices: The Value Relevance of Historical Cost, Price Level, and Replacement Cost Accounting in Mexico

ELIZABETH A. GORDON

Received 22 December 1997; accepted 18 April 2000

ABSTRACT

This paper investigates the value relevance of historical cost, price level and replacement cost accounting using a sample of Mexican firms from 1989 to 1995. It contributes to prior research by distinguishing between two distinct aspects of changing prices: (1) the change in the general price level, and (2) the change in the value of specific non-monetary assets. I select Mexico to examine because it is unique in requiring and disclosing separately price level and replacement cost adjustments. A sample of Mexican firms also addresses a key reason cited for mixed results in previous assessments of the usefulness of price level and replacement cost accounting using United States data: the effects of inflation are too weak to detect. High rates of inflation in Mexico,

Rutgers University. This paper is based on my dissertation at Columbia University. I am grateful to Trevor S. Harris, my dissertation advisor, and for the helpful comments of Eli Amir, Charles Calomiris, Won Choi, Peter Easton, Jennifer Francis, Mike Kirschenheiter, Mark Lang, Linda Vincent, Kristen Willard, and an anonymous referee. I appreciate the comments and suggestions of workshop participants at New York University, Rutgers University, University of Chicago, University of Minnesota, University of North Carolina, University of Pennsylvania, University of Washington, Villanova University, and Yale University and at the Big 10 + 1 Accounting Research Conference. I also gratefully acknowledge the financial support received from the Arthur Andersen & Co., SC Foundation, the Center for International Business Education, the Jerome A. Chazen Institute of International Business at Columbia University, and the Graduate School of Business at the University of Chicago.

ranging between 7% and 52% during the sample period, mitigate that potential problem. Results indicate that replacement cost adjustments are relatively and incrementally relevant beyond historical cost and price level measures while price level adjustments are incrementally value relevant beyond historical measures.

1. Introduction

This paper investigates the value relevance of historical cost (HC), price level (PL), and replacement cost (RC) accounting using a sample of Mexican firms from 1989 to 1995. It contributes to prior research by distinguishing between two distinct aspects of changing prices (1) the change in the general price level, and (2) the change in the value of specific non-monetary assets (Edwards and Bell [1961]; Moonitz and Sprouse [1962]; May, Mueller, and Williams [1980]).

To assess value relevance, I test for a statistical association between level and changes in HC, PL, and RC earnings and annual returns (Easton and Harris [1991]). Tests of the association between earnings and returns provide evidence on whether the earnings measure effectively summarizes the firm's activities over the reporting period and can be viewed as tests of the timeliness of earnings (Easton [1998]).[1] I test both relative and incremental value-relevance of HC, PL, and RC accounting (Biddle, Seow, and Siegel [1995]). To test relative value relevance, I examine the association of returns with earnings and changes in earnings under the three sets of accounting principles—HC, PL, and RC—and compare the explanatory power of each set of accounting principles using Vuong's [1989] likelihood ratio tests. Tests of relative value relevance provide evidence on the timeliness of reporting under one set of accounting principles. To test incremental value relevance of PL and RC accounting, I disaggregate reported earnings and changes in earnings into HC measures an adjustment between HC and PL, and an adjustment between PL and RC and test the significance of each adjustment. Additionally, I test key components of disaggregated earnings adjustments, such as monetary gains/losses and RC asset revaluation increments. Results indicate that RC adjustments are relatively and incrementally relevant beyond HC and PL measures while PL adjustments are incrementally value relevant beyond HC measures during the period examined.

[1] I operationalize value relevance as the timeliness of accounting earnings similar to recent studies by Ball, Kothari, and Robin [2000]; Bushman, Chen, Engel, and Smith [2000]; and Francis and Schipper [1999]. As noted by Ball, Kothari, and Robin [2000], there is a demand for accounting earnings with properties other than timeliness. Therefore, accountants incorporate only a subset of the value-relevant information available at the time. Factors such as the delay with which accounting numbers capture growth and investment opportunities, the lag with which accounting numbers reflect changes in the value of a firm's tangible and intangible assets, and alternative sources of information, such as other disclosures and analysts, will decrease the timeliness of earnings. These factors work against my finding an association between earnings and annual returns.

I select Mexico to examine because it is unique in requiring and disclosing separately PL and RC adjustments, so I can consider the timeliness of each for a single sample of firms. A sample of Mexican firms also addresses a key reason cited for mixed results in previous assessments of the usefulness of PL and RC accounting using United States (U.S.) data: the effects of inflation are too weak to detect. High rates of inflation in Mexico, ranging between 7% and 52% during the sample period, mitigate that potential problem. The range of inflation also allows for insights about the importance of the magnitude of inflation.

In selecting an emerging market such as Mexico to study, it is important to assess whether the assumption of informational efficiency underlying capital market–based accounting research is valid. Recent research using event study methods provides evidence on the informational efficiency of the Mexican equity market. Bhattacharya *et al.* [2000] do not observe share price or trading volume reactions to firm-specific news announcements that they attribute to unrestricted insider trading, implying a strong form of market informational efficiency. Davis-Friday *et al.* [2000] find weak evidence of trading volume reaction to earnings announcements, implying that the accounting system provides value-relevant information to certain classes of investors and markets are semi-strong efficient. Davis-Friday *et al.* also find that book value and earnings explain approximately 60% of the variation in Mexican stock prices. Neither of these studies contradicts adopting a capital market–based approach to examine Mexican accounting. Additionally, by using long-window returns rather than short-window returns, I rely on information about firm performance reaching the market, regardless of the channel. This approach is less prone to misidentifying announcement dates and less dependent on the exact timing of when information reaches the market.

Internationally, significant interest and debate exist on the use of PL and RC accounting. For example, a recent comparison by accounting standards setters in Canada, Mexico, and the U.S. identifies inflation accounting as one of the most significant accounting differences impeding harmonization among the countries. The Association for Investment Management and Research advocates current cost in the U.S. Standard setters in the United Kingdom are questioning the use of current cost accounting while Mexico recently disallowed RC accounting, but maintained price level accounting. Many emerging markets still experience high rates of inflation and need to select appropriate measures.

This paper is organized as follows. The next section discusses related research. Section 3 provides an overview of accounting and reporting in Mexico. Research design and methodology are presented in section 4. Section 5 describes the sample selection and data while section 6 discusses results. A summary and conclusions are in section 7.

2. *Related Research*

This paper is related to two streams of existing research: research on PL and RC accounting, (Beaver, Griffin, and Landsman [1982]; Beaver and

Landsman [1983]; Davis-Friday [1999]), and research on asset revaluations in countries such as Australia (Easton, Eddey, and Harris [1993]) and the United Kingdom (Aboody, Barth, and Kaznik [1998]). While PL and RC accounting have been extensively studied using data from the U.S. disclosed under Accounting Series Release No. 190, "Disclosure of Certain Replacement Cost Data" (ASR 190), and SFAS No. 33, "Financial Reporting and Changing Prices" (SFAS 33), limited empirical research has been conducted using a sample of firms from a high inflation country (Rivera [1987], Davis-Friday [1999]).

My study is most closely related to research by Davis-Friday [1999] that investigates the relation between reported accounting earnings and book values in Mexico and market values. Davis-Friday [1999] finds that aggregate reported earning and book values as well as disaggregated earnings, except monetary gains/losses, are related to market value. In contrast, I use reported and disclosed information in Mexico to examine earnings under three different measurement principles: HC, PL, and RC. Unlike Davis-Friday, I investigate the relation between returns and earnings under HC, PL, and RC accounting as if the choice to report under one set of accounting principles is mutually exclusive (section 4.1) as well as test whether the adjustment between HC and PL and the adjustment between PL and RC earnings are incrementally informative to HC earnings (section 4.2). The two papers are complementary in the sense that I examine reporting under three distinct sets of accounting principles whereas Davis-Friday [1999] examines current accounting that combines both PL and RC accounting in Mexico.

Our studies also differ in time periods examined and sources of data. Davis-Friday [1999] examines the years 1987–1990 while I examine the period 1989–1995, which provides a greater range of inflation rates over which to test the relevance of PL and RC accounting. Davis-Friday's financial statement data are obtained from the *Anuario Financiero,* an annual publication of the Mexican Stock Exchange summarizing each company's results. I gathered my data from annual reports because the *Anuario Financiero* may use different classifications of earnings and book value components than used in the annual reports and because interim rather than year-end information is presented for some companies.

Rivera [1987] also uses a sample of Mexican firms to investigate PL and RC accounting from 1981 to 1983, a period when Mexican GAAP required disclosures of PL and RC adjustments. He obtains conflicting results on the information content of PL earnings although he finds that the PL earnings are better predictors of returns than historical cost earnings.

Results of studies using data from the U.S. have been mixed. Most studies take an information perspective and focus on the cross-sectional relation between earnings (or unexpected earnings) and returns (or unexpected returns). Beaver, Griffin, and Landsman [1982] and Beaver and Landsman [1983] find PL and/or RC earnings provide no incremental information beyond HC. However, Bublitz, Frecka, and McKeown [1985], defining usefulness as an increase in adjusted *R*-squareds, conclude that the market uses the information. Event studies by Beaver, Christie, and Griffin [1980] and Gheyara and Boatsman [1980] find no reaction to the announcement of ASR 190 inflation information.

Haw and Lustgarten [1988] find that RC holding gains, realized holding gains, and an adjustment for net monetary position are significantly associated with market returns although the coefficients indicate measurement error in the variables. Research using a time-series approach provides evidence that RC adjustments are useful in certain industries where the correlation between HC and RC earnings is low (Bernard and Ruland [1987]). However, industry trends in both HC and RC earnings are anticipated by the market months earlier than firm-specific earnings, most likely due to availability of outside information (Freeman [1983]). These studies do not distinguish between PL and RC adjustments.

Research on asset revaluations outside of the U.S. indicates that asset revaluations are value relevant (Amir, Harris, and Venuti [1993]; Easton, Eddey, and Harris [1993]; Barth and Clinch [1998]) and are related to *actual* future earnings and cash flows (Aboody, Barth, and Kasnik [1998]). Prior work finds the total revaluation amount is value relevant whereas I find that both the PL (nominal) and RC (real) components of asset revaluations in Mexico are timely measures.

3. *Accounting for Changing Prices Under Mexican GAAP*

Accounting for changing prices in Mexico is prescribed in Bulletin B-10, "Recognition of the Effects of Inflation on Financial Information," issued by the Mexican Institute of Public Accountants. The bulletin, as amended, requires PL accounting for all entities and allows the use of RC accounting. Until 1997, the Mexican National Banking and Securities Commission required RC accounting for publicly traded companies.[2]

PL accounting as applied in Mexico requires estatement of all transactions to the year-end price level. In essence, an exchange rate" of the year-end price level divided by the price level when the transaction occurred is applied to all transactions occurring during the year. Prior year's financial statements are also restated to the current year price level.

Aggregate monetary position gains (losses) arise from the effects of inflation on maintaining a net monetary liability (asset) position. These gains/losses are calculated by applying the National Consumer Price Index to a company's monthly net monetary position. Monetary gains/losses are included on the income statement as part of comprehensive financing costs (CFC). Other items included in CFC are interest income, interest

[2] The Fifth Amendment of Bulletin B-10, effective for fiscal years beginning after January 1, 1997, eliminates the recognition of specific asset revaluations. However, replacement cost amounts are allowed to be disclosed in the footnotes.

expense, and foreign exchange gain/loss. CFC are detailed on the face of the financial statements or in a footnote.

Non-monetary assets, mainly inventory and property, plant, and equipment (PPE), were generally stated at net replacement costs until 1997. For publicly traded companies, independent appraisers registered with the Mexican National Banking and Securities Commission determine the replacement cost. Revaluations of PPE are disclosed in annual filings with the Commission and may be disclosed in the financial statements.

The difference between RC and PL values of non-monetary assets is included in stockholders' equity. It is commonly called the "excess (deficit) in equity restatement" or "excess (deficit) from holding non-monetary assets."[3] The change in the revaluation, the RC asset revaluation increment, is booked directly to shareholders' equity: it does not flow through the income statement. Mexican accounting standards are not clear on other items that may affect the change in the revaluation such as impairment of long-lived assets, deferred taxes relating to non-monetary assets, or consolidation of subsidiaries. Therefore, treatment of such items varies by company. A numerical example of the relations between HC, PL, and RC accounting is presented in the appendix.

4. *Research Design and Methodology*

4.1 TESTS OF RELATIVE VALUE RELEVANCE OF HC, PL, AND RC ACCOUNTING

To test relative value relevance of HC, PL, and RC accounting, the general form of the model I use is based on Easton and Harris [1991]. This model is also similar to other studies examining asset revaluations such as Easton, Eddey, and Harris [1993] and Barth and Clinch [1998], where returns are expressed as a function of earnings and changes in earnings:

$$RET_t = \alpha_0 + \alpha_1 E_t^* + \alpha_2 \Delta E_t^* + e_t \qquad (1)$$

Where:

- RET_t annual market return for the year ending 5 months after year-end.
- E_t clean surplus earnings over lagged market value for the period ended at time, t.
- ΔE_t change in clean surplus earnings over lagged market value over the period ended at time, t.
- e_t error term at time, t.
- $*$ accounting measures used: HC, PL, or RC.

Firm-specific subscripts are omitted in this, and all, equations.

---

[3] Amounts reported in equity may include the original adjustment (restated to current purchasing power) for the net monetary position when B-10 was adopted. This component will be included for only those companies in existence when B-10 was adopted. In the data, I include only the component related to the non-monetary asset replacement cost revaluation.

As noted by Easton [1998], a returns regression specification eliminates the concern over a spurious relation between the dependent and independent variables due to firm size or per share scaling that could be present in price models. Easton [1998] also discusses deflating price specifications by book values, rather than lagged price, as another method of addressing the scale effect. Because HC book values of many firms in the sample are near zero or negative, which could lead to inflated R^2s and t-statistics, I choose to examine returns.

While the model in equation (1) is applicable to any set of accounting principles, I use Vuong's [1989] likelihood ratio test to provide evidence on whether one set of accounting principles has greater explanatory power. The Vuong test essentially compares the R^2s of two non-nested regressions in order to select the model with the greater explanatory power. These tests provide evidence on timeliness under each set of accounting principles.

If HC earnings and changes in earnings are closely aligned with market returns then reporting under PL or RC accounting may not explain a greater amount of the variation in returns than HC accounting. In this case, R^2s of HC, PL, and RC regressions will not be significantly different. If PL and/or RC accounting capture information in a more timely manner than HC, the PL and/or RC measures will be more closely related to returns.

Since HC accounting does not adjust for the change in the unit of account, HC earnings are dependent on the price level at the time a firm makes investment and financing decisions. Consider the case of investment in long-lived equipment. Assume that one firm acquired a piece of long-lived equipment two years ago and another firm acquired a similar piece of equipment one year ago. If the general inflation rate was 100% during the year and if the value of equipment changes with the general inflation rate, the acquisition cost of equipment acquired one year ago is twice that of the acquisition cost of equipment acquired two years ago. Using straight-line accounting for depreciation, depreciation expense of the firm that acquired equipment one year ago would be higher even though the productive capacity used was the same. Assuming that the market adjusts stock prices for the change in the unit of account and recognizes the use of productive capacity using the same unit of account for both firms, neither firms' HC earnings will align well with market returns. However, if PL accounting is used to remeasure all earnings to the same unit of account, depreciation expense will be the same for both firms. Then, PL earnings will align with changes in market values. Because PL accounting measures all transactions in the same unit of account, I expect that PL earnings will explain a greater portion of the variation in stock returns than HC earnings. Therefore, R^2s of cross-sectional regressions are predicted to be greater for PL than HC accounting.

To consider the implication of RC accounting, continue the case of accounting for long-lived equipment but now assume that the value of the long-lived equipment changes at a rate other than the rate of general inflation. Here PL depreciation no longer accurately recognizes the productive capacity used. If the market impounds the change in the value of the equipment but PL depreciation is reported, PL earnings will not be as highly associated with stock returns. If the market learns of the change in the value of equipment during the same period as RC accounting recognizes the change and if the recognized RC amount is reliable, I expect that RC earnings will explain a greater portion of the variation in stock returns than both PL and HC earnings. Therefore, R^2s of cross-sectional regressions are predicted to be greater for RC than PL and HC earnings.

4.2 TESTS OF INCREMENTAL VALUE RELEVANCE OF PL AND RC ACCOUNTING

While tests of relative value relevance offer evidence on reporting under one set of accounting principles, tests of incremental timeliness provide evidence of the significance of each adjustment beyond HC accounting. To test incremental timeliness of PL and RC adjustments, I disaggregate reported earnings and changes in earnings into HC measures, an adjustment between HC and PL, and an adjustment between PL and RC:

$$RET_t = \gamma_0 + \gamma_1 E_t^{HC} + \gamma_2 E_t^{PL\text{-}HC} + \gamma_3 E_t^{RC\text{-}PL} + \gamma_4 \Delta E_t^{HC} + \gamma_5 \Delta E_t^{PL\text{-}HC} + \gamma_6 \Delta E_t^{RC\text{-}PL} + \nu_t \quad (2)$$

Where:

$E_t^{PL\text{-}HC}$	adjustment between PL and HC earnings over lagged market value for the period ending time, t.
$E_t^{RC\text{-}PL}$	adjustment between RC and PL earnings over lagged market value for the period ending time, t.
$\Delta E_t^{PL\text{-}HC}$	change in the adjustment between PL and HC earnings over lagged market value for the period ending time, t.
$\Delta E_t^{RC\text{-}PL}$	change in the adjustment between RC and PL earnings over lagged market value for the period ending time, t.

Because PL and RC adjustments are expected to capture timely information about current performance, I predict the adjustments to be significantly and positively associated with returns. If PL accounting is timely then γ_2 and γ_5 will be significant and positive. If RC accounting is timely then γ_3 and γ_6 will be significant and positive.

In addition to testing incremental versus relative relevance, the specification in equation (2) allows for testing the equality of estimated coefficients on HC earnings and the adjustments to PL and RC earnings. Equation (2) can be viewed as an unrestricted form of a regression equation that examines the association between annual returns and reported RC earnings. Disaggregating RC earnings into the components of HC earnings, the adjustment between HC and PL, and the adjustment between PL and RC relaxes the restriction that all components of RC earnings components have the same estimated coefficient. Relaxing this restriction allows me to test whether HC earnings, the adjustment between HC and PL, and the adjustment between PL and RC exhibit similar relations with stock returns and thus have estimated coefficients that are not significantly different. Therefore, I test the equality of estimated coefficients on the earnings variables: $\gamma_1 = \gamma_2 = \gamma_3$.

I expect the magnitudes of the estimated coefficients to depend on several factors including persistence of the earnings component, conservatism in accounting for the earnings component, and reliability of the earnings measure. If these factors vary across components, then the estimated coefficients will be significantly different. For example, PL adjustments are based on the government's estimate of the general inflation rate while RC adjustments are based on appraisals made by independent appraisers. If the market does not perceive that the RC adjustments based on the appraisals are as reliable as PL adjustments based on general inflation, then the estimated coefficient on the adjustment between HC and PL earnings and the estimated coefficient on the adjustment between PL and RC earnings will not be equal. However, I do not have specific predictions as to how these factors affect each of the components. I also test the equality of the estimated coefficients on changes in earnings to determine if the changes in earnings variables are valued similarly: $\gamma_4 = \gamma_5 = \gamma_6$.

A second hypothesis relating to magnitude of the estimated coefficient examines whether reported earnings components measure economic earnings. If reported earnings measure economic earnings and changes in market values reflect economic earnings during the period, then reported earnings components should be valued "dollar for dollar" by the market. In a regression of stock returns on earnings, the expected estimated coefficient on earnings is one (Easton and Harris [1991]). I test whether the magnitude of estimated earnings coefficients is equal to one, $\gamma_1 = 1, \gamma_2 = 1, \gamma_3 = 1$. There are several reasons why estimated coefficients will not equal the theoretical value of one such as conservative accounting, information reaching the market prior to being recognized in earnings, or earnings not being measured reliably.

4.3 ADDITIONAL TESTS OF PL AND RC ADJUSTMENTS

I disaggregate earnings adjustments to further investigate key earnings components in PL and RC earnings. The difference between PL and HC earnings includes three components: monetary gains/losses, restatement of earnings components (such as sales, cost of goods and depreciation expense to the year-end price level), and restatement of the beginning book value. Since monetary gains/losses, MGL_t, measure purchasing power gains/losses, I expect the estimated coefficient to be positively and significantly related to market returns. The restatement of sales, cost of goods sold and depreciation expense are difficult to estimate individually with the available data, so I include them in a single variable called other differences in earnings, $ODE_t^{RC\text{-}PL}$, which is also expected to be positively and significantly associated with market returns. The restatement of beginning book value, $REST_t$, is an adjustment due to the change in the unit of account. To the extent that book values map into price, the restatement should correspond to a one-to-one change in price.

The difference between RC and PL earnings is composed of the RC asset revaluation increment, RI_t^{RC}, and a nominal restatement of the beginning asset revaluation. While the RC asset revaluation increment, RI_t^{RC}, is not included on the income statement, it is considered an earnings component in the Hicksian sense that it represents a change in wealth during the period. If the RC asset revaluation increment provides information about current performance not captured under HC or PL accounting, then it is expected to be positively and significantly related to returns. I combine the nominal restatement of the beginning asset revaluation with the restatement of the beginning PL book value into the variable, $REST_t$, and estimate the following equation:

$$RET_t = \lambda_0 + \lambda_1 E_t^{HC} + \lambda_2 ODE_t^{PL\text{-}HC} + \lambda_3 MGL_t + \lambda_4 REST_t + \lambda_5 RI_t^{RC} + \lambda_6 \Delta E_t^{HC} + \lambda_7 \Delta ODE_t^{PL\text{-}HC} + \lambda_8 \Delta MGL_t + \lambda_9 \Delta REST_t + \lambda_{10} \Delta RI_t^{RC} + \upsilon_t \quad (3)$$

To determine whether HC earnings and the adjustments are valued similarly, I test equality of estimated coefficients on earnings variables: $\lambda_1 = \lambda_2 = \lambda_3 = \lambda_4 = \lambda_5$. Rejection of equality of estimated coefficients implies that earnings components contain different information about a firm's current activities. Additionally, I test equality of estimated coefficients on changes in earnings: $\lambda_6 = \lambda_7 = \lambda_8 = \lambda_9 = \lambda_{10}$. I also examine whether there is perfect alignment between earnings and returns by testing whether the magnitude of estimated earnings coefficient is equal to one, $\lambda_1 = 1, \lambda_2 = 1, \lambda_3 = 1, \lambda_4 = 1, \lambda_5 = 1$.

5. *Sample Data*

5.1 SAMPLE SELECTION

Pooled cross-sectional models with fixed year effects are estimated for the years 1989 through 1995. I used fixed year effects to control for changes in other factors, such as macroeconomic conditions, that could affect the relation between earnings and returns over time.[4] Prior to 1989, sample size is constrained by lack of market prices due to infrequent trading. Companies are selected based on availability of prices in early years of the sample. Additional companies are included as prices become available. A total of 260 firm years is included in the sample, as shown in table 1.

[4] I also estimate all regressions by year with similar qualitative and quantitative results, except that the difference between replacement cost and price level earnings in equation (2) is significant at the 0.05 level or better in 4 of 7 years. The lower level of significance may be attributable to decreased sample sizes. I did not observe a systematic relation between the level of significance and inflation rates.

TABLE 1
Sample Selection

	1989	1990	1991	1992	1993	1994	1995
Inflation rate	20%	30%	19%	12%	8%	7%	52%
Sample							
Publicly traded non-financial companies	121	130	135	134	133	134	124
Price not available	74	76	70	68	50	42	16
Available for sample	47	54	65	66	83	92	108
Year-end not November or December	4	2	0	0	0	0	0
Missing variables	8	3	8	6	3	3	2
Major reorganization	0	2	0	0	0	0	1
Outliers deleted	2	2	4	5	4	6	4
Not included in sample	5	14	19	17	33	38	60
Sample	28	31	34	38	43	45	41

To be included in the sample, companies are required to have a fiscal year-end of November or December.[5] Firms are excluded from the sample in the year they change year-end, if variables are missing, or due to major reorganizations during the year. Outliers are excluded based on plots of the dependent variable against each independent variable. The analyses are also performed excluding those observations with significant influence as measured by an *r*-student greater than (less than) three (-three). The results are not sensitive to these specifications.

Sixty-one companies are included in the sample although a maximum of 45 are used in regressions in any year. Forty-eight firms are in the sample for four or more years. The sample includes firms in 25 two-digit SIC codes with six firms each in the metals and mining category and the cement and related products category.

5.2 DATA COLLECTION AND VARIABLE ESTIMATION

Financial statement data are collected from various sources: financial reports, the Mexican Stock Exchange (MSE), and commercial databases. Financial statement information is primarily from annual financial statements or filings with the MSE and includes book value, dividends, earnings, asset revaluation, changes in the asset revaluation, monetary gains/losses, net property, plant and equipment, depreciation, other changes in owners' equity, and shares outstanding.

To estimate HC and PL earnings, I first calculate book values and then use the clean surplus relation to calculate earnings. HC book value is calculated as reported RC book value less the difference between RC net book value of PPE and HC net book value of PPE. HC net book value of PPE is obtained from Schedule 4 of the annual filing with the MSE.[6] Information on the

[5] Starting in 1990, the Mexican National Banking and Securities Commission required all firms to have December year-ends.

[6] If Schedule 4 could not be obtained, HC net book value of PPE is estimated as prior year's historical PPE plus current year's capital expenditures minus estimated HC depreciation. As

revaluation of inventory and other non-monetary items is not available consistently. Therefore, only differences in property, plant, and equipment are considered in calculating HC book value. Although the exclusion of other variables may distort the measure of historical cost, the calculated HC book value should suffice as a comparison to PL and RC accounting.[7] The clean surplus relation is relied on to calculate comprehensive HC earnings. HC earnings are calculated as the change in HC book value adjusted for capital transactions such as dividends and stock issues. PL book value is calculated as RC book value minus the asset revaluation reported in shareholders' equity; the clean surplus relation is used to estimate comprehensive PL earnings.

A firm is included in the sample if it was traded 15 days prior to or 15 days subsequent to 5 months after year-end. The trading price per share closest to month-end is used to calculate the market value as price per share times shares outstanding. In Mexico, several series of common stock exist. The most prevalent are "A," which can be purchased only by Mexican citizens, and "B," which can be purchased by any investor. Dividend and voting rights are the same for "A" and "B" shares.[8] Where prices for each type of share are available, the market value is calculated based on the sum of the market value of each type of share. Where the price for only one type of share is available, that price is multiplied by the total number of all shares outstanding to obtain the market value. Returns are calculated as the total market value plus dividends divided by lagged market value.

5.3 DESCRIPTIVE STATISTICS

Descriptive statistics are provided in table 2. The first three ratios are presented to offer an understanding of the basic summary measures of the Mexican firms in the sample. Under combined PL and RC accounting, the return on restated equity aims to measure real profitability. During this period, the Mexican return on restated beginning equity is 8.5%, compared to the U.S. with a median profitability of approximately 11%.[9] The median

---

a robustness check, analyses were also performed using observations for which the HC PPE amounts are available (approximately 75% of the observations). Results and conclusions do not significantly change from those presented.

[7] By measurement error, I mean the difference between the variable I estimate and the actual accounting measure, which is unobserved in this case. With measurement error, the coefficient on the variable I estimate is biased toward zero, which works against finding positive results. In a multivariate regression, other coefficients are biased as well, though in unknown directions (Greene [1993]). A second form of measurement error, present in many capital market–based accounting studies, is that the independent variables in the regression (i.e., accounting earnings) are different from the unobserved construct implicit in stock prices (i.e., permanent earnings). To address this form of measurement error, I re-estimate all equations including lagged returns as an instrumental variables. The results do not change quantitatively.

[8] Shares with characteristics of preferred stock, such as the L shares, are excluded from the calculation of market value. Trust shares ("C" or "CPO"), which are comprised of mainly "A" and "B" shares, but may include shares with limited rights, are included.

[9] Calculated using 1996 COMPUSTAT industrial database.

TABLE 2

Descriptive Statistics

Variable	Mean	Std. Dev.	Median
Net income over restated beginning replacement cost (RC) book value, $NI_t^{RC}/(BV_{t-1}^{RC} \times \textit{inflation rate}_t)$	0.038	0.457	0.085
Market value over RC book value, P_t/BV_t^{RC}	1.409	1.030	1.161
Price over net income, P_t/NI_t^{RC}	16.196	150.424	11.964
Annual market returns, RET_t	0.363	0.658	0.225
Earnings and changes in earnings:[a]			
Historical cost (HC) earnings, E_t^{HC}	0.063	0.420	0.050
Change in historical cost earnings, ΔE_t^{HC}	−0.032	0.464	0.010
Price level (PL) earnings, E_t^{PL}	0.359	0.404	0.237
Change in price level earnings, ΔE_t^{PL}	0.033	0.442	0.002
Replacement cost earnings, E_t^{RC}	0.223	0.405	0.166
Change in replacement cost earnings, ΔE_t^{RC}	0.011	0.407	0.019
Adjustments between PL & RC earnings and HC earnings:[a]			
Adjustment between PL and HC earnings, E_t^{PL-HC}	0.324	0.447	0.219
Adjustment between RC and PL earnings, E_t^{RC-PL}	−0.137	0.417	−0.064
Changes in:			
Adjustment between PL and HC earnings, ΔE_t^{PL-HC}	0.049	0.674	0.001
Adjustment between RC and PL earnings, ΔE_t^{RC-PL}	−0.015	0.506	−0.001
Other adjustments to earnings:[a]			
Other differences in earnings, ODE_t^{PL-HC}	−0.011	0.485	−0.006
Monetary gains/losses, MGL_t	0.087	0.186	0.030
RC asset revaluation increment, RI_t^{RC}	−0.060	0.395	−0.039
Restatement due to inflation, $REST_t$	0.177	0.376	0.095
Changes in:			
Other differences in earnings, ΔODE_t^{PL-HC}	−0.055	0.773	−0.003
Monetary gains/losses, ΔMGL_t	0.021	0.176	0.001
RC asset revaluation increment, ΔRI_t^{RC}	0.032	0.382	−0.002
Restatement due to inflation, $\Delta REST_t$	0.032	0.381	0.013

[a] Variables are divided by lagged market values.

RC market-to-book ratio of 1.16 is lower than the 1.49 median market-to-book value in the U.S. during the same period.[10] Annual data (untabulated) indicates that RC market-to-book values in Mexico are low in early years and approach levels similar to the U.S. in later years. While the pooled median price earnings ratio is 11.96, annual medians of price earnings ratios (untabulated) are increasing until 1995, consistent with the decrease in interest rates and inflation over the time period.[11]

Nominal mean (median) annual returns of 0.36 (0.23), exceed the 21% average inflation rate over the period. Mean (median) HC earnings over lagged market value of 0.06 (0.05) are lower than both PL and RC earnings

[10] Calculated using 1996 COMPUSTAT industrial database.

[11] The benchmark "earnings multiple" is commonly expressed as one plus the risk-free interest rate divided by the risk-free interest rate. If the risk-free interest rate is the only factor affecting the multiple, then as the rate decreases, the multiple will increase. However, other factors such as earnings persistence or the existence of negative earnings will impact the value of the multiple.

over lagged market value of 0.36 (0.24) and 0.22 (0.17), respectively, most likely due to the absence of price level adjustments and monetary gains. The mean (median) of PL earnings over lagged market value of 0.36 (0.24) is higher than RC earnings of 0.22 (0.17), in line with the negative mean (median) RC asset revaluation increment of −0.06 (−0.04). Additionally, the coefficient of variation, a measure of dispersion calculated as a variable's standard deviation over its mean, is higher for HC earnings (6.67) than for both PL and RC earnings (1.13 and 2.00, respectively), implying that HC earnings are more variable than both PL and RC earnings.

Table 3, panel A, presents Pearson (Spearman) correlations for variables used in equation (1). The magnitude of Pearson (Spearman) correlations between the returns and RC earnings of 0.56 (0.44) is higher than that of both PL and HC earnings at 0.32 (0.27) and 0.36 (0.32), respectively, although all correlations are significant with *p*-values of 0.00. Interestingly, the Pearson (Spearman) correlation between RC and HC earnings of 0.52 (0.45) is higher than that between PL and HC earnings of 0.34 (0.36) while the correlation between RC and PL earnings is 0.49 (0.66), suggesting that PL and RC earnings are correlated with different aspects of HC earnings.

For variables used in equation (2), table 3, panel B, presents Pearson (Spearman) correlations. The adjustment between PL and HC earnings is not significantly correlated with returns while the adjustment between RC and PL earnings is significantly correlated with returns with Pearson (Spearman) correlations of 0.19 (0.11) and *p*-value of 0.00 (0.08).

Table 3, panel C, details Pearson (Spearman) correlations for variables used in equation (3). The RC asset revaluation increment, RI_t^{RC}, and the restatement of book value, $REST_t$, are highly and significantly correlated (Pearson correlation = 0.78, $p = 0.00$; Spearman correlation = 0.58, $p = 0.00$), which implies that the two contain overlapping information. The Pearson (Spearman) correlation between returns and other differences in earnings, ODE_t^{PL-HC}, is unexpectedly negative, suggesting the PL adjustment, which increases items such as depreciation expense and costs of goods sold, conveys negative information to the equity markets about future firm performance. ODE_t^{PL-HC} is, however, negatively related to HC earnings as expected since higher HC earnings generally require a larger PL adjustment to items such as depreciation expense. The monetary gains/losses, restatements, and revaluation increment are positively related to returns although significance varies.

6. *Test Results*

6.1 RESULTS OF TESTS OF RELATIVE VALUE RELEVANCE OF HC, PL, AND RC ACCOUNTING

Results of return regressions of HC, PL, and RC earnings and changes in earnings are presented in table 4. Differences across the three regressions are interesting to observe. While earnings coefficients in the three

TABLE 3

Correlations with Probabilities (Pearson Correlations above Diagonal and Spearman Correlations below Diagonal)

Panel A: Correlations of variables used in equation (1)

	RET_t	E_t^{HC}	ΔE_t^{HC}	E_t^{PL}	ΔE_t^{PL}	E_t^{RC}	ΔE_t^{RC}
RET_t	1.00	0.36	0.30	0.32	0.08	0.56	0.32
	(0.00)	(0.00)	(0.00)	(0.00)	(0.19)	(0.00)	(0.00)
E_t^{HC}	0.32	1.00	0.61	0.34	−0.13	0.52	0.44
	(0.00)	(0.00)	(0.00)	(0.00)	(0.04)	(0.00)	(0.00)
ΔE_t^{HC}	0.26	0.53	1.00	0.09	0.09	0.51	0.56
	(0.00)	(0.00)	(0.00)	(0.18)	(0.16)	(0.00)	(0.00)
E_t^{PL}	0.27	0.36	0.20	1.00	0.33	0.49	0.27
	(0.00)	(0.00)	(0.00)	(0.00)	(0.00)	(0.00)	(0.00)
ΔE_t^{PL}	0.05	0.09	0.28	0.35	1.00	0.11	0.46
	(0.46)	(0.16)	(0.00)	(0.00)	(0.00)	(0.09)	(0.00)
E_t^{RC}	0.44	0.45	0.29	0.66	0.29	1.00	0.66
	(0.00)	(0.00)	(0.00)	(0.00)	(0.00)	(0.00)	(0.00)
ΔE_t^{RC}	0.27	0.31	0.51	0.29	0.49	0.57	1.00
	(0.00)	(0.00)	(0.00)	(0.00)	(0.00)	(0.00)	(0.00)

Panel B: Correlations of variables used in equation (2)

	RET_t	E_t^{HC}	E_t^{PL-HC}	E_t^{RC-PL}	ΔE_t^{HC}	ΔE_t^{PL-HC}	ΔE_t^{RC-PL}
RET_t	1.00	0.36	0.12	0.19	0.30	−0.14	0.17
	(0.00)	(0.00)	(0.24)	(0.00)	(0.00)	(0.03)	(0.01)
E_t^{HC}	0.32	1.00	−0.44	0.24	0.60	−0.51	0.56
	(0.00)	(0.00)	(0.00)	(0.00)	(0.00)	(0.00)	(0.05)
E_t^{PL-HC}	0.13	−0.28	1.00	−0.69	−0.36	0.58	−0.54
	(0.28)	(0.00)	(0.00)	(0.00)	(0.00)	(0.00)	(0.00)
E_t^{RC-PL}	0.11	0.07	−0.64	1.00	0.38	−0.44	0.51
	(0.08)	(0.26)	(0.00)	(0.00)	(0.00)	(0.00)	(0.00)
ΔE_t^{HC}	0.27	0.53	−0.20	0.06	1.00	−0.59	0.33
	(0.00)	(0.00)	(0.00)	(0.39)	(0.00)	(0.00)	(0.00)
ΔE_t^{PL-HC}	−0.14	−0.31	0.43	−0.32	−0.42	1.00	−0.71
	(0.03)	(0.00)	(0.00)	(0.00)	(0.00)	(0.00)	(0.00)
ΔE_t^{RC-PL}	0.12	0.18	−0.32	0.48	0.10	−0.66	1.00
	(0.04)	(0.00)	(0.00)	(0.00)	(0.11)	(0.00)	(0.00)

See Table 2 for notation.

regressions are significantly positive at the 0.01 level, only the RC earnings coefficients is insignificantly different from one at the 0.01 level. Additionally, the change in RC earnings is not significantly different from zero (while the change in PL and HC earning are) indicating that it adds no incremental information beyond RC earnings.

As expected, results of Vuong tests indicate that the explanatory power of RC accounting, with an R^2 of 0.33, is significantly greater than that of both PL and HC accounting with R^2s of 0.20 and 0.18 and probabilities of 0.00 and 0.03, respectively. However, the explanatory power of PL accounting is not significantly different from HC accounting. These results suggest that RC accounting captures value relevant information in a more timely manner than PL and HC accounting while the timeliness of PL accounting and HC accounting are similar.

TABLE 3—*Continued*

Panel C: Correlations of variables used in equation (3)

	RET_t	E_t^{HC}	ODE_t^{PL-HC}	MGL_t	RI_t^{RC}	$REST_t$	ΔE_t^{HC}	ΔODE_t^{PL-HC}	ΔMGL_t	ΔRI_t^{RC}	$\Delta REST_t$
RET	1.00	0.36	−0.26	0.10	0.21	0.29	0.30	−0.24	−0.09	0.23	0.23
	(0.00)	(0.00)	(0.00)	(0.12)	(0.00)	(0.00)	(0.00)	(0.00)	(0.16)	(0.00)	(0.00)
E_t^{HC}	0.32	1.00	−0.38	−0.25	−0.01	0.01	0.61	−0.49	−0.34	0.22	0.21
	(0.00)	(0.00)	(0.00)	(0.00)	(0.89)	(0.82)	(0.00)	(0.00)	(0.00)	(0.00)	(0.00)
ODE_t^{PL-HC}	−0.07	−0.33	1.00	−0.07	−0.68	−0.65	−0.50	0.59	−0.09	−0.57	−0.63
	(0.27)	(0.00)	(0.00)	(0.27)	(0.00)	(0.00)	(0.00)	(0.00)	(0.17)	(0.00)	(0.00)
MGL_t	0.03	−0.22	−0.02	1.00	−0.07	0.19	−0.04	−0.10	0.47	(0.00)	0.16
	(0.61)	(0.00)	(0.81)	(0.00)	(0.28)	(0.00)	(0.51)	(0.12)	(0.00)	(0.95)	(0.01)
RI_t^{RC}	0.18	0.11	−0.60	−0.26	1.00	0.78	0.20	−0.18	(0.00)	0.58	0.60
	(0.00)	(0.08)	(0.00)	(0.00)	(0.00)	(0.00)	(0.00)	(0.00)	(0.97)	(0.00)	(0.00)
$REST_t$	0.18	0.11	−0.60	0.05	0.58	1.00	0.23	−0.22	0.11	0.52	0.63
	(0.00)	(0.09)	(0.00)	(0.41)	(0.00)	(0.00)	(0.00)	(0.00)	(0.10)	(0.00)	(0.00)
ΔE_t^{HC}	0.26	0.53	−0.34	−0.05	0.11	0.14	1.00	−0.60	0.08	0.06	0.12
	(0.00)	(0.00)	(0.00)	(0.40)	(0.09)	(0.03)	(0.00)	(0.00)	(0.19)	(0.34)	(0.07)
ΔODE_t^{PL-HC}	−0.08	−0.20	0.62	−0.06	−0.41	−0.32	−0.38	1.00	0.10	−0.55	−0.53
	(0.21)	(0.00)	(0.00)	(0.36)	(0.00)	(0.00)	(0.00)	(0.00)	(0.11)	(0.00)	(0.00)
ΔMGL_t	−0.04	−0.27	−0.01	0.39	−0.19	0.04	0.04	0.01	1.00	−0.43	−0.30
	(0.57)	(0.00)	(0.91)	(0.00)	(0.00)	(0.57)	(0.52)	(0.89)	(0.00)	(0.00)	(0.00)
ΔRI_t^{RC}	0.16	0.14	−0.43	−0.06	0.52	0.32	0.01	−0.67	−0.27	1.00	0.78
	(0.01)	(0.03)	(0.00)	(0.37)	(0.00)	(0.00)	(0.85)	(0.00)	(0.00)	(0.00)	(0.00)
$\Delta REST_t$	0.03	0.06	−0.56	0.09	0.54	0.65	0.08	−0.49	(0.00)	0.58	1.00
	(0.68)	(0.36)	(0.00)	(0.15)	(0.00)	(0.00)	(0.21)	(0.00)	(0.98)	(0.00)	(0.00)

See Table 2 for notation.

TABLE 4

Results of Tests of Relative Value Relevance: Historical Cost, Price Level, and Replacement Costs Regressions and Vuong Tests[b]

$$RET_t = \alpha_0 + \alpha_1 E_t^* + \alpha_2 \Delta E_t^* + e_t \quad (1)$$

Panel A: Regression results

	α_0	α_1	α_2	Adj. R^2
Historical Cost	0.23	0.36	0.18	0.18
	(2.35)**	(3.40)***	(2.52)**	
Price Level	−0.10	0.40	0.23	0.20
	(−0.09)	(4.10)***	(2.53)**	
Replacement Cost	−0.02	0.86	−0.13	0.33
	(−0.84)	(7.45)***	(−1.39)	

Panel B: Results of Vuong tests

	Price Level	Replacement Cost
Historical Cost	PL = HC	RC > HC
Z statistic	0.06	2.83
probability	0.95	0.00
Price Level		RC > PL
Z statistic		2.09
probability		0.03

Notes:

RET_t annual market return for the year ending 5 months after year-end.
E_t clean surplus earnings for the period ended at time, t, over lagged market value.
ΔE_t change in clean surplus earnings over the period ended at time, t, over lagged market value.
e_t error term at time, t.
* accounting measures used: historical cost (HC), price level (PL), or replacement cost (RC).
***, ** significant at 0.01 level, significant at the 0.05 level.

[b]t-statistics in parentheses.

6.2 RESULTS OF TESTS OF INCREMENTAL VALUE RELEVANCE OF PL AND RC ACCOUNTING

Results of estimating equation (2), presented in table 5, confirm the expectation that adjustment between HC and PL earnings and the adjustment between PL and RC earnings are positively and significantly related to annual returns. Differences in earnings are positive and significant at the 0.01 level, indicating the adjustments are related to returns. Results of F-tests reject the equality of estimated coefficients on HC earnings, the adjustment between HC and PL earnings and the adjustment between PL and RC earnings, $\gamma_1, \gamma_2, \gamma_3$, at the 0.02 level, implying that the earnings are valued differently due to factors such as persistence of the earnings component, conservatism in accounting for the earnings component, and reliability of the earnings measure.

F-tests also indicate that the coefficients on both HC earnings and the adjustment between HC and PL earnings are insignificantly different from one with F-values of 1.07 and 0.22, respectively, and probabilities of 0.30 and 0.63, respectively. This finding suggests that, on average, the variables reliably summarize firm performance. The coefficient on the adjustment to

TABLE 5

Results of Tests of Incremental Value Relevance of Price Level and Replacement Cost Accounting and Additional Tests of Price Level and Replacement Costs Adjustments[b]

$$RET_t = \gamma_0 + \gamma_1 E_t^{HC} + \gamma_2 E_t^{PL-HC} + \gamma_3 E_t^{RC-PL} + \gamma_4 \Delta E_t^{HC} + \gamma_5 \Delta E_t^{PL-HC} + \gamma_6 \Delta E_t^{RC-PL} + v_t \quad (2)$$

$$RET_t = \lambda_0 + \lambda_1 E_t^{HC} + \lambda_2 ODE_t^{PL-HC} + \lambda_3 MGL_t + \lambda_4 REST_t + \lambda_5 RI_t^{RC} + \lambda_6 \Delta E_t^{HC} + \lambda_7 \Delta ODE_t^{PL-HC} + \lambda_8 \Delta MGL_t + \lambda_9 \Delta REST_t + \lambda_{10} \Delta RI_t^{RC} + v_t \quad (3)$$

Panel A: Regression results

Equation (2)	γ_0	γ_1	γ_2	γ_3	γ_4	γ_5	γ_6					Adj. R^2
	−0.16	1.23	0.97	0.82	−0.13	−0.12	−0.38					0.36
	(−1.60)	(7.55)***	(6.66)***	(5.80)***	(1.04)	(1.03)	(1.65)					
Equation (3)	λ_0	λ_1	λ_2	λ_3	λ_4	λ_5	λ_6	λ_7	λ_8	λ_9	λ_{10}	
	−0.33	1.10	0.84	0.69	1.05	0.14	0.09	−0.01	0.52	0.44	−0.31	0.37
	(−2.38)***	(6.48)***	(4.52)***	(2.93)***	(4.45)***	(0.47)	(0.69)	(0.14)	(2.12)***	(1.37)	(−1.10)	

Panel B: Tests of coefficient magnitudes

Equation (2)	Tests of Coefficients	F-value	Prob.	Equation (3)	Tests of Coefficients	F-value	Prob.
	$\gamma_1 = \gamma_2 = \gamma_3$	3.87	(0.02)		$\lambda_1 = \lambda_2 = \lambda_3 = \lambda_4 = \lambda_5$	5.53	(0.00)
	$\gamma_1 = 1$	1.07	(0.30)		$\lambda_1 = 1$	0.23	(0.63)
	$\gamma_2 = 1$	0.22	(0.63)		$\lambda_2 = 1$	0.63	(0.42)
	$\gamma_3 = 1$	3.15	(0.08)		$\lambda_3 = 1$	1.94	(0.16)
	$\gamma_4 = \gamma_5 = \gamma_6$	3.94	(0.02)		$\lambda_4 = 1$	0.00	(0.93)
					$\lambda_5 = 1$	8.08	(0.00)
					$\lambda_6 = \lambda_7 = \lambda_8 = \lambda_9 = \lambda_{10}$	2.86	(0.02)

Notation:

RET_t annual market return for the period ending 5 months after year-end.
E_t^{HC} clean surplus earnings over lagged market value for the period ended at time, t.
E_t^{PL-HC} adjustment between HC and PL earnings for the period ending time, t, over lagged market value.
E_t^{RC-PL} adjustment between RC and PL earnings for the period ending time, t, over lagged market value.
ODE_t^{RC-PL} other differences in earnings over lagged market values for the period ending time, t. It is the estimate of the restatement of sales, cost of goods sold, and depreciation expense.
MGL_t monetary gains/losses over lagged market value for the period ending time, t.
$REST_t$ restatement of beginning book value over lagged market value for the period ending time, t.
RI_t^{RC} replacement cost asset revaluation increment over lagged market value for the period ending time, t.
Δ change in variable.
*** significant at 0.01 level.

[b] t-statistics in parentheses.

RC earnings is significantly different from one, with an F-value of 3.15 and probability of 0.08, indicating some non-alignment of the change in the RC asset values with returns during the period.

None of the changes in earnings variables are significantly related to returns nor are the coefficients similar.

6.3 RESULTS OF ADDITIONAL TESTS OF PL AND RC ADJUSTMENTS

Results of equation (3), which tests key earnings components, are presented in table 5. Earnings adjustments, except the RC asset revaluation increment, RI_t^{RC}, are positively and significantly associated with price, which implies that they summarize the firm's performance over the reporting period. The insignificance of the RC asset revaluation increment, RI_t^{RC}, contrasts with the significant relation between returns and RC earnings found in equation (2). A possible explanation for the lack of significance is disaggregated components of earnings contain information that overlaps with that in the RC asset revaluation increment, RI_t^{RC}. Another possible explanation is a high and significant correlation between RI_t^{RC} and $REST_t$. When $REST_t$ is removed from equation (3), RI_t^{RC} becomes significant at the 0.01 level.

Tests of whether earnings coefficients equal one cannot be rejected for HC earnings (F-value = 0.23, probability = 0.63), other differences in earnings (F-value = 0.63, probability = 0.42), monetary gains/losses (F-value = 1.94, probability = 0.16) and the restatement of beginning book value (F-value = 0.00, probability = 0.93), indicating that these measures reliably summarize firm performance over the period. The F-test of the equality of the estimated earnings coefficients with an F-value of 5.53 and probability of 0.00, indicates that the magnitude of earnings coefficients are not equal, implying that the timeliness of earnings measures differ due to factors such as persistence of the earnings component, conservatism in accounting for the earnings component, or reliability of the earnings measure. The non-rejection is most likely due to the insignificance of RC asset revaluation increment.

Of the change variables, only the change in monetary gains/losses is positively and significantly, at the 0.01 level, related to returns. A possible reason for its significance is that the monetary gains/losses convey information about expected inflation and/or a firm's financing activities that are expected to persist.

The overall positive and significant association between returns and monetary gains/losses differs from Davis-Friday's [1999] results in price regressions. Davis-Friday [1999] finds a negative and significant association between price and monetary gains/losses. The difference can be attributed to differences in sample firms and/or sources of data. While my sample mean (median) monetary gains/losses are positive overall as shown in table 2 and in each year, Davis-Friday [1999] documents both mean (median) monetary losses in each year.

7. *Conclusions*

The analyses in this paper support the conclusion that price level and replacement cost accounting adjustments are value relevant beyond historical cost. Results indicate that replacement cost adjustments are relatively and incrementally relevant beyond both historical cost and price level measures while price level adjustments are incrementally value relevant beyond historical cost measures during the period examined. These results imply that price level and replacement cost accounting earnings and changes in earnings are timely, in the sense that they summarize a firm's current performance. Further, since the data include seven years from 1989 to 1995 when inflation ranged between 7% and 52%, results imply that adjustments are significant regardless of the inflation rate. Thus, results suggest that the decision by the Mexican Institute of Public Accountants to discontinue the revaluation to replacement costs eliminated value-relevant information.

While results of this study support the value relevance of PL and RC measures, at least three main limitations exist. First, the sample size is small. Results may differ from those obtained for a larger sample. Second, some of the variables were estimated and may therefore contain measurement error. Although results are robust to alternative approaches, some other methods may provide different findings. Finally, results from a sample of Mexican companies may not apply to other contexts.

APPENDIX

A Numerical Example of the Relation Between Historical Cost, Price Level, and Replacement Cost Accounting

This example numerically illustrates relations among historical cost (HC), price level (PL), and replacement cost (RC) book values and earnings. Table A starts with an HC balance sheet and income statement at year 1, shows adjustments to PL accounting and adjustments between PL and RC accounting.

To adjust from HC to PL accounting, all balances and transactions are adjusted to a common currency; here, the value of the currency at year-end. To adjust to PL accounting, an "exchange rate" of the price level at year-end over the price level when the transaction occurred is created. Assume that the beginning price level is 100, the average for the year is 125 and the year-end price level is 150.

First, start with the balance sheet and identify monetary and non-monetary items. Monetary items, such as cash and debt are already valued in the year-end currency and do not need to be adjusted. Non-monetary items such as property, plant, and equipment (PPE) and capital need to be adjusted. If PPE and capital were last valued at the beginning of the year when the price level was 100, then to value them at the year-end currency an exchange rate of 150/100 is used. The difference between the HC book value

TABLE A

A Numerical Example of the Relation Between Historical Cost, Price Level, and Replacement Cost Book Values and Earnings

	Historical	Price Level Adjustment Factor*	Price Level	Replacement Cost Amounts	Replacement Cost
BALANCE SHEET					
Cash	200		200		200
Property, plant and equipment					
Cost	1000	150/100	1500	1400	1400
Accumulated depreciation	(200)	150/100	(300)	−280	(280)
Net	800		1200		1120
Total assets	1000		1400		1320
Debt	500		500		500
Capital	400	150/100	600		600
Net income	100		300		320
Result of holding non-monetary assets					(100)
Total equity	500		900		820
Total liabilities & equity	1000		1400		1320
INCOME STATEMENT					
Income	200	150/125	240		240
Depreciation expense	(100)	150/100	(150)	−130	(130)
Monetary gain			210		210
Net income	100		300		320
Comprehensive income	100		300		220
*Price levels					
Beginning of year	100				
Average	125				
Ending of year	150				

and PL book value is 400, the same as the PL adjustment of non-monetary assets.

Moving to the income statement, assume that all sales occur evenly throughout the year so the appropriate exchange rate to use is the year-end price level over the average price level, 150/125. Depreciation expense is tied to the underlying non-monetary asset so the same exchange rate used for PPE of 150/100 is applied.

Monetary gains (losses) arise from maintaining a net monetary liability (asset) position. During the year, the company maintained a net monetary liability position. It held debt of 500 throughout the year and acquired the cash balance of 200 evenly throughout the year. The monetary gain of 210 is calculated as the gain on the 500 debt during the year of 250 ((500*150/100) – 500) plus the loss of 40 on holding the cash acquired evenly throughout the year ((200*150/125) – 200). To summarize, the difference of 200 between the HC and PL earnings is attributable to the 40 increase due to restatement of sales, the 50 decrease due to the difference in depreciation expense and the monetary gain of 210. Here earnings and comprehensive earnings are the same since there are no earnings items that by-pass the income statement.

To adjust from PL to RC accounting, non-monetary assets are valued at replacement cost. In this example, the replacement cost of the PPE is 1,120, calculated as 1,400 less the accumulated depreciation of 280. Depreciation expense is also adjusted to a replacement cost value. The resulting adjustment in the revaluation appears as part of equity under the caption, result of holding non-monetary items. The adjustment between the PL and RC book value is (80), the same as the difference between the RC and PL value of non-monetary assets. The adjustment between the PL and RC comprehensive earnings is (80), the same as the change in the RC revaluation during the year.

The equations below define the relations among HC, PL, and RC book values and earnings. Numbers from the example in table A are inserted into the equations as an illustration.

BOOK VALUES:

$$BV_t^{RC} = BV_t^{HC} + BV_t^{PL-HC} + BV_t^{RC-PL}$$

$$820 = 500 + 400 + (80)$$

EARNINGS:

$$E_t^{RC} = E_t^{HC} + SALES_t^{PL\text{-}HC} + COGS_t^{PL\text{-}HC} + DEPN_t^{PL-HC}$$
$$+ MGL_t + BV_{t-1}^{RC-PL} \cdot i_t + \Delta RV_t^{RC}$$

$$220 = 100 + 40 + 0 + (50) + 210 + 0 + (80)$$

Where:

BV_t^{HC}	HC book value at time, t
BV_t^{PL-HC}	adjustment between PL and HC book values at time, t.
BV_t^{RC-PL}	adjustment between RC and PL book values at time, t.
E_t^{HC}	clean surplus earnings over the period ended at time, t.
$SALES_t^{PL-HC}$	PL adjustment to sales over the period ended at time, t.
$COGS_t^{PL-HC}$	PL adjustment to cost of goods sold over the period ended at time, t.
$DEPN_t^{PL-HC}$	PL adjustment to depreciation over the period ended at time, t.
MGL_t	monetary gain/loss over the period ended at time, t.
i_t	inflation rate over the period ended at time, t.
ΔRV_t^{RC}	change in RC asset revaluation over the period ended at time, t.

REFERENCE

ABOODY, D.; M. E. BARTH; AND R. KASNIK. "Revaluations of Fixed Assets and Future Firm Performance: Evidence from the UK." *Journal of Accounting and Economics* 26 (1999): 149–78.

AMIR, E.; T. S. HARRIS; AND E. K. VENUTI. "A Comparison of Value-Relevance of U.S. Versus Non-U.S. GAAP Accounting Measures Using Form 20-F Reconciliations." *Journal of Accounting Research* (International Accounting Supplement 1993): 230–64.

ASSOCIATION FOR INVESTMENT MANAGEMENT AND RESEARCH (AIMR), *Financial Reporting in the 1990s and Beyond*, 1993.

BALL, R.; S. P. KOTHARI; AND A. ROBIN. "The Effect of International Institutional Factors on Properties of Accounting Earnings." *Journal of Accounting and Economics* 29 (2000): 1–51.

BARTH, M. E., AND G. CLINCH. "International Accounting Differences and Their Relation to Share Prices: Evidence from U.K., Australian, and Canadian Firms." *Contemporary Accounting Research* 13 (1996): 135–170.

BARTH, M. E., AND G. CLINCH. "Revalued Financial, Tangible, and Intangible Assets: Associations with Share Prices and Non-Market-Based Value Estimates" *Journal of Accounting Research* (Supplement 1998): 199–248.

BEAVER, W. H.; A. A. CHRISTIE; AND P. A. GRIFFIN. "The Information Content of SEC Accounting Series Release No. 190." *Journal of Accounting and Economics* 2 (1980): 127–157.

BEAVER, W. H.; P. A. GRIFFIN; AND W. R. LANDSMAN. "The Incremental Information Content of Replacement Cost Earnings." *Journal of Accounting and Economics* 4 (1982): 15–29.

BEAVER, W. H., AND W. R. LANDSMAN. *Incremental Information Content of Statement 33 Disclosures*. Research Report. Stamford, CT: FASB, 1983.

BELSLEY, D; E. KUH; AND R. WELSCH. "Regression Diagnostics: Identifying Influential Data and Sources of Collinearity." New York: Wiley, 1980.

BERNARD, V. L. "Cross-Sectional Dependence and Problems of Inference in Market-Based Accounting Research." *Journal of Accounting Research* (1987): 1–48.

BERNARD, V. L., AND R. G. RULAND. "The Incremental Information Content of Historical Cost and Current Cost Income Numbers: Time-Series Analyses for 1962–1980." *Accounting Review* (October 1987): 707–22.

BHATTACHARYA, U.; H. DAOUK; B. JORGENSON; AND C. KEHR. "When and Event Is Not an Event: The Curious Case of an Emerging Market." *Journal of Financial Economics* (2000): 69–101.

BIDDLE, G. C.; G. S. SEOW; AND A. F. SIEGEL. "Relative Versus Incremental Information Content." *Contemporary Accounting Research* 12 (1995): 1–23.

BILDERSEE, J. S., AND J. RONEN. "Stock Returns and Real Activity in an Inflationary Environment: The Informational Impact of FAS No. 33" *Contemporary Accounting Research* 4 (1987): 89–110.

BUBLITZ, B.; T. J. FRECKA; AND J. C. MCKEOWN. "Market Association Tests and FASB Statement No. 33 Disclosures: A Reexamination." *Journal of Accounting Research* (Supplement 1985): 1–27.

BUSHMAN, R. M.; Q. CHEN; Q. E. ENGEL; AND A. SMITH. "The Sensitivity of Corporate Governance Systems to the Timeliness of Accounting Earnings." Working paper, University of Chicago. 2000.

DAVIS-FRIDAY, P. "Equity Valuation and Current Cost Disclosures: The Case of Mexico." *Journal of International Financial Management and Accounting* (2001): Forthcoming.

EASTON, P. D. "Discussion of Revalued Financial, Tangible, and Intangible Assets: Associations with Share Prices and Non-Market-Based Value Estimates." *Journal of Accounting Research* (Supplement 1998): 235–47.

EASTON, P. D.; P. H. EDDEY; AND T. S. HARRIS. "An Investigation of Revaluations of Tangible Long-lived Assets." *Journal of Accounting Research* (International Accounting Supplement 1993): 1–38.

EASTON, P. D., AND T. S. HARRIS. "Earnings as an Explanatory Variable for Returns." *Journal of Accounting Research* (1991): 19–36.

EDWARDS, E. O., AND P. W. BELL. *The Theory and Measurement of Business Income*. Berkeley: University of California Press, 1961.

FINANCIAL ACCOUNTING STANDARDS BOARD (FASB). *Statement of Financial Accounting Standards No. 33, Financial Reporting and Changing Prices*. Stamford, CT: FASB, 1979.

FINANCIAL ACCOUNTING STANDARDS BOARD (FASB). *Financial Reporting in North America: A Joint Study Undertaken by: Canadian Institute of Chartered Accountants, Instituto Mexicano de Contadores Públicos, A.C. and Financial Accounting Standards Board*. Norwalk, CT: FASB, 1995.

FRANCIS, J., AND K. SCHIPPER. "Have Financial Statements Lost Their Relevance?" *Journal of Accounting Research* 37 (1999): 319–352.

FREEMAN, R. N. "Alternative Measures of Profit Margin: An Empirical Study of the Potential Information of Current Cost Accounting." *Journal of Accounting Research* (1983): 42–64.

GHEYARA, K., AND J. BOATSMAN. "Market Reaction to 1976 Replacement Cost Disclosures." *Journal of Accounting and Economics* 2 (1980): 107–25.

HAW, I. M., AND S. LUSTGARTEN. "Evidence on Income Measurement Properties of ASR No. 190 and SFAS 33 Data." *Journal of Accounting Research* (Autumn 1988): 331–52.

HOPWOOD, W., AND T. SCHAEFER. "Firm-Specific Responsiveness to Input Price Changes and the Incremental Information in Current Cost Income." *Accounting Review* (April 1989): 313–43.

MAY, R. G.; G. G. MUELLER; AND T. H. WILLIAMS. *A New Introduction to Financial Accounting*, 2nd ed. Englewood Cliffs, NJ: Prentice-Hall, 1980.

MOONITZ, M. *Accounting Research Study 1: The Basic Postulates of Accounting*. American Institute of Certified Public Accountants. 1961. Report in *The Accounting Postulates and Principles Controversy of the 1960s*, Edited by Stephen A. Zeff. New York: Garland, 1982.

MOONITZ, M., AND R. T. SPROUSE. *Accounting Research Study 3: A Tentative Set of Broad Accounting Principles for Business Enterprises*. American Institute of Certified Public Accountants, 1962.

MURDOCH, B. "The Information Content of FAS 33 Returns on Equity." *Accounting Review* (April 1986): 273–87.

RIVERA, J. M. "Price-adjusted Financial Information and Investment Returns in a Highly Inflationary Economy: An Evaluation." *Advances in International Accounting* (1987): 287–304.

VUONG, Q. "Likelihood Ratio Test for Model Selection and Non-tested Hypotheses," *Econometrica* 57 (1989): 307–33.

WHITE, H. "A Heteroskedasticity-Consistent Covariance Matrix Estimator and a Direct Test for Heteroskedasticity." *Econometrica 40* (1980): 817–38.

ZEFF, S. A. "Sitting on the Fence: The UK Standard-setter Is Wrong to Abandon What Looked Like a Commitment to Current Value Accounting," *Accountancy International* (July 1999): 68–69.

[14]

Accounting Horizons
Vol. 14 No. 2
June 2000
pp. 113–135

Inflation Accounting and 20-F Disclosures: Evidence from Mexico

Paquita Y. Davis-Friday and Juan Rivera

Paquita Y. Davis-Friday is a visiting Assistant Professor at Emory University, and Juan M. Rivera is an Associate Professor at the University of Notre Dame.

SYNOPSIS: This paper analyzes features of the Mexican accounting model and describes the effect of the accounting differences between Mexico and the U.S. on the relation between equity prices and accounting information reported in the two countries. The influence of U.S. accounting in Mexico is evident in several areas, partly due to the presence of numerous affiliates of U.S. multinational corporations, and also due to the prominence of local representatives of the Big 5 international accounting firms. Still, the Mexican accounting and reporting model addresses special issues—such as inflation accounting—in a manner different from that of the U.S. Using the population of Mexican firms listed on U.S. exchanges as American Depositary Receipts (ADRs), we assess the relationship between Mexican ADR prices and Mexican vs. U.S. GAAP earnings and equity. We find that although Mexican ADR firms are not required to reconcile their inflation accounting to U.S. GAAP, ADR prices are significantly related to Mexican GAAP net income. However, we find no significant relation between the ADR price and net income and equity reconciliations from Mexican to U.S. GAAP. Our results call into question once again the validity and usefulness of the SEC's required reconciliations to U.S. GAAP.

Key Words: American depositary receipts, Inflation accounting, Mexico, 20-F reconciliations.

Data Availability: Data used in this study are available from public sources.

INTRODUCTION

The capital market globalization experienced in the 1980s and 1990s has spawned new and intriguing areas for research. These cover a wide range of issues, from general

This paper was formerly titled "The Impact of Inflation Accounting on U.S. Investors: Evidence from Mexican Firms Traded as American Depositary Receipts (ADRs)." The authors are grateful to the AICPA for financial support. Professor Davis-Friday also appreciates the financial support of Arthur Andersen. The comments of Sudipta Basu, Elizabeth Gordon, Joe Weintrop (the discussant), two anonymous reviewers, and participants at the 1999 AAA/KPMG International Accounting Research Conference, the 1999 AAA International Accounting Section Midyear Meeting, and the 1998 IAAER/CIERA International Accounting Research Conference are also gratefully appreciated.

Submitted: November 1998
Accepted: October 1999
Corresponding author: Paquita Y. Davis-Friday
Email: Paquita_Davis-Friday@bus.emory.edu

topics like the debate on the integration, or segmentation, of international markets to more specific ones such as listing requirements for foreign stock registration or trade. In the case of the U.S., accounting research has concentrated on the relevance of U.S. GAAP-reconciled accounting information required of foreign companies whose shares trade in the U.S. capital markets. Typically, the foreign companies included in these studies are those that list or trade their stock under the American Depositary Receipt (ADR) format. When a foreign company wishes to list or trade its shares in the U.S. through the ADR mechanism, it either has to file its financial statements according to U.S. accounting principles, or it must include the Securities and Exchange Commission's (SEC) required reconciliations to U.S. GAAP in its annual Form 20-F filings.[1]

This paper investigates foreign GAAP accounting and required compliance with U.S. GAAP disclosures for a set of Mexican firms whose shares trade as ADRs in the U.S. capital markets. Prior studies have addressed the value of accounting information when different though closely linked GAAP reporting models are competing for acceptance. Particularly relevant here are the papers by Bandyopadhyay et al. (1994) and Bandyopadhyay et al. (1998) on Canadian firms reporting in the U.S. markets. However, most of the previous research on U.S. GAAP reconciliations has included, solely or predominantly, companies from developed countries. Analyzing the financial information of Mexican firms is justifiable because of the close economic interdependence between the U.S. and Mexico resulting from the North American Free Trade Agreement (NAFTA) and because Mexico is an emerging market.[2] U.S. capital markets provide significant sources of financing for expanding Mexican firms that otherwise encounter limited domestic resources. Investigating the financial-reporting practices of Mexican firms should help in assessing the relative differences between accounting standards in two economically and geographically linked countries, an issue that has only been addressed previously at a more conceptual level.[3] Thus, this paper extends the inquiry on the validity of U.S. GAAP reconciliations for a particular set of firms that operate in an environment close to that of the U.S.

Using the population of Mexican firms listed on U.S. exchanges as of December 1995, we analyze the Mexican-U.S. GAAP reconciliations reported in their 20-F forms for the years 1995 and 1996. We then consider the reporting implications of Mexican-U.S. GAAP differences by analyzing the relation between the firms' market value and their domestic and U.S. GAAP-reconciled net income and equity. Our results indicate that, on average, our sample firms' net income and equity measured under Mexican GAAP are less conservative than under U.S. GAAP. In addition, results from association tests demonstrate that both Mexican and U.S. net income are significantly related to the ADR firms' market value of equity, but the required 20-F reconciliations from Mexican to U.S. GAAP are not significant factors in the determination of those values. This can be explained by the fact that the SEC does not require Mexican firms to reconcile what may be the most significant reporting difference between the two countries—inflation accounting. Therefore, our results

---

[1] For a review of the registration procedures required of foreign firms registering their shares in U.S. markets, see Fordham International Law Review Symposium (1994). For a summary of the content of the 20-F form required by the SEC for foreign registrants, see McQueen (1995).

[2] Analyses of monthly stock indices comparing the U.S. S&P 500 index and the corresponding indices from foreign stock markets during a span of five years have shown Mexico's to be among those with the highest correlation with the U.S. (Chan and Seow 1996, 152–153).

[3] A study by the accounting standard setters from the U.S., Canada, and Mexico reports on the major similarities and differences in the accounting norms among those three countries (FASB et al. 1995).

suggest that either the remaining differences between Mexican and U.S. GAAP income and book value are immaterial or that U.S. investors can discern U.S. GAAP measures from Mexican GAAP measures.

In general, prior studies dealing with foreign financial reporting and U.S. GAAP reconciliations have been inconclusive regarding the information content and significance of the required adjustments. Nevertheless, SEC-prescribed accounting disclosures and reconciliations are still required, despite the fact that in a survey of foreign companies conducted by Fanto and Karmel (1997) they were found to be the leading obstacle to U.S. listing. Because of these requirements, financial markets in the U.S. might be at a competitive disadvantage to attract more foreign listings when compared to non-U.S. security markets. Given the lack of value-relevance for the reconciliations reported by the Mexican ADR firms examined in the study, policymakers should probably reconsider the nature and extent of the required reconciliations and possibly consider eliminating them altogether.

Our study begins with a discussion of the background for this research and a review of previous literature. The subsequent sections describe the Mexican financial-reporting environment and the Mexican capital market. The following section discusses the sample of Mexican firms, the nature of their reconciliations from Mexican to U.S. GAAP, and the effect of these differences on the relative values of Mexican and U.S. GAAP net income, book value, and return on equity. The closing section provides concluding comments on the implications of our study and the differences between Mexican and U.S. GAAP as determinants of ADR prices.

BACKGROUND AND PRIOR RESEARCH

From the standpoint of U.S. investors, the opportunity to participate in the capital of foreign firms has been well received, as evidenced by the expansion of this segment in the U.S. market. Holdings of foreign equity securities by U.S. investors increased from $150 billion in 1991 when they represented 3.5 percent of the total equity market in the U.S. to $600 billion in 1997, or 6.5 percent of the total U.S. market.[4] In this last year, about 1,300 foreign companies had their shares listed for trading on the New York Stock Exchange (NYSE), American Exchange (AMEX), National Association of Securities Dealers' Automation Quotation (NASDAQ), or over-the-counter, and this number reflected a 75 percent increase over 1991 (Foerster and Karolyi 1999). Even among institutional investors, ADRs are a popular choice, as reported by a survey of 1,200 of these institutions conducted by Georgeson and Company in 1995 (Karolyi 1998). According to this survey, 70 percent of those investors owned ADRs, and 50 percent owned only ADRs.

The ADR mechanism represents an effective and attractive option for portfolio diversification for U.S. investors, and it also brings benefits to the foreign issuers. In a survey of the academic literature, Karolyi (1998) finds that listed foreign companies in the U.S. have experienced a decrease in their domestic market risk and a reduction in their costs of capital. In addition, as a rule, liquidity of the trading shares also improves because of a highly liquid secondary market such as the NYSE.[5] However, counterbalancing these benefits are the stringent disclosure requirements imposed by the U.S. on foreign issuers. This is the most important impediment to the growth of this segment of the market.

One could argue that for the case of foreign security markets, whose stock price indices are highly correlated with those in the U.S., the foreign firms' GAAP earnings

[4] New York Stock Exchange (1997).

[5] See, for example, the *Wall Street Journal* (1999).

could be as good a signal as a U.S. GAAP-reformulated number when valuing ADR shares of foreign firms in the U.S. On the other hand, there might be some peculiar characteristics of the foreign environment (e.g., exchange rate volatility, steep inflation, import controls, etc.) that are better reflected in the foreign GAAP financial disclosures and not captured by the U.S. GAAP adjustments, in which case the SEC-required reconciliation may be unwarranted.

Research in the area of accounting information for foreign registrants in the U.S. capital markets has focused on the information content of financial reports and disclosures required of foreign firms. The key approach has been to measure the responsiveness of the value and returns of a company's stock to information reported in the SEC's Form 20-F applicable to foreign issuers. Meek (1993) examines 26 firms from five countries and finds no significant relation between security prices and earnings reported in the information equivalent to the current 20-F reports. Apparently, the information had already been impounded into earnings in the companies' disclosures prior to the SEC-required annual filings.

The issue of the value-relevance of foreign income and equity reconciliations to U.S. GAAP has also been investigated by Amir et al. (1993). Using a sample of 101 firms from 20 countries they observed that earnings and shareholders' equity reconciliations to U.S. GAAP included in 20-F statements were indeed value-relevant, even at the level of specific reconciling items (e.g., goodwill, asset revaluations, and taxes). However, they still questioned the usefulness of the 20-F reconciliations after arguing that a careful investor could reconstruct a similar U.S. GAAP information set by solely incorporating the most relevant adjustments to the foreign-based accounting data.[6] Chan and Seow (1996) examine a sample of 45 foreign firms, 40 with ADRs and five with direct common stock listing in the U.S., and find that foreign-GAAP reported earnings were more closely associated with U.S.-measured stock returns than U.S. GAAP reconciled earnings. Possible explanations for the greater information content of foreign GAAP earnings point toward the relevance of specific legal, business, and economic conditions in foreign countries. Thus, the peculiar characteristics of these foreign environments might not be translatable through reconciliations to U.S. GAAP. In summary, the empirical studies assessing the relevance of 20-F reconciliations for prices and returns of ADRs stocks do not provide strong and compelling arguments in support of the usefulness and enforceability of those reconciliations.

Research on non-U.S. accounting has also covered other issues related to the SEC requirements of financial disclosures for foreign issuers. Alford et al. (1993) address the comparative usefulness of accounting earnings information in various countries against a U.S. benchmark, while Frost and Kinney (1996) review the different filing options and corresponding required disclosures of foreign firms in the U.S. Biddle and Saudagaran (1991, 1995) examine the perceived benefits and costs faced by foreign firms when choosing to list in alternative foreign stock exchanges, and at the theoretical level, Huddart et al. (1999) develop an expectations model of international stock exchange listing choices by corporate management on the basis of public disclosure requirements. However, the U.S. accounting literature on foreign firms has been very limited in covering issuers from developing or "emerging" countries. In the case of Mexico, the Amir et al. (1993) study is one of the few known to include a handful of observations from three Mexican companies with ADRs.

[6] Similar studies addressing the potential value-added information resulting from 20-F reconciliations include McQueen (1995), Pope and Rees (1993), and Rees and Elgers (1997).

Focus on Mexican Accounting

In 1992, the importance of comparative accounting within the context of the NAFTA region attracted the attention of accounting standard setters from the three countries. In that year, the Canadian Institute of Chartered Accountants (CICA), the Mexican Institute of Certified Public Accountants (IMCP) and the Financial Accounting Standards Board (FASB) undertook a project whose objectives were to (1) analyze similarities and differences in the three countries, (2) identify areas where harmonization could be advanced, and (3) provide users of financial statements with information that would increase their ability to compare businesses in the three countries (FASB et al. 1995). The joint study by FASB and its Mexican and Canadian counterparts concluded that the differences in accounting standards were due in part to a lack of a standard on a particular subject, especially for the case of Mexico. For those few areas where significant differences exist, such as inflation accounting in Mexico or the treatment of specific foreign exchange gains or losses in Canada, the joint study recommends the standard-setting bodies to work toward reducing or eliminating those differences. The study, however, did not attempt to and could not identify the specific reasons for the particular differences in the accounting standards compared.

Other than in a few areas where a Mexican accounting norm is not available (such as in earnings per share disclosures), Mexican accounting principles are, in substance, similar to those followed in the U.S. and Canada. The main areas of difference are in the accounting restatement for inflation and in deferred taxes. Regarding the first one, Mexico's inflation has abated in the two most recent years and its standard setters have considered revising the standard on inflation accounting. However, the measurable differences caused by inflation accounting are not even subject to reconciliation to U.S. GAAP when the SEC collects the information required of foreign firms in their 20-F annual filings. Thus, the need for empirical research on the usefulness of foreign accounting reconciliation to U.S. GAAP in SEC filings remains a valid inquiry. Since inflation accounting for Mexican firms is not altered for U.S. investors, one can argue whether the remaining required reconciliations actually help investors to compare businesses from different countries, the third objective stated in the joint study. This is particularly important because the FASB, CICA and IMCP study group was well aware of the increased cost that these required reconciliations impose on companies (FASB et al. 1995, 1).

THE MEXICAN FINANCIAL REPORTING ENVIRONMENT

In Mexico, the institution in charge of issuing accounting standards is an organized profession, represented by the Mexican Institute of CPAs (Instituto Mexicano de Contadores Públicos or IMCP). The IMCP is a federation of state and local associations of registered public accountants. The IMCP is an independent, nongovernmental professional association, and through its standing committees, it formulates accounting principles, auditing standards, and professional rules of ethics for Mexico. Its Accounting Principles Commission, composed predominantly of prominent professional practitioners, has issued 37 bulletins (statements) and circulars (amendments) on generally accepted accounting principles.[7] Generally speaking, Mexican GAAP are less specific and detailed than their U.S. counterparts, and some significant accounting issues have not yet been addressed.[8]

[7] For a complete discussion of Mexican GAAP, see Instituto Mexicano de Contadores Públicos (1994) and Martinez (1994). See also Davis (1996) and Rivera (1998).

[8] The issues not yet addressed include, but are not limited to, earnings per share, segment reporting, interest on receivables and payables, and specialized industry practices.

Although there are some differences between financial reporting in the U.S. and Mexico, Mexican GAAP have been heavily influenced by U.S. accounting practices so that the financial statements of the two countries are similar in many respects. The influence of U.S. accounting is probably due to the presence of numerous affiliates of U.S. multinational corporations, and to the prominence of local representatives of the Big 5 international accounting firms. For those areas where a Mexican accounting principle is not yet available, such as earnings per share or line-of-business disclosures, it is customary to find the corresponding U.S. GAAP or International Accounting Standard being applied. Still, there are characteristics of the economy that call for addressing special accounting issues, such as inflation. There are also distinctive accounting practices and disclosures for regulated industries (banking and insurance, for example) that extend the scope of accounting principles as currently known. Looking specifically at information available in the domestic Mexican stock market, Chow and Wong-Boren (1987) find that the extent of voluntary financial disclosure by Mexican firms is associated with the size of the company, as measured by the value of their combined equity and debt.

Inflation Accounting

One characteristic of the Mexican economy, inflation, leads to the primary difference between Mexican accounting principles and those applied in the U.S.: the restatement for inflation.[9] Mexican accounting standard B-10, on the effects of inflation, became compulsory for all Mexican companies in 1984. Its five amendments since then have served to fine-tune the basic structure laid down in the prescribed accounting treatment. The standard is built around three angular concepts, namely, the effect of inflation on the net monetary position (assets minus liabilities), the gains or losses resulting from holding nonmonetary assets, and the preservation of capital in financial terms. The method requires restating all financial data in monetary units as of the end of the current reporting period. All comparative financial statements from prior years should also be restated to constant pesos as of the date of the most recent balance sheet.

A novel concept introduced by the accounting for inflation in Mexico is the "integral cost of financing," which is included in the income statement. This is the net result of the nominal interest expense, the gain or loss due to price level changes on the company's net monetary position, and the differences due to variations in exchange rates for the company's monetary assets and liabilities denominated in foreign currencies. Thus, capital maintenance in constant peso units is achieved through inflation and exchange-rate effects on net income for the year, and through the cumulative result of holding nonmonetary items reported in a special account within the owners' equity section of the balance sheet.

In summary, after several attempts, Mexican accountants have developed a generally accepted system of accounting for inflation through a comprehensive mechanism that adheres to the idea of capital maintenance in real terms. Reporting the inflation adjustments on the cost of financing is similar to the integral correction method used

[9] Other differences between U.S. GAAP and Mexican GAAP (which generally follows International Accounting Standards) include: the extent of information required to be disclosed in financial statements; prior period items and changes in accounting policies; related-party disclosures; and accounting for research and development, deferred income taxes, accrued vacations, pensions, changes in foreign exchange rates, extraordinary items, investments, and capitalization of interest. Additionally, some Mexican companies include minority interest in the net assets of subsidiaries as an element of consolidated owners' equity.

until 1994 in Brazil, with the added benefit that the various elements impacting that cost are separately disclosed in the Mexican accounting model. The consumer price index published by the central bank is the inflation factor that is used, thus standardizing the adjustment applied by all reporting firms and enhancing comparability across companies.

Business Operations

The operations of publicly owned corporations in Mexico are overseen by a number of federal agencies, the most prominent of which, in the area of financial disclosures, is the National Banking and Securities Commission (CNBV), an equivalent of the U.S. SEC. The CNBV, a semi-independent unit of the Ministry of Finance, administers Mexico's Securities Market Law and regulates the operation of securities markets. The current version of the Mexican Securities Law was enacted in 1975.[10] This law covers the public offering and trading of securities, the operation of the Mexican Stock Exchange, and the activities of securities brokers and traders. Annual financial statements of listed firms must be audited by a Mexican Certified Public Accountant, filed with the CNBV, and published in a nationally circulated medium.

Before 1990, companies could choose any fiscal year, provided it ended on the last day of the month. However, the law was changed in 1990, and now all fiscal years must coincide with the calendar year, as is customary in countries that follow the Napoleonic Code. All companies incorporated under Mexican law (Sociedades Anónimas, S.A.) are required to appoint one or more statutory auditors. The statutory auditors' report must include, at a minimum, their opinion as to whether (1) the accounting and reporting policies followed by the company are appropriate and adequate in the circumstances and have been consistently applied, and (2) the information presented by management gives a true and adequate picture of the company's financial position and operating results. Statutory auditors need not be public accountants, however when a company has independent auditors, a member of the auditing firm frequently serves as statutory auditor.

THE MEXICAN CAPITAL MARKET

Mexico has one stock exchange, located in Mexico City. The Mexican stock exchange (Bolsa) is a private institution that is equally owned by 32 brokerage houses. The Mexican Stock Exchange is operated by a corporation whose shareholders are the brokers and broker-dealers registered to do business through the Exchange. Just like in its U.S. counterparts, the principal requirement for listing a company's securities is the prior approval of the CNBV. Also, each listed company is required to provide annual audited consolidated financial statements as well as unaudited interim statements on a quarterly basis. Listed companies must also file with the CNBV the audited financial statements of all companies in which they hold 25 percent or greater control. Nevertheless, there are important institutional differences between the Mexican Bolsa and the U.S. exchanges. For example, no over-the-counter securities market exists in Mexico for listed companies, and in the Bolsa, stock transactions are currently only permitted in cash and must be settled within 48 hours. Margin operations and

[10] The Securities Market Law of January 2, 1975 contains all the rulings and reporting requirements for Mexican public corporations and it was published in the *Mexican Government's Official Gazette* (1975). Some amendments to this law, especially regarding foreign investment, were introduced at the end of 1993.

term operations were suspended in the Bolsa following the 1987 crash. Short sales, which were first introduced in 1991, are only permitted in stocks with high liquidity.[11] In addition, capital gains are fully nontaxable.

Shares of Mexican firms are denominated into series which all have full participation in the earnings of the firm, but some have restrictive ownership and voting rights. Typically, series "A" can only be held by Mexican nationals, and these shares hold at least 51 percent of voting rights. Series "B" is open to foreigners and institutional investors and may only account for up to 49 percent of ownership.[12] Foreigners are authorized to participate (buy and sell) in the Mexican Stock Exchange with certain restrictions that depend on the industry or sector of each listed entity and the series of shares. This is usually done in Mexico through the trading of Series "B," which is open to all investors, or through the purchase of "neutral" ("N" series) via a trust mechanism designed for foreign investors.[13] These shares are those that were previously held exclusively by Mexican nationals, and while the foreign investors might not have voting rights, the ownership rights are fully preserved (Instituto Mexicano del Mercado de Capitales and Bolsa Mexicana de Valores 1990). Currently, foreigners, primarily U.S. nationals, hold over 27 percent of the Mexican market, and on occasions, have accounted for 75 percent of the trading.

The Mexican Bolsa has two trading floors: Mercado de Capitales (Capital Market) and Mercado de Dinero (Money Market). Private sector equities and fixed income securities are traded in the capital market, and government debt and private commercial paper are traded in the money market. At the close of 1996, the capitalization value of the Bolsa totaled 838.7 billion new pesos (106.8 billion U.S. dollars), representing an increase of 20 percent over the previous year. The Bolsa is much smaller and less liquid than the large markets in the U.S. At the end of 1996, there were only 193 issuers (excluding mutual funds) listed on the exchange with a market capitalization of approximately $106 billion.

DATA ANALYSIS

Sample Selection

Our sample consists of the population of Mexican firms registered as American Depositary Receipts (ADRs) and listed on U.S. exchanges. At the end of 1995, there were 22 Mexican ADRs listed on the New York Stock Exchange (NYSE); three traded on the NASDAQ, and two on the American Stock Exchange (AMEX). We use the actual 1995 and 1996 20-F reports filed with the SEC by the Mexican firms as the data source for this study. In addition, stock market prices at December 31 (fiscal year-end) and June 30 (the date the 20-F becomes available in the U.S.) were collected from Dow

[11] Only a few academic studies investigating the institutions of the Mexican stock market have been conducted. In addition to Chow and Wong-Boren (1987), Herrera-Saizar (1992) finds evidence that the "January" effect and "size" effect exist in the Mexican stock market.

[12] The primary difference between the shares is the voting right, but this difference does not always appear to make the share more valuable since, in some cases, there is no difference between the market value of a firm's Series A and B shares.

[13] Mexico's most recent version of its Foreign Investment Law, which went into effect in January 1994, created this modality of shares. The law contains an investment mechanism that allows Mexican companies to issue these series "N" shares with no voting rights or with limited corporate rights. Such participation is not taken into account when computing the foreign investment percentage in the capital stock of Mexican corporations.

Jones News Retrieval. Of the 26 sample firms,[14] 11 of the companies belong to the heavy machinery industrial sector, this being the segment of the Mexican economy represented most in the sample. Of the remaining firms, five are in construction, three in communications, two in retail, two in banking, one in transportation services, and the last two are holding corporations. A list of these companies is presented in Table 1.

Our first analysis centers on measuring the differences between net income and equity calculated under Mexican and U.S. GAAP. Since Mexican firms provide reconciliations to U.S. GAAP (except for inflation accounting) in their 20-F forms, we are able to analyze how an inflation accounting model, with and without reconciliations, affects the relation between accounting information and the market value of the sample firms. Given NAFTA, the close proximity of the Mexican Stock Market to the U.S., and their similar hours of operation, one would expect the markets to be well integrated. Therefore, the purpose of the following analysis is to provide evidence of the effect of the Mexican accounting and reporting model on firm valuation.

The Analysis of Mexican-U.S. GAAP Differences

We identify the reconciliations from Mexican to U.S. GAAP in the 20-F reports to determine their dollar value and directional impact on U.S.-based net income and stockholders' equity. Table 2 reports the major categories of net income and equity reconciliations from Mexican to U.S. GAAP for the two years represented in the sample.[15, 16]

During 1995–1996 our sample firms reported 236 adjustments from Mexican GAAP net income to U.S. GAAP net income. The largest number of adjustments is for deferred taxes, compensation, and intangible assets. The results in Table 2 for the year 1995 indicate that the total dollar amount of negative adjustments exceeds that of the positive adjustments by almost one and one-half billion dollars. This implies that overall, Mexican-based net income is usually larger or less conservative than U.S. GAAP-based net income. In 1996, the direction of the adjustment is reversed and Mexican GAAP net income becomes more than two billion dollars less than U.S. GAAP net income.

During the two-year period, our sample firms made 224 adjustments to Mexican GAAP stockholders' equity to arrive at the U.S. GAAP stockholders' equity balance. Among the differences, the largest number of adjustments is for deferred taxes and compensation. The total adjustments are very similar for 1995 and 1996. Overall, Mexican GAAP equity is almost 41 billion dollars higher than U.S. GAAP equity for our sample firms.

Description of the Main Sources of Reconciling Items

A review of the Mexican firms' 20-F reconciliations summarized in Table 2 reveals that "Income and Deferred Taxes" are the main differences to be reconciled. Following that, the next significant reconciling item is for "Compensation" expenses. These differences are closely related and have a peculiar recognition in the Mexican accounting model. Under Mexican GAAP, deferred income taxes result from the partial liability method of accounting whereby only identifiable, nonrecurring temporary differences

[14] There are 26 sample firms and 27 series since Teléfonos de Mexico has shares traded on the NASDAQ and NYSE.

[15] The foreign currency amounts in the tables have been translated to U.S. dollars using year-end exchange rates.

[16] Transportación Marítima Mexicana provides reconciliations from International Accounting Standards to U.S. GAAP.

TABLE 1
Mexican ADRs Listed in the U.S. as of December 1995

Company Name	Exchange – Symbol	Sector
Banca Quadrum, S.A.[a]	NASDAQ – QDRMY	Financial Services
Bufete Industrial, S.A.	NYSE – GBI	Construction
Coca-Cola FEMSA, S.A. de C.V.	NYSE – KOF	Food, Beverages, and Tobacco
Consorcio G Grupo Dina, S.A. de C.V.	NYSE – DIN	Transport Machinery and Equipment
Desc, S.A. de C.V.	NYSE – DES	Holding Company
Elamex, S.A. de C.V.[a]	NASDAQ – ELAMF	Electronics
Empresas ICA-Sociedad Controladora, S.A. de C.V.	NYSE – ICA	Construction
Empresas la Moderna, S.A. de C.V.	NYSE – ELM	Food, Beverages, and Tobacco
Grupo Casa Autrey, S.A. de C.V.	NYSE – ATY	Retail
Grupo Elektra, S.A. de C.V.	NYSE – EKT	Retail
Grupo Embotellador de México, S.A. de C.V.	NYSE – GEM	Food, Beverages, and Tobacco
Grupo Financiero Serfin, S.A.[a]	NYSE – SFN	Financial Services
Grupo Industrial Durango, S.A. de C.V.	NYSE – GID	Paper Products
Grupo Industrial Maseca, S.A. de C.V.	NYSE – MSK	Food, Beverages, and Tobacco
Grupo Iusacell, S.A. de C.V.	NYSE – CEL	Communications
Grupo Mexicano de Desarrollo, S.A. de C.V.	NYSE – GMD	Construction
Grupo Radio Centro, S.A. de C.V.	NYSE – RC	Communications
Grupo Sidek, S.A. de C.V.	NYSE – SDK	Holding Company
Grupo Simec, S.A. de C.V.	AMEX – SIM	Steel
Grupo Televisa, S.A.	NYSE – TV	Communications
Grupo Tribasa, S.A. de C.V.	NYSE – GTR	Construction
Internacional de Ceramica, S.A. de C.V.	NYSE – ICM	Construction
Teléfonos de Mexico, S.A. de C.V.[b]	NASDAQ – TFONY	Communications
Teléfonos de Mexico, S.A. de C.V.[b]	NYSE – TMX	Communications
Transportación Marítima Mexicana, S.A. de C.V.	NYSE – TMM	Transportation
Tubos de Acero de Mexico, S.A.	AMEX – TAM	Steel
Vitro, S.A.	NYSE – VTO	Mineral Products

[a] Elamex files a 10k and Banca Quadrum and Grupo Financiero Serfin report using U.S. GAAP. Therefore, because they do not provide reconciliations to U.S. GAAP, they are excluded from subsequent analyses.

[b] Teléfonos de Mexico's shares are traded as two separate ADR issues. Those on the NASDAQ represent "A" shares and those on the NYSE represent "L" shares.

TABLE 2
Net Income and Stockholders' Equity Reconciling Items: Mexican to U.S. GAAP (Amounts in Thousands of U.S. Dollars)[a]

	Net Income Net Adjustments				Stockholders' Equity Net Adjustments			
	1995		1996		1995		1996	
Reconciling Item	**Firms**	**Amount**	**Firms**	**Amount**	**Firms**	**Amount**	**Firms**	**Amount**
Basis of Accounting: Effects of Changing Prices	10	$ 5,950,872	11	$5,536,421	1	$ 459,000	1	$ 355,000
Business Combinations	3	(18,310)	4	(191,882)	3	10,694	2	(63,949)
Changes in Accounting Principles	0	0	1	(212,387)	0	0	0	0
Consolidation and Equity Accounting	3	(226,164)	5	(26,754)	2	(167,078)	2	(1,229,044)
Foreign Currency Translation	3	(5,940)	3	196,428	2	(1,338,175)	2	(1,191,003)
Government Assistance	0	0	0	0	1	(863,413)	1	(680,983)
Income and Deferred Taxes	21	(7,086,775)	23	(2,780,389)	23	(24,537,419)	23	(23,256,204)
Compensation	19	(879,836)	19	(179,931)	20	(4,207,785)	19	(3,429,890)
Discontinued Operations	0	0	1	(50,000)	0	(50,000)	1	0
Extraordinary Items	1	44,000	2	247,501	1	0	0	(120,000)
Postemployment Benefits	3	8,120	5	12,798	8	(261,736)	8	(236,187)
Pension Accounting	4	(90,628)	3	640,548	1	(5,701,939)	1	(5,837,268)
Capitalization of Interest	5	162,232	7	(81,403)	5	2,107,432	5	1,156,456
Debt	0	0	0	0	0	(124,000)	1	0
Deferred or Capitalized Costs	2	(7,318)	3	54,976	2	(1,182,359)	3	(303,087)
Intangible Assets	13	(336,594)	12	996,042	15	(3,219,776)	13	(2,951,021)
Inventory	1	(1,748)	1	890	1	4,707	1	2,989
Investments	2	(156,116)	4	(1,466,065)	3	(2,395,350)	4	(1,061,347)
Property, Plant, and Equipment	3	366,504	4	830,964	2	(424,147)	3	(797,936)
Research and Development	0	0	1	(822,705)	0	0	0	0
Receivables	0	0	0	0	1	(12,531)	1	(1,619)
Shareholders' Equity	12	(398,051)	13	(745,971)	16	1,244,510	15	(454,916)
Other	5	1,211,772	4	123,664	5	(270,311)	6	(701,756)
Total Firms	23		23		23		23	
Total Firm Adjustments	110	$(1,463,980)	126	$2,082,745	112	$(40,929,677)	112	$(40,801,764)

[a] Dollar amounts represent the arithmetic totals of each reconciling item found in the 20-F reports for the companies in the sample.

(those expected to reverse over a definite period of time) are accounted for. They are recorded using the tax rates expected to be in effect when the temporary differences reverse. On the other hand, SFAS No. 109, *Accounting for Income Taxes* in the U.S. requires deferred income tax to be determined by the liability method for all temporary differences between the financial reporting and tax bases of assets and liabilities, with the differences measured at the tax rates expected when such taxes will be payable or refundable. The overall result of this reconciliation is a decrease in the reported Mexican income to arrive at U.S. GAAP income. This difference is also reflected, on a cumulative basis and with the same sign, on the reconciliations to owners' equity reported in the 20-Fs.

The adjustment for compensation expense that is normally subtracted from Mexican companies' income in the 20-F reconciliations derives from the annual employee profit sharing that Mexican firms are required to provide. The basis for determining this profit sharing is not the reported financial income but rather the income as defined by the corresponding legislation on profit sharing, an amount that approximates the taxable profits of the firm. This is why the compensation expense is tied to the reportable deferred taxes. Here again, any deferred employee profit sharing is determined by the partial liability method of accounting, which recognizes only those temporary differences that will be reversed in the future. Consequently, the impact of this treatment in the Mexican accounting model causes the needed reconciliations to a U.S.-based income. Another common adjustment to reported Mexican income to reflect differences with U.S. GAAP is the one for "Intangible Assets." This results from the differences due to the recognition criteria of intangibles, and more importantly, from the differences in the amortization lives assigned to those assets. The cumulative effect caused by these differences is also reported in the reconciliations to equity for the sample of firms represented in Table 2.

Another significant item among those listed in Table 2, both in terms of recurrence as well as amount, is the "Basis of Accounting: Effect of Changing Prices." One could argue that the reconciling item should be absent because an inflation accounting model is admissible for foreign companies seeking registration with the SEC. However, the reconciling item does not result from the inflation accounting model *per se*, but is due to the compounded inflation effect from the U.S. GAAP adjustment to the original Mexican-based data. The reconciliation to U.S. GAAP uses the reported data originally presented by the Mexican firms, hence those reconciliation numbers would have to be "deflated" to bring them back to a U.S. norm. The impact of those reconciliations on the reported accounts would cause additional inflationary gains or losses, which require adjustment to avoid double counting. For example, the difference derived from deferred taxes would create an increase in the deferred tax liability in Mexican pesos. Because of the Mexican accounting model, assuming inflationary trends, increases in liabilities would create an unrealized "inflation gain" reportable in the income statement and in the owners' equity accounts. Consequently, these effects of inflation accounting on U.S. GAAP adjustments would have to be undone. Hence the reconciliations for the effect on changing prices in the 20-F reports.

Mexican vs. U.S. GAAP Net Income and Equity

Table 3, Panels A and B, present net income and equity, respectively, measured under Mexican and U.S. GAAP in 1995 and 1996. On average, net income measured under Mexican GAAP is about 26 percent greater than the U.S. GAAP measure of net income for our sample of Mexican ADR firms. This difference is about 4 percent of

TABLE 3
Comparability of Mexican vs. U. S. GAAP
(Amounts in Thousands of U.S. Dollars)

Panel A: Net Income: Mexican vs. U.S. GAAP (by company)

		Net Income			
Company	**Date**	**Mexican GAAP**	**U.S. GAAP**	**Percentage Difference[a]**	**Difference as a Percentage of Mexican Equity**
Bufete Industrial	1995	(60,017)	(51,462)	16.62	9.63
	1996	(7,356)	(12,031)	–38.86	–4.29
Coca-Cola FEMSA	1995	41,186	28,640	–43.81	–4.07
	1996	63,290	62,208	–1.74	–0.28
Consorcio G Grupo Dina	1995	(59,806)	(32,105)	86.28	102.50
	1996	2,446	2,781	12.02	0.17
Desc	1995	33,531	(41,920)	–179.99	–10.77
	1996	239,821	249,495	3.88	1.01
Empresas ICA Sociedad Controladora	1995	85,424	91,728	6.87	0.53
	1996	67,948	68,342	0.58	0.03
Empresas la Moderna	1995	96,763	113,724	14.91	3.91
	1996	114,282	11,707	–876.17	–18.61
Grupo Casa Autrey	1995	14,364	15,127	5.04	0.59
	1996	24,242	28,415	14.68	2.29
Grupo Elektra	1995	39,275	29,575	–32.80	–5.80
	1996	38,988	28,449	–37.04	–7.54
Grupo Embotellador de México	1995	(18,256)	(41,126)	–55.61	–6.18
	1996	48,645	32,969	–47.55	–3.77
Grupo Industrial Durango	1995	32,627	(19,607)	–266.40	–13.63
	1996	119,103	122,840	3.04	0.89
Grupo Industrial Maseca	1995	57,877	74,102	21.90	4.98
	1996	83,781	97,449	14.03	3.20
Grupo Iusacell	1995	(74,055)	(33,815)	119.00	9.53
	1996	(43,395)	(16,905)	156.70	6.66
Grupo Mexicano de Desarrollo	1995	(50,410)	(93,999)	–46.37	–11.42
	1996	87,397	(64,923)	–234.62	–28.76
Grupo Radio Centro	1995	3,237	2,402	–34.80	–1.40
	1996	4,491	4,512	0.47	0.02
Grupo Sidek	1995	(245,048)	(90,836)	169.77	43.91
	1996	(308,620)	(138,378)	123.03	67.73
Grupo Simec	1995	(21,257)	(19,443)	9.33	0.96
	1996	51,766	47,569	–8.82	–2.04
Grupo Televisa	1995	122,663	64,495	–90.19	–4.57
	1996	(75,981)	(119,458)	–36.39	–3.36
Grupo Tribasa	1995	(44,204)	(42,518)	3.97	0.23
	1996	7,855	83,003	90.54	8.49
Internacional de Ceramica	1995	(23,743)	(29,413)	–19.28	–11.86
	1996	11,973	18,040	33.63	41.12
Teléfonos de México	1995	1,211,155	1,006,671	–20.31	–1.99
	1996	1,472,693	1,605,700	8.28	1.18
Transportación Marítima Mexicana	1995	51,473	31,583	–62.98	–6.13
	1996	42,978	56,778	24.31	4.07
Tubos de Acero de Mexico	1995	16,896	38,831	56.49	3.70
	1996	211,379	171,467	–23.28	–5.73
Vitro	1995	71,575	98,644	27.44	18.86
	1996	42,439	27,499	–54.33	–3.08
Total (All firm-years)	46	3,581,414	3,466,809		
Average		77,857	75,365	–25.84	3.93
Median		36,259	27,957	1.81	0.10
N < 0%				21	21

(Continued on next page)

Table 3 (Continued)
Comparability of Mexican vs. U. S. GAAP
(Amounts in Thousands of U.S. Dollars)

Panel B: Stockholders' Equity: Mexican vs. U.S. GAAP (by company)

Company	Date	Stockholders' Equity Mexican GAAP	Stockholders' Equity U.S. GAAP	Percentage Difference[a]	Difference as a Percentage of Mexican Equity
Bufete Industrial	1995	88,866	70,742	–25.62	–20.39
	1996	108,882	79,494	–36.97	–26.99
Coca-Cola FEMSA	1995	308,001	253,670	–21.42	–17.64
	1996	385,251	317,708	–21.26	–17.53
Consorcio G Grupo Dina	1995	27,026	29,998	9.91	10.99
	1996	196,204	209,537	6.36	6.80
Desc	1995	700,748	502,685	–39.40	–28.26
	1996	953,239	714,899	–33.34	–25.00
Empresas ICA Sociedad Controladora	1995	1,178,857	978,291	–20.50	–17.01
	1996	1,358,852	1,180,168	–15.14	–13.15
Empresas la Moderna	1995	434,012	319,747	–35.74	–26.33
	1996	551,121	357,082	–54.34	–35.21
Grupo Casa Autrey	1995	128,463	87,560	–46.71	–31.84
	1996	182,210	139,350	–30.76	–23.52
Grupo Elektra	1995	167,307	113,893	–46.90	–31.93
	1996	139,737	77,396	–80.55	–44.61
Grupo Embotellador de México	1995	369,875	279,206	–32.47	–24.51
	1996	415,747	323,370	–28.57	–22.22
Grupo Industrial Durango	1995	383,174	87,509	–337.87	–77.16
	1996	418,850	131,744	–217.93	–68.55
Grupo Industrial Maseca	1995	325,629	257,646	–26.39	–20.88
	1996	427,682	352,414	–21.36	–17.60
Grupo Iusacell	1995	422,432	357,388	–18.20	–15.40
	1996	397,638	359,305	–10.67	–9.64
Grupo Mexicano de Desarrollo	1995	381,636	157,604	–142.15	–58.70
	1996	529,687	93,885	–464.19	–82.28
Grupo Radio Centro	1995	59,591	55,411	–7.54	–7.01
	1996	131,655	125,317	–5.06	–4.81
Grupo Sidek	1995	351,240	(46,980)	–847.65	–113.38
	1996	(251,365)	(397,867)	–36.82	–58.28
Grupo Simec	1995	189,695	112,740	–68.26	–40.57
	1996	205,668	79,321	–159.28	–61.43
Grupo Televisa	1995	1,273,516	774,793	–64.37	–39.16
	1996	1,295,105	686,387	–88.68	–47.00
Grupo Tribasa	1995	735,938	532,987	–38.08	–27.58
	1996	885,127	923,726	4.18	4.36
Internacional de Ceramica	1995	47,799	19,677	–142.92	–58.83
	1996	(14,754)	(8,414)	75.35	42.97
Teléfonos de México	1995	10,284,479	8,352,369	–23.13	–18.79
	1996	11,236,017	9,341,724	–20.28	–16.86
Transportación Marítima Mexicana	1995	324,318	328,221	1.19	1.20
	1996	338,683	356,386	4.97	5.23
Tubos de Acero de Mexico	1995	592,155	329,821	–79.54	–44.30
	1996	696,816	422,498	–64.93	–39.37
Vitro	1995	1,435,450	945,316	–51.85	–34.14
	1996	485,682	469,962	–3.34	–3.24
Total (All firm-years)	46	41,283,939	31,235,681		
Average		897,477	679,037	–74.09	–28.25
Median		384,213	298,457	–32.91	–24.76
N < 0				40	40

[a] The percentage difference is calculated as [(U.S. GAAP amount – Mexican GAAP amount)/ | U.S. GAAP amount |].

Mexican GAAP equity and is consistent with the magnitude of reconciliations found in Rueschhoff and Strupeck (1998) who also investigate reconciliations from a sample of firms from developing countries. The median difference between Mexican and U.S. GAAP net income is about 2 percent (0.10 percent of Mexican equity), but unlike the mean, the median Mexican net income is less than U.S. GAAP net income. As is consistent with such a large difference between the mean and median, there is a wide range of differences across the firms (Mexican GAAP income ranges from almost ten times greater to two and one-half times less than U.S. GAAP income). Additionally, in 11 of the 23 pairs of observations, there was a switch in the sign of the difference between the U.S. and Mexican GAAP net income.

Panel B of Table 3 reports equity calculated under Mexican and U.S. GAAP. Mexican GAAP equity is on average 74 percent greater than U.S. GAAP equity. The median difference between the two is 33 percent. As a percentage of equity, these differences are 28 percent and 25 percent, respectively. Overall, equity measured under Mexican GAAP is greater than under U.S. GAAP (there are only six observations where equity is greater under U.S. GAAP).

We now consider the combined effects of net income and stockholders' equity differences by examining returns on equity (ROEs) measured under Mexican and U.S. GAAP. The results, presented in Table 4, indicate that although Mexican GAAP net income and equity are on average less conservative than their U.S. GAAP amounts for the sample firms (see Table 3), the average (median) U.S. GAAP ROE is 0.69 percent (0.53 percent) greater than the Mexican GAAP mean (median) ROE. Additionally, both the mean and median differences are significant at the 10 percent level. Thus, while Table 3 indicates that Mexican GAAP appears to inflate the firms' net income and equity, the results in Table 4 show the firms in a more favorable light with U.S. GAAP reporting. A plausible explanation for the higher return with U.S. GAAP-adjusted data is that the cumulative reconciled differences from Mexican to U.S. GAAP stockholders' equity substantially reduce the U.S. equity amount used in the comparisons.

The Value Relevance of Mexican vs. U.S. GAAP Income and Equity

Table 5 summarizes the descriptive statistics for the firms' ADR prices and Mexican and U.S. GAAP net income and equity. Overall, the average (median) ADR price per share is $19.64 ($12.90) for the two years examined. The average (median) total market value of equity is 6.0 (4.0) billion dollars. Consistent with the results in Table 3, which indicate that the Mexican accounting model is generally less conservative than U.S. GAAP, we find that the average Mexican GAAP book value per share for the pooled sample is $2.86 ($897 million in total) while the U.S. GAAP book value per share is $1.83 ($679 million in total). On average, Mexican GAAP net income is $0.24 per share ($78 million in total) and the mean U.S. GAAP net income is $0.13 per share ($75 million in total). Finally, on average U.S. GAAP equity is $1.03 per share ($218 million in total) less than Mexican GAAP equity and U.S. GAAP net income is on average $0.10 per share ($2 million in total) less than Mexican GAAP net income. Except for the book value and net income differences, the totals and per share amounts are greater in 1996 than in 1995.

The individual associations between ADR prices and income and equity measured under Mexican and U.S. GAAP are reported in Table 6.[17] The results indicate that

[17] We use Pearson and nonparametric Spearman correlation coefficients to identify statistically significant associations.

TABLE 4
Return on Equity: Mexican vs. U.S. GAAP (by company)

Company	Date	Return on Equity Mexican GAAP	Return on Equity U.S. GAAP	Difference[a]
Bufete Industrial	1995	–67.54%	–72.75%	–5.21%
	1996	–6.76	–15.13	–8.38
Coca-Cola FEMSA	1995	13.37	11.29	–2.08
	1996	16.43	19.58	3.15
Consorcio G Grupo Dina	1995	–221.29	–107.02	114.26
	1996	1.25	1.33	0.08
Desc	1995	4.78	–8.34	–13.12
	1996	25.16	34.90	9.74
Empresas ICA Sociedad Controladora	1995	7.25	9.38	2.13
	1996	5.00	5.79	0.79
Empresas la Moderna	1995	22.30	35.57	13.27
	1996	20.74	3.28	–17.46
Grupo Casa Autrey	1995	11.18	17.28	6.09
	1996	13.30	20.39	7.09
Grupo Elektra	1995	23.48	25.97	2.49
	1996	27.90	36.76	8.86
Grupo Embotellador de México	1995	–4.94	–14.73	–9.79
	1996	11.70	10.20	–1.51
Grupo Industrial Durango	1995	8.51	–22.41	–30.92
	1996	28.44	93.24	64.81
Grupo Industrial Maseca	1995	17.77	28.76	10.99
	1996	19.59	27.65	8.06
Grupo Iusacell	1995	–17.53	–9.46	8.07
	1996	–10.91	–4.70	6.21
Grupo Mexicano de Desarrollo	1995	–13.21	–59.64	–46.43
	1996	16.50	–69.15	–85.65
Grupo Radio Centro	1995	5.43	4.33	–1.10
	1996	3.41	3.60	0.19
Grupo Sidek	1995	–69.77	193.35	263.12
	1996	122.78	34.78	–88.00
Grupo Simec	1995	–11.21	–17.25	–6.04
	1996	25.17	59.97	34.80
Grupo Televisa	1995	9.63	8.32	–1.31
	1996	–5.87	–17.40	–11.54
Grupo Tribasa	1995	–6.01	–7.98	–1.97
	1996	0.89	8.99	8.10
Internacional de Ceramica	1995	–49.67	–149.48	–99.81
	1996	–81.15	–214.39	–133.24
Teléfonos de México	1995	11.78	12.05	0.28
	1996	13.11	17.19	4.08
Transportación Marítima Mexicana	1995	15.87	9.62	–6.25
	1996	12.69	15.93	3.24
Tubos de Acero de Mexico	1995	2.85	11.77	8.92
	1996	30.33	40.58	10.25
Vitro	1995	4.99	10.44	5.45
	1996	8.74	5.85	–2.89
Average (All firm-years)		–0.08	0.62	0.69
Median (All firm-years)		8.63	9.18	0.53

[a] The Return on Equity (ROE) difference is calculated as (U.S. GAAP ROE – Mexican GAAP ROE).

TABLE 5
Descriptive Statistics of ADR Prices and Mexican and U.S. GAAP Net Income and Equity[a,b]

	Pooled (n = 46)			1995 (n = 23)			1996 (n = 23)		
Variable	**Mean**	**Std. Dev.**	**Median**	**Mean**	**Std. Dev.**	**Median**	**Mean**	**Std. Dev.**	**Median**
MVE	$19.64	$22.28	$12.90	$17.30	$17.00	$11.00	$21.76	$26.42	$14.30
	(5,990)	(6,905)	(4,005)	(5,398)	(6,576)	(3,897)	(6,532)	(7,296)	(4,213)
BV^{MEX}	2.86	3.70	0.88	2.75	3.40	0.94	2.96	4.06	0.81
	(897)	(2,162)	(384)	(879)	(2,087)	(370)	(916)	(2,283)	(416)
BV^{US}	1.83	2.60	0.72	1.72	2.32	0.69	1.94	2.89	0.74
	(679)	(1,790)	(298)	(648)	(1,703)	(258)	(710)	(1,910)	(323)
NI^{MEX}	0.24	0.69	0.10	0.04	0.43	0.09	0.44	0.85	0.12
	(78)	(289)	(36)	(56)	(263)	(17)	(100)	(317)	(43)
NI^{US}	0.13	0.70	0.07	−0.04	0.54	0.02	0.31	0.80	0.10
	(75)	(282)	(28)	(48)	(217)	(2)	(103)	(338)	(28)
BV^{US-MEX}	−1.03	2.01	−0.19	−1.03	1.71	−0.25	−1.02	2.31	−0.15
	(−218)	(396)	(−84)	(−231)	(400)	(−91)	(−206)	(400)	(−75)
NI^{US-MEX}	−0.10	0.56	0.00	−0.08	0.34	0.00	−0.13	0.73	0.00
	(−2)	(62)	(0)	(−8)	(61)	(1)	(−1)	(64)	(0)

[a] The top numbers are measured on a per-share basis. Amounts in parantheses are totals in terms of millions of U.S. dollars.
[b] There are 23 firms in the sample. The sample includes all Mexican firms listed on the AMEX, NASDAQ, and NYSE as of December 1995 with Form 20-F reconciliations available for 1995 and 1996. All of the sample firms have 12/31 fiscal year-ends.

Variable Definitions
MVE = June 30 market value of equity;
BV^{MEX} = Book value of equity, measured under Mexican GAAP;
BV^{US} = Book value of equity, measure under U.S. GAAP;
NI^{MEX} = Net income, measured under Mexican GAAP;
NI^{US} = Net income, measured under U.S. GAAP;
BV^{US-MEX} = Difference between U.S. GAAP and Mexican GAAP equity;
NI^{US-MEX} = Difference between U.S. GAAP and Mexican GAAP net income.

TABLE 6
Correlations among Mexican and U.S. GAAP Net Income, Equity, and ADR Prices[a]
(1995–1996)

	USEQ	MEXEQ	EQDIFF	USNI	MEXNI	NIDIFF	ADRPRICE[b]
USEQ		0.85	–0.28	0.40	0.43	–0.04	0.41
		(0.01)	(0.06)	(0.01)	(0.01)	(0.79)	(0.01)
MEXEQ	0.92		–0.74	0.23	0.60	–0.45	0.47
	(0.01)		(0.01)	(0.13)	(0.01)	(0.01)	(0.01)
EQDIFF	–0.38	–0.60		0.10	–0.53	0.78	–0.33
	(0.01)	(0.01)		(0.51)	(0.01)	(0.01)	(0.03)
USNI	0.46	0.34	0.06		0.67	0.41	0.58
	(0.01)	(0.02)	(0.71)		(0.01)	(0.01)	(0.01)
MEXNI	0.60	0.59	–0.31	0.72		–0.40	0.69
	(0.01)	(0.01)	(0.04)	(0.01)		(0.01)	(0.01)
NIDIFF	–0.10	–0.18	0.22	0.33	–0.11		–0.13
	(0.49)	(0.23)	(0.14)	(0.02)	(0.45)		(0.41)
ADRPRICE[b]	0.58	0.58	–0.28	0.36	0.50	–0.13	
	(0.00)	(0.00)	(0.07)	(0.02)	(0.01)	(0.39)	

[a] Upper (Lower) Diagonal: Pearson (Spearman) Correlation Coefficients (n = 46). The correlations are based on per-share amounts and the numbers in parentheses represent p-values, two-tailed tests.

[b] These and subsequent analyses were also performed with December 31 prices. Thre results were very similar.

Variable Definitions:

USEQ ≡ Equity, measured under U.S. GAAP;
MEXEQ ≡ Equity, measured under Mexican GAAP;
EQDIF ≡ Difference between U.S. GAAP and Mexican GAAP equity;
USNI ≡ Net income, measured under U.S. GAAP;
MEXNI ≡ Net income, measured under Mexican GAAP;
NIDIFF ≡ Difference between U.S. GAAP and Mexican GAAP net income;
ADRPRICE ≡ June 30 market value of equity.

Mexican GAAP and U.S. GAAP book value per share are highly correlated. Additionally, Mexican GAAP and U.S. GAAP income per share are also correlated, but less so than Mexican and U.S. GAAP book values. In addition, all of the variables, except the net income reconciliation, are significantly correlated with the June 30 ADR price. These results suggest that the relation between inflation-adjusted net income measured under Mexican and U.S. GAAP may be strong enough that the reconciliations, which do not eliminate the effects of inflation, may not provide investors with much information beyond that in Mexican GAAP financial statements.

Research has shown that international GAAP differences may affect the capitalization factor applied to earnings reported under differing accounting regimes (Pope and Rees 1993). In the final analyses, we consider whether the reconciliations from Mexican to U.S. GAAP are incrementally value-relevant (related to ADR prices) beyond the reported Mexican GAAP net income and equity. The results from the regression analyses are presented in the Appendix.

Table A1, Panel A in the Appendix describes the results from association tests between the ADR price and Mexican and U.S. GAAP book value and net income. We find that Mexican GAAP net income is significantly related to the ADR price in 1995, 1996, and in the combined analysis. Mexican GAAP equity is significantly related to the ADR price only in 1995. In comparison, the results for the U.S. GAAP measures are similar, except U.S. GAAP equity is significantly related to the ADR price in the pooled analysis and in 1995. The lack of significant associations in 1996 may be the result of the peso devaluation that occurred at the end of 1995 but whose effects were felt throughout 1996.

The final models estimated include Mexican or U.S. GAAP net income and equity along with the differences between the Mexican and U.S. GAAP measures. The results, presented in Panel B of Table A1 in the Appendix, show that the reconciliations are not significantly related to the ADR prices in 1995, 1996, nor in the pooled analysis for either regression model. However, Mexican GAAP net income continues to be significantly related to the ADR price in the 1996 and pooled analyses and the results for U.S. GAAP net income and equity are similar.

Given the small sample size, especially for the annual analyses, these results should only be viewed as descriptive. However, they do suggest that Mexican GAAP and U.S. GAAP net income are impounded in the ADR price. Additionally, it appears that the reconciliations from Mexican GAAP to U.S. GAAP are not significantly related to the ADR price and therefore do not provide any additional information beyond the Mexican GAAP income and equity measures. Overall, the regression results indicate that while both the Mexican and U.S. GAAP numbers are value-relevant, the reconciliations do not add any additional information as far as price associations are concerned. Therefore, once you have one set of numbers, either Mexican or U.S. GAAP, there is no incremental gain to adding the second set.[18] This suggests that investors consider the difference between Mexican and U.S. GAAP income and book value immaterial or that U.S. investors can discern U.S. GAAP measures from Mexican GAAP measures. Since these reconciling items might be a deterrent to foreign issuers desiring to list or trade their securities in the U.S. markets, an argument can be made for the elimination or simplification of the adjustments currently required of Mexican firms in their 20-F reports.

---

[18] We thank the reviewer for this insight.

SUMMARY AND CONCLUSION

This paper provides an assessment of the validity and value-relevance of accounting disclosures produced by the Mexican inflation accounting model that differs from accounting principles in the U.S. Using the population of Mexican firms listed on U.S. exchanges as American Depositary Receipts (ADRs), we assess the impact of financial reporting differences on the relationship between Mexican ADR prices and Mexican vs. U.S. GAAP net income and stockholders' equity. The evidence presented here suggests that overall, U.S. investors are able to price the Mexican ADR shares despite their only having Mexican income and equity calculated using inflation accounting procedures.

Our results indicate that reconciliations from Mexican to U.S. GAAP have no significant impact on the ADR prices of the Mexican firms in the sample. Therefore, given NAFTA, Mexico's close proximity to the U.S. and the fact that the SEC does not require reconciliation of the most important difference between Mexican and U.S. GAAP-inflation accounting, it appears that the SEC could eliminate or further simplify the required reconciliations for Mexican firms filing form 20-F. Therefore, we provide additional evidence for the need to re-evaluate the U.S. GAAP reconciliations required in form 20-F of foreign issuers in the U.S.

APPENDIX
REGRESSION RESULTS

Our final tests are multivariate analyses to determine whether the reconciliations from Mexican to U.S. GAAP are incrementally value-relevant beyond the reported Mexican GAAP net income and equity. We estimate the following regression models to investigate this relation:

$$MVE_{it} = \gamma_0 + \gamma_1 BV_{it}^{MEX} + \gamma_2 NI_{it}^{MEX} + \varepsilon_{it} \tag{1}$$

$$MVE_{it} = \gamma_0 + \gamma_{1\bullet} BV_{it}^{US} + \gamma_{2\bullet} NI_{it}^{US} + \varepsilon_{it} \tag{2}$$

$$MVE_{it} = \gamma_0 + \gamma_1 BV_{it}^{MEX} + \gamma_2 NI_{it}^{MEX} + \gamma_3 BV_{it}^{US-MEX} + \gamma_4 NI_{it}^{US-MEX} + \varepsilon_{it} \tag{3}$$

$$MVE_{it} = \gamma_0 + \gamma_{1\bullet} BV_{it}^{US} + \gamma_{2\bullet} NI_{it}^{US} + \gamma_3 BV_{it}^{US-MEX} + \gamma_4 NI_{it}^{US-MEX} + \varepsilon_{it} \tag{4}$$

where MVE_{it} denotes the June 30 market value of common equity (closing ADR price) of firm i at time t; BV_{it}^{MEX} is the book value of equity, measured under Mexican GAAP; BV_{it}^{US} is the book value of equity, measured under U.S. GAAP; NI_{it}^{MEX} is net income, measured under Mexican GAAP; NI_{it}^{US} is net income, measured under U.S. GAAP; BV_{it}^{US-MEX} is the difference between U.S. GAAP and Mexican GAAP equity; and NI_{it}^{US-MEX} is the difference between U.S. GAAP and Mexican GAAP net income.

The results from the analyses are presented in Table A1. Panel A describes the results from association tests between the ADR price and Mexican and U.S. GAAP book value and net income. The final models tested include Mexican or U.S. GAAP net income and equity along with the differences between the Mexican and U.S. GAAP measures. The results, presented in Panel B, show that the reconciliations are not significantly related to the ADR prices in 1995, 1996, or in the pooled analysis for either regression model.

TABLE A1

The Value-Relevance of Mexican vs. U. S. GAAP Equity and Income

Panel A: Relation between ADR Prices and Mexican and U.S. GAAP Equity and Income

Regression 1: $MVE_{it} = \gamma_0 + \gamma_1 BV_{it}^{MEX} + \gamma_2 NI_{it}^{MEX} + \varepsilon_{it}$

Regression 2: $MVE_{it} = \gamma_0 + \gamma_{1^*} BV_{it}^{US} + \gamma_{2^*} NI_{it}^{US} + \varepsilon_{it}$

		Regression 1 (t-statistic)			Regression 2 (t-statistic)		
Variable	**Coefficient**	**Pooled**	**1995**	**1996**	**Pooled**	**1995**	**1996**
Sample year Intercept	γ_0	12.940 ***(4.772)	8.789 **(2.408)	13.939 ***(4.270)	13.751 ***(5.135)	6.926 **(2.291)	12.303 ***(3.762)
BV_{it}^{MEX}	γ_1	0.901 (1.274)	3.347 ***(3.549)	−0.555 (−0.518)			
BV_{it}^{US}	γ_1^*				1.576 *(1.742)	7.850 ***(5.837)	2.730 (1.699)
NI_{it}^{MEX}	γ_2	9.058 **(2.001)	17.420 **(2.592)	14.582 **(2.298)			
NI_{it}^{US}	γ_2^*				6.781 *(1.802)	9.972 **(2.327)	8.077 *(1.789)
Adjusted R^2		0.19	0.50	0.24	0.15	0.66	0.30

Panel B: Relation between ADR Prices and Mexican to U.S. GAAP Reconciliations

Regression 3: $MVE_{it} = \gamma_0 + \gamma_1 BV_{it}^{MEX} + \gamma_2 NI_{it}^{MEX} + \gamma_3 BV_{it}^{US-MEX} + \gamma_4 NI_{it}^{US-MEX} + \varepsilon_{it}$

Regression 4: $MVE_{it} = \gamma_0 + \gamma_{1^*} BV_{it}^{US} + \gamma_{2^*} NI_{it}^{US} + \gamma_3 BV_{it}^{US-MEX} + \gamma_4 NI_{it}^{US-MEX} + \varepsilon_{it}$

		Regression 3 (t-statistic)			Regression 4 (t-statistic)		
Variable	**Coefficient**	**Pooled**	**1995**	**1996**	**Pooled**	**1995**	**1996**
Sample year Intercept	γ_0	12.074 ***(3.774)	11.238 **(2.361)	12.092 ***(3.445)	12.864 ***(4.006)	11.731 **(2.513)	12.963 ***(3.707)
BV_{it}^{MEX}	γ_1	0.796 (0.725)	1.729 (0.898)	−1.442 (−0.789)			
BV_{it}^{US}	γ_1^*				0.745 (0.684)	1.664 (0.878)	−1.581 (−0.883)
NI_{it}^{MEX}	γ_2	21.133 ***(4.763)	10.968 (1.160)	32.219 **(2.444)			
NI_{it}^{US}	γ_2^*				21.418 ***(4.865)	11.790 (1.271)	33.146 **(2.568)
BV_{it}^{US-MEX}	γ_3	−0.872 (−0.323)	−0.582 (−0.134)	−4.906 (−0.490)	−1.446 (−0.664)	−2.192 (−0.716)	−3.580 (−0.416)
NI_{it}^{US-MEX}	γ_4	10.228 (1.408)	4.244 (0.300)	15.018 (0.565)	−11.528 (−1.418)	−8.111 (−0.521)	−17.914 (−0.812)
Adjusted R^2		0.47	0.09	0.19	0.48	0.11	0.22

Each estimated coefficient is expected to be positive. All variables are measured on a per share basis. MVE ≡ June 30 ADR price; BV^{MEX} ≡ Equity, measured under Mexican GAAP; NI^{MEX} ≡ Net income, measured under Mexican GAAP; BV^{US} ≡ Equity, measured under U.S. GAAP; NI^{US} ≡ Net income, measured under U.S. GAAP; BV^{US-MEX} ≡ The difference between U.S. GAAP and Mexican GAAP equity; NI^{US-MEX} ≡ The difference between U.S. GAAP and Mexican GAAP net income. There are 44 observations in the pooled sample and 22 in 1995 and 1996.

*, **, *** Statistically significant coefficients at < .10, < .05, < .01, respectively, two-tailed.

[a] The results reported here exclude Teléfonos de Mexico (Telmex), which has two ADR issues. Analyses including the Telmex "LADR" price yield results that are similar, except four of the adjusted R^2s are negative. Results including the Telmex "AADR" price are not economically meaningful. Finally, it is impossible to include a weighted ADR price for Telmex since we are unable to separate the number of shares represented by the "A" and "L" shares from the total reported shares.

REFERENCES

Alford, A., J. Jones, R. Leftwich, and M. Zmijewski. 1993. The relative informativeness of accounting disclosures in different countries. *Journal of Accounting Research* 31 (Supplement): 183–233.

Amir, E., T. Harris, and E. Venuti. 1993. A comparison of the value-relevance of U.S. versus non-U.S. GAAP accounting measures using Form 20-F reconciliations. *Journal of Accounting Research* (Supplement): 230–264.

Bandyopadhyay, S., J. Hanna, and G. Richardson. 1994. Capital market effects of U.S.-Canada GAAP differences. *Journal of Accounting Research* 32: 262–277.

———, D. Dover, and G. Richardson. 1998. The valuation relevance of Canadian-U.S. GAAP differences revisited. An examination of shareholders' equity differences. Working paper, University of Waterloo.

Biddle, G., and S. Saudagaran. 1991. Foreign stock listings: Benefits, costs, and the accounting policy dilemma. *Accounting Horizons* 5 (3): 113–124.

———, and ———. 1995. Foreign listing location: A study of MNCs and stock exchanges in eight countries. *Journal of International Business Studies* 26 (2): 319–334.

Chan, K., and G. Seow. 1996. The association between stock returns and foreign GAAP earnings vs. earnings adjusted to U.S. GAAP. *Journal of Accounting and Economics* 21 (February): 139–158.

Chow, C., and A. Wong-Boren. 1987. Voluntary financial disclosure by Mexican corporations. *The Accounting Review* (July): 533–541.

Davis, P. 1996. An inflation specification of an accounting-based valuation model with empirical evidence from Mexican accounting disclosures. Ph.D. dissertation, University of Michigan.

Fanto, J., and R. Karmel. 1997. A report on the attitudes of foreign companies regarding U.S. listing. Working paper 97–01, New York Stock Exchange.

Financial Accounting Standards Board, Canadian Institute of Chartered Accountants, and Instituto Mexicano de Contadores Públicos, A.C. 1995. *Financial Reporting in North America.* Stamford, CT: FASB.

Foerster, S., and G. Andrew Karolyi. 1999. The effects of market segmentation and investor recognition on asset prices: Evidence from foreign stock listings in the U.S. *Journal of Finance* 54 (3): 981–1013

Fordham International Law Review Symposium. 1994. Entering the U.S. securities markets: Opportunities and risks for foreign companies. Vol. 17. New York, NY: Fordham University.

Frost, C., and W. Kinney, Jr. 1996. Disclosure choices of foreign registrants in the United States. *Journal of Accounting Research* 34 (1) (Spring): 67–84.

Herrera-Saizar, M. 1992. Examination of anomalies in the Mexican stock market (seasonality). Ph.D. dissertation, University of Texas at Arlington.

Huddart, S., J. Hughes, and M. Brunnermeier. 1999. Disclosure requirements and stock exchange listing choice in an international context. *Journal of Accounting and Economics* 26 (1–3): 237–269.

Instituto Mexicano de Contadores Públicos, A.C. 1994. *Principios de Contabilidad Generalmente Aceptados.* Mexico City, Mexico: Instituto Mexicano de Contadores Públicos.

Instituto Mexicano del Mercado de Capitales and Bolsa Mexicana de Valores. 1990. *Annual Statistics.* Mexico City, Mexico: Instituto Mexicano del Mercado de Capitales and Bolsa Mexicana de Valores.

Karolyi, G. A. 1998. Why do companies list shares abroad? A survey of the evidence and its managerial implications. *Financial Markets, Institutions and Instruments* 7 (1) (February): 1–60.

Martinez, J. 1994. *Normas Internacionales de Contabilidad Supletorias (Como Principios de Contabilidad Generalmente Aceptados).* Mexico City, Mexico: Instituto Mexicano de Contadores Públicos.

McQueen, P. 1995. The information content of foreign and U.S. GAAP earnings in SEC Form 20-F. Working paper, Association for Investment Management and Research.

Meek, G. 1993. U.S. securities market responses to alternative earnings disclosures of non-U.S. multinational corporations. *The Accounting Review* (April): 394–402.

Mexican Federal Government. 1975. *Official Gazette (Diario Oficial de la Federacion)*. Mexico City, Mexico: Mexican Federal Government.

New York Stock Exchange. 1997. *The Exchange Monthly Report*. 4 (5): (July). New York City, NY

Pope, P., and W. Rees. 1993. International differences in GAAP and the pricing of earnings. *Journal of International Financial Management and Accounting*: 190–219.

Rees, L., and P. Elgers. 1997. The market's valuation of non-reported accounting measures: Retrospective reconciliations of non-U.S. and U.S. GAAP. *Journal of Accounting Research* (Spring): 115–127.

Rivera, J. 1998. Mexico under NAFTA: Accounting information in a changing economy. *University of Puerto Rico Forum Empresarial* 3 (1) (May): 2–16.

Rueschhoff, N., and C. Strupeck. 1998. Equity returns: Local GAAP versus U.S. GAAP for foreign issuers from developing countries. *Journal of International Accounting* 33 (3): 377–389.

Wall Street Journal. 1999. U.S. listings offer greater liquidity, lower fees for Latin American stocks. (October 27).

Part III
Far East

A
China

[15]

Journal of International Financial Management and Accounting 11:2 2000

Timeliness of Annual Report Releases and Market Reaction to Earnings Announcements in an Emerging Capital Market: The Case of China

*In-Mu Haw**

Texas Christian University and The Chinese University of Hong Kong

Daqing Qi and Woody Wu

The Chinese University of Hong Kong

Abstract

This paper examines the relation between firm performance and the timing of annual report releases in an emerging capital market. Based on the population of listed Chinese firms with A-shares for 1994–1997, we find that good news firms release their annual reports earlier than bad news firms, and loss firms release their annual reports the latest. Moreover, consistent with Chambers and Penman (1984) and Begley and Fischer (1998), these firms unexpectedly accelerate the release of good news and delay the disclosure of bad news relative to their previous reporting pattern. We also observe a significant price reaction to the annual earnings announcements for both early (good news) and late (bad news) reporting firms. Similar results are found for those A-share firms which have also issued B- or H-shares to foreign investors. Our study documents a systematic timing pattern of annual report disclosures, which is useful for investors to predict future earnings, especially in anticipating bad news in China's emerging market where information about future earnings is very limited.

1. Introduction

Since the reactivation of stock exchanges in early 1990, the stock market in China has grown rapidly. Such a growth has contributed to China's economic reform and particularly to the privatization of state-owned enterprises (SOEs). At the same time, it has also outpaced the development of the informational and regulatory infrastructure of the market. While accounting standards and practices in China are still at the developmental stage, recent studies have found that earnings prepared under Chinese GAAP are value relevant for investors in China's emerging stock market (Haw et al., 1998; Abdel-khalik et al., 1999; Bao and Chow, 1999; Haw

* Correspondence: In-Mu Haw, School of Accountancy, The Chinese University of Hong Kong, Shatin, NT, Hong Kong. We would like to thank two anonymous reviewers and Frederick D. S. Choi (the editor) for helpful comments. We also wish to acknowledge the financial assistance of the Chinese University of Hong Kong.

et al., 1999). However, little firm-specific information is available prior to the annual report release for investors to make accurate forecasts for future earnings in China.[1] Most listed Chinese firms fulfill only the minimum disclosure requirements mandated by the Chinese Securities Regulatory Commission (CSRC) and seldom provide earnings forecasts or voluntary information. Moreover, financial analysts and the financial press are still at their infancy and cannot act effectively as the information intermediaries between listed firms and investors. Consequently, investors have little information available to predict earnings and especially no warning of bad news before it is officially released. The following news sheds light on this issue:

> "Chengdu Hongguang Co. Ltd. made public the abstract of its 1997 annual report today, the statutory deadline for the release of its annual results. The company lost 198.4 million yuan in fiscal year 1997, almost half of the 410.2 million yuan of the proceeds it raised through its May 1997 initial public offering." (*Shanghai Securities Daily*, April 30, 1998)

The market was surprised by the extent of the losses and its share prices dropped by more than 16% immediately after the announcement.

The objective of this paper is to examine the relationship between firms' operating and market performance and the timing of annual report releases by listed Chinese firms. This study documents empirical regularities in anticipating the type of earnings news (good or bad) based on the timing pattern of disclosure (early or late) in the emerging market of China. Our analysis is based on the well documented timing pattern of earnings announcements in mature markets such as the US and Australia that firms accelerate the release of good news and delay the disclosure of bad news (e.g., Pastena and Ronen, 1979; Whittred, 1980; Patell and Wolfson, 1982; Givoly and Palmon, 1982; Chambers and Penman, 1984; Kross and Schroeder, 1984; Begley and Fischer, 1998).

Extensive literature in timing behavior has been developed for US firms. For instance, Pastena and Ronen (1979) analyzed the relative timing of firms' Form 8-K disclosures and their related press releases and suggested that management acts as if it intends to delay the release of negative information. Kross (1981), Givoly and Palmon (1982), and Kross and Schroeder (1984) found a significant statistical relationship between earnings forecast error and timeliness of the earnings announcement. Chambers and Penman (1984) also reported that the earliest announcements exhibit statistically significant positive announcement date abnormal returns and, in general, observed that early (late) announcements are associated with positive (negative) announcement date abnormal returns. Although Skinner (1994) argued that management and auditors faced intensified litigation risks during the 1980s so that the relationship documented in the earlier studies may no longer exist, a recent study by Begley and Fischer (1998) found consistent evidence of the good news early and bad news late relationship for a sample drawn from the 1980s and early 1990s. In the context of Australia, Whittred (1980) observed delays in the issuance of Australian corporate annual reports containing audit qualifications.[2] While the literature has accumulated findings of the association between the timing of earnings disclosure and the type of earnings in mature markets, the association in emerging capital markets has yet to be determined. We extend this line of inquiry to an emerging capital market in the transitional economy of China.

Our empirical results are consistent with prior evidence in mature markets such as the US and Australia. Based on 1,890 annual report releases by listed Chinese firms with A-shares and a subsample of 288 annual report releases of A-share firms which also issued B- or H-shares during fiscal years 1994–1997, we find that good news firms tend to release their annual reports earlier than bad news firms, and loss firms release their annual reports the latest.[3] The reporting lag times of firms are quite regular and predictable. Moreover, consistent with Chambers and Penman (1984) and Begley and Fischer (1998), firms unexpectedly accelerate the release of good news and delay the disclosure of bad news, relative to the reporting date in the prior year. We also find that accounting earnings measured under the Chinese accounting standards provide useful information to investors for firm valuation in China even if the release of the annual report is delayed. There are significant price reactions to the annual earnings announcements for both early (good news) and late (bad news) reporting firms. Similar results are found for a subgroup of A-share firms which have also issued B- or H-shares to foreign investors.

The rest of this paper proceeds as follows. Section 2 discusses the institutional background. Section 3 presents the hypotheses. Section 4 describes sample and variables. Section 5 reports empirical findings, followed by concluding remarks in section 6.

2. Institutional Background

2.1 Development of the Chinese Stock Market

The history of the present Chinese stock markets can be traced back to 1984 when the Shanghai Municipal Government approved the first regulation on securities in China. Subsequently, Feilo Electronics Ltd. issued China's first stock in November 1984, which began trading in August 1986 on the OTC market. In the following years, more SOEs were "incorporated" through the selling of shares to their employees, other stock companies, and other SOEs. However, the stockholding system did not become a significant vehicle for the SOE reform until the reactivation of the Shanghai Stock Exchange (SHSE) in 1990 and the establishment of Shenzhen Stock Exchange (SZSE) in 1991. The CSRC was set up in July 1992 as the Chinese equivalent of the Securities and Exchange Commission in the US to monitor and regulate the stock market. Since then, the stock market has expanded rapidly. In 1991, there were only eight and five stocks listed on the SHSE and SZSE, respectively. By the end of 1997, the number of firms listed on these two exchanges has increased to 383 and 362, respectively (as shown in panel A of Table 1). The total market capitalization has also increased significantly (as shown in panel B). By the end of June 1998, the total market capitalization rose to Renminbi 2.112 trillion yuan (equivalent to about US$257 billion).

2.2 *The Accounting and Reporting Framework in China*

To facilitate the development of stock markets, the Ministry of Finance of China promulgated the *Accounting System for Selected Shareholding*

Table 1. *Development of the Chinese Stock Market*

Year	*1991*	*1992*	*1993*	*1994*	*1995*	*1996*	*1997*
Panel A. Number of Listed Firms							
SHSE	8	29	105	171	188	293	383
SZSE	5	23	76	120	135	237	362
Total	13	52	181	291	323	530	745
Panel B. Market Capitalization							
SHSE	2.9	71.5	218.8	259.7	252.6	547.8	921.8
SZSE	8.0	49.0	133.5	109.1	94.9	436.5	831.1
Total	10.9	120.5	352.3	368.8	347.5	984.3	1,752.9
Panel C. The Composite Index of Chinese Stock Market							
SHSE	293.7	780.4	833.8	647.9	555.3	912.0	1,194.1
SZSE	110.4	241.2	238.3	140.7	113.3	312.9	381.3

Source: *Securities Markets Herald*, 1995–1997
SHSE is the Shanghai Stock Exchange.
SZSE is the Shenzhen Stock Exchange.
Market capitalization is in billion yuan. One US dollar is about 8.3 yuan.

Companies in May 1992. This marked the first time that listed Chinese firms were required to prepare their balance sheet, income statement, and statement of changes in financial positions in conformance with international accounting practices.[4] Moreover, these financial statements have to be made available to the public in audited annual reports within four months after the fiscal year-end. By law, all Chinese firms use the same fiscal year-end as of December 31. Thus, listed Chinese companies are required to release their audited annual reports no later than April 30 of the next calendar year. Since these firms are not required to make preliminary earnings announcements, they rarely disclose earnings before the filing of their annual reports to the CSRC. Therefore, the publication of the abstracts of annual reports on the CSRC-designated newspapers normally represents the first pubic announcement of their annual results.

In addition to the annual report, listed Chinese firms are required to make timely disclosures of significant events that may have material impacts on their share prices, as stipulated in the *Provisional Regulations on the Administration of the Issuing and Trading of Stock*. However, anecdotal evidence indicates that most firms tend to delay the disclosures of significant events until the release of annual reports.[5] While listed firms are required to provide semiannual reports by the end of August, it is not mandatory that they be audited. As a result, the annual report has become the most significant and reliable source of information on listed Chinese firms for domestic and foreign investors, with both annual operating results and some significant events disclosed for the first time.

3. Hypotheses on the Timing of Annual Report Release

Prior studies on developed markets indicate that managers release good news earlier and bad news later than expected (see, for example, Chambers and Penman, 1984; Begley and Fischer, 1998). Their findings are consistent with two theories, the stakeholder theory and the internal reporting hypothesis. The "stakeholder theory" suggests that, in the absence of an opportunity to hide bad news because of mandatory disclosure requirements, managers have incentive to delay its release (Watts and Zimmerman, 1990). By delaying the release of bad news so that the news filters into stock prices slowly, managers can influence stakeholders who use stock prices to monitor the firm. Similarly, announcing good news early will ensure that it is not preempted by other sources. In addition, managers can influence investors that rely on the media for firm-specific news by emphasizing good news while attempting to mitigate bad news (Bowen et al., 1992). Because a delay in the release of information may cause the news to be impounded gradually, it is advantageous to delay bad news until other industry-wide bad news is released. The firm-specific bad news is then expected and its eventual release receives less notice. Conversely, firms have the incentive to disclose good news before others to vie for the most media attention.

Alternatively, the "internal reporting hypothesis" maintains that managers are concerned about internal performance evaluation (Laurie and Pastena, 1975). If performance evaluation and/or compensation is related to earnings performance, managers at various levels are motivated to delay reporting bad news within the firm until it is verified, justified, and/or restated. Managers may thus benefit by getting more time to prepare responses to criticism and time to prepare a plan to reverse the poor performance. Kross (1981, 1982) also cited this argument as an explanation for his observed tendency of managers to delay reporting of bad news. On the other hand, good news receives relatively less scrutiny and passes through quickly. As a result, good news tends to be announced earlier than bad news.

While the two theories differ in managerial motivations for timing decisions, they both predict the same behavior by managers—delay the release of bad news and accelerate good news. Such timing behavior by managers has been well documented in developed stock markets. However, no empirical evidence exists for emerging capital markets. Although it is unclear whether these two theories developed in the US are applicable to the Chinese environment, anecdotal evidence suggests that the Chinese financial press highlights news containing large unexpected earnings in magnitude, and managers have been fired because of poor performance. Thus, we extend the existing literature based on developed markets to the emerging stock market of China by empirically testing the following two hypotheses based on the population of listed A-share Chinese companies and a subgroup of A-share firms which also issued B- or H-shares to foreign investors:

H1: Bad-news firms release their annual reports later than good news firms.

H2: Bad (good)-news firms delay (accelerate) the release of their annual reports relative to their expected reporting dates.

Moreover, we also empirically examine whether the market reacts to the annual report disclosures across different reporting lag groups.

4. Sample and Variables

Our sample consists of 1,890 annual report releases by listed A-share Chinese firms and a subsample of 288 annual report releases by A-share firms which also issued B- or H-shares for 1994–1997. We hand-collected all the release dates of annual reports from *Shenzhen Securities Times* and *Shanghai Securities Daily*. Following prior research in this area (e.g., Chambers and Penman, 1984), we define the timeliness of earnings reports in the following two ways, the reporting lag and the unexpected reporting lag. First, the reporting lag is defined as the number of days from the fiscal year-end to the annual report release date. Secondly, the unexpected reporting lag is defined as the difference between the actual and expected reporting dates.

As panel A of Table 2 shows, the mean (median) reporting lag for the full sample is 95.84 (102) days.[6] The median reporting date is April 12. Of the 1,890 announcements, only five were released after the April 30 reporting deadline. Three of them were announced on Tuesday, May 2, 1995. However, they were not in technical violation of the CSRC disclosure requirements because April 30 of 1995 was a Sunday and May 1 of 1995 was a national holiday when the securities newspapers did not publish. The other two were on May 1, 1996 and 1997 respectively, which were in technical noncompliance with the CSRC disclosure requirements. By contrast, about 20% of 10-K reports were filed with the SEC after the 90-day statutory period in the US (Alford et al., 1994).

To examine the relation between the timeliness of annual reports and the type of earnings news, we measure the earnings news by annual net income change in percentage (NIC):

$$NIC_{it} = (NI_{it} - NI_{it-1})/|NI_{it-1}|, \qquad (1)$$

where NI_{it} (NI_{it-1}) is net income for firm i in year t (t-1) as reported in the Taiwan Economic Journal (TEJ) China Data Base. We use the random walk model to proxy for the market expectation because no earnings forecasts are publicly available in China. We use the percentage change because listed Chinese firms are mandated by the CSRC to highlight such information in the annual report. For the 1,890 observations, the mean NIC is 0.709 while the median NIC is 0.120, suggesting the existence of large outliers. We therefore winsorize NIC at 1 and –1 to mitigate the outlier problem. Panel A of Table 2 reports that the average (median) winsorized NIC is 0.11 (0.12).[7] About two-thirds of our sample observations

Table 2. *Sample Description of 1,890 Annual Report Releases for Fiscal Years 1994–97*

Panel A. Full Sample

Variable	*Mean*	*Q1*	*Median*	*Q3*
Reporting Lag	95.84	79	102	115
Reporting Date	N/A	3/20	4/12	4/25
NIC	0.11	–0.19	0.12	0.47
Earnings	65.13	17.60	36.80	73.00

Panel B. Sample Description by Year

Variable	*1994*	*1995*	*1996*	*1997*	*Prob. of F*	*Prob. of* X^2
Number of Announcements	289	300	549	752		
Mean Reporting Lag	95.7	108.1	101.3	87.0	0.001	0.001
1st Quartile Reporting Date	3/25	4/13	3/31	3/12		
Median Reporting Date	4/11	4/25	4/18	3/24	0.001	0.001
3rd Quartile Reporting Date	4/25	4/28	4/26	4/17		
Mean NIC	0.224	–0.176	0.148	0.152	0.001	0.001
% of Positive NIC	70.59	40.00	67.21	69.15	0.001	0.001
% of Incurring Loss	0.35	5.00	6.56	5.72	0.001	0.001

Panel C. Sample Description by Stock Exchange

Variable	*Shanghai*	*Shenzhen*	*Prob. of F*	*Prob. of* X^2
Number of Announcements	1025	865		
Mean Reporting Lag	93.71	98.38	0.001	0.001
1st Quartile Reporting Date	3/18	3/25		
Median Reporting Date	4/9	4/16	0.001	0.001
3rd Quartile Reporting Date	4/24	4/26		
Mean NIC	0.137	0.077	0.020	0.041
% of Positive NIC	66.05	61.97	0.065	0.065
% of Incurring Loss	4.00	6.24	0.026	0.026

NIC is defined as the percentage change in net income. Earnings are in million of Chinese yuan. Reporting lag is defined as the number of days from the fiscal year-end to the report release date.

experienced an earnings increase. Among our sample firms, 95 firm-year observations incurred a loss during our sample period (not reported in Table 2).

Panel B of Table 2 reports sample distribution and descriptive statistics by fiscal year. The number of observations increases from 289 in 1994 to 752 in 1997 as more A-shares have been listed over time. Year-to-year comparisons reveal two major findings. First, for fiscal years from 1994 to 1996 many firms delayed the releases of their annual reports until the very end of April. More than 30% of listed firms released their annual reports in the last week of April. To alleviate this problem, the CSRC instructed the two stock exchanges to arrange for the even releases of annual reports from 1997 and limited the maximum number of releases per stock exchange per day to ten. Under this new rule, listed companies have to release their annual reports within a range of dates pre-set by the stock exchanges, but they can negotiate with the stock exchanges for later releases if they provide evidence of compliance hardship. As a result, the reporting lag decreased substantially in fiscal year 1997, with the median reporting date advancing by more than three weeks to March 24, 1998.

Second, the majority of firms experienced a decline in reported earnings in 1995, reflecting one of the most serious setbacks suffered by the overall Chinese economy since the beginning of the economic reform. While about 70% of firms reported an earnings increase in other years, 60% of listed firms reported an earnings decline in 1995 and the proportion of loss firms rose to 5%, from 0.35% in 1994. Both parametric and non-parametric tests indicate that the four years differ significantly in reporting lag, net income, and net income change.

Panel C of Table 2 reports sample distribution and descriptive statistics by stock exchange. Our sample consists of 1,025 A-share firm-years on the SHSE and 865 firm-years on the SZSE. Both parametric and nonparametric tests show that the mean reporting lag of 98.38 days for the SZSE companies is significantly longer than 93.71 days for the SHSE companies. Firm performance measured by NIC is also significantly lower for the SZSE firms than for the SHSE firms.

5. Empirical Results

5.1 Testing Hypothesis 1

Hypothesis 1 predicts that good news firms release their annual reports earlier than bad news firms. In this section, we define timeliness as the reporting lag from the end of the fiscal year to the date of the report release. We also define good (bad) news firms as the firms experiencing an earnings increase (decrease) in year t relative to year t-1. Empirical results for the full sample are reported in Table 3. In panel A, we divide the sample into four groups based on the quartiles of the reporting lags and examine firm performance in each reporting group based on NIC, the percentage of positive NIC, and the proportion of loss firms. Panel A indicates that as the reporting lag increases, both mean and median NIC monotonically decrease. The mean NIC of the earliest reporting group (dates for 1/13–3/19) is 0.38, significantly positive at the 0.001 level. By contrast, for the latest reporting group (dates for 4/25–5/02), it is –0.19 and significantly negative at the 0.001 level. Both parametric and non-parametric tests reject the null hypothesis that the NIC distributions are identical among the four reporting groups. Similar results are observed with firm performance measured by the percentage of positive NIC and the proportion of loss firms. For example, 87.3% (0.22%) of firms in the earliest reporting group experienced an earnings increase (loss), compared with 39.2% (15.38%) for the latest reporting group.

We then divide the sample into two groups based on the sign of NIC and examine whether the reporting lag differs between them. Panel B of Table 3 indicates that out of the statutory reporting period of 120 days, the average reporting lag for the firms experiencing earnings increases is about 90 days, and half of these firms released their annual reports by April 1. On the other hand, the firms experiencing earnings decreases released their annual reports after an average of 106 reporting days, 16 days later than the firms experiencing earnings increases. Half of them did not release their annual reports until April 24. Both parametric and non-parametric tests indicate that the reporting lag is significantly different between the two earnings groups at the 0.001 level.

In panel C of Table 3, we examine the difference in reporting lag between firms reporting a profit and firms reporting a loss. The average reporting lag for the 95 loss firms is 116.5 days, compared with about 95 days for the profit firms. About three-quarters of the loss firms did not release the annual results until the last week of the statutory reporting period. Both parametric and non-parametric tests indicate that the loss firms exhibit reporting lags significantly longer than those of the profitable firms at the 0.001 level.

Since the reporting lag varies significantly across the years (as shown in panel B of Table 2), we further analyze the relation between firm performance and the reporting lag by year to investigate if our full sample results are consistent over different time periods. Table 4 reports empirical results, indicating that the reporting lag is significantly negatively associated with firm performance in each of the four years.[8] This empirical regularity even holds for 1997, when the CSRC instructed the two stock exchanges to arrange for even releases of annual reports. As reported in panel D of Table 4, the first three reporting groups have significantly positive mean and median NIC, while the latest reporting group has a

Table 3. *Association between Timeliness and Earnings News for the Full Sample*

Panel A. Earnings Change by Reporting Lag

Reporting Date	*# of Obs.*	*Mean NIC*	*Median NIC*	*% of Positive NIC*	*% of Loss Firms*
1/13–3/19	450	0.38[a]	0.31[b]	87.3[b]	0.22
3/20–4/11	492	0.24[a]	0.20[b]	74.4[b]	0.81
4/12–4/24	428	0.04	0.07[b]	58.4[b]	2.34
4/25–5/02	520	–0.19[a]	–0.19[b]	39.2[b]	15.38
Test Statistics		F = 118.9[c]	X^2 = 293.7[c]	F = 106.7[c]	F = 59.5[c]

Panel B. Reporting Lag by Direction of Earnings Change (NIC)

			Reporting Date		
Direction of NIC	*# of Obs.*	*Mean Reporting Lag*	*Q1*	*Median*	*Q3*
Earnings Increase	1,213	89.96	3/15	4/1	4/21
Earnings Decrease	677	106.38	4/10	4/24	4/28
Test Statistics		F = 280.2[c]		X^2 = 222.3[c]	

Panel C. Reporting Lag by Profit or Loss Firms

			Reporting Date		
Earnings Level	*# of Obs.*	*Mean Reporting Lag*	*Q1*	*Median*	*Q3*
Profit	1,795	94.75	3/19	4/10	4/24
Loss	95	116.50	4/26	4/29	4/30
Test Statistics		F = 93.4[c]		X^2 = 80.4[c]	

Reporting date ranges are based on the distribution of the reporting dates in panel A of Table 2.
NIC is defined as the percentage change in net income.
[a]The two-sided t-test is significant at the 1% level.
[b]The sign test is significant at the 1% level.
[c]Significant at the 1% level.

significantly negative mean (median) NIC of –0.171 (–0.12) and contains most of the loss firms. This result suggests that the CSRC mandate has done little in altering the timing pattern of the annual report release between the good news and bad news firms.

We also examine the relationship between firm performance and the reporting lag by stock exchange, with empirical results reported in panels

Table 4. *Association between Timeliness and Earnings News by Year*

Reporting Date	*# of Obs.*	*Mean NIC*	*Median NIC*	*% of Positive NIC*	*% of Loss Firms*
Panel A. Earnings Change in 1994 by Reporting Lag (289 firms)					
95/1/13–3/24	71	0.383[a]	0.29[b]	87.3[b]	0
95/3/25–4/10	68	0.413[a]	0.37[b]	88.2[b]	0
95/4/11–4/24	73	0.186[a]	0.15[b]	67.1[b]	0
95/4/25–5/02	77	–0.054	–0.08	42.9	1.3
Test Statistics		F = 17.1[d]	X^2 = 46.1[d]	F = 19.3[d]	F = 0.9
Panel B. Earnings Change in 1995 by Reporting Lag (300 firms)					
96/1/24–4/12	74	0.135[a]	0.10[b]	64.9[b]	1.35
96/4/13–4/24	70	–0.126[a]	–0.07	41.4	1.43
96/4/25–4/27	74	–0.313[a]	–0.24[b]	31.1[b]	8.11
96/4/28–5/01	82	–0.376[a]	–0.48[b]	24.4[b]	8.54
Test Statistics		F = 18.0[d]	X^2 = 47.9[d]	F = 10.9[d]	F = 2.6
Panel C. Earnings Change in 1996 by Reporting Lag (549 firms)					
97/1/21–3/30	135	0.392[a]	0.37[b]	85.9[a]	0.74
97/3/31–4/17	128	0.274[a]	0.22[b]	78.1[b]	0.00
97/4/18–4/25	117	0.106[a]	0.14[b]	63.3[b]	1.71
97/4/26–5/01	169	–0.114[a]	–0.09	46.8	19.50
Test Statistics		F = 24.6[d]	X^2 = 60.2[d]	F = 61.2[d]	F = 25.4[d]
Panel D. Earnings Change in 1997 by Reporting Lag (752 firms)					
98/1/15–3/11	178	0.435[a]	0.37[b]	90.5[b]	0.00
98/3/12–3/23	185	0.267[a]	0.20[b]	80.5[b]	0.54
98/3/24–4/16	191	0.113[a]	0.11[b]	65.5[b]	1.05
98/4/17–4/30	198	–0.171[a]	–0.12[b]	42.9[c]	20.20
Test Statistics		F = 50.9[d]	X^2 = 113.7[d]	F = 44.6[d]	F = 40.4[d]

Reporting date ranges are based on the distribution of the reporting dates in panel B of Table 2.
NIC is defined as the percentage change in net income.
[a]The two-sided t-test is significant at the 1% level.
[b]The sign test is significant at the 1% level.
[c]The sign test is significant at the 5% level.
[d]Significant at the 1% level.

A (for the SHSE) and B (for the SZSE) of Table 5. For both exchanges, the NIC declines monotonically from the earliest reporting group to the latest, and both F and chi-square tests reject the null hypothesis that the mean and median of the NIC are the same among the four reporting groups. In sum, our results show that in China's emerging market, good news firms release their annual reports significantly earlier than bad news firms. This empirical regularity is robust across years and stock exchanges. We also observe that as the reporting lag increases, the earnings change monotonically decreases and becomes negative.

Table 5. *Sensitivity Analysis of the Association between Timeliness and Earnings News by Stock Exchange*

Reporting Date	*# of Obs.*	*Mean NIC*	*Median NIC*	*% of Positive NIC*	*% of Loss Firms*
Panel A. Earnings Change (NIC) for the SHSE Firms by Reporting Lag					
1/13–3/17	233	0.410[a]	0.35[c]	89.3[c]	0.43
3/18–4/08	279	0.271[a]	0.23[c]	77.8[c]	0.36
4/09–4/23	236	0.058[b]	0.07[c]	58.9[c]	0.85
4/24–5/01	277	–0.161	–0.15[c]	40.8[c]	13.40
Test Statistics		F = 66.1[d]	X^2 = 162.7[d]	F = 61.7[d]	F = 31.4[d]
Panel B. Earnings Change (NIC) of the SZSE Firms by Reporting Lag					
1/19–3/27	246	0.337[a]	0.29[c]	83.7[c]	0.00
3/28–4/15	181	0.176[a]	0.15[c]	69.1[c]	0.55
4/16–4/25	199	0.021	0.05	55.3	6.53
4/26–5/02	239	–0.218[a]	–0.23[c]	39.8[c]	16.70
Test Statistics		F = 47.5[d]	X^2 = 120.1[d]	F = 40.6[d]	F = 25.8[d]

Reporting date ranges are based on the distribution of the reporting dates in panel B of Table 2. NIC is defined as the percentage change in net income. SHSE is the Shanghai Stock Exchange and SZSE is the Shenzhen Stock Exchange.

[a]The two-sided t-test is significant at the 1% level.

[b]The two-sided t-test is significant at the 10% level.

[c]The sign test is significant at the 1% level.

[d]Significant at the 1% level.

5.2 Testing Hypothesis 2

Hypothesis 2 posits that good (bad) news firms unexpectedly accelerate (delay) the release of their annual reports. Following Chambers and Penman (1984), we assume that the reporting lag follows a random walk process and define unexpected reporting lag (URL) as the difference between the actual reporting lag time and the expected reporting lag time. The expected lag time was estimated as the lag time in the previous year. Hypothesis 2 predicts URL to be negative for good news firms (i.e., before the date expected) and positive for bad news firms (i.e., after the date expected).

Because there exist no earnings forecasts for listed Chinese firms, we are not able to construct unexpected earnings as defined in Patell and Wolfson (1982). Instead, we define good (bad) news firms as those experiencing an earnings increase (decrease) in year t after a decrease (increase) in year t-1 to increase the power of the tests. This measure is more conservative than the earnings changes used in the previous section and reduces our sample to 445 firm-years, consisting of 254 bad news and 191 good news observations.

Empirical results are reported in Table 6. Panel A compares the unexpected reporting lags (URL) between the good news and bad news firms. The average reporting lag for the bad news group is 104.8 days, significantly longer than 99.9 days for the good news group. Furthermore, for the bad news group, the average URL is 4.95 days and significantly positive (p = 0.002, two-tailed), suggesting that bad news firms release their reports about five days later than the date in the previous year. The last column indicates that more firms delay than accelerate the annual reports containing bad news (146:101). On the contrary, for the good news group, the average URL is –7.57 days and significantly negative at the 0.001 level, indicating that the good news firms release their annual reports about 8 days earlier than the expected date of release. Moreover, more firms accelerate than delay the annual reports containing good news (115:55). Both the parametric and non-parametric tests show that the URL differs significantly between the good and bad news groups.

To investigate the timing pattern of earnings announcement release, Chambers and Penman (1984) divide their sample into nine groups based on the URL and examine mean unexpected earnings for each group. We conduct similar tests and report our results in Panel B of Table 6. Because of our smaller sample size, we divide our sample into four groups. For the first URL quartile, which unexpectedly accelerated the annual report release the most, both the t- and sign tests indicate that they experienced a significant earnings increase. Their mean NIC is 0.242 and about 60% of firms reported good news. On the other hand, the URL quartile that unexpectedly delayed the annual report the most had a significant earnings decline. Their mean NIC is –0.186 and only 21.7% of firms reported good news. Moreover, both mean NIC and the frequency of good news firms decline monotonically from the most accelerated group to the most delayed group. Both the parametric and non-parametric tests show that the NIC and the frequency of good news firms differ significantly among the four URL groups.

Panel C of Table 6 reports the results of sensitivity analyses by year and stock exchange.[9] Overall, the results exhibit a pattern similar to those in panel A of Table 6, indicating that more firms delay (accelerate) the annual reports containing bad (good) news than accelerate (delay) them. However, the reporting pattern is not consistent for the bad news firms in 1997, which could be influenced by the CSRC's requirement for the even release since 1997. The Chi-square tests provide evidence that a significant association exists between the good (bad) news content and the acceleration (delay) of the news release in each of the three years. We

Table 6. *Association between Unexpected Reporting Lag and News Content*

Panel A. Unexpected Reporting Lag (URL) for Good News and Bad News Firms

News Content	*# of Obs.*	*Mean Reporting Lag*	*Mean URL*	*# of Delay: # of Advance*
Bad News	254	104.8	4.95[a]	146:101[b]
Good News	191	99.9	–7.57[a]	55:115[b]
Test Statistics		F = 6.9[d]	F = 27.1[d]	X^2 = 34.0[d]

Panel B. Earning News Content by Level of Unexpected Reporting Lag (URL)

Extent of URL	*# of Obs.*	*Range of URL*	*Mean of NIC*	*% of Good News*
Accelerated Most	104	12 to 98	0.242[a]	59.6%[b]
Accelerated	112	0 to 11	0.006	47.3%
Delayed	114	–9 to –1	–0.007	44.7%
Delayed Most	115	–96 to –10	–0.186[a]	21.7%[b]
Test Statistics		F = 10.4[d]		X^2 = 39.6[d]

Panel C. Sensitivity Analyses by Year and Stock Exchange

	# of Bad News	*# of Delay: # of Advance*	*# of Good News*	*# of Delay: # of Advance*	X^2
1995	112	79:23[b]	23	13:7	4.04[e]
1996	40	23:15	80	25:46[c]	7.75[d]
1997	102	34:63[b]	88	17:62[b]	4.25[e]
SHSE	127	82:41[b]	105	29:62[b]	32.67[d]
SZSE	127	64:60	86	26:53[b]	6.31[d]

Unexpected reporting lag (URL) is defined as the difference in reporting lag between year t and year t-1. Good (Bad) news firms are those experiencing an earnings increase (decrease) in year t after an earnings decrease (increase) in year t-1. NIC is defined as the percentage change in net income. SHSE is the Shanghai Stock Exchange and SZSE is the Shenzhen Stock Exchange.
[a]The two-sided t-test is significant at the 1% level.
[b]The sign test is significant at the 1% level.
[c]The sign test is significant at the 5% level.
[d]Significant at the 1% level.
[e]Significant at the 5% level.

observe similar results for both the SHSE and SZSE.[10] Overall, the relation between unexpected reporting lag and news content for our full sample holds for each year and for each of the two stock exchanges.

In sum, our results on the emerging market of China for the association between earnings news and timeliness (defined as the reporting lag and the unexpected reporting lag, respectively) are consistent with those in the developed markets. The results are also consistent with the stakeholder theory and the internal reporting hypothesis.

5.3 Price Reaction to Earnings Announcement

In the US, there is evidence that early (late) announcements are associated with positive (negative) abnormal returns (e.g., Chambers and Penman, 1984; Begley and Fischer 1998).[11] In the emerging market of China, Haw et al. (1998) find a significant price reaction to the announcement of annual earnings prepared under Chinese GAAP in a three-day window centered on the announcement date (see also Abdel-khalik et al., 1999; Bao and Chow, 1999). However, there has been no study examining the value-relevance of earnings in the timing context in an emerging capital market. If accounting earnings are value-relevant even if they are released late, then investors can utilize the timing pattern we have documented in their investment decision-making process. Since we observe that bad news firms release their annual reports later than good news firms and unexpectedly delay the release, investors can reduce their holdings of these firms' securities by anticipating bad news when the release of their annual report is delayed.

In this section, we examine market reactions to the releases of annual reports among different reporting lag groups through the following regression model:

$$CAR_{it} = \alpha + \beta\ UE_{it} + \varepsilon_{it} \qquad (2)$$

In equation (2), CAR_{it} is the cumulative 3-day market-adjusted return centered on the annual report release (earnings announcement) date, obtained from the TEJ China Data Base. We use market-adjusted return because Fama and French (1992) show that the "relation between market beta and average return is flat" and the static version of the CAPM may not be able to explain the cross-sectional variation in average returns. UE_{it} is the change in net income divided by share price at the beginning of the three-day period. Because earnings forecasts for listed Chinese A-share firms are not available, we rely on the random walk model to proxy for the market expectation of earnings before the annual report release. Because of missing data on the TEJ database, our sample is reduced to 1,158 observations.

Table 7 presents regression results for the pooled sample in fiscal years 1994 to 1997.[12] Panel A indicates that the market reacts to the annual

Table 7. *Price Reactions to Earnings Announcements by Timeliness of Annual Report Releases*

$$CAR_{-1,+1} = \alpha + \beta\, UE + e \qquad (2)$$

Sample	*# of Obs.*	α	β	*Adj-R²*
Panel A. Full Sample	1,158	–0.016	0.388	5.31%
		(–6.386)[a]	(8.120)[a]	
Panel B. By Earnings Change (NIC) as in Panel B of Table 3				
Earnings Increase	644	–0.003	0.265	1.91%
		(0.121)	(1.952)[c]	
Earnings Decrease	514	–0.042	0.295	2.54%
		(–5.496)[a]	(2.628)[a]	
Panel C. By Reporting Lag as in Panel A of Table 3				
Earliest Reporting Group	205	–0.004	0.251	2.01%
[1/13–3/19]		(–0.952)	(2.278)[b]	
Early Reporting Group	276	–0.009	0.091	0.16%
[3/20–4/11]		(–2.312)[b]	(1.197)	
Late Reporting Group	331	–0.014	0.540	5.54%
[4/12–4/24]		(–2.638)[a]	(4.512)[a]	
Latest Reporting Group	346	–0.025	0.413	5.52%
[4/25–5/2]		(–4.203)[a]	(4.600)[a]	
Panel D. By Unexpected Reporting Lag as in Panel B of Table 6				
Accelerated Most	56	0.007	0.554	2.09%
		(0.740)	(1.475)	
Accelerated	70	–0.017	0.349	2.92%
		(–1.718)[c]	(1.754)[c]	
Delayed	76	–0.013	0.614	11.52%
		(–1.219)	(3.300)[a]	
Delayed Most	78	–0.019	0.434	3.55%
		(–1.921)[b]	(1.959)[b]	

UE is defined as change in net income deflated by share price at the beginning period of the 3-day period. Numbers reported in parenthesis are t statistics. NIC is defined as the percentage change in net income.

[a]Significant at the 0.01 level (two-tailed).
[b]Significant at the 0.05 level (two-tailed).
[c]Significant at the 0.10 level (two-tailed).

report releases (earnings announcements). For the pooled sample, the β coefficient of 0.388 is significantly positive at the 1% level and the adjusted R^2 is 0.053. Panel B reports regression results for the earnings increase and decrease groups, separately. The earnings coefficients of the two groups are similar and positively significant at the conventional levels, which suggests that good (bad) earnings news is associated with positive (negative) returns.

We then divide the sample into four groups based on the reporting lag and unexpected reporting lag quartiles respectively and estimate the regression for each group. Panels C and D summarize results for each reporting lag and unexpected lag group, respectively. As shown in Panel C, a significant association exists between stock return and earnings changes for three of the four reporting lag groups. This indicates that the annual reports contain information useful to investors for share valuation despite the differences in the reporting lag. Panel D reports a similar pattern.[13,14]

5.4 Further Analysis of Firms which have also Issued B- or H-Shares

The Chinese stock market is unique in that some of the selected A-share firms are allowed to issue B- or H-shares to foreign investors.[15] Because these firms have additional regulatory and reporting requirements, we further analyze the reporting pattern and market reactions of 288 A-share firm-year observations (97 firms) that have also issued B- or H-shares. Panel A of Table 8 summarizes descriptive statistics. Compared with the results for the full sample in panel A of Table 2, the B/H share firms experienced a lower earnings increase and released their annual reports later. Panels B and C report that, consistent with the results in Table 3, the firms experiencing earnings increases release the news significantly earlier than the firms experiencing earnings decreases. Similarly, a significant association exists between the unexpected reporting lag and the nature of news content as shown in panels D and E. Consistent with the results in Table 6, B/H share firms unexpectedly accelerate (delay) the release of their annual reports containing good (bad) news. Finally, panel F reports regression results for the price reaction of B/H shares to earnings announcements. The earnings coefficients are positively significant at the conventional levels for each of the reporting lag groups, similar to those for the full A-share sample in Table 7.[16] Overall, the timing pattern of the earnings release and the market responses to the earnings announcements are similar between the full sample and A-share firms that have also issued B/H-shares.

6. Conclusion

In this paper, we investigate the relationship between reporting behavior and financial and market performance in the emerging capital market of China. Our empirical results are consistent with prior evidence in mature markets such as the US and Australia. Based on the population of listed Chinese firms with A-shares for 1994–1997, we observe that good news firms tend to release their annual reports earlier than bad news firms, and loss firms release their annual reports the latest. The reporting lag times of listed Chinese firms are quite regular and predictable. Moreover, consistent with Chambers and Penman (1984) and Begley and Fischer (1998), firms unexpectedly accelerate the release of good news and delay the

Table 8. *Analyses for the Subsample of B/H Shares on Timeliness, Earnings News, and Price Reactions*

Panel A. Descriptive Statistics for 288 B/H share firm-year observations

Variable	*Mean*	*Q1*	*Median*	*Q3*
Reporting Lag	106.74	101	112	117
Reporting Date	N/A	4/11	4/22	4/27
NIC	–0.05	–0.37	0.02	0.25
Earnings	134.65	35.24	82.03	164.63

Panel B. Earnings Change (NIC) by Reporting Lag

Reporting Date	*# of Obs.*	*Mean NIC*	*Median NIC*	*% of Positive NIC*	*% of Loss Firms*
2/18–4/10	70	0.24[a]	0.22[d]	75.7[d]	0.00
4/11–4/21	67	–0.05	–0.02	49.2	1.49
4/22–4/27	90	–0.09	–0.03	47.5	5.57
4/28–5/02	61	–0.31[a]	–0.24[d]	35.0[d]	9.84
Test Statistics		F = 14.0[e]	X^2 = 38.1[e]	F = 8.67[e]	F = 3.26[f]

Panel C. Reporting Lag by Direction of Earnings Change (NIC)

			Reporting Date		
Direction of NIC	*# of Obs.*	*Mean Reporting Lag*	*Q1*	*Median*	*Q3*
Earnings Increase	150	102.41	4/ 5	4/18	4/25
Earnings Decrease	138	111.46	4/17	4/24	4/28
Test Statistics		F = 31.4[e]		X^2 = 27.8[e]	

Panel D. Unexpected Reporting Lag (URL) for Good News and Bad News Firms

News Content	*# of Obs.*	*Mean URL*	*# of Delay: # of Advance*
Bad News	53	4.02[b]	29:22
Good News	30	–4.97[a]	8:22
Test Statistics		F = 8.3[e]	X^2 = 7.0[e]

continued overleaf

Table 8. *Continued*

Panel E. Earnings News Content by Delay or Acceleration

	# of Obs.	*Range of URL*	*Mean of NIC*	*% of Good News*
Accelerated	42	−1 to −40	0.053	47.6%
Delayed	41	0 to 61	−0.219[a]	24.4%[d]
Test Statistics		F = 6.3[f]		$X^2 = 3.7$[f]

Panel F. Price Reactions to Earnings Announcements

$$CAR_{-1,+1} = \alpha + \beta\, UE + e \qquad (2)$$

Sample	*# of Obs.*	*α (t-statistics)*	*β (t-statistics)*	*Adj-R^2*
Full sample	234	−0.024 (−5.77)[a]	0.519 (4.36)[a]	7.17%
Early Reporting Group	116	−0.014 (−3.20)[a]	0.208 (1.68)[c]	1.58%
Late Reporting Group	118	−0.031 (−4.16)[a]	0.684 (3.35)[a]	8.01%
Accelerated	37	−0.028 (−2.01)[b]	0.556 (1.68)[c]	4.84%
Delayed	37	−0.006 (−0.49)	1.366 (2.79)[a]	15.80%

NIC is defined as the percentage change in net income. Earnings are in million of Chinese yuan. Reporting lag is defined as the number of days from the fiscal year-end to the report release date. URL is the difference in reporting lags between year t and year t-1. Good (Bad) news firms are those experiencing an earnings increase (decrease) in year t after an earnings decrease (increase) in year t-1. Early and late reporting groups are based on reporting lag. Accelerated and delayed groups are based on unexpected reporting lag.

[a]The two-sided t-test is significant at the 1% level.
[b]The two-sided t-test is significant at the 5% level.
[c]The two-sided t-test is significant at the 10% level.
[d]The sign test is significant at the 1% level.
[e]Significant at the 1% level.
[f]Significant at the 5% level.

disclosure of bad news relative to the reporting date in the previous year. The reporting patterns for B/H share firms are similar to those for the full sample. These results are consistent with the stakeholder theory and the internal reporting hypothesis. We also find that accounting earnings prepared under the Chinese accounting standards are useful for firm valuation across different reporting lag groups.

This study adds to the existing financial reporting literature. First, it documents a systematic timing pattern of annual report disclosures in the emerging capital market of China. While the Chinese stock market is playing an increasingly important role in the reform of Chinese economy, information is very limited for investors to predict future earnings of listed companies. Listed Chinese firms rarely disclose any voluntary information before the annual report releases. Thus, the timing pattern this study has documented can be useful to domestic and foreign investors in forecasting listed Chinese firms' future earnings, and especially in anticipating bad news. Second, since this study is the first to document the reporting behavior in an emerging market, it extends our understanding of the timing pattern of earnings announcements to capital markets beyond mature markets such as the US.

Notes

1. Listed Chinese companies do not make preliminary earnings announcements. Their annual operating results are first released to the public through the publication of the abstracts of their annual reports in the newspapers designated by the Chinese Securities Regulatory Commission.

2. See also Dyer and McHugh (1975) and Davis and Whittred (1980) for further analysis of the timeliness of Australian annual reports in the context of audit process.

3. The SOEs listed in Chinese security exchanges were originally authorized to issue common shares only to Chinese citizens (which are called "A-shares"). Since 1992, some of the selected A-share companies have been allowed to issue shares to foreign investors (which are called "B-shares"). In addition, foreign investors may acquire H-shares of other Chinese firms traded through the Hong Kong Stock Exchange.

4. Since then, China has promulgated the conceptual framework for accounting standards and several detailed accounting standards. The appendix summarizes the latest development of Chinese accounting standard setting. See also Haw et al. (1999) and Xiang (1998) for detailed discussions. This *Accounting System for Selected Shareholding Companies* was in effect until the end of 1997. In January 1998, the Ministry revised it substantially and formalized it as *Accounting System for Shareholding Companies*. Currently, all listed Chinese firms prepare financial statements in accordance with this new system along with the promulgated detailed accounting standards as shown in the Appendix.

5. For example, Chengdu Hongguang Co. Ltd. stated in its May 1997 Prospectus that it would invest most of its IPO proceeds, totaling 412 million yuan, on production capacity expansion. However, it invested only 67.7 million yuan on expansion projects and used 235.45 million yuan for loan repayment. Such dramatic departure from its stated intention for the IPO proceeds was not made public until the release of its annual report on April 30, 1998.

6. The number of observations in 1996 and 1997 is greater than the total number of firms listed by the year-end because the sample includes firms that became listed and then released their first annual results during the first four months of the next year.

7. Out of 1,890 obserations, 302 (16%) firm-years are winsorized at the 100% cut-off point. Alternatively, we use the 200% cut-off point by winsorizing 158 firm-years (8%). The results are quite similar to those reported in tables. We also deleted such outliers from the analysis. The results are again similar.

8. The mean and median NIC decline monotonically by the reporting lag and are significantly different from zero in all four reporting groups in each of the four years (except one in 1994). For the latest reporting group, more firms experienced negative NIC in each of the four years but the frequency of positive NIC is statistically significant only for 1995 and 1997.

9. Since we measure good (bad) news based on an earnings increase (decrease) in year t after an earnings decrease (increase) in year t-1, our analysis is limited to 1995–1997.

10. We also performed sensitivity analyses for mean NIC among the four URL groups by stock exchange. The results are very similar to those in panel B of Table 6.

11. However, none of the prior timing studies controlled for the magnitude of the earnings forecast error in their annual earnings announcement studies. In the quarterly earnings study, Kross and Schroeder (1984) examined the association between quarterly announcement timing and stock returns after controlling for the magnitude of the earnings forecast error.

12. We also estimate equation (2) for each of the four years 1994–1997 and for each of the two stock exchanges. The regression results are qualitatively the same.

13. We test whether the β coefficients are equal among the reporting lag groups. While the coefficients are not statistically different at the conventional level ($F = 1.599$) among the unexpected reporting lag groups in panel D, the coefficients between the early and late reporting groups in panel C are statistically different at the 1% level.

14. Consistent with Chambers and Penman (1984) and Begley and Fischer (1998), we also find that there is a negative market reaction to unexpectedly late announcements around the "expected" date. The mean (median) 3-day CAR around the "expected" date is –1.78% (–2.36%) and statistically different from zero. Furthermore, there is evidence of market anticipation for good news prior to the annual report release as the estimated cumulative market-adjusted returns for the pre-earnings announcement period (–10 to –2 day) is +1.6% and significant at the conventional level. This price runup could provide a partial explanation for the insignificant earnings response coefficients for the most accelerated reporting group in panel D of table 7.

15. See Haw et al. (1998) for detailed discussion about the institutional background of B-share and H-share markets.

16. We further examine the reporting patterns and market reactions to earnings announcements for B/H share firms by year and stock exchange. The results are generally consistent with those in Table 8.

References

Abdel-khalik, A. R., K. Wong and A. Wu, "The Information Environment of China's A and B Shares: Can We Make Sense of the Numbers?," *International Journal of Accounting*, 34 (1999), pp. 467–489.

Alford, A. W., J. J. Jones and M. E. Zmijewski, "Extensions and Violations of the Statutory SEC 10-K Filing Requirements," *Journal of Accounting and Economics*, 17 (January 1994), pp. 229–254.

Bao, B. and L. Chow, "The Usefulness of Earnings and Book Value for Equity Valuation in Emerging capital Markets: Evidence from Listed Companies in the People's Republic of China," *Journal of International Financial Management and Accounting*, 10 (1999), pp. 85–104.

Begley, J. and P. E. Fischer, "Is there Information in an Earnings Announcement Delay?" *Review of Accounting Studies*, 3 (1998), pp. 347–363.

Bowen, R. M., M. F. Johnson, T. Shevlin and D. Shores, "Determinants of the Timing of Quarterly Earnings Announcements," *Journal of Accounting, Auditing & Finance*, 7 (1992), pp. 395–422.

Chambers, A. E. and S. H. Penman, "Timeliness of Reporting and Stock Price Reaction to Earnings Announcements," *Journal of Accounting Research*, 22 (Spring 1984), pp. 21–47.

Davis, B. and G. Whittred, "The Association Between Selected Corporate Attributes and Timeliness in Corporate Reporting: Further Analysis," *Abacus* (June 1980), pp. 48–60.

Dyer, J. and A. McHugh, "The Timeliness of the Australian Annual Report," *Journal of Accounting Research* (Autumn 1975), pp. 204–219.

Fama, E. and K. F. French, "The Cross-section of Expected Stock Returns," *Journal of Finance,* 47 (1992), pp. 427–465.
Givoly, D. and D. Palmon, "Timeliness of Annual Earnings Announcements: Some Empirical Evidence," *The Accounting Review,* 57 (July 1982), pp. 486–508.
Haw, I. M., D. Qi and Y. W. Wu, "Value-Relevance of Financial Reporting Disclosures in an Emerging Capital Market: The Case of B-shares and H-shares in China," Working paper, The Chinese University of Hong Kong (1998).
Haw, I. M., D. Qi and Y. W. Wu, "Value-Relevance of Earnings in an Emerging Capital Market: The Case of A-Shares in China," *Pacific Economic Review*, 4 (October 1999) pp. 337–347.
Kross, W., "Earnings Announcements and Time Lag," *Journal of Business Research* (September 1981), pp. 267–281.
Kross, W., "Profitability, Earnings Announcement Time Lags, and Stock Prices," *Journal of Business Finance and Accounting,* 22 (Spring 1982), pp. 313–328.
Kross, W. and D. A. Schroeder, "An Empirical Investigation of the Effect of Quarterly Earnings Announcement Timing on Stock Returns," *Journal of Accounting Research,* 22 (Spring 1984), pp. 153–176.
Laurie, A. and V. Pastena, "How Promptly do Corporations Disclose their Problems," *Financial Analysts Journal,* 31 (September–October 1975), pp. 55–61.
Pastena, V., and J. Ronen, "Some Hypotheses on the Pattern of Management's Informal Disclosures," *Journal of Accounting Research,* 17 (Autumn 1979), pp. 550–564.
Patell, J. and M. A. Wolfson, "Good News, Bad News, and the Intraday Timing of Corporate Disclosures," *The Accounting Review,* 57 (1982), pp. 509–527.
Skinner, D, "Why Firms Voluntarily Disclose Bad News," *Journal of Accounting Research,* 32 (Spring 1994), pp. 38–60.
Xiang, B. "Institutional Factors Influencing China's Accounting Reforms and Standards," *Accounting Horizons,* 12 (June 1998), pp. 105–119.
Watts, R. L. and J. L. Zimmerman, "Toward a Positive Theory of the Determination of Accounting Standards," *Accounting Review,* 65 (1990), pp. 131–156
Whittred, G., "Audit Qualification and the Timeliness of Corporate Annual Reports," *The Accounting Review* (October 1980), pp. 563–577.

Appendix: Development of Chinese Accounting Standard Setting

July 1, 1993	The conceptual framework *Accounting Standard for Business* Enterprises became effective	
Feb. 1994	The first exposure draft of detailed accounting standard for *Payables* released	
July 1994	The second batch exposure drafts of detailed standards released, including:	
	Receivables	
	Inventories	
	Investments (revised later)	became effective from 1999
	Capitalization of borrowing costs	
	Balance sheet	
	Income statement	
April 1995	The third batch exposure drafts of detailed standards released, including:	
	Fixed assets	
	Intangible assets	
	Owners equity	
	Long-term construction contracts	became effective from 1999
	Research and development	
	Statement of cash flow	became effective from 1998
	Banking industry	
July 1995	The fourth batch exposure drafts of detailed standards released, including:	
	Deferred charges	
	Revenue recognition	became effective from 1999
	Foreign exchange	
	Income taxes	
	Consolidated financial statements	
	Accounting policy and estimates	became effective from 1999
	Subsequent events	became effective from 1998
Nov. 1995	The fifth batch exposure drafts of detailed standards released, including:	
	Contingencies and commitments	
	Donations and government grants	
	Related party disclosures	became effective from 1997
	Employee benefits	
	Reorganizations and liquidations	became effective from 1999
March 1996	The sixth batch exposure drafts of detailed standards released, including:	
	Barter trade and other non-monetary transactions	
	Business combination	
	Futures contracts	
	Insurance industry	
	Investments, revised	became effective from 1999
	Leases	
Jan. 1, 1997	The first detailed accounting standard became effective	
	Related party disclosures	
Jan. 1, 1998	The second batch accounting standards became effective, including:	
	Subsequent events	
	Statement of cash flow	
Jan. 1. 1999	The third batch accounting standards became effective, including:	
	Investments	
	Reorganizations and liquidations	
	Accounting policy and estimates	
	Revenue recognition	
	Long-term construction contracts	

Source: Ministry of Finance, People's Republic of China.

[16]

Journal of Accounting Research
Vol. 38 No. 1 Spring 2000
Printed in U.S.A.

Research Reports

Financial Packaging of *IPO* Firms in China

JOSEPH AHARONY,* CHI-WEN JEVONS LEE,†
AND T. J. WONG‡

1. *Introduction*

This paper examines the earnings patterns of initial public offering (*IPO*) firms in China to shed light on the role of earnings management in the "financial packaging" of Chinese state-owned enterprises (*SOE*s) for public listing.[1] Our sample contains the entire population of 83 Chinese *SOE*s that issued to foreign investors B-Shares in Chinese domestic stock exchanges or H-Shares in the Hong Kong stock exchange during

*Tel Aviv University and Hong Kong University of Science and Technology; †Hong Kong University of Science and Technology and Tulane University; ‡Hong Kong University of Science and Technology. This research was funded by the Hong Kong Research Grants Council Competitive Earmarked Research Grant No. HKUST524/95H. We appreciate the helpful comments of an anonymous referee, participants in the 1997 Chinese Accounting Professor Association Conference, the 1998 International Conference of Finance, and the 1998 Hong Kong University of Science and Technology summer symposium. Price Waterhouse LLP (Hong Kong) kindly provided part of the data for this study. Hao Xu and Douglas Li provided excellent research assistance. All opinions and errors are our own.

[1] The term "Financial Packaging" (*cai wu bao zhuang* in Mandarin Chinese) is used by practitioners to describe the restructuring of an *SOE* from a quasi-government agency, wholly owned by the state, to a corporation whose common shares are partially privately owned (see Lee [1996; 1997] for more discussion).

1992–95.[2] These *IPO*s mark the beginning of the stock market in China and signify an important step in Chinese economic reform. We find that the *SOE* manager's incentives and opportunities for earnings management vary across industries and listing locations.

We classify 16 of the 83 sample firms into "protected" industries and the remaining 67 firms into "unprotected" industries. The protected industries include petrochemicals, energy, and raw materials, while all other industries are considered unprotected industries. Firms in protected industries are large monopolies under the direct supervision of the State Council. Their managers often held important government positions before and some have political ambition for the future; thus they act more as bureaucrats or politicians than businessmen. Furthermore, protected firms' close relation with the State Council enables them to receive special treatment from the state regulatory agencies for public listing. For example, protected firms are subject to less stringent profitability requirements for new equity issues than unprotected firms. Unprotected industries are usually under the supervision of provincial or local governments. Their managers are professional managers, who have more freedom to set prices than their counterparts in protected industries. Their products compete in the Chinese domestic markets and some even in international markets. Firms in unprotected industries have to compete openly for the listing privilege.

We examine the pre- and post-*IPO* earnings patterns for the entire sample, and separately for firms in protected versus unprotected industries and for B-Shares versus H-Shares. We find a statistically significant post-issue earnings decline for unprotected industry firms. This earnings decline is most significant for unprotected B-Share firms, marginally significant for protected B-Share and unprotected H-Share firms, but not significant for protected H-Share firms. In addition, we find some evidence that the accounting accruals of sample firms in unprotected industries decline, whereas their cash flows from operations increase, after the *IPO*. Taken together, earnings management in the process of financial packaging seems to depend on the firm's relation with the central government and on where its securities are listed. The evidence also suggests that the *SOE*s in unprotected industries may manage accounting accruals to boost earnings and/or list those business units with temporarily high profits resulting from high accounting accruals during the process of financial packaging.

---

[2] The Shanghai Securities Exchange (*SHSE*) was officially opened in December 1990, followed by the Shenzhen Stock Exchange (*SZSE*) in July 1991. The first batch of *IPO*s was restricted to citizens of the People's Republic of China (*PRC*). These are called "A-Shares." In January 1992, Chinese companies began to issue "B-Shares" restricted to foreign investors on the two domestic stock exchanges. The availability of shares solely for foreign investors was expanded in the following year when Chinese companies issued "H-Shares" on the Stock Exchange of Hong Kong (*SEHK*). See Bei, Koontz, and Lu [1992] and World Bank [1995].

Financial packaging is a crucial step before a Chinese *SOE* offers shares to foreigners. Its primary purpose is to make the *SOE* more marketable to investors, especially foreign investors. It involves both accounting and organizational changes. To attract international investors for their *IPO*s, many *SOE*s list only their profitable business units for public offering and keep the nonproductive and unprofitable units in the state-owned entity. The financial reports of the to-be-listed business units must be converted from a cash basis to an accrual basis in accordance with international accounting standards. Since Chinese *SOE* managers often lack expertise in modern corporate finance and accrual-based accounting principles, they hire international underwriters, accounting firms, and lawyers to design and implement the financial packaging.

The literature has mainly documented accrual earnings management by U.S. *IPO* firms.[3] For Chinese *IPO* firms, the financial packaging process allows firms not only to adjust accounting accruals in the course of accounting conversion but also to carve out for listing temporarily profitable business units during the restructuring. Therefore, for the Chinese *IPO* context, we use a broader definition of earnings management to include both accrual earnings management and the carve-out of temporarily profitable units. In addition, Chinese *SOE* managers may not have the same incentives to manage earnings as their U.S. counterparts. Owning essentially no shares of the firm and with no stock options, Chinese *SOE* managers have no immediate incentive to manage earnings, and they may also lack the accounting sophistication to do so.

Nevertheless, the manager in the Chinese *IPO* firm may have indirect incentives to manage earnings. Unlike the United States, where earnings management is initiated by the issuing firm, the Chinese government may direct the *SOE* managers toward earnings management, hoping to obtain as high an offering price and as much foreign currency as possible. To appear fair to all participants, the regulatory bureaucrats need to use an objective criterion for selecting *SOE*s for public offering—accounting earnings. A major listing requirement is that the applicant must have at least two consecutive years of operating profits. The *SOE* manager may manage earnings upward to increase the possibility of his firm being selected for listing, as this can result in higher prestige and other nonpecuniary benefits. However, *SOE*s are chosen for public listing not only on the basis of their future earnings prospects but also on

[3] Aharony, Lin, and Loeb [1993] find weak support for the hypothesis that entrepreneurs select accounting methods to increase reported net income in the period up to two years prior to the *IPO*. Friedlan [1994], examining unaudited interim data of an *IPO* sample from an earlier period than that used by Aharony, Lin, and Loeb [1993], finds significant evidence of earnings management in the most recent interim period prior to the *IPO*. Teoh, Wong, and Rao [1998] and Teoh, Welch, and Wong [1998*a*] find that both accounting earnings and total accruals are unexpectedly high around the *IPO* year and decline thereafter. Similar accruals patterns are documented in seasoned equity issues in the United States by Teoh, Welch, and Wong [1998*b*] and Loughran and Ritter [1997].

other considerations. In particular, firms in protected industries receive relatively favorable treatment in accessing the equity market, so *SOE* managers in these industries may have relatively less incentive to manage earnings to increase their chances in the *IPO* selection process.

Section 2 describes the institutional background of financial packaging and the incentives and opportunities for earnings management by Chinese *IPO* firms. Data collection and summary statistics of the sample are presented in section 3. The empirical analysis is discussed in section 4. Section 5 contains the summary and conclusion of the study.

2. *Institutional Background*

2.1 EMERGING STOCK MARKET

The Chinese stock market was organized by the government as a vehicle to convert its socialist planned economy into a market economy. The majority shareholders for most listed *SOE*s are state agencies that lack experience in monitoring and controlling public firms. Securities regulations are less rigorous than in many developed markets. Investors, financial analysts, and government officials are often uncertain about the real meanings and the true enforceability of regulatory codes and decrees. In China, auditor legal liability is not well defined. Up to 1998, all domestic auditors were public employees, and there was no reward for high-quality audits and no explicit penalty for audit failure. Foreign auditors typically handle the financial packaging of B-Share and H-Share firms, partially to boost the credibility of audited financial statements. Moreover, the socialist-style fund accounting used in *SOE*s does not provide useful information for investors. China has not yet promulgated its first complete set of generally accepted accounting principles.[4] The apparent lack of control and monitoring from investors, regulatory agencies, and auditors and the lack of transparency in financial disclosure have provided considerable discretion for managing earnings.

Capital markets in a transitional economy like China are segmented. For example, A-Shares, B-Shares, and H-Shares are issued by Chinese companies to different constituencies. All three types of shares have the same rights and obligations, the only differences being the type of investors permitted to own and trade them and the currencies used for trading and cash dividends. There is no transferability among A-Shares and B-Shares or H-Shares, and thus the prices can (and do) vary substantially. A-Shares are listed on domestic exchanges and traded in *RMB*; 70 of the 311 A-Share firms have been permitted to issue B-Shares to foreign in-

[4] The *PRC* adopted the socialist fund accounting system in 1949. A more commercially oriented system was introduced in 1985 for foreign joint venture firms. In 1993, new accounting rules were introduced for all enterprises. A more comprehensive set of accounting standards, more in line with International Accounting Standards, is in preparation. For details, see Davidson, Gelardi, and Li [1996], Winkle, Huss, and Chen [1994], and Zhou [1998].

vestors as of December 1995. B-Shares are traded in either U.S. dollars in Shanghai or Hong Kong dollars in Shenzhen, and they may be held only by foreign entities and foreign individuals. H-Shares, listed and traded only on the *SEHK*, are issued by Chinese companies which may or may not have also issued A-Shares (but which have not issued B-Shares to date). Only foreigners may purchase and trade H-Shares (in Hong Kong dollars).

2.2 FINANCIAL PACKAGING OF *IPO* FIRMS

Financial packaging is idiosyncratic to Chinese *IPO*s because the *IPO* firm is a set of business units carved out of a much larger *SOE*. The State Council in China is the ultimate owner of the *SOE* and the overseer of the *IPO* process. The *SOE* manager is of course a government employee, not an entrepreneur. The China Securities Regulatory Commission (*CSRC*), an executive branch of the State Council Securities Committee, simultaneously assists with and monitors the financial packaging of *IPO* firms. These aspects of financial packaging provide *SOE* managers with highly specific incentives and opportunities for earnings management.

Financial packaging brings the *IPO* firm's accounting system in line with international practices and converts its organization form into a limited liability corporation. Prior to public listing, the *SOE*'s financial statements were based on socialist fund accounting rules. Financial packaging prepares financial reports for B-Shares in accordance with International Accounting Standards (*IAS*) and H-Shares in accordance with either *IAS* or the Hong Kong Statement of Standard Accounting Practice (*HKSSAP*). To increase the confidence of foreign investors in the quality of the financial reports, international auditing firms are hired during the financial packaging process.

In a typical financial packaging, the original *SOE* carves out selected profitable business units for public offering. The unprofitable units are either retained by the original *SOE*, which becomes the parent holding company, or absorbed by a municipal government agency which serves as a holding company of various *IPO* firms in the municipality. For example, the Shanghai Asset Administration Bureau and the Shenzhen Special Economic Zone Investment Administration Company are the controlling shareholders of various *IPO* firms. The *IPO* firm keeps only selected commercial assets; noncommercial assets, such as hospitals and schools for employees and their families, are retained by the parent companies or government agencies. Some *IPO* firms also obtain discharge as guarantor for loans taken out by the parent or other subsidiaries of the parent firms.

A firm seeking listing must also go through a multi-step, tightly controlled selection process. The first step is approval from the *CSRC* followed by permission from the relevant local and national authorities to reorganize from a company owned by the state into one owned by shareholders. For example, Inner Mongolia Erdos Cashmere Products Co., Ltd., a regional *SOE* listed in Shenzhen, obtained approval from the Economic Restructuring Commission of Inner Mongolia to reorganize. Maanshan

Iron & Steel Company Ltd., a nationwide *SOE* listed in Hong Kong, was approved by the Anhui Provincial Government and the Ministry of Metallurgical Industries. The next step is examination by the listing committees of the stock exchanges, followed by a formal announcement of the *IPO*.

A major listing requirement for *IPO*s is at least two consecutive years of operating profit; additionally, B-Share and H-Share firms must be able to generate enough foreign exchange income in the future to pay dividends in foreign currencies. The State Council sets a stringent quota for new issues in each category annually. For instance, in 1993, the quota for B-Shares was 800 million shares; there were hundreds of *SOE* applicants but only 24 B-Share *IPO*s were approved. Each *IPO* is small and the competition among *SOE*s to be listed is fierce. The state and regional authorities are subjected to lobbying and political pressure.[5]

A major complaint about this selection process is that noncommercial factors play too big a role.[6] In particular, the State Council and the *CSRC* are suspected of favoring *SOE*s in the "protected" industries in their selection decisions.[7] Firms in protected industries (petrochemicals, energy, and raw materials) are state monopolies, under the direct supervision and control of the State Council. They are a major component of the central government's budget, and several *CEO*s in these industries held cabinet-level positions before their current posts. Likewise, most cabinet ministers who regulate the protected industries have worked in the same industries as managers. Not only do these protected *SOE*s control output prices, they receive, among other benefits, direct subsidies from the central government (*Far Eastern Economic Review* [November 11, 1993]). Firms in unprotected industries, mostly under the supervision of provincial or local governments, do not receive direct aid from the central government. Most of them compete in domestic markets and some even in international markets. Managers in unprotected industries exercise more freedom to set prices and act more as businessmen than politicians or bureaucrats, compared with their counterparts in pro-

[5] To satisfy provincial political pressure, the *CSRC* has selected firms from each geographic region for overseas listing. The 17 H-Share firms in our sample came from 14 different provinces or special economic zones. The 66 B-Share firms operate mainly in the Shanghai and Quangdong regions.

[6] Numerous articles in the financial press in Hong Kong have suggested that *IPO* firms are chosen not only on the basis of their future earnings prospects but also on political connections. See *Ming Poa Daily News* [December 31, 1996, B2], *China Law and Practice* (Roell [1996]), *China Securities Handbook* [1997, pp. 27–29] for more detailed discussions.

[7] The *CSRC* published a new set of requirements for rights issues in 1996. Companies in protected (unprotected) industries must have an after-tax return on equity of at least 9% (10%) in each of the past three years to qualify for new share offerings. Although the *CSRC* made no public statement about differential profitability requirements for listing protected versus unprotected firms, the mean and median *ROA* in the year prior to *IPO* are smaller for the protected than for the unprotected firms in our sample. The mean (median) difference is –4% (–2.4%) and it is statistically significant at less than 0.1%.

tected industries. Thus, the incentives and opportunities for earnings management in unprotected industries are different from those in protected industries.

2.3 INCENTIVES AND OPPORTUNITIES FOR EARNINGS MANAGEMENT

The Chinese *SOE* manager does not gain any direct benefit from a high *IPO* price, since the average share ownership of all employees in B-Share and H-Share companies is less than 0.05%. The manager may lack sufficient knowledge of *IAS* or Hong Kong accounting rules to manipulate earnings. Furthermore, the international investment banks and external auditors that assist in financial packaging have a reputation-based incentive to reduce earnings manipulation.

Some *SOE* managers may, however, have indirect economic incentives for earnings management, based on the increased autonomy and decreased government interference that accompany listed status. To the extent that *SOE* managers value listed status for its nonpecuniary benefits, and because earnings performance is a stated criterion for choosing *IPO* candidates, an *SOE* manager may attempt to manage earnings to boost his firm's chance of being selected for an *IPO*. Furthermore, the state, which remains the majority shareholder of the *IPO* firm, may instruct the manager to manage earnings to influence the offering price.[8]

Financial packaging provides opportunities for the *SOE* manager to boost earnings at the *IPO*. The process of converting the accounting rules and standards from socialist fund accounting to western accounting requires considerable judgment, which in turn creates opportunities for earnings management. The *SOE* can carve out the temporarily profitable business units for the *IPO* and retain unprofitable units.[9] As the controlling shareholder, the parent *SOE* may boost the earnings of its listed subsidiary in the year of the *IPO* and then siphon these profits back in future years.[10] Therefore, it is an open empirical question whether

[8] Underwriters commonly use the price–earnings multiple of a listed firm in the same industry to set the offering price. This generalization is based on discussions with the leading analyst of China research at a large investment bank in Hong Kong. Also, the offering price is positively related to reported earnings per share in the year before and the year of the *IPO* in our sample, with Spearman correlation coefficients of 0.53 and 0.75, respectively. However, these statistics may be driven by size effects and are reported for descriptive purposes only.

[9] Retaining the noncommercial assets in the parent *SOE*s or state agencies is common among B-Share and H-Share companies. In our sample of 83 firms, 31 (45) have a municipal government agency (parent *SOE*) as the majority shareholder. Only 7 have a joint venture company as the majority shareholders and these usually do not have noncommercial assets.

[10] A research report called *Darkness before Dawn* [May 1996] by Credit Lyonnais Securities, a leading underwriter for Chinese B-Shares and H-Shares, documents that ten of the B-Share and H-Share firms declared generous dividends while experiencing poor earnings and cash flows in 1995. They claimed the parent company's need for cash determined the high payout ratios.

TABLE 1

The Effect of Industry Membership and Listing Location on the Incentives and Opportunities for Earnings Management of Chinese IPO Firms

	Protected Industries	Unprotected Industries	
Listing in Hong Kong	**Weakest Effect** 1. High market monitoring and better investor sophistication reduce the opportunity for stock price boosting 2. Favorable access to equity market reduces the incentive for winning *IPO* approval	**Mild Effect** 1. High market monitoring and better investor sophistication reduce the opportunity for stock price boosting 2. The need for competing for *IPO* approval increases incentive	**Less Opportunity**
Listing in Shanghai and Shenzhen	**Mild Effect** 1. Low market monitoring and less investor sophistication increase the opportunity for stock price boosting 2. Favorable access to equity market reduces the incentive for winning *IPO* approval	**Strongest Effect** 1. Low market monitoring and less investor sophistication increase the opportunity for stock price boosting 2. The need for competing for *IPO* approval increases incentive	**More Opportunity**
	Weak Incentive	**Strong Incentive**	

Chinese *SOE* managers manipulate earnings around the time of an *IPO*. This is the first issue we address.

Under the direct supervision of the State Council, an *SOE* in a protected industry operates more like a government agency than a commercial enterprise and receives relatively favorable access to the *IPO* market. On the other hand, an *SOE* in an unprotected industry is more like a commercial enterprise, and receives relatively less favorable access to the *IPO* market. The incentives for earnings management may therefore vary between protected and unprotected industries. In addition, the listing location can affect the opportunities for earnings management. B-Shares are traded in domestic markets where market regulating and policing mechanisms are new and weak, while H-Shares are traded in the well-established Hong Kong stock market where market regulating mechanisms are more mature. We summarize the effects of industry membership and listing location on the incentives and opportunities for earnings management in a 2 × 2 matrix in table 1. We will examine how these two factors separately and jointly affect earnings management of Chinese *IPO* firms.

Financial packaging also affects the method of earnings management in China. For example, because the government sets depreciation rates for the *SOE*s, it is difficult to use depreciation accruals to manipulate the earnings number. However, the credit sales offer an opportunity for earnings management. Under a socialist planned economy, all *SOE*s exchange goods and services according to government plan. Thus, the major domestic customers of an *SOE* are other *SOE*s. Since all accounts receivable from *SOE*s are guaranteed by the state, allowances for bad debt are very small.[11] An *SOE* might therefore boost income by accelerating its credit sales prior to the *IPO*. A sharp post-*IPO* decline in the change in accounts receivable over cash sales would suggest that the *IPO* firm has accelerated credit sales to boost earnings temporarily. Since flexibility in the interaction between financial packaging and Chinese government rule provides an earnings management opportunity in the form of accelerated credit sales to *SOE*s, we analyze receivables accruals in the period surrounding the *IPO*.

3. Data

Our sample consists of 83 Chinese *IPO* firms that issued shares to foreign investors from the opening of this market (January 1, 1992) to the cutoff date for our data collection (September 1, 1995). Sixty-six firms issued B-Shares (35 on the *SHSE* and 31 on the *SZSE*) and 17 firms issued H-Shares. We obtained financial data from *IPO* prospectuses (three years of pre-*IPO* income statements and the latest balance sheet) and annual financial statements (data for the *IPO* year and the following two fiscal years). Price Waterhouse LLP (Hong Kong) provided all the published prospectuses and some of the annual reports. We acquired additional financial data from the publications of Wardley Investments Co. (*Wardley Cards*); the *Taiwan Economic Journal* (*TEJ*) electronic database; and the *EXTEL* on-line database. Table 2 presents the sample composition by share type, year of *IPO*, and industry.

Data on accruals and other operating numbers, not available from published sources, were collected manually from working papers filed (before and after the *IPO*) with the *CSRC*. These working papers were prepared in order to generate financial statements in accordance with either *IAS* or *HKSSAP*. To establish consistency, we compared the working paper data and the published financial reports.[12] Because some data required for our analyses were not available for all sample firms in all years, the number of firms analyzed varies from year to year according to data availability.

---

[11] Lee [1997] shows that all the accounts receivable in Shanghai Sunve Co. arose from credit sales to other *SOE*s. It is not traditional for Chinese *SOE*s to estimate bad debt expense. The new Chinese accounting system, put forth in 1993, required a standard provision for bad debt, set at 0.3% to 0.5% of the ending balance of accounts receivable. Numerous newspaper articles discussed the bad debt problems in H-Share and B-Share companies in 1994. Large H-Share companies such as Maanshan Iron and Steel, Kunming Machine Tool, and Tsingtao Brewery were named as having bad debt problems in 1994. See *Asian Wall Street Journal* [April 25, 1995*a*, pp. 1 and 24].

[12] *CSRC* data include cash, accounts receivable, inventory, total current assets, total assets, accounts payable, current maturity of long-term debt, total current liability, net sales, depreciation expense, pretax income, and net income from the year before the *IPO* to the year after the *IPO*.

TABLE 2

Sample Composition of Chinese IPOs, 1992–95[1]

Panel A: By Year of *IPO*

	Year of *IPO*				
Type of Common Shares	1992	1993	1994	1995[2]	Total
B-Shares[3]	18	24	16	8	66
H-Shares[3]	0	6	9	2	17
Total	18	30	25	10	83
(%)	(21.7%)	(36.1%)	(30.1%)	(12.1%)	

Panel B: By Industry

	Type of Common Shares		
Industry	B-Shares	H-Shares	Total
Protected Industries[4]			
Petrochemicals	2	5	7
Energy	2	3	5
Raw Materials	3	1	4
Total	*7*	*9*	*16*
Unprotected Industries[4]			
Machinery	7	2	9
Auto and Motorcycle	2	1	3
Glass	2	1	3
Transportation	5	2	7
Textiles	5	0	5
Consumer Goods	18	1	19
Property and Construction	9	0	9
Commercial Sector	6	0	6
Telecommunication and Electronics	5	1	6
Total	*59*	*8*	*67*
Entire sample	**66**	**17**	**83**

[1]This table presents the distribution of Chinese *IPOs* to foreign investors by calendar year (panel A) and by industry membership (panel B), for each type of shares.

[2]The sample includes all Chinese *IPOs* to foreign investors completed between January 1992 and September 1995.

[3]"B-Shares" are issued to foreign investors on the two Chinese domestic stock exchanges. "H-Shares" are issued to foreign investors on the Stock Exchange of Hong Kong.

[4]Firms in protected industries are state monopolies, under the direct supervision and control of the State Council, which permits these firms to control prices and provides them with direct subsidies. Firms in unprotected industries operate in a relatively more competitive market environment, under the supervision of local government.

Each *SOE* can issue only one type of shares (either B or H) to foreign investors. Table 2 shows that B-Share companies are more likely to operate in competitive/unprotected industries than are H-Share companies. Of the 66 B-Share companies, 59 are from unprotected industries, with 18 in the very competitive consumer goods industry, whereas the 17 H-Share companies are almost equally divided between the protected and unprotected industry categories, with 5 firms in the monopolistic petrochemical industry. This is consistent with the view that privileged (i.e., protected) *SOEs* have a better chance of being chosen for H-Share listing.

TABLE 3

Time Sequence of Securities Offerings to Domestic (Chinese) and Foreign (Non-Chinese) Investors by Chinese IPO Firms, 1992–95[1]

		B-Shares (66 firms)	H-Shares (17 firms)
A-Share Offering **before or in the Same Month as the** B/H-Share Offering[3]	N^2	52	3
	Median	3	3
	Mean	6.71	4.33
	Std. Dev.	8.25	5.13
	Min.	0	0
	Max.	30	10
A-Share Offering **after** the B/H-Share Offering	*N*	5	8
	Median	3	7
	Mean	4.60	8.00
	Std. Dev.	3.65	6.19
	Min.	1	1
	Max.	9	16
Firms without A-Share Offering	*N*	9	6

[1]This table presents the different time sequence of Chinese *IPOs* to Chinese domestic investors (A-Shares) and to foreign investors, either on the two Chinese domestic exchanges (B-Shares) or the Stock Exchange of Hong Kong (H-Shares), from January 1992 to September 1995. The B-Share and H-Share companies are examined separately.

[2]*N* indicates the number of observations.

[3]The median, mean, standard deviation, minimum, and maximum are all measured in number of months between the domestic and foreign offerings.

Table 3 shows how the Chinese stock market has evolved. The Chinese government first experimented with a stock market on a small scale with domestic investors only, then expanded to foreign investors, using B-Shares. Finally the government was ready to list some of its favored *SOE*s as H-Shares using a market outside the Chinese government's jurisdiction. After the H-Shares proved successful, the government allowed some H-Share companies to issue A-Shares to domestic investors, which completed the Chinese experiment with the stock market. The mean waiting time for the government to observe the experiment was about seven months and the median waiting time was about three months.

In table 3, 86% (57 out of 66) of the B-Share firms and 65% (11 out of 17) of the H-Share firms also have A-Shares, which can be held only by Chinese citizens. Most of the B-Share firms are given permission to issue shares to foreign investors after they have proved successful in the domestic market. However, the H-Share firms are often chosen directly for foreign share issuance. As shown in table 3, 82% (14 out of 17) of the H-Share firms are chosen for foreign share issuance before any A-Share issuance, compared to only 21% (14 out of 66) of the B-Share firms that issue foreign shares before issuing any A-Shares. Eight of the 11 H-Share firms issued A-Shares on average eight months *after* the H-Share offering, whereas 52 of the 57 B-Share firms listed A-Shares on average seven months *before* the B-Share offering.

Table 4 reports summary financial data for the sample firms. H-Share companies are, on average, larger than B-Share companies in terms of total assets and net sales. The differences in median (mean) total assets and net sales are *RMB* 3.2 billion (4.7 billion) and *RMB* 1.9 billion (2 billion), respectively (all statistically significant at the 1% level). Also, the median total proceeds received from issuing H-Shares are about 4.7 times the median proceeds from issuing B-Shares. Both median and mean differences are statistically significant at the 1% level. H-Share companies are larger and more likely to be protected than B-Share companies; and firms in protected industries are about four times larger in terms of total assets, net sales, and *IPO* proceeds than those in unprotected industries. The profitability of B-Share and H-Share companies does not differ; however, the median (mean) *ROA* of the unprotected industry firms in the *IPO* year is larger than that of the protected industry firms by 2.89% (3.52%), statistically significant at the 1% level. This evidence is consistent with unprotected industries having a higher profitability requirement for listing.

One purpose of financial packaging is to convert the *SOE*'s ownership structure from the pure state ownership into as many as five types of ownership as described in table 5, panel A: state ownership, domestic investor ownership (A-Shares), foreign investor ownership (B/H-Shares), Chinese institutional ownership, and foreign institutional ownership. The *SOE* issues a specific type of shares to each type of owner. A-Shares are issued to the *PRC* citizens and B-Shares and H-Shares to "foreigners" (including Hong Kong residents). A, B, and H-Shares can be traded only in their designated stock markets. Institutional shares owned by Chinese government agencies or by foreign corporations can be traded only in a private market by authorized institutions. In addition, government agencies can convert their institutional shares into other assets. State shares cannot be traded.

Panel B of table 5 summarizes majority ownership. It shows that 76 of the 83 sample firms are controlled by the state (represented by an *SOE* or a municipal government agency); 7 firms are controlled by joint ventures. Only one of these joint-venture-controlled firms belongs to a protected industry and none has issued any H-Shares. While state control is primarily represented by the *SOE* in about half (30 out of 59) of the B-Share companies, it is primarily represented by the *SOE* in 15 out of 17 H-Share companies. Slightly more than half (35 out of 61) of the unprotected firms have the *SOE* as the majority shareholder, while two-thirds (10 out of 15) of the protected firms have the *SOE* as the majority shareholder. This evidence, together with the data in table 3, suggests that B-Share firms and unprotected firms are relatively small enterprises administered by local governments, while H-Share firms and protected firms are relatively large enterprises administered by the central government.

The maximum state share ownership is about 74% among all 76 state-controlled firms. However, the minimum state share ownership is 14% in B-Shares or unprotected firms, compared to 43% in H-Share firms and

TABLE 4

Financial Attributes of Chinese IPO Firms, 1992–95[1]

		B-Shares (66 Firms)	H-Shares (17 Firms)	Difference[2]		Unprotected (67 Firms)	Protected (16 Firms)	Difference[2]	
Total Assets in Year of *IPO* (*RMB* Million)[3]	Median	1,006	4,192	-3,186	**(0.000)**	981	4,097	-3,116	**(0.000)**
	Mean	1,363	6,016	-4,653	**(0.002)**	1,486	5,795	-4,309	**(0.005)**
	Std. Dev.	1,278	5,026			1,564	5,176		
	Min.	71	708			71	239		
	Max.	6,509	16,503			8,673	16,503		
Net Sales in Year of *IPO* (*RMB* Million)	Median	511	2,394	-1,883	**(0.000)**	509	1,493	-983	**(0.000)**
	Mean	676	2,693	-2,016	**(0.003)**	724	2,621	-1,897	**(0.008)**
	Std. Dev.	609	2,411			700	2,493		
	Min.	9	137			9	110		
	Max.	3,615	7,583			3,615	7,583		
Net Income in Year of *IPO* (*RMB* Million)	Median	62	188	-126	**(0.000)**	72	171	-98	**(0.002)**
	Mean	94	355	-262	**(0.003)**	103	332	-229	**(0.014)**
	Std. Dev.	93	309			105	327		
	Min.	4	73			4	11		
	Max.	417	978			522	978		
ROA[4] in Year of *IPO* (%)	Median	9.51	7.16	2.35	(0.410)	9.60	6.71	2.89	**(0.014)**
	Mean	9.88	9.57	0.31	(0.856)	10.50	6.98	3.52	**(0.003)**
	Std. Dev.	5.29	6.32			5.70	3.38		
	Min.	0.10	2.45			0.10	1.75		
	Max.	26.51	25.57			26.51	12.69		
Proceeds[5] (*RMB* Million)	Median	171	804	-634	**(0.000)**	179	672	-492	**(0.000)**
	Mean	249	1,137	-888	**(0.004)**	274	1,087	-813	**(0.013)**
	Std. Dev.	252	1,096			296	1,146		
	Min.	38	143			38	64		
	Max.	1,260	4,390			1,740	4,390		

[1]This table reports firm characteristics, such as total assets, net sales, net income, *ROA* in year of the *IPO*, and *IPO* proceeds, of Chinese *SOEs* that issued shares to foreign investors from 1992 to 1995. The sample is partitioned into B-Share and H-Share and unprotected and protected subgroups. The differences in means and medians of the firm characteristics between the subgroups are also presented. B-Shares are issued to foreign investors on the two Chinese domestic stock exchanges. H-Shares are issued to foreign investors on the Stock Exchange of Hong Kong. Firms in protected industries are state monopolies, under the direct supervision and control of the State Council, which permits these firms to control prices and provides them with direct subsidies. Firms in unprotected industries operate in a relatively more competitive market environment, under the supervision of local government. The list of protected and unprotected industries is given in table 2, panel B.

[2]The p-values of the t-test of the difference in mean and the Wilcoxon signed-rank test of the difference in median are reported in brackets. Bold print indicates significance (two-tailed) at the 1% level or better.

[3]Exchange rates: US$1:*RMB* 8.3 as of June 1996.

[4]Net income over total assets minus cash in the year of the *IPO*.

[5]Offering price per share × total number of B-Shares or H-Shares issued.

TABLE 5

Ownership Structure as a Result of Financial Packaging of Chinese IPO Firms, 1992–95[1]

Panel A: Ownership Structure by Share Classes[2] (Unit: %)

Share Class		B-Share Firms	H-Share Firms	Unprotected Firms	Protected Firms
	N[3]	66	17	67	16
State Shares	Median	49	56	47	56
	Mean	39	51	39	49
	Min.	0	0	0	0
	Max.	74	75	75	75
A-Shares	Median	9	5	10	5
	Mean	12	7	12	6
	Min.	0	0	0	0
	Max.	54	26	54	17
B/H-Shares	Median	27	32	28	27
	Mean	28	33	29	29
	Min.	9	25	9	11
	Max.	50	49	50	39
Chinese Institutions	Median	8	1	6	7
	Mean	17	9	16	14
	Min.	0	0	0	0
	Max.	68	60	68	60
Foreign Institutions	Median	0	n.a.[4]	0	0
	Mean	4	n.a.	4	2
	Min.	0	n.a.	0	0
	Max.	73	n.a.	73	27

Panel B: Ownership Structure by Majority Shareholders (Unit: %)

Majority Shareholder		B-Share Firms	H-Share Firms	Unprotected Firms	Protected Firms
SOE	*N*	30	15	35	10
	Median	52	60	53	61
	Mean	50	59	50	61
	Min.	14	43	14	49
	Max.	71	75	72	75
Municipal Government Agency	*N*	29	2	26	5
	Median	54	43	54	54
	Mean	54	43	53	57
	Min.	24	42	24	49
	Max.	74	44	74	70
Joint Venture	*N*	7	0	6	1
	Median	73		73	72
	Mean	73		75	72
	Min.	64		72	72
	Max.	87		87	72

[1]This table presents in four subgroups (B-Share firms versus H-Share firms, unprotected firms versus protected firms) the ownership structure of the Chinese *IPO* firms by share classes in panel A and by majority shareholder type in panel B. B-Shares are issued to foreign investors on the two Chinese domestic stock exchanges. H-Shares are issued to foreign investors on the Stock Exchange of Hong Kong. Firms in protected industries are state monopolies, under the direct supervision and control of the State Council, which permits these firms to control prices and provides them with direct subsidies. Firms in unprotected industries operate in a relatively more competitive market environment, under the supervision of local government. The list of protected and unprotected industries is given in table 2, panel B.

[2]The ownership of shares is broken down into five share classes. The government owns the state shares, which cannot be traded. An *SOE* can hold the state shares on behalf of the government. Chinese citizens hold A-Shares traded on the *SHSE* or *SZSE*. Foreign investors hold B-Shares and/or H-Shares, the former being traded on the *SHSE* or *SZSE* and the latter on the *SEHK*. Chinese institutions such as *SOE*s or Investment Trusts hold Chinese institutional shares. Foreign institutions such as partners in joint ventures hold foreign institutional shares.

[3]*N* indicates the number of firms.

[4]n.a. indicates data are not available.

49% in protected firms. Hence, the Chinese government more tightly controls H-Share and protected firms than it does B-Share and unprotected firms. Overall, table 5 shows that the firm's relation to the government and where the new shares are listed affect the restructuring process in the financial packaging.

4. *Empirical Analysis*

We use earnings performance, measured as return on assets (*ROA*), surrounding the *IPO* year to document evidence of earnings management for our sample. ROA_t is net income (NI_t) in year t divided by total assets (TA_t) excluding total cash ($CASH_t$) at the end of year t. Total cash is excluded to remove the cash effect of the *IPO*.[13] We compare the *ROA* of the *IPO* fiscal year ($t = 0$) with the *ROA* in each of the two preceding years ($t = -2$ and $t = -1$, respectively) and in each of the three subsequent years ($t = +1$, $t = +2$, and $t = +3$, respectively). The sample median *ROA* (not reported in the tables) increases from 5.60% in $t = -2$ to 8.28% in $t = -1$, and to 9.25% in the *IPO* year (the sample mean *ROA* is 9.90% in $t = -2$, and it increases from 9.56% in $t = -1$ to 9.80% in the *IPO* year). The median (mean) falls to 2.87% (5.30%) in year +3. Figure 1, panel 1 shows that median *ROA* peaks in the *IPO* year for the entire sample. This pattern also holds for B-Shares and H-Shares, as shown in panel 2, and for protected and unprotected firms (panel 3). The pattern is clearer for the unprotected than for the protected firms and is clearer for the B-Share than for the H-Share companies.[14] This pattern alone does not provide conclusive evidence of earnings management. In the rest of this section we generate other corroborating evidence and conduct formal statistical tests. Because our samples are small, all results should be interpreted cautiously.

The difference in *ROA* between the *IPO* year ($t = 0$) and each surrounding year t is defined as $DROA_t = [NI_t/(TA_t - CASH_t)] - [NI_0/(TA_0 - CASH_0)]$. Table 6 presents mean and median *DROA* for the entire sample and for four subsamples: B-Share versus H-Share firms; firms in protected industries versus unprotected industries; B-Share firms in protected versus unprotected industries; and H-Share firms in protected versus unprotected industries. Two-tailed t-tests of significance of means

---

[13] Financial analysts have alleged that new issuers retain large amounts of *IPO* proceeds on deposit after flotation (see *Asian Wall Street Journal* [April 27, 1995*b*] and *South China Morning Post* [April 18, 1995]). A more accurate adjustment than subtracting total cash would subtract only the unused *IPO* proceeds, but these data are not available. The median ratios of $CASH_t$ to the *IPO* proceeds are 25.3%, 96.8%, 74.6%, 76.8%, and 75.0%, in years $t = -1, 0, +1, +2, +3$, respectively. This evidence increases our confidence that subtracting $CASH_t$ from TA_t provides a reasonable proxy for operating assets. The results in table 6 are qualitatively similar when TA_t is used as the deflator.

[14] Mean *ROA* patterns are qualitatively similar for B-Shares and H-Shares, and for protected and unprotected industries.

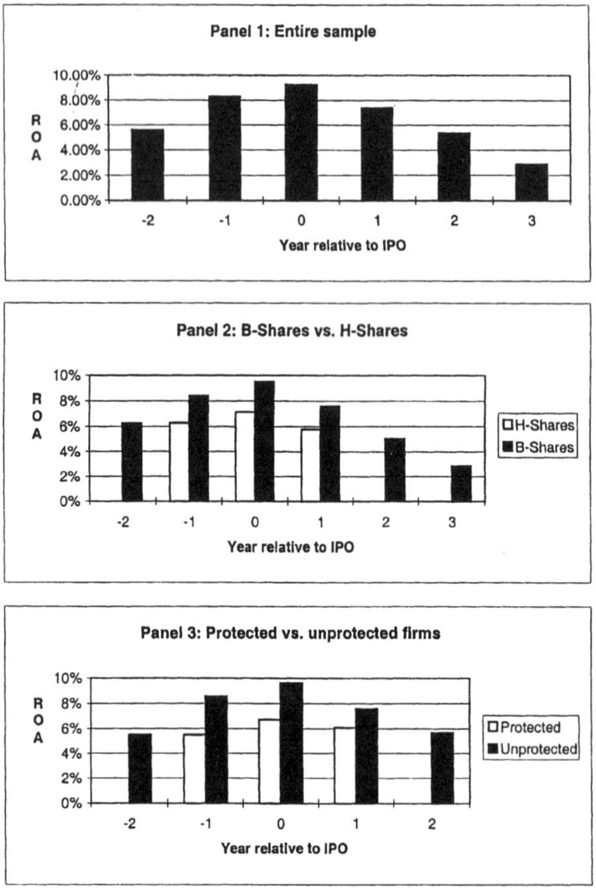

FIG. 1.—Earnings performance surrounding the *IPO* year of Chinese *IPO* firms, 1992–95. Figure 1 presents the time-series profiles of the *ROA* level from two years before the offering to three years after the offering, using the entire sample (panel 1), B-Shares versus H-Shares (panel 2), and protected versus unprotected industries (panel 3). B-Shares are issued to foreign investors on the two Chinese domestic stock exchanges. H-Shares are issued to foreign investors on the Stock Exchange of Hong Kong. Firms in protected industries are state monopolies, under the direct supervision and control of the State Council, which permits these firms to control prices and provides them with direct subsidies. Firms in unprotected industries operate in a relatively more competitive market environment, under the supervision of local government. The ROA_t is net income in year t ($t = -2, -1, 0, +1, +2, +3$, where $t = 0$ designates the *IPO* year) divided by total assets minus cash as of the end of year t. Each median *ROA* is computed with at least ten firm-year observations.

The number of observations for *ROA* varies across the years preceding and following the *IPO* year according to data availability. *ROA* data are available only up to the 1996 calendar year. Thus, ROA_1 is based on *IPOs* during 1992–94 (calendar years). ROA_2 is based on *IPOs* in 1992 and 1993 (calendar years). ROA_3 is based on *IPOs* in 1992 (calendar year). ROA_{-2}, ROA_{-1}, and ROA_0 are based on the entire sample of *IPOs*. The number of *IPOs* in each calendar year is shown in table 2.

are reported, as well as Wilcoxon signed-rank tests of significance of medians. The number of observations varies according to data availability.

For the entire sample, we detect significant *DROA* after the *IPO* but no significant *DROA* prior to the *IPO*. The median (mean) *DROA* are -1.76%, -4.14%, and -4.15% (-2.22%, -4.24%, and -5.64%) in years +1, +2, and +3, respectively, all significant at the 1% level or better. These results suggest that earnings management is associated with Chinese *IPO*s. Moreover, this earnings management may take the form of borrowing future earnings in order to boost profits in the *IPO* year.

The post-issue decline in earnings is much more significant for B-Share companies than for H-Share companies. The median (mean) *DROA* in the year after the *IPO* is −1.81% (−2.08%) for B-Shares, significant at the 1% level. The decline in earnings performance for B-Shares also persists in the two subsequent years, as evidenced by the highly significant negative median (mean) *DROA* of −4.32% and −4.15% (−4.45% and −5.64%), respectively. The median (mean) *DROA* for H-Share companies in the year after the *IPO* is −1.70% (−3.29%), with a *p*-value of 7%, and it is statistically insignificant (p = 0.625 for median and 0.493 for mean) in the subsequent year.

Partitioning the sample by protected versus unprotected industries indicates that the post-*IPO* decline in earnings performance is concentrated among unprotected firms. The median (mean) *DROA* for unprotected firms are −1.95%, −4.20%, and −3.86% (−2.71%, −4.74%, and −5.32%) in years +1, +2, and +3, respectively, all significant at the 1% level or better. Furthermore, this decline is driven more by the B-Share firms than by the H-Share firms. Although we identify a post-*IPO* decline in earnings performance for protected firms, the results are not statistically significant, possibly because of the small sample size. Taken as presented, however, the results suggest more pre-*IPO* earnings management among unprotected firms, consistent with the prediction in table 1. Perhaps the protected *IPO* firms were selected for political reasons and did not need to boost earnings. In addition, firms in protected industries can use price controls and subsidies to mitigate or avert a sharp decline in post-*IPO* earnings even if they engage in earnings management.

By further partitioning the B-Share firms into unprotected and protected industries, we find that evidence of earnings management is much stronger in unprotected industries than in protected industries for B-Share firms. The decline in earnings performance persists in years +2 and +3 for the unprotected B-Share firms (all significant at the 1% level or better) but not for the protected B-Share firms (*p*-values range from 0.168 to 0.625). For the H-Share firms, we find significant earnings decline for the unprotected firms but not for the protected firms. The median (mean) *DROA* for the unprotected H-Share firms is −4.22 (−6.87) in year +1, significant at the 4% level or better, while the median (mean) *DROA* for the protected H-Share firms is −0.61 (0.28) in year +1 with

TABLE 6

Differences in ROA between the IPO Year and Surrounding Years for Chinese IPO Firms, 1992–95[1]

	Years Relative to *IPO* Year (0)									
	−2		−1		+1		+2		+3	
Entire Sample										
Mean[2](%)	−0.06	(0.980)	−0.42	(0.416)	−2.22	**(0.000)**	−4.24	**(0.000)**	−5.64	**(0.002)**
Median[2](%)	−2.33	(1.000)	−0.65	(0.383)	−1.76	**(0.000)**	−4.14	**(0.000)**	−4.15	**(0.001)**
N[3]	11		81		72		42		11	
B-Shares										
Mean (%)	0.73	(0.761)	−0.53	(0.340)	−2.08	**(0.000)**	−4.45	**(0.000)**	−5.64	**(0.002)**
Median (%)	1.03	(0.770)	−0.20	(0.477)	−1.81	**(0.000)**	−4.32	**(0.000)**	−4.15	**(0.001)**
N	10		66		58		37		11	
H-Shares										
Mean (%)			0.12	(0.948)	−3.29	**(0.069)**	−4.02	(0.493)		
Median (%)			−0.86	(0.489)	−1.70	**(0.068)**	−2.23	(0.625)		
N	n.a.[4]		15		14		5		n.a.	
Protected Firms										
Mean (%)			−1.18	(0.197)	−0.68	(0.349)	−1.13	(0.730)	−6.48	(0.168)
Median (%)			−1.45	(0.130)	−0.98	(0.216)	0.82	(1.000)	−4.15	(0.250)
N	n.a.		16		13		5		3	
Unprotected Firms										
Mean (%)	−0.69	(0.777)	−0.17	(0.785)	−2.71	**(0.000)**	−4.74	**(0.000)**	−5.32	**(0.011)**
Median (%)	−3.16	(0.846)	−0.03	(0.920)	−1.95	**(0.000)**	−4.20	**(0.000)**	−3.86	**(0.008)**
N	10		65		59		37		8	
B-Shares/Protected										
Mean (%)			−0.55	(0.790)	−1.79	**(0.080)**	−3.32	(0.310)	−6.48	(0.168)
Median (%)			−3.86	(1.000)	−1.47	**(0.094)**	−1.95	(0.625)	−4.15	(0.250)
N	n.a.		7		6		4		3	

B-Shares/Unprotected										
Mean (%)	0.11	(0.967)	−0.50	(0.403)	−2.12	**(0.000)**	−4.58	**(0.000)**	−5.32	**(0.011)**
Median (%)	−2.33	(1.000)	−0.17	(0.586)	−1.81	**(0.000)**	−4.32	**(0.000)**	−3.86	**(0.008)**
N	9		59		52		33		8	
H-Shares/Protected										
Mean (%)			−1.67	**(0.004)**	0.28	(0.786)				
Median (%)			−1.44	**(0.004)**	−0.61	(0.938)				
N	n.a.		9		7		n.a.		n.a.	
H-Shares/Unprotected										
Mean (%)			2.81	(0.555)	−6.87	**(0.038)**	−6.94	(0.316)		
Median (%)			5.03	(0.563)	−4.22	**(0.031)**	−2.50	(0.250)		
N	n.a.		6		7		4		n.a.	

[1]This table reports the differences in *ROA* (encoded *DROA*) from two years before to three years after the offering relative to the *IPO* year. This time-series pattern of *DROA* is tested against a null of zero using the entire sample and eight subgroups: B-Share firms, H-Share firms, protected firms, unprotected firms, B-Share firms in protected industries, B-Share firms in unprotected industries, H-Share firms in protected industries, and H-Share firms in unprotected industries. B-Shares are issued to foreign investors on the two Chinese domestic stock exchanges. H-Shares are issued to foreign investors on the Stock Exchange of Hong Kong. Firms in protected industries are state monopolies, under the direct supervision and control of the State Council, which permits these firms to control prices and provides them with direct subsidies. Firms in unprotected industries operate in a relatively more competitive market environment, under the supervision of local government. ROA_t is net income (NI_t) in year t ($t = -2, -1, 0, +1, +2, +3$, where $t = 0$ designates the *IPO* year) divided by total assets (TA_t) minus total cash ($CASH_t$) as of the end of year t. The difference in *ROA* between the *IPO* year ($t = 0$) and a specific year $t \neq 0$ prior to or following year $t = 0$ is defined as: $DROA_t = [NI_t / (TA_t - CASH_t)] - [NI_0 / (TA_0 - CASH_0)]$.

[2]The *p*-value of the *t*-test of mean *DROA* and the Wilcoxon signed-rank test of median *DROA* are reported in brackets. Bold print indicates significance (two-tailed) at the 10% level or better.

[3]The number of observations for *DROA* varies across the years preceding and following the *IPO* year according to data availability. *ROA* data are available only up to the 1996 calendar year. Thus, $DROA_1$ is based on *IPOs* during 1992–94 (calendar years). $DROA_2$ is based on *IPOs* in 1992 and 1993 (calendar years). $DROA_3$ is based on *IPOs* in 1992 (calendar year). $DROA_{-2}$, $DROA_{-1}$, and $DROA_0$ are based on the entire sample of *IPOs*. The number of *IPOs* in each calendar year is shown in table 2.

[4]Data is not available.

$p = 0.938$ (0.786).[15] To the extent that unprotected firms are less politically favored by the State Council, they have more need to manage earnings, and to the extent that the B-Share market provides less monitoring of accounting practices, unprotected B-Share firms have the best opportunity and the most incentives to manage earnings. However, our small sample sizes preclude drawing any conclusions from these results.

Although the *ROA* patterns in table 6 provide evidence consistent with earnings management, they cannot distinguish between earnings manipulations and timing the *IPO* to coincide with high transitory earnings. Also, these patterns may be caused by the sample selection bias since one of the selection criteria for *IPO* is high *ROA*. The subsequent decline in *ROA* may simply be a mean reversion of high *ROA* in the *IPO* year. These two issues are addressed in table 7, which analyzes four earnings components for unprotected firms only: total accruals (TAC_t), operating cash flows (OCF_t), annual change in accounts receivable (ΔAR_t), and annual change in inventory (ΔINV_t). Each component is scaled by net cash sales (NCS_t) in year *t*, defined as $[NS_t - (AR_t - AR_{t-1})]$, where NS_t designates net sales in year *t*.[16] The difference in the earnings components between the *IPO* year ($t = 0$) and a surrounding year is $DX_t = X_t/(NCS_t) - X_0/(NCS_0)$, where *X* designates any of the four earnings components: *TAC*, *OCF*, ΔAR, and ΔINV.

Given sample size and data limitations, we use a variant of the unexpected accruals estimates described in Aharony, Lin, and Loeb [1993] and Friedlan [1994]. The change in accounts receivable measures whether firms accelerate their credit sales in the year of the *IPO*.[17] A sharp *decline* in the change in accounts receivable over cash sales post-issue would suggest that issuers use accelerated credit sales to boost earnings temporarily. If new issuers reduce their credit sales after the *IPO*, accounts receivable will drop and inventory will *rise*. On the other hand, inventory

[15] The analysis undertaken so far has focused on the time-series patterns in the sample's median *ROA*. However, if a few strong performers maintain their high *ROA* and also greatly expand in size (so that they are as big as all the other firms combined after a few years), the entire sample portfolio might do very well in a buy-and-hold investment strategy. The reason is that the median ratio does not capture the covariation of changes in scale and profitability, which is crucial from a portfolio performance perspective. As a diagnostic check, we also examine post-*IPO* earnings performance using Fama and French's [1995] portfolio methodology. Our results in table 6 are robust with respect to this check. Detailed results may be obtained upon request.

[16] Total accruals are defined as Δcurrent assets − Δcash − [Δcurrent liabilities − Δcurrent maturity of long-term debt] − depreciation expense. Operating cash flows are defined as net income minus total accruals. Friedlan [1994] uses net sales as the deflator. In our sample, median net sales rose from *RMB* 470 million in year −2 to *RMB* 640 million in year 0 and declined to *RMB* 500 million in year +3. We remove credit sales, proxied by the change in accounts receivable from net sales, so that our deflator is less likely to be affected by earnings management.

[17] Lev and Thiagarajan [1993] used the ratios of change in accounts receivable to cash sales and the change in inventory variable to cash sales to measure earnings quality.

TABLE 7

Methods of Earnings Management of Chinese IPO Firms in Unprotected Industries, 1992–95[1]

		Years Relative to *IPO* Year (0)									
		-2		-1		+1		+2		+3	
$D\Delta AR_t$	Mean (%)[2]	-1.57	(0.925)	6.20	(0.645)	-5.81	**(0.060)**	1.31	(0.807)	-17.36	(0.111)
	Median (%)[2]	-9.42	(1.000)	-6.44	(0.952)	-3.35	**(0.063)**	-5.19	(0.410)	-10.79	**(0.078)**
	N[3]	5		11		57		37		8	
$D\Delta INV_t$	Mean (%)	17.67	**(0.048)**	-12.56	(0.464)	-0.86	(0.816)	-4.84	(0.461)	4.86	(0.502)
	Median (%)	11.15	**(0.063)**	0.15	(0.810)	0.35	(0.811)	-1.88	(0.652)	-0.62	(0.844)
	N	5		11		57		37		8	
$DTAC_t$	Mean (%)	-11.90	(0.476)	13.75	(0.428)	-0.11	(0.990)	1.76	(0.897)	-35.87	**(0.032)**
	Median (%)	-22.04	(0.625)	23.51	(0.354)	-3.60	(0.781)	-7.25	(0.315)	-27.70	**(0.031)**
	N	5		11		57		37		7	
$DOCF_t$	Mean (%)	-19.22	(0.643)	-2.08	(0.916)	-3.07	(0.689)	-8.99	(0.507)	31.67	**(0.078)**
	Median (%)	19.36	(1.000)	0.81	(1.000)	3.61	(0.922)	4.86	(0.717)	10.10	**(0.078)**
	N	5		11		57		37		7	

[1]This table compares earnings components of the *IPO* year with the earnings components starting two years before the offering to three years after the offering, using the Chinese *IPO*s from unprotected industries between 1992 and 1995. Firms in unprotected industries operate in a competitive market environment and are controlled by local government. The list of unprotected industries is given in table 2, panel B. Each of the four earnings components in year t is standardized by net cash sales = $[NS_t - (AR_t - AR_{t-1})]$ as of the end of year t. The difference in each standardized earnings component DX_t between the *IPO* year ($t = 0$) and a surrounding year is defined as: $DX_t = X_t / [NS_t - (AR_t - AR_{t-1})] - X_0 / [NS_0 - (AR_0 - AR_{-1})]$, where X represents any of these four components—ΔAR: change in accounts receivable, ΔINV: change in inventories, TAC: total accruals, or OCF: operating cash flows.

[2]The p-values of the t-test of mean DX and Wilcoxon signed-rank test of median DX are reported in brackets. Bold print indicates significance (two-tailed) at the 10% level.

[3]N is the sample size.

buildups can increase current earnings at the expense of future earnings by absorbing overhead costs. If the issuers use inventory accruals to manage earnings upward during the *IPO* year, we will observe a *decline* in inventory accruals after the *IPO*.

The medians and means of the differences in earnings components, $D\Delta AR_t$, $D\Delta INV_t$, $DTAC_t$, and $DOCF_t$, are presented in table 7. The results indicate a statistically significant negative *DΔAR* in year $t = 1$ (for both mean and median tests) and year $t = 3$ (for the median test). The median *DTAC* is negative for all three post-*IPO* periods but significant ($p = 0.031$) only in year $t = 3$. The median *DΔINV* does not follow a particular pattern in the post-issue period, whereas the median *DOCF* mirrors the pattern of *DTAC*, showing a positive ($p = 0.078$) *DOCF* in year $t = 3$. These results, together with the earnings results in table 6, suggest that new issuers in unprotected industries may have engaged in accrual management by accelerating credit sales in the year of the *IPO*. If the *IPO* firms were purely timing their issues, or if the decline in *ROA* were strictly a result of mean reversion, both *DOCF* and *DTAC* would be negative in the post-issue period. However, the results in table 7 are also consistent with Chinese *SOE*s carving out business units with temporarily high profits from high accounting accruals in the *IPO* year.

The weight of the evidence on the patterns of *ROA*, accruals, and cash flows from operations suggests that the high *ROA* during the *IPO* year comes mainly from accruals, not cash flows from operations. After the *IPO*, the decline in *ROA* is associated with a decline in accruals and, more specifically, a decline in accounts receivable but not cash flows from operations. These results suggest there is earnings management among Chinese *IPO* firms and that accounting accruals are used for this purpose.

5. *Conclusions*

This study examines earnings management in the process of financial packaging preceding *IPOs* in which Chinese state-owned enterprises (*SOEs*) issue shares to foreign investors. For a sample of 83 *IPOs* completed between 1992 and 1995, we analyzed the behavior of return on assets (*ROA*) and selected earnings components in the two years preceding and the three years following the *IPO*. We found that the median firm *ROA* peaks in the *IPO* year and declines thereafter.

The post-*IPO* decline in *ROA* is statistically significant in unprotected (more competitive) industries, but not in protected industries such as petrochemicals, energy, and raw materials. This suggests that firms in the protected industries are favored by the state in the selection process. Thus, their chance of being selected for an *IPO* is not necessarily based on profitability, and they need not boost earnings in the *IPO* year. Even if they have managed earnings upward, they are more capable of maintaining the high earnings level after the *IPO* through political connections than are the unprotected firms. The post-*IPO* decline in *ROA* also is more significant for the B-Share companies than for H-Share companies. Further partitioning shows that unprotected B-Share firms exhibit the largest post-*IPO ROA* decline, while the protected H-Share firms exhibit the smallest post-*IPO ROA* decline. Because the primary customers of *SOE*s are *SOE*s and the state is ultimately responsible for all the *SOE*s' debts, we find that accelerating credit sales is a low-cost method for earnings management in China and is widely used by unprotected *SOE*s. There is evidence that the total accruals of unprotected *SOE*s decline, whereas the cash flows from operations increase, after the *IPO*. Taken together, this evidence suggests that the Chinese *IPO* firms engage in earnings management, and the pattern of earnings management depends on each firm's relation with the government and on where its shares are listed.

Among this study's limitations, the most significant is small sample size. All test results are exploratory and should be interpreted with caution. Another significant limitation is time clustering; earnings patterns may be affected by macroeconomic factors. These limitations notwithstanding, we do observe a systematic pattern of earnings management that varies according to incentives and opportunities idiosyncratic to China.

REFERENCES

AHARONY, J.; C. J. LIN; AND M. LOEB. "Initial Public Offerings, Accounting Choices, and Earnings Management." *Contemporary Accounting Research* (Fall 1993): 61–81.

Asian Wall Street Journal. "H-Share Firms Stumble as Fears of Bad Debt Rise." (April 25, 1995*a*): 1, 24.

_____. "Tsingtao's Profit Falls 42% on Higher Costs in China." (April 27, 1995*b*).

BEI, D.; A. KOONTZ; AND L. LU. "The Emerging Securities Market in the PRC." *China Economic Review* 3 (Spring 1992): 149–72.

China Securities Handbook, 1995–1996. Hong Kong: Philip Jay Publishing, 1997.

CREDIT LYONNAIS SECURITIES. *Darkness before Dawn.* Hong Kong: China Research Report, May 1996.

DAVIDSON, R. A.; A. GELARDI; AND F. LI. "Analysis of Conceptual Framework of China's New Accounting System." *Accounting Horizons* (March 1996): 58–73.

FAMA, E., AND K. FRENCH. "Size and Book-to-Market Factors in Earnings and Returns." *Journal of Finance* (March 1995): 131–55.

FRIEDLAN, J. "Accounting Choices of Issuers of Initial Public Offerings." *Contemporary Accounting Research* (Summer 1994): 1–32.

GOLDSTEIN, C. "Spared the Test." *Far Eastern Economic Review* (November 11, 1993).

LEE, C. J. "Restructuring China's State-Owned Enterprises." *China Review* (1996): 243–61.

_____. "Financial Packaging of State-Owned Enterprises in China." *Review of International Accounting and Finance* (1997): 1–20. [In Chinese.]

LEV, B., AND S. R. THIAGARAJAN. "Fundamental Information Analysis." *Journal of Accounting Research* (Autumn 1993): 190–215.

LOUGHRAN, T., AND J. RITTER. "The Operating Performance of Firms Conducting Seasoned Equity Offerings." *Journal of Finance* (December 1997): 1823–50.

Ming Pao Daily News. "The New IPO List, Revealing Regional Political Pressure." (December 1996): B2.

ROELL, S. "What Does the Future Hold for B and H Shares?" *China Law and Practice* (September 1996): 17–19.

South China Morning Post. "Machine Tool Firm Profits Take Tumble." (April 18, 1995).

TEOH, S.; I. WELCH; AND T. J. WONG. "Earnings Management and the Long-Term Underperformance of Initial Public Stock Offerings." *Journal of Finance* (December 1998*a*): 1935–74.

______. "Earnings Management and the Post-Issue Underperformance of Seasoned Equity Offerings." *Journal of Financial Economics* (October 1998*b*): 63–99.

TEOH, S.; T. J. WONG; AND G. RAO. "Are Accruals during Initial Public Offerings Opportunistic?" *Review of Accounting Studies* (May 1998): 175–208.

WINKLE, G. M.; H. F. HUSS; AND X. CHEN. "Accounting Standards in the People's Republic of China: Responding to Economic Reforms." *Accounting Horizons* (September 1994): 48–57.

WORLD BANK. *China: The Emerging Capital Market.* Vols. 1 and 2. Washington, D.C.: World Bank, 1995.

ZHOU, Z. H. "Chinese Accounting Systems and Practices." *Accounting, Organizations, and Society* 2 (1988): 207–24.

[17]

The International Journal of Accounting

The Information Environment of China's A and B Shares: Can We Make Sense of the Numbers?

A. Rashad Abdel-khalik,* Kie Ann Wong,† and Annie Wu‡
**University of Florida, Gainesville, FL, USA; †National University of Singapore, Singapore, Singapore; and ‡National Chengchi University, Taiwan, People's Republic of China*

Key Words: Emerging markets; Information content; Market segmentation

Abstract: *In 1990, three stock exchanges were opened in Shanghai, Shenzhen and Beijing. Partial privatization of China's enterprises began with offering two types of shares: A shares are sold only domestically to locals and are denominated in local currency; B shares are denominated in dollars and are sold only to foreign investors. All listed firms offer A shares, but to qualify for offering B shares, the firm must prepare financial statements in accordance with International Accounting Standards and also meet other requirements. Firms issuing A shares only adopt domestic accounting regulations.*

As a way of generating capital funds, market segmentation has been a success. Both types of shares, however, have two different information environments. The environment of A shares appears to be dominated by local regulations and customs at the time of offering or trading. The information environment of A shares appears to be relatively unstructured and is affected by informal communication between various groups. Other than the roles played by state officials and appointed managers, external monitoring of A shares appears to be limited. Independence and social acceptance of auditing appear to be making slow progress, especially when the majority of domestic CPA firms are government owned. In contrast, the information environment for the B shares is more structured because (1) financial reporting adheres to International Accounting Standards, (2) financial statements are audited by CPA firms with international practice; and (3) foreign investors — mainly large financial institutions — also act as external monitors.

We elaborate on the differences between these two information environments and suggest that accounting earnings and A share prices are not correlated, but earnings and share prices are correlated for B shares. In an event-study approach, we find results inconsistent with both hypotheses — for 1994 and 1995 we find that earnings and unexpected returns are correlated for A shares but not for B shares. The high price volatility, the significant and continuing dominance of government officials, and the thinness of trade in B shares are offered as possible explanation for these results.

Once the People's Republic of China (PRC) allowed its citizens to own and operate business firms; actions were undertaken to facilitate capital formation. Reactivating the

Direct all correspondence to: Dr. A. Rashad Abdel-khalik, Fisher School of Accounting, University of Florida, PO Box 117166, Gainesville, FL 32611, USA; E-mail: rashad@notes.cba.ufl.edu

The International Journal of Accounting, Vol.34, No. 4, pp. 467-489 ISSN: 0020-7063.

stock exchange after having been abandoned for 4 decades was accompanied by regulatory reforms and by a move to partially privatize state-owned enterprises. PRC currently operates three stock exchanges, with the two most active stock exchanges being the Shanghai Stock Exchange (SSE) and the Shenzhen Stock Exchange (SEZ). The third, Beijing Stock Exchange has, at the time of this writing, two stock trading centers for institutional holders of equity shares of 17 companies only. Our analysis concentrates on SSE and SEZ.

The newly privatized firms were authorized to issue various types of shares. Most common are A shares that are sold only to Chinese in the mainland, B shares that are sold only to foreign investors. More recently, a few firms issued H and N shares that are sold to foreign investors through listing on the Hong Kong stock exchange and on the New York Stock Exchange, respectively. H and N shares are relatively new instruments and only a few were able to offer these types of shares.

All firms listed on SSE and SEZ issue A shares, but less than one-fifth of those firms issue B shares. As of November 1996 there were 467 listed companies, of which 82 (17.5%) had issued B shares and prepared financial statements in accordance with International Accounting Standards (IASs issued by the International Accounting Standards Committee [IASC]). These requirements are intended to signal a degree of reliability and assurance to foreign investors. Segmenting capital markets in this fashion allows firms to finance their capital requirements from local savings as well as international funds and, as a result, large amounts of foreign funds had flowed into China.

In recent years listed firms have published their financial statements bi-annually in the newspapers; there are no other known systematic or organized means of disseminating the information to investors.

THE RESEARCH QUESTION

We began this project with the anticipation that the emergence of stock exchanges in PRC creates an interesting setting for studying the role of information in emerging capital markets. Because of their recent origin, different emerging capital markets are at different stages and do not have information systems of the types known in the more developed capital markets. Of particular interest to us is the role of accounting information in pricing common stocks. The unbiased and fast assimilation of accounting information in security prices is a phenomenon that is well documented in developed capital markets beginning with the work of Ball and Brown (1968) (for reviews, see Bernard, 1990 and Beaver, 1998), but has not been well examined in developing economies.

Breaking with conventional methods of research in capital markets, we view the role of information in emerging capital markets to be dominated by domestic institutional arrangements, cultural norms of communication and local customs of doing business. These factors interact to reduce data reliability at both transaction and aggregate levels. The maturation of markets and the financial sophistication of participants in those markets are not likely to have evolved to the level that can facilitate formulating historical trends and relationships between stock prices and accounting information.

RESEARCH PLAN

To build a case for the issues of relevance in studying emerging capital markets, we first highlight some basic conditions that must exist in order to conduct information content analysis. Those conditions often remain in the background and are always assumed to be satisfied. This is followed by a brief discussion of the extent to which we believe these conditions to be satisfied in emerging capital markets. A discussion of capital markets and the role of the accounting profession in PRC begins by distinguishing the information environments for A and B shares. Finally, using data from the Shanghai and Shenzhen stock exchanges, the association between accounting disclosures and share prices is examined in each of these two information environments separately. Because the firms issuing B shares adhere to a relatively higher standard of information-reporting reliability than those issuing A shares only, we hypothesize that the association between unexpected rates of return and accounting information differ for those two types. In particular, that the pattern for B shares is more likely to be similar to what we know in the extant literature, but no particular pattern was expected for those issuing A shares only. We use data for 1994 and 1995 in an event study design to test this hypothesis. *The results are inconsistent with expectations* in that the pattern of unexpected returns around earnings announcements for B shares appears to be random but, surprisingly, the results for the A shares are similar to those obtained in developed capital markets.

After reflecting on the information environment of A shares and on the extent to which the conditions for studying information efficiency are satisfied, we could not interpret these results as reflecting a causal relationship between accounting numbers and share prices. We realize that others might use the same results to make different inferences, but analysis of the setting and information obtained directly from market participants does not support making inferences about the information content of accounting numbers. As is elaborated below, most CPA firms are government owned and a corporate governance culture is evolving although the state continues to be the majority shareholder (of about 80% of equity) in privatized firms (Zhang, 1996). This structure does not provide for the independence of information producers and market makers.

Relevant Factors for Information Content Analysis

Basic and Necessary Conditions

The research on information content in the setting of developed and mature capital markets implicitly assumes some necessary conditions that must prevail in the information environment in order to give credence to any market tests of information content. Some of these conditions can be stipulated as follows:

1. Transaction-related data and source documents of accounting systems are the outcome of arms-length exchanges.
2. Transaction data are consistently aggregated in accordance with a known set of rules.
3. Effective internal controls are in place to safeguard the company's assets and to reduce opportunistic behavior.

4. Internal audits are implemented to ensure the integrity of the information system, input data and produced information.
5. Market prices reflect the preferences of market participants.
6. Capital markets are free of manipulation by regulators, individuals in power or capricious government interference.
7. Insiders do not use their informational advantage for their own gain before allowing equal access to other investors.

These conditions are generally satisfied for listed firms in developed economies where financial and accounting institutions, the public, the press and regulators act as external monitors or "watch dogs" that assure the integrity of the data reported to the public. In addition, enforcement agencies exist for dealing with serious departures from the expected norms. In that setting, researchers can reasonably assume that investors vote with their feet, capital markets operate efficiently, and prices reflect all publicly available information. To make reliable inferences about accounting information content, markets must operate with the least possible friction, a case that is difficult to make for many emerging capital markets.

Information Content in Emerging Capital Markets

There are various reasons why share prices in emerging capital markets may not satisfy the conditions listed above. Indeed, the efficiency of emerging capital markets has not been established because reported data and recorded stock prices may not reflect the free expression of the preferences of all market participants. Unique factors of local customs, bureaucratic regulation, the absence of a developed accounting and auditing profession, undue influence of state officials, and loose insider trading constraints do interact to impact the operation of capital markets.

A couple of illustrations might help to highlight this problem. Prior to May 1992, regulators of the SSE imposed tight controls over all share prices and trading volume. Although much of the underlying motives remain behind the scenes, to public observers these controls were manifested by imposing two constraints on trading in A shares, both aimed at reducing volatility. These constraints were: (1) the maximum allowed daily fluctuation in the price of any listed share cannot exceed 1%, and (2) trading prices should not change if volume of trade does not exceed 0.3% of the number of outstanding shares. On May 5, 1992, the allowed maximum daily fluctuation in prices was increased from 1% to 8%, but restrictions on the minimum volume required to trigger price changes were retained. On May 21, 1992 both measures of control were abolished. While the imposition of such regulatory controls on market forces has prevented share prices from reflecting the true preferences of market participants, it also has artificially maintained low levels of volatility. Upon lifting the restrictions on May 21, 1992, share prices more than doubled and the SSE price index increased by 105.3% in one day.

Another case of conspicuous regulatory interference with market processes in emerging capital markets was observed at a stock exchange in an Eastern European country (the "Exchange") at the early stages of privatizing business. One of the authors witnessed a slice of the operations on that exchange in 1992 when the exchange had only 12 listed companies and trading shares took place on Tuesdays and Thursdays only. Fifteen minutes before the official closing time, the chairman of the "Exchange" went to the trading floor, rang a bell and a bulletin board revealed the 12 closing prices for the day. On that particular day, the then chairman, a Western-educated man, went to the floor and, with news reporters and other observers looking on, unilaterally changed the prices of two stocks that he felt to be out of "acceptable ranges." The closing price of what he perceived to be an "over priced" stock was lowered, and the price of another stock that he perceived to be "underpriced" was increased. The newly dictated prices became the opening prices for the next trading day.

It was evident that the chairman of that "Exchange" saw his role as a market maker and a smoothing agent whose task was to reflect what he thought to be the "true" price. While it was never made clear, as far as we know, how the chairman of the exchange had individually arrived at those so-called "true" prices, making these changes could conceivably signal to other market participants that the chairman was in position of private information. In that event, this unilateral act might exacerbate a trend the chairman of the "Exchange" has independently charted irrespective of other market forces. Because of this action, opening prices on a given trading day differ from closing prices for the same stocks on the preceding trading day. Thus, reported share prices in those markets would not have the same attributes of prices generated from the interplay of normal market forces.

The PRC Setting

Stock Exchanges

Two major PRC stock exchanges began operations in 1990 — these are the SSE and the SEZ. Both exchanges trade A and B shares. According to market reports, the SSE draws more capital from the local and Taiwanese Chinese, while SEZ, which is located in south China near the border of Hong Kong, draws funds from investors in Hong Kong and the West (Kaye, 1992; Sender, 1992b).

These stock exchanges were established to facilitate trading the portion of equity shares (estimated at about 20% of equity) of the newly privatized firms whose ownership the government had decided to release to private investors. In all cases, however, "land" continues to be owned only by the state and is valued as an intangible (Zhang, 1996). Although problems arise in the valuation of state-owned companies because of the lack of market price information to value their assets, the movement toward privatization was followed by a steady growth in the number of privatized firms. As of October 1994, stocks of 164 firms were traded on SSE, and of 103 firms were traded on SEZ. The numbers increased to 184 and 127 in 1995 for the SSE and SEZ, respectively.

As indicated earlier, we will concentrate on the two common types of equity instruments that can be owned by individuals: A and B shares and are traded only on domestic exchanges. The former is denominated in yuans (the domestic currency) and is owned and traded *only* by citizens, while the latter is denominated in US dollars and is owned and traded by foreign investors *only*. As of December 1995, of the 184 listings on SSE, only 36 had issued B shares, and of the 127 listed on SEZ, only 34 had issued B shares. In December 1995, market capitalization had reached estimated levels of about US$40 billion for A shares and US$2 billion for B shares (Shanghai Securities News, SSE, January 7,

1996). Additionally, because of the size difference between these two markets, in August 1994, the government announced its intent to facilitate trading in A shares by foreign investors, but only through fund management organizations (Hansell, August 1994).

This segmentation of capital markets has succeeded in raising capital from citizens and foreigners, but it is not at all clear why *the price of an A share is more than three times the price of a B share in the same firm.* This disparity might, for example, be reflecting the effects of two distinct demand functions for stocks, with three factors could be stipulated as enhancing the demand for ownership of A shares: (1) industries in the southern region where SEZ is located are relatively young and are growing at fast rates; (2) the enormous pent-up demand for consumer and durable goods assures the ability of these firms to convert all of their production into revenues; and (3) allowing prices to change with market conditions heightens the expectations that producers will share more of the consumer surplus and earn abnormal profits, especially since the PRC economy is estimated to have been growing at more than 8% a year.

The Accounting Profession

For four decades, the communist rule prohibited private ownership, organized and free capital markets and the operation of a market price system, which has impeded the development of accounting and the infrastructure required for the flow of price relevant information. Prior to the recent move to allow private ownership of capital and to operate a market economy, the accounting focus had been on a few tangible measures: i.e., the existence of physical assets, growth in sales and cash flows. This focus emanated from the government's policies that measured firms' success by growth in output and employment statistics. Also, the focus on cash flows was considered essential in order to account for the enterprise's use of the funds appropriated by the state.

Although the information available about accounting as both a process and a profession in PRC is often incomplete, accounts of recent developments can be found in Zhang (1996), Qing et al. (1998) and Xiang (1998). Historically, conflicting descriptions appeared in the financial press. On the one hand, it is reported that, under prior systems, all transactions were recorded and "meticulously supported by vouchers" (Sender, 1992a) in a manner consistent with the Confucian philosophy of keeping historical records. On the other hand, the magnitude of missing controls were not reassuring:

> In most cases, there is no independent verification of critical items such as bank balances or account receivables. Prices charged from one month to the next for the same inputs are frequently inconsistent. In other cases, blank checks are presigned and written for amounts up to certain ceilings — the assumption being that if the actual cost is less, it will be refunded down the line. And there is no formal monitoring of stocks (inventory) either. (Sender, 1992a, p. 59)

Upon switching from a purely state-owned enterprise to a system of sharing ownership with private investors, the assets and liabilities of the firms being privatized had to be assigned some values in order to determine the extent of ownership equity. Additionally, special problems arose when the firm's debt included funds borrowed from foreign financial institutions since translating debt into the domestic currency at the prevailing exchange rates has very often led to much higher obligations than the numbers recognized on the books. Against this background, it is understandable why preparing credible financial statements could be an extensive and highly costly undertaking of reconstructing financial statements from vouchers, appraisals and estimates. Even then, all appraisals have to be authorized and it is argued that the required "procedure is perceived as having too much government intervention, which may impair the independence of the valuation (appraisal) firms" (Zhang, 1996, p. 8).

Of the firms that the government had permitted to issue B shares (and adhere to IASs), "it took the Hong Kong-based office of Arthur Andersen about 6000 man hours in January and February 1992 to ready the financial statements of Shanghai Vacuum Electronic Device, China's leading television maker for its B-share flotation in February" (Fairlamb, 1993, p. 37). The encountered difficulties are explicitly noted by the Arthur Andersen's partner in the Hong Kong office who was in charge of about 50% of the B shares privatization (quoted in Fairlamb, 1993, p. 37):

> Valuing a firm can be a nightmare. It is often unclear whether enterprises actually own some of the assets — such as land, which is not generally tradable in China — included in their balance sheets. Working out the value of goodwill in a socialist context is also difficult, as is assessing the true worth of stockpiled goods. And predicting future profitability in an environment where many prices were until recently controlled and where the domestic currency is not freely convertible is highly risky.

Similarly, it took more than 30 Hong Kong-based accountants with Arthur Andersen (who spent over 11,000 man-hours) to prepare the financial statements of *Brilliance China Automotive Holdings*, (Sender, 1992b).

In recent years, the PRC's government has established China's Institute of Certified Public Accountants to regulate and govern the conduct of professional CPAs. the Institute is a quasi-government organization that proclaimed independence, fairness, and objectivity as the three most fundamental professional rules of conduct. Since then, Fang and Tang (1991) report an apparent acceleration of development in accounting standards. In 1993, the government issued *Enterprise Accounting Standards No. 1*, which mandated desirable accounting qualities to adhere to "authenticity, relevance, comparability, consistency, timeliness, distinctiveness and materiality." Although these characteristics have the tone of the qualitative criteria adopted by the US Financial Accounting Standards Board as part of its conceptual framework, it is not clear they have been put into action. For example, Xiang (1998) reports that the implementation of the 13 accounting standards that were issued in 1992 has been postponed in spite of the assertion that they are considered transitory because of their concentrating on the mechanical processes of recording.

Zhang (1996) offers a lucid description of some major problems in accounting in PRC. He highlights the major difficulty business firms encounter in valuing their receivables and debt. First, payment of obligations is very slow-paced; firms "have not yet developed the habit of confirming the amounts of receivables requested by auditors" (p. 3); "and the government arbitrarily dictated that allowance for bad debt should not exceed the range of only 0.3% – 0.5% of the total amounts" (p. 3). Zhang details other serious shortcomings in the accounting system, but most general institutional concerns arise from the fact that the majority of CPA firms are government owned, the Ministry of Finance is in charge of making accounting and auditing standards, and auditors independence is at issue. In addition, the shortage of CPAs in China is critical; it is estimated that "78% are over 60 years old and 80% are retired personnel. Nearly all ... did not go through the CPA examination which was only introduced a couple of years ago" (Zhang, 1996, p. 23). According to Qing et al. (1998, p. 8), the biggest challenge facing the system is that the persistent ailment of lack [of] fidelity [faithful representation] about accounting information [which is] widespread in China."

Creating an accounting profession and culture cannot be done in a short period of time, especially when the basic elements of arms-length exchanges remain to be developed. However, optimism and high expectations accelerate with every new proposal that offer hope for improved disclosure and information environment. For example, Xiang (1998) describes some cases of the planned transition that give rise to those expectations:

> The selection of depreciation methods and the estimation of useful life were administered by government regulations; further, the amount of the provision for doubtful accounts could not exceed a maximum percentage of the amount of year-end accounts receivable. These regulations are no longer required under the [proposed] detailed standards. The proposed detailed accounting standards intend to be more prudent with the application of the LCM rule, as well as to be more flexible in the choice of accounting policies and estimates. These proposed detailed accounting standards will move China's accounting practice closer to IAS. (Xiang, 1998, p. 115)

The slow development of a reliable information structure in China has not been without cost to the economy. Information problems seem to be a major reason in delaying many firms from being traded; an estimated 4400 enterprises are waiting to develop the capacity to issue A shares and most firms are allowed to issue A shares. In addition, the relative scarcity of reliable financial information has been considered a major contributor to the speculative nature of the market for A shares. Chow et al. (1995) offer additional insights on the role of various cultural factors in influencing the development of accounting in China (see also Hall and Hall (1987) for assessment of some broad differences in culture).

Types of Information Environments

The Relatively More Formal Environment

B shares are denominated in US dollars and are sold only to foreign investors, cannot be owned by citizens and their registration requires that financial statements be prepared according to IASs. Although the IASC has representatives from over 140 countries, it is a voluntary standard-setting body having only a professional advisory capacity and no enforcement mechanism. To accommodate a variety of cultures the IAS are less stringent and leave more for judgment than the corresponding professional standards in the United States of America (USA) or in the United Kingdom (UK). While IASs constitute the lower bound for the set of accounting principles about which there could be general acceptance across nations, they are well developed by comparison to most domestic accounting standards in countries with emerging capital markets.

Beyond the comprehensiveness of the standards, there are also qualitative differences between applying either USA or UK accounting standards and IASs. In spite of those differences, the London Stock Exchange allows foreign registrants to use IASs in their filings. To this date, no evidence exists of major financial problems arising from granting this privilege to foreign-based companies, suggesting that IAS standards have met a threshold of credibility that satisfies the rigorous demands of a field test.

The information environment for Type B shares includes disclosure of financial statements in the documentation of the initial public offering and semi-annually for the related fiscal periods. In addition, the investment funds that own B shares represent sophisticated foreign investors who monitor the issuing firms' activities and decisions. Since Chinese citizens are not allowed to own or trade B shares, these shares are relatively insulated from trade manipulation by insiders or state officials.

To summarize, the main features of the information environment of B shares are as follows:

1. financial reporting must follow IASs;
2. these standards require a level of documentation and system quality that ensures the credibility of aggregated numbers;
3. financial statements are audited by internationally recognized audit firms to assure compliance with IASs;
4. almost all B shares are owned by institutional investors; because of the need to continue the inflow of foreign investments, state officials are likely to avoid burdening the B share firms with domestic problems;
5. in the final analysis, investors, auditors and state officials perform different functions in monitoring the activities and performance of B share firms.

From these features, as well as the earlier statements by the Hong Kong-based Arthur Andersen, we conclude that the information environment of firms issuing B shares is relatively formalized and is not too dissimilar to other information environments in more developed capital markets.

The Relatively More Informal Environment

In contrast with B shares, the information environment for A shares (available only for domestic investors) is much less formalized in terms of both reporting requirements and external monitoring. Osland (1990, p. 7) claims that "because of the extensive networks of relationships with significant interaction between people, communications among Chinese customers for a given product may be diffused very quickly. Word-of-mouth publicity takes on greater importance in China than in most Western nations."

This informality has become more apparent in connection with the procedures of making initial public offering of A shares. The informal communication networks of family and friends in the processing and execution of the initial public offerings of A shares was almost invited by the institutional arrangements that prevailed in the first few years of market operations. Until 1994, to offer new A shares to the public, the government had a complex system requiring prospective investors to purchase certificates of entitlement (CE, hereafter) that would entitle them to buy shares. The privatization agency's role in the initial offering was to announce (1) the type of enterprise being privatized, (2) the location and date of the sale of these CEs to the public, and (3) the location and times allowed for exchanging CEs for actual shares. Typically, the announcements appeared in newspapers, which were posted in visible places for the public to read and to spread the word through their informal networks. Because of the huge demand and the cumbersome process, the locations used to issue CEs were typically large public arenas such as football fields. Until the end of 1993, to acquire one A share, a person had to present 10 consecutively numbered CEs. Yet, each person was allowed to purchase only a limited number of CEs per identification card (ID). This arrangement created a market for relatives, friends and others to pool their IDs and to strategically position the holders of their ID pools in waiting lines to maximize the number of 10 serially-numbered bundles of CEs. College students, including the one who helped with an early draft of this paper, found temporary jobs standing in lines for CEs, sometimes for as long as 3 days, which created serious problems.

> Lining up for three days in front of the Shenzhen Stock Exchange to buy overpriced share-application forms (certificates of entitlement) on 9–11 August (1992) was bad enough for the 1 million people from throughout China who had flocked to the SEZ [Schenzhen Exchange] for the occasion. But when it became clear that **insiders** had taken the forms, their patience ran out. In the rampage among themselves and with police that followed, more than 200 people were hospitalized. (Clifford, 1992, p. 53).

From the account of Chun Wang (a PhD student in agronomy who was once hired to pool IDs of different individuals), the CEs for a privatized auto company were dispensed at a football stadium in order to accommodate the large crowd that showed up to subscribe, with individuals holding onto each other to keep their places in line and to keep their pools of IDs together. Because of the allegations that insiders, party members and favored officials scooped a larger percentage of the initial public offering prior to making it available to others, the government has taken steps to reduce the ratio of required CEs for purchasing shares as well as some other controls, which were not specified in reporting to the public.

In this type of information environment, even if the accounting system is well developed, accounting disclosures would not be expected to be informative to the public because state officials actions could impound that information in prices prior to its release. This environment coupled with growth of unsupported rumors has led the government in December 1996 to threaten taking action against speculators. Some of that speculation was attributed to information leakage through insider trading and personal contacts.

Implications of the Two Different Environments

The most tangible outcome of the differences between the two information environments is the difference in the prices of A and B shares for the same firm as well as the varying degrees of their price volatility. As one observer reports: "The Chinese markets are quite volatile because trading volume is low and because they are dominated by individual speculators often operating without access to the most basic corporate reports or financial statements" (Hansell, 1994). In 1995, the average price of shares traded on the

SSE ranged from a high of US$13.742 to a low of US$6.055 and the turnover rate for that year was 483.6%. For B shares, the average price fluctuation ranged between a high of US$0.482 and a low of US$0.267 and the turnover rate was 58.2% (Shanghai Securities News, January 7, 1996, p. 7).

Relative to A shares, the market for B shares on SSE is small because the high transaction cost of trading in the latter is affordable mainly by institutional investors who tend to hold most of B shares. The total volume of B shares issued over the period from 1992 to 1995 was estimated to be US$1.5 billion. At the end of 1995, the B shares traded on the SSE accounted for 3.64% of total market capitalization. Over the period from 1992 to 1995, the B shares trading ranged from 4.6% to 1.5% of the total volume on SSE. These shares are thinly traded because investors in B shares hold stocks for reasons other than making short-term gains. Thinness of trade deprives analysts from constructing trading profiles that could help in explaining the reasons for pricing A Shares at about one-third to one-fifth of the price of B shares.

As with other developing capital markets, the need to draw capital funds from abroad provided incentive to enhance the markets' international reputation and public image. Preparing financial statements of firms issuing B shares in accordance with IASs is one devise to show that the reported statements are less influenced by state-mandated actions in accounting and auditing or by other bureaucratic management discretion. Consequently, these financial statements can be viewed as providing a relatively more accurate description of the activities of the firms upon which they report. Increasing confidence in the publicly disclosed information about the 70 privatized companies (36 listed on SSE and 34 listed on SEZ) that issued B shares could only increase the likelihood that accounting numbers are utilized by external investors in share pricing. In contrast, firms that did not improve their information structure to the level of adopting IASs, either because of reluctance to incur high cost of conversion to IASs or other reasons, are forbidden from seeking foreign capital. We consider the differences in the information environment noted in the preceding as one of the reasons underlying this segmentation of capital markets. Furthermore, the accounting environment described in Zhang (1996) and Xiang (1998) and summarized above suggests that the relevance, objectivity and consistency of applying domestic accounting standards are of a much lower threshold than what is required by IAS.

These implications lead to the following two hypotheses:

H_1: Changes in stock prices for the firms issuing B shares are associated with the disclosure of accounting earnings based on IASs.

H_2: Disclosure of accounting earnings based on domestic accounting procedures has no observable effect on share prices for firms issuing only A shares.

Preliminary Empirical Analysis

Data on PRC firms have not found their way out of the country in a manner that would facilitate their accessibility to researchers. Even for firms issuing B shares, the data seem to be the province of a few large sophisticated (institutional) traders. In recent years, a Taiwanese consulting firm began collecting published financial information

Table 1. Number of Firms Disclosing Public Information Compared to Total Listing

Stock exchange types of shares	*Shanghai* A	*Shanghai* B	*Shenzhan* A	*Shenzhan* B
1993 (not used for analysis)				
Total traded	164	28	103	22
# disclosing	26	4	22	2
1994				
Total traded	164	28	103	22
# disclosing	109	13	45	8
1995				
Total traded	184	36	127	34
# disclosing	170	33	120	23

Notes: Type A Shares are sold to local investors only.
Type B Shares are sold to foreign investors only.

(sales and earnings), security prices, and trading volume (in addition to macro data) from PRC publications and all available financial press reports. Using this information and other macro-type data, the consulting firm compiled a data bank for sale to interested investors and businesses. The partners of the consulting firm have granted the National Chengchi University (Taiwan) the right to use the data bank for research purposes only, including this project.

Table 1 shows the number of firms disclosing financial information for the period 1993–1995. The year 1993 has poor data; public information can be found for less than 25% of listed A shares and only for 2% of listed B shares because most were privately placed directly with institutions. For this reason, 1993 is not part of the empirical analysis that follows. By 1995, the listing of both types of shares has almost doubled. For the SSE, 170 of 184 listed companies publicly disclosed performance information; of those companies, 33 also issued B shares. For Shenzhen, 120 of 127 listed companies have publicly disclosed financial performance information in 1995. Of those companies, 23 had issued B shares. Due to data limitations, the empirical analysis that follows is carried out for 1994 and 1995 only.

Characteristics of Trade

Table 2 presents summary information about trading on both the Shanghai and Shenzhen stock exchanges. Panel A shows total volume of trade per year for the period 1993–1995. The highest volume during the period under study was in 1994 when total trade amounted to 812 billion yuans. Less than 2% of the traded volume was due to trading in B shares, which is consistent with the view that foreign institutions invest in B shares for the long-term more so than for profiting from the market's short-term volatility. As a reflection of the speculative era of 1994, the volume of trade in 1995 was only 50% of that in 1994 in spite of the fact that additional firms were added to the listing on both exchanges.

Faced with limited opportunities to diversify their investments, domestic investors rushed to invest in the newly privatized firms, which spurred heavy demand for A shares,

Table 2. Statistics Related to Volume and Prices

Panel A: Trading Volumes for Both the SSE and SEZ (Turnover Volume of A–B Share Markets in China [Billion Yuan])

	1992	*1993*	*1994*	*1995*
Total volume	68.124	366.703	812.763	411.374
A share volume	65.016	356.237	800.308	403.585
B share volume	3.108	10.466	12.455	7.789

Panel B: Comparison of A and B Share Prices for Some Major Companies (Selected Closing Prices of A and B Shares in the SSE on September 2, 1996)

	B share price			
Share company	*In US$*	*In Yuan*	*A share price in Yuan*	*Price ratio of A to B*
Shanghai Vacuum	0.140	1.162	4.38	3.77
Shanghai No. 2 Textile Machine	0.106	0.879	3.85	4.37
Shanghai Alkai Chemical	0.224	1.859	8.35	4.48
Shanghai Heqiao	0.378	3.137	13.85	4.32
Shanghai Outer Gaoqiao	0.380	3.154	17.38	5.51
Shanghai Lujiashui	0.930	7.719	34.70	4.49

Sources: Zhuoji (1996), Investment Value of B Shares in China, *Lianhe Zaobao* (October 1996).

as can be discerned from Panel B of Table 2, which presents information about six major firms. Converted into yuans, an A share was traded at more than four times the trade value of a B share in the same company. While both A and B shares have inelastic supply, their demand functions differ significantly, and the artificial segmentation of funding sources appears to have given rise to price differentiation in the two different markets. Because of regulatory restraints, domestic investors have limited opportunities to diversify their investments. Domestic savings could not be used to invest in securities other than A shares and the ensuing competition for a limited stock of A shares has led to this price discrimination between the domestic and foreign markets.

Estimating the Market Model

Testing the two hypotheses stated earlier is based on an event-study research design. Given the above description of the information environment, we believed that applying more rigorous research designs could not be justified by the quality of the published financial data or the information system generating those data.

As a first step in generating unexpected returns, we estimated Sharpe's market model. Using all available security prices, daily and weekly rates of return were computed for each stock as in Equation (1):

$$r_{jt} = \log[(p_{jt} + d_{jt})/p_{jt-1}] \quad (1)$$

where p is for closing prices, d is for dividends, j is for the firm, and t is the relevant time period (day for daily and week for weekly). These returns were used to compute two

Table 3. Summary of Market Return Betas for 1994 and 1995

Stock market share type	*Shanghai*		*Shenzhen*	
	A	*B*	*A*	*B*
1994				
Firms in the sample	90	13	34	7
Mean daily return betas (standard deviation)	1.01 (0.24)	0.87 (0.46)	0.98 (0.15)	1.10 (0.53)
Mean weekly return betas (standard deviation)	1.07 (0.23)	0.80 (0.47)	1.07 (0.14)	0.91 (0.39)
1995				
Firms in the sample	166	32	117	21
Mean daily return betas (standard deviation)	1.02 (0.17)	1.04 (1.08)	1.07 (0.20)	0.96 (0.62)
Firms in the sample	166	21	116	15
Mean weekly return betas (standard deviation)	0.97 (0.25)	0.91 (0.43)	1.04 (0.24)	0.45 (0.42)

market indices: one is equally weighted and the other is value weighted using the capitalized values of outstanding shares as weights. A market index, r_{mt}, was computed separately for A and B shares and for each stock exchange. Rates of returns of all traded shares, including those for which we have prices but do not have the financial reporting information, were used in computing the related market index. Because of the large difference in the price relatives of A and B shares (see Table 1), a different market index was deemed necessary for each type.

Market rates of return were used in various regressions to estimate a market model for each share type on each exchange. For the daily returns, the market model was estimated using 60 days prior to the earnings announcements (from −71 to −10). The corresponding estimation period for the weekly model was −20 to −3. The estimated models took the form of Equation (2):

$$r_{jt} = \alpha_j + \beta_j r_{mt} + e_{jt} \tag{2}$$

where α_j is the intercept term and β is the estimated systematic risk, e is an error term with expectations zero and a variance s_e^2.

The market model could not be estimated for all disclosing firms due to missing observations. (After extensive search, it appeared that data were missing either because they were not reported or were not archived.) Table 3 includes the various samples of firms disclosing accounting information and those included in the analysis. The analysis is reported for 1994 and 1995 only since available information for 1993 yielded too small a sample to be useful for estimation.

For all models, β estimates are very small and are not statistically significant; this is generally true whether we use equal- or value-weighted rates of return for market indices. By construction, average β estimates are expected to approach unity. The number of firms used to construct market return indexes includes all of the listed firms for which price data can be collected, but the empirical analysis is done for the disclosing firms only. For the 1994 data, average β values ranged from 0.80 to 1.09. However, the distribution of β values for that year suggests a much wider dispersion for B shares than for A shares. The standard deviation of the distribution of estimated β for B shares is at least twice as much as that of A shares. A similar pattern is observed

Table 4. Beaver's *U* for Equally Weighted Index (1994 Return Data)

	Shanghai				*Shenzhen*			
	A - Shares		*B - Shares*		*A - Shares*		*B - Shares*	
Day with respect to announcement	*Mean*	*(t)*	*Mean*	*(t)*	*Mean*	*(t)*	*Mean*	*(t)*
−5	2.58	(2.46)[a]	1.04	(0.06)	1.36	(0.87)	0.67	(−0.66)
−4	1.71	(2.33)[a]	0.53	(−2.04)[b]	5.43	(1.12)	0.32	(−5.34)
−3	3.01	(2.44)[a]	1.23	(0.50)	1.49	(0.86)	0.76	−0.41
−2	1.96	(2.62)[a]	0.69	(−1.0)	1.56	(1.45)	0.70	(−0.91)
−1	2.51	(2.34)[a]	0.57	(−1.49)	1.17	(0.42)	0.57	(−1.58)
0	2.31	(2.09)[b]	0.26	(−6.20)[a]	5.8	(1.50)	0.96	(−0.13)
1	1.95	(2.77)[a]	0.56	(−1.80)[b]	4.34	(2.29)[a]	3.72	(0.82)
2	1.46	(1.88)[b]	2.75	(0.99)	2.19	(1.45)	0.20	(−9.80)[a]
3	3.06	(1.97)[b]	0.41	(−3.78)	1.65	(1.64)	0.89	(0.30)
4	2.39	(1.23)	1.38	(0.70)	6.0	(1.01)	3.43	(1.81)
5	1.30	(1.41)	0.93	(−0.21)	3.77	(1.11)	2.42	(1.00)
6	2.30	(2.20)[a]	1.37	(−0.91)	5.12	(1.01)	4.27	(1.75)
7	1.87	(2.01)[b]	0.93	(−0.93)	1.68	(1.72)	3.90	(0.90)
8	1.32	(1.45)	1.92	(0.13)	1.21	(0.61)	1.42	(0.71)
9	1.48	(1.48)	0.54	(−1.83)	5.11	2.28	1.05	(0.14)

Notes: [a]Statistically significant below 0.01.
[b]Statistically significant below 0.05.

for 1995. This is obtained for both daily and weekly estimates. However, the low efficiency of these estimates is largely due to the thinness of trading B shares as indicated earlier.

Hypotheses Testing

To test the two hypotheses stated above, the estimated α and β were used to estimate unexpected rates of return. A window of 32 trading days (-10 to $+20$, where 0 is the date of disclosure) was used for daily analysis, and a window of 5 weeks [-2 to $+2$] was used for weekly analysis.

The hypotheses being tested are not directional since we did not have a way of unambiguously identifying good and bad news. Thus, we used Beaver's *U* as a test statistic that does not distinguish between positive and negative reactions but takes account of the variation attributable to good and bad news relative to prior information. For each firm and share type, *U* statistics were estimated as in Equation (3):

$$U_j = s_j^2(\text{it})/s_j^2(\text{e}) \tag{3}$$

where $s^2(\text{it})$ is the average sum-of-squared residuals during the *i*th day of test period (days -10 to $+20$), $s^2(\text{e})$ is the average sum of the squared residuals during the estimation period, and *j* is for the *j*th stock.

In the absence of changes in the underlying return-generating process, the expected value of *U* would be unity. A large deviation of *U* values from unity implies a structural change consistent with the existence of an earnings announcement effect. A

Table 5. Beaver's *U* for Equally Weighted Index for 1995

	Shanghai				*Shenzhen*			
	A - Shares		*B - Shares*		*A - Shares*		*B - Shares*	
Day with respect to announcement	*Mean*	*(t)*	*Mean*	*(t)*	*Mean*	*(t)*	*Mean*	*(t)*
−5	1.26	(1.25)	0.60	(−4.01)[a]	2.42	(1.19)	1.01	(0.007)
−4	1.66	(1.39)	0.58	(−3.51)[a]	1.52	(0.88)	0.14	(−11.37)[a]
−3	1.15	(1.00)	0.85	(−0.80)	0.64	(−0.82)	0.54	(−1.07)
−2	1.22	(1.15)	0.54	(−4.20)[a]	1.27	(0.71)	0.52	(−0.95)
−1	1.49	(1.89)[b]	1.36	(0.83)	6.90	(1.24)	0.04	(−60.89)[a]
0	2.29	(2.93)[a]	2.26	(1.46)	25.11	(3.44)[a]	3.52	(0.72)
+1	2.34	(4.20)[a]	3.57	(1.71)[b]	7.20	(2.40)[a]	1.31	(0.30)
+2	2.86	(1.44)	5.51	(2.16)[a]	1.38	(1.00)	0.14	(−14.02)[a]
+3	1.45	(1.68)[b]	4.55	(1.69)[b]	1.13	(0.48)	2.05	(0.78)
+4	0.91	(−0.76)	9.27	(1.50)	2.88	(0.84)	0.46	(−2.04)[a]
+5	1.19	(1.04)	3.06	(1.87)[b]	0.74	(−0.30)	3.86	(0.84)
+6	0.29	(−0.59)	2.01	(1.18)	2.89	(1.34)	4.20	(1.15)
+7	0.98	(−0.09)	1.53	(0.73)	1.75	(1.19)	0.54	(−1.00)
+8	0.96	(−0.20)	0.38	(−6.04)[a]	0.64	(−1.46)	3.31	(0.80)
+9	0.91	(−0.55)	1.27	(0.81)	1.51	(0.94)	0.48	(−1.56)
Sample size	168	–	32	–	120		23	

Notes: [a]Statistically significant below 0.01.
[b]Statistically significant below 0.05.

significantly smaller *U* also implies a change in structure but one that might be attributed to lack of trading activity in the announcement period. Four portfolios were formed for each day of 1994 and 1995 in the test period. As shown in Table 4, these are: (1) Shanghai A shares; (2) Shanghai B shares; (3) Shenzhen A shares; and (4) Shenzhen B shares.

For each portfolio, the average values of the estimated *U*, denoted $\mu U(\mathrm{A})$, and $\mu U(\mathrm{B})$ for A and B shares, respectively, were tested against unity. The two hypotheses offered earlier can then be restated in operational terms as follows:

H$_1$: $\mu U(\mathrm{B}) > 1$

H$_2$: $\mu U(\mathrm{A}) = 1$

Tables 4 and 5 report the test results for unexpected daily returns for 1994 and 1995, respectively. For the first hypothesis concerning B shares, $\mu U(\mathrm{B})$ is generally below its expected value of unity for the shares traded on SSE. $\mu U(\mathrm{B})$ is significantly less than 1 for 1994 for trading days −4, 0 and +1. As to B shares traded on SEZ, $\mu U(\mathrm{B})$ is significantly less than unity for day +2. For 1995, also significantly negative average $\mu U(\mathrm{B})$ values are observed for stock trades on SSE for days −5, −4, and −2, and for shares traded on SEZ for days −4, −1, +2, and +4. The only results that appear consistent with the expectations presented in the first hypothesis are observed for B shares that were traded on SSE for post-earnings announcement. However, post-disclosure, positive $\mu U(\mathrm{B})$ values are obtained for B shares on the SSE in 1995 with days +1 and +5 are significant at 0.10, and day +2 significant at 0.01. This positive pattern did not extend to trades on SEZ and

Table 6. Beaver's *U* for Weekly Unexpected Rates of Return (for 1995)

	A - Shares		*B - Shares*	
	Mean	*Probability*	*Mean*	*Probability*
Panel A: Shanghai stock exchanges				
−2 weeks	1.32	0.89	1.07	0.15
−1 week	0.94	0.31	1.48	0.86
0: disclosure week	2.69	0.65	0.78	0.37
+ 1 week	1.05	0.12	1.48	0.167
+ 2 weeks	1.88	0.76	3.66	0.33
Panel B: Shenzhen stock exchanges				
−2 weeks	0.98	0.008	3.77	0.26
−1 week	0.57	0.95	1.74	0.28
0: disclosure week	0.87	0.002	2.11	0.35
+ 1	1.56	0.42	1.29	0.24
+ 2	0.99	0.015	1.04	0.64

they are not consistent enough to reverse the conclusion that the findings for 1994 and 1995 are inconsistent with H_1. Furthermore, the obtained finding of positive daily abnormal returns did not extend to analysis of weekly data as reported in Table 6. As shown in the weekly analysis, none of the average values of $\mu U(B)$ on either exchange is significantly different from unity. In general, these results are inconsistent with H_1.

In summary, for both exchanges (SSE and SEZ), the evidence does not support the hypothesis that accounting numbers in the relatively better information quality environment (the environment of B shares) are correlated with changes in share prices.

As to the second hypothesis concerning A shares, we find mean values of $U(A)$ to be significantly higher than unity using daily unexpected returns for both SSE and SEZ and for 1994 and 1995. For the shares traded on SSE, $\mu U(A)$ is significantly higher than one in every day of the period -5 through $+3$ for 1994, and for the period -1 to $+1$ for 1995. The results for SEZ show significant positive values $\mu U(A)$ on the day $+1$ for 1994, and on trading days 0 and $+1$ for 1995. In contrast with 1994, no significant negative values of $\mu U(A)$ are obtained for 1995.

The results of analyzing daily trades in A shares do not hold up when weekly returns are examined. For 1995, Table 6 shows significantly positive $\mu U(A)_w$ for weeks 0 and $+2$ for shares traded on SSE. However, the daily results are opposite of the expected findings for the information environment of A shares and suggest rejecting hypothesis H_2.

Interpretation of Results

The results reported in Tables 4 and 5 do not support either hypothesis. It is counterintuitive to suggest that accounting disclosures have information content in setting security prices for the low quality information environment (of A shares), but not for the high quality information environment (B shares). It is tempting, however, to celebrate and jump to the conclusion that accounting earnings are value relevant in pricing A shares.

Given the previous discussion of the differing information environments, four possible explanation for these findings are suggested:

1. Insider trading in A shares.
2. Thinness of trade in B shares.
3. The high volatility of trading prices.
4. Effects of other information channels.

Insider Trading

Without the necessary ingredients for market efficiency and allowing equal access to information prior to using it in trading, it is not defensible to conclude that the statistical results obtained for A shares are consistent with market efficiency. These results are consistent with several possible reasons because information is reflected in security prices when any trader, including insiders, acts on it. Given the information environment described earlier and the cases reported in Zhang (1996), a scenario can be advanced that insider trading and manipulation of trade by officials might be responsible for impounding accounting information in share prices prior to making public disclosure. Another scenario is that the obtained results are a statistical artifact because (a) the findings about A shares are not consistent across the two stock exchanges (SSE and SEZ), and (b) the obtained results for daily returns are not confirmed by the results of the less noisy weekly returns. Since these explanations cannot be ruled out given this analysis, we are unwilling to conclude that some of the observed findings reflect the reaction to accounting numbers.

Thinness of Trade

The data reported in Table 1 reveal that about 50% to 60% of all listed firms in 1994 disclosed accounting reports to the public, with this percentage increasing to over 90% in 1995, suggesting an improved reporting system. The annual volume of trade (in yuan) for both A and B shares is reported in Table 2. We also know from earlier citation (Shanghai Securities News, SSE, January 7, 1996) that total capitalization of A shares at that time was about 20 times that of B shares. At average currency conversion rates of 1995, this volume amounts to about US$40 billion in 1994 as compared to US$2 billion in December 1995. These two tables present conflicting signals, however, the trading volume presented in Table 2 shows the ratio of A shares to B shares during 1995 to be about 52% and the corresponding ratio in 1994 to be about 65%. Thus, while the number of listed firms has increased in 1995 over 1994, A shares were traded much more heavily in 1995 as compared to 1994. In addition, the SSE publication reports significant variation in turnover rates of A and B shares:

	Turnover Ratios	
	Type A	Type B
1994	20	6
1995	10	3.5

These ratios reveal the extent to which B shares are thinly traded as compared to A shares. As a result, analysis of the association between unexpected returns and accounting information is not likely to reveal the true information linkage — investors in B shares do not trade for short-term gains.

Analysis of Volatility

A further analysis of thinness of trade and relative market volatility of B shares is examined using relative volume movements. Using volume data, an equally weighted index of changes in the volume of trades, $\mathrm{v_{mt}}$, was constructed for each market using all listed shares in a manner analogous to constructing the market return portfolios. And, as in Beaver (1968) and Bamber (1987), a linear function of the following form (Equation [4]) was estimated for each firm in each market:

$$\mathrm{v}_{jt} = a_j + b_j \mathrm{v}_{\mathrm{mt}} + u_{jt} \tag{4}$$

where v_{jt} is the volume of trade for firm j during the trading period t, which is a day for the daily analysis and a week for the weekly analysis, a_j is an intercept term, b_j is the slope coefficient reflecting the covariation of the trading volume of the firm and market, $\mathrm{v_{mt}}$ is the index of market volume, and u is an error term. This model was estimated for daily and weekly volumes of trade for each share type and each exchange.

Table 7 provides some indication of the pattern of the estimated b coefficients for the firms that disclosed earnings. Using b estimates to denote relative volume volatility, it appears that the volume of trade for the firms disclosing financial information is less volatile than the volume for the market as a whole. Averages of b coefficients are consistently below unity for 1994 and 1995. (The data for the 1993 volume of trade is reported here for comparison only.) The estimated b coefficients show a widely dispersed distribution showing high standard deviations, sometimes as large as the mean (e.g., Table 7, Shanghai Exchange in 1994).

Efficiency and Sources of Market Friction

A likely explanation of the results relates to the operation of capital markets — can we take informational efficiency as a maintained hypothesis? As indicated earlier, unless markets are taken to be informationally efficient, the unexpected variation in market return reflects the joint effect of two hypotheses: market efficiency and information content. Testing for the information content of accounting numbers, or any other news, is contingent on satisfying market efficiency. As indicated earlier in this paper, emerging capital markets are not known to be efficient because of the numerous institutional frictions imposed by regulatory processes and unequal access to information. Some of the institutional features that characterize the PRC's stock exchanges are relevant to this issue.

First, the government remains the majority shareholder, and a sizable percentage of the privatized portions of A shares are owned by state officials, party members and other insiders. Because laws restricting insider trading are not known to be

Table 7. Relative Market Volume Volatility

Stock market share type	*Shanghai*		*Shenzhen*	
	A	*B*	*A*	*B*
1994				
For daily				
Number of firms used	90	14	34	7
Mean daily betas	0.54	0.59	0.75	0.93
(standard deviation)	(0.57)	(0.61)	(0.40)	(0.48)
For weekly				
Number of firms used	64	11	17	7
Mean volume betas	0.84	0.21	0.70	0.73
(standard deviation)	(0.78)	(0.07)	(0.35)	(0.56)
1995				
For daily				
Number of firms used	170	33	120	23
Mean daily betas	1.08	0.90	1.36	0.84
(standard deviation)	(1.254)	(0.654)	(1.74)	(1.85)
For weekly				
Number of firms used	170	33	120	23
Mean weekly betas	0.98	0.74	1.16	1.05
(standard deviation)	(0.402)	(0.74)	(0.88)	(0.44)

enforced, it is very likely that insiders act on the information prior to its public release and, as a result, the information content of disclosure would have been impounded in prices prior to the public release of annual reports. Second, given that PRC is at the "take off" stage of economic development and growth, which averaged more than 8% a year since 1979 except for 1990 (Fairlamb, 1993, p. 35), financial statements and short-term earnings may not be good indicators or predictors of future performance. The question that appears to be problematic is how to channel the huge pool of local savings that remain liquid into capital markets while keeping the markets orderly and avoiding severe volatility. In 1992, for example, these local savings were estimated at yuan 60 billion in the city of Shanghai alone (Kaye, 1992, p. 50).

Third, the history of trading shares to absentee investors in a public forum and of disclosing information about business firms' performance has been too brief to develop association measures and rules-of-thumb connecting reported numbers and subsequent events.

Fourth, the size of pent-up demand for products in PRC is such that the products of any firm will sell, and given the relative increase in the freedom to set prices, there are expectations of a continued long-term profitability irrespective of short-term profit volatility.

Finally, the novelty of the information and the extent to which pre-disclosure of accounting earnings are issues that need more research and validation.

Summary

In this paper we address the relevance of the information environment in understanding and interpreting published data about share pricing in the People's Republic of China. Two major stock exchanges opened in Shanghai and Shenzhen in 1990 to trade two types of stocks: A and B shares. The former is to be owned and traded only by citizens, while the latter is to be traded and owned only by foreign investors. Privatization of business in PRC has been growing but the state remains the majority owner; it is estimated that only about 20% of shares in privatized firms are held by private investors.

Although both types are traded on the same exchange, an A-type share is priced at three to four times the price of a B-type share. Because of the institutional arrangements, both types of shares face different demand preferences for investment and liquidity. While this aspect might explain the unusual difference in the prices of A and B shares, we attempt in this paper to examine the varying information environment that appear to characterize the markets for A and B share types. With respect to the A-type shares, several issues are of particular interest: (1) the process of making initial public offering, (2) the role of state officials in share ownership and management of the newly privatized firms, and (3) the structure of the accounting and auditing profession in PRC. While the official requirement is to have financial statements audited, most of the CPAs in PRC are trained under the state-owned and operated system and most of the CPA firms are owned by the government. Accounting standards are issued by a quasi-independent body that is under the jurisdiction of the Ministry of Finance. Few of those standards exist and their implementation is often delayed. Financial statements are issued at most twice a year and are published in the newspapers for public dissemination. In addition, cultural acceptance of independent audits is in its early stage of development.

In contrast, the information environment that characterize B-type shares is distinct by (1) requiring that financial statements be prepared according to IASs, (2) having CPAs who are qualified internationally to audit and offer audit opinions on financial statements, (3) foreign investors, consisting mainly of financial institutions, act as added external monitoring agents, and (4) state officials have little (if any) role to play in stock trading of B shares.

Because of these differences, we posited that A and B share prices react differently to accounting information. The varying elements of the environment discussed for A-type shares led us to hypothesize that accounting numbers are soft description of the underlying economics and would not be associated with security prices as these prices are determined by many other institutional and trade factors. A similar reasoning led us to hypothesize an association between accounting numbers and B-type share prices.

A preliminary analysis of trades on both exchanges in 1994 and 1995 led us to reject both hypotheses. While the evidence could be construed differently by different readers, we would like to point out that the results of daily and weekly return data lead to inconsistent inferences. In particular,

	In Table 5	In Table 6
Hypothesis 1	consistent	inconsistent
Hypothesis 2	inconsistent	consistent

This contradictory pattern led us to question the data quality and the factors that drive price changes. In attempting to explain this pattern, we speculated on the thinness of trading of B-type shares, the role of state officials, the role of insider trading and speculators, and the slow development of accounting and auditing. However, much more work is needed to further our understanding of these issues.

This conclusion is inconsistent with the findings reported by Haw et al. (1998). They find that the Chinese GAAP is more associated with returns than the information reported under the IASs. They even express surprise at their findings, which could fall in the class of anomalies, but they offer those results as exploratory without sufficiently detailed explanation.

Acknowledgments: We appreciate the encouragement of Chee Chow and would like to thank Chun Wang (a participant in a PRC public offering), Pierre Liang, and participants at Workshops at National University of Singapore, Wilfred Lurier University (Canada), the 1997 Asia–Pacific Conference in Korea, and IAAER/CIERA 1998 conference in Chicago.

REFERENCES

Ball, Ray and P. Brown. 1968. "An Empirical Evaluation of Accounting Income Number." *Journal of Accounting Research*, (Fall) 159–178.

Bamber, Linda S. 1987. "Unexpected Earnings, Firm Size and Trading Volume Around Quarterly Earnings Announcements." *The Accounting Review, 62* (July): 510–532.

Beaver, William H. 1968. "The Information Content of Annual Earnings Announcements." *Journal of Accounting Research*, (Supplement) 67–92.

Beaver, William H. 1998. *Financial Reporting: An Accounting Revolution*. NY: Prentice-Hall.

Bernard, Victor L. 1990. "Capital Markets Research in Accounting During the 1980s: A Critical Review." In: Frecka, T. J. ed. *The State of Accounting Research as We Enter the 1990s*. Urbana-Champaign, IL: The University of Illinois, Department of Accountancy, pp. 72–120.

Chow, L., G. Chau, and S. Gray. 1995. "Accounting Reforms in China: Cultural Constraints on Implementation and Development." *Accounting and Business Research, 26*(1): 29–49.

Clifford, Mark. 1992. "After Shenzhen Chaos: China Mulls Better Ways to Allocate Shares." *Far Eastern Economic Review*, (27 August): 53.

Fairlamb, David. 1993. "Surging, Churning China." *Institutional Investor*, (January): 33–44.

Fang, Zhilong and Yunwei Tang. 1991. "Recent Accounting Developments in China: An Increasing Internationalization." *The International Journal of Accounting*, (January): 87–103.

Hall, E. T. and M. R. Hall. 1987. *Hidden Differences*. New York: Anchor Press.

Hansell, Saul. 1994. "Chinese Stock Markets Bounce Back Rising 30%." *The New York Times*, (August 2).

Haw, In-Mu, Daqing Qi, and Woody Wu. 1998. Value-relevance of Financial Reporting Disclosures in an Emerging Capital Market: The Case of B-shares in China. Working paper. The Chinese University of Hong Kong.

Kaye, Lincoln. 1992. "Waiting for Godot." *Far Eastern Economic Review*, (16 July): 50–52.

Osland, Gregory E. 1990. "Doing Business in China: A Framework for Cross-cultural Understanding." *Marketing Intelligence and Planning*, 4–14.

Qing, He Mao, Jin Xiu Zhang, and Tao Yang Jian. 1998. The Accounting of China Towards the 21st Century (abstracts). A working paper (Wuhan, China) presented at the IAAER/CIERA International Accounting Conference, Chicago, IL, October 2–3.

Sender, Henney. 1992a. "Pin-striped Pioneers." *Far Eastern Economic Review*, (12 November): 59–60.

Sender, Henney. 1992b. "How Not to Profit: Investors Count the Pitfalls of China's B Shares." *Far Eastern Economic Review*, (10 December): 55–56.

Shanghai Securities News. Shanghai Stock Exchange, various issues.

Xiang, Bing. 1998. "Institutional Factors Influencing China's Accounting Reform and Standards." *Accounting Horizon, 12,* (June): 105–119.

Zhang, W. G. 1996. Corporatization of State-owned Enterprises and Revaluation of Assets. Working Paper. Shanghai University of Finance and Economics. Presented at the Asia–Pacific International Accounting Conference held in Seoul, Korea in October 1996.

Zhuoji, Xiao. 1996. "Investment Value of B Shares in China." *Lianhe Zaobao,* (October).

[18]

Journal of International Financial Management and Accounting 10:2 1999

The Usefulness of Earnings and Book Value for Equity Valuation in Emerging Capital Markets: Evidence From Listed Companies in the People's Republic of China

*Ben-Hsien Bao**
The Hong Kong Polytechnic University

Lynne Chow
Lingnan College

Abstract

This paper examines the *relative* value relevance in equity valuation of two sets of accounting information of listed Chinese companies which issued the so-called B shares to foreign investors on the Chinese stock exchanges. These firms are required to prepare two sets of financial statements: one based on China's accounting regulations (domestic GAAPs) and the other based on International Accounting Standards (IASs). The study adopted the Ohlson (1995) model and used the Davidson-MacKinnon J-test to assess which one of these two competing sets of accounting information is more closely associated with the share prices. The results showed that earnings and book value reported based on IASs have greater information content than those based on domestic GAAPs. The results of yearly regression analysis generally suggested that the explanatory power of these earnings and book values for share prices increased over time.

1. Introduction

This paper investigates the relevance of accounting earnings and book value in equity valuation in emerging capital markets using the data of listed companies in the People's Republic of China (PRC). Our inquiry is motivated by the rapid development in China in its capital markets and accounting infrastructure, and by the dual financial reporting requirements for different segments of capital markets. Since the official opening of the stock exchanges in Shanghai and Shenzhen in 1990 and 1992 respectively, China's stock market, with a total market capitalization of over US$200 billion by December 1997, has become increasingly important for state-owned

* Correspondence concerning this paper should be sent to: Dr. Ben-Hsien Bao, Department of Accountancy, The Hong Kong Polytechnic University, Hung Hom, Kowloon, Hong Kong. We thank the anonymous reviewer and Professor Michael Firth for their helpful comments and suggestions. Financial support obtained from The Hong Kong Polytechnic University (Research Grant Account Nos. 353 124 A3 210, 353 121 A3 210, and A 21 56 PA14) is gratefully acknowledged. The usual disclaimer applies.

enterprises in raising capital (Zhang, 1998). To foster the smooth and efficient operations of its capital markets, the Chinese government initiated accounting reforms since the late 1980s in order to establish a comprehensive regulatory framework for financial reporting with the aim of enhancing the usefulness of accounting information for the users of financial statements.

Starting from 1992, the government began to select companies for selling shares to foreign investors on the two domestic stock exchanges to attract foreign capital. These shares are called "B" shares, traded in foreign currencies and distinguished from those shares issued to PRC citizens, called "A" shares. The "A" share and "B" share markets are rigidly segmented, although both shares have the same rights and obligations. Companies which issued "B" shares are required to prepare two sets of financial statements, one based on PRC accounting regulations and the other based on International Accounting Standards (IASs). This institutional framework provides a unique opportunity for researchers to examine the relative relevance of accounting information reported based on domestic GAAPs versus that reported based on IASs to equity valuation. This study examines the following two main issues: (1) which set of accounting summary measures, reported earnings and book value based on domestic accounting regulations or those based on IASs, are more closely associated with stock prices; and (2) whether the value-relevance of earnings and book value increased over time given the consistent efforts made by the Chinese government to enhance the quality of financial information disclosed by listed companies. To compare the relative information content of earnings and book values reported based on different accounting requirements, we conducted association tests between stock prices and the two sets of earnings and book values reported by the Chinese enterprises which issued "B" shares to foreign investors.

Using the Ohlson (1995) model, the study found that both earnings and book value based on domestic GAAPs are significantly associated with the "B" share prices, explaining jointly 21% of the variations of share prices. The reported earnings based on IASs are significantly related to stock prices; book value based on IASs is not significant at the conventional level (5%); and both jointly explain about 24% of the variations in share prices. The study adopted the Davidson-MacKinnon J-test to assess which one of these two competing sets of accounting information is more closely associated with the share prices. The results showed that the IAS reporting model has additional explanatory power beyond that contributed by the domestic reporting model. This indicates that earnings and book value based on IASs jointly have greater information content than those based on domestic GAAPs. The results of yearly regression using IASs as well as domestic GAAPs reported earnings and book value generally suggested that the explanatory power of earnings and book value for share prices increased over time.

In the next section, we discuss the institutional background of China's capital markets and the financial reporting framework. We then present the research design and the data collection method in section 3. The empirical results are discussed in session 4. In the last section, we conclude the study.

2. Capital Market and the Evolution of Financial Reporting Framework in China

2.1 Development of Capital Markets in China

The economic reforms implemented in China since 1978 have brought significant growth in GDP and in individual personal savings. The establishment of two stock exchanges aimed to channel individual savings to enterprises which desperately needed funds for productive business activities. Issuing shares by enterprises to individual investors also caused a change in the ownership structure whereby the government intended to separate management of enterprises from ownership with an aim to improve the performance of state-owned enterprises. In the 15th National Congress of the Communist Party of China held in September 1997, the government reaffirmed that a joint stock company is a form of capital organization of modern enterprises, which facilitates the separation of ownership from management and helps to increase the efficiency of business operations. The establishment of a modern enterprise system in the form of a joint stock company remains the most important means to reform state-owned enterprises in China.

Chinese listed companies initially issued shares to the citizens of PRC. These shares, generally called "A" shares, are classified into three categories: state shares, institutional shares and individual shares. State shares are issued to the governmental agencies representing the government fund invested in an enterprise; institutional shares are held by domestic legal entities which have associations with governmental organizations or agencies; and individual shares are held by public investors. The state shares are not tradable in the stock exchanges, and the institutional shares are traded among institutions through a nationwide computer system called Securities Trading Quotation System. Only individual shares are circulated and traded in the two domestic stock exchanges. According to

Chinese regulations, individual shares should represent no less than 25% of the total share capital of a company (NPC, 1993, Article 152).

Starting from 1992, selected companies were allowed to issue shares to non-domestic investors, including foreigners as well as residents of Hong Kong and Taiwan. These shares, generally called "B" shares, are traded in US dollars in the Shanghai Stock Exchange and in Hong Kong dollars in the Shenzhen Stock Exchange. Listed companies may issue both "A" and "B" shares or may issue either one type of shares only. As "A" shares and "B" shares of a company have the same voting and distribution rights, they should be in theory of the same value. However, due to the rigid segmentation of "A" and "B" share markets which prohibits inter-flow of capital, the prices of these two types of shares have been significantly different in practice, with "B" share prices being consistently much lower than those of "A" shares. Since 1992, to further assess to foreign capital, selected Chinese companies were allowed to issue and list shares, generally called "H" shares, on the Hong Kong Stock Exchange. A few were also listed in London, New York and Singapore stock exchanges. As of December 1997, there were 730 "A" shares and 101 "B" shares listed on the domestic stock exchanges and 39 shares listed on the Hong Kong Stock Exchange.

2.2 The Evolution of Financial Reporting Framework

As pointed out by Lee (1987), developing an effective accounting infrastructure is essential for the efficient operations of emerging capital markets. In China, the development of capital markets becomes a major force which triggers the accounting reforms in the late 1980s. These reforms aimed to develop a comprehensive accounting infrastructure which is adaptable to China's socialist market economy. As part of these reforms, in 1992 the Ministry of Finance issued the "Accounting Regulation for Experimental Joint Stock Enterprises". This regulation abolishes the Russian-style fund accounting system[1] which was traditionally used by Chinese state enterprises for over four decades. Instead, the financial reporting system widely used in the Western countries was adopted. This Regulation was revised in 1998 to further bring the accounting practices for listed Chinese companies in line with international practices.[2]

In the early 1990s, the government determined to adopt the Anglo-Saxon approach in regulating financial reporting and launched an ambitious project to develop Chinese accounting standards. In November 1992, the first accounting standard, entitled the Accounting Standard for Business

Enterprises, was promulgated by the Ministry of Finance and became applicable to all enterprises in China starting 1 July 1993. The Standard broadened the users of accounting information and stated explicitly that accounting information should meet not only the needs of the State in macro-economic management, but those of relevant parties in understanding the financial position and operating results of enterprises. Eight new accounting standards were further issued: Disclosure of Related Party Relationships and Transactions in 1997 and seven more accounting standards including Cash Flow Statements and Post-Balance Sheet Events in 1998. It is expected that eventually more than 20 exposure drafts of accounting standards developed earlier will be promulgated either in 1999 or afterwards.

For companies which listed shares on stock exchanges, accounting information disclosure is further governed by the Chinese Securities Regulatory Commission (CSRC), a government agency similar to the Securities and Exchanges Commission (SEC) in the United States. A number of regulations relating to accounting information disclosure issues were promulgated by the CSRC since 1993, specifying the content and format of prospectus, interim reports and annual reports (CSRC, 1993, 1995, 1996, 1997). According to these regulations, a company should prepare an annual report within 120 days after the end of an accounting year, which falls on December 31 of each calendar year. The financial statements in the annual report should be prepared in compliance with relevant accounting regulations and standards issued by the Ministry of Finance, and should be audited by Chinese certified public accountants who are qualified to engage in the auditing of joint stock companies. A company should publish its summarized annual report in a newspaper designated by the CSRC by the end of April of the next year. It should also place copies of the complete annual reports at the company's registered office and the stock exchange where shares are listed for investors' inspection (CSRC, 1993).

In addition, a company which issued "B" shares should also prepare financial reports in accordance with the International Accounting Standards (IASs) and disclose them in an overseas (including Hong Kong) newspaper on the same date when the annual report based on domestic accounting regulations are published in Chinese newspapers. Should significant differences exist between these two sets of financial reports, explanations should be provided (CSRC, 1995). Distribution of dividends should be determined by referring to the lower distributable profit reported in the two sets of financial statements.

Differences between the domestic financial reports and IAS-based financial reports arise mainly due to the following three reasons:

(1) Differences between PRC accounting regulations and IASs. An example is accounting for provision for doubtful debts. Chinese accounting regulations restrict the provision to a proportion of accounts receivable prescribed by the State, e.g., 3% of the outstanding accounts receivable for enterprises with foreign capital, 1% for enterprises engaged in agriculture, construction and real estate development, and 0.3–0.5% for enterprises in other industries. IASs do not impose such restrictions and managers use their judgement in making the provisions based on the evidence available about the likely outcome of debt collection. Bad debts have been a major concern for companies operated in China, and a significant portion of trade debtors is overdue. Therefore the provisions made based on IASs are normally much greater than those based on domestic accounting requirements.

For fixed asset depreciation, the Chinese regulations prescribe the straight-line method with residual value ranging from 3% to 5% of the cost of a fixed asset. An approval from tax bureaus is needed for adopting accelerated depreciation methods and the depreciation rate should not exceed 30%. According to IASs, depreciation for fixed assets should be provided on a systematic basis during the useful lives of the assets. Several depreciation methods are allowed, and estimated residual value and depreciation rates are determined by management.

For valuation of inventory, the Chinese accounting regulations require inventory to be reported at historical cost, while according to the IASs inventory is reported at the lower of cost and net realizable value. The adjustment to inventory valuation and the recognition of inventory losses are one of the major items in the reconciliation of reported profits under these two different accounting requirements.

(2) Differences arising because of specific government policy. An example is the implementation of a far-reaching policy by the government on 1 January 1994 to unify the official exchange rate of local currency, *Renminbi,* with the market rates. This effectively devalued the official rate of *Renminbi* to US dollars by about 50%. Substantial gains and

losses were reported by enterprises when translating their assets or liabilities denominated in foreign currencies using the new official rate. According to the accounting regulations corresponding to this government policy, these gains or losses should be amortized over five years, while under IASs such exchange gains or losses are credited or charged to current profits.

According to the government policy, enterprises are required to provide for staff welfare at 14% of total salaries paid, regardless of the actual expenditure incurred. This provision proved inadequate to cover staff fringe benefits, including medical expenditure due to increasing medical costs in China. According to IASs, such expenditure is charged as periodic expenses at the actual amount incurred.

(3) Differences in professional judgements by domestic auditors versus those by international auditors (Lee, 1997). These are mainly referred to the timing of revenue and expense recognition. Both Chinese regulations and IASs require that sales revenue should be recognized when the goods have been transferred and rights to collect the invoiced amount have been confirmed. However, discrepancies may exist between Chinese and overseas auditors in determining whether the ownership of goods has been transferred.

Consistent with IASs, Chinese accounting regulations require an enterprise to consolidate an affiliated company when it holds over 50% of the affiliate's share capital or when it has effective control over the affiliated company. Differences in professional judgements may arise between domestic and overseas auditors regarding the determination of "effective control".

Major differences between the Chinese domestic accounting regulations and IAS-based financial reports are summarized in Table 1. A number of differences between the two will be eliminated with the implementation of the 1998 revisions of accounting regulation for joint stock companies.

2.3 The Development of the Auditing Profession

In view of the demand for auditing services which emerged as a result of influx of foreign investments and development of joint stock companies, the Chinese government revived the certified public accountant system in

Table 1. *Major Differences between PRC-GAAP and IASs*

Items	*PRC requirement*	*IASs*
Provision for doubtful debts	Maximum ceiling imposed, for example, 3% of accounts receivable for companies with foreign capital, and 0.3–0.5% for industrial companies	No maximum requirement; determined based on management judgments
Inventory	Reported at historical cost; provision for inventory obsolescence not permitted unless an approval is obtained	Reported at the lower of cost or net realizable value
Short-term investment	Reported at historical cost	Reported at the lower of cost or market
Depreciation for fixed assets	Straight-line with residual value averaging from 3 to 5% of costs; accelerated depreciation at a rate of not more than 30% needs approval from tax bureaus	Several methods are allowed, estimated residual value and useful life determined by management
Construction of fixed assets	Depreciation commences after the completion certificate has been issued, normally much later than the actual completion of the fixed assets	Depreciation commences when the construction of an asset is completed and the asset is put into effective use
Borrowing cost	Interest on loan to finance the construction of a fixed asset is capitalized until the completion certificate has been issued	Capitalization of interest should cease when the asset is put into effective use
Revaluation of fixed assets	Normally not permitted	Revaluation is permitted
Long-term investment	Equity method is used if the holding is at least 25% of investee's capital	Equity method is used if holding is at least 20% of investee's capital
Intangible assets	Minimum amortization period is prescribed	Amortization period is determined by an estimate of the period over which benefits accrue
Foreign exchange gains and losses	Foreign exchange gains or losses arising on 1 January 1994 due to the unification of exchange rates is amortized over 5 years. Exchange losses during operating period should be amortized over 5 years, exchange gains can be amortized or can be carried to set off future operating losses	Exchange gains or losses should be credited or charged to current profit
Staff welfare	Provision at 14% of total salaries is required; in addition, a fixed percentage of after-tax profit is transfer to reserve for staff welfare fund	Actual expenditure is charged
Staff quarter	Losses on sale of staff quarters should be recorded to a "staff quarter turnover fund" account	Such losses should be recognized as period costs

1980 after a suspension of it for more than 30 years. A national accountancy professional organization, the Chinese Institute of Certified Public Accountants (CICPA), was established in 1987. In the early 1990s, the Chinese government took the decision to allow foreign accounting firms to operate in China in the form of joint ventures with local firms. The authorities hoped that exposures to international accounting firms would assist local accountants to upgrade their professional standards. By 1997, around 6,700 accounting firms were established, employing about 58,000 qualified accountants (Yan and Yang, 1998). Of these, only those firms designated by the CSRC are eligible for providing audit services to listed companies. The CICPA also endeavored to develop auditing standards which are comparable to international practices. Two batches of Independent Auditing Standards were issued in 1996 and 1997 respectively.

Public accounting firms in China have been sponsored by or attached to government administrative agencies. For example, a number of universities have established public accounting firms, and seconded their faculty members to work for these firms. The Ministry of Finance and finance bureaus in various provinces also have sponsored a number of accounting firms. Most businesses and clients of these CPA firms are referred by the sponsoring units. This institutional setting is detrimental to the perceived independence of the auditing profession. Although the Auditing Law of the PRC enacted in 1994 requires auditors to avoid conflicts of interest, there have been no further regulations or guidelines to assist auditors to integrate the concept of independence into their practices. To promote auditor's independence, the government initiated a reform since 1997 to re-structure the accounting firms by requiring these firms to detach themselves from their sponsoring organizations (Yan and Yang, 1998). These efforts aimed to strengthen the function of auditing services and to enhance the credibility of audited financial statements.

Companies, which issued "B" shares, may engage international accounting firms which meet the requirements of the state regulations for auditing the financial reports issued to foreign investors. To minimize the overlap of work, these international accounting firms worked closely with their Chinese counterparts which performed the statutory audit for the same company. Because of the collaboration between these Chinese and international accounting firms, it is thus generally perceived that the audited financial statements released by companies which issued both "A" and "B" shares have greater credibility than those released by "A" share companies which are audited by Chinese accounting firms only.

3. Research Design

3.1 Model Specification

The information content of reported earnings has been a major focus of accounting research since the late 1960s in Western countries (Ball and Brown, 1968; Beaver et al., 1979; Bowen, 1981; Daley, 1984; Lipe, 1986; Fairfield et al., 1996). These studies found positive associations between stock returns and reported earnings or components of earnings. The association between book value and equity valuation, however, did not attract much researchers' attention until Ohlson (1995) considered both earnings and book value as major determinants in equity valuation. His valuation model, derived based on the clean surplus accounting assumption, is a linear additive function of earnings and book value. Bernard (1993, 1995) empirically tested various valuation functions which used earnings and book value as determinants and found that, on average, book value explained 55% of the cross-sectional variance in stock prices.

Some recent studies, however, reported a steady decline in the value relevance of earnings over time (Ramesh and Thiagarajan, 1995; Lev, 1997). The studies by Ely and Waymire (1996) and Francis and Shipper (1997) concluded that that there is no consistent evidence that combined value-relevance of earnings and book values has declined over time. Collins et al. (1997) found that the combined relevance of earnings and book value have actually increased slightly over the past forty years. They showed that the value-relevance of "bottom line" earnings has declined over time, but the value-relevance of book value has increased over the same period.

Some studies examined the incremental and relative information content of foreign GAAP earnings versus earnings adjusted to US GAAPs by foreign companies with shares or American Depository Receipts (ADRs) traded in U.S. exchanges (Amir et al., 1993; Bandyopadhgay et al., 1994; Chan and Seow, 1996). These studies generally provided empirical evidence that earnings based on domestic GAAPs are value-relevant. However, the results of these studies provided mixed evidence on the value-relevance of aggregated earnings reconciliation from non-U.S. to U.S. GAAPs. Alford et al. (1993) studied the relative informativeness of accounting earnings for several non-U.S. countries and found that accounting earnings prepared in accordance with domestic GAAPs in some countries are more value-relevant than accounting earnings based on U.S.-GAAPs. They concluded that it is unlikely that one set of standards is optimal for all firms because the characteristics of investors differ across various capital markets.

For this study, we used data of the financial reports of listed Chinese companies which issued "B" shares, and examined the relative information content of reported earnings and book value based on PRC GAAPs versus earnings and book value adjusted to follow IASs. This is an issue of relative information content as discussed by Biddle et al. (1995). We adopted the Ohlson model framework (1995) and conducted association tests between "B" share prices and the two sets of earnings and book values reported by the same company. The following valuation model, consistent with that used by Collins et al. (1997), which stated that stock price is positively associated with both earnings and book value, is employed:

$$P_{jt} = Y_0 + Y_1 E_{jt} + Y_2 BV_{jt} + \theta_{jt}$$

Where:

P_{jt} : "B" share price of firm *j* four months after fiscal year end of year *t*, i.e., on 30 April in *year t*+1, translated into *Renminbi* using the exchange rate at that date

E_{jt} : earnings per share for firm *j* for year *t*

BV_{jt} : Book value per share for firm *j* at 31 December of year *t*

θ_{jt} : error term

We estimated cross-sectional regressions for a 5-year period spanning from 1992 to 1996. For the dependent variable, the stock prices for "B" shares at 30 April are used as all companies are required to disclose their annual reports by this date, and most companies disclose these in newspapers in April annually.

To examine the relative information content of earnings and book value reported based on domestic accounting regulations versus those based on IASs, we applied the Davidson-MacKinnon J-test. A similar approach was used by Chan and Seow (1996) in studying the relative association between stock returns and earnings based on foreign GAAP versus earnings adjusted to U.S. GAAPs. The following pair of models is tested:

$$\mathbf{H_{10}}: \quad P_{jt} = \alpha_0 + \alpha_1 E^d_{jt} + \alpha_2 BV^d_{jt} + \varepsilon_t$$
$$\mathbf{H_{1a}}: \quad P_{jt} = \beta_0 + \beta_1 E^i_{jt} + \beta_2 BV^i_{jt} + \theta_t$$

Where:

P_{jt} : "B" share price of firm *j* four months after fiscal year end of year *t,* i.e., on 30 April in year *t*+1, translated into *Renminbi* using the exchange rate at that date

E^d_{jt}: Reported earnings per share based on China's domestic accounting regulations for firm *j* for fiscal year *t*

E^i_{jt} : Reported earnings per share based on IASs for firm *j* for fiscal year *t*

BV^d_{jt} : Reported book value per share based on China's domestic accounting regulations for firm *j* on 31 December of fiscal year *t*

BV^i_{jt} : Reported book value per share based on IASs for firm *j* on 31 December of fiscal year *t*

The purpose of the J-test is to assess which one of the two competing sets of independent variables is more closely associated with the dependent variable. To perform the test we first estimated the model using IAS reported earnings and book value, and from it we obtained the estimated stock prices, i.e., $Price^i_{jt}$. We added the predicted $Price^i_{jt}$ as an additional regressor to the model using domestically reported earnings and book value and estimated the following model:

$$P_{jt} = \alpha_0 + \alpha_1 E^d_{jt} + \alpha_2 BV^d_{jt} + \alpha_3 Price^i_{jt} + \varepsilon_t$$

The first hypothesis ($\mathbf{H_{10}}$) uses the PRC model as the reference model and tests that α_3 is not significantly different from zero. $\mathbf{H_{10}}$ will be rejected if the estimated coefficient of α_3 is significantly different from zero, indicating that the IAS model, representing the influence of variables not included in the domestic model, has additional explanatory power beyond that contributed by the domestic model.

A reversed pair of models stated below is also tested:

$$\mathbf{H_{20}}: P_{jt} = \beta_0 + \beta_1 E^i_{jt} + \beta_2 BV^i_{jt} + \theta_t$$
$$\mathbf{H_{2a}}: P_{jt} = \alpha_0 + \alpha_1 E^d_{jt} + \alpha_2 BV^d_{jt} + \varepsilon_t$$

A similar testing procedure is followed. We first estimated the domestic model coefficients and obtained the estimated $Price^d_{jt}$. We then used the estimated $Price^d_{jt}$ values as a third regressor in the IAS model and estimated the following model:

$$P_{jt} = \beta_0 + \beta_1 E^i_{jt} + \beta_2 BV^i_{jt} + \beta_3 Price^d_{jt} + \theta_t$$

We tested the second hypothesis ($\mathbf{H_{20}}$) that β_3 is not significantly different from zero. If this hypothesis is not rejected, it indicates that the domestic model has no additional explanatory power over the IAS model. Using joint results based on these tests, we can obtain the relative value relevance of the two models. On the other hand, if we reject $\mathbf{H}_{20}$ but can not reject $\mathbf{H}_{10}$, then the domestic model is more value relevant.

3.2 Sample and Data Collection

The sample of listed Chinese companies used in this study is obtained from the Taiwan Economic Journal (TEJ) database. It consisted of enterprises which issued "B" shares on domestic stock exchanges from 1992 to 1996, selected using the following criteria:

(1) Earnings per share data based on domestic accounting regulations and IASs are available;
(2) Book value per share data based on domestic accounting regulations and IASs are available; and
(3) Stock price data on 30 April following the fiscal year-end are available.

To ascertain the accuracy of the data, companies were randomly selected and relevant data items from the TEJ database are compared with those from published financial reports of the same firms. To control for the possible effects of extreme values, we removed observations that are in the extreme left or right 1% in the sample for either earnings-to-price or book value-to-price ratio. This yielded a final sample size of 213 firm-year observations.

4. Statistical Results

Descriptive statistics of the variables used in the study are presented in Table 2. The average earnings per share are ¥ 0.350 based on domestic accounting regulations and ¥ 0.321 based on IASs. The average book values per share are ¥ 2.719 based on domestic accounting regulations and ¥ 2.663 based on IASs (Table 2, Panel A). These statistics indicated that on average domestic GAAPs are less conservative than IASs. A paired sample two-tailed t-test and Wilcoxon Signed Ranks test suggested that the mean differences between these two sets of earnings and book values are statistically significant at 1% (Table 2, Panel B).

Regression results for both PRC and IAS models are shown in Table 3. In Panel A, both earnings and book value based on domestic accounting regulations are significantly associated with the stock prices, explaining jointly about 21% of the variations in stock prices. In Panel B, earnings

Table 2. *Descriptive Statistics for Firm-year Observations for the Years 1992–1996*

Panel A

Variables	*Mean*	*Standard deviation*	*Median*
P^t	3.161	1.989	
E^i	0.321	0.301	0.310
E^d	0.350	0.269	0.310
BV^i	2.663	0.831	2.504
BV^d	2.719	0.770	2.548

Panel B

	Test of significance of differences in mean scores			
	Two-tailed t test		*Wilcoxon signed ranks test*	
Variables	*t-value*	*p-value*	*Z-value*	*p-value*
E^i vs E^d	3.132	0.002	3.383	0.001
BV^i vs BV^d	3.661	0.001	5.384	0.000

based on IASs are significant while book value based on IASs is not statistically significant at a 5% significance level. The adjusted R^2 for the IASs model is greater than that for the domestic model.

The J-test results are reported in Table 4. In Panel A, the PRC model is the benchmark model to test the null hypothesis that the IAS model has no additional explanatory power in equity valuation. The test showed that the regression coefficient of the estimated price, i.e., $Price^i$, from the IAS model is statistically significant in the revised domestic model, indicating that the IAS model has additional explanatory power beyond that contributed by the domestic model. The null hypothesis that the PRC model is the true model is thus rejected. In Panel B, the IAS model is the assumed true model. The estimated price from the domestic model, i.e., $Price^d$, is added to the IAS model as an additional independent variable. The coefficient of $Price^d$ is not significantly different from zero in the modified IAS model, indicating that the domestic model has no additional explanatory power over the original IAS model. The null hypothesis that the IAS model is the true model cannot be rejected. The joint results in Panels A and B suggest that earnings and book value based on IASs have greater information content than those based on domestic GAAPs. This indicates

Table 3. *Regression Results of Yearly Cross-sectional Regressions of Stock Prices on Earnings and Book Value*

Panel A: $P_{jt} = \alpha_0 + \alpha_1 E^d_{jt} + \alpha_2 BV^d_{jt} + \varepsilon_t$

	α_1	α_2	*Adjusted* R^2
Coefficient	2.846	0.356	0.211***
t-Value	(5.504)***	(1.973)**	

Panel B: $P_{jt} = \beta_0 + \beta_1 E^i_{jt} + \beta_2 BV^i_{jt} + \theta_t$

	β_1	β_2	*Adjusted* R^2
Coefficient	3.020	0.141	0.236***
t-value	(6.307)***	(0.814)	

P_{jt}: "B" share price of firm *j* four months after fiscal year end of year *t*, i.e., on 30 April year *t*+1, translated into *Renminbi* using the exchange rate at that date
E^d_{jt}: Reported earnings per share based on China's domestic accounting regulations for firm *j* for fiscal year *t*
E^i_{jt}: Reported earnings per share based on IASs for firm *j* for fiscal year *t*
BV^d_{jt}: Reported book value per share based on domestic accounting regulations for firm *j* on 31 December of fiscal year *t*
BV^i_{jt}: Reported book value per share based on IASs for firm *j* on 31 December of fiscal year *t*
*** significant at 1% level; ** significant at 5% level.

that relatively the earnings and book value reported based on IASs are more closely associated with the stock prices of "B" shares issued by Chinese enterprises.

To eliminate any potential impact of initial public offering (IPO) on share prices, similar tests were performed using the data which exclude the observations for the year of IPO. Consistent results were obtained. A plausible explanation of these findings is that the Chinese regulation requires company's dividend distribution to be based on the lower profits reported in the two sets of financial statements based on different accounting requirements. As the earnings based on IASs are significantly lower than those based on domestic GAAPs, they are more relevant for dividend decisions and thus more useful for equity valuation.

To examine the association between accounting information and stock prices over time, yearly regression using IAS reported earnings and book value was performed. Data in 1992 were deleted for analysis due to a small number of observations. Results in Table 5 demonstrated that earnings have been significantly associated with stock prices with increasing

Table 4. *J test Results using Earnings and Book Value Reported based on PRC Accounting Regulations and based on IASs*

Panel A: PRC model as the reference hypothesis
$P_{jt} = \alpha_0 + \alpha_1 E^d_{jt} + \alpha_2 BV^d_{jt} + \alpha_3 Price^i_{jt} + \varepsilon_t$

	α_1	α_2	α_3	*Adjusted R^2*
Coefficient	0.141	0.175	0.891	0.234***
t-value	(0.721)	(0.157)	(2.684)**	

Panel B: IAS model as the reference hypothesis
$P_{jt} = \beta_0 + \beta_1 E^i_{jt} + \beta_2 BV^i_{jt} + \beta_3 Price^d_{jt} + \theta_t$

	β_1	β_2	β_3	*Adjusted R^2*
Coefficient	2.580	0.085	0.188	0.233***
t-value	(2.626)***	(0.413)	(0.513)	

P_{jt}: "B" share price of firm *j* four months after fiscal year end (FYE), i.e., on 30 April, in year *t*+1 translated into *Renminbi* using the exchange rate at that date
$Price^i_{jt}$: Estimated share prices for firm *j* on 30 April in year *t*+1 from the IAS model shown in Table 3
$Price^d_{jt}$: Estimated share prices for firm *j* on 30 April in year *t*+1 from the domestic model shown in Table 3
E^d_{jt}: Reported earnings per share based on China's domestic accounting regulations for firm *j* for fiscal year *t*
E^i_{jt}: Reported earnings per share based on IASs for firm *j* for fiscal year *t*
BV^d_{jt}: Reported book value per share based on domestic accounting regulations for firm *j* on 31 December of fiscal year *t*
BV^i_{jt}: Reported book value per share based on IASs for firm *j* on 31 December of fiscal year *t*
*** significant at 1% level; ** significant at 5% level.

R^2 by years, indicating that the explanatory power of earnings for stock prices increased over time. In contrast, book value is not significant until 1995. Consistent observations were obtained when analyzing earnings and book values reported based on domestic GAAPs.

In Table 6, alternative yearly regression analyses using book value at the beginning of a fiscal year as the deflator for all variables are presented. This excludes observations which do not have corresponding prior year book value, i.e., IPO-year observations. The analyses showed that while IAS earnings are significantly associated with the share prices, book value is not significant until 1995. The adjusted R^2 has increased since 1993. These results are generally consistent with those obtained in Table 5. The insignificance of book value revealed by these analyses may be due to the

Table 5. *Yearly Regression Analysis 1993–1996 based on IAS Earnings and Book Value*

$$P_{jt} = \alpha_0 + \alpha_1 E^i_{jt} + \theta_t$$
$$P_{jt} = \beta_0 + \beta_1 BV^i_{jt} + \varepsilon_t$$
$$P_{jt} = \gamma_0 + \gamma_1 E^i_{jt} + \gamma_2 BV^i_{jt} + \upsilon_t$$

Year	*N*	α_1	*Adj* R^2	β_1	*Adj* R^2	γ_1	γ_2	*Adj* R^2
1993	35	1.767**	0.086	0.213	0.012	1.925*	–0.015	0.057
1994	52	2.626***	0.312	0.310	0.032	2.858***	–0.116	0.305
1995	58	2.636***	0.476	0.593***	0.233	2.404***	0.126	0.473
1996	64	6.544***	0.694	1.787***	0.303	6.127***	0.282	0.694

P_{jt}: "B" share price of firm *j* four months after fiscal year end (FYE), i.e., on 30 April, in year *t*+1 translated into *Renminbi* using the exchange rate at that date
E^i_{jt}: Reported earnings per share based on IASs for firm *j* for fiscal year *t*
BV^i_{jt}: Reported book value per share based on IASs for firm *j* on 31 December of fiscal year *t*
*** significant at 1% level; ** significant at 5% level; * Significant at 10% level.
Note: Yearly analysis for data of 1992 was not performed due to small sample size.

Table 6. *Yearly Regression Analysis 1993–1996 based on IAS Earnings and Book Value (Beginning IAS Book Value is used as the Deflator)*

$$P_{jt}/BV^i_{jt-1} = \alpha_0 + \alpha_1 E^i_{jt}/BV^i_{jt-1} + \theta_t$$
$$P_{jt}/BV^i_{jt-1} = \beta_0 + \beta_1 BV^i_{jt}/BV^i_{jt-1} + \varepsilon_t$$
$$P_{jt}/BV^i_{jt-1} = \gamma_0 + \gamma_1 E^i_{jt}/BV^i_{jt-1} + \gamma_2 BV^i_{jt}/BV^i_{jt-1} + \upsilon_t$$

Year	*N*	α_1	*Adj* R^2	β_1	*Adj* R^2	γ_1	γ_2	*Adj* R^2
1993	21	4.730***	0.430	1.218***	0.293	3.979***	0.303	0.410
1994	43	3.427***	0.427	1.081***	0.272	2.903***	0.293	0.425
1995	54	3.602***	0.505	1.887***	0.529	1.751***	1.247***	0.614
1996	62	7.763***	0.618	3.735***	0.565	5.337***	1.854***	0.686

P_{jt}: "B" share price of firm *j* four months after fiscal year end (FYE), i.e., on 30 April, in Year *t*+1, translated into *Renminbi* using the exchange rate at that date
E^i_{jt}: Reported earnings per share based on IASs for firm *j* for fiscal year *t*
BV^i_{jt}: Reported book value per share based on IASs for firm *j* on 31 December of fiscal year *t*
BV^i_{jt-1}: Reported book value per share based on IASs for firm *j* on 31 December of fiscal year *t*-1
*** significant at 1% level.

high inflation rates in 1993 and 1994. The inflation rates in major cities in China rose to over 20% in 1993, with some cities having inflation as high as 35% (Liu, 1994). In 1994, inflation rates in Chinese large cities continued to run over 20% (*Eastern Express*, 1994). The book value of equity based on historical cost could not reflect the current value of assets employed.

5. Conclusion

To transform its centralized planned economy to a market-oriented economy, the Chinese government experimented with the share capital system which allowed state-owned enterprises to issue shares to individual investors through stock markets. The Chinese capital markets, witnessed by their rapid development since the early 1990s, have become an important vehicle to channel the society's resources to productive business activities. To achieve an optimal resource allocation objective and to protect the interests of individual investors, the government has endeavored to improve the accounting infrastructure with an aim of enhancing the quality of accounting information disclosed.

This study referred to the unique characteristics of capital market in China where listed companies issued shares to foreign investors, i.e., "B" shares, are required to prepare two sets of financial reports—one based on PRC accounting regulations and audited by Chinese certified accountants, and the other based on IASs and certified by international accounting firms. The study examined the relative information content of these two sets of accounting reports for the valuation of "B" share prices. Using the Ohlson (1995) model, the empirical results indicate that earnings and book value based on IASs are more closely related to "B" share prices versus those based on domestic GAAPs. Yearly analyses of the association between "B" share prices and reported earnings and book value suggest that the explanatory power of both earnings and book value for stock prices has been increased over time.

These findings are significant as they provide a valuable reference for accounting policy makers in regulating financial reporting practices in view that the Chinese authorities have endeavored to harmonize China's accounting standards with international practices. It is expected that differences in earnings and book values reported according to different requirements will be eventually reduced. The results of this study also add to literature by providing an insight into how the value-relevance of accounting information evolves in light of the evolution of accounting infrastructure in an emerging market.

Notes

1. Russian-style fund accounting system was basically developed for a centrally controlled economy, under which all funds required by enterprises were appropriated from the government with stipulated purposes. The approach emphasizes fund sources and applications. Funds appropriated by the government for acquiring fixed assets must be fully utilized to acquire fixed assets employed by the enterprises. Similar requirements are

applicable for funds for acquiring current assets and for earmarked projects. This accounting system has been adopted in China since the founding of the People's Republic, and has been gradually abolished during the period of accounting reforms.

2. This new accounting regulation made several changes in order to further harmonize China's accounting regulations and practices with international practices. It removes the maximum ceiling for provision for doubtful debts, allows the adoption of lower of cost and net realizable value for inventory and short-term investment, and requires the equity method for long-term investment when the shareholding represents at least 20% of investee's share capital (See Table 1 for the differences between PRC accounting regulations and IASs before the introduction of this new regulation). With the implementation of this new regulation in 1998, it is foreseen that the differences between the earnings and book values reported based on IASs and those based on domestic GAAPs will be narrowed.

References

Alford, A., J. Jones, R. Leftwich and M. Zmijewski, "The Relative Informativeness of Accounting Disclosures in Different Countries," *Journal of Accounting Research* 31 (Supplement 1993), pp. 183–223.

Amir, E., T. S. Harris and E. Venuti, "A Comparison of the Value-relevance of U.S. Versus Non-U.S. GAAP Accounting Measures using Form 20-F Reconciliations," *Journal of Accounting Research* 31 (Supplement 1993), pp. 230–263.

Ball, R. and P. Brown, "An Empirical Evaluation of Accounting Income Numbers," *Journal of Accounting Research* (1968), pp. 159–178.

Bandyopadhgay, S. P., J. D. Hanna and G. Richardson, "Capital Market Effects of U.S.-Canada GAAP Differences," *Journal of Accounting Research* (Autumn 1994), pp. 262–277.

Beaver, W. H., R. Clark and W. Wright, "The Association between Unsystematic Security Returns and The Magnitude of Earnings Forecast Errors," *Journal of Accounting Research* (Autumn 1979), pp. 316–340.

Bernard, V., "Earnings Quality, Book Value, and the State of Financial Statement Analysis," in *Earnings Quality*, S. A. Butler, ed. (OK: The University of Oklahoma, 1993), pp. 174–183.

Bernard, V., "The Feltham-Ohlson Framework: Implications for Empiricists," *Contemporary Accounting Research* (Spring 1995), pp. 733–747.

Biddle, G., G. Seow and A. F. Siegel, "Relative Versus Incremental Information Content," *Contemporary Accounting Research* 12 (1995), pp. 1–23.

Bowen, R. E., "Valuation of Earnings Components in the Electric Industry," *The Accounting Review* (January 1981), pp. 1–22.

Chan, K. and G. Seow, "The Association between Stock Returns and Foreign GAAP Earnings Versus Earnings Adjusted to U.S. GAAP," *Journal of Accounting and Economics* 21 (1996), pp. 139–158.

China Securities Regulatory Commission (CSRC), *Detailed Implementation Rules for Information Disclosure by Public Companies (Provisional)* (1993).

China Securities Regulatory Commission (CSRC), *Standard for Content And Format for Information Disclosure by Public Companies—No. 2: Content And Format for Annual Reports* (1995).

China Securities Regulatory Commission (CSRC), *Standard for Content And Format for Information Disclosure by Public Companies—No. 3: Content And Format for Interim Reports* (1996).

China Securities Regulatory Commission (CSRC), *Standard for Content And Format for Information Disclosure by Public Companies—No. 1: Content And Format for Prospectus* (1997).

Collins, D., E. Maydew and I. Weiss. "Changes in the Value-Relevance of Earnings and Book Values over the Past Forty Years," *Journal of Accounting and Economics* (December 1997), pp. 39–67.

Daley, L. A., "The Valuation of Reported Pension Measures for Firms Sponsoring Defined Benefit Plans," *The Accounting Review* (April 1984), pp. 177–198.

Eastern Express, "Cut Prices: State Bank 'Gift' Fuel Inflation" (28 August 1994).

Ely, K. and G. Waymire, "Accounting Standard Setting Organizations and Earnings Relevance," *Working paper* (Atlanta, GA: Emory University, 1996).

Fairfield, P. M., R. J. Sweeney and T. L. Yohn, "Accounting Classification and the Predictive Content of Earnings", *The Accounting Review* (July 1996), pp. 337–356.

Francis, J. and K. Shipper, "Have the Financial Statements Lost their Relevance?" *Working paper* (Chicago, IL: University of Chicago, 1997).

Lee, J., "Accounting Infrastructure and Economic Development," *Journal of Accounting and Public Policy* 6 (1987), pp. 75–85.

Lee, S. H., "An Analysis of the Differences in After-tax Profits between those Audited by Domestic Accountants and those Audited by International Accountants", *The Chinese Accounting Review* (1997), pp. 18–23.

Lev, B., "The Boundaries of Financial Reporting and how to Extend them," *Working paper* (New York, NY: New York University, 1997)

Lipe, R. C., "The Information Contained in the Components of Earnings," *Journal of Accounting Research* 24 (Supplement 1986), pp. 36–64.

Liu, A., "Inflation in China Hits 20 Percent," *Hong Kong Standard* (23 February 1994).

Ohlson, J. A., "Earnings, Book Values, and Dividends in Equity Valuation," *Contemporary Accounting Research* (Spring 1995), pp. 661–687.

NPC (National People's Congress, PRC), *The Company Law of the People's Republic of China* (1993).

Ramesh, K. and R. Thiagarajan, "Inter-temporal Decline in Earnings Response Coefficients," *Working paper* (Evanston, IL: Northwestern University, 1995).

Yan, H. Y. and W. Yang, "An Overview of Accounting Firm Reforms in China," The Tenth Annual Conference of Accounting Academics (June 1998), Hong Kong.

Zhang, W. G., (Chief Accountant of China Securities Regulatory Commission), "Emerging Stock Market and its Impact on China's Accounting Standard Setting," Keynote speech at The Tenth Annual Conference of Accounting Academics (June 1998), Hong Kong.

B
Japan

[19]

Journal of International Financial Management and Accounting 7:3 1996

The Influence of the Keiretsu on Japanese Corporate Disclosure

*T. E. Cooke**

Department of Economics, University of Exeter, Amory Building, Exeter EX4 4RJ

Abstract

This paper represents a contribution to testing whether the extent of disclosure in Japanese corporate annual reports varies according to group structure. Consideration is given to keiretsu (group interfirm networks) classification and the mechanism for monitoring by a main bank or main company. This topic is of interest because the Japanese system of corporate governance is fundamentally different from those prevailing in Anglo-Saxon countries and this distinction may impact on corporate disclosure policy. Attention is focused on the exclusionary theory of corporate disclosure in which information is disseminated within group members but specifically excludes others. Regression analysis is undertaken to assess the importance of group structure in explaining variability in the extent of disclosure after controlling for known factors such as size, stock market listing, industry, borrowings, and type of business. The results suggest that companies within a keiretsu with a main-bank or main-company monitor and which are therefore less subject to capital market discipline do not disclose less information than other companies in their annual reports. It appears that whatever type of corporate governance mechanism is adopted in Japan there exists a monitor that places approximately equal demands on information disclosure in corporate annual reports.

1. Introduction

Comparative corporate governance is a popular subject both within government circles and the academic community (Gilson and Roe, 1993). Interest stems from a consideration of the productive efficiency of North American business organizations vis-à-vis Japanese enterprises. The North American traditional model of corporate governance is based on the Berle-Means model (1932) of the corporation in which there is a separation of ownership and management with the shareholder being the main stakeholder. In contrast, the Japanese system is a complex network of implicit and explicit contracts among many different stakeholders (Kester, 1991). On the one hand there are companies that act as independent entities and on

* The author is professor of accounting at the University of Exeter, England. He would like to thank Professors M. Kikuya, M. Isoyama, and H. Tatebe for their advice. The financial support of the Canon Foundation in Europe and Institute of Chartered Accountants in England and Wales is acknowledged.

the other hand there are those that are part of keiretsu (group interfirm relationships). Features of Japanese corporate governance within keiretsu include reciprocal shareholding and trading agreements, implicit contracting, selective intervention, placement of personnel within the group, and information sharing. Some argue that the keiretsu are anti-competitive and exclusionary (see, for example, Sheard, 1992). Keiretsu seek to have one company, but only one, in each major industry (Miyazaki, 1976) and control participation to achieve this aim. Thus, the group networks exercise exclusionary rules to ensure that competition within the group does not occur. Such has been the concern in North America about the Japanese keiretsu that the US has explicitly introduced the subject into bilateral trade talks, specifically in the Structural Impediments Initiative (SII). The SII reiterates the view that keiretsu are very productive but are exclusionary.

The US was not alone in its concern over the keiretsu. In the early 1980s the EC Commission, acting for the nine member states of the Community, began to prepare a legal case that Japan's market structures were the source of the country's "unfair trade practices". The plan was to argue that the whole structure of Japan's economy and trade violated the principles of free trade under the General Agreement on Tariffs and Trade. The case was to be based on government support for industry and the exclusionary nature of the keiretsu system. The EC dropped the GATT case when Japan agreed to a period of general restraint.

This paper considers the exclusionary theory in relation to corporate disclosure within keiretsu entities in which information is disseminated within group members but specifically excludes others, including non-keiretsu shareholders. The dissemination process within the keiretsu is one in which privileged information cascades but much of that information is not disclosed in the corporate annual reports of Japanese companies. This is because the keiretsu are information clubs in which information is exchanged within but withheld from those outside the group relationship.[1] Further, those outside the keiretsu are unable to gain by observing the behaviour of those within the network because group companies do not trade on their privileged knowledge. This is due to shareholdings being held for long-term business reasons (Cooke and Kikuya, 1992b) and further, any trading on such information may be in breach of insider trading legislation (Sakakibara et al., 1988). In contrast, independent companies (i.e., those not belonging to keiretsu) are subject to the normal market pressures for disclosure of information in corporate annual reports, not least because funding derives from the capital markets. Thus, the theory suggests that companies belonging to keiretsu disclose less information in their corporate annual reports than non-keiretsu companies, other things being equal.

The rest of the paper is divided into six sections. In the next section, certain characteristics of Japanese corporate groups are considered. This is followed by a discussion of the benefits of keiretsu formation in Japan and specifically on corporate governance issues relating to keiretsu groups and independent corporations. The next section summarizes some of the disclosure of information literature and relates earlier findings with the purpose of the present study. The independent and dependent variables are enumerated and operationalized. This is followed by sections on research method including data collection, analysis and results, and the final section concludes.

2. Japanese Corporate Groups

2.1 Corporate Groups in a Market Economy

The formation of corporate groups is not unique to Japan and exists in many industrialized countries including Germany, France and Sweden in Europe and in Chinese societies like Taiwan and Hong Kong. An aspect of the Japanese enterprise system that differs from Anglo-Saxon countries is that there are no holding companies and no parent headquarters to receive profits and allocate resources (Fruin, 1994). While core companies do exist in Japan they are often smaller than their counterparts in the US (Gerlach, 1992; Prowse, 1992). The US group structure is characterized by multidivisional form (M-form) in which the parent company allocates capital and is thought by some (Chandler, 1980; Williamson, 1970) to be the most efficient form of industrial organization. In contrast, group companies in Japan often raise their own capital and make decisions within a framework of pursuing common group interests.

That such groups exist in Japan may be explained in terms of minimizing transaction costs. The existence of a firm, acting as organizing agency, may be explained by reducing the costs of direct negotiations and measurements that would result from direct dealings between owners of factors of production and the market (Coase, 1937). However, as firm size increases so monitoring costs increase and there is a tendency to make more incorrect decisions so that the optimum size of a firm or group is that in which these costs equal the implicit costs of operating in the market. Williamson (1975) developed the concept of transaction-cost economics in which within firms such costs are normally represented as transfer prices whereas between firms transaction costs are defined contractually in the market. The corporate group acts as an intermediary between firms and the market in which the benefits to the group include savings on transaction costs, such as the negotiation and enforcement of contracts, as well as the information collection costs. The benefits of being a group member are discussed later.

2.2 Cultural Aspects of Keiretsu

Family-based network organizations exist in Chinese societies such as Taiwan and Hong Kong. However, the Japanese keiretsu differ from the family-based networks in a number of respects (Fukuyama, 1995). First, the Japanese keiretsu centred around a main bank (called horizontal or intermarket keiretsu) have an average of 31 companies (Gerlach, 1992), whereas in Taiwan the average is only six. Secondly, an intertwined keiretsu normally trades in oligopolistic rather than monopolistic markets. Furthermore, companies within keiretsu trade with network members on favourable terms and the closeness of such business entities is based on trust. Fukuyama (1995) stresses the importance of a high level of trust within Japanese society which leads to lower transaction costs than those that could be concluded "... in a low-trust society like Hong Kong" (p. 202). Another aspect of Japanese society in general is the emphasis given to interdependency rather than independence. As McKinnon (1984, p. 27) summarizes "... corporate group associations in Japan reflect that nation's historical and cultural determinants of interpersonal and intergroup relationships".

The cultural aspect of interdependency is apparent in the extent of cross-shareholdings, an important characteristic of the Japanese keiretsu. For example, nearly 69 per cent (in 1993) of the shares of Japanese listed corporations were held by the financial institutions (44.5%) and other business corporations (24.4%). These shareholdings are maintained, in part, to consolidate business relationships. Another aspect is that the proportionate holding by the financial institutions and other business corporations has remained very constant for the last 15 years. Indeed, the trend since the dismembering of the zaibatsu after World War II has been for a decline in the number of shares being held by individuals and an increase in institutional ownership. Shareownership by business corporations increased from 11.0 per cent in 1951 to 17.8 per cent in 1961 and has remained fairly constant through the rest of the period. These trends led Sakakibara et al. (1988, p. 138) to suggest that "on the average, less than

30 per cent of outstanding shares of Japanese common stocks are available to the ordinary investor".

Most of the institutional shareholding is intra- rather than inter-group in nature (Okumura, 1982) making hostile takeovers in Japan very difficult to achieve (Cooke, 1991). Furthermore, Japanese businesses tend to pay a certain fixed rate of dividend based on the par value of the stock regardless of changes in profits. Thus, the payout ratio drops when after-tax profits are up and the converse is also true so that shareholders are almost treated as fixed interest debt-holders.

2.3 Aspects of Japanese Corporate Governance

The keiretsu emerged as a response by the Japanese to the dismembering of the zaibatsu (family financial combines) and the introduction of the Anti-Monopoly Law 1947 during the occupation of Japan by the Allied forces at the end of World War II. The aim of the Anti-Monopoly Law was to liquidate holding companies, dispose of the securities and other properties "with a view to democratizing the ownership and management of enterprises" (Article 1). While the holding companies could be abolished it was impossible to dismantle the huge network of binding relationships that had developed (Bison, 1954).

Once the Occupation Forces left Japan in April 1952 the Ministry of International Trade and Industry (MITI) began to permit the formation of cartels among small businesses as an exception to the Anti-Monopoly Law (Johnson, 1982). As a result the old zaibatsu names were restored and MITI encouraged the formation of keiretsu. Since the old banking system remained intact when the Occupation Forces left, industries were able, quite easily, to reform around a bank. Old members of the zaibatsu were favoured and the six main banking groups that emerged were the old groups of Mitsubishi, Sumitomo, Mitsui and Fuji (often referred to as Fuji Bank of the Fuyo group but formerly Yasuda) as well as the newer groups of Sanwa and Dai-Ichi Kangyo Group (DKB).

Those large companies centred around the main banks (DKB, Sakura, Sumitomo, Fuji, Sanwa, Mitsubishi) are referred to as horizontal keiretsu[2] as they share common ties with the bank including shared stockholdings as well as normal bank trading relations. In contrast, a vertical keiretsu normally involves one very large trading company with many small entities subservient to it e.g., Toyota Motor Corporation.

The commercial relationships that had developed during the rise of the zaibatsu, primarily in the second half of the nineteenth century, were hard to disband and formed the basis of subsequent contractual relationships between companies and their bankers, as well as with suppliers and subcontractors.

2.4 Role of the Main Bank in Horizontal Keiretsu

The main focus in the literature on corporate governance in Japanese horizontal keiretsu has been the role of the main bank as monitoring agent. The banks may be thought of as financial intermediaries who minimize the cost of monitoring and resolve incentive problems between borrowers and lenders (Diamond, 1984). This may be a more efficient solution than the disruptive monitoring by capital markets (Gilson and Roe, 1993).

Sheard (1989) has argued that the Japanese main bank system may be a substitute for screening and monitoring institutions such as bond- and credit-rating institutions as well as security analysts. The main banks are likely to have inside information on the company because they offer loans and are shareholders and therefore the demands for the disclosure of information in the corporate annual reports may be less than for other "independent" companies. The very stability of the relationship gives the bank access to superior information about its clients (Imani, 1986). Similarly, the incentives for corporate managers to disclose to those outside the keiretsu are less than on those managers in independent companies because the capital market pressures are greater in the latter. Indeed, such keiretsu banks may lobby against the disclosure of certain information on the grounds that they wish to retain their comparative information advantage. Consistent with this is the work by Hoshi et al. (1990a,b,c) in finding that companies in horizontal keiretsu have better access to capital because of the quality of information given to the banks.

It has been argued also that the main bank system acts as an alternative to the takeover market (Sheard, 1989). An important aspect of the main bank system is the close information-sharing relationship that exists between the bank and the firm. Information exchange is often facilitated by the main bank having a director link with the firm or through membership of a "presidents' club" in which the bank and other affiliated firms participate. Information is available to the main bank that is not available to the capital markets other than at high cost. The main bank's monitoring arising from superior information has been relied upon by other banks, even as a form of quasi-guarantee (Takagi, 1993).

The structure of these groups is such that they may be considered to be information clubs in which "... coordination is secured by a set of tacit, informal rules that emerge through a long history of exchange of information and recognition of interdependence, substantiated by financial linkages and interlocking directorates" (Goto, 1982, p. 61). Such clubs serve the information needs of insiders (keiretsu members) but exclude those outside including non-keiretsu shareholders. The information exchange is based on trust in which "cooperation is achieved by a coalition of self-interested individuals under implicit threats of expulsion" (Berglöf and Perotti, 1994, p. 281).

It is possible that information sharing within a club may be more efficient than the market mechanism which creates incentives to disclose information. First, information sharing may help to reduce fraud and misrepresentation. Secondly, while some managers are able to manipulate the timing of information disclosure and smooth earnings, monitoring by the bank and sharing of information within a group may make this more difficult. As such, this information sharing may be of some significance in Japan particularly because the audit function is relatively weak (McKinnon, 1985) and its culture is not litigious, in complete contrast to the situation prevailing in the US.[3]

Another aspect is that the main bank also has a role as the provider of funds and retains a shareholding to consolidate business relations. As pointed out by Gerlach (1992, p. 186) "the keiretsu serve as collective monitors, thereby permitting higher debt-to-equity ratios and reducing liquidity constraints on member firms". The bank monitors the "group" companies, shares information and acts as risk taker (for a more detailed analysis of risk sharing by keiretsu see Nakatani, 1984; Aoki, 1988; Sheard, 1991; Osano and Tsutsui, 1986; Sheard, 1986; Kawasaki and McMillan, 1987; and Sheard, 1989). Consistent with this theory is the notion that if a company gets into financial difficulties the main bank accepts the risk of bankruptcy and bails out the ailing corporation (Miyashita and Russell, 1994, p. 50). Further, it has been found that those with a main bank that have had financial difficulties have been protected and been able to recover their earnings better than non-main bank companies (Hoshi et al., 1990a; Abegglen and Stalk, 1985; McCauley and Zimmer, 1989).

As well as risk-sharing advantages, Goto (1982, p. 63) argues that Japanese firms can secure more broad investment opportunities than multidivisional firms. Further, that more information is provided about investment such that "member firms have access to information about other members which is not available to general investors" (Goto, 1982, pp. 63–64). Thus, because of the nature of Japanese groups the demands from members of that keiretsu for disclosure in corporate annual reports will be lower than for independent firms.

The Japanese group coalitions have a number of mechanisms that bind members including presidents' council meetings and cross-shareholdings. Presidents' council meetings (shacho-kai) normally take place on a monthly basis (every three months for the DKB group) (Gerlach, 1992). In practice the meetings are not restricted to group presidents only, with company chairmen being invited as well. Not all companies within a group are invited so that there is an "inner-group" and "outer-group". While minutes of the shacho-kai meetings are taken they are not formally distributed or made available to outsiders. Information is treated on a strictly confidential basis and members are not allowed to take notes to avoid unauthorized written records of the proceedings (Miyashita and Russell, 1994).

2.5 Role of the Main Company in Vertical Keiretsu

An alternative form of keiretsu group structure to the main-bank organization is one in which there is a very large company e.g., Hitachi, with many smaller companies subservient to it (main-company, vertical or pyramid). Such groupings are more common in manufacturing industries, for example in the electronics and automobile industries, in which it may be difficult for sub-contractors to work for more than one keiretsu because of conflicts of loyalty. "Within the vertical keiretsu, exchange between the parent and satellite firms is embedded in a dense network of ongoing relationships, as various forms of information, technical and financial assistance, and managerial expertise are provided on a reciprocity basis" (Gerlach, 1992, p. 70). With the horizontal keiretsu the main bank acts as monitor whereas in the vertical keiretsu the main company accepts the "obligation" to monitor companies within its keiretsu not through a legal document but rather as an acceptable business practice within Japan (Takagi, 1993). However, vertical keiretsu differ from horizontal keiretsu in that in the latter there is the binding lender/banker relationship. This may have implications for the extent of information exchanged and also disclosed in corporate annual reports.

2.6 Independent Firms

Those firms that are not part of keiretsu rely on arms-length relationships with customers, financiers and suppliers in which there is a tendency for large shareholders to monitor management (Prowse, 1992). It is a characteristic of Japan that ownership concentration is greater than in US firms and therefore monitoring by a main shareholder is somewhat easier (Prowse, 1992). Independent companies are subject to market driven disclosures. With respect to mandatory disclosures, Gibbins, Richardson and Waterhouse (1992) have argued that regulations can be avoided at some cost depending upon the opportunistic behaviour of management. Further, voluntary disclosure can improve shareholders' welfare by reducing information asymmetries among investors leading to improved risk-sharing. This led Gerlach (1992, p. 259) to conclude that "the quality of information that alliance partners have at their disposal is clearly different from that available to outside investors".

2.7 Theoretical Summary

The Japanese keiretsu (both vertical and horizontal) are characterized by stable shareholdings held for long-term business purposes and cross-shareholdings in which information is shared within their respective networks. The keiretsu act as information sharing clubs in which outside shareholders are excluded. The keiretsu are based on trust which recognizes mutual existence and offers advantages in terms of sharing risks and protection against takeovers. Whilst individual cross-shareholdings may be small they are in aggregate sufficiently large to lead to an effective dominant shareholding position of the keiretsu since the network acts in concert. This has the effect that a shareholding in a keiretsu company by a non-keiretsu entity may have little influence over the company. Because voting at annual general meetings is based on a follow-the-leader basis, where the leader is the dominant shareholding, non-keiretsu shareholders investing in keiretsu companies are effectively disenfranchised.

What unites both the horizontal and vertical keiretsu is control and influence, over and above that commensurate with their shareholdings. The main-bank and the main-company act as monitor and information conduits within their respective keiretsu. As a result of these monitoring activities and stable shareholdings, there is asymmetry of information between keiretsu members and non-keiretsu outside shareholders. Listed companies within keiretsu do not suffer the same pressures or have the same economic incentives to disclose information in corporate annual reports than their non-keiretsu counterparts. In effect, certain aspects of disclosure are intertwined within the keiretsu and therefore the demand for disclosure in corporate annual reports is lower than for independent companies. Information asymmetry exists because keiretsu members have access to information that non-keiretsu shareholders do not. This has been possible because "Japanese standards of financial accounting and reporting have always been loose" (Horsley and Buckley, 1990, p. 54). Thus, the exclusionary theory suggests that the information asymmetry leads to keiretsu companies disclosing less information in their corporate annual reports than non-keiretsu companies. The empirical part of this paper seeks to test the exclusionary theory.

3. Empirical Investigation

3.1 Prior Research

Previous research that attempts to explain variability in the extent of disclosure suggests that size, gearing, listing status and industry type are influential factors that need to be controlled for in any assessment of the relationship between the extent of disclosure and keiretsu classification.

(i) Size. Size may be important because of the need to raise capital, because of the greater pressure from shareholders themselves and their agents and investment analysts for increased disclosure (Schipper, 1981) and because large firms are also more likely to disclose information to customers, suppliers and even the public in general (Cooke, 1989b). Other factors of importance include the need to raise capital at the lowest cost (Choi, 1973), large firms are also likely to be more complex and require efficient management information systems to meet the needs of financiers and meet the needs for managerial control, and large corporations are also more closely monitored by the regulatory authorities (Firth, 1979).

Size has been found to be a significant variable in other research studies (see, for example, Cerf, 1961; Singhvi, 1967; Singhvi and Desai, 1971; Stanga, 1976; Belkaoui and Kahl, 1978; Firth, 1979, 1980; and Cooke, 1989a, 1992a). Sales has been used as the measure of size in this study and has been adopted in several studies (Cooke, 1989a,c, 1992a; Ahmed and Nicholls, 1994; Wallace et al., 1994).

(ii) Gearing/Borrowings. Gearing has been found to be an important explanatory variable by Belkaoui and Kahl (1978), Malone et al. (1993) and Wallace et al. (1994). In capital market based economies it might be hypothesized that companies with a higher proportion of their assets financed by bank borrowings will disclose more information in their annual reports to meet some of the needs of their lenders. Information might

be disclosed to assure bondholders that shareholders and management are less likely to bypass their covenant claims (Myers, 1977; Schipper, 1981). This view is consistent with Jensen and Meckling (1976) who suggest that firms with high gearing ratios will incur high monitoring costs and that this problem may be alleviated by more comprehensive levels of disclosure.

In a capital market based economy in the US it may be assumed that "expenditure on monitoring is an increasing function of the proportion of the firm's assets that is financed by outside capital, because the incidence of agency costs is higher for firms of the same size with a greater proportion of outside capital" (Leftwich et al., 1981, p. 56). However, in the case of Japan's credit based financial system this relationship may not hold true because the greater the proportion of total assets financed by bank borrowings the lower the incentive to disclose information if they belong to a keiretsu. For non-keiretsu companies the situation in the US may well prevail in Japan. As a result it was thought appropriate to control for the proportion of total assets financed by bank borrowings (referred to as the borrowing ratio hereafter) although the directional relationship may depend on the organizational structure of the company.

(iii) Listing Status. Listing status can also be a factor in explaining variability in the extent of disclosure because of the need to raise capital at the lowest cost. Thus, multiple listed corporations, raising capital on the international markets, may have a higher level of disclosure than purely domestically listed enterprises if the requirements of overseas stock markets are greater than those of their domestic exchanges. Research supporting this includes Singhvi and Desai (1971), Choi (1973), Spero (1979), Firth (1979), Cooke (1989a), Cooke (1992a) and Wallace et al. (1994). Companies in this survey are classified as being multiple listed (those with at least one overseas listing) or domestically listed.

(iv) Industry type. Levels of disclosure in corporate annual reports may well vary according to industry-type, perhaps where there is a bandwagon effect as a result of a leading influential company or perhaps for historical reasons (Stanga, 1976; Belkaoui and Kahl, 1978; Cooke, 1989c). In the case of Japan, it is true to say that its post-war economic success has been founded on manufacturing industry in which the "... economy prospers because areas of industry that show promise are stimulated by fiscal policies favoring investment" (van Wolferen, 1989, p. 7). Since manufacturing is of fundamental importance to Japan it is possible that levels of disclosure in their corporate annual reports may differ from other business sectors. Consequently, corporations included in this survey are

categorized as either manufacturing (21 firms) or non-manufacturing (14 firms).

3.2 Research Method and Definitions of Variables

(i) Definition of Disclosure. Disclosure refers to 165 items that may be included in Japanese corporate annual reports prepared in accordance with the Securities and Exchange Law (SEL). The introduction of the SEL was a major change in the orientation of corporate financial reporting since disclosure required under this Act is orientated to general investors (Japanese Institute of Certified Public Accountants, JICPA, 1984). The requirements of the SEL affect about 3000 of the largest corporations out of a total of about one million joint stock corporations.

(ii) Definition of Keiretsu. The early discussion has made a distinction between horizontal and vertical keiretsu. However, the boundaries are not well delineated and in practice a company may belong to more than one keiretsu. The six main horizontal keiretsu normally have a main trading company in the group as well as being bank-centred. However, while companies such as Matsushita, Toyota, Nissan, Honda, Hitachi and Mitsubishi may be identified with a main bank, in many respects they may be classified as independent of the main banks with their own vertical keiretsu. Indeed, the Hitachi Group may be classified as having its own vertical group although the company is a member of the Fuyo, Sanwa and DKB horizontal keiretsu.

Gerlach (1992, pp. xv + xvi) confirms that research is complicated by the variety of alliances that exist and the terminologies employed, by difficulties in defining membership, and by misconceptions concerning their nature and purposes. Thus, the groups are not clearly defined because of the blurring of boundaries and overlapping affiliations.

Since the boundaries are blurred, two different classifications are considered in this paper. The first is based on those companies that may be identified with the big six banks and are classified as belonging to a horizontal keiretsu with the rest belonging to the "other group". Using this classification 16 were included as horizontal keiretsu and 19 in the alternative category and is referred to as keiretsu classification 1. The second classification for the keiretsu was in terms of a three-way split. First, companies were classified as horizontal keiretsu if they were related to a main bank but were not part of a vertical keiretsu centred around a main bank. For example, in the first classification Hitachi was allocated to the horizontal group whereas in the second classification it was allocated to the vertical group since the group has its own satellite companies. As a result, the second classification (keiretsu classification 2) consisted of the horizontal group (10 cases), nine cases in the vertical group (dominated by manufacturing companies) with the third group being independent/ family owned (16 cases).

The preceding discussion leads to our hypothesis:

> Other things being equal, there is an association between keiretsu classification and the extent of disclosure by Japanese corporations.

3.3 Data Collection

The Annual Report Sample. This research uses the database on Japanese financial reports developed and used by Cooke (1992a). Thirty five corporations are considered compared with much smaller samples included in work by Choi (1973), Barrett (1977), Cairns, Lafferty and Mantle (1984), Stilling, Norton and Hopkins (1984), Campbell (1985), and Tonkin (1989). A sample of 100 Japanese corporations was selected and contacted by letter (letters were sent in English and Japanese) to request the 1988 annual reports.[4] The corporations were selected by simple random sampling without replacement from the entire population of listed companies which are published in the Japan Company Handbook. The overall response rate was 35 per cent.[5]

A major task is the selection of items of information that might be expected to be reported in corporate reports. Since the focus of this paper is disclosure of information to a wide range of users, an extensive (165) list of items, including both voluntary and mandatory disclosures, is included in the scoring sheet.[6] The selection of items to include is influenced by previous research studies, recommended disclosures by the International Accounting Standards Committee, accounting standards issued by the Business Advisory Deliberation Council, Ordinances of The Ministry of Finance, statements and opinions issued by the Japanese Institute of Certified Public Accountants and the law. Thus, the list of disclosures is not directed at specific user groups, is not constrained by exclusion of items likely to be irrelevant to a user group (Barrett, 1977) or constrained by the exclusion of statutorily required items (Firth, 1980).

The disclosure scoring sheet was pre-tested on three Japanese corporate annual reports and after consultation with Japanese accounting professionals the research instrument was modified. Such a wide-ranging approach to the measurement of the extent of disclosure has been adopted by

Spero (1979), Wallace (1987), and Cooke (1989a). The split between mandatory and voluntary disclosure items was as follows:

	Securities and Exchange Law accounts
Voluntary	76 (46%)
Mandatory	89 (54%)
Total	165 (100%)

Scoring the Disclosure Items. The approach to scoring items is essentially dichotomous in which an item scores one if disclosed and zero if it is not disclosed in the SEL accounts. However, where an item of disclosure is clearly not relevant to a particular company, the entity is not penalized for non-disclosure. Whilst this introduces a judgemental element into the scoring procedure this was considered to provide a more realistic assessment of corporate disclosure than a strict dichotomous approach. Judgement in the dichotomous procedure was made after reading the entire contents of the SEL and annual reports. Failure to adopt such a procedure would have meant that larger more diversified enterprises would be able and likely to disclose more information. A modified dichotomous approach was adopted also by Buzby (1972), Wallace (1987), and Cooke (1989a).[7]

The disclosure index I_j for a set of accounts is defined as:

$$I_j = \frac{\sum_{i=1}^{n_j} x_{ij}}{n_j}$$

where, n_j = number of relevant items for jth firm,
$n_j \leqslant 165$
x_{ij} = 1 if ith (relevant) item disclosed
= 0 if ith (relevant) item not disclosed
so that $0 \leqslant I_j \leqslant 1$

The implied assumption when an item is relevant is that each item of disclosure is equally important although clearly one class of user will attach different weights to an item of disclosure than another class of user. However, the focus of this research is not on one particular user group but rather all users of corporate annual reports. An approach which tried to encapsulate the subjective weights of a multitude of user groups would be difficult to operationalize. Thus, the approach here is in effect to assume that the subjective weights will average each other out. Support for not attaching weights can be found in Spero (1979), Robins and Austin (1986) and Wallace et al. (1994). Spero found that attaching weights was irrelevant because those enterprises that are better at disclosing "important items" are also better at disclosing "less important items" i.e., firms are consistent in their disclosure policies.

3.4 Analysis and Results

Multivariate model. A linear model[8] is used to assess whether keiretsu classification is associated with the extent of disclosure in corporate annual reports, other things being equal. Since keiretsu classification and the control variables, industry type and overseas listing, are categorical variables, dummy variables are used. The basic equation is:

$$Yi = \beta_1 + \beta_2 X_{2i} + \beta_3 X_{3i} + \beta_4 X_{4i} + \beta_5 X_{5i} + \beta_6 X_{6i} + \beta_7 X_{7i} + \beta_8 X_{8i} + \beta_9 X_{9i} + \varepsilon_i$$

Y = disclosure index scores

Size

X_2 = Sales

Borrowings ratio

X_3 = proportion of total assets financed by bank borrowings

Industry sector

X_4 = the company is a manufacturing company, 0 if otherwise

Listing status

X_5 = the company has at least one overseas listing, 0 if otherwise

Keiretsu classification

X_6 = the company is in a horizontal (main bank) group for classification 1, 0 if otherwise

X_7 = the company is in a horizontal (main bank) group for classification 2, 0 if otherwise

X_8 = the company is in a vertical (main company) group, 0 if otherwise

X_9 = the company is in an independent/family owned group, 0 if otherwise

ε = error term

i = 1, ... 35

β = parameters (where the constant $\beta 1$ adjusts for any excluded dummy variables)

and where at least one of X_7 to X_9 is zero.[9] In the first model X_7 to X_9 are excluded (keiretsu classification 1) and in the second model X_6 is excluded (keiretsu classification 2). The correlation matrix for the variables in keiretsu classification 1 are shown in Table 1 and for keiretsu classification 2 in Table 2.

Results. The overall disclosure index had a mean of 0.561 (standard deviation 0.061) with a minimum of 0.460 and maximum of 0.680. The multiple regression routines were tested using an unrestricted model in which no assumptions are made about any of the regression coefficients. The regression is then rerun with the q coefficients representing the keiretsu classification equal to zero giving a restricted model. In the case of the first keiretsu classification the appropriate test is the t-test because the keiretsu classification is dichotomous.

Using the second keiretsu classification the q dummy variables are dropped from the unrestricted model UR so that the error sum of squares of the restricted model (ESS_R) must be larger than the error sum of squares of the unrestricted model (ESS_{UR}). In this case the correct measure to test the joint significance of the keiretsu regression coefficients is:

$$\frac{(ESS_R - ESS_{UR})/q}{ESS_{UR}/(N-k)}$$

with $(N-k)$ degrees of freedom in the denominator and q omitted parameters in the numerator.[10]

Keiretsu classification 1

Table 3 shows the entered multiple regression routine with the R^2 (adjusted R^2) for the unrestricted model being 0.66194 (0.60305) whereas for the restricted model it was 0.65923 (0.61379). The t-statistic for the keiretsu coefficient was negative indicating that those in the keiretsu disclose less information than non-keiretsu companies but this difference was not significant at the 5% level. Thus, the hypothesis that there is an association between the extent of disclosure and keiretsu classification is rejected.

With respect to the unrestricted model, the industry variable has a positive coefficient that is significant at the 5% level indicating that manufacturing companies disclose significantly more information than non-manufacturing companies. In addition, the listing status variable has a

Table 3. *Multiple linear regression*

	Keiretsu classification 1		*Keiretsu classification 2*
	Unrestricted	*Restricted*	*Unrestricted*
Constant (β_1)	0.484376	0.476992	0.470829
	(22.431)	(31.736)	(30.752)
X_2 = sales	1.74699E-08	1.881560E-08	9.906935E-09
	(2.030)	(2.341)*	(1.017)
X_3 = bank borrowings/total assets	0.089350	0.98795	0.093963
(borrowing ratio)	(2.013)	(2.512)*	(2.121)*
X_4 = manufacturing or not	0.054358	0.054619	0.057341
	(3.500)*	(3.565)*	(3.769)*
X_5 = overseas listing or not	0.042290	0.043434	0.017280
	(2.265)*	(2.376)*	(0.720)
X_6 = horizontal (classi.1) or not	–0.007756		
	(–0.482)		
X_7 = horizontal (classi.2) or not			0.017013
			(0.949)
X_8 = vertical or not			0.052645
			(1.645)
X_9 = independent/family owned or not			1.0000
R^2	0.66194	0.65923	0.68995
Adjusted R^2	0.60365	0.61379	0.62352
F	11.35664	14.50882	10.38487

t-statistics are in parentheses
* significant at the 5% level

positive coefficient that is also significant at the 5% level showing that those with at least one overseas listing disclose significantly more information than those with a domestic listing only. In contrast to the previous model, the restricted model has all four independent variables (sales, borrowing ratio, industry type, and overseas listing) significant at the 5% level.

Keiretsu classification 2

With the second keiretsu classification the R^2 (adjusted R^2) for the unrestricted model was 0.68995 (0.62352) whereas for the restricted model it was, as previously stated, 0.65923 (0.61379). The difference in the error sum of squares between the restricted and unrestricted models is 0.0039 giving an F-statistic of 1.39037 which at the 5% level is not significant. This suggests that the association between the extent of disclosure and keiretsu classification is not significant.

Table 1. *Correlation Matrix: Classification 1 Variables*

	Index	*Keiretsu main-bank*	*Keiretsu other*	*Sales*	*Manufact.*	*Japan listing*	*Overseas listing*	*Borrowing*
Index	1.000							
Keiretsu-main bank	0.435	1.000						
Keiretsu-other	–0.435	–1.000	1.000					
Sales	0.619	0.424	–0.424	1.000				
Manufacturing	0.552	0.146	–0.146	0.280	1.000			
Japan listing only	–0.580	–0.308	0.308	–0.620	–0.227	1.000		
Overseas listing	0.580	0.308	–0.308	0.620	0.227	–1.000	1.000	
Borrowing	0.189	0.358	–0.358	–0.358	–0.068	0.138	–0.138	1.000

Table 2. *Correlation Matrix: Classification 2 Variables*

	Index	*Keiretsu main-bank*	*Keiretsu vertical*	*Keiretsu family*	*Sales*	*Manufact.*	*Japan listing*	*Overseas listing*	*Borrowing*
Index	1.000								
Keiretsu-main bank	0.044	1.000							
Keiretsu-vertical	0.589	–0.372	1.000						
Keiretsu-family	–0.556	–0.580	–0.540	1.000					
Sales	0.619	–0.149	0.752	–0.525	1.000				
Manufacturing	0.552	–0.062	0.197	–0.116	0.280	1.000			
Japan listing only	–0.580	0.120	–0.786	0.580	–0.620	–0.227	1.000		
Overseas listing	0.580	–0.120	0.786	–0.580	0.620	0.227	1.000	1.000	
Borrowing	0.189	0.486	–0.224	–0.244	–0.068	–0.036	0.138	–0.138	1.000

Both the borrowing ratio and industry type are significant at the 5% level with the coefficient being positive (as with keiretsu classification 1) indicating greater disclosure by those with higher borrowing ratios. The finding with respect to the borrowing ratio is consistent with work undertaken in capital market-based economies (see for example, Malone et al., 1993).

4. Concluding Comments

The exclusionary theory has been discussed to explain the dissemination of information within group alliances and its impact on disclosure in corporate annual reports in Japan has been analysed. Two corporate governance systems appear to operate side by side in Japan. The one in which members are part of a keiretsu group in which there is complex monitoring and control by interacting stakeholders in which information is shared to the exclusion of non-members. In contrast, the independent firms have mechanisms of corporate governance in which arms-length relationships are more typical.

The research hypothesis was developed and consideration given to the relationship between the extent of disclosure in annual reports and keiretsu classification after controlling for size, stock market listing, industry, borrowing ratio, and type of business. What has been found is that the association between keiretsu classification and the extent of disclosure in Japanese company reports is not statistically significant. There is no evidence that those companies belonging to a keiretsu disclose significantly less information than non-keiretsu companies. Further, detailed scrutiny of the 165 items of disclosure on an item-by-item basis did not reveal any systematic pattern between keiretsu and non-keiretsu firms.

In considering weaknesses of this study, it could be argued that the small sample is not representative of the population although it may be stated that the coefficients of the control variables are as expected and in line with the extant literature. A second limitation is that the disclosure indexes may have changed over time. This issue was addressed by conducting interviews in Japan, by reviewing the literature, and by checking the results of two of the sample companies. Using the same research instrument it was found that there were no material differences in disclosure index scores over time of the two companies suggesting applicability of the indexes. Another weakness might be misspecification of the keiretsu variable because of the non-uniqueness in membership to one group.

These limitations are important although it was found that the explanatory power of the models is good and two possible keiretsu classifications were tested and cross-checked with specialists in this area in Japan.[11] Thus, the evidence suggests that members of keiretsu do not exclude information in their corporate annual reports when compared with independent corporations. Whatever type of corporate governance mechanism is adopted in Japan there appears to exist a monitor that places approximately equal demands on information disclosure in corporate annual reports. In horizontal keiretsu the main bank acts as the main monitor, in vertical keiretsu the main company acts likewise, and in independent listed corporations it is the principal institutional shareholders. This finding is consistent with work by Prowse (1992) who found that institutional shareholders actively monitor the firms in which they invest.

Notes

1. The premise is that it would be unfair on non-keiretsu shareholders of keiretsu companies to receive less information in the annual reports of companies in which they had invested in compared with investments in independent corporations.

2. The term "horizontal" should not be confused with its normal usage in the West when referring to companies with similar business lines.

3. Perhaps Japan is not litigious because of the absence of anything similar to common law and especially because of the emphasis on harmony and conciliation in a Confucian culture.

4. It may be thought that the financial statements produced by Japanese corporations have changed since 1988 but causal empiricism together with interviews conducted in Japan in 1994, including interviews at the Japanese Institute of Certified Public Accountants, suggest that changes that have occurred could not materially affect the results reported in this paper. This is mainly because the disclosure index was based on a very extensive list of 165 items. To substantiate this point, two out of the sample of 35 companies were selected at random and the 1995 SEL accounts obtained. Disclosure by the two companies, Minolta and Ohkura, was assessed using the same research instrument. It was found that there was no substantial difference in the extent of disclosure between the 1988 SEL accounts and those for 1995. The difference over time in disclosure scores was less than 4% for both companies. However, improved disclosure was noted in accounting for lease transactions, segmental information and market prices of marketable securities.

5. The low response rate may yield a non-response bias to the results given here, inasmuch that it may be considered that corporations which did not respond may be reluctant to disclose information generally. Thus, responding corporations are likely to disclose more information in their annual reports and hence the indices of disclosure calculated are likely to be biased upwards. However, there is no reason to believe that the bias varies between corporations in the different groups or has any effect on the interrelationship between the dependent variable and the independent variables. Thus, the sample is considered to be satisfactory.

6. A copy of the research instrument may be obtained from the author.

7. The number of non-relevant items to any individual company included in the sample was less than 5% of the total disclosure items.

8. While ordinary least regression is robust tests were undertaken to ensure that the data are approximately normal. Standard tests (see Stuart and Ord, 1983, p. 144) of the data

set on the skewness and kurtosis for the values of 0 and 3 respectively indicate the acceptance of the hypothesis that the data are normally distributed.

9. Given the characteristics of the data, a first approximation of the relationship between the independent and dependent variables is a linear response function. Since this is a pilot study with no prior information as to the distribution of the residuals a reasonable assumption is that the errors have a homoscedastic independent structure which enables t-statistics to be derived.

10. See for example Pindyck and Rubinfield (1987, pp. 117–118).

11. I am grateful for the help of Professor Isoyama and Mr Sawa in this respect.

References

Abegglen, J. and J. Stalk, *Kaisha: the Japanese Corporation* (New York: Basic Books, 1985).

Ahmed, K. and D. Nicholls, "The Impact of Non-financial Company Characteristics on Mandatory Disclosure Compliance in Developing Countries: The Case of Bangladesh," *International Journal of Accounting* 29 (1994), pp. 62–77.

Aoki, M., *Information, Incentives, and Bargaining in the Japanese Economy* (Cambridge: Cambridge University Press, 1988).

Barrett, M. E., "The Extent of Disclosure in Annual Reports of Large Companies in Seven Countries," *The International Journal of Accounting* (Spring 1977), pp. 1–25.

Belkaoui, A. and A. Kahl, *Corporate Financial Disclosure in Canada*, Research Monograph No. 1 of the Canadian Certified General Accountants Association (Vancouver: Canadian Certified General Accountants Association, 1978).

Berglöf, E. and E. Perotti, "The Governance Structure of the Japanese Financial Keiretsu," *Journal of Financial Economics* 36 (1996), pp. 259–284.

Berle, A. A. and G. C. Means. *The Modern Corporation and Private Property* (London: Macmillan, 1932).

Bison, T. A., *Zaibatsu Dissolution in Japan* (Westport, CT: Greenwood Press, 1954).

Buzby, S. L., "An Empirical Investigation of the Relationship between the Extent of Disclosure in Corporate Annual Reports and Two Company Characteristics," Pennsylvania State University, unpublished doctoral dissertation, 1972.

Cairns, D., M. Lafferty and P. Mantle, *Survey of Accounts and Accountants 1983–84* (London: Lafferty Publications, 1984).

Campbell, L. G., *Accounting and Financial Reporting in Japan* (London: Lafferty Publications, 1985).

Cerf, A. R., *Corporate Reporting and Investment Decisions* (University of California, 1961).

Chandler, A. D., *Scale and Scope* (Boston: Harvard University Press, 1980).

Choi, F. D. S., "Financial Disclosure and Entry to the European Capital Market," *Journal of Accounting Research* (Autumn 1973), pp. 159–175.

Coase, R. H., "The Nature of the Firm," *Economica* 4 (1937), pp. 386–405.

Cooke, T. E., "Disclosure in the Corporate Annual Reports of Swedish Companies," *Accounting and Business Research* (Spring 1989a), pp. 113–124.

Cooke, T. E., *An Empirical Study of Financial Disclosures by Swedish Companies* (New York: Garland Publishing, 1989b).

Cooke, T. E., "Voluntary Corporate Disclosure by Swedish Companies," *Journal of International Financial Management and Accounting* (Summer 1989c), pp. 171–195.

Cooke, T. E., "Environmental Factors Influencing Mergers and Aquisitions in Japan," *Journal of International Financial Management and Accounting* (Summer 1991), pp. 160–188.

Cooke, T. E., "The Impact of Size, Stock Market Listing and Industry Type on Disclosure in the Annual Reports of Japanese Listed Corporations," *Accounting and Business Research* (Summer 1992a), pp. 229–237.

Cooke, T. E. and M. Kikuya, *Financial Reporting in Japan: Regulation, Practice and Environment* (Oxford: Blackwell Publishing, 1992b).

Diamond, D. W., "Financial Intermediation and Delegated Monitoring," *Review of Economic Studies* 51 (1984), pp. 393–414.

Firth, M., "Raising Finance and Firms' Corporate Reporting Policies," *Abacus* (December 1980), pp. 100–115.

Firth, M., "The Impact of Size, Stock Market Listing and Auditors on Voluntary Disclosure in Corporate Annual Reports," *Accounting and Business Research* (Autumn 1979), pp. 273–280.

Fruin, W., *The Japanese Enterprise System* (Oxford: Clarendon Press, 1994).

Fukuyama, F., *Trust: The Social Virtues and the Creation of Prosperity* (London: Hamish Hamilton, 1995).

Gerlach, M., *Alliance Capitalism* (Berkeley: University of California Press, 1992).

Gibbons, M., A. J. Richardson and J. Waterhouse, *The Management of Financial Disclosure: Theory and Perspectives* (Vancouver: The Canadian Certified General Accountants' Research Foundation, 1992).

Gilson, R. J. and M. J. Roe, "Understanding the Japanese Keiretsu: Overlaps between Corporate Governance and Industrial Organization," *The Yale Law Journal* (January 1993), pp. 871–906.

Goto, A., "Business Groups in a Market Economy," *European Economic Review* 19 (1982), pp. 53–70.

Horsley, W. and R. Buckley, *Nippon: New Superpower* (London: BBC Books, 1990).

Hoshi, T., A. Kashyap and D. Scharfstein, "Bank Monitoring and Investment: Evidence from the Changing Structure of Japanese Corporate Banking Relationships," in *Asymmetric Information, Corporate Finance, and Investment*, R. G. Hubbard, ed. (Chicago: Chicago University Press, 1990a), pp. 105–124.

Hoshi, T., A. Kashyap and D. Scharfstein, "Corporate Structure, Liquidity, and Investment: Evidence from Japanese Industrial Groups," *Quarterly Journal of Economics* 106 (1990b), pp. 33–60.

Hoshi, T., A. Kashyap and D. Scharfstein, "The Role of Banks in Reducing the Costs of Financial Distress in Japan," *Journal of Financial Economics* 27 (1990c), pp. 67–88.

Imai, K., "The Corporate Network in Japan," *Japanese Economic Studies* (Winter 1987–8), pp. 3–37.

Jacobson, R. and D. Aaker, "Myopic Management Behavior with Efficient, but Imperfect, Financial Markets: A Comparison of Information Asymmetries in the U.S. and Japan," *Journal of Accounting and Economics* 16 (1993), pp. 383–405.

Japanese Institute of Certified Public Accountants, *Corporate Disclosure in Japan: Reporting* (Tokyo: JICPA, 1984).

Jensen, M. and W. H. Meckling, "Theory of the Firm: Managerial Behavior, Agency Costs and Ownership Structure," *Journal of Financial Economics* 3 (1976), pp. 305–360.

Johnson, C. *MITI and the Japanese Miracle* (Stanford, CA: Stanford University Press, 1982).

Kawasaki, S. and J. McMillan, "The Design of Contracts: Evidence from Japanese Subcontracting," *Journal of the Japanese and International Economies* 1 (1987), pp. 327–349.

Kester, W. C., *Japanese Takeovers: The Global Contest for Corporate Control* (Boston: Harvard Business School Press, 1991).

Leftwich, R., R. L. Watts and J. L. Zimmerman, "Voluntary Corporate Disclosure: The Case of Interim Reporting," *Journal of Accounting Research* (supplement 1981), pp. 50–77.

Malone, D., C. Fries and T. Jones, "An Empirical Investigation of the Extent of Corporate Financial Disclosure in the Oil and Gas Industry," *Journal of Accounting, Auditing and Finance* (Summer 1993), pp. 249–273.

McCauley, R. and S. Zimmer, "Explaining Difference in the Cost of Capital," *Federal Reserve Bank of New York Quarterly Review* (Summer 1989), pp. 7–28.

McKinnon, J. L., "Application of Anglo-American Principles of Consolidation to Corporate Financial Disclosure in Japan," *Abacus* 20 (1984), pp. 16–33.

McKinnon, J. L., "Cultural Constraints on Audit Independence in Japan," *The International Journal of Accounting* 21 (1988), pp. 17–43.

Miyashita, K. and D. Russell, *Keiretsu: Inside the Hidden Japanese Conglomerates* (New York: McGraw-Hill, 1994).

Miyazaki, Y., *Enterprise Groups in Postwar Japan* (Tokyo: Nihon Keizai Shinbushi, 1976).

Myers, S. C., "Determinants of Corporate Borrowing," *Journal of Financial Economics* (November 1977), pp. 147–175.

Nakatani, I., "The Economic Role of Financial Corporate Groupings" in *The Economic Analysis of the Japanese Firm*, M. Aoki, ed. (Amsterdam: North-Holland, 1984).

Okumura, H., "Interfirm Relations in an Enterprise Group: the Case of Mitsubishi," *Japan Economic Studies* 12 (1982), pp. 53–82.

Osano, H. and Y. Tsutsui, "Credit Rationing and Implicit Contract Theory," *International Journal of Industrial Organization* 4 (1986), pp. 419–438.

Pindyck, R. S. and D. L. Rubinfeld, *Econometric Models and Economic Forecasts* (Tokyo: McGraw-Hill Kogakusha, 1987).

Prowse, S. D., "Institutional Investment and Corporate Finance in the U.S. and Japan," *Journal of Financial Economics* 27 (1990), pp. 67–88.

Prowse, S. D., "The Structure of Corporate Ownership in Japan," *The Journal of Finance* (July 1992), pp. 1121–1140.

Robins, W. A. and K. R. Austin, "Disclosure Quality in Governmental Financial Reports," *Journal of Accounting Research* (Autumn 1986), pp. 412–421.

Sakakibara, S., H. Yamaji, H. Sakurai, K. Shiroshita and S. Fukuda, *The Japanese Stock Market* (Westport, CT: Praeger, 1988).

Schipper, K., "Discussion of Voluntary Corporate Disclosure. The Case of Interim Reporting," *Journal of Accounting Research* 19 (supplement 1981), pp. 85–88.

Sheard, P., *Keiretsu and Closedness of the Japanese Market: An Economic Appraisal* (Institute of Social and Economic Research, Osaka University Discussion Paper No. 273, 1992).

Sheard, P., "Main Banks and Internal Capital Markets in Japan," *Shoken Keizai* 157 (1986), pp. 255–285.

Sheard, P., "The Japanese General Trading Company as an Aspect of Interfirm Risk-Sharing," *Journal of the Japanese and International Economies* 3 (1989), pp. 308–322.

Sheard, P., "The Role of Firm Organization in the Adjustment of a Declining Industry in Japan: The Case of Aluminium," *Journal of the Japanese and International Economies* 5 (1991), pp. 14–40.

Singhvi, S. S. and H. Desai, "An Empirical Analysis of the Quality of Corporate Financial Disclosure," *The Accounting Review* (January 1971), pp. 621–632.

Singhvi, S. S., Corporate Disclosure through Annual Reports in the U.S.A. and India," Columbia University, unpublished doctoral dissertation (1967).

Spero, L. L., "The Extent and Causes of Voluntary Disclosure of Financial Information in Three European Capital Markets: An Explanatory Study," Harvard University, unpublished doctoral dissertation (1979).

Stanga, K., "Disclosure in Published Annual Reports," *Financial Management* (Winter 1976), pp. 42–52.

Stilling, P., R. Norton and L. Hopkins, *World Accounting Survey* (London: Financial Times, 1984).

Stuart, A. and J. K. Ord, *Kendall's Advanced Theory of Statistics* (London: Financial Times, 1983).

Takagi, S., *Japanese Capital Markets* (Cambridge, MA: 1993).

Tonkin, D. J., *World Survey of Published Accounts: An Analysis of 200 Annual Reports from the World's Leading Companies* (London: Lafferty Publications, 1989).

van Wolferen, K., *The Enigma of Japanese Power* (London: MacMillan, 1989).

Wallace, R. S. O., "Disclosure of Accounting Information in Developing Countries: A Case Study of Nigeria," Exeter University, unpublished doctoral thesis, (1987).

Wallace, R. S. O., K. Naser and A. Mora, "The Relationship Between the Comprehensiveness of Corporate Annual Reports and Firm Characteristics in Spain," *Accounting and Business Research* (Winter 1994), pp. 41–53.

Williamson, O. E., *Corporate Control and Business Behavior: An Inquiry into the Effects of Organizational Form on Enterprise Behavior* (Englewood Cliffs, NJ: Prentice Hall, 1970).

Williamson, O. E., *Markets and Hierarchies: Analysis and Antitrust Implications* (New York: Free Press, 1975).

Pergamon

The International Journal of Accounting
37 (2002) 95–111

The International Journal of Accounting

The changing nature of financial disclosure in Japan

W.R. Singleton*, Steven Globerman

College of Business and Economics, Western Washington University, Bellingham, WA 98225-9170, USA

Accepted 31 December 2001

Abstract

This paper investigates whether Japanese companies listed on the Tokyo Stock Exchange (TSE) altered their voluntary accounting disclosure behavior over the period of the 1990s. It implicitly tests for whether the collapse of Japan's "Financial Bubble" in the late 1980s altered the incentives of Japanese managers to be more forthcoming about corporate information. Previous research on Japanese disclosure practices highlights the "secretive" nature of Japanese managers and suggests that cultural preferences strongly discourage disclosure. Our findings suggest that Japanese disclosure practices are sensitive to economic conditions. © 2002 University of Illinois. All rights reserved.

Keywords: Empirical study; Financial disclosure; Japanese companies

1. Introduction

The Japanese economy in the 1990s was subjected to recessionary pressures that were unprecedented in the post-WWII period. In particular, large-scale capital losses among Japanese banks and other financial companies, as well as the collapse of Japanese asset prices, including stock prices, contributed to a significant contraction in the ability (and willingness) of Japanese companies to raise capital in domestic capital markets. As a consequence, an increasing number of Japanese companies turned to foreign companies as equity-based partners, or sold assets and operating businesses to foreign investors.[1] Japanese

* Corresponding author.

E-mail addresses: ron.singleton@wwu.edu (W.R. Singleton), steven.globerman@wwu.edu (S. Globerman).

[1] By way of illustration, foreign direct investment inflows into Japan in 1994 totaled approximately US$1.9 billion. They totaled close to US$5 billion in 1999 (Phillips, 2000). Developments related to inward FDI in Japan are discussed in Globerman and Kokko (1999).

PII: S0020-7063(02)00138-3

companies seeking foreign capital faced strong competition to attract and retain that capital given the very strong performances of American and European stock markets over the period.

In light of an increased reliance on foreign capital, one might expect Japanese companies to undertake initiatives to improve the "marketability" of their debt and equity securities in international capital markets. One potential initiative is to "improve" disclosure practices as they are relevant to foreign investors. There is some theoretical and empirical support for the assertion that increased disclosure, in circumstances characterized by asymmetric information between company officials and potential lenders and investors, can reduce a company's cost of capital.[2] All other things constant, one might expect Japanese companies to incur additional costs associated with improved disclosure to the extent that any resulting favorable impacts on capital costs are expected to exceed the additional costs associated with altering historical disclosure practices.

It seems likely that the profound and widely publicized industrial and financial problems experienced by Japan in the 1990s would have increased the perceived "nonsystematic" risks associated with investing in Japanese assets. For example, news of recession and corporate bankruptcies arguably increased perceived bankruptcy risks across a range of Japanese industrial sectors. Moreover, foreign investors may have perceived an even greater risk of Japanese companies holding back economic "bad news" from foreign investors during the 1990s than during the boom times of the 1970s and 1980s. That is, concerns about opportunistic behavior related to asymmetric information are likely to have grown during the 1990s.

It therefore seems plausible that Japanese companies may have seen it in their economic self-interest to alter their disclosure practices during the 1990s. Haskins, Ferris, and Selling (2000) assert that as an increasing number of large Japanese companies place more emphasis on foreign equity markets for meeting their capital needs, they will be subjected to more stringent disclosure requirements. The plausibility of this development is tempered by at least two considerations. One is that financial analysts' report and other sources of information about Japanese companies may be sufficiently informative and forthcoming about the earnings prospects of those companies such that "additional" disclosure by the latter would have little impact on their costs of capital.[3] Put in other words, the informational efficiency of markets in which Japanese corporate assets are traded may not have been significantly and adversely affected by economic developments in the 1990s, and, as a consequence, corporate incentives to disclose may have been little changed from earlier periods. A second consideration is that reduced needs for financial capital, given reductions in planned investment levels, may have mitigated the pressures of increasing costs of capital facing Japanese companies.

The broad purpose of this paper is to examine whether the "voluntary" disclosure of Japanese companies changed over the 1990s. In this context, it addresses a relatively narrow

[2] See, for example, Botosan (1997), Drake and Peavy (1995), Krishnan, Sankaraguruswamy, and Shin (1996), and Sengupta (1998). For a contradictory argument, see Penno (1997).

[3] In this regard, Botosan (1997) finds for a sample of US companies that there is no association between her measure of disclosure level and the cost of equity capital for firms with high analyst following.

aspect of a much broader issue: how have Japanese institutions changed over recent years in the face of increased global competition for final outputs, as well as for inputs such as skilled labor and financial capital? For several samples of Tokyo Stock Exchange (TSE)-listed companies, we evaluate, using statistical analyses, whether voluntary-disclosure practices changed systematically from the late-1980s to the late-1990s. Our evidence supports the conclusion that voluntary disclosure increased when comparing the later period to the earlier period.

This finding is a contribution to the literature, which currently provides relatively little evidence on the stability of disclosure practices over time. Moreover, our finding contradicts assertions in the literature that Japanese disclosure practices are relatively rigid and insensitive to capital market pressures. A broader inference suggested is that economic circumstances can influence financial "reforms" in Japan.

The paper proceeds as follows. Section 2 offers a brief overview of corporate disclosure practices in Japan, including a review of academic research on those practices. Section 3 describes the approach we have taken to identify changes in disclosure practice during the 1990s. Section 4 analyzes the data described in the preceding section to determine whether voluntary-disclosure practices of Japanese firms have changed over time. Section 5 offers a summary and conclusion.

2. Disclosure practices in Japan

A number of studies have directly or indirectly focused on accounting and related disclosure practices of Japanese companies. Most notably, Cooke (1991, 1992) examines firm-specific characteristics of disclosure among survey samples of Japanese companies. In the process, he notes earlier studies that point to a strong resistance among Japanese companies toward disclosure, per se. He ascribes his own relatively low-survey response rates to the fact that "...the Japanese are inherently secretive and corporations are unwilling to supply accounts to non-shareholders..."[4] Conversely, Choi, Frost, and Meek (1999), while agreeing that Japanese companies are generally reluctant to disclose information, argue that the traditionally low disclosure levels of Japanese firms are due to managers' perceptions that the costs of additional disclosure are greater than the benefits. In this regard, they are proposing the hypothesis that cultural influences can be significantly modified by economic incentives.

Several features of Japanese culture have been cited in the literature as contributing to limited disclosure. One is the keiretsu ownership structure of Japanese industry. In this structure, "insiders" are major sources of financing and are well informed about the earnings prospects of keiretsu partners. Hence, a strong linkage between public disclosure and favorable access to capital allegedly does not exist (Morck, Nakamura, & Shivdasani,

[4] See Cooke (1991, p. 178). For an earlier study pointing to the reluctance of Japanese companies to disclose information, see McKinnon and Harrison (1985).

2000). However, Cooke (1996) finds that companies within a keiretsu with a main bank or main company monitor do not disclose less information than other companies in their annual reports. A second feature discussed in the literature is the alleged reluctance of Japanese borrowers to disclose negative information to outside lenders and investors (Lincoln, 1999). A third is an allegedly less-demanding attitude toward corporate financial reporting on the part of Japanese shareholders as compared to, say, Western shareholders (Haskins et al., 2000, p. 339).

To the extent that "inherent" secrecy of Japanese managers is a durable determinant of corporate disclosure practices in Japan, the dramatic change in that country's economic environment over the 1990s, as described above, might be expected to have little impact on the voluntary-disclosure practices of Japanese businesses. On the other hand, to the extent that segmented and wealthy domestic capital markets shielded Japanese companies from the need for large-scale involvement with international lenders and investors, disclosure practices may not have been so much culturally based, as tied to a relatively small estimated payoff to disclosing more information.[5]

In fact, research efforts examining specific determinants of disclosure behavior of Japanese companies obtain results that are not substantially different from those obtained for companies headquartered in other countries. For example, the single most important determinant of variations in voluntary disclosure among Japanese companies is size (Cooke, 1991, 1992). This is a ubiquitous finding in the disclosure literature.[6] Another finding is that Japanese companies listed on multiple stock exchanges disclose more information than companies listed only on the TSE (Cooke, 1992). This relationship has also been identified for non-Japanese companies. For example, Gray, Meek, and Roberts (1995) find that internationally listed US and UK multinational companies voluntarily disclose more information in their annual reports than domestically listed multinational companies, ceteris paribus.

This similarity between Japanese and non-Japanese companies in terms of the main determinants of disclosure practice belies the notion that cultural differences render Japanese disclosure practices completely idiosyncratic; however, cultural differences discussed earlier could still result in generally lower levels of disclosure in Japan, other things being constant.[7] A focus on whether and how Japanese corporate disclosure practices changed over the 1990s would provide an additional perspective on the strength of cultural influences. In particular, an indirect finding that pressures to integrate more closely into world capital markets were associated with increased information disclosure would be consistent with an interpretation that accounting practices are influenced by global economic imperatives, insofar as Japanese management is concerned.

[5] There is abundant evidence that companies using international capital markets engage in significantly more voluntary disclosure than their counterparts that raise capital primarily in domestic markets (see, for example, Choi & Levich, 1991; Cooke, 1991; Meek, Roberts, & Gray, 1995; Meek & Saudagaran, 1990; Saudagaran & Meek, 1997). A number of these studies point out that participation in international capital markets encourages increased disclosure, primarily of financial information.

[6] See, for example, Foster (1986), Frost and Pownall (1994a), and the studies reviewed in Meek et al. (1995).

[7] See Lincoln (1999) for examples of culturally specific disclosure practices in Japan.

In fact, there have been few studies examining the stability of disclosure behavior over time, particularly for Japan. Botosan (1997) references several non-Japanese studies and concludes that firms' disclosure policies appear to remain constant over time. Cooke (1991) suggests that the need for Japanese companies to raise considerable sums of money from international capital markets in the late 1980s may have encouraged increased disclosure, but he does not formally test this hypothesis. Our study differs from previous studies in its focus on the stability of Japanese company disclosure practices over time. Given the significant change in Japan's economic environment over the 1990s, a focus on this period provides a relatively strong test of the temporal stability of disclosure practices in Japan.

In the following section, we describe our sample selection and the methodology employed to test whether Japanese companies did, in fact, significantly alter their disclosure practices in response to the economic pressures of the 1990s.

3. Sample selection and methodology

3.1. Disclosure instrument and scores

Various methods have been used in the literature to measure the extent of a firm's disclosure.[8] For purposes of this study, the disclosure index developed by Botosan (1997) is used. It was chosen principally because the measurement categories more closely reflect voluntary-disclosure behavior for the sample firms of this study than do the instruments in other studies. For example, the focus of Botosan's index is on voluntarily disclosed information with high predictive value as opposed to disclosure of various historical accounting issues for regulatory purposes. In addition to the focus on voluntary disclosure, the reliability and validity of Botosan's disclosure instrument is the most rigorously tested of those cited in the literature. A copy of the instrument used to measure the disclosure score for each firm is attached as Appendix A.

The major components of the index are classified into the following five categories: background information, 10- or 5-year summary of historical results, key nonfinancial statistics, projected information, and management discussion and analysis of operations. Disclosure items can be both quantitative and qualitative. Points for each individual firm (j) are awarded for specific disclosure items within each category (i) for a given sample year (t). Hence, the final disclosure score ($DISC_{jt}$) measures the total points awarded for disclosure by the (j) firm in time period (t).[9] The maximum DISC score using this instrument is 127—the total value of the disclosure items.

[8] See, for example, Botosan (1997), Cooke (1991, 1992), Frost and Pownall (1994a), Gray et al. (1995), Sengupta (1998). Also, Marston and Shrives (1991) provide an extensive analysis and discussion of the limitations and use of disclosure indices.

[9] The points and scores assigned treat each disclosure item equally; i.e., they are unweighted. However, since there are more disclosure items for some categories of information than for others, Botosan's (1997) instrument implicitly weights information categories differently.

The disclosure index score is based upon information in each firm's annual report to shareholders. Specifically, annual reports were reviewed to determine whether or not to award points for the disclosure items identified in Appendix A. Although the annual report is not the only source or means of disclosure, as noted by Knutson (1992), it is typically the most important source of information for most analysts. In addition, Lang and Lundholm (1993) noted a high, positive correlation between annual-report disclosure and disclosure in other sources (such as press releases or regulatory filings). The annual reports for our sample of firms are the English-language version for each firm. Disclosure by Japanese firms in the English language further qualifies the revealed disclosure as "voluntary," since Japanese firms do not have to translate materials into English for Japanese regulatory purposes. Moreover, reporting in English might be seen as a direct attempt to reduce asymmetric information problems with potential foreign investors and/or customers.

The annual reports for each sample firm were obtained from the TSE. Each annual report was analyzed and assigned points by one of the authors. The same author assigned scores for all firms for internal consistency. The scores from each annual report constituted the disclosure score ($DISC_{jt}$) for each firm for a given year.

3.2. Sample firms

Our sample firms were randomly selected from a stratified sample of firms listed in the Nikkei 225 Index. The Nikkei 225 Index includes 225 of the major firms listed on the "first section" of the TSE. We excluded firms in industries that are highly regulated, for example, banking, insurance, and securities, since their levels of disclosure will be primarily conditioned by regulatory practices. We also excluded service-related firms that are less likely than their manufacturing counterparts to compete in international input and output markets. The sample firms are therefore drawn primarily from manufacturing-related industries.

Three overlapping, albeit not identical, initial samples were created. Their characteristics are summarized in Table 1, and encompass 109 firms for 1996–1998, 113 for 1993–1995, and 48 for 1989.[10] These sample sizes are comparable to those of other disclosure studies.[11] Since these samples are not identical in terms of the identities of the included firms, changes in the calculated disclosure indices over time may reflect changes in the composition of firms across the samples, rather than any "uniform" influence of time, per se, on disclosure behavior. This would be true if individual firms differ in their disclosure practices for reasons unrelated to characteristics "held constant" by our statistical analysis, described below.

[10] While admittedly somewhat arbitrary, we select 1989 as a year representative of Japan's financial and economic bubbles encompassing the second half of the 1980s.

[11] Sample sizes of firms for related studies are as follows: Botosan (1997), 122; Cooke (1991), 48; Cooke (1992), 35; Frost and Pownall (1994b), 93; Gray et al. (1995), 116 US, 64 UK; Sengupta (1998), 103.

Table 1
Summary of sample selection procedures

	Time period		
	1996–1998	1993–1995	Pre-1990
Firms in Nikkei Index	225	225	225
Less firms in regulated, specialized, or service-related	78	78	78
Available for selection	147	147	147
English-language annual report not issued or incomplete	38	34	99
Total	109	113	48
Sample classified by industry:[a]			
Chemicals (4)	15	16	5
Electrical machinery (11)	16	16	11
Foods (1)	10	10	1
Glass and ceramics (2)	8	7	3
Machinery (8)	13	14	9
Nonferrous metals (2)	8	9	3
Pharmaceuticals (4)	5	5	4
Precision instruments	3	3	0
Pulp and paper	4	3	1
Rubber	1	2	1
Steel	4	5	1
Textiles (2)	9	10	2
Transportation equipment (7)	13	13	7
Total sample	109	113	48

[a] The number of firms in the homogeneous sample is parenthetically noted for each industry.

We attempt to hold constant the influence of the identities of firms in our time-series panel, at least in part, by developing an identical sample of firms for each of the three periods. This sample consists of the subset of firms for which annual reports were available for each time period. Focusing on this sample implicitly holds constant interfirm differences that may influence disclosure behavior. That is, it implicitly holds constant the influences of differences in disclosure behavior that are related to a firm's identity and that do not change over time. Forty-one firms had annual reports available for each of the three time periods. The sample of 41 firms is henceforth referred to as the "homogeneous sample."

For the overlapping samples of nonidentical firms (henceforth, "heterogeneous samples"), changing industry mixes might influence overall disclosure behavior to the extent that propensities to disclose differ across industries.[12] A number of studies have identified industry disclosure effects (Botosan, 1997; Cooke, 1992; Sengupta, 1998).[13] If the industrial

[12] The homogeneous sample implicitly holds constant the influences of "industry mix," since no firm's industrial classification changed over the sample period.

[13] In a (unreported) statistical analysis, we also identified differences in the propensities of firms in different industries to disclose for any given time-period sample. These unreported results are available from the authors upon request.

mix of firms varied across our three sample periods (for the heterogeneous samples), we would presumably need to account explicitly for industry affiliation in our subsequent analysis. However, any such analysis is unnecessary, since the industrial compositions of our heterogeneous samples did not change across our three time-period samples.[14] Put in other words, the unchanged industrial mix of firms for our three time-period samples ensures that industry mix does not affect the *change* in disclosure behavior *over time*, which is our focus of interest.

3.3. Time periods

Analysis of the question of the temporal stability of firms' disclosure practices requires a sample time period. Given the time consuming and costly nature of the data collection process, the sample consisted of discrete years instead of a continuous time series. Our implicit assumption is that changes in disclosure are not reversible and proceed relatively deliberately, such that the observed changes between discontinuous years do not mask significant (and possibly contradictory) unobserved changes between nonsample years. Partitioned time periods to capture disclosure behavior have been used in related studies (e.g., Sengupta, 1998) of the incentive effects of disclosure on the firm's cost of capital.

Three specific time periods are selected to represent different economic environments in Japan: 1996–1998, 1993–1995, and 1985–1990. The pre-1990 period was characterized as the "Bubble" economy and was represented by relatively high economic and asset–price growth rates compared with the rest of the decade, as well as relatively abundant domestic sources of capital. The 1993–1995 period saw an "Adjustment" in Japan's economy as it began to experience bankruptcies, business failures, and extensive losses in the stock and real estate markets. For example, bankruptcies in the Tokyo area increased 106% between 1989 and 1995 (source of calculations, Teikoku Data Bank, 1998). A major recession and economic restructuring marked the 1996–1998 period, referred to as the "Current" period. Firms faced increasingly competitive global-product markets, while a banking crisis forced many firms to seek capital outside Japan. The three time periods arguably reflect three distinctive economic environments faced by Japanese firms, although the trend over the entire period was arguably one of Japanese companies facing stronger incentives to integrate into global financial markets, as well as to increase sales in foreign markets.[15] To the extent that increased disclosure improves access to foreign capital, Japanese companies' incentive to disclose information could be expected to increase over the 1990s.

A finding would provide further support for our hypothesis that increased disclosure by Japanese companies did indeed lower their cost of capital. We are unaware of any specific

[14] Using chi-square tests, we cannot reject the hypothesis that the distribution of sample firms by industrial classification is identical when comparing each paired time period.

[15] These periods were also convenient in the sense that the pre-1990 period is comparable with Cooke (1991) and the 1993–1995 relatively comparable with Botosan (1997); thus, the sample has benchmark studies for comparative purposes.

studies providing such a link.[16] However, there is anecdotal evidence supporting the existence of a linkage between disclosure and the cost of capital. For example, one article discusses the experience of Fuji Bank. Executives at Fuji Bank had long insisted that their bank's problems were not as bad as critics suggested. Nevertheless, the media seemed convinced it was hiding problems, and its shares were leading the market down. In late September 1998, the bank decided that it needed to be more forthcoming in its disclosures. In particular, it disclosed that it had US$19.3 billion in "gray area" loans, i.e., assets that did not fit the narrow regulatory definition of bad loans but were ones that prudent investors would want to know about. The bank hired the US accounting firm, Ernst & Young, to check its books and vouch for the accuracy of the bank's accounting. Fears of hidden losses seemed to vanish. Its shares recovered and the premium paid over other banks for funding all but disappeared (Sapsford, 1999).

Data were collected for one year for each time period. The specific years selected were 1989 (for the "Bubble" period), 1994 (for the "Adjustment" period), and 1998 (for the "Current" period). When annual reports for specific companies were not available for the specific year, the next closest preceding year was used, with 1987 as a cut-off year. While it is possible that the use of average-disclosure-index values for two or more years of any subperiod might eliminate purely transitory variations in "equilibrium" disclosure behavior, the individual years chosen are sufficiently separated in time as to capture meaningful changes in disclosure behavior over the decade of the 1990s.

4. Disclosure behavior and determinants

In this section, we report observed changes in disclosure behavior over time for our heterogeneous and homogeneous samples. We also identify the factors that seem to be associated with any observed changes.

4.1. Temporal shifts in levels of disclosure

Table 2 reports mean disclosure scores in each period for the heterogeneous samples, where the sample firms are stratified by industry. Simple comparisons of the average disclosure index values of the heterogeneous samples across the various time periods (the first row in Table 2) suggest that voluntary disclosure increased consistently over time. Specifically, the average value for $DISC_{jt}$ increased from 22.3 (the "Bubble" years) to 23.8 (the "Adjustment" period) to 28.6 ("Current" period). The increase in disclosure values between the first two time periods (Bubble and Adjustment) is modest, and a difference of means test indicates that the average disclosure index values are not significantly different from each other. However, the differences between the average disclosure index values in

[16] We are currently examining the statistical relationship between disclosure and the cost of capital for our sample of Japanese companies.

Table 2
Mean disclosure scores by industry classification (standard deviations in parenthesis)

	Time period					
Industry	*n*	1996–1998	*n*	1993–1995	*n*	Pre-1993
Heterogeneous samples	109	28.6 (10.2)	113	23.8 (7.3)	48	22.3 (7.0)
Chemicals	15	27.3 (11.2)	16	20.8 (6.4)	5	19.6 (4.4)
Electrical machinery	16	31.8 (8.6)	16	26.4 (6.7)	11	27.2 (6.2)
Foods	10	33.5 (9.5)	10	24.1 (7.8)	1	33.0 (–)
Glass and ceramics	8	23.1 (11.3)	7	18.4 (6.1)	3	19.3 (1.5)
Machinery	13	22.5 (6.4)	14	21.6 (5.1)	9	16.3 (6.2)
Nonferrous metals	8	33.8 (12.6)	9	25.6 (7.0)	3	20.7 (3.1)
Pharmaceuticals	5	35.4 (7.2)	5	27.4 (5.7)	4	27.0 (5.6)
Pulp and paper	4	26.8 (6.3)	3	17.7 (8.7)	1	18.0 (–)
Steel	4	24.8 (7.9)	5	30.4 (5.0)	1	11.0 (–)
Textiles	9	27.9 (12.3)	10	24.1 (6.0)	2	20.5 (9.2)
Transportation equipment	13	28.1 (11.5)	13	24.9 (9.5)	7	23.6 (5.4)
Homogeneous sample	41	30.9 (9.2)		25.8 (6.9)		22.8 (7.0)

The samples for precision instruments and rubber are not reported as they were comprised of three or fewer firms.

the Current period and both prior periods are significantly different at conventional significance levels.[17] These observations are further illustrated by the pattern for individual industries. In most cases, disclosure scores in the current period are higher than in the two preceding periods. Disclosure behavior change is somewhat less consistent industry-by-industry between the Bubble and Adjustment periods, although, the small sample sizes for many of the industries make it difficult to infer whether the observed differences are statistically significant.[18]

The average $DISC_{jt}$ values for each time period for the homogeneous sample is reported at the bottom of Table 2. The results again indicate consistently increasing disclosure over time similar to the sample results reported for the heterogeneous samples. Paired sample comparisons of the mean disclosure scores (for the identical 41 firms) indicate significant differences between successive paired time periods. Thus, the average disclosure scores for all firms in the homogeneous sample indicate significant increases in disclosure over the selected time periods.

[17] Strictly speaking, the use of a parametric difference of means test may not be appropriate as the three panels are not strictly independent. Specifically, there are some identical firms in each panel. Nevertheless, the disclosure index for any firm is a random variable over time. Moreover, the disclosure index values are normally distributed in each sample year. The results of relaxing the assumptions for parametric tests and using a Wilcoxon signed ranks nonparametric test are that the relative ranks of all time periods were significantly different from each other (including the first two periods).

[18] As discussed above, since the industry mix of firms is relatively constant over time, our conclusions with respect to overall changes in disclosure behavior should not be sensitive to differences in the disclosure practices of specific industries.

4.2. Analysis of temporal shifts holding determinants constant

The summary evidence presented to this point suggests that voluntary disclosure increased over time for various subsets of Japanese manufacturing companies, as well as across the Japanese manufacturing sector as a whole. A remaining issue to consider is whether the change in disclosure behavior reflects changes in underlying "determinants" of disclosure not implicitly held constant by the composition of our samples, or whether disclosure behavior increases even after the underlying determinants are held constant. Even within the homogeneous sample, the characteristics of firms may be changing in a way that "encourages" increased mean disclosure. For example, it has been widely observed that larger firms disclose more information than their smaller counterparts. Therefore, if our sample of homogeneous firms grew larger, on average, over our sample time period, disclosure could be expected to increase independently of any hypothesized pressures related to changing economic conditions in Japan.

The determinants of voluntary disclosure most often and consistently identified in the literature are firm size, equity market listing, and category of industry. Assets are usually the best indicator of firm size in empirical studies. Hence, we use asset size as a measure of changing firm size over time. Since all firms in both the homogeneous and heterogeneous samples were selected from the Nikkei 225, market listing in the home country is implicitly held constant over time. Moreover, none of the sample firms that were listed (or unlisted) on US stock exchanges changed their foreign-listing status over the sample period. Thus, market listing was effectively held constant through sample selection. Since firms were consistently classified to a given manufacturing industry over the time period considered, industry effects are also effectively held constant.

In other studies, the ownership structure of Japanese companies has been found to influence investment behavior and stock-price valuations in complex ways (Morck et al., 2000). However, as noted earlier, Cooke (1996) found that main company ownership within a keiretsu has no influence on a company's disclosure practices. Moreover, it is likely that ownership structure was relatively stable over time for our sample of large companies. In the event, we did not collect sufficiently detailed data on ownership to permit us to incorporate an ownership variable into our statistical analysis.

To hold firm size constant while examining changes in disclosure behavior over time, we rely upon regression analysis (ordinary least squares). Specifically, we employ two pooled (over time) cross-sections: the 41-firm (homogeneous) sample and the heterogeneous sample of Japanese manufacturing companies. The cross-sections are pooled for the three sample time periods for each sample. The estimating equation is given as Eq. (1):

$$\mathrm{DISC}_{jt} = a + b_1 \ln\mathrm{ASSET}_{jt} + b_2\mathrm{TIME}_t + e_{jt} \quad (1)$$

The dependent variable is defined as above. Values for ASSET are from each company's annual report or from the Japan Company Handbook (various years). The natural log specification is used to mitigate potential problems of heteroscedasticity. The TIME variable is a dummy variable taking a value of zero for our first time period, a value of unity for the second time period, and a value of two for the third time period. This specification embodies the assumption that incentives to disclose increased in a linear fashion over our three time periods. Hence, the dummy variable should have a positive sign.

Since the summary data reported in Table 2 suggest that incentives to disclose may not have increased in a uniform fashion over the sample period, we also use an alternative specification for the TIME variable. Specifically, separate time regimes are identified. One dummy variable ($TIME_2$) takes a value of unity for all sample observations in Period 2 and zero otherwise. A second ($TIME_3$) takes a value of unity for all sample observations in Period 3 and zero otherwise. The base period is therefore the "Bubble" period whose influence is

Table 3
Regression results

Panel A : Heterogeneous sample

$DISC_{jt}$ =	a	+	$b_1 \ln ASSET_{jt}$	+	$b_2 TIME_t$	+	e_{jt} (1)
Coefficients	23.9		3.40		3.17		
Standard error	0.3		39		0.63		
t statistic	− 4.55		8.75		5.03		
P value	.000		.000		.000		
Adj. R^2 = .277	F = 52.25 (prob. .000)				Durbin–Watson statistic = 1.77		
No. of observations = 128							

$DISC_{jt}$ =	a	+	$b_1 \ln ASSET_{jt}$	+	$b_2 TIME_2$	+	$b_3 TIME_3$	+	e_{jt} (2)
Coefficients	− 22.6		3.40		1.14		5.72		
Standard error	5.3		0.39		1.30		1.31		
t statistic	− 4.28		8.74		0.88		4.38		
P value	.000		.000		.380		.000		
Adj. R^2 = .283	F = 36.18 (prob. .000)				Durbin–Watson statistic = 1.79				
No. of observations = 128									

Panel B: Homogeneous sample

$DISC_{jt}$ =	a	+	$b_1 \ln ASSET_{jt}$	+	$b_2 TIME_t$	+	e_{jt} (1)
Coefficients	− 19.4		3.11		3.06		
Standard error	8.1		0.59		0.78		
t statistic	− 2.39		5.24		3.95		
P value	.019		.000		.00		
Adj. R^2 = .297	F = 26.39 (prob. .000)				Durbin–Watson statistic = 1.94		
No. of observations = 121							

$DISC_{jt}$ =	a	+	$b_1 \ln ASSET_{jt}$	+	$b_2 TIME_2$	+	$b_3 TIME_3$	+	e_{jt} (2)
Coefficients	− 19.5		3.16		1.67		6.09		
Standard error	8.13		0.60		1.56		1.56		
t statistic	− 2.40		5.30		1.08		3.93		
P value	.018		.000		.283		.000		
Adj. R^2 = .298	F = 17.97 (prob. .000)				Durbin–Watson statistic = 1.96				
No. of observations = 121									

implicit in the constant term. If disclosure does increase uniformly over time, the coefficients of $TIME_2$ and $TIME_3$ should be positive. The estimating equation is therefore:

$$DISC_{jt} = a + b_1 \ln ASSET_{jt} + b_2 TIME_2 + b_3 TIME_3 + e_{jt} \tag{2}$$

The results of estimating Eqs. (1) and (2) for both the heterogeneous and homogeneous samples are presented in Table 3. The results are fairly robust, with a similar general story to tell across the samples. Namely, voluntary disclosure increased significantly over time. More specifically, the insignificant t statistics for the $TIME_2$ coefficients in both the homogeneous and heterogeneous samples corroborate our earlier inference that there was a modest increase in disclosure comparing the Bubble and Adjustment periods, with the main increase in disclosure coming after the adjustment period. It is noteworthy that the regression coefficients are virtually identical in the homogeneous and heterogeneous samples. This result suggests that firm-specific influences, such as ownership differences, are not exerting a significant influence over time on the disclosure behavior of our heterogeneous sample of firms.

5. Summary and conclusion

This study examines whether disclosure on the part of Japanese firms increased over the 1990s. For three specific time periods, disclosure indices are constructed for different samples of TSE-listed firms. Statistical analysis indicates that average voluntary disclosure increases for our samples when comparing the initial and end time periods. This finding is statistically significant for both our heterogeneous sample and our homogeneous sample of firms. While disclosure is also modestly higher in the middle time period compared to the initial time period, the difference is not statistically significant in either the heterogeneous or the homogeneous sample.

Our basic findings are consistent with suggestions found in the literature that economic incentives tied to changing capital-market conditions will alter traditional disclosure practices, even in Japan. Specifically, they are consistent with the notion that cultural factors contributing to relatively limited voluntary disclosure on the part of Japanese companies are mutable in the face of economic incentives.

Whether the return of more robust economic conditions in Japan will stall or even reverse the trend towards more disclosure is an open question; however, policymakers in other countries might draw some comfort from the fact that large Japanese firms apparently acknowledge the managerial imperatives created by global competition for customers and financial capital.

Acknowledgments

The authors wish to thank the Center for International Business at Western Washington University for financial support and Thomas Miller for research assistance. Tom Roehl and two unidentified reviewers supplied helpful comments and suggestions.

Appendix A. Disclosure index scoring sheet

Disclosure level and the cost of equity capital (Christine A. Botosan, *Accounting Review*, vol. 72, no. 3, July 1997)

Company Name:
Report Type: Annual report/10-k/Summary annual report
Year end:

Background Information:	**Qual.**	**Quan.**
a. A statement of corporate goals or objectives is provided.		
b. A general statement of corporate strategy is provided.		
c. Actions taken during the year to achieve the corporate goal is discussed.		
d. Planned actions to be taken in future years are discussed.		
e. A time frame for achieving corporate goals is provided.		
f. Barriers to entry are discussed.		
g. Impact of barriers to entry on current profits is discussed.		
h. Impact of barriers to entry on future profits is discussed.		
i. The competitive environment is discussed.		
j. The impact of competition on current profits is discussed.		
k. The impact of competition on future profits is discussed.		
l. A general description of the business is provided.		
m. The principal products produced are identified.		
n. Specific characteristics of these products are described.		
o. The principal markets are identified.		
Specific characteristics of these markets are described.		
Summary of historical results:	**10 or more years**	**Fewer than 10 years**
a. Return-on-assets or sufficient information to compute return-on-assets (i.e. net income, tax rate, interest expense and total assets) is provided.		
b. Net profit margin or sufficient information to compute net profit margin (i.e. net income, tax rate, interest expense and sales) is provided.		

c. Asset turnover or sufficient information to compute asset turnover (i.e. sales and total assets) is provided.
d. Return-on-equity or sufficient information to compute return-on-equity (i.e. net income and stockholders equity) is provided.

	Yes	**No**
e. A summary of sales and net income for at least the most recent eight quarters is provided.		

Key nonfinancial statistics:	Amount
a. Number of employees.	
b. Average compensation per employee.	
c. Order backlog.	
d. Percentage of order backlog to be shipped next year.	
e. Percentage of sales in products designed in the last five years.	
f. Market share.	
g. Dollar amount of new orders laced this year.	
h. Units sold.	
i. Unit selling price.	
j. Growth in units sold.	
k. Rejection/defect rates.	
1. Production lead-time.	
m. Age of key employees.	
n. Sales growth in key regions not reported as geographic segments.	
o. Break-even sales US$.	
p. Volume of materials consumed.	
q. Prices of materials consumed.	
r. Ratio of inputs to outputs.	
s. Average age of key employees.	
t. Growth in sales of key products not reported as product segments.	

Projected information:	**Pos., Neg. or Neutral**	**Qual. or Quan.**
a. A comparison of previous earnings projections to actual earnings is provided.		
b. A comparison of previous sales projections to actual sales is provided.		
c. The impact of opportunities available to the firm on future sales or profits is discussed.		
d. The impact of risks facing the firm on future sales or profits is discussed.		

e. A forecast of market share is provided.			
f. A cash flow projection is provided.			
g. A projection of capital expenditures or R&D is provided.			
	Pos., Neg. or Neutral	**Qual. or Quan.**	**Wgt.**
h. A projection of future profits is provided.			
i. A projection of future sales is provided.			
Management discussion and analysis: (explanations for changes must be provided)	**Qual. or Quan.**	**Prod seg.**	**Tot. firm**
a. Change in sales.			
b. Change in operating income.			
	Qual. or Quan.	**Total firm**	
c. Change in cost of goods sold.			
d. Change in cost of goods sold as a percentage of sales.			
e. Change in gross profit.			
f. Change in gross profit as a percentage of sales.			
g. Change in selling and administrative expenses.			
h. Change in interest or interest income.			
i. Change in net income.			
j. Change in inventory.			
k. Change in accounts receivable.			
l. Change in capital expenditures or R&D.			
m. Change in market share.			

References

Botosan, C. (1997, July). Disclosure level and the cost of equity capital. *Accounting Review, 20* (3), 323–439.

Choi, F. D. S., Frost, C., & Meek, G. (1999). *International accounting* (3rd ed.). Englewood Cliffs: Prentice-Hall.

Choi, F. D. S., & Levich, R. M. (1991, June). Behavioral effects of international accounting diversity. *Accounting Horizons*, 1–13.

Cooke, T. E. (1991). An Assessment of voluntary disclosure in the annual reports of Japanese corporations. *International Journal of Accounting, 26* (3), 174–189.

Cooke, T. E. (1992). The impact of size, stock market listing and industry type on disclosure in the annual reports of Japanese listed corporations. *Accounting and Business Research, 22* (87), 229–237.

Cooke, T. E. (1996). The influence of the keiretsu on Japanese corporate disclosure. *Journal of International Financial Management and Accounting, 7* (3), 191–212.

Drake, P. D., & Peavy, J. W. (1995, Spring). Fundamental analysis, stock prices and the demise of the miniscribe corporation. *Journal of Portfolio Management*, 68–73.

Foster, G. (1986). *Financial statement analysis* (2nd ed.). Englewood Cliffs: Prentice-Hall.

Frost, C. A., & Pownall, G. (1994a). Accounting disclosure practices in the United States and United Kingdom. *Journal of Accounting Research, 32* (1), 73–102.

Frost, C. A., & Pownall, G. (1994, Summer). A comparison of the stock price response to earnings disclosure in the US and UK. *Contemporary Accounting Research, 11* (1), 59–83.

Globerman, S., & Kokko, A. (1999). *A new millennium for Japanese–North American economic relations?* Western Washington University, Center for International Business Discussion Paper Series, Number 3.

Gray, S. J., Meek, G. M., & Roberts, C. B. (1995). International capital market pressures and voluntary annual report disclosures by US and UK multinationals. *Journal of International Financial Management and Accounting, 6* (1), 45–68.

Haskins, M. E., Ferris, K. R., & Selling, T. I. (2000). *International financial reporting and analysis: a contextual emphasis* (2nd ed.). Boston: Irwin McGraw-Hill.

Japan Company Handbook, various years. New York: Toyo Keizai American.

Knutson, P. (1992). *Financial reporting into the 1990s and beyond.* New York: Association for Investment Management and Research.

Krishnan, M., Sankaraguruswamy, S., & Shin, H. (1996). *Skewness of earnings and the believability hypothesis: how does the financial market discount accounting disclosures?* Working Paper, University of Minnesota.

Lang, M., & Lundholm, R. (1993, Autumn). Cross-sectional determinants of analyst ratings of corporate disclosures. *Journal of Accounting Research, 32* (2), 246–271.

Lincoln, E. J. (1999, August). *The social consistency of the Japanese economic system and the implications for institutional transformation.* The Brookings Institution, mimeo.

Marston, C., & Shrives, P. (1991). The use of disclosure indices in accounting research: a review article. *British Accounting Review, 23*, 195–210.

McKinnon, J. L., & Harrison, G. L. (1985, Autumn). Cultural influence on corporate and governmental involvement in accounting policy determination in Japan. *Journal of Accounting and Public Policy*, 201–223.

Meek, G. K., Roberts, C. B., & Gray, S. J. (1995, 3rd Quarter). Factors influencing voluntary annual report disclosures by US, UK and continental European multinational corporations. *Journal of International Business Studies*, 555–572.

Meek, G. K., & Saudagaran, S. M. (1990). A survey of research on financial reporting in a transnational context. *Journal of Accounting Literature, 9*, 145–182.

Morck, R., Nakamura, M., & Shivdasani, A. (2000, July). *Bank equity ownership and firm value in Japan.* University of Alberta, mimeo.

Penno, M. C. (1997). Information quality and voluntary disclosure. *Accounting Review, 77*, 275–284.

Phillips, M. M. (2000, January 24). U.S. firms see Japan as hot investment. *Wall Street Journal, A2.*

Sapsford, J. (1999, March 31). Fuji Bank's stock symbolizes recovery play on Japan. *Wall Street Journal, B4.*

Saudagaran, S. M., & Meek, G. K. (1997). A review of research on the relationship between international capital markets and financial reporting by multinational firms. *Journal of Accounting Research, 16*, 127–159.

Sengupta, P. (1998). Corporate disclosure quality and the cost of debt. *Accounting Review, 73*, 459–474.

Teikoku Data Bank (1998). *Teikoku News*, (Tokyo, Japan).

Journal of International Financial Management and Accounting 11:1 2000

The Persistence and Forecast Accuracy of Earnings Components in the USA and Japan

*Don Herrmann**
Oregon State University

Tatsuo Inoue
Kwansei Gakuin University

Wayne B. Thomas
University of Utah

Abstract

Not all components of earnings are expected to provide similar information regarding future earnings. For example, basic financial statement analysis indicates that the persistence of ordinary income should be greater than the persistence of special, extraordinary, or discontinued operations. Because the market assigns higher multiples to earnings components that are more persistent, differentiating earnings components on the basis of relative persistence would appear to be useful. A focus on relative predictive value is consistent with research findings and user recommendations on separating earnings components that are persistent or permanent from those that are transitory or temporary. This paper examines the persistence and forecast accuracy of earnings components for retail and manufacturing companies listed in the world's two largest equity markets; the USA and Japan. We find the forecast accuracy of earnings in both the USA and Japan increases with greater disaggregation of earnings components. The results further indicate that the improvements in forecast accuracy due to earnings disaggregation are greater in the USA than in Japan. The greater emphasis and more detailed guidelines for reporting earnings components in the USA produce a better differentiation in the persistence of earnings components resulting in greater forecast improvements from earnings disaggregation.

Introduction

The Financial Accounting Standards Board (FASB) recently issued a Special Report entitled "Reporting Financial Performance: Current Developments and Future Directions" (FASB, 1998). The Special Report was prepared jointly by members of the Australian, Canadian, New Zealand,

* Address for correspondence: Don Herrmann, Department of Accounting, Finance & Information Management, Oregon State University, Corvallis, OR 97331–2603. We wish to acknowledge the helpful comments of Sudipta Basu, Bruce Behn, Ray Brooks, Roger Graham, Chandra Mishra, Keith Sellers, and Joeseph Weintrop. We also thank seminar participants at Oregon State University, the International Accounting Section 1998 Midyear Meeting, the American Accounting Association's 1998 Annual Meeting, and the Asian-Pacific Conference on International Accounting Issues for their useful comments.

UK, and US Accounting Standards Boards and the International Accounting Standards Committee and "is mainly concerned with the *presentation* or *reporting* of profit or income rather than its *recognition* and *measurement*" (FASB, 1998, para. 1.1). The Special Report emphasizes the importance of income presentation to many user groups and the need for international comparability in this area.

> Performance reporting is one of the central features of financial reporting, and many view it as the most important feature. Because of its importance and because of the growing pressures for financial reporting to be more comparable internationally, performance reporting is an area in which it would be particularly desirable for standard setters to coalesce in terms of their requirements (FASB, 1998, para. 6.1).

While the need for reporting earnings is widely accepted, the format for reporting earnings is not clear and varies widely across countries. The Special Report suggests that disaggregating earnings components according to differences in *persistence* would be one useful format for reporting income (FASB, 1998, para. 4.4). Similar suggestions have been made by the American Accounting Association's Financial Accounting Standards Committee which proposes that earnings components be reported on the basis of how current income relates to future income (AAA, 1997). In other words, earnings components should be presented according to relative earnings persistence. Separating earnings components according to relative earnings persistence would appear to be useful since several studies have shown that the market assigns higher (lower) multiples to earnings components that are more (less) persistent (Lipe, 1986; Ohlson and Penman, 1992; Strong and Walker, 1993).

The ability to distinguish components of earnings on the basis of how they indicate future earnings is closely related to forecast accuracy. As pointed out in the FASB's Special Report, a focus on relative predictive value is consistent with separating components of income that are persistent or permanent from those that are transitory or temporary (FASB, 1998, para. 4.28). Consistent with this view, the Association for Investment Management and Research (AIMR), the UK Institute of Investment Management and Research (IIMR), and the Jenkins Committee Report recommend that earnings be presented in such a way as to enhance its predictive value (FASB, 1998, ch. 4). Academic research has also re-emphasized the importance of earnings predictability in valuing the firm (see Ohlson, 1991, 1995; Penman, 1992; and Bernard, 1995).

Thus, based on the criteria set forth by the FASB and many other groups, this study evaluates and compares the income *reporting* practices of retail and manufacturing firms in the USA and Japan by (1) estimating the persistence coefficients of earnings components and (2) measuring the improvement in forecast accuracy achieved by earnings disaggregation. The persistence of an earnings component is defined as the extent to which an earnings component maps into future earnings, while controlling for other earnings components. Persistence is measured by the coefficients in regressions of next period's return on equity (ROE) on the various components of current period's ROE. The persistence of earnings components in the USA and Japan is estimated over five models representing progressively greater disaggregations of earnings.[1] Forecast accuracy is then used to measure the informativeness of progressively greater disaggregations of earnings.[2] Comparing the improvements in forecast accuracy caused by disaggregation of earnings components provides an indication of the relative benefits of current income reporting practices in the USA versus Japan.

The results demonstrate that the informativeness of earnings in both the USA and Japan consistently increases with greater disaggregation of earnings components. The adjusted R^2s for both the US and Japanese models progressively increase with greater disaggregations of ROE, indicating that greater disaggregations of ROE improve the ability to explain next period's ROE. Furthermore, the accuracy of earnings forecasts for both the US and Japanese firms significantly improves with each successive disaggregation of earnings.

The results also provide evidence that the benefits of earnings disaggregation are greater in the USA than in Japan. The increase in the adjusted R^2s between the most aggregated and most disaggregated models and the magnitude of the F-test for the equality of the persistence of all earnings components suggest that there are greater benefits from disaggregating earnings as reported in the USA than from disaggregating earnings as reported in Japan. Moreover, the improvement in forecast accuracy from the least to the most disaggregated models is greater for the US firms than for the Japanese firms, providing evidence that the benefits of earnings disaggregation, via improved forecast accuracy, are greater in the USA than in Japan. The results are consistent with US reporting guidelines producing a better differentiation in the persistence of earnings components resulting in relatively greater improvements in forecast accuracy from earnings disaggregation.

The remainder of the paper is organized as follows. The next section discusses the related literature on earnings components. The third section describes the five earnings component models. The fourth section provides sample information and descriptive statistics. The fifth section contains the empirical analysis and the final section concludes the paper.

Related Literature

The persistence and predictive ability of earnings components are directly relevant to financial statement users given that prior research has demonstrated that earnings components are differentially related to firm value. Lipe (1986) identifies significant variation in the stock return reactions associated with the unexpected changes in six commonly reported components of earnings indicating that the decomposition of earnings provides additional information to the market that would be lost if only earnings were reported. Swaminathan and Weintrop (1991), using analysts' forecasts to proxy for market expectations, find that revenue and expense components have information content beyond that of earnings. Ohlson and Penman (1992) evaluate empirically how disaggregated accounting data explain returns. They find that, over shorter return intervals from 1 to 5 years, the stock return reactions varied across the earnings components. They also examined the disaggregation of book value into balance sheet components. In contrast to the disaggregation of earnings, there appears to be less information content from the disaggregation of the balance sheet. Strong and Walker (1993) find a significant increase in the returns-earnings association for a sample of firms in the UK by allowing parameter values to vary across different components of earnings. A primary factor in this research is earnings persistence (Lev, 1989; Penman, 1991). The greater the earnings persistence, the greater the multiplier of current earnings (or its components) in the determination of stock price (Kormendi and Lipe, 1987; Easton and Zmijewski, 1989; Collins and Kothari, 1989).

In this study, we estimate the persistence of increasingly disaggregated components of earnings. We then examine whether greater disaggregation of earnings enhances the ability to forecast future earnings. If the components of earnings differ in persistence, then disaggregation of these earnings components should increase the ability to forecast future earnings. Givoly and Hayn (1992) show that backing out nonrecurring items (extraordinary items and discontinued operations) improves forecasts of earnings. Fairfield et al. (1996) find forecast improvements from progressively disaggregating US earnings up to the components of operating income, non-operating income plus taxes, special items, and nonrecurring items. In contrast to our findings, they find that disaggregation beyond this level does not further improve forecast accuracy. Kinney and Trezevant (1997) provide evidence that special items are used to manage income especially when earnings are well above or well below earnings reported in the prior year. They advise analysts to pay careful attention to special items in determining a firm's recurring earnings power.

We examine the persistence and forecast accuracy of earnings components in the world's two largest capital markets: the USA and Japan. These two countries provide a strong contrast in financial reporting requirements and financial regulatory environments (Herrmann, Inoue and Thomas, 1996, p. 64). Prior research has not estimated the persistence of earnings components or examined the benefits of earnings disaggregation in forecasting earnings in a Japanese setting. Furthermore, comparing the persistence of earnings components for the US and Japanese firms may provide information useful for financial statement analysis purposes. The earnings persistence of firms in one country may differ from the earnings persistence of firms in another country, especially when the earnings measurement and reporting practices are as different as those in the USA and Japan. Finally, comparing the improvements in forecast accuracy from earnings disaggregation between the two countries should provide insight into the appropriateness of the income statement format in the USA versus that found in Japan. For example, we find that the more narrow definition of extraordinary income in the USA results in a correspondingly greater differentiation in the persistence of ordinary and extraordinary income.

Earnings Component Models

ROE is regarded as the primary summary measure in traditional ratio analysis (Penman, 1991, p. 233). ROE is defined as earnings divided by beginning of period stockholders' equity. Deflating earnings and its various components by beginning stockholders' equity also serves to control for size effects (Foster, 1986, p. 267) and heteroscedasticity. Thus, the discussion of earnings components in this paper refers specifically to earnings components scaled by equity, not earnings components alone. To determine whether the results are sensitive to the use of stockholders' equity as the scale variable, we also ran all tests using total assets and total sales as the scale variable. The results using these alternative scale measures are similar to those reported and do not affect any of the conclusions. We also estimated all persistence coefficients and measured improvement in forecast accuracy using *unscaled* earnings. Once again, the results using no scale variable are very similar to those reported and none of the primary conclusions is affected.

Figures 1 and 2 provide a summary of the five earnings component models for the US and Japanese firms, respectively. The ROE model represents the fully aggregated benchmark model whereby next period's ROE is regressed on current ROE. The remaining four models, EBT, ORD, OPER, and FULL, represent progressively greater disaggregation of earnings scaled by equity. The earnings components included in each US model were matched as closely as possible with comparable earnings components for each Japanese model.

Earnings before Taxes and Corporate Taxes

The EBT model separates ROE into earnings before taxes, corporate taxes, minority interest, and either nonrecurring items for the US sample

Model				
ROE	EBT	ORD	OPER	FULL
ROE				
	EBT			
		ORD		
			OPER	
				SALES
				COGS
				SGA
			NONOPER	
				OTHINC
				INTEXP
		SPEC	SPEC	SPEC
	TAX	TAX	TAX	TAX
	MIN	MIN	MIN	MIN
	NONREC	NONREC	NONREC	
				DIS
				EXT

Figure 1. Models and Earnings Components for US Firms

ROE = return on equity, EBT = earnings before tax, TAX = income tax expense, MIN = minority interest, NONREC = nonrecurring items, ORD = ordinary income, SPEC = special items, OPER = operating income, NONOPER = nonoperating income, SALES = sales, COGS = cost of goods sold, SGA = selling, general, and admin. expenses, OTHINC = other revenues and expenses, INTEXP = interest expense, DIS = discontinued operations, and EXT = extraordinary items. All variables are earnings components in period t scaled by beginning of period stockholders' equity (t–1). The dependent variable is ROE in period t+1 (i.e., net income_{t+1}/ stockholders' equity_t).

		Model		
ROE	EBT	ORD	OPER	FULL
ROE				
	EBT			
		ORD		
			OPER	
				SALES
				COGS
				SGA
			NONOPER	
				OTHREV
				INTINC
				OTHEXP
				INTEXP
		EXT	EXT	
				EXTGAIN
				EXTLOSS
	TAX	TAX	TAX	TAX
	MIN	MIN	MIN	MIN
	OTHER	OTHER	OTHER	OTHER

Figure 2. Models and Earnings Components for Japanese Firms

ROE = return on equity, EBT = earnings before tax, TAX = income tax expense, MIN = minority interest, OTHER = other items, ORD = ordinary income, EXT = extraordinary items, OPER = operating income, NONOPER = nonoperating income, SALES = sales, COGS = cost of goods sold, SGA = selling, general, and admin. expenses, OTHREV = other revenue, INTINC = interest income, OTHEXP = other expenses, INTEXP = interest expense, EXTGAIN = extraordinary gain, and EXTLOSS = extraordinary loss. All variables are earnings components in period t scaled by beginning of period stockholders' equity (t–1). The dependent variable is ROE in period t+1 (i.e., net income_{t+1} / stockholders' equity_t).

or other items for the Japanese sample. Nonrecurring items for the US firms include discontinued operations and extraordinary items, reported net-of-tax. Other items for the Japanese firms represent income adjustments due to consolidation reporting such as the amortization of goodwill, income from non-consolidated subsidiaries, and foreign currency translation amounts. Two aspects of Japanese tax accounting are distinct from that found in the USA. First, in contrast to the differences in financial and tax reporting found in the USA, there is a high level of alignment between financial reporting and tax reporting in Japan. Second, intra-period tax allocation is not allowed in Japan. In the USA, nonrecurring items such as discontinued operations or extraordinary items are reported on a net-of-tax basis. In contrast to the practice in the USA, Japanese firms are not allowed to report individual line items on a net-of-tax basis. Rather, Japanese Generally Accepted Accounting Principles (GAAP) require corporate tax expense to be reported as a single line item just before net income.

Ordinary and Special/Extraordinary

The ORD model divides earnings before taxes into ordinary income and special items for the US sample while dividing earnings before taxes into ordinary income and extraordinary items for the Japanese sample. In the USA, special items are defined as unusual or infrequent items presented before taxes. In Japan, extraordinary items are defined in a much broader manner than in the USA, encompassing more than the US equivalent of special items and extraordinary items combined. Extraordinary items in Japan include prior period adjustments, gains/losses on sales of fixed assets, write-off of assets with no expected future benefit, and certain extraordinary foreign exchange gains/losses (BADC, 1982, p. 5; JICPA, 1991, pp. 14–15). The broader definition in Japan is more consistent with current international accounting standards. The US definition is more restrictive than most other countries in that extraordinary items must be both unusual and infrequent.[3] The persistence of extraordinary items in Japan may exceed the persistence of either special or extraordinary items in the US because the Japanese definition of extraordinary is more inclusive containing some items reported as operating income in the USA.

Operating and Nonoperating

The OPER model further separates ordinary income into operating and nonoperating income. Operating income consists of sales, cost of goods sold, and selling, general and administrative expenses in both countries. Nonoperating items in Japan include financing costs such as interest revenue, interest expense, dividend income, gains/losses on sales of marketable securities, and other miscellaneous items such as bond issue expense (JICPA, 1991, pp. 14–15). Nonoperating items in the USA are defined in a similar manner, except that some of the items reported as nonoperating in the USA are more likely to be reported as extraordinary items in Japan (e.g., gains/losses on sales of fixed assets).

Full Disaggregation

The FULL model disaggregates operating income into sales, costs of goods sold, and selling, general and administrative expenses for both countries. For the US sample, nonoperating income is divided into interest expense and the net of other nonoperating revenues and expenses. Nonrecurring items in the USA are divided into discontinued operations and extraordinary items. For the Japanese sample, nonoperating income is disaggregated into interest income, interest expense, other revenues, and other expenses. Japanese extraordinary income is divided into extraordinary gains and extraordinary losses. Japanese GAAP requires revenues, expenses, gains, and losses to be stated at gross amounts such that revenues and expenses cannot be excluded from the income statement by offsetting against one another (BADC, 1982, p. 2). US accounting standards permit the offsetting of certain items in the income statement. For instance, US GAAP allow the offsetting of gains and losses on discontinued operations. The FULL model examines whether revenues and gains indicate future earnings differently than expenses and losses for the operating, non-operating, and extraordinary categories, respectively. If persistence varies among revenues and expenses in the same category, an argument can be made that revenues and expenses should not be offset in a particular reporting category since they provide different information regarding future earnings.

Sample Information and Descriptive Statistics

Consolidated US data were collected from COMPUSTAT. Data for the consolidated[4] Japanese firms were collected from the NEEDS/MICRO database at the Kwansei Gakuin University Information Processing Research Center. This comprehensive Japanese database contains accounting information for all Japanese listed companies beginning in 1984. Financial, insurance, real estate, transportation, utilities, and service industries were excluded as reported earnings in these industries often do not conform to the common income statement format. Observations were deleted for the following reasons: (1) the components of ROE did not sum to within 1% of reported ROE, (2) beginning of period stockholders' equity, used in scaling the components of ROE, was negative, (3) ROE_{t+1} or ROE_t fell in the top or bottom 1% of the sample observations, and (4) observations had R-studentized residuals with a magnitude greater than 2 in the fully disaggregated model (Belsey, Kuh and Welsch, 1980). The four controls resulted in approximately 8.5% of the possible observations being eliminated from each sample. The final samples consist of 12,334 observations for the US sample and 7,564 observations for the Japanese sample for the 10-year period from 1985 to 1994.[5]

Descriptive statistics on the components of ROE for the US sample and the Japanese sample are provided in Tables 1 and 2, respectively. Consistent with prior research (Choi et al., 1983), the mean ROE in Japan (0.068) is significantly lower than in the USA (0.112). In fact, earnings at each level of aggregation (expressed as a percentage of shareholders' equity) are systematically lower for Japanese firms than for US firms. The mean ROE, EBT, ORD, and OPER are all approximately 4–5% (of stockholders' equity) lower in Japan. This may be attributable in part to the close relationship between financial and tax reporting in Japan. With few exceptions, expenses can only be deducted for tax purposes in Japan if they are also reported as expenses for financial reporting purposes. Due to the strong influence of taxes, there is a tendency towards conservative financial reporting in Japan (Radebaugh and Gray, 1997, p. 114).

Table 1. *Descriptive Statistics on the Components of ROE for US Firms for the 10 year period from 1985 to 1994* (n = 12,334)

Variable	*Mean*	*Std. dev.*	*Q1*	*Median*	*Q3*	*% = 0*	*% > 0*
ROE	0.112	0.189	0.037	0.121	0.196	0	82.8
EBT	0.194	0.269	0.065	0.189	0.313	0	84.5
ORD	0.205	0.244	0.075	0.194	0.313	0	86.7
OPER	0.264	0.305	0.111	0.233	0.359	0	90.0
SALES	3.958	4.743	1.859	2.864	4.471	0	100
COGS	2.838	4.034	1.094	1.891	3.191	0	100
SGA	0.857	0.937	0.391	0.656	1.046	0.2	99.8
NONOPER	–0.059	0.178	–0.074	–0.027	0.004	0.3	28.1
OTHINC	0.031	0.062	0.004	0.018	0.041	6.7	83.7
INTEXP	0.090	0.180	0.020	0.048	0.095	4.4	95.6
SPEC	–0.011	0.123	0.000	0.000	0.000	63.1	14.4
TAX	0.079	0.096	0.019	0.067	0.119	4.3	85.3
MIN	0.002	0.014	0.000	0.000	0.000	85.9	11.5
NONREC	–0.001	0.108	0.000	0.000	0.000	72.4	14.7
DIS	–0.002	0.052	0.000	0.000	0.000	89.2	4.8
EXT	0.001	0.097	0.000	0.000	0.000	79.9	11.7

ROE = return on equity, EBT = earnings before tax, TAX = income tax expense, MIN = minority interest, NONREC = nonrecurring items, ORD = ordinary income, SPEC = special items, OPER = operating income, NONOPER = nonoperating income, SALES = sales, COGS = cost of goods sold, SGA = selling, general, and admin. expenses, OTHINC = other revenues and expenses, INTEXP = interest expense, DIS = discontinued operations, and EXT = extraordinary items. All variables are earnings components scaled by beginning of period stockholder's equity.

Table 2. *Descriptive Statistics on the Components of ROE for Japanese firms for the ten year period from 1985 to 1994* (n = 7,564)

Variable	*Mean*	*Std. dev.*	*Q1*	*Median*	*Q3*	*% = 0*	*% > 0*
ROE	0.068	0.080	0.031	0.063	0.100	0	90.1
EBT	0.154	0.142	0.073	0.136	0.215	0	90.7
ORD	0.157	0.148	0.074	0.138	0.218	0	92.5
OPER	0.202	0.218	0.089	0.159	0.260	0	94.8
SALES	6.021	11.317	2.175	3.493	6.201	0	100
COGS	5.019	10.820	1.581	2.662	5.049	0	100
SGA	0.800	0.796	0.368	0.585	0.962	0	100
NONOPER	–0.046	0.129	–0.063	0.018	0.009	0	33.7
OTHREV	0.047	0.067	0.016	0.028	0.052	0	100
INTINC	0.046	0.099	0.016	0.028	0.046	0	100
OTHEXP	0.029	0.055	0.020	0.048	0.094	0.5	99.5
INTEXP	0.109	0.195	0.026	0.056	0.117	0.1	99.9
EXT	–0.002	0.050	–0.011	–0.002	0.002	6.9	32.8
EXTGAIN	0.028	0.228	0.000	0.004	0.018	18.4	81.6
EXTLOSS	0.030	0.224	0.003	0.010	0.025	10.2	89.8
TAX	0.087	0.074	–0.005	0.072	0.475	0.1	98.8
MIN	0.002	0.007	0.000	0.000	0.002	34.1	54.1
OTHER	0.002	0.016	0.000	0.000	0.004	27.6	46.9

ROE = return on equity, EBT = earnings before tax, TAX = income tax expense, MIN = minority interest, OTHER = other items, ORD = ordinary income, EXT = extraordinary items, OPER = operating income, NONOPER = nonoperating income, SALES = sales, COGS = cost of goods sold, SGA = selling, general, and admin. expenses, OTHREV = other revenue, INTINC = interest income, OTHEXP = other expenses, INTEXP = interest expense, EXTGAIN = extraordinary gain, and EXTLOSS = extraordinary loss. All variables are earnings components scaled by beginning of period stockholder's equity.

Sales and cost of goods sold as a percentage of beginning stockholder's equity are much higher in Japan than in the USA. However, gross margin as a percentage of beginning stockholder's equity is about 11% greater in the US (1.117) than in Japan (1.002). This is consistent with a relatively greater emphasis on market share in Japan, as opposed to earnings performance in the USA. Interest expense as a percentage of beginning stockholder's equity is also higher in Japan. This may be explained by the greater reliance on debt financing in Japan (Nobes and Parker, 1995, p. 293) offset to some extent by the lower interest rates in Japan.

The relative frequency of reporting the income statement components is similar between the two samples with the exception of extraordinary items and minority interest. A much higher proportion of Japanese firm-year observations report extraordinary items (93%) in comparison to US firm-year observations (20%) consistent with the much broader definition of extraordinary items used in Japan. Similarly, minority interest is reported more often in Japan (66%) than in the USA (14%). This is likely due to both differences in corporate structure and differences in the definition of minority interest between the two countries. Relative to the USA, the corporate group in Japan consists of an intricate group of cross holdings where there may be no dominant parent company resulting in a higher proportion of firms reporting minority interest.

Empirical Analysis

Persistence Coefficients of Earnings Components

ROE_{t+1} is regressed first on ROE_t and then on progressively greater disaggregations of ROE_t to estimate the persistence coefficients of the earnings components. Panel A of Tables 3 and 4 report the adjusted R^2s and the persistence coefficients (t-statistics) for the US and Japanese firms, respectively. The models in Panel A of Tables 3 and 4 are presented from the least disaggregated model (ROE model) to the most disaggregated model (FULL model). Panel B of Tables 3 and 4 provides F-tests for differences in the estimated persistence coefficients for the US and the Japanese firms, respectively. A significant F-test indicates there are differences in persistence coefficients.

Multicollinearity is a concern since the independent variables in the regressions are earnings components which may be highly correlated. In the presence of multicollinearity, the variance of the ordinary least squares coefficient estimates are large causing the coefficient estimates to be less precise. To determine the extent of multicollinearity, we calculate variance inflation factors (VIFs) for the independent variables. Kennedy (1992, p. 183) states that a VIF greater than 10 indicates harmful collinearity. For the US sample, no variable had a VIF greater than 10 in the EBT, ORD, or OPER model. In the FULL model, sales, cost of goods sold, and selling, general and administrative expenses each had a VIF greater than 10. For the Japanese sample, no variable had a VIF greater than 10 in the EBT or ORD model and only operating income had a VIF greater than 10 in the OPER model. In the FULL model, sales, cost of goods sold, selling, general and administrative expenses, interest expense, extraordinary gain, and extraordinary loss each had a VIF greater than 10.

Even in the presence of multicollinearity, coefficient estimates remain unbiased and continue to represent the best linear unbiased estimator. The adjusted R^2 statistic is also unaffected by multicollinearity. More importantly,

Table 3. *Estimated Coefficients (t-statistics) and F-statistics for Regressions of ROE_{t+1} on Components of ROE_t for US Firms from 1985 to 1994* (n = 12,334)

Panel A: Estimated Coefficients (t-statistics)

	ROE	*EBT*	*ORD*	*OPER*	*FULL*
Adjusted R^2	0.351	0.384	0.460	0.463	0.471
Intercept	0.046 (33.8)	0.032 (22.0)	0.019 (13.1)	0.021 (14.8)	0.031 (18.5)
ROE	0.501 (81.6)				
EBT		0.434 (50.6)			
ORD			0.580 (66.1)		
OPER				0.574 (65.4)	
SALES					0.582 (65.4)
COGS					–0.583 (–65.2)
SGA					–0.587 (–64.7)
NONOPER				0.629 (61.6)	
OTHINC					0.420 (21.8)
INTEXP					–0.630 (–58.5)
SPEC			0.124 (11.3)	0.118 (10.8)	0.126 (11.2)
TAX		–0.163 (–7.0)	–0.407 (–18.0)	–0.387 (–17.1)	–0.377 (–16.4)
MIN		–0.625 (–7.8)	–0.744 (–9.9)	–0.723 (–9.7)	–0.653 (–8.8)
NONREC		0.246 (20.8)	0.085 (7.3)	0.081 (7.0)	
DIS					0.066 (3.3)
EXT					0.099 (7.4)

ROE = return on equity, EBT = earnings before tax, TAX = income tax expense, MIN = minority interest, NONREC = nonrecurring items, ORD = ordinary income, SPEC = special items, OPER = operating income, NONOPER = nonoperating income, SALES = sales, COGS = cost of goods sold, SGA = selling, general, and admin. expenses, OTHINC = other revenues and expenses, INTEXP = interest expense, DIS = discontinued operations, and EXT = extraordinary items. All variables are earnings components scaled by beginning of period stockholder's equity.

Panel B: F-tests for differences in persistence coefficients in Panel A

Model	*Coefficients*	*F-statistic*
EBT	EBT = –TAX	267.87
	EBT = –TAX = –MIN = NONREC	225.16
ORD	ORD = SPEC	1,720.52
	ORD = SPEC = –TAX = –MIN = NONREC	622.55
OPER	OPER = NONOPER	84.85
	OPER = NONOPER = SPEC = –TAX = –MIN = NONREC	518.40
FULL	SALES = –COGS = –SGA	11.19
	OTHINC = –INTEXP	144.85
	DIS = EXT	1.96
	SALES = –COGS = –SGA, OTHINC = –INTEXP, DIS = EXT	46.31
	SALES = –COGS = –SGA = OTHINC = –INTEXP = SPEC = –TAX = –MIN = DIS = EXT	312.82

Table 4. *Estimated Coefficients (t-statistics) and F-statistics for Regressions of ROE_{t+1} on Components of ROE_t for Japanese Firms from 1985 to 1994* (n = 7,564)

Panel A: Estimated Coefficients (t-statistics)

	ROE	*EBT*	*ORD*	*OPER*	*FULL*
Adjusted R^2	0.519	0.552	0.574	0.578	0.581
Intercept	0.016 (23.1)	0.006 (7.3)	0.006 (7.7)	0.006 (8.1)	0.006 (6.1)
ROE	0.596 (90.4)				
EBT		0.448 (49.8)			
ORD			0.494 (54.4)		
OPER				0.488 (53.9)	
SALES					0.492 (54.2)
COGS					–0.491 (–54.2)
SGA					–0.489 (–54.0)
NONOPER				0.525 (54.3)	
OTHREV					0.536 (36.9)
INTINC					0.507 (38.7)
OTHEXP					–0.508 (–33.4)
INTEXP					–0.546 (–52.0)
EXT			0.291 (24.5)	0.278 (23.3)	
EXTGAIN					0.282 (23.6)
EXTLOSS					–0.278 (–22.9)
TAX		–0.229 (–13.4)	–0.314 (–18.2)	–0.291 (–16.7)	–0.306 (–17.3)
MIN		–0.059 (–0.7)	–0.229 (–3.0)	–0.068 (–0.9)	–0.113 (–1.4)
OTHER		0.558 (17.8)	0.540 (17.6)	0.537 (17.7)	0.542 (17.7)

ROE = return on equity, EBT = earnings before tax, TAX = income tax expense, MIN = minority interest, OTHER = other items, ORD = ordinary income, EXT = extraordinary items, OPER = operating income, NONOPER = nonoperating income, SALES = sales, COGS = cost of goods sold, SGA = selling, general, and admin. expenses, OTHREV = other revenue, INTINC = interest income, OTHEXP = other expenses, INTEXP = interest expense, EXTGAIN = extraordinary gain, EXTLOSS = extraordinary loss. All variables are earnings components scaled by beginning of period stockholder's equity.

Panel B: F-tests for differences in persistence coefficients in Panel A.

Model	*Coefficients*	*F-statistic*
EBT	EBT = –TAX	514.24
	EBT = –TAX = –MIN = OTHER	186.42
ORD	ORD = EXT	387.53
	ORD = EXT = –TAX = –MIN = OTHER	243.87
OPER	OPER = NONOPER	78.37
	OPER = NONOPER = EXT = –TAX = –MIN = OTHER	212.77
FULL	SALES = –COGS = –SGA	17.21
	OTHREV = –INTINC = –OTHEXP = –INTEXP	8.89
	EXTGAIN = –EXTLOSS	3.40
	SALES = –COGS = –SGA, OTHREV = –INTINC = –OTHEXP = –INTEXP, EXTGAIN = –EXTLOSS	7.98
	SALES = –COGS = –SGA = OTHREV = INTINC = –OTHEXP = –INTEXP = EXTGAIN = –EXTLOSS = –TAX = –MIN = OTHER	101.59

forecasts in the presence of multicollinearity are unaffected as long as the multicollinearity pattern is expected to prevail in the situations to be predicted (Kennedy, 1992, pp. 177–181). Therefore, we proceed with a brief discussion of the persistence coefficients bearing in mind that for the FULL model several of the coefficient estimates are less precise due to the presence of multicollinearity. The persistence coefficients and statistical tests presented in Tables 3 and 4 should be interpreted as descriptive statistics. The emphasis of the study is on the forecast accuracy of the earnings components which, as stated above, is unaffected by multicollinearity.

All of the persistence coefficients have the expected sign: positive for revenues and gains and negative for expenses and losses. The coefficients are all significant with the exception of MIN in Japan. The persistence coefficients on ORD greatly exceed those on SPEC/EXT for both US and Japanese firms. Also, note that the persistence of EXT (0.291) for Japanese firms is much higher than the persistence of SPEC (0.124) and NONREC (0.085) for US firms. This likely is related to the broader definition of extraordinary items used in Japan. It appears that a better distinction is being made in the USA than in Japan between ordinary income, expected to recur in the future, and non-ordinary income, affecting only the current period. The coefficient on interest expense in the USA is significantly greater than the coefficient on nonoperating income excluding interest expense (F-test = 144.85), providing support for reporting interest expense as a separate component of income. With this one exception, the results for both countries indicate that within each of the three categories of operating, nonoperating, and extraordinary, revenues and gains provide similar information to expenses and losses regarding future earnings. Offsetting revenues and expenses within the operating or nonoperating sections or offsetting gains and losses in the nonrecurring (i.e., discontinued operations or extraordinary items) section, as sometimes occurs under current US GAAP, does not appear to hinder the informativeness of those earnings components in explaining next period's ROE.

Beginning with the ROE model and moving to the right in Panel A of Tables 3 and 4, the adjusted R^2s progressively increase with greater disaggregations of ROE for both the US and Japanese samples. Greater disaggregations of ROE improve the ability of earnings components to explain next period's ROE. The adjusted R^2s in Japan are consistently higher than in the US for all five models indicating that the proportion of next period's ROE explained by the components of the current period's ROE is greater in Japan.

One way to measure the benefit of earnings disaggregation is by comparing the increase in the adjusted R^2s. The adjusted R^2 for the US sample increased from 0.351 for the ROE model to 0.471 for the FULL model (a 34% increase). The adjusted R^2 for the Japanese sample increased from 0.519 to 0.581 (a 12% increase). The benefits of disaggregation can also be seen by testing whether the coefficients on earnings components differ. If the coefficients on earnings components do not differ, then disaggregation provides no additional explanatory power for next period's earnings. The equality of coefficients is tested using the standard F-tests and the results are reported in Panel B of Tables 3 and 4. For each successive model, the null hypothesis that earnings coefficients are equal (i.e., the more disaggregated model does not outperform the less disaggregated model) can be rejected at the 0.01 level or better. Each progressive disaggregation of earnings provides significantly more explanatory power for next period's earnings than the previous model. The F-statistics are generally greater for the US sample than for the Japanese sample. Even though we are able to break Japanese earnings into slightly finer components than US earnings, the results suggest that there are greater benefits from disaggregating earnings as reported in the USA than from disaggregating earnings as reported in Japan.

Forecast Accuracy of Earnings Components

In this section, the primary emphasis of the paper, we test whether the perceived benefits from earnings disaggregation result in improved forecasts of next period's earnings. The earnings forecasts are performed in the following manner. Cross-sectional relations are estimated by regressing ROE in 1986 on the components of ROE in 1985. The estimated persistence coefficients are then applied to earnings components in 1986 to forecast ROE in 1987. This forecast procedure is then repeated each year resulting in a total of nine years of earnings forecasts (1987 through 1995). We delete influential observations independently for each forecasting year using the procedures discussed previously in the section on sample data and descriptive statistics. Influential observations are deleted only in developing the annual coefficient estimates used in the forecast models. Out-of-sample forecast observations are not deleted in order to avoid any potential hindsight bias.

Table 5 presents the absolute forecast errors for the US firms (Panel A) and the Japanese firms (panel B) for a naive model and each of the five progressively more disaggregated models defined earlier. The naive model

Table 5. *Absolute Forecast Errors for US Firms* (n = 10,656) *and Japanese Firms* (n = 6,182)

	Naive	*ROE*	*EBT*	*ORD*	*OPER*	*FULL*
Panel A: US Firms						
Mean	0.1467	0.1433	0.1403	0.1366	0.1360	0.1347
Std	1.3128	1.3133	1.3135	1.3126	1.3120	1.3118
25%	0.0208	0.0278	0.0261	0.0254	0.0246	0.0239
Median	0.0577	0.0612	0.582	0.0556	0.0548	0.0542
75%	0.1427	0.1274	0.1229	0.1170	0.1162	0.1144
95%	0.4191	0.3938	0.3900	0.3812	0.3823	0.3774
Panel B: Japanese Firms						
Mean	0.0442	0.0409	0.0403	0.0397	0.0388	0.0382
Std	0.0907	0.0891	0.0889	0.0885	0.0881	0.0864
25%	0.0089	0.0093	0.0096	0.0093	0.0087	0.0085
Median	0.0223	0.0213	0.0208	0.0205	0.0194	0.0196
75%	0.0488	0.0426	0.0416	0.0407	0.0404	0.0403
95%	0.1529	0.1336	0.1302	0.1306	0.1312	0.1276

The naive model forecasts next period's return on equity to be the current period's return on equity (i.e., a random walk forecast). See Figures 1 and 2 for other model definitions.

estimates ROE for firm i in period t + 1 to be equal to firm i's reported ROE in period t (i.e., a random walk model). For both the US and Japanese samples, the mean absolute forecast error for each of the five progressively more disaggregated models is lower than that found for the naive model. The same holds true for the median absolute forecast errors in Japan, while for the US sample, only the median absolute forecast errors for the ORD, OPER, and FULL models outperform the naive model.

Beginning with the ROE model and moving to the right in Panel A, the mean and median absolute forecast errors consistently decrease from the most aggregated to the most disaggregated model for US firms.[6] For the Japanese sample in Panel B, the mean absolute forecast error declines for each successive disaggregation from the ROE model to FULL model. The same is true for the median absolute forecast error with the exception that the median of the OPER model is slightly lower than the median of the FULL model. These findings also hold, in general, for both countries in the 25, 75 and 95 percentile values of absolute forecast errors indicating that forecast improvements are not restricted to one end of the distribution. In summary, the general decline in absolute forecast errors for the progressively more disaggregated models provides evidence that the income reporting formats in the USA and Japan provide useful information.

Absolute forecast errors are much lower in Japan than in the USA in each of the six models presented. The mean (median) absolute forecast error for the ROE model is 0.1433 (0.0612) for the US sample compared to 0.0409 (0.0213) for the Japanese sample. The lower forecast errors in Japan are related to the lower variability of Japanese income. The average absolute change in ROE, as shown by the mean for the naive model, is 0.1467 in the USA compared to only 0.0442 in Japan. Furthermore, the standard deviation for the naive model is 131% for US firms compared to a remarkably low 9% for Japanese firms providing additional descriptive evidence as to the significantly lower variability of earnings in Japan.

Table 6 reports the significance of the mean and median improvement in forecast accuracy between progressively more disaggregated models for US firms (Panel A) and Japanese firms (Panel B). The mean difference is tested using a paired t-test and the median difference is tested using a non-parametric Wilcoxon signed rank test. The nonparametric sign test was also computed. The results of the sign test closely follow those of the Wilcoxon signed rank tests and are discussed only when differences occur. For each pair of models, the absolute forecast error of the more disaggregated model is subtracted from the less disaggregated model. Therefore, positive values indicate that, on average, forecasting improves with greater disaggregation. Table 6 also reports the number of years (out of nine) in which the more disaggregated model has a smaller (mean or median) absolute forecast error than the less disaggregated model.

As shown in the first column of the results, the ROE model outperforms the naive model in terms of mean difference in absolute error. The median difference in absolute error for the US sample, however, indicates that the naive model outperforms the ROE model. The Wilcoxon test is not significant but a sign test is significant at approximately the 0.03 level. Next, beginning with the ROE model versus EBT model and moving to the right, the accuracy of earnings forecasts for both the US and Japanese firms improves with each successive disaggregation of earnings in terms of both mean and median values and is significant at the 0.001 level or better. The sign test for the ORD model versus the OPER model for the Japanese sample is significant at approximately the 0.04 level. For the US sample, the largest mean improvement in successive models is from disaggregating EBT into ORD and SPEC. For the Japanese sample, the largest mean improvement in successive models is from disaggregating ORD into OPER and NONOPER. Table 6 also shows that, on a yearly basis, the more disaggregated model generally outperforms the less disaggregated model. The exceptions are the median differences of the OPER model

Table 6. *Forecast Improvements from Disaggregating Earnings for US Firms* (n = 10,656) *and Japanese Firms* (n = 6,182)

	Naive vs. ROE	*ROE vs. EBT*	*EBT vs. ORD*	*ORD vs. OPER*	*OPER vs. FULL*	*ROE vs FULL*
Panel A: US Firms						
Mean	0.0034*	0.0030*	0.0036*	0.0006*	0.0013*	0.0086
(t-statistic)	(4.616)	(12.097)	(11.818)	(3.620)	(5.412)	(17.329)
#years[a]	7	9	9	7	9	9
Median	–0.0005	0.0019*	0.0012*	0.0001*	0.0008*	0.0060*
#years[a]	3	9	9	7	3	9
Panel B: Japanese Firms						
Mean	0.0034*	0.0006*	0.0005*	0.0008*	0.0006*	0.0026*
(t-statistic)	(9.128)	(3.589)	(3.247)	(6.702)	(3.922)	(9.449)
# years[a]	9	6	8	8	8	9
Median	0.0013*	0.0003*	0.0003*	0.0003*	0.0004*	0.0017*
# years[a]	7	5	5	5	4	9
Panel C: Difference in Forecast Improvement between US and Japanese Firms[b]						
Mean	0.0000	0.0024	0.0031	–0.0002	0.0007	0.0060
(p-value)	(0.970)	(0.001)	(0.001)	(0.235)	(0.017)	(0.001)
Z (p-value)	–4.805	10.458	7.571	–2.575	2.983	11.788
of Mann-Whitney U	(0.001)	(0.001)	0(.001)	(0.010)	(0.001)	(0.001)

The naive model forecasts next period's return on equity to be the current period's return on equity (i.e., a random walk forecast). See Figures 1 and 2 for other model definitions.
*Significant at <.001 level using the paired t-test for means and the Wilcoxon signed rank test for medians.
[a]"# of years" indicates the number of years out of nine that the more disaggregated model has a lower (mean or median) absolute forecast error than the less disaggregated model.
[b]The mean difference is defined as the mean forecast improvement for US firms minus the mean forecast improvement for Japanese firms. The significance of the mean difference is determined using an approximate t-test (Satterthwaite, 1946). Results of the nonparametric Mann-Whitney U Test are also provided as a test of difference in forecast improvement between the two samples.

versus FULL model for both samples. The total benefits of earnings disaggregation for improving forecasts can be seen in the final column in Table 6. This column reports the difference in absolute forecast accuracy of the most aggregated model (ROE) versus the most disaggregated model (FULL). For both the US and Japanese samples, the mean and median improvement in forecast error is positive and significant, and the FULL model outperforms the ROE model in all nine years.

Panel C of Table 6 provides tests of the differences in forecast improvement between the US and Japanese firms. The mean difference is defined as the mean forecast improvement for US firms minus the mean forecast improvement for Japanese firms. Since the variances of the two groups are unequal, the significance of the mean difference is determined using an approximate t-test (Satterthwaite, 1946). Results of the nonparametric Mann-Whitney U Test are also provided as a test of difference in forecast improvement between the two samples. The difference of means t-test indicates that there is no difference in the forecast improvement of the naive model versus ROE model or the ORD model versus OPER models between the two samples. The significant differences between all other models provide evidence that the forecast improvement is greater in the USA than in Japan. For the ROE versus FULL model, the difference in forecast improvement is 0.006 and is significant at better than the 0.001 level. Based on forecast improvement from disaggregation of earnings, these results indicate that the income reporting format in the USA is superior to that in Japan.

Results for the nonparametric Mann-Whitney U Test are generally similar to the difference of means t-test. The Mann-Whitney U Test shows that the forecast improvement of the naive model versus ROE model and the ORD model versus OPER model is greater in Japan. The forecast improvements for the other model comparisons are greater in the USA. Examining the final column in Panel C, the forecast improvement of the ROE versus FULL model shows further evidence in favor of improved forecast accuracy in the United States as a result of earnings disaggregation.[7]

Conclusion

We examine the persistence and forecast accuracy of earnings components for retail and manufacturing companies in the USA and Japan. The results demonstrate that the forecast accuracy of earnings in both the USA and Japan consistently increases with greater disaggregation of earnings components.[8] The results further indicate that the improvements in forecast accuracy from earnings disaggregation are greater in the USA than in Japan. This is consistent with US reporting guidelines producing a better differentiation in the persistence of earnings components resulting in greater forecast improvements from earnings disaggregation.

A comparison of descriptive statistics on the components of ROE between the USA and Japan reveal several interesting items. Earnings, earnings before taxes, ordinary income, and operating income, scaled by beginning of period stockholder's equity, are all approximately 4–5% (of stockholders' equity) lower in Japan. This may be attributed to the close relationship between tax and financial reporting in Japan, creating a tendency towards more conservative reporting. Sales and COGS as a percentage of beginning stockholder's equity are higher in Japan consistent with a relatively greater emphasis placed on market share in Japan. Earnings are more predictable in Japan. The ability to explain next period's earnings, measured by adjusted R^2s in regressions of next period's ROE on components of ROE, is greater in Japan. Similarly, earnings forecast errors and the variability of earnings forecast errors are lower in Japan.

While earnings are more predictable in Japan, the benefits of earnings disaggregation appear to be greater in the USA. The increase in the adjusted R^2s between the most aggregated and most disaggregated models and the related F-tests for differences in persistence coefficients suggest the benefits from disaggregating earnings may be greater in the USA. The greater improvement in forecast accuracy for US firms provides evidence that the benefits of earnings disaggregation are greater in the USA than in Japan.

Notes

1. In all cases, earnings are scaled by beginning of period stockholders' equity. Therefore, when earnings components are discussed in this paper they represent earnings components scaled by beginning of period stockholders' equity.

2. The superiority of forecasting earnings or cash flows is subject to debate. Ball, Kothari and Robin (1998, p. 15) and Dechow (1994) argue convincingly that cash flows are noisier than earnings in reflecting contemporaneous value-relevant information. Ball et al. (1998) find that earnings are superior (from the perspective of timeliness) to cash flow from operations in incorporating current value-relevant information in all seven countries examined including the USA and Japan.

3. US firms include gains or losses on voluntary early retirement of debt. Some US firms report extraordinary items year after year. This may help explain why the empirical results report a small, yet significant, persistence coefficient for extraordinary items.

4. The empirical analysis was also performed using Japanese parent company financial data. The findings are generally consistent with those using Japanese consolidated financial data. Therefore, only the results using Japanese consolidated data are reported in this paper.

5. Data for consolidated Japanese companies were not available before 1984. Since all variables are scaled by beginning of period stockholders' equity, 1985 is the first year of available data. In addition, at the time data were collected, 1995 (i.e., Japanese year-end of March 1996) was the most recent year available. Therefore, the last year available to calculate the dependent variable (i.e., ROE_{t+1}) was 1994.

6. In contrast to our findings, Fairfield et al. (1996) find that for their sample of US firms, disaggregation of earnings beyond the components of operating income, non-operating income and taxes, special items, and nonrecurring items does not further improve forecasts of next period's ROE. One difference between their study and ours is the number of years used in estimating forecast model parameters. Fairfield et al. (1996) use

the relation between earnings components and next period's ROE over the previous seven years to forecast next period's ROE. We use data only from the previous year to estimate this relationship. We replicated our forecast model using seven years of data as in Fairfield et al. (1996). Using a longer interval, however, reduces the number of earnings forecast years from nine (1987–95) to three (1993–95). The results for this smaller time period are very similar to those reported over the nine-year period and none of our conclusions are affected. In addition, our procedure for eliminating influential observations is similar to that of Fairfield et al. (1993). Thus, the slight difference between our results and the results of Fairfield et al. (1996) is likely due to sample composition and/or time period. Fairfield et al. (1993) include all nonfinancial firms over the 1973–90 period while we include only manufacturing and retail firms over the 1985–94 period.

7. The improvements in forecast accuracy are reported relative to beginning stockholders' equity. The average stockholder's equity for the US sample is $669 million and for the Japanese sample is ¥63,164 million. A reduction in forecast error of 0.0086 for the US sample, as shown in Panel A of Table 6 in the comparison of the FULL model and the ROE model, represents an average error reduction in forecasting earnings alone of $5.753 million. For the Japanese sample, the average error reduction in forecasting earnings alone would be ¥164.226 million.

8. The conclusions are restricted to retail and manufacturing companies. Whether decomposition of earnings components are beneficial in other industries such as financial, insurance, real estate, transportation, utilities, or service industries is left for future research.

References

AAA—American Accounting Association's Financial Accounting Standards Committee, "An Issues paper on Comprehensive Income," *Accounting Horizons* (June 1997), pp. 120–126.

Ball, R., S. P. Kothari and A. Robin, "The Effect of International Institutional Factors on Properties of Accounting Earnings," Working Paper, University of Rochester (1998).

Belsey, D. A., E. Kuh and R. E. Welsch, *Regression Diagnostics* (New York: Wiley, 1980).

Bernard, V., "The Feltham-Ohlson Framework: Implications for Empiricists," *Contemporary Accounting Research* (Spring 1995), pp. 733–747.

BAR—Business Accounting Deliberation Council, *Financial Accounting Standards for Business Enterprises* (1982).

Cairns, D., *A Guide to Applying International Accounting Standards* (Accountancy Books, 1995).

Choi, F. D. S. et al., "Analyzing Foreign Financial Statements: The Use and Misuse of International Ratio Analysis," *Journal of International Business Studies* (Spring 1983), pp. 113–131.

Collins, D. W. and S. P. Kothari, "An Analysis of Intertemporal and Cross-sectional Determinants of Earnings Response. Coefficients," *Journal of Accounting and Economics* (July 1989), pp. 143–182.

Dechow, P., "Accounting Earnings and Cash Flows as Measures of Firm Performance: The Role of Accounting Accruals," *Journal of Accounting & Economics* 18 (1994), pp. 3–42.

Easton, P. D. and M. E. Zmijewski, "Cross-sectional Variation in the Stock Market Response to Accounting Earnings Announcements," *Journal of Accounting and Economics* (July 1989), pp. 117–141.

Fairfield, P. M., R. J. Sweeney and T. L. Yohn, "Accounting Classification and the Predictive Content of Earnings," *The Accounting Review* (July 1996), pp. 337–355.

FASB—Financial Accounting Standards Board, "Reporting Financial Performance: Current Developments and Future Directions," (Norwalk, CT: Financial Accounting Series, January 1998).

Foster, G., *Financial Statement Analysis* (Prentice Hall, 2nd ed., 1986).

Givoly, D. and C. Hayn, "Transitory Accounting Items: Information Content and Earnings Management," Working Paper, University of California at Irvine (1992).

Herrmann, D., T. Inoue and W. B. Thomas, "Are There Benefits to Restating Japanese Financial Statements According to U.S. GAAP?" *The Journal of Financial Statement Analysis* (Fall, 1996), pp. 61–73

JICPA—Japanese Institute of Certified Public Accountants, *Corporate Disclosure in Japan–Reporting*, (JICPA, 3rd ed., 1991).

Kennedy, P., *A Guide to Econometrics* (MIT Press, 3rd ed., 1992).

Kinney, M. and R. Trezevant, "The U.S.e of Special Items to Manage Earnings and Perceptions," *The Journal of Financial Statement Analysis* (Fall 1997), pp. 45–54.

Kormendi, R. and R. Lipe, "Earnings Innovations, Earnings Persistence and Stock Returns," *Journal of Business* (July 1987), pp. 323–345.

Lev, B., "On the Usefulness of Earnings and Earnings Research: Lessons and Directions from Two Decades of Empirical Research," *Journal of Accounting Research* Vol. 27 (Supplement 1989), pp. 153–192.

Lipe, R., "The Information Contained in the Components of Earnings," *Journal of Accounting Research* (Supplement 1986), pp. 37–64.

Nobes, C. W. and R. H. Parker (eds), *Comparative International Accounting* (Prentice Hall, 4th ed., 1995).

Ohlson, J. A., "The Theory of Value and Earnings, and an Introduction to the Ball-Brown Analysis," *Contemporary Accounting Research* (Fall 1991), pp. 1–19.

Ohlson, J. A., "Earnings, Book Values, and Dividends in Equity Valuation," *Contemporary Accounting Research* (Spring 1995), pp. 661–687.

Ohlson, J. A. and S. H. Penman, "Disaggregated Accounting Data as Explanatory Variables for Returns," *Journal of Accounting, Auditing, & Finance* (Fall 1992), pp. 553–573.

Penman, S. H., "An Evaluation of Accounting Rate-of Return," *Journal of Accounting, Auditing & Finance* (Spring 1991), pp. 233–255.

Penman, S. H., "Return to Fundamentals," *Journal of Accounting, Auditing & Finance* (Fall 1992), pp. 465–483.

Radebaugh L. and S. Gray, *International Accounting and Multinational Enterprises* (Wiley, 4th ed., 1997).

Satterthwaite, H., "An Approximate Distribution of Estimates of Variance Components," *Biometrics Bulletin* (1946), pp. 110–114.

Strong, N. and M. Walker, "The Explanatory Power of Earnings for Stock Returns," *The Accounting Review* (April 1993), pp. 385–399.

Swaminathan, S. and J. Weintrop, "The Information Content of Earnings, Revenues, and Expenses," *Journal of Accounting Research* (Autumn 1991), pp. 418–427.

The International Journal of Accounting

Relevance of U.S.-GAAP for Japanese Companies

Joseph H. Godwin, Stephen R. Goldberg, and Edward B. Douthett
Grand Valley State University and Texas Christian University

Key Words: Book value equity, Earnings, Foreign registrants, Japanese-GAAP, U.S.-GAAP, Value-relevance.

Abstract: *We use differences in U.S.-GAAP and Japanese-GAAP accounting measures to evaluate the value-relevance of U.S.-GAAP reports. We show data provided in U.S.-GAAP financial statements of Japanese firms is value-relevant beyond that contained in domestic-GAAP statements. Our results complement extant research and support the proposition that U.S. reporting methods provide value-relevant data. Understanding the value-relevance of data from Japanese firms is important in its own right because of the major role these firms play in international markets. We also provide evidence on significant transnational firms that voluntarily provide U.S.-GAAP statements.*

This paper reports on an analysis of the value-relevance of Japanese firms' financial statements that are prepared with U.S. generally accepted accounting principles (GAAP). Value relevance is defined as a significant association between earnings or stockholders' equity and security returns. Our findings suggest that U.S.-GAAP financial statements provide value-relevant data beyond Japanese-GAAP statements. These findings, therefore, support the reporting requirements imposed on transnational firms by the U.S. Securities and Exchange Commission (SEC).

Non-U.S. companies listed on a primary U.S. exchange may choose to either provide their U.S. shareholders with financial statements prepared according to their domestic (non-U.S.) GAAP or provide them with U.S.-GAAP statements. The SEC requires non-U.S. firms that elect to provide domestic-GAAP financial statements to also provide a reconciliation of domestic earnings and shareholders' equity to their U.S.-GAAP counterparts. Both reporting alternatives imply a testable SEC hypothesis that U.S.-GAAP measures provide value-relevant data beyond domestic-GAAP measures.

Amir, Harris, and Venuti (1993) [henceforth AHV] provide evidence that reconciliations of domestic earnings and shareholders' equity to U.S.-GAAP are associated with price

Direct all correspondence to: Edward B. Douthett, Department of Accounting, M.J. Neeley School of Business, Texas Christian University, Fort Worth, TX 76129; 817-257-7921; Fax: 817-257-7227; E.Douthett@TCU.edu.

(returns) which they interpret as an indication of value-relevance. Their result holds for both aggregate reconciliations and for some specific reconciliation components. This evidence is important to the continuing policy debate over the SEC requirement that foreign companies provide either reconciliations or U.S.-GAAP statements with Form 20-F in order to be listed on a U.S. securities exchange. AHV assert it would be difficult to argue for the requirement if it could not be shown that the reconciliation data were value-relevant.

Since foreign companies can also meet SEC requirements by providing U.S.-GAAP financial statements and are thus not considered by AHV, the question arises whether such U.S.-GAAP data have value-relevance beyond data contained in firms' domestic-GAAP financial statements. While specific differences in GAAP are not highlighted as they are when reconciliations are provided, aggregate differences can be determined by an examination of both U.S. and domestic-GAAP earnings and shareholders' equity line items. Thus, U.S. and non-U.S.-GAAP measures can be used in statistical tests to evaluate the value-relevance of U.S.-GAAP financial statement data.

The purpose of this paper, therefore, is to examine the value-relevance of U.S.-GAAP earnings and shareholders' equity data of non-U.S. companies (Japanese firms, in particular) that prepare U.S.-GAAP financial statements. This paper is of interest for several reasons. First, we suggest, in the spirit of AHV, that it would be difficult to argue for requirements to provide costly data in the form of either reconciliations or complete U.S.-GAAP statements if it could not be shown that the data were value-relevant. Second, the SEC allows non-U.S. firms to choose from two alternative reporting protocols which could have value-relevance implications. If one protocol has differential advantages, firms should consider those advantages. Thus, comparing our results with AHV could give additional insight into reconciling domestic-GAAP to U.S.-GAAP earnings and stockholders' equity numbers as compared to preparing statements in U.S.-GAAP. Third, evidence of value relevance could provide an explanation of why some firms prepare U.S.-GAAP financial statements even when they are not required to do so by listing or registration requirements. Fourth, AHV examine only firms that provide domestic statements along with reconciliations and thereby omit significant transnational firms from a country with a different industrial structure and different methods of preparing financial statements.[1] Thus, our results should be viewed in conjunction with AHV's results to draw conclusions about SEC reporting requirements.[2] Fifth, as Zmijewski (1993) points out, research on cross-country comparisons of the role of earnings and other information is important because we can provide information to regulators and investors grappling with the issues related to globalization of the world's capital markets.

The next section provides additional details and describes some institutional background. We then describe sample selection and research design in the sections 3 and 4. Results are presented in section 5 and concluding remarks are in section 6.

INSTITUTIONAL BACKGROUND

There has been a recent surge in the number of transnational firms that are SEC registrants and trade in U.S. markets. Between October 1989 and May 1993, 208 registrants from foreign countries entered the U.S. market for the first time and approximately $80 billion of

Table 1. Sampling Scheme to Determine Japanese Firms That Prepare U.S. GAAP Statements

Firm Name	*12g3-2(b) exempt[2]?*	*U.S. GAAP per JCH[1]*	*Observations used = 253*
NYSE Firms:			
Hitachi, Ltd.	No	Yes	9
Honda Motor Co., Ltd	No	Yes	7
Kubota Corporation	No	Yes	9
Kyocera Corporation	No	Yes	9
Matsushita Electric Ind.	No	Yes	9
Mitsubishi Bank, Ltd.	No	No[1]	0[3]
Pioneer Corporation	No	Yes	8
Sony Corporation	No	Yes	7
TDK Corporation	No	Yes	7
Nippon Telegraph & Telephone	No	No[1]	0[4]
NASDAQ Firms:			
CSK Corporation	Yes	Yes	10
Canon, Inc.	No	Yes	9
Dai'ie, Inc.	Yes	No[2]	0
Fuji Photo Film Co.	Yes	Yes	10
Ito-Yokado Co.	No	Yes	10
Japan Airlines Co.	Yes	No[2]	0
Kirin Brewery	Yes	No[2]	0
Makita Corporation	No	Yes	7
Mitsui & Co. Ltd.	No	Yes	9
NEC Corporation	No	Yes	9
Nissan Motor Co., Ltd.	Yes	No[2]	0
Sanyo Electric Co., Ltd.	Yes	Yes	9
Tokio Marine & Fire Ins.	No	No[1]	0[3]
Toyota Motor Corp.	Yes	No[2]	0
Wacoal Corp.	No	Yes	7
OTC Firms:			
Ricoh	No	Yes	9
Komatsu	No	Yes	9
Marubeni	Yes	Yes	9
Mitsubishi	Yes	Yes	9
Mitsubishi Elect. Ind.	No	Yes	9
Dai Nippon Printing	No	Yes	7
Omron	Yes	Yes	9
Not in ADR Universe:			
Asahi Optical	No	Yes	9
Itochu	No	Yes	9
Murata	No	Yes	7
Nippon Meat Packers	No	Yes	7
Orix Corp.	No	Yes	6
Toshiba	No	Yes	9

Notes: [1] Firm prepares U.S. GAAP statements but Japanese GAAP used in Japan Company Handbook (JCH).
[2] Exempt from registration provisions under Rule 12g3-2(b) and does not provide U.S. GAAP statements.
[3] Excluded from sample because firm is financial institution.
[4] Excluded because Japanese Government has significant ownership.

the securities were registered for sale in the U.S. (USSEC, 1993a). The number of transnational SEC registrants reporting U.S.-GAAP data increased from 528 to 625 between May 1993 and June 1994 (USSEC, 1994a).

Shares of foreign firms usually trade in the U.S. through American Depository Receipts (ADRs). ADRs are negotiable receipts issued by a depository (normally a bank or trust company) in the U.S. to represent ownership of the underlying shares of a foreign firm. A custodian bank in the firm's home country typically holds the underlying shares in trust.[3] ADRs are sold, registered, and transferred in the U.S. in the same manner as any share of stock. Each ADR represents some multiple of shares of the underlying stock such that the trading price of each ADR is in a generally accepted range of $10 to $30.

An ADR facility can be created with or without a company's sponsorship. If the facility is created without sponsorship, trading occurs over-the-counter (OTC) and the ADR (or firm) is not subject to SEC reporting requirements. Sponsorship of an ADR facility occurs at one of three levels that are unofficially coined as sponsored level-I, II, or III.

Sponsored level-I ADRs trade in the OTC "pink-sheet" market and can neither be listed nor make a public offering in the U.S. The sponsoring company often obtains a 12g3-2(b) exemption from 1934 Exchange Act reporting requirements. This ADR level is often used by foreign firms to test their reception in U.S. markets.[4]

Sponsored level-II ADRs trade on NASDAQ or an exchange but are not associated with a public offering. Level-III classification is associated with listing and a public offering. Both level-II and III ADR sponsorship involve meeting SEC reporting requirements to either provide domestic-GAAP statements with reconciliations or provide U.S.-GAAP financial statements.[5] The question we address is whether earnings and shareholders' equity reported on a foreign firm's U.S.-GAAP financial statements have value-relevance after controlling for earnings and equity determined with non-U.S.-GAAP.

SAMPLE SELECTION

Japanese firms make up the fourth largest group of foreign SEC registrants subject to reporting provisions of the Securities Exchange Act of 1934. They are the largest group, however, that unanimously provides U.S.-GAAP financial statements rather than reconciliations to U.S.-GAAP (SEC, 1993a).[6] Since 100% of Japanese SEC registrants and several other Japanese firms prepare U.S.-GAAP statements, we are afforded a useable sample of commonly domiciled firms which reduces concern that returns-earnings coefficients might not be constant across countries.[7] Thus, Japanese firms provide a unique opportunity to examine the value- relevance of one SEC reporting option.

We examine a pooled cross-section of Japanese firms that prepare U.S.-GAAP financial statements either because they wish to list or issue securities or because they deem it otherwise advantageous. A search of the Japan Company Handbook (Toyo Keizai, 1993) [hereafter JCH] identified thirty firms that report U.S.-GAAP data. We also identified two additional Japanese firms listed on the New York Stock Exchange (NYSE) and six additional firms listed on NASDAQ since these firms are most likely to provide U.S.-GAAP financial data.[8] These sources yield the 38 firms listed in Table 1.

JCH reports only Japanese-GAAP data for firms that employ both U.S. and Japanese-GAAP to prepare consolidated statements. We obtained U.S.-GAAP annual reports for the three NYSE and NASDAQ firms listed in Table 1 for which JCH did not report U.S. data. Subsequently, we dropped these three firms from the analysis because they were financial institutions or, in Nippon Telegraph & Telephone's case, significantly owned by the Japanese Government. We dropped these firms because of difficulty collecting consistent U.S.-GAAP data and uncertainty over effects of their regulatory environment.

Five other NASDAQ firms were dropped because they do not provide U.S.-GAAP statements. Non-U.S. firms traded in the U.S. do not necessarily meet SEC registration and reporting requirements. Thirty-two Japanese firms are exempt from registration requirements under Rule 12g3-2(b) (SEC, 1994b).[9] Eight of the exempt firms are NASDAQ traded.[10] Three NASDAQ firms and three OTC firms prepare U.S.-GAAP financial statements despite the exemption. Six sample firms do not trade in the U.S.

The last column of Table 1 shows the number of firm-year observations each firm contributes to the final sample. We collected sample-firm data for the period 1983 to 1992. We excluded one or two observations for seven firms that reported partial-year data when they changed to March 31 fiscal year ends in the late-eighties to coincide with the government's fiscal year-end (Toya Keizai, Inc, 1993). Additional firm-years were lost because of missing data in the Global Vantage data base (Compustat-PC, Plus, 1993). We have a maximum of 253 observations representing thirty firms for which we have domestic stock price (returns) data and both Japanese-GAAP and U.S.-GAAP financial data.

We collected annual returns and U.S.-GAAP financial data from Global Vantage and from JCH. Global Vantage reports U.S.-GAAP consolidated data for those firms that provide U.S.-GAAP data and Japanese-GAAP consolidated data for those firms that do not provide U.S.-GAAP data.

We collected Japanese-GAAP financial data from JCH which reports both parent company data and consolidated data. The parent company data is prepared via Japanese-GAAP and the consolidated data is prepared with either U.S. or Japanese-GAAP. AHV point out that "most Japanese companies listed on a U.S. exchange use U.S.-GAAP because at the time they originally listed in the United States, Japan did not require consolidated financial statements. Since the companies had no domestic equivalent, they chose U.S.-GAAP and were allowed to retain this for Japanese reporting purposes once Japan adopted full consolidation" (p. 233).

One limitation of allowing Japanese firms to use U.S.-GAAP data for domestic purposes is that we are constrained to compare U.S. consolidated data to Japanese unconsolidated data. Thus, we perform a joint test that consists of the value-relevance of U.S.-GAAP over Japanese-GAAP and the value-relevance of U.S. consolidated over Japanese unconsolidated data. Our approach seems reasonable for several reasons. First, Japanese financial reporting has traditionally emphasized unconsolidated financial statements. For example, the Commercial Code (Shoho) of Japan does not require consolidated statements (Renketsu Zaimushohyo) and the Japan Securities and Exchange Law (Shokentorihikiho) requires consolidation only as supplemental information (Campbell, 1991; Coopers & Lybrand, 1991). Second, Darrough and Harris (1989) provides evidence that unexpected unconsolidated earnings of Japanese firms are more closely associated with returns than unexpected consolidated earnings. Third, U.S.-GAAP consolidated data displays high correlation (.70) with Japanese-GAAP unconsolidated data which is similar to the correlation between consolidated and unconsolidated data (.86) of an industry-matched sample of firms that do not prepare U.S. consolidated data. We provide additional specification checks on this issue through other comparisons of sample firms with match firms. Nevertheless, Japanese-GAAP unconsolidated and U.S.-GAAP statements are the available inputs to decision models and the value-relevance of the U.S.-GAAP data is an important issue for the reasons enumerated previously.

Another potential limitation is there could be something economically different about firms that choose to prepare U.S.-GAAP which could preclude generalization of results. We do not address motivations of sample firms for preparing U.S.-GAAP. We do, however, attempt to measure differences by comparing our sample with a matched sample of firms that do not prepare U.S.-GAAP. This comparison provides some evidence that sample firms behave similarly to other firms.

RESEARCH DESIGN

Following AHV,[11] we use two approaches to evaluate the value-relevance of U.S.-GAAP disclosures by Japanese firms. The first approach considers the association between stock market returns and accounting earnings determined under two different accounting practices. The second approach considers whether differences between Japanese and U.S.-GAAP measures explain the market (P) to book-value of shareholders' equity (BV) ratio. AHV assert that most earnings announcements contain domestic-GAAP income only, show that most firms do not file annual reports at the same time as Form 20-F, discuss other challenges of isolating the news and date of information releases to the market (p. 237) and find no significant association between short-window market returns and U.S.-GAAP disclosures. Therefore, because of the difficulties of identifying the timing of information releases in two or more markets, we do not use an event-study methodology to evaluate the value-relevance of U.S.-GAAP disclosures by Japanese firms.

Return–Earnings Association

Securities of most firms in this study trade in at least two countries (Japan and the U.S.) and currencies (yen and dollars) and this fact raises the issue of where to measure returns. We follow AHV and run all tests using domestic market prices to calculate returns. One advantage of this approach is that we can admit six firms to the sample that do not trade in the U.S. and thus do not have U.S. prices (returns). AHV find the correlation between U.S. and non-U.S. returns is in excess of .99 and point out that arbitrage conditions suggest equal domestic and U.S. prices unless thin trading in one market or the other creates a transaction cost barrier.

We examine the association between returns and earnings over a twelve-month window corresponding with the firm's fiscal year.[12] The earnings variables follow from the relationship:

$$EARN_{j,Jpn,¥,t} = EARN_{j,US,¥,t} + DEARN_{j,¥,t} \quad (1)$$

where *EARN* is reported earnings per share (excluding extraordinary items) for firm *j*, the subscripts *Jpn* and *US* show which country's GAAP is employed, the subscript ¥ shows the currency, and *t* shows the year. We drop the subscript ¥ since we use reported Yen measures for both U.S.-GAAP and domestic-GAAP data in this study. *DEARN* shows the difference between earnings reported under U.S. and Japanese-GAAP that balances the equation. A review of annual reports indicates that major differences exist between U.S. and Japanese accounting for deferred taxes, currency translation, accrual of expenses, post employment benefits, leases, and stock purchase warrants.

We continue with the model:

$$R_{j,t} = \alpha_0 + \alpha_1\ EARN_{j,Jpn,t}/P_{j,t-1} + \alpha_2\ \Delta EARN_{j,Jpn,t}/P_{j,t-1} + \alpha_3\ V_{jt} + e_{j,t} \qquad (2)$$

where $R_{j,t}$ is $(P_{j,t} - P_{j,t-1}+dividends_{j,t})/P_{j,t-1}$; $\Delta EARN_{j,Jpn,t}$ is the earnings change under Japanese- GAAP from period t-1 to t; P denotes share price at the subscripted time; V_{jt} represents nonrandom additional information that explains returns for firm j at time t; and $e_{j,t}$ is an i.i.d. random error term.

If U.S.-GAAP earnings reflect the additional information associated with returns, then equation (2) can be rewritten as:

$$R_{j,t} = \alpha_0 + \alpha_1\ EARN_{j,Jpn,t}/P_{j,t-1} + \alpha_2\ \Delta EARN_{j,Jpn,t}/P_{j,t-1} + \alpha_{31}\ DEARN_{j,t}/P_{j,t-1} + \alpha_{32}\ \Delta DEARN_{j,t}/P_{j,t-1} + e_{j,t} \qquad (3)$$

where $DEARN_{j,t}$ is as defined in equation (1), and $\Delta DEARN_{j,t}$ is the change in the difference in earnings from the prior period (i.e., $DEARN_t - DEARN_{t-1}$).

Our general hypothesis, implied by SEC reporting requirements, is that accounting measures prepared under U.S.-GAAP are value-relevant after controlling for accounting measures prepared under Japanese-GAAP. Evidence supporting this hypothesis suggests that SEC disclosure requirements provide benefits, net of costs, to transnational firms and investors.[13] We provide evidence to support the SEC hypothesis if we are able to reject either the statement α_{31} or α_{32} = zero or the joint null hypothesis that $\alpha_{31} = \alpha_{32}$ = zero .

Price-to-Book Analysis

Our second approach to evaluate the value-relevance of U.S.-GAAP disclosures considers whether they help explain the price-to-book-value ratio. Goodwill is the difference between the market and book-value of an asset and is related to market perceptions of expected earnings. AHV points out that P and BV may also differ because of accounting differences, suggesting a higher ratio when firms use conservative practices. We examine whether or not aggregate differences between Japanese and U.S.-GAAP measures help explain the P to BV ratio when BV is measured in Japanese-GAAP (See AHV, Bernard, Merton, and Palepu [1992]; Easton, Eddey, and Harris [1993]; Feltham and Ohlson [1993]; Ou and Penman [1992]). We continue with the model:

$$P_{j,t}/BV_{j,Jpn,t} = \beta_0 + \beta_1\ EARN_{j,Jpn,t}/BV_{j,Jpn,t,} + \beta_2\ W_{j,Jpn,t} + e_{j,t} \qquad (4)$$

where $BV_{j,Jpn,t}$ is the book-value per share determined via Japanese-GAAP for firm j at time t, and $W_{j,Jpn,t}$ is nonrandom additional information explaining the price-to-book ratio of firm j at time t. Assuming the difference between U.S.-GAAP and Japanese-GAAP earnings and equity is the additional information contained in $W_{j,Jpn,t}$, equation (4) can be rewritten as:

$$P_{j,t}/BV_{j,Jpn,t,} = \beta_0 + \beta_1\, EARN_{j,Jpn,t}/BV_{j,Jpn,t,} + \beta_{21}\, DBV_{J,t}/BV_{j,Jpn,t,} + \beta_{22}\, DEARN_{j,t}/BV_{j,Jpn,t,} + e_{j,t} \quad (5)$$

where DBV is U.S. minus Japanese-GAAP measures of book-value for firm j at time t and other variables are as defined.

β_1 reflects the association between Japanese-GAAP return on equity (ROE) and the P to BV ratio. The variable $DBV_{j,Jpn,t}/BV_{j,Jpn,t}$, equals $((BV_{j,US,t}/BV_{j,Jpn,t}) - 1)$. If the U.S.-GAAP measure of BV is more closely aligned with price than the Japanese-GAAP measure, then β_{21} will be positive. The coefficient β_{22} reveals how incorporating U.S.-GAAP practices in earnings incrementally explains the P/BV ratio based on Japanese-GAAP. If the U.S.-GAAP measure of earnings reflects a measurement of ROE closer to that used by the market, then β_{22} will be positive.

AHV assert the price-to-book model in (5) is a function of practices implicit in domestic GAAP. The right-hand-side variables in (5) reflect both future profitability and adjustment of measurement differences implicit in Japanese measures of shareholders' equity and earnings. We also define the price-to-book ratio in terms of U.S.-GAAP to distinguish the two effects. Rewriting equation (5) as:

$$P_{j,t}/BV_{j,U.S.,t} = \theta_0 + \theta_1\, EARN_{j,Jpn,t}/BV_{j,U.S.,t} + \theta_{21}\, DBV_{j,t}/BV_{j,U.S.,t} + \theta_{22}\, DEARN_{j,t}/BV_{j,U.S.,t} + e_{j,t} \quad (6)$$

where $BV_{j,U.S.,t}$ can be rewritten as $BV_{j,Jpn,t} + DBV_{j,t}$. This measure alters the P/BV ratio in equation (5) to account for differences between U.S. and Japanese-GAAP measurement practices. If these differences are value-relevant, then the P/BV ratio based on U.S.-GAAP measures should be closer to one and have a lower variance than Japanese measures.[14]

AHV provide arguments (p. 243) that we can expect θ_1 to be positive if Japanese-GAAP earnings reflect firms' profitability. If U.S.-GAAP shareholders' equity reduces the measurement error component, however, θ_1 should be smaller than the coefficient β_1 in (5).

A nonzero coefficient β_{22} could result from differences between Japanese and U.S. protocols to determine earnings or from the measurement error inherent in Japanese-GAAP shareholders' equity. If U.S.-GAAP reduces the measurement error, then the value-relevance of a difference in earnings can still be evaluated. A nonzero coefficient, θ_{22}, will indicate that earnings determined under U.S.-GAAP provides value-relevant information beyond that contained in differences between shareholders' equity.

Finally, if the additional information contained in U.S.-GAAP BV is value-relevant while Japanese-GAAP BV provides no incremental information, then $DBV_{j,t}/BV_{j,U.S.,t}$ should not help explain the price-to-book ratio based on U.S.-GAAP. In this case, θ_{21} is expected to be zero.

Table 2. Summary Statistics for Japanese Firms Preparing U.S. GAAP $N = 245^1$

	Median	*Mean*	*Std. Dev.*	*Quartile 1*	*Quartile 3*
R_t	0.0035	0.0754	0.3335	−0.1701	0.3052
$EARN_{j,Jpn,t}/P_{j,t-1}$	0.0247	0.0280	0.0148	0.0186	0.0340
$\Delta EARN_{j,Jpn,t}/P_{j,t-1}$	0.0007	0.0011	0.0010	0.0004	0.0014
$DEARN_{j,t}/P_{j,t-1}$	0.0061	0.0079	0.0182	0.0000	0.0139
$\Delta DEARN_{j,t}/P_{j,t-1}$	0.0005	−0.0001	0.0158	−0.0037	0.0053
$EARN_{j,US,t}/P_{j,t-1}$	0.0338	0.0361	0.0251	0.0221	0.0468
$\Delta EARN_{j,US,t}/P_{j,t-1}$	0.0014	−0.0002	0.0192	−0.0053	0.0078
$EARN_{j,Jpn,t}/BV_{j,Jpn,t}$	0.0658	0.0675	0.0297	0.0467	0.0848
$DBV_{J,t}/BV_{j,Jpn,t,}$	0.1216	0.2023	0.3004	0.0184	0.3035
$DEARN_{j,t}/BV_{j,Jpn,t,}$	0.0139	0.0232	0.0424	0.0000	0.0394
$EARN_{j,Jpn,t}/BV_{j,U.S.,t}$	0.0546	0.0599	0.0553	0.0397	0.0725
$DBV_{j,t}/BV_{j,U.S.,t}$	0.1084	0.1281	0.1930	0.0181	0.2328
$DEARN_{j,t}/BV_{j,U.S.,t}$	0.0134	0.0145	0.0371	0.0000	0.0310
P_{Jpnt}/BV_{Jpnt}	2.3769	2.6251	1.1361	1.8353	3.2136
P_{Jpnt}/BV_{ust}	1.9894	2.4058	2.6733	1.598	2.8794
$^2EARN_{j,US,t}$	42.04	66.22	68.39	20.48	88.4
$^2EARN_{j,Jpn,t}$	37.7	54.01	51.97	15.8	64.9
$^2BV_{us}$	574	841	738	359	1030
$^2BV_{jpn}$	517	759	645	312	940

Notes: $R_{j,t}$ is the annual return of firm j for the period ending at fiscal year-end;
$P_{j,t}$ is the domestic price per share of firm j at fiscal year end;
$EARN_{j,t}$ is fiscal year earnings per share of firm j reported in the subscripted GAAP;
$\Delta EARN_{j,t}$ is the change in subscripted GAAP fiscal year earnings;
$DEARN_{j,t}$ is U.S. GAAP earnings – Japanese GAAP earnings per share for firm j;
$\Delta DEARN_{j,t}$ is the change in *DEARN* from time $t-1$ to t for firm j.
$BV_{j,t,}$ is the book value per share of shareholders' equity of firm j at time t reported in the subscripted GAAP.
[1]Sample excludes observations where R-student values > |3| in regressions.
[2]Statistics for these items are for full sample of 253 firms.

RESULTS

Table 2 contains descriptive statistics for the primary variables used in our analysis and for the earnings and book-value numbers used to calculate those variables. The median (mean) annual stock return is .35 (7.54)%. The high variance of returns reflects the roller-coaster ride taken by Japan's stock market during the period. Average return on Japanese-GAAP equity is 6.75%. Mean U.S.-GAAP (Japanese-GAAP) earnings are 3.6 (2.8)% of price. The difference between earnings is 1.45 (2.32)% of U.S.-GAAP (Japanese-GAAP) book-value. Both U.S.-GAAP consolidated earnings and book-value are greater and have more variability than Japanese unconsolidated figures. The P/BV ratio based on U.S.-GAAP measures is closer to one than P/BV based on Japanese measures, providing some evidence that U.S.-GAAP measures are more closely aligned with price.

Return–Earnings Analysis

The results for the returns model in equation (3) are reported in Table 3. We estimate the model for the full sample (1983-1992), for the years 1983 through 1987, for the years 1988 through 1992, and for each year in the sample period.[15] We delete from regressions any

Table 3. *Regression Results for Annual Returns-Earnings Associations for U.S. and Japanese GAAP Differences for Experimental Sample:*[1] *1983-1992*

$R_{j,t} = \alpha_0 + \alpha_1 EARN_{j,Jpn,t}/P_{j,t-1} + \alpha_2 \Delta EARN_{j,Jpn,t}/P_{j,t-1} + \alpha_{31}\, DEARN_{j,t}/P_{j,t-1} + \alpha_{32}\, \Delta DEARN_{j,t}/P_{j,t-1} + \in_{j,t}$

	α_0	α_1	α_2	α_{31}	α_{32}	Adj. R^2	N	$N^{\#}$
1983-92	−0.131***	4.061***	76.465***	1.530	1.730	0.121	253	248
	−2.960	*3.119*	*3.157*	*1.104*	*1.237*			
1983-87	0.033	1.854	4.866	1.765	−0.472	−0.001	121	118
	0.605	*1.384*	*0.570*	*1.323*	*−0.461*			
1988-92	−0.436***	11.469***	253.790***	−1.497	13.142***	0.466	132	130
	−6.218	*4.602*	*6.051*	*−0.886*	*3.698*			
1983-84	0.082	0.914	−8.407	9.493***	1.426	0.017	34	34
	0.536	*0.241*	*−1.672*	*3.068*	*0.544*			
1985	−0.201**	4.003***	23.470	2.101	−0.082	0.176	30	29
	−2.418	*2.802*	*1.455*	*0.850*	*−0.026*			
1986	−0.276***	7.284*	120.750***	−3.128	2.371	0.320	29	28
	−3.147	*2.024*	*3.993*	*−1.645*	*1.344*			
1987	−0.102	7.262*	102.160**	6.135**	0.837	0.248	28	28
	−0.968	*1.925*	*2.378*	*2.432*	*0.459*			
1988	0.086	4.458	98.685	8.982	3.819	0.072	24	24
	0.438	*0.671*	*1.538*	*1.449*	*0.578*			
1989	−0.603***	15.379***	362.750***	1.730	19.977**	0.509	24	23
	−3.746	*2.891*	*4.439*	*0.239*	*2.497*			
1990	−0.240**	12.803**	-137.990	−1.399	16.416***	0.342	26	25
	−2.585	*2.479*	*−1.419*	*−0.331*	*3.936*			
1991	−0.360***	5.755***	135.460***	1.863	4.008	0.205	29	28
	−6.810	*3.918*	*4.099*	*1.349*	*0.622*			
1992	−0.472***	9.268***	71.679	−0.017	1.866	0.387	29	29
	−7.840	*3.854*	*1.389*	*−0.011*	*0.870*			

Notes: [1] Sample firms are Japanese firms that prepare U.S. GAAP financial statements.
N is the number of observations available for each regression.
$N^{\#}$ is the number of observations that enter each regression after removing those with R-student scores>|3|.
t-statistics are *italicised*.

Notes: ***Significant at < .01 level. **Significant at < .05 level. *Significant at <.10 level.

$R_{j,t}$ is the annual return of firm *j* for the period ending at fiscal year-end;
$P_{j,t}$ is the domestic price of firm *j* at fiscal year end;
$EARN_{j,Jpn,t}$ is fiscal year earnings per share of firm *j* reported in Japanese GAAP;
$\Delta EARN_{j,Jpn,t}$ is the change in Japanese GAAP fiscal year earnings;
$DEARN_{j,t}$ is U.S. GAAP earnings - Japanese GAAP earnings per share for firm *j*;
$\Delta DEARN_{j,t}$ is the change in *DEARN* from time *t-1* to *t* for firm *j*.

observation that yields an *R*-student ratio with an absolute value greater than three.[16] The second to last column in Table 3 indicates the number of available observations for each sample period and the last column reports the number of observations entering the regression after excluding those with large *R*-student ratios. We use White's (1980) covariance-matrix estimator in all regressions to adjust for heteroscedasticity.

Coefficients on earnings levels (α_1) and change in earnings (α_2) determined with Japanese- GAAP are positive and significant for the full sample, for the last five years of the sample, and for most of the individual-year sub-samples. Coefficients on differences between U.S.-GAAP and Japanese-GAAP earnings (α_{31}) or change in difference in earnings (α_{32}) are significant at the .01 level for the second five year sub-sample and for a few

Table 4. Results for Price-to-Book Regressions for Aggregate Differences between U.S. and Japanese GAAP Measures for Experiemental Sample:[1] 1983-1992

$P_{j,t}/BV_{j,Jpn,t,} = \beta_0 + \beta_1 EARN_{j,Jpn,t}/BV_{j,Jpn,t,} + \beta_{21} DBV_{J,t}/BV_{j,Jpn,t,} + \beta_{22}\ DEARN_{j,t}/BV_{j,Jpn,t,} + {}_{j,t}$

	β_0	β_1	β_{21}	β_{22}	Adj. R^2	N	N#
Panel A: Japanese GAAP Measure of Book Value:							
1983-92	1.677***	12.580***	–0.240	7.160***	0.188	253	251
	12.862	5.508	*–0.931*	*3.081*			
1983-87	1.594***	11.577***	0.013	5.083**	0.164	121	120
	9.017	*4.149*	*0.042*	*2.140*			
1988-92	1.496***	17.607***	–0.900**	14.487***	0.279	132	131
	7.575	*5.356*	*–2.339*	*3.382*			
1983-84	1.278***	12.194***	0.275	9.353	0.221	34	33
	3.946	*3.012*	*0.363*	*1.417*			
1985	1.497***	5.959	0.182	6.510**	0.251	30	29
	4.811	*1.466*	*0.298*	*2.509*			
1986	1.122***	21.275***	–0.997	0.587	0.212	29	28
	4.025	*3.992*	*–1.650*	*0.195*			
1987	1.446***	23.714**	–1.073**	14.601*	0.351	28	28
	3.035	*2.144*	*–2.138*	*1.930*			
1988	2.593***	7.081	–0.019	15.057	0.075	24	24
	4.437	*0.735*	*–0.036*	*1.633*			
1989	2.544***	4.375	–0.537	26.571***	0.350	24	23
	9.684	*1.013*	*–0.924*	*5.510*			
1990	1.227***	19.815***	–1.173	21.480***	0.534	26	25
	4.774	*3.392*	*–1.580*	*3.362*			
1991	1.344***	15.154**	–0.236	4.700	0.213	29	29
	3.265	2.281	*–0.430*	*0.730*			
1992	0.830***	19.325***	–0.170	0.032	0.641	29	28
	9.389	*9.000*	*–0.657*	*0.018*			
	θ_0	θ_1	θ_{21}	θ_{22}	Adj. R^2	N	N#
$P_{j,t}/BV_{j,U.S.,t} = \theta_0 + \theta_1 EARN_{j,Jpn,t}/BV_{j,U.S.,t} + \theta_{21} DBV_{j,t}/BV_{j,U.S.,t} + \theta_{22}\ DEARN_{j,t}/BV_{j,U.S.,t} + \in_{j,t}$							
Panel B: U.S. GAAP Measure of Book Value:							
1983-92	1.682***	11.574***	–1.102***	4.200*	0.884	253	251
	4.494	*5.424*	*–5.207*	*1.753*			
1983-87	1.595***	11.577***	0.013	5.826**	0.164	121	120
	9.022	*4.149*	*0.041*	*2.453*			
1988-92	1.550***	16.842***	–2.858***	17.524***	0.388	132	129
	9.882	*5.540*	*–8.211*	*4.843*			
1983-84	1.244***	11.622***	–1.220***	14.114**	0.130	34	33
	4.394	*3.348*	*–3.024*	*2.288*			
1985	1.353***	7.439**	–0.819	5.273***	0.190	30	29
	5.298	*2.220*	*–1.624*	*2.749*			
1986	0.895***	26.430***	–1.932*	1.344	0.336	29	29
	2.948	*4.025*	*–1.909*	*0.371*			
1987	1.289***	26.715**	–2.196***	12.531*	0.419	28	28
	2.881	*2.417*	*–4.845*	*1.942*			
1988	2.156***	8.721	–2.150**	25.505***	0.345	24	23
	3.825	*0.888*	*–2.388*	*4.123*			
1989	2.705***	2.125	–2.717***	22.071***	0.572	24	23
	10.953	*0.401*	*–4.038*	*4.966*			
1990	1.262***	21.142***	–3.206***	22.766***	0.531	26	25
	5.057	*3.711*	*–4.636*	*3.742*			

(continued)

Table 4. (Continued)

1991	1.665***	9.959**	−1.119***	−0.262	0.995	29	29
	6.111	*2.247*	*−8.819*	*−0.041*			
1992	0.840***	18.416***	−0.818**	−0.715	0.649	29	28
	10.167	*8.390*	*−2.305*	*−0.332*			

Notes: [1]Sample firms are Japanese firms that prepare U.S. GAAP financial statements.
N is the number of observations available for each regression.
$N^{\#}$ is the number of observations that enter each regression after removing those with R-student scores>|3|.
t-statistics are *italicised.*
***Significant at < .01 level. **Significant at < .05 level. *Significant at <.10 level.
$P_{j,t}$ is the domestic price of firm j at fiscal year end;
$BV_{j,Jpn,t.}$ is book value per share of shareholders' equity of firm j at time t in Japanese GAAP.
$BV_{j,U.S.,t}$ is book value per share of shareholders' equity of firm j at time t in U.S. GAAP.
$EARN_{j,Jpn,t}$ is fiscal year earnings per share of firm j reported in Japanese GAAP;
$EARN_{j,US,t}$ is U.S. GAAP earnings per share for firm j;
$DEARN_{j,t}$ $= EARN_{j,US,t} - EARN_{j,Jpn,t}$.
$DBV_{j,t}$ $= BV_{j,U.S.,t} - BV_{j,Jpn,t}$.

of the individual years. For the full sample, however, coefficients on the differences are not significant.[17]

Price-to-book Analysis

We report results for the regression analysis using aggregate differences between U.S. and Japanese measures in Table 4. Panel A reports results with the price-to-book ratio measured in Japanese-GAAP. The adjusted R^2 is .188 for the full sample and coefficients on both ROE (β_1) and difference in earnings (β_{22}) measures are positive and significant at the .01 level. These results generally hold for many of the sub-samples, including 1983-1987. Thus, it appears that incorporating U.S.-GAAP practices in earnings reflects a measurement of ROE closer to that used by the market.

The coefficient β_{21} is not positive for any sample period and is significant and negative for the 1988-1992 and the 1987 sub-samples. These results taken alone, provide mixed support for U.S.-GAAP measures of BV being more closely aligned with price than Japanese-GAAP measures.

We also define the price-to-book ratio in terms of U.S.-GAAP to distinguish the effects of future profitability and implicit measurement differences of Japanese-GAAP. Results for regressions using U.S.-GAAP shareholders' equity to determine price-to-book ratios are reported in panel B of Table 4. The adjusted R^2 is .884 for the full sample and all coefficients on earnings and book-value measures are significantly different from zero.

The coefficient θ_1 is smaller than β_1 (reported in Panel A) for the full sample, the 1988-1992 sub-sample, and for four of nine annual subsamples. This is consistent with U.S.-GAAP shareholders' equity reducing the measurement error component in Japanese-GAAP book-value.

Significant negative coefficients for the difference in BV variable (θ_{21}) suggest that Japanese-GAAP measures of book value are value-relevant beyond U.S.-GAAP measures.[18] The nonzero coefficient, θ_{22}, for the full sample and for most sub-samples, suggests earnings determined under U.S.-GAAP provides value-relevant information beyond that contained in differences between shareholders' equity. Overall, these results suggest that adjusting book-value to comply with U.S.-GAAP captures value-relevant information beyond that contained in Japanese-GAAP. The stronger results for the price-to-book tests than for the returns analysis could be due to a small impact of accounting differences on earnings compared with their impact on book-value in which differences accumulate over time. It is also possible that measurement differences are value-relevant regarding price levels that have less effect on price changes.

Additional Analysis

We compare AHV's results for a sample that is mostly European with our results on Japanese companies. AHV find mixed support for the value-relevance of earnings reconciliations. We also find mixed support (Table 3) for U.S.-GAAP earnings providing incremental value-relevant data. AHV's results provide support for the value-relevance of differences in book value of stockholders' equity. Our results also support an hypothesis that U.S.-GAAP book-value measures provide value-relevant data (Table 4, Panels A, and B).

AHV find no support for the hypothesis that earnings differences explain the price-to-book ratio. Our results, however, support the hypothesis that earnings differences explain the price-to-book ratio. U.S.-GAAP earnings in our sample are higher than Japanese-GAAP earnings. The reverse is true in AHV's sample. The standard deviation of earnings differences is smaller in our sample (.018) than in AHV's sample (.12). An interpretation of these contrasting results is that the differences between Japanese-GAAP earnings and U.S.-GAAP earnings provide more precise value-relevant disclosures for explaining the price to book ratio than the differences between a cross-section of various domestic-GAAPs and U.S.-GAAP. The AHV sample consists of firms from 20 countries. Value relevance is likely to differ by country. Treating sample companies as if earnings result from the same protocol is likely to result in greater measurement error.

It is possible that firms that choose to list their shares in the U.S. or otherwise choose to report U.S.-GAAP data may be substantially different than other Japanese companies. We examine a separate sample of 244 observations from twenty-nine Japanese firms matched to our sample on SIC code to shed some light on whether firms in our sample are representative of other Japanese companies.

Experimental firms are significantly larger than firms in the control sample. For the experimental (control) sample, mean unconsolidated sales is ¥3.45 trillion (¥1.13 trillion) and mean unconsolidated total assets is ¥1.97 trillion (¥1.10 trillion).[19] The correlation of consolidated with unconsolidated sales for both groups is greater than .989. The correlation of consolidated with unconsolidated income is also high for both groups, .70 for the experimental group and .86 for the control group. These high correlation coefficients support, to an extent, our joint test for differences across GAAPs and entities. Experimental and control firms also have similar international sales characteristics. A comparison of mean export ratios of the experimental (33%) and control (29%) samples yields an insignificant t-test p-value of .49.

We estimate models relating price (returns) to earnings for both groups. A comparison of coefficients (not reported) provides some evidence that the two groups behavior is similar for the period 1988–1992 but dissimilar for the 1983–1987 period.

CONCLUDING COMMENTS

We use aggregate differences in U.S.-GAAP and Japanese-GAAP accounting measures to evaluate the value-relevance of U.S.-GAAP reports. Our results are of interest for several reasons. We show data provided in U.S.-GAAP financial statements of Japanese firms is value-relevant beyond that contained in domestic-GAAP statements. Our results complement AHV and support the proposition that both SEC reporting methods (reconciliations or full U.S.-GAAP reports) provide value-relevant data such that a firm's choice might be predicated on local custom or other factors. We also provide evidence on a significant portion of transnational firms that elect to provide U.S.-GAAP statements rather than reconciliations. Moreover, understanding the value-relevance of data from Japanese firms is important in its own right because of the major role these firms play in international markets.

The stronger results for book-value measures raise the possibility that value-relevance studies that rely on earnings measures only may reach different conclusions. In summary, our findings provide additional evidence to support the implied SEC hypothesis that U.S.-GAAP data has value-relevance beyond domestic-GAAP data. It is possible, however, that similar value-relevant data could be reconstructed from other data available in a firm's home country.

Acknowledgments: We thank participants at the congress of The European Accounting Association and the annual meeting of the American Accounting Association for their helpful comments.

NOTES

1. Five of the worlds ten largest public companies are Japanese. Two of these provide U.S.-GAAP statements (WSJ, 1994). In addition, eighty-four of the 528 SEC registrants provided U.S.-GAAP statements in 1993 (SEC, 1993a).
2. Neither AHV's nor our methodology precludes the possibility that U.S.-GAAP earnings and equity are redundant to other information available in the market.
3. This arrangement between domestic and U.S. banks and trust companies is commonly termed an ADR facility.
4. As of August 1994, 996 firms hold the 12g3-2(b) exemption (SEC, 1994b).
5. As of July 1994, 625 foreign firms are subject to SEC registration and reporting requirements (SEC, 1994a).
6. The five countries with the most SEC reporting registrants (U.S.-GAAP statement preparers) are: Canada, 291 (22); United Kingdom, 53 (2); Israel, 36 (3); Japan, 19 (19); and Australia, 19 (1) (SEC, 1993a). Because Canadian and U.S. practices are similar, we would expect the value-relevance of the differences between the two countries to be minimal.
7. AHV examine 467 observations representing 101 firms in 20 countries.
8. The ADR Universe (Bankers Trust, 1993) lists 155 ADRs for Japanese firms traded in U.S. markets. Ten ADRs trade on the NYSE, fifteen trade on NASDAQ, and the remainder trade OTC or in the "pink sheets."
9. The exemption from registration is provided a foreign issuer that submits information about which investors ought to be informed and which the issuer makes public in its country of domicile, files with stock exchanges, or distributes to shareholders.

10. On October 6, 1983, the SEC revised Rule 12g3-2(b) by terminating availability of the exemption rule for certain foreign issuers with securities traded on an automated inter-dealer quotation system (which includes NASDAQ). Securities of non-Canadian issuers then in compliance were grandfathered indefinitely.
11. AHV base their approach on Easton and Harris (1991), Ohlson (1989), and Ball and Brown (1968).
12. We estimate returns-earnings associations for 12-month windows ending from one to six months after the fiscal year-end for the sub-sample of firms that are SEC registrants. The results (not reported) are qualitatively equivalent to those reported.
13. This could also explain why some firms provide U.S.-GAAP data without being required by the SEC to do so.
14. See Bernard, Merton, and Palepu (1992) and Easton, Eddey, and Harris (1993) for a discussion of this argument.
15. We combined the five observations from 1983 with twenty-nine 1984 observations.
16. See Belsley, Kuh, and Welsch (1980) for a discussion about measurement and investigation of influential observations.
17. We also estimate a model (not reported) which includes both Japanese and U.S. earnings levels and changes to consider relative versus incremental value-relevance of the two measures. For the full sample, neither Japanese nor U.S. levels are significant. Earnings changes are significant for both GAAPs. The results are otherwise similar to Table 3 for subperiods.
18. The variable $DBV/BV_{U.S.}$ equals $1\text{-}(BV_{JPN}/BV_{U.S.})$
19. Unconsolidated data are the only common items available for firms in both groups.

REFERENCES

Amir, E., T. Harris, and E. Venuti. 1993. "A Comparison of the Value-Relevance of U.S. versus Non-U.S.-GAAP Accounting Measures Using Form 20-f Reconciliations." *Journal of Accounting Research,* (Supplement): 230–264.

Ball, R. and P. Brown. 1968. "An Empirical Evaluation of Accounting Income Numbers." *Journal of Accounting Research,* (Autumn): 159,331–378.

Bankers Trust Company. 1993. *The ADR Universe* (January).

Belsley, D., E. Kuh, and R. Welsch. 1980. *Regression Diagnostics.* New York: Wiley.

Bernard, V., R. Merton, and K. Palepu. 1992. A Mark-to-Market Accounting for U.S. Banks and Thrifts: Lessons from the Danish Experience. Working Paper, University of Michigan.

Campbell, W. 1991. *Comparative International Accounting.* (edited by C. Nobes and R. Parker). New York: Prentice-Hall International.

Compustat-PC Plus. 1993. Global Vantage, Standard and Poors.

Coopers & Lybrand. 1991. *International Accounting Summaries, a Guide for Interpretation and Comparison.* New York: John Wiley & Sons.

Darrough, M. N. and T. S. Harris. 1989. "Tests of the Association Between Management Forecasts of Earnings and Stock Returns in Japan." Working Paper, Columbia University.

Easton, P., P. Eddey, and T. Harris. 1993. "An Investigation of Revaluations of Long-Lived Tangible Fixed Assets," *Journal of Accounting Research,* (Supplement): 1–38.

Easton, P.D. and T.S. Harris. 1991. "Earnings as an Explanatory Variable for Returns." *Journal of Accounting Research* (Spring): 19–36.

Feltham, G. and J. Ohlson. 1993. "Valuation of Clean Surplus Accounting for Operating and Financial Activities." Working Paper, Columbia University. (March)

Ohlson, J.A. 1989. "Accounting Earnings, Book Value and Dividends: The Theory of the Clean Surplus Equation (Part 1)." Working Paper, Columbia University.

Ou, J. and S. Penman. 1992. "Financial Statement Analysis and the Evaluation of Market-to-Book Ratios." Working Paper, University of California, Berkeley, (August).

Toyo Keizai Inc. 1993. *Japan Company Handbook.* (Spring).

U.S. Securities and Exchange Commission. May 1993a. "Survey of Financial Statement Reconciliations by Foreign Registrants." Division of Corporate Finance.

U.S. Securities and Exchange Commission. June 1994a. "Weekly Statistical Package."

U.S. Securities and Exchange Commission. August 1994b. "List of Foreign Issuers Which Have Submitted Information Required by the Exemption Relating to Certain Foreign Securities." Release No. 34-34477: Federal Register: Vol 58, No. 158.

Wall Street Journal (WSJ). 30, 1994: R26. (September)

White, H. 1980. "A Heteroscedasticity-Consistent Covariance Matrix Estimator and a Direct Test for Heteroscedasticity." *Econometrica*, 48: 817–838.

Zmijewski, M. 1993. "Comments on 'Earnings forecasting research: its implications for capital markets research,' by L. Brown." *International Journal of Forecasting*, 9: 337–342.

[23]

Journal of International Financial Management and Accounting 11:1 2000

The Value Relevance of Earnings and Cash Flows: Empirical Evidence for Japan

Andreas Charitou
University of Cyprus
Colin Clubb
Imperial College of Science, Technology and Medicine, University of London, UK
Andreas Andreou
University of Cyprus and Arthur Andersen

Abstract

The Japanese equity market is one of the largest in the world. In recent years, fund managers worldwide have substantially increased their exposure to the Japanese capital markets. In spite of the Japanese capital market's rapid growth and its increasing importance in the international financial world, there has been limited empirical evidence linking security returns to earnings and cash flows. This study extends the growing empirical literature on the association of earnings and cash flows with security returns by using a Japanese dataset consisting of 6,662 firm-year observations for the period 1984–93. We hypothesize that (i) earnings and cash flows are jointly associated with stock returns, and (ii) the association between cash flows (earnings) and security returns increases (decreases) when earnings are transitory. This study provides empirical evidence (i) that cash flows (earnings) have information content beyond earnings (cash flows) in explaining security returns, and (ii) that cash flows (earnings) play a more (less) important role in the marketplace when earnings are transitory. Moreover, results show that the explanatory power of our Japanese models is similar to the evidence provided in prior US studies, indicating that Japanese investors utilize earnings and cash flows in their pricing of equities as their US counterparts.

1. Introduction

In the past two decades there has been extensive research examining the relevance of financial reporting differences for valuation of securities in international capital markets (Choi and Levich, 1990). Yet, in marked

* Address for correspondence: Andreas Charitou, Department of Business Administration, University of Cyprus, P.O.Box 537, Nicosia, CY 1678, Cyprus. Email: charitou@atlas.pba.ucy.ac.cy

The authors would like to thank P. Hadgicostas, G. Hadginikolas, E. Karahanna, E. Liatsos, A. Soteriou, L. Trigeorgis, and N. Vafeas for their useful comments, and K. Polynikis for valuable research assistance. The paper has benefited from workshop participants at the European Accounting Association conference, University of Cyprus and University of Toronto. This project was partly supported by the Institute of Certified Public Accountants of Cyprus (Arthur Andersen Chrysanthou and Christoforou, KPMG Metaxas Loizides Syrimis, Ernst and Young Russel Lakoufis; PriceWaterhouse Coopers; Deloitte and Touche; Pavlou and Poyiatzis) and by the University of Cyprus. Remaining errors are the responsibility of the authors.

contrast to the USA, there is little empirical evidence linking fundamental accounting variables with security returns in Japan and the association of cash flows with security returns has generally been overlooked in research on the Japanese capital market.[1] Among the studies focusing on accounting information in the Japanese capital market, Hall, Hamao and Harris (1994) examine the association between earnings and security returns in Japan and the USA over varying return windows and conclude that Japanese investors make less use of accounting information than do their US counterparts. Alford et al. (1993) compare and contrast the information content of accounting earnings in several countries using the USA as a benchmark and provide some evidence of lower explanatory power of earnings for security returns in Japan compared to the USA. Chan et al. (1991) provide evidence that net income plus depreciation (scaled by market value of equity) is more useful than the earnings-price ratio for predicting future security returns in the Japanese capital market, possibly reflecting distortions in reported earnings, but do not consider cash flow from operations as an alternative fundamental variable for this purpose. In summary, prior research on the relationship between security prices and fundamental variables in Japan has focused on earnings and suggests that the relationship between returns and earnings is weaker in Japan than in the USA. This supports the view that Japanese financial reporting is conservative and more concerned with the protection of creditors than the provision of information to investors (Wagasugi, 1988).

The increased importance of the Japanese capital market, the sparse empirical evidence linking stock returns to earnings and cash flows in Japan, the recent emphasis on cash flow reporting worldwide and the inconclusive results of prior studies provide motivation for the present study. This study differs from prior studies in that it examines not only the incremental information content of cash flows beyond earnings, but also the role of cash flows and earnings in capital markets when earnings are transitory. We hypothesize that (i) cash flows (earnings) have incremental information content beyond earnings (cash flows), and (ii) the incremental information content of cash flows (earnings) beyond earnings (cash flows) increases (decreases) when earnings are transitory. Thus far, no other study has examined these hypotheses using Japanese data.[2] Our results provide support for the hypotheses and show that the explanatory power of our Japanese models incorporating both earnings and cash flow data is similar to that in prior US studies.

The remainder of the study is organized as follows: section (II) discusses financial reporting in Japan; section (III) motivates the study and develops the hypotheses; section (IV) describes sample selection procedures and the empirical models; section (V) discusses the empirical results, and section (VI) provides summary and conclusions.

II. Financial Reporting in Japan

Significant accounting, economic, tax, institutional and cultural differences exist between Japan and the USA and these differences are reflected in security prices and market derived indicators such as price-earnings (PE) ratios, market-book (MB) ratios and dividend yields.[3] The accounting practices in Japan are the furthest removed from global norms and this departure from these norms is manifested in substantially underreported earnings (i.e., average PE ratios are relatively high). This is partially due to the Japanese conservative accounting practices which are driven to a large extent by the legal requirement that expenses claimed for tax purposes correspond to those claimed for financial reporting purposes (Bildersee, Cheh and Lee, 1990).[4] A review of the Japanese GAAP also reveals that, relative to the USA GAAP, several current income-reducing practices exist (i.e., depreciation methods, bad debts, contingent reserves, etc.).[5] US managers, on the other hand, may have little incentive to aggressively anticipate such charges against earnings, given the stock market's preference for higher reported earnings and the preponderance of executive compensation plans linked to security prices and to earnings.

In addition, a longer term view on profitability, with less emphasis on the annual financial statements, may be taken by Japanese managers because: (i) corporate shares are typically held largely by related commercial banks, trade suppliers, and corporate customers, who are more interested in maintaining and strengthening functional business ties than stock market gains; (ii) banks have direct access to their clients' accounting information and therefore have relatively little interest in external financial reporting, and (iii) corporate earnings in Japan are seen as the source of funds that can be distributed as dividends if the shareholders so desired (Choi et al., 1983). In general, there is therefore a widespread belief that less effort may be made in Japan to provide earnings and other financial information useful to making economic decisions.

Because operating cash flows inherently remove many differences that exist between the accounting practices in different countries (e.g., depreciation and other noncash revenues and expenses), financial analysts and fund managers have used the price to cash flow ratio and cash flow per share instead of the traditional PE ratio as a benchmark to compare investments in different countries (Haskins et al., 1996). Although in recent years there has been increased interest in cash flow reporting worldwide, the commercial code in Japan does not require the preparation of a cash flow statement.[6] Nevertheless, corporations whose securities are traded on a Japanese stock exchange are required to disclose extensive (but unaudited) cash flow information in the supplementary schedules filed with the Ministry of Finance (Nissan et al., 1995).

Undoubtedly, from the previous discussion, there are substantial differences between Japanese and US financial reporting systems and there is some evidence of weak association between fundamental variables and security returns in Japan: for example, the great volatility in the Japanese stock market prices in the 1980s was unrelated to fundamental variables (French and Poterba, 1991; Hall et al., 1994; Zielinski and Holloway, 1991; Viner, 1988). However, there is also a belief that fundamental variables, such as earnings, are associated with security returns because: (i) there exists some empirical evidence that Japanese reported accounting earnings and management forecasts have information content around earnings announcements (Darrough and Harris, 1991; Sakakibara et al., 1988), and (ii) there exists some evidence that earnings are associated with security returns, especially during the early 1990s (Hall et al., 1994). In general, therefore, the issue of whether Japanese investors utilize earnings and cash flows more or less in their valuation of securities than do US investors requires examination.

In summary, empirical research has not quite kept pace with the Japanese stock market's rapid growth. Studying a market as important as the Japanese stock market is of interest in its own right. Our results, when combined with those from the USA and other countries, may also be useful in evaluating empirical models of the association of stock returns with earnings and cash flows. For example, finding that the same financial variables are associated with stock returns in the USA and Japan would strengthen our confidence in the US evidence provided thus far. On the other hand, finding that different factors affect stock returns in the two countries would suggest further research exploring institutional or behavioural differences between the two countries.

III. Motivation and Development of the Hypotheses

The research hypotheses to be tested in the present study are:

H1: *Operating cash flows (earnings) are associated with security returns given operating earnings (cash flows).*

H2: The incremental impact of operating cash flows (earnings) on security returns increases (decreases) when earnings are transitory.

A discussion on each of the above hypotheses follows.

Hypothesis 1: Operating cash flows (earnings) are associated with security returns, given operating earnings (cash flows)[7]

Hypothesis 1 predicts that cash flows (earnings) are associated with security returns given earnings (cash flows). Regulatory bodies in the USA, UK, Australia, Canada and the International Accounting Standards Committee (IASC) support the notion that information about cash flows, in addition to earnings, is useful in assessing share value. The objective of this hypothesis is to examine the role of cash flows in explaining security returns in Japan and thus provide support for the propositions made by the aforementioned regulatory bodies. This hypothesis was tested in prior US studies with mixed and inconclusive results (Wilson, 1986; Bowen et al., 1986; Bernard and Stober, 1989; Livnat and Zarowin, 1990) and the explanatory power of these earnings and cash flow models has been typically very low (Lev, 1989).[8] While cash flows are influenced by timing and matching problems that cause them to be a noisy measure of firm performance (Dechow, 1994), we believe that the financial reporting practices previously discussed may limit the usefulness of reported earnings numbers in Japan and result in significant incremental information content for cash flows in explaining security returns. The extent to which the Japanese stock market makes use of earnings and cash flow data is therefore an important question which is addressed by this hypothesis.

Hypothesis 2: The incremental impact of operating cash flows (earnings) on security returns increases (decreases) when earnings are transitory

We expect that the less (more) permanent are unexpected accounting earnings, the lower (higher) the security return response associated with unexpected earnings and the higher (lower) the security return response associated with unexpected cash flow from operations, when unexpected earnings and cash flow data are used jointly to explain security returns (Cheng et al., 1996). Lev (1989) and Ali and Zarowin (1992) argue that the underlying assumption that investors react identically to earnings and cash flows of all firms (implying constant response coefficients) may not be realistic and this has led researchers to examine the impact of earnings permanence and persistence on security returns (Easton and Zmijewski, 1989; Collins and Kothari, 1989; Kormendi and Lipe, 1992). In particular, Cheng et al. (1996) showed that cash flows play a more important role in the US capital market when earnings are transitory. A major motivation of this paper is to extend this prior US research to examine the information content of earnings and cash flows in the Japanese stock market using a contextual model that incorporates the possible effects of earnings permanence on earnings and cash flow response coefficients. This hypothesis implies that earnings may contain transitory elements with limited valuation implications because (i) management compensation contracts and debt covenants are usually based on reported earnings and managers have the incentive to introduce transitory elements in earnings, and (ii) earnings may include large transitory accruals, such as restructuring losses and earnings effects from changes in accounting standards (Cheng et al., 1996). To the extent that such factors are present in the Japanese capital market, we expect our tests of the earnings permanence hypothesis to result in a better explanatory model for security returns.

IV. Research Design

This section describes (i) the dataset and measurement of variables, and (ii) the empirical models.

(a) Dataset and Measurement of Variables

The sample firms are selected from the Global Vantage database (1995 version) using the following criteria: (i) availability of data to calculate earnings (E) and cash flows (CFO) for the period 1985–93, and (ii) availability of monthly market price and monthly dividend data to calculate security returns for the period 1985–93. Japanese industrial firms with data available for the above period are included in the sample. This selection procedure resulted in a sample of 6,662 firm-year observations.[9]

The analysis focuses upon security returns and their relationship to the level and changes of earnings and cash flow measures. The variables used in the present study are defined as follows:

- Security returns (RET): Annual security return for the fiscal year defined as cash dividends plus capital gains (losses), divided by security price at the beginning of the fiscal year.[10]

- Operating earnings (E): Net income before extraordinary items, discontinued operations, special and non-operating items.
- Cash flow from operations (CFO): Operating earnings (E) adjusted for all non-current accruals not affecting working capital (e.g., depreciation, amortization, deferred taxes, equity earnings), plus net changes in all working capital accounts related to operations, except for changes in cash, marketable securities, and debt in current liabilities.[11]

All independent variables (level and changes) used in the empirical models are deflated by the security price of the firm at the beginning of the fiscal year.[12]

Panel A of Table 1 presents descriptive statistics (mean, median, standard deviation, upper and lower quartile, minimum and maximum) for all variables (level and changes of earnings and cash flows and security returns) used in the regression models. Descriptive statistics results indicate that (i) the variability of the cash flow measures is greater than the variability of the earnings measures, (ii) the mean and median of the cash flow levels variable are greater than the equivalent earnings levels statistics, (iii) the mean and median for the changes in earnings and changes in cash flows are approximately the same. Panel B of Table 1 presents Pearson correlation

Table 1.
Panel A: Descriptive Statistics (N = 6,662)

	Mean	*Median*	*St. dev*	*Minimum*	*Maximum*	*Lower quintile*	*Upper quintile*
E	0.047	0.043	0.046	–0.341	0.501	0.025	0.067
ΔE	0.001	0.001	0.031	–0.315	0.471	–0.011	0.01
CFO	0.072	0.061	0.113	–1.094	1.321	0.024	0.109
ΔCFO	0.002	0.001	0.127	–0.969	0.989	–0.038	0.039
R	0.091	0.009	0.432	–0.924	4.826	–0.178	0.259

Panel B: Correlation Analysis (N = 6,662)

	E	*ΔE*	*CFO*	*ΔCFO*	*RET*
E	1	0.377	0.332	0.092	0.253
ΔE		1	0.023	0.103	0.297
CFO			1	0.573	0.137
ΔCFO				1	0.004
RET					1

Where: E: operating earnings, ΔE: change in E; CFO: cash flow from operations; ΔCFO: change in CFO; RET: security returns.

coefficients for all level and changes of earnings, cash flows and returns variables. These results indicate that (i) the correlation between returns and earnings is greater than the association between returns and cash flows, (ii) the correlation between the level (changes) of earnings and the level (changes) of cash flows is 0.332 (0.103), and (iii) the correlation between the level of earnings (cash flows) and the changes of earnings (cash flows) is 0.377 (0.573). These Japanese descriptive statistics and correlation results are consistent with prior US evidence.

(b) Empirical Models

The association of operating earnings and operating cash flows with security returns is tested using the following multivariate regression models:

Model 1: $RET_{it} = b_0 + b_1E_{it} + b_2\Delta E_{it} + e_{it}$
Model 2: $RET_{it} = b_0 + b_3CFO_{it} + b_4\Delta CFO_{it} + e_{it}$
Model 3: $RET_{it} = b_0 + b_1E_{it} + b_2\Delta E_{it} + b_3CFO_{it} + b_4\Delta CFO_{it} + e_{it}$
Model 4: $RET_{it} = b_0 + b_1E_{it} + b_2\Delta E_{it} + b_5E_{it}{*}D + b_6\Delta E_{it}{*}D + e_{it}$
Model 5: $RET_{it} = b_0 + b_3CFO_{it} + b_4\Delta CFO_{it} + b_7CFO_{it}{*}D + b_8\Delta CFO_{it}{*}D + e_{it}$
Model 6: $RET_{it} = b_0 + b_1E_{it} + b_2\Delta E_{it} + b_3CFO_{it} + b_4\Delta CFO_{it} + b_5E_{it}{*}D + b_6\Delta E_{it}{*}D + e_{it}$
Model 7: $RET_{it} = b_0 + b_1E_{it} + b_2\Delta E_{it} + b_3CFO_{it} + b_4\Delta CFO_{it} + b_7CFO_{it}{*}D + b_8\Delta CFO_{it}{*}D + e_{it}$
Model 8: $RET_{it} = b_0 + b_1E_{it} + b_2\Delta E_{it} + b_3CFO_{it} + b_4\Delta CFO_{it} + b_5E_{it}{*}D + b_6\Delta E_{it}{*}D + b_7CFO_{it}{*}D + b_8\Delta CFO_{it}{*}D + e_{it}$

where RET_{it}, E_{it} and CFO_{it} represent security returns, earnings and cash flows respectively for firm i in period t, Δ denotes the change in a variable, e_{it} is the error term for firm i in period t and D (in models 4–8) is a dummy variable taking a value of one when earnings are transitory and zero otherwise. Similar to Cheng et al. (1996), we use two alternative definitions to determine D. Under one approach, D equals 1 (0) when $|\Delta E_{it}/P_{it-1}|$ is greater than (less than) its yearly cross-sectional median (Ali, 1994; Freeman and Tse, 1992). Under the second approach, we rank firms each year according to their E_{it}/P_{it-1}, placing firms with positive E_{it}/P_{it-1} into the first nine groups with equal number of firms per group and firms with negative earnings in the tenth group. We classify earnings in the bottom two and top two groups as transitory (D = 1) and earnings in the middle six groups as permanent (D = 0) (Ali and Zarowin, 1992; Ou and Penman, 1989).

Hypothesis 1 is tested by comparing the relative explanatory power of models 1 and 3 and models 2 and 3 using partial F-tests and by examining the t-statistics for the combined coefficients ($b_1 + b_2$) and ($b_3 + b_4$) in model 3. The rationale for examining the combined coefficients ($b_1 + b_2$) and ($b_3 + b_4$) is that they represent estimates of the coefficients of the unexpected operating earnings and cash flows respectively (Easton and Harris, 1991; Ali and Zarowin, 1992; Cheng et al., 1996). If both the cash flow and accrual components of earnings are positively valued and if the cash flow component is more highly valued than the accrual component we would expect ($b_1 + b_2$) > 0 and ($b_3 + b_4$) > 0 in model 3.

Hypothesis 2 is tested by comparing the relative explanatory power of models 3 and 8 using a partial F-test and by examining the t-statistics for the combined coefficients ($b_5 + b_6$) and ($b_7 + b_8$) in model 8, where ($b_5 + b_6$) < 0 and ($b_7 + b_8$) > 0 indicates support for the earnings permanence hypothesis (Cheng et al., 1992). The partial F-test from comparing models 3 and 8 indicates whether the identification of *both* earnings and cash flows for firm-year observations where earnings are transitory *jointly* provides additional explanatory power beyond the basic incremental information content model (i.e., model 3). We also carry out two further partial F-tests to consider the separate implications of the earnings permanence hypothesis for earnings and cash flow response coefficients. Thus, a partial F-test comparing models 7 and 8 provides evidence on the extent to which transitory earnings realisations are differentially valued in comparison to more permanent earnings realisations and a further partial F-test comparing models 6 and 8 provides evidence on any additional differential impact of cash flows on security returns resulting from transitory earnings. Rejection of the null in the case of a partial F-test suggests that the coefficients of the additional variables in the extended model are not jointly equal to zero.

Finally, we also examine the extent to which our results in relation to the incremental information content of earnings and cash flows (hypothesis 1) apply to the case where temporary and permanent earnings (and associated cash flows) are separately identified. Thus, a partial F-test comparing models 4 and 8 provide evidence on the extent to which cash flows have incremental information content beyond temporary and permanent earnings variables (separately identified). The motivation for this is that if a comparison of models 1 and 3 supports incremental information content for cash flows beyond earnings, it does *not* necessarily follow that cash flows will have incremental information content beyond model 4 which allows temporary and permanent earnings variables to be separately identified. Similarly, a comparison of model 5 and model 8 provides evidence on the robustness of tests of the incremental information content of earnings beyond cash flows provided by a comparison of models 2 and 3. These tests are briefly discussed in relation to our empirical tests of hypothesis 1 in the next section.

V. Empirical Results

This section discusses the empirical results that relate to the tests of the research hypotheses.

(a) The Association of Earnings and Cash Flows with Security Returns (Hypothesis 1)

Hypothesis 1 states that cash flows (earnings) are associated with security returns, given earnings (cash flows). This hypothesis is examined by regressing returns (RET) on the level and changes of earnings (E, ΔE) and cash flows (CFO, ΔCFO) for the period 1985–93.

Table 2 presents pooled results for model 1 which indicate that earnings are positively associated with security returns. The sum of the coefficients of earnings ($b_1 + b_2$) over the period 1985–93 is 4.196 and statistically significant at $a = 0.01$ ($t = 28.608$). The R^2 for model 1 is 11.40%. Table 2 also presents the pooled results for model 2 which indicate a positive association between cash flows and security returns. The sum of the coefficients of cash flows ($b_3 + b_4$) is equal to 0.297 and is statistically significant at $a = 0.01$ ($t = 8.762$). The R^2 for model 2 is 2.90%. In summary, consistent with prior US and international evidence, the combined earnings coefficient in model 1 is considerably higher than the combined cash flow coefficient in model 2 and the explanatory power of the earnings model is much greater than that of the cash flow model.[13]

Table 3 presents annual, pooled and mean results for model 3. Annual results show that (i) the sum of the coefficients of the level and changes in earnings ($b_1 + b_2$) is positive and statistically significant in all years tested, and (ii) the sum of the coefficients of the level and changes in cash flows ($b_3 + b_4$) is positive and statistically significant in four years. Aggregate (mean and pooled across time) regression results also indicate that (i) there exists a strong positive association between earnings (level and changes) and security returns and (ii) there exists incremental information content for cash flows. The sum of the coefficients of the level and changes in earnings is 4.12 and statistically significant at $a = 0.01$. Results also show that the sum of the coefficients of the level and changes in cash flows ($b_3 + b_4$) is 0.185 and statistically significant at $a = 0.01$. The R^2 for model 3

Table 2. *Summary of Pooled Regression Results of the Association of Earnings and Cash Flows with Security Returns over the Period 1985–93*

Full Model: $RET = a + b_1E + b_2\Delta E + b_3CFO + b_4\Delta CFO + b_5D*E + b_6D*\Delta E + b_7 D*CFO + b_8D*\Delta CFO$ (where D equals 1 (0) when $|\Delta E_{it}/P_{it-1}|$ is greater than (less than) its yearly cross-sectional median). N = 6,662

	Intercept	*E*	*ΔE*	*CFO*	*ΔCFO*	*D*E*	*D*ΔE*	*D*CFO*	*D*ΔCFO*							
	b_0	b_1	b_2	b_3	b_4	b_5	b_6	b_7	b_8	$b_1 + b_2$	b_3+b_4	$b_5+ b_6$	b_7+b_8	*SSE*	*F-value*	*R^2-adj %*
MODEL 1	0.004 (0.140)	1.437*** (14.911)	2.759*** (18.856)							4.196*** (28.608)				751.6	429.80 ***	11.40
MODEL 2	0.023*** (4.305)			0.605*** (14.229)	0.308 (–9.491)						0.297*** (8.762)			823.5	101.60 ***	2.90
MODEL 3	–0.015** (–2.4)	1.035*** (10.185)	3.085*** (20.633)	0.501*** (11.705)	–0.316*** (–10.047)					4.12*** (29.132)	0.185*** (6.166)			735.3	256.6 ***	13.31
MODEL 4	0.009 (1.411)	0.852*** (5.795)	6.383*** (6.223)			0.738 (5.257)	–3.733*** (–3.603)			7.235*** (7.125)		–2.99*** (–2.923)		747.6	224.9 ***	11.90
MODEL 5	0.024*** (4.539)			0.501*** (6.951)	–0.400*** (–6.865)			0.149* (1.936)	0.143** (2.137)		0.101* (1.802)		0.292*** (4.417)	821	55.96 ***	3.20
MODEL 6	–0.0075 (–1.151)	0.49*** (3.346)	6.849*** (6.743)	0.497*** (11.626)	–0.312*** (–9.944)	0.68*** (4.897)	–3.875*** (–3.78)			7.350*** (7.31)	0.190*** (5.59)	–3.2*** (–3.15)		731.6	177.48 ***	13.7
MODEL 7	–0.12* (–1.869)	1.029*** (10.136)	3.09*** (20.657)	0.327*** (4.708)	–0.322*** (–5.813)			0.239*** (3.278)	0.024 (0.385)	4.12*** (28.24)	0.01 (0.09)		0.26*** (4.21)	733.18	174.67 ***	13.5
MODEL 8	–0.007 (–0.122)	0.504*** (2.9)	6.97*** (6.878)	0.455*** (5.542)	–0.39*** (–6.642)	0.667*** (3.678)	–4.008*** (–3.911)	0.054 (0.561)	0.118* (1.699)	7.474*** (7.459)	0.065 (1.151)	–3.34*** (–3.306)	0.172** (2.447)	724.5	135.4 ***	13.91

Where: E: operating earnings, ΔE: change in E; CFO: cash flow from operations; ΔCFO: change in CFO; RET: security returns; ***, **, * = statistically significant at a = 0.01, 0.05, 0.10, respectively.

Table 3. *Regression Results of the Association of Earnings and Cash Flows with Security Returns (N = 6,662)*

Model 3: RET = $a + b_1E + b_2\Delta E + b_3CFO + b_4\Delta CFO$

	Intercept	*E*	*ΔE*	*CFO*	*ΔCFO*				
Year	b_1	b_1	b_2	b_3	b_4	$b_1 + b_2$	$b_3 + b_4$	*F-value*	R^2*-adj*
1985	0.039	1.048**	1.292**	0.664**	–0.379**	2.341***	0.285	11.1***	13.83
t-value	0.946	2.215	2.275	2.453	–1.997	4.398	1.443		
1986	0.088**	1.923***	0.855	0.267	–0.064	2.778***	0.203	7.48***	11.22
t-value	2.06	2.979	1.31	0.911	–0.219	4.118	1.435		
1987	0.28***	1.353***	3.939***	0.398***	–0.153*	5.292***	0.245***	63.9****	24.75
t-value	13.803	4.631	9.424	3.222	–1.924	13.573	2.582		
1988	0.153***	0.269	4.629***	0.477***	–0.197	4.898***	0.28*	29.3***	12.21
t-value	7.474	0.704	8.141	2.877	–1.609	9.479	1.807		
1989	0.061***	2.632***	3.538***	–0.014	–0.116	6.17***	–0.13	30.3***	11.57
t-value	2.971	5.977	4.484	–0.075	–0.611	9.249	–1.37		
1990	–0.277***	2.57***	0.441	–0.009	0.013	3.011***	0.004	42.5***	15.14
t-value	–25.458	9.987	1.003	–0.101	0.213	8.076	0.051		
1991	–0.312***	0.957***	2.542***	0.43***	–0.242***	3.499***	0.188***	38.9***	14.02
t-value	–28.697	4.758	7.149	4.812	–3.679	10.647	4.203		
1992	–0.108***	0.536***	0.838***	0.224***	–0.025***	1.374***	0.199***	21.1***	7.98
t-value	–10.816	3.99	4.081	5.432	–2.697	6.87	4.469		
1993	0.107***	0.336***	1.802***	0.058	–0.041	2.138***	0.017	24.4***	9.18
t-value	10.871	2.623	8.546	0.904	–1.095	9.708	0.347		
MEAN	0.003	1.291***	2.208***	0.277***	–0.134***	3.501***	0.143***		13.32
t-value	0.429	10.581	13.176	4.907	–2.775	22.63	3.834		
POOLED	–0.015**	1.035***	3.085***	0.501***	–0.316***	4.12***	0.185***	256.6***	13.31
t-value	–2.4	10.185	20.633	11.705	–10.047	29.132	6.166		

Where: E: operating earnings, ΔE: change in E; CFO: cash flow from operations; ΔCFO: change in CFO; RET: security returns; ***, **, * = statistically significant at a = 0.01, 0.05, 0.10, respectively.

is 13.3% for the pooled dataset over the period 1985–93 and partial F-tests reported in Table 5 confirm that earnings have incremental information content beyond cash flows (the F-statistic from comparing models 2 and 3 is 399.47 which is highly statistically significant) and that cash flows have incremental information content beyond earnings (the F-statistic from comparing models 1 and 3 is 76.004 which is also highly statistically significant). These results therefore provide support for the hypothesis of incremental information content for both earnings and cash flows and indicate that the operating cash flow component of earnings is more highly valued than the accruals component.

Finally, as noted previously, a further test of the incremental information content of earnings and cash flow which takes account of the possible impact of earnings permanence on earnings and cash flow response coefficients is provided by a comparison of models 4 and 5 with model 8. Thus, while we reserve a detailed discussion of the coefficients in model 8 to the next section dealing with the earnings permanence hypothesis, it is relevant to note here that the change in R^2 between model 4 and model 8 is 2.01% (with a corresponding F-statistic of 52.948 which is significant at $a = 0.01$) and that the change in R^2 between model 5 and model 8 is 10.71% (with a corresponding F-statistic of 221.436 which is significant at $a = 0.01$). We conclude that further support for hypothesis 1 is provided by a comparison of models 4, 5 and 8 which permits earnings and cash flow coefficients to vary with the degree of earnings permanence.[14]

In summary, even though there have been several concerns in the literature regarding the quality of Japanese earnings, our results show that earnings are positively valued in the Japanese marketplace. The explanatory power of our model, as measured by the R^2, is also similar to the results presented in prior US studies.[15] As expected, the combined earnings coefficients are greater than the combined cash flow coefficients ($b_1 + b_2 > b_3 + b_4$) and again these results are consistent with prior US and international evidence. Finally, our findings of incremental information content for cash flows should be of interest to the Japanese standard setting body and to the Ministry of Finance, since, as previously discussed, Japanese public firms are not currently required to prepare cash flow statements.

(b) The Earnings Permanence Hypothesis (Hypothesis 2)

The earnings permanence hypothesis states that the incremental impact of operating cash flows (earnings) on security returns increases (decreases) when earnings are transitory. Panel A of Table 4 presents detailed annual

Table 4. *Regression Results of the Association of Earnings and Cash Flows with Security Returns when Earnings are Transitory (N = 6,662)*

Panel A: Model 8: RET = a + b_1E + b_2ΔE + b_3CFO + b_4ΔCFO + b_5D*E + b_6 D*ΔE + b_7D*CFO + b_8D*ΔCFO; where D equals 1 (0) when $|\Delta E_{it}/P_{it-1}|$ is greater than (less than) its yearly cross-sectional median.

	Intercept	*E*	*ΔE*	*CFO*	*ΔCFO*	*D*E*	*D*ΔE*	*D*CFO*	*D*ΔCFO*						
Year	b_0	b_1	b_2	b_3	b_4	b_5	b_6	b_7	b_8	$b_1 + b_2$	$b_3 + b_4$	$b_5 + b_6$	$b_7 + b_8$	*F-value*	*R^2-adj %*
1985	0.029	1.299	3.172	0.764	–0.109	–0.287	–1.98	–0.126	–0.288	4.471	0.655	–2.267	–0.414	5.8***	13.16
t-value	*0.043*	*1.442*	*0.495*	*1.339*	*–0.212*	*–0.297*	*–0.308*	*–0.195*	*–0.519*	*0.711*	*1.274*	*–0.358*	*–0.742*		
1986	0.051	4.692***	14.269*	–0.411	0.53	–3.341**	–13.76*	0.841	–0.521	18.961**	0.119	–17.101**	0.32	5.3***	14.27
t-value	*0.044*	*3.453*	*1.804*	*–0.72*	*0.955*	*–2.315*	*–1.736*	*1.258*	*–0.783*	*2.388*	*0.698*	*–2.144*	*1.027*		
1987	0.294	0.541	1.799	0.311	–0.306*	0.866	1.787	0.245	0.191	2.34	0.005	2.653	0.436**	33.9***	25.56
t-value	*0.022*	*0.962*	*0.496*	*1.446*	*–1.729*	*1.427*	*0.489*	*0.93*	*0.97*	*0.654*	*0.007*	*0.741*	*2.297*		
1988	0.16***	0.066	–2.999	0.585	–0.321	0.507	7.29**	–0.138	0.151	–2.933	0.264	7.797**	0.013	15.8***	12.65
t-value	*7.33*	*0.097*	*–0.911*	*1.618*	*–1.465*	*0.718*	*2.178*	*–0.341*	*0.575*	*–0.922*	*0.927*	*2.447*	*0.038*		
1989	0.085***	2.363***	5.224*	–0.598*	0.279	–0.273	–1.372	1.062***	–0.84**	7.587***	–0.319	–1.645	0.213	14.8***	10.99
t-value	*4.265*	*4.121*	*1.904*	*–1.89*	*1.049*	*–0.435*	*–0.476*	*2.587*	*–2.229*	*2.821*	*–1.426*	*–0.604*	*0.9*		
1990	–0.028***	2.951***	4.061***	–0.219	0.055	–0.531	–3.746**	0.362*	–0.049	7.012***	–0.164	–4.277***	0.313**	23.3***	16.06
t-value	*–24.763*	*7.971*	*2.775*	*–1.248*	*0.366*	*–1.495*	*–2.444*	*1.706*	*–0.3*	*5.047*	*–1.386*	*–2.982*	*2.063*		
1991	–0.315***	1.249***	5.909***	0.256**	–0.183**	–0.402	–3.491**	0.294	–0.097	7.158***	0.073	–3.893** *	0.197*	21.0***	14.69
t-value	*–28.209*	*4.444*	*4.511*	*1.992*	*–2.182*	*–1.369*	*–2.575*	*1.638*	*–0.699*	*5.472*	*0.942*	*–2.873*	*1.783*		

Table 4. *continued*

Year	Intercept	E	ΔE	CFO	ΔCFO	D*E	D*ΔE	D*CFO	D*ΔCFO						
	b_0	b_1	b_2	b_3	b_4	b_5	b_6	b_7	b_8	$b_1 + b_2$	$b_3 + b_4$	$b_5 + b_6$	$b_7 + b_8$	F-value	R^2-adj %
1992	−0.114***	0.309	5.567***	0.635***	−0.119	0.219	−4.97***	−0.47***	0.1	5.876***	0.516***	−4.751***	− 0.372***	12.9***	9.34
t-value	*−10.869*	*1.258*	*3.283*	*4.957*	*−1.477*	*0.875*	*−2.934*	*−3.526*	*1.238*	*3.458*	*5.16*	*−2.777*	*−3.546*		
1993	0.101***	0.217	7.424***	0.352***	−0.025	0.061	−5.74***	−0.33***	−0.027	7.641***	0.327***	−5.676***	−0.356***	14.8***	10.66
t-value	*9.847*	*0.791*	*4.183*	*2.607*	*−0.378*	*0.203*	*−3.221*	*−2.276*	*−0.35*	*4.292*	*2.763*	*−3.165*	*−2.73*		
Pooled 85–93	−0.007	0.504***	6.97***	0.455***	−0.39***	0.667***	−4.008***	0.054	0.118*	7.474***	0.062	−3.341***	0.172**	135.4***	13.91
t-value	*−0.122*	*2.9*	*6.878*	*5.542*	*−6.642*	*3.678*	*−3.911*	*0.561*	*1.699*	*7.459*	*1.151*	*−3.306*	*2.447*		

Panel B: Model 8: RET= a + b_1E + b_2ΔE + b_3CFO + b_4ΔCFO + b_5D*E + b_6D*ΔE + b_7D*CF O + b_8D*ΔCFO
Where D = 0 if it has its earnings in one of the six middle groups, and D = 1 if it has its earnings in one of the two highest or lowest groups

Year	b_0	b_1	b_2	b_3	b_4	b_5	b_6	b_7	b_8	$b_1 + b_2$	$b_3 + b_4$	$b_5 + b_6$	$b_7 + b_8$	F-value	R^2-adj %
Pooled 85–93	−0.03***	1.453***	4.197***	0.447***	−0.36***	−0.427**	−1.769***	0.1164	0.047	5.65***	0.086	−2.196 ***	0.163**	136.8***	13.92
t-value	*−4.225*	*8.17*	*16.92*	*6.416*	*−6.416*	*−2.29*	*−5.764*	*1.323*	*0.699*	*20.77*	*1.58*	*−6.82*	*2.4*		

Where: E: oper. earnings, ΔE: change in E; CFO: oper. cash flows; ΔCFO: change in CFO; RET: sec. returns; ***, **, * = stat. significant at a = 0.01, 0.05, 0.10, respectively.

results for model 8 where earnings permanence is measured by the magnitude of $|\Delta E_t/P_{t-1}|$. The coefficients of $(b_1 + b_2)$ and $(b_3 + b_4)$ represent estimates of the coefficients of the unexpected operating earnings and cash flows, respectively, when earnings are permanent. The coefficients of $(b_5 + b_6)$ and $(b_7 + b_8)$ provide estimates of the impact of transitory earnings on the magnitude of these coefficients. We hypothesize that $(b_5 + b_6) < 0$ (negative) and $(b_7 + b_8) > 0$ (positive).

Our results support both predictions of the earnings permanence. More specifically, the pooled results for the period 1985–93 show that (i) the sum of the coefficients of earnings $(b_1 + b_2)$ is 7.474 and statistically significant at a = 0.01, (ii) the sum of the coefficients of transitory earnings $(b_5 + b_6)$ is negative (–3.341) and statistically significant at a = 0.01, (iii) the sum of the coefficients of the level and changes of cash flows $(b_3 + b_4)$ is 0.062 and statistically insignificant, (iv) the sum of the coefficients of cash flows when earnings are transitory $(b_7 + b_8)$ is 0.172 and statistically significant at a = 0.01, and (v) the R^2-adj. is 13.91% and is slightly larger than the R^2 of 13.31% for the basic incremental information content model represented by model 3. These results therefore show a large and highly significant fall in the earnings response coefficient associated with transitory earnings and a significant positive coefficient for cash flows only in the case of transitory earnings $(b_7 + b_8)$. These findings are reinforced by the pooled results for models 6 and 7 reported in Table 2 which also indicate that (i) the impact of transitory earnings on the earnings coefficient is –3.2 $(b_5 + b_6)$ and significant at a = 0.01 (model 6) and (ii) the impact of transitory earnings on the cash flow coefficient is 0.26 $(b_7 + b_8)$ and significant at a = 0.01 (model 7).

Moreover, a partial F-test comparing models 3 and 8 in Table 5 rejects the hypothesis that the four additional variables in model 8 are jointly equal to zero at a = 0.01 (F = 24.790). Table 5 also indicates that a partial F-test comparing models 7 and 8 rejects the null hypothesis that b_5 and b_6 in model 8 are jointly equal to zero at a = 0.01 (F = 39.853). Similarly, a partial F-test comparing models 6 and 8 rejects the null hypothesis that b_7 and b_8 in model 8 are jointly equal to zero at a = 0.01 (F = 32.599).

In summary, these results indicate that the marginal impact of earnings on security returns is smaller and that the marginal impact of cash flows on security returns is greater when earnings are transitory, the latter results also suggesting that the positive incremental value of cash flows in our results for model 3 (see previous sub-section) are largely due to cases of transitory earnings. While the increase in R^2 associated with the earnings hypothesis is small, t-tests and partial F-tests provide statistical support

Table 5. *Summary of Partial F-test Results for Assessing the Value Relevance of Earnings and Cash Flows when these Variables are Introduced in a Series of Nested Models*

Partial F-test	*F-value*	*Δ in R-square*
F-test (Model 1, Model 3)	76.004***	1.91
F-test (Model 1, Model 4)	17.899***	0.50
F-test (Model 2, Model 3)	399.469***	10.41
F-test (Model 2, Model 5)	10.045***	0.30
F-test (Model 3, Model 8)	24.790***	0.61
F-test (Model 4, Model 8)	52.948***	2.01
F-test (Model 6, Model 8)	32.599***	0.20
F-test (Model 7, Model 8)	39.853***	0.40
F-test (Model 5, Model 8)	221.436***	10.71

$F = ((SSE_R - SSE_F)/(k-g))/(SSE_F/n-k-1))$, where SSE_R, SSE_F = sum of square errors of the reduced and full model, respectively, k, g = number of dependent variables in the full and reduced model, respectively; n = number of observations; Reject Ho if $F > F(a, k-g, n-k-1)$; a = level of significance; ***, **, * = statistically significant at a = 0.01, 0.05, 0.10, respectively.

for the predictions of the hypothesis. Moreover, these Japanese results are consistent with the existing US evidence provided by Cheng et al. (1996).[16]

The earnings permanence hypothesis was also tested using an alternative definition of transitory earnings, as described in the previous section. Results in Panel B of Table 4 confirm the results of our first approach i.e., that the marginal effect of earnings (cash flows) on security returns is decreasing (increasing) when earnings are transitory. More specifically, the pooled results show that (i) the sum of the coefficients of earnings variables ($b_1 + b_2$) is 5.65 and statistically significant at a = 0.01, (ii) the sum of the coefficients of transitory earnings ($b_5 + b_6$) is negative (–2.196) and statistically significant at a = 0.01, (iii) the sum of the coefficients of the level and changes of cash flows ($b_3 + b_4$) is 0.086 and statistically insignificant (t = 1.58), (iv) the sum of the coefficients of cash flows when earnings are transitory ($b_7 + b_8$) is 0.163 and statistically significant at a = 0.05 (t = 2.4). The R^2 is 13.92%. Again, these results corroborate (i) the evidence provided under the first alternative approach, (ii) the evidence provided under our first hypothesis, and (iii) the existing US evidence.

In summary, our results support the predictions of the earnings permanence hypothesis that the marginal effect of earnings on security returns is smaller and that the marginal effect of cash flows on security returns is greater when earnings are transitory. These results represent a useful extension to the results on the basic incremental information content model reported in the previous sub-section and are broadly consistent with prior US evidence.

VI. Conclusions

This study provides Japanese empirical evidence on the association of earnings and cash flows with security returns. More specifically, we hypothesize that (i) cash flows (earnings) are associated with security returns given earnings (cash flows), and (ii) the market valuation of earnings diminishes and the incremental valuation of cash flows increase when earnings are transitory. In relation to the first hypothesis, the results suggest that earnings (cash flows) are valued in the Japanese capital markets, given cash flows (earnings). Consistent with prior US and other international evidence, earnings are also shown to have a stronger statistical association with security returns than cash flows. In relation to the second hypothesis, results indicate that cash flows (earnings) play a more (less) important incremental role in the marketplace when earnings are transitory. These results usefully extend the evidence in relation to our first hypothesis and are consistent with prior US evidence.

Even though we identified several differences between the Japanese and the US systems (i.e., conservatism, under-reported earnings), these Japanese results corroborate prior US empirical evidence and support the view that both earnings and cash flows play an important role in the Japanese capital markets. Although in recent years there has been increased attention on cash flow reporting worldwide, the commercial code in Japan does not require the preparation of a cash flow statement. Since the present study provides empirical support for the usefulness of cash flows in the Japanese marketplace, our results are expected to provide guidance (i) to the Japanese standard setting body and to the ministry of finance regarding the usefulness of the cash flows, and (ii) to the Japanese and worldwide investors regarding the usefulness of cash flows in explaining security returns.

Finally, this study also encourages further research that may improve our understanding of the role of earnings and cash flows in explaining security returns. While our analysis suggests similarities between the USA and Japan in relation to the incremental information content of earnings and cash flows and the relevance of the earnings permanence hypothesis in both capital market settings, there are also some differences between our results and previous US results which may reflect differences between Japan and US accounting practices. For example, our tests on

Japanese data generated higher earnings response coefficients than the tests on prior US data, possibly reflecting greater conservatism in income measurement in Japan. Furthermore, if earnings quality is lower in Japan than in the USA, we might expect cash flow data to have greater incremental information content in Japan than in the USA, an issue not addressed in the current study. We conclude that future research could usefully compare the joint role of earnings and cash flows in explaining security returns in these and other capital markets using methodologies which permit a more detailed assessment of the impact of accounting practice on earnings and cash flow response coefficients.

Notes

1. In the USA, the cross-sectional relationship between security returns and earnings has been extensively studied. The earnings usefulness in returns studies has also been examined recently in conjunction with cash flows (Cheng et al., 1996; Ali and Zarowin, 1992; Dechow, 1994; Charitou and Ketz, 1990). Thus far, US empirical research provided evidence to support that earnings is valued more in the marketplace than cash flows. Evidence on the incremental information content of cash flows beyond earnings has been inconclusive.
2. A comparable US study that was conducted by Cheng et al. (1996) examined only a very short period (four years only). In the present study we examine all nine years of data that were available in the Global Vantage database (1985–93).
3. Differences in financial ratios such as liquidity and solvency are not just the result of accounting differences but also differences in the financial systems and norms of these countries. In Japan for example, higher levels of liquidity and solvency are considered normal relative to the USA because of longer-term relationships with bankers and suppliers. The conservative valuation of debt and the propensity to finance debt tend to cause Japanese companies to appear to be substantially less solvent than their US counterparts. For more information about financial reporting differences between Japan and the USA see Haskins et al., 1996; Cooke, 1993; Nobes and Parker, 1996; Choi and Hiramatsu, 1987.
4. Bildersee et al. (1990) show that historically there have been significant differences in the PE ratios between Japan and the USA. These researchers showed that these differences can be reduced by adjustments to earnings due to differences in depreciation, leverage and ownership policies in the two countries.
5. Japanese firms with large capital investments tend to have distorted earnings because they predominantly use accelerated depreciation methods.
6. Standard setting bodies in Canada (CICA No. 1540, 1985), USA (SFAS No. 95, 1987), Australia (ASB, 1991), UK (FRS No. 1, 1991) as well as the IASC (IAS No. 7, 1995) require that a statement of cash flows be prepared by all public companies.
7. In the present study, we examine the role of operating earnings and operating cash flows in explaining security returns. For simplicity, we use the terms "earnings" and "cash flows" throughout the study.
8. UK research is also consistent with prior US evidence (Ali and Pope, 1995; Clubb, 1995; McLeay et al., 1997). Moreover, recent studies showed that as the return interval increases, the explanatory power of the model increases (Easton et al., 1992; Hall et al., 1994, among others).
9. Utilities, banks, insurance companies and real estate trusts are excluded from the sample. In order to also ensure that the results are not affected by outliers, extreme

observations of the independent variables (approximately 1%) are excluded from the sample. This is consistent with similar prior empirical studies (Ali and Pope, 1995; Alford et al., 1993; Easton and Harris, 1991, among others).

10. Other 12-month return intervals were used ending 3–6 months after the fiscal year end. These alternative definitions did not alter the substance of the results.

11. Similar to Wilson (1986), Bernard and Stober (1989) and Charitou and Vafeas (1998), our calculation of CFO adjusts E for current and non-current accruals consistently across all firms.

12. For more information about earnings level and change specifications see Kothari, 1992; Easton and Harris, 1991; Harris, Lang and Moller, 1994; and Ali and Zarowin, 1992.

13. Annual results for models 1 and 2 are consistent with the pooled results. The annual results are not reported in the paper but can be obtained from the authors on request.

14. We also tested (a) the incremental information content of the combined earnings coefficients ($b_5 + b_6$) beyond the level and changes of earnings by comparing model 1 with model 4 (the partial F-statistic is 17.899 and significant at a = 0.01), and (b) the incremental information content of the combined cash flow coefficients ($b_7 + b_8$) beyond the level and changes of cash flows by comparing model 2 with model 5 (the partial F-statistic is 10.045 and significant at a = 0.01).

15. The adjusted R^2 for model 3 of 13.3% compares with a corresponding R^2 of 12% reported by Cheng et al. (1996) for their US data.

16. The explanatory power of our model, as measured by the R^2, is also similar to the US results (the R^2 for model 8 of 13.91% compares with a comparable figure of 12% reported by Cheng et al.).

References

Accounting Standards Board, *Financial Reporting Standard 1. Cash Flow Statements* (London, 1991).

Alford, A., J. Jones, R. Leftwich and M. Zmijewski, "The Relative Informativeness of Accounting Disclosures in Different Countries," *Journal of Accounting Research* Vol. 31 (Supplement 1993), pp. 183–229.

Ali, A., "The Incremental Information Content of Earnings, Working Capital from Operations and Cash Flows," *Journal of Accounting Research* Vol. 32 (Spring 1994), pp. 61–74.

Ali, A. and P. Pope, "The Incremental Information Content of Earnings, Funds Flow and Cash Flow: The UK Evidence," *Journal of Business Finance and Accounting* Vol. 22 (January 1995), pp. 19–34.

Ali, A. and P. Zarowin, "The Role of Earnings Levels in Annual Earnings-Returns Studies," *Journal of Accounting Research* Vol 30 (Autumn 1992), pp. 286–296.

Ali., A. and P. Zarowin, "Permanent Versus Transitory Components of Accounting Earnings and Estimated Error in Earnings Response Coefficients," *Journal of Accounting and Economics* (1992), pp. 249–264.

Belsley D., E. Kun and R. Welsh, *Regression Diagnostics: Identifying Influential Data and Sources of Collinearity* (New York, Wiley, 1980).

Bernard, V. L. and T. L. Stober, "Nature and Amount of Information in Cash Flows and Accruals," *The Accounting Review* Vol. 64 (October 1989), pp. 24–52.

Bildersee, J., J. Cheh and C. Lee, "The International Price-Earnings Ratio Phenomenon: A Partial Explanation," *Japan and the World Economy* Vol. 2 (1990), pp. 263–282.

Bowen, R., D. Burgstahler and L. Daley, "The Incremental Information Content of Accruals Versus Cash Flows," *The Accounting Review* Vol. 62 (October 1986), pp. 723–747.

Canadian Institute of Chartered Accountants, *CICA Statement 1540: Statement of Cash Flows* (1985).

Chan, L., Y. Hamao and J. Lakonishok, "Fundamentals and Stock Returns in Japan," *Journal of Finance* (December 1991), pp. 1739–1764.

Chan, L.,Y. Hamao and J. Lakonishok, "Can Fundamentals Predict Japanese Stock Returns?" *Financial Analysts Journal* (August 1993), pp. 63–9.

Charitou, A. and C. Clubb, "Earnings, Cash Flows and Security Returns over Long Return Intervals: Analysis and UK Evidence," *Journal of Business Finance and Accounting* Vol. 26 (March 1999).

Charitou, A. and N. Vafeas, "The Association between Operating Cash Flows and Dividend Changes: An Empirical Investigation," *Journal of Business Finance and Accounting* Vol. 25, Nos. 1 & 2 (January–March 1998) pp. 225–249.

Charitou A. and E. Ketz, "Valuation of Earnings and Cash Flows and their Components," *Journal of Accounting, Auditing and Finance* Vol. 5, (1990), pp. 475–497.

Cheng, C. S. A., C. Liu and T. Schaefer, "Earnings Permanence and the Incremental Information Content of Cash Flows from Operations," *Journal of Accounting Research* Vol. 34 (Spring 1996), pp. 173–181.

Cho, J. Y. and K. Jung, "Earnings Response Coefficients: A Synthesis of Theory and Empirical Evidence," *Journal of Accounting Literature* Vol. 10 (1991), pp. 85–116.

Choi, F. and K. Hiramatsu, *Accounting and Financial Reporting in Japan* (Van Nostrand Reinhold, Princeton NJ, 1987).

Choi, F., H. Hino, S. Min, S. Nam, J. Ujiie and A. Stonehill, "Analyzing Foreign Financial Statements: The Use and Misuse of International Ratio Analysis," *Journal of International Business Studies* (Spring 1983), pp. 113–131.

Choi, F. and Levich, *The Capital Market Effects of International Accounting Diversity* (Himewood, IL, Dow Jones-Irwin, 1990).

Christie, A., "On Cross-Sectional Analysis in Accounting Research," *Journal of Accounting and Economics* Vol. 9 (December 1987), pp. 231–258.

Clubb, C., "An Empirical Study of the Information Content of Accounting Earnings, Funds Flows and Cash Flows in the UK," *Journal of Business Finance and Accounting*, Vol. 22 (January 1995), pp. 35–52.

Cooke T., "The Impact of Accounting Principles on Profits: The US Versus Japan," *Accounting and Business Research* Vol. 23, No. 92 (1993), pp. 460–476.

Constand R., L. Freitas and M. Sullivan, "Factors Affecting Price Earnings Ratios and Market Values in Japanese Firms," *Financial Management* (Winter 1991), pp. 68–79.

Collins, D. W. and S. P. Kothari, "An Analysis of Intertemporal and Cross-sectional Determinants of Earnings Response Coefficients," *Journal of Accounting and Economics* (July 1989), pp. 143–182.

Darrough, M. and T. Harris, "Do Management Forecasts of Earnings Affect Stock Prices in Japan?" In *Japanese Financial Market Research*, W. Ziemla, W. Bailey and Y. Hamao, eds. (North Holland, 1991), pp. 197–229.

Dechow, P., "Accounting Earnings and Cash Flows as Measures of Firm Performance: The Role of Accounting Accruals," *Journal of Accounting and Economics* Vol. 18 (1994), pp. 3–42.

Dielman, T., *Applied Regression Analysis for Business And Economics* (Duxbury Press, 2nd ed. 1996).

Easton P. and T. Harris, "Earnings as an Explanatory Variable for Returns," *Journal of Accounting Research* Vol. 29 (Spring 1991), pp. 19–36.

Easton, P., T. Harris and J. Ohlson, "Aggregate Accounting Earnings Can Explain Most of Security Returns," *Journal of Accounting and Economics* Vol. 15 (1992), pp. 119–142.

Easton, P. D. and M. E. Zmijewski, "Cross-sectional Variation in the Stock Market Response to Accounting Earnings Announcements," *Journal of accounting and Economics* (July 1989), pp. 117–141.

Fama, E. and K. R. French, "The Cross-Section of Expected Stock Returns," *Journal of Finance* Vol. 47 (June 1992), pp. 427–465.

Financial Accounting Standards Board, *Statement of Financial Accounting Standards No. 89: Statement of Cash Flows* (Stamford CT FASB, 1987).

Freeman, R. N. and S. Y. Tse, "A Non-Linear Model of Security Price Responses to Unexpected Earnings," *Journal of Accounting Research* Vol. 30 (Autumn 1992), pp. 185–209.

French, K. and J. Poterba, "Were Japanese Stock Price Too High?" *Journal of Financial Economics* Vol. 29 (1991), pp. 337–363.

Hall, C., Y. Hamao and T. Harris, "A Comparison of Relations Between Security Market Prices, Returns and Accounting Measures in Japan and the United States," *Journal of International Financial Management and Accounting* Vol. 5, No. 1 (1994), pp. 47–73.

Harris, T., M. Lang and H. P. Moller, "The Value Relevance of German Accounting Measures: An Empirical Analysis," *Journal of Accounting Research* Vol. 32, No. 2 (Autumn 1994), pp. 187–209.

Haskins, M., K. Ferris and T. Selling, *International Financial Reporting and Analysis: A Contextual Emphasis* (Irwin, 1996).

Kormendi, R. and R. Lipe, "Earnings Innovations, Earnings Persistence, and Stock Returns," *Journal of Business* Vol. 60 (July 1987), pp. 323–346.

Kothari, S. P., "Price-Earnings Regressions in the Presence of Prices Leading Earnings; Earnings Level Versus Change Specifications and Alternate Definitions," *Journal of Accounting and Economics* Vol. 15 (1992), pp. 173–202.

Livnat, J. and P. Zarowin, "The Incremental Information Content of Cash-Flow Components," *Journal of Accounting and Economics* Vol. 13 (May 1990), pp. 25–46.

Lev, B., "On the Usefulness of Earnings and Earnings Research: Lessons and Directions from Two Decades of Empirical Research," *Journal of Accounting Research* Vol. 27 (Supplement 1989), pp. 153–192.

Mcleay, S., J. Kassab and M. Helan, "The Incremental Information Content of Accruals: Evidence Based on the Exponential Smoothing of Levels and Trends in Pre-Tax Earnings, Funds Flow and Cash Flow," *Journal of Business Finance and Accounting* (September 1997), pp. 1147–1167.

Nissan, S., N. Kamata and R. Otaka, "Cash Reporting in Japan," *The International Journal of Accounting* (1995), pp. 168–180.

Nobes, C. and R. Parker, *Comparative International Accounting* (Prentice Hall, 4th ed., 1995).

Rayburn, J., "The Association of Operating Cash Flow and Accruals With Security Returns," *Journal of Accounting Research* (Supplement 1986), pp. 112–133.

Rao, R., R. Aggarwal and T. Hiraki, "Dividend Yields and Stock Returns: Evidence from the Tokyo Stock Exchange," *Journal of Economics and Business* (1992), pp. 187–200.

Radebaugh, L. and S. Gray, *International Accounting and Multinational Enterprises* (Wiley, 4th ed., 1996).

Sakakibara, S., H. Yamaji, H. Sakurai, K. Shiroshita and S. Fukuda, *The Japanese Stock Market: Pricing Systems and Accounting Information* (Praeger, 1988).

Wilson, G., "The Relative Incremental Information Content of Accruals and Cash Flows: Combined Evidence at the Earnings Announcement and Annual Report Date," *Journal of Accounting Research* Vol. 24 (Supplement 1986), pp. 165–200.

Zielinski, R. and N. Holloway, *Unequal Equities: Power and Risk in Japan's Stock Market* (Tokyo: Kodansha International, 1991).

[24]

Journal of International Financial Management and Accounting 12:2 2001

Japanese Corporate Groupings (*Keiretsu*) and the Informativeness of Earnings

Edward B. Douthett, Jr.
M. J. Neeley School of Business, Texas Christian University
Kooyul Jung
Graduate School of Management, Korea Advanced Institute of Science and Technology

Abstract

This paper examines the effect of Japanese corporate groupings, *keiretsu*, on the informativeness of earnings. *Keiretsu* firms maintain close financial and personal ties through cross-shareholding, credit holding, interlocking corporate directorates, and various business transactions. We propose that the strong interrelations of the *keiretsu* ownership structure enhance the informativeness of earnings through efficient monitoring of managerial performance. Our empirical results show that *keiretsu* firms have higher earnings response coefficients than those of non-*keiretsu* firms, the earnings response coefficient increases as the strength of the *keiretsu* relationship increases, and discretionary accruals by *keiretsu* firms are smaller than discretionary accruals of non-*keiretsu* firms. All of these results suggest that the monitoring ability of the *keiretsu* improves the informativeness of earnings.

1. Introduction

The ownership structure of Japanese firms is typically highly concentrated among corporate stockholders with financial institutions occupying a majority of the stock holdings. A significant portion of Japanese industrial firms' ownership is represented by small groups of enterprises (*keiretsu*) composed of firms in different industries. These firms are interrelated through cross holdings of equity ownership and generally rely on a large commercial bank for their primary banking needs. The *keiretsu* firms maintain close financial and personal ties through cross-shareholding, credit holding, interlocking corporate directorates within the group, and a variety of business transactions.

We propose that the strong interrelations of the Japanese *keiretsu* affect the informativeness of earnings in various ways.[1] First, the *keiretsu* relationship increases the monitoring of managerial performance (Kang

The authors appreciate the comments provided by participants at the 1999 Annual Meeting of the American Accounting Association, Texas Christian University, and two anonymous referees. The authors are also grateful for the financial support of the Charles Tandy American Enterprise Center of the M. J. Neeley School of Business, Texas Christian University.

and Shivadasani, 1995, 1997; Kaplan and Minton, 1994), limits discretion for earnings management, and therefore enhances the quality and predictability of accounting earnings.[2] Also, the close financial and business ties between the member firms allow a credible exchange of information (Kester, 1991) or coordination of research efforts through direct or indirect participation in management or the coordination meeting. We expect that this relationship will reduce the agency problem and information asymmetry between managers and stockholders, thereby increasing the informativeness of earnings. In support of this, Jacobson and Aaker (1993) compared the return-earnings relation between Japanese and the US firms and found that Japanese investors are better informed about the future prospect of a firm than are US investors. They suggested that the result could be due to the reduction in information asymmetry that arises from the prevalent cross-shareholdings in Japan.

Alternatively, the *keiretsu* relationship may decrease the effectiveness of monitoring. Managers under the *keiretsu* relationship may entrench in an inefficient, low-effort arrangement in which managers protect each other in the market for corporate control, resulting in an anti-competitive and exclusionary environment, thereby decreasing the effectiveness of Japanese corporate performance (Sheard, 1991). In an accounting context, the exclusionary theory posits that information is disseminated within group members but specifically excludes others. Also, since these companies are less subject to market discipline, there is a possibility that *keiretsu* companies disclose less information than other companies in their annual reports (Cooke, 1996).[3] Under these conditions, the informativeness of earnings would be low. Although we expect that the *keiretsu* relationship would serve as an active monitoring vehicle (as evidence predominantly suggests), how management entrenchment in the *keiretsu* would mitigate the effectiveness of monitoring and the informativeness of earnings is an empirical question.

In this study, we investigate the informativeness of earnings by examining earnings response coefficients in the regression of stock returns on earnings. To examine the effect of the *keiretsu* on earnings informativeness, we separate the Japanese firms into *keiretsu* and non-*keiretsu* independent firms, and compare the coefficients of earnings variables after controlling for agency and earnings quality related variables. These regressions are performed using consolidated earnings and unconsolidated earnings separately following evidence by Harris et al. (1994) who report that the return-earnings relation is different according to the degree of consolidation in Germany.

As additional evidence on the effect of *keiretsu* relationship on the informativeness of earnings, we investigate the association between the strength of the *keiretsu* relationships and the informativenss of earnings. If the *keiretsu* relationship indeed increases the informativeness of earnings, then the informativeness of earnings should be higher given a stronger *keiretsu* relationship. This is examined using a power variable that measures the strength of the *keiretsu* relationship as explained later. Further, we examine differences in the manager's accounting choice decision between *keiretsu* and non-*keiretsu* firms. If the monitoring rationale for *keiretsu* firms limits the managers' discretion in the choice of accounting methods for their self-interests, the accounting choices (as manifested by discretionary accruals) should be also different between *keiretsu* and non-*keiretsu* firms.

The results show that *keiretsu* firms have higher earnings response coefficients than those of non-*keiretsu* firms after controlling for earnings quality and other agency costs, supporting the proposal that the *keiretsu* relationship serves as an active monitoring mechanism. These results are robust to whether consolidated or unconsolidated earnings are used. Also, we find a significant relationship between earnings informativeness and the strength of the *keiretsu* relationship. This is additional evidence that it is the monitoring ability of *keiretsu* that improves the informativeness of earnings. Finally, the results show that there are significant differences in the accrual behavior between *keiretsu* and non-*keiretsu* firms, suggesting that the manager's accounting choices are different between *keiretsu* and non-*keiretsu* firms.

The remainder of the paper is organized as follows. Section 2 explains Japanese ownership structure. Section 3 describes the sample and data. Section 4 presents the hypotheses and the methodology and section 5 presents the results. Section 6 concludes the paper.

2. Japanese Ownership Structure

Japanese ownership structure is a complex network of implicit and explicit contracts among many different stakeholders (Kester, 1991).[4] An interesting aspect of Japanese ownership structure is the industrial groupings known as the *keiretsu*.[5] The *keiretsu* is a successor of prewar *zaibatsu*, which originated as family-controlled concerns such as Yasuda banking complex, Mitsubishi shipping conglomerate, and Mitsui trading company, and existed as early as the 1870s. After the *zaibatsu* were dissolved by the Anti-Monopoly Law (1947) during the occupation of Japan by the

Allied forces following World War II, the pre-existing inter-firm relations gradually reemerged as *keiretsu* through coordination by the previous *zaibatsu* banks and other large commercial banks.

After the Occupation forces left Japan in April 1952, the Ministry of International Trade and Industry (MITI) began to permit the formation of cartels among small businesses as an exception to the Anti-Monopoly Law (Johnson, 1982). As a result, the old *zaibatsu* names were restored and MITI encouraged the formation of *keiretsu*. Banks continued to be the major nexus of interlocking shareholding ties in these "financial *keiretsu*". The main banking groups of Mitsubishi, Sumitomo, Mitsui and Fuyo as well as the newer groups of Sanwa and Dai-Ichi Kangyo Group (DKB) were the initial six financial *keiretsu*. These financial *keiretsu* are referred to as horizontal *keiretsu* since the member firms have common ties with a main bank, including shared stockholdings as well as normal banking relations. In contrast, a vertical *keiretsu* normally involves a very large trading company with many small, subservient companies such as Toyota Motor Corporation.

Firms in financial groups are usually related to each other by the following mechanisms: (a) The main bank is the principal lender to the group members, it owns a significant number of shares in group firms, and it often takes part in their management;[6] (b) Group firms cross-hold shares and occasionally exchange personnel as well; and (c) "President Club" (*shacho-kai*) meetings are regularly scheduled between presidents or directors of *keiretsu* firms. The President Clubs are often mentioned as a mechanism of intra-group coordination (*Industrial Groupings in Japan*, 1994).

These groups of firms operating in different industries, but engaged in long-term relationships, exchange equity stakes in each other, creating reciprocal voting rights. A credible mutual commitment is achieved once another firm in the group obtains a controlling stake in one firm. By pooling voting rights, the coalition can exercise control over any firm's strategic decisions, and ensure that a manager acting opportunistically is fired or demoted. Management control is held in hostage in the *keiretsu* coalition to ensure commitment to efficient, cooperative behavior (Berglof and Perotti, 1994).

Such a *keiretsu* relationship is not without costs, however. Nakatami (1984) highlights some of the costs associated with these arrangements. In the typical, diffusely held corporation, the disciplining effect of the market serves to reduce the potential managerial inefficiencies that arise from latent agency conflicts within a corporation. This discipline may be less effective, however, when group members own a large block of shares. The practice of reciprocal shareholdings within a *keiretsu* may lead to interlocking corporate directorates and thereby dampen the disciplinary effectiveness of the market for corporate control. Therefore, group members may attempt to maximize the wealth of employees and management rather than that of the shareholders. Consistent with such behavior, Nakatani as well as Prowse (1992), and Brown et al. (1994) find that the return on assets is lower (but more stable) for *keiretsu* firms when compared to non-*keiretsu* firms.

Of course, there is also a mechanism that monitors such inefficient, low-effort coalitions. The main bank plays an important role in monitoring. The *keiretsu* main bank, as a creditor and shareholder, has strong incentives to become informed about firms and their investment opportunities and to use the information to ensure that efficient choices are made. The main banks may be considered a financial intermediary who minimizes the cost of monitoring and resolves incentive problems between borrowers and lenders (Diamond, 1984). Sheard (1989) argues that the Japanese main bank system may be a substitute for screening and monitoring institutions such as credit rating institutions and security analysts, or act as an alternative to the takeover market.

Another aspect of main bank system is the information sharing relationship between the bank and the firm. The main bank has better access to inside information on the firm. The main bank's monitoring based on superior information is relied upon by other banks. This information sharing within a group may help to reduce fraud and misrepresentation of accounting information. It can also help prevent management's manipulation of earnings by curbing discretionary accruals. As such, this information sharing may be of some significance in Japan where external audit is relatively weak.

The main bank's role becomes more important if the firm is in financial distress. When a *keiretsu* firm's profit is poor, the main bank, representing the creditors, may try to take control. This makes the management responsive to poor performance. Evidence indicates that, despite a virtual absence of takeovers, managerial turnover is very responsive to poor performance, perhaps even more so than in the US (Kaplan, 1994). In fact, when a firm's stock market performance is poor, both the main bank and other *keiretsu* member firms tend to appoint external directors to the board of the troubled firm.[7] The appointment of directors from banks increases with negative current earnings as well (Kaplan and Minton, 1994). Kang and Shivdasani (1995) also report that the sensitivity of management turnover to earnings performance is higher for firms with ties to a main bank system than for firms without such ties. The intensity of these monitoring activities is positively correlated with shareholder concentration and *keiretsu* affiliation.

This paper focuses on how the close financial and personal ties mentioned above may increase monitoring and reduce agency problems between managers and shareholders, and consequently enhance the informativeness of earnings.

3. Sample and Data

Sample firms were obtained from *The Japan Company Handbook* (1988 and 1994). It provides ownership data for all the firms listed in the First Sections of the Tokyo, Osaka and Nagoya stock exchanges. 1,182 firms are listed in both years of 1988 and 1994. These firms constitute our initial sample. We then eliminate the firms not in *Global Vantage*, financial companies, and firms in the three industries (air transportation, communications, and electric power and city gas supply) in which few *keiretsu* companies exist. This procedure resulted in 911 firms.

These firms are then classified into 402 *keiretsu*-affiliated firms and 509 non-*keiretsu* independent firms according to *Industrial Groupings in Japan*, which identifies those firms that are associated with each of eight horizontal *keiretsu*—Mitubishi, Fuyo, Sumitomo, Sanwa, Dai-Ichi Kangyo Bank, Mitsui, Tokai, and Industrial Bank of Japan.[8,9] The book provides information on whether a stockholder is a member firm in the same *keiretsu* group, and the names and stockholdings of the ten largest stockholders. This provides information on the cross-shareholding also.

Table 1. *Sample Selection of Japanese Firms*

	No. of Firms	Firm Years
Japanese Firms Available in the Japanese Handbook	1,182	
Minus:		
Not in Global Vantage	(231)	
Air transport, finance, utility, & communication companies	(40)	
Total Exclusions	(271)	
Final Sample of Japanese Firms	911	7,283
Keiretsu Members	402	3,213
Non-*Keiretsu* Members	509	4,070

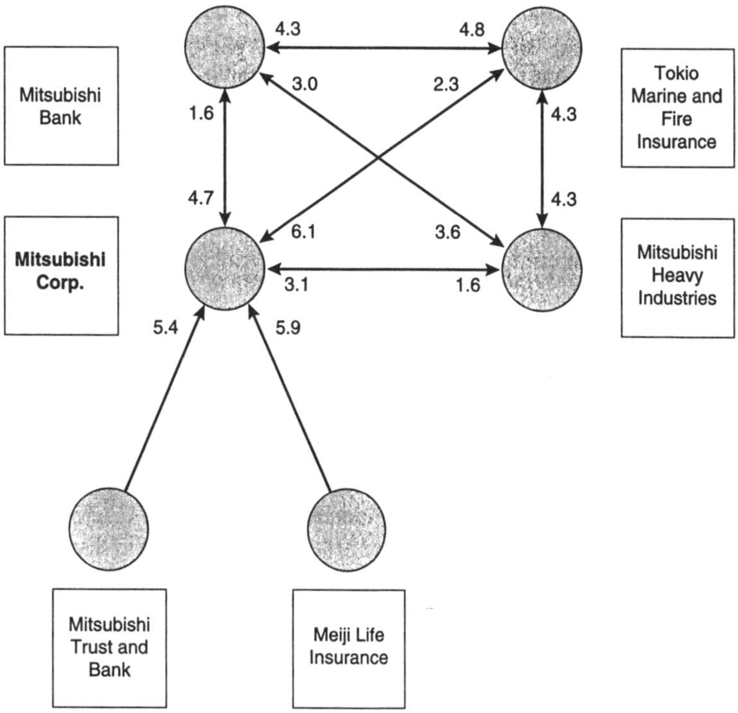

Figure 1. Crossholding of Shares for Mitsubishi Corp. by Group Firms

The Industrial Groupings in Japan also provides information to compute a measure of influential power of *keiretsu* member firms. Influential power is computed by dividing the holdings of the member firms that belong to the same group with the total holdings of the ten largest stockholders listed in the book. This construct measures the coalition power of a *keiretsu* on the member firm. Figure 1 shows the cross-shareholding among four major Mitsubishi group firms in 1994. For example, Mitsubishi Corporation holds 1.6 per cent of The Mitsubishi Bank while The Mitsubishi Bank holds 4.7 per cent of Mitsubishi Corporation; Mitsubishi Corporation also holds 2.3 per cent of Tokio Marine & Fire Insurance while Tokio Marine & Fire Insurance holds 6.1 per cent of Mitsubishi Corporation, etc. From this cross-shareholding information we calculate the influential power of a *keiretsu* on a particular firm. For Mitsubishi Corporation, 5 *keiretsu* group firms within the largest 10 shareholders hold 25.2 per cent of Mitsubishi Corporation's shares. Since the total holdings of the largest 10 shareholders are 42 per cent, the power variable is computed as 60 per cent (25.2 / 42.0).

4. Hypotheses and Methodology

4.1 Keiretsu *Membership and the Informativeness of Earnings*

As described in the previous sections, the *keiretsu* grouping improves the monitoring of managerial performance. For US corporations, Warfield et al. (1995) examine the relationship between managerial ownership and the informativeness of earnings. They suggest that demand for accounting-based constraints is higher when managerial ownership (insider holdings) is lower, and that managers are expected to respond to the contractual environment in their self-interest, increasing managerial discretion in choosing accounting methods (as manifested in the increase in discretionary accrual) and therefore, decreasing the explanatory power of earnings for returns. On the other hand, discretionary accruals will be lower and earnings explanatory power higher if insider holdings are higher. If the *keiretsu* relationship plays a monitoring role similar to that of insiders, earnings management for self-interest will be reduced and/or accounting policies will be selected in such a way as to better reflect the economic reality of the company under *keiretsu* relationships than it is for non-*keiretsu* companies.

For *keiretsu* companies, the main bank largely performs monitoring. As discussed in section 3, the *keiretsu* main bank, as a creditor and shareholder, has a strong incentive to monitor managerial performance. The main bank's monitoring and information sharing may help to reduce fraud and misrepresentation of accounting information, and prevent management's manipulation of earnings by curbing discretionary accrual. This will make earnings quality higher than non-*keiretsu* independent firms. The active monitoring for *keiretsu* firms is evidenced in the pattern of earnings also. Prowse (1992) and Brown et al. (1994) report that *keiretsu* earnings are lower but less variable than those of independent firms. The stable earnings increase the predictability of earnings and its informativeness.

Further, *keiretsu* membership facilitates information sharing through interlocking directorates, president clubs, and the general trading company in the *keiretsu* (Sheard, 1989). Jacobson and Aaker (1993) report that stock prices of Japanese firms incorporate information about future profitability earlier than do stock prices of US firms. They suggest that this could be due to prevalent cross-shareholding in Japan. We investigate the contemporaneous relationship between earnings and returns between *keiretsu* and non-*keiretsu* firms as in hypothesis 1.

Hypothesis 1: The informativeness of earnings is greater for *keiretsu* firms than non-*keiretsu* independent firms.

In our tests we start with the following basic return-earnings model:

$$R_{it} = a_0 + a_1E_{it} / P_{it-1} + a_2E_{it} * D_{it} / P_{it-1} + a_3E_{it} * Y90 / P_{it-1} + e_{it} \quad (1)$$

where

R_{it} = Returns of firm i for 12-month period for fiscal year t. The return is computed as $(P_{it} + d_{it} - P_{it-1}) / P_{it-1}$. d_{it} represents dividends of firm i during fiscal year t.
E_{it} = Primary earnings per share for firm i in fiscal year t.
P_{it-1} = Stock price per share of firm i at the end of fiscal year t–1.
D_{it} = Dummy variable for *keiretsu* membership, 1 for *keiretsu* and 0 for non-*keiretsu*.
Y90 = 1 for the period from 1990 and 0 before 1990.

The return is computed for the fiscal 12-month operating period. We use the level of earnings[10] as an explanatory variable and add a year dummy variable, Y90, on the basic return-earnings model to control time effects between the pre- and post-1990 periods. The Japanese stock market started to plunge in 1990 after booming periods during 1980s.

4.2 Consolidation versus Non-consolidated Earnings

The return-earnings relation is influenced by the accounting policy of the company. For example, previous research shows differences in consolidation are correlated with differences in the return-earnings association. Harris et al. (1994) report that consolidated earnings possess greater value relevance than unconsolidated earnings in Germany. Godwin et al. (1998) report that data provided in US-GAAP financial statements is value relevant beyond that contained in Japanese domestic-GAAP statements.

Additionally, filing and disclosure exceptions exist for many Japanese companies. Most Japanese listed companies should follow filing requirements under both the commercial code (administrated by the Ministry of Justice) and the Securities and Exchange Law (SEL, administrated by the Ministry of Finance). Statutory filing under the commercial code does not require consolidated financial statements. On the other hand, SEL requires the companies to report consolidated earnings from 1977. A significant number of firms still report unconsolidated financial statements because certain exceptions exempt the companies from filing consolidated statements. For instance, companies are not required to prepare consolidated financial statements if the subsidiary's sales are less than 10 per cent of the sales of the parent company. Another reason that many firms file unconsolidated financial statements is that the requirement is not strictly enforced.[11] For the reasons mentioned above, earnings are likely to be mismatched if we compare consolidated earnings of *keiretsu* firms with parent only earnings of non-*keiretsu* firms or vice versa. Therefore, we analyze the return-earnings equation (1) separately between consolidated and non-consolidated firms.

4.3 Agency and Earnings Quality Variables

The basic return-earnings relationship is influenced by agency and earnings quality variables. Variables from agency theory include firm size, risk and debt. Numerous studies report that these variables affect the firm's accounting choice decisions (see Watts and Zimmerman, 1990, for a review of the literature). Firm size is motivated by political cost theory. Watts and Zimmerman (1978, 1990) argue that managers of large corporations are politically sensitive and are more likely to exploit accounting discretion to reduce political costs. Risk is considered because high-risk firms possess greater incentives to exploit accounting discretion (Zmijewski and Hagerman, 1981). Evidence indicates that leverage is positively related to accounting choice decision. The higher the leverage, the more likely managers choose income-increasing methods. Also, the leverage variable captures the firm's default risk that is not captured by the equity beta (Billings, 1999). Size and leverage have been found to be significant determinants of accounting choices in Japan also (Inoue and Thomas, 1996). Inoue and Thomas report that these variables are significant even for *keiretsu* firms, which have a close relationship with banks and are presumably protected from the risk of bankruptcy and takeover.

For earnings quality control, we include variables for growth, earnings variability, and earnings persistence. These variables have been found to affect the informativeness of earnings (Kormendi and Lipe, 1987; Collins and Kothari, 1989; Easton and Zimijewski, 1989). We also control for insider holdings and industry following Warfield et al. (1995). For industry effects, we separate manufacturing versus non-manufacturing industry. Van Wolferen (1989) argues that economies can prosper because areas of industry that show promise are stimulated by fiscal policies that favor investment. In Japan, manufacturing has been of fundamental economic importance. Including all the control variables, equation (1) is now expanded as follows:[12]

$$R_{it} = a_0 + a_1E_{it} / P_{it-1} + a_2E_{it} * D_{it} / P_{it-1} + a_3E_{it} * SIZ_{it} / P_{it-1} + a_4E_{it} * RISK_{it} / P_{it-1} + a_5E_{it} * DEBT_{it} / P_{it-1} + a_6E_{it} * GRW_{it} / P_{it-1} + a_7E_{it} * VAR_{it} / P_{it-1} + a_8E_{it} * PER_{it} / P_{it-1} + a_9E_{it} * INS_{it} / P_{it-1} + a_{10}E_{it} * Y90 / P_{it-1} + a_{11}E_{it} * MFG_i / P_{it-1} + e_{it} \quad (2)$$

where

SIZ_{it} = Firm size measured as total assets.
$RISK_{it}$ = Risk of the firm measured as market beta.
$DEBT_{it}$ = Leverage of the firm measured as total debt divided as total assets.
GRW_{it} = Growth prospects of the firm, measured as Tobin's' Q ratio. The Q ratio is computed as market value of equity / book value of equity.
VAR_{it} = Variability of earnings measured as the standard deviation of EPS during the test periods, 1988–96.
PER_{it} = Persistence of earnings measured as the auto correlation coefficient of earnings during the test periods, 1988–96.
INS_{it} = Insider holdings by the chairman, president, and his family.
MFG_i = 1 if a firm is in the manufacturing industry, 0 otherwise.
e_{it} = i.i.d. random error.
Other variables are previously defined.

4.4 Keiretsu *and Discretionary Accrual*

Warfield et al. (1995) argues that incentives for opportunistic behavior increase when managerial ownership is low. In light of the findings by Warfield et al., the extent to which managers' accounting choices are constrained by contractual provisions and the motivation of managers to opportunistically respond to those constraints suggests that the size of accrual adjustments will be inversely related to managerial ownership. A similar relationship is posited between *keiretsu* versus *non-keiretsu* firms. We expect that due to the high level of monitoring and coordination among the member firms and the main bank, managers of *keiretsu* firms will have less discretion in the choice of accounting methods for self-interest than those of non-*keiretsu* firms. Although managers' accounting choice potentially involves more than discretionary accruals, we expect that the manager's accounting behavior will be manifested in the discretionary accrual.

It is also possible that the opportunistic choice of accounting method by managers could increase for *keiretsu* firms if managers of *keiretsu* firms collude with corporate shareholders in the same *keiretsu*. We empirically investigate the discretionary accrual behavior between *keiretsu* and non-*keiretsu* firms in hypothesis 2.

Hypothesis 2: The magnitude of the discretionary accrual is smaller for *keiretsu* firms than non-*keiretsu* firms.

The discretionary accrual is calculated by subtracting the nondiscretionary, or expected, accrual from the total accrual. The total accrual in the previous year is treated as the non-discretionary accrual of the current year following DeAngelo (1986).[13] Therefore,

$$DA_{it} = TA_{it} - NDA_{it} \qquad (3)$$

where

DA_{it} = Discretionary accrual for year t.
TA_{it} = Total accrual in year t.
NDA_{it} = Nondiscretionary accrual in year t ($NDA_{it} = TA_{it-1}$).

Total accrual is calculated as:

$$TA_{it} = (\Delta CA_{it} - \Delta CL_{it} - \Delta Cash_{it} + \Delta STD_{it} - Dep_{it}) / A_{it-1} \qquad (4)$$

where

ΔCA_{it} = Change in current assets
ΔCL_{it} = Change in current liabilities

$\Delta Cash_{it}$ = Change in cash and cash equivalents
ΔSTD_{it} = Change in debt included in current liabilities
Dep_{it} = Depreciation and amortization expense
A_{it-1} = Total assets.

The difference in discretionary accruals is examined using the following regression.

$$|DA_{it}| = a_0 + a_1 D_{it} + a_2 SIZ_{it} + a_3 RISK_{it} + a_4 DEBT_{it} + a_5 INS_{it} + a_6 MFG_{it} + e_{it} \quad (5)$$

Size, risk, and leverage are motivated by the agency theories. As explained above, agency variables affect the firm's accounting choice decisions. Insider holding is included following Warfield et al. (1995) who report that the (absolute) magnitude of discretionary accruals is inversely related to the managerial holdings. Unlike equation (2), we do not include earnings quality variables—growth, variability, and persistence—because they are not relevant to accrual behavior. The year variable is not included also because there is no reason, *a priori*, to expect a difference in the accruals between pre- and post-1990 period.

4.5 Full Model with Accrual Included

Since accrual behavior is hypothesized to be related to *keiretsu* membership, equation (2) is now expanded as below including the accrual variable.

$$R_{it} = a_0 + a_1 E_{it} / P_{it-1} + a_2 E_{it} * D_{it} / P_{it-1} + a_3 E_{it} * SIZ_{it} / P_{it-1} + a_4 E_{it} * RISK_{it} / P_{it-1} + a_5 E_{it} * DEBT_{it} / P_{it-1} + a_6 E_{it} * GRW_{it} / P_{it-1} + a_7 E_{it} * VAR_{it} / P_{it-1} + a_8 E_{it} * PER_{it} / P_{it-1} + a_9 E_{it} * INS_{it} / P_{it-1} + a_{10} E_{it} * |DA|_{it} / P_{it-1} + a_{11} E_{it} * Y90 / P_{it-1} + a_{12} E_{it} * MFG_i / P_{it-1} + e_{it} \quad (6)$$

Equation (6) is used as a full model to test Hypothesis 1. We separately run the regression for consolidated firms and unconsolidated firms.

4.6 Strength of Keiretsu Relationship and the Informativeness of Earnings

Equation (6) tests whether the informativeness of earnings differs between *keiretsu* and non-*keiretsu* firms after controlling for all relevant variables including accruals. If it is primarily the *keiretsu* relationship that increases the informativeness of earnings, then it is possible that the informativeness of earnings will be greater the stronger the *keiretsu* relationship. Hence, we have the following hypothesis.

Hypothesis 3: For *keiretsu* firms, the informativeness of earnings is greater, the stronger the *keiretsu* relationship.

Hypothesis 3 is tested for *keiretsu* firms only using equation (7) below. We use the power variable as previously described as a measure of the strength of the *keiretsu.*

$$\begin{aligned} R_{it} = {} & a_0 + a_1E_{it} / P_{it-1} + a_2E_{it} * POW_{it} / P_{it-1} + a_3E_{it} * SIZ_{it} / \\ & P_{it-1} + a_4E_{it} * RISK_{it} / P_{it-1} + a_5E_{it} * DEBT_{it} / P_{it-1} + a_6E_{it} * GRW_{it} / \\ & P_{it-1} + a_7E_{it} * VAR_{it} / P_{it-1} + a_8E_{it} * PER_{it} / P_{it-1} + a_9E_{it} * INS_{it} / \\ & P_{it-1} + a_{10}E_{it} * |DA|_{it} / P_{it-1} + a_{11}E_{it} * Y90 / P_{it-1} + a_{12}E_{it} * MFG_i / \\ & P_{it-1} + e_{it} \end{aligned} \tag{7}$$

where

POW = Influential power of *keiretsu* as a percentage of holdings by the same *keiretsu* member firms (see pages 139 and 140 for details). All other variables are defined as before for equation (6).

5. Results

5.1 Descriptive Statistics

Table 2 provides descriptive statistics for *keiretsu* and non-*keiretsu* firms separately. The mean values of total assets are 450.325 billion Yen for *keiretsu* firms and 195.325 billion Yen for non-*keiretsu* firms, indicating that *keiretsu* companies are significantly larger than non-*keiretsu* companies. *Keiretsu* firms show lower profitability than non-*keiretsu* firms. The mean return on total assets (ROA) for *keiretsu* firms is 14.5 per cent, which is significantly lower than 24.3 per cent for non-*keiretsu* firms. Consistent with previous evidence, *keiretsu* firms show lower variability in earnings (15.388 for *keiretsu* firms, 51.139 for non- *keiretsu* firms). In market returns, *keiretsu* firms experienced an average annual return of negative 5.4 per cent during the period compared with a negative 4.4 per cent for non-*keiretsu*, the difference being statistically significant. The

Table 2. *Descriptive Statistics (Mean, Standard Deviation, and Median)*

(1) Variable	*(2) All Obs*	*(3) Non-Keiretsu*	*(4) Keiretsu*	*(5) Difference test*[1]
R	–0.048	–0.044	–0.054	–1.88**
(fiscal year return[2])	0.241	0.240	0.241	
	–0.073	–0.063	–0.081	–2.23**
E	0.014	0.015	0.013	–1.84**
(ratio of eps to price)	0.035	0.038	0.033	
	0.017	0.018	0.015	–8.52***
SIZ	307.842	195.325	450.325	8.86***
(assets in billions)	749.735	364.380	1,034.000	
	107.731	94.590	135.015	8.20***
RISK	1.013	0.967	1.071	11.72***
(beta)	0.380	0.389	0.360	
	1.014	0.967	1.067	11.84***
DEBT	0.357	0.328	0.392	15.34***
(ratio of total debt to assets)	0.181	0.180	0.175	
	0.351	0.318	0.390	15.26***
GRW	2.969	2.919	3.033	1.42*
(ratio of market to book equity)	3.527	3.983	2.845	
	2.209	2.130	2.311	6.05***
VAR	35.364	51.139	15.388	–2.87***
(standard deviation	594.219	794.503	15.885	
of earnings per share)	10.694	11.412	9.956	–6.32***
PERS	0.464	0.485	0.438	–4.10***
(persistence of earnings)	0.491	0.525	0.442	
	0.517	0.546	0.481	–6.19***
|DA|	0.063	0.068	0.058	–2.71***
(absolute value of	0.146	0.188	0.064	
discretionary accruals)	0.040	0.041	0.039	1.53*
CON	0.182	0.152	0.220	7.39***
(1:0 indicator for	0.386	0.359	0.414	
consolidated or not)	0	0	0	7.48***
INS	0.015	0.023	0.004	19.72***
(proportion of inside	0.046	0.058	0.018	
ownership)	0	0	0	19.82***
Y90	0.822	0.795	0.856	6.96***
(1:0 indicator for post	0.382	0.403	0.350	
or pre-1990)	1.000	1.000	1.000	6.83***

Table 2. *Continued*

(1) Variable	*(2) All Obs*	*(3) Non-Keiretsu*	*(4) Keiretsu*	*(5) Difference test*[1]
MFG	0.578	0.567	0.593	2.17**
(1:0 indicator for	0.494	0.495	0.491	
manufacturer or not)	1.000	1.000	1.000	2.16**
ROA	0.200	0.243	0.145	−7.76***
(return on assets)	0.554	0.608	0.473	
	0.125	0.174	0.073	−18.49***
P/E	88.427	76.550	103.466	2.29**
(price-earnings ratio)	470.684	346.379	591.464	
	44.856	42.648	47.267	2.28***
POW			0.479	
(Proportion of *Keiretsu*	NA	NA	0.223	NA
holdings)			0.462	

[1]The first test provides a t-statistic for difference in means (column 4 minus column 3), the second test provides a z-statistic for difference in medians (Wilcoxon rank-sum).
[2]Currency in Yen for all variables.

Variable Definitions:

R = Fiscal year stock return.
E = Ratio of earnings per share to stock price at t−1.
SIZ_{it} = Firm size measured as total assets.
$RISK_{it}$ = Risk of the firm measured as market beta.
$DEBT_{it}$ = Leverage of the firm measured as total debt divided as total asset.
GRW_{it} = Growth prospect of the firm, measured as Tobin's' Q ratio. The Q ratio is computed as market value of equity / book value of equity.
VAR_{it} = Variability of earnings measured as the standard deviation of EPS during the test period 1988–1996.
PER_{it} = Persistence of earnings measured as the auto correlation coefficient of earnings during the test period 1988–1996.
$|DA_{it}|$ = Absolute value of discretionary accruals (see table 6 definitions).
CON_{it} = 1 for the firms reporting consolidated earnings and 0 otherwise.
INS_{it} = proportion of insider holdings for the chairman, president, and their family.
Y90 = 1 for the period from 1990 and 0 before 1990.
MFG_i = 1 if a firm is in a manufacturing industry, 0 otherwise.
ROA_{it} = Return on assets calculated as earnings per share divided by total assets.
P/E = Stock price divided by earnings per share at fiscal year end.

negative returns for both sets of firms reflect the overall economic downturn in Japan during the sample period.

The agency variables debt and risk are significantly different between *keiretsu* and non-*keiretsu* firms. *Keiretsu* firms show a statistically higher debt ratio (total debt divided by total assets) of 0.392 compared with 0.328 for non-*keiretsu* firms. The higher debt ratio for *keiretsu* firms is consistent with evidence presented by Hoshi et al. (1991) and Flath (1993).

Risk, measured by market beta, is also higher for *keiretsu* firms (1.071 for *keiretsu* versus 0.967 for non-*keiretsu* firms).

For the earnings quality control variables, *keiretsu* firms have higher growth potential (measured as price to book value ratio), lower earnings variability, lower persistence, and lower accruals. *Keiretsu* firms have lower insider holdings than non-*keiretsu* firms. Interestingly, the majority of firms have no insider holdings, indicating that insider holdings may not be important for corporate governance in Japan (Prowse, 1992). Descriptive statistics further show that *keiretsu* membership contains a larger percentage of companies in a manufacturing industry (59.3 for *keiretsu* versus 56.7 per cent for non-*keiretsu* firms).

The mean power (a proxy for *keiretsu* influence) for *keiretsu* firms is 47.9 per cent, suggesting that the *keiretsu* group, on average, exercises a significant influence over its member firms.

5.2 Regression Results

5.2.1 Keiretsu *and the informativeness of earnings.* The informativeness of earnings is first tested by examining the coefficient on the level of earnings variable in regression model (1) partitioned by whether earnings are consolidated or not (see Table 3). The models are highly significant with an F-value of 261.57 and adjusted R-square of 11.6 per cent for non-consolidated firms, and 26.13 and 5.40 per cent for consolidated firms, respectively. Both the earnings variable and the interaction between earnings and the keiretsu dummy are positive and significant at conventional significance levels for consolidated and non-consolidated firms, indicating that earnings response coefficients are greater for *keiretsu* than non-*keiretsu* firms.[14] The larger coefficient on earnings suggests that the earnings of non-consolidated firms are more informative than the earnings of consolidated firms in Japan. This is inconsistent with evidence in Harris et al. (1994) for German firms, but consistent with the finding in Beckman (1998) that parent-only earnings are generally more predictable than consolidated earnings in Japan. The year dummy interaction variable is negative and highly significant, indicating that the informativeness of earnings is smaller in the post-1990 period than the pre-1990 period.

The model with control variables is reported in Table 4 (model (2)). For the agency variables, firm size is generally positive and significant, and risk and debt are significant with negative signs. The size variable will be negative if large firms manage earnings more than small firms to avoid political costs. On the other hand, it will be positive if more information is

Table 3. *Multivariate Regression Results. (Basic Returns Model for All Observations, Consolidated, or Non-Consolidated Only.)*

$R_{it} = a_0 + a_1E_{it} / P_{it-1} + a_2E_{it} * D_{it} / P_{it-1} + a_3E_{it} * Y90 + e_{it}$

Variable	*Predicted Sign*	*Parameter Estimate (t-statistic)* *All Observations*	*Consolidated Only*	*Non-Consolidated Only*
Intercept	+/–	–0.083	–0.072	–0.089
		(–27.69)***	(–9.62)***	(–26.95)***
E / P	+	7.700	3.655	8.418
		(26.75)***	(4.65)***	(27.26)***
E * D/P	+	0.435	0.716	0.333
		(3.00)***	(1.94)**	(2.11)**
E * Y90/P	+/–	–7.290	–2.246	–8.156
		(–25.37)***	(–2.87)***	(–26.45)***
Adj R-Sq		0.096	0.054	0.116
F-Stat		259.58***	26.13***	261.57***
N		7,283	1,324	5,959

One tail p-values (***, **, * indicates .01, .05, or .10 significance level, respectively).
Variables defined in Table 2.

available for the large firms during the year than the small firms. The positive size variable suggests that large firms produce more information during the year and, therefore, have greater earnings response coefficients, consistent with Chaney and Jeter (1992). Negative signs for the risk and debt variables indicate that earnings response coefficients are smaller for riskier firms and firms with higher leverage, as predicted. These firms are more likely to have more accounting constraints and therefore use discretion in the choice of accounting methods in response to the constraints, lowering earnings quality. The leverage variable can be also interpreted as a risk measure that captures a firm's default risk (Billings, 1999). Billings reports that the leverage ratio captures firm default risk that is not captured by equity risk and is negatively related to the earnings response coefficient.

For the earnings quality variables, the growth variable is positive and marginally significant for consolidated firms, and the persistence variable is significant for non-consolidated firms only. Earnings variability has inconsistent signs between consolidated and non-consolidated firms. The results for the agency and earnings quality variables are generally consistent with those reported in Warfield et al. (1995) except for earnings variability. The insider holdings variable has a negative sign, but is only

Table 4. *Multivariate Regression Results. (Returns Model Including Control Variables for All Observations, Consolidated, or Non-Consolidated.)*

$R_{it} = a_0 + a_1E_{it} / P_{it-1} + a_2E_{it} * D_{it} / P_{it-1} + a_3E_{it} * SIZ_{it} / P_{it-1} + a_4E_{it} * RISK_{it} / P_{it-1} + a_5E_{it} * DEBT_{it} / P_{it-1} + a_6E_{it} * GRW_{it} / P_{it-1} + a_7E_{it} * VAR_{it} / P_{it-1} + a_8E_{it} * PER_{it} / P_{it-1} + a_9E_{it} * INS_{it} / P_{it-1} + a_{10}E_{it} * Y90_{it} / P_{it1} + a_{11}E_{it} * MFG / P_{it-1} + e_{it}$

		Parameter Estimate (t-statistic)		
Variable	*Predicted Sign*	*All Observations*	*Consolidated Only*	*Non-Consolidated Only*
Intercept	+/–	–0.103	–0.099	–0.105
		(–31.09)***	(–12.99)***	(–28.49)***
E / P	+	4.706	6.994	5.281
		(5.31)***	(2.21)**	(4.86)***
E * D/P	+	0.421	0.646	0.278
		(2.86)***	(1.67)**	(1.70)**
E * SIZ/P	+/–	0.479	0.080	0.465
		(7.22)***	(0.39)	(5.40)***
E * RISK/P	–	–1.323	–3.554	–1.074
		(–6.14)***	(–5.37)***	(–4.60)***
E * DEBT/P	–	–2.422	–2.815	–1.962
		(–5.87)***	(–2.44)***	(–4.13)***
E * GRW/P	+	0.033	0.181	0.026
		(1.53)*	(1.29)*	(1.16)
E * VAR/P	–	0.002	0.0001	–0.004
		(1.38)*	(1.09)	(–1.97)**
E * PER/P	+	0.207	–0.350	0.261
		(1.63)*	(–0.85)	(1.94)**
E * INS/P	+	–0.023	–0.012	–0.021
		(–1.61)*	(–0.27)	(–1.38)*
E * MFG/P	+/–	–0.156	0.791	–0.172
		(–1.10)	(1.78)**	(–0.83)
E * Y90/P	+/–	–6.947	–2.517	–7.581
		(–24.05)***	(–3.21)***	(–23.97)***
Adj R-Sq		0.120	0.1012	0.131
F-Statistic		91.34***	14.19***	82.69***
N		7,283	1,324	5,959

One tail p-values (***, **, * indicates .01, .05, or .10 significance level, respectively).
Variables defined in Table 2.

marginally significant. As previously explained, insider holdings is measured as stockholdings by the president or the chairman (reported in the *Japan Company Handbook*). The majority of our sample firms do not have insider holdings within the largest 10 stockholders. Prowse (1992) also reports that insider holdings do not play an important role in Japan.

Thus, we do not expect that its effect on earnings informativeness will be significant. The overall results support hypothesis 1 that *keiretsu* firms' earnings are more informative than non-*keiretsu* firms' earnings.

5.2.2 Discretionary Accrual and the Keiretsu. Hypothesis 2 proposes that due to the high level of monitoring and coordination among member firms and main banks, managers of *keiretsu* firms will be more restricted in the opportunistic accounting choice than non-*keiretsu* firms, decreasing discretionary accruals. Table 5 reports discretionary accruals between *keiretsu* and non-*keiretsu* firms using equation (5), which regresses the absolute amount of discretionary accrual on agency and control variables used in the informativeness of earnings model. The results show that *keiretsu* firms have significantly smaller discretionary accruals than non-*keiretsu* firms whether or not consolidated or non-consolidated earnings are used, supporting hypothesis 2. The control variables are not generally significant.

Table 6 reports the regression results for the full model, including a variable for discretionary accruals.[15] The result shows that the earnings informativeness (E*D/P) of *keiretsu* firms is higher for both consolidated and non-consolidated firms. The discretionary accrual variable is negative as expected and highly significant for consolidated firms. The significance of the persistence variable is higher in the non-consolidated partition. The coefficient of the earnings variable for consolidated firms is negative, but not significant. The variable was positive and highly significant in Tables 3 and 4. We believe that the negative coefficient on the earnings variable is caused by the high correlation between earnings and accrual variables for consolidated firms. The results for all other variables are similar to those reported in Table 4. The results in Table 6 further support hypothesis 1.

5.2.3 The strength of the Keiretsu *relationship and the informative of earnings.* Hypothesis 3 proposes that within *keiretsu* firms, the informativeness of earnings is greater, the stronger the *keiretsu* relationship. The strength of the *keiretsu* relationship is measured by the power variable as previously described.

Table 7 reports the results using the full model for keiretsu firms.[16] The interaction variable between power and earnings variables measures the informativeness of earnings according to the strength of the *keiretsu* relationship. It is positive and significant, indicating that earnings informativeness

Table 5. *Multivariate Regression Results. (Accrual Model for All Observations, Consolidated, and Non-Consolidated Only.)*

$|DA_{it}| = a_0 + a_1D_{iti} + a_2SIZ_{it} + a_3RISK_{it} + a_4DEBT + a_5INS_{it} + a_6MFG_{it} + e_{it}$

		Parameter Estimate (t-statistic)		
Variable	*Predicted Sign*	*All Observations*	*Consolidated Only*	*Non-Consolidated Only*
Intercept	+/–	0.214	0.164	0.214
		(13.49)***	(5.84)***	(10.76)***
D	–	–0.005	–0.007	–0.005
		(–1.99)**	(–2.12)**	(–1.70)**
SIZ	+	–0.013	–0.009	–0.013
		(–10.50)***	(–5.01)***	(8.02)***
RISK	+	0.004	0.011	0.003
		(1.06)	(1.92)**	(0.77)
DEBT	+	–0.016	–0.016	–0.015
		(–2.15)**	(–1.60)*	(–1.78)**
INS	+/–	–0.0001	0.002	–0.0003
		(–0.28)	(5.11)***	(–0.88)
MFG	+/–	0.004	0.0004	0.005
		(1.49)*	(0.12)	(1.56)*
Adj R-Sq		0.0208	0.104	0.013
F-Statistic		22.27***	16.17***	12.55***
N		5,996	785	5,211

One tail p-values (***, **, * indicates .01, .05, or .10 significance level, respectively).
Variables defined in Table 2 except $|DA_{it}|$, which is defined below.
$|DA_{it}|$ = Absolute value of discretionary accrual.
Discretionary accrual constructed as follows:
$DA_{it} = TA_{it} - NDA_{it}$
where
DA_{it} = Discretionary accrual for year t.
TA_{it} = Total accruals in year t.
NDA_{it} = Nondiscretionary accrual in year t ($NDA_{it} = TA_{it-1}$).
TA, total accrual, is calculated as: $TA_{it} = (\Delta CA_{it} - \Delta CL_{it} - \Delta Cash_{it} + \Delta STD_{it} - Dep_{it} / A_{it-1}$
where
ΔCA_{it} = Change in current assets (Compustat item 4).
ΔCL_{it} = Change in current liabilities (Compustat item 5).
$\Delta Cash_{it}$ = Change in cash and cash equivalents (Compustat item 1).
ΔSTD_{it} = Change in debt included in current liabilities (Compustat item 34).
Dep_{it} = Depreciation and amortization expense (Compustat item 14).
$A_{it\ 1}$ = Total assets (Compustat item 6).

is higher, the greater the strength of the *keiretsu* relationship. The trends of all other variables are similar to those reported in Table 6. The significance of the power variable supports hypothesis 3. If we assume that the monitoring ability of *keiretsu* is related to the strength of the *keiretsu*,

Table 6. *Multivariate Regression Results. (Returns Model Including Accrual Variable (DA), for All Observations, Consolidated, or Non-Consolidated Only.)*

$R_{it} = a_0 + a_1E_{it} / P_{it-1} + a_2E_{it} * D_{it} / P_{it-1} + a_3E_{it} * SIZ_{it} / P_{it-1} + a_4E_{it} * RISK_{it} / P_{it-1} + a_5E_{it} * DEBT_{it} / P_{it-1} + a_6E_{it} * GRW_{it} / P_{it-1} + a_7E_{it} * VAR_{it} / P_{it-1} + a_8E_{it} * PER_{it} / P_{it-1} + a_{10}E_{it} * |DA|_{it} / P_{it-1} + a_{11}E_{it} * INS_{it} / P_{it-1}\ a_{12}E_{it} * Y90_{it} / P_{it1} + a_{13}E_{it} * MFG / P_{it-1} + e_{it}$

Variable	Predicted Sign	*Parameter Estimate (t-statistic)* All Observations	Consolidated Only	Non-Consolidated Only
Intercept	+/–	–0.111	–0.083	–0.113
		(–30.93)***	(–7.74)***	(–29.98)***
E / P	+	5.569	–1.626	7.205
		(5.39)***	(–0.41)	(5.97)***
E * D/P	+	0.404	0.688	0.335
		(2.56)***	(1.44)*	(1.97)**
E * SIZ/P	+/–	0.546	0.574	0.452
		(7.47)***	(2.25)**	(4.98)***
E * RISK/P	–	–1.270	–0.102	–1.223
		(–5.46)***	(–1.27)	(–4.98)***
E * DEBT/P	–	–2.740	–4.878	–2.632
		(–6.03)***	(–3.29)***	(–5.37)***
E * GRW/P	+	0.019	0.460	0.084
		(0.87)	(2.85)***	(0.37)
E * VAR/P	–	–0.002	–0.008	–0.002
		(–0.93)	(–0.12)	(–1.23)
E * PER/P	+	0.324	0.352	0.274
		(2.42)***	(0.64)	(1.97)**
E * |DA|/P	–	–1.200	–17.579	–0.764
		(–1.36)*	(–3.51)***	(–0.84)
E * INS/P	+	–0.018	–0.007	–0.016
		(–1.17)	(–0.11)	(–1.01)
E * MFG/P	+/–	–0.159	0.751	–0.252
		(–1.07)	(1.45)*	(–1.57)*
E * Y90/P	+/–	–8.199	–2.096	–8.809
		(–18.65)***	(–1.31)*	(–19.07)***
Adj R-Sq		0.102	0.099	0.103
F-Statistic		57.77***	8.12***	51.17***
N		5,996	785	5,211

One tail p-values (***, **, * indicates .01, .05, or .10 significance level, respectively).
Variables defined in Table 2 (except |DA|, which is defined in Table 5).

the significance of the power variable suggests that it is indeed the monitoring ability that improves the informativeness of earnings for *keiretsu* firms.

Table 7. *Multivariate Regression Results. (Returns Model Including Accrual Variable (DA), for Keiretsu Members Only, Consolidated, and Non-Consolidated.)*

$$R_{it} = a_0 + a_1E_{it} / P_{it-1} + a_2E_{it} * POW_{it} / P_{it-1} + a_3E_{it} * SIZ_{it} / P_{it-1} + a_4E_{it} * RISK_{it} / P_{it-1} + a_5E_{it} * DEBT_{it} / P_{it-1} + a_6E_{it} * GRW_{it} / P_{it-1} + a_7E_{it} * VAR_{it} / P_{it-1} + a_8E_{it} * PER_{it} / P_{it-1} + a_{10}E_{it} * |DA|_{it} / P_{it-1} + a_{11}E_{it} * INS_{it} / P_{it-1}\ a_{12}E_{it} * Y90_{it} /P_{it1} + a_{13}E_{it} * MFG / P_{it-1} + e_{it}$$

		Parameter Estimate (t-statistic)		
Variable	*Predicted Sign*	*All Observations*	*Consolidated Only*	*Non-Consolidated Only*
Intercept	+/–	–0.108	–0.082	–0.113
		(–19.81)***	(–6.19)***	(–18.87)***
E / P	+	3.393	12.999	4.173
		(1.86)**	(1.67)**	(1.96)**
E * POW/P	+	0.016	0.342	0.015
		(2.42)***	(1.80)**	(2.08)**
E * SIZ/P	+/–	0.549	–0.521	0.508
		(4.57)***	(–1.33)*	(3.33)***
E * RISK/P	–	–0.549	–1.086	–0.458
		(–1.30)*	(–0.91)	(–0.99)
E * DEBT/P	–	–3.310	–8.519	–2.955
		(–4.24)***	(–3.86)***	(–3.46)***
E * GRW/P	+	0.029	0.808	0.019
		(0.55)	(2.82)***	(0.34)
E * VAR/P	–	–0.006	–0.050	–0.010
		(–1.06)	(–2.25)**	(–1.66)**
E * PER/P	+	0.291	1.676	0.212
		(1.33)*	(1.75)**	(0.92)
E * |DA|/P	–	0.154	–30.874	1.502
		(0.09)	(–4.04)***	(0.80)
E * INS/P	+	–0.056	0.630	–0.107
		(–0.59)	(2.10)**	(–1.01)
E * MFG/P	+/–	0.348	0.714	0.224
		(1.38)*	(0.90)	(0.82)
E * Y90/P	+/–	–7.346	–2.555	–7.734
		(–8.91)***	(–0.55)	(–8.95)***
Adj R-Sq		0.069	0.111	0.066
F-Statistic		17.13***	5.35***	13.85***
N		2,639	457	2,182

One tail p-values (***, **, * indicates .01, .05, or .10 significance level, respectively).
Variables defined in Table 2 (except |DA|, which is defined in Table 5).

5.2.4 Additional tests. We performed various sensitivity tests to further confirm the results using alternative models or measures. First, we used an alternative return window of 18 months in lieu of 12 months. Japanese firms are required to file annual reports within 6 months after the fiscal year-end. An 18-month return window allows for information in the delayed filing to be impounded in stock price. Also, we used earnings changes instead of earnings levels. The earnings change variable has been used more widely in previous research. Further, we used the log of absolute discretionary accruals and long-term debt as alternative measures for discretionary accruals and leverage. We also used 6 financial *keiretsu* in place of 8 *keiretsu* groups, eliminating Tokai and Industrial Bank of Japan *keiretsu*. The six financial *keiretsu* are the major financial *keiretsu* in Japan. The results for all these sensitivity tests are not qualitatively different from those reported and lead us to the same conclusion.

6. Conclusion

This paper examines the informativeness of earnings between *keiretsu* and non-*keiretsu* firms. The *keiretsu* relationship improves monitoring due to the cross-shareholding of ownership interests and financial and personnel ties between member firms and main banks. We propose that the close relationships within the *keiretsu* group increase the informativeness of *keiretsu* earnings.

The results support the hypothesis that the informativeness of earnings is greater for *keiretsu* firms than non-*keiretsu* firms. Within *keiretsu* firms, we also find a positive and significant association between the informativeness of earnings and the strength of *keiretsu* relationships. This further suggests that it is indeed the monitoring ability of the *keiretsu* membership that strengthens the informativeness of earnings.

We also compare the manager's use of discretionary accruals between *keiretsu* and non-*keiretsu* firms. For the same rationale as above, we find that the absolute amount of discretionary accruals is smaller for *keiretsu* firms. Our overall results show that the *keiretsu* relationship in Japan improves the informativeness of earnings of Japanese firms. This result adds to the finding that the *keiretsu* relationship improves the overall economic efficiency of Japanese firms by improving information efficiency.

Notes

1. The economic efficiency of Japanese *keiretsu* has been examined by Gilson and Roe (1993), Weinstein and Yafeh (1995), Nakatami (1984), and Hoshi et al. (1991), among others. However, few studies examine the effect of *keiretsu* on informational efficiency in an accounting context.

2. Warfield et al. (1995) proposed a similar argument for the relationship between managerial ownership and the informativeness of earnings. They suggest that demand for accounting-based constraints is higher when managerial ownership (insider holdings) is lower, and accordingly, managers are expected to respond to the contractual environment in their self-interest, causing the quality of earnings to decline. They report that discretionary accrual is greater and earnings explanatory power is lower when managerial holdings are lower. If the *keiretsu* relationship plays a role similar to that of insiders, we can expect higher earnings quality in a *keiretsu* arrangement.

3. Cooke (1996) finds, however, that *keiretsu* companies do not disclose less information than other companies.

4. The discussion on the history and main bank system of *keiretsu* has benefited from Cooke (1996).

5. The term, *keiretsu*, is often used in a variety of different ways. We focus on financial (horizontal) *keiretsu*. There are also production-based (vertical) corporate groups called a capital *keiretsu*. Financial *keiretsu* are more prevalent in Japan. For more details about financial *keiretsu*, see Aoki (1994), Sheard (1994), and Berglof and Perotti (1994).

6. Unlike in the US, stockholdings by banks in Japan has long been permitted. The ownership limit was set at 5 per cent in 1987.

7. The directors could be outside directors external to the troubled firms or to the *keiretsu* membership.

8. Membership in a *keiretsu* is not clearly definable. Some use *Keiretsu no Kenkyu* classification, or a refinement of it used by Nakatani (1984). He classified a firm as affiliated with a *keiretsu* if, for three consecutive years, more than 40 per cent of the firm's total debt was borrowed from financial institutions of the *keiretsu* and 20 per cent of the firm's stock was held within the *keiretsu*, or historically it was associated with the *keiretsu* by a long membership in the *keiretsu* presidents' council. *Industrial Groupings in Japan* provides more recent classification, which was used by Kang and Shivdasani (1995) also.

9. *The Industrial Groupings in Japan* is published biannually and the 1994/1995 is the last issue published. It lists eight horizontal groups. Many studies use six largest financial groups (the first six). We used eight horizontal groups following *Industrial Groupings in Japan*. The use of six largest groups does not change the result significantly.

10. The basic return-earnings model has limitations because it does not control other variables that affect earnings quality. We add other control variables in equations (2) and (6). Also, the dependent variable can be regressed on the change in earnings variables. The use of the change in earnings variable does not change the results qualitatively.

11. Beckman (1998) reports that a significant number of companies listed on the Tokyo Stock Exchange do not submit consolidated reports to the exchange. Recently, the exchange announced that Japanese markets will soon fully enforce the requirement for consolidated financial reporting by all listed companies. In our sample, only 1,361 observations (18.6 per cent) have consolidated financial statements. This ratio is lower than we expected. According to our discussion with the staff at Global Vantage (including a local representative in Japan) where we obtained the data, Global Vantage reports all the consolidated financial statements that are available to them. We conjecture that the unconsolidated companies include those companies that i) have no controlling subsidiaries, ii) have controlling subsidiaries but with no significant sales, and iii) are required to file consolidated financial statements but do not file them.

12. It can be argued that some agency and earnings quality variables are **endogenous** to the *keiretsu* membership. To the extent that these variables motivate the formation of *keiretsu* group, the endogeneity problem occurs. We do not examine what motivates the formation of the *keiretsu*. Our paper examines the effect of the *keiretsu* on earnings informativeness, **given** the *keiretsu* relationship.

13. We use DeAngelo's model because it only requires two years of data per observation. Other discretionary accrual models are more demanding on the data since they require extended time series of earnings information. Dechow et al. (1995) report that DeAngelo's model performed as well as other models of earnings management detection, including the Jones model.

14. We report significance level in the regressions using a one-tailed test.

15. The sample size dropped to 5,996 observations for data unavailability for the accrual variable.

16. We performed the regression analysis for other reduced models also. The results are similar and therefore we only report the results for the full model.

References

Aoki, M., *Information, Incentives and Bargaining in the Japanese Economy* (Cambridge: Cambridge University Press, 1994).

Beckman, J., "A Comparison of Consolidated and Parent-only Earnings Forecasts for Japanese Firms," *The Journal of Financial Statement Analysis* (Spring 1998), pp. 17–28.

Berglof, E. and E. Perotti, "The Governance Structure of the Japanese Financial Keiretsu," *Journal of Financial Economics* 36 (1994), pp. 259–284.

Billings, B., "Revisiting the Relation between the Default Risk of Debt and the Earnings Response Coefficients," *Accounting Review* (1999), pp. 509–522.

Brown, P., V. Soybel and C. Stickney, "Comparing U.S. and Japanese Corporate—Level Operating Performance Using Financial Statement Data," *Strategic Management Journal* (1994).

Dodwell Marketing Consultants, *Industrial Groupings in Japan* (Tokyo: Dodwell Marketing Consultants, 1988, 1990, 1992, 1994).

Chaney, P. K. and D. C. Jeter, "The Effect of Size on the Magnitude of Long-Window Earnings Response Coefficients," *Contemporary Accounting Research* 8 (1992), pp. 540–560.

Cooke, T. E., "The Influence of the *Keiretsu* on Japanese Corporate Disclosure," *Journal of International Financial Management and Accounting* 8 (1996), pp. 191–214.

Collins, D. and S. P. Kothari, "An Analysis of Intertemporal and Cross-Sectional Determinants of Earnings Response Coefficients," *Journal of Accounting and Economics* (July 1989), pp. 139–157.

DeAngelo, L. E., "Accounting Numbers as Market Valuation Substitutes. A Study of Management Buyouts of Public Stockholders." *The Accounting Review* 61 (1986), pp. 400–420.

Diamond, D. W., "Financial Intermediation and Delegated Monitoring," *Review of Economic Studies* 51 (1984), pp. 393–414.

Dechow, P. M., R. G. Sloan and A. P. Sweeney, "Detecting Earnings Management," *The Accounting Review* (April 1995), pp. 193–225.

Easton, P. D. and M. E. Zmijewski, "Cross-Sectional Variation in Stock Market Response to Accounting Earnings Announcements," *Journal of Accounting and Economics* (July 1989), pp. 117–141.

Flath, D., "Shareholding in the Keiretsu, Japan's Financial Groups," *The Review of Economics and Statistics* (1993), pp. 249–256.

Gilson, R. and M. Roe, "Understanding the Japanese Financial Keiretsu: Overlaps between Corporate Governance and Industrial Organization," *Yale Law Journal* 102 (1993), pp. 871–920.

Godwin, J. H., S. R. Goldberg and E. B. Douthett, "Relevance of U.S.-GAAP for Japanese Companies," *The International Journal of Accounting* 33 (1998), pp. 589–604.

Harris, T., M. Lang and H. P. Moller, "The Value Relevance of German Accounting Measures: An Empirical Analysis," *Journal of Accounting Research* 32 (1994), pp. 187–209.

Hoshi, T., A. Kashyap and D. Scharfstein, "Corporate Structure, Liquidity and Investment: Evidence from Japanese Panel Data," *Quarterly Journal of Economics* 106 (1991), pp. 33–60.

Inoue, T. and W. B. Thomas, "The Choice of Accounting Policy in Japan," *Journal of International Financial Management and Accounting* 7 (1996), pp. 1–23.

Jacobson, R. and D. Aaker, "Myopic Management Behavior with Efficient, but Imperfect Financial Markets: A Comparison of Information Asymmetries in the U.S. and Japan," *Journal of Accounting and Economics* (1993), pp. 383–405.

Japan Company Handbook, (Tokyo: Oriental Economist, 1988, 1994).

Johnson, C., "MITI and the Japanese Miracle" (Stanford, CA: Stanford University Press, 1982).

Kang, J. K. and A. Shivdasani, "Firm Performance, Corporate Governance, and Top Executive Turnover in Japan," *Journal of Financial Economics* 38 (1995), pp. 29–58.

Kang, J. K. and A. Shivdasani, "Corporate Restructuring during Performance Decline in Japan," *Journal of Financial Economics* 46 (1997), pp. 29–65.

Kaplan, S. N., "Top Executive Rewards and Firm Performance: A Comparison of Japan and the U.S.," *Journal of Political Economy* 102 (1994), pp. 510–546.

Kaplan, S. N. and B. A. Minton, "Appointments of Outsiders to Japanese Boards: Determinants and Implications for Managers," *Journal of Financial Economics* 36 (1994), pp. 225–258.

Kester, W. C., "Japanese Takeovers: The Global Contest for Corporate Control" (Boston: Harvard Business School Press, 1991).

Kormendi, R. and R. Lipe, "Earnings Innovation, Earnings Persistence and Stock Returns," *Journal of Business* (1987), pp. 323–346.

Nakatami, I., "The Economic Role of Corporate Financial Grouping," in *Economic Analysis of Japanese Firms*, M. Aoki ed. (New York: Elsevier, 1984).

Prowse, S., "The Structure of Corporate Ownership in Japan," *The Journal of Finance* (1992), pp. 1121–1140.

Sheard, P., "The Japanese General Trading Company as an Aspect of Inter-Firm Risk Sharing," *Journal of the Japanese and International Economies* 3 (1989), pp. 308–322.

Sheard, P., "The Role of Firm Organization in the Adjustment of a Declining Industry in Japan: The Case of Aluminium," *Journal of Japanese and International Economies* 5 (1991), pp. 14–40.

Sheard, P., "The Economics of Interlocking Shareholding in Japan," in *The Japanese Firm: The Sources of Competitive Strength*, M. Aoki and R. Dore, eds. (Oxford: University Press, 1994)

Van Wolferen, K., *The Enigma of Japanese Power* (London: MacMillan, 1989).

Warfield, T., J. J. Wild and K. Wild, "Managerial Ownership, Accounting Choices, and Informativeness of Earnings," *Journal of Accounting and Economics* (1995) pp. 61–91.

Watts, R. L. and J. L. Zimmerman, "Positive Accounting Theory: A Ten Year Perspective," *The Accounting Review* 65 (1990), pp. 131–156.

Watts, R. L. and J. L. Zimmerman, "Towards a Positive Theory of Determination of Accounting Standards," *The Accounting Review* 53 (1978), pp. 112–134.

Weinstein, D. E. and Y. Yafeh, "Japan's Corporate Groups: Collusion or Competitive? An Empirical Investigation of Keiretsu Behavior," *Journal of Industrial Economics* 43 (1995), pp. 359–376.

Zmijewski, M. and R. Hagerman, "An Income Strategy Approach to the Positive Theory of Accounting Standards Setting/Choice, *Journal of Accounting and Economics* 3 (1981), pp. 129–149.

Journal of Business Finance & Accounting, 28(9) & (10), Nov./Dec. 2001, 0306-686X

The Relation Between Incremental Subsidiary Earnings and Future Stock Returns in Japan

DON HERRMANN, TATSUO INOUE AND WAYNE B. THOMAS*

1. INTRODUCTION

Our paper is motivated by the widely held view that parent-only data, as opposed to consolidated data, provide a more reasonable basis for valuing the consolidated Japanese firm.[1] Some suggest that because of the unique Japanese business environment, consolidated financial statements, which are prepared using largely US-based consolidation practices, result in less meaningful information (McKinnon, 1984; and Lowe, 1990). We investigate the extent to which parent-only earnings and subsidiary earnings in the current year persist into consolidated earnings in the next year. We then examine whether the market understands these time-series behaviors. If subsidiary earnings are important in predicting next year's consolidated earnings and market participants do not fully understand this, then stock prices will lag reported subsidiary earnings.

The results indicate that the Japanese stock market adjusts correctly for the persistence of parent-only earnings, but the

* The authors are respectively from Oregon State University; Kwansei Gakuin University; and the University of Oklahoma. This paper has benefited greatly from the comments of Bruce Behn, Neil Bhattacharya, Ray Brooks, Christine Botosan, Barry Cushing, Roger Graham, Ilene Kleinsorge, Bob Lipe, Marlene Plumlee, Peter Pope, Grace Pownall, Lynn Rees, David Senteney, and an anonymous referee for the 2001 ACCA/ICAEW/JBFA Capital Markets Conference, as well as workshop participants at Oregon State University, the University of Utah, the 2000 American Accounting Association International Section Mid-year Meeting, and the 2000 American Accounting Association Annual Meeting.

Address for correspondence: Don Herrmann, Oregon State University, College of Business, 200 Bexell Hall, Corvallis, OR 97331-2603, USA.
e-mail: hermann@bus.orst.edu

market appears to underestimate the persistence of subsidiary earnings in current stock prices. Consequently, stock prices correct in a predictable manner in the subsequent year, resulting in a significant, positive relation between returns in year $t+1$ and subsidiary earnings in year t. The results continue to hold after controlling for firm size, book-to-market ratio, debt-to-asset ratio, market beta, earnings-to-price ratio, cash flow-to-price ratio, and dividend yield.

Further analysis indicates that the anomalous results are more likely attributable to market mispricing than failure to control for cross-sectional differences in risk. If subsidiary earnings proxy for risk characteristics, then the relation between subsidiary earnings and stock returns may persist in years beyond year $t+1$. We find that subsidiary earnings in year t are *not* related to stock returns in year $t+2$ or $t+3$. The market appears to correct fully in year $t+1$ so that stock returns are no longer predictable beyond year $t+1$. We also form zero-investment hedge portfolios based on firms' subsidiary earnings. These hedge portfolios earn an average annual abnormal return of 7.06% with positive abnormal returns in 12 of the 13 years in the test period. If the positive abnormal returns are attributable to risk (i.e., the hedge portfolio strategy is risky), then the hedge portfolio should result in positive returns in some years and negative returns in others. The finding of positive returns year after year makes it less likely that the abnormal returns are attributable solely to risk factors.

The findings of this study contribute to the growing literature that questions the market's efficiency with respect to earnings and other accounting information (e.g., Bernard and Thomas, 1989 and 1990, for quarterly earnings series; Sloan, 1996, for accruals; Abarbanell and Bushee, 1997 and 1998, for certain fundamental signals; and Thomas, 1999, for foreign earnings of multinational firms).[2] This line of research is centered on the premise that the market fails to understand fully how earnings (or its components) persist into future earnings. The market then corrects for its error in a predictable manner in the subsequent period. To date, this research has focused almost exclusively on the US capital markets.

An investigation of the Japanese market's efficiency in incorporating publicly available information is important not only to financial analysts and market regulators in Japan, but also to financial analysts and market regulators worldwide due to the tremendous size and global influence of the Japanese stock market. Japan is the world's second largest economy. At one point during our sample period, the Tokyo Stock Exchange was the largest stock exchange in the world measured in terms of market capitalization of listed firms. Therefore, understanding how the Japanese market prices (or fails to price) securities relative to publicly available accounting information has significant global implications.

The paper proceeds as follows. A background on consolidated and parent-only earnings in Japan is provided in the next section. The research design is outlined in Section 3. The sample, variable measurement, and descriptive statistics are discussed in Section 4. The empirical results are reported in Section 5. Tests to distinguish between market mispricing and failure to control for risk are discussed in Section 6. The paper concludes in Section 7.

2. BACKGROUND ON CONSOLIDATED AND PARENT-ONLY EARNINGS

The Japanese Securities and Exchange Law began requiring the submission of consolidated financial statements in addition to parent-only financial statements for fiscal years ending March 31, 1978, although full consolidation reporting did not become mandatory until 1984 (Hall et al., 1994). The addition of consolidated financial information was driven externally by foreign capital markets and internally by several well-publicized bankruptcies in Japan. Externally, as Japanese companies began listing their securities abroad, they began preparing consolidated financial statements in conformance with foreign listing requirements. Similarly, when US companies began listing on the Tokyo Stock Exchange in 1973, the Japanese Ministry of Finance accepted the consolidated financial statements used for reporting in the United States (Beckman, 1998). Internally, several bankruptcies in Japan were subsequently related to questionable earnings recognition practices between the parent and their subsidiaries. The circumstances surrounding these bankruptcies became well publicized, pointing out the need for better financial reporting of transactions between parent and subsidiaries.

The Japanese financial markets have historically perceived parent-only statements as the primary financial statements, while consolidated financial statements have traditionally been regarded more as supplemental information (Lowe, 1990; French and Poterba, 1991; and Hall et al., 1994).[3] Furthermore, Japanese financial analysts have traditionally valued securities using parent-only statements (Ely and Pownall, 1999; Conroy et al., 2000; and Conroy and Harris, 1995). This is in contrast to most of the other major capital markets in the world where consolidated financial statements represent the primary format for presenting and evaluating a firm's financial results. The main reason given as to why consolidated financial statements have not attained the same level of status in Japan is that consolidation, based on the Western concept of legal ownership, inadequately reflects the business structure of many Japanese firms. Control in Japan has been related to items in addition to legal ownership such as interlocking directorships, common business transactions, and mutual shareholdings that may not be fully reflected in the consolidated financial statements. However, it should be noted that in recent years Japanese standard setters have begun to place greater importance on the reporting of consolidated financial statements.[4]

Japanese companies are currently required to file both their parent-only and consolidated financial statements with the Ministry of Finance within three months after year-end. Prior to 1989, parent-only financial statements were due within three months after year-end, whereas consolidated financial statements were due within four months after year-end. Earnings announcements commonly precede the formal filing of the financial statements. Parent-only earnings are announced in the brief report '*Kessan-tanshin*' normally between 40–70 days after year-end. Consolidated earnings are announced in the brief report '*Renketsu-kessan-tanshin*' either concurrently with or within 1–2 weeks after parent-only earnings.[5]

Consolidated earnings consist of parent company earnings, subsidiary earnings, and earnings under the equity method for unconsolidated subsidiaries. This total is adjusted downward for any income assigned to minority interests, consolidation adjustments such as goodwill amortization, and inter-company income. The amount reported for parent-only earnings represents the separate earnings of the parent company plus income from dividends received from subsidiaries and affiliated companies under the cost method. Thus, in contrast to consolidated earnings, parent-only earnings can be more easily managed through the use of inter-company transactions and the timing of dividend payments by subsidiaries and affiliated companies. Subsidiary earnings are defined in this paper as the difference between consolidated earnings and parent-only earnings. This measure of subsidiary earnings represents the incremental earnings beyond parent-only earnings due to the application of consolidation practices. To make this apparent, we refer to subsidiary earnings as 'incremental subsidiary earnings' in the remainder of the paper.

Subsidiary earnings represent an important component of total consolidated earnings for Japanese firms. Cross-holdings through subsidiaries are very common in Japan. Hirose (1992) examined the number of subsidiaries held by 828 Japanese listed companies. While the median number of subsidiaries was in the 11–20 range, 198 firms in the sample (24%) had 20–50 subsidiaries, 90 firms (11%) had 51–100 subsidiaries, 40 firms (5%) had 101–200 subsidiaries, 9 firms had 201–300 subsidiaries, and 12 Japanese companies reported over 300 subsidiaries. Thus, over 40% of the sample firms reported 20+ subsidiaries. Subsidiary earnings also exhibit wide variation. The standard deviation of the change in incremental subsidiary earnings for our sample is approximately 50% of the standard deviation of parent-only earnings, indicating that incremental subsidiary earnings represents an important contribution to consolidated earnings for our sample of firms. Finally, as reported in Section 4, the actual persistence of subsidiary earnings changes exceeds parent-only earnings changes providing evidence that subsidiary earnings are not transitory, but rather, are an important element in determining firm value in Japan.

3. RESEARCH DESIGN

As parent-only financial statements have traditionally been the primary financial statements for decision-making purposes in Japan, this study investigates the possibility that the Japanese financial markets have relied too extensively on parent-only earnings, underestimating the role of incremental subsidiary earnings in the total performance of the consolidated entity. Mishkin (1983) develops an empirically testable framework to determine whether the market rationally prices information. The Mishkin framework has been used in the accounting literature to examine whether the market rationally prices the implications of current accounting earnings and its components for future stock returns (e.g., Sloan, 1996; Kasznik and McNichols, 1999; Thomas, 1999; Hribar, 2000; and Xie, 2000). In the context of our study, the framework examines whether the price reaction to subsidiary and parent-only earnings is consistent with the empirical relation between future earnings and subsidiary/parent-only earnings components. The test for market rationality involves simultaneously estimating the following two equations:

$$\Delta \mathrm{CE}_{t+1} = \alpha_0 + \alpha_S \Delta \mathrm{SE}_t + \alpha_P \Delta \mathrm{PE}_t + v_{t+1}$$

$$\mathrm{ARET}_{t+1} = \beta_0 + \beta_1(\Delta \mathrm{CE}_{t+1} - \alpha_0 - \alpha_S^* \Delta \mathrm{SE}_t - \alpha_P^* \Delta \mathrm{PE}_t) + \varepsilon_{t+1}.$$

Where $\Delta \mathrm{CE}_{t+1}$ = the change in consolidated earnings in year $t+1$; $\Delta \mathrm{SE}_t$ = the change in incremental subsidiary earnings in year t; $\Delta \mathrm{PE}_t$ = the change in parent-only earnings in year t; and ARET_{t+1} = the abnormal (or unexpected) stock return in year $t+1$. The Mishkin test involves simultaneously estimating the two equations using non-linear least squares. Non-linear least squares is necessary to estimate the coefficients in the second equation. The estimation procedure is similar to full information maximum likelihood estimation, but empirically more tractable (Sloan, 1996).[6]

The first equation represents the *actual* time-series relation of the change in incremental subsidiary and parent-only earnings to next year's change in consolidated earnings. α_S estimates the persistence of the change in incremental subsidiary earnings (controlling for parent-only earnings) and α_P estimates the persistence of the change in parent-only earnings (controlling for incremental subsidiary earnings). A zero coefficient suggests that earnings changes follow a random walk process (i.e., changes in earnings tend to be permanent). The more negative the coefficient, the less persistent the change in earnings.

The second equation provides an estimate of the market's *perceived* time-series behavior of incremental subsidiary and parent-only earnings. Since unexpected movements in stock prices are related to unexpected earnings information received in the same period, the extent to which the market perceives parent-only and incremental subsidiary earnings to persist into consolidated earnings can be estimated. α_S^* estimates the market's perceived persistence of the change in incremental subsidiary earnings and α_P^* estimates the market's perceived persistence of the change in parent-only earnings, controlling for one another. If $\alpha_S \neq \alpha_S^*$ or $\alpha_P \neq \alpha_P^*$, then the market's perception of earnings persistence differs from the historical time-series pattern. For instance, an $\alpha_S^* < \alpha_S$ implies that the market perceives the persistence of changes in incremental subsidiary earnings to be less than it actually is.

The relation between incremental subsidiary earnings and parent-only earnings and year-ahead stock returns can also be tested using raw returns as the dependent variable and controlling for common risk factors as additional independent variables:

$$\text{RET}_{t+1} = \beta_0 + \beta_1 \Delta\text{SE}_t + \beta_2 \Delta\text{PE}_t + \beta_3 \text{SIZE}_t + \beta_4 \text{BM}_t + \beta_5 \text{DA}_t + \beta_6 \text{BETA}_t + \varepsilon_{t+1}.$$

Raw returns in year $t+1$ are regressed on the change in incremental subsidiary earnings in year t, the change in parent-only earnings in year t, and four control variables in year t. In a market that rationally prices information, a variable in year t should not be related to returns in year $t+1$, unless that variable represents cross-sectional differences in risk. However, if the Japanese market underestimates the persistence of incremental subsidiary earnings, as suggested in the previous analysis, incremental subsidiary earnings should exhibit a significant, positive coefficient as prices correct in the following annual period. The coefficient on parent-only earnings is expected to be zero, consistent with a market that correctly prices these earnings in year t.

4. SAMPLE, VARIABLE MEASUREMENT, AND DESCRIPTIVE STATISTICS

The sample includes all Japanese listed firms having the necessary financial and stock return data. Financial data were obtained from the NEEDS/MICRO database at the Kwansei Gakuin University Information Processing Research Center. Stock return data were obtained from Nihon Keizai Shimbun, Inc. Financial, insurance, real estate, transportation, utilities, and service industries are excluded to increase the cross-sectional comparability of firms, as these represent regulated or semi-regulated industries in Japan. Firms were required to report financial data on a parent-only basis and a consolidated basis. The final sample consists of 8,490 firm-year observations over the period 1985–1997.[7] To control for differences in size across firms and over time, earnings variables are scaled by average consolidated assets. Scaling all earnings variables by average consolidated assets allows the incremental subsidiary and parent-only components of consolidated earnings to sum to consolidated earnings.[8]

Abnormal returns are measured as the twelve-month buy-and-hold security return minus the equally-weighted buy-and-hold return of a comparable portfolio. Comparison portfolios are defined according to three firm characteristics: capitalization value, book-to-market ratio, and debt-to-asset ratio. In each year, all listed Japanese firms are sorted evenly into quartiles based on the natural log of their market value of equity. Then, within each size quartile, firms are sorted evenly into quartiles based on their book-to-market ratios.[9] The book-to-market ratio is measured as the log of the firm's book-to-market ratio minus the long-run industry average. Finally, within each of the 16 size/book-to-market portfolios, firms are sorted evenly into quartiles based on their debt-to-asset ratios. The debt-to-asset ratio is measured as the log of the firm's debt-to-asset ratio minus the long-run industry average. Firms were classified in industries based on their three-digit industry classification. The industry adjustment for the book-to-market ratio and the debt-to-asset ratio should increase the cross-sectional comparability of the ratios (Cohen and Polk, 1995; and Daniel et al., 1997). Thus, 64($4 \times 4 \times 4$) size/book-to-market/debt-to-asset portfolios are created each year with approximately the same number of firms in each portfolio. Size, book-to-market, and debt-to-asset ratios for each firm are measured at the most recent fiscal year end before the return accumulation period begins. Abnormal returns are then measured as security *i*'s twelve-month return beginning four months after the fiscal year end (e.g., beginning August 1 for March 31 year-end firms) minus the equally-weighted return of the comparison portfolio (excluding security *i*) over the same twelve-month period. All of the information related to consolidated and parent-only earnings in year *t* is publicly available by the beginning of the year $t + 1$ return interval. We also control for a firm's market beta, computed as the slope estimate from the usual market model. Estimates are obtained using monthly returns and an equally-weighted market index over a 60-month period ending with the fiscal year end. Observations are required to have at least 30 monthly returns to estimate beta.

Panel A of Table 1 presents distributions of the variables used in this study. The mean abnormal return is close to zero. Also, the mean change in both subsidiary earnings and parent-only earnings is close to zero. The mean industry-adjusted book-to-market ratio is negative, indicating that consolidated firms tend to have lower book-to-market ratios than their industry counterparts. This is consistent with consolidated firms having less risk than non-consolidated firms. The mean debt-to-asset ratio is slightly positive. Panel B of Table 1 reports the correlations for the variables used in the study. The correlation between changes in parent-only and incremental subsidiary earnings is relatively small (−0.0641), indicating that incremental subsidiary earnings can potentially provide value-relevant information different from parent-only earnings.

Panel C of Table 1 presents averages of selected variables when firms are sorted annually into deciles based on the magnitude of the change in incremental subsidiary earnings. The first column shows that the change in incremental subsidiary earnings (scaled by average consolidated assets) ranges from −0.0169 for the lowest decile to 0.0175 for the highest decile. The second column shows that while there is some correlation between incremental subsidiary and parent-only earnings at the portfolio level, the range of the change in parent-only earnings across changes in subsidiary earnings is somewhat limited. The average amount of parent-only earnings is −0.0002 for the lowest incremental subsidiary earnings decile and 0.0000 for the highest incremental subsidiary earnings decile.[10] The SIZE, BM, DA, and BETA columns reveal that the variation in the control variables is

Table 1

Descriptive Statistics ($n = 8{,}490$)

Panel A: Distributions

Variables	*Mean*	*Standard Deviation*	*Min*	*Q1*	*Median*	*Q3*	*Max*
$ARET_{t+1}$	−0.0019	0.2636	−0.8597	−0.1443	−0.0298	0.0990	2.426
ΔCE_{t+1}	0.0000	0.0275	−0.4454	−0.0015	0.0004	0.0064	0.3480
ΔCE_t	0.0002	0.0266	−0.4454	−0.0062	0.0006	0.0067	0.3480
ΔSE_t	0.0000	0.0126	−0.3130	−0.0024	0.0000	0.0024	0.2427
ΔPE_t	0.0002	0.0243	−0.4502	−0.0040	0.0005	0.0049	0.3633
$SIZE_t$	25.12	1.341	21.13	24.17	25.03	25.99	29.74
BM_t	−0.0589	0.6061	−5.722	−0.3747	−0.0191	0.3486	6.667
DA_t	0.0088	0.3070	−1.851	−0.1187	0.0674	0.2156	0.7180
$BETA_t$	1.067	0.4060	−1.488	0.8301	1.069	1.309	3.731

Panel B: Correlations

	ΔCE_{t+1}	ΔSE_t	ΔPE_t	$SIZE_t$	BM_t	DA_t	$BETA_t$
$ARET_{t+1}$	0.1097	0.0551	0.0081	0.0107	0.0219	0.0045	−0.0273
ΔCE_{t+1}		−0.0892	−0.3041	−0.0076	−0.0875	0.0398	−0.0176
ΔSE_t			−0.0641	0.0005	−0.0165	0.0029	−0.0006
ΔPE_t				0.0368	−0.0935	0.0115	0.0236
$SIZE_t$					−0.0747	−0.0499	−0.2651
BM_t						−0.4104	−0.1005
DA_t							0.0789

Panel C: Mean values of selected variables when firms are sorted annually into deciles based on the magnitude of the change in subsidiary earnings (ΔSE_t).

Decile	ΔSE_t	ΔPE_t	ΔCE_t	$SIZE_t$	BM_t	DA_t	$BETA_t$	*Asset Ratio*$_t$	*Sales Ratio*$_t$
1	−0.0169	−0.0002	−0.0171	25.01	−0.0772	0.0281	1.098	0.8371	0.8366
2	−0.0049	−0.0021	−0.0070	25.04	−0.0355	0.0324	1.075	0.8475	0.8467
3	−0.0025	−0.0004	−0.0029	25.06	−0.0208	0.0043	1.069	0.8619	0.8595
4	−0.0011	−0.0011	−0.0022	25.15	−0.0075	−0.0096	1.045	0.8765	0.8773
5	−0.0003	0.0007	0.0004	25.12	0.0463	0.0063	1.060	0.8866	0.8922
6	0.0004	0.0012	0.0016	25.18	−0.0353	−0.0115	1.044	0.8855	0.8844
7	0.0012	0.0009	0.0021	25.27	−0.0585	0.0175	1.054	0.8655	0.8699
8	0.0025	0.0013	0.0038	25.23	−0.0673	−0.0209	1.068	0.8640	0.8644
9	0.0047	0.0017	0.0064	25.12	−0.0906	0.0077	1.064	0.8471	0.8428
10	0.0175	0.0000	0.0175	24.98	−0.1510	0.0334	1.092	0.8465	0.8310

Notes:
$ARET_{t+1}$ = twelve-month buy-and-hold security return beginning four months after the fiscal year end minus the equally-weighted return of a comparable portfolio of firms based on size, book-to-market ratio, and debt-to-equity ratio over the same twelve-month period (the return on security *i* is excluded from the equally-weighted comparison portfolio return); $\Delta CE_{t(t+1)}$ = the change in consolidated earnings in fiscal year $t(t+1)$, scaled by average consolidated assets; ΔSE_t = the change in incremental subsidiary earnings in fiscal year *t*, scaled by average consolidated assets; ΔPE_t = the change in parent-only earnings in fiscal year *t*, scaled by average consolidated assets; $SIZE_t$ = natural log of market value of equity (in yen) at the end of fiscal year *t*; BM_t = natural log of the ratio of consolidated book value of equity to market value of equity at the end of the fiscal year *t* minus the long run industry average; DA_t = natural log of the ratio of consolidated total debt to consolidated total assets at the end of fiscal year *t* minus the long run industry average; $BETA_t$ = slope estimate from a regression of monthly security returns of security *i* on an equally-weighted market return over the 60-month period ending with the fiscal year end; Asset Ratio = ratio of parent-only assets to consolidated assets; Sales Ratio = ratio of parent-only sales to consolidated sales.

somewhat limited across portfolios, with a slight tendency for firms in the extreme portfolios to appear riskier. The final two columns report the ratio of parent-only assets to consolidated assets and parent-only sales to consolidated sales. The lower and higher deciles of ΔSE exhibit lower parent to consolidated ratios or higher subsidiary to consolidated ratios. Companies with a higher proportion of subsidiary assets or sales have more extreme changes in subsidiary earnings.

5. EMPIRICAL ANALYSIS

The results of the Mishkin (1983) test are presented in Table 2. Results are reported using the Fama-McBeth (1973) procedure, where the reported coefficients represent the mean of the annual regression coefficients and the standard errors are based on the time-series variation of the annual coefficients. There are twelve annual regressions for the test period (1985–1996). The corresponding *p*-values from the two-tailed *t*-test that the mean coefficient is equal to zero are shown in parentheses. Assuming independence through time, the Fama-MacBeth procedure has the advantage of controlling for cross-sectional correlation in the residuals. In the presence of positive cross-correlation in the residuals, the standard errors can be biased downward and the *t*-statistics biased upward in the pooled regression.[11]

In the first equation, changes in consolidated earnings in year $t+1$ are regressed on changes in incremental subsidiary earnings and changes in parent-only earnings in year t. The coefficient on incremental subsidiary earnings (α_S) is -0.2139 and the coefficient on parent-only earnings (α_P) is -0.3966. Changes in incremental subsidiary earnings are more persistent (less negative) than changes in parent-only earnings. The difference in the persistence coefficient for incremental subsidiary earnings and parent-only earnings is significant (p-value $= 0.0514$). Both coefficients are significantly different from zero. These results suggest that incremental subsidiary earnings provide information beyond parent-only earnings in explaining next year's consolidated earnings. Contrary to criticism leveled against consolidation practices in Japan, incremental subsidiary earnings are more persistent than parent-only earnings for next year's

Table 2

Nonlinear Least Squares Regression of the Relation Between Future Abnormal Stock Returns and Information in Current Changes in Incremental Subsidiary Earnings and Changes in Parent-only Earnings About Future Changes in Consolidated Earnings ($n = 8,490$)

$$\Delta CE_{t+1} = \alpha_0 + \alpha_S \Delta SE_t + \alpha_P \Delta PE_t + v_{t+1}$$

$$ARET_{t+1} = \beta_0 + \beta_1(\Delta CE_{t+1} - \alpha_0 - \alpha_S^* \Delta SE_t - \alpha_P^* \Delta PE_t) + \varepsilon_{t+1}$$

	Estimate[a]	*p-value*[b]
α_0	0.0003	0.8726
α_S	−0.2139	0.0195
α_S^*	−1.112	0.0001
α_P	−0.3966	0.0001
α_P^*	−0.4137	0.0749
β_0	−0.0032	0.3145
β_1	1.326	0.0001
Test of Equal Persistence:[c]		
H_0: $\alpha_S = \alpha_P$		0.0514
Test of Market Efficiency:[c]		
H_0: $\alpha_S^* = \alpha_S$		0.0007
H_0: $\alpha_P^* = \alpha_P$		0.9375

Notes:
$ARET_{t+1}$ = twelve-month buy-and-hold security return beginning four months after the fiscal year end minus the equally-weighted return of a comparable portfolio of firms based on size, book-to-market ratio, and debt-to-equity ratio over the same twelve-month period (the return on security i is excluded from the equally-weighted comparison portfolio return); ΔCE_{t+1} = the change in consolidated earnings in fiscal year $t+1$, scaled by average consolidated assets; ΔSE_t = the change in incremental subsidiary earnings in fiscal year t, scaled by average consolidated assets; ΔPE_t = the change in parent-only earnings in fiscal year t, scaled by average consolidated assets.

[a] Amounts shown represent averages of annual coefficients.
[b] Amounts shown represent p-values from two-tailed t-tests that the average coefficient is equal to zero, where the standard error is computed using the inter-temporal variation of the annual coefficients.
[c] p-values for these tests are calculated using a two-tailed difference of means t-test that the coefficients are equal.

consolidated earnings. If market participants place less emphasis on incremental subsidiary earnings, then stock prices should lag changes in incremental subsidiary earnings.

Examining the second equation, estimates of the market's perceived persistence of incremental subsidiary earnings (α_S^*) and parent-only earnings (α_P^*) are −1.112 and −0.4137, respectively. The coefficient on subsidiary earnings α_S^* is significantly different from zero (p-value = 0.0001) and not significantly different than negative one (p-value = 0.5801), indicating that the market appears to ignore the impact of changes in incremental subsidiary earnings in setting its expectations for future changes in consolidated earnings (i.e., the market perceives changes in subsidiary earnings to be transitory). The difference between the historical time-series pattern of incremental subsidiary earnings and the market's perception of the time-series pattern of incremental subsidiary earnings is significant (p-value = 0.0007). In contrast, the historical time-series pattern for parent-only earnings and the market's perception of the time-series pattern are not significantly different (p-value = 0.9378).[12] The results indicate the Japanese market understands the time-series behavior of parent-only earnings and prices securities appropriately.[13]

The mean coefficients from cross-sectional regressions using raw returns as the dependent variable are reported in Table 3. The first and second columns report the results from regressing returns separately on changes in incremental subsidiary earnings and changes in parent-only earnings, respectively, along with the four control variables. The third column reports the results from a regression of returns on changes in both incremental subsidiary earnings and parent-only earnings and the four control variables. The final column excludes the control variables.

The results indicate that changes in incremental subsidiary earnings are significantly positively related to year-ahead returns with or without the inclusion of parent-only earnings. The findings are consistent with the results of the Mishkin test. The market appears to underestimate the extent to which current changes in incremental subsidiary earnings persist to next year's consolidated earnings. Prices then correct in a predictable manner in the following period. Changes in parent-only earnings are not related to year-ahead returns under any of the model

Table 3

Mean Coefficients (*p*-values in parentheses) of Cross-sectional Regressions of Raw Returns in Year $t+1$ on Changes in Incremental Subsidiary Earnings, Changes in Parent-only Earnings, and Other Control Variables in Year $t (n = 8{,}490)$[a]

$$RET_{t+1} = \beta_0 + \beta_1 \Delta SE_t + \beta_2 \Delta PE_t +_3 SIZE_t + \beta_4 BM_t + \beta_5 DA_t + \beta_6 BETA_t + \varepsilon$$

β_0	0.3513 (0.3522)	0.3527 (0.3486)	0.3561 (0.3403)	0.0816 (0.2907)
β_1	1.307 (0.0166)		1.210 (0.0293)	1.184 (0.0276)
β_2		0.1123 (0.6341)	0.1254 (0.5897)	0.0169 (0.9527)
β_3	−0.0096 (0.4756)	−0.0096 (0.4741)	−0.0098 (0.4627)	
β_4	0.0836 (0.0002)	0.0824 (0.0002)	0.0831 (0.0002)	
β_5	0.0886 (0.0625)	0.0898 (0.0588)	0.0897 (0.0600)	
β_6	−0.0158 (0.4655)	−0.0178 (0.4279)	−0.0169 (0.4541)	
R^2	0.0313	0.0296	0.0313	0.0118

Notes:
RET_{t+1} = twelve-month buy-and-hold security return beginning four months after the fiscal year end; ΔSE_t = the change in incremental subsidiary earnings in fiscal year t, scaled by average consolidated assets; ΔPE_t = the change in parent-only earnings in fiscal year t, scaled by average consolidated assets; $SIZE_t$ = natural log of market value of equity (in yen) at the end of fiscal year t; BM_t = natural log of the ratio of consolidated book value of equity to market value of equity at the end of the fiscal year t minus the long run industry average; DA_t = natural log of the ratio of consolidated total debt to consolidated total assets at the end of fiscal year t minus the long run industry average; $BETA_t$ = slope estimate from a regression of monthly security returns of security i on an equally-weighted market return over the 60-month period ending with the fiscal year end.

[a] Amounts reported represent mean coefficients of cross-sectional regressions. Amounts in parentheses are *p*-values from two-tailed *t*-tests that the mean coefficient is equal to zero where the standard error is computed using the inter-temporal variation of the annual coefficients.

specifications. The Japanese market incorporates the time-series trend of parent-only earnings and prices securities appropriately. Two of the four control variables are also significantly related to year-ahead returns. The coefficients on the book-to-market ratio and the debt-to-asset ratio are both positive and significant. The coefficients on size and beta are negative and not significant.

6. DISTINGUISHING BETWEEN MARKET MISPRICING AND FAILURE TO CONTROL FOR RISK

The positive relation between changes in incremental subsidiary earnings and year-ahead stock returns provides evidence consistent with market mispricing. However, the relation is also consistent with incremental subsidiary earnings being a proxy for, or source of, risk. If changes in incremental subsidiary earnings are positively correlated with some unidentified risk variable, this could explain the relation between incremental subsidiary earnings and year-ahead stock returns. While our tests control for commonly identified risk factors, there may be additional unidentified risk factors.[14] However, since the firm's intrinsic value is unobservable, one cannot know with certainty whether the results are due to market mispricing or failure to control for cross-sectional differences in risk. What the researcher is able to do is to conduct tests whose results are either more or less consistent with market mispricing versus risk mismeasurement (Bernard et al., 1997). To better distinguish between market mispricing and failure to control adequately for risk, we investigate (1) the relation between changes in incremental subsidiary earnings and long-term stock returns and (2) the pattern of future annual returns to zero-investment hedge portfolios created using firms' changes in incremental subsidiary earnings.

(i) Relation With Long-Term Stock Returns

The first test involves estimating the relation between changes in incremental subsidiary earnings and long-term stock returns, defined as returns two and three years into the future. If market mispricing occurs because the market understates the contribution of changes in incremental subsidiary earnings in the current year to changes in consolidated earnings in the subsequent year, then prices should correct in the subsequent year as additional information becomes available to the market. It is not likely that the market would take more than one year to correct any mispricing. If, however, changes in incremental subsidiary earnings are related to cross-sectional differences in risk, then we could expect the relation between current incremental subsidiary earnings and future returns to exist over several subsequent periods. For example, Stober (1992) finds that the abnormal returns to Ou and Penman's (1989) *Pr* trading strategy continue for up to 72 months, concluding the result is consistent with the *Pr* trading strategy proxying for omitted risk factors, rather than market mispricing.

Table 4 estimates the relation between future returns and changes in incremental subsidiary and parent-only earnings using, as the dependent variable, two-year-ahead and three-year-ahead returns. The mean coefficients of cross-sectional regressions are presented with and without controlling for risk factors. The results provide little evidence that the relation between current changes in incremental subsidiary earnings and future returns persists beyond one year. For all model specifications, changes in incremental subsidiary earnings and parent-only earnings are not significantly related to two-year-ahead or three-year-ahead stock returns. The evidence is consistent with the market adjusting for the mispricing of incremental subsidiary earnings in the subsequent year so that abnormal returns are no longer present beyond year $t + 1$. Note that the book-to-market ratio is significantly related to two-year-ahead and three-year-ahead stock returns, consistent with this variable being a cross-sectional measure of risk as in Chan et al. (1993).

(ii) Hedge Portfolios

The second test measures the year-ahead abnormal returns to a zero-investment hedge portfolio consisting of a long position in stocks expected to perform well and a short position in stocks expected to perform poorly. If the market underestimates the

Table 4

Mean Coefficients (*p*-values in parentheses) of Cross-sectional Regressions of Returns in Year $t + \tau$ on Changes in Incremental Subsidiary Earnings, Changes in Parent-only Earnings, and Other Control Variables in Year t[a]

$$RET_{t+\tau} = \beta_0 + \beta_1 \Delta SE_t + \beta_2 \Delta PE_t + \beta_3 SIZE_t + \beta_4 BM_t + \beta_5 DA_t + \beta_6 BETA_t + \varepsilon$$

	$\tau = 2(n = 7{,}259)$		$\tau = 3(n = 6{,}181)$	
β_0	0.0616 (0.4377)	0.2834 (0.4673)	0.0029 (0.9691)	0.0567 (0.8855)
β_1	−0.1704 (0.5002)	−0.2556 (0.3654)	0.2553 (0.4700)	0.2740 (0.4118)
β_2	0.2903 (0.2635)	−0.2190 (0.3456)	−0.4625 (0.2233)	−0.3197 (0.4021)
β_3		−0.0083 (0.5585)		−0.0013 (0.9251)
β_4		0.0558 (0.0184)		0.0271 (0.0112)
β_5		0.0576 (0.2606)		0.0322 (0.0641)
β_6		−0.0042 (0.8351)		0.0145 (0.7618)
R^2	0.0004	0.0128	0.0028	0.0112

Notes:

$RET_{t+\tau}$ = twelve-month buy-and-hold security return beginning four months after the fiscal year end, where $\tau = 2$ or 3; ΔSE_t = the change in incremental subsidiary earnings in fiscal year t, scaled by average consolidated assets; ΔPE_t = the change in parent-only earnings in fiscal year t, scaled by average consolidated assets; $SIZE_t$ = natural log of market value of equity (in yen) at the end of fiscal year t; BM_t = natural log of the ratio of consolidated book value of equity to market value of equity at the end of the fiscal year t minus the long run industry average; DA_t = natural log of the ratio of consolidated total debt to consolidated total assets at the end of fiscal year t minus the long run industry average; $BETA_t$ = slope estimate from a regression of monthly security returns of security i on an equally-weighted market return over the 60-month period ending with the fiscal year end.

[a] Amounts reported represent mean coefficients of cross-sectional regressions. Amounts in parentheses are *p*-values from two-tailed *t*-tests that the mean coefficient is equal to zero where the standard error is computed using the inter-temporal variation of the annual coefficients.

persistence of subsidiary earnings in year *t*, then stocks with large positive (negative) changes in incremental subsidiary earnings are expected to perform well (poorly) in year $t + 1$. The hedge portfolio abnormal return is measured over the twelve-month period beginning four months after the March 31 fiscal year-end. Firms with year-ends other than March 31 are excluded in this analysis so that the variables used to construct the hedge portfolios (i.e., changes in parent-only and incremental subsidiary earnings) coincide chronologically. Abnormal returns are defined as the twelve-month buy-and-hold security return beginning four months after the fiscal year end minus the equally-weighted return of a comparable portfolio of firms based on size, book-to-market ratio, and debt-to-equity ratios over the same twelve-month period. The return on the security being examined is excluded from the equal-weighted comparison portfolio return. Comparison portfolios are sorted evenly into size quartiles based on their market value of equity. Then, within each size quartile, firms are sorted evenly into quartiles based on their book-to-market ratios. Finally, within each of the sixteen size/book-to-market portfolios, firms are sorted evenly into quartiles based on their debt-to-asset ratios. Thus, sixty-four ($4 \times 4 \times 4$) size/book-to-market/debt-to-asset portfolios are created each year with approximately the same number of firms in each portfolio. Size, book-to-market, and debt-to-asset ratios are measured at the end of each fiscal year in creating the comparison portfolios, and the portfolio return is then measured over the twelve-month period beginning four months after year-end.[15]

In an efficient market, a return significantly different from zero must be attributable to differences in risk when equal amounts are invested in the long and short positions of the hedge portfolio. However, a *risky* zero-investment hedge portfolio, while exhibiting an overall average positive return, should result in positive returns in some periods and negative returns in others. Positive returns period after period are not likely to be attributed solely to omitted risk factors (Bernard et al., 1997).

The long and short positions of the hedge portfolio are created each year by first sorting firms evenly into deciles based on current changes in parent-only earnings. Then, within each of these deciles, firms are sorted evenly into deciles based on current changes in incremental subsidiary earnings. Creating the portfolios in this manner allows sorting based on changes in incremental subsidiary earnings, while controlling for changes in parent-only earnings. Changes in parent-only earnings will be approximately equal across the deciles based on changes in subsidiary earnings. A long position is taken in firms in the highest decile of changes in incremental subsidiary earnings and a short position is taken in firms in the lowest decile of changes in incremental subsidiary earnings.[16] If the Japanese market underestimates the persistence of incremental subsidiary earnings, then the hedge portfolios should produce positive abnormal returns year after year. Evidence consistent with failure to control for cross-sectional differences in risk would be found if the hedge portfolios produce both positive and negative returns across years.

The annual returns to the hedge portfolios are illustrated in Figure 1. The hedge portfolio abnormal returns are positive in 12 of the 13 years. The single outlier is a return of −1.21% in 1986. The average abnormal return over the 13-year period is 7.06% (p-value = 0.0013). The average abnormal return to the long position is 2.35% (p-value = 0.1953) and the average abnormal return to the short position is −4.71% (p-value = 0.0052).[17] The returns to the long position are positive in 9 of the 13 years and the returns to the short position are negative in 12 of the 13 years. The consistent pattern of positive hedge portfolio abnormal returns is characteristic of a market that underestimates the persistence of incremental subsidiary earnings. Stock prices move in a predictable manner in the subsequent period as next period's consolidated earnings become known.[18] Furthermore, abnormal returns do not persist beyond year $t+1$. The average abnormal returns to the hedge portfolios in year $t+2$ (1.69%) and year $t+3$ (0.91%) are not significantly different from zero. These results are consistent with those reported in Table 4 and further reinforce the conclusion that the market corrects fully for its mispricing of incremental subsidiary earnings in year t as consolidated earnings in year $t+1$ become known.[19]

Figure 1

Annual Returns to Hedge Portfolios

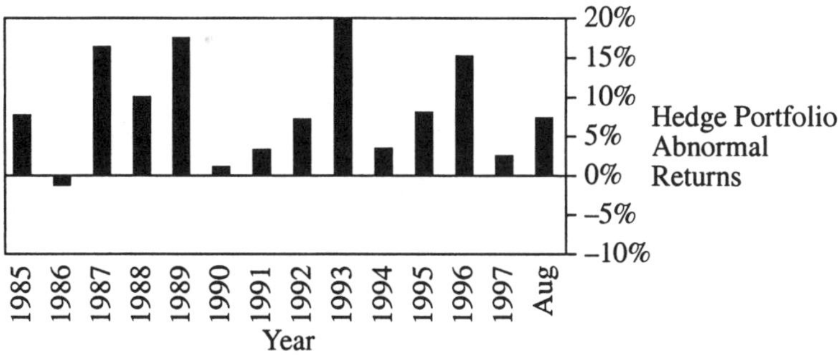

Notes

The figure shows abnormal returns to a hedge portfolio taking a long (short) position in firms in the top (bottom) decile of changes in incremental subsidiary earnings. Firms are sorted evenly in each year into deciles based on changes in parent-only earnings. Then within each of these deciles, firms are sorted evenly into deciles based on changes in incremental subsidiary earnings. Abnormal returns are defined as the twelve-month buy-and-hold security return beginning four months after the fiscal year end minus the equally-weighted return of a comparable portfolio of firms based on size, book-to-market ratio, and debt-to-equity ratio over the same twelve-month period. The return on security *i* is excluded from the equally-weighted comparison portfolio return. The calendar year is the year in which the portfolio is formed and the return interval begins four months after the year end (e.g., for 1985, changes in subsidiary earnings for the fiscal year ending March 1985 are used to form the long and short positions of the hedge portfolio and abnormal returns are then measured for the twelve-month period beginning August 1, 1985, and ending July 31, 1986).

7. CONCLUSION

A growing body of research finds evidence consistent with the market not fully understanding the time-series behavior of earnings or its components (e.g., Bernard and Thomas, 1989 and 1990; and Sloan, 1996; Abarbanell and Bushee, 1998; and Thomas, 1999). As a result, stock prices appear to misstate the value of the firm and then correct in a predictable manner. Our study builds on this line of research by investigating whether returns in the Japanese stock market accurately reflect the information in parent-only earnings and incremental subsidiary earnings (defined as consolidated earnings minus parent-only earnings) for future consolidated earnings. The study is motivated by the widely-held view that parent-only data are superior to consolidated data in Japanese firm valuation. Some have even questioned whether there is any relevance to consolidated financial statements in the unique Japanese business environment.

The results provide evidence that incremental subsidiary earnings provide information beyond parent-only earnings in forecasting next period's consolidated earnings. However, security prices do not fully reflect the persistence of incremental subsidiary earnings in the current period, resulting in a significant positive relation between changes in incremental subsidiary earnings and year-ahead stock returns. These results are consistent with consolidated financial statements providing value-relevant information beyond parent-only financial statements that is not fully utilized by the Japanese stock market in a timely manner.

Two additional tests are performed to help distinguish between the competing hypotheses of market mispricing and the failure to control adequately for risk. First, the relation between incremental subsidiary earnings and long-term stock returns is examined. The results indicate that the relation between incremental subsidiary earnings and future returns does not persist beyond the subsequent year. Second, zero-investment hedge portfolios are constructed based on incremental subsidiary earnings. The hedge portfolios result in an average annual abnormal return of 7.06% in the year following the hedge portfolio formation with positive returns in 12 of the 13 years examined. In the second and third year following the hedge portfolio formation, the average abnormal returns were not significantly different from zero.

Taken collectively, these results are consistent with market mispricing rather than the failure to control adequately for cross-sectional differences in risk. The results suggest that current stock prices lag reported changes in incremental subsidiary earnings and then correct in the following period as abnormal returns are not available beyond the subsequent year. On the other hand, risk-based explanations cannot be ruled out completely. The results may even be attributable to a combination of both market mispricing and unobservable risk characteristics. Therefore, we conclude only that the supplemental tests are more consistent with mispricing than mismeasurement of risk characteristics.

NOTES

1 In contrast to the consolidated financial information required in the US and the UK, Japanese firms report both parent-only and consolidated financial statements. Parent-only financial statements are prepared in conformity with the Japanese Commercial Code and consolidated financial statements are prepared in compliance with the Japanese Securities and Exchange Law (Choi, Frost and Meek, 1999).

2 For a complete review of this literature, see Kothari (2000).

3 The Commercial Law considers parent-only financial statements to be the primary financial statements for Japanese companies. Under the provisions of the Commercial Law, Japanese companies are not required to prepare consolidated financial statements.

4 Beginning March 1995, the Ministry of Finance required companies to widen disclosure of consolidated subsidiaries and affiliates (e.g., consolidated statements can no longer exclude subsidiaries that have consolidated assets or sales less than 10% of the parent's) as part of a move to bring accounting standards more into line with international practice. On February 19, 1999, the Business Advisory Deliberation Council, an advisory board of the Ministry of Finance, finalized its implementation guidance on review of forms of annual reports. The review takes the position that annual reports should focus on consolidation-based information. Beginning in March 2000, the Japanese Securities and Exchange Law requires consolidated financial statements to be the primary financial statements and parent-only statements to be secondary in the annual report filed with the Ministry of Finance. The Japanese Commercial Code, however, will continue to consider the parent-only statements as the primary financial statements.

5 Any timing difference in the announcement of parent-only or consolidated earnings will not affect the results or conclusions of this study. As discussed below, the future abnormal return period begins four months after the fiscal year end. By this time, both parent-only earnings and consolidated earnings have been announced and are public information.

6 For a more extensive, generalized discussion of this test, see Mishkin (1983), Sloan (1996) or Kraft et al. (2001).

7 At the time of data collection, consolidated data from 1984 to 1997 and stock return data from 1984 to 1998 were available. Since the tests require changes in earnings and average total assets, 1985 is the first year of usable observations. Most firms do not provide consolidated financial information prior to 1984 (Hall et al., 1994). Since earnings in year $t + 1$ are required to estimate earnings persistence, 1996 is the final year of usable observations. Observations for 1997 can be used in the hedge portfolio analysis as only future stock returns are required.

8 To determine whether the choice of scale variable affects the results, tests were run with all earnings variables scaled by average parent-only assets. The results are very similar to those reported. There is a high correlation between average consolidated assets and average parent-only assets (0.9768).

9 Observations that had negative book values were excluded.

10 When firms are sorted annually into deciles based on parent-only earnings, the average amount of parent-only earnings ranges from −0.0363 for the lowest decile to 0.0359 for the highest decile.

11 Using simulated data, Kraft et al. (2001) question the applicability of the Mishkin test in accounting studies when observations are pooled across firms and through time. The Fama-McBeth procedure estimates regression coefficients each year to avoid pooling over time. We also ran the regressions in Table 3 separately by industry. The results continue to hold when the regression models, as suggested by Kraft et al. (2001), are estimated by industry and year.

12 The joint test of the equality of the two sets of coefficients is significant at the 0.0001 level ($\chi^2 = 26.38$).

13 The Mishkin test was also performed using the change in parent-only earnings as the only earnings variable. In this model, the market's perception of the persistence of parent-only earnings is not significantly different from the actual times-series pattern.

14 Tests were also conducted after controlling for the earnings-to-price ratio, cash flow-to-price ratio, and the dividend yield. None of these variables was significant and including them had no qualitative impact on the results.

15 The comparison portfolios successfully control for differences in size, book-to-market ratio, and debt-to-asset ratio in the long and short positions of the hedge portfolios. For the long position, the average size (25.17), book-to-market ratio (−0.1380), and debt-to-asset ratio (0.0456) are approximately equal to the averages for the comparison portfolios (25.15, −0.1600, 0.0435, respectively). Similarly, for the short position, the average size (25.11), book-to-market ratio (−0.0804), and debt-to-asset ratio (0.0482) are approximately equal to the averages of the comparison portfolios (25.80, −0.1371, 0.0496, respectively). Therefore, any differences in returns of the long and short positions should not be due to differences in these firm characteristics.

16 The average change in parent-only earnings for the long (short) position was 0.0011 (0.0012).

17 The average market beta of firms in the long (short) position is 1.100 (1.127).

18 Hedge portfolio returns to a parent-only strategy were also computed by taking a long (short) position in stocks with the most positive (negative) change in parent-only earnings. For this strategy the annual returns are quite volatile. The hedge portfolio abnormal returns are positive in 6 of the 13 years with an overall average return of 0.76%, which is not significantly different from zero (p-value = 0.7383). The yearly returns range from 17.5% to −9.65%. Neither the mean abnormal return to the long position (0.57%) nor to the short position (−0.19%) were significantly different from zero. Thus, there is no evidence of market mispricing with respect to parent-only earnings.

19 An additional test to distinguish between market mispricing and failure to control for differences in risk suggested in Bernard et al. (1997) is to measure the market's reaction to future quarterly earnings announcements of firms in the long and short positions of the hedge portfolio. Such a test, however, is very problematic in the Japanese environment. First, Japanese firms do not announce quarterly earnings or publish quarterly financial statements. Japanese firms are required to file only semi-annual financial statements. Japanese firms generally announce semi-annual earnings around eight months after the beginning of the fiscal year. Therefore, a host of other information sources will be received and incorporated in security prices before semi-annual earnings are announced. Second, as

discussed in Section 2 of the paper, parent-only and consolidated earnings are announced in separate reports and often not announced concurrently. At the time semi-annual earnings are announced, firms are also required by the stock exchanges to report many other items (e.g., sales, dividends, holding gains and losses, shareholders' equity, forecasts of consolidated and parent-only sales, forecasts of consolidated and parent-only earnings, and forecasts of dividends). Thus, it is not possible to isolate the market's reaction due solely to the earnings surprise at the time of the earnings announcement.

REFERENCES

Abarbanell, J. and B. Bushee (1997), 'Fundamental Analysis, Future Earnings, and Stock Prices', *Journal of Accounting Research* (Spring), pp. 1–24.

_______ _______ (1998), 'Abnormal Returns to a Fundamental Analysis Strategy', *The Accounting Review* (January), pp. 19–45.

Beckman, J. (1998), 'A Comparison of Consolidated and Parent-only Earnings Forecasts for Japanese Firms', *The Journal of Financial Statement Analysis* (Spring), pp. 17–27.

Bernard, V. and J. Thomas (1989), 'Post-earnings-announcement Drift: Delayed Price Response or Risk Premium?' *Journal of Accounting Research* (Supplement), pp. 1–36.

_______ _______ (1990), 'Evidence that Stock Prices Do Not Fully Reflect the Implications of Current Earnings for Future Earnings', *Journal of Accounting and Economics*, pp. 387–404.

_______ _______ and J. Whalen (1997), 'Accounting-based Stock Price Anomalies: Separating Market Inefficiencies From Risk', *Contemporary Accounting Research* (Summer), pp. 89–136.

Chan, L., Y. Hamao and J. Lakonishok (1993), 'Can Fundamentals Predict Japanese Stock Returns?' *Financial Analysts Journal*, 49 (July/August), pp. 63–69.

Choi, F. D. S., C. Frost and G. Meek (1999), *International Accounting* (Prentice-Hall, Upper Saddle River, NJ).

Cohen, R. and C. Polk (1995), 'An Investigation of the Impact of Industry Factors in Asset-pricing Tests', Working Paper (University of Chicago).

Conroy R. and R. Harris (1995), 'Analysts' Earnings Forecasts in Japan: Accuracy and Sell-side Optimism', *Pacific-Basin Finance Journal*, Vol. 3, pp. 392–408.

_______ K. Eades and R. Harris (2000), 'A Test of the Relative Pricing Effects of Dividends and Earnings: Evidence From Simultaneous Announcements in Japan', *Journal of Finance*, Vol. 55, pp. 1199–227.

Daniel, K., M. Grinblatt, S. Titman and R. Wermers (1997), 'Measuring Mutual Fund Performance with Characteristic-based Benchmarks', *Journal of Finance* (July) pp. 1035–58.

Ely, K. and G. Pownall (1999), 'The Value Relevance of Consolidated vs. Unconsolidated Earnings and Book Values for Japanese Firms: Evidence From Crosslisted and Non-crosslisted Firms', Working Paper (Emory University).

Fama, E. and J. MacBeth (1973), 'Risk, Return and Equilibrium: Empirical Tests', *Journal of Political Economy*, Vol. 71 (May/June), pp. 607–36.

French, K. and J. Poterba (1991), 'Were Japanese Stock Prices Too High?' *Journal of Financial Economics*, Vol. 29, pp. 337–63.

Hall, C., Y. Hamao and T. Harris (1994), 'A Comparison of Relations Between Security Market Prices, Returns, and Accounting Measures in Japan and the United States', *Journal of International Financial Management and Accounting*, Vol. 5, pp. 47–73.

Hribar, P. (2000), 'The Market Pricing of the Components of Accruals', Working Paper (Cornell University).

Kasnik, R. and M. McNichols (1999), 'Does Meeting Expectations Matter? Evidence From Analyst Forecast Revisions and Share Prices', Working Paper (Stanford University).

Kothari, S.P. (2000), 'Capital Markets Research in Accounting', Prepared for the Journal of Accounting & Economics Conference (April 28–29).

Kraft, A., A. Leone and C. Wasley (2001), 'On the Use of Mishkin's Rational Expectations Approach to Testing Efficient-Markets Hypotheses in Accounting Research', Working Paper (University of Rochester).

Lowe, H. (1990), 'Shortcomings of Japanese Consolidated Financial Statements', *Accounting Horizons*, Vol. 4, pp. 1–9.

McKinnon, J. (1984), 'Application of Anglo-American Principles of Consolidation to Corporate Financial Disclosure in Japan', *Abacus*, Vol. 20, pp. 16–33.

Mishkin, F. (1983), *A Rational Expectations Approach to Macroeconomics: Testing Policy Effectiveness and Efficient Markets Models* (Chicago, IL: University of Chicago Press for the National Bureau of Economic Research).

Ou, J. and S. Penman (1989), 'Financial Statement Analysis and the Prediction of Stock Returns', *Journal of Accounting and Economic*, pp. 295–329.

Sloan, R. (1996), 'Do Stock Prices Fully Reflect Information in Accruals and Cash Flows About Future Earnings?' *The Accounting Review* (July), pp. 289–315.

Stober, T. (1992), 'Summary Financial Statement Measures and Analysts' Forecasts of Earnings', *Journal of Accounting and Economics*, pp. 347–72.

Thomas, W.B. (1999), 'A Test of the Market's Mispricing of Domestic and Foreign Earnings', *Journal of Accounting and Economics*, pp. 243–67.

Xie, H. (2000), 'Are Discretionary Accruals Mispriced? A Reexamination', Working Paper (University of Arizona).

C
Other Asian Countries

Journal of International Financial Management and Accounting 9:3 1998

Corporate Accounting Disclosure in ASEAN

*Russell Craig and Joselito Diga**
The Australian National University

Abstract

This article analyses corporate annual report disclosure practices in five ASEAN countries: Singapore, Malaysia, Indonesia, the Philippines and Thailand. The purpose is twofold. First, to ascertain the extent, pattern and nature of corporate disclosure in ASEAN. Second, to reveal whether existing disclosure requirements would be conducive to accounting harmonisation in the ASEAN region. Data sources are the annual reports of 145 public companies listed on ASEAN stock exchanges, and disclosure requirements in companies legislation and stock market regulations. A disclosure checklist and a model are used to analyse disclosure practices. The results reinforce and extend extant international studies of disclosure practices. They are thought likely to benefit those seeking to operate public companies in ASEAN and those contemplating accounting harmonisation in ASEAN.

I. Introduction

This paper analyses existing corporate disclosure regulations in five Association of South East Asian Nations (ASEAN) countries: Singapore, Malaysia, the Philippines, Indonesia and Thailand. The aim is to catalogue the nature and extent of existing disclosure requirements and to identify common regional patterns and differences in both financial and non-financial disclosures required by various company laws, securities market regulations and accounting standards as at 31 December 1993.

The principal data sources relied upon for each country were:

For Singapore:	The Institute of Certified Public Accountants' Statements of Accounting Standards (ICPAS), and The Singapore *Companies Act* (Ninth Schedule)
For Malaysia:	Malaysian Association of Certified Public Accountants' and Malaysian Institute of Accountants' Malaysian Accounting Standards, and The Malaysian *Companies Act* (Ninth Schedule)

* Russell Craig is a Professor of Accounting and Joselito Diga is a Research Associate of the Department of Commerce, The Australian National University, Canberra, ACT 0200, Australia.

For Indonesia:	Indonesian Institute of Accountants' Indonesian Accounting Principles, and *Bapepam* Regulations on the Form and Content of Financial Statements
For the Philippines:	Accounting Standards Council Statements of Financial Accounting Standards, and Philippine Securities Exchange Commission Regulations on the Form and Content of Financial Statements
For Thailand:	Institute of Certified Accountants and Auditors of Thailand Financial Accounting Standards, and Thai Stock Exchange Commission Regulations on Financial Statements.

Thus, Companies Acts requirements were relied upon principally in Malaysia and Singapore whilst in Indonesia, Thailand and the Philippines, the more detailed guidelines of the relevant securities market laws were the principal data sources.[1]

There are two principal motivating forces for the paper. First, to extend understanding of the explanators for corporate disclosures in annual reports. Unlike the *national* focus of almost all previous similar studies, the paper focuses on disclosures in a *regional grouping* of countries (ASEAN): it also provides the first major analysis of the nature and level of non-financial and social disclosures in the ASEAN region. Second, to help determine the extent to which accounting disclosure rules and practices might impede accounting harmonisation in ASEAN. This is an important contemporary policy issue, for success in achieving harmonisation seems likely to help economic development in the region. Whether *measurement* harmony should be given preferential emphasis over *disclosure* harmony is not addressed here.[2] Nonetheless, it is important to acknowledge that establishment of an appropriate and harmonious disclosure regime is important to the success of ASEAN's emerging capital markets.

Method

The authoritative sources cited above were scrutinised to identify specific disclosures required in at least one of the five ASEAN countries. The 530 items noted were compiled into a disclosure checklist which is available on request to the second author. The extent of compliance with these disclosure requirements was determined from an examination of the consolidated annual reports of 145 companies selected randomly from companies listed on principal national stock exchanges as at 31 December

Table 1. *Sample ASEAN Companies—Industry Classification*

Industry	*Indonesia (n = 30)*	*Malaysia (n = 30)*	*Philippines (n = 30)*	*Sing. (n = 30)*	*Thailand (n = 25)*	*Total (n = 145)*
1. Diversified holdings	2	11	6	9	2	30
2. Banking & finance	4	4	3	2	13	26
3. Manufacturing	15	6	6	7	5	39
4. Utilities	0	2	2	1	0	5
5. Natural resources	1	1	5	0	1	8
6. Property development	3	4	6	4	2	19
7. Other services	5	2	2	7	2	18

1993 (30 companies each were chosen from Singapore, Malaysia, The Philippines, and Indonesia, and 25 were chosen from Thailand). The companies sampled were from the seven industry groups shown in Table 1 and reflect the industry-mix of each country's stock exchange.

Indonesia was represented strongly by manufacturing-type entities; Malaysia and Singapore by diversified conglomerates; and Thailand by banks and financial institutions. The proportion of companies in the sample group with one or more overseas subsidiaries was highest in Singapore (20%), followed by Malaysia (19%), Thailand (9%), Indonesia (5%) and the Philippines (4%).

Some important caveats need to be mentioned immediately. First, exclusive use of publicly-listed companies limits the generalisability of the results. However, there are advantages in limiting the study in this way. From an international investment perspective, it is the financial reporting behaviour of publicly-listed companies that is of primary importance to international portfolio investors and creditors. Further, the selection of publicly-listed companies automatically controls for the potential confounding effects of differences between listed and unlisted companies, thus simplifying the interpretation of results. A second limitation is that of cross-sectionality: only the reporting practices for the financial year ended 1993 were examined.

II. Extent and Nature of Disclosure Requirements

De Jure Disclosure

Details of the items required to be disclosed in each country, and as a consequence of what regulatory authority, are available on request to the second author. Table 2 provides a summary, in aggregate, of how many of

Table 2. *Extent and Sources of ASEAN Disclosure Regulation*

	Items required Max = 530		*By accounting standards*		*By government regulations*	
	n	%	*n*	%	*n*	%
Indonesia	275	52	165	31	233	44
Malaysia	388	73	330	62	218	41
Philippines	358	68	314	59	189	36
Singapore	393	74	330	62	203	38
Thailand	345	65	312	59	200	38

the 530 items were required to be disclosed in each country, together with a summary of the authoritative source requiring each disclosure.

Singapore had the most extensive set of specific disclosure requirements: 393 of the 530 items (74%) were to be disclosed. It was followed closely by Malaysia (73%), the Philippines (68%), Thailand (65%) and Indonesia (52%). The obligation to disclose in most countries appeared to stem principally from the imprimatur given through Companies Acts and other legislation to accounting standards promulgated by professional accounting bodies. The extent to which disclosure requirements were sourced in professionally-derived accounting standards was lowest in Indonesia (31%), which lagged well behind the other four countries. Only in Indonesia did the proportion of government-sourced requirements (44%) exceed those emanating from a professional accounting body (31%).

There was a relatively high degree of consensus among the five countries in terms of shared disclosure requirements. About 33% (n = 177) of the 530 disclosure items were common to all five countries. In comparison, only 18% (n = 95) of these requirements were unique to any one country. The proportion of total disclosure items common to at least three countries was 68% (n = 359).

Table 3 cross-tabulates the proportion of requirements shared between any two particular ASEAN countries. The *columns* show the proportion of requirements in each country that are common with another. Thus, from the bottom row, 83% of Indonesia's requirements are common with those of Malaysia, the Philippines, Singapore and Thailand. The similar statistic for Thailand is (80%), for Malaysia (75%), Singapore (74%) and the Philippines (71%). The higher percentage for Indonesia reflects the smaller total of disclosure requirements in that country. The *rows* display the proportion of requirements in each country that is required also in the other ASEAN countries. Thus, from the extreme right hand column, 61% of requirements in Malaysia, the Philippines, Singapore, and Thailand are identical with those in Indonesia.

Singapore shares the highest proportion of its requirements with other ASEAN countries (85%), closely followed by Malaysia (84%), Thailand (78%), the Philippines (73%), and then Indonesia (61%). This suggests that some ASEAN countries "obtain" their disclosure requirements from Singapore or from the same sources which Singapore uses. The high proportions for Malaysia, Singapore and Thailand appear to reflect the way these countries have strongly incorporated International Accounting Standards (IAS) disclosure requirements into their domestic rules. To confirm the extent to which ASEAN countries rely on IAS-prescribed requirements, a checklist comprising 200 specific IAS disclosures was prepared.[3] Specific disclosure requirements in each country, whether government or privately-sourced, were compared to this IAS disclosure checklist. Results are presented in Table 4.

As expected, in Malaysia (89%), Singapore (93%) and Thailand (86%), IAS disclosure requirements reflected significantly greater input than for the Philippines (69%) and Indonesia (55%). However, the data

Table 3. *Correlation Matrix of Disclosure Requirements in ASEAN*

	Indonesia	*Malaysia*	*Philippines*	*Singapore*	*Thailand*	*Average (Row)*
Indonesia	–	59	63	58	66	61
Malaysia	83	–	74	92	90	84
Philippines	82	68	–	67	75	73
Singapore	83	93	74	–	90	85
Thailand	83	80	72	79	–	78
Average (Column)	83	75	71	74	80	–

Table 4. *Use of IAS Disclosure Requirements in ASEAN*

Country	*No. of IAS Disclosures Required (n = 200)*	*Proportion of IAS Disclosures (%)*
Indonesia	110	55
Malaysia	178	89
Philippines	138	69
Singapore	186	93
Thailand	172	86

reported in Table 4 are drawn from annual reports for the year ending prior to 31 December 1993 and do not necessarily reflect developments since then. For example, Indonesia's adoption of IAS in 1995 would almost inevitably have caused the proportion of IAS disclosure requirements in that country to rise.

Stock Exchange Requirements. ASEAN stock exchanges are often a significant source of disclosure requirements: they determine company listing criteria, impose continuing reporting obligations, and mandate specific items of disclosure. Stock exchange requirements in the five countries have much in common, but important differences as well, as evidenced by Table 5.

Disclosure requirements imposed by ASEAN stock exchanges range over both financial and non-financial information. Commendably, they specify the need to provide interim financial reports and forecast information. However, co-ordination of stock exchange disclosure requirements in ASEAN would enhance prospects of accounting harmony. There appears ample scope to harmonise disclosure requirements on R&D (1c), corporate social responsibility (1f), management information (2a/b), prospective investors (3e), interim reports (4d), and segment information (4g). In view of the growing importance of competitive capital markets as a source of finance, ASEAN stock exchanges will probably play an increasingly important role in shaping the development of financial reporting in ASEAN.

Summary. A high level of harmony exists in the disclosure requirements of the five ASEAN countries. Nonetheless, there are important national differences in the volume and extent of disclosure, and in sources of authority. The influence of IAS in Malaysia, Singapore and Thailand is reflected in their similar disclosure requirements. Other than in Indonesia, the extent of disclosure requirements appears to be determined largely by the accounting profession. ASEAN governments appear disposed to delegate the formulation of detailed accounting requirements to professional accounting bodies or to stock exchanges. However, in some cases, government-based regulations overlap professionally recommended requirements, thus reinforcing the authoritativeness of extant professional regulations. In other cases, regulatory agencies promulgate requirements distinct from those established by professional bodies, particularly in areas where governments are seeking to enforce and monitor progress towards specific regulatory objectives.[4]

Overall, the level of *de jure* disclosure harmony (that is, harmony in terms of what is *required* to be disclosed) in ASEAN is high. It does not

Table 5. *ASEAN Stock Exchanges Disclosure Requirements**

Requirements	*INDO (JSE)*	*MAL (KLSE)*	*PHIL (PSE)*	*SING (SES)*	*THAI (SET)*
1. GENERAL INFORMATION					
(a) Company history	YES	YES	YES	YES	YES
(b) Outline of business	YES	YES	YES	YES	YES
(c) Research and development	NO	YES	NO	YES	YES
(d) Employee-labour relations	YES	YES	YES	YES	YES
(e) Capital expenditures	YES	YES	YES	YES	YES
(f) Corporate social responsibility	NO	NO	NO	YES	YES
(g) Pending or potential litigation	Pending	Pending	Pending	Pending	Pending
(h) Dependence on major customers	YES	YES	YES	YES	YES
2. INFORMATION ON MANAGERS/DIRECTOR					
(a) Names, salaries and functional responsibilities of managers	YES (Not salaries)	YES	YES (Not salaries)	YES	YES (Not salaries)
(b) Names, salaries and major outside affiliations of directors	YES (Not salaries)	YES	YES (Not salaries)	YES	YES (Not salaries)
3. INFORMATION ON COMPANY'S CAPITAL					
(a) General information on capitalisation	YES	YES	YES	YES	YES
(b) Statement of changes in share capital	YES	YES	YES	YES	YES
(c) Number and types of shareholders	YES	YES	YES	YES	YES
(d) Names and size of holdings of largest stockholders	YES	YES	YES	YES	YES
(e) Names and particulars of parties seeking to obtain substantial interest	NO	YES	NO	YES	NO
4. FINANCIAL INFORMATION					
(a) Historical summary of important operating and financial data	YES	YES	YES	YES	YES
(b) Audited financial statements (balance sheet and profit and loss statement)	YES	YES	YES	YES	YES
(c) Statement of cash flows	YES	YES	YES	YES	YES
(d) Interim reports (quarterly or semi-annually)	Quarterly	Semi-annual	Quarterly	Semi-annual	Quarterly
(e) Post-balance sheet events	YES	YES	YES	YES	YES
(f) Consolidated statements	YES	YES	YES	YES	YES
(g) Segment information	NO	YES	NO	YES	NO
(h) Pro forma statements of any major financing,recapitalisation, acquisition, or reorganisation	NO	NO	NO	NO	NO
5. RECENT DEVELOPMENT AND PROSPECTS					
(a) Significant information that may affect the market for a company's securities	YES	YES	YES	YES	YES
(b) Discussion of major factors which will influence next year's results	YES	YES	YES	YES	YES
(c) Profit forecast	YES	YES	YES	YES	YES

Sources: Stock Exchange Listing Manuals: Jakarta Stock Exchange (JSE); Kuala Lumpur Stock Exchange (KLSE); Philippine Stock Exchange (PSE); Stock Exchange of Singapore (SES); Stock Exchange of Thailand (SET).

*Table format adapted from Choi and Mueller (1992)

follow, however, that actual or *de facto* disclosure practices (that is, what *is* disclosed) also enjoy a high level of harmony. The following section highlights the gap between regulatory harmony (*de jure* harmony), reported above, and practice harmony (*de facto* harmony).

III. Disclosures of Commonly Required Items: *De Facto* Disclosure

Financial

The extent to which ASEAN companies disclosed "substantially common" requirements was determined from scrutiny of disclosures made in the 145 sampled annual reports. These "substantially common" items comprised 270 specific disclosure requirements which were common to at least four of the five ASEAN countries.[5] Results are presented in Table 6.

The mean level of disclosure ranged from 51% (Indonesia) to 61% (Singapore). That is, on average, only just over one-half of substantially common requirements across ASEAN are disclosed routinely in the annual reports of any ASEAN country. "Between country" differences are revealed as very highly statistically significant. These differences possibly reflect different conclusions about whether expected regulatory costs (e.g., audit costs) associated with the 270 specific disclosures exceed the perceived benefits of ensuring all items are disclosed.

ASEAN policy-makers need to consider whether the reported levels of disclosure of common requirements signal a need to strengthen their regulatory and enforcement activities. Clearly, the cost of doing so needs to be weighed against the benefits of improved levels of disclosure. If the likelihood of achieving disclosure practice harmony is increased, then this seems conducive to improving the climate for investment.

Table 6. *Compliance with 270 Common Disclosure Requirements in ASEAN (in %)*

Country	*Min*	*Max*	*Mean*	*Std Dev*
Indonesia (n = 30)	35.2	75.9	50.9	10.3
Malaysia (n = 30)	44.8	70.4	58.7	7.1
Philippines (n = 30)	33.7	69.6	55.2	8.4
Singapore (n = 30)	41.5	73.7	61.3	9.4
Thailand (n = 25)	46.3	73.0	56.4	5.9
ANOVA (F-ratio)	6.36 ($p < .001$)			
KW (Chi-square)	21.2 ($p < .001$)			

Social and non-financial

There have been few studies of disclosure of social and non-financial information by ASEAN companies. One exception is Teoh and Thong's (1984) study of corporate social reporting in Malaysia, which generally indicated that few disclosures were made about social responsibility issues. More information about corporate disclosure performance would be timely and useful. In the absence of an agreed upon checklist of desirable social and non-financial disclosures, the minimum disclosure items recommended by the United Nations (UN) (1977) Intergovernmental Group of Experts on International Standards of Accounting and Reporting are invoked here as an evaluative benchmark of disclosure performance. The UN (1977) recommended nine sets of non-financial and social disclosures, (a) to (i) below. A tenth set of items, "production and operational statistics" [(j) below], is added here for completeness. Scrutiny of the 145 ASEAN company annual reports revealed substantial variations in disclosure of social and non-financial items *within* each country and *between* the countries generally (see Table 7).

(a) Value-added statement. Only Singaporean companies (47%) disclosed value-added statements in the normal course of reporting, presumably in accordance with RAP 3 (*Reporting Value Added Information*), issued by ACPAS. Other ASEAN countries might contemplate providing such information.

(b) Organisational structure. All ASEAN companies surveyed disclosed some information on this matter. The most extensive disclosures were by Malaysian and Singaporean companies who provided biographical profiles of each director (including posts held in other companies).

(c) Ownership. In general, disclosure of ownership information was high in Singapore (100%), Malaysia (97%) and Indonesia (90%). Details of principal shareholders were often provided. However, disclosure levels were very low in the Philippines (17%) and Thailand (16%). The UN (1977) recommended that information on the ultimate parent company and major shareholders be disclosed. This information is required by company laws in Malaysia and Singapore and by stock exchange regulations in Indonesia, the Philippines and Thailand. Nonetheless, in Indonesia and Malaysia, some companies did not disclose this information in their annual reports, possibly because the conduit for disclosure of ownership information to securities agencies and stock exchanges is by means other than annual reports.

(d) Transfer pricing and related party transactions. The UN (1977) recommended disclosure of the amount of intra-group transactions and

Table 7. *Incidence of Social and Non-Financial Disclosures in ASEAN*

	Indonesia n = 30		*Malaysia* n = 30		*Philippines* n = 30		*Singapore* n = 30		*Thailand* n = 25		*Total* n = 145	
Type of Information	*n*	%	*n*	%	*n*	%	*n*	%	*n*	%	*n*	%
Value added statements	0	0	0	0	0	0	14	47	0	0	14	10
Organisational structure	30	100	30	100	30	100	30	100	25	100	145	100
Ownership details	27	90	29	97	5	17	30	100	4	16	95	66
Transfer pricing policies	13	43	0	0	2	7	0	0	0	0	15	10
Labour and employment	17	57	7	23	15	50	13	43	14	56	66	46
Technology transfers	18	60	13	43	7	23	8	27	3	12	49	34
Government subsidies	1	3	0	0	8	27	0	0	0	0	9	6
Environmental measures	7	23	3	10	7	23	5	17	3	12	25	17
Investment program and future plans	30	100	30	100	29	97	27	90	23	92	139	96
Production and operational statistics	15	50	20	67	18	60	15	50	6	24	74	51

group policy with regard to transfer price determination. Few ASEAN companies surveyed disclosed this information. An exception was in Indonesia, where 47% of companies provided information about intra-group transfers made at market rates. The disclosure performance of ASEAN companies on this matter is poor, particularly in view of the probability that many maintain detailed records of transfer pricing arrangements to comply with tax regulations. Anecdotal evidence suggests that enforcement of transfer pricing tax regulations is quite lax.[6]

(e) Labour and employment. The UN (1977) recommended disclosure of information on trade unions, employees, employee training programs and other labour relations issues. About half of the companies surveyed disclosed some form of employee information, although not necessarily in accord with the UN's recommendations. For example, none of the disclosures dealt with company policy on recognising workers' "rights to organise".[7] The disclosures made were generally of a "public relations" nature concerning company training programs, incentive schemes and company-provided fringe benefits. A few companies, particularly those in manufacturing and primary industries, also disclosed information on employee health and safety.

(f) Technology transfers. Levels of disclosure of inward and outward transfers of technology were fairly modest, except in Indonesia and Malaysia, where they are influenced by stringent government regulations. As a pre-condition for sanctioning joint-venture agreements, the Indonesian government usually wants to be satisfied that there is an agreement for technology transfers to flow to Indonesia from the foreign joint-venture partner. The Malaysian government is also very interested in ascertaining whether companies with foreign equity are engaged in higher value-added activities: it requires many affected companies to disclose information about licensing and technology agreements with foreign companies.

(g) Government Subsidies. The UN (1977) recommended disclosure of accounting policies relating to government grants and subsidies (nature, extent, unfulfilled conditions and project coverage). Specific guidelines based on IAS 20 are recommended in Indonesia, Malaysia and Singapore, but, as evidenced by the low level of disclosure, are adopted infrequently. This finding could indicate that companies do not receive any form of government assistance or that they are reluctant to disclose such information because of political sensitivities.

(h) Environmental measures. The UN (1977) proposed that companies disclose information on their environmental activities and relevant cost data, where available. However, only 17% of the ASEAN companies disclosed

any information on environmental programs. Those who did were engaged in manufacturing, mining, utilities and transport activities. They provided information on their attempts to reduce waste discharges, restore the physical environment (e.g., through reforestation programs), and raise the level of environmental consciousness among employees (e.g., through support for relevant staff training). There were no disclosures of specific financial data relating to environmental programs and activities.

(i) Investment program. A very large proportion (96%) of ASEAN companies disclosed information on future capital expenditures and on-going projects. Most companies discussed future strategies in the context of their response to economic and market changes.

(j) Production and operational statistics. A slim majority (51%) of ASEAN companies provided some operational and production statistics. The style of presentation and the nature of the information disclosed varied widely. Some companies reported specific developments for each major division or product line whereas others provided only a general discussion of group production activities. Those most inclined to provide comprehensive disclosures of specific operational data were utility and transport companies, whereas manufacturing companies were more inclined to provide only highly aggregated data.

Overall, ASEAN companies appear to disclose non-financial and social information that they perceive to provide a sound basis for evaluating their future financial performance and capability (*viz.*, the more frequent disclosure of information on organisational structure and management, investment programs, and operational and production achievements). Understandably, companies appeared reluctant to disclose information that was perceived to be politically or socially sensitive (*viz.*, information relating to labour and employment activities, environmental programs, transfer pricing policies, government subsidies received and distribution of enterprise value added). These results are generally consistent with the findings of Teoh and Thong (1984) and point to corporate financial reporting in ASEAN being oriented strongly towards the information needs of capital providers, rather than the needs of a broader set of stake-holders (including employees, government agencies, and the general community).

IV. An Explanatory Model of ASEAN Disclosure Levels

This section reports on our development and testing of a model of factors influencing levels of disclosure in ASEAN. The model has several unique features, including a "country of origin" variable. It seeks to explain and help predict variation in levels of *de facto* disclosure observed within each ASEAN country and to assist those seeking to improve corporate accounting disclosure in ASEAN. The results reinforce and extend previous disclosure model studies, such as those of Wallace (1988), Cooke (1989), and Ahmed and Nicholls (1994).

(1) Dependent Variable.

The dependent variable, D, disclosure level, was measured using the checklist of 530 individual items of financial disclosures which are required in at least one of the five ASEAN countries. The individual disclosure items were treated as dichotomous and additive, such that the total disclosure score or index, D, of a company is:

$$D = \sum_{i=1}^{530} d_i$$

where $d_i = 1$ if the *i*th item is disclosed
$d_i = 0$ if the *i*th item is not disclosed.

The disclosure index was unweighted,[8] assumed all items applied with relevance to all companies,[9] and was based on raw scores.[10] The most specific or disaggregated disclosure requirement of any country was used in the checklist to improve the sensitivity of the index.[11]

(2) Independent Variables

(i) Company Size. Size is believed to be correlated positively with levels of disclosure. A large enterprise is generally more complex than a small one, resulting in a need to report more information. Further, the larger a company, the higher its political costs will be and the greater will be the threat of adverse regulatory action (Watts and Zimmerman, 1978). Large companies seem likely to respond to regulatory threats by "voluntarily" increasing their level of disclosure. Two size proxies were used for each company: "total assets" and "sales (net of sales returns)".[12] The asset amounts were unadjusted because of insufficient data to reflect the impact of different accounting methods of asset valuation and revenue recognition. The specific hypothesis tested was:

H1: The level of disclosure by a publicly-listed ASEAN company is associated *positively* with the company's *size* measured in financial terms.

(ii) Degree of leverage. As a company's debt level increases relative to shareholders' equity, it is likely that levels of disclosure will increase to provide greater assurance to debt holders of the company's ability to satisfy its debt obligations (Watts and Zimmerman, 1990). The degree of leverage was measured here by the company's debt-to-equity ratio (computed by dividing total liabilities by total shareholders' funds). The specific hypothesis tested was:

H2: The level of disclosure by a publicly-listed ASEAN company is associated *positively* with the company's *degree of leverage.*

(iii) Industry Membership. This has been suggested as a more appropriate proxy for political cost sensitivity than size measured in accounting terms (Ball and Foster, 1982). For example, specific industries, such as banking, are politically more sensitive than others, thereby encouraging greater levels of disclosure by firms in that industry. Further, a company with diversified interests seems likely to have a greater volume of financial information to report than an undiversified company. The specific hypothesis tested was:

H3: The level of disclosure by a publicly-listed ASEAN company is associated with the company's *industry.*

(iv) International operations. It seems likely that a company's presence in international markets will increase its level of disclosure. Zarzeski (1996) found that companies with high levels of foreign sales to total sales provided significantly high levels of investor-oriented disclosures. Because companies in Indonesia, the Philippines and Thailand did not routinely disclose segment information to allow the proportion of foreign sales to total sales to be determined, a different proxy variable was used: whether or not a company had an overseas-based subsidiary. The specific hypothesis tested was:

H4: The level of disclosure by a publicly-listed ASEAN company is associated *positively* with whether the company *operates internationally* through an overseas-based subsidiary.

(v) Foreign Ownership. This has been suggested as an important influence on disclosure behaviour (Cooke, 1992; Ahmed and Nicholls, 1994). Differences in disclosure levels between foreign-owned and locally-owned companies could arise because a foreign subsidiary is required to report in accordance with the regulations of both the host country and the country in which its parent company is domiciled as well. Also,

political cost arguments suggest that the relationship between MNCs and host country governments would encourage additional disclosures (Dunning 1993; Gray et al., 1984). The specific hypothesis tested was:

H5: The level of disclosure by a publicly-listed ASEAN company is associated with whether the company is *locally-owned* or *foreign-owned.*

(vi) Country of origin. A company's country of origin or the location of its headquarters is likely to be an important factor explaining disclosure levels. This view is consistent with the "culturally grounded" view of international accounting practice which argues that factors in the national environment directly affect disclosure levels. The specific hypothesis tested was:

H6: The level of disclosure by a publicly-listed ASEAN company is associated with the *country* where the company has its headquarters.

Statistical methods

Univariate. Parametric and non-parametric tests determined whether there were statistically significant differences among countries in terms of their disclosure scores, assets, turnover and debt-to-equity ratios. The Kruskall-Wallis test was used for untransformed variables because it did not require the assumption of normality. One-way ANOVA was used after the continuous variables were log-transformed and satisfied normality assumptions. Multiple range tests using Tukey's procedure were applied to discern pairwise differences between countries.

Multivariate. Multiple regression analysis revealed that the dependent and independent variables were exponential. The model was simplified by logarithmic transformation to establish a linear model of the form

$$\log Y = \alpha + \beta_1 \log X_1 + \beta_2 \log X_2 + \beta_3 \log X_3 + \log \varepsilon$$

for analysis using OLS regression. This transformation provided a more parsimonious model with greater explanatory power. ANOVA tests for possible interactions between the continuous and dummy variables were not statistically significant ($p \leqslant 0.05$).

The assumptions underlying the regression model were tested for multicollinearity, heteroscedasticity, non-normal distribution of residuals, outliers and influential observations. A plot of the studentised residuals against predicted values did not show any unusual distribution pattern, thus supporting the assumption of constant variance in the error distribution. The Breusch-Pagan (1979) test statistic of 2.36 ($p = 0.14$) supported the assumption of homoscedasticity. A histogram and normal probability plot of the studentised residuals showed that the distribution of residuals did not differ markedly from a normal distribution. The Kolmogorov-Smirnov Lilliefors (KSL) test statistic of 0.052 ($p \leq 0.01$) also supported a conclusion that the residuals were normally distributed. A casewise plot of standardised residuals revealed one case with a relatively high residual. However, the computed Cook's Distance statistic of this observation (Cd = 0.12) indicated that it was not highly influential,[13] and thus it was not necessary to revise the multiple regression equation to account for its effects separately.

Multicollinearity in explanatory variables was diagnosed through analyses of correlation factors and variance inflation factors (VIF), consistent with Weisberg (1985, pp. 196–200). Table 8 presents the correlation matrix of the dependent and continuous independent variables, including statistics regarding the Multiple R, Adjusted R^2 and VIFs.

There was some evidence of multicollinearity. Asset size and turnover, not surprisingly, were highly correlated (Pearson $r = 0.8072$), consistent with Buzby (1975), Wallace (1988), Cooke (1989a, 1991, 1992), and Ahmed and Nicholls (1994). Also, the debt-to-equity (DE) ratio was correlated significantly with both asset size and turnover ($p \leq 0.05$). VIFs were computed to check whether inclusion of these independent variables in the regression model would inflate the variance of regression coefficient estimators.[14] The VIFs of asset size and turnover confirmed that

Table 8. *Pairwise Pearson Correlation Coefficients Among Dependent and Continuous Explanatory Variables*

	Disclosure (ln)	*Asset size (ln)*	*Turnover (ln)*	*Debt-to-equity ratio (ln)*
Disclosure (ln)	1.0000			
Asset size (ln)	0.4685**	1.0000		
Turnover (ln)	0.5002**	0.8072**	1.0000	
Debt-to-equity (ln)	0.1637*	0.5469**	0.3584**	1.0000
Multiple $R^\dagger$		0.853	0.813	0.565
R^2 (Adjusted)		0.724	0.657	0.309
VIF		3.623	2.915	1.447

** Significant at $p \leq 0.01$ (two-tailed prob.).
* Significant at $p \leq 0.05$ (two-tailed prob.).
† Obtained by regressing each explanatory variable by the other explanatory variable.

multicollinearity would be a problem if both size variables were included. However, the VIF for the DE ratio did not indicate a significant multicollinearity problem if the DE ratio variable was included with the size variable.[15] The DE ratio variable was therefore retained in the regression model.

Principal components analysis (PCA) was used to preserve the explanatory contribution of asset size and turnover (Weisberg, 1985; Maddala, 1992).[16] Eigenvalues and the percentage of variance explained by each principal component of "latent" variable were computed to determine which latent variables would be useful in the multiple regression analysis. Asset size and turnover loaded highly on the first principal component (eigenvalue = 1.797), accounting for 90% of the original variables' total variance. While all the principal components could be used in the regression, such an approach would lack explanatory parsimony and would not guarantee better estimates of the coefficient in the original regression equation (Maddala, 1992). Also, while the first principal component was found to proxy for "size" in financial terms, it was not apparent what the second principal component was a proxy for. Using a decision rule suggested by Kaiser (1985) and Jolliffe (1972), only the first principal component (the only one whose eigenvalues exceeded 0.7) was selected. Finally, factor loadings between the principal components and the original variables were computed (Table 9).

These factor loadings represent correlations between the principal components and the original variables. Since only the first principal component was to be used as a proxy for size, the equation for this was derived:

$$\text{Size measure} = 0.948*\text{Turnover} + 0.948*\text{Asset size}$$

In summary, the first principal component could be interpreted as the latent variable that incorporates the effects of the original collinear variables of asset size and turnover. This derived variable, computed for each

Table 9. *Factor Loadings of Variables*

	Correlation Matrix of Variables	
Variables	*First p.c.*	*Second p.c.*
Turnover (ln)	0.948	0.319
Asset size (ln)	0.948	–0.319

company, was used as a proxy for company size in the regression equation. After incorporating the derived size measure, the regression model used to test the hypotheses was:

$$D = c + a_1 S + b_1 L + \sum_{i=1}^{6} w_i I_i + \sum_{j=1}^{2} x_j F_j + \sum_{k=1}^{2} y_k O_k + \sum_{l=1}^{4} z_l N_l + \varepsilon$$

where

Dependent variable

D *Disclosure* score (1n)

Company-specific variables

S *Size* measure derived using PCA

L *Leverage* measured using debt-to-equity ratio (1n)

I_i *Industry group*

0 = Diversified holding (default level)
1 = Banks and financial institutions
2 = Manufacturing
3 = Utilities (power, water, telecom)
4 = Natural resources (mining, agriculture, fishing)
5 = Real estate and property development
6 = Other services (construction, transport, hotels)

F_j *Foreign operation*

0 = No foreign subsidiary (default level)
1 = One or more foreign subsidiaries

O_k *Ownership group*

0 = Locally-owned (default level)
1 = Foreign-owned or controlled

Country-of-origin variable

N_l *Nation or country of origin*

0 = Indonesia (default level)
1 = Malaysia
2 = Philippines
3 = Singapore
4 = Thailand

Other terms

$c, a_l, b_l, w_i, x_j, y_k, z_l$ Coefficients to be estimated

ε Stochastic disturbance term: that part of D not explained by other explanatory variables.

The disclosure model assumes an additive effect of the indicator (dummy) variables on the dependent variable. In general, most regression studies assume additivity since the alternative of having to consider the interaction effects between one or more continuous independent variables and dummy variables expands the model's complexity. Use of four dummy variables (industry, international operations, ownership and country) and two continuous variables (company size and degree of leverage) as independent variables requires a formal test of the "homogeneous slopes" hypothesis for each set of dummy variables.[17] ANOVA testing for homogeneous slopes indicated that none of the interaction effects are significant.[18] Hence, the assumption that the effects of size and leverage is homogeneous across countries, international operation, industry groups and ownership categories was supported. As such, no interaction term needed to be included in the regression model.

Results

Descriptive statistics. Skewness and kurtosis were significant, particularly for reported assets, turnover, and DE ratios. These variables were transformed using natural logs. Normality tests of the transformed variables indicated that the resulting distribution was not markedly different from a normal distribution. The Shapiro and Wilk test (Shapiro and Wilk, 1965) and KSL test (Lilliefors, 1969) accepted the normality assumption for the log-transformed variables ($p \leq 0.05$).

Univariate Tests. Results of multiple range tests using Tukey's Pairwise Comparison are shown in Table 10.

Statistically significant differences existed among companies in terms of their disclosure scores, asset sizes, turnover or sales, and DE ratios. In terms of *disclosure scores*, Indonesian companies (46) disclosed significantly less than Malaysian (87), Singaporean (103) and Thai companies (66). Philippine companies (62) disclosed significantly less than companies in Malaysia (87) and Singapore (103), while Thai companies (66)

Table 10. *KW, ANOVA and Tukey Tests of Country Differences*

	Indo	*Mal*	*Phil*	*Sing*	*Thai*	*n*	*Chisq*	*Anova*	*Tukey sig diff pairs***
Disclosure score	46	87	62	103	66	145	33.9*	12.2*	*Indo-Thai, Indo-Mal, Indo-Sing, Phil-Mal, Phil-Sing, Thai-Sing*
Assets	60	87	47	86	88	145	24.1*	7.2*	*Indo-Mal, Indo-Sing, Indo-Mal, Phil-Mal, Phil-Sing, Phil-Thai*
Turnover	65	91	47	89	72	145	22.3*	6.6*	*Phil-Mal, Phil-Sing, Phil-Thai*
DE ratio	82	63	56	61	109	145	28.2*	9.7*	*Indo-Phil, Indo-Thai, Mal-Thai, Phil-Thai, Sing-Thai*

* Significant at $p \leq 0.01$ (two-tailed probability).
** Significant at $p \leq 0.05$ (two-tailed probability).

disclosed significantly less than those in Singapore (103). Overall, except for Malaysian companies, publicly-listed companies in all other ASEAN countries disclosed less, on average, than Singapore companies. A distinct pattern emerged. Malaysia and Singapore, whose financial accounting systems have been influenced strongly by the U.K., had higher levels of financial disclosure, on average, than the non-British group (Indonesia, the Philippines and Thailand). However, these results do not account for the impact of differences in characteristics of reporting companies.

The average *assets* of Indonesian (60) and Philippine (47) listed companies (as measured by total assets) were significantly less than companies in Malaysia (87), Singapore (86) and Thailand (88). This is possibly because Malaysia and Singapore had a greater number of diversified holding companies in the sample (20 as opposed to 10 for Indonesia, Thailand and the Philippines combined). Nonetheless, the dichotomisation of ASEAN companies in terms of their asset size is matched also by two other broad characteristics of the ASEAN countries: size of capital markets, and macroeconomic policy environment. Indonesian and Philippine stock markets are much smaller and less sophisticated than those in Thailand, Malaysia and Singapore. This suggests that the size and stage of development of a country's capital market influences the average size of companies in that capital market. Ambient national macroeconomic policy environments also appear to contribute to observed size differences. The Indonesian and Philippine governments have traditionally pursued an import-substitution, inward-looking economic growth strategy, offering strong protection from foreign competition through tariff and other trade barriers. In contrast, Malaysia, Singapore and Thailand have pursued an export oriented, outward-looking macroeconomic strategy. As competition increases, industries are forced to rationalise through buy-outs and mergers, resulting in larger entities with greater operational and financial capabilities.

In terms of *turnover*, sales of Philippine companies (47) were significantly less than those in Singapore (89), Malaysia (91) and Thailand (72). This pattern is consistent with the asset size differences reported previously and partly appears to reflect differences in the macroeconomic environment of the Philippines compared with other ASEAN countries.

Finally, the degree of leverage of Thai companies (109) was significantly higher than the companies in other countries. This characteristic is explained by the greater proportion of banks and other financial institutions in the Thai sample. Additionally, it reflects the high economic growth rates in Thailand during the late 1980s and early 1990s when the Bank of

Thailand made credit available freely to Thai companies.[19] The leverage of Indonesian companies (82) was significantly higher than for the Philippines (56), but accorded with that of Malaysia (63) and Singapore (61). It is noteworthy that from about 1988, Indonesia revamped its financial sector and deregulated its banking system. The resultant competition among banks and financial institutions encouraged Indonesian firms to expand debt levels.[20] Philippine companies were less levered than their ASEAN counterparts, reflecting the country's tight credit environment from 1990 to 1993.

Multivariate Tests

Results from the multiple regression model are presented in Table 11.

The adjusted R^2 of 0.487 compares favourably with similar studies using disclosure indices.[21] Lower adjusted R^2 statistics were reported by

Table 11. *ASEAN Disclosure Model*

Variable	*Expected Relationship*	*Estimated Coefficient*	*Standard error*	*t-statistic*	*p-value*
Constant *(c)*	NA	4.380	0.217	20.17	<0.001**
Size *(S)*	+	0.026	0.006	4.44	<0.001**
Degree of leverage *(L)*	+	0.023	0.013	1.72	0.089*
Industry (I)					
Banks	?	–0.202	0.047	–4.31	<0.001**
Manufacturing	?	–0.113	0.039	–2.97	0.004**
Utilities	?	–0.209	0.077	–2.80	0.006**
Natural resources	?	–0.132	0.061	–2.16	0.032*
Property development	?	–0.104	0.045	–2.32	0.022*
Miscellaneous services	?	–0.139	0.045	–3.07	0.003**
Foreign Operation (F)					
One or more foreign subsidiaries	+	0.050	0.033	1.49	0.138
Ownership (O)					
Foreign owned	?	–0.102	0.041	–2.51	0.013*
Country (N)					
Malaysia	?	0.093	0.047	1.99	0.049*
Philippines	?	0.106	0.043	2.49	0.014*
Singapore	?	0.201	0.047	4.30	<0.001**
Thailand	?	0.077	0.043	1.80	0.074*
F-value: 10.75 ($p \leq 0.01$)		Adj. R^2 = 0.487			

** Significant at $p \leq 0.01$ (two-tailed prob.).
* Significant at $p \leq 0.10$ (two-tailed prob.).

Singhvi (1968) in India (0.42), Singhvi and Desai (1971) in the USA (0.43), and Wallace (1988) in Nigeria (0.07). In comparison, higher adjusted R^2 were reported by Cooke (1989a) in Sweden (0.60) and Ahmed and Nicholls (1994) in Bangladesh (0.52), possibly due to the inclusion of extra independent variables in regression models: for example, for multiple listing status, number of subsidiaries owned by the parent company, and number of shareholders (Cooke, 1989a) and for qualifications of principal accounting officer and size of audit firm (Ahmed and Nicholls, 1994).

H1: ***Size.*** As predicted, the effect of company size on disclosure level was positive and highly statistically significant ($p \leq 0.01$), consistent with previous studies in the USA, U.K., Canada, India, Nigeria, Sweden and Japan. These results strengthen the argument that size, measured in financial terms, is important in determining corporate disclosure levels regardless of a company's country of origin. However, the actual reason why size is important could vary from one country to another. Size could proxy for the breadth and complexity of company operations in one country and for political cost in another.

H2: ***Degree of Financial Leverage.*** The sign of the correlation coefficient, as predicted, was positive, consistent with the view that more highly levered companies disclose significantly more financial information. However, the result, whilst strong, was not statistically significant ($p = 0.089$). The positive correlation was consistent with Courtis (1979) for New Zealand, Chow and Wong-Boren (1987) for Mexico, and Ahmed and Nicholls (1994) for Bangladesh, but was inconsistent with Belkaoui and Kahl (1978) for Canada. The corpus of these results suggests that degree of leverage influences the amount of financial disclosure in a way which is country-specific.

H3: ***Industry Group.*** The industry effects were all statistically significant ($p \leq 0.05$) or highly statistically significant ($p \leq 0.01$), consistent with an association between industry group and financial disclosure levels. The signs of the correlation coefficients for individual industry categories revealed that companies with diversified interests disclosed significantly more than non-diversified companies who were engaged in one principal activity only, as surmised. The potential influence of political cost, where industry group proxies for political cost, was discernible also. Companies with higher political cost, in terms of threat of increased regulatory scrutiny, such as banks and utilities, were argued to be likely to disclose more than companies with lower political cost. However, surprisingly, "banks" and "utilities" were the industry groups with the lowest levels of disclosure, despite being very highly regulated in ASEAN. The results are consistent with conjecture that highly regulated companies probably use alternative channels for communicating financial and other information (e.g., through special reports to government) thereby obviating the need to make extensive disclosures in general-purpose financial reports.

H4: ***International operations.*** As predicted, companies with at least one overseas subsidiary disclosed more than those with no overseas subsidiary. The result is not statistically significant ($p \leqslant 0.138$), but is consistent generally with the findings of Saudagaran (1988) and Zarzeski (1996). It can be explained by three factors: first, the different proxy variable used (i.e., presence of an overseas subsidiary rather than proportion of foreign sales to total sales); second, by the relatively small contribution of overseas subsidiaries to overall financial results (e.g., segment disclosures in Malaysia revealed that over 50% of enterprise revenues were generated domestically); and third, that the overseas subsidiaries are usually financed by the parent entity. ASEAN companies with overseas subsidiaries are generally not cross-listed in the country where their subsidiary is located.[22]

H5: ***Foreign Ownership.*** The effect of foreign ownership was highly statistically significant ($p = 0.013$), but, somewhat curiously, the sign of the coefficient was the opposite of that reported for Bangladesh by Ahmed and Nicholls (1993). That is, foreign-owned companies in ASEAN tend to disclose *less* than locally-owned companies. This suggests that ASEAN governments are disposed to accommodate foreign interests through more lenient regulatory enforcement, possibly as an inducement to attract foreign investment. The climate for foreign investment in ASEAN appears to be more "foreign investor–friendly" than in many developing countries outside ASEAN. The push to create the ASEAN Free Trade AREA (AFTA) provides further evidence that

ASEAN governments have adopted a concerted policy to attract more foreign direct investment (Yuan, 1994).

H6: ***Country of Origin.*** The effect of country of origin was statistically significant for all countries other than Thailand. Singapore companies provided the highest levels of disclosure. Malaysian, Philippine and Thai companies all provided moderate levels of disclosure. These findings are consistent with the hypothesis that factors in the national environment are significant explanatory variables, even after controlling for the effects of enterprise-specific characteristics. They also highlight the need for in-depth analysis of *how* and *why* various institutional and environmental factors influence the development of financial accounting systems in ASEAN.

V. Conclusions

Corporate disclosure regimes and practices in ASEAN, both *de jure* and *de facto*, are unlikely to impede the achievement of accounting harmonisation. There is a high degree of *de jure* disclosure harmony in ASEAN, which stems from the preponderant influence of IASC-sanctioned accounting standards on national accounting standards issued by domestic professional accounting bodies. A relatively high level of common disclosure requirements exists within ASEAN: 68% of disclosure requirements were common to three or more countries. Nonetheless, this study has identified several areas where national disclosure requirements could be reviewed to engender a better and more harmonious regional disclosure environment. For example, as highlighted in Table 5, regional stock exchanges might review disclosure requirements with respect to research and development activities, corporate social responsibility, management information, interim reporting, and segmental information.

With respect to *de facto* disclosure, actual disclosure practices are much more diverse. There were statistically significant differences in actual disclosure levels among the five countries, indicating that disclosure practice harmony will be achieved with some difficulty because of the effects of national environmental differences. While levels of disclosure differed among the five countries, these differences are not large in practical terms. Compliance with common financial disclosure requirements was rather low throughout the region, raising questions about the effectiveness of national enforcement mechanisms. Policy-makers in ASEAN need to consider whether current levels of disclosure are acceptable. Better enforcement procedures appear warranted, although mandatory disclosure requirements may prove costly and ineffective. Whether market discipline, through competition in capital markets, will ultimately act to increase the level of "voluntary" disclosure in individual enterprises is an issue for exploration in future research.

Non-financial and social disclosures appear to be accorded fairly cursory attention in ASEAN. Disclosure practices varied considerably within each country and between ASEAN countries. There was considerable reluctance to disclose information on labour and employment, environmental activities, transfer pricing policies, government subsidies and value added. The "stakeholder" view of corporate accountability did not appear to have been widely accepted. Clearly, unique political, economic and social-cultural considerations underpin preferences for specific types of social and non-financial disclosures. This will make it more difficult for disclosure harmony to be achieved in the absence of specific regulatory compulsion.

A model of the variables influencing ASEAN disclosure levels produced results consistent with previous research of this genre: an adjusted R^2 of 0.487 and disclosure levels in ASEAN correlated positively with size ($p < 0.001$), degree of leverage ($p = 0.089$), and foreign operation ($p = 0.138$). But of greater note were the pronounced industry effects and country-of-origin effects revealed. A surprising result was that despite their *high* political cost exposures "banks" and "utilities" were the industry groups with the *lowest* levels of disclosure. Country of origin was found to be an important variable influencing disclosure levels too, even after controlling for enterprise-specific characteristics. A peculiar result observed was that unlike previous studies and conjecture which posits that "foreign-owned" companies will disclose more information than locally-owned companies, the reverse was the case. In ASEAN, the correlation between the variable "foreign ownership" and disclosure level was negative ($p = 0.013$), indicating that foreign-owned companies disclose less than local companies. Whether such accommodation continues to be necessary in order to attract foreign investment appears to be a policy matter worthy of immediate review.

Notes

1. For a review of the nature and form of regulation in each of the five nations, see Craig and Diga (1996).

2. To capture some of the debate on this matter see IASC (1983, 1990) and Grove and Bazley (1993).

3. This checklist is available on request to the second author.

4. Examples include disclosures of the level of statutory reserves (Thailand), export activities (Indonesia), ethnic composition of ownership (Malaysia), internal controls (Singapore) and reasons for non-distribution of retained profits as dividends (Philippines).

5. Of the 270 items, 177 (66%) were common to all five countries and 93 (34%) were common to four of them.

6. One factor attractive to multinational corporations setting up operations in ASEAN is the relatively liberal rules which exist in ASEAN with respect to transfer pricing.

7. This is a particularly sensitive matter in most ASEAN countries because of tensions between government agencies and labour rights groups. See Limqueco et al. (1989) for an in-depth analysis.

8. Items have not been weighted because of potential scoring bias and scaling problems, consistent with Firth (1979), Chow and Wong-Boren (1987), Wallace (1988), Cooke (1989), and Ahmed and Nicholls (1994).

9. We have not adopted Cooke's (1989) recommendation that a judgement be made regarding an item's applicability in a disclosure index because that would increase the chances of a systematic overstatement bias in the scoring process, particularly if non-disclosure is interpreted to mean lack of relevance.

10. Ahmed (1993) recommended normalising raw scores using a logarithm transformation of the odds ratio to avoid estimation problems using OLS regression. This transformation facilitates logit modelling (using OLS) on the transformed dependent variable, but was not undertaken here because actual disclosure scores ($114 \leqslant D \leqslant 306$) made it improbable that predicted values for the dependent variable would approach the maximum possible score of 530.

11. For example, if one country specified that the year-end inventory amount be disclosed (without indicating the valuation method), whereas another country required both the cost and net realisable value of inventory to be disclosed, then the latter, more specific, requirement was used.

12. It was not possible to obtain a measure of size in non-financial terms for all countries because data (e.g., number of shareholders or employees) were unavailable for some countries.

13. The outlying observation was a Philippine resources-based company whose disclosure score was quite small relative to similar companies. Shares of the company were considered high-risk and were not traded actively. It was a small, closely held company in comparison to its competitors.

14. VIF measures the variance of an estimator compared to what the variance would have been if the independent variable was not collinear with any of the other explanatory variables (Aczel, 1993).

15. VIF = 1 means that the variable is not collinear with any of the other explanatory variables.

16. PCA aims to decompose the information content of a set of variables into information about an inherent set of "latent" components (Aczel, 1993). The components were orthogonal (i.e., had zero correlation) and captured the variance of the original variables.

17. This test analyses whether the effect of continuous variables (company size and leverage) are the same regardless of country of origin, presence of foreign subsidiary, industry group or ownership. A non-significant result indicates that the assumption of homogeneous slopes between different levels of a specific dummy variable can be accepted.

18. The F-ratios and p-values for each hypothesised interaction effect are as follows: Industry by Size (1.0; 0.4); Foreign Subsidiary by Size (2.7; 0.1); Ownership by Size

(0.7; 0.4); Country by Size (0.65; 0.63); Industry by Leverage (0.8; 0.56); Foreign Subsidiary by Leverage (0.16; 0.69); Ownership by Leverage (0.07; 0.79); Country by Leverage (1.65; 0.17).

19. During this period, the Thai economy's average GDP growth rate exceeded 7% per annum.

20. Banking deregulation helped to curb the oligopolistic power enjoyed by large, state-owned banks prior to 1988. Moreover, the JSE was revived after 1988 by policies which made share investments more competitive. See Hewison (1988), Ng (1989) and Financial Times (1993).

21. A reviewer has observed that the adjusted R^2 might have been higher had the model included another independent variable which captured whether the items disclosed were required, or not required, to be disclosed.

22. Exceptions exist in Malaysia and Singapore where companies are usually listed in the KLSE and SES (Woon, 1995).

References

Aczel, A. D., *Complete Business Statistics*, 2nd ed. (Homewood, Illinois: Irwin, 1993).

Ahmed, K., *An Empirical Study of the Quality of Disclosure in Corporate Annual Reports in Developing Countries: The Case of Bangladesh.* Unpublished PhD Thesis, The Australian National University, 1993.

Ahmed, K. and D. Nicholls, "The Impact of Non-financial Company Characteristics on Mandatory Disclosure Compliance in Development Countries: The Case of Bangladesh," *International Journal of Accounting* (1994) Vol. 29, No. 1, pp. 62–77.

Ball, R. and G. Foster, "Corporate Financial Reporting: A Methodological Review of Empirical Research," *Journal of Accounting Research* (1982) Vol. 20, Supplement, pp. 161–234.

Belkaoui, A. R. and A. Kahl, "Corporate Financial Disclosure in Canada," CCGA *Research Monograph No. 1* (Vancouver: Canadian Certified General Accountants Association (CCGA), 1978).

Breusch, T. S. and A. R. Pagan, "A Simple Test for Heteroscedasticity and Random Coefficient Variation," *Econometrica* (1979) Vol. 47, No. 5, September, pp. 1287–1294.

Buzby, S. L. "Company Size, Listed Versus Unlisted Stocks, and the Extent of Financial Disclosure," *Journal of Accounting Research* (1975) Vol. 13, No. 1, pp. 16–37.

Choi, F. D. S. and G. G. Mueller, *International Accounting*, 2nd edition (Englewood Cliffs, NJ: Prentice Hall, 1992).

Chow, C. W. and A. Wong-Boren, "Voluntary Financial Disclosure by Mexican Corporations," *Accounting Review* (1987) Vol. 62, No. 3, July, pp. 533–541.

Cooke, T. E., "Disclosure in the Corporate Annual Reports of Swedish Companies," *Accounting and Business Research* (1989a) Vol. 19, No. 74, pp. 113–124.

Cooke, T. E., "Voluntary Corporate Disclosure by Swedish Companies," *Journal of International Financial Management and Accounting* (1989b) Vol. 1, No. 2, pp. 171–195.

Cooke, T. E., "An Assessment of Voluntary Disclosure in the Annual Reports of Japanese Corporations," *International Journal of Accounting* (1991) Vol. 26, No. 3, pp. 174–189.

Cooke, T. E., "The Impact of Size, Stock Market Listing and Industry Type on Disclosure in the Annual Reports of Japanese Listed Corporations," *Accounting and Business Research* (1992) Vol. 22, No. 87, pp. 229–237.

Cooke, T. E., "The Impact of Accounting Principles on Profits: the US versus Japan," *Accounting and Business Research* (1993) Vol. 23, No. 92, pp. 460–476.

Courtis, J. K., "Annual Report Disclosure in New Zealand: Analysis of Selected Corporate Attributes," *UNE Research Study No. 8* (Armidale, NSW: University of New England at Armidale, 1979).

Craig, R. J. and J. G. Diga, "Financial Reporting Regulation in ASEAN: Features and Prospects," *International Journal of Accounting* (1996) Vol. 31, No. 2, pp. 239–259.

Dunning, J. H., *Multinational Enterprises and the Global Economy* (Reading, Massachusetts: Addison-Wesley, 1993).

Financial Times *Banking in the Far East 1993: Structures and Sources of Finance* (London: Financial Times Business Information, 1993).

Firth, M., "The Impact of Size, Stock Market Listings, and Auditors on Voluntary Disclosure in Corporate Annual Reports," *Accounting and Business Research* (1979) Vol. 9, No. 36, pp. 237–280.

Gray, S. J., L. B. McSweeney and J. C. Shaw *Information Disclosure and the Multinational Corporation* (New York: John Wiley, 1984).

Grove, H. D. and J. D. Bazley, "Disclosure Strategies for Harmonization of International Accounting Standards," *International Journal of Accounting* (1993) Vol. 28, No. 2, pp. 116–128.

Hewison, K., "The Structure of Banking Capital in Thailand," *Southeast Asian Journal of Social Science* (1988) Vol. 16, No. 1, pp. 81–91.

International Accounting Standards Committee (IASC), *Objectives and Procedures* (London: IASC, 1983).

International Accounting Standards Committee (IASC), *Statement of Intent on the Comparability of Financial Statements* (London: IASC, 1990).

Joliffe, I. T., "Discarding Variables in Principal Component Analysis 1: Artificial Data," *Applied Statistics* (1972) Vol. 21, No. 2, pp. 160–173.

Kaiser, H. F., "The Varimax Criterion for Analytic Rotation in Factor Analysis," *Psychometrika* (1958) Vol. 23, pp. 187–200.

Lilliefors, W. H., "On the Kolmogorov-Smirnov Test for Normality with Mean and Variance Unknown," *Journal of American Statistical Association* (1969) Vol. 64, pp. 387–389.

Limqueco, P., B. McFarlane and J. Odhnoff, *Labour and Industry in ASEAN* (Manila: Journal of Contemporary Asia Publishing, 1989).

Maddala, G. S., *Introduction to Econometrics,* 2nd edition (New York: MacMillan, 1992).

Ng, B. K., ed. *The Development of Capital Markets in the SEACEN Countries* (Kuala Lumpur: Southeast Asian Central Banks Training Centre (SEACEN), 1989).

Saudagaran, S. M., "An Empirical Study of Selected Factors Influencing the Decision to List on Foreign Stock Exchanges," *Journal of International Business Studies* (1988) Vol. 19, No. 1, pp. 101–127.

Shapiro, S. S. and M. B. Wilk, "An Analysis of Variance Test for Normality (Complete Samples)," *Biometrika* (1965) Vol. 52, no. 3/4, pp. 591–611.

Singhvi, S., "Characteristics and Implications of Inadequate Disclosure: A Case Study of India," *International Journal of Accounting* (1968) Vol. 3, No. 2, pp. 29–43.

Singhvi, S. and H. B. Desai, "An Empirical Analysis of the Quality of Corporate Financial Disclosure," *Accounting Review* (1971) Vol. 46, No. 1, pp. 120–138.

Teoh; H. Y. and G. Thong, "Another Look at Corporate Social Responsibility Reporting: An Empirical Study in a Developing Country (Malaysia)," *Accounting, Organizations and Society* (1984) Vol. 9, No. 2, pp. 189–206.

United Nations (UN), *International Standards of Accounting and Reporting by Transnational Corporations: Report of the Secretary-General and Report of the Group of Experts on International Standards of Accounting and Reporting* (E/C.10/33) (New York: UN Commission on Transnational Corporations, 1977).

Wallace, R. S. O., "Corporate Financial Reporting in Nigeria," *Accounting and Business Research* (1988) Vol. 18, No. 72, pp. 352–362.

Watts, R. and J. Zimmerman, "Towards a Positive Theory of the Determination of Accounting Standards," *Accounting Review* (1978) Vol. 53, No. 1, January, pp. 112–134.

Watts, R. and J. Zimmerman, "Positive Accounting Theory: A Ten Year Perspective," *Accounting Review* (1990) Vol. 65, No. 1, January, pp. 131–156.

Weisberg, S., *Applied Linear Regression,* 2nd edition (New York: John Wiley, 1985).

Woon, W. C., "Regionalisation of Corporate and Securities Law: The Singapore and Malaysia Experience," *Australian Journal of Corporate Law* (1995) Vol. 5, pp. 356–363.

Yuan, L. T., "The ASEAN Free Trade Area: The Search for a Common Prosperity," *Asian-Pacific Economic Literature* (1994) Vol. 8, No. 1, pp. 1–7.

Zarzeski, M. T., "Spontaneous Harmonization Effects of Culture and Market Forces on Accounting Disclosure Practices," *Accounting Horizons* (1996) Vol. 10, No. 1, March, pp. 18–37.

[27]

The International
Journal of
Accounting

Accounting Practices and the Market Valuation of Accounting Numbers: Evidence from Indonesia, Korea, Malaysia, the Philippines, Taiwan, and Thailand

Roger C. Graham* and Raymond D. King†
**Oregon State University, Corvallis, OR, USA and †University of Oregon, Eugene, OR, USA*

Key Words: International accounting practices; Valuation; Asia; Clean surplus; Conservatism

Abstract: *This study examines the relation between stock prices and accounting earnings and book values in six Asian countries: Indonesia, South Korea, Malaysia, the Philippines, Taiwan, and Thailand. The analysis is based on a residual earnings model that expresses the value of the firm in terms of book value and residual income. The model holds for any clean surplus accounting system. However, for finite time horizons, biased accounting may affect model estimates. The six countries examined in this study differ in faithfulness to clean surplus accounting as well as bias (conservatism). The study addresses two questions. First, are there systematic differences across countries in the value relevance of accounting, and are these differences related to accounting differences? Second, are there systematic differences in the incremental and relative information content of book value per share (BVPS) and abnormal (residual) earnings per share (REPS) across the countries, and are such differences related to accounting differences? We find differences across the six countries in the explanatory power of BVPS and REPS for firm values. Explanatory power for Taiwan and Malaysia is relatively low while that for Korea and the Philippines is relatively high. These differences are generally consistent with differences in accounting practice; however, since Korean accounting practice is strongly influenced by tax law, we did not expect the high association for Korea. Second, with respect to the incremental and relative explanatory power of BVPS and REPS, we find BVPS to have high explanatory power in the Philippines and Korea but little in Taiwan. In all six countries REPS has less explanatory power than BVPS in most years. Again, the evidence may be interpreted as suggesting accounting practice affects valuation (with Korea again as the exception). Finally, we provide evidence on the sensitivity of the timing of comparisons of stock prices and accounting values. We find that comparing prices at year-end (even though annual accounting information has not been released at that time), in general, provides the highest correlation between market and accounting numbers.*

Differences in accounting practices across countries are a major concern to investors, accounting standard setters, stock exchanges, and financial analysts. The International

Direct all correspondence to: Raymond D. King, Lundquist College of Business, University of Oregon, Eugene, OR 97403, USA; E-mail: rking@oregon.uoregon.edu

The International Journal of Accounting, Vol. 35, No. 4, pp. 445–470 **ISSN: 0020-7063.**

Accounting Standards Committee (IASC) and the International Organization of Securities Commissions (IOSCO) have devoted considerable effort to standardization or harmonization of accounting practices across countries. Investment professionals claim that accounting differences may impede international capital flows (Choi and Levich, 1991). This study examines the relation between accounting numbers and firm market values in six Asian countries with diverse accounting practices: Indonesia, Korea, Malaysia, the Philippines, Taiwan, and Thailand. We focus on the incremental and relative explanatory power of book value and residual earnings. Because accounting systems differ across the six countries, we examine whether those differences are related to the valuation usefulness of accounting measures. Our objective is to provide evidence on the value relevance of accounting numbers from different accounting systems. Such evidence should inform the current debate over international accounting standards and practices.

Our analysis follows a model developed by Preinreich (1938), Edwards and Bell (1961), and Peasnell (1982) and formalized by Ohlson (1991, 1995) and Feltham and Ohlson (1995) sometimes termed the *Residual Earnings (Income)* model. The model formally states a simple concept: firm value is a function of book value and future residual earnings. A key aspect of the model is that its valuation accuracy does not depend on a particular set of "good" accounting procedures. The only requirement on accounting procedures is *clean surplus accounting*, that is, book value of equity changes only with income or loss and net capital investments and withdrawals (dividends) by owners. In addition, empirical applications of the model to finite horizons are potentially affected by bias in the accounting system. Therefore, comparisons across countries with different accounting practices are one way to investigate the value relevance of different accounting practices.

Across the six countries, accounting systems vary in their faithfulness to clean surplus accounting and in the extent to which they exhibit bias (conservatism). Hence, it is possible that accounting values from some of the countries may provide better estimates of firm value than accounting values from the other countries. Therefore, the usefulness of accounting for firm valuation may differ across countries as well. On the other hand, the accounting standards developed in these countries may be partly based on International Accounting Standards (IAS) or US GAAP. This would tend to make accounting procedures and their value relevance similar. Saudagaran and Diga (1997) report that of our six countries, only Korea has not adopted some or all of IAS.

We investigate the value relevance of different accounting practices using an empirical model that regresses current book value and current residual earnings on market prices. In contrast, the residual income model is based on *expected* residual earnings. Considerable prior research, as discussed in the next section, examines the contemporaneous relation between accounting and market values. In this study, we examine that relation for six Asian countries. However, our interest is in the relation between accounting practices and the value relevance of accounting numbers. We focus on differences in accounting procedures across the six countries that affect book value and residual earnings.[1] The accounting procedures selected: accounting for goodwill, asset revaluations, leases, research and development (R&D) expenditures, and the equity method of accounting for affiliated companies each may be categorized in terms of faithfulness to clean surplus and extent of conservatism.

We address the implications of these accounting procedures for the value relevance of accounting information. Philippine firms, for example, record goodwill and revalue assets, but firms in Taiwan do neither. This means that book values in the Philippines will reflect market values of assets more closely than in Taiwan. Therefore, we expect the explanatory power of book value will be greater for Philippine firms than for Taiwanese firms. As another example, only Indonesian and Malaysian firms capitalize leases and R&D expenditures and use the equity method for affiliated companies. These are less conservative accounting practices than alternatives used in other counties.

We find accounting in Korea and Taiwan to be least faithful to clean surplus accounting. Korea does not capitalize goodwill and asset revaluations are amortized to equity according to tax law. Taiwan does not capitalize goodwill nor allow asset revaluations. Korea is also the only country not to use the equity method for affiliated companies. Thus, the earnings of Korean firms do not include the earnings of affiliated firms. Philippine firms, however, amortize both goodwill and asset revaluations to income. Recall that violations of clean surplus accounting occur when income does not reflect changes in equity value. Thus, violations of clean surplus bias empirical calculations of residual earnings. Therefore, we expect the explanatory power of residual earnings will be highest for Philippine firms and least for Korean and Taiwan firms.

Overall, our results show significant differences across countries in the value relevance of accounting earnings and book values. Explanatory power over all firm-years ranges from $R^2 = .17$ in Taiwan to $R^2 = .68$ for Korea. The incremental explanatory power of book value per share (BVPS) and residual earnings per share (REPS) is similarly diverse. Incremental explanatory power of BVPS over all firm-years ranges from 7.2 percent (Taiwan) to 65.3 percent (Philippines). For REPS, the incremental explanatory power over all firm-years ranges from 1.4 percent (Korea) to 13.2 percent (Thailand).

Generally, we find differences in accounting appear to be related to differences in value relevance. We find that the explanatory power of book value is highest in the Philippines and lowest in Taiwan. This is consistent with our expectations based on the accounting differences in the two countries. Indonesia and Malaysia have accounting systems that are less conservative than other countries. However, we find the incremental explanatory power of book value does not stand out as high in Indonesia or in Malaysia. This result is only partly consistent with our expectations. We also expected that the relative explanatory power of residual earnings would be high in the Philippines and low in Korea and Taiwan, and the results support this prediction. Our comparisons across countries should be viewed with caution because the number of years of data available ranges from only 2 years for the Philippines to 10 years for Malaysia.

The next section of the article briefly reviews related research and this is followed by the section discussing accounting differences in the six Asian countries. This is followed by the description of the sample and development the study design. The section presenting the analysis of our data and reporting the results of our tests follows. A final section summarizes our findings.

RELATED RESEARCH

Research concerned with the relation of accounting numbers and stock prices covers decades. In this brief review we summarize recent research with study designs and research methods similar to ours. We see two principal strains: first, research focused on explaining stock prices with accounting book value and earnings; and second, research examining the *incremental* explanatory power of book value and earnings in the presence of the other.

Stock Prices Explained by Book Value and Earnings Per Share

Examining a large set of US firms, Bernard (1993) found that book values explain 55 percent of the cross-sectional variation in market prices. When current return on equity (ROE; ranks) was added to the regression, these two accounting measures explain about 64 percent of the variation in market prices. Bernard (1994) finds that return on common equity (ROE) is mean reverting over time so that firms with the highest (lowest) current ROEs tend to have lower (higher) ROEs in later years.

King and Langli (1998) examine the explanatory power of BVPS and earnings per share (EPS) for three European countries: Germany, Norway, and the UK. They find significant differences in the valuation power of accounting book value and earnings across the three countries, and they interpret some of the differences as consistent with diversity in accounting practices. They also find future earnings realizations as proxies for expected earnings do not have incremental explanatory power beyond that of current earnings and book value.

Frankel and Lee (1999) look at the relation between accounting values, earnings forecasts and market prices across 20 countries (including Korea and Thailand) for 8 years, 1987–1994. Sample sizes for Korea and Thailand are small with 3 to 8 observations per year (33 total firm-years) for Korea and 1 to 40 observations per year (162 total firm-years) for Thailand. They find that estimates of value based on the residual earnings model have incremental explanatory power beyond book value and earnings in explaining market value in all countries. In addition, they find evidence of superior returns to trading strategies based on an estimate of value from a residual earnings model.

Joos and Lang (1994) relate book value and earnings to stock prices for France, Germany, and the UK. Their sample covers 1982 to 1990, and they focus on the effects of implementing the accounting related directives of the European Union. They find the explanatory power of book value and earnings together ranges from 20 to 38 percent for Germany, from 48 to 78 percent for France, and from 14 to 42 percent for the UK. They do not examine incremental explanatory power. Evidence on changes over time is ambiguous, probably because the time periods for the sample are relatively short.

Harris et al. (1994) examine the value relevance of accounting numbers for German firms compared to that for a matched set of US firms for 1982–1991. They find little difference in overall value relevance (R^2) between German and US firms. However, coefficients (multiples) on book value and on earnings for German firms are greater than for matched US firms. Further, they find that consolidation increases the value relevance of accounting numbers, and restatements of earnings to adjust for transitory elements in German accounting also increases explanatory power.

Incremental Explanatory Power of Book Value and Earnings Per Share

Collins et al. (1997) examine the incremental explanatory power of book value and earnings across a 41-year time period (1953–1993) for US firms. They find a decline in the ability of earnings to explain market prices over this period. But the explanatory power of book values increases such that total explanatory power is actually higher in more recent periods. Average adjusted R^2 for a model regressing BVPS and EPS on stock price for the first 10 years (1953–1962) was .50 increasing to .69 for their most recent 10-year period (1984–1993). Collins et al. (1997) investigated possible reasons for these changes. They find the reduced explanatory power of earnings is explained by an increase in the incidence of one-time items and reported losses as well as a decrease in the size of firms in the sample.

King and Langli (1998) examine a 15-year period (1982–1996) for Germany, Norway, and the UK. They find that for Germany the incremental explanatory power of book value increases significantly while that for EPS decreases. There is no significant change in their common information. For Norway, there is no significant change in the incremental explanatory power of book value or EPS over time. While for the UK, the incremental explanatory power of book value increases and the incremental explanatory power of EPS is unchanged over the time period.

Harris et al. (1994) also examine the separate explanatory power of book value and of earnings using simple regressions with only one variable. They do not report the test statistics. However, they say that while the explanatory power of EPS in Germany is approximately equal to that in the US, the explanatory power of book value is much lower. This contrasts sharply to the King and Langli (1998) results for a longer time period. The Harris et al. (1994) results are not, however, tests of incremental explanatory power since the simple regressions use only one variable.

This study extends the evidence summarized above. We examine the value relevance of accounting numbers for companies in Asian countries. Prior financial reporting research in English language journals has been limited.

ACCOUNTING DIVERSITY ACROSS THE SIX COUNTRIES

The accounting systems in all six countries have developed relatively recently. The six accounting systems differ on some dimensions but are similar on others. Two dimensions that we examine are (1) the model on which the accounting systems are based and (2) the type of standard setting body. Table 1 shows these characteristics for the six countries. IAS was the primary basis for accounting standards in Indonesia, Malaysia, and Thailand (although Thailand has also been influenced by US GAAP). US GAAP, on the other hand, was the primary basis in the Philippines and Taiwan (although Philippine GAAP is secondarily based on tax law). Korean accounting standards are unique in that they are based on Korean tax law that, like tax law in all countries, emphasizes cash realization. Different accounting models may lead to differences in the value relevance of the resulting accounting numbers. We have no prior expectations concerning the relative value relevance of IAS versus US GAAP. It is likely, however, that tax law is more susceptible to political influence than other accounting bases. To the extent that such political influence might serve to make accounting less informative, Korean accounting may be less value relevant because it is based on tax law.

The standard setting bodies in four of the six countries are independent of the government. In Korea and Taiwan, however, standard setting is not independent. Where

Table 1. Accounting Standards and Standard Setting in the Six Countries

Country	*Primary basis for accounting standards*	*Independent accounting standards setting body?*
Indonesia	IAS	yes
Korea	Tax Law	no
Malaysia	IAS	yes
Philippines	US GAAP	yes
Taiwan	US GAAP	no
Thailand	IAS	yes

standard setting is influenced or controlled by government there is greater potential for political influence in the standards setting process. As where accounting follows tax law, this may lead to lower value relevance of accounting numbers.

We analyzed the accounting standards and practices for each country using a variety of sources including Akathaporn (1995), Graham and Wang (1995), and publications from the AICPA (1989, 1990, 1992), CIFAR (1995), Deloitte Touche Tohmatsu International (1995a,b, 1996a,b, 1997), Price Waterhouse (1995a,b, 1996a,b,c,d), and Mathew Bender & Co.(1996). Under the residual earnings model the only crucial accounting characteristics are *unbiased accounting* and *clean surplus accounting*. Conservative accounting practices are biased since value changes are reflected asymmetrically, value declines are recognized more quickly than value increases. The clean surplus relation (CSR) allows book value of equity to change only with income or loss and net capital investments and withdrawals (dividends) by owners. CSR is violated if changes in book value can by-pass income. We focus our analysis on the effects of accounting differences on book value and on residual (abnormal) earnings, the accounting arguments in the residual earnings model. However, accounting differences affect valuation only when they are violations of unbiased accounting or clean surplus accounting.

Differences Across Countries Affecting Book Value

Revaluing assets is a violation of CSR if the accompanying credit is taken directly to equity. Yet asset revaluations bring book value nearer to market value. Immediate write-off of goodwill violates CSR and usually moves book values farther from market values. In summary, both recognizing goodwill (consistent with CSR) and revaluing assets (violating CSR) bring book value nearer to market value. Hence, developing predictions on the effects of specific accounting treatments on value relevance is not always clear. Conservative accounting (bias) is expected to generally reduce the value relevance of both book value and earnings since the essence of conservatism is delay in reflecting certain events in the accounting records.

Recording goodwill is common practice in Indonesia and the Philippines, and uncommon but allowed in Malaysia and Thailand. Korea and Taiwan do not allow goodwill to be recorded. Asset revaluations are common in all countries except Indonesia and Taiwan where they are allowed but restricted in practice. Table 2 presents a summary of our analysis of these accounting practices.

Table 2. Goodwill and Asset Revaluations on the Balance Sheet

Country	*Goodwill recorded on balance sheet?*	*Asset revaluation on balance sheet?*
Indonesia	yes	uncommon
Korea	no	common
Malaysia	some	common
Philippines	yes	common
Taiwan	no	uncommon
Thailand	some	common

Table 3. Other Asset Values on the Balance Sheet

Country	*Capital leases on balance sheet?*	*R&D expenditures on balance sheet?*	*Equity method used for affiliates?*
Indonesia	yes	yes	yes
Korea	some	yes	no
Malaysia	yes	yes	yes
Philippines	no	no	yes
Taiwan	some	no	yes
Thailand	not until 1996	yes	yes

Asset revaluation and goodwill are both recorded only in the Philippines, and neither is recorded in Taiwan. The other four countries allow one procedure or the other but not both. We expect the incremental explanatory power of book value to be high in the Philippines and low in Taiwan relative to the other five countries. However, the effect of these accounting practices on the incremental explanatory power of book value for the other countries is ambiguous.

The six countries also differ in other accounting practices, including capitalizing leases, capitalizing research development costs, and applying the equity method to affiliated firms. Firms that capitalize and use the equity method are likely to have book values that are closer to market values than firms that do not.[2] Table 3 presents a summary of our analysis of these accounting practices.

Only Indonesia and Malaysia allow or require all three accounting procedures. The effect of these accounting differences on incremental explanatory power is ambiguous for the other countries. However, we expect the explanatory power of book value in Indonesia and Malaysia to be higher than in Thailand and Taiwan.

Differences Across Countries Affecting Residual Earnings

As explained in the previous section, conservatism is expected to reduce the value relevance of both book value and residual earnings. In addition, we can make some predictions about the effects of clean surplus accounting for goodwill and asset revaluations on the value relevance of book value. However, the effects of these accounting practices on the value relevance of residual earnings are less clear.

The Philippines is the most faithful to clean surplus accounting as both goodwill and asset revaluations are amortized to income over their useful lives. The other

Table 4. Goodwill and Asset Revaluation Amortization

Country	*Goodwill amortized to?*	*Amortization period*	*Revaluations amortized to?*	*Amortization period*
Indonesia	income	useful life	–	–
Korea	–	–	shareholder equity	per tax law
Malaysia	–	immediate write-off	shareholder equity	useful life
Philippines	income	no more than 40 years	income	useful life
Taiwan	–	–	–	–
Thailand	–	immediate write-off	shareholder equity	useful life

countries (1) do not record goodwill (Korea and Taiwan), (2) do not record asset revaluations (Indonesia and Taiwan), (3) immediately write-off goodwill to equity (Malaysia and Thailand), or (4) amortize asset revaluation increments to equity (Korea, Malaysia, and Thailand). Korea and Taiwan are least faithful to clean surplus accounting. Korea does not capitalize goodwill and asset revaluations are amortized to equity according to schedules mandated by tax law. Taiwan does not capitalize goodwill nor allow asset revaluations. Korea is also the only country that does not use the equity method for affiliated companies; therefore the earnings of Korean firms do not include the earnings of affiliated firms. We expect the relative explanatory power of residual earnings to be high in the Philippines and low in Korea and Taiwan. The effect on the explanatory power of residual earnings for the other countries is ambiguous. Table 4 presents a summary of the amortization practices.

Summary of the Research Questions

Our examination of accounting practices reveals some systematic differences across the six countries. While the differences appear to be substantial, it is an empirical question whether they result in meaningful violations of the CSR or in significant accounting bias (conservatism), the important factors for the residual earnings model. Accounting bias will likely reduce the explanatory power of both book value and earnings. Furthermore, violations of the CSR may either increase or decrease the explanatory power of book value depending on whether the violation moves book value toward or away from market values. Because countries differ on both dimensions, ex ante hypotheses on which effect will dominate are problematic. Even so, we expect that bias and CSR violations will affect the value relevance of accounting numbers in systematic ways. Particularly because Philippine firms record both goodwill and asset revaluations and Taiwan firms do neither, we expect the value relevance of book value to be greatest in the Philippines and least in Taiwan. Because both Indonesian and Malaysian firms capitalize leases and R&D expenditures and use the equity method we expect the value relevance of their book values to exceed the value relevance of book value in Thailand and Taiwan. Because Philippine firms amortize both goodwill and asset revaluations to income, we expect the value relevance of residual earnings to be high in the Philippines.

In addition, we investigate changes in the value relevance of accounting numbers over time. Our sample contains 3,655 firm-years across six countries. We have sufficient data for only 2 years of yearly regressions for the Philippines but 10 years for Malaysia. We

Table 5. Sample Countries and Firm-Years

Sample selection	*Firm-years*
Indonesia	338
Korea	902
Malaysia	1,311
Philippines	139
Taiwan	369
Thailand	596
Sample size	3,655

trace the total explanatory power of accounting earnings and book value and the incremental explanatory power of each earnings and book value in the presence of the other across time for each country.

SAMPLE AND STUDY DESIGN

Our sample covers publicly traded firms in Indonesia, Korea, Malaysia, the Philippines, Taiwan, and Thailand across the period from 1987 to 1996. The stock prices and accounting data for this study are from the *Worldscope Global Researcher.* The sample selection criteria are:

1. Accounting data is from consolidated financial statements.
2. Financial firms are excluded (insurance, banks, and other miscellaneous financial firms). Accounting practices for these firms are so distinct that their valuation parameters are likely to be substantially different from those for industrial firms.
3. Firms with negative book values are deleted. These firms are likely to be in financial distress and may be interesting in their own right. However, the focus of this study is the across country differences in value relevance of accounting numbers derived under different accounting practices. Hence, restricting our sample to firms with positive book values will allow us to focus on firms where differences are mostly likely to reflect accounting differences.
4. Twelve firms with EPS greater than their BVPS are deleted since data on those firms is likely to contain errors. These firms constituted less than 1 percent of the sample.
5. Twenty firm-years with excessive statistical influence in our regressions were deleted. The firm-years showed undue influence by the diagnostics and cutoff rules described in Belsley et al. (1980).

These restrictions on the sample will have several effects. First, the model will appear to "fit" better than it would fit unrestricted data. That is, the explanatory power of book value and of residual earnings information in the sample is likely to be greater than for an unrestricted sample. Second, the samples across the six countries will be more homogeneous and the effects of different business cycles in the six countries will be reduced. This should allow a better focus on the effects of accounting differences. Table 5 shows the countries and number of firm-years.

Table 6. Descriptive Statistics on Variables for Six Southeast Asian Countries

Variable	*N*	*Mean*	*Standard deviation*	*5th Percentile*	*Median*	*95th Percentile*
Panel A: Indonesia						
Price	338	2,813	2,261	556	2,236	6,500
BVPS	338	1,668	1,175	361	1,374	4,394
EPS	338	242	305	43	154	765
REPS	338	− 75	272	− 474	− 52	180
ROE	340	0.15	0.09	0.03	0.14	0.30
Panel B: Korea						
Price	902	25,629	34,972	8,002	18,100	63,921
BVPS	902	21,019	31,375	6,282	14,104	50,225
EPS	902	1,353	4,324	− 979	786	5,007
REPS	902	− 372	3,334	− 3,291	− 398	2,389
ROE	902	0.07	0.14	− 0.09	0.06	0.26
Panel C: Malaysia						
Price	1,311	5.16	5.99	0.94	3.84	13.96
BVPS	1,311	1.71	1.11	0.53	1.44	3.72
EPS	1,311	0.18	0.21	− 0.03	0.15	0.56
REPS	1,311	0.06	0.19	− 0.17	0.04	0.37
ROE	1,311	0.13	0.15	− 0.04	0.12	0.38
Panel D: Philippines						
Price	139	19.06	31.65	0.17	6.37	81.37
BVPS	139	7.91	12.00	0.17	2.54	38.68
EPS	139	0.97	1.71	− 0.08	0.37	4.94
REPS	139	− 0.14	1.32	− 2.75	− 0.01	1.30
ROE	139	0.16	0.14	− 0.04	0.14	0.40
Panel E: Taiwan						
Price	369	30.55	13.21	14.95	27.89	53.83
BVPS	369	12.43	2.81	7.80	12.19	17.51
EPS	369	1.20	1.25	− 0.79	1.16	3.16
REPS	369	− 0.18	1.25	− 2.17	− 0.21	1.84
ROE	369	0.10	0.11	− 0.06	0.09	0.26
Panel F: Thailand						
Price	596	95.79	102.39	18.25	59.59	330.00
BVPS	596	41.35	35.05	11.05	31.09	117.83
EPS	596	5.93	8.32	− 1.14	3.59	21.24
REPS	596	− 0.23	5.10	− 6.41	− 0.78	7.48
ROE	596	0.12	0.14	− 0.06	0.13	0.34

Price = Stock price at the end of year t. BVPS = Book value of shareholders' equity at the end of year t. EPS = Earnings per share for year t. REPS = Residual (abnormal) earnings per share = $EPS_t - r^*((BVPS_t + BVPS_{t-1})/2)$ where r is the country average lending rate in year t taken from the International Financial Statistics Yearbook. Price, book value, EPS, and REPS amounts are in nominal local currency. ROE = Return on equity = $EPS_t/((BV_t + BV_{t-1})/2)$.

Table 6 provides descriptive statistics for the sample. Per share values are in nominal currency of the countries, so comparisons are difficult. However, we can compare ROE (the ratio of EPS to average book value) across countries and the differences are substantial. Median ROE ranges from 6 percent (over 8 years) in Korea to 14 percent

Table 7. Correlation Statistics on Variables for Six Asian Countries (*p* values in parentheses)

			Spearman			
Variable	*N*	*Price*	*EPS*	*BV*	*ROE*	*REPS*
Pearson						
Panel A: Indonesia						
Price	338		.6164 (.0001)	.5685 (.0001)	.2255 (.0001)	.0662 (.2252)
EPS	338	.5741 (.0001)		.6915 (.0001)	.5066 (.0001)	.2846 (.0001)
BV	338	.4777 (.0001)	.6418 (.0001)		−.1406 (.0097)	−.3028 (.0001)
ROE	338	.3423 (.0001)	.6118 (.0001)	−.0130 (.8119)		.8904 (.0001)
REPS	338	.2498 (.0040)	.6262 (.0001)	−.1012 (.0631)	.7768 (.0001)	
Panel B: Korea						
Price	902		.5328 (.0001)	.6021 (.0001)	.3095 (.0001)	.1727 (.0012)
EPS	902	.6894 (.0001)		.5552 (.0001)	.8285 (.0001)	.6624 (.0001)
BV	902	.8177 (.0001)	.7438 (.0001)		.1374 (.0001)	−.0681 (.0408)
ROE	902	.1667 (.0001)	.4769 (.0001)	.0865 (.0093)		.7442 (.9190)
REPS	902	.3395 (.0001)	.8529 (.0001)	.2766 (.0001)	.5963 (.0001)	
Panel C: Malaysia						
Price	1,311		.6224 (.0001)	.5572 (.0001)	.3272 (.0001)	.4496 (.0001)
EPS	1,311	.4171 (.0001)		.5419 (.0001)	.7678 (.0001)	.8697 (.0001)
BV	1,311	.5031 (.0001)	.5552 (.0001)		.0160 (.5619)	.1774 (.0001
ROE	1,311	.1093 (.0001)	.6042 (.0001)	.0117 (.6730)		.9252 (.0001)
REPS	1,311	.2564 (.0001)	.9093 (.0001)	.2102 (.0001)	.7218 (.0001)	
Panel D: Philippines						
PRICE	139		.8133 (.0001)	.8601 (.0001)	.1725 (.0423)	.1177 (.1676)
EPS	139	.7593 (.0001)		.7726 (.0001)	.4577 (.0001)	.3776 (.0001)
BV	139	.7906 (.0001)	.7790 (.0001)		−.0654 (.4441)	−.0715 (.4027)
ROE	139	.0169 (.8439)	.2416 (.0042)	−.1081 (.2052)		.8089 (.0001)
REPS	139	.0727 (.3949)	.4301 (.0001)	−.1866 (.0278)	.4931 (.0001)	
Panel E: Taiwan						
Price	369		.5043 (.0001)	.3056 (.0001)	.4399 (.0001)	.4431 (.0001)
EPS	369	.3618 (.0001)		.2487 (.0001)	.9499 (.0001)	.9291 (.0001)
BV	369	.2639 (.0001)	.2422 (.0001)		−.0010 (.9853)	−.0390 (.4548)
ROE	369	.3048 (.0001)	.9353 (.0001)	.0276 (.5972)		.9804 (.0001)
REPS	369	.3116 (.0001)	.9609 (.0001)	−.0151 (.7731)	.9909 (.0001)	
Panel F: Thailand						
Price	596		.7308 (.0001)	.5639 (.0001)	.6144 (.0001)	.5523 (.0001)
EPS	596	.6284 (.0001)		.7144 (.0001)	.8625 (.0001)	.7757 (.0001)
BV	596	.5145 (.0013)	.8121 (.0001)		.3443 (.0001)	.2411 (.0001)
ROE	596	.4415 (.0001)	.5912 (.0001)	.2494 (.0001)		.9362 (.0001)
REPS	596	.5166 (.0001)	.8068 (.0001)	.3405 (.0001)	.7237 (.0001)	

Price = Stock price at the end of year t. EPS = Earnings per share for year t. BVPS = Book value of shareholders' equity at the end of year t. ROE = Return on equity = $EPS_t / ((BVPS_t + BVPS_{t-1})/2)$. REPS = Residual (abnormal) earnings per share = $EPS_t - r^*((BVPS_t + BVPS_{t-1})/2)$ where r is the country average lending rate in year t taken from the International Financial Statistics Yearbook.

(over 5 and 2 years) in Indonesia and the Philippines. For comparison, King and Langli (1998) find ROE over the 1980s and 1990s to be about 6 percent in Germany, 10 percent in Norway, and 13 percent in the UK. In the US, this measure has averaged around 13 percent over the last 20 years. Prior research has speculated that such differences across countries may reflect differences in conservatism of accounting methods. As noted above, for example, Taiwan does not record either goodwill asset revaluations (most conservative) while both are recognized in the Philippines (least conservative).

Table 7 reports the pair-wise correlation between stock price and accounting variables for all countries. For all countries except Korea the rank (Spearman) correlations are greater than the product–moment (Pearson) correlations. However, the patterns and significance of the parametric (Spearman) and non-parametric (Pearson) correlations are similar. Stock prices are strongly correlated with BVPS and with EPS for all countries. The pair-wise correlations between price and EPS are approximately the same as between price and BVPS. The correlation (Pearson) between BVPS and EPS is high in Thailand (.81), the Philippines (.78), and Korea (.74), and relatively low for Taiwan (.24). If EPS is used as a proxy for residual earnings, the high correlation between BVPS and EPS (they are related by size) may make it difficult to partition value relevance between book value and earnings. However, the pair-wise correlations between BVPS and REPS are far smaller, significant in some cases, insignificant in others, and sometimes negative. This is anticipated since there is no reason to expect residual (unexpected) per share earnings to be related to book value. One important reason for using REPS in the empirical analysis is to avoid the high correlation between BVPS and EPS.

TESTS AND ANALYSIS

Our analysis is based on contemporaneous cross-sectional regressions of accounting book values and residual earnings on stock prices (dependent variable). We analyze both the *relative* and the *incremental* explanatory power of book value and residual earnings using an approach applied previously in accounting by Biddle et al. (1995) and Collins et al. (1997).

Empirical specification of the residual earnings model requires estimates of book value, residual earnings, and the horizon for residual earnings. For residual earnings estimated to terminate at time T, the model would be:

$$\text{Price}_{it} = a_0 + a_1\text{BVPS}_{it} + a_2\text{RE}_{it+1} + a_3\text{RE}_{it+2} + a_4\text{RE}_{it+3} + \ldots + a_k\text{RE}_{iT} + e_{it} \quad (1)$$

where Price_{it} is the price per share of firm i at the end of period t, BVPS_{it} is the book value per share of firm i at the end of period t, and RE_{it} is the residual earnings per share of firm i for year $t+k$.

The coefficient a_1 would have an expected value of 1.0 while the coefficients a_2 to a_4 would have expected values of $(1+r)^{-t}$. Finally, the expected value of coefficient a_k would be $(1/r)$*$(1+r)^{-T}$.[3] Residual earnings horizons will differ cross-sectionally; therefore, parsimonious cross-sectional representations of Equation (1) will have only a few terms. For example Frankel and Lee (1999) use $T=2$ because analysts' forecasts used to predict future residual earnings were only available for 2 years.

Our first tests are concerned with the incremental explanatory power of book value and residual earnings. As in Collins et al. (1997) we compare the results of three regression equations to address the question of relative and incremental explanatory power. Equation (2) below provides the most parsimonious empirical specification of the residual earnings model on a per share basis (the horizon is only one period). Current period residual earnings is the proxy for future expected residual earnings. Residual earnings are estimated by subtracting an estimate of normal (expected) earnings from reported earnings. Expected earnings is the product of the estimated rate of return (r) and book value. Like Frankel and Lee (1999), we derive the estimated rate of return from interest rates in the *International Financial Statistics Yearbook* published by the International Monetary Fund (1997). Frankel and Lee (1999), however, are able to calculate a risk-adjusted return by adding a risk premium to long-term government bond rates Government bond rates are not available for four of the countries; therefore, we use commercial lending rates. Conceptually, this rate is the sum of a riskless rate and the average commercial lending risk premium. In the residual earnings model, book value and firm value are taken at time t while future abnormal earnings are for periods after time t. In our empirical analysis residual earnings (RE_t) are for the period ending at time t. Hence, as in Bernard (1994) and Collins et al. (1997), current earnings is a proxy for expected future earnings.

$$\text{Price}_{it} = b_0 + b_1\text{BVPS}_{it} + b_2\text{REPS}_{it} + e_{it} \tag{2}$$

where Price_{it} is the stock price per share of firm i at the end of year t, BVPS_{it} is the book value of shareholders' equity of firm i at the end of year t, REPS_{it} is the residual earnings per share, which is equal to $\text{EPS}_{it} - r^*(\text{BVPS}_{t-1})$[4] (proxy for expected REPS in period $t+1$), EPS_{it} is the earnings per share of firm i for year t, and r is the country's average commercial lending rate in year t taken from the International Financial Statistics Yearbook.

Book values and earnings are, of course, unobservable until some weeks after the end of the fiscal year. This raises the question of the timing of the market value measure to be associated with the accounting variables. As discussed by Barth et al. (1996), choice of contemporaneous versus lagged market values is a trade-off. The advantage to using a lagged market price is that it may reasonably reflect the accounting results since sufficient time has passed for these results to be public information. However, lagged market values will include effects of information and events occurring after the end of the fiscal year. Collins et al. (1997), examining associations between market and accounting numbers for US firms, take prices 3 months after the end of the fiscal period. In cross-country studies, however, this is problematic since the time lag between fiscal year-ends and report dates can vary widely. For this reason, our tests examine the relation between accounting numbers (book value and residual EPS for a fiscal year) and stock prices at the end of the fiscal year. Later, we analyze the sensitivity of our results using stock prices lagged 0 to 6 months following the end of the fiscal year.

Equation (2) expresses price as a function of book value and residual earnings. Examining the relative and incremental explanatory power of book value and of residual earnings requires two additional equations expressing price as a function of book value alone, Equation (3), and residual earnings alone, Equation (4).[5]

$$\text{Price}_{it} = c_0 + c_1\text{BVPS}_{it} + e_{it} \tag{3}$$

$$\text{Price}_{it} = d_0 + d_1\text{REPS}_{it} + e_{it} \tag{4}$$

Following Theil (1971), we define the incremental explanatory power of the book value and residual earnings variables in terms of differences in the coefficient of determination (R^2). These differences are sometimes called the *semi-partial coefficient of determination* (Cohen and Cohen, 1975, pp. 79–84). They are a measure of the incremental explanatory power of one variable given the remaining independent variables.

Define the R^2 statistics from Equations (2), (3), and (4) as R_b^2, R_r^2, and $R_{b,r}^2$, respectively. Then the incremental explanatory power is defined as:

$R_{b|r}^2 = R_{b,r}^2 - R_r^2$ The incremental explanatory power of book value is the total explanatory power of book value and residual earnings less the explanatory power of residual earnings alone.

$R_{r|b}^2 = R_{b,r}^2 - R_b^2$ The incremental explanatory power of residual earnings is the total explanatory power of book value and residual earnings less the explanatory power of book value alone.

$R_{com}^2 = R_{b,r}^2 - R_{b|r}^2 - R_{r|b}^2$ The explanatory power common to book value and residual earnings is the total explanatory power of book value and residual earnings less the incremental explanatory power of book value and the incremental explanatory power of residual earnings.[6]

We can also assess the ***relative*** explanatory power of book value and residual earnings by comparing the conditional (incremental) power as shown above (Biddle et al., 1995).[7] That is, we can also address the question of whether book values or residual earnings have greater explanatory power for each country.

Explanatory Power of BVPS and REPS Across the Six Countries

Table 8 reports summaries of regressions (2), (3), and (4) as well as incremental R^2 for each year with 30 or more observations and for all years together for the six countries. First, we focus on the coefficients and the significance of regressions (2), (3), and (4), and then we analyze the relative and incremental explanatory power.[8]

Coefficients on BVPS are positive for all countries. They are significant overall and for most years. BVPS coefficients are greater than 1.0 for Malaysia (2.75), the Philippines (2.17), Taiwan (1.26), and Thailand (1.41) in regression (2). BVPS coefficients are less than 1.0 for Indonesia (.82) and Korea (.89). Coefficients on REPS are positive and significant for all countries except the Philippines. Coefficients on REPS for regression (4) range from 1.26 for Malaysia to 10.90 for Thailand.[9]

We find significant differences in the value relevance of accounting across countries. The explanatory power of book value and residual earnings is quite high for Korea and the Philippines, near to what is found for Anglo-American markets. However, the explanatory power for Taiwan is well below that found for most other countries. Table 9 presents a

Table 8. Incremental and Relative Information Content of Book Values and Residual Earnings: Regressions of Book Value and Residual Earnings on Price by Year (*t*-statistics in parentheses)

$$\text{Price}_{it} = b_0 + b_1\text{BVPS}_t + b_2\text{REPS} + e_{it} \quad R^2_{b,r}$$

$$\text{Price}_{it} = c_0 + c_1\text{BVPS}_t + e_{it} \quad R^2_b$$

$$\text{Price}_{it} = d_0 + d_1\text{REPS} + e_{it} \quad R^2_r$$

where Price_{it} is the price per share of firm *i* at time *t*, BVPS_t is the book value per share of firm *i* at the end of period *t*, and REPS_t is the residual earnings per share of firm *i* for year *t*.

$R^2_{b\|r} = R^2_{b,r} - R^2_r$	The incremental explanatory power of book value is the total explanatory power of book value and residual earnings less the explanatory power of residual earnings alone.
$R^2_{r\|b} = R^2_{b,r} - R^2_b$	The incremental explanatory power of residual earnings is the total explanatory power of book value and residual earnings less the explanatory power of book value alone.
$R^2_{com} = R^2_{b,r} - R^2_{b\|r} - R^2_{r\|b}$	The explanatory power common to book value and residual earnings is the total explanatory power of book value and residual earnings less the incremental explanatory power of book value and the incremental explanatory power of residual earnings alone.

Year	*N*	b_0	b_1BV	b_2REPS	$R^2_{b,r}$	c_1BV	R^2_b	d_1REPS	R^2_r	$R^2_{b\|r}$	$R^2_{r\|b}$	R^2_{com}
Panel A: Indonesia												
All	338	1,400 (7.83)	0.96 (10.90)	2.49 (6.57)	.308	0.90 (9.69)	.219	2.07 (4.73)	.062	.246	.089	−.027
1991	46	698 (2.12)	1.62 (7.38)	6.08 (3.82)	.559	1.16 (5.52)	.409	−0.34 (−0.17)	.001	.558	.150	−.149
1992	61	596 (1.82)	1.75 (8.80)	5.66 (8.82)	.564	1.32 (5.43)	.358	2.46 (1.80)	.052	.542	.236	−.184
1993	63	1,864 (6.19)	1.04 (6.54)	0.86 (1.78)	.419	0.99 (6.22)	.388	0.34 (0.55)	.005	.414	.031	−.026
1994	70	1,495 (3.41)	0.79 (3.98)	3.07 (3.53)	.332	0.90 (4.22)	.208	3.59 (3.78)	.173	.159	.124	.049
1995	80	1,526 (3.61)	0.63 (3.32)	3.41 (3.99)	.266	0.66 (3.13)	.114	3.50 (3.86)	.161	.105	.152	.009
Mean[a]	64	1,236	1.17	3.82	.434	1.01	.295	1.91	.078	.356	.139	−.060

(continued)

Table 8. (Continued)

Year	N	b_0	b_1BV	b_2REPS	$R^2_{b,r}$	c_1BV	R^2_b	d_1REPS	R^2_r	$R^2_{b\mid r}$	$R^2_{r\mid b}$	R^2_{com}
Panel B: Korea												
All	901	7,746 (9.48)	0.87 (40.07)	1.29 (6.27)	.683	0.91 (42.61)	.669	3.56 (10.83)	.115	.568	.014	.101
1988	48	15,983 (10.36)	0.21 (2.43)	1.94 (2.41)	.182	0.18 (1.96)	.077	1.62 (1.93)	.075	.107	.105	−.030
1989	61	19,043 (16.22)	0.31 (4.26)	1.44 (2.53)	.241	0.22 (3.32)	.157	0.25 (0.45)	.000	.241	.084	−.084
1990	67	13,791 (17.12)	0.24 (4.49)	0.89 (2.11)	.240	0.18 (3.87)	.187	−0.10 (−0.26)	.001	.239	.053	−.052
1991	82	9,826 (9.51)	0.27 (5.08)	0.73 (2.09)	.261	0.26 (4.75)	.220	0.50 (1.25)	.019	.242	.041	−.022
1992	106	9,383 (5.75)	0.50 (7.13)	1.99 (5.53)	.584	0.67 (9.42)	.461	3.13 (7.97)	.379	.205	.123	.256
1993	145	11,318 (4.75)	0.74 (9.49)	3.26 (4.60)	.820	1.05 (23.44)	.794	8.91 (18.64)	.709	.111	.026	.683
1994	180	13,979 (8.06)	0.81 (18.06)	1.61 (3.48)	.816	0.91 (26.96)	.803	7.27 (12.73)	.477	.339	.013	.464
1995	182	3,266 (2.25)	0.92 (28.72)	0.32 (1.02)	.843	0.91 (30.87)	.842	−3.22 (−4.81)	.115	.728	.001	.114
Mean[a]	109	12,074	0.51	1.52	.498	0.55	.442	2.92	.222	.276	.056	.166
Panel C: Malaysia												
All	1,311	0.51 (2.00)	2.53 (19.54)	5.07 (6.55)	.277	2.71 (21.06)	.253	8.25 (9.60)	.067	.210	.024	.043
1987	42	0.66 (1.77)	1.38 (4.08)	2.57 (2.59)	.300	0.82 (2.97)	.180	−0.04 (−0.04)	.000	.300	.120	−.120
1988	50	0.59 (1.89)	1.24 (4.88)	2.33 (3.00)	.391	1.18 (4.20)	.269	1.90 (2.08)	.083	.308	.122	−.039
1989	59	1.76 (4.54)	0.75 (2.65)	4.28 (3.78)	.322	0.98 (3.16)	.149	4.89 (4.21)	.237	.085	.173	.064
1990	67	1.74 (4.27)	0.85 (2.75)	6.00 (4.71)	.381	1.24 (3.59)	.166	6.92 (5.37)	.307	.074	.215	.092
1991	102	0.92 (3.69)	0.99 (6.35)	9.33 (9.96)	.637	1.32 (6.13)	.273	10.58 (9.78)	.489	.148	.364	.125
1992	169	0.16 (0.66)	1.72 (12.57)	8.30 (8.36)	.532	1.45 (9.17)	.335	5.32 (3.96)	.086	.446	.197	−.111
1993	172	−1.11 (1.30)	4.31 (9.70)	5.09 (1.62)	.371	4.37 (9.80)	.361	7.30 (1.88)	.020	.351	.010	.010
1994	183	0.86 (1.04)	3.03 (7.84)	2.41 (0.91)	.264	3.07 (7.98)	.260	4.58 (1.50)	.012	.252	.004	.008
1995	258	0.80 (1.33)	2.38 (8.77)	3.25 (1.90)	.263	2.48 (9.30)	.253	0.64 (3.30)	.041	.222	.010	.031
1996	201	4.21 (4.02)	1.37 (5.21)	7.64 (3.33)	.157	1.97 (4.95)	.110	10.73 (5.04)	.113	.044	.047	.066
Mean[a]	130	1.06	1.80	5.12	.362	1.89	.236	5.28	.139	.223	.126	.013

continued overleaf

Panel D: Philippines												
All	139	2.44 (1.32)	2.20 (16.75)	5.49 (4.60)	.680	2.08 (1.30)	.625	1.74 (0.85)	.005	.675	.055	−.050
1994	31	0.45 (0.15)	2.92 (14.63)	13.76 (6.67)	.885	2.41 (8.27)	.702	2.27 (0.41)	.010	.875	.183	−.173
1995	49	−0.23 (−0.16)	2.58 (22.99)	18.72 (10.09)	.921	1.89 (10.88)	.716	−3.37 (−0.68)	.010	.911	.205	−.195
Mean[a]	40	0.11	2.75	16.24	.903	2.15	.709	−0.55	.010	.893	.194	−.184
Panel E: Taiwan												
All	369	15.57 (5.43)	1.26 (5.64)	3.34 (6.63)	.169	1.24 (5.24)	.070	3.30 (6.28)	.097	.072	.099	−.002
1993	42	9.30 (0.84)	2.20 (2.38)	1.32 (0.65)	.135	2.19 (2.40)	.126	1.30 (0.60)	.009	.126	.009	.000
1994	98	15.39 (3.82)	1.68 (5.08)	3.63 (3.79)	.272	1.52 (4.36)	.164	3.03 (2.84)	.077	.195	.108	−.031
1995	179	9.35 (3.43)	1.35 (6.63)	2.19 (5.21)	.300	1.41 (6.47)	.191	2.35 (5.02)	.125	.175	.109	.016
Mean[a]	106	11.35	1.74	2.38	.236	1.71	.160	2.23	.070	.166	.076	−.006
Panel F: Thailand												
All	596	51.28 (9.71)	1.28 (11.29)	7.76 (11.38)	.397	1.50 (14.63)	.265	10.37 (14.70)	.267	.130	.132	.135
1991	40	18.63 (2.25)	1.81 (11.06)	2.84 (3.49)	.848	2.06 (12.24)	.798	6.67 (4.48)	.345	.503	.050	.295
1992	74	27.59 (3.45)	1.68 (10.53)	5.55 (4.92)	.727	1.93 (11.15)	.635	9.42 (5.55)	.300	.427	.092	.208
1993	130	102.78 (6.72)	0.57 (1.91)	12.64 (5.39)	.300	1.33 (4.55)	.139	14.74 (7.05)	.280	.020	.161	.119
1994	166	47.66 (5.60)	1.10 (6.80)	9.18 (8.39)	.512	1.53 (8.39)	.300	11.56 (9.88)	.373	.139	.212	.161
1995	175	38.21 (2.80)	1.12 (6.64)	7.14 (5.65)	.369	1.38 (7.62)	.251	9.33 (6.91)	.216	.153	.118	.098
Mean[a]	117	46.97	1.26	7.47	.551	1.65	.425	10.34	.303	.248	.126	.177

[a]The mean coefficient is the average of yearly regression coefficients, and the *t*-statistic is the average coefficient divided by its time-series standard error. The mean R^2 is the average of yearly R^2.

Table 9. Explanatory Power of Book Value and Residual Earnings

Country	R^2 all firm-years	*Country*	*Mean yearly* R^2	*Number of years*
Korea	.683	Philippines	.903	2
Philippines	.680	Thailand	.551	5
Thailand	.397	Korea	.498	8
Indonesia	.308	Indonesia	.434	5
Malaysia	.277	Malaysia	.362	10
Taiwan	.169	Taiwan	.236	3

ranking from the highest to lowest explanatory power for the samples pooled over all years and for the yearly average.

The mean yearly R^2 are greater than the pooled firm-years for all countries except Korea. Fitting the model for each year allows for yearly variation in the relation and results in a better fit than pooled firm-years. Table 8 reveals considerable year to year variation in the coefficients.

The following initial conclusions seem warranted. First, coefficients on book value and earnings are not greatly different from those found for European and American markets. Second, there is a high level of cross-country variation in explanatory power of accounting earnings and book values for stock prices. The six Asian countries in this study differ more than European and North American countries in prior studies. Third, earlier in this article we predicted, based on accounting differences, that accounting values in the Philippines would have high explanatory power for firm value but low explanatory power in Taiwan. Both of these predictions are substantiated. However, contrary to our predictions Korean accounting values have high explanatory power. This appears anomalous given the reliance of accounting practice on tax law in Korea.

Incremental Value Relevance of BVPS and REPS

Next, we examine the incremental explanatory power of BVPS beyond that for REPS, $R_{b|r}^2$, and the incremental explanatory power of REPS beyond that of BVPS, $R_{r|b}^2$. Relative explanatory power can be addressed by comparing $R_{b|r}^2$ and $R_{r|b}^2$ to each other (Biddle et al., 1995). Table 8 reports these results for each year and for all years together. Fig. 1 shows the patterns across time. Focusing on the incremental explanatory power of BVPS, $R_{b|r}^2$, we find the incremental power of BVPS ranges widely across the six countries, from a low of .070 in Taiwan to a high of .669 for Korea. Except for Taiwan, BVPSs have higher explanatory power than in prior studies. Prior studies (Harris et al., 1994; Collins et al., 1997; King and Langli, 1998) have used EPS rather than REPS to measure abnormal future earnings. EPS is typically highly correlated with BVPS and hence, the incremental explanatory power of book value is reduced. REPS is not highly correlated with BVPS and as a consequence BVPS has relatively more explanatory power. Table 10 lists from highest to lowest the incremental explanatory power for BVPS for the samples pooled over all years and for yearly means.

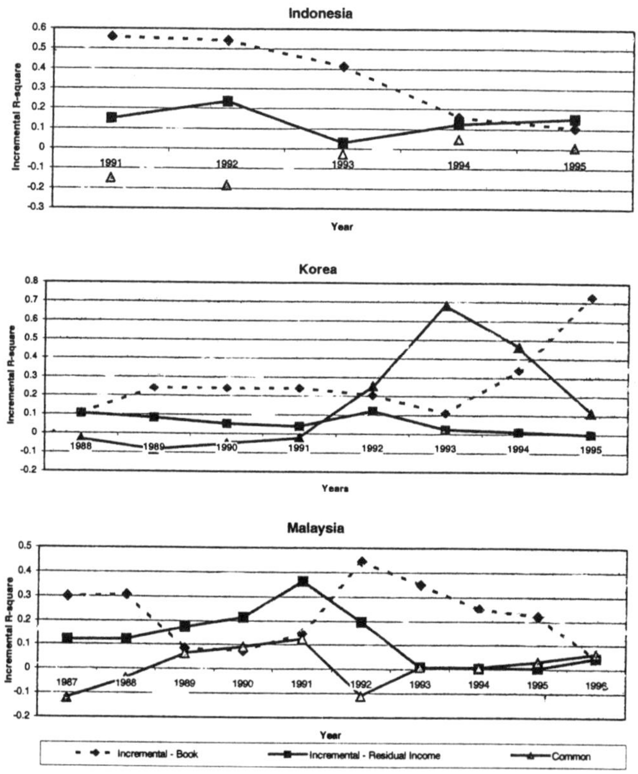

Figure 1. Incremental Explanatory Power of Book Value and Residual Earnings for Prices.

In the section of this article discussing the accounting diversity across the six countries, we predicted that the Philippines, Indonesia, and Malaysia would have high incremental explanatory power for book value with low explanatory power in Taiwan and Thailand. Our expectation that the explanatory power of book value would be highest in the Philippines and the lowest in Taiwan is supported. However, the incremental explanatory power of book value in Indonesia and Malaysia do not stand out as high.

Focusing on the incremental explanatory power of REPS, $R_{r|b}^2$, we find the incremental power of REPS is much lower than that for BVPS. Furthermore, $R_{r|b}^2$ appears more stable over time. Table 11 lists the highest to lowest incremental explanatory power for REPS for the samples pooled over all years.

Thailand ranks first (third) in incremental explanatory power for residual earnings for pooled firm-years (yearly average). The Philippines shows some evidence (yearly

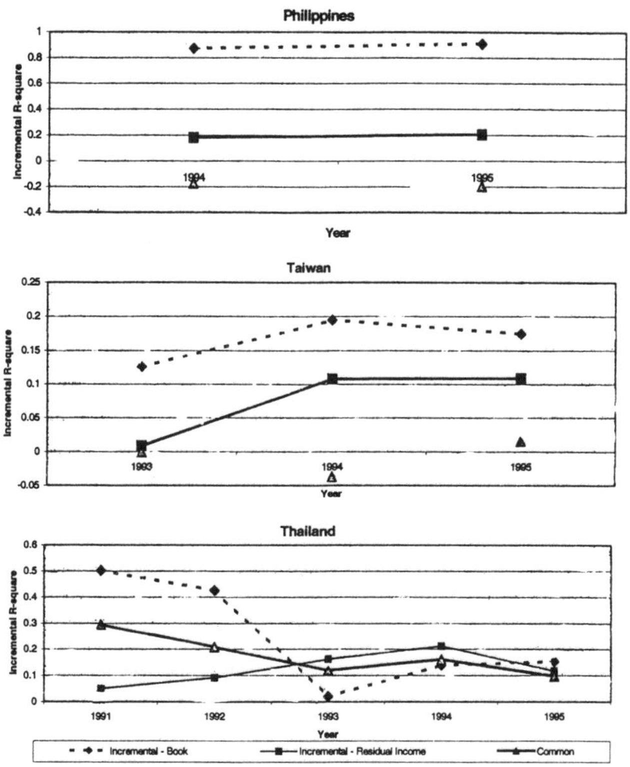

Figure 1. (continued)

average) of the hypothesized high incremental explanatory power. Residual earnings have little explanatory power for Korea. Since prior studies have examined EPS rather than REPS, these results are not strictly comparable. We also ran the regressions using EPS and find marginally lower incremental explanatory power for EPS than for REPS. However, the incremental power of BVPS was lower as well. Our results reflect the difficulty in making predictions about the explanatory power of residual earnings across countries.

Explanatory Power of BVPS and REPS Over Time

Following Collins et al. (1997) and King and Langli (1998), we examine changes across time in the explanatory power of book value and residual earnings. The incremental explanatory power of BVPS and REPS differ greatly over time and across countries. The

Table 10. Incremental Explanatory Power of BVPS

Country	$R^2_{b\|r}$ *all firm-years*	*Country*	*Mean yearly* $R^2_{b\|r}$	*Number of years*
Philippines	.653	Philippines	.893	2
Korea	.568	Indonesia	.356	5
Indonesia	.246	Korea	.277	8
Malaysia	.211	Thailand	.248	5
Thailand	.130	Malaysia	.223	10
Taiwan	.072	Taiwan	.165	3

Table 11. Incremental Explanatory Power of Residual Earnings

Country	$R^2_{r\|b}$ *all firm-years*	*Country*	*Mean yearly* $R^2_{r\|b}$	*Number of years*
Thailand	.132	Philippines	.194	2
Taiwan	.099	Indonesia	.139	5
Indonesia	.089	Thailand	.127	5
Philippines	.055	Malaysia	.126	10
Malaysia	.024	Taiwan	.075	3
Korea	.014	Korea	.056	8

time patterns revealed in the regressions are illustrated in Fig. 1. The time patterns show that the overall explanatory power is increasing for Korea, the Philippines, and Taiwan, and declining for Indonesia and Thailand and mixed for Malaysia. Similarly, the incremental explanatory power of BVPS is increasing for Korea, the Philippines, and Taiwan, decreasing for Indonesia and Thailand, and mixed for Malaysia. For the incremental explanatory power of residual earnings, results show increases in the Philippines, Taiwan, and Thailand, decreases for Korea, and mixed patterns for Indonesia and Malaysia.

Sensitivity to the Timing of Price

We examined the sensitivity of our results to the date at which the stock price is taken. At the end of the fiscal year, information in the financial reports including book values and earnings are not available to investors. Use of lagged stock prices would allow for that financial statement information to be impounded into price. On the other hand, later prices will include information concerning events subsequent to the fiscal year thereby confounding the relation between accounting and firm value. To test the sensitivity of the price date, we run the regressions for lags of 0 to 5 months. Table 12 reports the total and incremental explanatory power for BVPS and for REPS for these six price dates.[10] Only Indonesia and Korea show higher R^2s for prices lagged after fiscal year-end. Total explanatory power for Indonesian (Korean) firms is greatest when prices are measured 4 (2) months after the fiscal year-end. The differences in R^2 are not large, and the higher R^2s do not affect the ordering of countries in Tables 9–11.

Table 12. The Information Content of Book Values and Residual Earnings: Regressions of Book Value and Residual Earnings on Lagged Prices

Dependent variable	*N*	$R^2_{b,r}$	R^2_b	R^2_r	$R^2_{b\|r}$	$R^2_{r\|b}$
Panel A: Indonesia						
Price at year-end	338	.308	*.219*	.062	.246	.089
Price after 1 month	284	.280	.181	.069	.211	.099
Price after 2 months	319	.296	.196	.075	.221	.100
Price after 3 months	319	.310	.212	.073	.237	.098
Price after 4 months	318	*.366*	.212	.115	*.251*	.154
Price after 5 months	322	.355	.194	*.125*	.230	*.161*
Panel B: Korea						
Price at year-end	902	.683	.669	.115	.568	.014
Price after 1 month	884	.729	.717	.114	.615	.012
Price after 2 months	884	*.773*	*.754*	.139	.634	.019
Price after 3 months	884	.764	.741	*.150*	.614	*.023*
Price after 4 months	884	.755	.744	.115	*.640*	.011
Price after 5 months	884	.751	.739	.117	.634	.012
Panel C: Malaysia						
Price at year-end	1,311	*.277*	*.253*	*.066*	*.211*	*.023*
Price after 1 month	1,310	.151	.133	.043	.108	.018
Price after 2 months	1,310	.159	.150	.033	.126	.009
Price after 3 months	1,310	.147	.133	.036	.111	.014
Price after 4 months	1,310	.135	.123	.032	.103	.012
Price after 5 months	1,310	.137	.122	.037	.100	.015
Panel D: Philippines						
Price at year-end	139	*.680*	*.625*	.005	*.675*	.055
Price after 1 month	139	.410	.354	*.015*	.395	*.056*
Price after 2 months	139	.438	.411	.002	.436	.027
Price after 3 months	139	.445	.435	.001	.444	.010
Price after 4 months	139	.420	.413	.001	.419	.007
Price after 5 months	139	.323	.308	.000	.323	.015
Panel E: Taiwan						
Price at year-end	369	*.169*	*.070*	*.097*	*.072*	*.099*
Price after 1 month	366	.138	.057	.078	.060	.081
Price after 2 months	366	.130	.057	.072	.058	.073
Price after 3 months	366	.108	.050	.057	.051	.058
Price after 4 months	366	.092	.059	.036	.056	.033
Price after 5 months	366	.091	.052	.037	.054	.039

The highest explanatory power is in italics. See Table 8 for definitions and regression models.

SUMMARY AND CONCLUSIONS

In this study, we examine the accounting systems in six Asian countries to assess whether they differ in their value relevance under the residual earnings model. The countries selected: Indonesia, Korea, Malaysia, the Philippines, Taiwan, and Thailand, differ in the conservatism of their accounting practices, as well as in their adherence to clean surplus accounting. The study addresses two questions. First, are there systematic differences across countries in the value relevance of accounting numbers? Second, are there systematic differences in the incremental and relative contribution of book values and residual earnings to value across the countries related to accounting differences?

Our results indicate first, that accounting book value and residual earnings are positively and significantly related to current stock prices across all six countries consistent with King and Langli's (1998) findings for European countries and Bernard's (1994) results for US firms. Our results also show significant differences in the relation between accounting numbers and stock prices across the six countries and across time. We find some consistency between our predictions of explanatory power of accounting for firm value based on accounting practice in the six countries; however, the predictions are incomplete and some results are not consistent. While this study suggests that differences in the explanatory power of accounting are related to accounting differences across the countries, more evidence is needed. Second, when we focus on the relative and incremental explanatory power of book value and residual earnings, the empirical results again vary across countries more than for European and American markets in prior studies. Again, there are some tantalizing hints that accounting practice is related to these differences, but more evidence is needed.

The extent to which accounting differences are related to valuation differences is of concern in the debate on international accounting standards and practices. The body of research examining the value relevance of accounting includes North American (Bernard, 1994; Collins et al., 1997), European (Joos and Lang, 1994; King and Langli, 1998), and now Asian countries. The evidence seems clear that strongly conservative (biased) accounting is less value relevant. The evidence concerning violations of the CSR is less clear. Conceptually, violations of CSR that cause book values to be closer to market values, e.g., asset revaluation, increase the value relevance of book value. However, CSR violations that move book value away from market value, e.g., immediate write-offs of goodwill, will decrease the value relevance of book value. Evidence to date is broadly consistent with these expectations. Less clear are the predicted and actual effects of CSR violations on the value relevance of residual earnings.

The study makes two additional contributions. First, we compute incremental explanatory power for residual earnings (the appropriate value under the residual earnings model) rather than for earnings as in prior studies. Residual earnings have little correlation with book value and allow a better separation of the explanatory power of book value and earnings. Second, we investigate the effects of different price dates in the relation. We find that year-end stock prices are more highly correlated with accounting variables in most countries and are near to the highest correlation in all countries.

NOTES

1. The explanatory power of book value and residual earnings will not be affected if a bias is constant across firms and time. However, the accounting procedures examined are unlikely to be constant either across firms or across time.
2. Each of these accounting procedures will be relevant to only a subset of firms. Hence, the cross-sectional effect will be smaller than for accounting procedures affecting all or most firms.

3. The expected coefficients in Equation (1) can be see from the equation for firm value with a finite horizon (for example, see Equation (5) in King and Langli, 1998).
4. We use *average* book value to calculate our proxy for abnormal earnings rather than *beginning* book value as defined by the residual earnings model. Since we use actual earnings as the proxy for expected future earnings, average book values represent the book values in place that generated those earnings. Regression results for residual earnings calculated from beginning book values (not reported) are essentially equal to, but have slightly less explanatory power than, the results reported in this study.
5. The coefficients b_2 and d_1 in Equations (2) and (4) are *not* equal to the a_2 coefficient in Equation (1). The earnings proxy used in Equations (2) and (4) is residual earnings for the current year rather than future expected residual earnings. The exact relationship in the coefficients in Equations (2) and (3) relative to that in Equation (1) is difficult to specify. However, it is easy to show that b_2 and d_1 must be smaller than a_2.
6. Theil (1971, pp. 167–171) shows that where the independent variables are not orthogonal, the sign of the difference between total R^2 ($R^2_{b,r}$) and the sum of the incremental R^2s ($R^2_{r|b}+R^2_{b|r}$) is not determined. That is, R^2_{com} may be either positive or negative.
7. Biddle et al. (1995) show that this procedure is equivalent to comparing the explanatory power of single regressions. In other words, whether book value or residual earnings has greater relative explanatory power can be determined either comparing the R^2s from Equations (3) and (4) or by comparing the incremental R^2s (i.e., $R^2_{b|r}$ to $R^2_{r|b}$).
8. To compare with prior research, all of the analyses in this article were repeated with EPS replacing REPS. EPS has greater explanatory power than REPS in most years for all countries. REPS has a lower (sometimes negative) correlation with book value than EPS. Consequently, book value has greater incremental explanatory power in the presence of REPS than with EPS. However, the general tenor of the results and the time-series patterns are quite similar.
9. Multicollinearity is not a problem in our regressions. None of the regressions containing both book value and residual earnings has variance inflation factors greater than 2. Heteroscedasticity in the error terms was detected, however, in the Indonesia and Malaysia regressions containing both book value and residual earnings. We report White's adjusted t-statistics for those two countries.
10. We do not have share price data for Thailand for months beyond year-end, so Table 12 covers only five countries.

REFERENCES

Akathaporn, Parporn. 1995. *Accounting Practice in Thailand.* Unpublished Manuscript, Bangkok, Thailand.

American Institute of Certified Public Accountants. 1989. *The Accounting Profession in the Philippines*. New York: American Institute of Certified Public Accountants.

American Institute of Certified Public Accountants. 1990. *The Accounting Profession in Korea.* New York: American Institute of Certified Public Accountants.

American Institute of Certified Public Accountants. 1992. *The Accounting Profession in Taiwan, Republic of China.* New York: American Institute of Certified Public Accountants.

Barth, Mary E., William H. Beaver, and Wayne R. Landsman. 1996. "Value Relevance of Banks' Fair Value Disclosures Under SFAS No. 107." *Accounting Review,* (October) *71*(4): 513–538.

Belsley, David, Edwin Kuh, and Roy Welsch. 1980. *Regression Diagnostics*. New York: Wiley.

Bernard, Victor L. 1993. "Earnings Quality, Book Value, and the State of Financial Statement Analysis." In S. Butler, ed. *Earnings Quality*. Norman, OK: The Center for Economic and Management Research, pp. 174–183.

Bernard, Victor L. 1994. *Accounting-Based Valuation Methods, Determinates of Market-to-Book Ratios, and Implications for Financial Statement Analysis*. Working Paper, University of Michigan, (January).

Biddle, Gary C., Gim S. Seow, and Andrew Siegel. 1995. "Relative Versus Incremental Information Content." *Contemporary Accounting Research*, (Fall) *12*(1): 1–23.

Center for International Financial Analysis & Research. 1995. *International Accounting and Auditing Trends*, 4th edition, vol. I. Princeton, NJ: CIFAR Publications.

Choi, Frederick D.S. and Richard M. Levich. 1991. "International Accounting Diversity and Capital Market Decisions." In F.D.S. Choi, ed. *Handbook of International Accounting*. New York: Wiley, pp. 7.1–29.

Cohen, Jacob and Patricia Cohen. 1975. *Applied Multiple Regression/Correlation Analysis for the Behavioral Sciences*. Hillsdale, NJ: Lawrence Erlbaum Associates.

Collins, Daniel W., Edward L. Maydew, and Ira S. Weiss. 1997. "Changes in the Value-Relevance of Earnings and Book Values over the Past Forty Years." *Journal of Accounting and Economics*, (December) *24*(4): 39–68.

Deloitte Touche Tohmatsu International. 1995a. *Indonesia: International Tax and Business Guide*. New York: Deloitte Touche Tohmatsu International.

Deloitte Touche Tohmatsu International. 1995b. *Korea: International Tax and Business Guide*. New York: Deloitte Touche Tohmatsu International.

Deloitte Touche Tohmatsu International. 1996a. *Philippines: International Tax and Business Guide*. New York: Deloitte Touche Tohmatsu International.

Deloitte Touche Tohmatsu International. 1996b. *Taiwan: International Tax and Business Guide*. New York: Deloitte Touche Tohmatsu International.

Deloitte Touche Tohmatsu International. 1997. *Malaysia: International Tax and Business Guide*. New York: Deloitte Touche Tohmatsu International.

Edwards, Edward O. and Philip W. Bell. 1961. *The Theory and Measurement of Business Income*. Berkeley: University of California Press.

Feltham, Gerald and James A. Ohlson. 1995. "Valuation and Clean Surplus Accounting for Operating and Financial Activities." *Contemporary Accounting Research*, (Spring) *11*(2): 689–732.

Frankel, Richard and Charles M.C. Lee. 1999. *Accounting Diversity and International Valuation*. Working Paper, Cornell University, (May).

Graham, Roger C. and Chin-hsin Coco Wang. 1995. "Taiwan and International Accounting Standards: A Comparison." *International Journal of Accounting*, *30*: 149–167.

Harris, Trevor S., Mark Lang, and Hans Peter Möller. 1994. "The Value Relevance of German Accounting Measures: An Empirical Analysis." *Journal of Accounting Research*, (Autumn) *32*(2): 187–209.

International Monetary Fund. 1997. *International Financial Statistics Yearbook*, vol. XLV. Washington, DC: IMF Publication Services.

Joos, Peter and Mark Lang. 1994. "The Effects of Accounting Diversity: Evidence from the European Union." *Journal of Accounting Research*, (Supplement) *32*: 141–168.

King, Raymond D. and John Christian Langli. 1998. "Accounting Diversity and Firm Valuation." *International Journal of Accounting*, *33*(5): 529–567.

Mathew Bender & Co. 1996. *World Accounting*. New York: Mathew Bender & Co.

Ohlson, James A. 1991. "The Theory of Value and Earnings, and an Introduction to the Ball–Brown Analysis." *Contemporary Accounting Research*, (Fall) *8*(1): 1–19.

Ohlson, James A. 1995. "Earnings, Book Values, and Dividends in Security Valuation." *Contemporary Accounting Research*, (Spring) *11*(2): 661–687.

Peasnell, Kenneth V. 1982. "Some Formal Connections Between Economic Values and Yields and Accounting Numbers." *Journal of Business Finance and Accounting*, (October) *9*(3): 61–381.

Preinreich, Gabriel. 1938. "Annual Survey of Economic Theory: The Theory of Depreciation." *Econometrica,* (January) *6*(3): 219–231.

Price Waterhouse. 1995a. *An Introduction to Malaysian GAAP.* Kuala Lumpur, Malaysia: Price Waterhouse.

Price Waterhouse. 1995b. *Financial Reporting—An International Survey.* Washington, D.C.: Price Waterhouse, (May).

Price Waterhouse. 1996a. *Doing Business in Indonesia.* Jakarta, Indonesia: Price Waterhouse.

Price Waterhouse. 1996b. *Doing Business in Malaysia.* Kuala Lumpur, Malaysia: Price Waterhouse.

Price Waterhouse. 1996c. *Doing Business in Taiwan.* Taipei, Taiwan: Price Waterhouse.

Price Waterhouse. 1996d. *Doing Business in the Republic of Korea.* Seoul, Korea: Price Waterhouse.

Saudagaran, Shahrokh M. and Joselito G. Diga. 1997. "Financial Reporting in Emerging Capital Markets: Characteristics and Policy Issues." *Accounting Horizons,* (June) *11*(2): 41–64.

Theil, Henri. 1971. *Principles of Econometrics.* New York: Wiley.

ELSEVIER Journal of Accounting and Economics 33 (2002) 401–425

JOURNAL OF Accounting & Economics

www.elsevier.com/locate/econbase

Corporate ownership structure and the informativeness of accounting earnings in East Asia ☆

Joseph P.H. Fan[a], T.J. Wong[b,*]

[a] *Department of Finance, School of Business and Management, The Hong Kong University of Science and Technology, Clear Water Bay, Hong Kong*

[b] *Department of Accounting, School of Business and Management, The Hong Kong University of Science and Technology, Clear Water Bay, Hong Kong*

Received 23 February 2000; received in revised form 12 January 2002

Abstract

This study examines the relations between earnings informativeness, measured by the earnings–return relation, and the ownership structure of 977 companies in seven East Asian economies. Our results are consistent with two complementary explanations. First, concentrated ownership and the associated pyramidal and cross-holding structures create agency conflicts between controlling owners and outside investors. Consequently, controlling owners are perceived to report accounting information for self-interested purposes, causing the reported earnings to lose credibility to outside investors. Second, concentrated ownership is associated with low earnings informativeness as ownership concentration prevents leakage

☆ We appreciate helpful comments from Ray Ball, Gary Biddle, Charles Chen (the referee), Ellen Engel, Masaharu Hanazaki, Hasung Jang, Steve Matsunaga, Jevons Lee, Jody Magliolo, Randall Morck, Suil Pae, Enrico Perotti, Terry Shevlin, Megumi Suto, Sheridan Titman, John Wei, Joanna Wu, Takeshi Yamada, Ross Watts (the editor), Jerold Zimmerman, an anonymous referee, and workshop participants at the Asian Development Bank Institute, the Chinese University of Hong Kong, Hitotsubashi University, The Hong Kong University of Science and Technology, the Polytechnic University of Hong Kong, National Chengchi University of Taiwan, Nanyang Technological University at Singapore, and Shanghai University of Finance and Economics, and conference participants at the 2000 Conference on Accounting in Transition Economics at the William Davidson Institute, the 2000 HKUST Accounting Symposium, the 2000 AAANZ Conference, the 2000 Shanghai APFA Conference, the 2000 London EFA Conference, the 2001 AFA annual meeting at New Orleans, the 2001 AAA annual meeting at Atlanta, and the 2001 Conference on Designing Financial Systems in East Asia and Japan organized by IMF and Hitotsubashi University. T.J. Wong acknowledges the financial support of the Wei Lun Fellowship.

*Corresponding author. Tel.: +852-2358-7574; fax: +852-2358-1693.

E-mail address: actjwong@ust.hk (T.J. Wong).

PII: S0165-4101(02)00047-2

of proprietary information about the firms' rent-seeking activities.

JEL classification: G32; M41

Keywords: Ownership concentration; Transparency; Earnings informativeness; Emerging market

1. Introduction

Public corporations in East Asia typically have low levels of transparency and disclosure quality. Some commentators and policy advisors believe that a closer adherence to international disclosure rules and the adoption of international accounting standards are essential for improving corporate transparency in the region (World Bank, 1998). Despite efforts to impose stricter reporting rules and standards, the general perception is that corporate transparency has been declining (Asian Wall Street Journal, 1999). While the new accounting rules may have increased the quantity of accounting information, investors have reservations about the quality of the reported numbers.[1] Therefore, it is important for regulators and policy makers to understand the causes of the low quality of reported accounting information in the region.

This paper focuses on the relations between corporate ownership structure and the quality of accounting information in seven East Asian economies excluding Japan. More specifically, we use the informativeness of accounting earnings to investors as a measure of the quality of accounting information. We develop two complementary arguments pertaining to the relations between ownership structure and earnings informativeness. The first argument is related to the entrenchment effect of ownership concentration (Morck et al., 1988). Corporate ownership is highly concentrated in East Asia. As the controlling owners are entrenched by their effective control of the firms, their decisions that deprive the rights of minority shareholders are often uncontestable in the weak legal systems in the region and by ineffective corporate governance mechanisms such as boards of directors and the market for corporate control (Shleifer and Vishny, 1997; La Porta et al., 1999; Johnson et al., 2000b). Moreover, due to the complicated pyramidal and cross-holding ownership structures typical in East Asian companies, a significant number of controlling owners in the region actually possess more control than their equity ownership indicates, which further exacerbates the entrenchment effect.[2] The

[1] This view of low information quality was shared among business professionals at the recent World Bank Meeting. For example, a local lawyer from Thailand remarked that "the major difference (in accounting disclosure) between the past and today is that statements of accounts now carry more qualifications, not better information". See the report by Sender (1999).

[2] Claessens et al. (2002) report that the concentrated control and the divergence between ownership and control in public corporations in eight East Asian economics diminish firm value, indicating the economic significance of the agency problem associated with ownership structures. Consistent evidence is also found in several other studies. La Porta et al. (2002) examine over 300 firms from 27 wealthy economies and

entrenchment effect of the ownership structure potentially affects firms' financial reporting. Because the controlling owner oversees the accounting reporting policies and is perceived to have strong opportunistic incentives to hold up minority shareholders, the market expects that the owner will not report high-quality accounting information. This market perception will reduce the credibility of accounting earnings reports and consequently the informativeness of those earnings.

The second argument is related to proprietary information and specific human capital. By concentrating ownership, decision rights can be given to individuals who possess specific knowledge (Jensen and Meckling, 1992; Christie et al., 2002). One benefit of co-locating decision rights with specific knowledge is that the leakage of the specific knowledge to competitors is prevented and the transferring cost of the specific knowledge is avoided. This benefit is great in East Asia where political lobbying activities are common and lucrative. As concentrating ownership limits information flows to the public, political rent-seekers are able to avoid potential competition and social sanctions. Thus, this information effect argument predicts that concentrated ownership is associated with opacity and low informativeness of accounting earnings.

Our empirical evidence is broadly consistent with the predictions of the entrenchment and information effects arguments. We find that earnings informativeness, measured by the earnings–return relation, is significantly negatively related to the ultimate owner's control level, conditional on the owner having gained effective control. This evidence is consistent with the information effect. We also find that earnings informativeness is significantly negatively related to the degree of divergence between the ultimate owner's control and the equity ownership level. This lends support to the entrenchment effect argument. The result is also consistent with the information effect argument, provided that controlling owners who want to protect proprietary information use stock pyramids or cross-shareholdings to leverage their control, thus creating divergence between ownership and control. These empirical results are robust to controls for firm size, market-to-book assets, leverage, the number of industry segments operated by the firm and to varying the starting and ending dates of the stock return window.

This analysis of East Asian corporations allows us to study the subject of earnings informativeness in a different ownership context from that of the research on U.S. corporations. Our research results are also rich in policy implications. In general, our results support Ball et al. (2000) by finding that policy makers should consider a country's overall institutional environment before prescribing a comprehensive set of rules and regulations for corporate reporting. Also, it is important for policy makers and regulators to understand how the concentrated share ownership structure in East Asia is associated with incentives for firms to reduce accounting information quality. Blindly adopting international accounting standards and disclosure rules

(*footnote continued*)
report that firms with higher ownership by controlling owners have higher valuation. Johnson et al. (2000a) document that levels of shareholder protection explain the extent of stock market decline in many emerging markets during the Asian financial crisis.

without considering the institutional environment in East Asia will not improve the corporate transparency in this region. Last, the paper illustrates that it would be fruitful for future research to focus on how ownership structures shape accounting policies in emerging markets and transition economies.

The paper proceeds as follows. In Section 2, we discuss the causes and effects of ownership structures in East Asia and develop our hypothesis on the relation between ownership structure and earnings informativeness. In Section 3, we describe our sample and data, report statistics on the ownership structures of East Asian firms, and present our empirical analyses. We conclude this paper in Section 4.

2. Development of hypothesis

The ownership of listed companies in East Asia is typically concentrated in the hands of large shareholders. This concentrated control is achieved through complicated ownership arrangements, i.e., stock pyramids and cross-shareholdings.[3] In this section, we discuss the forces that shape the ownership structure. We then discuss how the ownership structure shapes the firms' agency problems, through its entrenchment and incentive alignment effects on controlling owners. We finally discuss the entrenchment and the information arguments, which lead to a hypothesis pertaining to the relation between ownership structure and earnings informativeness.

2.1. Causes of concentrated ownership

The body of property rights literature provides a general framework for analyzing the determinants of corporate share ownership structures.[4] The literature emphasizes the roles of customs, social norms, and law and legal systems in shaping the structure of property rights and their governance systems. Corporate share ownership can be viewed as a property rights arrangement through which the owner of the share is entitled to three categories of property rights. First, the owner has the decision right of deploying corporate assets, i.e., the control or voting right. Second, the owner has the right to earn income, i.e., the cash flow right. Third, the owner has the right to transfer the share and the associated control and cash flow rights to another party. The value of the share depends on how well its property rights are enforced. The enforcement of property rights is usually undertaken by both individual owners and the state. In economies where the state does not effectively enforce property rights, the enforcement by individual owners plays a relatively more important role. The structure of share ownership affects the degree to which corporate contracts are

[3] Dual-class shares are rare in East Asia. Among the seven economies that we investigate, only South Korea allows dual-class listings. They are completely prohibited in Hong Kong and Singapore. The remaining economies prohibit dual-class shares, but allow certain preferred shares to have dual-class characteristics. See Nenova (1999).

[4] The literature was pioneered by Coase (1960), Demsetz (1964), Alchian (1965, 1977), and Cheung (1970, 1983). Interested readers are referred to Eggertsson (1990) for a survey of the literature.

enforced, because it affects the owners' abilities and incentives to enforce the property rights delineated by the contracts.

One prediction from the property rights framework is that concentrated ownership will be observed in economies where property rights are not well enforced by the state. Controlling owners obtain the power (through high voting rights) and the incentives (through high cash flow rights) to negotiate and enforce corporate contracts with various stakeholders, including minority shareholders, managers, laborers, material suppliers, customers, debtholders, and governments. The various parties in the nexus of corporate contracts share the benefits of trade as a result.[5] Shleifer and Vishny (1997) elaborate on this point and suggest that the benefits from concentrated ownership are relatively larger in countries that are generally less developed, where property rights are not well defined and/or protected by judicial systems. To test this proposition, La Porta et al. (1999) investigate the ownership concentration by the three largest shareholders of the largest corporations in countries around the world and find that weak legal and institutional environments (laws and enforcement) are associated with the highly concentrated share ownership of listed companies. The private enforcement of property rights is a probable reason for the concentrated ownership of East Asian corporations, which often confront weak legal systems, poor law enforcement, and corruption.

2.2. *Incentive effects of ownership concentration*

The degree of ownership concentration affects the nature of contracting, creating agency problems between managers and outside shareholders. When ownership is diffuse, as is typical in the U.S. and the U.K., agency problems stem from the conflicts of interest between outside shareholders and managers who own an insignificant amount of equity in the firm (Berle and Means, 1932; Jensen and Meckling, 1976; Roe, 1994). On the other hand, when ownership is concentrated to a level at which an owner obtains effective control of the firm, as is the case in East Asia and most other locations outside the U.S. and the U.K., the nature of the agency problem shifts away from manager–shareholder conflicts to conflicts between the controlling owner (who is also the manager) and minority shareholders.

2.2.1. *The entrenchment effect*

Gaining effective control of a corporation enables the controlling owner to determine how profits are shared among shareholders. Although the minority shareholders are entitled to the cash flow rights corresponding to their share investments, they face the uncertainty that the entrenched controlling owner may

[5] Large owners can be beneficial in diffusely held firms, too. The existence of large owners mitigates the free-rider problem associated with the diffuse ownership structure in monitoring managers. Demsetz and Lehn (1985) provide evidence that ownership concentration in the U.S. is positively related to the control potential of firms, among other factors. They argue that distortions in the market for corporate control along with the managerial labor market increase the control potential of shareholders, which leads to increases in ownership concentration. Shleifer and Vishny (1986) argue that large shareholders monitor managers, which in turn increases firm value. This argument is supported by U.S. evidence (Holderness and Sheehan, 1988; Barclay and Holderness, 1989).

opportunistically deprive them of their rights. The effects of entrenchment by the controlling shareholder include outright expropriation, i.e., the controlling shareholder benefits from self-dealing transactions in which profits are transferred to other companies he/she controls.[6] The controlling shareholder can also exercise de facto expropriation through the pursuit of objectives that are not profit-maximizing in return for personal utilities. The entrenchment problem created by the controlling owner is similar to the managerial entrenchment problem discussed by Morck et al. (1988). Increasing managerial ownership may entrench managers, as they are increasingly less subject to governance by boards of directors and to discipline by the market for corporate control.

2.2.2. The alignment effect

One way to mitigate the problem of controlling owner entrenchment is to increase further the controlling shareholder's ownership stake, or even to go private if the problem is sufficiently severe. A higher ownership stake gives a controlling owner stronger voting and cash flow rights in the firm. Once the controlling owner obtains effective control of the firm, any increase in voting rights does not further entrench the controlling owner, but his/her higher cash flow rights in the firm mean that it will cost more to divert the firm's cash flows for private gain. The high ownership concentration can also serve as a credible commitment that the controlling owner is willing to build a reputation for not expropriating minority shareholders (Gomes, 2000). The commitment is credible because minority shareholders know that if the controlling owner unexpectedly extracts high levels of private benefits when he/she still holds a substantial amount of shares, they will discount the stock price accordingly, and the majority owner's share value will be reduced. In equilibrium, the majority shareholder will hold a large ownership stake and the stock price of the company will be higher. Thus, ownership concentration has an incentive alignment effect: increasing an owner's share ownership beyond the minimum level needed for effective control improves the alignment of interests between the controlling owner and the minority shareholders and reduces the effects of entrenchment.

2.2.3. Entrenchment effect when control exceeds ownership.

In addition to the characteristic concentrated ownership, the ownership arrangements of East Asian corporations are further complicated by pyramidal and cross-holding structures. These ownership arrangements allow controlling owners to commit low equity investment while maintaining tight control of the firm, creating a separation in control (voting rights) and ownership (cash flow rights).[7]

[6] Scott (1999) studies the role of corporate governance in four Asian countries that were in financial crisis: Indonesia, Malaysia, South Korea and Thailand. He concludes by recommending that strengthening the effective limits on self-dealing transactions of controlling owners would be the priority task for these countries.

[7] Separation between cash flow and voting rights is common among public corporations around the world (La Porta et al., 1999). In the context of diffuse ownership, Stulz (1988) suggests that there exist various contractual arrangements that allow managers to increase their voting power to a degree beyond

One consequence of the divergence between voting and cash flow rights is that the controlling owner becomes entrenched with high levels of control, while the low equity ownership level provides only a low degree of alignment between the controlling owner and minority shareholders.[8] A controlling owner in this situation could extract wealth from the firm, receive the entire benefit, but only bear a fraction of the cost.[9] We offer a simple pyramidal structure to illustrate this point. An entrepreneur owns 25% of the stock in publicly traded Firm A, which in turn owns 32% of the stock in Firm B. In the most modest scenario, we note that the entrepreneur controls 25% of Firm B—the weakest link in the chain of voting rights. At the same time, the entrepreneur owns about 8% of the cash flow rights of Firm B, the product of the two ownership stakes along the chain. Given this ownership structure, it costs the entrepreneur only $8 for every $100 expropriated from Firm B. Clearly, if stock pyramids or cross-shareholdings were used to consolidate control, they would also result in a separation between ownership and control, which exacerbates the entrenchment problem of controlling owners.

In summary, once controlling owners achieve effective control, their ownership concentration has two incentive effects on them: entrenchment and alignment. When there is no separation between voting and cash flow rights, concentrating ownership beyond the minimum level for effective control enhances the alignment of interest and hence mitigates the entrenchment effect. When the voting rights and cash flow rights diverge, however, the lower cash flow rights may fail to provide sufficient incentive alignment to curtail the entrenchment effect.

2.3. Ownership structure and earnings informativeness

We now discuss the relations between ownership structure and earnings informativeness in East Asia. We provide two potential arguments that may explain the relations. The first argument is based on the entrenchment effect discussed above. The second argument is related to the firms' proprietary information and specific human capital effect, which will be detailed below.

(*footnote continued*)
their equity ownership. Such arrangements may lead to changes in capital structures or differential voting rights, which in turn provide managers more control than what they are entitled to by their equity ownership. What causes the separation between voting and cash flow rights is a subject not adequately addressed in the literature. It is potentially related to both controlling owners' financing constraints and their desires to maintain control. Owners may not have sufficient personal wealth or loans to finance the investment projects that they desire to control. With limited amounts of cash, owners could leverage their control by way of stock pyramids or cross-shareholdings. The ownership arrangements, which help in the formation of business groups, also allow the controlling owners to create internal capital and factor markets and hence to bypass underdeveloped external markets.

[8] Controlling owner entrenchment as an agency cost of the separation of cash flow rights from voting rights plays a key role in the theoretical models of Burkart et al. (1997, 1998), Bebchuk et al. (2000), and Wolfenzon (1999).

[9] Although minority shareholders appear to have been expropriated by the controlling owner, they may be price-protected when they bought the shares. That is, if the minority shareholders purchased the shares after control existed, the stock price should be discounted for this action and the discount would on average pay for the apparent transfer.

2.3.1. The entrenchment argument

Just as the share ownership structure delineates a firm's agency problem, it also impacts the firm's reporting. When an owner effectively controls a firm, he/she also controls the production of the firm's accounting information and reporting policies. When the controlling owner is entrenched by his/her voting power and there is a large separation of the voting and cash flow rights, the credibility of the accounting information is reduced. That is, outside investors pay less attention to the reported accounting numbers, because they expect that the controlling owner reports accounting information out of self-interest rather than as a reflection of the firm's true underlying economic transactions. In particular, outside investors may not trust the firm's reported earnings because the controlling owner may manipulate earnings for outright expropriation. In addition, outside investors know that the controlling owner has an incentive to avoid reporting accounting information that would attract close monitoring by outside shareholders. This does not always mean that there is outright earnings manipulation to cover up possible earnings effects of wealth extraction. The controlling owner may simply bury the wealth effects of his/her expropriation activities in the aggregate earnings numbers without reporting them as separate income statement items. The loss of credibility in earnings reports lowers the stock price informativeness of the earnings. Prior studies have noted the importance of the effects of earnings credibility. Teoh and Wong (1993) report that the market perception of the quality of accounting earnings, as proxied by the size of the firm's auditor, positively affects the stock price informativeness of earnings.

2.3.2. The information argument

Concentrating ownership allows firms to limit their information disclosure to the public. Opacity is a good strategy because it prevents leakage of proprietary information to competitors and allows firms to avoid unwanted political or social scrutiny. Firms with proprietary knowledge and specific human capital tend to concentrate their ownership and decision rights in the individuals who possess the specific knowledge (Jensen and Meckling, 1992; Christie et al., 2002). Assigning control to individuals without specific knowledge can lead to suboptimal decisions or a high cost of transferring knowledge to necessary individuals. Moreover, if firms with proprietary knowledge give more individuals decision rights, they also have to give those individuals the proprietary knowledge to allow them to make informed decisions. The larger the set of informed individuals, the larger the likelihood that the proprietary information leaks to the public and potential competitors. This scenario is common among firms that engage in political rent-seeking activities, which are prevalent and highly profitable in East Asia.[10] Morck (1996) argues that there are two reasons why closely held firms are better able to engage in political lobbying than widely held firms. First, the concentrated decision rights within the

[10] Fisman (2001) conducted an event study on the stock price effects of the news announcements of Suharto's illness. He analyzed the value drops in the firms connected to Suharto and reported that the proportion of these firms' share values attributed to Suharto connections was very large—about a quarter of each firm's share value. Political connections were valued by investors in this case.

firms allow them to operate in greater secrecy. A politician may desire more secrecy in order to maintain a reputation of integrity. The firms also prefer operating in secret in order to discourage entry by competitors. Second, compared to a hired manager in a widely held firm, a controlling owner is more secure in his position in the firm and thus has more credibility on which to trade favors with the government. In order to trade favors with politicians and bureaucrats in secret, firms generally have highly concentrated ownership that allows them to have tight control of information flows to the public, which in turn reduces corporate transparency. In this business environment, it is in the interest of both the controlling owners and the minority shareholders to release as little accounting information to the public as possible. This information effect argument suggests that high ownership concentration is associated with *low* earnings informativeness.

2.3.3. Predicted relations

The relation between ownership concentration and earnings informativness is affected by the several factors discussed earlier. On the one hand, there are two incentive effects of ownership concentration that impact earnings informativeness. First, the entrenchment effect predicts that concentrated ownership leads to weak earnings informativeness. However, as the degree of ownership concentration exceeds the minimum level needed for effective control, the alignment effect may mitigate the entrenchment effect. At such level, further increasing the ownership concentration can improve earnings informativeness. On the other hand, the information argument suggests a negative relation between ownership concentration and earnings informativeness. As these two incentive effects have opposing predictions and could coexist with the information effect, the relation between ownership concentration and earnings informativeness is ambiguous and needs to be addressed empirically.

Attempting to disentangle the two incentive effects of ownership concentration on earnings informativeness, we employ the degree of divergence between voting and cash flow rights as a proxy for controlling owner entrenchment. We expect that the credibility of a firm's accounting information and consequently the informativeness of this information to outside investors decreases with an increase in the degree to which the level of voting rights exceeds the associated level of cash flow rights. Formally, our hypothesis is: *an increase in the degree of divergence between the controlling owner's cash flow rights and voting rights decreases the informativeness of the firm's earnings*.

We acknowledge that the divergence measure may also reflect the information effect. That is, a controlling owner who has proprietary information to protect may use stock pyramids and cross-shareholdings to leverage his/her control concentration; and the divergence of these rights may tend to increase with the firm's desired opacity. Finding a negative relation between earnings informativeness and the level of divergence between the two rights, although consistent with the entrenchment argument, is also consistent with the information argument.

3. Empirical analysis

In this section, we describe the sample, data sources, and the ownership structures of the sample firms. We then test the hypothesis developed in the previous section by analyzing the relations between the corporate ownership structure and earnings informativeness.

3.1. Sample and data

We select our sample firms from seven East Asian economies—Hong Kong, Indonesia, Malaysia, Singapore, South Korea, Taiwan and Thailand. We include firms that have sufficient ownership, stock returns, earnings and other financial data for empirical analysis. Below is a description of the sample and data sources.

3.1.1. Ownership data

Most prior studies of ownership structures focus on immediate ownership—common shares directly owned by individuals or institutions. Immediate ownership is not sufficient for characterizing the ownership and control structure of East Asian firms, as these firms are generally associated with complicated indirect ownership. As a departure from these prior studies, we focus on ultimate ownership. We use data assembled by Claessens et al. (2000), which identifies the ultimate owners of 2,980 firms in nine East Asian economies, along with their shares of cash flow and voting rights. The ownership data is available for 1996. The procedure of identifying ultimate owners is similar to the one used in La Porta et al. (1999). An ultimate owner is defined as the shareholder who has the determining voting rights of the company and who is not controlled by anybody else. If a company does not have an ultimate owner, it is classified as widely held. To economize on the data collection task, the ultimate owner's voting right level is set at 50% and not traced any further once that level exceeds 50%. Although a company can have more than one ultimate owner, we focus on the largest ultimate owner. As our definition of ownership relies on both cash flow and voting control rights, the cash flow rights that support the control by ultimate owners are further identified. Firm-specific information on pyramid structures and cross-holdings are used to make the distinction between cash flow and voting rights. To facilitate the measurement of the separation of cash flow and voting rights, the maximum cash flow rights level associated with any ultimate owner is also set at 50%. However, there is no minimum cutoff level for cash flow rights.

From the 2,980 firms, we exclude 1,240 Japanese firms from our analysis because Japan's institutional environment and its firms' ownership structures are quite different from the other East Asian economies.[11] We further exclude 319 firms whose

[11] Different from the East Asian firms that are typically family controlled, the dominant ultimate owners of Japanese firms are institutions, typically the main banks of industrial groups. Japanese firms' ownership structures are also quite different from those of the East Asian firms in both the degree of control and cash-vote divergence.

largest ultimate owners have less than 20% of voting rights. This restriction allows us to focus on firms with controlling shareholders and is expected to increase the power of our test since the entrenchment and information arguments are more applicable to ultimate owners that have already secured effective control. La Porta et al. (1999) also use the 20% cutoff level to define control. Bradley and Kim (1985) report that tender offers rarely occur in firms with control at the 20% level.

3.1.2. Stock return and financial data

We merge the ownership data with the PACAP electronic database, which is commercially distributed by the University of Rhode Island. PACAP contains the financial and stock return data of publicly traded companies of the seven East Asian economies analyzed here. We select 1991 through 1995 as the period of analysis and retrieve the stock return and financial data for that period. An exception is Korea, for which we have data up to 1994 only. We do not include 1996 because the data are not available to us for that year. We also exclude pre-1991 data because we are concerned that the ownership structures earlier than 1991 may differ too much from the structures documented in 1996. Although we have ownership data for the Philippines, we do not include firms from that country because they are not covered by the PACAP database. The merging of the 1996 ownership data and the 1991–1995 stock return and financial data requires us to assume that the ownership and control structures of the firms did not change substantially during that period. This is a reasonable assumption since the economic and political conditions were relatively stable at the time. The final sample has 977 firms with a total of 3,572 firm-years.[12]

3.2. Basic statistics of ownership structures

Table 1 presents the descriptive statistics of the cash flow and voting rights of the largest ultimate owners of the final sample. Broken down by economies, the sample covers 282 Hong Kong firms, 91 Indonesian firms, 177 Malaysian firms, 133 Singaporean firms, 95 South Korean firms, 66 Taiwanese firms, and 133 Thai firms. The sample covers 30% of all publicly traded firms in the region.[13] Panel A of the Table shows that the mean voting rights of the East Asian corporations is 30.44%. In a quarter of the East Asian companies, more than 40% of the voting rights are in the hands of the largest ultimate owner. Thai firms display the most concentrated voting rights, 36.32% on average, followed by Indonesian firms (34.51%), Malaysian firms (30.73%), Hong Kong firms (29.68%), Singaporean firms (28.95%), South Korean firms (26.11%), and Taiwanese firms (24.70%). The high control concentration is not surprising, given the 20% voting rights restriction imposed on the sample. However, the control concentration remains high when the

[12] The two extreme percentiles of firm-year observations of annual stock returns and net earnings over market value of equity (see Section 3.3 for the two variable definitions) are eliminated from the sample.

[13] As of December 1996, the numbers of listed firms in these economies were: 583 in Hong Kong, 267 in Indonesia, 760 in Korea, 621 in Malaysia, 266 in Singapore, 382 in Taiwan, and 454 in Thailand.

Table 1
Cash flow and voting rights of the largest ultimate owners of East Asian corporations[a]

	Firm no.	Mean	Std. err.	First quartile	Median	Third quartile	Minimum	Maximum
Panel A: voting rights (%)								
Hong Kong	282	29.68	10.91	20.00	30.00	40.00	20.00	50.00
Indonesia	91	34.51	9.92	30.00	30.00	40.00	20.00	50.00
Malaysia	177	30.73	10.17	20.00	30.00	40.00	20.00	50.00
Singapore	133	28.95	9.40	20.00	30.00	40.00	20.00	50.00
South Korea	95	26.11	7.48	20.00	20.00	30.00	20.00	50.00
Taiwan	66	24.70	7.49	20.00	20.00	30.00	20.00	50.00
Thailand	133	36.32	11.18	30.00	40.00	50.00	20.00	50.00
East Asia	977	30.44	10.53	20.00	30.00	40.00	20.00[b]	50.00[c]
Panel B: cash flow rights (%)								
Hong Kong	282	25.60	11.19	20.00	20.00	30.00	3.00	50.00
Indonesia	91	26.08	10.81	18.00	25.00	32.00	4.00	50.00
Malaysia	177	26.03	11.45	20.00	22.00	30.00	5.00	50.00
Singapore	133	22.96	10.48	16.00	20.00	30.00	6.00	50.00
South Korea	95	21.36	8.16	18.00	20.00	30.00	4.00	50.00
Taiwan	66	21.46	8.76	16.00	20.00	24.00	8.00	50.00
Thailand	133	34.23	11.68	24.00	30.00	40.00	4.00	50.00
East Asia	977	25.84	11.37	20.00	21.00	30.00	3.00	50.00[c]
Panel C: the ratio of cash flow rights over voting rights[d]								
Hong Kong	282	0.87	0.22	0.80	1.00	1.00	0.13	1.00
Indonesia	91	0.77	0.24	0.60	0.80	1.00	0.13	1.00
Malaysia	177	0.84	0.22	0.70	1.00	1.00	0.17	1.00
Singapore	133	0.78	0.22	0.60	0.80	1.00	0.27	1.00
South Korea	95	0.83	0.25	0.60	1.00	1.00	0.13	1.00
Taiwan	66	0.86	0.17	0.73	1.00	1.00	0.40	1.00
Thailand	133	0.95	0.16	1.00	1.00	1.00	0.20	1.00
East Asia	977	0.85	0.22	0.70	1.00	1.00	0.13	1.00

Sample: The sample consists of 977 firms from Hong Kong, Indonesia, Malaysia, Singapore, South Korea, Taiwan, and Thailand. To be included in the sample, a firm must have at least 1 year of stock returns and financial data from the PACAP database between 1991 and 1995, its ultimate ownership data must be available from Claessens et al. (2000), and its largest ultimate owner must have at least 20% of voting rights.

[a] An ultimate owner is defined as an owner that is not controlled by anybody else. Although a firm can have more than one ultimate owner, only the one with the largest voting rights is reported.

[b] Sample firms are restricted to have a largest ultimate owner with at least 20% voting rights.

[c] The voting rights and cash flow rights level of an ultimate owner is set at 50% and not traced any further once that level exceeds 50%.

[d] The ratio of cash flow rights over voting rights is defined as the level of cash flows rights divided by the level of voting rights. The value of this ratio ranges from zero to one.

restriction is relaxed. Claessens et al. (2000) employ a lower minimum voting rights cutoff, 5% (instead of 20%), and report that the mean voting rights of the seven economies range from 35.25% (Thailand) to 17.78% (South Korea).

Panel B reports the basic statistics for levels of cash flow rights. The cash flow rights patterns are similar to the voting rights patterns in Panel A. The overall average concentration is 25.84%. Note particularly that the mean levels of cash flow rights are lower than the corresponding levels for voting rights in Panel A, indicating the divergence between cash flow and voting rights. In Panel C, we report the basic statistics of the ratio of cash flow rights over voting rights (CV). The ratio, by definition, ranges between zero and one. If a firm is widely held, i.e., it has zero cash flow and voting rights, its CV ratio is set to one. The CV ratio indicates the degree of divergence between cash flow and voting rights. The closer the ratio is to zero, the larger the divergence. In East Asia, the mean CV ratio is 0.85. The mean CV ratios are rather similar across the seven East Asian economies, ranging between 0.77 (Indonesia) and 0.95 (Thailand). Over a quarter of the East Asian firms display cash-vote divergence ($CV < 1$). The minimum CV ratio is 0.13. The Pearson correlation coefficient between the voting rights and CV is only −0.07, suggesting that CV is not simply a proxy for voting rights.

The actual degree of ownership concentration in East Asia should be higher than the statistics reported here for several reasons. First, the 50% ceiling for the ownership data and the inability to trace some hidden control chains would bias our statistics downward. In addition, small firms tend to have more concentrated ownership, but our sample mainly consists of larger firms due to the limited availability of ownership data of small firms. However, we expect that the understatement of ownership data and the large firm bias in our sample would weaken but not systematically bias the data in favor of our hypothesis. Notwithstanding the data limitation, it is sufficient to conclude from Table 1 that the typical ownership and control structure of the East Asian firms is highly concentrated, in contrast to the diffuse ownership in the U.S., as documented in prior research. The East Asian firms also differ from U.S. firms in that they are characterized by a separation of ownership and control resulting from the controlling owner's possession of more voting power than cash investment.

3.3. Regression analysis

We next perform regression analysis to examine the relations between corporate ownership structure and earnings informativeness in East Asia.

3.3.1. Basic relations between returns and earnings

Before we focus on the role of the ownership structure, we perform a set of ordinary least squares regressions to determine the basic relations between stock returns and earnings in East Asia:

$$\mathrm{CAR}_{it} = a_0 + a_1 \mathrm{NI}_{it} + (\text{Fixed effects}) + u_{it}, \tag{1}$$

where, for sample firm i, CAR_{it} is the cumulative net-of-market 12-month stock returns at year t, NI_{it} the net earnings at year t divided by the market value of equity at the beginning of year t, fixed effects the dummy variables controlling for fixed effects of calendar years and/or economies, and u_{it} the error term at year t.

The regressions are performed year by year, economy by economy, and pooling all of the years and economies. The results are reported in Table 2. Because we generally find heteroskedasticity problems in the regressions, we report White-adjusted t-statistics for all the coefficients. Fixed effects of calendar years and/or economies, where appropriate, are included as dummy intercepts in the regressions. For simplicity, they are not reported in the table. The estimated coefficients of earnings (NI) are positive and statistically significant across all the years and economies, suggesting that earnings have an information role in East Asia.

3.3.2. The effects of ownership structure

We next test the informativeness of earnings conditional on ownership structure using the following pooled time-series cross-sectional regression model:

$$\begin{aligned}\text{CAR}_{it} = {} & a_0 + a_1\text{NI}_{it} + a_2\text{NI}_{it}\text{SIZE}_{it} + a_3\text{NI}_{it}Q_{it} + a_4\text{NI}_{it}\text{LEV}_{it} + a_5\text{NI}_{it}\text{SEG}_i \\ & + a_6\text{NI}_{it}V_i + a_7\text{NI}_{it}\text{CV}_i + (\text{Fixed effects}) + u_{it},\end{aligned} \quad (2)$$

where, for sample firm i, CAR_{it} is the cumulative net-of-market 12-month stock returns at year t, NI_{it} the net earnings at year t divided by the market value of equity at the beginning of year t, SIZE_{it} the natural logarithm of the market value of equity in millions of U.S. dollars at the beginning of year t, Q_{it} the market value of equity divided by the book value of total assets at the beginning of year t, LEV_{it} the total liability divided by total assets at the beginning of year t, SEG_i the number of industry segment(s) in which the firm operates, V_i the voting rights level of the largest ultimate owner, CV_i the ratio of cash flow rights over voting rights of the largest ultimate owner, fixed effects the dummy variables controlling for fixed effects of calendar years and economies, and u_{it} the error term at year t.

We include a set of variables to control for observed variations in the earnings–return relation that are likely due to causes other than voting rights or divergence of cash flow and voting rights.

The ratio of market value of equity to the book value of total assets (Q) is included to control for the effects of growth on the earnings–return relation.[14] Growth opportunities are likely to be positively associated with future earnings levels and/or earnings persistence (Collins and Kothari, 1989). The higher the market-to-book assets, the larger the expected earnings growth and/or earnings persistence, the stronger the earnings–return relation.[15] On the other hand, the market-to-book ratio may also be affected by firm risk. High growth firms may be more risky, which weakens the earnings–return relation. Also, fast growing firms are likely to be young firms with less informative earnings. Given these countervailing effects, the net effect of growth on the earnings–return relation is therefore an empirical issue.

We also incorporate leverage (LEV) in the regression. Leverage could be a proxy for the riskiness of debt or default risk (Dhaliwal et al., 1991). Highly levered firms are associated with high risk and hence their earnings–return relation is weakened.

[14] The use of the market-to-book value of equity produces qualitatively similar results in our regressions.

[15] We do not include a separate control for earnings persistence because the earnings history is inadequate for its empirical estimation in our sample.

Table 2
Simple regressions of stock returns on earnings[a]

	Intercept	NI	Adjusted R^2	Number of observations
1991	−0.23***	1.26***	0.15	652
	(−6.90)[b]	(6.19)		
1992	−0.05	0.76***	0.04	727
	(−1.39)	(3.77)		
1993	−0.25***	1.09***	0.10	784
	(−8.19)	(6.08)		
1994	−0.25***	1.06***	0.17	817
	(−12.12)	(7.51)		
1995	−0.14***	0.76***	0.11	772
	(−8.25)	(6.20)		
Hong Kong	−0.17***	0.73***	0.10	1045
	(−6.57)	(7.36)		
Indonesia	−0.07	0.73***	0.06	259
	(−1.26)	(3.85)		
Malaysia	−0.12***	0.80***	0.04	684
	(−4.52)	(3.25)		
Singapore	−0.04	0.64***	0.07	561
	(−1.58)	(2.89)		
South Korea	−0.00	1.67***	0.16	346
	(−0.08)	(6.62)		
Taiwan	0.14***	1.65**	0.23	311
	(3.87)	(2.56)		
Thailand	−0.13***	2.62***	0.17	546
	(−3.16)	(7.99)		
Pooled	−0.18***	0.99***	0.08	3752
	(−10.79)	(13.01)		

Model specification: $\text{CAR}_{it} = a_0 + a_1\text{NI}_{it} + (\text{Fixed effects}) + u_{it}$.
Variable definitions: CAR_{it} = the cumulative net-of-market 12-month stock returns for firm i at year t. The annual returns are continuously compounded from monthly stock returns starting from 12 months before the latest date, as required by law or listing rules, that the firm discloses its annual report. NI_{it} = the net earnings at year t divided by the market value of equity at the beginning of year t for firm i.
Sample: The sample includes 3,752 firm-year observations, spanning between 1991 and 1995 and covering 977 firms from Hong Kong, Indonesia, Malaysia, Singapore, South Korea, Taiwan, and Thailand. To be included in the sample, a firm must have at least 1 year of stock returns and financial data from the PACAP database between 1991 and 1995, its ultimate ownership data must be available from Claessens et al. (2000), and its largest ultimate owner must have at least 20% of voting rights. Observations with largest and smallest 1% values of CAR and NI are excluded from the sample.
***Indicates significant at 1% (two-tailed).
**Indicates significant at 5% (two-tailed).
[a] Simple OLS regressions of annual stock returns on earnings are run year by year, economy by economy and pooling across years and economies (pooled). Fixed-effects of calendar years and/or economies are included for each regression when appropriate, but not reported.
[b] White-adjusted t-statistics are in parentheses.

On the other hand, Smith and Watts (1992) suggest that leverage can proxy for a firm's investment opportunity set. Mature firms with low growth opportunities generally have high leverage and are likely to have informative earnings. Hence firms with high leverage may have higher earnings–return sensitivity than firms with low leverage. Taking the risk and the growth effects together, the net effect of leverage on the earnings–return relation is to be determined empirically.

In addition, we include the number of industry segments (SEG) in which each sample firm operates as another control. Conglomerate firms, due to their relatively more complex earnings-generating process, may have weaker earnings–return relations than firms operating in a single industry.[16]

Finally, we include firm size (SIZE) as a control for other missing factors that affect the earnings–return relation. For example, prior literature on the U.S. case (Atiase, 1985; Freeman, 1987) has documented that public disclosure and private development of non-earnings information are increasing functions of firm size.

The summary statistics of the dependent and independent variables of the regression are reported in Table 3. The mean CAR is −1.12% and the mean NI is 7.27%, but they are statistically insignificantly different from zero due to their large standard errors. Both CAR and NI display large dispersion in value in the sample. The summary statistics of *V* and CV are consistent with those reported in Table 1. The owners on average possess high voting control: 30% of voting rights. They also control significantly more votes than those determined by their ownership positions. Specifically, the mean CV is 0.85, indicating that the controlling owners' levels of cash flow rights are on average 15% lower than their corresponding levels of voting rights. Also shown in the basic statistics, the values of the control variables are mostly distributed within reasonable ranges, suggesting that the regression results are unlikely to be plagued by outliers.

We employ the ordinary least-squares method to regress CAR on voting rights level (*V*), the degree of separation between cash flow and voting rights (CV), and the control variables.[17] The regression results are presented in Eq. (1) of Table 4. We report White-adjusted *t*-statistics for all the coefficients due to heteroskedasticity. For simplicity, we omit reporting fixed effects of calendar years and economies. Larger firms' earnings are more informative, as indicated by the significantly positive estimated coefficient of NI∗SIZE. The coefficient of NI∗Q is insignificant, suggesting that the risk and the growth effects are offset by each other. The estimated coefficient of NI∗LEV is significantly positive, consistent with the view that highly levered firms tend to be mature firms that have more informative earnings. The coefficient of NI∗SEG is significantly negative, suggesting that conglomerate firms report less informative earnings than more focused firms.

The coefficient of NI is insignificantly negative. It does not suggest that earnings are uninformative because the simple regressions in Table 2 show that stock returns

[16] The 1996 company segment data were collected from Worldscope and supplemented with additional data from the Asian Company Handbook. Since companies report their segment data with different degrees of detail, the companies' segments are grouped according to the two-digit Standard Industry Classification system.

[17] We also try adjusting *V* by subtracting the median voting rights of the economy in which it operates because firms in different economies are associated with different levels of ultimate voting control and the results are qualitatively similar. For simplicity, we report only the results with the unadjusted *V*.

Table 3
Summary statistics of regression variables

Variables	Mean	Std. err.	First quartile	Median	Third quartile	Minimum	Maximum
CAR (%)	−1.12	33.46	−23.35	−6.96	14.02	−62.53	147.49
NI (%)	7.27	8.32	3.53	6.31	10.40	−45.20	461.70
SIZE	12.03	1.37	11.07	11.99	12.87	7.13	17.05
Q	1.09	0.95	0.41	0.83	1.47	0.02	7.98
LEV (%)	46.83	23.57	28.52	44.16	62.59	0.08	259.95
SEG	2.55	1.61	1.00	2.00	4.00	1.00	9.00
V (%)	29.93	10.37	20.00	30.00	40.00	20.00	50.00
CV	0.85	0.22	0.70	1.00	1.00	0.13	1.00

Variable definitions: CAR = the cumulative net-of-market 12-month stock returns. The annual returns are continuously compounded from monthly stock returns starting from 12 months before the latest date, as required by law or listing rules, that the firm discloses its annual report. NI = the net earnings divided by the market value of equity at the beginning of the year. SIZE = the natural logarithm of the market value of equity in millions of U.S. dollar at the beginning of the year. Q = the market value of equity divided by the book value of total assets at the beginning of the year. LEV = the total liability divided by total assets at the beginning of the year. SEG = the number of industry segment(s). V = the voting rights level of the largest ultimate owner. CV = the ratio of cash flow rights over voting rights of the largest ultimate owner. *Sample*: The sample includes 3,752 firm-year observations, spanning between 1991 and 1995 and covering 977 firms from Hong Kong, Indonesia, Malaysia, Singapore, South Korea, Taiwan, and Thailand. To be included in the sample, a firm must have at least 1 year of stock returns and financial data from the PACAP database between 1991 and 1995, its ultimate ownership data must be available from Claessens et al. (2000), and its largest ultimate owner must have at least 20% of voting rights. Observations with largest and smallest 1% values of CAR and NI are excluded from the sample.

are significantly positively associated with earnings. Their relation becomes insignificant in Eq. (1) because the inclusion of the additional independent variables may have controlled for most of the variation of NI and lowered its explanatory power. The intercept remains significantly negative as in the regression results in Table 2. The negative intercept could be caused by the omitted expected earnings component. When we include lagged earnings as expected earnings by replacing NI with the change in earnings (current year earnings minus lagged earnings all divided by the lagged market value of equity) in the regression, the magnitude of the intercept drops by more than half.

The focus of Table 4 is the role of the ownership structure. The result in Eq. (1) shows that the estimated coefficient of NI $*$ V is negative and statistically significant at the 5% level. This result is consistent with the information effect that high voting rights are associated with secrecy and low earnings informativeness. The result also suggests that the information effect dominates the incentive alignment effect, which predicts that additional ownership concentration beyond the minimum level of effective control increases earnings informativeness. To gain understanding of the economic importance of the result, we use the estimated regression of Eq. (1), set all of the independent variables at their mean, and then estimate how much CAR would change given that V increases by a magnitude of one standard deviation. We find

Table 4
Pooled time-series cross-sectional regressions with interactions for corporate ownership structure[a]

	(1)[b]	(2)[c]
Intercept	−0.18***	−0.17***
	(−10.39)[d]	(−9.09)
NI	−0.59	−0.99*
	(−1.17)	(−1.79)
NI * SIZE	0.10***	0.12***
	(2.67)	(2.89)
NI * Q	−0.00	−0.03
	(−0.05)	(−0.34)
NI * LEV	1.03***	0.99***
	(4.09)	(3.71)
NI * SEG	−0.09***	−0.11***
	(−2.71)	(−2.83)
NI * V	−1.20**	−0.21
	(−2.47)	(−0.29)
NI * CV	0.69***	0.74***
	(3.49)	(3.44)
Adjusted R^2	0.10	0.10
Number of observations	3752	3284

Model specification: $\text{CAR}_{it} = a_0 + a_1\text{NI}_{it} + a_2\text{NI}_i * \text{SIZE}_{it} + a_3\text{NI}_{it} * Q_{it} + a_4\text{NI}_{it} * \text{LEV}_{it} + a_5\text{NI}_i * \text{SEG}_i + a_6\text{NI}_{it} * V_i + a_7\text{NI}_{it} * \text{CV}_i + (\text{Fixed effects}) + u_{it}$.

Variable definitions: CAR_{it} = the cumulative net-of-market 12-month stock returns for firm i at year t. The annual returns are continuously compounded from monthly stock returns starting from 12 months before the latest date, as required by law or listing rules, that the firm discloses its annual report. NI_{it} = the net earnings at year t divided by the market value of equity at the beginning of year t for firm i. SIZE_{it} = the natural logarithm of the market value of equity in millions of U.S. dollar at the beginning of year t for firm i. Q_{it} = the market value of equity divided by the book value of total assets at the beginning of year t for firm i. LEV_{it} = the total liability divided by total assets at the beginning of year t for firm i. SEG_i = the number of industry segment(s) of firm i. V_i = the voting rights level of the largest ultimate owner of firm i. CV_i = the ratio of cash flow rights over voting rights of the largest ultimate owner of firm i.

Sample: The sample includes 3,752 firm-year observations, spanning between 1991 and 1995 and covering 977 firms from Hong Kong, Indonesia, Malaysia, Singapore, South Korea, Taiwan, and Thailand. To be included in the sample, a firm must have at least 1 year of stock returns and financial data from the PACAP database between 1991 and 1995, its ultimate ownership data must be available from Claessens et al. (2000), and its largest ultimate owner must have at least 20% of voting rights. Observations with largest and smallest 1% values of CAR and NI are excluded from the sample.

***Indicates significant at 1% (two-tailed).

**Indicates significant at 5% (two-tailed).

*Indicates significant at 10% (two-tailed).

[a] Two OLS regressions are run pooling across years and economies. Fixed-effects of calendar years and economies are included in the regressions but not reported.

[b] Eq. (1) uses the final sample that excludes observations with $V < 20\%$.

[c] Eq. (2) uses the sub-sample that excludes both $V < 20\%$ and $V \geqslant 50\%$.

[d] White-adjusted t-statistics are in parentheses.

that when V increases from its mean, 30%, by one standard deviation to 40%, the level of CAR decreases by 1%, representing a 9% change relative to its previous level.

We now turn to investigate the effect of separation of cash flow and voting rights on earnings informativeness. CV, by definition, is inversely related to cash-vote divergence. To be consistent with the entrenchment effect and/or the information effect, we should observe a significantly positive estimated coefficient of CV. Consistent with our conjecture, the coefficient of CV is positive and statistically significant at the 1% level. In terms of economic significance, when all of the independent variables are set at their mean, decreasing CV from its mean (0.85) by one standard deviation to 0.63 is associated with a 1% decrease in the level of CAR, representing an 11% drop relative to its previous level.[18]

In summary, when ultimate owners effectively control their firms, their voting rights levels are negatively related to the informativeness of the firms' reported earnings. This suggests that the information effect dominates the incentive alignment effect. We also find evidence supporting our hypothesis that after controlling for the level of voting rights, cash-vote divergence significantly weakens earnings informativeness. This evidence is consistent with the entrenchment effect. However, the result is also consistent with the information effect, provided that controlling owners tend to employ pyramidal or cross-holding ownership structures to protect the information about their rent-seeking activities.

3.3.3. *Checks of robustness*

Since all voting and cash flow rights that exceed 50% are capped, the effects of any variation in voting and cash flow rights of these firms would not be captured by our measure. Moreover, if actual voting and cash flow rights both exceed 50%, their divergence would not be captured by the CV measure, as it would be recorded as one, which indicates no divergence. As a sensitivity test of any possible bias in our results, we rerun the regression by excluding observations associated with voting rights equal to or more than 50% from the full sample. As reported in Eq. (2) of Table 4, the sign of the coefficient of $\mathrm{NI} * V$ becomes statistically insignificant. On the other hand, the sign, magnitude, and significance level of the coefficient of $\mathrm{NI} * \mathrm{CV}$ remains qualitatively similar to results in Eq. (1). We thus confirm that the 50% ceiling for our ownership data would not have biased the results in favor of our hypothesis.

As further diagnostic checks,[19] we have estimated the regression models using cumulative abnormal returns calculated from two fixed annual windows: nine (six) months prior to and three (six) months after the current fiscal year end. We have also used cumulative raw returns, instead of net-of-market returns, and used the two-year cumulative net-of-market returns, starting 21 months before to three months after the fiscal year-end, as an alternative dependent variable. The two-year returns, which

[18] We have also run the same regression by including firms with the largest ultimate owners having <20% voting rights. The results support our hypothesis that firms with a larger separation between their cash flow and voting rights have less informative earnings. Consistent with our conjecture that the information and entrenchment effects are weaker among firms without owners commanding effective control, the magnitude (*t*-statistics) of the coefficients of $\mathrm{NI} * V$ and $\mathrm{NI} * \mathrm{CV}$ in this regression has (have) dropped from −1.2 to −0.60 (−2.47 to −1.43) and 0.69 to 0.47 (3.49 to 2.46), respectively.

[19] The results of the diagnostic checks are not reported in the tables but are available upon request.

include both current and lagged-year returns, attempt to adjust for any differences in price efficiency in capturing future earnings between highly concentrated (high V) and less concentrated ownership (low V) firms (Jacobson and Aaker, 1993; Ali and Hwang, 2000). In addition, instead of using NI in our regression model, we have also used ΔNI, change in earnings (current earnings minus lagged earnings all divided by lagged market value of equity). Our results for V and CV remain qualitatively similar after using ΔNI or these alternative measurements of CAR.

We provide a further test of whether or not the effects of voting control and cash-vote divergence on East Asian firms cluster in time and/or economies. Table 5 presents the results of a set of year-by-year regressions. These regressions include NI * V and NI * CV, in addition to the control variables. We find that the coefficients of NI * V and NI * CV are mostly of the expected signs, and NI * CV is statistically significant in all years but 1995, while NI * V is significant in 1991 and 1994. Table 6 presents the results of a set of economy-by-economy regressions using the same model. We find ownership effects in several economies. The effect of V on earnings informativeness is negative and significant in Hong Kong, Malaysia, and Taiwan. The effect of CV is positive and significant in Hong Kong, Malaysia, Taiwan and Thailand. From the year-by-year and economy-by-economy results, we find that the effects of the ownership variables are not concentrated in any given year or economy.

The above diagnostic checks have demonstrated that our empirical results are robust to the measurement bias in the ownership variables and to the various specifications of cumulative stock returns and earnings. In addition, the ownership effects are generally found in our sample, not just in any single year or economy.

4. Conclusion

The Asian financial crisis has caused East Asian economies to re-examine the adequacy of their corporate financial reporting. Despite efforts to improve corporate transparency by imposing new accounting and disclosure rules in East Asia, the perception is that the financial reporting quality of corporations remains low.

We hypothesize that the high ownership concentration and the large separation of ownership and control, which are common in East Asia, weaken the informativeness of reported earnings to outside investors. We provide two explanations for this relation. The first explanation is based on the controlling owners' entrenchment. The earnings credibility is weakened because minority shareholders anticipate that the ownership structure gives the controlling owners both the ability and incentive to manipulate earnings for outright expropriation or to report uninformative earnings to avoid detection of their expropriation activities. The second explanation is related to proprietary information. As rent-seeking activities are prevalent and highly profitable in this region, it is in the best interest of rent-seekers to concentrate ownership and decision rights, so that the specific knowledge about their activities can be concealed from potential competitors and the public. This information effect

Table 5
Year-by-year regressions with interactions for corporate ownership structure[a]

	1991	1992	1993	1994	1995
Intercept	−0.26***	−0.01	−0.27***	−0.25***	−0.13***
	(−7.51)[b]	(−0.28)	(−8.35)	(−10.97)	(−6.34)
NI	−1.28	1.25	−2.61**	0.24	−0.45
	(−1.03)	(1.05)	(−2.08)	(0.23)	(−0.48)
NI * SIZE	0.29***	−0.18*	0.33***	−0.01	0.03
	(3.39)	(−1.94)	(3.61)	(−0.12)	(0.38)
NI * Q	−0.32	−0.13	−0.22	0.26*	0.34*
	(−1.43)	(−0.61)	(−1.22)	(1.79)	(1.80)
NI * LEV	0.44	1.46**	−0.10	1.54***	2.03***
	(1.09)	(2.13)	(−0.19)	(3.42)	(4.70)
NI * SEG	−0.14*	−0.06	−0.12*	0.04	−0.11*
	(−1.87)	(−0.67)	(−1.77)	(0.55)	(−1.84)
NI * V	−3.14***	0.07	−0.85	−2.30**	0.05
	(−3.26)	(0.06)	(−0.76)	(−2.42)	(0.06)
NI * CV	0.99**	1.13**	0.88*	0.77*	−0.01
	(2.17)	(2.19)	(1.89)	(1.82)	(−0.03)
Adjusted R^2	0.20	0.06	0.12	0.19	0.13
Number of observations	652	727	784	817	772

Model specification: $\text{CAR}_{it} = a_0 + a_1\text{NI}_{it} + a_2\text{NI}_{it} * \text{SIZE}_{it} + a_3\text{NI}_{it} * Q_{it} + a_4\text{NI}_{it} * \text{LEV}_{it} + a_5\text{NI}_{it} * \text{SEG}_i + a_6\text{NI}_{it} * V_i + a_7\text{NI}_{it} * \text{CV}_i + (\text{Fixed effects}) + u_{it}$.

Variable definitions: CAR_{it} = the cumulative net-of-market 12-month stock returns for firm i at year t. The annual returns are continuously compounded from monthly stock returns starting from 12 months before the latest date, as required by law or listing rules, that the firm discloses its annual report. NI_{it} = the net earnings at year t divided by the market value of equity at the beginning of year t for firm i. SIZE_{it} = the natural logarithm of the market value of equity in millions of U.S. dollar at the beginning of year t for firm i. Q_{it} = the market value of equity divided by the book value of total assets at the beginning of year t for firm i. LEV_{it} = the total liability divided by total assets at the beginning of year t for firm i. SEG_i = the number of industry segment(s) of firm i. V_i = the voting rights level of the largest ultimate owner of firm i. CV_i = the ratio of cash flow rights over voting rights of the largest ultimate owner of firm i.

Sample: The sample includes 3,752 firm-year observations, spanning between 1991 and 1995 and covering 977 firms from Hong Kong, Indonesia, Malaysia, Singapore, South Korea, Taiwan, and Thailand. To be included in the sample, a firm must have at least 1 year of stock returns and financial data from the PACAP database between 1991 and 1995, its ultimate ownership data must be available from Claessens et al. (2000), and its largest ultimate owner must have at least 20% of voting rights. Observations with largest and smallest 1% values of CAR and NI are excluded from the sample.

***Indicates significant at 1% (two-tailed).

**Indicates significant at 5% (two-tailed).

*Indicates significant at 10% (two-tailed).

[a]OLS regressions are run separately for each of the sample year from 1991–1995. Fixed-effects of economies are included in the regressions but not reported.

[b]White-adjusted t-statistics are in parentheses.

argument predicts that high ownership concentration is associated with low earnings informativeness.

Our empirical results are generally consistent with the entrenchment and the information effect arguments. Our results are robust to controls for firm size,

Table 6
Economy-by-economy regressions with interactions for corporate ownership structure[a]

	Hong Kong	Indonesia	Malaysia	Singapore	South Korea	Taiwan	Thailand
Intercept	−0.19***	−0.13**	−0.10***	−0.04	0.00	0.17***	−0.17***
	(−7.00)[b]	(−1.96)	(−3.49)	(−1.39)	(0.08)	(5.13)	(−3.95)
NI	−0.93	−0.65	5.50***	1.36	7.12***	11.83**	−7.33***
	(−1.15)	(−0.62)	(2.77)	(0.74)	(2.80)	(2.35)	(−3.10)
NI*SIZE	0.14***	0.13	−0.38***	−0.09	−0.10	−0.40	0.36**
	(2.61)	(1.35)	(−2.61)	(−0.68)	(−0.59)	(−1.18)	(2.05)
NI*Q	0.19	0.41	−0.56***	0.03	−2.82***	−1.85***	0.66**
	(1.46)	(0.86)	(−2.58)	(0.13)	(−2.82)	(−3.71)	(2.21)
NI*LEV	0.44	0.67	−0.08	0.49	−3.13**	−5.01**	4.65***
	(1.31)	(0.96)	(−0.16)	(0.73)	(−2.46)	(−2.15)	(4.24)
NI*SEG	−0.03	0.14	−0.02	−0.14	−0.41**	−0.42	0.00
	(−0.72)	(1.51)	(−0.21)	(−1.50)	(−2.48)	(−1.55)	(0.01)
NI*V	−1.57***	−1.70	−2.75*	1.83	−3.40	−12.77**	−1.20
	(−2.60)	(−1.37)	(−1.70)	(1.02)	(−1.08)	(−2.28)	(−0.67)
NI*CV	0.45*	0.16	1.48**	−0.07	0.38	4.73**	2.99**
	(1.65)	(0.35)	(2.17)	(−0.11)	(0.47)	(2.33)	(2.31)
Adjusted R^2	0.11	0.07	0.07	0.07	0.17	0.26	0.24
Number of observations	1045	259	684	561	346	311	546

Model specification: $\text{CAR}_{it} = a_0 + a_1\text{NI}_{it} + a_2\text{NI}_{it}*\text{SIZE}_{it} + a_3\text{NI}_{it}*Q_{it} + a_4\text{NI}_{it}*\text{LEV}_{it} + a_5\text{NI}_{it}*\text{SEG}_i + a_6\text{NI}_{it}*V_i + a_7\text{NI}_{it}*\text{CV}_i + \text{(Fixed effects)} + u_{it}$.

Variable definitions: CAR_{it} = the cumulative net-of-market 12-month stock returns for firm i at year t. The annual returns are continuously compounded from monthly stock returns starting from 12 months before the latest date, as required by law or listing rules, that the firm discloses its annual report. NI_{it} = the net earnings at year t divided by the market value of equity at the beginning of year t for firm i. SIZE_{it} = the natural logarithm of the market value of equity in millions of U.S. dollar at the beginning of year t for firm i. Q_{it} = the market value of equity divided by the book value of total assets at the beginning of year t for firm i. LEV_{it} = the total liability divided by total assets at the beginning of year t for firm i. SEG_i = the number of industry segment(s) of firm i. V_i = the voting rights level of the largest ultimate owner of firm i. CV_i = the ratio of cash flow rights over voting rights of the largest ultimate owner of firm i.

Sample: The sample includes 3,752 firm-year observations, spanning between 1991 and 1995 and covering 977 firms from Hong Kong, Indonesia, Malaysia, Singapore, South Korea, Taiwan, and Thailand. To be included in the sample, a firm must have at least 1 year of stock returns and financial data from the PACAP database between 1991 and 1995, its ultimate ownership data must be available from Claessens et al. (2000), and its largest ultimate owner must have at least 20% of voting rights. Observations with largest and smallest 1% values of CAR and NI are excluded from the sample.

***Indicates significant at 1% (two-tailed).

**Indicates significant at 5% (two-tailed).

*Indicates significant at 10% (two-tailed).

[a] OLS regressions are run separately for each of the seven economies. Fixed-effects of calendar years are included in the regressions but not reported.

[b] White-adjusted t-statistics are in parentheses.

market-to-book assets, leverage, number of industry segments operated by the firm, and to various specifications of earnings and stock returns.

This paper makes several contributions. First, it provides an analysis that contrasts with those in prior research focusing on U.S. and U.K. corporations. The prior research documents that an increase in managerial ownership (Warfield et al., 1995) or institutional ownership (Rajgopal et al., 1999) would reduce the principal–agent problem between managers and shareholders, which would in turn lower the incentives and opportunities for managers to control earnings while raising the price informativeness of earnings. However, this relation between share ownership and accounting information is not applicable to East Asian corporations due to differences in the degree of ownership concentration and in the associated type of agency problems. Also, compared with the results from this body of research, our results are more generalizable to other parts of the world because concentrated corporate ownership in East Asia as compared to diffuse corporate ownership in the U.S. and the U.K. is a more representative corporate share structure throughout the world.

Second, several recent accounting studies (Ball et al., 2000, 1999; Ali and Hwang, 2000) have provided evidence that in addition to accounting standards, features of the institutional environment such as corporate governance as well as legal and financial systems can also explain the differences in the properties of accounting information across countries. We extend their work by examining ownership structure as one of the channels through which a country's institutional environment influences each individual firm's reporting quality.

Third, this research may have implications for East Asian economic reformers and regulators who are striving to improve corporate governance and transparency in their countries.

References

Alchian, A., 1965. Some economics of property rights. Il Politico 30, 816–829. (Originally published in 1961 by the Rand Corporation. Reprinted in Alchian, A., 1977. Economic Forces at Work. Liberty Press, Indianapolis, IN.)

Alchian, A., 1977. Economic Forces at Work. Liberty Press, Indianapolis, IN.

Ali, A., Hwang, L.S., 2000. Country-specific factors related to financial reporting and the value relevance of accounting data. Journal of Accounting Research 38, 1–21.

Asian Wall Street Journal, 1999. Business transparency in region has worsened, survey shows, November 24, 5.

Atiase, R.K., 1985. Predisclosure information, firm capitalization and security price behavior around earnings announcements. Journal of Accounting Research 23, 21–36.

Ball, R., Robin, A., Wu, J., 1999. Properties of accounting earnings in four East Asian countries. Working paper, University of Rochester and Rochester Institute of Technology.

Ball, R., Kothari, S.P., Robin, A., 2000. The effect of institutional factors on properties of accounting earnings: International evidence. Journal of Accounting and Economics 29, 1–52.

Barclay, M., Holderness, C., 1989. Private benefits from control of public corporations. Journal of Financial Economics 25, 371–395.

Bebchuk, L., Kraakman, R., Triantis, G., 2000. Stock pyramids, cross-ownership, and dual class equity: the creation and agency costs of separating control from cash flow rights. In: Morck, R.K. (Ed.), Concentrated Corporate Ownership. University of Chicago Press, Chicago, IL.

Berle, A., Means, G., 1932. The Modern Corporation & Private Property. Hartcourt, Brace & World. (Reprinted in 1991. Transaction Publishers, NJ.)

Bradley, M., Kim, E.H., 1985. The tender offer as a takeover device: its evolution, the free rider problem and the prisoner's dilemma. Working paper, University of Michigan.

Burkart, M., Gromb, D., Panunzi, F., 1997. Large shareholders, monitoring, and the value of the firm. Quarterly Journal of Economics 112, 693–728.
Burkart, M., Gromb, D., Panunzi, F., 1998. Why high takeover premia protect minority shareholders. Journal of Political Economy 106, 172–204.
Cheung, S., 1970. The structure of a contract and the theory of a non-exclusive resource. Journal of Law and Economics 13, 49–70.
Cheung, S., 1983. The contractual nature of the firm. Journal of Law and Economics 26, 1–21.
Christie, A., Joye, M., Watts, R., 2002. Decentralization of the firm: theory and evidence. Journal of Corporate Finance, forthcoming.
Claessens, S., Djankov, S., Lang, L.H.P., 2000. The separation of ownership and control in East Asian corporations. Journal of Financial Economics 58, 81–112.
Claessens, S., Djankov, S., Fan, J.P.H., Lang, L.H.P., 2002. Disentangling the incentive and entrenchment effects of large shareholdings. Journal of Finance, forthcoming.
Coase, R.C., 1960. The problem of social cost. Journal of Law and Economics 3, 1–44.
Collins, D.W., Kothari, S.P., 1989. An analysis of intertemporal and cross-sectional determinants of earnings response coefficient. Journal of Accounting and Economics 11, 143–181.
Demsetz, H., 1964. The exchange and enforcement of property rights. Journal of Law and Economics 3, 1–44.
Demsetz, H., Lehn, K., 1985. The structure of ownership: causes and consequences. Journal of Political Economy 93, 1155–1177.
Dhaliwal, D., Lee, K., Fargher, N., 1991. The association between unexpected earnings and abnormal security returns in the presence of financial leverage. Contemporary Accounting Research 8, 20–41.
Eggertsson, T., 1990. Economic Behavior and Institutions. Cambridge University Press, Cambridge.
Fisman, R., 2001. Estimating the value of political connections. American Economic Review 91, 1095–1102.
Freeman, R., 1987. The association between accounting earnings and security returns for large and small firms. Journal of Accounting and Economics 9, 195–228.
Gomes, A., 2000. Going public without governance: managerial reputation effects. Journal of Finance 55, 615–646.
Holderness, C., Sheehan, D., 1988. The role of majority shareholders in publicly held companies. Journal of Financial Economics 20, 317–346.
Jacobson, R., Aaker, D., 1993. Myopic management behavior with efficient, but imperfect, financial markets. Journal of Accounting and Economics 16, 383–405.
Jensen, M.C., Meckling, W.H., 1976. Theory of the firm: managerial behavior, agency costs and ownership structure. Journal of Financial Economics 3, 305–360.
Jensen, M.C., Meckling, W.H., 1992. Specific and general knowledge, and organizational structure. In: Werin, L., Wijkander, H. (Eds.), Contract Economics. Blackwell, Oxford, pp. 251–274.
Johnson, S., Boone, P., Breach, A., Friedman, E., 2000a. Corporate governance in the Asian financial crisis. Journal of Financial Economics 58, 141–186.
Johnson, S., La Porta, R., Lopez de Silanes, F., Shleifer, A., 2000b. Tunnelling. American Economics Review 90, 22–27.
La Porta, R., Lopez-De-Silanes, F., Shleifer, A., 1999. Corporate ownership around the world. Journal of Finance 54, 471–518.
La Porta, R., Lopez-De-Silanes, F., Shleifer, A., 2002. Investor protection and corporate valuation. Journal of Finance, forthcoming.
Morck, R., 1996. On the economics of concentrated ownership. Canadian Business Law Journal 26, 63–75.
Morck, R., Shleifer, A., Vishny, R.W., 1988. Management ownership and market valuation: an empirical analysis. Journal of Financial Economics 20, 293–315.
Nenova, T., 1999. The value of a corporate vote and private benefits: cross-country analysis. Working paper, Harvard University.
Rajgopal, S., Venkatachalam, M., Jiambalvo, J., 1999. Is institutional ownership associated with earnings management and the extent to which stock prices reflect future earnings? Working paper, University and Washington and Stanford University.

Roe, M.J., 1994. Strong Managers, Weak Owner—The Political Roots of American Corporate Finance. Princeton University Press, Princeton, NJ.

Scott, K., 1999. Corporate governance and East Asia. Working paper No. 176, Stanford Law School.

Sender, H., 1999. Smoke and mirrors. Far Eastern Economic Review 30, 34–38.

Shleifer, A., Vishny, R., 1986. Large shareholders and corporate control. Journal of Political Economy 94, 461–488.

Shleifer, A., Vishny, R., 1997. A survey of corporate governance. Journal of Finance 52, 737–783.

Smith, C., Watts, R., 1992. The investment opportunity set and corporate financing, dividend and compensation policies. Journal of Financial Economics 32, 263–292.

Stulz, R.M., 1988. Managerial control of voting rights, financing policies and the market for corporate control. Journal of Financial Economics 20, 25–54.

Teoh, S.H., Wong, T.J., 1993. Perceived auditor quality and the earnings response coefficients. The Accounting Review 68, 346–367.

Warfield, T., Wild, J.J., Wild, K., 1995. Managerial ownership, accounting choices, and informativeness of earnings. Journal of Accounting and Economics 20, 61–91.

Wolfenzon, D., 1999. A theory of pyramidal structures. Working paper, Harvard University.

World Bank, 1998. East Asia: The Road to Recovery. World Bank, Washington DC.

Name Index